Libya: From Repression to Revolution

International Criminal Law Series

Editorial Board

Series Editor

M. Cherif Bassiouni (*USA/EGYPT*)

Distinguished Research Professor of Law Emeritus, President Emeritus, International Human Rights Law Institute, DePaul University College of Law; President, International Institute of Higher Studies in Criminal Sciences; Honorary President, Association Internationale de Droit Pénal; Chicago, USA

VOLUME 5

The titles published in this series are listed at brill.com/icls

Libya: From Repression to Revolution

A Record of Armed Conflict and International Law Violations, 2011–2013

Edited by

M. Cherif Bassiouni

MARTINUS

NIJHOFF

PUBLISHERS

LEIDEN • BOSTON

2013

Library of Congress Cataloging-in-Publication Data

Libya from repression to revolution : a record of armed conflict and international law violations, 2011–2013 / edited by M. Cherif Bassiouni.
        pages cm. — (International criminal law series ; volume 5)
        Includes index.
        ISBN 978-90-04-25734-4 (hardback : alk. paper) — ISBN 978-90-04-25735-1 (e-book) 1. Libya—History—Civil War, 2011—Law and legislation—Sources. 2. Libya—History—Civil War, 2011—Atrocities—Sources. 3. War crimes—Libya. I. Bassiouni, M. Cherif, 1937– editor.

        KZ6795.L53L53 2013
        961.205—dc23

                                                                                2013033819

This publication has been typeset in the multilingual "Brill" typeface. With over 5,100 characters covering Latin, IPA, Greek, and Cyrillic, this typeface is especially suitable for use in the humanities. For more information, please see www.brill.com/brill-typeface.

ISSN 2213-2724
ISBN 978-90-04-25734-4 (hardback)
ISBN 978-90-04-25735-1 (e-book)

This book is printed on acid-free paper.

PRINTED BY DRUKKERIJ WILCO B.V. – AMERSFOORT, THE NETHERLANDS

CONTENTS

PART ONE

THE LIBYAN CONFLICT IN CONTEXT: HISTORY OF
REPRESSION AND THE AFTERMATH OF REVOLUTION

PART TWO

THEATERS OF MILITARY OPERATIONS

ABOUT THE EDITOR

M. Cherif Bassiouni is Emeritus Professor of Law and Honorary President of the International Human Rights Law Institute at DePaul University College of Law, Chicago (USA) where he taught for 45 years, from 1946 to 2009, and remained as an active professor *emeritus* until 2012. He is also the President of the International Institute of Higher Studies in Criminal Sciences in Siracusa, Italy from 1989 to date and previously served as Dean from 1972 to 1989. He is also the Honorary President of the International Association of Penal Law, Paris (France). He served an unprecedented three five-year terms as Secretary General and another three five-year terms as President, from 1974 to 2005.

He is the author of twenty-four books and editor of forty-four books, and also the author of 265 law articles on a variety of subjects, including international criminal law, comparative criminal law, human rights, U.S. criminal law and Islamic law. These publications have been written in Arabic, English, French, Italian and Spanish. Some of his works have been translated into various languages including Arabic, Chinese, Farsi, French, German, Hungarian, Italian, Portuguese and Spanish.

Professor Bassiouni has played an important role in the development of international criminal law and was nominated for the Nobel Peace Prize in 1999 for his role in the establishment of the International Criminal Court. He has also served as Chair, Commissioner, or Independent Expert of: three United Nations Commissions, respectively for the Former Yugoslavia, Afghanistan, and Libya; one National Commission, Bahrain; and one National Project, Iraq. He was also the UN Independent Expert on Human Rights, on The Rights to Restitution, Compensation and Rehabilitation for Victims of Grave Violations of Human Rights and Fundamental Freedoms.

He is the recipient of eight honorary doctorates of law degrees from the following universities: Salzburg (Austria); Tirana (Albania); Ghent (Belgium); Case Western Reserve (USA); Catholic Theological Union (USA); National University of Ireland, Galway (Ireland); Niagara University (USA); University of Pau (France); University of Torino (Italy). He has also received medals from: Austria, Egypt, France, Germany, Italy, and the United States.

THE CONTRIBUTORS

The staff members who participated in the general researching, drafting and editing of this book are Douglass K. Hansen, Jesse M. Franzblau, Sara Parikh Drar and Angela Mudukuti. The project also benefited from the assistance of Yousuf S. Khan and Haydeh Eftekhar, and the military expertise of Marc Garlasco.

Douglass K. Hansen holds a BA in Philosophy and Peace & Justice Studies from Tufts University, a JD from the University of Connecticut School of Law and an LLM from the School of Oriental and African Studies at the University of London. He has worked as a criminal mediator for domestic courts in the United States, and as a lawyer at the Extraordinary Chambers in the Courts of Cambodia, the Special Court for Sierra Leone and the International Criminal Tribunal for Rwanda. Most recently he served as the Chief Administrative and Financial Officer of the Bahrain Independent Commission of Inquiry.

Jesse M. Franzblau holds a BA in International Affairs form the University of Colorado and an MPP from the University of Michigan. He specializes in analysis of government archives pertaining to national security and human rights policy. Before joining the project, he was an associate with the National Security Archive, a research and analysis center based in Washington, D.C., where he worked on researching human rights violations in a number of Latin American countries.

Sara Parikh Drar holds a BA in Arabic and Law from the School of African and Oriental Studies at the University of London, in conjunction with the University of Alexandria, Egypt. She oversaw staff conducting evidence collection and database entry of reported violations. Before joining ISISC, she was a team leader in the Bahrain Independent Commission of Inquiry in 2011.

Angela Mudukuti holds an LLB from the University of Pretoria, South Africa, and an LLM from the University of the Western Cape in South Africa, in conjunction with Humboldt University. Before joining the project, she was an assistant to the Immediate Office of the Prosecutor, Public Information Unit at the International Criminal Court and has assisted in civil and criminal cases as part of a defense counsel in Zimbabwe.

ACKNOWLEDGEMENTS

The International Institute of Higher Studies in Criminal Sciences (ISISC) project received support from three external academics whose contributions are gratefully acknowledged. Professor Feisal Amin Rasoul Istrabadi, who provided access to the Indiana University database, is Director of the Center for the Study of the Middle East at Indiana University School of Law, Bloomington, Indiana. Professor William C. Banks, director of the Institute for National Security and Counterterrorism (INSCT) at Syracuse University, provided assistance to the CoI and to this project by preparing a history of Qadhafi's support for international acts of terrorism with the assistance of Dr. Corri Zoli.[1] Professor David Crane, of Syracuse University School of Law, provided information on issues of accountability in relation to the Qadhafi regime.

The project also received technical and research assistance from Yousuf S. Khan, Haydeh Eftekhar and Marc Garlasco.

Yousuf S. Khan holds a JD from the University of Wisconsin-Madison, and an LLM (Adv.) in Public International Law from Leiden University. He previously clerked with the International Criminal Tribunal for the former Yugoslavia.

Haydeh Eftekhar holds an MA in Middle Eastern Studies, Political Science and Psychology from the University of Hamburg and spent two post-graduate terms at the University of London's School of Oriental and African Studies. Her thesis on Iranian foreign policy entailed in-depth research in Iran's nuclear politics and national interests. She has previously worked on issues of social justice and development in Iran as well as Germany.

Marc Garlasco was the senior military advisor to the United Nation's Independent Commission of Inquiry for Libya. Previously, he led the office on civilian protection at the UN mission in Afghanistan (UNAMA) in Kabul.

---

[1] Corri Zoli, Sahar Azar & Shani Ross, *Patterns of Conduct, Libyan Regime Support for and Involvement in Acts of Terrorism*, 3 INSTITUTE FOR NATIONAL SECURITY AND COUNTERTERRORISM-INSCT, Apr. 27, 2011.

Before joining the United Nations, he worked for many years in conflict zones investigating war crimes for Human Rights Watch. Marc began his career in the Pentagon where he was Chief of High Value Targeting.

ISISC staff members Filippo Musca and Christina Abraham also provided important assistance to the project. This manuscript was reviewed for editorial and transliteration purposes by Naira Antoun. All three are gratefully acknowledged for their contribution.

GENERAL INTRODUCTION

Initiated by the International Institute of Higher Studies in Criminal Sciences (ISISC) in January 2012, the Libya Project ("Project") was to provide external research support to the Commission of Inquiry (CoI) established by the United Nations Human Rights Council on 25 February 2011 to investigate and report on human rights violations in Libya.[1] The Project, however, operated independently of the CoI, and did not have access to its files, witness testimony, internal evidence, or internal findings. The ISISC staff worked without interaction, whether direct or indirect, with the CoI staff and relied on government reports, individual expert reports, NGO publications, and media accounts. Seven researchers worked on the Project from January 2012 to December 2012 and some worked until June 2013. The Project first availed itself of a database housed at Indiana University (IU) School of Law until February 2012, and after that it set up its own database along with the use of CaseMap – management software.

Initially, the Project was designed to compile information and produce analysis for the benefit of the CoI on the history and evolution of the conflict and on international human rights law (IHRL) and international humanitarian law (IHL) violations committed during the period between February 2011 and March of 2012. The work done between January 2012 and February 2012 was compiled in a 300-page report that was submitted to the CoI. It focused on seven regions of Libya that experienced the heaviest fighting and most extensive violations allegedly committed by *thuwar* and Qadhafi forces.

Subsequent to the completion of the CoI's mandate in March 2012, I undertook the task of reviewing the work of the Project, and to edit it for inclusion in this book.[2] In the course of that work it became obvious that

---

[1] The UN Commission of Inquiry on Libya was dispatched during a special session held by the UN Human Rights Council. *See* H.R.C. Res. S-15/1, U.N. Doc. A/HRC/RES/S-15/1 (Feb. 25, 2011).

[2] I was appointed by the UN Human Rights Council to be Chairperson of the Commission on 15 March 2011, and served in this capacity until I resigned the post in October of the same year, at which time I continued as a member of the CoI. In my capacity as Chair and as a member of the CoI, during that time I refrained from communicating with the contributors to the ISISC Project in order to ensure that the findings of ISISC were independent of those of the CoI. ISISC's Acting Scientific Director, Dr. Filippo Musca, was the ISISC Officer-in-Charge of the project, and he first offered assistance to the CoI, in a

the reports produced by the CoI[3] and the Project's work, preceding and subsequent to the production of the CoI reports, were complementary. Consequentially, it became desirable to integrate some of the material contained in the CoI's reports into the text of this book in order to avoid redundancies and make this work more comprehensive.[4] To supplement the work of the ISISC researchers, I sought the consultancy of an outside expert on military operations who provided analysis on the military structures of both the Qadhafi and *thuwar* forces, and reviewed military questions, including the role of NATO.[5]

The CoI carried out its last field mission in January 2012 and produced its final report in March of the same year under the direction of Judge Philippe Kirsch, who succeeded me as Chairperson. We both served as members for the Commission for the entire duration of its mission. The CoI's mandate, however, ended at a time when much was still unfolding in Libya. The conflict and its aftermath were still ongoing and much more needed to be reported. For this reason, the ISISC Project continued

---

letter dated 15 November 2011, in the nature of preparing a database of information on Libya. In a letter of 4 December 2011, Judge Philippe Kirsch, the incoming Chairperson of the CoI, welcomed the offer of assistance and the contribution of an overall analytical report from ISISC to be used in preparation of the CoI's final report. ISISC sent its report to the Commission on 22 February 2012, which was subsequently acknowledged by Judge Kirsch in an email dated 24 February 2012. Judge Kirsch expressed his gratitude for the report and for ISISC's efforts in support of the CoI.

[3] The CoI produced two reports, one as A/HRC/17/44 and the other as A/HRC/19/68. The ISISC Project reviewed and incorporated information from every version of these reports. The first CoI report, A/HRC/17/44, was first published to the website of the Office of the High Commissioner for Human Rights (OHCHR) in June 2011 as an "Advance Unedited Version," and again in January 2012 without designation. The latter, A/HRC/19/68, was published to the OHCHR website twice in March 2012, both times with a designation as an "Advance Unedited Version." The two versions of these reports that are heavily sourced throughout this book are; (1) The Report of the United Nations International Commission of Inquiry to investigate all the alleged violations of international human rights law in the Libyan Arab Jamahiriya, U.N. HRC. 17th Sess. U.N. Doc. A/HRC/17/44 (January 12, 2012) and (2) The Report of the United Nations International Commission of Inquiry on Libya, U.N. HRC. 19th Sess., U.N. Doc. A/HRC/19/68, advance unedited version (March 2, 2012). For more on the UN practices with regards to the release of the Libya CoI reports, *see infra* Reports of the International Commission of Inquiry Reports on Libya.

[4] References made throughout this book to the CoI reports are either paraphrased or quoted verbatim. Every CoI reference includes a footnote that cites the paragraph of the respective report to enable the reader to easily identify the exact location of the given information. The footnotes in this book are consecutive with respect to each chapter.

[5] The consultant, Marc Garlasco, had served as the military expert for the CoI, and was consulted by ISISC after his work with the CoI and the UN was completed. His consultancy ensured that the ISISC project's findings in terms of military analysis were complementary to those of the CoI.

until June 2013, and this led to the preparation of this book.[6] The Project, which since March 2012 came under my direction, continued to document and produce analysis of ongoing country developments, and make assessments on internal challenges in the post-conflict period. This additional work provides a more extensive examination of the conflict and its consequences than what the CoI reports contain. But, as stated above, the two efforts are complementary.

The ISISC Project faced many of the same difficulties that confronted the CoI, but from different perspectives. The CoI, as a United Nations official fact-finding body, was limited by its mandate and constrained by its designated mission that was executed in accordance with United Nations rules and practices. The ISISC Project, on the other hand, was research and analysis focused and relied on multiple sources that the CoI may or may not have relied upon. As an academic research project, it was free to draw on whatever sources it deemed credible from a research perspective, and to draw its own conclusions based on its own analysis.

Along with the difficulty of analyzing the different aspects of Libya's highly complex post-conflict environment, the Project confronted a number of other challenges, chief among them the quality and reliability of the data sources it consulted. These materials had inaccuracies and discrepancies that required time and effort to fact-check in order to make the description of events as accurate as possible. The researchers also had to address the question of vague and inconsistent terms used by various sources. For example, media accounts tended to characterize the post-conflict violence as committed along tribal lines, whereas it should have been understood as a result of regional, social, political and ethnic divisions.[7] More importantly, media and other reports tended to describe the various armed factions that formed during and after the war as "militias," thus oversimplifying the complex nature of the many state and non-state actors that operated in Libya.[8] Distinguishing between the many groups of armed actors is essential in order to provide an accurate understanding

---

[6] The ISISC Project ended in April 2013.

[7] For information on the post-conflict violence that ensued after the fall of the Qadhafi, *see* Ch. V, Secs. 5 & 6.

[8] This research provides an analysis of the composition of the so-called militias that incorporated both armed groups that evolved out of the war and armed factions that took shape in the post-conflict period. In describing these non-state armed actors, we chose to adopt the term used by the source, along with providing context on the type of armed groups involved in the reported incident.

of the conflict, and avoid misrepresentation and confusion, particularly with respect to matters of accountability.[9]

The Project describes the many groups of combatants as well as where and how they operated.[10] This was particularly difficult with respect to the operations of the Qadhafi forces during the conflict, which consisted of combatant units in the regular military forces, semi-autonomous military brigades, the police, security bodies, and militia affiliated with the regime. The *thuwar* forces were equally varied and the composition of its armed actors was different in the various theaters of military operations as discussed in Chapter II and in Part Two. Whether on the part of regime or *thuwar* side of the conflict, this situation made it difficult to identify units and individuals responsible for IHL violations during the war and for ICL violations committed in the post-conflict period.[11]

The project used the same terminology of the CoI's reports, whereby "Qadhafi forces" is used collectively to designate any military units and non-state actors that fought for the Qadhafi regime against the insurgents, and the term "*thuwar*" to describe those forces that took up arms with the aim of realizing their common purpose of overthrowing the Qadhafi regime. The word *thuwar* means revolutionaries in Arabic and was adopted by opposition forces at the time of the uprising and thereafter into the post-conflict period. It refers specifically to those who took up arms against the Qadhafi regime during the military phase of the conflict and does not include demonstrators or opposition supporters, even though many have since claimed that honorific title.[12]

The context provided throughout the book should hopefully minimize the reader's confusion over certain contradictions in terms used by various sources to describe the different armed actors involved in the conflict and in the post-conflict environment. With regard to incidents where it was not possible to identify the perpetrator of IHL violations as directly affiliated with either the Qadhafi or *thuwar* forces, the research employs

---

[9] For information on the post-conflict challenges to accountability, *see* Ch. IV, Secs. 5 & 6.

[10] *See* Ch. II & Part Two.

[11] For more on ICL violations, *See* M. CHERIF BASSIOUNI, INTRODUCTION TO INTERNATIONAL CRIMINAL LAW: SECOND REVISED EDITION, 137–284 (Leiden, The Netherlands: Brill Publications, 2d ed., 2013).

[12] Report of the International Commission of Inquiry, advance unedited version (Mar. 2012), *supra* note 3 at n. 21.

the terminology provided by the source, along with a contextual description of the armed actor's involvement in the given incident.[13]

After the killing of Qadhafi on 20 October 2011, the media, NGOs and the international community shifted their focus to other areas of conflict in the Arab world, in particular to Egypt and Syria.[14] The attacks on the U.S. consulate in September 2012 that resulted in the killing of Ambassador Christopher Stevens and three other Americans[15] rekindled international attention toward Libya, which resulted in increased media coverage and analysis of the country. However, the coverage often concentrated on the security challenges, overlooking other important dynamics taking place within the country's political, social, judicial and economic structures.[16]

The ISISC Project undertook factual research concerning the conflict and its aftermath in order to address as many issues as possible. The Project's salient contributions are its detailed description of: the various theaters of operations; the strategy (or more aptly the absence of a strategy, save for NATO's) by both sides of the conflict, the tactics employed by the two opposing sides; the identification of the different groups of combatants on each side; what occurred in different theaters of operations; the chronology of events; the manner in which combat evolved in each territory; accountability for IHL and ICL violations; the outcomes following the end of combat operations; and last but not least an examination of NATO's role and its legality.

It is noteworthy that the post-conflict justice description and analysis of contextual events is not contained in any other work presently available on Libya. The result of this research and analysis is reflected in the five chapters of Part One and in the eleven chapters of Part Two of this book, as briefly described below.

---

[13] As discussed in the glossary of terms, the term "*kata'ih*" meaning "brigades," is generally used to describe certain military units belonging to both the Qadhafi and *thuwar* forces. It does not correspond to a particular military standard describing such units in the armed forces of different countries.

[14] M. Cherif Bassiouni, *The "Arab Revolution" and Transitions in the Wake of the "Arab Spring,"* UCLA JOURNAL OF INTERNATIONAL LAW AND FOREIGN AFFAIRS. (forthcoming 2013); ESAM AL-AMIN, THE ARAB AWAKENING: UNDERSTANDING TRANSFORMATIONS AND REVOLUTIONS IN THE MIDDLE EAST (American Educational Trust, 2013); MARC LYNCH, THE ARAB UPRISING: THE UNFINISHED REVOLUTIONS OF THE NEW MIDDLE EAST (Public Affairs, 2012).

[15] *See* Ch. V, Sec. 4.

[16] *See generally* Ch. V.

PART ONE – THE LIBYAN CONFLICT IN CONTEXT:
HISTORY OF REPRESSION AND THE AFTERMATH OF REVOLUTION

Chapter I – Historical Background. This chapter draws upon historical texts going back to the ancient and classical periods, through colonization, independence and up to the end of Qadhafi's rule. It provides an overview of Libya's history, with a special focus on the Qadhafi era. For the sections relating to this period, the researchers were able to cross-reference secondary texts with primary sources – declassified and leaked U.S. government records – in order to compile a detailed, referenced analysis of Libya's political and social structure under Qadhafi.

Following the completion of the first ISISC Report submitted to the CoI in February 2012, the researchers expanded on this chapter by producing a detailed analysis of the period of rapprochement between the Qadhafi regime and western governments from 2001–2011. The normalization of relations with the United States, the United Kingdom and other NATO states brought about new opportunities for Qadhafi's family and inner circle to regain some apparent legitimacy. In a cynical way, these and other governments gave their security and economic interests precedence over human rights abuses, past and ongoing in Libya. It was not until the February 2011 uprising, when the wanton violence against civilians at the hand of the regime became too much for the international community to ignore, that western governments abandoned Qadhafi and intervened to end his rule. The era of normalized relations with western governments is placed within the context of the events leading up to the 2011 civil war. The final section of the chapter looks at Qadhafi's mental state as well as the psycho-social trauma that his policies and cult of personality had on Libyan society. The section concludes with a synopsis of the history of Qadhafi's support for international acts of terrorism, drawing on declassified CIA cables on the 1988 Pan Am flight 103 bombing, and provides an overall assessment of the Lockerbie affair.

Chapter II – The Evolution of the Armed Conflict: 2011–12. This chapter provides an overview of the conflict. It introduces several themes followed throughout the book, in particular the nature and evolution of the conflict. It also includes an analysis of the Libyan military and structure of the Qadhafi forces, and provides insight into the formation and composition of the *thuwar* forces and how they operated. It describes, to the extent known, the relationship between the diverse *thuwar* forces across the country. The composition of the armed actors that emerged during the war is essential to understanding the conflict, and has bearing on the post-conflict situation, as described in Chapter V.

The chronology and military analysis presented in this chapter shows the capability of the Qadhafi forces to deploy weaponry and troops across the country, and how that was curtailed by NATO bombings (*see* Chapter III). It also looks at the unconventional and personalized command and control structure of the Qadhafi regime, and the diversity of the military units that took part in the war. When examining these events it becomes clear that the war was fought in a manner that was unplanned and which became more chaotic as new theaters of operation were opened (as described in Part Two). The Qadhafi regime had not prepared contingency plans, let alone a strategic approach for confronting an internal uprising or a foreign intervention of the sort that developed in 2011. Its military leaders were kept in the dark with regard to any overall strategy, if ever one existed, on how to deal with an uprising or foreign intervention and were not provided with even basic battle plans at the tactical level. There were no clear strategic objectives on the part of the Qadhafi regime; rather, military actions were reactive and intent on punishing civilian populations in areas where there was a strong *thuwar* presence.[17]

Chapter III – The NATO Campaign. The chapter includes an overview of the Law Of Armed Conflict (LOAC) and an assessment of the legal basis used to justify the use of military force to intervene in the Libyan conflict, including a brief history of the use of Chapter VII of the UN Charter by the Security Council to authorize the use of armed force that led to Security Council Resolution 1973 (UNSCR 1973). The resolution sanctioned foreign military engagement for humanitarian reasons, but the interpretation of the mandate to justify NATO's direct involvement in the conflict continues to be subject to debate. NATO's rules of engagement allowed for conducting targeted strikes against Qadhafi's security forces that were involved in attacking civilians or threatening to attack civilians. Some of the actions taken by NATO and non-NATO states, however, such as providing direct

---

[17] The historical differences between the 2011 conflict and past wars that have been fought over the same territory are noteworthy. As discussed in the historical narrative of Chapter I, the 1940–42 WWII Western Desert Campaign was fought from Cyrenaica, to the city of Tobruq, and into Egypt. During this campaign, Allied and Axis powers operated with planning and foresight, fighting for control of strategically important areas, such as Tobruq, which served as a fortress between Libya and Egypt. The nature of the 2011 war was entirely different.

support for the rebel forces, calls into question the legitimacy and justification of the foreign intervention into the Libyan conflict.

The chapter then looks at the application of the principles of IHL to the
intervening forces engaged in the 2011 conflict. The CoI recorded several
incidents of NATO airstrikes that resulted in civilian casualties or destroyed
targets where no clear military objective could be identified. Other independent investigations have documented civilian deaths resulting from
airstrikes, and human rights groups continue to express concern about
NATO's unwillingness to investigate, and in some cases even acknowledge, the NATO strikes that caused civilian casualties.[18] Concentrating on
these strikes, this chapter provides an assessment of the NATO campaign
and evaluates its outcomes in Libya. It also addresses the principles of
IHL and the obligation of NATO to investigate all potentially unlawful
attacks as well as IHL violations. It closes with a conclusion and analysis of NATO's conduct during the Libya campaign and its significance for
similar future interventions.

The material contained in this chapter goes beyond what little is contained in the CoI reports on this subject, even though it only touches the
surface of what needs to be addressed in connection with NATO's actions
in Libya.

Chapter IV – Accountability Issues. During the course of the Libyan conflict, there were violations of international human rights law (IHRL),
international humanitarian law (IHL) and international criminal law
(ICL).[19] These three international legal regimes overlap in certain respects,
although they are legally distinct characterizations of particular illegal
acts. IHRL is the broadest category of violations and applies during times
of peace and armed conflict, but does not entail criminal sanction. IHL
is the law of armed conflict that criminalizes certain conduct in armed
conflicts of an international and non-international character. Violations
of IHL are considered war crimes. ICL includes a number of international
crimes that criminalize certain violations of IHRL irrespective of whether

---

[18] *Libya: Slow Pace of Reform Harms Rights,* HUMAN RIGHTS WATCH, Feb. 6, 2013, *avail-able at* http://www.hrw.org/news/2013/02/06/libya-slow-pace-reform-harms-rights.

[19] *See* M. CHERIF BASSIOUNI, 1 INTERNATIONAL CRIMINAL LAW: INTERNATIONAL CRIMES 10 (Leiden, The Netherlands: Martinus Nijhoff, 3d rev. ed. 2008). *See also* M. CHERIF BASSIOUNI, CRIMES AGAINST HUMANITY IN INTERNATIONAL CRIMINAL LAW 568 (The Hague, The Netherlands: Kluwer Law International, 2d rev. ed. 1999).

there is an armed conflict or not, and – most relevant to the conflict – it includes torture and crimes against humanity.

Throughout the course of the Libyan conflict and into the post-conflict period, acts that qualify as violations of all three legal regimes have been committed. Some of the practices of the Qadhafi regime can be characterized as crimes against humanity, while others can be characterized as war crimes, irrespective of whether the conflict is ultimately deemed in whole or in part to be of an international or non-international character. On the part of the rebel forces, some of the acts and practices of the *thuwar* groups can be characterized as war crimes and violations of international human rights law.[20] More particularly, whether or not the conflict is characterized as a conflict of a non-international character that became a conflict of an international character,[21] the three international legal regimes apply.[22] For purposes of the general description of the conflict in this book, its theaters of military operations, and the command structure, the term "violations" is used in reference to breaches of IHL, ICL, and IHRL.

This Chapter includes a section on accountability and the prospects for post-conflict justice in Libya. Under Qadhafi, there were no mechanisms for holding individuals accountable for violations of international law norms. In post-Qadhafi Libya, submitting persons to accountability on an equal basis presents a serious obstacle to the government. The *thuwar* simply see themselves as justified in what they did when it comes to opposing the regime. They are not unlike other revolutionary groups who see the legitimacy of their goals and claims as overriding the illegality of their actions. As it now appears, accountability is not likely for the *thuwar*, and only likely for some high level symbols of the Qadhafi regime. Instead of accountability the *thuwar* are using their estimated 3,000 prisoners for leverage, as they ransom them for release or negotiate for their political support.

---

[20] The CoI concluded that *thuwar* anti-Qadhafi forces committed serious violations, including war crimes and breaches of international human rights law, the latter continuing at the time of its March 2012 report.

[21] *See* Legal Consequences of the Construction of a Wall in the Occupied Palestinian Territory, Advisory Opinion, 2004 I.C.J. Reports 136 (July 9). *See also* M. Cherif Bassiouni, *The Future of Human Rights in the Age of Globalization, in* 40 DENVER J. INT'L L. & POL'Y 22 [PERSPECTIVES ON INTERNATIONAL LAW IN AN ERA TIME OF CHANGE] (Anjali Nanda and Alissa Mundt eds., 2012).

[22] *See Prosecutor v. Dusko Tadić*, Case No. IT-94-1-A, Appeal Judgement (Int'l Crim. Trib. for the Former Yugoslavia, July 15, 1999).

Human rights groups continue to voice concern over the slow pace of reform, and affirm the need for accountability for serious crimes through fair trials that respect international best practices. The chapter discusses the importance of building a fully functioning and fair judicial system that can carry out effective accountability measures for past and ongoing international and domestic law violations.

Chapter V – The Post-Conflict Period. This chapter identifies important aspects of the political, social, military and economic factors existing in Libya in the wake the conflict. It places emphasis on the non-state armed groups that emerged during the war and held influence in its aftermath, the political landscape after the fall of the Qadhafi regime, and the regional security challenges posed by weapons proliferation and terrorist activity. The issues that emerged in the post-Qadhafi environment were in part an outgrowth of the conflict itself, and in part new problems resulting from a crisis of governance. As the interim government sought to establish its control it was faced by many difficulties, including but not limited to: political, social, an absence of functioning institutions, a lack of trained personnel, and a fragmented society. These and other factors made it quite challenging to bring about effective governance. In this climate a host of new or unsuspected political actors emerged, including Islamic groups that sought to fill the power vacuum through organizing and recruiting. The existence of non-state armed factions holding sway over parts of the country and parts of Tripoli is by no means a small part of the overall problem of governability.

Influential non-state armed actors that grew out of the revolutionary experience also played a pivotal role in the formation of the country's post-conflict security apparatus. Understanding their nature and composition is essential for confronting the challenges facing the new government. After the fall of Qadhafi, the transitional government established security bodies but failed to effectively demobilize and disarm the non-state armed groups. As the non-state armed actors refused to surrender their weapons, consolidating their control over territory and security installations, the government sought to co-opt them by including them in the police and military forces. That experience failed, however, because the actors were not disciplined enough, nor willing to accept being part of a disciplined system. Some also had their own political agenda. Throughout the post-conflict period human rights concerns intensified. Torture and abuse continued to take place by such groups in detention centers outside of government control. Human rights groups reported that deaths in prison custody continued, and that as of October 2012 nearly 8,000 people remained in detention, with an estimated 3,000 of these still outside even the nominal control of government ministries or the military.[23]

The chapter highlights how Libya's security challenges are international in scope, as demonstrated by the 11 September 2012 attack on the U.S. consulate in Benghazi. As weapons continue to flow out of Libya and allegedly into the hands of insurgents and rebel forces in countries such as Syria and Mali, the broader consequences of the Libyan war become increasingly relevant. The chapter provides a context for understanding the unintended consequences of arming an insurgency to overthrow a government, and the emerging security, political and social challenges stemming from the 2011 decision by the international community to intervene and help remove the Qadhafi regime.

The material contained in this chapter, as in Chapter IV, is a significant contribution to understanding post-conflict events in Libya.

Part Two – The Theaters of Military Operations

Chapters VI–XVI. Part Two of the book is divided into ten chapters based on the different regions that experienced the heaviest fighting during the conflict. Every chapter of Part Two follows the same format, which includes background information, a description of events, information on IHL violations allegedly committed by Qadhafi and *thuwar* forces,[24] a section on the role of NATO,[25] and a conclusion. These chapters follow the same pattern as the CoI reports but add substantially to its contents,

---

[23] Human Rights Watch, World Report 2013: Libya (Feb. 2013), *available at* http://www.hrw.org/world-report/2013/country-chapters/libya.

[24] The CoI reports identify certain specific military units and individuals, but they withheld the names of individuals believed responsible for certain violations in order to prevent reprisal violence and avoid prejudicing future trials. Readers may, however, find in this book the names of the specific military unit suspected for the IHL violations, but not the name of the alleged responsible individual. *See* Report of the International Commission of Inquiry, advance unedited version (Mar. 2, 2012), *supra* note 3 at ¶ 14. The Commission provided a list of names of suspected perpetrators to the High Commissioner for Human Rights.

[25] While each Section contains a brief assessment on the role of NATO in that particular theater of military operations, the larger analysis on the NATO campaign is devoted to Chapter III.

namely additional facts to events contained in these reports and over one year of facts and events not included in these reports.[26]

In conclusion, all of us who worked on this project and others, particularly those who worked on the CoI and those from the UN and NGO community concerned with Libya, hope that accountability will be realized in the country, and that the apparent trend of impunity will be reversed. The principal aim of this book is to provide a historical accounting on Libya in order to promote accountability for the violations recorded herein. There must be accountability for all those who have committed violations of IHL, irrespective of who they are or in which military group they may have participated. The international community must not be distracted by the cases generating the most media attention, such as the trials of Saif al-Islam Qadhafi and 'Abdullah al-Senussi. It is essential not to overlook the many unresolved cases stemming from the violations of IHL committed by those on all sides of the conflict. Those of us who are committed to international criminal justice as a means of enforcing international law and as a means of reducing human harm must not allow a "politics as usual" approach to divert our attention from this conflict and the need to hold those responsible for violations of IHL accountable to justice. We owe it to the victims of this conflict, to future victims, and to our fellow human beings. This is why we found it important to go beyond the work of the CoI, which came to an end in March 2012. We hope that the documentation produced by this project will prove useful to Libyans and non-Libyans who care for human rights and international criminal justice.

M. Cherif Bassiouni
Chicago, May 1, 2013

---

[26] The events covered in the CoI reports are paraphrased and referred to in footnotes in order to add additional facts and continue where the CoI ended. These additions, as stated above, cover a period of time equal to that covered by the CoI, and it extends into the post-conflict period. This chapter, therefore, completes the work of the CoI, albeit as an academic work.

GLOSSARY OF TERMS

Abu Salim Prison	A maximum-security prison in Tripoli that became a symbol of repression during the Qadhafi era. Under the authority of the Internal Security Agency (ISA), the facility was used to hold political prisoners, along with suspected militants and regime opponents. In 1996, regime security forces killed over 1,200 inmates following a protest demanding better prison conditions in what became known as the Abu Salim Prison massacre.
Al-lejna al-Amniya al-'Ulya	The Supreme Security Committee (SSC) was created by the Ministry of Interior in October 2011 to incorporate the *thuwar kata'ib* into a police force in the post-conflict period. The SSC units operated under the nominal authority of the Ministry of Interior, but functioned as parallel police forces without accountability mechanisms and composed of mainly civilian revolutionary brigades, and members of the disbanded security units from the Qadhafi regime. The SSC was utilized by the interim government as an auxiliary force to carry out security detail, and grew rapidly in size and strength in the months following the fall of the Qadhafi regime.
Amazigh	An ethnic group in Libya, also known as Berbers. The Amazigh were the largest group in northwest Africa before the arrival of Arabs in the seventh century CE. In contemporary Libya, the Amazigh have largely mixed with the Arab population and the majority live in the west of the country.
Ansar al-Shari'a	A non-state armed group that formed during the 2011 war and a prominent actor in the wake of the fall of Qadhafi. The group advocates the implementation of strict shari'a law in Libya, and its members are accused of involvement in planning politically disruptive acts of violence in the post-conflict period.
Baltaji/Baltajiyya	Plain-clothed police officers. These officers worked alongside security forces to disrupt demonstrations, sometimes using batons and firearms or driving through crowds in vehicles.

Cyrenaica

One of Libya's three provinces, along with Fezzan and Tripolitania, with Benghazi as its capital. It is the largest province in terms of territory, taking up most of the eastern half of the country. The region was home to the Senussi religious order and the base of King Idris al-Senussi's support during the Kingdom of Libya (1951–69).

Falaqa

A torture method that entails beating the soles of the victim's feet.

Fezzan

One of the three provinces of Libya, Fezzan is located in the southwest of the country, with the city of Sabha as its capital. It is the second largest province after Cyrenaica but has the smallest population due to its harsh terrain and large territory that spans into the Sahara. The Magarha, one of the largest tribes of Fezzan, supported Qadhafi during the civil war. The region is also home to the minority Tebu people.

General National Congress (GNC)

The GNC is the Libyan legislative body, and was established through national elections held on 7 July 2012. It is comprised of 200 elected representatives, with 120 seats reserved for independents and 80 seats reserved for representatives of political parties. The GNC officially took over from the National Transitional Council on 9 August 2012, and elected the first President of the Congress on 10 August 2012. The GNC elected the Prime Minister on 12 September 2012.

Al Haras al-Sha'abi

The Popular Guard (also referred to as the People's Guard) was a security force that served as a regime protection unit. It was tasked with suppressing internal dissent, particularly in response to political Islamist activities in the eastern part of the country in the 1990s.

Al-Haras al-Thawri

The Revolutionary Guard (also known as the Republican Guard) was one of the principal paramilitary and political organizations operating during the Qadhafi era. Its members served to protect the Qadhafi regime, and comprised brigades and special forces units.

Hayat Amn al-Jamahiriyya

The Jamahiriyya Security Organization (JSO) was responsible for internal and external security under Qadhafi. Its two main organs were the Jihaz al-Amn al-Dakhili or the Internal Security Agency (ISA) and the Jihaz al-Amn al-Khariji or the External Security Agency (ESA).

'Ibadi Muslims

A branch of Islam originating in the early days of Islam when a minority group broke away from mainstream Islam in rejection of the Sunni-Shi'a split. 'Ibadis are based primarily in Oman, but also live across North and East Africa. In Libya, 'Ibadis are concentrated in the Nafusa Mountains region among the Amazigh.

Jamahiriyya

The word Jamahiriyya is an Arabic neologism approximately meaning "the state of the masses." The word was coined by Qadhafi during a speech in Sabah on 2 March 1977, when the country's name was changed to the Socialist People's Libyan Arab Jamahiriyya.

Jihaz al-Amn al-Dakhili

The Internal Security Agency (ISA), an arm of the Hayat Amn al-Jamahiriyya. In control of the country's internal security under Qadhafi, the ISA was the most powerful security organ of the regime. It functioned as a political policing force, was responsible for internal repression and controlled several of the regime's detention facilities, such as the Abu Salim Prison.

Jihaz al-Amn al-Khariji

The External Security Agency (ESA), an arm of the Hayat Amn al-Jamahiriyya. The ESA dealt with Libya's foreign intelligence operations, including targeting Libyan exiles for assassination and planning and carrying out terrorist attacks abroad.

Jihaz al-Amn al- 'Askari or Istikhbarat

The Military Intelligence Service of the Libyan Armed Forces that operated under the Qadhafi regime.

Katiba (sing.) / Kata'ib (pl.)

The word katiba has been loosely translated into English as brigade. The word does not imply any specific size or position within the organization of the military. In relation to the Qadhafi forces, the word describes a special uniformed brigade under the command of individuals with a special connection or degree of loyalty to Qadhafi. They were heavily armed and estimated to number as many as 3,000 men each. During the civil war, the word was also used to describe opposition *thuwar* forces, often with geographical markers.

The Khamis 32nd Katiba

The 32nd Katiba (also called the Khamis Katiba) was commanded by Khamis Qadhafi, the youngest son of Qadhafi. The Khamis Katiba was the most elite and well-equipped fighting force in the regime's arsenal, and deployed primarily in western Libya during the civil war. It is claimed that Khamis himself was killed during attacks in Bani Walid in October 2011.

Al-Lijan al-Thawriyya	The Revolutionary Committees were established by Qadhafi through proclamation in 1977. The committees were created to safeguard the Qadhafi regime and spread his revolutionary ideas. Making up the regime's most ardent supporters, they received special privileges over the decades for serving as ideological and security enforcers.
Libyan Islamic Fighting Group (LIFG)	An Islamist militant group formed in 1994 in opposition to the Qadhafi regime. The LFIG were violently suppressed and hundreds of LIFG members were arrested and imprisoned in Abu Salim Prison, many of whom were killed in the 1996 prison massacre. The LIFG was listed as a terrorist organization by the U.S. government in 2004 due to its links with Al-Qaʿida. The group was later dissolved, but some of its fighters went on to join the *thuwar* forces in 2011. ʿAbd al-Hakim Balhaj, who had been the general commander of the LIFG, later became the leader of the Tripoli Military Council.
Mashashiyya	A tribe located primarily in the western Nafusa Mountains region. Its members were accused of supporting the Qadhafi regime during the 2011 war, and were subjected to violent attacks from some of the rebel forces.
Mujahid(s) / Mujahidin (pl)	Mujahidin generally refers to persons who are engaged in militant activity, in the service of Islam. The LIFG are an example of a Libyan Mujahidin group.
National Front for the Salvation of Libya (NFSL)	Created in 1981 by anti-Qadhafi Libyan exiles, the NFSL became one of the most important Libyan opposition groups operating abroad. Its military wing, the Salvation Forces, received U.S. and French support in the 1980s, and carried out a number of attacks against the Qadhafi regime and its officials overseas.
National Transitional Council (NTC)	Established in Benghazi on 27 February 2011, the NTC became the political body representing the Libyan opposition movement. It was dissolved on 8 August 2012 when the General National Congress took power. The members of the council were mainly former Qadhafi regime officials, defectors, Cyrenaican politicians and Libyan exiles.
North Atlantic Treaty Organization (NATO)	NATO is a military alliance founded in 1949 to provide for the collective defense of its members. While initially founded as a Cold War device to put military pressure on the Soviet Union, it has become increasingly involved in humanitarian and other military

operations since the early 1990s, first in Bosnia & Herzegovina, and subsequently in a number of countries including Afghanistan, Kosovo, Iraq and off the coast of Somalia. One of its most prominent post Cold War operations was Operation Unified Protector in Libya.

Operation Odyssey Dawn	The U.S. military operation in Libya that ensued immediately following UN Security Council Resolution 1973. Operation Odyssey Dawn started on 19 March 2011, and continued until 31 March when it was replaced by the NATO-mission Operation Unified Protector. The purpose of Operation Odyssey Dawn was to enforce a no-fly zone, maritime arms embargo and protect civilians on the ground from advancing regime forces.
Operation Unified Protector	The NATO mission that took over the Libya operation after the end of military operations by individual states. The operation began on 23 March 2011 and assumed full control over international military intervention in Libya on 31 March. The Operation ended on 31 October 2011.
Quwat Dira' Libya	The Libyan Shield Force (LSF) was created by a network of *thuwar kata'ib* that had participated in the conflict to operate as a unified army in the post-conflict period. The LSF brigades were given official sanction by Chief of Staff of the Armed Forces Major General Yusuf al-Mangush in April 2012, and were used to protect strategic infrastructure and were deployed to the country's conflict zones. The LSF brigades operated parallel to the regular armed forces, serving as reserve forces and as army auxiliary units. The General National Congress ordered the LSF disbanded after deadly clashes between its forces and demonstrators took place in Benghazi in June 2013.
Al-Qa'ida	A radical Sunni Islamist group classified as a terrorist organization by the U.S. government. Al-Qa'ida was founded in the 1980s by Osama bin Laden in Afghanistan. The group later extended its operations into the Middle East and North Africa.
Al-Qa'ida in the Islamic Maghreb (AQIM)	An extension of Al-Qa'ida, the group is said to operate in the Northern Africa Maghreb region.
Quryna	A privately owned Libyan newspaper, based in Benghazi. Quryna was previously owned by Saif al-Islam Qadhafi.

Quwat al-Daʿm
al-Markazi

The riot police that operated under the jurisdiction of Qadhafi's Ministry of Interior. They were involved in repression during the Qadhafi years, and reportedly carried out attacks against demonstrators during the 2011 uprising.

Tebu

A minority community that lives in southern Libya, northern Chad, Niger and Sudan. Although the Tebu have lived in Libya for decades, the group was discriminated against and marginalized under the Qadhafi regime.

Thawrat al-Fatah

Also known as the Al-Fatah Revolution, it marks Qadhafi's ascension to power on 1 September 1969.

Thuwar

The Arabic term for revolutionaries. It was used to describe the forces fighting against the Qadhafi regime as well as armed groups during the post-conflict period.

Tripolitania

One of the three major regions in Libya, located on the northwest coast. It is the country's smallest region in terms of territory, but its most populous. Several major Libyan cities are located in Tripolitania, including Tripoli, Misrata and Zawiyya.

Tuareg

A semi-nomadic Berber group that lives in northwest Africa, including the southwest of Libya and the southwest Sahara in Algeria, Mali, and Niger.

United Nations Security
Council Resolution
(UNSCR) 1970

On 26 February 2011, the UN Security Council passed Resolution 1970, which established an arms embargo, imposed a travel ban on regime officials and compelled member states to freeze the financial assets of six regime figures and members of the Qadhafi family. The resolution also gave the International Criminal Court jurisdiction over all war crimes and crimes against humanity committed in Libya after 15 February 2011.

United Nations Security
Council Resolution
(UNSCR) 1973

On 17 March 2011, the UN Security Council passed UNSCR 1973, which granted member states the authority to use "all necessary measures" to protect Libyan civilians threatened by Libyan military forces. It also authorized a no-fly zone and arms embargo.

A NOTE ON TRANSLITERATION

Arabic names and terms have been transliterated according to the guidelines of the *International Journal of Middle East Studies* (*IJMES*). Technical terms and nouns are transliterated with diacritics and italicized. In accordance with the *IJMES* guidelines, diacritical marks are not applied to the transliteration of proper nouns. The transliteration of Libyan Arabic presented a few challenges and the Libyan pronunciation of Arabic was taken into consideration. This includes a change of the letter q to g, which applies to proper nouns, e.g. Al-Qamudi, which is transliterated Al-Gamudi. However, an exception was made for the name Qadhafi. The *IJMES* system suggests that the Arabic letter *ye*, whenever representing a diphthong, to be transliterated to the letter y, *e.g.* Hussayn and not Hussain or Hussein. However, commonly known personal names are not transliterated in this manner, *e.g.* Saif al-Islam. Furthermore, the suffix -h, whenever it represents the Arabic *tā'marbūṭa*, is not retained. The character *hamza*, at the beginning of a word, will be omitted, e.g. *iǧtihād* instead of *'iǧtihād*. Expect for the initial *hamza*, which is dropped, the letters *ʿayn* and *hamza* are preserved and transliterated with a superscript letter c and with an apostrophe, respectively.

A NOTE ON THE REPORTS OF THE INTERNATIONAL COMMISSION OF INQUIRY ON LIBYA

The UN Human Rights Council adopted Resolution S-15/1 on 25 February 2011, which provided for the establishment of the International Commission of Inquiry (CoI). The CoI produced two reports, one as A/HRC/17/44 and the other as A/HRC/19/68. The former, A/HRC/17/44, was first published to the website of the Office of the High Commissioner for Human Rights (OHCHR) in June 2011 as an "Advance Unedited Version," and again in January 2012 without designation. The latter, A/HRC/19/68, was published to the OHCHR website twice in March 2012, both times with the designation of "Advance Unedited Version."

The OHCHR webpage for Libya[1] lists both A/HRC/17/44 and A/HRC/19/68, the former without any designation and the latter as the "Advance Unedited Version" of the CoI's report. The inclusion of the designation for A/HRC/19/68 allows for the inference that the A/HRC/17/44 published there is the final edited version. However, the A/HRC/17/44 link on the Libya page leads to the "Advance Unedited Version" of June 2011 and not the final version of January 2012.

The OHCHR Libya webpage also provides a link to a "Full list of documents in the Charter-based bodies Database" for Libya,[2] which provides a listing for the "Final Version" of A/HRC/17/44 from January 2012, but not the earlier version from June 2011. The "Full List" does not, however, provide a listing for either version of A/HRC/19/68.

As indicated above, there are two versions of A/HRC/19/68, one from 2 March 2012 and the second from 8 March 2012. The 2 March and 8 March versions are substantially the same, the difference being that the 2 March version is significantly longer than the 8 March version. In this book the longer 2 March version is used, and not the subsequent, shorter version from 8 March.

The 8 March version is listed on the cover page of the OHCHR Libya webpage; the 2 March version is not listed on the OHCHR Libya webpage.

---

[1] *Libya*, OFFICE OF THE HIGH COMMISSIONER FOR HUMAN RIGHTS, *available at* http://www.ohchr.org/en/countries/menaregion/pages/lyindex.aspx.

[2] *Documents on Libyan Arab Jamahiriya*, OFFICE OF THE HIGH COMMISSIONER FOR HUMAN RIGHTS, *available at* http://ap.ohchr.org/documents/dpage_e.aspx?c=104&su=110.

The 2 March version of the report can, however, be found on the OHCHR website using a Google search.[3] This search yields a Microsoft Word version of the report, whereas the 8 March version of A/HRC/19/68, and the January 2012 and June 2011 version of A/HRC/17/44 are reproduced in Adobe's portable document format (PDF). The 2 March version of A/HRC/19/68 is available on the websites of two other UN entities, namely the Office of the High Commissioner for Refugees[4] and the United Nations Regional Information Centre (UNRIC) in Brussels.[5] Both of these versions are in PDF format, and designated as the "Advance unedited Version" of the report, as is the Word version on the OHCHR website. It is unclear whether the PDFs were made from the available Word document, or were received via another channel.

In short, the Libya webpage of the OHCHR provides three of the four available versions of the CoI's reports, namely:

1. A/HRC/17/44 from June 2011 ("Advance Unedited Version"),
2. A/HRC/17/44 from January 2012; and
3. A/HRC/19/68 from 8 March ("Advance Unedited Version").

The 2 March version of A/HRC/19/68 is not available on the Libya webpage of the OHCHR.

---

[3] *Google search "2 March A/HRC/19/68"*, GOOGLE.

[4] *Report of the International Commission of Inquiry on Libya*, REFWORLD, *available at* http://www.refworld.org/cgi-bin/texis/vtx/rwmain?page=topic&tocid=4565c2254a&toid=4565c25f593&publisher=&type=&coi=&docid=4ffd19532&skip=0.

[5] *UNRIC Library Backgrounder: Libya*, UNITED NATIONS REGIONAL INFORMATION CENTRE, *available at* http://www.unric.org/en/unric-library/26483.

BASIC FACTS ABOUT LIBYA

Libya derives its name from the word Libu, an ancient Amazigh tribe that existed in what is modern day Cyrenaica and were closely related to ancient Egyptians. The name was later adopted by Greek settlers, who applied it to Cyrenaica as well as to northwestern Africa in general.

Located in North Africa on the Mediterranean Sea, Libya is bordered on the west by Tunisia and Algeria, on the south by Niger, Chad and the Sudan, and on the east by Egypt. Libya's closest northern neighbor is the island-state Malta, approximately 350 kilometers away and beyond that Italy. With a total landmass of 1,759,540 square kilometers, it ranks as the fourth largest country in Africa and the 17th largest in the world. The country's coastline extends some 1,770 kilometers (1,100 miles) from Tunisia to Egypt.[1]

Libya is made up of three provinces – Tripolitania in the northwest, Cyrenaica in the East and Fezzan in the southwest. Cyrenaica is the largest of the three provinces in terms of size, while Tripolitania has the largest population. The total population of Libya is estimated at 6.5 million, with a third below the age of 15. It is estimated that 90 percent of the people live in less than ten percent of the land area, overwhelmingly along the coast. Libya's population is small relative to the country's landmass, with more than half concentrated in urban centers, mostly in Tripoli and Benghazi,[2] which are located in Tripolitania and Cyrenaica, respectively. Tripoli, the capital, is estimated to have an urban population of 1.1 million, with nearly 2 million in greater Tripoli.[3]

Most of Libya is arid desert, except for a narrow strip of land along the Mediterranean coast. As such, only one percent of Libya's total landmass is suitable for farming and less than a fifth of that is suitable for growing permanent crops.[4] Most of the country is uninhabited desert. Notably, the major provinces of Libya – Tripolitania, Cyrenaica and Fezzan – are

---

[1] *The World Factbook: Libya*, CENTRAL INTELLIGENCE AGENCY (May 7, 2013), *available at* https://www.cia.gov/library/publications/the-world-factbook/geos/ly.html [hereinafter, "CIA, *Libya*"].

[2] *Information about Libya*, UNITED STATES EMBASSY, TRIPOLI, LIBYA, *available at* http://libya.usembassy.gov/libya2.html.

[3] *Tripoli*, WOLFRAMALPHA, *available at* http://www.wolframalpha.com/input/?i=tripoli.

[4] CIA, *Libya*, *supra* note 1.

divided by desert, which historically limited interaction between the three regions.

The geographic divides led to the provinces developing distinctly from one another, each maintaining a separate identity. Tripolitania was traditionally the metropolis, with connections to northwest Africa, including Morocco, Algeria and Tunisia. Cyrenaica was historically oriented more towards Egypt, and heavily influenced by the Muslim political-religious order, the Senussi. Fezzan, with a nomadic population, maintained closer links to Sub-Sahara Africa.[5]

The Libyan population is comprised of different ethnic communities, the majority of mixed Arab and Amazigh origin. The Amazigh – also known as Berber – are indigenous to North Africa and pre-date Arab influence in the region.[6] The Arab-Amazigh community is the product of intermarriage between the indigenous Amazigh population and the Bani Hilal and Bani Sulaym groups that moved into what is modern day Libya in the 11th century CE.[7] The Amazigh population is predominantly located in the western Nafusa Mountains region, with some ethnically Amazigh communities living in Tripolitania, and smaller indigenous Tuareg communities living in the far south of the country.[8] The Tuareg are a semi-nomadic group, inhabiting southwestern Libya as well as the southwestern Sahara in Algeria, Mali and Niger.[9]

The Amazigh suffered from discrimination during the Qadhafi era. Denied recognition as a minority, they were prevented from preserving and expressing their cultural and linguistic identity.[10] Other populations, such as the Tebu in southern Libya, were either granted or denied rights

---

[5] *Country Profile: Libya*, U.S. LIBRARY OF CONGRESS – FEDERAL RESEARCH DIVISION (Apr. 2005), *available at* http://lcweb2.loc.gov/frd/cs/profiles/Libya.pdf.

[6] ANTHONY BELL ET AL., INSTITUTE FOR THE STUDY OF WAR, 4 THE LIBYAN REVOLUTION: THE TIDE TURNS 13 (Nov. 2011), *available at* http://www.understandingwar.org/sites/default/files/Libya_Part4.pdf [hereinafter "THE TIDE TURNS"].

[7] DIRK VANDEWALLE, A HISTORY OF MODERN LIBYA 16 (Cambridge, UK: Cambridge University Press, 2006).

[8] INTERNATIONAL CRISIS GROUP, DIVIDED WE STAND: LIBYA'S ENDURING CONFLICT 6 (Sept. 14, 2012), *available at* http://www.crisisgroup.org/~/media/Files/Middle%20East%20North%20Africa/North%20Africa/libya/130–divided-we-stand-libyas-enduring-conflicts [hereinafter "DIVIDED WE STAND"].

[9] Report of the International Commission of Inquiry on Libya, U.N. HRC. 19th Sess., Annex I, ¶ 686. U.N. Doc. A/HRC/19/68, advance unedited version (Mar. 2, 2012).

[10] BELL ET AL., THE TIDE TURNS, *supra* note 6 at 14; Oliver Holmes, *Excluded from Cabinet, Libya's Berbers fear isolation*, REUTERS, Nov. 25, 2011, *available at* http://af.reuters.com/article/libyaNews/idAFL5E7MO0KJ20111125.

based on the shifting policies of the Qadhafi regime.[11] At times the Qadhafi government openly declared that the Tebu were indigenous to other countries, such as Chad, Sudan and Niger, and went so far as to threaten them with deportation.[12] In accordance with the 1954 citizenship law, and as part of Qadhafi's strategy to "Arabize" Libya, non-Arab groups such as the Tebu lacked official documentation, and were denied access to education, skilled jobs, housing and health care.[13]

Tribes and the tribal system have traditionally played a significant role in Libyan politics and society. There are roughly 140 tribes in Libya, and around 30 of these carry significant political influence.[14] The Warfalla are considered the largest and most influential tribe in Libya, located mostly in the Bani Walid region, and comprising roughly 15% of the country's population.[15] Along with the Qadhadhfa and Magarha tribes, the Warfalla were generally strong supporters of the Qadhafi government.[16] Qadhafi's tribe, the Qadhadhfa, were dominant in the city of Sirte, Qadhafi's hometown.[17] While relatively small, the Qadhadhfa took on a prominent political role under Qadhafi. Following his assumption of power, a number of members of the Qadhadhfa, Magarha and Warfalla tribes took key positions in the security apparatus, such as the armed forces, police and intelligence services.[18] The Arab Mashashiyya and Qawalish tribes are also prominent in the Nafusa Mountains region, and were conventionally loyal to the Qadhafi regime.[19]

---

[11] At times the Qadhafi regime treated the Tebus as allies, recruiting Tebu fighters to aid Libya in the war in Chad. See ANTHONY BELL & DAVID WITTER, INSTITUTE FOR THE STUDY OF WAR, 1 THE LIBYAN REVOLUTION: THE ROOTS OF REBELLION 18 (Sep. 2011) [hereinafter "THE ROOTS OF REBELLION"], available at http://www.understandingwar.org/sites/default/files/Libya_Part1_0.pdf. See also INTERNATIONAL CRISIS GROUP, DIVIDED WE STAND, supra note 8 at 3.

[12] U.S. Embassy in Tripoli, Confidential Cable, Tribal Violence in Kufra, Nov. 16, 2008, available at http://www.telegraph.co.uk/news/wikileaks-files/libya-wikileaks/8294878/TRIBAL-VIOLENCE-IN-KUFRA.html.

[13] Rebecca Murray, Libya's Tebu tribe hopes for lasting peace, AL JAZEERA, Dec. 3, 2012, available at http://www.aljazeera.com/indepth/features/2012/11/20121118115735549354.html.

[14] BELL & WITTER, THE ROOTS OF REBELLION, supra note 11 at 17.

[15] Gaddafi stronghold Bani Walid falls, THE GUARDIAN, Oct. 17, 2011, available at http://www.guardian.co.uk/world/2011/oct/17/libyan-rebels-capture-bani-walid.

[16] BELL & WITTER, THE ROOTS OF REBELLION, supra note 11 at 19.

[17] BELL ET AL., THE TIDE TURNS, supra note 6 at 11, 26.

[18] Uprising in Libya: Survival Hinges on Tribal Solidarity, SPIEGEL ONLINE, Feb. 23, 2011, available at http://www.spiegel.de/international/world/0,1518,747234,00.html.

[19] Giorgio Cafiero, Beyond Libya's election, FOREIGN POLICY IN FOCUS, Jul. 18, 2012, available at http://www.fpif.org/articles/beyond_libyas_election.

The large expanse and terrain of Libya led to the tribes looking inward. Survival in the deserts of Libya demanded strong familial ties and communal ownership to protect resources and defend precious commodities from outsiders. The tribes of Libya are essentially extended families that merged together to form social, economic, political and military units to secure internal harmony and external vigilance.[20] The country's three provinces are comprised of numerous tribes, whose relations are characterized by varying degrees of fraternity and enmity. Some of the tribes spill over into bordering countries, further complicating alliances and national identities. The discord between the tribes of Libya is reflective of the macro-divisions that developed between Tripolitania, Cyrenaica and Fezzan.

In Libya, as in many other African countries, in recent years factors such as urbanization have caused the influence of the tribal system to diminish and tribal affinity to weaken. Regional allegiances and ethnic divides have instead become more prominent social forces.[21] While there is still overlap between tribal allegiances and ethnicity, migration patterns and demographic shifts have changed these dynamics. The 2011 civil war highlighted the racial and ethnic divisions within the country. Rebel forces, in particular, carried out violations based on ethnicity, targeting black Libyans and Sub-Saharan Africans. Violence fueled by ethnic differences erupted between Arab and Tebu communities, as well as between Arab and Amazigh groups, such as the Tuaregs.[22] These divisions, along with the proliferation of non-state armed actors and renewed militarism in the country, became important aspects of post-Qadhafi Libya.

Unequal development and distribution of resources over the decades also led to regional differences along socio-economic lines. The substantial income from oil, coupled with a small population (approximately 6.5 million), gives Libya one of the highest per capita GDPs in Africa, at approximately $11,000.[23] The country's development has been uneven, however, and the economic wealth shared unequally across the provinces.

---

[20] ALI ABDULLATIF AHMIDA, THE MAKING OF MODERN LIBYA: STATE FORMATION, COLONIZATION, AND RESISTANCE 15, 23 & 47 (Albany, USA: SUNY Press, 2009).

[21] Mohamed Hussein, *Libya crisis: what role do tribal loyalties play?*, BBC, Feb. 21, 2011, *available at* http://www.bbc.co.uk/news/world-middle-east-12528996.

[22] *See* Ch. VI, Sec. 3.4.

[23] *Libya Economic Indicators*, ECONOMY WATCH, *available at* http://www.economy-watch.com/economic-statistics/country/Libya.

Despite its oil wealth, Libya lacked modern infrastructure and 28% of the population suffered from lack of access to improved water sources.[24]

The extraction of Libyan oil and natural gas reserves grew rapidly in the years after oil was discovered in commercial quantities in 1959, and the extractive sector grew from 20,000 barrels per day in 1960 to 3 million by September 1969. This expansive growth in hydrocarbon exports propelled the Libyan economy to 20% annual growth rates of GDP during the 1960s.[25] The economy has been overly dependent on income from oil and natural gas, which contributes to nearly 95% of export earnings and 80% of government revenue.[26]

The rapid increase in oil exports had a profound effect on the Libyan population. At the time of independence in 1951, Libya was one of the poorest countries in the world with a per capita annual income of $25–35. This grew exponentially after the first oil exports began in 1961, rising to $2,000 in 1969 and to more than $10,000 a decade later.[27] After the 1 September 1969 coup that brought the Revolutionary Command Council (RCC) to power, Libya invested significantly in education and health.[28]

Investment in health and education led to Libya obtaining the highest Human Development Index (HDI) score in the North African region (compared to Algeria, Egypt, Mauritania, Morocco and Tunisia) and 64th highest in the world.[29] In comparison to its North African neighbors, it has a high index for life expectancy, health, education, and income, and the lowest for gender inequality.[30] The Libyan state provided healthcare for children, and the country reached the highest literacy and educational enrollment rates in the region.[31]

---

[24] Report of the International Commission of Inquiry, advance unedited version (Mar. 2012), Annex I, ¶ 36, *supra* note 9.

[25] DIRK VANDEWALLE, A HISTORY OF MODERN LIBYA 62 (Cambridge, UK: Cambridge University Press, 2006).

[26] Report of the International Commission of Inquiry, advance unedited version (Mar. 2012), Annex I, ¶ 36, *supra* note 9.

[27] VANDEWALLE, A HISTORY OF MODERN LIBYA, *supra* note 25 at 62, 97.

[28] *Id.* at 88.

[29] *Libyan Arab Jamahiriya, Country Profile: Human Development Indicator*, UNITED NATIONS DEVELOPMENT PROGRAMME, *available at* http://hdrstats.undp.org/en/countries/profiles/LBY.html. Libya's HDI is .76. By comparison, the 2011 HDI rankings for the remaining North African states are: Algeria at .698 (96 in the UNDP's rankings), Egypt at .644 (113 in the UNDP's rankings), Morocco at .582 (130 in the UNDP's rankings), and Tunisia at .698 (94 in the UNDP's rankings).

[30] *Id.*

[31] Report of the International Commission of Inquiry, advance unedited version (Mar. 2012), Annex I, ¶ 35, *supra* note 9.

Despite Libya's success in providing education and healthcare for its citizens, the country's economic track record is mixed. Even with high levels of growth throughout the 1970s and early 1980s, the country was unable to significantly diversify its economy away from the hydrocarbon sector and suffered significant declines over the past 30 years. The regime was equally unsuccessful in creating jobs for Libyans, especially outside agriculture. Foreign workers continued to dominate the hydrocarbon industry and unemployment rose sharply, especially in the wake of economic stagnation and public sector employment reductions resulting from market liberalization. The country also continued to suffer from gender-based discrimination, where legislation does not provide for equal rights, particularly in terms of marriage, divorce and inheritance.[32]

Libya is a state party to all of the major international human rights treaties and conventions, namely:

1. International Convention on the Elimination of All Forms of Racial Discrimination (CERD);[33]
2. International Covenant on Economic, Social and Cultural Rights (ICESCR);[34]

---

[32] *Id.* at Annex I, ¶ 37.

[33] International Convention on the Elimination of All Forms of Racial Discrimination, G.A. Res. 2106 (XX), 660 U.N.T.S. 195 (Dec. 21, 1965). The Kingdom of Libya acceded to the convention on 3 July 1968, with the following Reservations: "(a) The Kingdom of Libya does not consider itself bound by the provisions of article 22 of the Convention, under which any dispute between two or more States Parties with respect to the interpretation or application of the Convention is, at the request of any of the parties to the dispute, to be referred to the International Court of Justice for decision, and it states that, in each individual case, the consent of all parties to such a dispute is necessary for referring the dispute to the International Court of Justice. (b) It is understood that the accession to this Convention does not mean in any way a recognition of Israel by the Government of the Kingdom of Libya. Furthermore, no treaty relations will arise between the Kingdom of Libya and Israel."

[34] International Covenant on Economic, Social and Cultural Rights, G.A. Res. 2200A (XXI), U.N. Doc. A/6316 (1966), 993 U.N.T.S. 3 (Dec. 16, 1966). The Libyan Arab Republic acceded on 15 May 1970 with the following Reservation: "The acceptance and the accession to this Covenant by the Libyan Arab Republic shall in no way signify a recognition of Israel or be conducive to entry by the Libyan Arab Republic into such dealings with Israel as are regulated by the Covenant." Libya is not a signatory to the ICESCR Optional Protocol.

3. International Covenant on Civil and Political Rights (ICCPR)[35] and the first Optional Protocol to the ICCPR;[36]

4. Convention on the Elimination of all Forms of Discrimination Against Women (CEDAW);[37]

5. The Convention against Torture and Other Cruel, Inhuman or Degrading Treatment (CAT);[38]

6. The Convention on the Rights of the Child (CRC),[39] as well as the first Optional Protocol on the Involvement of children in armed conflict[40] and the second Optional Protocol on the sale of children, child prostitution and child pornography;[41]

---

[35] International Covenant on Civil and Political Rights, G.A. Res. 2200A (XXI), U.N. Doc. A/6316 (1966), 999 U.N.T.S. 171 (Dec. 16, 1966). The Libyan Arab Republic acceded on 15 May 1970, lodging the following reservation: "The acceptance and the accession to this Covenant by the Libyan Arab Republic shall in no way signify a recognition of Israel or be conducive to entry by the Libyan Arab Republic into such dealings with Israel as are regulated by the Covenant." Libya is not a signatory to the second ICCPR Optional Protocol.

[36] First Optional Protocol to the International Covenant on Civil and Political Rights, G.A. Res. 2200A (XXI), U.N. Doc. A/6316 (1966), 999 U.N.T.S. 302. The Libyan Arab Jamahiriya acceded on May 16, 1989.

[37] Convention on the Elimination of All Forms of Discrimination against Women, G.A. Res. 34/180, U.N. Doc. A/34/46, 149 U.N.T.S. 13 (Dec. 18, 1979). The Libyan Arab Jamahiriya acceded on 16 May 1989, with the following reservations: "1. Article 2 of the Convention shall be implemented with due regard for the peremptory norms of the Islamic Shariah relating to determination of the inheritance portions of the estate of a deceased person, whether female or male. 2. The implementation of paragraph 16 (c) and (d) of the Convention shall be without prejudice to any of the rights guaranteed to women by the Islamic Shariah." Four countries objected to Libya's Reservation. Libya acceded to the CEDAW Optional Protocol on June 18, 2004. Optional Protocol to the Convention on the Elimination of All Forms of Discrimination against Women, U.N. Doc. A/RES/54/4, 2131 U.N.T.S. 83 (Oct. 6, 1999).

[38] Convention against Torture and Other Cruel, Inhuman or Degrading Treatment or Punishment, G.A. res. 39/46, U.N. Doc. A/39/51, 1465 U.N.T.S. 85 (Dec. 10, 1984) [hereinafter CAT]. The Libyan Arab Jamahiriya acceded on May 16,1989 without Reservation or Declaration. Libya is not a signatory to the CAT Optional Protocol.

[39] Convention on the Rights of the Child, G.A. Res. 44/25, U.N. Doc. A/44/49, 1577 U.N.T.S. 3 (Nov. 20, 1989). The Libyan Arab Jamahiriya acceded on Apr. 15 1993 without Reservation or Declaration.

[40] Optional Protocol to the Convention on the Rights of the Child on the Involvement of Children in Armed Conflict, U.N. Doc. A/RES/54/263, 2173 U.N.T.S. 222 (May 25, 2000). The Libyan Arab Jamahiriya acceded on Oct. 29, 2004, with the Declaration that "... the required legal age for volunteering to serve in the armed forces of the Great Socialist People's Libyan Arab Jamahiriya, according to the national legislation thereof, is eighteen years."

[41] Second Optional Protocol to the Convention on the Rights of the Child on the Sale of Children, Child Prostitution and Child Pornography, U.N. Doc. A/RES/54/263, 2171 U.N.T.S. 227 (May 25, 2000). The Libyan Arab Jamahiriya acceded on June 18, 2004.

7. International Convention on the Protection of the Rights of All Migrant Workers and Members of Their Families (ICRMW).[42]

Libya is also a state party to the Convention on the Prevention and Punishment of the Crime of Genocide,[43] the Convention on the Non-applicability of Statutory Limitations to War Crimes and Crimes Against Humanity,[44] the International Convention on the Suppression and Punishment of the Crime of Apartheid,[45] and the International Convention against Apartheid in Sports.[46] Libya has signed, but not ratified the Convention on the Rights of Persons with Disabilities.[47]

---

[42] International Convention on the Protection of the Rights of All Migrant Workers and Members of Their Families, U.N. Doc. A/RES/45/158, 2220 U.N.T.S. 3 (Dec. 18, 1990). The Libyan Arab Jamahiriya acceded on June 18, 2004 without Reservation or Declaration.

[43] Convention on the Prevention and Punishment of the Crime of Genocide, 78 U.N.T.S. 277 (Dec. 9, 1948). The Libyan Arab Jamahiriya acceded on May 16, 1989 without Reservation or Declaration.

[44] Convention on the Non-Applicability of Statutory Limitations to War Crimes and Crimes Against Humanity, G.A. Res. 2391 (XXIII), U.N. Doc. A/7218, 754 U.N.T.S. 73 (Nov. 26, 1968). The Libyan Arab Jamahiriya acceded on May 16, 1989 without Reservation or Declaration.

[45] International Convention on the Suppression and Punishment of the Crime of Apartheid, G.A. Res. 3068, U.N. Doc. A/9030, 1015 U.N.T.S. 243 (Nov. 30, 1973). The Libyan Arab Jamahiriya acceded on July 8, 1976 without Reservation or Declaration.

[46] International Convention against Apartheid in Sports, 1600 U.N.T.S. 161 (Dec. 10, 1985). The Libyan Arab Jamahiriya signed on May 16, 1986 and Ratified on June 29, 1988.

[47] Convention on the Rights of Persons with Disabilities, G.A. Res. 61/106, U.N. Doc. A/61/49, 2515 U.N.T.S. 3 (Dec. 13, 2006). The Libyan Arab Jamahiriya signed on May 1, 2008. Libya is not a signatory to the CRPD Option Protocol.

CHRONOLOGY OF EVENTS

- 15 February: The Qadhafi regime takes preemptive measures and detains activists planning the "Day of Rage" protest, scheduled for 17 February. The arrest of human rights activist in Benghazi on 15 February draws protesters into the streets earlier than planned, demanding their release.
- 16 February: Demonstrations in Benghazi become large, and spread to other cities in the east such as Al-Bayda, Al-Quba, Darna and Tobruq.
- 16–20 February: Protests continue to spread to Ajdabiya as well as Tripoli, Misrata, Zintan, Zawiyya, Bani Walid and Nalut in the west. Qadhafi responds with excessive use of force against protesters, resulting in hundreds of casualties and injuries of civilian demonstrators.
- 20 February: Interior Minister 'Abd al-Fattah Yunis is the highest-level official to defect and takes control of the Al-Fadil bin 'Umar Katiba from the Qadhafi regime on 20 February, thereby taking control of Benghazi.
- 21 February: Libya's deputy permanent representative at the Libyan mission to the United Nations, Ibrahim Dabbashi, breaks from the Qadhafi regime and condemns the use of violence against demonstrators.
- 22 February: The Arab League condemns the use of force against civilians and suspends Libya's participation in the League until it responds to calls to end the violence immediately.
- 25 February: The United Nations Human Rights Council holds an emergency session (15th Special Session on the Situation of human rights in the Libyan Arab Jamahiriya), condemning the violence in Libya, and adopting HRC Resolution S-15/1. As part of the resolution, the HRC dispatches an independent International Commission of Inquiry on Libya (CoI), and requests the UN Secretary-General and the High Commissioner provide all the administrative, technical, and logistical assistance required to enable the CoI to fulfill its mandate.
- 26 February: The United Nations Security Council (UNSC) adopts Resolution 1970 (UNSCR 1970) imposing an arms embargo, issuing a travel ban and freezing assets of senior members of the Qadhafi regime. Under Chapter VII of the UN Charter, the council refers the situation in

Libya to the International Criminal Court (ICC) to investigate all crimes against humanity committed after 15 February.

- 27 February: The National Transitional Council (NTC) officially establishes its headquarters in Benghazi.

MARCH 2011

- 1 March: The UNHCR warns of an impending humanitarian crisis as its emergency staff report on thousands of Libyans pouring into Tunisia daily. The Tunisian authorities estimate 70,000–75,000 people have arrived from Libya fleeing the violence since 20 February.
- 1 March: The UN General Assembly suspends Libya from the Human Rights Council in a unanimous vote, and expresses deep concern about the situation in the country.
- 1 March: The U.S. Senate unanimously passes Senate Resolution 85, condemning the Qadhafi regime for the violence in Libya.
- 3 March: The ICC Prosecutor Luis Moreno Ocampo announces that the Office of the Prosecutor (OTP) will open an investigation into alleged crimes against humanity committed in Libya since 15 February. A statement issued by the prosecutor identifies the worst incidents as taking place in Benghazi, Misrata, Al-Bayda, Darna, Zintan, Ajdabiya, Tripoli and Zawiyya, from 15–20 February 2011.
- 5 March: The NTC, led by former Minister of Justice Mustafa 'Abd al-Jalil, holds its first meeting in Benghazi and issues a statement declaring it to be the sole representative of all Libya.
- 10 March: France is the first country to recognize the National Transitional Council as the legitimate representative of Libya, pledging to exchange ambassadors between Paris and Benghazi.
- 12 March: The Council of the Arab League calls on the United Nations Security Council to impose a no-fly zone to protect civilians under attack in Libya.
- 15 March: The President of the Human Rights Council establishes the International CoI to begin its work in Libya. The Office of the United Nations High Commissioner for Human Rights (OHCHR) supports the Commission with a secretariat.
- 17 March: The United Nations Security Council adopts Resolution 1973 (UNSCR 1973), authorizing a no-fly zone over Libya and authorizing member states to take all necessary measures, short of foreign occupation, and notwithstanding the arms embargo imposed by UNSCR 1970, to protect civilians against Qadhafi forces.

- 18 March: U.S. President Obama states in a press release that in order to avert impending military intervention, Qadhafi must implement an immediate ceasefire, stop the attacks against civilians, and withdraw his forces from their advancement on Benghazi.
- 19 March: Qadhafi forces begin shelling Benghazi in a concerted campaign to retake the city. At the same time, military forces from France, the United Kingdom, and the United States begin conducting airstrikes within Libyan territory.
- 22 March: NATO officially begins to enforce the arms embargo against Libya, and member states dispatch warships to the region to intercept sea transport carrying equipment to Libya.
- 29 March: The UN Secretary-General gives a statement in which he backs the call of the United Kingdom's Prime Minister for a "Contact Group," to ensure close coordination between the United Nations, the League of Arab States, the African Union, the Organization of the Islamic Conference and the European Union.
- 31 March: NATO assumes command and control of operations to enforce all aspects of UNSCRs 1970 and 1973, marking the beginning of Operation Unified Protector.

April 2011

- 7 April: The Commander of the U.S. Africa Command General Carter Ham publicly warns that despite the military progress, recent advancements by the Qadhafi forces increase the likelihood that a stalemate will develop.
- 12–29 April: The UN CoI visits Libya as part of its investigations into serious violations of human rights and international humanitarian law committed by all parties to the conflict in the country. The field mission includes meetings with NTC officials in eastern Libya, as well as visits to detention facilities and hospitals in Benghazi. The Commissioners also meet with Libyan government officials and NGO's in Tripoli, along with detention centers in the region.
- 14 April: British and Qatari representatives organize the first Libya Contact Group meeting, involving Qatar, Italy, Kuwait, France and others that have agreed to provide financial support to the NTC.
- 19 April: Britain's Foreign Secretary William Hague announces the UK's diplomatic mission in Benghazi will expand to include an additional military liaison advisory team whose role will be to work with the NTC

to improve their military organizational structures, communications and logistics.

- 20 April: The UN High Commissioner for Human Rights condemns the reported use of cluster munitions and heavy weaponry by Qadhafi forces and warns that the attacks on civilians in Misrata may constitute international crimes.
- April 26: The United States approves $25 million in non-lethal commodities, equipment and services for the NTC.

MAY 2011

- 1 May: The Qadhafi regime deploys additional forces from the elite Khamis Katiba (under command of Qadhafi's son, Khamis) to the Nafusa Mountains region.
- 7–8 May: French and British navy ships strike Qadhafi forces they detect firing rocket launchers into Misrata.
- 16 May: The OTP of the ICC applies for arrest warrants for Mu'ammar Qadhafi, Saif al-Islam Qadhafi, and Libya's intelligence chief 'Abdullah al-Senussi.
- 30 May: Protests erupt in Tripoli and are dispersed by live fire from Qadhafi forces.

JUNE 2011

- 1 June: NATO announces that it will extend its mission in Libya for a further 90 days.
- 1 June: Pursuant to UN Human Rights Council Resolution S-15/1 of 25 February 2011, the UN Commission of Inquiry submits its report (A/HRC/17/44) to the UN HRC.
- 15 June: The UNHCR reports that thousands of Libyans continue to flee over the Egyptian border daily. Since February, more than 343,000 people are estimated to have entered Egypt through Al-Sallum; approximately 104,000 are of Egyptian origin, 163,000 Libyan and almost 77,000 are nationals from other countries.
- 10 June: The UN HRC decides to extend the mandate of the UN CoI in light of the extensive and on-going allegations of abuses, and requests the CoI to provide a second report at the Council's nineteenth session in March 2012.

- 27 June: The Pre-Trial Chamber of the ICC issues arrest warrants for Mu'ammar Qadhafi, his son Saif al-Islam, and Libya's intelligence chief Al-Senussi.

JULY 2011

- 1 July: French Foreign Affairs Minister Alain Juppe responds to concerns over France supplying weapons directly to Libya's rebel forces, declaring that the action is within the framework of UNSCRs 1970 and 1973.
- 15 July: The United States announces that it will officially recognize the NTC as the legitimate government of Libya, affirming the international commitment to seeing the end of the Qadhafi regime. This official recognition allows the United States to unfreeze Libyan assets in American banks and allow the money to be used by the NTC.
- 28 July: 'Abd al-Fattah Yunis, then-leader of the rebel front based in Benghazi (the Libyan National Army), is assassinated in unclear circumstances. Sulayman Mahmud assumes control of the Libyan National Army following Yunis' death.

AUGUST 2011

- 8 August: The head of the NTC 'Abd al-Jalil dissolves the Executive Board (the NTC's interim government) following the assassination of Yunis.
- 10 August: The Libyan Constitutional Declaration that was finalized by the NTC on 3 August is made public. It is intended to be in place until a permanent constitution is drafted. Members of civil society in Libya claim the Constitutional Declaration is drafted without popular consultation.
- 18 August: In the Nafusa Mountains region *thuwar* forces advance and take control of Al-Gharyan, thus securing control of the corridor between Wazin and Al-Gharyan. This marks the *thuwar* forces' nearly total control of the Nafusa Mountains region.
- 20 August: *Thuwar* forces surround Tripoli, with a combination of *kata'ib* moving in from Zawiyya to the west, Al-Gharyan to the south and Misrata to the east.
- 30 August: 'Abd al-Jalil of the NTC declares that the regime loyalists in Sirte – one of the last Qadhafi strongholds – have a four-day deadline to surrender or face military action.

- 6 September: NTC forces, combined with *thuwar kata'ib*, march on Sirte to begin the final battle of the war.
- 16 September: The UN General Assembly votes to give Libya's seat to the National Transitional Council. The UN Security Council adopts Resolution 2009 (2011), which eases economic sanctions on Libya, constitutes further international recognition of the interim government and gives the NTC access to previously frozen Libyan assets. The resolution also establishes the United Nations Support Mission in Libya (UNSMIL), headed by Ian Martin, the Special Representative of the UN Secretary-General.
- 21 September: NATO announces it will extend its mission for another 90 days. The decision to extend NATO's engagement in Libya is a result of the ongoing fighting in Sirte and other Qadhafi loyalist towns.

- 3 October: The NTC interim government is appointed.
- 20 October: A U.S. predator drone and French aircraft fire on a convoy of cars leaving the city of Sirte. The convoy is carrying Mu'ammar Qadhafi who flees his vehicle in an attempt to hide in a nearby concrete drain. *Thuwar* forces capture Qadhafi and he dies in their custody.
- 25 October: Mu'ammar Qadhafi and his son Mu'tassim are reportedly buried at a secret location.
- 21 October: The OHCHR calls for a full investigation into the killing of Qadhafi. The spokesperson for the UN High Commissioner for Human Rights Navanethem Pillay tells reporters an investigation is needed to determine whether Qadhafi was killed during fighting or by execution.
- 23 October: The Libyan transitional Prime Minister Mahmud Jibril declares the country's official liberation from the Qadhafi regime and sets a schedule for establishing a new government.
- 26 October: The NTC President 'Abd al-Jalil requests that NATO extends its mission in Libya.
- 27 October: the UN Security Council decides to end the NATO Civilian Protection Mandate over Libya.
- 31 October: The NTC appoints 'Abd al-Rahman Keib as prime minister.

NOVEMBER 2011

- 19 November: Members of the Zintan Katiba capture Saif al-Islam south of the town of 'Ubari. Saif is transferred to Zintan and held by the city's powerful *kata'ib* members. Representatives from the ICC declare that Libya has a legal obligation to hand Saif over to the ICC, based on its pending indictment for his arrest.
- 22 November: The NTC names the officials in the interim government that will lead the country until parliamentary elections are held. Prime Minister Keib tells a news conference that all of Libya is represented in the government.
- 22 November: The Pre-Trial Chamber (PTC) of the ICC terminates the case against Mu'ammar Qadhafi due to his death.
- 23 November: About 150 protesters gather in front of NTC office in Benghazi to voice dissatisfaction with the new government appointments, claiming a lack of representation of Benghazi's local tribes in the key positions of government.

DECEMBER 2011

- 31 November–16 December: The UN CoI visits Tripoli as part of its continuing investigations into serious violations of human rights and international humanitarian law committed by all parties to the conflict in the country. During the visit, the Commissioners meet with the Chairman of the NTC and other government officials, as well as NGO representatives and interview detainees at the Ma'atiga detention facility.
- 18 December: The NTC adopts Law Number 192 of 2011 on Transparency and Honesty, regarding future candidates to the election of the General National Congress (GNC).
- 20 December: The central authorities in Tripoli make several attempts to disarm the militias and urge them to leave the capital in the interests of encouraging stability and unified action under the central authorities.

JANUARY 2012

- 4 January: The NTC adopts Law Number 2 of 2012, which annuls the law criminalizing membership of political parties.

- 12 January: The UN CoI releases its final version of its report (A/HRC/17/44) on the alleged violations of international human rights law in the Libyan Arab Jamahiriya.
- 18 January: The NTC adopts Law Number 3 of 2012 establishing a National High Commission responsible for elections.
- 21 January: Armed protestors in Benghazi storm a government building where ʿAbd al-Jalil's office is working. He attempts to address the crowd but retreats after water bottles are thrown at him.
- 22 January: The interim government deputy head of the NTC, ʿAbd al-Hafiz Ghuga, resigns.
- 28 January: The NTC issues Law Number 4 for the year 2012 for the Election of the GNC, establishing the framework for upcoming elections. The law sets the provisions for the election of 200 members of the GNC.
- January: The UN CoI carries out its last of its three field missions to gather evidence for its final report.

February 2012

- 6 February: Heavily armed fighters from various militias from Misrata enter the Janzur Marine Academy where about 2,000 Tawerghans are being sheltered. Several are killed and injured, including women and children.
- 26 February: The NTC adopts Law Number 17 of 2012 on Transitional Justice.

March 2012

- 5 March: The NTC takes measures to gain control over the country's border crossings, setting a deadline for the former *thuwar kata'ib* to give up control over the strategic transnational gateways in the border cities.
- 6 March: Benghazi declares an autonomous governing council, the Cyrenaica Provincial Council, to manage political affairs independently from central authorities in Tripoli.
- 8 March: The UN CoI on Libya releases its final report (A/HRC/19/68) on the country's human rights situation, pursuant to UN HRC Resolution S-15/1. An earlier draft was released on 2 March.

- 13 March: The NTC adopts Constitutional Amendment Number 1 of 2012, which amends the constitutional declaration extending the time-frame for drafting the constitution.
- 17 March: Al-Senussi is apprehended at the airport in Mauritania with the assistance of French intelligence services.

APRIL 2012

- 6 April: A demonstration of 300 people and 50 military and police vehicles in Benghazi calls for the non-state armed actors to lay down their weapons.
- 10 April: Armed men target a UN convoy in Benghazi carrying the head of the UN Mission Ian Martin.
- 20 April: The interim government takes control of Tripoli International Airport from the Zintan Katiba.
- 27 April: A bomb explodes in a Benghazi courthouse, caused by three packages placed against the walls of the court, resulting in one injury.

MAY 2012

- 1 May: The Libyan government formally challenges the admissibility of the case against Saif al-Islam Qadhafi before the ICC.
- 2 May: NTC passes Law Number 36 of 2012 freezing the assets and properties of 260 individuals and 79 companies, including Qadhafi's family, numerous relatives and members of his inner circle.
- 8 May: Armed militia from the Nafusa Mountains occupy the office of the interim prime minister in Tripoli, 'Abd al-Rahman Keib, demanding payment from the interim government.
- 10 May: The Head of UNSMIL Ian Martin releases a statement about the challenges facing the interim government. Martin emphasizes the need for stronger coordination of plans for the demobilization and reintegration of non-state armed groups, and control of weapons.
- 17 May: Salam Furjani, a prominent heart surgeon, is accused of links to the former regime and is arrested by armed forces from the Supreme Security Committee (SSC) under violent circumstances. He is held for five days, and tortured before being released.
- 19 May: Local elections for a new city council are held in Benghazi.
- 22 May: The Benghazi headquarters of the International Committee of the Red Cross are attacked by rocket fired grenades.

JUNE 2012

- 1 June: The Pre-trial Chamber of the ICC postpones the surrender of Saif al-Islam to the ICC in order to assess the admissibility of the case.
- 4 June: The interim government loses control of Tripoli International Airport to militias from the town of Tarhun, belonging to the Al-'Awfiyya Katiba.
- 6 June: A bomb explodes outside a building used by the U.S. Diplomatic Mission in Benghazi.
- 11 June: A convoy escorting the UK Ambassador to Libya is attacked while visiting Benghazi.
- 14 June: Four members of an ICC delegation visiting Saif al-Islam in a Zintan detention center are detained and accused of spying and carrying suspicious documents for Saif al-Islam. They are released two weeks later.
- June 18: Armed gunmen storm the Tunisian consulate in Benghazi to protest an art exhibition in Tunisia perceived as offensive to Islam.
- 25 June: Tunisia extradites former Libyan prime minister, Al-Baghdadi 'Ali al-Mahmudi, to Libya.

JULY 2012

- 5 July: The NTC adopts Constitutional Amendment Number 3 of 2012 which modifies Constitutional Amendment Number 1 of 2012 and mandates that members of the constitutional assembly should be elected not appointed.
- 5 July: The NTC adopts Declaration Number 7 of 2012 recommending that the GNC consider Islam as the main source of legislation. It also suggests that the issue should be submitted to a referendum.
- 7 July: Elections are held for a 200-member GNC, which plans to name a new prime minister and draft a constitution.
- 17 July: The results of the elections are announced, with the National Forces Alliance (NFA) winning the majority of the seats, and the Justice and Development Party in second place.

AUGUST 2012

- 9 August: The NTC hands over power to the recently elected GNC.
- 10 August: Muhammad Yusuf al-Magarayf is elected president of the GNC.

- 16 August: The Libyan Justice Minister Ahmad al-Jahani declares that Saif al-Islam will face trial in September 2012 in Zintan, despite the demand from the ICC to bring him to trial at The Hague.
- 26 August: Libya's Interior Minister Fawzi 'Abd al-'Ali resigns in response to the severe criticism directed at him by the GNC in relation to his handling of the series of attacks on Sufi Muslim shrines.

SEPTEMBER 2012

- 4 September: Libya's largest oil refinery in Ra's Lanuf resumes production.
- 5 September: The Mauritania government complies with the Libyan request for the extradition of Al-Senussi. After arriving to Tripoli, Al-Senussi is taken to a detention center to await trial for crimes committed as the internal security chief during the Qadhafi regime.
- 11 September: The U.S. Ambassador to Libya Christopher Stevens and three other American officials are killed in an attack in Benghazi.
- 12 September: The GNC elects Mustafa Abu Shagur as prime minister.
- 19 September: Benghazi police officers revolt and refuse to take orders from the police chief appointed by the government in Tripoli.
- 21 September: Thousands take to the streets in Benghazi calling for militia groups to disarm, and seize control of several headquarters, including that of the Ansar al-Sharī'a militia.
- September: The U.S. Congress approves the appropriation of $8 million over the following year to fund the establishment of an elite security forces unit consisting of an estimated 500 soldiers.

OCTOBER 2012

- 7 October: Prime Minister Abu Shagur is dismissed after the GNC rejects his proposal regarding the formation of a new cabinet.
- 8 October: The Office of the Prosecutor general decides that the trial of Saif al-Islam is to be postponed by five months in order to take account of the testimony of Al-Senussi.
- 9–10 October: The Pre-Trial Chamber of the ICC conducts oral hearings concerning the admissibility of the case against Saif al-Islam.
- 14 October: The GNC elects 'Ali Zaydan as the new prime minister. He is sworn in on the same day.
- 17 October: Clashes break out in Bani Walid between government forces and Qadhafi loyalists accused of harboring individuals wanted

for crimes committed during the conflict, leaving 50 dead and displacing an estimated 10,000 families.

- 31 October: Militias occupy the parliament building in protest against the formation of the new government.

NOVEMBER 2012

- Early November: A series of attacks are carried out on police officials in Benghazi, including a car bomb attack on a police station.
- 14 November: The government of 'Ali Zaydan takes office.
- 21 November: Faraj al-Deirsy, the police chief of Benghazi, is assassinated by gunmen, pushing the death count for police officers in the city over 20.

JANUARY 2013

- 2 January: The head of the investigations unit of the Benghazi police is abducted, allegedly for investigating the murder of policy chief Faraj al-Deirsy.
- 16 January: The Italian consul to Benghazi is attacked, prompting the closure of the Italian Consulate in the city.
- January: The Head of UNSMIL, Tarek Mitri, reports that several thousand conflict-related prisoners remain in detention facilities where they face mistreatment and are denied due process.

FEBRUARY 2013

- 7 February: The ICC Pre-Trial Chamber orders the Libyan government surrender 'Abdullah al-Senussi to stand trial in The Hague.

MARCH 2013

- 5 March: The GNC parliament building is stormed by armed demonstrators demanding the exclusion of Qadhafi government regime officials from holding office.
- 26 March: Two former Qadhafi officials, Ali Mayra and Mohamed Ibrahim Momsour, are extradited to Libya from Egypt.

April 2013

- 2 April: The Libyan government challenges the admissibility of the ICC's jurisdiction over al-Senussi.
- 3 April: Egypt denies the extradition request for Ahmed Qaddaf al-Dam, Mu'ammar Qadhafi's cousin. Al-Dam remains in Egypt to stand trial for attempted murder in Cairo.
- 10 April: The UN Security Council's Panel of Experts on Libya release a report detailing how the precipitous spread of weapons from Libya are being used in a number of conflicts in the region, including Mali and Syria.
- 23 April: A bomb attack on the French Embassy in Tripoli destroys the building and injures several guards and visitors. It is the first attack in Tripoli since 2011.
- 28 April: The Benghazi police station is attacked by a car bomb, causing severe damage to the building but no casualties.
- Late April: Armed gunmen occupy the Ministries of Foreign Affairs and Justice in Tripoli in support of proposed law to ban Qadhafi era officials from holding office.

May 2013

- 5 May: The Libyan Parliament votes to ban former Qadhafi officials from holding public office.
- 13 May: A car bomb outside a hospital in central Benghazi kills at least three and injures an estimated 17.

PART ONE

THE LIBYAN CONFLICT IN CONTEXT: HISTORY OF REPRESSION AND
THE AFTERMATH OF REVOLUTION

INTRODUCTION TO PART ONE

Part One of this book is designed to provide the reader with an overview of the Libyan civil war, its causes, its participants, its major events and its aftermath, as well as the NATO intervention, a legal evaluation of the war itself and the accountability measures taken thus far, and the post-conflict period. As such, Part One differs from the localized factual and legal analysis of the various theaters of conflict found in Part Two.

It is impossible to understand Libya and the conflict that embroiled it in 2011 without an appreciation of the country's history, social and economic context, and the multitude of groups and interests at work in the country in February 2011 when the uprising against the Qadhafi regime began. While all armed conflicts have unique histories and causes, Libya's is distinct in a number of significant respects. Accordingly, Part One begins in Chapter I with a survey of Libyan history from its earliest days through the era of Arab domination, Ottoman control, Italian occupation, the formation of the Libyan monarchy in 1951 and the subsequent calamitous rules of King Idris and Mu'ammar Qadhafi.

One of the essential characteristics of Libya is that it has rarely, if ever, had a state in the common sense of the term, having been mostly controlled from afar or brutalized by outsiders, and never had a nation to go along with its state institutions and geographic boundaries. From its earliest days, Libya has been composed of groups of people with divergent histories and practices who were collected into an entity by foreigners. Its Libyan identity has been entirely imposed by external forces and has not developed to date. The primary salient division in Libya has been regional – Tripolitania to the west, Cyrenaica to the east, and Fezzan in the south – and within these regions into further sub-divisions based on social, tribal, political and religious identities. Any expression of these identities was severely suppressed during the four decades of Mu'ammar Qadhafi's rule, however, during which public expression was limited to allegiance to the revolutionary state, and loyalty to the regime was paramount not only for political survival, but also for social advancement and economic well-being. To that end, the regime privileged certain groups while subjugating others, thereby exacerbating existing divisions and fueling frustrations that boiled below the surface. Given the often fractious nature of Libya, it is difficult to speak of "Libyans" the way one might speak of Egyptians or Tunisians, notwithstanding the existence of the Libyan state. This is an issue that continues to befuddle and complicate the post-conflict phase and the country's attempts to rebuild itself.

The central figure in Libya's recent history has undoubtedly been Mu'ammar Qadhafi, the country's longstanding ruler, a man who polarized the population and ultimately served as the catalyst needed to bring together disparate opposition forces into a collective capable of overthrowing him. Qadhafi cast a long shadow over the country that he attempted to engineer in pursuit of his goals and interests. The nature of the 2011 uprising, the formation of the insurgent forces and the unfolding of the conflict was, in many ways, an outgrowth of these past divisions and a reaction to decades of repression under Qadhafi.

The complex social, cultural, economic and political dynamics of Libya under Qadhafi is evident in Chapter II, which identifies the antagonists in the conflict and the course of the conflict itself. The first section of Chapter II outlines the labyrinthine nature of the security forces under Qadhafi's control, which were based on allegiance and personality rather than formal structures and hierarchies. It similarly investigates the composition and makeup of the opposition forces, known as *thuwar*, which were locally organized militia and, similarly to the government's forces, operated outside conventional command structures.

To understand the patchwork quilt of the Qadhafi and *thuwar* forces, it is necessary to understand the privilege system that undergirded Qadhafi's rule: the groups that were privileged under Qadhafi remained loyal to the regime, giving the conflict an ethnic dimension as well. In effect, this meant that those groups that overthrew the regime did not represent all aspects of Libyan society, and certainly did not present a unified vision for Libya beyond the end of dictatorship. After the *thuwar* forces realized their common cause of defeating Qadhafi, these divisions became increasingly evident, as the country became fractionized along the regional, social, tribal, religious and political lines. Furthermore, those groups that supported the regime suffered reprisals after the conflict, an issue that continued well into the post-conflict period. Understanding the regime and *thuwar* forces described in Chapter II also plays an important role in identifying and analyzing the patterns of violence and violations described in Chapter IV, as well as the complex security situation in the post-conflict period, as described in Chapter V. In the wake of the 2011 conflict, the National Transitional Council, the body that assumed power after the fall of Qadhafi, at once tried to contain the power of various *thuwar* militias and absorb them into the new security apparatus, as these militia were the only truly capable fighting force in the country. Nevertheless, the allegiances of these militia invariably lay less with the central government than with the communities and structures out of which they developed.

The second section of Chapter II provides the reader with an overview of the different phases of the conflict, beginning with the protest phase in February 2011, continuing with the armed conflict phase and concluding with the post-Qadhafi phase after November 2011. The incidents described in Chapter II thus provide the reader with the meta-narrative and a global overview of the conflict to allow for a better understanding and contextualization of the individual theaters of military operation discussed in Part Two, as well as the specifics of the NATO intervention discussed in Chapter III and the accountability issues raised in Chapter IV.

Chapter III provides an analysis of the 2011 NATO campaign, known as Operation Unified Protector, with a special emphasis on the enabling Security Council resolution, the legal framework for intervention and an assessment of the particular air strikes carried out by NATO. Acting under the color of Security Council Resolution 1973, participating states involved themselves in the Libyan conflict in a number of ways, including by aiding the opposition political movement, by providing weapons and other materiel, by sharing intelligence, and by training *thuwar* forces on the ground, as well as by carrying out actual air strikes on Qadhafi forces. Invariably, given the wide-ranging nature of the intervention and its incisive impact on the outcome of the conflict, questions arose as to whether NATO violated the Security Council's mandate to protect civilians, in particular after it became clear that certain strikes had hit non-military sites and caused civilian casualties and damage. Chapter III also addresses NATO's failure to fully investigate and account for these strikes and the Security Council's failure to ensure necessary accountability measures. The chapter concludes with an assessment of NATO's need for accountability measures, and the UN Security Council's obligation to ensure these accountability measures are carried out.

Chapter IV contains an overview and assessment of the various accountability and impunity issues that face Libya in the aftermath of the 2011 conflict, and the domestic and international initiatives that have been taken to address them. As is detailed in Part Two, the 2011 conflict resulted in violations by Qadhafi and *thuwar* forces of the various legal regimes that applied to the conflict, namely domestic Libyan laws, international humanitarian law (IHL), international human rights law (IHRL) and international criminal law (ICL).

The particular violations identified in this book are: i) the use of excessive force against protestors and demonstrators; ii) unlawful killings; iii) arbitrary detentions and enforced disappearances; iv) torture and other forms of ill-treatment; v) denial of access to medical treatment; vi) continued restrictions on the freedom of expression; vii) attacks against civilians, civilian objects, protected persons and objects; viii) the prohibited use of weapons; ix) the recruitment of mercenaries; x) violations against specific groups; xi) sexual violence; and xii) the use of children and their treatment in armed conflict. It should be noted, however, that these characterizations are illustrative and not legal in nature, as discussed in Chapter IV.

Given the multitude of challenges facing Libya today, holding individuals accountable for violations remains a significant challenge. Several immediate problems present themselves, from the lack of political will to hold all sides accountable, to the lack of a stable and unified security situation, to a largely ineffective judiciary. For decades, the Qadhafi regime used courts as a tool to attack political opponents. As described in Chapter I, the extent to which any state institution existed during the Qadhafi era, it did so to repress and suppress any form of dissent. The security apparatus, judiciary and legislative bodies all worked to ensure the regime's total control over the population. This led to a deeply entrenched lack of trust in government institutions as a whole, creating an additional challenge to any attempt at legal accountability for past violations. Insofar as there is a Libyan judiciary, it is limited by the capacity of its judges, prosecutors, defense attorneys, investigators and staff, as well as by the lack of an effective, nation-wide security apparatus. Finally, even if the judiciary should wish to hold individuals accountable, the adoption of amnesty laws for *thuwar* seriously constrains its ability to do anything.

With respect to what has been done, Chapter IV reviews the cases against high-level Qadhafi government officials. These include Safi al-Islam Qadhafi and ʿAbdullah al-Senussi, both of whom have been charged by the International Criminal Court with crimes against humanity, but who nevertheless appear to be headed for prosecution in Libya. These figures, along with others from the Qadhafi regime – including Khamis and Muʿtassim Qadhafi, Musa Kusa – played a critical role shaping and carrying out policies during the Qadhafi era. Chapter IV also looks at a number of other important cases against individuals.

Finally, Chapter V looks at the ongoing developments in the post conflict period in Libya and the persistent challenges the country is facing as
it attempts to emerge from civil war and four decades of repression. The
Chapter begins with an assessment of the security challenges facing the
country in the post-conflict period, including the ongoing difficulties it
faces in dealing with heavily armed militia, who have yet to be brought to
heel or disarmed. In the vacuum left by an ineffective central government,
these local militias continue to dominate large swathes of the country and
exert influence even in the capital, where they have besieged and attacked
various ministries to get their way. Similarly, with respect to post-conflict
accountability, many of the militias continue to run their own detention
facilities and have yet to transfer custody to national authorities. Perhaps
the most notable example of this is the continued detention of Saif al-
Islam Qadhafi in Zintan despite ongoing proceedings before the ICC and
a looming domestic trial in Libya.

Perhaps the most pressing security challenge arising out of the post-
conflict era is the proliferation of weapons in the hands of non-state armed
groups and the continued inability of the Libyan government to assert
its authority throughout the country. During the Qadhafi era, the regime
acquired large amounts of conventional and unconventional weapons,
some of which were seized and used by the *thuwar* during the conflict or
left unguarded in the wake of the war. These weapons also included those
supplied by NATO and non-NATO states directly to the rebel groups during the conflict. These weapons have made their way into regional conflicts, including Mali and Syria, thus raising serious security concerns. The
proliferation of weapons and the hardening of some Islamist groups are
challenges in themselves, but are exacerbated by a government that is still
trying to establish itself in a divided society.

Finally, Chapter V evaluates the ongoing legislative and electoral developments, including the 2012 election that saw the rise of moderate parties against all expectations. Problems persist, however, as the General
National Congress, the body that was elected in 2012, has been unable to
build a working consensus and has been forced into various compromises
with *thuwar* militia, including the adoption of a law banning senior officials from the Qadhafi era from holding government positions, a law that
forced out the sitting President and which may cause serious problems
going forward.

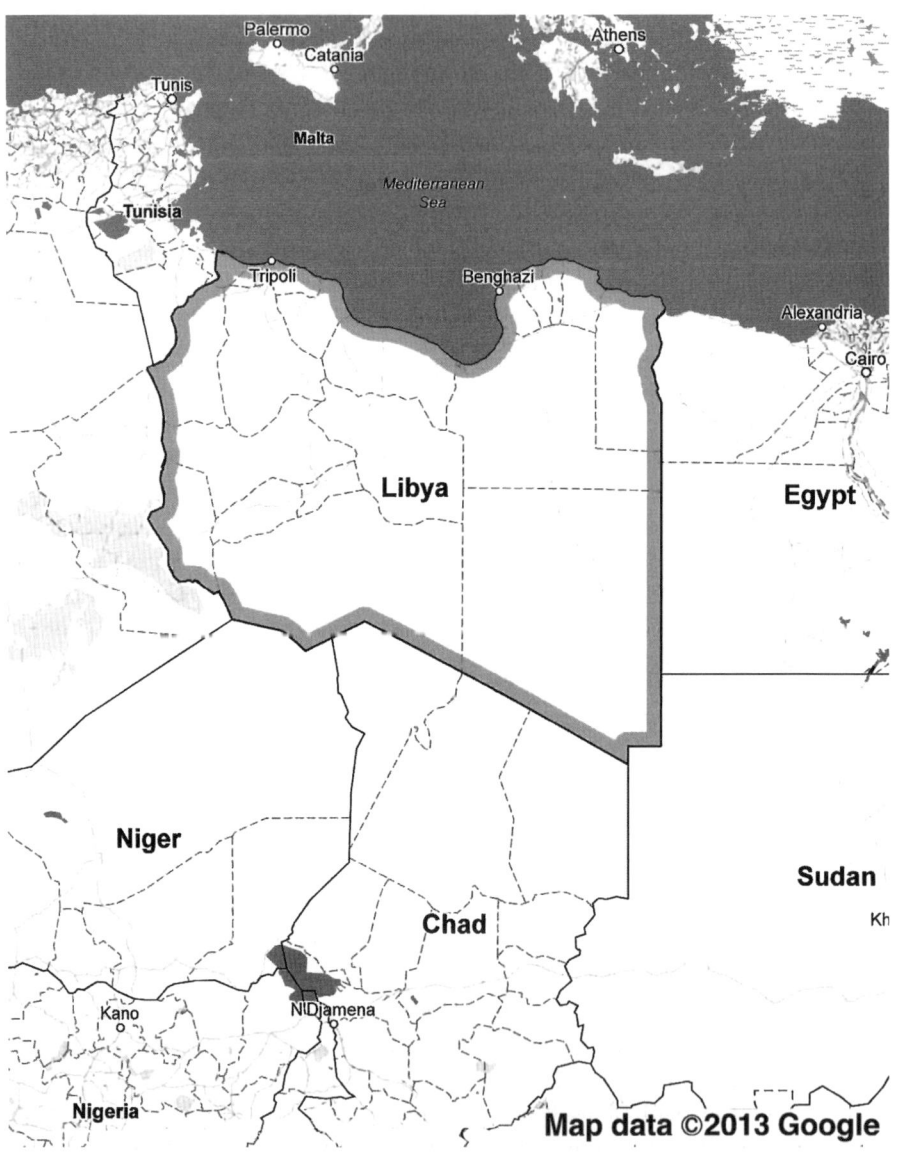

Map 1: Regional map of North Africa (Map data © 2013 Barasoft, Google, Mapa GISrael, ORION-ME, basado en BCN IGN España).

Map data ©2013 Google

Map 2: Map of northern Libya (Map data © 2013 Google).

CHAPTER ONE

HISTORICAL BACKGROUND

1. INTRODUCTION

The history of Libya is characterized by a pattern of external dominance and internal repression that has been met with resistance and rebellion in equal measure. The history of occupation over the territory of modern-day Libya began in the era of Arab domination, and continued through the Ottoman Empire and Italian colonization. Political violence remained a prominent feature of Libyan history before and after independence and the rise of the monarchy. Historical resistance fighters, such as 'Umar al-Mukhtar – leader of the struggle against Italian colonization – remain at the forefront of national consciousness. Resistance in the face of outside threats and internal oppressors brought about cohesion that contributed to the shaping of a nascent Libyan national identity, though it remained an unevenly defined patchwork and separated across regional divides.[1] The path towards independence was influenced by outside powers, and independence took the form of a political solution that imposed unification. The country's regional divisions did not disappear following independence, however; on the contrary, they continued to play an influential role during the government of King Idris, and throughout the Qadhafi era. After independence, marginalization, favoritism, and the practice of internal repression continued, reaching the highest levels and becoming a matter of policy during the Qadhafi years.

The coalescing of rebel groups during the 2011 uprising reflected the historical trend toward national unity taking shape in the face of external and internal oppression. The revolutionary cause transcended regionalism and other divisions to bring together disparate factions in the Cold War and would play a central role in the decision by the international community to intervene militarily in 2011. Correspondingly, the following chapter

---

[1] Historian Dirk Vandewalle argues, "in Libya the focus and rationale for a national identity would only materialize, intermittently and temporarily, when an outside threat appeared imminent." DIRK VANDEWALLE, A HISTORY OF MODERN LIBYA 23 (Cambridge, UK: Cambridge University Press, 2006) [hereinafter "A HISTORY OF MODERN LIBYA"].

pays particular attention to the country's trajectory after 1951, notably the overthrow of the monarchy and the era of Mu'ammar Qadhafi.

Libyan history, which can be divided into basic periods shaped by conquest, occupation, and rebellion, are traced in the sections below. The chapter begins with the ancient period of Berber domination, through to the classical period and the conquests by the Carthaginians, Greeks, Romans and Byzantines (Section 2), then looks at the period of Arab domination, stretching from 642 to 1517, including various Norman and Iberian occupations (Section 3). Next comes the first period of Ottoman domination from 1551 to 1835, including the rise and fall of the Qaramanli Dynasty in Tripolitania during the 18th and early 19th centuries (Section 4), and the second Ottoman domination from 1835 until 1911, including the growth of the Senussiya Order in Cyrenaica (Section 5). The chapter then turns to Italian colonial domination, lasting from 1911 to 1943, in particular the brutal war waged to crush the internal resistance movement and the rise of King Idris al-Senussi (Section 6), and political independence and the monarchy from December 1941 to September 1969, including the transformative discovery of oil (Section 7). The following section considers the rise of Mu'ammar Qadhafi, and the Libyan Arab Republic from September 1969 until March 1977, covering the failed Arab Socialist Union (Section 8), and the Great Socialist People's Libyan Arab Jamahiriyya from March 1977, including the fallout with the Western world. Section 10 analyzes the era of rapprochement with the West from 2001 until the 2011 uprising. The chapter ends with a brief section on the psychology of Qadhafi and a detailed look at the history of involvement of his regime in acts of terrorism.

There are several identifiable threads that run through Libyan history, one of which is the division between the peoples of Tripolitania, Cyrenaica and Fezzan. Not until 1835 did these three provinces begin to merge and a basic common identity emerge. But even this identity was weak and reactive. Well after Libya gained independence in 1951, it remained "a state in a minimalist and territorial sense" largely lacking "a distinct political community."[2] These divisions remained significant throughout the Qadhafi era and were evident during the 2011 war. It was in the eastern city of Benghazi that the uprising began, a city in the oil-rich Cyrenaica province defined by a history of separation and a strong sense of neglect by

---

[2] *Id.* at 73.

the central government, based in Tripolitania. The post-conflict landscape saw the same regional hostilities, stemming from decades of policies that meant the unequal distribution of resources across the provinces, particularly in the southern Fezzan region, the poorest region of the country.

Another thread is that of effective statelessness. A functioning centralized state did not exist until the 19th century, although there had been nominal state control for periods of Libyan history. The Libyan experience with the state has not been positive: the Ottoman state was anemic and more interested in taxation; the Italian state was repressive and brutal; the Kingdom of Libya was an extension of Cyrenaican power and vastly corrupt; and Qadhafi dismantled functioning state institutions and replaced them with a network of informal agencies and paramilitary structures. There has yet to exist a Libyan state that is the product of popular will, with a proper government committed to serving the Libyan people. This trend has left a history of deep distrust among the Libyan citizenry in the state and its governing officials, leading some historians to argue that the Libyan people have long been passive objects rather than active subjects.[3]

The final thread running through Libya's history identified in this chapter is that of entrenched political corruption and violence. Occupation and domination left a legacy of bloodshed that continues to permeate Libyan society today. The Libyan population experienced a campaign of genocide from 1929–1933 under Italian fascist colonial rule, involving concentration camps and mass murder.[4] The post-WWII Kingdom embodied a system of corruption, fueling a revolutionary wave that brought Mu'ammar Qadhafi to power. The country sustained four decades of the Qadhafi regime's internal repression characterized by systematic arbitrary arrests, forced disappearances, assassinations and torture. The prospects for a peaceful future, following a civil war and international intervention, will have to account for a traumatically violent past.

This chapter places modern Libya within the context of this history of oppression and resistance. The use of this historical lens brings into sharp focus the danger of simply glorifying revolution, as past events show that

---

[3] Dirk Vandewalle, *Libya's Revolution in Perspective*, in LIBYA SINCE 1969: QADHAFI'S REVOLUTION REVISITED 9 (Dirk Vandewalle ed., New York, USA: Palgrave McMillan, 2011) [hereinafter "QADHAFI'S REVOLUTION REVISITED"].

[4] As Ali Abdullatif Ahmida argues, at independence, "A Libyan state was created without strong Libyan nationhood." ALI ABDULLATIF AHMIDA, THE MAKING OF MODERN LIBYA: STATE FORMATION, COLONIZATION, AND RESISTANCE 146 (Albany, USA: SUNY Press, 2009) [hereinafter "AHMIDA. THE MAKING OF MODERN LIBYA"].

the overthrow of an oppressive system does not necessarily bring about peace and justice. History provides important lessons for independence and self-governance, such as the 1969 overthrow of King Idris that led to the Qadhafi regime. Qadhafi then institutionalized revolutionary policies that ushered in an era of repression and abuse worse than that which characterized monarchical rule. Understanding the lessons of history is important for Libyan society, its leaders, and all those involved in shaping policies that impact the country's trajectory in the post-revolution era.

2. Ancient Libya: 10th Century bce–642 ce

Historical and archaeological records, dating back to antiquity, show that Libya was once a verdant place with a well-established agricultural base, transformed over time by ecological changes into its current arid state.[5] The historical record indicates a fair amount of agricultural and pastoral wealth in Greek Cyrenaica, particularly in the wool and cattle trade,[6] but as Herodotus's *Histories* relate, by the 5th century bce, Libya was "wholly sand."[7]

As discussed above, Libyan climate and terrain created significant barriers between the three regions that make up modern Libya – Tripolitania, Cyrenaica and Fezzan – severely limiting interaction between the three areas. For instance, there is a nearly 500-km/300 mile stretch of desert between Misrata in eastern Tripolitania and Ajdabiya in western Cyrenaica. Equally imposing terrain and distances separate both Tripolitania and Cyrenaica from Fezzan. The conditions in the ancient and classical periods were such that travel times between the three were measured in weeks and months rather than days.[8]

Accordingly, the three regions turned their attention not towards each other, but towards their neighbors: Tripolitania towards Tunisia, Cyrenaica towards Egypt and Fezzan towards Sub-Saharan Africa, in particular Niger and the Lake Chad region.[9] As a result of these conditions these regional

---

[5] *See generally*, Ahmida, The Making of Modern Libya, *supra* note 4.

[6] Geoff Simons, Libya: The Struggle for Survival 94 (New York, USA: St. Martin's Press, 1996) [hereinafter, "Simons, Libya: The Struggle for Survival"]. *See also* Homer, The Odyssey (Bernard Knox ed., Penguin Classics, 2006).

[7] Vandewalle, A History of Modern Libya, *supra* note 1.

[8] *Id.* at 15.

[9] *Id.*

territories developed much stronger political, social, and economic ties with their neighbors than with one another.[10]

During this period, no powerful centralized "Libyan" state emerged like those of its more recognizable Egyptian or Carthaginian neighbors. The powers that did arise, for instance the Garamantes of Fezzan or Libu of Cyrenaica, were localized. A unified state encompassing Tripolitania, Cyrenaica and Fezzan made no economic, social or political sense given the circumstances and landscape of northern Africa at the time.

Very little is known about the earliest inhabitants of Libya, as most of the historical record is the product of observations by Egyptian, Greek and Arab outsiders.[11] The earliest mention of the inhabitants of modern-day Libya appears in the Egyptian records, and describes the Tjehenu and Tjemehu to the West. These early peoples may have been the antecedents of the Libu and Meshwesh cultures, although the historical record is patchy and it is difficult to definitively determine the relationship between them.[12] There are also records of the Garamantes of Fezzan, who established themselves around 1000 BCE and who, despite their relative isolation, resisted continual attempts by outsiders, particularly the Romans, to conquer them.[13] It was only in the aftermath of the Arab invasion in the 7th century that the last remnants of the Garamantes disappeared.[14] Finally, ancient historians also recorded the presence of "Ethiopians" in southern Cyrenaica, who may have been the forbearers of the modern Sudanese.[15]

The first continual foreign presence in the Libyan region came with the arrival of Phoenicians, who in the 9th century BCE occupied the area, including many of the coastal towns of Tripolitania, and founded Carthage in 814 BCE in modern day Tunisia. The Carthaginians eventually came to rule over much of North Africa, including Tripolitania, introducing more intensive agricultural practices for export.[16] As a regional trading power, the Carthaginians developed an extensive trade network with the indigenous populations throughout North Africa, although they themselves

---

[10] AHMIDA, THE MAKING OF MODERN LIBYA, *supra* note 4 at 12.

[11] Richard Smith, *What Happened to the Ancient Libyans? Chasing Sources across the Sahara from Herodotus to Ibn Khaldun*, 14 J. WORLD HIST. 459, 461 [hereinafter "Smith, *What Happened to the Ancient Libyans?*"].

[12] *Id.* at 459, 460–461.

[13] SIMONS, LIBYA: THE STRUGGLE FOR SURVIVAL, *supra* note 6 at 93, 98.

[14] *Id.* at 100.

[15] Smith, *What Happened to the Ancient Libyans?*, *supra* note 11 at 14.

[16] SIMONS, LIBYA: THE STRUGGLE FOR SURVIVAL, *supra* note 6 at 93.

stayed along the coast.[17] Carthaginian power waned in the aftermath of
the Punic Wars, with Rome entering the vacuum and assuming control
over the majority of western Libya in the 1st century BCE and control over
the rest of the territory a century later.[18] The Romans incorporated the
Phoenician cities Sabrata, Oea and Leptis Magna into a single entity in
146 BCE, adopting the name Tripoli (or three cities).[19]

Roman rule over North Africa was, as with Phoenician rule, limited
to economically productive areas along the coast, and concentrated economically on agricultural products. Perhaps the most important Roman
import was the camel, which was effectively introduced into inland trade,
greatly increasing travel capabilities.[20] Camels only came into broad use,
however, after the Arab conquest several centuries later, becoming the
primary mechanism for regional trade and along the great trans-Saharan
routes.[21]

Roman administration was limited to the coast, enforced with a strong
military dispatched to control the indigenous Berber communities and
prevent their free movement into Roman areas.[22] Roman control over
North Africa dissolved in the 4th century with the general breakdown of
the Roman Empire, allowing for increased Berber influence to move from
inland regions to the economically valuable coast.

Cyrenaica did not come under Phoenician or Roman control, but rather
grew as a Greek colony from the 7th century BCE. Cyrenaica itself takes
its name from the original Greek colony at Cyrene. Like the Phoenicians,
the Greeks developed significant inland trade routes, but were neither
able to fully establish themselves nor to keep out other foreign invaders.
Cyrenaica came under the control of Alexander of Macedon, otherwise
known as Alexander the Great, and upon his death, Cyrenaica was given,
along with Egypt, to Ptolemy.[23] Greek influence, however, persisted until
the 6th century CE.[24]

---

[17] *Id.* at 92–93.

[18] *Id.* at 99–101.

[19] *Id.* at 93.

[20] AHMIDA, THE MAKING OF MODERN LIBYA, *supra* note 4 at 18.

[21] Smith, *What Happened to the Ancient Libyans?, supra* note 11 at 459, 493.

[22] Eduardo Manzano Moreno, *The Iberian Peninsula and North Africa, in* THE NEW CAM-
BRIDGE HISTORY OF ISLAM VOLUME 1: THE FORMATION OF THE ISLAMIC WORLD SIXTH TO
ELEVENTH CENTURIES 581 (Chase F. Robinson ed., Cambridge University Press, 2010).

[23] SIMONS, LIBYA: THE STRUGGLE FOR SURVIVAL, *supra* note 6 at 93–94.

[24] *Id.* at 99.

After the split of the Roman Empire in 395 CE, Cyrenaica remained, by dint of its connection to Egypt, allied with the Eastern Roman Empire under Byzantine rule. Tripolitania remained under the control of the Western Roman Empire, although as the fortunes of Rome faded, it first came under the control of Vandal invaders and later the Byzantines.[25] The Byzantine Empire established control over all of modern-day Libyan territory after the Justinian conquest of North Africa in the 6th century. While the Byzantines, and the Vandals before them, were able to exert control and turn tribes against each other, neither was able to establish a strong base. Within a century Byzantium was itself displaced by Arab invaders in 642, heralding the introduction of Islam to the region.[26]

3. The Arab Domination Period: 642–1517 CE

Arab forces conquered Cyrenaica in 642 and Fezzan in 663, having subdued Byzantine Egypt just a few years before.[27] After this conquest, Cyrenaica was annexed to Egypt.[28] Muslim forces also took over Tripolitania from Egyptian control, but retreated after assuring the area's allegiance.[29] As frustration grew among the indigenous Berber population at their treatment by successive Roman and Byzantine occupiers, they established a connection with the new Arab arrivals in a shared desire to remove the occupiers from the West.[30] Cyrenaican tribal leaders made deals with their Arab counterparts, offering their allegiance in exchange for assurance of a certain degree of local control.[31] Tripolitania finally came under full control of Arab forces by the turn of the 8th century, in the wake of a movement to overtake the entire Maghreb region.[32]

---

[25] *Id.* at 101.

[26] Moreno, *The Iberian Peninsula and North Africa, supra* note 22 at 581–582.

[27] *Id.* at 102.

[28] Michael Brett, *Egypt in* THE NEW CAMBRIDGE HISTORY OF ISLAM VOLUME 1: THE FORMATION OF THE ISLAMIC WORLD SIXTH TO ELEVENTH CENTURIES 544 (Chase F. Robinson ed., Cambridge, UK: Cambridge University Press, 2010).

[29] Moreno, *The Iberian Peninsula and North Africa, supra* note 22 at 583.

[30] However, there is evidence as well that the Arab invaders both treated Libyan Berbers harshly and demanded the extraction of taxes, which was often accompanied by trading in child slaves. *Id.* at 590.

[31] *Id.* at 582–583.

[32] Paul M. Cobb, *The Empire in Syria, in* THE NEW CAMBRIDGE HISTORY OF ISLAM VOLUME 1: THE FORMATION OF THE ISLAMIC WORLD SIXTH TO ELEVENTH CENTURIES 705–763 (Chase F. Robinson ed., Cambridge, UK: Cambridge University Press, 2010).

The region quickly adopted Islam, and while there was no shortage of
religious differences and conflicts – especially between the Shiʻa Fatamids
of Egypt and the emerging Sunni of Libya – the process of integration
between Arabs and the local Berber tribes was relatively smooth and fast.
By the end of the 14th century, the people of Tripolitania, Cyrenaica and
Fezzan had adopted Islam and Arabic was widely spoken.[33] This process
of integration accelerated after the 11th century when the Bani Hilal and
Bani Sulaym tribes migrated from Egypt into the eastern Maghreb.[34] The
ability of the Bani Hilal and Sulaym to integrate may have been in part a
result of the similarity of their customs stemming from their own nomadic
origins in the Arab peninsula.[35]

The historical record provides varying descriptions of the entry of the
Bani Hilal into Tripolitania and the Bani Sulaym into Cyrenaica. Some historical accounts, following the work of Ibn Khaldun, describe their entry
as a military response by the Fatamid Caliphate to defeat a Sunni rebellion, with the Bani Hilal and Bani Sulaym tasked with subduing the native
population. Other accounts indicate that the Bani Hilal and Bani Sulaym
settled in Libya due to deteriorating economic and ecological conditions
in Egypt, and are better understood as migrants rather than mercenaries
or military fighters.[36]

The Bani Hilal were settlers, much like their Phoenician, Greek and
Roman predecessors. The difference, however, was the scale of the population influx: roughly 200,000 families moved into Western Libya from
Egypt, coming to constitute a very significant proportion of the local
population.[37] Consequently, the modern Libyan population is thought to
be a mix of the indigenous Berber populations and invading Arab tribes,
as well as the migrants that followed. By the 19th century, the indigenous
communities and Arab tribes had largely merged into the mixed Arab-
Berber population that largely exists today, with the exception of a number of Berber communities in Tripolitania.[38]

While there was antagonism between the indigenous Berbers and
Arabs, the Arab invasion precipitated a significant change in the politi-

---

[33] AHMIDA, THE MAKING OF MODERN LIBYA, *supra* note 4 at 17.

[34] VANDEWALLE, A HISTORY OF MODERN LIBYA, *supra* note 1.

[35] AHMIDA, THE MAKING OF MODERN LIBYA, *supra* note 4 at 17.

[36] *Id.*; SIMONS, LIBYA: THE STRUGGLE FOR SURVIVAL, *supra* note 6 at 102–103.

[37] SIMONS, LIBYA: THE STRUGGLE FOR SURVIVAL, *supra* note 6 at 102.

[38] VANDEWALLE, A HISTORY OF MODERN LIBYA, *supra* note 1 at 16; AHMIDA, THE MAK-
ING OF MODERN LIBYA, *supra* note 4 at 46.

cal, economic and social makeup of the Maghreb, allowing for greater interaction and trade than previously existed.[39] During the course of Arab rule, the trans-Saharan trade expanded dramatically from Tripolitania through Fezzan, and from Cyrenaica into sub-Saharan Africa, with two of the four great trans-Saharan trade routes originating in Tripoli and one in Benghazi.[40] The growth of the trans-Saharan caravan trade was due in large part to the introduction of commercial law into the region and the expansion of longer-distance trade routes. Under the Phoenicians, as there were no political or legal controls permitting long distance trade, Greek and Roman trade routes had operated as relays, with goods travelling smaller distances and sold along until reaching their final destination.

Arab control of the region was not continuous or harmonious, and there were regular local insurrections, fierce competition between various political factions and numerous incursions by European powers into Tripolitania and Cyrenaica during the Crusades.[41] The first notable European incursion was the Norman conquest of Tripoli in 1146. Having conquered the Emirate of Sicily, the Normans crossed the Mediterranean, first taking Malta and then the coastal region of Tripolitania. Norman control, however, lasted a brief 12 years until the Almohads of Morocco reclaimed the city and the region.[42] In the early 16th century, Spanish forces again captured Tripoli, holding the city and surrounding areas until 1551, when Ottoman forces captured Tripolitania, effectively unifying the Maghreb with Egypt and the Eastern Mediterranean under their rule.[43] After the establishment of Ottoman control in the middle of the 16th century European powers would be effectively locked out of the Maghreb until the rise of European colonialism in the 19th century.

---

[39] Smith, *What Happened to the Ancient Libyans?*, *supra* note 11 at 459, 471.

[40] SIMONS, LIBYA: THE STRUGGLE FOR SURVIVAL, *supra* note 6 at 103; AHMIDA, THE MAKING OF MODERN LIBYA, *supra* note 4.

[41] Michael Brett, *The Central Lands of North Africa and Sicily, until the Beginning of the Almohad Period, in* THE NEW CAMBRIDGE HISTORY OF ISLAM VOLUME 2: THE WESTERN ISLAMIC WORLD ELEVENTH TO EIGHTEENTH CENTURIES 48, 59–61 (Maribel Fiero ed., Cambridge, UK: Cambridge University Press, 2010); SIMONS, LIBYA: THE STRUGGLE FOR SURVIVAL, *supra* note 6 at 103.

[42] Michael Brett, *The Central Lands of North Africa and Sicily, until the Beginning of the Almohad Period, supra* note 41 at 59; MICHAEL DUMPER AND BRUCE STANLEY, CITIES OF THE MIDDLE EAST AND NORTH AFRICA: A HISTORICAL ENCYCLOPEDIA 367 (ABC-CLIO, 2006); AHMIDA, THE MAKING OF MODERN LIBYA, *supra* note 4 at 46.

[43] AHMIDA, THE MAKING OF MODERN LIBYA, *supra* note 4 at 22; SIMONS, LIBYA: THE STRUGGLE FOR SURVIVAL, *supra* note 6 at 103–104.

4. The First Ottoman Domination and the Qaramanli Dynasty:
1551–1835

Cyrenaica had long been linked to Egypt politically, economically and socially, and accordingly, when the Ottomans captured Egypt in 1517 they continued on into Cyrenaica with relative ease.[44] The Ottoman conquest of Tripolitania was driven in part by the need to push out the Christian knights who controlled both Malta and Tripoli – and who used Malta as a major base for piracy against Ottoman shipping – as well as the search for taxable lands.[45] The Ottomans were at the time engaged in a protracted war with the Hapsburgs in Europe and were in need of funds. Extensive administrative control and the consolidation of its dominion over the Maghreb were not part of the Ottoman government's designs. Ottoman rule of Libya was "slight and nominal" and consisted mostly of controlling the coast and extracting tribute for the Ottoman government in Istanbul.[46]

Accordingly, Ottoman rule in Libya was not consolidated and remained concentrated in those areas where the potential for tax collection was greatest. The interaction between Libyans and the Ottoman state was overwhelmingly driven by forcible tax collection.[47] The Ottoman presence moved inland and into Fezzan coming into contact with the Sultanate of Awlad Muhammad, an important trading state established by a family of nobility from Fezzan that survived until the second Ottoman period in the 19th century.[48] During the first Ottoman occupation, Awlad Muhammad alternated between paying taxes and opposing the attempts of Ottoman forces to collect tribute.[49]

The historical record documents the disproportionate use of military force by Ottoman governors against the native Arab-Berber population,

---

[44] Vandewalle, A History of Modern Libya, *supra* note 1 at 16.

[45] Colin Imber, *The Ottoman Empire (tenth/sixteenth century), in* The New Cambridge History of Islam Volume 2: The Western Islamic World Eleventh to Eighteenth Centuries 332, 341 (Maribel Fierro ed., Cambridge, UK: Cambridge University Press, 2010); Ahmida, The Making of Modern Libya, *supra* note 4 at 20–22.

[46] Vandewalle, A History of Modern Libya, *supra* note 1 at 16; Ahmida, The Making of Modern Libya, *supra* note 4 at 22.

[47] Simons, Libya: The Struggle for Survival, *supra* note 6 at 104–105; Vandewalle, A History of Modern Libya, *supra* note 1 at 16; Ahmida, The Making of Modern Libya, *supra* note 4 at 16.

[48] Ahmida, The Making of Modern Libya, *supra* note 4 at 22; H.J. Fisher, *The Eastern Maghrib and the Central Sudan, in* 3 The Cambridge History of Africa 314 (Roland Oliver ed., Cambridge, UK: Cambridge University Press, 1977).

[49] Ahmida, The Making of Modern Libya, *supra* note 4 at 22.

involving occasional acts of terror combined with diplomacy designed to play various tribes against each other. During the Ottoman period, the coastal mercantile class also became increasingly alienated from the local population, leading to further social discord and the exclusion of most locals in the organization and administration of Ottoman rule.[50] Ottoman control, like that of most of its predecessors, was limited to the coastal areas.

Beyond ensuring the remittance of taxes, the territories in the Maghreb were of little interest to the Ottoman government and were largely ignored. Remnants of the substantial military forces sent to oust European forces from North Africa took advantage of this general disinterest at the center of the Ottoman Empire, and their leaders began asserting regional autonomy in the wake of the gradual distancing of the colonies from the center.

In Libya, these conditions led to a declaration of independence in 1711 by the Ottoman governor in Tripoli, Ahmad Bay Qaramanli. His successors secured recognition from Istanbul, and later extended control over parts of Cyrenaica and Fezzan.[51] In general, however, the Qaramanli did not have the capacity to engage the Awlad Muhammad in Fezzan or incorporate the tribes of Cyrenaica into its fold. As with its Ottoman predecessors, the successive rulers of the Qaramanli Dynasty either granted local control to powerful tribal leaders in exchange for a portion of their taxable income or militarily subdued those tribes that refused to cooperate.[52] Outside of Tripoli, Qaramanli state power was therefore minimal and where it did exist, purely military.

Beyond internal taxation and control of trans-Saharan trade routes, the Qaramanli raised funds through the taxation of shipping routes.[53] This was especially contentious, as the increasingly formidable Qaramanli navy taxed all ships passing through its controlled waters, capturing and holding those ships that did not pay tribute. This policy brought the Qaramanli into open conflict with the United States during the Barbary Wars as well as with Europe, which in 1815 outlawed piracy, including

---

[50] SIMONS, LIBYA: THE STRUGGLE FOR SURVIVAL, *supra* note 6 at 105.

[51] VANDEWALLE, A HISTORY OF MODERN LIBYA, *supra* note 1 at 16–17; RONALD BRUCE ST. JOHN, LIBYA AND THE UNITED STATES: TWO CENTURIES OF STRIFE 20 (Philadelphia, USA: University of Pennsylvania Press, 2002).

[52] AHMIDA, THE MAKING OF MODERN LIBYA, *supra* note 4 at 23.

[53] *Id.* at 26.

Qaramanli practices, and the slave trade.[54] These changes proved fatal to the Qaramanli state. After reaching the apex of its power at the turn of the 19th century, the Qaramanli Dynasty rapidly faded, and by 1835 the break-away Ottoman province was again brought into the empire's fold. As with its predecessor states, neither the first Ottoman period nor the Qaramanli Dynasty produced any internal cohesion, or any semblance of a nation. While both engaged in trade and the Qaramanli engaged in power politics with various European states, these governments did not engage in any significant administration or regulation of their territories and certainly did not build a local political community or nation.

5. THE SECOND OTTOMAN DOMINATION: 1835–1911

Qaramanli rule came to an end in 1835 when Ottoman forces reasserted their influence over the region, and due to conflict with the United States. The impetus for Ottoman reoccupation was in part to curtail Qaramanli naval practices – which were considered piratical by the Europeans and the United States – and to stem increasing European colonial interest.[55]

Ottoman forces waged three military campaigns to subdue Libya, but were unable to establish full control over Tripolitania and Fezzan until 1858, Cyrenaica would never prove wholly governable.[56] Indeed, in Cyrenaica the Ottomans were only able to establish lasting control over four coastal towns, while the inland remained, for all intents and purposes, free of Ottoman control.

The new governors in Tripoli engaged in a concerted campaign to consolidate power, particularly over Tripolitania. After 1835, Ottoman control over trade routes into the Sahara were further expanded and grew significantly until displaced by Atlantic maritime trade, which was significantly cheaper than overland routes to the Mediterranean.[57] Beyond cutting Ottoman tax revenue, the rise of Atlantic maritime shipping had a devastating effect on the nascent mercantile class in Tripoli, leaving Libya without an indigenous bourgeoisie. Unlike many other colonized states,

---

[54] AHMIDA, THE MAKING OF MODERN LIBYA, *supra* note 4 at 27; VANDEWALLE, A HISTORY OF MODERN LIBYA, *supra* note 1 at 16–17.

[55] VANDEWALLE, A HISTORY OF MODERN LIBYA, *supra* note 1 at 17.

[56] *Id.* at 17; AHMIDA, THE MAKING OF MODERN LIBYA, *supra* note 4 at 79.

[57] AHMIDA, THE MAKING OF MODERN LIBYA, *supra* note 4 at 31–32, 34. Trade disruption due to maritime trade was significant in Tripolitania and Fezzan, but less so in Cyrenaica which traded more with the Sudan and Chad than with West Africa.

the stillborn mercantile class in Libya was accordingly unable to act as a unifying force or counterbalance the persistent power of tribes. This issue, along with the lack of an indigenous administrative corps, would be exacerbated under Italian rule and ultimately prove critical after independence.

The second period of Ottoman rule saw the first attempt by any single power to administer the entire territory of modern-day Libya as a unified state. It was motivated in large part by a larger economic shift in the Ottoman Empire towards capitalism. This necessitated the introduction of educational and legal systems, land registration, agricultural reform and development of infrastructure and, perhaps most importantly, the imposition of direct taxation without the use of feudal or tribal intermediaries.[58] These efforts were not well received, and local resistance to these measures was significant, particularly among the tribal intermediaries who had previously collected taxes and paid off the central Ottoman and Qaramanli leadership. This was especially true in Cyrenaica, where Ottoman forces controlled only Benghazi, Al-Marj, Darna and Al-Qayab, and were effectively prevented from collecting taxes by the tribes and the Senussiya – a Cyrenaican political and economic community that emerged in the 1840s.[59]

Ultimately, Libya proved "rebellious, difficult to govern and economically of little importance to Constantinople."[60] Indeed, the Ottoman government was unable to afford or justify outright military subjection of the tribes in the interior.[61] The government of the Ottoman Empire was also unable to find capable colonial officers willing to administer Libya; over the nearly eight decades after re-establishing control in 1835, more than 30 different leaders were dispatched to govern the territory.[62] The Ottomans also refrained from investing significant numbers of troops, focusing rather on the on-going conflicts in Europe. In a country where military might was the key to power, the bulk of the empire's troops were stationed in Tripolitanian coastal positions, leaving only a minimal military presence in the rest of the country – there were only 300 Ottoman soldiers, for instance, in the southern region of Fezzan.[63]

---

[58] *Id.* at 34, 58; VANDEWALLE, A HISTORY OF MODERN LIBYA, *supra* note 1 at 20.
[59] AHMIDA, THE MAKING OF MODERN LIBYA, *supra* note 4 at 74–75.
[60] VANDEWALLE, A HISTORY OF MODERN LIBYA, *supra* note 1 at 18.
[61] AHMIDA, THE MAKING OF MODERN LIBYA, *supra* note 4 at 51.
[62] VANDEWALLE, A HISTORY OF MODERN LIBYA, *supra* note 1 at 17.
[63] AHMIDA, THE MAKING OF MODERN LIBYA, *supra* note 4 at 51.

Despite the relative unimportance of Libya compared to other territories to either the Ottomans or to various European powers, the territory had symbolic and geographic significance. For the Ottomans, reasserting control over Libya was a mechanism for protecting the empire's gradual decline in power in North Africa and for collecting taxes urgently needed in other parts of the empire. For European states, North Africa was a means of extracting resources. For Italy, in particular, Tripolitania was a piece of readily available land to its immediate south that would relieve internal demographic problems and allow the fledgling Italian nation to recall earlier glory.

While the 1884–1885 Berlin Conference (the conference held in Germany to negotiate colonization and trade in Africa) did not assign Libya to any of the European states, North Africa was already divided between the various European powers by the beginning of the 1880s. France seized Algeria in 1830 and Tunisia in 1881, Britain took control of Egypt in 1882, and Morocco was recognized as within France's sphere of influence. After the establishment of French control of Tunisia in 1881, Libya remained the only "unclaimed" North African territory.[64]

Of singular importance to Libyan history was the emergence of the Senussiya Order during the second Ottoman occupation. The Senussiya were a Sufi political, social and economic movement based in Cyrenaica that over the course of the 19th century spread into eastern Algeria, western Egypt, northern Sudan and northern Chad. Like many of the Islamic revivalist movements in the 19th century, the Senussiya arose in response to the power vacuum left by the decline of the Ottomans and the encroachment of Europeans on Muslim lands.[65]

At the heart of the Senussiya was its founder, Sayyid Muhammad ibn 'Ali al-Senussi, an Algerian-born cleric and intellectual who had studied in his home country, as well as Morocco, Egypt and Saudi Arabia, lastly under the tutelage of the Sufi reformer Idris al-Fasi. Al-Senussi, who claimed descent from the prophet, settled in Cyrenaica in 1842 and soon gained a following among Cyrenaicans, both due to his ability to preach

---

[64] Vandewalle, A History of Modern Libya, *supra* note 1 at 11.

[65] Knut S. Vikør, *Sudan, Somalia and the Maghreb to the end of the First World War, in* The New Cambridge History of Islam, Volume 5: The Islamic World in the Age of Western Dominance 126 (Francis Robinson ed., Cambridge, UK: Cambridge University Press, 2010); Ahmida, The Making of Modern Libya, *supra* note 4 at 87; Vandewalle, A History of Modern Libya, *supra* note 1 at 19.

a simplified and accessible form of Islam and by minimizing inter-tribal conflict through a system of lodges he established.[66]

Al-Senussi, who would become known as the "Grand Senussi," had originally intended to establish himself in his Algerian homeland. However, by the time he left the Arabian Peninsula in 1837 after Al-Fasi's death, Algeria had been colonized by France. Egypt proved unreceptive to his heterodox teachings and Tripolitania's Ottoman government, while not effective overall, was strong enough to resist his alternative models of social and political organization.[67] Consequently, in 1842 Al-Senussi established himself in the Cyrenaican interior and began building his revivalist movement there.[68]

The Senussiya philosophy was built upon austerity, morality and anticolonial resistance, fused with a system of personal and inter-tribal support and solidarity.[69] Al-Senussi himself curried favor among the Cyrenaican tribes because he was a deeply religious intellectual who claimed to be a descendant of the prophet. His success was also significantly based on his ability to foster peace among Cyrenaican tribes, something he was able to do by showing the benefits of tribal cooperation, whether in the form of trade or in their increased capacity for resistance. That he was an outsider unaffected by a perceived bias towards any one tribe made this task easier.[70]

Al-Senussi's ideology resonated among the nomadic and semi-nomadic peoples of Cyrenaica and spread quickly throughout the Fezzan province, as well as parts of Sudan and Chad. It was not well received in "cosmopolitan" and settled areas like Tripolitania, where systems of government already existed.

At the center of the Senussiya movement was a system of Senussi lodges, designed as meeting places to address both the religious and worldly affairs of the communities in which they operated. All followers of Al-Senussi were required not only to perform strict religious duties, but also to study, train for defense and engage in trade.[71] The lodges themselves

---

[66] AHMIDA, THE MAKING OF MODERN LIBYA, *supra* note 4 at 86–87, 92.

[67] *Id.* at 88.

[68] *Id.* at 89.

[69] *Id.* at 91; VANDEWALLE, A HISTORY OF MODERN LIBYA, *supra* note 1 at 19.

[70] AHMIDA, THE MAKING OF MODERN LIBYA, *supra* note 4 at 92.

[71] Ahmad Dallal, *The Origins and Early Development of Islamic Reform, in* THE NEW CAMBRIDGE HISTORY OF ISLAM, VOLUME 6: MUSLIMS AND MODERNITY CULTURE AND SOCIETY SINCE 1800 137 (Robert Hefner ed., Cambridge, UK: Cambridge University Press, 2010).

were built at the intersection of tribal borders in order to gain maximum
exposure and facilitate cross-tribal interaction.

Senussi lodges served as religious centers and schools for the local communities, and also as quasi-judicial centers where Senussiya leaders mediated disputes between the various tribes.[72] The lodges, in effect, served
as community centers for a committed and disciplined following. Al-
Senussi was a proponent of self-determination and an outspoken critic of
foreign encroachment, particularly by non-Muslims. Having seen what
happened to his native Algeria, he attached military training institutes to
each lodge, creating a formidable armed force by the 1870s.[73] The movement became increasingly militarized following conflict with French colonial forces that sought to oust the Senussiya from Chad at the turn of the
20th Century.[74]

The Senussiya operated carefully and below the surface of formal tribal
affairs and functional Ottoman control. The Order worked hard to create
trans-tribal identities, promote inter-tribal fraternity, and minimize existing hierarchies and purely tribal identities. It also sought to secure growth
in eastern trans-Saharan trade and ease tensions between the tribes,
especially with regard to access to water sources.[75] Ultimately, power was
shared in most communities between the local leader and the Senussi
lodge leader. The lodges were "integrated into local communities but also
formed a coherent whole which shared economic interests, patterns of
social and political organisation and authority, as well as religious doctrine and practice. The lodges mediated between tribes and, more important, provided organisational principles that superseded tribal loyalties."[76]

In this way, the Order was able to use its trans-tribal identity to become
a powerful political, economic and social force not only in Cyrenaica, but
also in Fezzan, Sudan, Chad, western Egypt, parts of Tripolitania and
eastern Algeria.[77] By the 1870s, the Senussiya had built a *de facto* state in
Cyrenaica, although the territory remained *de jure* a part of the Ottoman
Empire.[78] Al-Senussi himself tolerated the Ottomans, although he was not

---

[72] AHMIDA, THE MAKING OF MODERN LIBYA, *supra* note 4 at 92.

[73] *Id.* at 88, 97.

[74] Vikør, *Sudan, Somalia and the Maghreb to the end of the First World War, supra* note
65 at 127.

[75] *Id.* at 125; AHMIDA, THE MAKING OF MODERN LIBYA, *supra* note 4 at 78.

[76] Dallal, *The Origins and Early Development of Islamic Reform, supra* note 71 at 138.

[77] Vikør, *Sudan, Somalia and the Maghreb to the end of the First World War, supra* note
65 at 126; AHMIDA, THE MAKING OF MODERN LIBYA, *supra* note 4 at 95.

[78] AHMIDA, THE MAKING OF MODERN LIBYA, *supra* note 4 at 93.

friendly towards them, both because of their anemic response to European encroachment into North Africa, and out of a sense of Arab nationalism that rejected the notion that either a Turk or a non-descendent of the
prophet could lead the Muslim peoples.[79]

Although Al-Senussi and his successors were officially the heads only
of the Senussiya Order, they slowly established themselves as the *de facto*
leaders of the Cyrenaican tribes.[80] Indeed, the Grand Senussi's grandson,
Idris, would rise to become first the Emir of Cyrenaica in 1920, then Emir
of Tripolitania in 1922 and finally King of Libya at independence in 1951.

The Senussiya would also produce the bulk of anti-Italian resistance
after 1911. Senussiya fighters resisted Italian colonization for more than
20 years in a variety of ways, especially under the leadership of 'Umar al-
Mukhtar who would go on to occupy a central place in the Libyan imagination, providing a symbolic reference point for both Mu'ammar Qadhafi
and his opponents.

6. ITALIAN COLONIAL DOMINATION AND THE SHAPING OF THE LIBYAN NATION: 1911–1943

6.1. *Occupation and Resistance*

Italian claims on North Africa in the modern period date to the 1830s,
when early Italian nationalists started agitating for annexation of Libya. In
1838, Giuseppe Mazzini, a prominent republican, declared in no uncertain
terms that "North Africa must belong to Italy."[81] Mazzini's views became
ubiquitous in Italy, especially after unification of the country in 1861.

Italian claims were grounded in part by invoking a Roman imperial
past. Furthermore, with France controlling much of North Africa, Britain – the dominant naval power – in control of Egypt, and the Ottomans
holding sway over the eastern Mediterranean, Italy sought to protect
itself from being "squeezed" in the Mediterranean. Italy's colonial thirst
for Libya was also fueled by the desire to diminish internal Italian political
pressures, including suffrage and the division of power between northern
industrialists and southern large landholders.[82] The annexation of Libya

---

[79] *Id.* at 89–90.

[80] *Id.* at 101.

[81] SIMONS, LIBYA: THE STRUGGLE FOR SURVIVAL, *supra* note 6 at 103, 110.

[82] AHMIDA, THE MAKING OF MODERN LIBYA, *supra* note 4 at 103–104; SIMONS, LIBYA:
THE STRUGGLE FOR SURVIVAL, *supra* note 6 at 110.

was seen as a way not only to project power and reclaim national honor in the wake of unification, but also to ease political tensions and relocate landless peasants from the south.

Italy began its policy of "peaceful penetration" into Libya in the 1880s, engaging in industrial development, property development, and investment banking.[83] Engineers and planners were sent to study the possibility of agricultural development, while others worked on opening various Italian newspapers and cultural and educational institutions.[84] Italian migrants started crossing the Mediterranean for Tripolitania in a steady trickle.

On the diplomatic front, in 1899 Italy secured French and British acknowledgement that Libya lay within its sphere of influence.[85] Within the next decade, the Italian government struck agreements with France, Britain, Germany and Russia recognizing Italy's claim to Tripolitania, Cyrenaica and Fezzan.[86] By the time of the 1911 military invasion of Tripolitania, Italy had succeeded in laying the economic and political foundations for annexation and the transformation of Libya into Italy's so-called "fourth shore."

Popular clamor for the annexation of Libya increased in Italy during the first decade of the 20th century, as it began preparing for the military conquest of Libya. The Ottomans responded to these Italian moves by dispatching a supply ship loaded with guns and ammunition to Tripoli in September 1911, an act Rome proclaimed would destabilize the region and constitute a threat to the Italians of Libya.[87] Accordingly, on 26 September the Italian government declared its intention to annex Tripolitania and Cyrenaica, rejecting the Ottoman government's offer to peacefully transfer control.

Italian forces invaded and occupied Tripoli, Benghazi, Darna, Khums and Tobruq in October 1911. Although Italy declared its takeover of Tripolitania and Cyrenaica on 5 November 1911 and formal annexation on 25 February 1912, Libya remained largely beyond its control, with both

---

[83] SIMONS, LIBYA: THE STRUGGLE FOR SURVIVAL, *supra* note 6 at 111.

[84] AHMIDA, THE MAKING OF MODERN LIBYA, *supra* note 4 at 37–41; VANDEWALLE, A HISTORY OF MODERN LIBYA, *supra* note 1 at 21.

[85] SIMONS, LIBYA: THE STRUGGLE FOR SURVIVAL, *supra* note 6 at 111.

[86] VANDEWALLE, A HISTORY OF MODERN LIBYA, *supra* note 1 at 21; SIMONS, LIBYA: THE STRUGGLE FOR SURVIVAL, *supra* note 6 at 113.

[87] SIMONS, LIBYA: THE STRUGGLE FOR SURVIVAL, *supra* note 6 at 114.

Ottoman and tribal forces offering stiff resistance.[88] The Ottomans did not formally withdraw from Libya until the conclusion of the Treaty of Lausanne in 1923. While the language of the treaty indicated that Libyans had technically received their freedom, sovereignty was officially transferred to Italy.[89]

The Italian forces that arrived in October 1911 proved successful in Tripolitania, as they were able to control the open terrain and exploit a disorganized resistance.[90] Despite the continued supply of Ottoman materiels, the Italians were able to take effective control of Tripolitania by 1914.[91] The Italian advance stalled in Fezzan and Cyrenaica, however, largely due to the stiff resistance waged by Senussiya fighters. In guerrilla warfare these fighters had advantages in terms of mobility, tribal supply chains and local terrain. The difficulty of the terrain, in particular, taxed the mechanized Italian forces and brought their offensive to a virtual standstill.[92]

World War I broke out in July 1914. As part of the negotiations to bring Italy into the Allied camp, Libya was again promised to Italy at the 1915 Treaty of London.[93] During WWI Libya was a sideshow of the conflict in Europe, with the Ottomans, Germans, Italians, and later the British engaging with various tribal leaders to undercut one another.[94]

Once Italy was fully engaged in WWI in 1915 it largely retreated from Libya and effectively permitted home rule in its territories.[95] Nevertheless, outside forces continued to determine the course of Libya's history, as the Ottomans persuaded the Senussiya to attack British Egypt in 1916. The move failed and had historical consequences, as it prompted the ascent of Idris al-Senussi,[96] the grandson of the Great Senussi, to the leadership of the Senussiya Order. Idris would prove to be a willing partner in the pursuit of British interests, and in exchange for Senussiya support the British elevated Idris to representative of Cyrenaica.

---

[88] VANDEWALLE, A HISTORY OF MODERN LIBYA, *supra* note 1 at 24–26; AHMIDA, THE MAKING OF MODERN LIBYA, *supra* note 4 at 103.

[89] SIMONS, LIBYA: THE STRUGGLE FOR SURVIVAL, *supra* note 6 at 115; VANDEWALLE, A HISTORY OF MODERN LIBYA, *supra* note 1 at 25.

[90] VANDEWALLE, A HISTORY OF MODERN LIBYA, *supra* note 1 at 26.

[91] SIMONS, LIBYA: THE STRUGGLE FOR SURVIVAL, *supra* note 6 at 115.

[92] VANDEWALLE, A HISTORY OF MODERN LIBYA, *supra* note 1 at 26.

[93] *Id.* at 28.

[94] AHMIDA, THE MAKING OF MODERN LIBYA, *supra* note 4 at 130.

[95] *Id.* at 105.

[96] *Id.* at 122.

The October 1917 Akrama Agreement between Italy and Idris formally recognized Idris as the representative of Cyrenaica and the Senussiya as having legitimate control over the Cyrenaican interior.[97] Three years later, in October 1920, Idris was elevated again, this time to the position of Emir of Cyrenaica through the Al-Rajma Agreement, which also formalized the autonomous status of the region.[98]

As Emir of Cyrenaica, Idris was given a monthly salary and direct control over various regions in Cyrenaica in exchange for recognizing Italian police power and the implementation of the *Legge Fondamentale*. Adopted in October 1919, the *Legge Fondamentale* granted Tripolitania and Cyrenaica their own parliaments. This allowed for relatively significant local control, exemption from military service and the provision of dual citizenship for all Cyrenaicans and Tripolitanians.[99]

Idris and the Senussiya, expressing territorial interests of their own, attempted to use their status in Cyrenaica as a basis to establish control over Tripolitania and Fezzan. Tripolitanian tribes, however, resisted and ultimately fought a battle at Bani Walid in 1917 in which the Senussiya were forced to retreat back to Cyrenaica.[100]

Tripolitanians had also set out on a different track from Cyrenaica, establishing the first Arab republic in 1918. The Tripolitanian Republic was the culmination of several earlier attempts at Tripolitanian unity that had been aborted. The establishment of the Tripolitanian Republic was prompted by an increasing awareness that Cyrenaican unity enabled the region to extract important concessions, while the internal divisions in Tripolitania undermined the possibility of self-rule.[101]

The Tripolitanian Republic, however, was doomed almost from the start. Despite progressive institutions and the granting of rights, such as suffrage and press freedoms, the Republic foundered under the weight of internal political squabbles, in particular between Arab-Berber and non-Arab-Berber tribes. These conflicts were exacerbated by Italian intervention. Lacking both a unifying social and political force comparable to

---

[97] Vandewalle, A History of Modern Libya, *supra* note 1 at 27; Ahmida, The Making of Modern Libya, *supra* note 4 at 106; Simons, Libya: The Struggle for Survival, *supra* note 6 at 116.

[98] Vandewalle, A History of Modern Libya, *supra* note 1 at 28.

[99] *Id.* at 28.

[100] *Id.*

[101] *Id.* at 29.

the Senussiya and a steadying influence like the British, the Tripolitanian Republic folded without having held a single election.[102]

With the end of WWI, Italian interests turned back to Libya. Giuseppe Volpi was appointed the Italian governor of Tripoli in July 1921. At the time, Italy controlled very little of Tripolitania, leaving the anemic Republic to administer and tax as much as it could.[103] Determined to reassert control, Volpi in short order nullified the Tripolitanian *Legge Fondamentale* of 1919, imposed martial law and aggressively reasserted control over the province, in part through military campaigns against rebellious tribes in Misrata.[104] Upon the victory over Misrata in January 1922, the ascendant Volpi declared, "Italy is forever destined to bathe the assertion of her rights in blood!"[105] His declaration would foreshadow Italy's conduct in the coming decade as it established control over the rest of the country.

By mid-1922, Tripolitanian leaders, in the face of pressure from Volpi and amidst significant internal discord, determined that the only path forward was through unification with Cyrenaica, although under unfavorable terms. In July 1922, representatives officially presented the offer of extension of Idris's mandate into the western province as Emir of both Tripolitania and Cyrenaica, something they had fiercely resisted in 1917. This offer put Idris in the precarious position of balancing Italian and Cyrenaican interests with his own ambitions. In November 1922, Idris accepted the proposal but went into exile in Egypt a month later, leaving the military wing of the Senussiya to resist the inevitable Italian response.[106] Out of this resistance emerged 'Umar al-Mukhtar, who would lead the Senussiya for nearly ten years against the Italians.

1922 also saw the election of Benito Mussolini, who oversaw a radical hardening of Italian colonial policy. In the period 1911–1922, Italian policy had been designed to incorporate Libyans into the Italian system, by extending local control to the Emirate of Cyrenaica and the Tripolitanian Republic and the provision of comparatively progressive rights in the *Legge Fondamentale*. The pre-fascist leadership had even moved farmers from southern Italy to Libya to ease internal tensions, though

---

[102] AHMIDA, THE MAKING OF MODERN LIBYA, *supra* note 4 at 106; VANDEWALLE, A HISTORY OF MODERN LIBYA, *supra* note 1 at 29.

[103] SIMONS, LIBYA: THE STRUGGLE FOR SURVIVAL, *supra* note 6 at 120.

[104] VANDEWALLE, A HISTORY OF MODERN LIBYA, *supra* note 1 at 30; SIMONS, LIBYA: THE STRUGGLE FOR SURVIVAL, *supra* note 6 at 121; AHMIDA, THE MAKING OF MODERN LIBYA, *supra* note 4 at 133.

[105] *Quoted in* SIMONS, LIBYA: THE STRUGGLE FOR SURVIVAL, *supra* note 6 at 121.

[106] VANDEWALLE, A HISTORY OF MODERN LIBYA, *supra* note 1 at 29.

this policy was limited in scope. Following fascist ascendance in 1922, this policy shifted to unwavering Italian domination of Libya through military subjugation, as well as the transfer of vast numbers of settlers across the Mediterranean.[107]

The commander of Italian forces in Libya was Rodolfo Graziani, whose heavy-handed tactics would earn him infamy in both Libya and Ethiopia.[108] Graziani, who later became a Field Marshal in WWII, served as deputy governor of Cyrenaica, and became known as the "Butcher of Fezzan," for ordering executions and overseeing the massacres of entire communities.[109] By 1924, Graziani's forces had routed Tripolitanian resistance fighters, pushing them into Fezzan, which was not itself subjugated until 1930.[110] However, it was in Cyrenaica where the most fierce fighting took place, with Al-Mukhtar leading small groups of rebels in hit and run guerrilla actions. Italians were not able to defeat these fighters until 1932.

Graziani dealt with Cyrenaican resistance by engaging in a war of attrition and the imposition of collective punishment, with the aim of forcing the population into submission. Pietro Badoglio, Field Marshal of the Italian Army who governed Libya from 1928–1934, proclaimed that unless the resistance ceased, "I will wage war with powerful systems and means, which they will long remember. No rebel will be left in peace, neither he nor his family nor his herds nor his heirs. I will destroy everything, men and things."[111] Along with Graziani, Badoglio played a central role in defeating the insurrection.

Italian collective punishment entailed sealing wells, confiscating tribal herds, destroying crops and, in 1931, the forcible transfer of at least 85,000 Libyans to concentration camps. Two years later, only 35,000 of these were still alive.[112] This organized and administrative killing foreshadowed the extermination policies of WWII. In 1930 and 1931, some 12,000 Cyrenaicans

---

[107] *Id.*; AHMIDA, THE MAKING OF MODERN LIBYA, *supra* note 4 at 135.

[108] AHMIDA, THE MAKING OF MODERN LIBYA, *supra* note 4 at 135.

[109] *Italy memorial to Fascist hero Graziani sparks row*, BBC, Aug. 15, 2012, *available at* http://www.bbc.co.uk/news/world-europe-19267099; Rory Carroll, *Italy's Bloody Secret*, THE GUARDIAN, June 24, 2001, *available at* http://www.guardian.co.uk/education/2001/jun/25/artsandhumanities.highereducation.

[110] VANDEWALLE, A HISTORY OF MODERN LIBYA, *supra* note 1 at 30. A small resistance held out in the deserts of Sirte until 1928. *See* SIMONS, LIBYA: THE STRUGGLE FOR SURVIVAL, *supra* note 6 at 122; AHMIDA, THE MAKING OF MODERN LIBYA, *supra* note 4 at 107.

[111] *Quoted in* SIMONS, LIBYA: THE STRUGGLE FOR SURVIVAL, *supra* note 6 at 127.

[112] AHMIDA, THE MAKING OF MODERN LIBYA, *supra* note 4 at 107, 139; SIMONS, LIBYA: THE STRUGGLE FOR SURVIVAL, *supra* note 6 at 123; VANDEWALLE, A HISTORY OF MODERN LIBYA, *supra* note 1 at 31.

were also summarily executed.[113] After carrying out forced deportations in 1931, General Graziani declared that Italy was "calmly determined to reduce the people to [the] most miserable starvation" should Al-Mukhtar and his followers refuse to submit.[114] To that end, Italian forces began a process of random confiscation of property and killing of livestock. By 1933 the sheep population in Cyrenaica was reduced from 800,000 to 100,000, the camel population from 75,000 to 3,000 and the horse population from 4,000 to 1,000.[115] Graziani also sealed Libya's eastern border with fences and continual armed patrols, effectively cutting off the traditional escape route of Cyrenaicans into Egypt.[116]

By 1931, 'Umar al-Mukhtar's Senussiya resistance was limited to a few enclaves as the Italians methodically destroyed each in turn, pursuing the fleeing fighters and civilians into the desert with their air force.[117] Al-Mukhtar was captured on 11 September 1931, and following interrogation on an Italian warship off the coast was condemned to death after a trial lasting 30 minutes. Five days after his capture, Al-Mukhtar was hung at an Italian concentration camp near Benghazi before 20,000 Cyrenaicans assembled by force to witness the execution.[118] For the first time since the 1911 invasion, Italy was able to proclaim an official end to any internal resistance in Libya.

Reliable estimates place the number of non-natural deaths over the 30 years of Italian domination at between 250,000 and 300,000, out of a population of less than 1 million.[119] Italian colonial policy towards Libya was aimed not simply at defeating the Senussiya and securing the territory. Italy looked upon Libya as a viable way to absorb its industrial and population surpluses. Libya also served as a convenient mechanism for alleviating the growing pressures within the Italian polity, and increasing numbers of settlers to Libya.

---

[113] VANDEWALLE, A HISTORY OF MODERN LIBYA, *supra* note 1 at 31.

[114] SIMONS, LIBYA: THE STRUGGLE FOR SURVIVAL, *supra* note 6 at 130.

[115] *Id.* at 136. *See also* VANDEWALLE, A HISTORY OF MODERN LIBYA, *supra* note 1 at 31; AHMIDA, THE MAKING OF MODERN LIBYA, *supra* note 4 at 107.

[116] SIMONS, LIBYA: THE STRUGGLE FOR SURVIVAL, *supra* note 6 at 128; AHMIDA, THE MAKING OF MODERN LIBYA, *supra* note 4 at 138.

[117] VANDEWALLE, A HISTORY OF MODERN LIBYA, *supra* note 1 at 31.

[118] SIMONS, LIBYA: THE STRUGGLE FOR SURVIVAL, *supra* note 6 at 131–133; VANDEWALLE, A HISTORY OF MODERN LIBYA, *supra* note 1 at 32.

[119] VANDEWALLE, A HISTORY OF MODERN LIBYA, *supra* note 1 at 31.

Pre-colonial propaganda painted a romantic image of Libya and visitors described the place as an indispensable agricultural asset.[120] The policy of dispatching agricultural experts to Libya accelerated with the ascent of Mussolini and the fascists in 1922. The fruits of Italian agricultural policy lay in the conversion of large areas of desert into productive agricultural zones, entailing subjugation of the countryside. By 1929, Italian engineers had converted 180,000 hectares of arid land for farming. Nearly two thirds of all funds invested in Libya went towards agricultural development, with the remainder going towards infrastructural projects such as a coastal highway.[121]

The social and economic consequences were enormous for Libyans, who were forced to cede land and resources for Italian use. Unlike the prefascist period, after 1922 Libyans were also systematically excluded from participating in government or administration, foreclosing the formation of a generation of civil servants who could have played an important role in independent Libya.

Italy also promoted immigration on a large scale, although this did not accelerate until the late 1930s. By 1941, 110,000 settlers had migrated from Italy to Libya, and came to constitute more than a tenth of the total population. Two thirds of these immigrants lived in Tripolitania, with the rest settling in Cyrenaica. Mussolini's plans called for a doubling of the settler population in 1942 and a fivefold increase by the 1960s.[122]

As with the majority of African states, the Libyan encounter with European colonialism in the 20th century was overwhelmingly negative. The brutality of Italian military policy towards the Cyrenaicans precipitated a sea change in Libyan attitudes towards Europe and the West. While Libyans had been suspicious of the Ottomans, their rule had been comparatively benign and had not faced significant resistance.[123] The victory of the Italians in 1932 marked the end of Libyan appreciation of the West,[124] sparking not only resentment of Italy but also "reinforce[ing]

---

[120] SIMONS, LIBYA: THE STRUGGLE FOR SURVIVAL, *supra* note 6 at 111; VANDEWALLE, A HISTORY OF MODERN LIBYA, *supra* note 1 at 32.

[121] VANDEWALLE, A HISTORY OF MODERN LIBYA, *supra* note 1 at 32–33.

[122] *Id.* at 33–34; Kenneth Perkins, *North Africa from the First World War*, *in* THE NEW CAMBRIDGE HISTORY OF ISLAM VOLUME 5: THE ISLAMIC WORLD IN THE AGE OF WESTERN DOMINANCE 424 (Francis Robnson ed., Cambridge, UK: Cambridge University Press, 2010).

[123] VANDEWALLE, A HISTORY OF MODERN LIBYA, *supra* note 1 at 22.

[124] AHMIDA, THE MAKING OF MODERN LIBYA, *supra* note 4 at 155.

local perceptions that statehood itself was at best a mixed blessing."[125] As Dirk Vandewalle argues

> For Libyans, their perception of their first encounter with the mechanisms of a modern state was that of an authoritarian and domineering adminis-tration that could be used, seemingly unchecked, to subjugate and often dispossess them. In contrast, the ethos of the tribe, with its promises of egalitarianism and inclusion would – as subsequent events were to show – not surprisingly remain firmly lodged as a positive factor in the imagination of many Libyans.[126]

Italian colonialism not only destroyed communities and indigenous economic and administrative capacity, but also actively drove Libyans away from a modern, administrative state. As such, political, economic and social values that had predominated since at least the beginning of recorded history in Libya, were reinforced.

6.2. *WWII and the Western Desert Campaign*

Under the authority of the Italian colonial empire, Libya officially declared war on Britain and France on 10 June 1940, and aligned itself with Nazi Ger-many in the fight for Northern Africa.[127] Italy had approximately 250,000 troops stationed in Libya, with the 5th Army based in Tripolitania facing the French forces in Tunisia, and the 10th Army based in Cyrenaica fac-ing the British forces in Egypt. During the war, Libya became a strategic point in the Western Desert Campaign, and was used as a launching pad for the Italian incursion into Egypt. The goal was to take the Suez Canal, but the Italian and Axis forces met with considerable resistance and never reached the main British defense positions.[128]

In August 1940, Mussolini ordered Field Marshal Rodolfo Graziani, then-Commander-in-Chief of Italian North Africa, to invade Egypt. Graziani expressed concern that his forces were ill-equipped, but ulti-mately obeyed the orders, and moved the Italian 10th Army into Egypt

---

[125] VANDEWALLE, A HISTORY OF MODERN LIBYA, *supra* note 1 at 23.

[126] *Id.* at 34.

[127] MAJ. GEN. IAN STANLEY ORD PLAYFAIR ET AL., MEDITERRANEAN AND MIDDLE EAST VOLUME I: THE EARLY SUCCESSES AGAINST ITALY (TO MAY 1941), HISTORY OF THE SECOND WORLD WAR, UNITED KINGDOM MILITARY SERIES (Butler, J.R.M. ed., Uckfield, UK: Naval & Military Press, 2007).

[128] MAJ. KENNETH MACKSEY, BEDA FOMM: CLASSIC VICTORY, BALLENTINE'S ILLUSTRATED HISTORY OF THE VIOLENT CENTURY, BATTLE BOOK NUMBER 22 35 (New York, USA: Ballan-tine Books, 1971).

on 13 September 1940. Graziani marched four divisions in an epic deployment that inched its way from Benghazi into Egypt before meeting the British Royal Navy. While the Italian forces were split between the 10th and 5th armies, Graziani's forces nevertheless outnumbered British forces in Egypt, which consisted of an estimated 36,000 troops.[129] The terrain was difficult, however, and many of the Italian soldiers, accustomed to fighting colonial wars in Abyssinia and Libya, were ill-prepared for European-style warfare.

By November 1940, the British counter-offensives, part of Operation Compass, had nearly destroyed the entire 10th Army, and around 130,000 Italian troops had been taken prisoner.[130] Graziani resigned his commission and General Italo Gariboldi took over as Governor-General of Libya.

Hitler determined that the Italians could not single-handedly face the Allied forces in Egypt, which consisted of a mixture of Australians, New Zealanders, Indians, South Africans, UK forces, a French contingent of Free French volunteers, and later American troops. In February 1941, Germany sent an expeditionary force into Libya and Tunisia, called the Afrika Korps.[131] Under the command of German General Erwin Rommel, the Afrika Korps conducted rapid movement tank battles in the desert, pushing the British forces into Egypt. These Blitzkrieg tactics became notorious, earning Rommel the moniker "Desert Fox."[132]

Rommel's forces were defeated, however, in the Siege of Tobruq, which began in April 1941 and lasted 240 days, marking the first failure of his Blitzkrieg tactics. The Allies pushed back against Rommel's forces, halting his advance just 66 miles from Alexandria at the historic First Battle of El Alamein (July 1942). The Allies then went on the offensive during the Second Battle of El Alamein (October–November 1942), forcing Rommel's forces to withdraw. This battle was a decisive and marked the success of the Allied powers in the Western Desert Campaign, turning the tide against the Axis forces. The withdrawal of the Afrika Korps from Egypt meant that the Suez Canal – a vital connection between the Mediterranean

---

[129] EDDY BAUER, THE HISTORY OF WORLD WAR II 93 (Peter Young ed., London, UK: Orbis Publishing, 2000).

[130] *Id.* at 118.

[131] *Id.* at 121.

[132] ERWIN ROMMEL & LIDDELL HART, THE ROMMEL PAPERS (B.H. ed., New York, USA: Da Capo Press, 1982); ERWIN ROMMEL, ROMMEL AND HIS ART OF WAR (John Pimlott ed., London, UK: Greenhill Books, 2006).

and the Indian sub-continent – was no longer under threat from the Axis powers.

While the WWII battles of the Northern Africa front were hard fought, all sides saw something chivalrous, if not romantic, in the war in Libya and Egypt. In fact, this romantic image captured the imagination of most people in the world who compared what was happening in this theater of war to what was happening in many parts of Europe and the Far East. A particularly extraordinary element was that both sides were respectful of international humanitarian law in a way that had never occurred in modern conflict. Treatment of POWs by both sides was humane and decent, not to say even respectful well before the 1949 Geneva Conventions were adopted. There were practically no attacks on civilian populations by the air forces of either side, as the only town that was heavily bombarded was Tobruq, which was an important port and fortress city on the Mediterranean.

This type of respect for civilian populations and enemy soldiers stands in stark contrast to the treatment of the Libyan population by Italian colonial forces. The period preceding Libyan independence was characterized by sustained violence on the part of the Italians, particularly during the counter-insurgency campaign aimed at liquidating supporters of the Al-Mukhtar-led rebellion. This history is deeply engrained in the Libyan national identity, and was fresh in the nation's consciousness as it moved towards independence and statehood.

7. Independence and the Establishment of the Kingdom of Libya: 1943–1969

7.1. *Establishing Independence*

Italy lost control of Libya in 1943 when Allied forces defeated the Axis powers in North Africa. Tripolitania, Cyrenaica and Fezzan were quickly absorbed into the colonial administration of Britain and France, with Britain assuming control of the coastal provinces and France of Fezzan.[133]

Libya's future was determined largely by the strong relationship Idris had with the United Kingdom. Independence was the carrot dangled by the British in exchange for Libyan support during World War II. Despite

---

[133] Vandewalle, A History of Modern Libya, *supra* note 1 at 38.

widespread antipathy towards the Italians, this support could not be assumed. In the run-up to the war, the leadership of Tripolitania and Cyrenaica met on several occasions to discuss the question of political allegiance. Support for the Allies wavered, with parts of the Tripolitanian leadership concerned that it would strengthen Idris's position as Britain's chosen leader of Libya. By August 1940, Idris had convinced Libyan delegates to support the Allied cause with the understanding that Britain would continue to support Libya after the war.[134]

At the August 1940 meeting, the Libyan delegates also agreed to the formation of a joint Cyrenaican and Tripolitanian Emirate, with Idris as its leader and representative to the British.[135] Idris, in this capacity, worked to have Libyan independence recognized in the midst of growing concerns that neither Britain nor France would relinquish control over the provinces after 1943 – France was seeking a buffer to Chad and Britain was looking to establish an extended defense of the Suez Canal.[136]

With the end of World War II, Libya faced a political crisis: the political unity that had been achieved in 1940 between the three provinces was coming under significant strain in the years after 1943. Free from Italian occupation and endowed with some political freedom, Tripolitanian leaders, concerned by the power of Idris, began exerting their independence from Cyrenaica. Indeed, the Cyrenaican leadership dominated the 1946 National Congress, whose strongly federalist designs for an independent nation diverged radically from the interests of Tripolitanian leaders. While the Cyrenaicans demanded a unified leadership with Idris as Emir, Tripolitanians called for a revival of the Tripolitanian Republic and the principles of nascent Arab nationalism.

The planned state essentially suffered a breakdown when Tripolitanians agitated for a more progressive and modern political system than the Emirate they had agreed to in 1940. The Cyrenaicans, based on historical precedent, sought a federal system that would grant most power to the individual provinces with a minimum of centralized control. The only things the three provinces could agree upon were the principle of independence itself, the unity of the three provinces, and membership in the Arab League.[137]

---

[134] *Id.* at 36.
[135] SIMONS, LIBYA: THE STRUGGLE FOR SURVIVAL, *supra* note 6 at 140.
[136] *Id.* at 141, 147; VANDEWALLE, A HISTORY OF MODERN LIBYA, *supra* note 1 at 36.
[137] VANDEWALLE, A HISTORY OF MODERN LIBYA, *supra* note 1 at 37–38.

The differing interests were clear, as Tripolitanians favored a unitary government, which they would dominate based on their sizable population advantage. Cyrenaicans and Fezzanis, on the other hand, cognizant of the advantage Tripolitania would enjoy under a unitary state, argued forcefully for a federal model. By 1948, the question of the form and structure of the future Libyan state had come to a head, prompting the referral of the matter to a Four Powers Commission early that year. At issue was the hardening of political positions in each of the provinces that threatened to unravel the Libyan state before it even came into existence. Cyrenaica would only support a unified government controlled by Al-Senussi, the Tripolitanians would not accept this, and the Fezzani were divided over joining Tripolitania and Cyrenaica in a Libyan state or aligning with French colonial territories in Chad and Niger.[138] Deeply entrenched regional and tribal identities played a major factor in negotiations surrounding the governmental structure of the future Libyan state.

Ultimately, independence came through the UN General Assembly, which had been tasked in 1948 with resolving the matter when the Four Powers and the Libyans themselves could not agree to an outcome. The General Assembly issued a declaration in November 1949, declaring that Libya should gain independence by 1 January 1952.[139]

Despite their differences, Tripolitanian and Cyrenaican leaders rallied around the Declaration when confronted with the unpalatable alternative proposed by the Anglo-Italian Bevin-Sforza Plan, which called for Libya to be placed under European trusteeship for ten years. Under the plan, Italy would assume responsibility for Tripolitania, the United Kingdom for Cyrenaica, and France for Fezzan. Libyan leaders joined together to defeat the Bevin-Sforza Plan at the General Assembly, despite uncertainty about the alternative.[140]

The imposition of the 1 January 1952 deadline was a significant strain on the Libyans and their external advisors, including the United Nations and the United Kingdom. Adrian Pelt, the UN High Commissioner for Libya, was tasked in December 1949 with overseeing the transition to statehood in just 24 months. There were various options on the table, but

---

[138] *Id.* at 38.
[139] VANDEWALLE, A HISTORY OF MODERN LIBYA, *supra* note 1 at 39; SIMONS, LIBYA: THE STRUGGLE FOR SURVIVAL, *supra* note 6 at 145.
[140] *Id.*

by that time the provinces had already assumed local control and were effectively operating independently of one another.[141]

One of Pelt's first acts was to convene a National Assembly, made up of representatives he selected after consulting with leaders from the three provinces.[142] The assembly was empowered to draft the constitution and lay the foundations for the nascent Libyan state.[143] Despite significant external concern, the National Assembly was thus constituted with British and American backing, and tasked with creating the new Libyan state.[144]

The National Assembly convened for the first time on 25 November 1950, and on 2 December determined that Libya should become a constitutional monarchy with an elected parliament, and Idris as king. Two days later, the assembly established a committee tasked with preparing the draft constitution for ratification by the assembly.[145] Tripolitanians, wary of a seemingly inevitable federal Libya, took to the streets and hundreds were arrested.[146]

The question of federalism was the single greatest issue confronting the National Assembly and its supervisor, Pelt. Beyond the question of federalism, the constitutional committee grappled with the powers of the parliament vis-à-vis the king and the location of the capital. On both of these issues, the Tripolitanians and Cyrenaicans clashed. While the Tripolitanian leadership insisted on a parliament with law making powers and a capital located in Tripoli, the Cyrenaican leadership called for law-making powers to reside with the king and for Benghazi to be the capital.

The committee finally determined that legislative power should reside with the elected parliament, and that the capital would be shared between Tripoli and Benghazi.[147] A split capital, combined with the federalism of the government, would prove to be a great burden on Libya. There would be four governments in Libya, one federal and one in each of the provinces. With the king, parliament and the three provinces, there were five seats of power for a population of 1 million.[148]

---

[141] SIMONS, LIBYA: THE STRUGGLE FOR SURVIVAL, *supra* note 6 at 148–150; VANDEWALLE, A HISTORY OF MODERN LIBYA, *supra* note 1 at 39.

[142] VANDEWALLE, A HISTORY OF MODERN LIBYA, *supra* note 1 at 46–47.

[143] SIMONS, LIBYA: THE STRUGGLE FOR SURVIVAL, *supra* note 6 at 151.

[144] *Id.* at 151–152.

[145] *Id.* at 152.

[146] *Id.* at 151.

[147] *Id.* at 153.

[148] VANDEWALLE, A HISTORY OF MODERN LIBYA, *supra* note 1 at 48.

The National Assembly promulgated a constitution with a strongly federal character on 7 October 1951 in Benghazi. The following month, on 6 November, the assembly passed an elections law and then ceased to exist.[149] Independence came on 24 December 1951. Ultimately, Libya's founding document reflected the fundamental problems facing Libya at the time, along with the unwillingness of Idris and the Libyan political elite to engage with these problems and build a proper state. It was an unhappy compromise, whose only positive attribute was that it secured independence.

Despite the behind-the-scenes political wrangling, the United Kingdom of Libya was proclaimed in Benghazi on 24 December 1951, just a week before the General Assembly's deadline. It represented a rushed and "uneasy compromise" by Libyan stakeholders that was more reflective of their overriding desire for independence – as well as the wishes of the British and the Americans – than any affirmative desire for unification.[150]

The 1951 Libyan Constitution was distinguished by its strong federalist character. Indeed, Article 38 provided the federal government no powers of implementation. Consistent with the devolved powers favored by Cyrenaica, the federal government could only pass legislation, thereby leaving implementation entirely in the hands of the provinces. Such was the independence of the provinces that under Article 200 each province had its own border controls and required visas for entry.

While the 1951 Constitution gave legislative power to the parliament, the King and his royal court effectively controlled it, as laid out in the constitution. This was later complemented by electoral manipulation. In the Senate, the King appointed half of the 24 senators himself, while the other half were elected. The second chamber of parliament was the House of Representatives, with one delegate for every 20,000 males. It could, however, be dissolved by the King.

The most important federalist provision of the constitution was Article 38, which conferred executive powers upon the regional governments in Tripolitania, Cyrenaica and Fezzan. This allowed the provinces to determine the means and mechanisms for the implementation of legislation passed by the parliament and promulgated by the king. The constitution also conferred upon the King the power to appoint provincial governors,

---

[149] SIMONS, LIBYA: THE STRUGGLE FOR SURVIVAL, *supra* note 6 at 154.
[150] VANDEWALLE, A HISTORY OF MODERN LIBYA, *supra* note 1 at 44.

allowing him to influence the implementation of legislation through his appointed provincial leaders.[151]

7.2. *The Early Independence Period*

King Idris emerged as Libya's leader, receiving the royal crown after effectively being elevated from his role as emir of Tripolitania and Cyrenaica. As the first king of Libya, he presented the people with an unfamiliar title to go along with the new status of independence. King Idris set the stage for things to come by issuing his first proclamations from the city of Benghazi, in Cyrenaica, emphasizing early on his political aloofness from Tripoli. Indeed, much of King Idris's nearly 18-year reign would find him in Cyrenaica, and after 1955, he was mostly at his palace in Tobruq in eastern Cyrenaica close to the Egyptian border. The palace also stood next to a British naval base, arguably pointing in a more fundamental sense to where the king's most firm allegiance lay.[152]

At its birth in December 1951, Libya was the least developed country in North Africa, both politically and economically.[153] It was one of the poorest countries in the world and was almost completely reliant on foreign aid for survival.[154] Libya faced three significant problems, namely the lack of infrastructure and economic development, the absence of a unifying political or economic class to guide the state, and the lack of a common polity or national identity.

Libya inherited an infrastructure destroyed by years of warfare – a countryside covered in mines, an economy suffering from high unemployment, minimal trade and a per capita annual income of approximately $25, a population that was more than 90 percent illiterate, and a healthcare system with a 40 percent infant mortality rate.[155] Libya also lacked a unifying elite, both in the public and private sectors. Italian colonial policies effectively destroyed administrative capacity within the country, and its exclusionary economic policies reinforced the effects of the collapse of the Tripolitanian mercantile class in the late 19th century.[156] Taken

---

[151] *Id.* at 48–49; SIMONS, LIBYA: THE STRUGGLE FOR SURVIVAL, *supra* note 6 at 152–154.
[152] AHMIDA, THE MAKING OF MODERN LIBYA, *supra* note 4 at 154.
[153] *Id.* at 53.
[154] VANDEWALLE, A HISTORY OF MODERN LIBYA, *supra* note 1 at 51–52.
[155] *Id.* at 41; SIMONS, LIBYA: THE STRUGGLE FOR SURVIVAL, *supra* note 6 at 141.
[156] AHMIDA, THE MAKING OF MODERN LIBYA, *supra* note 4 at 69.

together, this left Libya with neither an internal administrative caste nor an economic middle class to anchor the post-colonial system.[157]

Beyond these material and administrative problems, the country lacked the broad-based positive national identity and social cohesion necessary to operate a modern state. Whatever Libyan identity the nation possessed was negative, or rather reactive to outside intervention, whether the struggle against the imposition of a territorial identity by the Ottomans in the 19th century, resistance to Italian brutality in the first half of the 20th century, or opposition to continued external control as proposed, for instance, by the Bevin-Sforza plan.[158] Even when a negative common identity bound Libyans together, however, it remained heavily influenced by regional interests and values, which were often incompatible with one another.

King Idris was largely disinterested in governing Libya, and more concerned with returning to his Cyrenaican homeland to live a tranquil life. His political loyalties, at least initially, were squarely with Cyrenaica.[159] Where his concerns extended beyond Cyrenaica, they were mostly aligned with British and American interests. King Idris certainly did not place much faith in the federal government. By 1959, it had a mere 12,000 civil servants; 6,000 in Tripolitania, 4,000 in Cyrenaica, and 2,000 in Fezzan.[160] King Idris was equally wary of popular sovereignty. Even before the first parliamentary election in February 1952, he banned the major Tripolitanian and Cyrenaican political parties, ostensibly to preserve unity and avoid political discord. This left the smaller political parties to contest the first elections. While they were technically multi-party elections, the fairness and freedom of the February 1952 vote is dubious. In any case, shortly thereafter Idris had all remaining political parties banned.[161]

After this, only well-connected individuals would be able to stand for office, further cementing the power of King Idris. Without any organized opposition, the king and his supporters manipulated the next general

---

[157] VANDEWALLE, A HISTORY OF MODERN LIBYA, *supra* note 1 at 41.

[158] The Bevin-Sforza plan was the plan introduced by Italian foreign minister, Count Carlo Sforza and the British foreign secretary, Ernest Bevin, to grant trusteeship of Cyrenaica to Britain, Tripolitania to Italy, and Fezzan to France, for a ten year period, after which Libya would become independent. The plan was met with hostility in Libya and rejected by the UN General Assembly in May 1949.

[159] VANDEWALLE, A HISTORY OF MODERN LIBYA, *supra* note 1 at 50.

[160] VANDEWALLE, A HISTORY OF MODERN LIBYA, *supra* note 1 at 48.

[161] *Id.* at 49; SIMONS, LIBYA: THE STRUGGLE FOR SURVIVAL, *supra* note 6 at 160–161.

election that took place in January 1956.[162] The 1952 electoral experiment would be the closest, therefore, that Libya would come to free and fair elections, whether under the monarchy or in the era of Mu'ammar Qadhafi.[163]

The king's control of parliament and manipulation of elections had direct effects on the country's political and social structure. Idris was able to exclude the majority of the population from meaningful participation in government, subsequently blocking Tripolitania from having any role in the state.[164] The arrangement functioned to ensure that power rested almost wholly with the king and his royal court, which was in the main composed of Cyrenaican elites who shared his political interests.[165] King Idris also appointed Cyrenaicans to his Council of Ministers and as heads of all federal agencies.[166] Cyrenaica effectively controlled Libya.

The state that King Idris helped to build was largely incapable of resolving the complex problems the country faced. Indeed, problems in education, healthcare, the rule of law, and economic development – which required sustained government attention – were ignored by the king's government. Instead, The United Kingdom of Libya survived through the export of castor oil and esparto grass, and the sale of scrap metal left over from WWII.[167] The government also reaped large sums from the rent of military bases to the United Kingdom and the United States, as well as foreign aid from these states. During this period, Libya was rewarded in kind for serving as an important Cold War client state to United Kingdom and the United States.[168]

Throughout his reign, King Idris would prove intolerant of both political opposition and civil society, targeting those who attempted to organize political parties, trade unions and students. In 1962, 78 Libyans were tried for membership in a Ba'thist party and sentenced to jail terms of up to 32 months.[169] Crackdowns on trade unions were severe, particularly after the discovery of oil in 1959 when the government worked hard to suppress labor organizing.[170] Throughout the 1960s, students were attacked

---

[162] SIMONS, LIBYA: THE STRUGGLE FOR SURVIVAL, *supra* note 6 at 160–161.
[163] VANDEWALLE, A HISTORY OF MODERN LIBYA, *supra* note 1 at 49.
[164] *Id.* at 41.
[165] *Id.* at 49.
[166] *Id.* at 50.
[167] *Id.* at 44, 50–51; SIMONS, LIBYA: THE STRUGGLE FOR SURVIVAL, *supra* note 6 at 157.
[168] VANDEWALLE, A HISTORY OF MODERN LIBYA, *supra* note 1 at 44.
[169] SIMONS, LIBYA: THE STRUGGLE FOR SURVIVAL, *supra* note 6 at 161.
[170] *Id.* at 161, 167.

for their support of the Palestinian cause and their opposition to the U.S. war in Vietnam, with mass trials against students in 1967.[171]

Without a viable middle class or functional civil society, the Libya of King Idris soon fell sway to favoritism within the court, the abuse of authority and widespread corruption. The king himself appeared incapable of addressing the problem, being a man who preferred contemplation and solitude in Cyrenaica to the difficult work of addressing the significant problems confronting Libya.[172] He was unable or unwilling to address the problems of federalism. Indeed, his attempts prior to 1963 to make concessions regarding his strong federalist position were blocked by his Cyrenaican allies.[173] Consequently, Libya was regionally divided and structurally unprepared for the discovery of significant quantities oil and natural gas in the late 1950s – a discovery that would radically transform the country.[174]

The discovery of oil in commercial quantities instigated a marked shift in the country's economy. Between 1960 and 1969, oil exports grew from 20,000 to nearly 3 million barrels a day. The economy grew by 20 percent annually and per capita annual income increased from as little as $25 to $2,000.[175] The discovery of oil, however, produced an irreconcilable political problem in the country, stemming from its federalist arrangement. While all sub-surface resources belonged to the federal government according to the 1951 Constitution, the permits required to drill and explore belonged to the provinces. Even with the existence of business-friendly legislation, Libya was not an easy business climate.[176]

The discovery of oil necessitated and expedited political change,[177] and in 1963 the king abrogated the federal system with a new constitution.[178] The 1963 Constitution centralized power, and by removing Article 38 all executive functions were allocated to the federal government. Provincial legislative assemblies were banned and judicial organs were federalized. After 1963, the federal government assumed authority over customs enforcement, ports management, finance, transportation, development

---

[171] *Id.* at 167.
[172] VANDEWALLE, A HISTORY OF MODERN LIBYA, *supra* note 1 at 43; SIMONS, LIBYA: THE STRUGGLE FOR SURVIVAL, *supra* note 6 at 158.
[173] VANDEWALLE, A HISTORY OF MODERN LIBYA, *supra* note 1 at 63.
[174] *Id.* at 53; SIMONS, LIBYA: THE STRUGGLE FOR SURVIVAL, *supra* note 6 at 156.
[175] VANDEWALLE, A HISTORY OF MODERN LIBYA, *supra* note 1 at 62.
[176] *Id.* at 64.
[177] *Id.* at 62.
[178] SIMONS, LIBYA: THE STRUGGLE FOR SURVIVAL, *supra* note 6 at 161.

and taxation – all matters that had previously been within the jurisdiction of the provinces.[179] King Idris and his court effectively maintained control over the overall system, with the only fundamental change being the dismantling of obstacles to the efficient extraction and export of oil.[180]

The 1955 Libyan Petroleum Law provided for a powerful National Oil Corporation. It also contained a number of features that created significant problems. In order to promote rapid infrastructural development and extraction, Libyan oil concessions were time limited and small. This led to fast paced investment and drilling, but also prevented investors and oil companies from investing significantly in long-term infrastructure and the maintenance of the oil fields.[181] The Petroleum Commission, also provided for in the 1955 Libyan Petroleum Law, proved effective at employing the best minds in the country and ensuring that the government benefited from the oil industry.[182] Not only was Libya able to rise within a few years to become the fourth largest producer of oil globally, but it was able to do so in a way that generated significant returns for the government and some development for the country in the form of "sweeteners," in which oil companies were given contracts only after agreeing to invest in special development projects.[183]

The advent of oil had other effects, including increased corruption on the part of King Idris and his advisors. Corrupt practices included undermining regulatory and enforcement mechanisms such as tax collection, and misappropriating development projects attached to oil contracts. A vast political patronage system also developed, favoring the Cyrenaican elite, to the exclusion of non-Cyrenaicans, the middle classes and the poor.[184] A minimal bureaucratic elite did emerge in Tripolitania, especially around the Petroleum Commission, but did not signal a larger shift from a regionally divided country.[185] The distribution of oil profits was unequal across the provinces, further exacerbating the tribal and socio-economic divisions that would continue into the Qadhafi era.

Vast oil revenue also allowed the government to avoid real economic development and, in some respects, undermined existing efforts toward this end. Massive oil revenues allowed for the emergence of a dual

---

[179] VANDEWALLE, A HISTORY OF MODERN LIBYA, *supra* note 1 at 65.
[180] *Id.* at 66.
[181] *Id.* at 58.
[182] *Id.* at 61.
[183] *Id.* at 58–9.
[184] *Id.* at 68.
[185] *Id.* at 69.

economy in which oil provided the majority of the country's wealth and propped up inefficient businesses that had connections to the royal court. It also meant that government agencies had no interest in diversifying the economy or engaging in infrastructural development. By the early 1960s, oil extraction produced 99 percent of the country's revenues but employed only 1 percent of the population. The majority of the population was economically unproductive, working mostly as subsistence farmers and herders, and the government failed to meaningfully address development for the country as a whole.[186] Government agencies, with the notable exception of the Libyan Petroleum Company, were little more than instruments for distributing money and paying off clients.[187]

Finally, the influx of massive oil rents retarded the development of a tax base or tax authority that a functional state requires. As with most oil-rich states, Libya quickly converted itself into an economy based purely on oil, to the detriment of other necessary sources of income or mechanisms of government. Oil revenues quickly filled government coffers, and were used to paper over internal problems and promote political patronage, undermining the development of a properly functioning state.[188] Moreover, the government essentially operated as an extension of the Cyrenaican elite that still dominated the government and the police, and failed to engage or incorporate the majority of the population.

By the end of the 1960s, the situation had become untenable. Idris's government had developed into a corrupt plutocracy propped up by patronage schemes in which power was controlled by a small clique around the king. Flush with oil rents, the government was able to continue operating while avoiding the difficult problems of integrating Tripolitanians, Cyrenaicans and Fezzani into a coherent polity or of developing a modern diversified economy.

The government also appeared fundamentally unwilling to move away from its support of the West – and by extension, the state of Israel – which proved especially problematic after the 1967 Arab-Israeli War. King Idris and his entourage failed to recognize the fundamental shift in popular attitudes stemming from the rise of Arab nationalism in the region.[189]

---

[186] Vandewalle, *Libya's Revolution in Perspective, in* QADHAFI'S REVOLUTION REVISITED, *supra* note 3 at 13.

[187] VANDEWALLE, A HISTORY OF MODERN LIBYA, *supra* note 1 at 45.

[188] SIMONS, LIBYA: THE STRUGGLE FOR SURVIVAL, *supra* note 6 at 166; VANDEWALLE, A HISTORY OF MODERN LIBYA, *supra* note 1 at 75.

[189] Ethan Chorin, *The Future of the U.S.-Libyan Commercial Relationship*, in QADHAFI'S REVOLUTION REVISITED, *supra* note 3 at 158–159; VANDEWALLE, A HISTORY OF MODERN

Throughout, King Idris refused to lead as head of state, deferring instead to his royal court and handlers.[190] By outlawing and repressing dissent, whether in politics, civil society or education, the government cut off relief valves for the country's mounting pressures.[191] Political change was largely superficial and a function of court intrigue: in his 17-year reign, the king presided over 11 governments and more than 200 ministers.[192] By the end of his rule, King Idris himself enjoyed support only in Cyrenaica,[193] and so it was no great shock that in September 1969 long-circulating rumors of a coup were actually realized.[194]

8. The Libyan Arab Republic and the Rise of Mu'ammar Qadhafi: 1969–1977

8.1. *The Free Unionist Officers Movement and the 1969 Coup*

The origins of the 1969 coup can be traced back to the early 1960s when Mu'ammar Qadhafi brought like-minded young officers into a group that would congeal into the Free Unionist Officers Movement and later the Revolutionary Command Council (RCC).[195] Colonel Qadhafi's revolutionary ambitions developed in an international political and ideological climate defined by popular upheavals, anti-imperialism, nationalism and pan-Arabism. From a young age, Qadhafi looked up to Jamal 'Abd al-Nasser – the Egyptian colonel who overthrew the Egyptian monarchy, promoted Arab nationalism and rejected subservience to the West. In secondary school, Qadhafi regularly listened to Nasser on the Egyptian radio broadcast "Voice of the Arabs,"[196] and recited his speeches in front of his classmates.[197] He modeled himself after the Egyptian president,[198]

Libya, *supra* note 1 at 69–71; Simons, Libya: The Struggle for Survival, *supra* note 6 at 174–175.

[190] Vandewalle, A History of Modern Libya, *supra* note 1 at 78.

[191] *Id.* at 69–71.

[192] Anthony McDermott, *Qaddafi and Libya*, 29 (9) The World Today 398, 404 (1973).

[193] Vandewalle, A History of Modern Libya, *supra* note 1 at 77.

[194] *Id.* at 77–78.

[195] Hanspeter Mattes, *Formal and Informal Authority in Libya since 1969*, *in* Qadhafi's Revolution Revisited, *supra* note 3 at 62.

[196] McDermott, *Qaddafi and Libya*, *supra* note 192 at 398.

[197] Pargeter, Libya: The Rise and Fall of Qaddafi 64 (New Haven, USA: Yale University Press, 2012).

[198] Vandewalle, *Libya's Revolution in Perspective*, *in* Qadhafi's Revolution Revisited, *supra* note 3 at 10.

developing a fervently anti-imperialist mentality and strong opposition to Libya's monarchical system and its ruling elite.

Qadhafi participated in demonstrations in the 1960s, and began organizing students into a nascent underground opposition movement. He then entered the military academy along with other revolutionary-minded students, such as 'Abd al-Salam Jallud and 'Umar 'Abd al-Salam al-Mahayshi, who would both come to occupy important positions in Qadhafi's inner circle.[199]

On 1 September 1969 a group of roughly 70 Libyan junior military officers, led by the young Mu'ammar Qadhafi, launched a bloodless coup that quickly toppled the existing government.[200] The king's guards did not resist, and King Idris was himself outside the country receiving medical treatment. The Free Unionist Officers leaders, while not initially announcing their identities, assumed leadership of the country under the auspices of the RCC and issued an interim constitution on 11 December 1969 upon which they based their authority.[201] Qadhafi immediately stood out as the head of the RCC, and after a series of internal political struggles, would assume *de facto* rule of Libya until 2011. While the Free Officers were technically equal in rank, Qadhafi was the leader and engineer of the coup.[202]

The identities of the remaining members of the RCC were made public in early 1970, and consisted of Major 'Abd al-Salam Jallud, Major Bashir Hawadi, Captain Mukhtar 'Abdullah Gerwi, Captain 'Abd al-Mun'im Tahir al-Huni, Captain Mustafa al-Kharubi, Captain Al-Khawayldi al-Hamadi, Captain Muhammad Nijm, Captain 'Ali 'Awad Hamza, Captain Abu Bakr Yunis Jabr and Captain 'Umar 'Abd al-Salam al-Mahayshi.[203]

Like many lower- and middle-class Libyans, the Free Officers were hostile to the monarchy and King Idris because of their social marginalization. Its members came from poor or lower-middle class backgrounds, and from less prominent tribes who were not affiliated with the Senussi family or other powerful Cyrenaican families. 'Umar al-Mahayshi, from a well-connected wealthy Misratan family, was the only exception.[204] The

---

[199] PARGETER, LIBYA: THE RISE AND FALL OF QADDAFI, *supra* note 197 at 49–50.

[200] Nathan Alexander, *Libya: The Continuous Revolution*, 17(2) MIDDLE EASTERN STUDIES 210, 211 (1981).

[201] 1969 Libyan Constitution, Adopted Dec. 11, 1969, *available at* http://www.servat.unibe.ch/icl/ly00000_.html.

[202] Mattes, *Formal and Informal Authority in Libya since 1969*, in QADHAFI'S REVOLUTION REVISITED, *supra* note 3 at 56.

[203] VANDEWALLE, A HISTORY OF MODERN LIBYA, *supra* note 1 at 79.

[204] AHMIDA, THE MAKING OF MODERN LIBYA, *supra* note 4 at 156.

remainder had studied at the military academy because they had not been able to secure the requisite certificate to attend university.[205] Six years after they graduated, the Free Unionists were at the helm of the Libyan state. They stood as a clear change from contemporary Libyan politics, representing not only a tribal and class alternative to the dominance of King Idris and Cyrenaica, but also in a larger sens an Arab alternative to the staunchly western orientation of the Kingdom.

This aspect became more important after the 1967 Arab-Israeli War, and in concert with the wave of Arab nationalism in the region, the Free Officers demanded "total political and economic independence from any kind of foreign (particularly non-Arab) influence, direction, control or constraint."[206] Under Qadhafi's leadership in the military academy and subsequently in the army, the Free Officers came to strongly reject the policies and principles of King Idris in favor of the militant Arab nationalism of Nasser. The formation of the Free Officers movement was taken directly from Nasser's revolutionary model.[207] The 1969 coup replicated the Egyptian coup to such an extent that following the ouster of the king, Qadhafi reached out to Nasser, reportedly telling his advisor: "We have carried out this revolution. Now it is for Nasser to tell us what to do."[208]

While young and lacking any experience in political affairs, Qadhafi and the Free Unionist officers were adept at capturing the mood of the times and tapping into growing popular frustration. The coup leaders situated themselves to fill the power vacuum that existed in the country as the old regime slowly lost its grip on power. The officers saw Libya as a fundamentally unfair and unequal country, abundant in resources but where the majority of the population was poor and unable to advance socially or economically.[209] Certain segments of society were marginalized based on their social standing, geographic location, or tribal affiliation.[210] Latent discontent was apparent from the large-scale demonstrations that erupted following the overthrow of the old regime.[211]

---

[205] Vandewalle, *Libya's Revolution in Perspective, in* QADHAFI'S REVOLUTION REVISITED, *supra* note 3 at 10.

[206] Alexander, *Libya: The Continuous Revolution, supra* note 200 at 212.

[207] PARGETER, LIBYA: THE RISE AND FALL OF QADDAFI, *supra* note 197 at 51.

[208] *Id.* at 68.

[209] AHMIDA, THE MAKING OF MODERN LIBYA, *supra* note 4 at 156.

[210] Mattes, *Formal and Informal Authority in Libya since 1969, in* QADHAFI'S REVOLUTION REVISITED, *supra* note 3 at 70.

[211] PARGETER, LIBYA: THE RISE AND FALL OF QADDAFI, *supra* note 197 at 59.

The Free Officers introduced policies based on a simple political platform that called for social justice, self-determination, Arab nationalism and anti-colonialism. The 1969 Interim Constitution articulated three important themes that marked a radical departure from the policies of the past. First, it sounded a call to Arab unity and support for Arabs everywhere. Indeed, as discussed below, throughout the early 1980s Libya would pursue a policy of unification and integration with fellow Arab states. Second, it provided for a "socialist" state, one that was based on Arab and Muslim values, particularly the values of Libyan society, as spelled out later in Qadhafi's Green Book. Third, it demanded economic and political independence from western dominance and exploitation.

Other specific values enshrined in the interim constitution included the provision of free primary, secondary and tertiary education (Article 14), the establishment of a healthcare system (Article 15) and the right to private property except where such ownership was exploitative (Article 8). The RCC's objection to private property was not simply ideological. During the reign of King Idris the privatization of property had been a mechanism for corruption and cronyism, and the young revolutionaries demanded public ownership also as a kind of mechanism for accountability.[212]

The implementation of these ideas demonstrated, however, that the new government was reluctant or unable to break with many aspects of the past system. For example, certain rights remained curtailed, notably the right to freedom of expression. Under Article 13 of the interim constitution, expression was only "guaranteed within the limits of public interest and the principles of the Revolution." Political parties were also banned in a subsequent legislative act. These measures were in keeping with the policies of the former regime, which was suspicious of political parties and had banned their operation just months into the establishment of the kingdom.[213]

Religion played an important, albeit complex role in the formation of the revolutionary state. Islamic values and Sharī'a principles are clearly present in the interim constitution, and Qadhafi discussed religion regularly in his speeches. These references are somewhat misleading, however, as Qadhafi and his comrades were initially wary of religion and viewed it as a private matter to be kept out of the operation of the state.[214] The fact

---

[212] VANDEWALLE, A HISTORY OF MODERN LIBYA, *supra* note 1 at 92.

[213] Vandewalle, *Libya's Revolution in Perspective, in* QADHAFI'S REVOLUTION REVISITED, *supra* note 3 at 11.

[214] VANDEWALLE, A HISTORY OF MODERN LIBYA, *supra* note 1 at 81.

that King Idris was a religious leader likely influenced this view. In their earlier and more pragmatic iteration, Qadhafi and the RCC attempted to appease religious opponents by giving formal homage to Islam, and closing churches, banning alcohol, closing nightclubs and introducing certain Islamic forms of punishment.[215] Qadhafi, nonetheless, came to harshly repress any signs of political Islam, which he saw as the most dangerous internal challenge to his rule.

As such, Qadhafi's references to Islam are best understood as a mechanism for incorporating religious critiques in order to deter the potential of religious figures to disrupt his revolutionary state.[216] Qadhafi viewed influential religious leaders as a threat to his authority and suppressed Islamic groups that sought to organize outside of his control. Islamist groups were particularly prominent in the eastern province of Cyrenaica, in cities such as Benghazi, Ajdabiya, and Darna, where the Senussiya had been a strong political force prior to 1969.[217] One of the most notable groups targeted by the regime was the local branch of the Muslim Brotherhood (Al-Ikhwan al-Muslimun). The group's history in Libya began in the 1940s when members of the Egyptian Muslim Brotherhood began to enter Libya to flee persecution from their own government.[218] The Libyan branch was founded in the 1950s, and its ranks soon filled with the country's educated middle-classes and university students.[219] Along with the Ba'thists, communists, and members of the Islamic Liberation Party (Hizb al-Tahrir), members of the Muslim Brotherhood became targets of Qadhafi's popular committees and police forces, and were subject to mass arrests in the early 1970s.[220]

---

[215] *Id.* at 81.

[216] Alison Pargeter, *Qadhafi and Political Islam in Libya, in* QADHAFI'S REVOLUTION REVISITED, *supra* note 3 at 83.

[217] ANTHONY BELL & DAVID WITTER, INSTITUTE FOR THE STUDY OF WAR, 2 THE LIBYAN REVOLUTION: THE ROOTS OF REBELLION 16–17 (Sept. 2011) [hereinafter "THE ROOTS OF REBELLION"], *available at* www.understandingwar.org/sites/default/files/Libya_Part2_0.pdf.

[218] CHRISTOPHER M. BLANCHARD, LIBYA: UNREST AND U.S. POLICY, CONGRESSIONAL RESEARCH SERVICE 23, Sept. 29, 2011 [hereinafter "UNREST AND U.S. POLICY"], *available at* http://fpc.state.gov/documents/organization/175868.pdf.

[219] *See* interview with Dr 'Abd al-Monim Harisha, prominent member of the Libyan Muslim Brotherhood based in London, in Paul Cruickshank & Tim Lister, *Energized Muslim Brotherhood in Libya eyes a prize,* CNN, Mar. 25, 2011, *available at* http://www.cnn.com/2011/WORLD/africa/03/25/libya.islamists/index.html.

[220] PARGETER, LIBYA: THE RISE AND FALL OF QADDAFI, *supra* note 197 at 79.

The Brotherhood was banned in Libya in 1972, along with other political and opposition groups.[221]

Qadhafi and the RCC also failed to break from the policies of the former regime when it came to economic dependence from foreign powers. The country's economy continued to depend on outside investment to maintain its state infrastructure and high levels of oil production. In 1969, Libya's economy was wholly reliant upon the oil industry, which constituted 99 percent of the country's revenues. By 1973, it was Libya's only export commodity, as the country's agricultural and industrial sectors made up a mere 4.4 percent of its GDP.[222] Despite calls for economic independence, there was no practical way for the country to divest itself from multinational oil companies. Libya was simply unable to provide the highly-skilled laborers required for the country's oil extraction, especially given the relative complexity of its oil infrastructure.[223]

Under King Idris, the administrative bodies charged with overseeing the oil industry had relied on foreign assistance, and pressed for international investment and development, but not for equal participation or the development of a national work force capable of managing its oil fields. Consequently, in 1969 very few Libyans possessed the skills necessary for a modern oil economy.[224] The post-Idris government therefore inherited an economy that relied on outside intervention for survival, and was compelled to adopt policies that would extend over the decades of Qadhafi's rule. Even had it wanted to force out the multinationals and nationalize the oil industry, the RCC could not have done so without forfeiting its only revenue stream.[225] While dissenting views would later divide the RCC, in the immediate aftermath of the coup, the oil sector remained outside the scope of any substantial socialist reforms.

The RCC focused instead on Libya's comparative advantage, given high global demand and oil speculation. In 1969, Libya was pumping 3 million barrels of oil a day and receiving among the lowest prices of any state in

---

[221] CHRISTOPHER M. BLANCHARD, LIBYA: BACKGROUND AND U.S. RELATIONS, CONGRESSIONAL RESEARCH SERVICE 23, Aug. 6, 2008 [hereinafter "BACKGROUND AND U.S. RELATIONS"], *available at* http://fpc.state.gov/documents/organization/109510.pdf.

[222] Vandewalle, *Libya's Revolution in Perspective*, in QADHAFI'S REVOLUTION REVISITED, *supra* note 3 at 13–15.

[223] VANDEWALLE, A HISTORY OF MODERN LIBYA, *supra* note 1 at 89.

[224] *Id.* at 92.

[225] Vandewalle, *Libya's Revolution in Perspective, in* QADHAFI'S REVOLUTION REVISITED, *supra* note 3 at 9; VANDEWALLE, A HISTORY OF MODERN LIBYA, *supra* note 1 at 79.

the world.[226] This was the case despite the fact that Libyan crude oil has a very low sulfur content that requires minimal refinement, and should therefore sell at a higher market rate than oil from many other countries. Libya is not only a major producer in terms of quantity, but produces a type of "sweet crude" that is known as "the world's only irreplaceable oil."[227] Instead of forcing out multinational oil corporations, therefore, Qadhafi and the RCC raised taxes on multinationals doing business in Libya and negotiated for greater concessions.[228] The new Libyan leadership was able to double the price of its oil, from $2.21 per gallon in 1969 to $4.58 in 1973, and even higher after the oil crisis in the mid-1970s. Qadhafi was able to use the oil windfall to shore-up his domestic support. He was also instrumental in helping other oil producing countries to achieve the same results.[229]

Thus, when it came to the oil sector, the RCC lacked the internal capacity to implement the more extensive elements of their platform. In other areas, such as independence from foreign military powers, the RCC had greater success in putting its rhetoric into practice. The government closed the British military base and then the U.S. Wheelus Air Base in June 1970.[230] The RCC foreign policy platform, spelled out in the interim constitution, called for the closing of British and American military bases on Libyan territory, removal of all foreign troops, and political neutrality in the Cold War.[231]

The new government's foreign military policy, and especially the speeches of Qadhafi, were militant, giving voice and renewed vigor to the Arab nationalism of the time. This meant not only attacking Israel, but also any state that appeased the West or that, in Qadhafi's rhetoric, ignored the needs of its people.[232] Qadhafi presented himself as the voice for a generation of people who had lived through marginalization, both within Libya and abroad. To the older generation, including those who had lived through anti-colonial struggles in the region, however, Qadhafi

---

[226] Ronald Bruce St. John, *The Libyan Economy in Transition, in* QADHAFI'S REVOLUTION REVISITED, *supra* note 3 at 128.

[227] Jason Pack, *Libya is Too Big to Fail*, Mar. 18, 2011, FOREIGN POLICY, *available at* http://www.foreignpolicy.com/articles/2011/03/18/libya_is_too_big_to_fail.

[228] VANDEWALLE, A HISTORY OF MODERN LIBYA, *supra* note 1 at 87, 91.

[229] McDermott, *Qaddafi and Libya, supra* note 192 at 403.

[230] *Id.* at 398.

[231] Vandewalle, *Libya's Revolution in Perspective, in* QADHAFI'S REVOLUTION REVISITED, *supra* note 3 at 11.

[232] VANDEWALLE, A HISTORY OF MODERN LIBYA, *supra* note 1 at 127.

was inexperienced and his ideas simplistic and ill-conceived. Moreover, during the 1970s political unions in the region were being forged along Islamic lines, and Qadhafi's calls for pan-Arabism appeared increasingly outdated.[233]

Ultimately, during this period, Libya followed a more moderate and pragmatic line than the rhetoric suggested, maintaining formal and economic relations with the West, including with the United States.[234] The relationship between Libya and the West continued to function, as it had previously, by mutual necessity: the West needed Libya's oil and was intent on maintaining its contracts within the country, and Libya needed western investors and a market to sell its oil. This was especially so with the United States, ostensibly Qadhafi's greatest antagonist. By 1977, the United States was Libya's largest trading partner.[235] While Qadhafi called Libya's independence in December 1951 a "false independence," the Libya of the early 1970s was in many ways fundamentally similar to the Libya it had replaced.[236]

It is also noteworthy that under the watch of the RCC, the state by no means withered away. Despite various failed attempts at introducing democratic accountability, the RCC did not release the levers of control. Unlike the more radical approach adopted after 1977 with the establishment of the Socialist People's Libyan Arab Jamahiriyya, the Libyan Arabic Republic maintained provisions for the institutions of a regular state. During this period, the government invested massively in education and healthcare, raised and enforced minimum wages, provided interest free loans and subsidies for home construction, and began a process of redistributing land controlled by Italians and the Senussi.[237] The RCC also initiated plans to diversify the economy by building petrochemical plants, turnkey cement and steel factories, expanding harbors, developing the electrical grid, and engaging in significant land reclamation and agricultural research.[238] Oil refineries were also built to develop domestic capacity and deepen Libyan influence over the oil industry.

Despite its rhetoric, the RCC was also relatively lenient with regard to the political opposition in the aftermath of the September 1969 coup.

---

[233] PARGETER, LIBYA: THE RISE AND FALL OF QADDAFI, *supra* note 197 at 121.

[234] VANDEWALLE, A HISTORY OF MODERN LIBYA, *supra* note 1 at 86.

[235] Chorin, *The Future of the U.S.-Libyan Commercial Relationship, in* QADHAFI'S REVOLUTION REVISITED, *supra* note 3 at 160.

[236] AHMIDA, THE MAKING OF MODERN LIBYA, *supra* note 4 at 157.

[237] VANDEWALLE, A HISTORY OF MODERN LIBYA, *supra* note 1 at 88.

[238] *Id.* at 93.

There were few arrests and short jail sentences for political opponents, in addition to sackings of supporters of the former regime.[239] This initial approach demonstrated openness and restraint, especially when compared to a decade later when Qadhafi would openly call for the killing of the regime's opponents.

A little more than a year after taking power, the RCC began taking steps towards creating a more participatory system of governance by making provisions for an elected legislature. The legislative body itself was to be comprised of representatives of "popular congresses" across the country. The parliament would in turn elect the country's president. Qadhafi announced the plan for this "popular rule" at a speech in January 1971 in Zawiyya.[240]

While political parties were not permitted, members of the RCC campaigned across the country to encourage popular participation. Election results were far from what Qadhafi and the RCC expected. Libyans expressed little interest in politics and paid scant attention to the government's democratic initiatives.[241] While some Libyans appreciated the RCC's economic platforms and Qadhafi's fiery tongue, they appear not to have cared much for organized political programs.[242] The popular congresses did succeed in mobilizing middle and upper class Libyans, which was the population that the RCC specifically sought to exclude from power by enfranchising impoverished and marginalized groups.

In the wake of the failure of the January 1971 initiative, on 11 June 1971 the RCC formed an Arab Socialist Union (ASU), based on the Egyptian model. Rather than calling for mass participation, the RCC would create a vanguard party to lead the people.[243] Formal leadership of the ASU belonged to Qadhafi as head of the RCC.[244] However, as with its predecessor, the ASU attracted young, upwardly mobile Libyans who were procedurally engaged but politically suspect, which is to say that they did not profess the radical attitudes and stances Qadhafi and the RCC were looking for. The more radical participants that the RCC had hoped to find – the lower

---

[239] *Id.* at 81–82.

[240] *Id.* at 82; Vandewalle, *Libya's Revolution in Perspective, in* QADHAFI'S REVOLUTION REVISITED, *supra* note 3 at 11.

[241] VANDEWALLE, A HISTORY OF MODERN LIBYA, *supra* note 1 at 82; Vandewalle, *Libya's Revolution in Perspective, in* QADHAFI'S REVOLUTION REVISITED, *supra* note 3 at 11.

[242] VANDEWALLE, A HISTORY OF MODERN LIBYA, *supra* note 1 at 89.

[243] *Id.* at 83; Vandewalle, *Libya's Revolution in Perspective, in* QADHAFI'S REVOLUTION REVISITED, *supra* note 3 at 11–12.

[244] Alexander, *Libya: The Continuous Revolution, supra* note 200 at 215.

classes downtrodden by occupation, the monarchy and capitalism – failed to materialize.[245]

While these moves did not effect major social or political change in the system, they did mark a turning point in the trajectory of Libyan history. The People's Court was created in 1971 to try members of the former royal family and others accused of corruption. This court came to be known for deterring dissent through its closed trials of political opponents, until it was abolished in January 2005.[246] All political activity outside the ASU was banned in May 1972.[247] What was new was not the ban on parties, but that after 1972 political expression outside certain controlled spaces was also illegal. This was the start of a policy of curbing freedom of expression that would be a defining characteristic of the Libyan state for decades to come.

As part of efforts to encourage engagement with the ASU, elections were held in December 1971 and January 1972. As far as the RCC and Qadhafi were concerned, the results for the ASU elections were catastrophic. Politically engaged moderates repeatedly took over the union, again derailing the revolutionary potential Qadhafi saw in the ASU and the Libyan people.[248] Disgusted and disgruntled, Qadhafi approached the matter head on when, on the occasion of the Prophet's birthday, he announced in a speech in the city of Zuwara a new phase of the revolution. Qadhafi was preparing to initiate the radical reformation of Libyan society for which he would become infamous.[249]

In its broadest terms, the period between 1 September 1969 and the April 1973 Zuwara speech marked a period of conventional revolutionary attitudes on the part of Qadhafi and the RCC. Qadhafi and his comrades had taken over Libya in order to increase the material well-being of the people and free it from the grip of western control symbolized by the American and British military bases located on its soil. For all its radical language, however, the RCC and Qadhafi were traditional in their outlook, and attempted to build a state and work with the existing global economic system to profit from Libya's oil.

---

[245] Amal Obeidi, *Political Elites in Libya Since 1969, in* QADHAFI'S REVOLUTION REVISITED, *supra* note 3 at 107.

[246] Report of the International Commission of Inquiry on Libya, U.N. HRC. 19th Sess., Annex I, ¶ 41. U.N. Doc. A/HRC/19/68, advance unedited version (Mar. 2, 2012).

[247] VANDEWALLE, A HISTORY OF MODERN LIBYA, *supra* note 1 at 83.

[248] *Id.* at 83.

[249] Alexander, *Libya: The Continuous Revolution, supra* note 200 at 216–217.

There was also an abiding faith in the early period in the ultimate unity of all Arabs. Qadhafi sought to enter political union with other states on five occasions, reaching preliminary agreements with Egypt and Sudan in 1969, Egypt and Syria in 1971, Egypt in 1972, Algeria in 1973, and Tunisia in 1974.[250] These efforts were stymied, however, by the reality that his fellow Arab leaders wanted solidarity, not a literal unification of political systems. As would be the case in many instances in the following decades, Qadhafi became increasingly frustrated when his visions clashed with reality.

Qadhafi and the RCC had been able to achieve a number of important goals, as they had dismantled the power of the Senussiya and the monarchical institutions from King Idris's reign.[251] But Qadhafi was repeatedly disappointed by his inability to convince Libyans and his fellow Arabs of the indispensability of his vision of an egalitarian and militantly anti-imperialist world. His disappointment fueled more radical changes in Libya's system, leading to the April 1973 proclamation of the Popular Revolution and the launching of 2,000 people's committees.[252]

8.2. Qadhafi's Popular Revolution

Qadhafi viewed Libya in 1973 in much the way he did in 1969 – as a state in which power was vested at the top and in which ordinary people were marginalized from political participation. Qadhafi maintained the mentality of an opposition leader; he did not think of himself as the head of the Libyan state, but rather saw his role as a figure outside the system constantly leading revolutionary movements with the aim of altering traditional governmental structures.[253] This view would bring him into conflict not only with the very essence of the Libyan state, but also with members of the RCC who may have shared his analysis but disagreed with his methods.

Qadhafi remained a believer in the people, even if they did not act the way he hoped.[254] He and the RCC were now determined that the state itself was the problem, and that the oil industry, in particular, would benefit from greater popular control. Therefore, in 1973 initiatives were

---

[250] VANDEWALLE, A HISTORY OF MODERN LIBYA, *supra* note 1 at 87. Libya reached preliminary agreement over union with Chad in 1981 and Morocco in 1984.

[251] *Id.* at 94–95.

[252] McDermott, *Qaddafi and Libya, supra* note 192 at 405.

[253] *Id.* at 404.

[254] VANDEWALLE, A HISTORY OF MODERN LIBYA, *supra* note 1 at 96.

introduced to diminish power of the formal institutions, while at the same time building up state control over economic enterprise. These initiatives have been characterized as the start of "a course of increasingly dramatic and contradictory policies that simultaneously aimed at putting the state in charge of all economic activity, and tried to make it irrelevant as a focus for political identity."[255]

In Qadhafi's 1973 Zuwara speech, he outlined a five-point program and emerging system that would come to dominate Libyan society for decades to come.[256] The five planks of the program were: first, the nullification of all existing laws and structures in favor of those that promoted the interests of the people and the commandments of Islam; second, that Libyan communists, atheists and members of the Muslim Brotherhood be purged; three, that the people be armed for popular resistance; four, that the bureaucracy be revolutionized so that the needs of the people would no longer be neglected; and five, that the country engage in a cultural revolution.[257] This five-point program was the outline of a plan that would effectively sweep away Libya's existing political structures.[258] The most important element of this radical vision and reformation of Libya came in the form of what Qadhafi called "popular revolution," later catalogued in the Green Book, which spelled out what Qadhafi called the "Third Universal Theory" that would serve as the ideological guideline for the revolutionary system.[259]

The RCC was already in many respects a populist organization, but in calling for popular revolution Qadhafi deepened his commitment to populist rule. No longer, as far as he was concerned, would government and bureaucrats stand in the way of popular power, as authority would reside directly with the people in the form of people's committees. This direct and immediate democracy would, by its very nature, render diversion away from the people's interests impossible.[260]

Qadhafi's popular revolution contained three important elements: firstly, it led to the dismantling of government institutions and structures,

---

[255] *Id.*

[256] *Id.* at 85.

[257] Mattes, *Formal and Informal Authority in Libya since 1969, supra* note 195 at 77; McDermott, *Qaddafi and Libya, supra* note 192 at 404.

[258] PARGETER, LIBYA: THE RISE AND FALL OF QADDAFI, *supra* note 197 at 49–50.

[259] VANDEWALLE, A HISTORY OF MODERN LIBYA, *supra* note 1 at 85.

[260] Vandewalle, *Libya's Revolution in Perspective, in* QADHAFI'S REVOLUTION REVISITED, *supra* note 3 at 12.

from the lowest to the highest rungs, including those that had been built up since 1969; secondly, it destroyed existing formal participatory mechanisms; and finally, it produced Qadhafi's Third Universal Theory.[261] In effect, Qadhafi's proposals set out to destroy any government or social forces that blocked the revolutionary potential of direct, local control of the people. The lower and middle classes, and especially the youth, would be handed power and their natural, radical inclinations would lead the way.[262]

The day after proclaiming his popular revolution, Qadhafi announced that direct democracy would be achieved in Libya through the election of popular congresses and committees at all levels of society: in cities, neighborhoods, schools and workplaces.[263] By August 1973, there were over 2,000 people's committees in operation.[264] The building block of the popular revolution was the Basic People's Congress, the fundamental organizational body to which every person belonged. Each elected a basic people's committee, which assumed executive and administrative responsibility for the Basic People's Congress, implementing its directives and enforcing its rules.[265] The members of the basic people's congress also elected working committees, which formed a general popular congress for each geographic district. The members of the general popular congresses then elected the General People's Congress, the national legislative body. The General People's Congress in turn elected a General People's Committee, which served as the government's cabinet.[266]

This structure placed every Libyan within a Basic People's Congress. It was, in theory, a system of direct participatory democracy, giving each citizen a voice and role in governing the country.[267] This new system replaced all existing political systems, as the ASU was refashioned in 1976 as the General People's Congress,[268] and laid the political foundation of the Libyan state that would exist until 2011.

In making these revisions and establishing people's committees, Libya abolished

---

[261] *Id.* at 12.

[262] *Id.* at 9, 12.

[263] Alexander, *Libya: The Continuous Revolution, supra* note 200 at 217.

[264] PARGETER, LIBYA: THE RISE AND FALL OF QADDAFI, *supra* note 197 at 79.

[265] VANDEWALLE, A HISTORY OF MODERN LIBYA, *supra* note 1 at 104–105.

[266] VANDEWALLE, A HISTORY OF MODERN LIBYA, *supra* note 1 at 104–105.

[267] Alexander, *Libya: The Continuous Revolution, supra* note 200 at 220.

[268] VANDEWALLE, A HISTORY OF MODERN LIBYA, *supra* note 1 at 105.

[t]he local government modernizing structures originally encouraged by the RCC and caused a significant reduction in the authority of modernizing officials. People's committees assumed local administrative functions, and the chairmen of the municipal and provincial people's committees became the chief administrative officials for the municipality and the province, respectively. In addition to their administrative functions, people's committees at the municipal level were also given legislative responsibility for such service functions as health clinics, minor roads, sewage, water, parks, clubs and so forth.[269]

Several important sectors, including essential government agencies, were not affected by these changes, however, and were not subject to popular control.[270] The RCC sat atop the decision-making chain and was still able to issue directives. Similarly, foreign policy, the military, and economic matters remained in the control of Qadhafi, the RCC and a number of specialized agencies. These changes, furthermore, did not apply to the oil sector, which remained the engine of Libya's economy managed by a tightly controlled bureaucracy.

While Qadhafi held the post of Chairman of the RCC and was its informal leader, his was not the only voice within the group during this period, and a number objected to his proposals. The massive oil reserves at Libya's disposal and the proactive manner with which the RCC went about increasing revenues meant the country was awash with money. By 1979, oil revenue brought $95 million annually into Libyan state coffers. For Qadhafi, this revenue provided the means for building a "just, egalitarian and participatory society – and to adopt an increasingly activist confrontation with the West."[271] Although the rest of the RCC generally shared this view, they did not agree that its achievement required the abolition of Libya's regulatory apparatus and the destruction of its bureaucracy.[272]

By the end of 1974 two clear factions had developed within the RCC. On the one hand were the technocrats who desired a strong central government to efficiently implement the RCC's political agenda, and who were skeptical of Qadhafi's foreign adventurism. On the other side stood Qadhafi and his staunch allies, ready to sacrifice development in the name of mass mobilization, both within Libya and the wider Arab world.[273] The debate was highly ideological and centered on a number of factors, but in

---

[269] Alexander, *Libya: The Continuous Revolution, supra* note 200 at 218.
[270] *Id.* at 210, 224.
[271] VANDEWALLE, A HISTORY OF MODERN LIBYA, *supra* note 1 at 97.
[272] *Id.* at 99.
[273] *Id.* at 100.

practical terms hinged on whether Libya would use its oil wealth to build a state or to deconstruct it.[274]

Qadhafi attempted to marginalize his opponents in the RCC by promoting non-politicians to important posts within the government.[275] This move was in keeping with his larger plan to devolve power to citizens and had the effect of marginalizing opposing voices. Throughout the end of 1974 and the first half of the following year, the two factions within the RCC fought for the upper hand. This instability was reflected on the streets of Tripoli, where students went on strike and workers seemed restless. In August 1975, the situation came to a head. 'Umar 'Abd al-Salam al-Mahayshi, the Minister of Planning and a leader of the technocratic wing of the party, refused to dispense funds for several Qadhafi-backed development projects. In short order, he and another RCC member, Bashir Hawadi, launched a coup against Qadhafi's leadership, bringing the two factions into open confrontation.

Ultimately, Qadhafi's faction emerged victorious after another influential RCC member, 'Abd al-Salam Jallud, sided with Qadhafi and forced Al-Mahayshi into exile, leaving the radicals within the RCC in control.[276] With the ouster of Al-Mahayshi and his supporters, only five RCC members remained within the fold just six years after its establishment: Qadhafi himself, Abu Bakr Yunis Jabr, Al-Khawayldi al-Hamadi, Al-Kharubi and Jallud.[277] Of the other 13 original members of the RCC, one died in a car crash, two were placed under house arrest by Qadhafi, one was relieved of his duties, and the remainder went into exile. Twenty-three non-RCC Free Officers were executed in the aftermath of the Al-Mahayshi failed coup.[278]

The historical importance of the August 1975 coup cannot be understated, as it marked the end of the revolutionary counterbalance to Qadhafi and the beginning of his consolidation of exclusive control over Libya's affairs of state. All political opponents were removed from military and political bodies, and tribal politics again assumed importance as Qadhafi increasingly relied on certain tribes for support, something that would have very unlikely in 1969. While the RCC was initially composed of a diverse and roughly proportionate mix of officers from Tripolitania, Cyrenaica and Fezzan, as well as a variety of tribes, after Al-Mahayshi's

---

[274] Vandewalle, *Libya's Revolution in Perspective, in* QADHAFI'S REVOLUTION REVISITED, *supra* note 3 at 18.

[275] VANDEWALLE, A HISTORY OF MODERN LIBYA, *supra* note 1 at 84.

[276] AHMIDA, THE MAKING OF MODERN LIBYA, *supra* note 4 at 158.

[277] VANDEWALLE, A HISTORY OF MODERN LIBYA, *supra* note 1 at 101.

[278] AHMIDA, THE MAKING OF MODERN LIBYA, *supra* note 4 at 158.

failed coup, Qadhafi turned inward to promote those whose personal connections and tribal loyalties put them beyond suspicion.[279]

Qadhafi and the surviving members of the RCC did not stop with purging the technocrats from positions of authority. In the aftermath of the failed coup, the existing policy of targeting political opponents was accelerated, as Marxists, communists, Ba'thists, trade unionists, government ministers and workers, businessmen and religious leaders were marginalized or simply eliminated.[280] The use of repression became widespread, as the revolutionary government began a policy of systematic violence to deter dissent, in sharp contrast to the relatively bloodless nature of the 1969 coup.[281] In April 1976, the regime forces entered college campuses in Tripoli and Benghazi to quell demonstrations, detaining hundreds of students. The following year there were public hangings on the campus of Tripoli's Al-Fatah University.[282] This type of public display of violence would become a trademark of the Qadhafi regime, reminding both opponents and non-politicized citizens that even speaking publicly entailed great risks.

The 1975 coup attempt also marked the beginning of Qadhafi's more extreme policies, characterized as the "breaking point in the politics of revolutionary Libya."[283] These policies would intensify culminating in March 1977, when the Libyan Arab Republic was replaced by the Socialist People's Libyan Arab Jamahiriyya. The Jamahiriyya signified the realization of Qadhafi's vision articulated at Zuwara, the values of the Third Universal Theory. It would entail seeking to integrate the revolution into Libyan society through more forceful measures than had been employed previously.

9. The Socialist People's Libyan Arab Jamahiriyya: 1977–2001

9.1. *The 1977 Declaration of the Establishment of the Jamahiriyya*

The General People's Congress formally announced the establishment of the Jamahiriyya on 2 March 1977, representing the formal enactment of a process that had been gaining momentum since 1973. In some respects, the announcement of the Jamahiriyya also completed the fundamental

---

[279] Mattes, *Formal and Informal Authority in Libya since 1969, supra* note 195 at 73; VANDEWALLE, A HISTORY OF MODERN LIBYA, *supra* note 1 at 101.

[280] Alexander, *Libya: The Continuous Revolution, supra* note 200 at 217; McDermott, *Qaddafi and Libya, supra* note 192 at 406.

[281] PARGETER, LIBYA: THE RISE AND FALL OF QADDAFI, *supra* note 197 at 94.

[282] *Id.*

[283] VANDEWALLE, A HISTORY OF MODERN LIBYA, *supra* note 1 at 101.

break Libya had made with its past after September 1969. The name was itself new, a neologism invented by Qadhafi, combining the Arabic words for "masses" and "state", indicating that the Jamahiriyya was a *sui generis* state of the people or state of the masses, distinct from the republic and monarchy that preceded it. The establishment of the Jamahiriyya signaled the beginning of the "era of the masses" as defined by Qadhafi.[284]

Some of the elements of the Jamahiriyya had already come into existence, such as the representative system announced in Zuwara in 1973, and the abolishment of the ASU in 1977. Now, with the 1977 Declaration on the Authority of the People, the RCC was also formally abolished, leaving Qadhafi as the Secretary General of the General People's Congress. In December 1978, Qadhafi resigned from this position, taking on the formal role of head of the military and the informal role of the "guide" of the revolution.

At the theoretical level, the Jamahiriyya represented a political community of inclusion in which "ordinary citizens own the country's resources, exercise authority, and directly manage the country's administration and its bureaucracy through a system of popular congresses and committees."[285] The idea behind the new system was to create a "stateless society" with popular rule carried out by the masses. In this new order, the state was no longer responsible for the social provisions it had provided since 1969, such as education and healthcare investments, minimum wage enforcements, interest-free loans, and subsidies.[286] The Jamahiriyya called for the people to organize and take on these responsibilities themselves, at the local level.

At its core, the Jamahiriyya embodied Qadhafi's quest for radical independence and the basic proposition that "the wealth of the nation should be shared equally, and this equality could only be established if no individual was dependent economically upon another."[287] As the 1970s progressed, Qadhafi published the three volumes of the Green Book, outlining his political theory and the basis for the Jamahiriyya state. The three volumes themselves were made up of a series of Qadhafi's speeches and

---

[284] Vandewalle, *Libya's Revolution in Perspective, in* QADHAFI'S REVOLUTION REVISITED, *supra* note 3 at 20.
[285] Vandewalle, *Libya's Revolution in Perspective, in* QADHAFI'S REVOLUTION REVISITED, *supra* note 3 at 19.
[286] VANDEWALLE, A HISTORY OF MODERN LIBYA, *supra* note 1 at 88.
[287] *Id.* at 107.

writings during the regime's increasingly radical period from 1973 onwards. According to Vandewalle, "The Green Book's central tenet is that ordinary citizens can directly manage the bureaucratic and administrative institutions that shape their lives, and devise their own solutions to their economic and social problems."[288]

The three volumes of the Green Book – Democracy, The Solution of the Economic Problem and The Social Basis of the Third Universal Theory – were published between September 1976 and June 1979. In them, Qadhafi laid out in progressive form how the preceding experiments in electoral democracy had not represented the will of the people (Book 1), because at the time Libyans had not been given control over their economic lives and still suffered from inequality (Book 2), and that this required a radical overhaul of the country's social structure (Book 3).[289]

Qadhafi's Third Universal Theory – the subject of the third volume of the Green Book – was particularly notable as it represented a stark alternative to both of the dominant political forces of the day, capitalism and communism. As Qadhafi explained in the Green Book, it represented a clear Libyan and Muslim "alternative to capitalist materialism and communist atheism."[290] Libya's leader argued that true democracy was not possible in capitalist states where inequality deprived large swathes of the population of their right to equality and equal participation. Democracy was also not possible in communist states, Qadhafi argued, where power was concentrated at the top, communicating itself through diktats and directives.

The Jamahiriyya was the embodiment of the Third Universal Theory – a state in which political and economic hierarchies were eliminated and where people approached each other as equals. It represented an alternative that was neither capitalist nor communist, and as Qadhafi propounded, was better suited to the values undergirding Libyan tribal life and Islam. As such, it also provided a design for uniting Muslim and Arab communities more broadly.[291] Indeed, for Qadhafi it would become a model for all developing countries.

---

[288] Vandewalle, *Libya's Revolution in Perspective, in* QADHAFI'S REVOLUTION REVISITED, *supra* note 3 at 19.

[289] *Id.* at 9, 19.

[290] *Quoted in* Oye Ogunbadejo, *Qaddafi's North African Design*, 8(1) INTERNATIONAL SECURITY 154, 155 (1983).

[291] *Id.* at 156.

In order to implement this vision, the regime dissolved formal government institutions and replaced them with hollowed-out administrative bodies alongside parallel power structures under Qadhafi's direct control. In September 1978, Qadhafi announced the formation of a "revolutionary authority" that would be separate from the "people's authority." The General People's Congress then introduced the Declaration on the Separation of Rule and Revolution on 2 March 1979, declaring that the "instruments of government" would function apart from the "instruments of the revolution." This formally separated Qadhafi and the military from the Basic and General People's Congresses.

Qadhafi still wielded supreme power in the country, ruling by proxy as he selected the heads of the General People's Committee, giving himself indirect control over the main administrative body of the state.[292] He also retained control by creating "endless committees and congresses as well as scores of regulatory and supervisory bodies" that fostered "a sense of orchestrated chaos" in which he was the voice of "wisdom and calm."[293] John Alterman provides a blunt assessment of Qadhafi's Libya, concluding, "The governmental system in Libya created committees upon committees – so much representation, in fact, that the system was merely a cover for despotism."[294]

In 1979, Qadhafi announced the Revolutionary Committees movement, which would function as the paramilitary wing of the revolutionary authority.[295] These Revolutionary Committees, composed of Qadhafi's most ardent supporters, were tasked with protecting Libya,[296] enforcing policy directives,[297] and serving "as instruments for further mobilization and indoctrination."[298] Qadhafi had first announced the intent to arm a "people's military" in order to protect the revolution during his April 1973 Zuwara speech, and revolutionary cells began operating as early as 1976. Qadhafi had indicated that the committees would function as a security mechanism for the revolution, and they did indeed become the

---

[292] VANDEWALLE, A HISTORY OF MODERN LIBYA, *supra* note 1 at 120.

[293] Alison Pargeter, *Libya: Reforming the Impossible?*, 33 REVIEW OF AFRICAN POLITICAL ECONOMY 225 (2006).

[294] John Alterman, *Foreward, in* QADHAFI'S REVOLUTION REVISITED, *supra* note 3 at xii.

[295] PARGETER, LIBYA: THE RISE AND FALL OF QADDAFI, *supra* note 197 at 95, 97.

[296] AHMIDA, THE MAKING OF MODERN LIBYA, *supra* note 4 at 158.

[297] Mattes, *Formal and Informal Authority in Libya since 1969, supra* note 195 at 67; Vandewalle, *Libya's Revolution in Perspective, in* QADHAFI'S REVOLUTION REVISITED, *supra* note 3 at 23.

[298] VANDEWALLE, A HISTORY OF MODERN LIBYA, *supra* note 1 at 120.

force behind the revolutionary authority.[299] The Revolutionary Committees carried out the task of eliminating all opposition to the regime, as daily suppression fell to them rather than the regular army forces.[300] This strategy allowed for a measure of separation between the Jamahiriyya and everyday political violence that, without official mechanisms for accountability, created a culture of impunity.

As the Revolutionary Committees expanded into all facets of Libyan society, they essentially became heavily-armed enforcers of Qadhafi's will.[301] At the behest of Qadhafi, the Revolutionary Committees would assume the role of the police (arresting and interrogating alleged counter revolutionaries) and the judiciary (through the revolutionary courts established after 1980).[302] Qadhafi specifically empowered the Revolutionary Committees to carry out extrajudicial killings of political opponents in order to "guarantee the revolutionary order."[303] The revolutionary authorities came to infiltrate every corner of Libyan society and exert ultimate control within the organs of government, allowing Qadhafi to dictate policies through the people's committees, and ensure compliance with their decisions through the Revolutionary Committees.[304]

Under Qadhafi's authority, the system came to rely on informal armed structures that operated parallel to the formal state apparatus to enforce the revolution. Revolutionary authority directly challenged the formal structures that Qadhafi had himself created.[305] The new directives and initiatives effectively rendered Libya's formal institutions impotent, as the country's legislative framework, judicial and national institutions all deteriorated.[306] The courts served as tools of repression through which to spread fear and quell dissent. The People's Court continued to pass harsh sentences against political opponents in closed trials. Qadhafi also created revolutionary courts staffed by members of the Revolutionary Committees. They were given free reign to conduct mass trials of political opponents, including retrials of prisoners who had been arrested after 1973.[307] Qadhafi's directives gave him control over the political, judicial and

---

[299] Id.
[300] Id. at 147.
[301] Mattes, *Formal and Informal Authority in Libya since 1969, supra* note 195 at 67.
[302] Id. at 68.
[303] Id. at 80.
[304] Id. at 66; VANDEWALLE, A HISTORY OF MODERN LIBYA, *supra* note 1 at 121.
[305] VANDEWALLE, A HISTORY OF MODERN LIBYA, *supra* note 1 at 119.
[306] PARGETER, LIBYA: THE RISE AND FALL OF QADDAFI, *supra* note 197 at 96, 100.
[307] Id. at 101.

economic institutions, and were of greater force and authority than any judicial ruling.[308]

The Jamahiriyya thus came to embody more a construction of Qadhafi's vision, and less the will of the masses. It is doubtful whether the majority of Libyan society wanted, or even understood the sweeping revolutionary policies Qadhafi was pursuing.[309] While some zealously embraced Qadhafi's ideas, the majority went along through coercion or out of fear. Qadhafi maintained that his course was the only path for Libya, and that if necessary he would "take people to paradise in chains."[310]

Although he held no formal position in the Jamahiriyya, Qadhafi was recognized as the "Guide to the Revolution" or "Brother Leader," a figure who simply "advised" on policies and then could conveniently blame any failures on institutions or "the people."[311] According to Alterman's analysis, Libya had become an authoritarian state with a mass of alienated and disinterested citizens, and an enforcement squad capable of subduing any opposition that did arise.[312]

While Qadhafi created parallel armed structures to ensure against dissent, he simultaneously invested heavily in the military sector, which remained Libya's most powerful formal institution. Qadhafi was familiar with the manner in which the military operated, and took measures to ensure loyalty from its leaders through providing them with access to a steady stream of resources. The Jamahiriyya's military spending reached such exorbitant levels in the 1970s–1980s that Libya acquired more equipment than the military could use.[313] Libya was importing an average of $3 billion in arms purchases annually.[314] This policy, along with other measures, helped keep the armed forces largely de-politicized throughout this period.[315]

To the extent that any discontent did develop within the military, the Revolutionary Committees served as a counterbalance to the formal security apparatus.[316] Additionally, Qadhafi created a number of security organizations that existed outside the regular military structures, such

---

[308] Report of the International Commission of Inquiry, advance unedited version (Mar. 2, 2012), Annex I, ¶ 43, *supra* note 246.

[309] PARGETER, LIBYA: THE RISE AND FALL OF QADDAFI, *supra* note 197 at 81.

[310] *Id.* at 80.

[311] Pargeter, *Libya: Reforming the Impossible?, supra* note 293 at 226.

[312] Vandewalle, *Libya's Revolution in Perspective, in* QADHAFI'S REVOLUTION REVISITED, *supra* note 3 at 33.

[313] PARGETER, LIBYA: THE RISE AND FALL OF QADDAFI, *supra* note 197 at 110.

[314] VANDEWALLE, A HISTORY OF MODERN LIBYA, *supra* note 1 at 148.

[315] *Id.* at 147.

[316] PARGETER, LIBYA: THE RISE AND FALL OF QADDAFI, *supra* note 197 at 80.

as the Revolutionary Guard (*Al-Haras al-Thawri*), the People's Guard (*Al-Haras al-Sha'bi*), and the Purification Committees (*lijan al-tathir*).[317] These bodies shared in the task of protecting the regime and the revolutionary order. In essence, these parallel structures served to ensure Qadhafi's power, by infiltrating and monitoring the formal security institutions and governing bodies.

United States intelligence agencies reported internally in 1986 that Qadhafi continued to emphasize the creation of popular militias as a "counterweight to the regular armed forces." The CIA assessed that the "revolutionary committees' campaign of backstabbing and political intrigue against military officers" had been a principal source of military discontent for several years. The creation of new irregular armed bodies confirmed, in the view of the CIA, the "expanded influence of the Revolutionary Committees at the expense of professional army officers."[318] The reliance on informal governing structures allowed for a system of governance tightly controlled by Qadhafi and his inner circle, as the posts of the Revolutionary Committees were filled with members of his family and tribe, the Qadhadhfa.[319]

Qadhafi also assigned members of his inner circle, family and tribe to positions of power within the regular armed forces,[320] and he appointed blood relatives to important positions. Brigadier Ahmad Qadhaf al-Dam, for instance, was appointed as Commander of the Tobruq military region, then Commander in Cyrenaica, and later as Qadhafi's Special Representative for Relations with Egypt, while Brigadier Sayyid Muhammad Qadhaf al-Dam served as an officer with political control functions, and as General Coordinator of the Social People's Leadership Committees, and Colonel Khalifa Hanaysh served early on as Qadhafi's personal bodyguard and Commander of the Presidential Guard, and in the 1990s began taking charge of armaments procurement for the regime.[321] Perhaps most notably, Qadhafi's son, Khamis Qadhafi, served as Commander of the elite 32nd "Khamis" Katiba. The 32nd Katiba became known as

---

[317] Hanspeter Mattes, *Challenges to Security Sector Governance in the Middle East: The Libyan Case* 15–16 (Geneva Centre for the Democratic Control of Armed Forces conference paper presented 12–13 July 2004), *available at* http://www.dcaf.ch/Event-Attachement/ Challenges-to-Security-Sector-Governance-in-the-Middle-East-the-Libyan-Case.

[318] *Libya: Qadhafi's Political Position Since the Airstrike*, U.S. Central Intelligence Agency, Directorate of Intelligence, secret report, July 17, 1986, *available at* http://www.foia.cia.gov/ docs/DOC_0000389192/DOC_0000389192.pdf.

[319] PARGETER, LIBYA: THE RISE AND FALL OF QADDAFI, *supra* note 197 at 98–99.

[320] VANDEWALLE, A HISTORY OF MODERN LIBYA, *supra* note 1 at 120.

[321] Mattes, *Challenges to Security Sector Governance in the Middle East*, *supra* note 317 at 7–8.

the most loyal military unit, referred to as a "primary regime protection element" by NATO in 2011.[322] Colonel Qadhafi turned to his brother-in-law, 'Abdullah al-Senussi to handle State intelligence and surveillance of political opponents.[323] Under his leadership, the Internal Security Agency (ISA) was tasked with monitoring both internal and external threats to the regime.[324]

The Qadhafi regime also instituted economic reforms in the 1970s and through the following decade, geared towards ensuring loyalty among the population. In sum, these reforms fundamentally realigned Libya's economic and social undergirding through a process of nationalization, expropriation and redistribution. As with the old regime, Qadhafi's Libya was built upon a "highly developed patronage network" on which the entire political power structure of the country was built.[325] Redistribution was therefore carried out according to the needs of the regime, as Qadhafi allocated privilege to the most loyal, including the informal security organizations, members of the security services and his inner circle. Members of Revolutionary Committees, for example, were given their own farms in the countryside, and security officers received expensive cars.[326]

Qadhafi used small handouts to keep the population obedient, and more substantial outlays for the regime's coalition of supporters that ensured its survival.[327] This system entailed privileging certain groups such as the Qadhadhfa and Warfalla tribes, while marginalizing others, such as the indigenous Berber population.

These economic reforms therefore dovetailed with Qadhafi's policies of differential treatment of different social groups. The Berbers had long been at odds with the regime, in particular because of Qadhafi's policy of Arabization, which entailed the banning of their native Amazigh

---

[322] VARUN VIRA & ANTHONY H. CORDESMAN, CENTER FOR STRATEGIC AND INTERNATIONAL STUDIES, THE LIBYAN UPRISING: AN UNCERTAIN TRAJECTORY, 18 (June 20, 2011) [hereinafter "THE LIBYAN UPRISING"], *available at* http://csis.org/files/publication/110620_libya.pdf

[323] David D. Kirkpatrick & Suliman Ali Zway, *Spy Chief for Qaddafi is Extradited to Libya*, Sept. 5, 2012, N.Y. TIMES, *available at* http://www.nytimes.com/2012/09/06/world/africa/senussi-qaddafi-spy-chief-is-extradited-to-libya.html.

[324] Report of the International Commission of Inquiry to investigate all the alleged violations of international human rights law in the Libyan Arab Jamahiriya, U.N. HRC. 17th Sess., ¶ 40. U.N. Doc. A/HRC/17/44 (Jan. 12, 2012).

[325] Pargeter, *Libya: Reforming the Impossible?, supra* note 293 at 228.

[326] PARGETER, LIBYA: THE RISE AND FALL OF QADDAFI, *supra* note 197 at 113.

[327] VANDEWALLE, A HISTORY OF MODERN LIBYA, *supra* note 1 at 115.

language.[328] In western Libya, the regime marginalized the Zintan tribe, while favoring the Mashashiyya.[329]

The Warfalla tribe, located mostly in Bani Walid in the Tripolitania region, was considered one of the most loyal to the Qadhafi regime.[330] Members of the Warfalla, Qadhadhfa and Magarha, conventionally loyal to the regime, held high-level positions within the security forces and Revolutionary Committees.[331] Leading figures from these tribes were often put in charge of politically unstable areas, including cities in eastern Libya such as Darna.[332] The deliberate policy of favoritism drew resentment from groups who felt mistreated and underrepresented by the regime, and divisions along tribal and ethnic lines were exacerbated.

As a result, the population was split into those who enjoyed positions of privilege and those among who there was growing discontent and opposition. Qadhafi maintained a systematic policy of repression to silence his opponents. In 1980 alone, there were 2,000 arrests and 800 executions for various political offenses.[333] Public hangings also continued, for instance the killing of a student in 1985 at the Faculty of Law, Ghar Yunis University in Benghazi.[334]

As repression grew more widespread and abusive in the 1980s, Libya's student movement became more radicalized, and opposition groups were driven out of the country or underground. Many professionals and members of the middle class left to study abroad in the 1970s and 1980s, often linking with moderate and militant Islamist opposition groups spreading throughout the region.[335] Libyan Islamists connected with the growing Muslim Brotherhood movement, particularly in Tunisia and Algeria, and some who returned, worked clandestinely to disseminate their ideology at home.[336]

---

[328] ANTHONY BELL ET AL., INSTITUTE FOR THE STUDY OF WAR, 4 THE LIBYAN REVOLUTION: THE TIDE TURNS 14 (Nov. 2011), *available at* http://www.understandingwar.org/sites/default/files/Libya_Part4.pdf [hereinafter "THE TIDE TURNS"].

[329] *Id.* at 13.

[330] PARGETER, LIBYA: THE RISE AND FALL OF QADDAFI, *supra* note 197 at 158.

[331] *Id.*

[332] VANDEWALLE, A HISTORY OF MODERN LIBYA, *supra* note 1 at 152.

[333] Ogunbadejo, *Qadhafi's North African Design*, *supra* note 290 at 159–160.

[334] Report of the International Commission of Inquiry (Jan. 12, 2012), ¶ 24, *supra* note 324.

[335] PARGETER, LIBYA: THE RISE AND FALL OF QADDAFI, *supra* note 197 at 163.

[336] INTERNATIONAL CRISIS GROUP, HOLDING LIBYA TOGETHER: SECURITY CHALLENGES AFTER QADHAFI, Dec. 14, 2011 [hereinafter "HOLDING LIBYA TOGETHER"], *available at* http://www.crisisgroup.org/~/media/Files/Middle%20East%20North%20Africa/North%20Africa/115%20Holding%20Libya%20Together%20-%20Security%20Challenges%20after%20Qadhafi.pdf.

Within Libya, young Islamists risked imprisonment by organizing to study radical religious teachings.[337]

Militant groups were also formed during this period, such as the National Front for the Salvation of Libya (NFSL) – created in 1981 by Muhammad al-Mugarayf, formerly a member of the Muslim Brotherhood.[338] The National Front became one of the most important exile opposition groups during the 1980s.[339] It maintained a military wing, the Salvation Forces, which received U.S. and French support, and carried out a number of attacks against the Qadhafi regime.[340] Al-Mugarayf lived in Atlanta during most of his years in exile, continuing to push for the overthrow of Qadhafi from the United States. Other National Front leaders also lived and organized in the United States, such as the prominent anti-Qadhafi dissident Jum'a Shawish, who became the NFSL representative of the West Coast.[341] The National Front was one of the more notable clandestine groups that also reportedly had the capacity to target Libyan government officials travelling outside Libya.[342]

The growing strength of clandestine militant groups abroad and the influence of political Islam fueled Qadhafi's paranoia, and the regime sought to track down Libyan opposition groups organizing overseas. In 1982, the regime created the International Center to Resist Imperialism, Racism, and Reactionary Force, known as the Mathaba, to spread the revolution, as well as deal with Libya's opposition abroad.[343] Libyan officials and intelligence operatives monitored, harassed, and in some instances assassinated expatriate dissidents, including in Europe and the United States.[344] The operations were headed by the widely feared intelligence chief, Musa Kusa, who coordinated the regime's intelligence operations in Libya's foreign embassies.[345] Kusa served as Libya's ambassador to the

---

[337] PARGETER, LIBYA: THE RISE AND FALL OF QADDAFI, *supra* note 197 at 164.

[338] Pargeter, *Qadhafi and Political Islam in Libya, in* QADHAFI'S REVOLUTION REVISITED, *supra* note 3 at 87.

[339] Mattes, *Challenges to Security Sector Governance in the Middle East, supra* note 317 at 26.

[340] Vandewalle, *Libya's Revolution in Perspective, in* QADHAFI'S REVOLUTION REVISITED, *supra* note 3 at 32.

[341] Marine Olivesi, *Libyan Exiles Return to Run for Office*, PRI'S THE WORLD, July 5, 2012, *available at* http://www.theworld.org/2012/07/libya-exiles-vote.

[342] BLANCHARD, BACKGROUND AND U.S. RELATIONS, *supra* note 221 at 23.

[343] PARGETER, LIBYA: THE RISE AND FALL OF QADDAFI, *supra* note 197 at 103.

[344] BLANCHARD, BACKGROUND AND U.S. RELATIONS, *supra* note 221 at 22.

[345] PARGETER, LIBYA: THE RISE AND FALL OF QADDAFI, *supra* note 197 at 103, 105.

United Kingdom, until he was expelled from the country in 1980 after speaking openly about targeting Libyans in London.[346]

Libya's Islamic opposition figures were forced to flee beyond the reach of Qadhafi's security apparatus, and many ended up in countries that welcomed them at the time, such as Pakistan and Afghanistan. Libya's Islamists were also drawn to the jihadist movement, and travelled to Afghanistan to fight with the Afghan mujahidin against the Soviet occupation in the 1980s.[347] Through their involvement in the U.S. and Saudi-backed fight in Afghanistan, many Libyans became further radicalized and committed to overthrowing the Qadhafi regime militarily. As discussed later in this chapter, many members of the Libyan Islamic Fighting Group (LIFG) and other opposition groups would be forcibly transferred back to Libya with the aid of U.S. and British intelligence services – extraordinary rendition – and held in Abu Salim prison. The systematic violence inflicted by the Qadhafi regime seemed to come full circle, as more Libyan exiles would return to take part in the uprising of 2011 and join the post-Qadhafi political process.[348]

9.2. *Exporting Revolution and Confrontation with the West*

Qadhafi conceived of Libya's problems as both internal and external, and his domestic prescription and logic applied equally to the rest of the world.[349] For Qadhafi, it was not enough to simply reform Libya's internal dynamic; the Jamahiriyya had ambitions to influence the international order at large. Libya's huge oil revenues provided Qadhafi with the ability to confront the West and challenge imperialism on all fronts, most notably through the support of terrorist violence and insurgent groups.[350]

The most notorious case of Libyan involvement in terrorism was the Lockerbie bombing in 1988, but even before that, over the course of the 1970s Libya supported – or was strongly suspected of supporting – a

---

[346] Musa Kusa spoke openly about killing dissidents overseas, telling THE TIMES on 11 June 1980: "we killed two in London and there were another two to be killed . . . I approved of this." *See* PARGETER, LIBYA: THE RISE AND FALL OF QADDAFI, *supra* note 197 at 103, 105.

[347] Numbers of estimated Libyans who fought in Afghanistan during the 1980s range from 800 and 1,000. PARGETER, LIBYA: THE RISE AND FALL OF QADDAFI, *supra* note 197 at 165.

[348] *See* Ch. VI, Sec. 5.

[349] George Joffé, *Prodigal or Pariah?*, *in* QADHAFI'S REVOLUTION REVISITED, *supra* note 3 at 198.

[350] *Id.*; VANDEWALLE, A HISTORY OF MODERN LIBYA, *supra* note 1 at 97.

number of terrorist groups.[351] As early as 1972, Libya was indirectly implicated in the killing of the Israeli Olympians in Munich, providing safe-
haven for the surviving perpetrators from the Black September group.
The next year, rumors surfaced about Libya's role in the death of the U.S.
ambassador to Sudan. By the late 1970s, Libya publicly endorsed a range
of groups accused of terrorism such as the Provisional Irish Republican
Army, and gave refuge to others, including the Palestinian Abu Nidal
Group, the Popular Front for the Liberation of Palestine – General Command (PFLP-GC) and the Palestinian Islamic Jihad.[352] By 1989, the United
States alleged that Libya was the benefactor of 30 terrorist groups.[353]

Support for terrorist activities and groups abroad fed into Qadhafi's
understanding of himself as the patron of a larger struggle.[354] Confrontation with the West, which led to crippling economic conditions for the
people of Libya, was at the same time an integral part of Qadhafi's image
as a leader in the global anti-imperialistic struggle. During the 1980s, the
heightened militaristic approach of the United States was at times coun-
terproductive in that it served to enhance Qadhafi's mass popular appeal,
and to feed the Colonel's inflated sense of self-power and influence.

The election of Ronald Regan in 1980 signaled a shift towards direct
confrontation as the United States adopted a more hardline approach
to Libya as part of its Cold War maneuverings.[355] United States policy
became tougher with the stated intention of convincing Qadhafi that
the United States would "not tolerate his support for terrorism."[356] This
included increased unilateral measures to isolate Libya economically and
politically. The United States drastically reduced economic ties with Libya,
while engaging in military actions against the regime.

When U.S. forces shot down a Libyan plane in 1981 in the Gulf of Sidra,
Qadhafi used the attack to justify the mass militarization of Libyan society that began the same year.[357] In 1986, the U.S. Defense Department
acknowledged that Qadhafi was succeeding in rallying Arab political

---

[351] *See infra* Sec. 11.2.

[352] VANDEWALLE, A HISTORY OF MODERN LIBYA, *supra* note 1 at 132.

[353] Vandewalle, *Libya's Revolution in Perspective, in* QADHAFI'S REVOLUTION REVISITED,
supra note 3 at 36.

[354] PARGETER, LIBYA: THE RISE AND FALL OF QADDAFI, *supra* note 197 at 136.

[355] AHMIDA, THE MAKING OF MODERN LIBYA, *supra* note 4 at 158; VANDEWALLE, A HIS-
TORY OF MODERN LIBYA, *supra* note 1 at 133.

[356] U.S. Secretary of Defense, Declassified (formerly Top Secret) Memorandum for the
President, *Military Measures Against Libya*, Feb. 10, 1986 (copy in editor's files).

[357] PARGETER, LIBYA: THE RISE AND FALL OF QADDAFI, *supra* note 197 at 138.

support as a result of stricter U.S. political-economic measures against Libya. A number of Arab governments told U.S. officials in private that the press surrounding American actions had "built Qadhafi up to the point where they, as brother Arabs, feel compelled to support him even though privately they hope[d] our [U.S.] actions will succeed in moderating his behavior or precipitating internal changes in Libya."[358]

The United States pursued its policy of direct confrontation throughout the 1980s, and carried out routine naval and air operations in the Gulf of Sidra and around Tripoli.[359] The tensions reached their peak on 15 April 1986, when the United States carried out a military strike on Tripoli following Libya's suspected involvement in a terrorist attack that killed U.S. servicemen in Berlin ten days earlier. According to U.S. intelligence reporting, three months after the raid, these actions had weakened Qadhafi internally and many Libyans hoped that continued U.S. pressure would eventually result in Qadhafi's demise.[360]

A number of measures led to further isolation of the country with a devastating impact on the population. By this point, Libya had been on the U.S. State Department list of state sponsors of terrorism since 1979, and in December 1981 the United States instituted a travel ban on its own citizens, and in March 1982 it banned the import of Libyan crude oil, before banning all Libyan oil products in November 1985.[361]

American sanctions had a dramatic effect on the Libyan's economy – a third of its foreign revenue was cut when the United States stopped importing Libyan crude. While Libya could still sell its oil to Europe, the lack of access to American technology and know-how made operations significantly more difficult and costly.[362] Since 1969, Libya had spent money with abandon on various development schemes with few or no returns. By the 1980s, the country was spending $10 billion on economic development and nearly as much on military defense and foreign "adventures"

---

[358] *Id.*

[359] *Id.*

[360] *Libya: Qadhafi's Political Position Since the Airstrike*, July 17, 1986, U.S. Central Intelligence Agency, Directorate of Intelligence, secret report, *available at* http://nsarchive.files .wordpress.com/2011/02/libya-cia-2.pdf.

[361] Vandewalle, *Libya's Revolution in Perspective, in* QADHAFI'S REVOLUTION REVISITED, *supra* note 3 at 9, 22; VANDEWALLE, A HISTORY OF MODERN LIBYA, *supra* note 1 at 133.

[362] Vandewalle, *Libya's Revolution in Perspective, in* QADHAFI'S REVOLUTION REVISITED, *supra* note 3 at 39–42.

whether through support of terrorist groups or waging a prolonged war with Chad.[363]

Following Qadhafi's rise to power, wealth had initially greatly increased for Libyans, as the per capita income rose from $2,000 to $10,000 during the first decade of the revolution.[364] Since Libya failed to diversify its economy, however, almost everything it consumed had to be imported. This caused great problems from the mid-1980s onwards when the value of the Libyan dinar dropped and inflation skyrocketed.[365] In 1990, agriculture still accounted for only 2 percent of the national budget, industry not much more, and neither could bridge the budget deficit.[366] Libya remained the dual economy that Qadhafi had inherited: a rich oil state without a complementary means for supporting itself or generating income. As such, it was vulnerable to the vagaries of the oil trade and the consequences of an oil embargo.

Ultimately Libya could not afford its domestic programs while simultaneously antagonizing much of the rest of the world through its foreign adventures. Libya managed well in the 1970s during a period of high oil prices, but without an alternative source of income, when oil prices fell precipitously in the 1980s, Libya's economy suffered. The insecurity surrounding American sanctions lowered the price of Libyan oil even further. In response, the government pumped more oil, leading to friction within OPEC.[367] Libyan oil fields were also growing increasingly outdated and, due to the American embargo, could not be modernized. By the 1990s, when the UN Security Council placed sanctions on Libya, the country's oil capacity was decreasing at a rate of 8 percent a year.[368]

Additionally, the 1986 bombing of Tripoli fuelled a sense of insecurity, further lowering the economic prospects of the country. The per capita income of Libyans began a steady decline; it was $5,896 in 1999, down from $10,000 in the first decade of the revolution.[369] Qadhafi responded to the bombing, which had also led to the death of one of his adopted children, by once again deciding to restructure the state. He blamed the

---

[363] *Id.* at 35.

[364] VANDEWALLE, A HISTORY OF MODERN LIBYA, *supra* note 1 at 96.

[365] Vandewalle, *Libya's Revolution in Perspective, in* QADHAFI'S REVOLUTION REVISITED, *supra* note 3 at 43.

[366] AHMIDA, THE MAKING OF MODERN LIBYA, *supra* note 4 at 160.

[367] Vandewalle, *Libya's Revolution in Perspective, in* QADHAFI'S REVOLUTION REVISITED, *supra* note 3 at 39.

[368] *Id.* at 43.

[369] *Id.* at 40.

state's security organizations publicly for not providing sufficient protection to the country.[370]

By the late 1980s, the damage to Libya's economy and society seemed irreversible. Libya's oil concessions were producing diminishing returns due to the American embargo and the cost of inducing other companies to invest. The revolutionary movement had torn apart Libya's social fabric, and the country was shaken after seeing foreign jets strike its territory undefended.

With the domestic situation deteriorating, and ostracized by the United States, Europe and his Arab neighbors, Qadhafi resorted to striking out in a remarkable and tragic way. In December 1988, Libyan agents orchestrated an attack that brought down Pan Am Flight 103 in Lockerbie, Scotland, and in September 1989 agents were involved in another attack that brought down French UTA Flight 772 in Niger.[371]

The international reaction to the Lockerbie and French UTA incidents led to the complete isolation of the country, and a non-binding but forceful UN Security Council Resolution. Ironically, the two terrorist acts that most isolated the country were a function of Qadhafi's weakening state, acting out and engaging the world through violence, the method he had long replied upon to solve problems.[372]

Libya also experienced a rise in insurgent organizing within the country in the 1990s, as militant groups sought to take advantage of the regime's weakening position in the face of economic and social instability. Mujahidin fighters returning from Afghanistan began establishing cells and gathering recruits across Libya.[373] The rebels formed the Libyan Islamic Fighting Group (LIFG) and began to build up a supply of small-scale arms through raids on security forces' supply stations across the country.[374] By 1994, the LIFG had an estimated 300 fighters in its ranks.[375] The Muslim Brotherhood also began re-establishing its presence in Libya, and was able to create a renewed, though limited, presence in a number of mosques across the country.[376] During this period some armed opposition groups, such as the Libyan Movement for Change and Reform

---

[370] *Id.* at 45.

[371] VANDEWALLE, A HISTORY OF MODERN LIBYA, *supra* note 1 at 140.

[372] *Id.*

[373] PARGETER, LIBYA: THE RISE AND FALL OF QADDAFI, *supra* note 197 at 168.

[374] Yasmine Ryan, *Libyans rise up against militias' dominance*, Sept. 24. 2012, AL JAZEERA, *available at* http://www.aljazeera.com/indepth/features/2012/09/2012922183801998go.html.

[375] PARGETER, LIBYA: THE RISE AND FALL OF QADDAFI, *supra* note 197 at 168.

[376] *Id.*

and the Libyan National Army, reportedly received support from western intelligence agencies.[377]

In the face of growing internal and external threats, the regime heightened its security and once again turned to extreme repressive measures. Internationally, the Jamahiriyya Security Organization (JSO) intensified its intelligence collaboration with Arab secret services to combat renewed militancy in the region.[378] Domestically, the regime targeted groups such as the Muslim Brotherhood with arbitrary arrests, detaining over 200 of its members in 1998, and forcing many more into exile.[379] Several of those detained reportedly died in custody, and two prominent Brotherhood members were given over 70 life sentences and sentenced to death in 2000.[380]

The regime carried out sweeping arrests of suspected LIFG members along with their suspected supporters and sympathizers, tasking the Revolutionary Committees with neutralizing the threat, by "liquidating" suspected Islamists.[381] Entire cities in the east where the fighting was concentrated were essentially turned into garrison zones as the security apparatus overpowered the insurgents, and hundreds of LIFG fighters were captured and held in Abu Salim prison. In 1996, the government carried out what became its most notorious attack on Libya's Islamists, carrying out a large-scale massacre at Abu Salim prison that left over 1,200 inmates dead.[382] The security forces buried the victims in mass graves, and kept the deaths secret from their families for years. The Islamist uprising was definitively crushed by 1998, as the remaining LIFG militants fled for Afghanistan, the United Kingdom, and other parts of Europe.[383]

Unrest grew among the population in part resulting from economic stagnation – by the late 1990s, official unemployment stood at 13 percent, with unofficial estimates reaching 40 percent.[384] Youth unemployment, in particular, brought with it a set of challenges that the regime was unable to address effectively. The Libyan state was no longer able to provide for

---

[377] BLANCHARD, UNREST AND U.S. POLICY, *supra* note 218 at 20.

[378] Mattes, *Challenges to Security Sector Governance in the Middle East, supra* note 317 at 18.

[379] INTERNATIONAL CRISIS GROUP, HOLDING LIBYA TOGETHER, *supra* note 336.

[380] BLANCHARD, BACKGROUND AND U.S. RELATIONS, *supra* note 221 at 23.

[381] PARGETER, LIBYA: THE RISE AND FALL OF QADDAFI, *supra* note 197 at 169.

[382] *Id.* at 170.

[383] Pargeter, *Qadhafi and Political Islam in Libya, in* QADHAFI'S REVOLUTION REVISITED, *supra* note 3 at 98.

[384] Pargeter, *Libya: Reforming the Impossible?, supra* note 293 at 223.

its citizens as it had before, and was paying the price with growing popular dissent.

A changing international landscape also clearly called for pragmatism. With the fall of Communism and the end of the Cold War, making peace with the United States and Europe seemed the only option for reviving Libya's flagging economy. While it had never been close to the Soviet Union or Eastern Europe ideologically, Libya had previously been able to turn to the East for oil sales and support. Now Libya had to make substantive peace with the powers it had greatly antagonized for decades.

Qadhafi set out in the 1990s on a path of public diplomacy in Africa and with the West. On the African continent, Qadhafi's campaign met with relative success: he came to be seen as an elder statesman and advocate for African cooperation and union, as a peacemaker and mediator. In Uganda and the Congo, he was able to broker peace accords, while in Sudan he worked with Egypt, a long-time foe, to broker a peace agreement. Libya also agreed to peacefully and legally settle the question of the ownership of the hotly contested Aouzou Strip in northern Chad by sending the matter to the International Court of Justice.[385]

Libya's reintegration with the West would require serious measures, including eliminating ties with militant groups and resolving accusations of supporting or executing acts of terrorism. As such, in the 1990s Qadhafi provided information on various Palestinian groups operating from Libya and agreed to support the Palestine Liberation Organization (PLO) instead of more radical groups.[386] United States intelligence assessments from this period, however, indicate that these were merely symbolic overtures and that Qadhafi continued to support a policy of political violence. The CIA warned in 1995 that despite measures to reduce its "terrorist profile" to avoid additional UN sanctions or a U.S. military strike, these measures were largely cosmetic and Libya was in fact renewing its support for terrorism.[387]

Qadhafi had a consistent track record of being unpredictable and willing to switch alliances based on shifting geo-political interests and goals. The Libyan government fluctuated between supporting insurgent groups

---

[385] Dirk Vandewalle, *From International Reconciliation to Civil War, in* QADHAFI'S REVO-LUTION REVISITED, *supra* note 3 at 221.

[386] *Id.* at 220.

[387] U.S. Central Intelligence Agency, Counterterrorist Center, *Secret Terrorism Review* (June 1995), *available at* http://www.foia.cia.gov/docs/DOC_0000918468/DOC_0000918468 .pdf.

and turning on them by providing information about their activities to different intelligence agencies.[388] United States officials produced extensive assessments on Qadhafi's erratic behavior, reporting that he was an "inconsistent sponsor of these [terrorist] groups" and often criticized for being "unreliable."[389] In 1999, after Qadhafi expelled the Abu Nidal organization from Libya, the U.S. State Department reported that Tripoli continued to retain ties to some Palestinian groups that used violence to oppose the U.S.-sponsored Middle East peace process.[390]

Notwithstanding these issues, western governments pursued a policy of normalization of relations with Libya. In 1999, Libya started secret discussions with the United Kingdom over a raft of issues, including Lockerbie and the killing of British police officer Yvonne Fletcher in 1984.[391] Qadhafi turned over two Libyans in 1999 accused of bombing Pan Am Flight 103 for trial in the Netherlands.[392] That same year, Libyan representatives met with U.S. officials for the first time in nearly two decades.[393] Qadhafi's Libya was edging onward on the path towards normalized relations with the West.

10. LIBYA AND THE WEST, A NEW ERA OF ECONOMIC, DIPLOMATIC AND SECURITY RELATIONS: 2001–2011[394]

When the United States and other western governments considered the prospects of rapprochement with Libya, they did so through the lens of their global security and economic interests. On the part of the Qadhafi regime, its economy was in dire need of foreign investment and technology to repair its crumbling energy sector and explore new oil reserves. The economic desolation wrought by crippling international sanctions and systemic mismanagement threatened the survival of the Qadhafi state. The

---

[388] SIMONS, LIBYA: THE STRUGGLE FOR SURVIVAL, *supra* note 6.

[389] U.S. Central Intelligence Agency, *Secret Terrorism Review, supra* note 387.

[390] U.S. DEPARTMENT OF STATE, PATTERNS OF GLOBAL TERRORISM: 1999 59 (Apr. 2000), *available at* http://www.higginsctc.org/patternsofglobalterrorism/1999pogt.pdf.

[391] Dirk Vandewalle, *From International Reconciliation to Civil War, in* QADHAFI'S REVOLUTION REVISITED, *supra* note 3 at 215, 221.

[392] PARGETER, LIBYA: THE RISE AND FALL OF QADDAFI, *supra* note 197 at 179.

[393] *Id.* at 219.

[394] While negotiations with the regime began well before 2001, and diplomatic relations were not fully normalized until after Libya's 2003 agreement to give up its WMD's, this book chooses 2001 as the turning point for Libya's relations with the West. This date is based on the enhanced collaboration with Libya's intelligence apparatus that took place immediately following the Sept. 11 2001 attacks.

government needed a new flow of oil wealth to fulfill its social contracts and maintain the security institutions that ensured its hold on authority. The regime could no longer ignore the economic hardships experienced inside the country and was determined to attract foreign investment and break Libya out of its international isolation.[395]

Ongoing sanctions, notably the strict unilateral sanctions imposed by the United States, blocked the technology and resources needed for economic development.[396] In order to get international sanctions fully removed, Libya agreed to certain stipulations, including compensation for victims for the Lockerbie bombing, elimination of its Weapons of Mass Destruction (WMD) and long-range missile program, and renouncing its support for terrorism.

Libya's long-standing support of international terrorism, in particular, was a deep-rooted point of contention. Libya remained on the State Department's list of state sponsors of terrorism, and according to U.S. intelligence, continued to engage with terrorist organizations. As late as 1999, the United States reported that Libya continued to maintain the "infrastructure and state institutions to support terrorism, despite its efforts to appear to be distancing itself from international terrorism to gain reprieve from the UN sanctions imposed in 1992."[397]

During the period of *détente* with Libya, the Qadhafi regime went from being an international pariah state to a crucial ally of the U.S. and UK governments on international security matters. Libya provided the United States and the United Kingdom with an important ally in the region as a source of intelligence on global terrorist activity.[398] The settlement satisfied the strategic interests of the United States and the United Kingdom, along with other governments, particularly those belonging to the European Union and NATO.[399]

---

[395] VANDEWALLE, A HISTORY OF MODERN LIBYA, *supra* note 1 at 186.

[396] PARGETER, LIBYA: THE RISE AND FALL OF QADDAFI, *supra* note 197 at 176.

[397] Central Intelligence Agency, Counterterrorist Center, *Libya Maintains Ties to International Terrorist Activity*, U.S. Central Intelligence Agency, *Secret Terrorism Review*, Jan. 1999, *available at* http://www.foia.cia.gov/docs/DOC_0000918472/DOC_0000918472.pdf.

[398] As discussed elsewhere, the reliability of this information was questionable, and in some cases engendered more enemies than it eliminated. *See* Ch. V, Sec. 5.

[399] For further analysis on the conflict between realpolitik and human rights, *see* M. Cherif Bassiouni, *The Perennial Conflict between International Criminal Justice and Realpolitik*, 22 GA. ST. U. L. REV. 541 (2006); M. Cherif Bassiouni, *Justice and Peace: The Importance of Choosing Accountability Over Realpolitik*, 35 CASE W. RES. J. INT'L L. 191 (2003); M. Cherif Bassiouni, *Searching for Justice in the World of Realpolitik*, 12 PACE INT'L L. REV. 213 (2000).

10.1. *The Post-9/11 Global War on Terrorism*[400]

Relations with Libya shifted dramatically in the wake of the 11 September 2001 terrorist attack (9/11) on the United States, as western governments saw Libya as a potential ally in the war on terror, and consequently began collaborating directly with Libya's intelligence chiefs.[401] Despite the Qadhafi regime's unpredictable support for terrorism, U.S. and UK intelligence services began working with Musa Kusa – director of Libya's foreign intelligence who was implicated in the Lockerbie bombing, UTA 772 airline bombing, and assassination of Libyan dissidents abroad.[402] Just one month after 11 September 2001, Musa Kusa, who had been expelled from the United Kingdom in 1980, travelled to London to share information on suspected Islamists militants, including Libyan dissidents living in exile around the world.[403] The CIA's top counterterrorism chief at the time, Ben Bonk, was also present during the meeting in London,[404] at which time Kusa reportedly presented information that led to the capture of suspected terrorist supporters.[405] Kusa also became closely involved in negotiations over financial settlements in terrorism cases, as well as over the abandonment of Libya's non-conventional weapons program.[406]

In an effort to end economic sanctions, and as part of the process of normalizing relations with western governments, the Qadhafi regime began to make concessions on terrorism cases. In 2003, Libya accepted responsibility for the Lockerbie bombing and agreed to pay compensation to the family members of the victims in exchange for the termination of UN and U.S. sanctions.[407] Libya issued payments of $4 million per victim

---

[400] The global "War on Terrorism" is a term used here to describe the policies adopted by the U.S. Government under the Presidency of George W. Bush. The term, as applied here, refers to the international military campaign to target and eliminate suspected members of Al-Qa'ida and other suspected militant organizations.

[401] PARGETER, LIBYA: THE RISE AND FALL OF QADDAFI, *supra* note 197 at 184.

[402] SUSKIND, THE ONE PERCENT DOCTRINE, *supra* note 402 at 44–45.

[403] PARGETER, LIBYA: THE RISE AND FALL OF QADDAFI, *supra* note 197 at 185.

[404] Timothy R. Smith and Jeff Stein, *Ben Bonk dies at 56; CIA official helped stem Libya's weapons development*, THE WASHINGTON POST, Mar. 10, 2011, *available at* http://www.washingtonpost.com/wp-dyn/content/article/2011/03/10/AR2011031006241.html.

[405] SUSKIND, THE ONE PERCENT DOCTRINE, *supra* note 402 at 44–45, 53.

[406] BLANCHARD, BACKGROUND AND U.S. RELATIONS, *supra* note 221 at 35.

[407] Letter from the Great Libyan Arab Jamahiriyah to the President of the Security Council, reprinted in United Kingdom Foreign & Commonwealth Office Release – "UK Calls for Lifting of UN Sanctions on Libya," Aug. 15, 2003; United Nations Security Council, Security Council Lifts Sanctions Imposed on Libya After Terrorist Bombing of Pan Am 103, UTA 772, 4820th Meeting (Part II) (AM), *available at* http://www.un.org/News/Press/docs/2003/sc7868.doc.htm.

following the termination of UN sanctions in September 2003, and a second payment of $4 million to each victim's family following the termination of U.S. sanctions in September 2004.[408] The settlements allowed for further deepening of relations between Libya and the West, particularly in the area of counterterrorism.

Direct cooperation with western governments in counterterrorism efforts opened up new opportunities for the Qadhafi regime. Qadhafi used the international threat of terrorism to enhance his internal security apparatus, giving the police forces military powers in April 2004.[409] The regime drafted hundreds of thousands of government employees into units of the security services created to combat terrorism. When it came to justifying police repression and violation of civil liberties in the name of security, Libyan officials cited the actions and policies of the American and European governments at the time.[410]

The extreme political environment of the war on terror also opened up new avenues to target Libyan opposition figures living overseas.[411] As part of the deepening collaboration between Libya and the West, the United States included anti-Qadhafi Islamist groups to its list of terrorist organizations. The United States froze the assets of the LIFG in September 2011, and placed the group on the list of Foreign Terrorist Organizations in 2004.[412] United States and Libyan officials claimed that the LIFG was a global threat to international security, citing such leaders as Ayman al-Zawahiri and Abu Layth al-Libi, who claimed a close LIFG affiliation with Al-Qaʿida.[413]

Some interpreted the policy as conciliation to the Qadhafi regime for providing information to assist the U.S.-led global counter-terrorism efforts.[414] Observers and former LIFG leaders point out that most of the LIFG militants who sought refuge in Pakistan and Afghanistan rejected

---

[408] Blanchard, Background and U.S. Relations, *supra* note 221 at 9.

[409] Pargeter, *Qadhafi and Political Islam in Libya, in* Qadhafi's Revolution Revisited, *supra* note 3 at 101.

[410] *Id.* at 100.

[411] Pargeter, *Libya: Reforming the Impossible?, supra* note 293 at 230.

[412] Blanchard, Unrest and U.S. Policy, *supra* note 218 at 23.

[413] *Id.*

[414] Then head of the British intelligence (MI6), Sir Richard Dearlove, later commented "It was a political decision, having very significantly disarmed Libya, for the [British] Government to co-operate with Libya on Islamist terrorism." *See* Leigh Day & Co Solicitors, press release *Libyan politician questioned by British police over rendition allegations,* July 19, 2012, *available at* http://www.leighday.co.uk/News/2012/July-2012/Libyan-politician-questioned-by-British-police-ove.

the globalist jihadi views of Al-Qaʿida, and were solely committed to fighting Qadhafi.[415] In the context of the global war on terror, however, members of militant Islamists groups such as the LIFG were perceived as a threat regardless of their objectives, and as such were targeted in counter-terror operations. Qadhafi seized on the opportunity to track down his political opponents living across the globe.

In the wake of the fall of the Qadhafi regime, new evidence emerged revealing the extent of the intimate collaboration between U.S. and Libyan intelligence during this period, and the systematic human rights violations that occurred as a result. This included the secret detention, rendition,[416] and torture of Libya's opposition figures, such as former LIFG leader, ʿAbd al-Hakim Balhaj (also known by his pseudonym, ʿAbdullah al-Sadiq).[417] Information on these extraordinary rendition operations came from files discovered in the office of Musa Kusa, abandoned after the fall of Tripoli.[418] According to the files and witness testimonies, Balhaj and his wife were arrested in Kuala Lumpur with the help of British intelligence (MI6) and detained for several days by the CIA in Thailand. From there, Balhaj was flown to Tripoli in March 2004, where Musa Kusa reportedly met him personally.[419] He was held in Abu Salim prison for seven years, where he was subjected to torture.[420]

Human Rights Watch documented over 15 cases where collaborative efforts between U.S., UK, and Libyan intelligence led to the capture,

---

[415] David D. Kirkpatrick, *Political Islam and the Fate of Two Libyan Brothers*, N.Y. TIMES, Oct. 6, 2012, a*vailable at* http://www.nytimes.com/2012/10/07/world/africa/political-islam-and-the-fate-of-two-libyan-brothers.html.

[416] For more on U.S. extraordinary rendition policy, *See* M. CHERIF BASSIOUNI, THE INSTITUTIONALIZATION OF TORTURE BY THE BUSH ADMINISTRATION: IS ANYONE RESPONSIBLE? 141–182 (Antwerp, Belgium: Intersentia, 2010).

[417] Balhaj later joined the opposition in the advent of the 2011 uprising, and became a prominent *thuwar* leader as the head of the Tripoli Military Council. *See* Ch. V, Sec. 5. *See also* Adrian Blomfield *'Rendition' Libyan commander Abdel Hakim Belhadj to form his own party*, THE TELEGRAPH, May 15, 2012, *available at* http://www.telegraph.co.uk/news/worldnews/africaandindianocean/libya/9267933/Rendition-Libyan-commander-Abdel-Hakim-Belhadj-to-form-his-own-party.html.

[418] *Secret Intelligence Documents Discovered in Libya*, HUMAN RIGHTS WATCH, Sept. 9, 2011, *available at* http://www.hrw.org/news/2011/09/08/secret-intelligence-documents-discovered-libya.

[419] HUMAN RIGHTS WATCH, DELIVERED INTO ENEMY HANDS: US-LED ABUSE AND RENDITION OF OPPONENTS TO GADDAFI'S LIBYA 9 (Sept. 2012) [hereinafter "HUMAN RIGHTS WATCH, DELIVERED INTO ENEMY HANDS"], *available at* http://www.hrw.org/sites/default/files/reports/libya0912webwcover_1.pdf.

[420] HUMAN RIGHTS WATCH, *Secret Intelligence Documents Discovered in Libya*, *supra* note 418.

rendition and torture of Libyans overseas. One of these cases is that of Ibn al-Shaykh al-Libi, who provided false information under coercion about Iraq that was later used by the Bush administration to garner international support for the Iraq war.[421] Al-Libi was captured on the Pakistani-Afghanistan border, held in Bagram detention center, and transferred to Egypt, where he provided false information linking the Saddam Hussein regime to Al-Qa'ida. While the information was discredited by the U.S. Defense Intelligence Agency, Colin Powell cited it as evidence during his speech garnering support for war against Iraq at the United Nations on 5 February 2003.[422] Al-Libi was later transferred to Libya, where he died in prison in May 2009.[423]

The rendition cases and the Kusa files reveal the depth of U.S. involvement with the Libyan government during the years of the Bush administration.[424] United States and UK intelligence services captured a number of LIFG members, interrogated them for information on suspected militants, and transferred them to Libya where they suffered further abuses at the hands of the Qadhafi authorities.[425] Speaking to Human Rights Watch, victims of the rendition policy claimed they were forcibly returned to Libya at a time when Libya's record on torture clearly showed they would face abuse upon their return.[426] The information also reveals that the Libyan government was cooperating directly with the United States on sensitive counterterrorism operations at a time when Libya was still on the U.S. State Department list of state sponsors of terrorism and states not fully cooperating with U.S. counterterrorism efforts.[427]

The U.S. State Department's Country Report on Terrorism for Libya in 2007 confirmed that the Libyan government "continued to cooperate closely with the U.S. and the international community on counterterrorism efforts," and this included support for U.S. efforts against the LIFG and Al-Qa'ida in the Islamic Maghreb (AQIM).[428] Reports also indicate that the United States was working towards extending its counterterrorism

---

[421] HUMAN RIGHTS WATCH, DELIVERED INTO ENEMY HANDS, *supra* note 419 at 120.

[422] *Id.* at 123.

[423] *Id.* at 128.

[424] *Id.* at 2.

[425] *See generally id.*

[426] HUMAN RIGHTS WATCH, DELIVERED INTO ENEMY HANDS, *supra* note 419 at 5.

[427] The United States did not remove Libya from the state sponsors of terrorism list until June 2006. BLANCHARD, BACKGROUND AND U.S. RELATIONS, *supra* note 221 at 7.

[428] U.S. DEPARTMENT OF STATE, OFFICE OF THE COORDINATOR FOR COUNTERTERRORISM, COUNTRY REPORTS ON TERRORISM – LIBYA 120 (Apr. 30, 2007), *available at* http://www.state.gov/documents/organization/105904.pdf.

assistance to Libya and regional countries, through the Trans-Sahara Counter Terrorism Initiative (TSCTI), which operated under the authority of the U.S. Africa Command (AFRICOM).[429]

In addition to issues related to terrorism, concern in U.S. policy circles over Libya's stockpile of non-conventional weapons also remained a major obstacle to the full normalization of relations.[430] While Qadhafi had not achieved the capability to build nuclear weapons, he had acquired the equipment enabling him to do so. In the late 1990s, Libya had begun purchasing centrifuges and nuclear weapons designs through a clandestine network headed by a Pakistani nuclear scientist, 'Abd al-Qadir Khan (the A.Q. Khan network).[431] Libya had moved to reinvigorate its nuclear, missile, and biological weapons program through the Khan network in 1999–2000, and through new sources in Europe.[432] United States intelligence had confirmed in 1999 that Qadhafi was continuing his pursuit of WMD and missiles.[433] The CIA provided a telling assessment of Qadhafi's pursuit of non-conventional weapons, describing the Colonel's decisions as reflective of his irrational and unpredictable behavior. The CIA noted that Tripoli did not appear to have a "strategic or tactical doctrine for the military employment of these [WMD] weapons and delivery systems," but Qadhafi continued these programs nonetheless for reasons of "deterrence, prestige, and terrorism."[434]

From August 2002 through December 2003, a secret dialogue took place between UK and U.S. officials and Libyan representatives regarding Libya's weapons of mass destruction program.[435] The negotiations intensified in

---

[429] BLANCHARD, BACKGROUND AND U.S. RELATIONS, *supra* note 221 at 16. The Trans-Sahara Counter Terrorism Initiative has been under the U.S. Africa Command since 2008, and involves U.S. forces working with African counterparts from Algeria, Chad, Mali, Mauritania, Morocco, Niger, Nigeria, Senegal, and Tunisia, on a range of counterterrorism efforts to improve intelligence, command and control, logistics, and border control. *See* Lauren Ploch, *Africa Command: U.S. Strategic Interests and the Role of the U.S. Military in Africa*, 19 CONGRESSIONAL RESEARCH SERVICE, Jan. 5, 2009, *available at* http://fpc.state.gov/documents/organization/116606.pdf.

[430] PARGETER, LIBYA: THE RISE AND FALL OF QADDAFI, *supra* note 197 at 183.

[431] *Id.*

[432] Arms Control Association, *Chronology of Libya's Disarmament and Relation with the United States*, Mar. 2011, *available at* http://www.armscontrol.org/factsheets/Libya Chronology.

[433] U.S. CENTRAL INTELLIGENCE AGENCY, TOP SECRET REPORT, PROLIFERATION DIGEST: LIBYA: PURSUING WMD AND MISSILE PROGRAMS IN SEARCH OF POWER AND PRESTIGE (Mar. 1999), *available at* http://www.foia.cia.gov/docs/DOC_0001123259/DOC_0001123259.pdf.

[434] *Id.*

[435] PARGETER, LIBYA: THE RISE AND FALL OF QADDAFI, *supra* note 197 at 186.

March 2003, following the Lockerbie settlement, as Saif al-Islam Qadhafi (Qadhafi's second oldest son) and intelligence chief Musa Kusa engaged in discussions with U.S. and UK intelligence authorities.[436] In December 2003, Qadhafi announced he would give up Libya's WMD program and welcome international inspectors into the country.[437]

The actual disposal of Libya's massive amounts of non-conventional weapons, however, was another challenge altogether. Libya's declaration of its chemical weapons stockpile given to the Organization for the Prohibition of Chemical Weapons (OPCW) in 2004 documented approximately 23 metric tons of mustard gas and more than 1,300 metric tons of precursor chemicals.[438] OPCW's report for 2009 estimated that Libya had destroyed 39 percent of its chemical weapons precursors but had not started destroying its 23 tons of mustard gas.[439] By 2010, Libya had only destroyed 13.5 tons of mustard gas.[440] This assessment provides grounds for serious concern over the large amounts of non-conventional weapons unaccounted for in the lead up to Libya's 2011 civil war.

Some policymakers and experts argue that it was the Iraq war that pushed Libya into compliance with the West, while others argue that it was the longstanding sanctions and diplomatic efforts (secret negotiations going back as early as 1992) that finally came to fruition.[441] What is certain is that this period saw major steps towards full normalization of relations with the United States, lifting of unilateral sanctions, and the opening of Libya's economy to foreign investment.

Indeed, the policy of rapprochement with the West can be interpreted as part of Qadhafi's skillful balancing of interests aimed at ensuring his political survival. Libya's engagement with the West ushered in a new period of economic development and other opportunities, such as weapons procurement through U.S., UK, and French defense contractors.[442] Many Libyans held high hopes that normalizing relations with the West would result in significant political openings, but the regime's unbridled

---

[436] BLANCHARD, BACKGROUND AND U.S. RELATIONS, *supra* note 221 at 35.

[437] *Id.*

[438] Arms Control Association, *Chronology of Libya's Disarmament and Relation with the United States, supra* note 432.

[439] *Id.*

[440] *Id.*

[441] PARGETER, LIBYA: THE RISE AND FALL OF QADDAFI, *supra* note 197 at 187.

[442] Vivienne Walt, *Gaddafi's Ghost: How the Tyrant Haunts Libya a Year After his Death,* TIME WORLD, Oct. 19, 2012, *available at* http://world.time.com/2012/10/19/gaddafis-ghost-how-the-tyrant-haunts-libya-a-year-after-his-death.

power and overall lack of accountability left little room for reform.[443] The
close diplomatic, security, and economic collaboration provided Qadhafi
and his regime with a new lease on life as U.S. assessments predicted the
Qadhafi family would continue to determine Libya's fate for the foresee-
able future.[444] Qadhafi's children took full advantage of the situation,
using Libya's new relative openness with the West to amass wealth, and to
position themselves to hold power in a post-Mu'ammar Qadhafi Libya.[445]

10.2. *Economic Incentives*

The economic incentives that came along with normalizing relations
with the West played an important role in Libya's concessions on WMD,
especially as western businesses set their sights on Libya's oil exploration
and distribution. By the time of the December 2003 agreement on WMD,
Libya had already undertaken significant reforms towards liberalizing its
economy, including measures to privatize a large part of its state-owned
enterprises.[446] Libya's National Oil Corporation had high ambitions of
doubling its 2003 outputs production from 1.5 to 3 million barrels per
day, which would require an estimated $30 billion in foreign investment.[447]
Libyan officials understood it would not be possible to reach these levels
until U.S. sanctions were fully lifted.

Western governments had, and continue to have, a strong interest in
Libya's oil exploration. In August 2004, Libya announced that it would
open up 15 new offshore and onshore locations for exploration and
production agreements.[448] The White House responded by fully lifting
economic sanctions just one month later, allowing for U.S. companies
to participate in the bidding process.[449] United States firms quickly put
in their bids for the lucrative oil contracts and won the exploration and

---

[443] VANDEWALLE, A HISTORY OF MODERN LIBYA, *supra* note 1 at 201.

[444] United States officials assessed which of the Qadhafi family would succeed
Mu'ammar. *See* U.S. Embassy in Tripoli, Secret Cable, *Libya's Succession Muddled as the
Al-Qadhafi Children Conduct Internecine Warfare*, Mar. 9, 2009, *available at* http://www
.guardian.co.uk/world/us-embassy-cables-documents/195954.

[445] PARGETER, LIBYA: THE RISE AND FALL OF QADDAFI, *supra* note 197 at 209–210.

[446] VANDEWALLE, A HISTORY OF MODERN LIBYA, *supra* note 1 at 185.

[447] *Id.* at 188.

[448] *Id.* at 189.

[449] BLANCHARD, BACKGROUND AND U.S. RELATIONS, *supra* note 221 at 6.

production rights for a majority of the contracts during the first round of bidding in January 2005.[450]

United States officials in Libya recognized the comparative advantage of American oil companies bidding on Libyan contracts. United States diplomats reporting from Tripoli on the 2004 oil bids commented that the U.S. edge was "clearly in the experience and technology they can bring to development of Libyan oil fields, not necessarily in being the ones offering the sweetest financial deal to the GOL [government of Libya]." The cable goes on to report that U.S. firms were looking at Libya as a "place where they expect to do business in the future."[451] The lifting of most international sanctions in 2003 and 2004, followed by economic liberalization, oil sales, and international investment also brought about new wealth to some in Libya.[452]

Over 100 international companies bid on the contracts, and U.S. companies began participating in economic conferences to compete for the lucrative deals. The U.S. Embassy reported that major U.S. companies, Marathon, Amereda Hass, ConocoPhillips, Occidental, were negotiating with Libya's National Oil Corporation on their re-entry into the country's oil market. ConocoPhillips, for example, told the Embassy they had initiated an agreement with the Libyans for re-entry based on the arrangement they had before pulling out in 1986.[453] The results of the first round of Libya's Exploration and Production Sharing Agreement (EPSA) were announced in January 2005, and 11 out of the 15 companies chosen were U.S.-based, including Occidental, Amerada Hess, and ChevronTexaco.[454]

Libya subsequently passed a law in 2005 to reform the banking sector to permit foreign banks to open subsidiaries in Libya, further opening up opportunities for international investment.[455] As Libya became increasingly important to American corporate interests, the U.S. Embassy in Tripoli sent a steady stream of information back to Washington, DC to keep policymakers up to speed with the latest developments. In 2007, Ambassador Christopher Stevens reported on the fourth in the series of EPSA rounds, the first to focus on natural gas. The cable highlighted data from the U.S. Energy Information Administration that estimated Libya

---

[450] U.S. Embassy in Tripoli, Secret Cable, *U.S. Oil Companies Persevere in Libya*, Dec. 14, 2004, *available at* http://wikileaks.org/cable/2004/12/04TRIPOLI28.html.

[451] *Id.*

[452] BLANCHARD, UNREST AND U.S. POLICY, *supra* note 218 at 25.

[453] U.S. Embassy, *U.S. Companies Persevere in Libya, supra* note 450.

[454] VANDEWALLE, A HISTORY OF MODERN LIBYA, *supra* note 1 at 189.

[455] Pargeter, *Libya: Reforming the Impossible?, supra* note 293 at 231.

had 52 trillion cubic feet of proven gas reserves, fourth among all African countries. The cable further reports that a dozen parcels comprising of 41 separate blocks of territory were offered for bidding, generating 19 offers by 13 companies for ten of the 12 parcels.[456] Clearly, there was a significant focus on future lucrative economic opportunities stemming from the vast resources in Libya that were just beginning to bare fruit.

10.3. *Military Relations and Weapons Procurement*

The period following Libya's agreement to abandon WMD in 2003 – and until the start of the uprising in February 2011 – marked an unparalleled era in United States-Libya military relations. This brought new opportunities for Libya to purchase the latest weaponry and military technology from the United States. As such, the Qadhafi regime had significant incentives to abandon its non-conventional weapons program and replenish the armed forces with newer defense equipment.

The security apparatus was the most powerful formal governmental structure within the Libyan state, receiving a steady flow of resources and employing a significant portion of the public sector. It was not subject to civilian authority and its high-ranking members enjoyed perks and privileges, with a number of them involved in private enterprise.[457] The Qadhafi regime had survived several decades in large part due to this extensive security sector, which itself persisted because of continued access to a steady revenue stream.[458] With a growing youth population and increasing unemployment, the Jamahiriyya required full military and intelligence capacity to ensure its continued authority. Moves towards liberalization of the economy and scaling back the public sector, did not affect the security apparatus. In fact, Qadhafi announced the creation of up to 200,000 security jobs in 2005 during a period when the state was seeking to reduce public sector employment.[459]

United States Embassy cables show how the Qadhafi regime relied on the security state, and placed a strong emphasis on weapons procurement, particularly for Libya's elite security units. In August 2005, during a

---

[456] U.S. Embassy in Tripoli, Confidential Cable, *Libya EPSA Gas Bidding Round: International Majors' Interest is Tempered*, Dec. 13, 2007, *available at* http://www.cablegatesearch .net/cable.php?id=07TRIPOLI1038.

[457] VANDEWALLE, A HISTORY OF MODERN LIBYA, *supra* note 1 at 205; PARGETER, LIBYA: THE RISE AND FALL OF QADDAFI, *supra* note 197 at 197.

[458] VANDEWALLE, A HISTORY OF MODERN LIBYA, *supra* note 1 at 205.

[459] PARGETER, LIBYA: THE RISE AND FALL OF QADDAFI, *supra* note 197 at 195.

visit by U.S. Senator Richard Lugar, Qadhafi made clear his strong desire to obtain "defensive equipment." Qadhafi argued that his security forces needed the weapons to guarantee Libya's "self protection" against emerging extremist elements within Libya and in neighboring countries. The cables reveal Qadhafi's repeated insistence that he had been promised to be rewarded for giving up WMD in 2003, reiterating that he was "still waiting for the promised benefits."[460]

The United States lifted most unilateral sanctions though a Presidential Executive Order issued in September 2004, permitting Libyan purchases of U.S.-built aircraft.[461] The European Union also lifted a 20-year arms embargo on Libya in October 2004, allowing European companies to export arms and other military equipment. In European policy, Libya was increasingly seen as the bulwark to prevent illegal immigration to Europe, and as such it was in their interests for Libya to have weapons for border security.[462] Due to its status on the U.S. State Department's list of state sponsors of terrorism, however, Libya was still subject to prohibitions on some arms exports and U.S. Defense Department contracts at this time.

Just over a month after Senator Lugar's meeting with Qadhafi, President Bush issued two waivers of Arms Export Control Act restrictions on the export of defense articles to Libya, allowing for the refurbishment of C-130 transport planes.[463] In June 2006, the U.S. State Department removed Libya from the list of state sponsors of terrorism, removing the export ban on U.S. defense items. Lethal weapons were still restricted, however, and certain dual-use technology exports also remained restricted by the U.S. Department of Commerce.[464]

Libyan officials continued to bring up the issue of compensation for its agreement on WMD, and in 2009, the Libyan government threatened to delay the disposal of its stockpile of non-conventional weapons. During a November 2009 meeting, Saif al-Islam told the American ambassador that Libya had halted a shipment of its remaining Highly Enriched Uranium (HEU) because it believed the United States was backtracking on its

---

[460] U.S. Embassy in Tripoli, Secret Cable, *Senator Lugar's Meeting with Qadhafi August 20*, Aug. 31, 2005, *available at* http://wikileaks.org/cable/2005/08/05TRIPOLI221.html.

[461] BLANCHARD, BACKGROUND AND U.S. RELATIONS, *supra* note 221 at 6.

[462] Arms Control Association, *Chronology of Libya's Disarmament and Relation with the United States, supra* note 432.

[463] BLANCHARD, BACKGROUND AND U.S. RELATIONS, *supra* note 221 at 7.

[464] *Id.*

commitments to bilateral cooperation.[465] Saif asserted that Libya's decision to give up its WMD program was contingent upon "compensation" from the United States, including the "purchase of conventional weapons and non-conventional military equipment; security cooperation; military cooperation; civil-nuclear cooperation and assistance, to include the building of a Regional Nuclear Medicine Facility; and the end of 'double taxation' and economic cooperation, such as the signing of a Trade and Investment Framework Agreement."[466]

Libya's desire to obtain U.S. weapons and technology also took a prominent role during diplomatic exchanges between Libyan political and military leaders. During a December 2009 meeting, for example, a representative from Saif al-Islam's staff requested approval for U.S. "Little Bird" attack helicopters, spare parts for their Jordanian 4x4 Tiger vehicles, and expressed interest in refurbishing their M113 armored personnel carrier (APC) holdings.[467] United States officials commented that Saif al-Islam made the request on behalf of the 32nd Katiba commanded by his younger brother, Khamis Qadhafi.[468]

The U.S. State Department approved millions of dollars in non-lethal weapons procurement for Libya, including over $60 million in 2008 and 2009.[469] According to the State Department Annual Military Assistance Reports, the sales approvals consisted mostly of aircraft equipment, but also included explosives, more than $1 million in 2008.[470] The Qadhafi regime's bet on disarmament of non-conventional weapons paid off, opening the way to a new policy that allowed Libya access to the latest weapons technology.

The Libyan regime continued to press for import approval of more armaments. The Libyan Minister of Defense and other high-level security officials believed the claims compensation agreement with the United States

---

[465] U.S. Embassy in Tripoli, Secret Cable, *Libyans Seek Renewed Commitment from U.S. in Return for Progress on HEU Shipment*, Nov. 30, 2009, *available at* http://www.nytimes.com/interactive/2010/11/28/world/20101128-cables-viewer.html#report/libya-09TRIPOLI941.

[466] *Id.*

[467] U.S. Embassy in Tripoli, Secret Cable, *Saif al Islam al-Islam's Staff Reaches out on Pol-Mil Relations*, Dec. 14, 2009, *available at* http://www.telegraph.co.uk/news/wikileaks-files/libya-wikileaks/8294701/SAIF-AL-ISLAMS-STAFF-REACHES-OUT-ON-POL-MIL-ISSUES.html.

[468] *Id.*

[469] U.S. Department of State, Directorate of Defense Trade Controls, *Section 665 Annual Military Assistance Reports, available at* http://www.pmddtc.state.gov/reports/655_intro.html.

[470] *Id.*

for the victims of the Lockerbie bombing had "paved the way for purchasing lethal weapons from the United States in the near future."[471] In other conversations, Libyan officials suggested having armament removed from U.S. helicopters so they could be classified as "non-lethal."[472] Qadhafi personally met with U.S.-based defense contractors, such as Lockheed Martin in 2008, and was adamant about securing U.S. government guarantees that export licenses would be granted for future weapons purchases.[473] By the end of 2008, high-level Libyan military officials were expressing their desire to shift away from purchasing military equipment from Russia and former Soviet Republics because they saw U.S. military hardware as "technically superior."[474] From the perspective of regime security, the benefits of acquiring the latest military technology from the West outweighed the costs of giving up outdated non-conventional weapons.

In part to stem immigration into Europe, EU countries also took advantage of the new era of openness to sell large amounts of weapons to the Qadhafi regime.[475] France sold an estimated $500 million in weapons to Libya between the lifting of the European arms embargo in 2004 up until the start of the uprising in 2011. Italy was also in negotiations with Tripoli for more than $1 billion worth of deals in 2010.[476] European Union countries granted export licenses for 834.5 million euros worth of arms exports in the first five years after the arms embargo was lifted. In 2009 alone, the European Union approved 343.7 million euros in arms exports.[477]

In this period prior to the NATO intervention in 2011, military relations reached unprecedented levels with the United States, and deepened with European Union countries. Throughout 2008, a Memorandum of

---

[471] U.S. Embassy in Tripoli, Secret Cable, *Libya Interested in U.S. Weapons, More Ambivalent on Other Military Cooperation*, Dec. 31, 2008, *available at* http://wikileaks.org/cable/2008/12/08TRIPOLI992.html.

[472] U.S. Embassy, *Saif al Islam al-Islam's Staff Reaches out on Pol-Mil Relations, supra* note 467.

[473] U.S. Embassy, *Libya Interested in U.S. Weapons, More Ambivalent on Other Military Cooperation, supra* note 471.

[474] *Id.*

[475] For more information about European military equipment sales to the Qadhafi regime, *see* Ch. II Secs. 2.1 & 2.2.

[476] *France, UK Have Differing Motives for Intervening in Libya*, FORBES, Mar. 29, 2011, *available at* http://www.forbes.com/sites/energysource/2011/03/29/france-u-k-have-differing-motives-for-intervening-in-libya.

[477] The data comes from an investigation published in THE GUARDIAN. *See* Simon Rogers, *EU arms exports to Libya: who armed Gaddafi?*, THE GUARDIAN, DataBlog, Mar. 1, 2011, *available at* http://www.guardian.co.uk/news/datablog/2011/mar/01/eu-arms-exports-libya.

Understanding (MOU) between Libya and the United States was a major
point of negotiations, and was signed at the beginning of 2009, providing
a "framework for a military-to-military relationship and cooperation on
programs of mutual interest."[478]

This led to the high profile visit in April 2009 by Libya's National Security Advisor Mu'tassim Qadhafi – son of Mu'ammar Qadhafi – to Washington where he met with U.S. Secretary of State, Hillary Clinton.[479] United
States officials described Mu'tassim as a potential successor to the leadership of the regime, though they noted that he had been described as
"a bloody man" who was "not terribly bright" by the Serbian ambassador to
Tripoli. During the press appearance with Mu'tassim, Clinton told reporters she was "very much looking forward" to broadening and strengthening
the relationship between the two nations.[480]

The MOU agreement led to joint meetings between U.S. and Libyan
military delegations. In September 2009, for example, U.S. AFRICOM
commanders hosted three senior Libyan military officers at the U.S.
Ramstein Air Base in Germany. An AFRICOM statement described the
visit as part of an orientation to explain the command's mission, and an
aspect of the efforts by the United States and Libya to "build their military
relationship."[481]

These deepening military relations entailed extending invitations to
military officers to visit the United States as part of an "exchange program." Khamis took up an offer to tour military installations in February 2011, and travelled to the United States on a trip organized by the
Los Angeles engineering company AECOM, with approval from the State
Department. During the trip, Khamis visited the U.S. Air Force Academy
and defense contractors including Northrop Grumman and Lockheed
Martin, where U.S. military officials were also present.[482] Khamis had

---

[478] U.S. Africa Command Public Affairs Document, *Libyan Delegation Makes Historic Visit to Africa Command*, Sept. 28, 2009, *available at* http://www.africom.mil/getArticle.asp?art=3486&.

[479] PARGETER, LIBYA: THE RISE AND FALL OF QADDAFI, *supra* note 197 at 189.

[480] U.S. Department of State, *Remarks with Libyan National Security Adviser, Dr. Mutas-sim Qadhafi Before Their Meeting*, Apr. 21, 2009, *available at* http://www.state.gov/secretary/rm/2009a/04/121993.htm.

[481] U.S. Africa Command Public Affairs Document, *Libyan Delegation Makes Historic Visit to Africa Command*, Sept. 28, 2009, *available at* http://www.africom.mil/getArticle.asp?art=3486.

[482] Brian Ross, *During Libya Protests Khamis Gadhafi Hurried Home . . . From Wall Street*, ABC NEWS, Mar. 28, 2011, *available at* http://abcnews.go.com/Blotter/khamis-gadhafis-us-tour-york-la-washington-wall/story?id=13237920#.UNNdDG_AeuI.

to cut his trip short, however, to return to Libya to command his troops against the uprising that was erupting in Benghazi.

The Khamis 32nd Katiba was an elite unit with access to the best of Libya's armament, including T-72 tanks, Armored Personnel Carriers (APCs), BM-21 122mm rocket launchers, and attack helicopters.[483] The unit also received the British-made Bowman tactical communications and data system in 2008.[484] During the uprising, however, NATO called the Khamis Katiba a "primary regime protection element" that "remained at the forefront of operations against civilians[485] and targeted it in an airstrike.[486] This brigade, along with Qadhafi's entire military, quickly went from being a major customer of western arms and technology, to becoming a target of NATO operations.

10.4. *Human Rights Considerations*

Engagement with the West meant increased security for the regime, but did not translate into security for Libya's citizens, who continued to live in fear of the repressive security apparatus. Amnesty International submitted a report to the United Nations in 2007 that detailed the abusive practices practiced by security forces and the Revolutionary Committees, such as extrajudicial detention, ill-treatment of political prisoners, and torture.[487] Qadhafi continued to use firing squads, and freedom of assembly and association were severely curtailed. Dissident voices were silenced through imprisonment and intimidation, and a culture of impunity prevailed. The Amnesty report concluded, "The legacy of gross human rights violations committed in the past, particularly during the 1970s, 1980s and 1990s, continues to cast a long shadow on Libya's human rights record."[488]

In 2007, the UN Human Rights Council noted documented cases of enforced disappearance and cases of extrajudicial, summary, or arbitrary executions. The HRC also expressed concerns about the lack of information concerning effective investigation and redress, and the absence of judicial

---

[483] *See* Ch. II, Sec. 2.2. *See also* VIRA & CORDESMAN, THE LIBYAN UPRISING, *supra* note 322 at 22.

[484] Andrew MacGregor, *Can African Mercenaries Save the Libyan Regime?*, JAMESTOWN FOUNDATION, Feb. 23, 2011, *available at* http://www.jamestown.org/programs/gta/single/?tx_ttnews%5Btt_news%5D=37551&cHash=4e5f37dc8755b53452b6de6c97eef96a.

[485] VIRA & CORDESMAN, THE LIBYAN UPRISING, *supra* note 322 at 23.

[486] *See* Ch. III, Sec. 6. *See also* BLANCHARD, UNREST AND U.S. POLICY, *supra* note 218 at 25.

[487] *Libyan Arab Jamahiriya: Briefing to the Human Rights Committee*, AMNESTY INTERNATIONAL, June 2007, *available at* http://www.amnesty.org/en/library/info/MDE19/008/2007/en.

[488] *Id.*

review following arbitrary detentions,[489] as well as the use of torture as a form of punishment. The UN Commission of Inquiry (CoI) on Libya reported

> During Libya's Universal Periodic Review in November 2010, members of the HRC raised concerns regarding serious human rights violations including arbitrary detention; torture and other forms of ill-treatment; constraints to freedom of expression, association and assembly; and impunity for gross human rights violations including enforced disappearances and the killings of over 1,200 prisoners in Abu Salim Prison in 1996. The Qadhafi Government of Libya dismissed the criticism, and rejected all recommendations regarding specific violations and steps to address them.[490]

In 2007, the regime established a replacement for the widely-feared People's Court, which had been dissolved two years previously. The Special Security Court served a similar function as its predecessor in using the legal system to target government opponents in trials that failed to meet minimum standards of fairness. These standards included, "the right to adequate defense, the right to be informed of charges, and the right to appeal...Even those limited safeguards guaranteed by Libyan law – such as the right to a lawyer – were routinely flouted in political cases." The courts remained under the authority of the regime, unable to act independently, and functional only to the extent that they served the political purposes of the regime. This left a judicial system that virtually collapsed in the wake of the 2011 revolution, and allowed for the continuation of abusive practices during the post-Qadhafi period.[491]

The UN Human Rights Committee commented in 2008 that since its 1998 examination of civil and political rights in Libya, "almost all subjects of concern remained unchanged."[492] Indeed, Libya's history of repression and violence would not easily be overcome. Qadhafi's intelligence services were notorious for tracking down and openly killing Libyans in exile on the streets of foreign capitals.[493] The Revolutionary Committees, along

---

[489] For more on the lack of accountability for past human rights violations committed during the Qadhafi era, *see* Ch. IV.

[490] Report of the International Commission of Inquiry, advance unedited version (Mar. 2, 2012), *supra* note 246 at Annex I, ¶ 32.

[491] *Id.* at Annex I, ¶ 41.

[492] AMNESTY INTERNATIONAL, AMNESTY INTERNATIONAL REPORT 2008: THE STATE OF THE WORLD'S HUMAN RIGHTS 193 (2008), *available at* http://report2008.amnesty.org/press-area/en/airo8-en-low-res.pdf.

[493] PARGETER, LIBYA: THE RISE AND FALL OF QADDAFI, *supra* note 197 at 105.

with other formal and informal security organizations, instilled a pervasive climate of fear and intimidation up until the 2011 uprising.[494]

Many Libyans were voicing their dissatisfaction that human rights were not taking a more prominent role in U.S. policy towards Libya.[495] The U.S. Embassy in Tripoli reported that some groups were frustrated with the absence of political pluralism years after relations had been established. A U.S. Embassy cable from 2008, for example, noted the disappointment of "a number of Libyans" that the United States did not "more publicly and directly urge greater respect for human rights."[496] The cable goes on to note, "Absent a clear message that engagement on human rights will be a necessary adjunct of an expanded United States-Libya relationship, meaningful progress in this area is unlikely."[497]

United States officials did pressure their Libyan counterparts over human rights concerns, but these efforts were met with limited success. United States officials raised, for instance, the issue of political prisoners, notably the detention and health deterioration of Fathi al-Jahmi – the country's most prominent dissident and political prisoner at the time. United States Embassy officers attempted to visit Al-Jahmi in the hospital in May 2008, but were prevented from doing so by Libyan security officials.[498] At the end of the year, U.S. officers spoke with Saif al-Islam and other representatives about the health of Al-Jahmi, who reportedly remained hospitalized with a heart condition.[499] After falling into a coma and being evacuated to Amman, Jordan for emergency medical treatment, Al-Jahmi died on 21 May 2009.[500]

---

[494] *Id.* at 102.

[495] U.S. Embassy, Secret Cable, *A Glimpse Into Libyan Leader Qadhafi's Eccentricities*, Sept. 29, 2009, *available at* http://www.guardian.co.uk/world/us-embassy-cables-documents/227491.

[496] U.S. Embassy, Secret Cable, *Scene-setter for Secretary Rice's Visit to Libya* (Aug. 29, 2008), *available at* http://www.guardian.co.uk/world/us-embassy-cables-documents/167961.

[497] *Id.*

[498] U.S. Embassy in Tripoli, Confidential Cable, *Embassy Denied Access to Detained Human Rights Activist Fathi El-Jahmi*, May 22, 2008, *available at* http://www.telegraph.co.uk/news/wikileaks-files/libya-wikileaks/8294817/EMBASSY-DENIED-ACCESS-TO-DETAINED-HUMAN-RIGHTS-ACTIVIST-FATHI-EL-JAHMI.html.

[499] U.S. Embassy, Confidential Cable, *Developments in El-Jahmi and Boufayed Human Rights Cases*, Dec. 12, 2008, *available at* http://www.telegraph.co.uk/news/wikileaks-files/libya-wikileaks/8294892/DEVELOPMENTS-IN-EL-JAHMI-AND-BOUFAYED-HUMAN-RIGHTS-CASES.html.

[500] *Libya: Libyan Dissident, Long Imprisoned, is Dead*, HUMAN RIGHTS WATCH, May 21, 2009, *available at* http://www.hrw.org/news/2009/05/21/libya-libyan-dissident-long-imprisoned-dead.

Saif al-Islam championed himself as a human rights advocate, and introduced measures that many perceived as steps towards reforming the system.[501] He was seen by many inside and outside of Libya as a leader with progressive ideas who could introduce initiatives to incorporate the country's forward-thinking intellectuals, and work to marginalize the old guard and members of the Revolutionary Committees. United States officials reported speaking with young Libyan contacts who expressed their hope that Saif al-Islam would be the successor to his father, particularly when faced with the alternative prospect of Mu'tassim, Hannibal Qadhafi or another family heir running the country.[502] United States officials also noted that some observers in Libya believed Saif al-Islam's role in the government would provide the Qadhafi regime with a "new lease on life" because he was reform-minded.[503]

Saif al-Islam was unable to operate independently, as each proposal was subject to approval by Mu'ammar Qadhafi, who allowed for little opening in the system. His human rights initiatives brought new hope to the country's reformers, and caused widespread disappointment when they languished or were rejected by the Colonel. It also became evident to outside observers and those inside Libya that Saif al-Islam's commitment to his own family took precedence over his proposed reforms. He profited from the new opportunities that came with privatization and was an active beneficiary of the patronage system, reportedly importing large numbers of new cars to hand out to regime supporters in cities such as Misrata.[504] Moreover, Saif demonstrated a commitment and allegiance to the security apparatus, as evidenced by his weapons requests for the regime's military units. United States Embassy officers commented that Saif al-Islam's requests for U.S. equipment in 2009 were meant particularly for the 32nd Katiba, and were part of Saif's "attempts to curry his youngest brother's favor."[505]

---

[501] PARGETER, LIBYA: THE RISE AND FALL OF QADDAFI, *supra* note 197 at 199, 204.

[502] U.S. Embassy, Secret Cable, *Qadhafi Children Scandals Spilling over into Politics*, Feb. 2, 2012, *available at* http://www.nytimes.com/interactive/2010/11/28/world/20101128-cables-viewer.html#report/libya-10TRIPOLI95.

[503] U.S. Embassy, Secret Cable, *What Passes for Political Ferment in Libya*, Oct. 26, 2009, *available at* http://www.telegraph.co.uk/news/wikileaks-files/libya-wikileaks/8294667/WHAT-PASSES-FOR-POLITICAL-FERMENT-IN-LIBYA.html.

[504] *Divided We Stand: Libya's Enduring Conflict, Middle East/North Africa Report N°130* 7, n. 39, INTERNATIONAL CRISIS GROUP, *available at* http://www.crisisgroup.org/~/media/Files/Middle%20East%20North%20Africa/North%20Africa/libya/130-divided-we-stand-libyas-enduring-conflicts.

[505] U.S. Embassy, Secret Cable, *Saif al Islam Al-Islam's Staff Reaches out on Pol-Mil Issues*, Dec. 14, 2009, *available at* http://www.telegraph.co.uk/news/wikileaks-files/libya-wikileaks/8294701/SAIF-AL-ISLAMS-STAFF-REACHES-OUT-ON-POL-MIL-ISSUES.html.

As the uprising began, Saif al-Islam cemented his allegiance to the regime. He delivered a chilling speech on 20 February 2011 that marked a definitive end to any lingering hope for reform from within the existing Qadhafi government. The militaristic speech included threats against protesters in Benghazi and allegations that deranged Islamists were influencing demonstrators.[506]

Many reformers who held hopes for Saif al-Islam were shocked at the role he played in the government violence. His family members and officials in the regime's inner circle, on the other hand, saw him as responsible for raising people's hopes through his proposed reforms and for fueling unrest when the proposals failed. In some aspects, Saif al-Islam was responsible for creating the space for dialogue that facilitated the popular demands for reform. He also brought officials into government who later became leaders in the opposition movement, such as Mustafa 'Abd al-Jalil, former justice secretary who became head of the National Transitional Council, and Mahmud Jibril, former chief of the National Planning Council, put in charge of the NTC's crisis management.[507]

Part of Saif al-Islam's efforts also involved attempts to "rehabilitate" Islamic militant prisoners by persuading them to renounce violence and agree to refrain from organizing against the regime.[508] He began discussions with former LIFG leaders such as Sami Mustafa al-Sa'di, and in 2009, 'Abd al-Hakim Balhaj was one of over 200 LIFG members who were released from prison after renouncing terrorism and violence against civilians.[509] These efforts on the part of Saif were meant as a gesture to the West that the regime was serious about human rights. The policy also served to divide and weaken opposition groups at home and abroad. The agreements with the prisoners fractured anti-Qadhafi organizing, as these negotiations were rejected by militants still active in Pakistan and Afghanistan.[510]

Some of the talks took place at Abu Salim prison itself,[511] the site of the 1996 prison massacre. Saif al-Islam worked with the families and lawyers

---

[506] PARGETER, LIBYA: THE RISE AND FALL OF QADDAFI, *supra* note 197 at 229.

[507] *Id.* at 232.

[508] *Id.* at 203–204.

[509] INTERNATIONAL CRISIS GROUP, HOLDING LIBYA TOGETHER, *supra* note 336.

[510] Pargeter, *Qadhafi and Political Islam in Libya, in* QADHAFI'S REVOLUTION REVISITED, *supra* note 3 at 100.

[511] U.S. Embassy, Confidential Cable, *Latest Round of Talks with Imprisoned LIFG Members Concludes, Next Round Scheduled for Late February,* Jan. 22, 2009, *available at* http://www.telegraph.co.uk/news/wikileaks-files/libya-wikileaks/8294915/LATEST-ROUND-OF-TALKS-WITH-IMPRISONED-LIFG-MEMBERS-CONCLUDES-NEXT-ROUND-SCHEDULED-FOR-LATE-FEBRUARY.html.

representing the victims of the massacre, one of the most notorious cases of state repression in Libya's modern history. The prison was run by the Internal Security Agency (ISA), and held between 1,600 and 1,700 prisoners at the time of the massacre. After prisoners had protested for better conditions, 'Abdullah al-Senussi,[512] Chief of State intelligence and in charge of the ISA, visited Abu Salim to negotiate with the prisoners. Rather than holding discussions, however, Al-Senussi sent troops onto the prison roof and ordered them to machinegun the men assembled in the courtyard.[513] Relatives of the prisoners provided testimony to the CoI corroborating the reports of the killings, and testifying that under the direction of Al-Senussi some 1,272 persons were killed by prison guards firing machine guns.[514]

The history of the Abu Salim prison massacre played an important role in the 2011 uprising – the trigger for the demonstrations in Benghazi came from the 15 February 2011 arrest of Fathi Terbil, a lawyer representing the victims of the massacre. Terbil, who himself had lost three brothers in the prison, was working with others to organize a "Day of Rage" demonstration on 17 February, to commemorate the anniversary of the 2006 shooting of peaceful demonstrators by security forces, when at least 12 people were killed.[515] Within 24 hours of the arrest of Terbil and the other organizers, thousands took to the streets of Benghazi in protest. As the government security forces responded violently, the demonstrations began to spread across the country, initiating the start of the revolution.

---

[512] 'Abdullah al-Senussi fled Libya in Aug. 2011, was detained in Mauritania, and then extradited to Libya on Sept. 5, 2012 to face charges for past crimes. He is wanted by the ICC for crimes against humanity committed during the 2011 conflict, by France for suspected involvement in the bombing of an Air France plane in 1989, and for questioning by Britain for the Lockerbie bombing. *See* Like Harding & Ian Black, *Mauritania extradites Gaddafi spy chief Senussi to Libya*, THE GUARDIAN, Sept. 5, 2012, *available at* http://www.guardian .co.uk/world/2012/sep/05/mauritania-gaddafi-senussi-libya. A U.S. Embassy cable from 2008 also describes Senussi as playing a "significant role" as an advisor to Saif Qadhafi, *see News-maker: Former Libyan intelligence chief Abdullah Senussi*, REUTERS, Nov. 20, 2011, *available at* http://www.reuters.com/article/2011/11/20/us-libya-senussi-idUSTRE7AJ0MT20111120.

[513] *Libya: Abu Salim Prison Massacre Remembered*, HUMAN RIGHTS WATCH, June 27, 2012, *available at* http://www.hrw.org/news/2012/06/27/libya-abu-salim-prison-massacre-remembered.

[514] Report of the International Commission of Inquiry (Jan. 12, 2012), ¶ 24, *supra* note 324.

[515] *Libya: Arrest, Assaults in Advance of Planned Protests*, HUMAN RIGHTS WATCH, Feb. 17, 2011, *available at* http://www.hrw.org/news/2011/02/16/libya-arrests-assaults-advance-planned-protests.

11. Qadhafi: A History of Political Terror

11.1. *The Legacy of Fear and Psycho-Social Trauma*

The UN Commission of Inquiry on Libya heard repeated accounts of unresolved human rights violations that had left a deep psycho-social impact on Libya. The most notable cases included the Abu Salim Prison massacre in June 1996 and the public hanging at the university of students accused of directly or indirectly opposing the government, with others forced to watch. The CoI report noted that this was "in addition to the widespread and systematic cases of torture, disappearance and extra-judicial executions perpetrated by the Qadhafi Government," that left families powerless to complain and often with no knowledge of what happened to their loved ones.[516]

Historians have documented how, in addition to the physical violence, the Qadhafi regime inflicted a type of psychological terror through a climate of fear and constant uncertainty, epitomized by his whimsical policy changes.[517] Long-time observers of Qadhafi's rule note that while Libyans may be able to recover from Qadhafi's corruption and brutality, the "falseness of life in the Great Socialist People's Libyan Arab Jamahiriyya will take a long time to fade."[518]

The lasting psycho-social impact of the years of dictatorship can be attributed, at least in part, to the cult of personality left behind by a psychologically imbalanced ruler. According to psychological profiles produced by U.S. intelligence agencies over the decades, Mu'ammar Qadhafi was known for being unstable and psychopathic, while at the same time possessing an unusual level of intelligence. This combination of intelligence and mental instability made Qadhafi dangerously unpredictable and capable of planning sensational acts of violence without remorse.[519] A 1981 CIA profile, for example, depicted the Colonel as dangerous and

---

[516] Report of the International Commission of Inquiry, advance unedited version (Mar. 2, 2012), *supra* note 246 at Annex I, ¶ 38.

[517] Mansour O. El-Kikhia, Libya's Qaddafi: The Politics of Contradiction 88–89 (Gainesville, USA, University Press of Florida, 1997).

[518] Andrew Solomon, *Enigmas and Lies in Libya*, The New Yorker, Aug. 21, 2011, *available at* http://www.newyorker.com/online/blogs/newsdesk/2011/08/libya-rebels-and-qaddafi.html.

[519] Adel al-Toraifi, *Qaddafi and the CIA*, Al Arabiya News, Aug. 24, 2011, *available at* http://www.alarabiya.net/views/2011/08/24/163901.html.

insecure,[520] and among leaders in the Middle East, he was known as the "madman of the desert." Former CIA director, Robert Gates, commented, however, that intelligence profiles led U.S. officials to believe Qadhafi was "crazy like a fox."[521]

Despite Qadhafi's history of irrational violence and unpredictable behavior, the United States developed and maintained close relations with his regime up until the 2011 uprising. The renewed relations with Libya offered western diplomats a closer view of Qadhafi's erratic behavior and eccentric personality. In August 2008, as Condoleezza Rice prepared for the first official visit by a U.S. Secretary of State since 1953, Ambassador to Libya, Christopher Stevens, warned Rice that Qadhafi was "notoriously mercurial." During the visit, Qadhafi reportedly showered Rice with expensive gifts, including a copy of his Green Book with the inscription expressing "respect and admiration."[522]

When Qadhafi visited the United States for the first time in September 2009 for a UN General Assembly in New York, U.S. officials gained further "rare insights" into Qadhafi's inner circles and "personal proclivities."[523] A 29 September 2009 U.S. Embassy report written following Qadhafi's trip again characterized him as both mercurial and eccentric, going on to warn that this should not be interpreted as a sign of weakness. On the contrary, the cable makes the important comment that the "longest standing dictator" managed to stay in power for 40 years through a "skillful balancing of interests and realpolitik methods."[524]

Despite his glaring idiosyncrasies, Qadhafi knew how to manipulate Libyan society to remain in power for over four decades.[525] Over time, however, it appeared that Qadhafi's mental state slipped further from reality, and he lost touch with events on the ground. The decades of absolute power and constant paranoia apparently took a toll on his mental ability

---

[520] The CIA profile was disclosed in the Los Angeles Times in 1981. Tomas Omestad, *Psychology and the CIA: Leaders on the Couch*, 118 FOREIGN POLICY 95 104–122 (Summer, 1994).

[521] *Id.*

[522] *Gaddafi's Condoleezza Rice Photo Album Found At Tripoli Compound*, HUFFINGTON POST WORLD, Nov. 12, 2012, *available at* http://www.huffingtonpost.com/2011/08/25/gaddafi-condoleezza-rice-album-_n_936385.html. After the fall of the regime, pictures of Condoleezza Rice were reportedly found in Qadhafi's ransacked compound.

[523] U.S. Embassy, Secret Cable, *A Glimpse Into Libyan Leader Qadhafi's Eccentricities*, Sept. 29, 2009, *available at* http://www.guardian.co.uk/world/us-embassy-cables-documents/227491.

[524] *Id.*

[525] PARGETER, LIBYA: THE RISE AND FALL OF QADDAFI, *supra* note 197 at 256.

to accurately perceive events in Libya. Professor Jerrold M. Post, founder of the CIA's Center for the Analysis of Personality and Political Behavior, wrote that he suffered from a borderline personality disorder, and that high levels of stress could trigger Qadhafi's mood swings that ranged from intense anger to euphoria.[526]

There were also numerous accounts of Qadhafi's addictive use of Viagra and his sexual obsessive behavior.[527] The Colonel was known for surrounding himself with a group of female bodyguards, known as the "nuns of the revolution," with whom he reportedly had sex and showered with lavish gifts.[528] Also known as the "Green Nuns," they were part of the Jamahiriyya Revolutionary Guard unit,[529] and they numbered around 40.[530] The incorporation of the "nuns" into Libya's revolutionary forces was indicative of Qadhafi's inability to separate political from personal life, and the nuns became a visible trademark of his bizarre behavior.

The combination of Viagra and other medication also reportedly had a damaging effect on Qadhafi's mental state, leading to even more unpredictable behavior and irrational actions.[531] Professor Jerrold Post noted that as the stress mounted during the uprising, Qadhafi seemed increasingly to have lost touch with reality, and predicted that the Colonel would fight to the bitter end before giving up his hold on power.[532]

It seems that after four decades under a cult of personality, it is likewise difficult for Libyan society to remove itself from the shadow of dictatorship.

---

[526] Jerrold M. Post, *Qaddafi Under Siege: A political Psychologist assesses Libya's mercurial leader*, FOREIGN POLICY, Mar. 15, 2011, *available at* http://www.foreignpolicy.com/articles/2011/03/15/qaddafi_under_seige.

[527] Vivienne Walt writes, "Qaddafi was notorious for summoning countless young women to his compound for sex" in Vivienne Walt, *Gaddafi's Ghost: How the Tyrant Haunts Libya a Year After his Death*, TIME WORLD, Oct. 19, 2012, *available at* http://world.time.com/2012/10/19/gaddafis-ghost-how-the-tyrant-haunts-libya-a-year-after-his-death. *See also* Marie Colvin, *Viagra-munching Gaddafi bedded five a day*, THE SUNDAY TIMES, Nov. 14, 2011, *available at* http://www.theaustralian.com.au/news/world/viagra-munching-muammar-gaddafi-bedded-five-a-day/story-e6frg6so-1226193941736; Craig Mackenzie, *Qaddafi 'bedded four women before holding trade talks with Prince Andrew'*, MAIL ONLINE, Nov. 13, 2011, *available at* http://www.dailymail.co.uk/news/article-2060940/Gaddafi-bedded-women-holding-trade-talks-Prince-Andrew.html.

[528] Colvin, *Viagra-munching Gaddafi bedded five a day, supra* note 527.

[529] Report of the International Commission of Inquiry, advance unedited version (Mar. 2, 2012), Annex I, ¶ 59, *supra* note 246.

[530] VIRA & CORDESMAN, THE LIBYAN UPRISING, *supra* note 322 at 28.

[531] Marc Lynch, *Cherif Bassiouni: The FP Interview*, FOREIGN POLICY, Apr. 18, 2012, *available at* http://lynch.foreignpolicy.com/posts/2012/04/18/cherif_bassiouni_the_fp_interview.

[532] Post, *Qaddafi Under Siege: A political Psychologist assesses Libya's mercurial leader, supra* note 526.

A year after the fall of the Qadhafi regime, for example, many Libyans
still expressed fear that Mu'ammar's youngest son and commander of the
feared 32nd Katiba, Khamis Qadhafi, was still alive, even though he was
reportedly killed on 24 August 2011.[533] The lingering fear that the Qadhafi
family could still pose a threat to Libya is as symptom of the lasting legacy
of the former regime. The case also demonstrates that it is easier to get rid
of a dictator than it is to shed the legacy of dictatorship. Truth and justice
measures will need to take into account of the psychological trauma of
the past four decades of dictatorship in order for peace and reconciliation
efforts to be successful in Libya.

11.2. *Support for International Terrorism*

Libya's involvement in terrorist activity surpassed most state-sponsors of
terrorism in its sustained level of commitment to political violence that
spanned decades. Terrorism and support of terrorist activities became a
predominant aspect of Libya's foreign policy.[534] Under the authority of
Mu'ammar Qadhafi, support for terrorism became institutionalized as a
primary function of Libya's foreign intelligence apparatus.[535] Over time,
Libya developed the infrastructure and institutions to plan and support
acts of terrorism across the globe. This infrastructure included deploying
a web of foreign agents in Libyan embassies (People's Bureaus) to target Libyan dissidents abroad, and plot acts of violence under diplomatic
cover. The identifiable patterns of Qadhafi-orchestrated terrorism led to
Libya becoming one of the world's most notorious supporters of terrorist
groups around the world.[536]

Annual U.S. State Department reports provide a rich source of information on the patterns of terrorism employed by the Qadhafi regime,
which generally included 1) providing material support, especially funds
and arms, for extremist groups that use terrorist tactics; 2) building and
operating numerous training sites for foreign dissident groups; 3) ensuring safe-haven in Libya for terrorist groups, networks, intelligence and

---

[533] Walt, *Gaddafi's Ghost: How the Tyrant Haunts Libya a Year After his Death, supra*
note 527.

[534] U.S. STATE DEPARTMENT, PATTERNS OF GLOBAL TERRORISM: 1985, OFFICE OF THE
AMBASSADOR AT LARGE FOR COUNTER-TERRORISM 4 (Oct. 1986), *available at* http://www
.higginsctc.org/patternsofglobalterrorism/1985pogt.pdf.

[535] U.S. Central Intelligence Agency, *Libya Maintains Ties to International Terrorist
Activity, supra* note 397.

[536] Post, *Qaddafi Under Siege: A political Psychologist assesses Libya's mercurial leader,*
supra note 526.

activities; 4) abusing diplomatic privilege by using embassies to plan and conduct terrorist acts; 5) building and organizing mercenary militias involved in non-international conflicts in Africa, the Middle East, and beyond; 6) targeting for assassination and attack exiles, *persona non grata*, internationally protected persons, and regime opposition groups; 7) orchestrating terrorist events, including passenger aircraft bombings, hijackings, and assassination of diplomats, to attract global media coverage and inspire public fear.[537]

It is difficult to determine the rationale behind Libya's pattern of conduct in relation to terrorist activity. The acts of political violence exhibited differing characteristics based on Qadhafi's shifting geopolitical and strategic interests and goals. At times, Qadhafi defended his actions as part of Libya's policy of providing support for anti-colonial, separatist, and insurgent groups engaged in struggles for self-determination.[538] Some observers explain Qadhafi's support for violence as a consequence of his desire for global influence and prestige, rather than as part of a strategic doctrine.[539] Indeed, the Colonel's decision to use political terror as a weapon was likely fuelled by his inflated sense of self-importance and desire to be a major figure on the international stage.

In some cases of terrorism, the motive was simply seen as revenge. The 1989 bombing of flight UTA 772, for example, was allegedly carried out in reprisal for French support of Chad during the war with Libya.[540] Additionally, the 1988 bombing of Pan Am Flight 103 was suspected to have been carried out as revenge for the downing of Iran Air Flight 655.[541] Qadhafi's support for violence was often a reactive response to acts of aggression by the United States or other forms of external pressures. The CIA noted in 1994, for example, that if Qadhafi believed external actors were

---

[537] Corri Zoli et al., *Patterns of Conduct, Libyan Regime Support for and Involvement in Acts of Terrorism*, 3 INSTITUTE FOR NATIONAL SECURITY AND COUNTERTERRORISM-INSCT, Apr. 27, 2011.

[538] BLANCHARD, BACKGROUND AND U.S. RELATIONS, *supra* note 221 at 4.

[539] The Central Intelligence Agency determined that Qadhafi's pursuit of nuclear weapons was based not on strategic or tactical doctrine, but rather on "deterrence, prestige, and terrorism." U.S. Central Intelligence Agency, Top Secret report, Proliferation Digest, Mar. 1999.

[540] Paul Reynolds, *UTA 772: The Forgotten Flight*, BBC, Aug. 19, 2003, *available at* http://news.bbc.co.uk/2/hi/uk_news/3163621.stm.

[541] HARVEY W. KUSHNER, ENCYCLOPEDIA OF TERRORISM 194 (Thousand Oaks, USA: Sage Publications, 2003).

engaging in activities that could threaten his regime's survival, he would resume his support for terrorism.[542]

The decades of political violence can therefore be explained as an extension of Qadhafi's paranoia stemming from real or perceived external and internal threats. In this context, it is important to note the distinction between acts of international terrorism targeting foreigners, and those acts of political terror aimed at Libyans at home and abroad. The attacks against international targets were often employed with the aim of gaining attention from the international community, or as an attempt to show strength in the face of a stronger power. The political violence directed at Libyans had a different objective. Qadhafi viewed his opponents as a threat to his own power, and was intent to hunt them down wherever they fled. The CIA noted that Qadhafi was "deeply worried about the opposition's ability to topple his regime and will continue to focus his terrorist resources against it."[543] Therefore, while the Qadhafi regime employed the same agents of the intelligence apparatus to carry out these attacks, they had different objectives in terms of intent and rationale.

United States government agencies closely monitored the actions of the Qadhafi regime over the decades, documenting Libya's connection to terrorist activities. The CIA produced regular reports, terrorism reviews, internal assessments, and station cables with information detailing Libya's links to terrorism.[544] The formerly secret, and later declassified, documents include details on the inner-workings of the Libyan foreign intelligence apparatus under Qadhafi, and evidence of support for international terrorist activities. These U.S. government documents were produced contemporaneously to the events, written for internal consumption and not subject to public scrutiny. Because of the mostly clandestine nature of terrorist planning, these records are particularly useful for illuminating the methods and agents behind Libyan operations.

---

[542] U.S. Central Intelligence Agency, Counterterrorism Center, *Terrorism Review: Special Edition-1993 in Review*, Mar. 21, 1994, *available at* http://www.foia.cia.gov/docs/DOC_0000407935/DOC_0000407935.pdf.

[543] U.S. CENTRAL INTELLIGENCE AGENCY, DIRECTORATE OF INTELLIGENCE, TERRORISM REVIEW (Jan. 13, 1986), *available at* http://www.foia.cia.gov/docs/DOC_0000258586/DOC_0000258586.pdf.

[544] The records, most of which were classified as Secret to Top Secret, include Terrorism Reviews, National Intelligence Daily reports, internal memorandums, talking points, cables, and situation reports, produced by the CIA counterterrorism section and foreign stations.

The U.S. State Department also produced regular unclassified reports relating to patterns of global terrorism, which discuss in detail Libya's involvement in political violence and links to insurgent groups. The following analysis on Libya's history of support for political violence includes information compiled from U.S. State Department and CIA records, as well as other sources.[545]

11.2.1. *Summary of Incidents*[546]

Over the course of the 1970s, the Qadhafi regime demonstrated a commitment to providing material support for terrorist and paramilitary groups that espoused the political use of violence – including the Provisional Irish Republican Army, U.S. Black Power movement, militant Palestinian splinter groups, as well as guerrilla insurgent movements based in the Philippines, Ethiopia, Somalia, Yemen, Chad, Morocco, Tunisia, Thailand and Panama.[547] Libyan patronage greatly contributed to this period's upsurge in transnational terrorism.

In one of the most visible acts of terrorism of the early 1970s, Libya was indirectly implicated in the killing of Israeli Olympians in Munich in 1972. The Black September operatives who carried out the attack were reportedly trained in Libya a month prior to the operation.[548] Three of the perpetrators who survived the attack were ultimately given refuge in Tripoli after Germany released the prisoners in response to demands made by hijackers of a Lufthansa passenger jet in October 1972.[549]

---

[545] This analysis follows the same methodology of the "Patterns of Conduct" report, which selected examples of Libya's involvement in international terrorism according to two general guidelines: 1) those that provide a comprehensive picture of the various ways Qadhafi mobilized terrorism, often as part of Libya's foreign policy approach, and 2) those that can be verified by at least one (but often more) reliable sources and where links could be determined between the terrorist activity and the sponsor, *i.e.*, Libya or Libyan agents and assets. The sources examined include, but were not limited to UN and U.S. government and official documents, academic scholarship and independent research, reports from human rights, humanitarian, and aid advocacy organizations (*i.e.*, Amnesty International) and think tanks, reputable news media reports and analysis, among others.

[546] Zoli et al., *Patterns of Conduct, Libyan Regime Support for and Involvement in Acts of Terrorism, supra* note 537.

[547] CENTRAL INTELLIGENCE AGENCY, INTERNATIONAL AND TRANSNATIONAL TERRORISM: DIAGNOSIS AND PROGNOSIS 20 (Apr. 1976), *available at* http://www.higginsctc.org/patterns ofglobalterrorism/1976PoGT-Research-Study.pdf.

[548] SIMON REEVE, ONE DAY IN SEPTEMBER: THE FULL STORY OF THE 1972 MUNICH OLYMPICS MASSACRE 43–44 (New York, USA: Arcade Publishing, 2000).

[549] *See* KAY SCHILLER AND CHRISTOPHER YOUNG, THE 1972 MUNICH OLYMPICS AND THE MAKING OF MODERN GERMANY 216–17 (Berkley and Los Angeles, USA: University of California Press, 2010).

By the late 1970s, Libya publicly endorsed a range of groups accused of terrorism, and gave refuge to others, including the Palestinian Abu Nidal Group, the Popular Front for the Liberation of Palestine – General Command (PFLP-GC) and the Palestinian Islamic Jihad.[550] Following the burning of the U.S. Embassy in Tripoli on 2 December 1979, the U.S. government designated Libya a state sponsor of terrorism.[551]

Libya's support for international terrorism shifted in the 1980s towards a focus on targeted assassinations campaigns, attacks on diplomats in the Middle East, hijacking, and regional interventions. Assassinations and assassination attempts increased steadily from 1975 onwards, and in 1980 there were almost twice as many incidents as in any previous year.[552] This increase was due, in part, to well-planned campaigns by Libyan officials targeting expatriates in Europe. It became stated policy to silence Libyan students suspected of resistance activity.[553] The creation of the International Mathaba, to spread the revolution, and track down Libya's opposition abroad also led to a significant spike in targeted assassinations of Libyan citizens outside of Libya.[554] Musa Kusa expanded his influence and prominence as he coordinated these operations in Libya's foreign embassies.[555]

Libya orchestrated its most high profile passenger aircraft bombings during the late 1980s. On 21 December 1988, Pan Am flight 103 went down over Lockerbie Scotland after it departed London en route to New York. A bomb detonated on board, causing the death of 244 passengers, 15 crewmembers, and another 11 people in the town of Lockerbie.[556]

In September 1989, Libyan agents were allegedly involved in another attack of a passenger airliner that went down over Niger.[557] On 20 September 1989, French UTA Flight 772 exploded in south-eastern Niger, killing

---

[550] VANDEWALLE, A HISTORY OF MODERN LIBYA, *supra* note 1 at 132.

[551] Zoli et al., *Patterns of Conduct, Libyan Regime Support for and Involvement in Acts of Terrorism, supra* note 537.

[552] CENTRAL INTELLIGENCE AGENCY, PATTERNS OF INTERNATIONAL TERRORISM: 1980 1, 9 (June 1981), *available at* http://www.higginsctc.org/patternsofglobalterrorism/1980PoGT .pdf.

[553] CENTRAL INTELLIGENCE AGENCY, PATTERNS OF INTERNATIONAL TERRORISM 1981 11 (July 1982), *available at* http://www.higginsctc.org/patternsofglobalterrorism/1981PoGT .pdf.

[554] PARGETER, LIBYA: THE RISE AND FALL OF QADDAFI, *supra* note 197 at 103.

[555] Musa Kusa, who was expelled from London for such acts, spoke openly about killing dissidents overseas, telling THE TIMES on 11 June 1980: "we killed two in London and there were another two to be killed...I approved of this." *See* PARGETER, LIBYA: THE RISE AND FALL OF QADDAFI, *supra* note 197 at 103, 105.

[556] BLANCHARD, BACKGROUND AND U.S. RELATIONS, *supra* note 221 at 8.

[557] VANDEWALLE, A HISTORY OF MODERN LIBYA, *supra* note 1 at 140.

all 171 passengers and crewmembers on board. Reports indicate that the Libyan government was involved in terms of planning, authorization, and support.[558] Less than a month after the UTA explosion, the CIA reported on evidence that suggested Tripoli's involvement. The CIA cited previous attacks on UTA flights where Libya was suspected of involvement and stated, "we cannot rule out the possibility that Tripoli supported an attack carried out by a client group."[559]

A French magistrate issued charges against Libyan officials on 30 October 1991. The charges stated that Al-Azraq, the First Secretary at the Libyan People's Bureau in Brazzaville, Congo, recruited three Libyan-trained Congolese to plant the suitcase bomb and provided them with the device. The bomb was brought into Congo in a Libyan diplomatic pouch.[560] The judge also issued international lookout notices against Musa Kusa and 'Abd al-Salam Zadma.[561]

In the wake of the highly sensational airliner bombings, the Qadhafi regime's tactics shifted towards more clandestine acts of violence and support for insurgent groups in order to reduce its international terrorist profile. In 1990, a CIA assessment on terrorism noted this shift, predicting a rise in Libyan-supported violence and warning that Qadhafi had "improved his ability to conceal Libyan involvement in terrorist operations."[562] The assessment opined that Qadhafi was getting restless, and impatient with "the results of his relatively moderate policies over the past year and recent political setbacks." The document cautioned that Qadhafi's moderate façade was part of his strategy to mask continued involvement in terrorist operations, and that Americans and West

---

[558] U.S. Department of State, International Institute for Counter-Terrorism, *Libya's Continuing Responsibility for Terrorism*, Apr. 15, 1992, *available at* http://212.150.54.123/documents/documentdet.cfm?docid=2. In 2008, Libya agreed to pay $1 million in compensation to relatives of each of the victims onboard the flight, but denied any linkage to the bombing. *See US court orders Libya to pay $6bn*, BBC, Jan. 16, 2008, *available at* http://news.bbc.co.uk/2/hi/americas/7191278.stm.

[559] U.S. CENTRAL INTELLIGENCE AGENCY, DIRECTORATE OF INTELLIGENCE, SECRET TERRORISM REVIEW (Oct. 5, 1989).

[560] NATIONAL MEMORIAL INSTITUTE FOR THE PREVENTION OF TERRORISM IN OKLAHOMA CITY, PATTERNS OF GLOBAL TERRORISM: 1990 35 (1990), *available at* http://www.higginsctc.org/patternsofglobalterrorism/1990pogt.pdf.

[561] U.S. State Department, Secret Cable, *Libyan Officials Indicted for Bombing Pan 103*, Nov. 14, 1991, *available at* http://wikileaks.org/cable/1991/11/91STATE374256.html#.

[562] U.S. CENTRAL INTELLIGENCE AGENCY, DIRECTORATE OF INTELLIGENCE, SECRET TERRORISM REVIEW (Jan. 25, 1990), *available at* http://www.foia.cia.gov/docs/DOC_0000258756/DOC_0000258756.pdf.

Europeans in Third World countries would be the most likely targets of any new round of Libyan-sponsored attacks.[563]

Qadhafi also began to focus more on exerting influence on regional affairs in order to spread his radical cause, particularly in West Africa. While Libya's diplomatic representation was diminishing in the Arab world, it increased dramatically in West Africa.[564] With the increase in diplomatic representation followed influx of cash and support for insurgent groups in the region. In the 1990s, Libya trained rebel groups involved in movements across Africa, including Foday Sankoh's Revolutionary United Front in Sierra Leone and Charles Taylor's National Patriotic Front of Liberia.[565] This support included training of hundreds of rebels from Charles Taylor's forces at a military base near Tripoli, involving instructions on how to fire an AK-47 and surface-to-air missiles.[566] Qadhafi's intervention in these countries led to further destabilization across the region.

United States intelligence continued to closely monitor the activity and threats coming from the Qadhafi regime, and in 1994 warned that Libya could be resuming terrorism for the first time since the indictments of the Lockerbie suspects three years earlier.[567] The assessment was made on the bases of incidents such as "Tripoli's probable abduction on 11 December [1993] of a prominent Libyan oppositionist [Mansur Kikhya] in Egypt."[568] Kikhya had served as Qadhafi's Foreign Minister before quitting, reportedly over objections to the regime's support for international terrorist activity. He represented Libya in the United Nations until 1980, before officially defecting from the regime and becoming one of Qadhafi's most outspoken critics. Kikhya had been a resident in the United States and only months away from gaining citizenship, before he was abducted during a visit to Cairo on 11 December 1993. Kikhya had travelled to Cairo to attend a meeting of the Arab Organization for Human Rights (an organization he helped establish) when he was kidnapped on the street by

---

563 *Id.*

564 *Qaddafi says farewell, Arabia, and sets his sights on Africa*, THE ECONOMIST, Apr. 22, 1999, *available at* http://www.economist.com/node/200915.

565 *Id.*

566 Lee Ferran, *Charles Taylor Defense: Why is Qadhafi Not on Trial for War Crimes?*, ABC NEWS, Mar. 9, 2011, *available at* http://abcnews.go.com/Blotter/charles-taylor-defense-gadhafi-trial-war-crimes/story?id=13094284.

567 U.S. Central Intelligence Agency, Counterterrorism Center, *Secret Terrorism Review: Special Edition-1993 in Review*, Mar. 21, 1994, *available at* http://www.foia.cia.gov/docs/DOC_0000407935/DOC_0000407935.pdf.

568 *Id.*

Egyptian government agent and turned over to the Qadhafi regime.[569] He was considered one of Libya's politically "disappeared," until his body was discovered in 2012 in a building that had been used by Libyan intelligence during the Qadhafi years.[570]

According to a CIA assessment from 1994, available evidence at the time suggested that Qadhafi's operatives had abducted Mansur Kikhya, who had "long been on Tripoli's short list for assassination."[571] The terrorism review also stated that Kikhya's disappearance, along with that of another Libyan dissident, was an indication that Qadhafi was intent on reactivating Tripoli's longstanding program to eliminate leading Libyan exiles.[572] The case of Mansur Kikhya is emblematic of the political terror inflicted by Qadhafi's intelligence apparatus against opposition figures outside of Libya's borders. Moreover, the operations foreshadowed the type of extraordinary rendition programs later adopted by the U.S. and UK governments during the post-9/11 era.[573]

In 1995, the CIA went on to report that Libya's intelligence apparatus continued to target Libyan dissidents in foreign territories. The same document calls attention to Musa Kusa's appointment in 1994 as head of the External Security Organization (ESO), making reference to his suspected involvement in past terrorist acts.[574] Despite Libya's overt measures to reduce its terrorist profile in order to avoid additional UN sanctions or a U.S. military strike, Libya was "reinvigorating support for terrorism."[575]

On 29 January 1998, the French completed their investigation into the 1989 bombing of UTA flight 772 and concluded that the Libyan intelligence service was responsible, naming Qadhafi's brother-in-law, and

---

[569] *The Disappearance of Mansour Kikhia*, N.Y. TIMES, Oct. 14, 1997, *available at* http://www.nytimes.com/1997/10/14/opinion/the-disappearance-of-mansour-kikhia.html.

[570] *Libya mourns Gaddafi opponent, body found after 19 years*, TIMES LIVE, Dec. 3, 2012, *available at* http://www.timeslive.co.za/africa/2012/12/03/libya-mourns-gaddafi-opponent-body-found-after-19-years.

[571] U.S. Central Intelligence Agency, Counterterrorism Center, *Secret Terrorism Review: Special Edition-1993 in Review*, Mar. 21, 1994, *available at* http://www.foia.cia.gov/docs/DOC_0000407935/DOC_0000407935.pdf.

[572] *Id.*

[573] For more on Libya's collaboration with the United States and the United Kingdom in the post-9/11 war on terrorism *see supra* Sec. 10.

[574] U.S. Central Intelligence Agency, Counterterrorism Center, *Secret Terrorism Review: Special Edition-1993 in Review*, June 1995, *available at* http://www.foia.cia.gov/docs/DOC_0000918468/DOC_0000918468.pdf.

[575] *Id.* The CIA referred to the foreign intelligence service as the External Security Organization (ESO), while other sources, such as the UN CoI reports, refer to it as the External Security Agency (ESA).

deputy head of intelligence, 'Abdullah al-Senussi, as the mastermind of the attack. Al-Senussi and five other Libyan officials were charged and found guilty in absentia in French courts in 1999 for their roles in the attack.[576]

As late as 1999, the United States reported that Libya continued to maintain the "infrastructure and state institutions to support terrorism, despite its efforts to appear to be distancing itself from international terrorism to gain reprieve from the UN sanctions imposed in 1992."[577]

11.2.2. *The Lockerbie Affair and its Aftermath*

The attack on Pan Am flight 103 has its origins in the 1988 downing of an Iranian civilian airliner over the Strait of Hormuz by a U.S. Navy Ship stationed in the Persian Gulf. On 3 July 1988, USS Vincennes shot down Iran Air Flight 655 as it flew from Bandar Abbas destined for Dubai, killing all 290 people on board.[578] Shortly after the attack, the CIA warned that Tehran would retaliate with an act of terrorism. The CIA outlined a number of scenarios, including that a group "backed by Iran will implement an operation that has long been in the planning stages but that will now be carried out as revenge for the downing of Iran Air Flight 655."[579]

Iran filed charges against the United States before the International Court of Justice,[580] and the victims of the attack received reparations in a 1996 settlement with the U.S. government.[581] However, in the immediate aftermath of the affair, the Iranian government apparently sought revenge

---

[576] Scott Steward, *Libya's Terrorism Option*, STRATFOR GLOBAL INTELLIGENCE, Mar. 23, 2011, *available at* http://www.stratfor.com/weekly/20110323-libyas-terrorism-option.

[577] U.S. Central Intelligence Agency, *Libya Maintains Ties to International Terrorist Activity, supra* note 397.

[578] George C. Wilson, *Navy Missle Downs Iranian Jetliner*, THE WASHINGTON POST, July 4, 1988, *available at* http://www.washingtonpost.com/wp-srv/inatl/longterm/flight801/stories/july88crash.htm.

[579] U.S. CENTRAL INTELLIGENCE AGENCY, TERRORISM REVIEW (July 28, 1988), *available at* http://www.foia.cia.gov/docs/DOC_0000258679/DOC_0000258679.pdf.

[580] Thee case concerning the *Aerial Incident of 3 July 1988 (Islamic Republic of Iran v. United States of America)*, entered on the Court's General List on May 17, 1989 under Number 79, and was removed from the List by an Order of the Court of Feb. 22 1996, following a discontinuance by agreement of the Parties. *See* Case Concerning the Aerial Incident of 3 July 1988 (Iran v. U.S.), 1996 I.C.J. Reports 9.

[581] In the 1996 settlement, the United States recognized the incident as a terrible human tragedy and expressed deep regret over the loss of life, and agreed in full the final settlement to pay 131 million in claims. *See* Settlement Agreement on the Case Concerning the Arial Incident of 3 July 1988 Before the ICJ, 1996 I.C.J. Reports, *available at* http://www.icj-cij.org/docket/files/79/11131.pdf.

in the form of political violence, as predicted by the CIA. It is believed that Iranian government officials contacted Syrian intelligence to leverage its influence and pressure Syrian officials into taking action against the United States. Iran was a major supporter of the Hafez al-Assad regime, and the Syrian government relied on oil from Iran at well below the rates of the international market. Iran also provided financial backing to the PFLP-GC – an organization with a strong base in Syria that had been involved in plane hijackings and attempted bombings of aircraft.[582]

While the Syrian regime was the main supporter of the PFLP-GC and provided it safe haven to operate from Damascus, Iranian and Libyan ties to the group also raised alarm in U.S. policy-making circles.[583] The Iranian Foreign Minister, for instance, met with the head of the PFLP-GC and former Syrian army captain, Ahmad Jibril, in Tripoli in December 1987.[584] Qadhafi was a long-time supporter of the organization, providing it bases in Libya, and financing the group to carry out terrorist acts. The circumstances surrounding the Lockerbie bombing led many observers to conclude that the PFLP-GC prepared the plan and collaborated with Libyan intelligence agents to execute it, in revenge for the 1988 downing of Iran Air Flight 655.[585] Investigators thought it was likely that Jibril was involved in the attack, at least in training the bombers.[586]

Most of what is known about the planning and implementation of the Lockerbie bombing comes from the Scotland Yard and FBI investigations that pieced together what happened through forensic evidence and witness questioning. What is known is that the plan entailed placing the bomb in a suitcase in the cargo area of an Air Malta flight for transfer in London onto Pan Am 103, which was to be arranged by the Air Libya station manager in Malta. A Libyan intelligence operative was to be sent to Malta to purchase a suitcase for carrying the bomb, and that suitcase was placed in a container that was identified as part of the cargo manifest, which was then to be transferred at London's Heathrow onto the Pan Am Flight. The bomb, which was set to explode over the Atlantic so that no remains of the plane would be found, detonated prematurely over land.

---

[582] David Tal, *The International Dimension of PFLP-GC Activity, in* INTER: A REVIEW OF INTERNATIONAL TERRORISM IN 1989 61 (Bolder, USA: Westview Press, 1990).

[583] U.S. DEPARTMENT OF STATE, PATTERNS OF GLOBAL TERRORISM: 1999 112 (Apr. 2000), *available at* http://www.higginsctc.org/patternsofglobalterrorism/1999pogt.pdf.

[584] Dr. Ludwig de Braeckeleer, *Ahmed Jibril and the PFLP-GC*, CANADA FREE PRESS, Sept. 4, 2008, *available at* http://www.canadafreepress.com/index.php/article/4812.

[585] KUSHNER, ENCYCLOPEDIA OF TERRORISM, supra *note* 541 at 194.

[586] *Id.*

Scotland Yard and the FBI collected remnants from the explosion and recovered pieces of the suitcase used to carry the bomb and its contents. Investigators also rebuilt a 20-meter section of the fuselage of the ruined jet. Forensic scientists collected 56 fragments from the bomb carrier, determining that the explosion came from within a brown Samsonite type suitcase – a type of suitcase that had only been sold in the Middle East and was discontinued. Pieces of the items that had been inside the suitcase, including a radio cassette player and clothing, were also collected.[587] From this evidence, the investigators were able to identify the source of the explosion as the cargo area where the suitcase was located. The investigators identified Malta as the provenance of the suitcase and its contents, leading them to a store on the island that sold the clothing recovered from the crash. The store's shopkeeper, Tony Gauci, later became an important witness in the case, identifying the purchaser of the clothing as a Libyan man. Investigators also determined that 7 December 1988 was the date that the clothes were bought.[588] According to information received by CIA agents stationed in Malta, a Libyan intelligence operative named 'Abd al-Basit 'Ali Muhammad al-Miqrahi had travelled to Malta on 7 December 1988 and passed through security with the assistance of a Libyan Arab Airlines (LAA) station manager at Luqa Airport named Al-Amin Fahima.[589]

Internal information received by the CIA in October 1988 also indicated that 'Abdullah al-Senussi, then head of intelligence operations, was involved in plotting the attack.[590] Due to widespread suspicion that the PFLP-GC was connected to the affair, U.S. officials later requested the CIA station in Malta to pass over any information that would indicate possible PFLP-GC involvement.[591] The U.S. State Department reported in secret correspondence in 1991

---

[587] H.M. Advocate v. Megrahi & Fhimah (2000) J.C. 555 (Scot.). The verdict was delivered by the High Court at Camp Zeist.

[588] *Id.*

[589] U.S. Central Intelligence Agency, Secret Cable, *Travel of Libyan External Security Organization Officers Through Malta in December 1988*, Dec. 22, 1988, *available at* http://www.foia.cia.gov/docs/DOC_0001518880/DOC_0001518880.pdf.

[590] U.S. Central Intelligence Agency, Malta Station, Secret cable, *Terrorism: Libyan External Security Organization Activities in Malta*, Oct. 11, 1988, *available at* http://www.foia.cia.gov/docs/DOC_0001518891/DOC_0001518891.pdf.

[591] U.S. Central Intelligence Agency, Malta Station, Secret Cable, *subject: [deleted]*, Sept. 1, 1989, *available at* http://www.foia.cia.gov/docs/DOC_0001518857/DOC_0001518857.pdf.

we believe Libya was responsible for the destruction of Pan Am Flight 103 over Lockerbie. Government officials involved in previous terrorist attacks around the world orchestrated the operations. Forensic evidence indicates that the bomb's timer was unique to Libyan inventories, and an official of the Libyan national carrier, Libyan Arab Airlines, used his credential to circumvent security procedures in Malta to assist in the operation.[592]

In November 1991, the U.S. and UK governments issued indictments for Al-Miqrahi and Fahima, for their alleged involvement in the Lockerbie bombing.[593] The indictments charged the two Libyan security officials with planting the explosives on the plane that led to the death of 259 passengers and 11 individuals on the ground. The U.S. and UK governments sought their extradition by criminally charging them in their respective jurisdictions, citing the Convention for the Suppression of Unlawful Acts Against the Safety of Civil Aviation. This convention provides for the duty to prosecute (Article 7), and for the duty to extradite in its (Article 8).[594] The Qadhafi government argued that it had the priority and right to prosecute domestically, while the United States and United Kingdom argued that no prosecution in Libya would be effective because Libyan authorities were themselves involved in the plot.

The United States and United Kingdom took the issue to the United Nations, and in 1992, the UN Security Council issued a resolution (UNSCR 731) incorporating U.S. and UK demands to turn over the suspects, condemning the destruction of Pan Am flight 103, and urging the Libyan government to immediately "provide a full and effective response to those requests so as to contribute to the elimination of international terrorism."[595] The resolution also called for Tripoli to cooperate with the French authorities in their separate investigation of the UTA 772 bombing of 1989.

Subsequently, Libya filed a case against the United States and the United Kingdom before the ICJ, claiming that pursuant the 1971 Montreal Convention Article, Libya had the right to handle the case domestically, since the obligation to prosecute preceded that of extradition.[596] Libya

---

[592] U.S. State Department, Secret Cable, *Libyan Officials Indicted for Bombing Pan 103*, Nov. 14, 1991, *available at* http://wikileaks.org/cable/1991/11/91STATE374256.html#.

[593] VANDEWALLE, A HISTORY OF MODERN LIBYA, *supra* note 1 at 170.

[594] Convention for the Suppression of Unlawful Acts Against the Safety of Civil Affairs [Montreal Hijacking Convention], Sept. 23, 1971, 24 US T. 564, 974 U.N.T.S. 177, 10 I.L.M 1151.

[595] S.C. Res. 731 (1992), Jan. 21, 1992, U.N. Doc. S/RES/731 (1992).

[596] Questions of Interpretation and Application of the 1971 Montreal Convention Arising from the Aerial Incident at Lockerbie (Lib. v. U.S.), Provisional Measures, 1992 ICJ Reports 114 (Apr. 14).

alleged that the United States was in violation of Article 5 of the Montreal Convention as a result of its threats and actions seeking to override Libya's legitimate jurisdiction to deal with the matter.[597] The ICJ decided in a preliminary opinion that it did not have the judicial supervisory power to review the decisions of the UN Security Council, which had the power to determine the court's own competence pursuant to Chapter VII.[598] Thus, the ICJ did not settle the issue, and a legal stalemate ensued for ten years, only to be settled through negotiations.[599]

In response to sustained pressure from the United States and the United Kingdom, the UN Security Council adopted another, stronger resolution in April 1992 that imposed sanctions on Libya (UNSCR 748).[600] These sanctions were crippling to the Libyan economy over the course of the 1990s, and in turn the Qadhafi regime began making overtures towards the West. Behind the scenes, Libya's top intelligence chief, Musa Kusa, played a central role in negotiations over Lockerbie and the lifting of UN sanctions. As discussed above, Kusa's relationship with the MI6 and CIA involved intelligence sharing as well as discussions that drew Libya closer to restoring relations with the U.S. and UK governments. Kusa helped negotiate the terms of the agreement, such that the Lockerbie trial would take place on neutral ground in the Netherlands, having helped to convince Qadhafi to allow the two Lockerbie suspects to be tried outside of Libya. In 1998, the Qadhafi government agreed to hand over the Lockerbie suspects to be tried under Scottish law, but in The Hague.[601] In April 1999, the trial began in a specially convened court, and in January 2001 Al-Miqrahi was found guilty and sentenced to life imprisonment, while Fahima was acquitted on lack of evidence.[602] The investigations determined that Al-Miqrahi carried the bomb in a suitcase that originated in Malta, and that the suitcase was transferred from Malta to Frankfurt, then London, where it was placed on Pan Am Flight 103.[603]

Investigators in the case also looked extensively into leads connecting members of the PFLP-GC to the bombing. The Scottish judges accepted evidence related to a PFLP-GC cell that was operating in Germany and had

---

[597] Id.

[598] M. Cherif Bassiouni, Introduction to International Criminal Law: Second Revised Edition 498 (Leiden, The Netherlands: Brill Publications, 2d ed., 2013).

[599] Id. at 499.

[600] S.C. Res. 748 (1992), Mar. 31 1992, U.N. Doc. S/RES/748 (1992).

[601] Vandewalle, A History of Modern Libya, supra note 1 at 195.

[602] Id. at 172

[603] Pargeter, Libya: The Rise and Fall of Qaddafi, supra note 197 at 164.

the "means and the intention to manufacture bombs which could be used to destroy civil aircraft." Two months before the Pan Am explosion, police in Frankfurt had made a number of arrests and raided a safe-house, finding radio cassette players, explosives, detonators, and other items, including airline timetables, one apparently a Pan Am timetable. The opinion of the Scottish judges concluded that while the PFLP-GC was engaged in terrorist activity at the time of the Lockerbie bombing, they found no conclusive evidence "from which to infer that they were involved in this particular act of terrorism and the evidence relating to their activities does not create a reasonable doubt in our minds about the Libyan origin of this crime."[604] There was no further investigation into the alleged Syrian links, and President Hafez al-Assad, Syria's head of intelligence, as well as the PFLP-GC leadership benefited from impunity surrounding the affair.

The pursuit of justice for the Lockerbie bombing slowly shifted to a focus on financial compensation for the family members of the victims. The Libyan regime had already started a round of secret talks over compensation with the UK government in 1999, coinciding with the suspension of multilateral economic sanctions following the handing over of the Lockerbie suspects.[605] A group of high-level Libyan officials, eager to benefit from closer ties to the West, were pushing Qadhafi to comply with these financial demands and settle the Lockerbie case. Kusa, becoming more of an asset to the MI6 and CIA in the wake of 9/11 and gaining the confidence of the West by providing information on Libya's WMD program, played a key role in brokering the compensation agreements. In addition to Kusa, this group of officials included Foreign Affairs Secretary ʿAbd al-Rahman Shalqam, Ambassador to London ʿAbd al-ʿAti al-ʿUbaydi, and Secretary of the Congress, Muhammad Zway.[606] The text of the UN Security Council resolution to lift sanctions against Libya was negotiated in London, and subsequently adopted by the Security Council.

The agreement contained a settlement for the victims of Lockerbie, and the United States undertook the task of convincing victims and groups representing victims to agree to the terms of the settlement and drop their claims in U.S. courts. The United States was represented at these London negotiations by the deputy legal advisor to the Department of State and

---

[604] H.M. Advocate v. Megrahi & Fhimah (2000) J.C. 555 (Scot.). The verdict was delivered by the High Court at Camp Zeist.

[605] Dirk Vandewalle, *From International Reconciliation to Civil War, in* QADHAFI'S REVOLUTION REVISITED, *supra* note 3 at 215.

[606] PARGETER, LIBYA: THE RISE AND FALL OF QADDAFI, *supra* note 197 at 181.

others. The UK government, acting through Foreign Office representatives, negotiated a similar settlement for the Scottish and British victims. In 2003, a settlement was reached, and Libya agreed to pay successive payments to the families of Pan Am 103 victims following the termination of UN and U.S. sanctions.[607]

Saif al-Islam, who also became an important young figure in the negotiations with the West over Libya's WMD and other issues,[608] is believed to have benefited from the Lockerbie financial settlement. Saif served as the chairmen of the quasi-governmental Qadhafi Development Foundation (QDF),[609] which served as the official representative organization for continuing talks after 2003 and distributing the agreed upon payments to the victims.[610] Serving in this capacity, Saif reportedly benefited by receiving some portion of the settlement either out of the Libya fund or through other means after the funds reached the U.S. law firm handling the disbursements of compensation money. The full details of that story should be examined, and considered as Saif faces future questioning for past abuses.[611]

The extensive role of Kusa as a negotiator with the West, and his close ties with UK intelligence, explains why he fled to London on 30 March 2011 during the insurrection. After reportedly being questioned by British police and Scottish prosecutors, he was permitted to leave freely, and fly to Qatar, where he lives at the time of this writing. The former spy chief, with crucial information on the historical acts of terrorism, seems to have averted the prospect of being prosecuted for the terrorist operations he oversaw, and the torture he authorized.[612]

The Egyptian government also played a role in the Lockerbie agreements. At the time of the negotiations on compensation, the foreign policy advisor to President Hosni Mubarak, 'Usama al-Baz, engaged in discussion with the cousin of Mu'ammar Qadhafi, Ahmad Qadhaf al-Dam.[613]

---

[607] BLANCHARD, BACKGROUND AND U.S. RELATIONS, *supra* note 221 at 9.

[608] Dirk Vandewalle, *From International Reconciliation to Civil War*, in QADHAFI'S REVOLUTION REVISITED, *supra* note 3 at 216.

[609] U.S. Embassy in Tripoli, Secret Cable, *Tweaking the Tigers' Tail: Saif Al-Islam Opens New Human Rights Organization in Libya*, Mar. 1, 2009, *available at* http://wikileaks.org/cable/2009/03/09TRIPOLI196.html.

[610] BLANCHARD, BACKGROUND AND U.S. RELATIONS, *supra* note 221 at 9.

[611] For more on Saif al-Islam, *see* Ch. IV, Sec. 6.3(b)(i).

[612] For more on Musa Kusa *see* Ch. V, Sec. 6.3(b)(iii).

[613] Al-Dam (a unique name, literally translated as "the blood") fled to Egypt during the uprising, and Libya's post-Qadhafi government sought his extradition to face charges of corruption. *See Libya demands Extradition of Qaddafi exiles from Egypt*, LIBYA HERALD,

Al-Dam often acted as a conduit between his cousin Muʿammar Qadhafi and Egyptian officials.[614] In this capacity, Qadhaf al-Dam would deal with the Egyptian head of general intelligence, General Omar Suleiman or al-Baz, and there were times when Al-Dam would meet with President Mubarak himself to convey personal messages from Muʿammar Qadhafi.[615]

The discussions between Al-Baz and Al-Dam resulted in essentially the same plan that was ultimately carried out by the United Kingdom and the United States: Libya would not admit to responsibility for blowing up Pan Am 103, but it would accept responsibility for the consequences, pay compensation, and surrender the two accused persons to be tried in Scotland under Scottish law, but with the guarantee that they would not be interrogated by the intelligence service of the United States, the United Kingdom, or any other country. The only differences between this proposition and what was agreed in London was that the trial took place in The Hague, the specific amount of compensation, and the specific language in the resolution of the Security Council, along with the text of the letter from the Libyan government.

Mubarak, who had offered his offices to Libya to help in its dealings with the United States and the United Kingdom, then learned that Muʿammar Qadhafi wanted to meet him in person to agree on the terms of a plan as hashed out by Qadhafi's cousin and Mubarak's foreign policy advisor, for which Egypt was going to be the mediator. A meeting was hastily arranged in a western oasis in Egypt, close to the Libyan border. Mubarak met Qadhafi at the airport, where to Mubarak's surprise, Qadhafi changed a terms of what had been agreed upon in Cairo. Mubarak immediately returned to Cairo furious over the affair, vowing never again to act as a mediator between Qadhafi and any other state, convinced that Qadhafi was a mercurial and unreliable person to deal with.[616]

Feb. 12, 2012, *available at* http://www.libyaherald.com/2012/02/29/qaddafi-exiles-living-in-egypt-under-false-identities.

[614] Ahmad Qadhaf al-Dam was referred to as the General Coordinator of Egyptian-Libyan Relations in Cairo in government circles. *See* Egyptian Embassy Press Release of Dec. 2009, *available at* http://www.egyptembassy.se/press/23dec09.pdf.

[615] This would of course get in the way of Musa Kusa relations with General Suleiman, but that was part of the *modus operandi* of Muʿammar Qadhafi.

[616] This is probably the most delicate way of expressing Mubarak's otherwise much stronger negative reactions towards Muʿammar Qadhafi.

12. Conclusion

The Lockerbie case and its outcome, including the establishment of relations with Libya, can only be explained through the prism of strategic
political, economic, and security interests. The efforts to resolve the Lockerbie case stemmed from the desire by the United States, United Kingdom,
and Libya to open-up avenues to pursue larger goals. During the period
of *détente* with Libya, the Qadhafi regime went from being an international pariah state to a crucial ally of the U.S. and UK governments on
international security matters, as Libyan officials agreed to give up their
WMD program and divulge further information about a clandestine procurement network.[617] Libya provided the United States and the United
Kingdom an important ally in the region as a source of intelligence on
global terrorist activity.[618] The settlement satisfied the strategic interests
of the United States and the United Kingdom, along with other governments, particularly those belonging to the European Union and NATO.
Realpolitik seems to have prevailed over justice once again.[619]

The economic interests in reaching a settlement on Lockerbie and
establishing relations grew stronger as western businesses set their sites
on Libya's oil exploration and distribution. The Economist reported how
a steady stream of business began flowing in following the Lockerbie settlement, and that in 1999 Libyan officials met with bankers, oil and gas
executives, and other foreign businessmen in Geneva to discuss the best
approach towards opening up Libya's economy.[620] When Libya announced
it was opening up new sites for oil exploration in August 2004, the White
House followed by fully lifting economic sanctions just one month later.
The U.S. Embassy in Tripoli closely followed the 'oil major' as U.S. firms
bid for the lucrative contracts and, as discussed above, U.S. companies
won the exploration and production rights for a majority of the oil contracts during the first round of bidding.[621]

---

[617] Jon B. Alterman, *Libya and the US: The Unique Libyan Case*, Middle East Quar-
terly 21–29 (Winter 2006), *available at* http://www.meforum.org/886/libya-and-the-us-
the-unique-libyan-case. *See* Section on Libya and the West, *supra*, for more details on the
"Khan Network" in reference to Pakistani nuclear scientist, Abdel Qader Khan.

[618] *See supra* Sec. 10.1. *See also* Ch. IV, Sec. 6.3.

[619] For further analysis on the conflict between realpolitik and human rights, *see* articles by M. Cherif Bassiouni, *supra* note 399.

[620] *Qaddafi says farewell, Arabia, and sets his sights on Africa*, The Economist, Apr. 22,
1999, *available at* http://www.economist.com/node/200915.

[621] *See supra* Sec. 10.2.

Economic benefits for Libyans mostly flowed from the private businesses that began entering the Libyan market after relations with the western world were restored.[622] A group of regime insiders, including members of the Qadhafi family, benefited most substantially from the business opportunities resulting from liberalization policies and rapprochement with the West. Qadhafi's children, in particular, used their positions of influence to take part in private business ventures and expand their personal wealth. Saif al-Islam channeled his business ventures through his One Nine investment company. Mu'tassim made a small fortune in various ways, even going so far as to demand his own oil fields.[623] The Qadhafi family also benefited from the use of international banks abroad, securing legal advice on how best to transfer funds to foreign banks. The new Libyan government has expressed its desire to recover assets of the Qadhafi regime, but the secret nature of the international banking system makes this extremely difficult.

There were mutually beneficial exchanges in the area of security cooperation as well, as Qadhafi's military sought to refurbish its old stockpiles and acquire the latest weapons technology from the West. International arms suppliers were more than willing to meet the demand of a new client. U.S. Embassy officials acted as an intermediary of sorts between U.S.-based defense contractors and the Qadhafi regime, in many instances fielding demands from high-level Libyan military officials to approve sales of the new weaponry.[624]

The revolutionary movements that spread through the Middle East in 2011 forced the United States and other western countries to re-consider their relationships with the dictators of the region. In the face of Libya's uprising, the international community took action, with France advocating for foreign intervention first. France's motivations have been characterized as stemming from domestic politics, regional agendas, economic goals, and the desire to reassert itself as a leader on foreign and military affairs. France was also a major supplier of weapons to Libya, and continued to do so as the conflict was underway. Whatever the specific interests of the different states that took part in military intervention, their actions helped secure the end of the Qadhafi regime. The assistance of western government's in bringing down the regime did not translate, however,

---

[622] Alterman, *Libya and the US: The Unique Libyan Case, supra* note 617.
[623] PARGETER, LIBYA: THE RISE AND FALL OF QADDAFI, *supra* note 197 at 181.
[624] *See supra* Sec. 10.3.

into assistance in the post-Qadhafi period.[625] Rebuilding the country through reconstruction and development projects were essentially left to the Libyan people to manage in the wake of the conflict. This presented an immediate challenge, as Qadhafi had cultivated a culture of fear and isolation that destroyed self-sufficiency in Libyan society. The international sanctions cut Libyans off from the world, denying them access to study foreign languages or interact with other cultures abroad. State institutions, including those charged with handling economic and social development, were hollow structures that had been deliberately stripped of any functional capacity. Qadhafi instead had used foreign contractors to deliver public services and development projects.

Material goods, such as weapons, trucks, generators, and other types of equipment remained un-maintained and went to waste. This conveyed to society a general sense that wastefulness should be tolerated and conservation was unnecessary. Decades of Qadhafi's policies also created reliance on a distributive state.[626] Along with human rights atrocities and impunity, this form of state reliance is a legacy that will present a significant challenge for Libyan society and its institutions in the post-Qadhafi era.

The international community should consider these factors and examine the history of relations with Libya when determining its future involvement in the country. The records of declassified and leaked U.S. documents show the progression of U.S. policy from the decades of confrontation with Qadhafi to his regime becoming an important ally and asset in the region. The files also expose how in the years leading up to the 2011 revolution, U.S. policy was shaped by the assumption that enhancing military and economic ties with Libya would translate into greater democratic opening and political reform. History demonstrated, however, that this assumption did not hold true. While there were overtures and limited gestures in the area of human rights, the promise of reform remained unfulfilled. It was, in reality, the frustration and boiling social and political unrest resulting from the lack of respect for human rights and denial of any real democratic opening that erupted into the uprising of February 2011.

---

[625] *See generally* Ch. VI.
[626] PARGETER, LIBYA: THE RISE AND FALL OF QADDAFI, *supra* note 197 at 195.

CHAPTER TWO

THE EVOLUTION OF THE ARMED CONFLICT: 2011–2012

1. INTRODUCTION

Transformative change arrived in Libya on the tide of popular demands for reform sweeping through the region. Libya's revolution had been long in the making, however, with stirring social unrest an outcome of 42 years of tyranny and oppression. The growing indignation spread so that a critical mass of the country's citizenry openly expressed their frustration with a corrupt, exploitative, and repressive regime controlled by an absolute ruler who was known for being deeply mentally imbalanced.

As described in Chapter One, Mu'ammar Qadhafi's patronage system of rewards and punishment created a divided society, and a government run by a corrupt inner circle of Qadhafi's family and their coterie. Corruption was endemic, spreading to all levels of governance, and into the private sector of the small oligarchy that was part of the leader's privileged network. The Libyan people not only suffered from oppression, exploitation, and abuse, but also lived in a state of historical limbo without clear direction whether at the national or individual level. The regime effectively reduced the population to dependency by removing any incentives to education, innovation, inventiveness, or entrepreneurship. Additionally, the despotic regime inflicted systematic violence against its own citizens, both within and beyond the country's borders. The regime's policy of violence entailed sustained support for international terrorism in addition to political terror against Libyan exiles living abroad.[1]

Revolutions historically arrive in the form of small events that ignite larger transformative episodes. That spark occurred when a group of lawyers representing the Abu Salim Prison massacre victims organized a protest in front of the Benghazi courthouse.[2] The family members of the victims had been politically active for years, demanding justice for the murder of 1,272 prisoners, executed by machine gun fire by security guards under the direct command and control of 'Abdullah al-Senussi, Qadhafi's

---

[1] See Ch. I, Sec. 11.
[2] *See infra* Sec. 3.2.

brother-in-law and then head of internal security.[3] Those killed at the prison were deemed enemies of the state and targeted by the security apparatus for their opposition to the regime.[4] They included individuals who employed militant means, along with those who were activists and critics of Qadhafi's rule. In making no distinction between militants and outspoken dissenters, the regime directly violated citizens' right to freedom of speech and expression, which are rights legally protected under the International Covenant on Civil and Political Rights (ICCPR).[5]

Subsequent to their arrest, detainees were placed in the prison of 1,600–1,700 inmates where they were harshly treated and kept in a row of cells without access to open air. Their general treatment and conditions were in violation of the United Nations' Standard of Minimum Rules for the Treatment of Prisoners.[6] Many had become ill, but their protests to the prison authorities went unheeded. They decided to go on a strike and captured two guards in an attempt to force the authorities to meet their demands for better conditions.[7] One of those captured was then killed when guards opened fire, killing six prisoners and wounding a further 20. Libyan security officials headed by Al-Senussi and Nasir al-Mabruk then negotiated with representatives of the prisoners,[8] and agreed to meet their demands, including the provision of medical care for 120 sick prisoners. Instead of receiving medical attention, however, many of the sick were taken away and killed. On 29 June, gunmen on the roofs opened fire on hundreds of prisoners gathered into a courtyard under the pretense that a settlement with the authorities was about to be finalized. By the time the shooting stopped, over 1,200 prisoners had been killed. In an act of cruelty for which he would become notorious, Al-Senussi gave the direct order to continue shooting until all the prisoners were executed.[9]

---

[3] *Libya: Abu Salim Prison Massacre Remembered*, HUMAN RIGHTS WATCH, June 27, 2012, *available at* http://www.hrw.org/news/2012/06/27/libya-abu-salim-prison-massacre-remembered.

[4] For more details on the Abu Salim prison and on political prisoners held by the Qadhafi regime, *see* Ch. I, Secs. 9, 10 & 11.

[5] Libya is a state party to the ICCPR and its first optional protocol. *See supra* Basic Facts about Libya, for more details on Libya's obligations under international law.

[6] Standard Minimum Rules for the Treatment of Prisoners, E.S.C. Res. 663 C (XXIV) UN Doc. E/3048, July 31, 1957, *amended by* E.S.C. res. 2076, UN Doc. E/5988 (May 13, 1977).

[7] HUMAN RIGHTS WATCH, *Libya: Abu Salim Prison Massacre Remembered, supra* note 3.

[8] Report of the International Commission of Inquiry to investigate all the alleged violations of international human rights law in the Libyan Arab Jamahiriya, U.N. HRC. 17th Sess., ¶ 24. U.N. Doc. A/HRC/17/44 (Jan. 12, 2012).

[9] For more on Al-Senussi, his extradition from Mauritania to Libya, and charges levied against him, *see* Ch. IV, Sec. 6.3(b)(ii). *See also* HUMAN RIGHTS WATCH, *Libya: Abu Salim Prison Massacre Remembered, supra* note 3.

There was no outrage following the massacre, simply because the regime kept the killings hidden. Family members continued to visit the prison on a weekly basis, leaving food and clothing in the belief that their relatives were alive, as the guards would accept the provisions.[10] The Qadhafi government kept the massacre a secret for years, and did not begin informing the families of the victims until mounting pressure finally led to information surfacing in 2001.[11] A wave of indignation swept the country when the truth about the affair became known, but the regime remained steadfast in its position, seemingly neither shaken nor troubled by the event.

The anger was most marked in Benghazi, where a large number of the prisoners had originated. In the face of demands for justice, the Qadhafi regime responded in typical fashion by attempting to quiet the family members with financial compensation. Lawyers from Benghazi representing the family members of the victims negotiated for several years, finally agreeing to a sum equivalent of $1 million for each victim. Shortly after the compensation settlement, however, news went public that the Libyan government offered $3 million for each victim of the bombing in the Lockerbie case.[12] The family members of the Abu Salim Prison massacre protested, and their lawyers demanded at least equal compensation for the Libyan victims as the Americans, British, and other Europeans. Some characterized the disparity as a larger analogy for the Libyan government's treatment of its citizens, suggesting that under Qadhafi, the life of a Libyan was worth a third of that of a European.

Frustration grew over the Qadhafi regime's intransigence in response to repeated calls for truth and reparations for the Abu Salim killings. The continual postponement of justice fueled a growing activism among lawyers and family members unified by a common struggle and a shared tragedy. It was the arrest of the lawyers representing the Abu Salim Prison victims, notably Fathi Terbil, which came to be the tipping point that led to the overthrow of the regime.[13] In reflecting on this progression of events, it becomes apparent that the advent of the 2011 revolution was deeply rooted in calls for justice and accountability for past human rights atrocities.

---

[10] Report of the International Commission of Inquiry (Jan. 12, 2012), *supra* note 8 at ¶ 24.

[11] HUMAN RIGHTS WATCH, *Libya: Abu Salim Prison Massacre Remembered, supra* note 3. See also *Libya: June 1996 Killings at Abu Salim Prison*, HUMAN RIGHTS WATCH, June 28, 2006, *available at* http://www.hrw.org/legacy/english/docs/2006/06/28/libya13636.htm.

[12] *See* Ch. I, Sec. 11.2.2.

[13] *See* Ch. VI, Sec. 2.

The events in Libya were inspired in part by similar popular uprisings in neighboring countries that had culminated with the resignation of President Zine al-ʿAbidine Ben ʿAli in Tunisia and President Hosni Mubarak in Egypt. As in Tunisia and Egypt, the demonstrations did not initially call for the overthrow of the government. Rather, the demonstrations that erupted in mid-February 2011 in Libya were part of long-standing demands by human rights activists for accountability for past violations and for political reforms. It was not until Qadhafi forces responded to the peaceful protests with brazen violence that the movement began to call for regime change, and turned into an armed rebellion. The regime crackdowns on the demonstrations fueled the flames of unrest, and galvanized the burgeoning insurgent movement. By the end of February 2011, the conflict had escalated into civil war.[14]

As the "Arab Spring" revolutions spread, the Qadhafi regime responded to calls for protests in Libya with heightened surveillance and repression. Security forces detained activists on 1 February 2011 for posting material online calling for demonstrations. The National Conference of Libyan Opposition, an opposition group of exiled activists, organized a separate online call for protests. Lawyers and activists in Benghazi began organizing a demonstration, and the movement coalesced into a coordinated plan for a large protest scheduled for 17 February 2011.[15] The "Day of Rage" demonstrations were scheduled to coincide with the commemoration of the five-year anniversary of a government crackdown on a demonstration outside an Italian consulate in Benghazi, in which 14 protesters were killed.[16] Other observers also note the importance of the 17 February date, going back to 1987, when nine people were executed on national television following charges of seditious plotting.[17] It was an important date commemorating resistance in the face of repression, and 17 February would again become a significant date, marking the start of the 2011 revolution.

Libyan authorities were intent on quelling the protests before they began, attempting to calm the situation by releasing twelve prisoners and meeting with local media and political activists. Regime officials issued threats to activists, pressuring them to call off the demonstrations.

---

[14] Report of the International Commission of Inquiry (Jan. 12, 2012), *supra* note 8 at ¶ 26.

[15] ANTHONY BELL & DAVID WITTER, INSTITUTE FOR THE STUDY OF WAR, 2 THE LIBYAN REVOLUTION: THE ROOTS OF REBELLION 24 (Sept. 2011) [hereinafter "THE ROOTS OF REBELLION"], *available at* www.understandingwar.org/sites/default/files/Libya_Part2_0.pdf.

[16] Report of the International Commission of Inquiry (Jan. 12, 2012), *supra* note 8 at ¶ 27.

[17] BELL & WITTER, THE ROOTS OF REBELLION, *supra* note 15 at 24.

Qadhafi sent his son Sa'adi, a special forces commander, and intelligence chief Al-Senussi to Benghazi in an attempt to avert the protests and ease the unrest. These moves, however, were met with a backlash, stirring up more anger among Cyrenaicans. A speech given by Sa'adi that promised reform exacerbated tensions due to its condescending nature, as he was seen not as a figure of reform but rather remembered for his role in the regime's historical repression against Benghazi's citizens and as a symbol of the corrupt Qadhafi family.[18] Al-Senussi directly questioned human rights activist and lawyer Terbil in an attempt to intimidate him into calling off the planned "Day of Rage" events. Terbil responded by telling Al-Senussi and other regime agents that it was out of his hands.[19] The arrests of Terbil and others on 15 February by the regime's internal security forces (Jihaz al-Amn al-Dakhili) sparked a mass protest in Benghazi, two days earlier than planned.[20] Within days, protests had spread across Libya.

Qadhafi failed to understand the transformative nature of the Arab Spring, making the same mistake as Ben 'Ali and Mubarak had before him. He did not recognize the full potential of the inchoate rebellion, viewing it simply as another wave of dissent that could be easily dealt with in the same manner as those that had come before. On this occasion, however, the decision to use violence in the face of discontent only served to spread the uprising, leading to military defections on the part of those who refused to carry out indiscriminate attacks against protesters. The defectors that joined the resistance helped organize the rebels as they began arming themselves with weapons seized from military depots, and the nascent revolution was underway.

2. Military Forces and Organizational Structure

2.1. *Background on the Libyan Military*

The military structure of the Qadhafi regime was comprised of a multi-layered and overlapping system of security organizations designed to provide protection from opposition.[21] The structure, mandate and reporting

---

[18] Alison Pargeter, Libya: The Rise and Fall of Qadhafi 218 (New Haven, USA: Yale University Press, 2012).

[19] *Id.* at 219.

[20] Report of the International Commission of Inquiry (Jan. 12, 2012), *supra* note 8 at ¶ 27.

[21] Dirk Vandewalle, A History of Modern Libya 149 (Cambridge, UK: Cambridge University Press, 2006).

lines of the country's various security agencies were opaque, making them unclear to outside observers. The UN Commission of Inquiry (CoI) expressed the view that "the amorphous system reflected a purposeful policy to obfuscate responsibility and minimize any threat to the central control of Colonel Qadhafi himself." It found that the security organizations were "controlled exclusively by the Revolutionary Leadership led by Colonel Qadhafi."[22]

The primary function of the country's security apparatus was to serve as an instrument for safeguarding the regime.[23] To counterbalance any potential threat from within the regular armed forces, Qadhafi created separate paramilitary forces, such as the Revolutionary Guard, Popular Guard, and Revolutionary Committees. Additionally, within the Jamahiriyya system, the Internal Security Agency (ISA) monitored and detained political opponents. These bodies were given the authority to carry out investigative as well as security functions. By controlling the judiciary, the Qadhafi regime allowed the security forces to exercise sweeping powers with no accountability.[24]

Libya's military spending reached extraordinary levels in the 1970s–1980s, such that the country had acquired more equipment than the military could use or absorb.[25] Libya was importing an average of $3 billion in arms purchases per year, and between 1979 and 1983 spent an estimated $12 billion.[26] Qadhafi sought support from foreign military advisers, from countries such as Russia, Pakistan, Cuba and the Czech Republic, in order to maintain the massive amounts of military equipment acquired during this period. There were upwards of 2,000 advisers from the Soviet Union in Libya in 1979.[27]

The Libyan state maintained massive amounts of weaponry, but Qadhafi chose to stockpile most of the weapons rather than distribute them among his armed forces, so as to not allow any one unit to develop too much power. International sanctions and the fall of the Soviet Union

---

[22] Report of the International Commission of Inquiry (Jan. 12, 2012), ¶ 43, *supra* note 8.

[23] Hanspeter Mattes, *Challenges to Security Sector Governance in the Middle East: The Libyan Case* (Geneva Centre for the Democratic Control of Armed Forces conference paper presented 12-13 July 2004), *available at* http://www.dcaf.ch/Event-Attachement/Challenges-to-Security-Sector-Governance-in-the-Middle-East-the-Libyan-Case.

[24] *See* Ch. IV Sec. 6. *See also* Report of the International Commission of Inquiry on Libya, U.N. HRC. 19th Sess., Annex I, ¶ 51. U.N. Doc. A/HRC/19/68, advance unedited version (Mar. 2, 2012).

[25] PARGETER, LIBYA: THE RISE AND FALL OF QADHAFI, *supra* note 18 at 110.

[26] VANDEWALLE, A HISTORY OF MODERN LIBYA, *supra* note 21 at 148.

[27] PARGETER, LIBYA: THE RISE AND FALL OF QADHAFI, *supra* note 18 at 110.

limited Libya's ability to acquire weapons during the 1990s, and left a large amount of military equipment to languish. After UN sanctions were lifted in 1999, Libya again turned to Russia, spending $100 million on contracts for arms and upgrades on its old weaponry.[28] After EU and U.S. sanctions were lifted in 2004, Libya spent billions of dollars on weapons and upgrades.[29]

In the years leading up to the civil war, Libya turned to western governments for military technology and refurbishment. While the United States and others had sought for decades to halt Qadhafi's non-conventional weapon programs, there were no such concerns over the acquisition of conventional weaponry, particularly if they were bought from Western manufacturers.[30] With extensive cash and oil reserves, once Libya halted its WMD weapons development and sanctions were lifted, it was again seen as a high-end military consumer. Although Russia presented Qadhafi with an immediate opening to military equipment, he turned first to the United States. High-level military officials made persistent requests to U.S. officials for the refurbishment and sales-approvals for spare parts for military equipment – M113 Armored Personnel Carriers (APC), attack helicopters and Jordanian-made 4×4 'Tiger' transport vehicles.[31] United States military advisers also provided education and training for the Libyan military, as part of a defense cooperation Memorandum of Understanding agreed upon between the two militaries in 2008.[32]

The U.S. Air Force sent teams of maintenance experts to carry out seminars and training programs to assist the Libyans in maintaining their C-130 cargo planes. The U.S. Coast Guard also visited Libya in 2009 as part of a bilateral security cooperation mission to strengthen the maritime partnership between the United States and Libya.[33] By the end of 2008, Libyan officials expressed their desire to move away from purchasing military

---

[28] VANDEWALLE, A HISTORY OF MODERN LIBYA, *supra* note 21 at 148.

[29] See *infra* Sec. 2.2.

[30] *See* Ch. I, Sec. 10.

[31] U.S. Embassy in Tripoli, Secret Cable, *Saif al Islam al-Islam's Staff Reaches out on Pol-Mil Relations*, Dec. 14, 2009, *available at* http://www.telegraph.co.uk/news/wikileaks-files/libya-wikileaks/8294701/SAIF-AL-ISLAMS-STAFF-REACHES-OUT-ON-POL-MIL-ISSUES .html.

[32] For more information on United States-Libyan military relations in the lead-up 2011, *see* Ch. I, Sec. 10.3.

[33] U.S. Embassy in Tripoli, Press Release, *The United States and Libya Conduct Military Maintenance Training Seminar*, n.d., *available at* http://libya.usembassy.gov/news-events/news-from-the-embassy2/the-united-states-and-libya-conduct-military-maintenance-training-seminar.html.

equipment from Russia and former Soviet Republics to pursuing "technically superior" equipment from the United States.[34] Nevertheless, Libya continued to purchase billions of dollars worth of weaponry from Russia in the years leading up to the civil war in 2011.[35]

In 2009, Libya's ground forces numbered an estimated 25,000 personnel, with an additional 25,000 conscripts. The International Institute for Strategic Studies reported that the ground forces were organized into 11 border defense and four security zones, one regime security brigade (the Khamis Katiba), ten tank battalions, ten mechanized infantry battalions, 18 infantry battalions, six commando battalions, 22 artillery battalions, four SSM brigades and seven air defense artillery battalions.[36] Other sources estimate that in 2010, the Libyan Armed Forces had approximately 76,000 personnel: roughly 50,000 in the Army, 18,000 in the Air Force, and 8,000 in the Navy.[37] Libya could only field 150 T-72 tanks, which were the most advanced tanks in the military's inventory, though they dated to 1979.

The Qadhafi regime began a massive modernization drive of the Armed Forces following the termination of UN, U.S. and EU sanctions. In 2007, Libya signed the first arms deal with a European nation since the lifting of the 2004 European arms embargo when France agreed to sell Libya $230 million worth of advanced Milan anti-tank missiles.[38] Two years later, in 2009, Belgium delivered €11.5 million worth of small arms and ammunition to the Khamis 32nd Katiba.[39] In 2010, Libya was preparing to purchase the advanced S-300 air defense system for the Army as well as several dozen T-90 tanks, Russia's most advanced export tank.[40]

---

[34] U.S. Embassy in Tripoli, Secret Cable, *Libya Interested in U.S. Weapons, More Ambivalent on Other Military Cooperation*, Dec. 31, 2008, *available at* http://wikileaks.org/cable/2008/12/08TRIPOLI992.html.

[35] For more on arms purchases for the Army and Air Force, *see infra* Sec. 2.2.

[36] THE INTERNATIONAL INSTITUTE FOR STRATEGIC STUDIES, THE MILITARY BALANCE 2009 256 (June 2009), *available at* http://www.iiss.org/publications/military-balance/the-military-balance-2009.

[37] BELL & WITTER, THE ROOTS OF REBELLION, *supra* note 15 at 7.

[38] Afaf Geblawi, *Libya and France Sign 168-Million_Euro Arms Deal*, AFP, Aug. 2, 2007, *available at* http://www.spacewar.com/reports/Libya_And_France_Sign_168_Million_Euro_Arms_Deal_999.html.

[39] Amnesty International reported that, according to news reports and court documents, Belgium delivered the arms to protect (according to the Walloon government) humanitarian convoys going to Darfur, in the Sudan. *See* AMNESTY INTERNATIONAL, ARMS TRANSFERS TO THE MIDDLE EAST AND NORTH AFRICA: LESSONS FOR AN EFFECTIVE ARMS TRADE TREATY (2011), *available at* http://www.amnesty.org/en/library/asset/ACT30/117/2011/en/049fdeee-66fe-4b13-a90e-6d7773d6a546/act3011720011en.pdf.

[40] *Russia set to sell $2B in arms to Libya*, UPI, Jan. 27, 2010, *available at* http://www.upi.com/Business_News/Security-Industry/2010/01/27/Russia-set-to-sell-2B-in-arms-to-Libya/UPI-76051264611600.

The Libyan civil war and NATO's support of it cost Russian defense firms over \$4 billion in military equipment sales.[41] Qadhafi also bought 100,000 Kalashnikov assault rifles from Ukraine and negotiated with China for a further 500,000.[42] Weapons manufacturers from many other countries took to selling weapons to Qadhafi during this period. Even though Qadhafi did not have the manpower to operate the military equipment he was buying, it appears that he had a thirst for modern weapons, believing that he would make Libya a regional power. Many of the stockpiled weapons were discovered by the rebel forces during the 2011 uprising, and those that had not deteriorated with age were used against Qadhafi forces.[43]

The Libyan Army not only suffered from outdated equipment but also from Qadhafi's paranoia. Even with his inner-circle and family members in firm positions of power within the military, Qadhafi sustained an unhealthy level of paranoia that translated into distrust for all of the security forces. Qadhafi promoted individuals within the military based upon tribal loyalties rather than merit, tended to rotate officers haphazardly to ensure no-one could accumulate too much influence, and limited training of units he considered a threat to his regime.[44] Given these systemic failures, it was unlikely the modernization program could have done more than provide window dressing for a hollow force. The Libyan Army was not a capable military and instead existed more to defend Qadhafi from his own people than to defend the country from external threats.

The nature of Qadhafi's military was an outcome of Libya's history. It may appear illogical from a western perspective, but is not as anomalous as it may initially appear. Qadhafi took a military tradition based on tribal and regional loyalties built up over decades of fighting external aggressors and tried to apply it to a divided nation. As discussed in Chapter One, Libya had never stood strong and independent whether under the Romans in ancient times, the Ottomans of the 19th Century, or Italian colonial rule. When Libya did gain independence in 1951, it owed much to the

---

[41] *UN sanctions on Libya to cost Russia US\$4 Billion*, RT, Feb. 27, 2011, *available at* http://rt.com/news/russia-arms-export-libya.

[42] Vivienne Walt, *Conflicting Priorities Imperil Effort to Gather Up Gaddafi's Discarded Arms*, TIME, Nov. 15, 2011, *available at* http://www.time.com/time/world/article/0,8599,2099549,00.html.

[43] For more on the weapons used during and after the conflict, *see infra* Sec. 2.3.

[44] ANTHONY H. CORDESMAN, CENTER FOR STRATEGIC AND INTERNATIONAL STUDIES, THE NORTH AFRICAN MILITARY BALANCE: FORCE DEVELOPMENTS IN THE MAGHREB (Mar. 28, 2005) [hereinafter "FORCE DEVELOPMENTS"], *available at* http://csis.org/files/media/csis/pubs/050328_norafrimibal%5B1%5D.pdf.

United Kingdom and was extremely poor and undeveloped. Oil wealth brought about uneven development and corruption under King Idris that fostered resentment and exacerbated regional divides.[45] The military crafted by Qadhafi and the Free Unionist Officers Movement after overthrowing the King in 1969 was a capable force in terms of its revolutionary nature in line with the pan-Arab themes of the time. It was a strong and respected institution with modern weapons and served as a unifying force for a divided nation, but just for a brief moment in history.

The Libyan military reacted to Qadhafi's corruption and poor policies with coup attempts. Just as Qadhafi had plotted to overthrow King Idris, so too did elements of his military attempt to remove the Colonel. Their failure sowed the seeds for a bifurcated military. On one hand the army provided strong regime security, and on the other, was a sad, leaderless "jobs program" that existed more to keep men in uniform content with steady employment but without any incentive to progress. This is not without precedent; Saddam Hussein did much the same with a brutal Republican Guard centered in Baghdad employed to protect him, while the rest of the army languished but kept men both employed and mollified. Qadhafi's military was organized illogically as a fighting force, but for decades it succeeded in its central role of protecting the regime. In the end, the policy of keeping the army inept for self-preservation would lead to the military's inability to protect Qadhafi from his demise.

The Qadhafi regime was aware that unrest was surfacing in the lead-up to the uprising, particularly in the east where the voices of the opposition were the strongest. U.S. Embassy contacts reported in October 2009 that there was a growing frustration among the younger generation, and that the regime was concerned about widespread frustration exploding into violence.[46] In the wake of the Egyptian and Tunisian uprisings, the regime took steps to enhance its security presence in the eastern regions. Qadhafi moved Revolutionary Committee members to the 7 April military camp, and sent top security chiefs, such as Al-Senussi, head of the Internal Security Agency, to Benghazi.[47] In the face of growing pressure from activists, the regime resorted to long-trusted tactics of intimidation, but the military

---

[45] *See* Ch. I, Secs. 6 & 7.

[46] U.S. Embassy in Tripoli, Secret Cable, *What Passes for Political Ferment in Libya*, Oct. 26, 2009, *available at* http://www.telegraph.co.uk/news/wikileaks-files/libya-wikileaks/8294667/WHAT-PASSES-FOR-POLITICAL-FERMENT-IN-LIBYA.html.

[47] PARGETER, LIBYA: THE RISE AND FALL OF QADHAFI, *supra* note 18 at 219.

apparatus and defense systems were not equipped to deter the full-scale internal rebellion and foreign intervention that unfolded in 2011.

2.2. *The Qadhafi Forces*

The CoI gathered information on the structure and composition of the Qadhafi military and *thuwar* groups to "obtain a better understanding of the armed forces involved during the conflict, and to be able to identify specific military or security units involved in specific incidents constituting violations."[48] As previously noted, however, the Qadhafi security apparatus had no clear organizational structure, and was comprised of multiple overlapping entities with little direct communication between the various agencies.[49] Moreover, during the course of the conflict, the regime employed both informal and formal security bodies, complicating efforts to identify the decision makers behind violations committed during the 2011 civil war. Nevertheless, the CoI was able in many instances to identify senior military officers or military units allegedly responsible for the violations. The information in this section is intended to provide a roadmap to help identify those individuals and groups responsible for the atrocities carried out during the conflict.

The Qadhafi forces were comprised of both formal security institutions (including the police and regular military forces) and irregular security organizations (under the umbrella of the national security apparatus). The Armed Forces included the Army, the Libyan Air Force (LAF) and the Navy. The national security apparatus was comprised of political bodies such as the National Security Council, and security agencies that carried out internal and foreign intelligence functions (the Internal Security Agency, and External Security Agency) along with informal paramilitary bodies (such as the Revolutionary Committees). Many of these bodies were created after the 1969 coup and Qadhafi's ascent to power in order to promote the revolution and safeguard the regime. The security organizations created by Qadhafi infiltrated and overlapped with the regular army forces, such as the Revolutionary Guard, which included both regular brigades and special forces units. The following section is therefore not an authoritative map of the organizational structure of Qadhafi's

---

[48] Report of the International Commission of Inquiry, advance unedited version (Mar. 2, 2012), *supra* note 24 at Annex I, ¶ 49.

[49] *Id.* at Annex I, ¶ 50.

military, but rather an outline of the Libyan forces that were employed by
the regime during the 2011 war.

2.2.1. *The Armed Forces*

THE MILITARY INTELLIGENCE SERVICE (Jihaz al-Amn al-'Askari or Istikhbarat): While the regular armed forces had been pushed aside over the years
and no longer handled internal security matters, Military Intelligence
continued to function as a powerful internal force.[50] The CoI gathered
extensive witness testimony regarding detention facilities run by Military
Intelligence during the conflict from victims as well as military officers,
including officers from the Search and Interrogation Office (Maktab al-
Taharyyat wa-l-Bahith). Intelligence units provided lists of people to be
arrested, and instructed ground forces to turn over suspected *thuwar* to
Military Intelligence.[51] The CoI noted that the systematic torture carried
out by Qadhafi forces was especially prevalent at the installations run by
internal security and Military Intelligence services.[52]

THE LIBYAN ARMY: Libya fielded the world's tenth largest tank force
and a massive and robust artillery force backed up by tactical ballistic
missiles and over 45,000 men in active service and 40,000 men in popular
militia forces. Over half of Libya's armament, however, was in storage due
to chronic understaffing and poorly trained recruits, in numbers and types
of vehicles that complicated logistics to the point of paralysis, and UN
sanctions. Equipment therefore aged, making its value questionable in a
modern war.[53] The Libyan Army did, though, have more than adequate
equipment to maintain internal security as it did for over four decades
and – had it been properly trained and directed – would have been able
to put down a popular uprising.

The Libyan Army had one regime security brigade[54] (the Khamis Katiba), ten tank battalions, 21 mechanized infantry battalions, 15 paratroop
battalions, five surface-to-surface missile brigades, 22 artillery battalions,

---

[50] *Id.* at Annex I, ¶ 52.

[51] *Id.* at Annex I, ¶ 49.

[52] Instances of torture were reported most extensively during the conflict in detention
facilities in Tripoli and surrounding cities. *See* Ch. XIII. *See also* Report of the International
Commission of Inquiry, advance unedited version (Mar. 2, 2012), *supra* note 24 at Annex I,
¶ 320, n. 460.

[53] CORDESMAN, FORCE DEVELOPMENTS, *supra* note 44.

[54] As discussed in the Introduction to this book and in the Glossary of Terms, both the
Qadhafi forces and the *thuwar* forces used the term *kata'ib*, or brigades, to identify their
fighting units.

and the army commanded Libya's SA-5 surface-to-air missiles.[55] The number of armored vehicles in Libya's Army was striking; 2,210 tanks, 2,520 armored personnel carriers, 2,400 artillery pieces, and over 3,000 anti-tank missiles.[56] However, many of these weapons were in storage and most were antiquated.[57]

THE QADHAFI BRIGADES *(KATA'IB)*: Each individual brigade (katiba) is estimated to have been comprised of up to 3,000 men and armed with heavy weaponry.[58] Membership in the Qadhafi *kata'ib* was based on loyalty, family, and tribal ties.[59] Other paramilitary organizations within the security apparatus, such as the Revolutionary Guard, also formed kata'ib that existed within the regular military structure (see details below on the Revolutionary Guard).

THE 32ND (KHAMIS) KATIBA: Headed by Khamis Qadhafi, the son of Mu'ammar Qadhafi, the 32nd Katiba was the only military unit that was fully manned, equipped with nominally modern weapons, and adequately trained and led.[60] Unlike other brigades, it also included "ground forces, Special Forces, artillery units, Grad missiles units, airborne units, in addition to the intelligence units."[61] The term "brigade" is somewhat of a misnomer when describing this unit as it was estimated to have at least 10,000 Libyan soldiers reinforced by foreign fighters, approximately the strength of a modern division (which typically has between two and four brigades).[62] While the Libyan Army was undermanned and underequipped, the 32nd Katiba had surplus strength.

---

[55] THE MIDDLE EAST STRATEGIC BALANCE 2002–2003 (Kam Ephraim & Yiftah S. Shapir eds., Tel Aviv, Israel: Center for Strategic Studies at Tel Aviv University, Dec. 28, 2009).

[56] *Id. See also* CORDESMAN, FORCE DEVELOPMENTS, *supra* note 44.

[57] *Libya: Secure Unguarded Arms Depots*, HUMAN RIGHTS WATCH, Sept. 10, 2011, *available at* http://www.hrw.org/news/2011/09/09/libya-secure-unguarded-arms-depots.

[58] This is on the low-end when compared to brigades from other militaries, such as a NATO Brigade that is typically 3,000–5,500 men.

[59] Report of the International Commission of Inquiry, advance unedited version (Mar. 2, 2012), *supra* note 24 at Annex I, ¶ 53.

[60] Colonel Qadhafi removed the initial commander of this brigade to place his son Khamis in charge, even though at the time, young Khamis was only a 1st lieutenant. The entire command structure of the brigade was made up of captains and lieutenants who were artificially promoted to higher ranks after young Lieutenant Khamis became a general.

[61] Report of the International Commission of Inquiry, advance unedited version (Mar. 2, 2012), *supra* note 24 at Annex I, ¶ 54.

[62] *Profile: Khamis Khaddafi*, BBC, Sept. 4, 2011, *available at* http://www.bbc.co.uk/news/world-africa-14723041.

The Khamis Katiba was the most well-known, though certainly not the only named katiba. Libyan Army *kata'ib* were usually named after their commanders, but there is scant information, if any, on the specific *kata'ib*, their equipment levels, or their garrison locations. Other Libyan Army *kata'ib* mentioned in press reports include the Hamza,[63] Husban,[64] Munawaba[65] and Tawergha *kata'ib*.[66]

THE LIBYAN NAVY: Although the Qadhafi regime had been trying to revive the Navy with new purchases, it remained a shell of its former regional glory when the civil war began in 2011. The Navy boasted 17 combat ships, 12 patrol craft, 4 amphibious landing craft, 13 auxiliary vessels and a force of some 8,000 sailors; a seemingly formidable force capable of defending the nation and the Gulf of Sidra.[67] Only half of its sailors were considered active or fit for service, however. Without foreign advisers they could not be relied upon to operate the ships or their weapons, especially as many of the ships were in a state of disrepair. The Libyan Navy was no longer able to conduct maneuvers at sea, and the ships remained moored. The Navy's two helicopter squadrons were defunct and incapable of firing weapons.[68] Libya's six Foxtrot submarines had also fallen into disrepair; only two were seaworthy, and neither been out to sea since 2005. The only offensive capability the regime could count on from the Navy was its mining vessels that could still effectively mine the Gulf. However, Qadhafi forces used inflatable rafts to plant mines during the civil war, demonstrating that it did not require dedicated mine vessels for the task. Beyond the poor state of their vessels, naval personnel were inadequately trained and could not be relied upon to perform their duties.[69] International sanctions in the 1990s contributed to the demise and all but decimation of the once great Libyan Navy of the 1980s.

---

[63] *Qadhafi Blames Uprising on Al-Qaeda*, AL JAZEERA, Feb. 24, 2011, *available at* http://www.aljazeera.com/news/africa/2011/02/201122414305498804.html.

[64] *Zawiyah in rebel hands, but under siege*, NEWS 24, Mar. 5, 2011, *available at* http://www.news24.com/Africa/News/Libya-Zawiyah-in-rebel-hands-but-under-siege-20110305.

[65] *See* Libyan Proud, *Zawiyya Hospital Aftermath of 11/06/2011*, YOUTUBE (June 12, 2011), *available at* http://www.youtube.com/watch?feature=player_embedded&v=EV5Kpvva9GM. A subtitled version is available at *Zawiyya Hospital Aftermath of 11/06/2011*, AMARA, *available at* http://www.universalsubtitles.org/en/videos/P2F7mQoXiJTw/en/117282.

[66] This statement is based on information provided to the ISISC Project by the consultant. *See also* Fatima AzZahra, *Misrata and Tawargha*, FEB 17th, Nov. 13, 2011, *available at* http://feb17.info/editorials/op-ed-misrata-and-tawargha.

[67] THE MIDDLE EAST STRATEGIC BALANCE 2002–2003, *supra* note 55.

[68] CORDESMAN, FORCE DEVELOPMENTS, *supra* note 44.

[69] *Id.*

Qadhafi recognized the challenges faced by the Navy, and embarked on a modernization program to improve its capabilities. Between 2005–2009, Libya received six MV115 Fast Patrol Boats from Italy,[70] a type of boat armed with a 30mm Oto Malera gun, capable of speeds in excess of 50 knots. From Croatia, Libya received six PV30 Patrol Boats with another six on order in June 2008. Libya sent five rocket gunboats to Croatia for overhaul in 2009, and was also in negotiation the same year for new Corvettes and ships for their Coast Guard from Croatia.[71]

The expansion of the Libyan Navy was well underway. However, purchasing new ships would not overcome the acute need for better training and capable manpower. Notwithstanding the lack of trained and capable personnel, the Navy forces were able to mount at least one successful attack during the civil war when they shelled Ra's Lanuf and conducted an amphibious assault on the city.[72]

THE LIBYAN AIR FORCE: Libya had the largest air force in North Africa.[73] In 2009, the Libyan Air Force (LAF) had 260 combat aircraft, 83 transport aircraft, 117 helicopters and various support aircraft in service. In addition, it had a significant reserve of hundreds of aircraft, used mainly for spare parts due to decades of arms embargos and neglect.[74] Air Force and defense personnel numbered some 18,000.[75] The vast majority of LAF aircraft were Cold War-era Soviet designs with a small number of Cold War-era French aircraft and some Vietnam-era American helicopters to supplement the mostly Russian and French helicopters in service. Although the LAF had a sizeable number of airplanes and helicopters, their ability to field them was severely limited due to poor training, inadequate maintenance, and a general lack of capable airframes to take on modern threats.[76]

Libyan Air Defense forces, which formed part of the LAF, operated a large, robust yet aging air defense system.[77] The system was comprised of

---

[70] THE MIDDLE EAST STRATEGIC BALANCE 2002–2003, *supra* note 55.

[71] *Libyan Navy – Modernization*, GLOBALSECURITY.ORG, *available at* http://www.global security.org/military/world/libya/navy-modernization.htm.

[72] *See* Ch. VIII. *See also Gaddafi forces launch offensive*, AL JAZEERA, Mar. 11, 2011, *available at* http://www.aljazeera.com/news/africa/2011/03/201131041228856242.html.

[73] *Libyan Air Force*, GLOBALSECURITY.ORG, *available at* http://www.globalsecurity.org /military/world/libya/af.htm.

[74] THE MIDDLE EAST STRATEGIC BALANCE 2002–2003, *supra* note 55.

[75] *Id.*

[76] LIBYA: A COUNTRY STUDY (Helen Chapin Metz ed., Washington, USA: Federal Research Division, Library of Congress, 1989).

[77] According to the Library of Congress Country Study the Libyan Army operated Libya's most modern air defense sites, the SA-5 purchased from Russia in 1980s. *See Id.*

at least 17 operational strategic early warning radar sites, a combination of Soviet and Italian Cold War-era designs, in addition to a layered air defense system based on critical target defense combining strategic and tactical Surface-to-Air Missiles (SAM) assets.[78] There were approximately 30 heavy SAM batteries, 17 medium SAM batteries, 55 light SAM batteries, and some 440 short-range air-defense guns.[79] While the Libyan air defense network was sizeable, it was also outdated and extremely susceptible to electronic countermeasures. Indeed, it failed to bring down a single NATO aircraft during the civil war.

Qadhafi greatly expanded the LAF after he took power, and during the Cold War it was designed and modernized by the Soviet Union. The LAF was organized into three fighter squadrons, five bomber squadrons, a counterinsurgency squadron, nine helicopter squadrons and three air defense brigades.[80] Libyan pilots were reportedly of such poor caliber that Qadhafi often employed foreign pilots to fly for him, mostly from Russia, North Korea, Pakistan, South Africa, and the former Yugoslavia. The LAF had a poor historical record, employed occasionally for ground support, but used mostly as a transportation asset. The LAF participated in the war in Chad but did not distinguish itself or play a prominent role beyond ferrying troops and providing occasional ground support.[81]

Qadhafi began a modernization program after the UN embargo was lifted in 1999, making the LAF a centerpiece of his renewal campaign by cutting deals with several countries worth billions of dollars for some of the world's most advanced aircraft and air defense systems.[82] France upgraded Libya's Mirage F1s in 2006, and over the next two years Libya purchased helicopters from Italy. Russia upgraded Libya's Su-24 ground attack aircraft in 2009, and Libya was slated to be the first export customer of Russia's advanced Su-35 multirole fighter, with delivery scheduled for 2012.[83] Needless to say, the ousting of the Qadhafi regime derailed this deal.

---

[78] *The Libyan Air Defense System: Libya's Surface to Air (SAM) Missile Network*, CENTRE FOR RESEARCH ON GLOBALIZATION, GLOBAL RESEARCH, Mar. 21, 2011, *available at* http://www.globalresearch.ca/the-libyan-air-defense-system-libya-s-surface-to-air-missile-sam-network/23841.

[79] THE MIDDLE EAST STRATEGIC BALANCE 2002–2003, *supra* note 55.

[80] LIBYA: A COUNTRY STUDY, *supra* note 76.

[81] GLOBALSECURITY.ORG, *Libyan Air Force, supra* note 73.

[82] *Libya Seeking Arms Deals*, DEFENSE INDUSTRY DAILY, Mar. 4, 2012, *available at* http://www.defenseindustrydaily.com/the-french-connection-libya-seeking-arms-deals-04417.

[83] *Id.*

2.2.2. *The National Security Apparatus*

THE NATIONAL SECURITY COUNCIL (MAJLIS AL-AMN AL-QAWMI): Established through Law Number 4 in 2007, the National Security Council (NSC) was meant to function as a policy-making and implementing body. Qadhafi appointed his son, Muʿtassim Qadhafi, to head the council as National Security Adviser. According to information received by U.S. Embassy officials, along with Muʻtassim at the head, membership of the council included the Prime Minister, Foreign Minister, Minister of Public Security, Minister of Economy and Trade and Chief of Defense.[84] The NSC was considered the primary link between the military and security agencies.[85]

THE JAMAHIRIYYA SECURITY ORGANIZATION (HAYAT AMN AL-JAMAHI-RIYYA): The Jamahiriyya Security Organization (JSO) was comprised of two main branches, the Internal Security Agency (Jihaz al-Amn al-Dakhili) and the External Security Agency (Jihaz al-Amn al-Khariji).[86] At the helm of these branches were two of the regime's most powerful and notorious figures, ʻAbdullah al-Senussi and Musa Kusa.[87] The CoI reported that, under the leadership of Al-Senussi, the ISA was tasked with "countering terrorism and monitoring anti-Qadhafi organizations, such as lawyers and doctors' unions and individuals to evaluate the extent of any internal threat to the regime."[88] The Internal Security Agency had jurisdiction over the Abu Salim and ʻAin Zara prisons, which held political prisoners for years without trial.[89] Sources also indicate that Al-Senussi was at

---

[84] U.S. Embassy in Tripoli, secret cable, *Libya's National Security Council: Experiencing Growing Pains*, Dec. 23, 2007, *available at* http://www.telegraph.co.uk/news/wikileaks-files/libya-wikileaks/8294769/LIBYAS-NATIONAL-SECURITY-COUNCIL-EXPERIENCING-GROWING-PAINS.html.

[85] Report of the International Commission of Inquiry, advance unedited version (Mar. 2, 2012), *supra* note 24 at Annex I, ¶ 55.

[86] *Id.* at Annex I, ¶ 57. *See also Jamahiriya Security Organization (JSO)*, GLOBALSECU-RITY.ORG, *available at* http://www.globalsecurity.org/intell/world/libya/jso.htm.

[87] Both Kusa and Al-Senussi changed hands as the second most powerful figures in the regime directly under Qadhafi. While Musa Kusa had international experience, studying in the United States and other countries, Al-Senussi did not travel and was reported to have a very Libya-centric view of the world. *See* Mattes, *Challenges to Security Sector Governance in the Middle East: The Libyan Case*, *supra* note 23 at 8, 12–13.

[88] According to the CoI's January 2012 report, the ISA commander for the eastern region at the time of the events in February 2011 was Senussi al-Waziri; and the commander for Tripoli was Brigadier General Tuhami Khalid. *See* Report of the International Commission of Inquiry (Jan. 12, 2012), *supra* note 8 at ¶ 40, n. 34.

[89] *See Truth and Justice Can't Wait*, HUMAN RIGHTS WATCH, Dec. 12, 2009, *available at* http://www.hrw.org/en/node/87096/section/8.

the head of the entire JSO apparatus, from 1992 onwards.[90] Kusa (who defected from the regime in February 2011) commanded the External Security Agency (ESA) from September 1994[91] until March 2009, at which time he was appointed foreign minister.[92] This ESA was the principal intelligence institution responsible for supporting terrorist organizations and perpetrating state sponsored acts of terrorism.[93] The agency also was involved in military intelligence matters and was responsible for overseas intelligence assessments.[94] While members of both the ISA and ESA often wore civilian clothes and drove unmarked vehicles, witnesses in the civil war claim to have been able to recognize their agents.[95]

Both the ISA and the ESA were involved in the 2011 war in various capacities. In the early days of the protests, the ISA engaged in planning meetings with members of the Revolutionary Committees to coordinate the regime response.[96] Additionally, the ESA also carried out operations near the Tunisian border during the conflict, compiling lists of individuals involved in anti-Qadhafi organizing in Tunisia.[97] Intelligence units were involved in carrying out summary executions, such as the Boy Scout camp killings in the Nafusa Mountains region.[98] Witness testimony also indicates that ISA and ESA military installations were used for interrogating and torturing arrested thuwar during the conflict.[99] The CoI found that the ISA as well as the Military Intelligence Service were primarily responsible for systematic torture upon those suspected of being *thuwar* and their supporters.[100]

---

[90] Mattes, *Challenges to Security Sector Governance in the Middle East: The Libyan Case,* *supra* note 23 at 12.

[91] U.S. Central Intelligence Agency, Counterterrorist Center, *Secret Terrorism Review* (June 1995).

[92] According to the January 2012 CoI Report, other ESA officials as of February 2011 included the head of the Special Operations Unit, Abu Zayid Durda. *See* Report of the International Commission of Inquiry (Jan. 12, 2012), *supra* note 8 at ¶ 40.

[93] GLOBALSECURITY.ORG, *Libyan Jamahiriya Security Organization (JSO), supra* note 86.

[94] Report of the International Commission of Inquiry, advance unedited version (Mar. 2, 2012), *supra* note 24 at Annex I, ¶ 57.

[95] *See* Chs. IX, XIII & XIV.

[96] *See* Report of the International Commission of Inquiry, advance unedited version (Mar. 2, 2012), *supra* note 24, Annex I, ¶ 110.

[97] *See* Ch. X, Sec. 3.2.

[98] *Libya: Mass Grave Yields 34 Bodies,* HUMAN RIGHTS WATCH, Sept. 14, 2011, *available at* http://www.hrw.org/news/2011/09/14/libya-mass-grave-yields-34-bodies.

[99] Report of the International Commission of Inquiry, advance unedited version (Mar. 2, 2012), *supra* note 24 at Annex I, ¶ 271.

[100] *See* Ch. III, Secs. 2 & 9. *See also* Report of the International Commission of Inquiry, advance unedited version (Mar. 2, 2012), *supra* note 24 at Annex I, ¶ 378.

THE REVOLUTIONARY COMMITTEES (AL-LIJAN AL-THAWRIYYA): Created by Qadhafi in 1977 to spread Qadhafi's revolutionary ideas to the masses, the Revolutionary Committees were tasked over the decades with securing the regime's policies through intimidation and force.[101] To the extent that discontent developed within the Armed Forces, the Revolutionary Committees served as a counterbalance to the formal security apparatus.[102] According to information collected by the CoI, "their members wore civilian clothes and were armed with light weapons (handguns and AK-47s)." They numbered in the tens of thousands, "possibly between 60,000 and 100,000 members" who were tasked with police functions, and given authority to intimidate, detain, and hold trials of regime opponents and political dissidents.[103]

The Revolutionary Committee offices were notorious symbols of the regime's repression, and were targeted by protesters during the early stages of the revolution. The committee members formed an integral part of the regime's loyalist supporters who carried out attacks against demonstrators and confronted the rebel forces.

THE REVOLUTIONARY GUARD (AL-HARAS AL-THAWRI): A structured political and paramilitary body that carried out the function of suppressing internal opposition, the Revolutionary Guard also included regular military units. Its members were believed to include individuals from the Revolutionary Committees who formed regular units within the Armed Forces.[104] According to information provided to the CoI, "the Revolutionary Guard included six brigades (a special forces brigade, an infantry brigade, an artillery brigade, and three tank brigades all stationed on the outskirts of Tripoli). It was thought to have been approximately 40,000 strong"[105] and "had access to battle tanks, armored personnel carriers, helicopters and possibly anti-aircraft artillery and guided weapons." The Revolutionary Guard, also known as the Republican Guard, was accused

---

[101] For more on the creation and history of the Revolutionary Committees, *see* Ch. I, Sec. 8. *See also* Evan Hill, *Under Qadhafi's Eyes*, AL JAZEERA, Apr. 17, 2011, *available at* http://www.aljazeera.com/indepth/features/2011/04/20114171045914762.html.

[102] PARGETER, LIBYA: THE RISE AND FALL OF QADHAFI, *supra* note 18 at 80.

[103] Report of the International Commission of Inquiry, advance unedited version (Mar. 2, 2012), *supra* note 24 at Annex I, ¶ 56.

[104] *See* Report of the International Commission of Inquiry (Jan. 12, 2012), *supra* note 8 at ¶ 42.

[105] *Revolutionary Guard*, GLOBALSECURITY.ORG, *available at* http://www.globalsecurity.org/intell/world/libya/rg.htm.

of numerous abuses during the 2011 war, including the shooting of protesters, detention of rebel fighters and occupation of hospitals.

THE POPULAR GUARD (AL-HARAS AL-SHAʿABI): Tasked with protecting the regime and the revolutionary order, the Popular Guard (also referred to as the People's Guard) was another organization that existed outside the formal security structure. Along with the other paramilitary bodies, it served to ensure Qadhafi's power, in part by infiltrating and monitoring the formal security institutions and governing bodies. The Popular Guard was created in 1990 in response to the escalating militant activities of the Libyan Islamic Fighting Group (LIFG), who took up arms in opposition to the Qadhafi regime, mostly in the eastern Cyrenaica province.[106] The Popular Guard also took part in summary executions of captured opposition forces and suspected *thuwar* supporters.[107]

Separate from the Armed Forces and the national security bodies, the security apparatus included police units under the control of the Interior Ministry. Some of these forces, such as the riot police force (Quwat al-Daʿm al-Markazi) took part in suppressing demonstrations.[108] The Special Forces police unit was another force involved in maintaining internal security, and was under the chain of command of the Ministry of Interior and headed by General ʿAbd al-Fattah Yunis prior to the conflict during which he defected.[109] As Interior Minister under the Qadhafi regime, Yunis was accused of involvement in the violent suppression of members of LIFG in the east in the 1990s. Former LIFG members formed part of the *thuwar* 17 February Martyr's Katiba, which was suspected of the killing of Yunis.[110]

2.3. *The* Thuwar *Forces*

The *thuwar* forces in the east soon recognized the need for a unified body to coordinate the rebellion and manage diplomatic relations with the international community. The National Transitional Council (NTC) was

---

[106] Mattes, *Challenges to Security Sector Governance in the Middle East: The Libyan Case*, *supra* note 23 at 15–16.

[107] For more information on the Boy Scouts camp massacre, *see* Ch. X, Sec. 3.2.

[108] *See* Ch. III, Sec. 9. *See also* Report of the International Commission of Inquiry (Jan. 12, 2012), *supra* note 8 at ¶ 41.

[109] Report of the International Commission of Inquiry, advance unedited version (Mar. 2, 2012) *supra* note 24 at Annex I, ¶ 58.

[110] ANTHONY BELL ET AL., INSTITUTE FOR THE STUDY OF WAR, 3 THE LIBYAN REVOLUTION: STALEMATE & SIEGE 34 n. 49 (Oct. 2011) [hereinafter "STALEMATE & SIEGE"], *available at* http://www.understandingwar.org/sites/default/files/Libya_Part3_0.pdf.

officially formed on 27 February 2011, stating its commitment to the end of the Qadhafi regime.[111] Led by former Minister of Justice Mustafa 'Abd al-Jalil, the NTC issued its first decree on 2 March in Benghazi, declaring itself the "sole representative of all Libya,"[112] thereby positioning itself to be the political body that would manage the transitional period. The NTC was comprised of former regime officials and Libyan expatriates, and included representatives from city councils in Cyrenaica and *thuwar*-held cities in the west.[113] Two representatives for foreign affairs were appointed, Mahmud Jibril and 'Ali al-'Issawi.[114] The NTC was quickly recognized by France, Gambia, Italy, Jordan, Kuwait, Maldives and Qatar as Libya's legitimate interim governing body and the UN General Assembly followed suit in September 2011.[115]

The rebel forces were coordinated by representative councils on several fronts, but eastern Libya and the NTC served as the international face of the uprising, with the NTC achieving broad international recognition early on. The NTC went on to provide a safe haven for defectors in Benghazi, a region known for anti-regime activity.[116] Many of the defectors who joined the eastern rebellion had military experience and, in addition to strengthening the *thuwar* in the east, degraded the regime's military capabilities in Cyrenaica.[117] The NTC leadership also created a military council, under the authority of 'Umar Hariri, and an operations center led by Brigadier General 'Abd al-Salam al-Hasi.[118]

The eastern rebellion, however, remained distant from the heavy fighting taking place in other parts of Libya. While the NTC garnered international support, its leadership was disconnected from other parts of the country, such as Misrata and the Nafusa Mountains region, where local rebels faced the regime forces on their own accord.[119] This dynamic,

---

[111] *The National Transitional Council in Benghazi*, AL JAZEERA, June 21 2011, *available at* http://cc.aljazeera.net/asset/language/arabic/national-transitional-council-benghazi.

[112] *See* Ch. VI, Sec. 2. *See also* Report of the International Commission of Inquiry, advance unedited version (Mar. 2, 2012), *supra* note 24 at Annex I, ¶ 82.

[113] BELL & WITTER, THE ROOTS OF REBELLION, *supra* note 15 at 28.

[114] *Id.* at 8.

[115] Report of the International Commission of Inquiry (Jan. 12, 2012), *supra* note 8 at ¶ 31.

[116] *See* Ch. VI, Sec. 2.

[117] *See id.* for more on the defection of regime officials such as General 'Abd al-Fattah Yunis. *See also* BELL & WITTER, THE ROOTS OF REBELLION, *supra* note 15 at 25.

[118] Report of the International Commission of Inquiry, advance unedited version (Mar. 2, 2012), *supra* note 24 at Annex I, ¶ 65.

[119] BELL & WITTER, THE ROOTS OF REBELLION, *supra* note 15 at 8; INTERNATIONAL CRISIS GROUP, HOLDING LIBYA TOGETHER: SECURITY CHALLENGES AFTER QADHAFI, Dec. 14,

which caused resentment from some of the *thuwar kata'ib* battling Qadhafi forces, manifested itself in mistrust of the NTC by many rebel groups
who refused to submit to their authority in the post-conflict period.

The *thuwar* were groups organized for the most part independently,
without any guiding central authority, and only some groups had organized command structures. This led to communication problems that
hindered the unification of the disparate armed factions and led to the
development of military structures and chains of command operating in
isolation from one another.[120] As noted in Chapter One, the geographic
differences, regional divides, and diverse terrain that historically imposed
barriers between Fezzan, Tripolitania, and Cyrenaica equally played a factor in shaping the rebel forces in 2011.

As a result, a number of "geographically-rooted armed *kataeb* proliferated across Libya. Such militias were responsible for taking control and
securing their own areas, and maintained their independence even after
the end of hostilities."[121] In the wake of the fall of Qadhafi, Libya was
divided into territories controlled by non-state armed factions, a product
not only of Libya's history but also specifically, the nature of the conflict
itself, and the manner in which it was fought by the rebel forces.

There was no uniformity in *thuwar kata'ib* of the kind one might look
for in a conventional military. Although they called themselves "brigades,"
the term had nothing to do with their actual size or composition and was
more an honorific marker. Early in the conflict, these brigades were geographic, made up of small groups of men from the same neighborhood or
locality with little or no command, control or central authority. The Misrata Military Council, for example, grew out of civilian youths who banded
together to repel the initial onslaught of Qadhafi troops.[122] The *thuwar
kata'ib* sought to establish some level of uniformity both to improve their
combat capabilities and to appeal to western powers. By April 2011, men in
these *kata'ib* carried photo identification and their weapons were marked
and recorded.[123] Many of these so-called brigades were small and unlikely

---

2011 [hereinafter "HOLDING LIBYA TOGETHER"], *available at* http://www.crisisgroup.org/~/
media/Files/Middle%20East%20North%20Africa/North%20Africa/115%20Holding%20
Libya%20Together%20--%20Security%20Challenges%20after%20Qadhafi.pdf.

[120] Report of the International Commission of Inquiry, advance unedited version (Mar.
2, 2012), *supra* note 24 at Annex I, ¶ 61.

[121] *Id.* at ¶ 62.

[122] INTERNATIONAL CRISIS GROUP, HOLDING LIBYA TOGETHER, *supra* note 119.

[123] Evan Hill, *Libyan rebels get organized*, AL JAZEERA, Apr. 19, 2011, *available at* http://
www.aljazeera.com/indepth/features/2011/04/201141942947854663.html.

to have reached the 3,000-man threshold to be considered a brigade in the technical sense.

That small groups of men defending their localities were understood as brigades or *kata'ib*, caused a great deal of confusion among the rebels regarding civilian status and the definition of a noncombatant. During interviews with the CoI and human rights organizations on the ground during the conflict, numerous rebels identified themselves as civilians. When pressed on the issue, they stated they had been civilians and considered themselves as such, even when armed. They were unfamiliar with the idea of combatant immunity or the issue of civilians losing protected status. This was at the root of problems the CoI found regarding *thuwar* attacks on civilians and civilian objects. The siege of Sirte was one such case where the *thuwar* made no attempt to differentiate between civilians and combatants because they considered everyone in the city a supporter of Qadhafi and therefore a legitimate target.[124] This also complicated the CoI investigation when *thuwar* identified individuals killed by Qadhafi forces as civilians when later investigations showed them to have been combatants.[125]

There was an early attempt to create a rebel army, the Libyan National Army, based in Benghazi, under a central command and led by General Yunis. The prominent role Yunis had previously played in the Qadhafi regime, however, fueled mistrust among the rebels in Cyrenaica. Yunis was also involved in a series of NATO airstrikes in the Ajdabiya and Brega region in early April 2011, when NATO accused him of failing to provide them with adequate intelligence.[126]

The Libyan National Army was unable to coordinate any unified resistance against the Qadhafi regime. Even in the east, where the NTC was based, the rebels organized on their own, forming independent *kata'ib* such as the influential 17 February Martyrs Katiba (Katiba Shuhada')

---

[124] *See* Ch. XV.

[125] This statement is based on information provided to the ISISC Project by the consultant based on discussions with Human Rights Watch and the Center for Civilians in Conflict.

[126] *See* Ch. VII. *See also* Craig Allen et al., *Errant NATO Airstrikes in Libya: 13 Cases (Brega)*, N.Y. TIMES, Dec. 16, 2011, *available at* http://www.nytimes.com/interactive/2011/12/16/world /africa/nato-airstrikes-in-libya.html?ref=africa#page/rebel-convoy. *See also* Press Release, Operational Media Update for 7 April 2011, NORTH ATLANTIC TREATY ORGANIZATION, Apr. 7, 2011, *available at* http://www.nato.int/nato_static/assets/pdf/pdf_2011_04/20110402_110402-oup-update.pdf; Press Release, Operational Media Update for 8 April 2011, North Atlantic Treaty Organization, Apr. 8, 2011, *available at* http://www.nato.int/cps/en/natolive /opinions_72150.htm.

in Benghazi,[127] along with other equally influential *kata'ib* in Al-Bayda, Darna and Ajdabiya.[128] In other regions of Libya, *kata'ib* continued to form around regional centers, acting autonomously and under local command.[129] Estimates of the number of *thuwar kata'ib* that operated throughout the country during the civil war range from 100 up to 300.[130]

The rebel forces had different experiences of fighting according to the level of engagement of Qadhafi forces in the different regions. The Misrata *thuwar* were forced to fight battles on several fronts as Qadhafi forces approached the city from every direction.[131] The CoI reported that in its "isolation during the conflict, Misrata developed its own leadership under the command of Khalifa Zway, who headed the local Misrata Council, and included representatives from the Misrata Military Council and Security Committee."[132] The Misrata *kata'ib* consisted of numerous smaller kata'ib *kata'ib*, such as the Swihli, the Lions of the Desert, the Tiger Katiba, and the 501st Katiba, named after the telephone prefix for Misrata.[133] These units were autonomous and had their own weapons and even identified themselves with their own logos on vehicles, although most employed the "Misrata camouflage scheme" of grey and black.[134] The *kata'ib* based in Misrata were the most well-armed and organized of the numerous *kata'ib* that fought in Libya. While fighters associated themselves with the Misrata Katiba, they more often identified with their individual fighting unit, which proved helpful for investigations. For instance, it would have been difficult to investigate the death of Qadhafi's son Mu'tassim at the hands of the Misrata Katiba, which was relatively large, but by

---

[127] *See* Ch. VI.

[128] *See id. See also* Report of the International Commission of Inquiry, advance unedited version (Mar. 2, 2012), *supra* note 24 at Annex I, ¶ 66.

[129] *See* Chs. X & XI. *See also* Report of the International Commission of Inquiry, advance unedited version (Mar. 2, 2012), *supra* note 24 at Annex I, ¶ 67.

[130] Report of the International Commission of Inquiry, advance unedited version (Mar. 2, 2012), *supra* note 24 Annex I, ¶ 67. *See also* INTERNATIONAL CRISIS GROUP, HOLDING LIBYA TOGETHER, *supra* note 119.

[131] *See* Ch. IX, Sec. 2.

[132] Report of the International Commission of Inquiry, advance unedited version (Mar. 2, 2012), *supra* note 24 at Annex I, ¶ 68.

[133] This statement is based on information provided to the ISISC Project by the consultant.

[134] For further information about violations carried out by members of Misrata-based brigades, *see* Ch. III, Secs. 5 & 9.

identifying the Tiger Katiba it became possible to narrow down the potential perpetrators.[135]

Some of the most powerful and well-equipped *thuwar* groups also formed in the Nafusa Mountains region, in cites such as Zintan, Nalut and Yafran.[136] As the CoI explained:

> As the conflict progressed, control was centralized around the Western Military Council based in Zintan, which not only coordinated operations in the Nafusa Mountains region, but also commanded *thuwar* in Zawiyya and the southern and western suburbs of Tripoli. The Nafusa Mountains region was also used as a training ground for *thuwar* who escaped from Qadhafi-controlled territory in Tripoli, Zowara and Zawiyya. The area was an important hub for supplies – weapons, food and medicines – smuggled across the Tunisian border, as well as flown in from Benghazi.[137]

The rebel forces, which mainly consisted of civilian volunteers with no combat training, initially relied primarily on weapons and vehicles taken from Qadhafi forces, such as AK-47 rifles, rocket propelled grenades (RPG) and the signature 14.5mm and 23mm anti-aircraft machine guns mounted on pick-up trucks, and known as "technicals."[138] Other weapons included homemade and jury-rigged weapons.[139] "As the conflict progressed, *thuwar* used heavy weapons seized in battle including tanks and Grad rockets, particularly in Sirte and Bani Walid."[140] *Thuwar* forces employed creative means in combat, modifying pickup trucks into armored vehicles, and constructing portable launchers for old Russian air-to-surface missiles.[141] Equipment was scarce, however, and compared to the government forces, the rebels were dramatically under-resourced.[142]

At a later stage, *thuwar* forces received equipment from foreign countries, notably Qatar and France, including uniforms and communication

---

[135] This statement is based on information provided to the ISISC Project by the consultant.

[136] *See* Ch. X.

[137] Report of the International Commission of Inquiry, advance unedited version (Mar. 2, 2012), *supra* note 24 at Annex I, ¶ 71.

[138] *Id.* at Annex I, ¶ 69.

[139] Alan Taylor, *DIY Weapons of the Libyan Rebels*, THE ATLANTIC, June 14, 2011, *available at* http://www.theatlantic.com/infocus/2011/06/diy-weapons-of-the-libyan-rebels/100086.

[140] *See* Chs. XIV & XV. *See also* Report of the International Commission of Inquiry, advance unedited version (Mar. 2, 2012), *supra* note 24 at Annex I, ¶ 69.

[141] PARGETER, LIBYA: THE RISE AND FALL OF QADHAFI, *supra* note 18 at 233.

[142] C.J. Chivers, *Inferior Arms Hobble Rebels in Libya War*, N.Y. TIMES, Apr. 20, 2011, *available at* http://www.nytimes.com/2011/04/21/world/africa/21rebels.html.

equipment.[143] As the CoI explained, "Weapons were smuggled into Libya through the Tunisia border, as well as distributed from Benghazi and Malta to the besieged city of Misrata by sea."[144]

NATO and non-NATO coalition members provided military trainers to the Libyan rebels during the war.[145] Both France and the United Kingdom, for instance, sent trainers to operate in Libya, initially to provide intelligence and logistics training.[146] The role of military trainers rapidly expanded, with the United Kingdom creating a Joint Operations Centre in Benghazi to assist the rebels in providing information to NATO.[147] Qatar provided military trainers to teach infantry skills, sending hundreds of military personnel to support the Libyan rebels, supervise them, and in some cases, to act as a direct link with NATO.[148] The *thuwar* also received body armor and advanced communication equipment from the United Kingdom and United States.[149]

The Libyan rebels provided NATO with targeting assistance throughout the war through direct communication.[150] NATO supported rebel operations with airstrikes, drone surveillance, and later on with special operations forces sent to Libya to directly target Qadhafi forces using NATO air assets. Initially, the rebels provided NATO with coordinates of

---

[143] *France airdropped arms to the rebels*, BBC, June 29, 2011, *available at* http://www.bbc .co.uk/news/world-africa-13955751; *Qatari weapons reaching rebels in the Libyan Mountains*, REUTERS, Mar. 31, 2011, *available at* http://www.reuters.com/article/2011/05/31/us-libya-weapons-idUSTRE74U3C520110531.

[144] Report of the International Commission of Inquiry, advance unedited version (Mar. 2, 2012), *supra* note 24 at Annex I, ¶ 70.

[145] *See* Ch. III, Sec. 7.1.

[146] *British Military Officers to be sent to Libya*, BBC, Apr. 19, 2011, *available at* http://www .bbc.co.uk/news/uk-13132654.

[147] Bruno Waterfield, *Libya: British military advisers set up 'joint operations centre' in Bengazi*, THE TELEGRAPH, May 18, 2011, *available at* http://www.telegraph.co.uk/news/ worldnews/africaandindianocean/libya/8521977/Libya-British-military-advisers-set-up-joint-operations-centre-in-Benghazi.html.

[148] Portia Walker, *Qatari military advisers on the ground, helping Libyan rebels get into shape*, THE WASHINGTON POST, May 12, 2011 *available at* http://articles.washingtonpost .com/2011-05-12/world/35233351_1_rebel-council-libyan-rebels-rebel-army. *See also* Ian Black, *Qatar admits sending hundreds of troops to support Libya rebels*, THE GUARDIAN, Oct. 26, 2011, *available at* http://www.guardian.co.uk/world/2011/oct/26/qatar-troops-libya-rebels-support.

[149] ROYAL UNITED SERVICES INSTITUTE, ACCIDENTAL HEROES: BRITAIN, FRANCE AND THE LIBYA OPERATION, AN INTERIM LIBYA CAMPAIGN REPORT 11 (Sept. 2011), *available at* http:// www.rusi.org/downloads/assets/RUSIInterimLibyaReport.pdf.

[150] *See* Ch. III, Sec. 7.1.

Qadhafi forces and expressed frustration that NATO did not act quickly enough.[151] By May 2011, former British SAS soldiers paid by Qatar were directly supporting NATO with intelligence from the ground.[152] By August, the relationship between the rebel forces and NATO was well-developed and operating smoothly, with direct communication between the rebels and NATO and French and British forces operating in Libya.[153]

NATO weapons were air-dropped into Libya, and trainers assisted rebel forces with rapid education in asymmetric warfare. The SAS provided forward air controllers to direct airstrikes; French, Qatari, and Jordanian special operations forces also played a role.[154] In addition, the CIA and MI6 worked with the rebels, gathered intelligence and assisted with targeting.[155]

This support provided the rebel forces with the necessary modern weapons and tactics to confront and ultimately defeat Qadhafi forces. By providing weapons and direct training, however, they may have acted in violation of the UN Security Council mandate to protect civilians.[156]

3. Stages of the Conflict

3.1. *Military Analysis and Overview*

The 2011 war was fought on three basic fronts. In the east, Cyrenaica was a seesaw stalemate for months, while in the west, Qadhafi's early victory Zawiyya turned into hit and run fighting in the Nafusa Mountains region. The uprising began in the east, but it was in the center, where the crucial

---

[151] *Libyan rebels 'disappointed' by NATO*, AL JAZEERA, Apr. 6, 2011, *available at* http://www.aljazeera.com/news/africa/2011/04/201145191641347449.html.

[152] Richard Norton Taylor and Chris Stephen, *Libya: SAS Veterans helping NATO identify Gaddafi targets in Misrata*, THE GUARDIAN, May 31, 2011, *available at* http://www.guardian.co.uk/world/2011/may/31/libya-sas-veterans-misrata-rebels.

[153] Eric Schmitt & Steven Lee Myers, *Surveillance and Coordination with NATO aided Rebels*, N.Y. TIMES, Aug. 21, 2011, *available at* http://www.nytimes.com/2011/08/22/world/africa/22nato.html.

[154] Julian Borger et al., *Battle for Tripoli: pivotal victory in the mountains helped big push*, THE GUARDIAN, Aug. 22, 2011, *available at* http://www.guardian.co.uk/world/2011/aug/22/battle-for-tripoli-libya-gaddafi.

[155] Mark Mazetti & Eric Schmitt, *C.I.A. agents in Libya Aid Airstrikes and Meet Rebels*, N.Y. TIMES, Mar. 30, 2011, *available at* http://www.nytimes.com/2011/03/31/world/africa/31intel.html.

[156] For more details on the foreign direct support for the Libyan opposition forces and the UN Security Council's civilian protection mandate, *see* Ch. III, Sec. 7.

battle was fought in Misrata, and the fate of the war ultimately decided. The Qadhafi forces became bogged down in part due to the uprisings in Misrata and Zawiyya that siphoned critical forces off to these regions. Only after the uprising in Zawiyya was put down by the Khamis 32nd Katiba,[157] did Qadhafi forces turn to Misrata. This delay was critical to giving Misrata time to arm and prepare its defenses.

Airpower was one of the deciding factors of the war, with the Qadhafi forces relying heavily on their air force capability. Early in the war, the Qadhafi forces were able to supplement ground forces with airstrikes. When ground troops met resistance from the *thuwar*, the regime sent airpower to support the ground assault. NATO neutralized Qadhafi's air and naval forces early in the war, placing the entire burden of the defense of the regime on an undermanned, poorly trained, ill-led army equipped with weapons that were decades-old.[158] Qadhafi forces, hamstrung with old and aging Cold War equipment, were notably unable to engage NATO with theater SAM assets. Once NATO destroyed the surface-to-air missile capability, the Qadhafi military had little more than tactical air defenses to protect their forces from airstrikes.

Evidence indicates that the regime's response to the uprising was initially organized and administered from the top. The CoI gathered witness accounts indicating that Qadhafi dispatched the head of Military Intelligence, and mobilized the Jamahiriyya revolutionary forces in Benghazi to swiftly suppress the protests with brute force.[159] Press accounts point to documents discovered in Misrata in June 2011 that contain evidence of Qadhafi giving direct orders, transmitted by his generals to attack cities, siege towns, and hunt down injured rebel fighters.[160]

As the conflict erupted into full-scale civil war, the lack of coordination between the Qadhafi regime's security agencies became increasingly apparent, as operations were often improvised and reactive. The regime relied on various informal mechanisms to deploy security forces to fight battles for control over cities and regions across the country. The conflict became increasingly chaotic as the resistance grew in strength, and the security forces at times took action outside the official command

---

[157] *See* Ch. XII.

[158] *See* Ch. I.

[159] Report of the International Commission of Inquiry, advance unedited version (Mar. 2, 2012), *supra* note 24 at Annex I, ¶ 110.

[160] *See* Ch. IX, Sec. 2. *See also* Chris Stephen, *Qadhafi Files Show Evidence of Murderous Intent*, THE GUARDIAN, June 18, 2011, *available at* http://www.guardian.co.uk/world/2011/jun/18/gaddafi-misrata-war-crime-documents.

and control mechanisms, relying on informal channels of communication. As such, the regime forces operated in an improvised manner, shifting to alternative tactics, such as using private trucks to transport artillery, and resorting to desperate measures to deploy forces to reclaim cities in rebel strongholds. Moreover, NATO airstrikes that damaged Libyan military communications had a marked impact on the regime's military operational abilities.[161]

After the regime's airpower was effectively neutralized, the Qadhafi military relied almost entirely on ground forces to combat the insurgency. The nature of the 2011 conflict therefore differed with geographic location, with each theater of conflict determined by the regime's capability to deploy to that region.[162] Qadhafi *kata'ib* from Tripoli, for example, had greater capacity to deploy large amounts of artillery and troops to cities near the capital, such as Zawiyya, 48 kilometers (30 miles) to the west, and Misrata, 185 kilometers (115 miles) from the capital, as opposed to cities in the east such as Benghazi, 643 kilometers (400 miles), from the capital and towns in the Nafusa Mountains region across difficult terrain.

How the civil war was fought was also determined by long-standing tribal affiliations and regional alliances. In several regions, Qadhafi forces used regime-loyalist towns as bases to attack *thuwar*-controlled territories, plundering regions and leaving behind internecine fighting.[163] This led to reprisal violence and fighting between communities that continued after the war.[164] This constitutes another dynamic of the war that made it difficult to adequately account for force structure, equipment levels, and the units involved in the fighting.

While the conflict varied according to geographic location, it is possible to determine certain patterns employed by both the regime's security units and *thuwar* throughout the country. The regime's security forces used heavy artillery weaponry against protesters,[165] while both Qadhafi

---

[161] *NATO targets Gadhafi Communications*, AFP, June 6, 2011, *available at* http://www.rawstory.com/rs/2011/06/06/nato-air-strike-targets-gaddafis-intelligence-headquarters.

[162] For more a more detailed description of the battles carried out in different cities across Libya, *see* Ch. III.

[163] For more information on the attacks against the Tawerghan community, *see* Ch. VI, Sec. 3. Ch. IX, Sec. 3, Ch. XI, Sec. 3, Ch. XIII, Sec. 3 & Ch. XV, Sec. 3.

[164] *See* Ch. V, Sec. 2.4.

[165] *See* Chs. VIII & IX. *See also Gaddafi blames unrest on al-Qaeda*, AL JAZEERA, Feb. 24, 2011, *available at* http://www.aljazeera.com/news/africa/2011/02/2011224143054988104.html.

forces[166] and *thuwar* besieged towns,[167] punished civilian populations
with indiscriminate shelling,[168] targeted and systematically executed suspected rebels/spies,[169] and displaced large populations from their homes.[170]
For example, the Qadhafi forces extracted a huge toll from Misrata, laying
siege to the town for months, using mines and cluster bombs, and targeting civilians. The Misrata *thuwar* depopulated the town of Tawergha in
August 2011 and participated in reprisal killings.[171] Specific security units
stand out in the conflict, such as the Khamis Katiba, along with informal
security organizations, such as the Revolutionary Guard and Revolutionary Committee forces.

Communication during the conflict employed a mix of informal and
formal channels. In some instances, Qadhafi sent orders to his commanders who transmitted them to the field units. Upon examination of the
communication employed by the Qadhafi regime, the CoI found that Qadhafi issued orders through satellite phone calls to commanders. The CoI
also reported that the informal lines of communication made it difficult
to trace orders and commands.[172] Later, Qadhafi switched to a courier
system to communicate out of fear that NATO would intercept his communications, thereby determining his location and killing him. In the final
weeks of the war, perhaps as early as late August 2011 when he went to
Sirte, Qadhafi began to lose touch with his military forces, although his
inner military circle remained operational. He expressed frustration with
his lack of understanding of how the conflict was unfolding and his inability to directly command forces.[173]

As security officials defected to the rebels and as NATO strikes hindered the advance of the regime troops, command and control responsibility became more improvised. The fighting became increasingly chaotic,
and armed forces carried out systematic and indiscriminate violence on a

---

[166] For sieges on towns by Qadhafi forces, *see* Ch. III, Secs. 3, 5, & 6.

[167] For attacks on towns by *thuwar* forces, *see* Ch. III, Secs. 5 & 11.

[168] For indiscriminate use of weapons, *see* Ch. III, Secs. 4, 5, 6 & 9.

[169] For more on instances of unlawful killings, *see* all sections of Ch. III.

[170] For more on large-scale displacement, *see* Ch. III, Secs. 5 & 6.

[171] *See* Ch. IX.

[172] Report of the International Commission of Inquiry (Jan. 12, 2012), *supra* note 8 at
¶ 44.

[173] This statement is based on information provided to the ISISC Project by the
consultant.

large scale, resorting to dirty-war tactics in an effort to liquidate the support for the rebel insurgency.[174]

These tactics involved the creation of "dirty operations" kata'ib formed by the Military Intelligence Service to arrest and interrogate suspected thuwar and transfer them to other facilities for further interrogation.[175] This was coupled with torture and systematic enforced disappearances. Hospitals were also targeted and medical supplies destroyed.[176] The sieges and indiscriminate shelling across the country targeting civilian populations formed part of counterinsurgency tactics intended to drain the fish from the sea of rebel support. As noted above, however, the use of force had adverse consequences and drove populations to support the growing rebellion.[177]

Both sides fought with little regard for the civilian population. While much has been made of the suffering of Misrata due to Qadhafi's siege, civilians in Sirte suffered a similar fate at the hands of the thuwar in September 2011.[178] There was a marked ignorance of combatant and non-combatant status. Rebel fighters, as discussed above, often identified themselves as civilians in interviews with human rights groups and the CoI, even when armed. Their understanding was based on their profession before the conflict and so diverges significantly from understandings derived from International Humanitarian Law (IHL). Qadhafi forces similarly saw anyone supporting the rebel movement as sympathizers or spies, and therefore a legitimate target. Once the battle for Misrata was won by the rebels, Qadhafi had effectively lost the war as the rebels' now battle-hardened and strongest units were able to turn their attention to Tripoli.[179] This was in addition to NATO's airpower, weapons, and foreign trainers, which enhanced the rebels' strength to fight the Qadhafi military.

---

[174] The term "dirty-war" is a common phrase used to describe the tactics employed by military dictatorships in Latin America during the Cold War against popular social movements and subversive insurgent groups. These tactics included surveillance, death-squad operations, massacres of civilian populations, secret kidnapping and enforced disappearance, systematic torture and summary executions.

[175] Report of the International Commission of Inquiry, advance unedited version (Mar. 2, 2012), supra note 24 at Annex I, ¶ 148.

[176] Lisa Schlein, People in Battle-Torn Libya Facing Critical Shortages, VOICE OF AMERICA, June 7, 2011, available at http://www.voanews.com/english/news/People-in-Battle-Torn-Libya-Facing-Critical-Shortages-123354293.html.

[177] See Chs. IV, IX, XII, XIII.

[178] See Ch. XV, Sec. 2.

[179] See Ch. XIII, Sec. 2.

The analysis that follows describes the phases of the war, and identifies patterns, tactics and strategies employed by the Qadhafi and *thuwar* forces during the conflict.

3.2. *The Protest Phase*

The popular uprisings in the Middle East spread as increasing numbers raised the call for protests in authoritarian states. On 4 February, calls were issued on social media for protests in Libya on 17 February, dubbed the "Day of Rage."[180] The arrest of prominent human rights activists and lawyers on 15 February, however, sparked protests in Benghazi two days earlier than planned calling for their release.[181]

The following day, on 16 February, protests spread to the cities of Al-Bayda, Al-Quba, Darna and Tobruq. The largest protests took place in Benghazi where thousands gathered in front of the courthouse.[182] Regime forces responded with teargas and batons, resulting in hundreds of casualties and injuries of civilian demonstrators. This aggressive show of force triggered further demonstrations, and as news of these events spread, protests grew in strength and size, spreading across Libya within the next few days, to cities including Ajdabiya, Misrata, Tripoli, Zawiyya and Zintan.[183]

The nature of injuries inflicted in several locations is indicative of a "shoot-to-kill" policy.[184] Between 16 and 21 February, protesters and bystanders were killed in Benghazi and Al-Bayda, and over 200 protesters were killed in Tripoli, with further casualties reported in Tobruq, Zawiyya and Misrata.[185]

The CoI received witness statements from former military commanders who testified that Qadhafi delivered orders to chiefs of police and internal security to suppress demonstrations "with all means necessary."[186] The conduct of the Qadhafi forces in many parts of the country indicate that

---

[180] Cajsa Wikstrom, *Calls for weekend protests in Syria*, AL JAZEERA, Feb. 4, 2011, *available at* http://www.aljazeera.com/news/middleeast/2011/02/201122171649677912.html.

[181] *See* Ch. VI. *See also* William Edwards, *Violent protests rock Libyan city of Benghazi*, FRANCE 24, Feb. 16, 2011 *available at* http://www.france24.com/en/20110216-libya-violent-protests-rock-benghazi-anti-government-gaddafi-egypt-tunisia-demonstration.

[182] *See* Ch. VI.

[183] *See* Ch. III, Secs. 3, 5, 6, 8, & 9. *See also* BELL & WITTER, THE ROOTS OF REBELLION, *supra* note 15 at 7; Report of the International Commission of Inquiry, advance unedited version (Mar. 2, 2012), *supra* note 24 at Annex I, ¶ 77.

[184] *Id.* at Annex I, ¶ 135.

[185] *Id.* at Annex I, ¶ 78.

[186] *Id.* at Annex 1, ¶ 111.

they were acting on orders to engage in the harsh crackdown of demonstrators.[187] These orders translated into Libya's police forces using lethal force against protesters, firing live ammunition at demonstrators.[188]

High-level Libyan officials, including Military Intelligence chiefs, were responsible for the planning and implementation of the regime's response during the early days of the protests. Senior military officers told the CoI that the chief of Military Intelligence and the head of the Wahda al-Amniyya[189] security units flew to Benghazi to deal with growing protests.[190] "The CoI reviewed a videotape of what appears to be the head of Military Intelligence in discussion with Revolutionary Committees members in Benghazi in February. In the video, "he is seen and heard giving instructions to them to 'crush' the demonstrators."[191]

The CoI reported that the General Prosecutor's office in Benghazi obtained interrogation records in which witnesses state that members of the security forces were given orders, by their commanding officers, to use force against demonstrators.[192] This was the case not only in Benghazi, but also in Al-Bayda, where military forces were deployed to deliberately disperse demonstrations using violence. *Kata'ib* commanders, notably Khamis Qadhafi, the head of the 32nd Katiba, delivered orders directly to field units during this period. A former security director told the CoI that he sought approval from high level ISA officials and senior political figures for the redeployment of officers outside Al-Bayda, but was told to take instructions only from Khamis Qadhafi.[193]

The Qadhafi regime deployed the Revolutionary Guard, which fired on protesters in Benghazi on 17 February. Witnesses reported seeing members of the unit, including the chief of the Revolutionary Guard who was

---

[187] Report of the International Commission of Inquiry (Jan. 12, 2012), *supra* note 8 at ¶ 89.

[188] *See also* Report of the International Commission of Inquiry, advance unedited version (Mar. 2, 2012), *supra* note 24 at Annex I, ¶ 76.

[189] These were primarily security units for the protection of the Qadhafi Government from possible military coup.

[190] Report of the International Commission of Inquiry, advance unedited version (Mar. 2, 2012), *supra* note 24 at Annex I, ¶ 110.

[191] *See* Summary of Events in Ch. VI. *See also* Report of the International Commission of Inquiry, advance unedited version (Mar. 2, 2012), *supra* note 24 at Annex I, ¶ 110.

[192] Report of the International Commission of Inquiry (Jan. 12, 2012), *supra* note 8 at ¶ 89.

[193] *Id.* at ¶ 87.

identified standing in front of the building where the Guard opened fire on the demonstrators.[194]

After being charged by Qadhafi with providing support to the overwhelmed ground forces in Benghazi, Interior Minister Yunis showed up on 19 February at the besieged barracks only to defect and join the *thuwar*.[195] The barracks thus came under *thuwar* control on 20 February, and effectively ended the fighting in Benghazi.[196] The defection of Yunis and his soldiers was an important advancement for the opposition forces. It came on the heels of a number of military defections in the preceding days as soldiers took to defending protesters,[197] and provided the *thuwar* with guns and other supplies.[198]

More defections further reduced Qadhafi's control of military assets stationed in the east. The commander of the army barracks in Tobruq publicly renounced his loyalty to Qadhafi on 17 February, and two Libyan Air Force colonels flew to Malta to request political asylum after protesters seized their base in Benghazi.[199] These defections weakened the regime's military capabilities in Cyrenaica and gave the growing rebel movement an important boost in morale.[200] Taking control over Benghazi also provided the rebels a base from which to form a transitional governing authority, the NTC, and to coordinate military operations in the eastern part of the country.

By late February, around 8,000 soldiers had defected from the Libyan Armed Forces, and there were moves to create an opposition national army led by former officers of the Qadhafi regime.[201] Regional divides, however, along with tribal affiliations and political differences kept a unified defector-led rebel army from establishing itself and taking hold across

---

[194] Report of the International Commission of Inquiry, advance unedited version (Mar. 2, 2012), *supra* note 24 at Annex I, ¶ 114.

[195] *See* Ch. VI. *See also* BELL & WITTER, THE ROOTS OF REBELLION, *supra* note 15 at 25.

[196] *Battle at army base broke Gadhafi hold in Benghazi*, WASHINGTON POST, Feb. 25, 2011, *available at* http://www.washingtonpost.com/wp-dyn/content/article/2011/02/25/AR 2011022505021.html.

[197] *Bloodshed as tensions rise in Libya*, BBC, Feb. 19, 2011, *available at* http://www.bbc .co.uk/news/world-middle-east-12513941; *Libya revolt spreads to Tripoli*, AL JAZEERA, Feb. 21 2011, *available at* http://www.aljazeera.com/news/africa/2011/02/20112213143929158g.htmls.

[198] *Libya revolt spreads to Tripoli*, AL JAZEERA, Feb. 21, 2011, *available at* http://www .aljazeera.com/news/africa/2011/02/20112213143929158g.htmls.

[199] John Hooper & Ian Black, *Libya defectors: Pilots told to bomb protesters flee to Malta*, THE GUARDIAN, Feb. 21, 2011, *available at* http://www.guardian.co.uk/world/2011/feb/21/ libya-pilots-flee-to-malta.

[200] BELL & WITTER, THE ROOTS OF REBELLION, *supra* note 15 at 25.

[201] INTERNATIONAL CRISIS GROUP, HOLDING LIBYA TOGETHER, *supra* note 119.

the country. Defections in the western part of the country were not as widespread as in Cyrenaica, and a defector-led army ended up operating significantly only in the east, while Qadhafi forces controlled the capital Tripoli in the west, and maintained a loyalist stronghold in Sirte about half-way between the capital and Benghazi.[202]

As protests spread across the country, similar events as occurred in Benghazi unfolded in other cities. In Misrata, government security forces used live ammunition against protesters, sending in riot-control police and armed *baltajiyya*[203] to fire on demonstrators.[204] Qadhafi forces used AK-47s and anti-aircraft weapons against demonstrators in Misrata, leading to numerous civilian deaths.[205]

Protesters targeted the regime's political and security installations, such as the Revolutionary Committee offices in Benghazi, and Misrata. "On 21 and 22 February, demonstrators attacked Revolutionary Committee offices in Misrata, as well as police stations and military barracks, taking arms and weapons from these locations."[206] The acquisition of weapons, along with growing support from among the population, meant *thuwar* forces were gaining in strength and capability.

The use of military sharpshooters to target demonstrators and deter further protests was widespread by Qadhafi forces, with Internal Security Agency (ISA) agents deployed to coordinate the assaults. A witness told the CoI that members of the ISA instructed snipers, stationed on the top of buildings, to fire on protesters in Darna on 17 February.[207] Witnesses also reported seeing ISA agents in the far eastern city of Tobruq, where protests in Al-Shuhadà Square "triggered an intervention, according to witnesses, from joint Government security agencies, including ISA, riot police, and Revolutionary Committees."[208]

Witness accounts from Benghazi and Tripoli testify to having seen four-by-four trucks roaming the streets with Qadhafi troops, and helicopters circling overhead. Students from Benghazi also reported on four-by-four

---

[202] *Id.*

[203] In describing these baltajiyya, witnesses referred to armed young men acting as groups in "gang-like" fashion to disrupt the demonstration. The word is used in the Egyptian context to describe armed "thugs."

[204] *See* Ch. IX.

[205] Report of the International Commission of Inquiry (Jan. 12, 2012), *supra* note 8 at ¶ 85.

[206] *See* Ch. IX. *See also* Report of the International Commission of Inquiry (Jan. 12, 2012), *supra* note 8 at ¶ 80.

[207] *Id.* at ¶ 80.

[208] *Id.* at ¶ 81.

vehicles,[209] and residents from Tripoli described armed Qadhafi loyalists on the streets in specially-equipped "four-wheel-drive cars with Qadhafi's photos on the doors and windows."[210]

As the demonstrations escalated, becoming more organized and better armed due to ambushes on military installations, the Qadhafi regime deployed its brigade units to the most restive cities. The Khamis Katiba was deployed to Zawiyya, and on 23 February, 20–30 military vehicles and 200-armed soldiers entered the city center.[211] Witnesses told the CoI that Qadhafi forces fired on predominately unarmed demonstrators using "rocket propelled grenades and heavy machine guns.[212] A mid-level officer told the CoI that Qadhafi forces used tanks, RPGs, and 14.5 mm anti-aircraft guns during its attacks on Zawiyah."[213]

The assault was part of the broader regime offensive developing across the country, entailing the shelling of cities, the targeting and torture of suspected rebels, and indiscriminate killings.

3.3. *The Armed Conflict*

The events of 17 February caught the Qadhafi regime by surprise, as did the rapid spread of protests throughout the country. Qadhafi's response was slow and disjointed at first as he attempted to quiet popular discontent in Benghazi and isolate the spreading demonstrations. Qadhafi's efforts failed and a popular uprising spread throughout the country. By 5 March, Cyrenaica had fallen to *thuwar* forces who were beginning an invasion of Tripolitania from the east. At the same time, the capital was in open revolt, and Zawiyya east of Tripoli in direct warfare with Qadhafi's troops. Meanwhile, the Nafusa Mountains region was in rebel hands, and Qadhafi found himself without access to most of the oil he would need to support his mechanized forces. In less than a month, Qadhafi was effectively surrounded and without decisive action he was on the verge of losing power.[214]

By late February, the Qadhafi and *thuwar* forces were embroiled in armed conflict. As rebels organized and formed political and military

---

[209] PARGETER, LIBYA: THE RISE AND FALL OF QADHAFI, *supra* note 18 at 233.

[210] *Id.* at 230.

[211] *See* Ch. XII. *See also* Report of the International Commission of Inquiry, advance unedited version (Mar. 2, 2012), *supra* note 24 at Annex I, ¶ 127.

[212] *Id.* at Annex I, ¶ 558.

[213] *Id.*

[214] BELL & WITTER, THE ROOTS OF REBELLION, *supra* note 15 at 25.

councils, they began capturing cities and claiming territory. In the western part of the country, the militias that made up the *thuwar* forces centered around neighborhoods, towns and cities, such as Misrata and Zintan.[215] They were self-armed and self-trained, and acted independently of NTC authority. Even in Benghazi where the NTC was based, local fighters formed resistance groups autonomously of the council, such as the 17 February Martyrs Katiba, which became a powerful fighting force. As with *kata'ib* in other cities, some of its leadership came from former members of the Libyan Islamic Fighting Group (LIFG).[216]

In the capital, fighters organized the Tripoli Military Council, to coordinate a group of *kata'ib* that operated regionally. The Tripoli Council included long-time opposition leaders, such as 'Abd al-Hakim Balhaj, former leader of the LIFG.[217] *Thuwar* from the capital also formed a Tripoli katiba made up of volunteers, and were able to establish an important foothold in the western city of Nalut. The katiba was initially relatively small, numbering in the low hundreds and headed predominantly by expatriates, notably the Irish-Libyan Mahdi al-Harati. With the support of several foreign governments, the katiba carried out basic military training.[218]

After the Qadhafi regime secured Tripoli in late February, its security forces embarked on a major offensive to secure regions and reclaim cities that had been captured by rebel forces.[219] The offensive involved deploying *kata'ib* to carry out heavy shelling of civilian areas and sieges of towns under *thuwar* control.[220]

Benghazi was the first city to come under opposition control as the Al-Fadil bin 'Umar military barracks in Benghazi were stormed on 19 February by rebel forces and Yunis and his elite units seized the building.[221]

---

[215] *See* Ch. III, Secs. 5 & 6.

[216] BELL ET AL., STALEMATE & SIEGE, *supra* note 110 at 34, n. 49.

[217] *See* Ch. XIII. *See also* Report of the International Commission of Inquiry, advance unedited version (Mar. 2, 2012), *supra* note 24 at Annex I, ¶ 72.

[218] This information concurs with multiple sources confirming Qatari support for Libya's rebels during this time. According to media sources, the Tripoli brigades received three weeks training from Qatari special forces. *See* Margaret Coker, *Length of Libya's standoff hinges on leader's militia*, WALL STREET JOURNAL, Aug. 24, 2011, *available at* http://online.wsj.com/article/SB10001424053111903327904576526642369893206.html. The Tripoli brigades were first trained in Benghazi, but relocated to the Nafusa Mountains to participate in the campaign for Tripoli from the west. *See* INTERNATIONAL CRISIS GROUP, HOLDING LIBYA TOGETHER, *supra* note 119 at 3, n. 21.

[219] BELL & WITTER, THE ROOTS OF REBELLION, *supra* note 15 at 25.

[220] *See* Ch. III, Secs. 3, 5 & 6.

[221] *See* Ch. VI.

With Benghazi in rebel hands on 20 February, the city of Brega also rose against Qadhafi, with part of the city falling the same day.[222] The city armed itself and held out long enough against repeated attacks by the Qadhafi forces for reserves to flow in from the surrounding region on 2 March.[223] By 24 February, media reports indicated that protesters were in control of Tobruq, Misrata and Zuwara.[224] On 4 March, the rebels pushed along the coastal highway to Ra's Lanuf, the site of Libya's largest oil refinery. After violent fighting, the city fell to the *thuwar* forces who then advanced to Bin Jawad.[225]

The Qadhafi regime was steadfast in its actions, contending that the use of force was necessary to counter attacks by the crowds. High-level officials in the regime delivered explicit threats, for instance, in the address by the son of Qadhafi, Saif al-Islam, on state television on 21 February, he declared "we will fight to the last man and woman and bullet." The following day, state television aired a speech by Qadhafi in which he pledged to lead "millions to purge Libya inch by inch, house by house, household by household, alley by alley, and individual by individual until I purify this land". He blamed foreigners for the situation and called the protesters "rats" that needed to be executed.[226]

The events in Libya provoked a strong response from the international community. On 25 February, United Nations Human Rights Council condemned the violence and ordered the formation of an independent international Commission of Inquiry (CoI) to investigate violations of international human rights.[227] The following day, in response to the escalating violence and reports of serious human rights violations, the United Nations Security Council passed Resolution 1970 imposing an arms

---

[222] *See* Ch. VII.

[223] Mitch Potter, *Rebels quash Gadhafi raid*, THE STAR, Mar. 2011, *available at* http://www .thestar.com/news/world/article/947638--the-star-in-libya-rebels-quash-gadhafi-raid; *Libya rebels on edge as Kadhafi rages*, AFP, Feb. 27, 2011, *available at* http://213.158.162.45/~egyptian /index.php?action=news&id=15494&title=Libya%20rebels%20on%20edge%20as%20 Gaddafi%20rages.

[224] Report of the International Commission of Inquiry (Jan. 12, 2012), *supra* note 8 at ¶ 28.

[225] Mohammed Abbas, *Libyan rebels take oil town in Ras Lanuf: Rebels*, REUTERS, Mar. 4, 2011 *available at* http://www.reuters.com/article/2011/03/04/libya-port-idUSLDE723204 20110304.

[226] Report of the International Commission of Inquiry (Jan. 12, 2012), *supra* note 8 at ¶ 28.

[227] For more details on the background of the UN Security Council authorization, *see* Ch. IV.

embargo and referring the situation in Libya to the International Criminal Court (ICC).[228]

March 2011

Rebellions in the western part of the country, in Misrata and Zawiyya, in addition to cities in the Nafusa Mountains region, such as Zintan and Nalut, were the most significant in March.[229] Qadhafi's military was geographically split, as his best unit, the Khamis Katiba, had been deployed to Zawiyya in order to defend against potential rebel advances on Tripoli. Less capable regular army forces stormed across Cyrenaica. This proved to be Qadhafi's first tactical mistake. Had the Qadhafi regime concentrated its military force on fighting Benghazi, it may have been able to crush the rebellion before the passing of UNSCR 1973, which paved the way for NATO intervention. Instead, Qadhafi was concerned with the proximity of the revolution to the capital, convinced that the rebels would not constitute a credible threat to his military. Though slow in repelling rebel advances, by 19 March Qadhafi forces were close to ending the rebellion. Qadhafi troops had brought rebel gains to a halt, retaken lost territory, subdued the uprising in Tripolitania, and sent tanks to Benghazi.

In March 2011, the war was being fought on three fronts. In the east, the rebels held Cyrenaica, in the center of the country Misrata was under siege, and in the west a battle for Zawiyya was underway.[230] March saw a paradigm shift in the conflict. Up to this point, the regime had been caught by surprise, and the rebels made rapid gains and took control over increasing amounts of territory. In Cyrenaica, the rebels had charged west from Benghazi, taking Ajdabiya, Brega, Ra's Lanuf, and extending their control to the edge of Bin Jawad.[231] In less than a month, there had been open protests in Tripoli, Zawiyya, and the Nafusa Mountains region, and in the east the rebels had charged within striking distance of Sirte, Qadhafi's hometown.[232] The front lines were almost encircling Qadhafi himself. On 6 March, however, the regime's forces began to erase the rebel gains in the east and simultaneously attacked Misrata and Zawiyya.[233]

---

[228] SC Res. 1970 (2011), Feb. 26, 2011, UN Doc. S/RES/1970 (2011).
[229] INTERNATIONAL CRISIS GROUP, HOLDING LIBYA TOGETHER, *supra* note 119.
[230] *See* Chs. IX & XII.
[231] *See* Chs. VII & VIII.
[232] *See* Ch. XV.
[233] *See* Chs. IX & XII. *See also* Mohammed Abbas, *supra* note 225.

On the morning of 6 March, rebel forces near Bin Jawad were attacked by planes and helicopters.[234] During intense fighting in the Bin Jawad area, the rebels faced a pro-Qadhafi population for the first time as well as incurred brutal artillery attacks from an organized military. Unable to sustain operations against Qadhafi forces without an organized base, the *thuwar* forces retreated to Ra's Lanuf.[235] Airstrikes and artillery barrages continued to hammer the rebels in Ra's Lanuf until their retreat to Brega on 10 March.[236] At the same time, they were experiencing losses in the west, in particular the fall of Zawiyya, which freed up the Khamis Katiba to reinforce the fight in Cyrenaica.

After bloody fighting, the second battle of Brega had ended by 13 March. The rebels were in full retreat to Ajdabiya, thereby giving up control of a critical road connecting the eastern cities, in what was seen at the time as a potential turning point in the war. The Qadhafi forces were advancing eastwards, approaching the *thuwar* stronghold in Benghazi. Rebel positions in Ajdabiya were hit by air, artillery and naval gunfire, which indicates how significant Qadhafi considered this strategic road to be.[237] Rebel air assets attacked and sunk the naval ships attacking Ajdabiya, but this was the only victory the *thuwar* forces would score as tanks surrounded the city on 15 March.[238] Having surrounded the city and established control over the road, Qadhafi forces conducted a run to Benghazi. Qadhafi promised amnesty to those who laid down their arms and death to those who did not.[239]

On 17 March, the United Nations Security Council adopted Resolution 1973, authorizing member states to enforce a no-fly zone over Libya and to take "all necessary measures," short of foreign occupation, and notwithstanding the arms embargo mandated in UNSCR 1970, to protect civilians

---

[234] *See* Ch. VIII. *See also* Kat Higgins, *Libya, Gaddafi Gunships Fire on Rebels*, SKY NEWS, Mar. 6, 2011, *available at* http://news.sky.com/story/841639/libya-gaddafi-gunships-fire-on-rebels.

[235] BELL & WITTER, THE ROOTS OF REBELLION, *supra* note 15.

[236] *Heavy Fighting in Libya as rebels advance toward capitol*, AP, Mar. 6, 2011, *available at* http://www.independent.co.uk/news/world/africa/heavy-fighting-in-libya-as-rebels-advance-toward-capital-2233947.html.

[237] *See* Ch. VII.

[238] Mohammad Abbas, *Gaddafi forces seize key town, G8 stalls on no-fly*, REUTERS, Mar. 15, 2011, *available at* http://in.reuters.com/article/2011/03/15/idINIndia-55582720110315; Anthony Shadid, *Libyan forces rout rebels as west's effort for no-flight zone stalls*, N.Y. TIMES, Mar. 15, 2011, *available at* http://www.nytimes.com/2011/03/16/world/africa/16libya.html.

[239] Douglas Stanglin, *Gadhafi vows to attack Bengazi and "show no mercy"*, USA TODAY, Mar. 17, 2011, *available at* http://content.usatoday.com/communities/ondeadline/post/2011/03/gadhafi-vows-to-retake-benghazi-and-show--no-mercy/1#.UM4OInPjlAE.

against Qadhafi forces. French, U.S. and UK forces began conducting air-strikes on 19 March, averting a possible recapture of Benghazi.

On the same day, Qadhafi forces bypassed Ajdabiya and attacked Benghazi in an attempt to end the rebellion before NATO could make use of UNSCR 1973.[240] Regime forces shelled the city and then attacked with a dozen T-72 tanks, the Libyan military's most modern and capable armor. By around 10:30 pm, the city appeared to be on the verge of falling to Qadhafi forces, until rebel counterattacks pushed them to the edge of the city.[241]

In Misrata, *thuwar* had taken control of the city during the initial phase of fighting in February, and throughout March rebel *kata'ib* in the city were engaged with Qadhafi forces. The rebels fielded some 3,000–5,000 men from at least three *brigades*, the Lions of the Desert, the Tiger Katiba, and the 501st Katiba.[242] The city faced unabated attacks from Qadhafi forces deployed from Tripoli and Sirte.[243] The Libyan military initially sent the Hamza Katiba to Misrata, later reinforced by a number of other *kata'ib*, including the Khamis Katiba on 12 March after the protests in Zawiyya were brought under control.[244] The CoI reported that evidence indicated that the Khamis Katiba was placed in charge of retaking Misrata, and remained in this role until early August.[245]

According to witnesses, 11 Qadhafi *kata'ib* took part in an attack on Misrata in mid-March. On 16 March, Qadhafi forces took up positions in neighborhoods on the outskirts of Misrata and moved tanks into the center of the city.[246] Qadhafi forces also set up positions to attack the

---

[240] *See* Ch. VI.

[241] Barbara Jones & Ian McIlgorm, *The Battle of Benghazi: City seemed lost to Gaddafi forces but was retaken by rebels*, DAILY MAIL, Mar. 20, 2011, *available at* http://www.daily mail.co.uk/news/article-1368030/Libya-Benghazi-lost-Gaddafis-forces-retaken-rebels.html.

[242] Marc Burleigh, *Snipers, cluster bombs panic Libya's Misrata*, AFP, Apr. 11, 2011, *available at* http://news.smh.com.au/breaking-news-world/snipers-cluster-bombs-panic-libyas-misrata-20110418-1dlhb.html.

[243] INTERNATIONAL CRISIS GROUP, HOLDING LIBYA TOGETHER, *supra* note 119.

[244] *Libyan forces shoot protesters*, AL JAZEERA, Feb. 25, 2011, *available at* http://www .aljazeera.com/news/africa/2011/02/201122513334597205.html; *Libyan troops defect near rebel-held Misrata*, REUTERS, Mar. 13, 2011, *available at* http://www.reuters.com/article /2011/03/13/libya-misrata-attack-idAFLDE72B0AO20110313; for video footage of the Hamza Katiba in Misrata, *see* miusrata17miusrata, مصراته في حمزة كتيبة, YouTube (Apr. 20, 2011), *available at* http://www.youtube.com/watch?feature=player_embedded&v=XK2UqU6Qprs.

[245] Report of the International Commission of Inquiry, advance unedited version (Mar. 2, 2012), *supra* note 24 at ¶ 117.

[246] Report of the International Commission of Inquiry, advance unedited version (Mar. 2, 2012), *supra* note 24 at ¶ 550. For more information on strength and locations of the Hamza Katiba during combat, *see* BELL ET AL., STALEMATE & SIEGE, *supra* note 110 at 18.

population with heavy shelling from the neighboring town of Tawergha.[247] Misratans maintained that Tawerghan inhabitants aided Qadhafi forces, and later targeted the town in a wave of reprisal violence.[248]

Misrata witnessed the most brutal, violent, and sustained attacks and fighting of the conflict,[249] lasting from early March until mid-May.[250] Reports indicate that orders were transmitted on 4 March to block cars, fuel, and other services from entering Misrata,[251] and Qadhafi forces from Sirte were deployed to the city to enforce the blockade and support the Hamza Katiba that had been stationed at the airport.[252] The indiscriminate shelling and siege on the civilian population in Misrata was a form of collective punishment, demonstrating an intent to starve and terrify the population into submission.[253]

The level of destruction in the city is evidence of the heavy-handed measures unleashed upon Misrata. "In surveying the damage to Misrata, the Commission's military expert noted that the damage to buildings was consistent with the use of small arms (7.62×39mm and other), heavy machine guns (12.7mm and 14.5mm), anti-aircraft guns (23mm), tube and rocket artillery, large caliber weapons (HEAT – 'high-explosive anti-tank' tank rounds and HESH – 'high explosive squash head' tank rounds), mortars (various from 60–120mm), rockets (122mm Grad entry holes were found with the rear of the rockets still protruding from ground), RPGs and recoilless rifles."[254] Qadhafi forces also employed a strategy of targeting doctors, medical facilities, and humanitarian services, including internationally recognized humanitarian agencies, such as the Red Cross. This was especially the case in Misrata, as well as in Yafran in the Nafusa Mountains region.[255]

---

[247] *See* Ch. IX, Sec. 3.3.

[248] INTERNATIONAL CRISIS GROUP, 28 HOLDING LIBYA TOGETHER, *supra* note 119.

[249] *See* Ch. IX.

[250] Report of the International Commission of Inquiry, advance unedited version (Mar. 2, 2012), *supra* note 8 at ¶ 554.

[251] *See also* Chris Stephen, *Qadhafi Files Show Evidence of Murderous Intent*, THE GUARDIAN, June 18, 2011, *available at* http://www.guardian.co.uk/world/2011/jun/18/gaddafi-misrata-war-crime-documents; PHYSICIANS FOR HUMAN RIGHTS, WITNESS TO WAR CRIMES: EVIDENCE FROM MISRATA, LIBYA 24 (Aug. 2011), *available at* https://s3.amazonaws.com/PHR_Reports/Libya-WitnesstoWarCrimes-Aug2011.pdf.

[252] BELL ET AL., STALEMATE & SIEGE, *supra* note 110 at 18.

[253] *See* Ch. IX.

[254] Report of the International Commission of Inquiry, advance unedited version (Mar. 2, 2012), *supra* note 24 at ¶ 74.

[255] *See* Ch. X, Sec. 2.6.

From early to mid-March, as the Qadhafi forces sought to retake control of Misrata, they carried out reprisal attacks against residents suspected of supporting the *thuwar*. People were taken into custody and subsequently disappeared.[256] Others were kidnapped from roads and other public places during advancements by Qadhafi forces.[257] The Commission also reported sexual violence against civilians in their private residences, especially in the towns of Tumina, Dafniyya and Karamin.[258]

Soldiers from the notorious Khamis Katiba arrived in Misrata on 12 March. After they failed to enter the city, fighting erupted around Misrata's perimeter.[259] Over the next few days, regime forces shelled Misrata as casualties mounted and the front line shifted deeper into the city. On 18 March, a short cease-fire went into effect in anticipation of NATO's role in the conflict.[260]

Securing energy supplies became a critical factor determining the deployment of Qadhafi forces. With the fall of Cyrenaica, Qadhafi had lost access to Libya's largest oil fields. Misrata was both a key shipping city and strategic point on the coastal road between Tripoli and Cyrenaica, complicating the movement of military forces to the east. For the regime, it was essential to put down the revolt in Zawiyya, due to the city's close proximity to the capital, but more importantly because it housed the country's second largest refinery.

As the fighting in Misrata continued, the Qadhafi regime deployed forces in early March to put down the growing rebellion in Zawiyya, 50 kilometers (31 miles) west of the capital.[261] Reports indicate that Brigadier General Mahdi al-'Arabi, Deputy Chief of Staff of the Armed Forces and resident of Zawiyya, commanded a deterrent battalion during the

---

[256] AMNESTY INTERNATIONAL, MISRATAH UNDER SIEGE AND UNDER FIRE 27 (May 6, 2011), *available at* http://www.amnesty.org/en/library/asset/MDE19/019/2011/en/4efa1e19-06c1-4609-9477-fe0f2f4e2b2a/mde190192011en.pdf.

[257] AMNESTY INTERNATIONAL, BATTLE FOR LIBYA: KILLINGS, DISAPPEARANCES AND TORTURE 58 (Sept. 13, 2011), *available at* http://www.amnesty.org/en/library/asset/MDE19/025/2011/en/8f2e1c49-8f43-46d3-917d-383c17d36377/mde190252011en.pdf.

[258] Report of the International Commission of Inquiry, advance unedited version (Mar. 2, 2012), *supra* note 24 at Annex I, ¶ 517.

[259] Souhail Karam et al., *Libyan troops defect near rebel-held Misrata*, REUTERS, Mar. 12, 2011, *available at* http://www.reuters.com/article/2011/03/13/libya-misrata-attack-idAFLDE72BoAO20110313; *Gadhafi forces shell oil town as troops advance*, AP, Mar. 13, 2011, *available at* http://www.huffingtonpost.com/2011/03/13/libya-gaddafi-forces-shell-brega_n_835032.html.

[260] *Report: Fighter jet shot down in Bengazi*, CNN, Mar. 19, 2011, *available at* http://www.cnn.com/2011/WORLD/africa/03/18/libya.civil.war/index.html.

[261] *See* Ch. XII.

initial attacks on the city.[262] Major General Al-Khawayldi al-Hamadi[263] also reportedly led a deterrent battalion from Surman in Zawiyya.[264]

Security forces moved in to Zawiyya on 4 March in full force, launching extensive artillery, rocket and anti-aircraft barrages, and using snipers to target *thuwar* fighters.[265] The same day, a battalion from the Khamis Katiba was deployed from Tripoli to reinforce the stationed troops, with 500 more soldiers, tanks, armored vehicles, and heavy artillery forces.[266] They were reinforced by the Husban Katiba attacking from the west.[267] The Qadhafi forces faced a ragtag rebel army made up of some 2000 men. Heavy shelling forced the rebels to retreat to the central square.[268]

Qadhafi forces attacked Zawiyya on 4 March, and by 9 March had free reign within the city, including control of the strategic town square and mosque.[269] Satellite imagery of Zawiyya from 8 March shows heavy artillery in the city, including 12 tanks, one self-propelled artillery, four possible armored personnel carriers, two possible infantry fighting vehicles, five heavy equipment transports, and 41 road block and/or barriers.[270] Witnesses who were formerly senior security officials in the Qadhafi regime, provided testimony of Qadhafi forces firing "Grad rockets and mortars into Zawiyya. They also used tanks, rocket launchers and 14.5mm anti-

---

[262] BELL & WITTER, THE ROOTS OF REBELLION, *supra* note 15 at 33.

[263] For more information on the NATO strike that hit the home of Al-Khawayldi al-Hamadi and his son Khalid on 20 June 2011, *see* Ch. III, Sec. 6.2.

[264] BELL & WITTER, THE ROOTS OF REBELLION, *supra* note 15 at 33.

[265] *See* Ch. XII, Sec. 8. *See also 37 dead as Gaddafi regime hits back*, PRESS ASSOCIATION, Mar. 4, 2011, *available at* http://www.independent.ie/breaking-news/world-news/37-dead-as-gaddafi-regime-hits-back-2565656.html.

[266] BELL & WITTER, THE ROOTS OF REBELLION, *supra* note 15 at 33.

[267] *Zawiyah in rebel hands, but under siege*, AFP, Mar. 6, 2011, *available at* http://news.smh.com.au/breaking-news-world/libyan-city-in-rebel-hands-but-under-siege-20110306-1bj3j.html.

[268] Vivienne Walt, *Gaddafi gets his revenge: The Price of Rebellion*, TIME, Mar. 17, 2011, *available at* http://www.time.com/time/world/article/0,8599,2059596,00.html; *At least 30 killed in Libya as Gaddafi forces fight to take back rebel-held town*, HAARETZ, Mar. 4, 2011, *available at* http://www.haaretz.com/news/world/at-least-30-killed-in-libya-as-gadhafi-forces-fight-to-take-back-rebel-held-town-1.347213.

[269] Report of the International Commission of Inquiry, advance unedited version (Mar. 2, 2012), *supra* note 24 at Annex I, ¶ 560; Maria Golovnina and Mohammad Abbas, *Gaddafi forces step up attack on western rebel town*, REUTERS, Mar. 5, 2011, *available at* http://www.reuters.com/article/2011/03/05/us-libya-protests-idUSTRE71G0A620110305; Paul Schemm, *Libyan warplanes strike rebels at oil port*, AP, Mar. 7, 2011 *available at* http://www.businessweek.com/ap/financialnews/D9LQHEPOo.htm.

[270] *Conflict Analysis: Zawiyah, Libya (as of 08 March 2011)*, UNITED NATIONS INSTITUTE FOR TRAINING AND RESEARCH, Mar. 23, 2011, *available at* http://reliefweb.int/sites/reliefweb.int/files/resources/7308EDFFF4FDA0478525785D00702BF7-map.pdf.

aircraft guns."[271] Pitched battles raged in Zawiyya for the coming days, but by 11 March the city was firmly in the control of Qadhafi forces, with much of the central city destroyed.[272] By 20 March, Qadhafi forces had destroyed the mosque used by *thuwar* forces as a makeshift hospital and headquarters.[273]

Many of Zawiyya's rebels fled to join the *thuwar* in the Nafusa Mountains region,[274] while others remained and organized underground resistance. Regime troops maintained control of the city from March until towards the end of the civil war when *thuwar* forces came from the Nafusa Mountains region and re-claimed the city with NATO support on 20 August.[275]

In response to the growing demonstrations in the west, the Qadhafi regime sent forces towards the Nafusa Mountains region and stationed troops in towns in between the major cities of Zintan, Nalut and Yafran. "Qadhafi forces began to enforce a siege against these towns, preventing food and fuel entering."[276] On 3 March, Qadhafi forces moved to re-take Zintan, the largest city in the Nafusa Mountains region.[277] Government troops also moved to counter the *thuwar* in the strategic city of Nalut, located near the main border crossing with Tunisia. The troops set siege to the town and began disrupting supplies by mid-March.[278]

Meanwhile, in Tripoli[279] and Zawiyya,[280] Qadhafi forces continued to detain large numbers of those suspected of being rebel supporters for interrogation and torture. They were detained at demonstrations,

---

[271] Report of the International Commission of Inquiry, advance unedited version (Mar. 2, 2012), *supra* note 24 at Annex I, ¶ 75.

[272] Michael Georgy & Maria Golovnina, *Rebels repel Gaddafi assault on Libys oil port*, REUTERS, Mar. 11, 2011, *available at* http://in.reuters.com/article/2011/03/11/idINIndia-55498020110311.

[273] *Satellite images appear to show destruction of Libya mosque*, CNN, Mar. 22, 2011, *available at* http://www.cnn.com/2011/WORLD/africa/03/21/libya.zawiya.mosque/index.html.

[274] *See* Ch. X.

[275] BELL & WITTER, THE ROOTS OF REBELLION, *supra* note 15 at 33.

[276] *See* Ch. XII. *See also* Report of the International Commission of Inquiry, advance unedited version (Mar. 2, 2012), *supra* note 24 at Annex I, ¶ 563.

[277] AMNESTY INTERNATIONAL, LIBYA – DISAPPEARANCES IN THE BESIEGED NAFUSA MOUNTAIN AS THOUSANDS SEEK SAFETY IN TUNISIA 7 (May 2011), *available at* https://www.amnesty.org/en/library/asset/MDE19/020/2011/en/aed13a1a-07b4-434b-bb28-0c0aa1d53069/mde1902020011en.pdf.

[278] Report of the International Commission of Inquiry, advance unedited version (Mar. 2, 2012), *supra* note 24 at Annex I, ¶ 564.

[279] *See* Ch. XIII. *See also* Report of the International Commission of Inquiry, advance unedited version (Mar. 2, 2012), *supra* note 8 at Annex I, ¶ 333.

[280] *See* Ch. XII, Sec. 8. *See also* Report of the International Commission of Inquiry, advance unedited version (Mar. 2, 2012), *supra* note 24 at Annex I, ¶ 270, n. 385.

checkpoints and elsewhere.[281] One notable case, documented by the CoI, involved an estimated 120 persons who were rounded up at checkpoints and sent to the Directorate of Military Intelligence in Tripoli where they were tortured, before being transferred to Abu Salim Prison.[282]

By 19 March, all of the rebel gains had crumbled. Rebel forces were on the brink of losing Benghazi, the symbolic center of the uprising, as they began an all-out retreat. The rebellion in Tripoli had been halted, with suspected rebels being disappeared, and the uprising in Zawiyya and towns in the western part of Libya towards Tunisia had been brought under control. The nascent Libyan rebellion appeared on the verge of collapse.

By the end of March the frontlines became relatively established and would change little until August. In the east, the war was fought in small seesaw battles from Ra's Lanuf to Brega and towards Ajdabiya.[283] In Tripolitania, Misrata settled into a protracted siege. NATO intervened in Misrata on 23 March, focusing its strikes on breaking the siege on the city.[284] In the west, there was fighting in the Nafusa Mountains region, and Qadhafi forces shelled the towns in the region through the end of March and into April, using a mixture of 106mm shells, tank rounds and Grad rockets.[285] For many months little ground would change hands.

Following UN Security Council Resolution 1973, the United States, United Kingdom and France began military operations in Libya on 19 March, concentrating in and around Benghazi, and striking targets to take out Libya's air defense systems.[286] NATO's intervention gave the rebels a lifeline. Had French airstrikes not immediately engaged Libyan government forces on that day, the rebellion would have been severely impeded. Benghazi, with army tanks in the city, had been particularly vulnerable.[287]

---

[281] *Id.* at Annex I, ¶ 270.

[282] *See* Ch. XIII. *See also* Report of the International Commission of Inquiry, advance unedited version (Mar. 2, 2012), *supra* note 24 at Annex I, ¶ 333.

[283] *See* Ch. VII.

[284] *See also* Chris McGreal et al., *Libya: Allied air strikes secure Misrata for rebels*, THE GUARDIAN, Mar. 24, 2011, *available at* http://www.guardian.co.uk/world/2011/mar/23/libya-allied-air-strikes-misrata.

[285] *See* Ch. X. *See also* Report of the International Commission of Inquiry, advance unedited version (Mar. 2, 2012), *supra* note 8 at Annex I, ¶ 563.

[286] For more details on the foreign intervention and coalition operations, *see* Ch. III.

[287] Liz Sly et al., *France fires first shots against Libya after Qadhafi's forces enter Bengazi*, THE WASHINGTON POST, Mar. 18, 2011 (updated Mar. 19, 2011), *available at* http://www.washingtonpost.com/world/us-allies-prepare-military-action-against-libya-as-gaddafi-forces-continue-attacks/2011/03/18/ABLAOfs_story.html.

NATO targeted surviving remnants of Qadhafi's air and naval defenses with follow-on raids as well as heavy attacks on ground forces.[288] Destroying Libya's air defenses served the dual purpose of enforcing the UN-authorized no-fly zone, while debilitating the most organized and well-equipped element of the regime's military forces. The Libyan Air Force had long been Qadhafi's most privileged security unit, and with its forces out of the picture, the fighting in defense of the regime fell to ground *kata'ib*. On March 31, NATO assumed control of the international military operation in Libya, an intervention that also saw the involvement of non-NATO states such as Jordan, Sweden, the UAE, and Qatar.

NATO focused on cities where Qadhafi troops were engaged with *thuwar* forces, such as in Misrata, Brega and Zintan.[289] They were able to stop Qadhafi forces in the east and allow the rebels to retake all the land they had lost as far as Ra's Lanuf and Brega.[290] Up until this point, the front lines had shifted rapidly and often in the east. By the end of March, however, an offensive by Qadhafi forces, coupled with bad weather that impeded NATO airstrikes, pushed the rebels out of Brega, forcing them to retreat to Ajdabiya, resulting in a stalemate that was to last until the end of July.[291] The rebel retreats were testament to their lack of equipment and experience, a constant problem, especially in the early months of the conflict.[292] In spite of the coalition strikes, by the end of March Qadhafi's ground forces were able to roll back the rebel advances that had progressed westward along the Libyan coastal road towards Sirte.[293]

---

[288] *See also* VARUN VIRA & ANTHONY H. CORDESMAN, CENTER FOR STRATEGIC AND INTERNATIONAL STUDIES, THE LIBYAN UPRISING: AN UNCERTAIN TRAJECTORY 18 (June 20, 2011) [hereinafter "THE LIBYAN UPRISING"], *available at* http://csis.org/files/publication/110620_libya.pdf.

[289] *See also* VIRA & CORDESMAN, THE LIBYAN UPRISING, *supra* note 288 at 18.

[290] Ben Brown, *Libya: Rebels take Ras Lanuf, Brega, Uqayla, Bin Jawad*, BBC, Mar. 27, 2011, *available at* http://www.bbc.co.uk/news/world-africa-12873434.

[291] Alexander Dziadosz, *Libya rebels beat rapid retreat east under fire*, REUTERS, Mar. 30, 2011, *available at* http://www.reuters.com/article/2011/03/30/libya-east-retreat-idUSWEA174420110330; Thomas Penny and Partick Donahue, *Libya Rebels seek cease-fire after U.S. vows to withdraw jets*, BLOOMBERG, Apr. 1, 2011, *available at* http://www.bloomberg.com/news/2011-04-01/libya-rebels-seek-cease-fire-after-u-s-vows-to-withdraw-jets-by-tomorrow.html.

[292] See also the battle for Qawalish on July 6, 2011. *See* Ch. X, Sec. 2.8. *See also* BELL ET AL., STALEMATE & SIEGE, *supra* note 110.

[293] CHRISTOPHER M. BLANCHARD, CONGRESSIONAL RESEARCH SERVICE, LIBYA: UNREST AND U.S. POLICY 5 (Apr. 25, 2011) [hereinafter "UNREST AND U.S. POLICY"], *available at* http://www.hsdl.org/?view&did=5616.

On 28 March, NATO announced that one of its airstrikes had hit the Khamis Katiba "regime security unit," which had reportedly remained "at the forefront of operations against civilians."[294] A significant strike, it was emblematic of NATO's ability to seriously damage the Qadhafi regime's tactical capabilities. Officials leading the NATO operations continued to report successes, such as on 25 March, when U.S. Joint Staff Director Vice Admiral Bill Gortney stated that, as a result of coalition military strikes, Qadhafi had

> no air defense left to him and a diminishing ability to command and sustain his forces on the ground. His air force cannot fly, his warships are staying in port, his ammunition stores are being destroyed, communication towers are being toppled, and his command bunkers are being rendered useless.[295]

These claims were not entirely accurate, however, and NATO continued to strike Libyan air defense assets into the final month of the conflict. Although LAF aircraft were destroyed at the end of March, there was still significant air defense for NATO to be concerned with. For example, as late as September, NATO was still engaging significant numbers of Libyan tactical surface-to-air missile systems and anti-aircraft artillery.[296] While NATO strikes were resulting in significant damage to the Qadhafi military, the regime continued fighting relentlessly, shifting tactics and employing extreme measures to defeat the rebel forces and their supporters.

April 2011

The main axis of the conflict in April was the fight for Misrata.[297] Regime forces had surrounded and laid siege to the city. The battle had dire consequences for the civilian population and the city became dependent upon a sealift for supplies. Once NATO entered the war, Qadhafi forces shifted from open maneuver to using civilian vehicles to mask their movements. In Misrata and other cities, Qadhafi forces started to operate largely in populated areas to protect their units from airstrikes. While this saved

---

[294] Bill Gortney, U.S. Department of Defense News Briefing, *Libya Operation Odyssey Dawn*, Mar. 28, 2011.

[295] *Id.*

[296] Operational Media Update for 31 August, NORTH ATLANTIC TREATY ORGANIZATION, *available at* http://www.nato.int/nato_static/assets/pdf/pdf_2011_09/20110901_110901-oup-update.pdf; Operational Media Update for 1 September, NORTH ATLANTIC TREATY ORGANIZATION, *available at* http://www.nato.int/nato_static/assets/pdf/pdf_2011_09/20110902_110902-oup-update.pdf.

[297] *See* Ch. IX.

their units from air attacks, it also compelled them to operate in areas where they were unable to maximize their military advantage over the rebels and were thus exposed to urban-style insurgent attacks. Tanks, for instance, cannot be fully utilized in dense cities because they are open to attack on weak armor on their top and rear. It is also difficult to navigate armor in narrow urban streets, thus diminishing their effectiveness.

Fighting on rebel-held territory took the advantage away from the Qadhafi forces, but the *thuwar* groups were still largely disjointed, with units operating autonomously with little or no central control. This improved marginally as the war progressed, but rebel forces continued to fight locally without a coordinated strategy and proved unable to plan combined attacks. This was in part the result of the composition of the *thuwar* forces, made up of civilians and poorly trained ex-Qadhafi soldiers. The month of April saw an entrenchment and solidifying of the front lines. In the east the war had bogged down around Brega, in the center the regime was focused on the siege of Misrata, and in the west low-level fighting in the Nafusa Mountains region remained in a in deadlock.

On 7 April, the commander of the U.S. Africa Command, General Carter Ham, testified that as a result of coalition strikes the Qadhafi regime had a "significantly degraded ability to continue to attack civilians." He also warned that a stalemate appeared more likely given recent developments.[298]

The battle for Cyrenaica continued in the east as Qadhafi forces pushed past Brega and began shelling Ajdabiya on 8 April.[299] The fighting intensified into street battles until NATO airstrikes and rebel reinforcements pushed Qadhafi forces out of the city. *Thuwar* and Qadhafi forces traded rocket fire over the following days, and the fighting reached a stalemate with Brega and Ajdabiya becoming the eastern frontline until August.[300]

General Ham also warned of difficulties created by shifts in tactics by Qadhafi forces that led to an intensification of civilian casualties, committed by all sides of the conflict, stating

> What has changed dramatically has been the tactics applied by the regime forces, where they have shifted from their traditional use of conventional

---

[298] BLANCHARD, UNREST AND U.S. POLICY, *supra* note 293 at 5.

[299] Greg Campbell, *Gadhafi forces push towards western gate*, USA TODAY, Apr. 8, 2011, *available at* http://usatoday30.usatoday.com/news/world/2011-04-08-libya_N.htm.

[300] Adrian Croft & Maria Golovnina, *Western, Arab nations say Gadhafi must go*, REUTERS, Apr. 13, 2011, *available at* http://www.thestar.com/news/world/article/974198--western-arab-nations-say-gadhafi-must-go.

armored equipment, which was easily identifiable as regime forces and therefore easily targeted. They now operate largely in civilian vehicles. And when those vehicles are intermixed with the opposition forces, it's increasingly difficult to discern which is which. Secondly, we have seen an increase tactic by the regime forces to put their military vehicles adjacent to civilian aspects, mosques, schools, hospitals, civilian areas, which would result in significant civilian casualties through the strike of those assets.[301]

As the conflict progressed, *thuwar* used "heavy weapons seized in battle including tanks and Grad rockets, particularly in Sirte and Bani Walid."[302] Third party countries played an increasing role in strengthening the *thuwar* forces through the provision of weapons, training, and advice. Qatar provided training and weapons, including shoulder-fired anti-tank weapons, greatly enhancing the ability of the rebel groups to counter the regime forces.[303] By early April, this translated into the strengthening of the Cyrenaican frontlines after the second retreat to Ajdabiya in early April.[304] In Misrata, the local NTC also reached out to coalition forces in April to open the port to the city, allowing the delivery of supplies and weaponry, such as assault weapons (Kalashnikov variants, FN FALs), PKM and DShK machine guns, French-made MILAN anti-tank missiles, ammunition, and artillery.[305]

Fighting continued in the western Nafusa Mountains region. Qadhafi forces attempted to enter Al-Qala' on 10 April but were pushed back. The CoI reported that "the town was then sealed off, with fuel, food and water supplies being prevented from entering through the installation of checkpoints by Qadhafi forces."[306]

By mid-April, Qadhafi forces occupied the towns south of Nalut, including Al-Ghazaya, and placed Nalut firmly under siege. "Rockets and artillery were fired from Al-Ghazaya towards Nalut."[307] There was also consider-

---

[301] Carter Ham, Hearing to Receive Testimony on U.S. Transportation Command and U.S. Africa Command In Review of The Defense Authorization Request For Fiscal Year 2012 and The Future Years Defense Program, Testimony before Senate Armed Services Committee, Apr. 7, 2011, *available at* http://www.armed-services.senate.gov/Transcripts/2011/04%20 April/11-26%20-%204-7-11.pdf.

[302] Report of the International Commission of Inquiry, advance unedited version (Mar. 2, 2012), *supra* note 24 at Annex I, ¶ 69.

[303] BELL ET AL., STALEMATE & SIEGE, *supra* note 110 at 15.

[304] *Id.*

[305] *Id.* at 24.

[306] For a description of Events in Al-Qala', *see* Ch. X, Sec. 2.7. *See also* Report of the International Commission of Inquiry, advance unedited version (Mar. 2, 2012), *supra* note 24 at Annex I, ¶ 160.

[307] *Id.* at Annex I, ¶ 564.

able destruction and civilian casualties in Al-Ghazaya, where a legion of the Popular Guard was among the Qadhafi ranks stationed in the town.[308]

A NATO airstrike on 30 April in Tripoli killed Qadhafi's son, Saif al-'Arab, and portended increased airstrikes on the capital as NATO shifted its focus to the city.[309] The CoI investigated the site of the strike that killed Saif al-'Arab, finding that the site had been a command bunker used by the Qadhafi regime.[310]

Throughout April, Qadhafi forces engaged in clashes with *thuwar* forces on the Tunisian border in Wazin.[311] There were incursions into Tunisia and shelling in Tunisian territory to disrupt rebel resupply routes. The Tunisian military became involved[312] and there were several flare-ups throughout the summer, but the indecisive nature of the clashes typified the fighting in the west, where the war in the Nafusa Mountains region was at a stalemate that would last until June.

May 2011

The month of May saw pressure mount on Qadhafi, with NATO airstrikes on significant regime facilities and reports of unrest in the capital.[313] The rebel forces started the war as a ragtag, untrained, poorly-armed force with no central command and control that should have been simple for Qadhafi forces to defeat. With NATO's support, however, the rebels were able to acquire arms as well as buy time in which to become better organized, such that they came to constitute a credible threat to the regime. They also had the world's most modern air forces on their side, and Qadhafi's forces were no match, even as they shifted tactics to hide

---

[308] For a description of Events in Nalut, *see* Ch. X, Sec. 2.2. Report of the International Commission of Inquiry, advance unedited version (Mar. 2, 2012), *supra* note 24 at Annex I, ¶ 566.

[309] Lin Noueihed, *Libyan leader's son Saif al-Arab killed in NATO strike*, REUTERS, Apr. 30, 2011 *available at* http://www.reuters.com/article/2011/04/30/us-libya-attack-idUSTRE73 T2HV20110430.

[310] This statement is based on information provided to the ISISC Project by the consultant. For NATO's claim that the target was a command bunker, *see* No evidence Qadhafi's son killed: NATO, MCCLATCHY-TRIBUNE INFORMATION SERVICES, May 2, 2011, *available at* http://news.brisbanetimes.com.au/breaking-news-world/no-evidence-gaddafis-son-killed-nato-20110502-1e3ko.html.

[311] For a description of Events in Wazin, *see* Ch. X, Sec. 2.1.

[312] Zoubeir Souissi, *Pro-Qadhafi forces clash with Tunisian military*, REUTERS, Apr. 29, 2011 *available at* http://www.reuters.com/article/2011/04/29/libya-tunisia-idAFLDE73S0Y 020110429.

[313] *See* Ch. XIII.

under civilian cover.[314] In tactical terms, both Qadhafi and *thuwar* forces fought a similar hit-and-run war. They would attack, often with indirect fire weapons, followed by ground forces, in a mixture of guerrilla-style insurgency and Soviet-style fighting. Both sides failed to consolidate on their advances and did not press to expand their attacks. The rebels did, however, improve greatly in this area later in the war due to help from foreign trainers. Other than minor attacks, both sides lacked the capability to operate at night, which contributed to an inability to follow up on advances, thus giving the adversary time to regroup. After a series of airstrikes against Qadhafi forces, NATO announced on 20 May that the siege of Misrata was over, freeing up hundreds of battle-tested *thuwar* to fight elsewhere. The war in the Nafusa Mountains region continued apace, while there were no appreciable changes in Cyrenaica. By the end of May, the tide was turning. In the east and west the stalemate continued, but in the center of the country Qadhafi was losing.[315]

The *thuwar* victory over Qadhafi forces in Misrata in mid-May 2011 was the most significant military event for the month of May, if not a turning point in the entire war, though Qadhafi forces withdrew to defensive positions. The city had been heavily targeted by Qadhafi forces, engaging in extreme measures to defeat the resistance, including attempts to mine the waters of the port of Misrata.[316] NATO strikes were able to deter these efforts through operations along the coast. On 19 May, for example, the UK air force carried out a strike on a naval base at Khums, hitting a facility that was being used to construct inflatable boats to mine the harbor of Misrata and attack nearby vessels.[317]

NATO airstrikes hammered Tripoli for two days, 24–25 May, targeting Qadhafi sites including his offices and regime security buildings at Bab

---

[314] *See* Chs. VII, XII, XIV & XV.

[315] *See also* Qadhafi losing firm grip on Western Libya too, AP, Apr. 26, 2011, *available at* http://www.cbsnews.com/2100-202_162-20057593.html. Andrew Harding, *Libya: Misrata breathes as Gaddafi siege lifted*, BBC, May 17, 2011, *available at* http://www.bbc.co.uk/news/world-africa-13421646; *Libyan Revolutionary Fighters Claim Gains Against Qadhafi Forces in Misurata, EU Opens Office in Bengazi*, AL JAZEERA, May 11, 2011, *available at* http://www.ccun.org/News/2011/May/11%20on/Libyan%20Revolutionary%20Fighters%20Claim%20Gains%20Against%20Qadhafi%20Forces%20in%20Misrata,%20EU%20Opens%20Office%20in%20Bani%20Ghazi,%20May%2011,%202011.htm.

[316] *See* Ch. IX.

[317] *See also* Christian F. Anrig, *Allied Air Power over Libya*, 91 AIR AND SPACE POWER JOURNAL 89 (Winter 2011).

al-'Aziziyya.[318] NATO did not strike his residence there, however. The strikes led Qadhafi to propose a cease-fire on 26 May, which was promptly rejected the next day.[319] By this time, NATO members would not agree to any deal that would allow Qadhafi to stay in power. Russia, which had initially opposed intervention, called for Qadhafi to step down on the same day, seemingly sealing his fate.[320] The regime's loss of Misrata meant it was no longer possible to hold off a *thuwar* incursion into Tripoli, as it freed up hundreds of *thuwar* to begin a fight for the capital.

At this point, the practice of extralegal detention and interrogation had become so widespread that the Qadhafi regime created new detention facilities in cities throughout the country to accommodate the growing number of prisoners. Detainees were mostly held in poor conditions, tortured and interrogated for information, and hundreds died in detention.[321]

By May, Qadhafi forces had established an ad hoc detention center in the town of Khums, 120 kilometers (75 miles) to the east of Tripoli.[322] A former senior intelligence official told the CoI that the site was under the control of Brigadier Muhammad Abu Bakr Dabub al-Qadhafi, the head of Military Intelligence's Search and Interrogation Office, which reported directly to the head of Military Intelligence. The second-in-command of the detention center was an officer from the Tripoli branch of Military Intelligence, who had been tasked by the head of Military Intelligence with creating a "dirty operation" katiba.[323] Suspected *thuwar* were interrogated in the Khums detention center, and then sent to the capital for further interrogation.[324]

---

[318] *See also* Diaa Hadid & Michelle Faul, *U.S. reaches out to Libya rebels amid airstrikes*, AP, May 24, 2011, *available at* http://www.msnbc.msn.com/id/43140642/ns/world_news-mideast_n_africa/#.ULeOROOe9AG.

[319] African Union, Press Release, *The African Union High-Level Ad Hoc Committee On Libya Convened Its 5th Meeting In Addis Ababa Press release*, May 26, 2011, *available at* http://www.au.int/en/sites/default/files/Press%20Release%20ad%20hoc%20committee%205th%20Meeting%2026%20MAy%202011.pdf; Joe Parkinson, *NATO allies reject Libyan cease-fire offer*, WALL STREET JOURNAL, May 27, 2011, *available at* http://www.shabablibya.org/news/nato-allies-reject-libyan-cease-fire-offer.

[320] Joseph Logan, *Russia joins western chorus for Gaddafi to go*, REUTERS, May 27, 2011, *available at* http://uk.reuters.com/article/2011/05/27/uk-libya-idUKTRE74E1I420110527.

[321] *See generally* Part Two.

[322] *See* Chs. XI & XIII.

[323] Report of the International Commission of Inquiry, advance unedited version (Mar. 2, 2012), *supra* note 24 at Annex I, ¶ 148.

[324] *Id.*

Qadhafi's brutality could not hide the reality of the regime's losses, which were apparent to increasing numbers of the country's population. On 30 May, protests erupted in Tripoli.[325] Though they were put down with force they signaled an end to whatever popularity Qadhafi may have had.

June 2011

June saw huge gains on the side of the rebels in the west due in part to NATO airstrikes and weapons supplies. The east remained mired in a stalemate even though NATO escalated its strikes in the area, most notably using attack helicopters in Libya for the first time.[326] The rebels began the war fighting with seized and homemade weapons, hindering their ability to make tactical progress or win decisive battles. This lack of weapons contributed to the rebels' failure to hold the gains made in March in the east. When modern weaponry and training were introduced, there were immediate results. France, for example, provided weapons in June that included machine guns, RPGs, and anti-tank missiles that greatly enhanced the arsenal of the *thuwar* forces.[327]

Once western support began to flow to the rebels, there was also a marked shift in the fighting in the Nafusa Mountains region.[328] NATO airstrikes enabled the Zintan rebels to break through loyalist lines on 2 June, and rebel fighters seized numerous towns in the Nafusa Mountains region in the following weeks.[329] As the rebels took control of the region, Qadhafi forces withdrew towards the Al-Mil'ab forest on 5 June where they used a Boy Scouts camp on the edge of Al-Qala' as a military base for the forces from Safiyyat.[330] Evidence and witness accounts indicate that Qadhafi forces summarily executed the prisoners at the base before their

---

[325] *Unprecedented protests have taken place in Libya*, AL JAZEERA, May 30, 2011, *available at* http://blogs.aljazeera.com/topic/libya/libya-may-30-2011-2350.

[326] Kim Sengupta, *NATO strike force in Libya enjoys quick success with Apache gunships*, THE GUARDIAN, June 5, 2011, *available at* http://www.guardian.co.uk/world/2011/jun/05/nato-libya-apache-gunships-success.

[327] Nick Hopkins, *Nato reviews Libya campaign after France admits arming rebels*, THE GUARDIAN, June 29, 2011, *available at* http://www.guardian.co.uk/world/2011/jun/29/nato-review-libya-france-arming-rebels.

[328] *See* Ch. X.

[329] BELL ET AL., STALEMATE & SIEGE, *supra* note 110 at 11.

[330] The transliteration of the name of this place was adopted from the reference. Report of the International Commission of Inquiry, advance unedited version (Mar. 2, 2012), *supra* note 24 at Annex I, ¶ 160.

retreat from the region.[331] Witnesses were able to provide some details to the CoI regarding the individuals in command at the site, but "were unable to specify to the Commission which military or intelligence units to which the soldiers at the Boy Scouts camp belonged."[332] Sources suggested it was run by a combination of security agencies, reporting on the presence of soldiers from the Popular Guard, Military Intelligence officers, and members of the External Security Agency.[333] Evidence also suggested links to Colonel Al-Senussi, former chief of the ISA.[334]

NATO airstrikes continued to bombard Tripoli and strike Qadhafi forces in early June.[335] The *thuwar* began an operation to retake Zawiyya on 11 June,[336] launched from the Nafusa Mountains region. A critical oil city and road link to Tripoli, Zawiyya had been lost by *thuwar* forces early in the war. The rebel June offensive forced the closure of a section of the Libyan coastal highway east of the city and also occupied the western part of Zawiyya, requiring the Qadhafi government to commit more troops to the city's defense.[337] Although Qadhafi forces regained the city the following day, the battle in the west was now pushing nearer to the capital. The town of Yafran fell to *thuwar* forces, and along with prior gains in the Nafusa Mountains region indicated the stalemate in the west had ended as the rebels edged closer to Tripoli.[338]

---

[331] *See* Ch. X, Sec. 3.

[332] Report of the International Commission of Inquiry, advance unedited version (Mar. 2, 2012), *supra* note 24 at Annex I, ¶ 168.

[333] *Libya: Mass Grave Yields 34 Bodies*, HUMAN RIGHTS WATCH, Sept. 14, 2011, *available at* http://www.hrw.org/news/2011/09/14/libya-mass-grave-yields-34-bodies.

[334] *Id.*

[335] *See* Ch. XIII.

[336] *See also* Nick Carey & Peter Graff, *Fighting in Zawiya shuts Libya road to Tunisia*, REUTERS, June 11, 2011, *available at* http://www.reuters.com/article/2011/06/11/us-libya-idUSTRE7270JP20110611.

[337] Carey & Graff, *Fighting in Zawiya shuts Libya coast road-resident, supra* note 336; Nick Carey, *Zawiyah's heart a ghost town after rebel advance*, REUTERS, June 12, 2011, *available at* http://www.reuters.com/article/2011/06/12/us-libya-zawiyah-idUSTRE75B2HJ20110612; *Libya: Rebels press Gaddafi on three fronts as southern tribe revolts*, SCOTSMAN, June 12, 2011, *available at* http://www.scotsman.com/news/libya_rebels_press_gaddafi_on_three_fronts_as_southern_tribe_revolts_1_1691903; *Rebels battle Gaddafi forces in western Libya*, AL JAZEERA, June 12, 2011, *available at* http://www.aljazeera.com/news/africa/2011/06/201 1612155350821500.html.

[338] *See also NATO strikes rock Libyan capitol*, AL JAZEERA, June 7, 2011, *available at* http://www.aljazeera.com/news/africa/2011/06/20116791428754691.html.

July 2011

Qadhafi's last hope for survival was the apparent turmoil in the rebel leadership, but this hope faded fast as regime forces continued to lose further ground in July. With June characterized by rebel gains and with a rebel breakthrough in August, the month of July came to be the last stand for the Qadhafi regime. July opened with the rebels advancing towards Tripoli. In the west the rebels had taken Kikla,[339] a city 160 kilometers (100 miles) southwest of Tripoli, and continued to fight for Zawiyya. In the center of the country, the Misrata *kata'ib* were fighting for Zlitan on the road to Tripoli. The stalemate in Brega continued unabated. NATO increased its airstrikes on military targets in the Nafusa Mountains region and Tripoli.[340]

As the conflict entered its sixth month of continual fighting, the splintering within the *thuwar* forces was becoming increasingly clear. The killing of Yunis on 28 July in Benghazi demonstrated the political infighting that hindered the *thuwar* forces from forming a unified national army.[341] These internal divisions foreshowed the challenges that would arise in post-Qadhafi Libya. Following the assassination of Yunis,[342] the head of the NTC, 'Abd al-Jalil, dissolved the NTC's interim government on 8 August, and called for Jibril, one of the council's representatives for foreign affairs, to select a new one. 'Abd al-Jalil said, "Administrative mistakes have been noted in the NTC bureau performance in the recent period, prompting the NTC to take the decision to dissolve the bureau," adding that "a newly formed bureau would be entrusted with reviewing the 'conspiracy' that involved the assassination of General Younes."[343]

By 6 July, the *thuwar* had halved the distance of their forces to the capital from the south, capturing Qawalish, just over 80 kilometers (50 miles) south of Tripoli. NATO airstrikes continued as Qadhafi forces

---

[339] *See* Ch. X.

[340] Adam Schreck, *NATO boosts airstrikes on military targets in Libya*, Reuters, July 3, 2011 *available at* http://www.boston.com/news/world/africa/articles/2011/07/03/nato_boosts_airstrikes_on_military_targets_in_libya.

[341] *See* Ch. VI. *See also* International Crisis Group, Holding Libya Together, *supra* note 119.

[342] *Libya*, Max Planck Institute for Comparative Public Law and International Law, *available at* http://www.mpil.de/ww/en/pub/research/details/know_transfer/constitutional_reform_in_arab_/libyen.cfm.

[343] *Libyan rebels reshuffle leadership*, Al Jazeera, Aug. 8, 2011, *available at* http://www.aljazeera.com/news/africa/2011/08/201188191426994446.html.

fell back closer to the capital.[344] As regime forces lost more ground, Qadhafi resorted to desperate tactics to maintain power, including the recruitment of mercenary forces. The CoI received reports that Qadhafi's head of Military Intelligence, for example, arranged for several hundred Sudanese fighters from the Justice and Equality Movement opposition group to be brought into Libya to fight on the side of the Qadhafi forces.[345]

In July, in the wake of retreating government forces in areas such as the Nafusa Mountains region, *thuwar* carried out systematic violence against towns and groups suspected of aiding the Qadhafi forces. This type of violence exemplified the pre-existing deep social divides that were exacerbated by the war, including divisions based on regional affiliation, ethnicity and race, and loyalties to the regime.[346] *Thuwar* forces from Zintan, for example, entered Zawiyyat al-Bajul in May and Awaniyya in July, targeting members of the Mashashiyya for their suspected support of the Qadhafi forces.[347] Similar attacks took place in Tiji in August when *thuwar* carried out attacks against the town's residents.[348] The rebel forces used the opportunity to settle old scores and displace targeted communities through attack and intimidation. Groups such as the Mashashiyya and Tawerghan community were forced from their homes and unable to return out of fear of further attacks.[349]

By mid-July, *thuwar* forces were trying to break the stalemate in Brega. There were repeated attempts to retake the city, with a fierce seesaw battle ensuing that lasted over five days.[350]

August 2011

August marked the end of Qadhafi forces military operations as the rebels surged into Tripoli and overcame the regime's defense. The surge was facilitated by outside intervention in the single clearest example of direct

---

[344] Mark Doyle, *Libyan rebels make most significant advance in the west*, BBC, July 7, 2011 *available at* http://www.bbc.co.uk/news/world-africa-14074069.

[345] For discussion on non-Libyan "mercenary" fighters, *see* Ch. IV. *See also* Report of the International Commission of Inquiry, advance unedited version (Mar. 2, 2012), *supra* note 24 at Annex I, ¶ 684.

[346] *See* Ch. VI.

[347] *See also* Report of the International Commission of Inquiry, advance unedited version (Mar. 2, 2012), *supra* note 24 at Annex I, ¶ 454.

[348] *See* Ch. III, Sec. 6.3. *See also* Report of the International Commission of Inquiry, advance unedited version (Mar. 2, 2012), *supra* note 24 at Annex I, ¶ 470.

[349] *Id.* at Annex I, ¶ 103.

[350] *Libyan rebels pushed back from Brega*, AL JAZEERA, June 19, 2011, *available at* http://www.aljazeera.com/news/africa/2011/07/201171922526752203.html.

support resulting in military gains when the Qatari resupply of the Misrata *kata'ib* during the fight for Zlitan turned the tide. Once weapons and
ammunition reached the front, the rebels made rapid gains, making their
way undeterred to Tripoli.[351]

August opened with *thuwar* pressure on Tripoli from the west and
south. The Misrata Katiba was still involved in heavy fighting in Zlitan.
It was only Zlitan that stood in the way of the heavily armed Misrata
Katiba from taking the highway to Tripoli. Qadhafi was close to being
surrounded.[352]

Qadhafi deployed the Khamis 32nd Katiba to defend Zlitan on 2
August.[353] The initial battle lasted for three days with all rebel gains
erased by the evening of 4 August when Qadhafi forces retook the town.[354]
The regime's future rested on Qadhafi's ability to hold Zlitan; once it fell,
the capital would likely soon follow. The battle was so critical that the
rebels landed a Qatari plane in Misrata loaded with ammunition to resupply the Misrata Katiba at the Zlitan front.[355] Qadhafi forces were using
Majer,[356] south of Zlitan, as a staging area when on 8 August a NATO
airstrike hit a number of residences. According to NATO, this was a key
military target but the CoI found it to be the single largest loss of civilian
lives from a NATO airstrike during the war, with 34 civilians killed.[357]

Fighting continued in Brega in the east.[358] On 15 August, Qadhafi
forces fired a SCUD tactical ballistic missile from Sirte aimed for Ajdabiya

---

[351] *See* Ch. XIII.

[352] Michael Georgy, *Libyan Rebels Say They Have Tripoli Surrounded*, REUTERS, August
15, 2011, *available at* http://news.nationalpost.com/2011/08/15/libyan-rebels-take-strongest-
position-yet-on-road-to-tripoli; Heba Saleh et al., *Rebels claim to have Qadhafi surrounded*,
FINANCIAL TIMES, Aug. 25, 2011 *available at* http://www.ft.com/cms/s/0/511e84f4-ce57-11e0-
99ec-00144feabdc0.html#axzz2JyKzKMh8.

[353] *Libya Live Blog*, AL JAZEERA, Aug. 2, 2011, *available at* http://blogs.aljazeera.com
/topic/libya/libya-aug-2-2011-1650.

[354] *Zlitan: Gaddafi forces say they control key town*, BBC, Aug. 4, 2011, *available at* http://
www.bbc.co.uk/news/world-africa-14413157.

[355] Mussab Al-Khairalla, *Qatari plane supplies ammunition to Libyan rebels*, REUTERS, Aug.
6, 2011 *available at* http://www.reuters.com/article/2011/08/06/libya-rebels-ammunition-
idAFLDE77505S20110806.

[356] The transliteration of this place names was adopted from the reference. Report of
the International Commission of Inquiry, advance unedited version (Mar. 2, 2012), *supra*
note 24 at Annex I, ¶ 87.

[357] *See* Report of the International Commission of Inquiry, advance unedited version
(Mar. 2, 2012), *supra* note 24 at Annex I, ¶ 87.

[358] *See* Ch. VII.

but it landed in the desert.[359] Misrata was under *thuwar* control and on 11 August, rebels from Misrata attacked Qadhafi forces in Tawergha, taking the city the following day.[360] Tawergha became the site of violent attacks by Misrata *thuwar* against the town's inhabitants.[361]

Thuwar battled Qadhafi forces for Zlitan from 13-20 August, closing the circle around Tripoli from the west.[362] Once it fell to the *thuwar* on 19 August the road to Tripoli from the west was open.[363] The capital was then open to attack on all sides.

The Tripoli Katiba, which had participated in the Nafusa Mountains region campaign, numbered roughly 1,200 fighters by mid-August.[364] Together with the *thuwar* from the Nafusa Mountains, it coordinated an offensive and advanced on Tripoli with NATO support. Fighting reached Tripoli suburbs on 20 August, including Tajura, Suq al-Juma' and Fashlum.[365] *Kata'ib* advanced from Misrata, Benghazi, Zawiyya and Zintan, meeting scattered resistance from Qadhafi forces as they moved into the center of the city. After several days of clashes, *thuwar* reached the Bab al-'Aziziyya military barracks in the southern suburbs of the city on 23 August. Sporadic fighting continued in various parts of the city.[366] By 27 August, Tripoli was officially in the hands of *thuwar* forces, and the battle for the capital was over.

After the fall of Tripoli, the *thuwar* escalated their attacks against perceived Qadhafi loyalists. The Berber communities in the region reportedly attacked Arabs perceived to have sided with Qadhafi during

---

[359] Damien McElroy & Richard Spence, *Col Qadhafi fires Scud missile at rebel territory as NATO braces itself for final violent showdown*, THE TELEGRAPH, Aug. 15, 2011, *available at* http://www.telegraph.co.uk/news/worldnews/africaandindianocean/libya/8703041/Col-Gaddafi-fires-scud-missile-at-rebel-territory-as-Nato-braces-itself-for-final-violent-show down.html.

[360] *See also Libya rebels eye Brega oil installations*, AL JAZEERA, Aug. 13, 2011, *available at* http://www.aljazeera.com/news/middleeast/2011/08/201181215510690602.html.

[361] Report of the International Commission of Inquiry, advance unedited version (Mar. 2, 2012), *supra* note 24 at Annex I, ¶ 218.

[362] *NATO says anti-Qadhafi forces make 'significant advances'*, XINHUA, Aug. 16, 2011, *available at* http://news.xinhuanet.com/english2010/world/2011-08/16/c_131053531.htm; *Libya Live Blog*, AL JAZEERA, Aug. 20, 2011, *available at* http://blogs.aljazeera.com/topic/libya /libya-aug-21-2011-0017.

[363] *Libyan rebels say 32 fighters killed in Zlitan*, REUTERS, Aug. 19, 2011, *available at* http:// www.reuters.com/article/2011/08/19/libya-zlitan-casualties-idUSLDE77I0PB20110819.

[364] INTERNATIONAL CRISIS GROUP, HOLDING LIBYA TOGETHER, *supra* note 119.

[365] *See* Ch. XIII.

[366] Report of the International Commission of Inquiry, advance unedited version (Mar. 2, 2012), *supra* note 24 at Annex I, ¶ 91.

the war, in the neighborhoods of Zultan,[367] Al-Jamil, Riqdalin and Abu Kammash.[368]

As regime forces retreated from the capital during the third week of August, they sought to cover their tracks and carry out systematic killings of suspected *thuwar* held in detention centers. Before abandoning sites used for holding and interrogating suspected *thuwar*, "Qadhafi forces executed prisoners at several detention facilities including Khilit al-Firjan in Yarmouk and Gargur in Tripoli."[369]

Qadhafi and his forces escaped to Sirte, one of the last regime holdouts. In late August, the *thuwar* sent the Ajdabiya Martyrs Katiba to Sirte to negotiate the surrender of Qadhafi and his forces.[370] On 30 August, 'Abd al-Jalil of the NTC gave the loyalist forces in Sirte a four-day deadline to surrender or face military action.[371]

September 2011

At the end of August, the war's only frontline was in the last Qadhafi stronghold of Sirte, with minor pockets of resistance throughout Libya. The *thuwar* had surrounded Qadhafi, and the war was now close to its end. Outside Sirte, the war devolved into celebration and in a number of places, victorious *thuwar* looted the spoils of war.

On 1 September, the *thuwar* extended an ultimatum to Sirte to surrender by a week to allow tribal mediators a chance to negotiate.[372] There were also apparent rifts in the regime, as one of Qadhafi's sons supported surrender while another of his sons, Saif al-Islam, vowed to continue fighting.[373] The negotiations ultimately failed and by 6 September, the *thuwar* marched on Sirte and the final battle of the Libyan civil war began.

---

[367] The transliteration of this place name was adopted from the reference. Report of the International Commission of Inquiry, advance unedited version (Mar. 2, 2012), *supra* note 24 at Annex I, ¶ 730.

[368] *See also* Report of the International Commission of Inquiry, advance unedited version (Mar. 2, 2012), *supra* note 24 at Annex I, ¶ 730.

[369] *Id.* at Annex I, ¶ 92.

[370] Kareem Fahim, *Qadhafi Forces Given Deadline to Surrender*, N.Y. TIMES, Aug. 30, 2011, *available at* http://www.nytimes.com/2011/08/31/world/africa/31libya.html.

[371] *Libyan rebels give 4-day ultimatum to Gadhafi forces*, VOICE OF AMERICA, Aug. 30, 2011, *available at* http://blogs.voanews.com/breaking-news/2011/08/30/libyas-rebels-give-4-day-ultimatum-to-gadhafi-forces.

[372] Kareem Fahim, *Qadhafi Forces Given Deadline to Surrender, supra* note 370.

[373] Richard Spencer, *Libya: Saif al-Islam vows to continue the war and retake Tripoli*, THE TELEGRAPH, Aug. 31, 2011, *available at* http://www.telegraph.co.uk/news/worldnews/africa andindianocean/libya/8734174/Libya-Saif-al-Islam-Gaddafi-vows-to-continue-the-war-and-retake-Tripoli.html.

The battle for Sirte was protracted and bloody, taking *thuwar* forces until late September to fight to the edges of the city. NATO continued a steady bombardment, focusing on the Qadhafi forces' air defense systems and C2 targets.[374] The *thuwar* conducted bombardments of the city throughout the siege, with tank and Grad rockets raining on the city with little care for civilians.[375] On 30 September, the NTC called for a two-day cease-fire to allow civilians to flee the city.

October 2011

The war was all but over, but there could not be full closure or serious post-conflict planning with Qadhafi still at large. The final operation set out to capture or kill Qadhafi, as well as the last remnants of the old regime. With the *thuwar* now in full control of Libyan territory and with the advantage of weapons, they had the power to carry out indiscriminate attacks at the expense of civilian populations. Qadhafi forces were reduced to several hundred men,[376] armed with what they had carried and could find. Unlike the rebels who had NATO's airpower, there was no force to support or save Qadhafi's men.

In early October, the *thuwar* began a major new offensive into Sirte, but they remained hampered by a lack of coordination.[377] Even in the last month of the war, the *thuwar* had difficulty effectively directing their forces or coordinate operations. Fighting *kata'ib* continued to act relatively autonomously, with *kata'ib* from Brega and Benghazi coming from the east, Misrata from the west and Zintan from the south, unable to fight together in a unified fashion. The battle was desperate and for the first time in the war the Qadhafi forces used a suicide bomber to attack *thuwar* forces.[378] The *thuwar* were finally able to launch a coordinated attack on three sides with hundreds of Grad rockets hitting the city. NATO began using electronic warfare aircraft to broadcast radio messages in

---

[374] *See* Ch. XV.

[375] Report of the International Commission of Inquiry, advance unedited version (Mar. 2, 2012), *supra* note 24 at Annex I, ¶¶ 575–81.

[376] *Id.* at Annex I, ¶ 237.

[377] *See also Opposition forces close in on Gaddafi stronghold*, INDEPENDENT, Oct. 4, 2011, *available at* http://www.independent.co.uk/news/world/africa/opposition-forces-close-in-on-gaddafi-stronghold-2365188.html.

[378] *Gaddafi uses, for the first time, a suicide bomber against combatants*, ENNAHAR ONLINE, Oct. 6, 2011, *available at* http://www.ennaharonline.com/en/international/7404 .html.

Sirte directing Qadhafi forces to surrender.[379] The attack foundered and rather than providing the anticipated final push in the battle for Sirte, it devolved into brutal urban fighting.

The battle for Sirte ended with the death of Qadhafi on 20 October[380] after an increasingly intense block-by-block battle lasting over three weeks. Civilians paid a particularly high price for Sirte. The CoI was unable to determine the total number of civilians killed in the fighting but noted a desperate humanitarian situation, indiscriminate attacks on civilians by both sides, and extensive damage to civilian structures. UNOSAT satellite analysis of Sirte showed little physical damage to the city as late as 16 October, but by 20 October there was widespread physical damage to the city visible on satellite imagery. The senior military adviser to the CoI estimates the damage to Sirte to be far more extensive than the damage inflicted upon Misrata by the Qadhafi forces.[381]

3.4. *The Post-Qadhafi Period*

A heavily militarized country, which was divided into factions based on regions and allegiances, presented an enormous challenge for the interim government in the wake of the fall of the Qadhafi regime.[382] The armed forces were divided among factions in control of regional territories, and the various *thuwar* units that entered Tripoli to help take control of the capital remained. In late November 2011, forces such as the Misrata Katiba maintained a presence across Tripoli and as far east as Sirte,[383] 250 kilometers (155 miles) southeast of the capital on the Mediterranean coast.[384] The Zintan Katiba held the Tripoli International Airport through March 2012, and in June of that year, it was briefly taken by a katiba from Tarhuna, highlighting the continued instability posed by the widespread presence of non-state armed groups and actors.[385]

---

[379] Ruth Sherlock, *Libyan rebels launch the final push for Surt and their crowning victory*, THE TELEGRAPH, Oct. 7, 2011, *available at* http://www.telegraph.co.uk/news/worldnews /africaandindianocean/libya/8813811/Libyas-rebels-launch-the-final-push-for-Surt-and-their-crowning-victory.html.

[380] *See* Ch. XV. *See also* Ch. IV, Sec. 6.3.

[381] This statement is based on information provided to the ISISC Project by the consultant.

[382] *See* Ch. VI, Sec. 2.

[383] *See* Ch. XV, Sec. 2.

[384] INTERNATIONAL CRISIS GROUP, HOLDING LIBYA TOGETHER, *supra* note 119.

[385] Hadi Fornaji, *Tripoli International Airport Still Held by Zintan Brigade*, LIBYA HERALD, Mar. 25, 2012, *available at* http://www.libyaherald.com/2012/03/25/tripoli-internation-al-airport-still-held-by-zintan-brigade; Rami al-Shaheibi, *Libya's Tripoli Airport Attacked by*

The former revolutionary *kata'ib* that liberated the country continued to operate independently, and did not submit to national authorities. There was no coordinated or centralized disarmament, demobilization, and reintegration program (DDR) in Libya although NATO had offered to assist.[386] *Kata'ib* continued to clash regularly.[387] In Misrata, members of *kata'ib* policed the streets at night, harassing and arresting men they accused of being Tawerghan, illegal migrants, and terrorists.[388] In one reported incident, a militia arrested a dozen men thought to be homosexual and threatened them with death.[389]

There were a number of various grievances the *thuwar* groups wanted addressed before they would submit to national authority. For example, they wanted to ensure medical treatment for the war-wounded and follow-up medical care. Their demands were also economic, calling for the provision of jobs. More than that, they demanded respect from a government they considered to be led by Libyans who had lived overseas for so long they had forgotten their Arabic. A number of *thuwar* indicated that after tasting power they could not return to a normal life. Many of the former fighters suffered from PTSD and were in need of treatment.[390]

There also existed regional tensions, linked to tribal affiliations and conflicting alliances that developed during the war. Residents in cities where Qadhafi forces had based their attacks were perceived as having supported the regime, and were the victims of reprisal violence.[391] Many Misratans, for example, were suspicious of, and openly hostile towards, of residents of the nearby town of Tawergha, who they claimed supported Qadhafi forces during the fighting.[392] Similarly, in the Nafusa Mountains

---

Disgruntled Militia, AP, June 4, 2012, *available at* http://www.huffingtonpost.com/2012/06/04/libyan-militia-takes-control-of-tripoli-airport_n_1567976.html.

[386] David Brunnstrom, *NATO worried by Libya armed groups, offers security help*, REUTERS, Sept. 27, 2012 *available at* http://www.reuters.com/article/2012/09/27/us-un-assembly-nato-libya-idUSBRE88Q1YO20120927.

[387] Ghaith Shennib, *Rival Libya militias battle on streets of Tripoli*, REUTERS, Nov. 4, 2012 *available at* http://www.reuters.com/article/2012/11/04/us-libya-attack-idUSBRE8A306420121104.

[388] This statement is based on information provided to the ISISC Project by the consultant.

[389] *Twelve men face execution by Libyan militia for allegedly being gay*, DAILY MAIL, Nov. 26, 2012, *available at* http://www.dailymail.co.uk/news/article-2238812/Twelve-men-face-execution-Libyan-militia-allegedly-gay.html.

[390] This statement is based on information provided to the ISISC Project by the consultant.

[391] *See generally* Part Two.

[392] *See* Ch. IX.

region, members of the Zintan tribe became actively engaged in violence against members of the Mashashiyya tribe, who had traditionally been pro-government.[393]

One major issue that arose after the end of the war was the large numbers of prisoners detained during the conflict, and the question of who had authority over the detention facilities.[394] The *thuwar* forces took thousands of prisoners during the war and continued to hold them in detention centers across Libya. As the interim government authorities sought to establish control, it was difficult to determine who was responsible for these detention facilities. Many of the prisoners were held for ransom, for financial gain or political favors. By May 2012, there were still an estimated 4,000 detainees still in the custody of *kata'ib*, with transfer to the custody of the Ministry of Justice extremely slow.[395]

4. Conclusion

The Libyan people revolted against Qadhafi in the face of brazenly violent attacks against protesters calling for political reform. The initial demonstrations were inspired by the Arab Spring revolutions, but were a culmination of years of grievances and longstanding demands for justice and accountability for decades of abuse. The frustration was widespread, and manifested in different ways throughout the country. In the east, human rights activists demanded justice for the Abu Salim Prison massacre and other atrocities. Cyrenaica also hosted political Islamists with a history of opposition and resistance against the Qadhafi regime. The communities and social groups that had been marginalized and suffered from Qadhafi's divisive policies were eager to join the rebellion. Four decades of dictatorship had led to an accumulation of resentment and a variety of enemies that coalesced into a myriad of fighting forces committed to the cause of overthrowing a tyrannical regime.

Libya's pre-war security structure had been shaped by Qadhafi's paranoia, in which the security forces were divided into manageable units and informal security organizations were created to serve as a counterbalance to the military. Within this system, high-level security officials demonstrated loyalty through acts of cruelty towards real or perceived enemies

---

[393] VIRA & CORDESMAN, THE LIBYAN UPRISING, *supra* note 288 at 66.
[394] *See* Ch. IV.
[395] U.N. SC, 6768th mtg, U.N. Doc. SC/10644 (May 10, 2012).

of the regime. This cultivated a culture that impacted the behavior of commanders and soldiers in the field during the 2011 conflict. In turn, this caused a comparable reaction among the *thuwar* forces, which committed atrocities in the wake of the war, especially against targeted communities perceived as having supported the Qadhafi regime.

Qadhafi's own methods of control created the seeds for the success of the revolution. He had marginalized the military to ensure his own power and prevent the success of any potential coups. The security forces were thus unable to stand up to the *thuwar* backed by advanced foreign military forces, and Libya was liberated from a 42-year-old repressive regime through violent insurrection and intervention. A number of challenges accompany rapid power changes, and after the revolution these challenges were magnified and manifested in a number of social issues.

The nature of the civil war will have lasting repercussions for the new Libya. The war was won by loosely associated regions, cities, communities and towns united in their desire to remove a dictator but with little shared vision of the new nation that would follow. Libya experienced a form of Balkanization of the country that was impacted by the city-state character of the internal conflict. Non-state armed groups from Misrata, Tripoli, Benghazi, Zintan and other regions held the weapons and real power, while the newly elected government attempted to navigate the complex relationships between these actors and organize effective government control over the country.

Foreign governments played an integral role in the overthrow of the Qadhafi regime, and maintain a strong interest in establishing security and economic relations with the new government. Libya's internal stability is critical to ensure that oil reserves are protected and oil flow to the international market is unhindered. For those nations concerned about internal stability, however, it will be essential to consider the promotion of human rights and the rule of law when developing any new security agreements. If the new Libyan government does not adhere to human rights standards or undergo security sector reform, it risks falling into the same cycle of repression and violence as embodied in the former regime.

To the extent that government institutions functioned under Qadhafi, they served as arbiters of repression, not to protect Libyans or enforce the law. The new government is thus faced with the task of reshaping the security apparatus and all the institutions that existed under a dictatorship. The civil war also saw grave violations of IHL and IHRL by the *thuwar* forces, with attacks carried out against civilians, and indefinite detention and torture remain important issues that need to be addressed by the post-war government.[396] The new judicial system will need to operate in order to ensure accountability and not to favor elites or only those who participated on the winning side of the war.

While the revolution succeeded in removing a dictator, it will require larger efforts to reform the country's institutions that are rooted in dictatorship, and reconcile a war-torn country. Numerous challenges emerged in the wake of the conflict, some of which stemmed from past grievances, were a direct outgrowth of war, or the result of the shortcomings of the interim government. The post-conflict challenges were determined by the circumstances and nature of conflict that differed across the country's large terrain. The following chapter examines the conflict through the lens of each region that experienced the war in different ways, and provides insight into the progression of the fighting within the different theaters of operations, and the resulting post-conflict environment that emerged in the wake of the war.

---

[396] *See* Ch. III, Secs. 5, 6, & 9. *See also* Ch. VI.

APPENDIX: GLOSSARY OF THE WEAPONS USED DURING THE CONFLICT[397]

Homemade Weapons

The *thuwar* made use of numerous homemade and jury-rigged weapons for which there are no conventional names. They also used several of the weapons listed below on homemade mounts and without the benefit of guidance or targeting systems. For instance, the *thuwar* regularly mounted UB-16 and UB-32 rocket pods on the back of pickup trucks. These weapons were designed to be fired from rotary-wing and fixed-wing aircraft. This occurred throughout the war as the *thuwar* improvised with weapons stockpiles they had looted. The manner in which they were mounted drastically reduced the accuracy of the rockets, leading to many civilian casualties.

Aerial Bombs

Laser-Guided Bombs: NATO reported using 3,644 laser-guided bombs during the conflict, the most common of which was the GBU-12 Paveway II 500-pound (226-kilogram) bomb. NATO also reported regular use of the GBU-24 Paveway III 2000-pound (907-kilogram) bomb.[398] "These are precision-guided bombs directed to the target by a laser carried in a targeting pod. The targeting pod can be carried by the attacking aircraft or by an assisting aircraft including unmanned aerial vehicles."[399]

GPS-Guided Bombs: Global Positioning System technology was an important component of NATO's operation planning. This type of technology was used by NATO-member states such as the United States, which provided unmanned drones for intelligence surveillance.[400] NATO reported using 2,844 GPS-guided bombs during the conflict, and the most commonly used was the GBU-31 Joint Direct Attack Munition 2000-pound (907-kilogram) bomb, according to CoI documentation. Additionally,

---

[397] For more on weapons used during the conflict, *see* Ch. IV.

[398] Letter to Philippe Kirsch, Chair of the International Commission of Inquiry, Jan. 23, 2012, in Report of the International Commission of Inquiry, advance unedited version (Mar. 2, 2012), *supra* note 24 at Annex II.

[399] Report of the International Commission of Inquiry, advance unedited version (Mar. 2, 2012), *supra* note 24 at Annex V; *Laser Guided Bombs*, FEDERATION OF AMERICAN SCIENTISTS, *available at* http://www.fas.org/man/dod-101/sys/smart/lgb.htm.

[400] *See* Ch. III, Sec. 2.1.

NATO reported regular use of the GBU-38 Joint Direct Attack Munition 500-pound (226-kilogram) bomb.[401]

Both laser and GPS-guided bombs may use hardened penetrating warheads or "bunker-busters" that allow the munitions to penetrate through concrete before exploding inside a structure or below ground. NATO used such warheads to target underground facilities, such as the Qadhafi Command Bunker at the Gargur Residence, and also to minimize collateral damage by containing blast and fragmentation damage.[402]

Guided Missiles

Tomahawk: The United States and United Kingdom launched Tomahawk cruise missiles from submarines and surface warships. These missiles have several variants with the most common warhead being a conventional 1,000-pound (453-kilogram) warhead.[403]

Hellfire: The United States and other NATO countries fired Hellfire anti-tank missiles from piloted and unmanned aircraft. The most common anti-armor warhead was the 20-pound (9-kilogram) variant, though others were also used. A U.S. Predator drone fired a Hellfire missile at Qadhafi's motorcade on 20 October 2011, narrowly missing its target.[404]

Hakim: The United Arab Emirates used the PGM 500 Hakim anti-tank missile. This was the first operational use of this weapon in history. It has a 500-pound (225-kilogram) warhead.[405]

---

[401] Report of the International Commission of Inquiry, advance unedited version (Mar. 2, 2012), *supra* note 24; Letter to Philippe Kirsch, Chair of the International Commission of Inquiry, Jan. 23, 2012, *in* Report of the International Commission of Inquiry, advance unedited version (Mar. 2, 2012), *supra* note 24 at Annex II; Joint Direct Attack Munition, FEDERATION OF AMERICAN SCIENTISTS, *available at* http://www.fas.org/man/dod-101/sys /smart/jdam.htm.

[402] *BLU-109/I-2000/HAVE VOID*, GLOBALSECURITY.ORG, *available at* http://www.global security.org/military/systems/munitions/blu-109.htm.

[403] David Kirkpatrick et al., *Allies Open Air Assault on Qaddafi Forces in Libya*, N.Y. TIMES, Mar. 19, 2011, *available at* http://www.nytimes.com/2011/03/20/world/africa/20libya .html. *See also* Colin Freeman & Sean Rayment, *Libya: British forces fire missiles at Gaddafi*, THE TELEGRAPH, Mar. 19, 2011 *available at* http://www.telegraph.co.uk/news/worldnews /africaandindianocean/libya/8393128/Libya-British-forces-fire-missiles-at-Gaddafi.html.

[404] Glynnis MacNichol, *REPORT: U.S. Drone Responsible for Initially Hitting Qaddafi Convoy*, BUSINESS INSIDER, Oct. 20, 2011, *available at* http://www.businessinsider.com/us-drone-killed-qaddafi-2011-10.

[405] *UAE Air Force on the offensive in Libya*, ARABIAN AEROSPACE, Aug. 24, 2011, *available at* http://arabianaerospace.aero/uae-air-force-on-the-offensive-in-libya.html.

Brimstone: The United Kingdom used the Brimstone anti-tank missile. The Brimstone was developed based on the American Hellfire, and while it resembles the Hellfire, it is different internally and carries a tandem high-explosive anti-tank warhead.[406]

Storm Shadow: The Storm Shadow is a tripartite UK, French and Italian cruise missile used extensively in Libya. Similar to the American Tomahawk it also has a 1,000-pound (453-kilogram) warhead and has a range in excess of 250 kilometers.[407]

Anti-tank Weapons

RPG-7: The RPG-7 is a shoulder-fired rocket propelled grenade launcher that has the capability to fire anti-tank and anti-personnel rockets, as well as a variety of other warheads, with a range above 200 meters.[408] The Qadhafi forces used this launcher throughout the conflict, and the *thuwar* forces began using it as they captured and looted weapons.[409] The rebels were short on ammunition and at times supplemented their stockpiles with homemade rockets.[410]

Milan: The Milan anti-tank missile was provided to the *thuwar* forces by western states during the war. It is an advanced wire-guided missile with night capability, requiring a trained operator and with a range of 2 kilometers and a high-explosive anti-tank warhead.[411] It is of Franco-German origin and manufactured by numerous European nations.

---

[406] Thomas Harding, *Libya: RAF fears over missile shortages*, THE TELEGRAPH, Apr. 20, 2011, *available at* http://www.telegraph.co.uk/news/worldnews/africaandindianocean/libya/8463799/Libya-RAF-fears-over-missile-shortages.html.

[407] Iain Drewry, *Tornado's Top Guns' 3,000 mile mission to hammer tyrant's military machine*, THE DAILY MAIL, Mar. 21, 2011, *available at* http://www.dailymail.co.uk/news/article-1368259/Libya-Tornado-Top-Guns-3-000-mile-mission-hammer-Gaddafis-military-machine.html.

[408] Report of the International Commission of Inquiry, advance unedited version (Mar. 2, 2012), *supra* note 24; *RPG-7, RPG-7V, Rocket Propelled Grenade*, GLOBALSECURITY.ORG, *available at* http://www.globalsecurity.org/military/world/russia/rpg-7.htm.

[409] Peter Layton & Kimberley Layton, *Long summer of civil war in Libya*, DEFENCE FOCUS, Aug. 29, 2011, *available at* http://www.academia.edu/1350056/A_long_summer_of_civil_war_in_Libya.

[410] C.J. Chivers, *Hidden Workshops Add to Libyan Rebels' Arsenal*, N.Y. TIMES, May 3, 2011, *available at* http://www.nytimes.com/2011/05/04/world/africa/04misurata.html.

[411] *Milan*, GLOBALSECURITY.ORG, *available at* http://www.globalsecurity.org/military/world/europe/milan.htm.

M40 106mm recoilless rifle: The CoI found "dozens of spent 106mm shells in Libya with HEAT (high-explosive anti-tank) and HESH (high-explosive squash head) warheads."[412] The Libyan Army had approximately 220 M40 launchers and an unknown number of munitions for these direct fire systems commonly mounted to vehicles.[413]

Assault Rifles

The weapons most commonly used during the war by the Qadhafi forces and the *thuwar* forces were assault rifles, including the AK-47, FNFAL and the F2000.[414] Belgium sold Libya advanced small arms, including the F2000 and ammunition, worth 6.9 million Euros in 2009 for the purpose of protecting "humanitarian aid convoys." These weapons were used exclusively by the Khamis Katiba against the *thuwar* forces as well as civilian populations.[415]

Armored Personnel Carriers (APC) and 4×4 vehicles

The Libyan forces maintained a fleet of M113 APCs, which Khamis al-Qadhafi expressed personal interest in refurbishing, making requests for spare parts in 2009.[416] Libya's security forces also maintained four-by-four Jordanian-made vehicles for internal security purposes. High-ranking officials, such as Saif al-Islam Qadhafi, requested spare parts for the vehicles during 2009 discussions with U.S. officials over approval for weapons sales.[417]

Helicopters

The Libyan military maintained Mi-17 helicopters, and demonstrators reported the use of helicopters during the early days of the protests,

---

[412] Report of the International Commission of Inquiry, advance unedited version (Mar. 2, 2012), *supra* note 24; *M40 106mm Recoiless Rifle*, GLOBALSECURITY.ORG, *available at* http://www.globalsecurity.org/military/systems/ground/m40rclr.htm.

[413] CORDESMAN, FORCE DEVELOPMENTS, *supra* note 44 at 63.

[414] Report of the International Commission of Inquiry, advance unedited version (Mar. 2, 2012), *supra* note 24.

[415] *Belgium probes arms sales to Qadafi regime*, EXPACTICA BELGIAN NEWS, Feb. 21, 2011, *available at* http://www.expatica.com/be/news/belgian-news/belgium-probes-arms-sales-to-kadhafi-regime_131541.html.

[416] U.S. Embassy, Secret Cable, *Saif al Islam al-Islam's Staff Reaches out on Pol-Mil Relations*, Dec. 14, 2009, *available at* http://www.telegraph.co.uk/news/wikileaks-files/libya-wikileaks/8294701/SAIF-AL-ISLAMS-STAFF-REACHES-OUT-ON-POL-MIL-ISSUES.html.

[417] *Id.*

before the enforcement of the no-fly zone.[418] This type of helicopter can be armed with machine guns and rocket pods.[419]

The Libyan Air Force (LAF) operated approximately 43 Mi-24/35 Russian attack helicopters.[420] These are armed with a chin-mounted 12.7mm machine gun and can carry a variety of weapons including bombs, machine guns, rockets and anti-tank missiles on external wings.[421]

The LAF operated American CH-47 Chinook transport helicopters. There were reports of Libyan rebels operating captured CH-47 in violation of the no-fly zone,[422] for instance when accompanying Qadhafi's body from Sirte to Misrata on 20 October 2011.[423] The United Kingdom operated Apache attack helicopters[424] and France operated Eurocopter Tiger attack helicopters.[425] These helicopters carry machine guns, rockets and missiles.

Machine Guns

Numerous types of man-portable machine guns, such as the PK, were used by both the Qadhafi and *thuwar* forces. The most common type of machine guns documented by the CoI are listed below.

DShK 12.7x108mm machine gun: This type of weapon was common in Libya. "It is a gas-operated heavy machine gun with a rate of fire of

---

[418] PARGETER, LIBYA: THE RISE AND FALL OF QADHAFI, *supra* note 18 at 222; Sudarsan Raghavan & Leila Fadel, *Military helicopters reportedly fire on protesters in Libya*, THE WASHINGTON POST, Feb. 21, 2011, *available at* http://www.washingtonpost.com/wp-dyn/content/article/2011/02/20/AR2011022004185.html.

[419] *Mi-17*, GLOBALSECURITY.ORG, *available at* http://www.globalsecurity.org/military/world/russia/mi-17-specs.htm.

[420] THE MIDDLE EAST STRATEGIC BALANCE 2004–2005 (Zvi Shtauber and Shapir Yiftah S. eds., Brighton, UK: Sussex Academic Press, 2009).

[421] *Mi-24 HIND, Mi-25 HIND D, Mi-35 HIND E*, GLOBALSECURITY.ORG, *available at* http://www.globalsecurity.org/military/world/russia/mi-24-specs.htm.

[422] *Libyan Government: We have shot down two US-built helicopters*, AP, Apr. 10, 2011, *available at* http://www.foxnews.com/world/2011/04/10/libyan-government-shot-2-built-helicopters.

[423] This statement is based on information provided to the ISISC Project by the consultant based on discussions with Human Rights Watch.

[424] *Libya: UK Apache helicopters used in NATO attacks*, BBC, June 4, 2011, *available at* http://www.bbc.co.uk/news/uk-13651736.

[425] Jim Bittermann, *French helicopters keep up pressure on Qadhafi*, CNN, June 15, 2011, *available at* http://www.youtube.com/watch?v=oHNnyHShq30.

600 rounds per minute and a 2000m effective range. The cartridge is 147.5mm in length."[426]

KPV 14.5x114mm machine gun: This "is a short-recoil operated heavy machine gun with a rate of fire of 600 rounds per minute and 3000m effective range. The cartridge is 155.8mm in length."[427]

ZU-23 23mm Anti-aircraft cannon machine gun: "It is a belt-fed auto-cannon with a rate of fire of 2000 rounds per minute and a 2.5km effective range."[428]

Man-portable Air Defense System Missiles (MANPADs)

Estimates of Libya's MANPADs (shoulder-launched surface-to-air missiles) stockpile ranged from 400 to 2,000, and suggest that much of the inventory was comprised of SA-7 missiles.[429] In April 2011, coalition forces estimated "as many as 20,000" MANPADs that were thought to be in Libya before the conflict started "are now not accounted for."[430] Other estimates suggest that much of the inventory was made up of legacy SA-7 missiles acquired from the Soviet Union in the late 1970s and early 1980s.[431]

Ballistic Missiles

SCUD-B: The SCUD-B is a tactical ballistic missile that is 11.25 meters in length and requires a dedicated vehicle for transport and firing. Libya reportedly had 500 SCUD-B missiles and 50 MAZ-543 launchers in 2009.[432] The CoI reported finding an emptied MAZ-543 launcher in Misrata. NATO reported that three were launched during the war, one that targeted

---

[426] Report of the International Commission of Inquiry, advance unedited version (Mar. 2, 2012), *supra* note 24; Jonathan Marcus, *Libya: How the opposing sides are armed*, BBC, Aug. 23, 2011, *available at* http://www.bbc.co.uk/news/world-africa-12692068.

[427] Report of the International Commission of Inquiry, advance unedited version (Mar. 2, 2012), *supra* note 24 at Annex V.

[428] *Id. See also ZU-23 23mm Antiaircraft Gun*, FEDERATION OF AMERICAN SCIENTISTS, *available at* http://www.fas.org/man/dod-101/sys/land/row/zu-23.htm.

[429] BLANCHARD, UNREST AND U.S. POLICY, *supra* note 293 at 5.

[430] For more on the presence of MANPAD's after the war, *see* Ch. V, Sec. 3. *See also* Testimony of U.S. AFRICOM Commander General Carter Ham, SENATE ARMED SERVICES COMMITTEE, Apr. 7, 2011, *available at* http://www.armed-services.senate.gov/Transcripts/2011/04%20April/11-26%20-%204-7-11.pdf.

[431] *Holy grails – Libya loses control of its MANPADS*, JANE'S INTELLIGENCE REVIEW, Apr. 15, 2011.

[432] THE MIDDLE EAST STRATEGIC BALANCE 2002–2003, *supra* note 55.

Misrata and two that targeted Brega. "The missile has a range of 300km and carries a 985kg warhead."[433]

FROG-7: Libya reportedly had 45 Free Rocket Over Ground (FROG-7) ballistic missiles on eight-wheeled transporter erector launcher (TEL) trucks. These were heavily targeted by NATO airpower during the war. These are often mistaken for SCUD-B missiles. At least one FROG-7 was launched by Libya during the war.[434]

Rockets

Type-63 multiple rocket launcher: This was the most commonly used by the *thuwar* and Qadhafi forces during the war.[435] "It fires a 107mm rocket with a maximum range of 8km."[436]

BM-21 Grad with 122mm M21 rocket: This rocket is particularly dangerous to civilian populations, as it is used to fire on general areas and not designed to hit specific targets. It can fire two rockets per second and reach a range of 20km.[437] Grad rockets were used first by the Qadhafi forces against populated areas and later by the rebels against Sirte.[438]

S-5: This is an unguided rocket that is fired from the air from either an aircraft or helicopter. The *thuwar* used these rockets on the back of pickup trucks with UB-32 and UB-16 rocket launchers.[439] The rockets are

---

[433] Report of the International Commission of Inquiry, advance unedited version (Mar. 2, 2012), *supra* note 24 at Annex V; *R-11/SS-1B SCUD A/ R-300 9K72 Elbrus/SS-1C SCUD-B*, FEDERATION OF AMERICAN SCIENTISTS, *available at* http://www.fas.org/nuke/guide/russia/theater/r-11.htm.

[434] *Libya: RAF Tornados destroy Libyan missile launchers*, BBC, May 8, 2011, *available at* http://www.bbc.co.uk/news/uk-13325389.

[435] Jonathan Marcus, *Libya: How the opposing sides are armed*, BBC, Aug. 23, 2011, *available at* http://www.bbc.co.uk/news/world-africa-12692068.

[436] Report of the International Commission of Inquiry, advance unedited version (Mar. 2, 2012), *supra* note 24 at Annex V; *Type-63 107mm Rocket Laucher*, FEDERATION OF AMERICAN SCIENTISTS, *available at* http://www.fas.org/man/dod-101/sys/land/row/type-63-r.htm.

[437] Report of the International Commission of Inquiry, advance unedited version (Mar. 2, 2012), *supra* note 24 at Annex V. *See also 9K51 BM-21 GRAD (HAIL)*, FEDERATION OF AMERICAN SCIENTISTS, *available at* http://www.fas.org/man/dod-101/sys/land/row/type-63-r.htm.

[438] David Kirkpatrick, *Western Libya Earns a Taste of Freedom as Rebels Loosen Qadhafi's Grip*, N.Y. TIMES, June 25, 2011, *available at* http://www.nytimes.com/2011/06/26/world/africa/26libya.html. *See also Libya: Protect Civilians in Sirte Fighting*, HUMAN RIGHTS WATCH, Oct. 12, 2011, *available at* http://www.hrw.org/news/2011/10/12/libya-protect-civilians-sirte-fighting.

[439] Alan Taylor, *DIY weapons of the Libyan rebels*, THE ATLANTIC, June 14, 2011, *available at* http://www.theatlantic.com/infocus/2011/06/diy-weapons-of-the-libyan-rebels/100086.

typically 1.4 meters in length and can carry a 5kg warhead and reach up to 4km in distance.[440]

SNEB: This is a French-designed unguided rocket that is designed to fire directly from air transport systems. As with the S-5, the *thuwar* forces mounted these rockets on pickup trucks on improvised mounts using MATRA rocket launchers.[441]

---

[440] Report of the International Commission of Inquiry, advance unedited version (Mar. 2, 2012), *supra* note 24 at Annex V. *See also S-5 (57mm) Aircraft Rockets (Russia) (Russian Federation), Air-launched rockets*, JANE'S INTELLIGENCE REVIEW, *available at* http://webcache .googleusercontent.com/search?q=cache:http://articles.janes.com/articles/Janes-Air-Launched-Weapons/S-5-57-mm-aircraft-rockets-Russia-Russian-Federation.html.

[441] Report of the International Commission of Inquiry, advance unedited version (Mar. 2, 2012), *supra* note 24 at Annex V.

CHAPTER THREE

THE NATO CAMPAIGN: AN ANALYSIS OF THE 2011 INTERVENTION

1. Introduction

As the violence against protesters grew worse and civilian casualties mounted in February 2011, it became increasingly apparent that the situation in Libya was going to solicit an international response. Within days of the start of the uprising, high level Libyan officials began to defect, and international actors – including UN Secretary-General Ban Ki-moon and Navanethem Pillay, the High Commissioner for Human Rights – began raising concerns and organizing efforts in response to the violent conduct of the Qadhafi regime.[1]

The UN Security Council reacted by adopting two Resolutions. Resolution 1970 was adopted on 26 February 2011, and imposed a number of measures on Libya, most notably a referral to the International Criminal Court (ICC) and the imposition of an arms embargo.[2] The second, Resolution 1973, was adopted on 17 March 2011, and authorized several additional actions, including the imposition of a no-fly zone over Libya and a civilian protection mandate, which resulted in foreign intervention by member states of the North Atlantic Treaty Organization (NATO).[3] The NATO intervention flew more than 26,500 air sorties[4] that provided critical support for the *thuwar* forces and hastened the eventual fall of the Qadhafi

---

[1] *Outraged Secretary-General Calls for Immediate end to Violence in Libya*, UN Secretary-General, Feb. 22, 2011, *available at* http://www.un.org/News/Press/docs/2011/sgsm13408 .doc.htm; *UN rights chief condemns violence against protesters in Middle East, North Africa*, UN News Centre, Feb. 18, 2011, *available at* http://www.un.org/apps/news/story.asp?New sID=37567&Cr=protests&Cr1.

[2] SC Res. 1970 (2011), Feb. 26 2011, UN Doc. S/RES/1970 (2011).

[3] SC Res. 1973 (2011), Mar. 17 2011, UN Doc. S/RES/1973 (2011). For a U.S. perspective on the NATO intervention, *see* Ivo H. Daalder and James G. Stavridis, *NATO's Victory in Libya: The Right Way to Run an Intervention*, Foreign Affairs, Mar./Apr. 2012, *available at* http://www.foreignaffairs.com/articles/137073/ivo-h-daalder-and-james-g-stavridis/natos-victory-in-libya.

[4] Operation Unified Protector Final Mission Stats, North Atlantic Treaty Organization, Nov. 2, 2011, *available at* http://www.nato.int/nato_static/assets/pdf/ pdf_2011_11/20111108_111107-factsheet_up_factsfigures_en.pdf.

regime. The intense bombing campaign also caused heavy destruction and civilian casualties in the process.[5]

Throughout its involvement in the conflict, NATO adopted an offensive posture by not only targeting Qadhafi military assets, but also by arming and training the *thuwar* opposition forces on the ground. Moreover, while casualties were small relative to the munitions expended, neither NATO nor the UN Security Council followed up with adequate accounting or made reparations for the destruction of property and civilian casualties resulting from the air campaign. For its part, NATO released detailed operational media updates, press briefings and fact sheets with information regarding its airstrikes that destroyed regime targets.[6] Yet, NATO was not entirely forthcoming and at times denied having any information regarding strikes that led to civilian deaths. This chapter highlights several instances where NATO failed to provide sufficient information, or provided inaccurate statements regarding operations that caused civilian destruction and/or civilian casualties.

The use of force by foreign actors in Libya is not without controversy, and questions have been raised over whether the intervention itself was legal pursuant to the resolution provided by the Security Council, and also whether particular strikes were consistent with the requirements of the resolution. This chapter provides a general assessment of the NATO intervention, and examines critical questions with regards to accusations that NATO exceeded its mandate, violated its own rules of engagement and failed to adhere to the specific laws of war while carrying out its operations.

This chapter first provides a factual overview of the NATO campaign and the events that gave rise to the authorization for foreign intervention. Next, a legal overview is provided of the law of armed conflict, along with an assessment of Security Council Resolutions 1970 and 1973, and NATO's

---

[5] HUMAN RIGHTS WATCH, UNACKNOWLEDGED DEATHS: CIVILIAN CASUALTIES IN NATO'S AIR CAMPAIGN IN LIBYA (May 2012) [hereinafter "UNACKNOWLEDGED DEATHS"], *available at* http://www.hrw.org/sites/default/files/reports/libya0512webwcover.pdf.

[6] Readers can access factsheets on NATO's overall operations as well as transcripts of its Press Briefings on the Libya campaign, *available at* http://www.nato.int/cps/en/natolive/topics_71652.htm. NATO also hosts an electronic library of its daily summaries of Operational Unified Protector operations, spanning from 1 April to 25 October 2011, *available at* http://www.nato.int/cps/en/natolive/news_71994.htm. For an example of a press briefing transcript with information on successful airstrikes, *see* Carmen Romero and Brigadier General Claudio Gabellini, Press Briefing on Libya, NORTH ATLANTIC TREATY ORGANIZATION (May 10, 2011), *available at* http://www.nato.int/cps/en/natolive/opinions_73660.htm.

interpretation of the Resolutions and its rules of engagement. The chapter concludes with an examination of a sample of NATO airstrikes conducted during the conflict, and closes with an assessment of NATO's operations and whether its humanitarian remit was exceeded. This chapter does not, however, endeavor to provide a clinical overview of each strike or determine conclusively whether NATO violated the laws of armed conflict.

2. OVERVIEW OF THE NATO CAMPAIGN

On 21 February 2011, Libya's Deputy Permanent Representative at the Libyan mission to the United Nations, Ibrahim Dabbashi, broke with the Qadhafi regime and condemned the use of violence against demonstrators in Benghazi.[7] The following day the Arab League condemned the use of force against civilians by the Qadhafi regime and suspended Libya's participation in the League until Libya met its demands to immediately put a stop to the violence.[8] On 25 February, the Human Rights Council (HRC) issued a resolution expressing "deep concern" and "condemn[ing]" the "gross and systematic violations of human rights by the Libyan authorities." The Security Council debated the situation and subsequently adopted Resolution 1970 on 26 February.[9] Most notably, acting under the powers conferred it by Chapter VII of the UN Charter, Resolution 1970 referred the situation in Libya to the ICC for all crimes occurring after 15 February,[10] imposed an arms embargo on the Jamahiriyya,[11] and issued a travel ban[12] and asset freeze[13] for senior members of the Qadhafi regime. It should be noted that, in light of Security Council Resolution 1973 and the later involvement of NATO, Resolution 1970 did not authorize the use of force by Member States.

The Security Council's reliance on Chapter VII is of particular importance, as it allows the body to take "action with respect to threats to the

---

[7] Colin Moynihan, *Libya's U.N. Diplomats Break With Qaddafi*, N.Y. TIMES, Feb. 21, 2011, *available at* http://www.nytimes.com/2011/02/22/world/africa/22nations.html.

[8] *Update Report No. 3: Libya*, UN SECURITY COUNCIL REPORT, Feb. 25, 2011, *available at* http://www.securitycouncilreport.org/update-report/lookup-c-glKWLeMTIsG-b-6586331 .php.

[9] SC Res. 1970 (2011), *supra*, note 2.

[10] *Id.* at ¶ 4.

[11] *Id.* at ¶ 9.

[12] *Id.* at ¶ 15.

[13] *Id.* at ¶ 17.

peace, breaches of the peace and acts of aggression,"[14] and thereby enti-
tles it to act in any fashion it deems relevant to preserve international
peace.[15] For instance, the Council had previously invoked Chapter VII to
establish the International Criminal Tribunal for Rwanda in the aftermath
of the Rwandan Genocide[16] and to authorize peacekeeping and stabiliza-
tion missions, including in East Timor[17] and Haiti.[18] By authorizing international intervention for the first time in the form of punitive measures
just shy of armed force (*e.g.*, sanctions), Resolution 1970 brought a new
international dimension to the Libyan conflict.[19]

On 1 March, the UN General Assembly voted to suspend Libya from
the HRC, and issued a statement expressing deep concern about the situation in Libya in the wake of Qadhafi's "violent crackdown on anti-Government protesters."[20] The same day, the U.S. Senate passed Resolution
85, strongly condemning "the gross and systematic violations of human
rights in Libya, including violent attacks on protesters demanding democratic reforms," and urging "the United Nations Security Council to take
such further action as may be necessary to protect civilians in Libya from
attack, including the possible imposition of a no-fly zone over Libyan
territory."[21]

On 3 March, Luis Moreno Ocampo, then Prosecutor of the ICC,
announced that his Office was opening an investigation into the situation in Libya, with particular reference to alleged crimes against humanity committed by forces under the command of Qadhafi, members of his
family and the regime's inner circle.[22] The following week, on 10 March,
France became the first country to recognize the leadership of the National

---

[14] United Nations, Charter of the United Nations, Oct. 24, 1945, 1 UNTS XVI [hereinafter
"UN Charter"] at Chapter VII.

[15] *See* Questions of Interpretation and Application of the 1971 Montreal Convention
arising from the Aerial Incident at Lockerbie (Lib. v. U.S.), Provisional Measures, 1992 ICJ
114 (Apr. 14, 1992).

[16] SC Res. 955 (1994), 8 Nov. 1994, UN Doc. S/RES/955 (1994).

[17] SC Res. 1272 (1999), 25 Oct. 1999, UN Doc. S/RES/955 (1999).

[18] SC Res. 1944 (2010), 14 Oct. 2010, UN Doc. S/RES/1944 (2010).

[19] *See infra* Sec. 4.

[20] UN Press Release, GA/11050, Mar. 1 2011, *available at* http://www.un.org/News/Press/
docs/2011/ga11050.doc.htm.

[21] S. Res. 85, 112th Cong. §§ 2, 3, 7 (as passed by Senate, Mar. 1, 2011). Referenced in
James C. Ho and Trevor W. Morrison, Editors, 1 J.L.: Periodical Laboratory of Leg. Scholarship 260, Apr. 1, 2011.

[22] For more on the ICC cases, *see* Ch. IV, Sec. 6.2. *See also* CHRISTOPHER M. BLANCHARD,
CONGRESSIONAL RESEARCH SERVICE, LIBYA: UNREST AND U.S. POLICY 4, Apr. 25, 2011, *available at* http://www.hsdl.org/?view&did=5616 [hereinafter "UNREST AND U.S. POLICY"].

Transitional Council (NTC). The recognition came shortly after defense ministers representing NATO gathered in Brussels to discuss the imposition of a no-fly zone over Libya.[23] By the middle of March, public opinion across the Arab world was turning rapidly against the Qadhafi regime as well, and on 12 March the Arab League announced its support for the proposed no-fly zone.[24] On 15 March, the HRC established the International Commission of Inquiry (CoI) to "investigate all alleged violations of international human rights law."[25] The CoI, with the support of the United Nations Office of the High Commissioner for Human Rights (OHCHR), sent the first international observers to Libya to investigate the ongoing violence.[26] The next day, on 16 March, Secretary-General Ban Ki-moon again expressed grave concern over the escalation of violence in Libya and called for an immediate cessation of hostilities between Qadhafi and opposition forces.[27]

On 17 March, the Security Council convened for a second time to discuss the continuing violence in Libya and adopted Resolution 1973.[28] Again acting under the color of Chapter VII of the UN Charter, the Security Council ratcheted up the pressure on the Qadhafi regime by authorizing Member States "to take all necessary measures . . . to protect civilians and civilian populated areas under threat of attack in the Libyan Arab Jamahiriya, including Benghazi, while excluding a foreign occupation force of any form on any part of Libyan territory,"[29] and requested other Member States and the League of Arab States to assist under the provisions stipulated in Chapter VIII (regional arrangements) of the UN Charter.[30]

The Resolution also created a no-fly zone "to establish a ban on all flights in the airspace of the Libyan Arab Jamahiriya in order to help protect

---

[23] Leela Jacinto, *Rebel Benghazi to get ambassador*, FRANCE 24, Mar. 11, 2011, *available at* http://www.france24.com/en/20110310-France-NTC-national-transitional-council-embassy-Libya.

[24] ROYAL UNITED SERVICES INSTITUTE, ACCIDENTAL HEROES: BRITAIN, FRANCE AND THE LIBYA OPERATION, AN INTERIM LIBYA CAMPAIGN REPORT 5 (Sept. 2011) [hereinafter "ACCIDENTAL HEROES"], *available at* http://www.rusi.org/downloads/assets/RUSIInterim LibyaReport.pdf.

[25] HRC Res. S-15/1, UN Doc. A/HRC/RES/S-15/1 (Feb. 25, 2011).

[26] Report of the International Commission of Inquiry on Libya, U.N. HRC. 19th Sess., Annex I, ¶ 2. U.N. Doc. A/HRC/19/68 (Mar. 2, 2012).

[27] Statement on Libya, Ban Ki-moon, United Nations (Mar. 16, 2011), *available at* http://www.un.org/sg/statements/?nid=5141.

[28] SC Res. 1973 (2011), *supra* note 3.

[29] *Id.* at ¶ 4.

[30] *Id.* at ¶ 5.

civilians"[31] and allowed for naval inspections of all ships bound for or departing from Libya to check for weapons.[32] The central element of Resolution 1973 was the authorization of the use of air power to "protect civilians." The ambit of this authorization is nebulous, a fact that caused significant disagreement during the subsequent NATO air campaign.

As the international intervention prepared to commence, U.S. President Obama issued an ultimatum to the Qadhafi government, stating in a press release on 18 March that, in order to avert the pending military intervention, it must "implement an immediate ceasefire, including by ending all attacks on civilians; halt his troops' advance on Benghazi; pull his troops back from three other cities; and establish water, electricity, and gas supplies to all areas."[33]

Immediately following the adoption of Resolution 1973, NATO countries began assembling forces to carry out strikes against Libya's military installations. United States, UK, and French officials took the lead, meeting in Paris from 17–19 March to plan the implementation of the no-fly zone, and discuss plans for airstrike operations.[34] French forces were the first to engage, sending planes to attack tanks and armed forces, thereby deterring the regime's military advance on Benghazi.[35]

During the initial phase of operations, states acted independently, the United States operating under the banner of Operation Odyssey Dawn, France under Operation Harmattan, the United Kingdom under Operation Bellamy and Canada under Operation Mobile. On 19 March, fighter planes from France, the United Kingdom, and the United States launched attacks in Libya.[36] After deliberations over command and control arrangements, the U.S. Africa Command (AFRICOM) took control of initial coalition operations.[37] The strikes were coordinated from AFRICOM, based in Stuttgart, Germany, with U.S. General Carter F. Ham serving as theater commander for U.S. Libya operations, and tactical U.S. operations coordinated by a Joint Task Force under Admiral Sam Locklear, Commander of U.S.

---

[31] *Id.* at ¶ 6.

[32] *Id.* at ¶ 13.

[33] Press Release, Office of the Press Secretary, The White House, Remarks by the President on the Situation in Libya, Mar. 18, 2011, available at http://www.whitehouse.gov/the-press-office/2011/03/18/remarks-president-situation-libya.

[34] ROYAL UNITED SERVICES INSTITUTE, ACCIDENTAL HEROES, *supra* note 24 at 4.

[35] *Id.*

[36] Report of the International Commission of Inquiry (Mar. 2012), *supra* note 26 at Annex I, ¶ 603.

[37] Christian F. Anrig, *Allied Air Power over Libya*, 91 AIR AND SPACE POWER JOURNAL 89 (Winter 2011).

Naval Forces in Europe and Africa.[38] Initially, French combat aircraft targeted armored vehicles outside of Benghazi, as U.S. Navy ships launched missiles targeting Libya's air force defense system.[39] United States Defense Department officials reported that the United States and the United Kingdom launched over 110 missiles at air defense systems across Libya while French fighter jets flew sorties striking the regime's military vehicles.[40]

On 23 March, NATO officially began to enforce the arms embargo against Libya, and member countries dispatched warships to the region to intercept sea transports carrying equipment to Libya. The next day, on 24 March, NATO formally enforced the no-fly zone.[41] On 31 March, NATO assumed sole command and control of the international military effort to enforce all aspects of Security Council Resolutions 1970 and 1973, as part of Operation Unified Protector (OUP),[42] thereby replacing the individual efforts and operation names. United States military forces remained directly engaged in these operations, while undertaking fewer missions than they had under the auspices of Operation Odyssey Dawn.[43]

On 14 April, the representatives of the countries participating in OUP agreed to commit all necessary resources for as long as necessary until "all attacks on civilians and civilian-populated areas have ended," "the Qadhafi regime withdraws all military and para-military forces to bases" and "the Qadhafi regime permits immediate, full, safe and unhindered access to humanitarian aid for the Libyan people."[44]

The goal of the Libyan mission expanded quickly as NATO and the international community committed to seeing Qadhafi step down. In April, U.S. President Barack Obama, French President Nicolas Sarkozy and British Prime Minister David Cameron published a joint pledge asserting that regime change must take place in order to achieve the stated humanitarian goal of protecting Libyan civilians.[45] The issue came to a head when, in May, Qadhafi offered a ceasefire with the rebels, thereby

---

[38] BLANCHARD, UNREST AND U.S. POLICY, *supra* note 22.

[39] Anrig, *Allied Air Power over Libya, supra* note 37 at 10.

[40] Allan Little, *Libya: US, UK and France attack Gaddafi forces*, BBC, Mar. 20, 2011, *available at* http://www.bbc.co.uk/news/world-africa-12796972.

[41] *NATO and Libya: Operation Unified Protector*, NORTH ATLANTIC TREATY ORGANIZATION, *available at* http://www.nato.int/cps/en/natolive/topics_71652.htm.

[42] *Id.*

[43] BLANCHARD, UNREST AND U.S. POLICY, *supra* note 22 at 7.

[44] Tony White, *A chronology of NATO's involvement in Libya*, ROYAL CANADIAN AIRFORCE, Apr. 12, 2011, *available at* http://www.rcaf-arc.forces.gc.ca/v2/nr-sp/index-eng.asp?id=12783.

[45] Amatai Etzioni, *The Lessons of Libya*, 92 MILITARY REVIEW 45, 49 (Jan.–Feb. 2012).

ending attacks against civilians, but which would allow him to stay in power. NATO rejected the Libyan offer, determined that regime change was the only solution.[46]

Warplanes from eight countries conducted airstrikes: Belgium, Canada, Denmark, France, Italy, Norway, the United Kingdom and the United States.[47] As of 22 August, French, British and American warplanes were responsible for approximately 60 percent of the strike sorties.[48] By the end of NATO's operations, sources reported higher figures for the percentage of strikes carried out by U.S. and UK forces: 19 and 21 percent of the total sorties, respectively.[49] The UAE was the only Middle Eastern state to reportedly have conducted airstrikes in Libya.[50]

At its peak, NATO deployed 20 ships and more than 250 aircraft to enforce Resolution 1973.[51] OUP ceased operations on 31 October 2011.[52] NATO's final mission statistics report that between 31 March and 31 October 2011, OUP carried out 26,500 sorties in Libya, 9,700 of which were strike sorties – strikes that are intended to identify and engage appropriate targets, but do not necessarily deploy munitions each time.[53] These strike sorties resulted in the destruction of more than 5,900 military

---

[46] *Id.*

[47] Norway reportedly withdrew from conducting strike sorties as of 1 August. Other countries, such as Sweden, Qatar, and the Netherlands, participated in other missions, enforcing the no-fly zone and conducting surveillance. *See* J. Benitez, *National Composition of NATO Strike Sorties in Libya*, ATLANTIC COUNCIL, Aug. 22, 2011, *available at* http://www.acus.org/natosource/national-composition-nato-strike-sorties-libya.

[48] According to the Atlantic Council, France carried out approximately 33 percent of all strike sorties, Denmark 11 percent, Britain 10 percent, the United States 16 percent, Canada 10 percent, Italy 10 percent, and Norway 10 percent. *See Id.*

[49] C.J. Chivers & Eric Schmitt, *In Strikes on Libya by NATO, an Unspoken Civilian Toll*, N.Y. TIMES, Dec. 17, 2011, *available at* http://www.nytimes.com/2011/12/18/world/africa/scores-of-unintended-casualties-in-nato-war-in-libya.html; HUMAN RIGHTS WATCH, UNACKNOWLEDGED DEATHS, *supra* note 5 at 20.

[50] The UAE used the PGM-500 "Hakim" guided bomb fired from Mirage 2000 aircraft. This was the first operational use of the "Hakim." For a photo of an unexploded "Hakim" destroyed by sappers, *see* David Cenciotti, *Photo: Unexploded MBDA PGM-500 500-lb guided bomb "Hakim" blown at Zintan, Libya*, THE AVIATIONIST, July 12, 2012, *available at* http://theaviationist.com/tag/uae-air-force/#.UMDQkJPjlAE. *See also Power Brokers – Qatar and the UAE take center stage*, JANE'S INTELLIGENCE REVIEW, Dec. 21 2011, *available at* http://articles.janes.com/articles/Janes-Intelligence-Review-2012/Power-brokers--Qatar-and-the-UAE-take-centre-stage.html.

[51] *NATO and Libya: Operation Unified Protector*, NATO, *available at* http://www.nato.int/cps/en/natolive/topics_71652.htm.

[52] *Id.*

[53] *Operation Unified Protector Final Mission Stats*, NORTH ATLANTIC TREATY ORGANIZATION, Nov. 2, 2011, *available at* http://www.nato.int/nato_static/assets/pdf/pdf_2011_11/20111108_111107-factsheet_up_factsfigures_en.pdf.

targets, including more than 400 artillery pieces or rocket launchers, and more than 600 tanks or armored vehicles.[54] According to NATO legal adviser Peter Olson, 25,944 strikes were made during the campaign. Of those, 25,011 were carried out by fixed-wing aircraft, 424 by rotary-wing aircraft (helicopters) and 509 by unmanned aerial vehicles (drones).[55] Of the 7,642 air-to-surface weapons used, 3,644 were laser-guided bombs, 2,844 were GPS-guided munitions, 1,150 were precision-guided direct fire weapons (such as electro-optically guided missiles), and four were miscellaneous precision-guided munitions.[56]

2.1. The U.S. Role in the NATO Operations

Domestic political conditions in the United States posed a challenge to the Obama administration's military's involvement in Libya. United States lawmakers maintained that the use of military force required Congress or Senate approval and introduced initiatives to challenge the President's continued action in Libya. The U.S. President provided a letter to Congress on 21 March 2011 citing his "constitutional authority to conduct U.S. foreign relations as Commander in Chief and Chief Executive," and stated he would "keep the Congress fully informed, consistent with the War Powers Resolution."[57] The President also made clear early on that the United States would not deploy ground forces, that the mission was not the overthrow of Qadhafi, and that "broadening the military operation to include regime change would be a mistake."[58]

As the mission dragged on, continued United States involvement in the operations reignited debate over longstanding questions concerning the President's constitutional authority to use military force without congressional authorization.[59] President Obama maintained that the White House did not need congressional authorization to continue the mission

---

[54] *Id.*

[55] Letter from Paul Olson to Philippe Kirsch, Chair of the International Commission of Inquiry (Jan. 23 2012), in Report of the International Commission of Inquiry (Mar. 2012), *supra* note 26 at Annex II.

[56] *Id.*

[57] BLANCHARD, UNREST AND U.S. POLICY, *supra* note 22 at 9.

[58] Barack Obama, President, United States of America, *Remarks by the President in Address to the Nation on Libya*, Mar. 28, 2011, *available at* http://www.whitehouse.gov/the-press-office/2011/03/28/remarks-president-address-nation-libya.

[59] MICHAEL JOHN GARCIA, CONGRESSIONAL RESEARCH SERVICE, WAR POWERS LITIGATION INITIATED BY MEMBERS OF CONGRESS SINCE THE ENACTMENT OF THE WAR POWERS RESOLUTION (June 22, 2011) [hereinafter "WAR POWERS LITIGATION"], *available at* http://www.fas.org/sgp/crs/natsec/RL30352.pdf.

because U.S. forces were not engaged in "hostilities" within the meaning of the War Powers Resolution.[60] Congressional representatives directly challenged this assertion, and on 15 June, ten members of the House of Representatives filed suit in the U.S. District Court for the District of Columbia challenging the lawfulness of U.S. participation in military actions in Libya.[61] In the face of such challenges from the legislature, by 20 June the United States was nearly forced to withdraw from OUP.[62]

United States military involvement was critical to the mission in Libya. President Obama stated that the U.S. military efforts were "focused on unique U.S. military capabilities."[63] The United States played an important role in the conflict, coordinating early NATO operations and providing drones for reconnaissance and intelligence gathering missions.[64] Even after handing over operational control to NATO, the New York Times, citing unnamed officials, reported that U.S. warplanes hit some 60 Libyan targets, while unmanned U.S. drones fired roughly 30 times.[65] Other sources confirm the operations included manned U.S. fighter aircraft along with unmanned U.S. aerial vehicles to conduct strikes against ground targets as part of the NATO mission.[66] United States Secretary of Defense Robert Gates announced the authorization of the use of Predator drones and explained their unique capabilities during a press conference in late April.[67]

United States Permanent Representative to NATO, Ambassador Ivo Daalder, gave a summary of the NATO operations in September 2011, emphasizing

---

[60] Charlie Savage & Thom Shanker, *In Libya, Scores of U.S. Airstrikes Followed Handoff to NATO*, N.Y. Times, June 20, 2011, *available at* http://www.nytimes.com/2011/06/21/world/africa/21powers.html.

[61] Garcia, War Powers Litigation, *supra* note 59.

[62] *Congress Threatens To Cut Off Funding For War In Libya; Obama Weighs US Troop Withdrawal From Afghanistan: Today's Q's for O's WH – 6/20/2011*, ABC News, June 20, 2011, *available at* http://abcnews.go.com/blogs/politics/2011/06/congress-threatens-to-cut-off-funding-for-war-in-libya-obama-weighs-us-troop-withdrawal-from-afghani.

[63] Blanchard, Unrest and U.S. Policy, *supra* note 22 at 9.

[64] C.J. Chivers & Eric Schmitt, *In Strikes on Libya by NATO, an Unspoken Civilian Toll*, *supra* note 49; David Cloud, *U.S. begins using Predator drones in Libya*, L.A. Times, Apr. 22, 2011 *available at* http://articles.latimes.com/2011/apr/22/world/la-fg-gates-libya-20110422.

[65] Charlie Savage & Thom Shanker, *In Libya, Scores of U.S. Airstrikes Followed Handoff to NATO*, *supra* note 60.

[66] Garcia, War Powers Litigation, *supra* note 59 at 14, n. 80.

[67] Andrew North, *Libya: US to Deploy Armed Drones – Robert Gates*, BBC, Apr. 22, 2011, *available at* http://www.bbc.co.uk/news/world-africa-13166441.

It was the United States that took out the air defense system in Libya in the opening part of this operation and continued to suppress enemy air defenses throughout the conflict as well as provided a critical precision targeting capability by deploying armed Predators. It was the United States that provided the bulk of the intelligence, surveillance and reconnaissance information that was critical for the conduct of this operation in all of its aspects, at sea and in the air. It was the United States that provided the critical targeters who were able to translate information into targets. And it was the United States that provided the critical air refueling capability that allowed countries to sustain their combat operations in the air.[68]

3. The Legal Framework for the Use of Force

The NATO intervention in Libya raised concerns over violations of international law, in particular also over the use of force by foreign actors. The use of armed force by states is regulated by customary and conventional international law. In general terms, two separate legal regimes apply to the use of force, each with its own set of rules. The first regime is the *jus ad bellum*, or law of the conflict, which deals solely with the legality of engaging in the use of force, and does not concern the means and methods by which belligerents use force. The *jus ad bellum* was the subject of a number of treaties in the 1920s, including most prominently the Kellogg-Briand Pact of 1928,[69] and was within the jurisdiction of the International Military Tribunal at Nuremberg (IMT).[70] In contemporary practice, the *jus ad bellum* is regulated and circumscribed by the customary law of self-defense and the provisions contained in the UN Charter.[71]

The second regime is the *jus in bello*, or law in the conflict, which deals solely with the means and methods used by belligerents in the course of fighting, and does not address the legality of the conflict itself. The *jus in bello* has been codified in a significant number of international instruments, including the Geneva Conventions,[72] which make up the corpus of

---

[68] Ivo Daalder, U.S. Ambassador to NATO, *Remarks to the Press on Libya and Operation Unified Protector*, Sep. 8, 2011, *available at* http://nato.usmission.gov/libya-oup-90811.html.

[69] General Treaty for Renunciation of War as an Instrument of National Policy, Aug. 28, 1928, 46 Stat. 2343, 94 L.N.T.S. 57.

[70] *See* Charter of the International Military Tribunal – Annex to the Agreement for the prosecution and punishment of the major war criminals of the European Axis, Aug. 8, 1945 [hereinafter "London Agreement"].

[71] *See generally* UN Charter, *supra* note 14.

[72] *See e.g.*, Geneva Convention Relative to the Treatment of Prisoners of War (Third Geneva Convention), Aug. 12, 1949, 75 UNTS 135; Geneva Convention Relative to the

international humanitarian law (IHL). The two fundamental precepts of the *jus in bello* is the rule of distinction, which require that belligerents distinguish between targets and only attack legitimate targets (*i.e.*, non-civilian objects), and the rule of proportionality, which requires that collateral or incidental loss of civilian life or damage to civilian objects not be excessive in relation to the military advantage gained from an attack.[73]

In essence, the *jus ad bellum* regulates when and why belligerents may lawfully engage in combat, while the *jus in bello* regulates how those belligerents shall fight. The legal analyses of the *jus ad bellum* and the *jus in bello* are based upon distinct sets of rules, and a determination that one has been violated does not affect the assessment of the other.[74] Stated another way, each set of rules is binding upon states: the legitimacy of the belligerents' initiation of war does not entitle them to intentionally violate IHL, or fail to prevent or punish violations of IHL by combatants. Accordingly, there are four conceivable types of conflicts: wars that are waged legitimately and whose combatants adhere to IHL norms; wars that are waged legitimately but whose combatants violate IHL norms; wars that are waged illegitimately but whose combatants adhere to IHL norms; and wars that are waged illegitimately and whose combatants violate IHL norms.

The clearest exposition of the *jus ad bellum* is found in Article 2(4) of the UN Charter, which provides that, "All Members shall refrain in their international relations from the threat or use of force against the territorial integrity or political independence of any state, or in any other manner inconsistent with the Purposes of the United Nations."[75] Further, Article 2(7) of the Charter provides that

> Nothing contained in the present Charter shall authorize the United Nations to intervene in matters which are essentially within the domestic jurisdiction of any state or shall require the Members to submit such matters to

---

Protection of Civilian Persons in Time of War (Fourth Geneva Convention), Aug. 12, 1949, 75 UNTS 287.

[73] The rules of distinction and proportionality are discussed in greater length in Sec. 5.2, *infra*.

[74] The contrary has been argued on occasion. For instance, the judgment of the International Military Tribunal held that a war of aggression, the *sine qua non* violation of the *jus ad bellum* injunction, "is not only an international crime; it is the supreme international crime differing only from other war crimes in that it contains within itself the accumulated evil of the whole." Nuremberg Judgment, p. 426, *available at* http://avalon.law.yale.edu/imt/09-30-46.asp.

[75] Art. 2(4), UN Charter, *supra* note 14.

settlement under the present Charter; but this principle shall not prejudice the application of enforcement measures under Chapter VII.[76]

There are only two recognized exceptions to Articles 2(4) and 2(7) in the UN Charter, namely self-defense under Article 51,[77] or when acting with authorization from the Security Council under the color of its Chapter VII powers to address "threats to the peace, breaches of the peace, and acts of aggression."[78] Formally, the UN Charter only recognizes the legitimacy of armed conflict in these very limited situations.[79] Armed conflicts outside these exceptions are not legitimate and are accordingly in breach of international law.

Notably, the UN Charter does not recognize the use of force for humanitarian grounds or for "regime change." Recent attempts to enlarge the formal sanction of the use of armed conflict for humanitarian reasons, most notably the so-called "Responsibility to Protect" doctrine,[80] have not affected the fundamental presumption against military action outside of the most limited set of circumstances, namely in self-defense against an act of aggression by another state, or when the Security Council invokes its Chapter VII mandate. The *jus ad bellum* is a fundamentally conservative doctrine that posits the inviolability of state sovereignty, and as such is a continuation of the Westphalian system of state sovereignty that arose after the end of the Thirty Years War in 1648.

The permissibility of self-defense recognized in Article 51 of the UN Charter is unquestioned, although it is subject to debate when an attack is only threatened or in an inchoate form. The contemporary debate over preemptive wars, most notably the U.S. invasion of Iraq or Israeli air strikes in Syria, very likely exceed permissible self-defense and qualify as aggressive conduct.

---

[76] *Id.* at Art. 2(7).

[77] *Id.* at Art. 51. Article 51 codifies the customary law "right of individual or collective self-defence if an armed attack occurs against a Member of the United Nations, until the Security Council has taken measures necessary to maintain international peace and security."

[78] *Id.* at Ch. VII.

[79] The now obsolete Article 107 of the UN Charter created an exception "in relation to any state which during the Second World War has been an enemy of any signatory to the present Charter, taken or authorized as a result of that war by the Governments having responsibility for such action." Art. 107, UN Charter, *supra* note 14.

[80] INTERNATIONAL COMMISSION ON INTERVENTION AND STATE SOVEREIGNTY, THE RESPONSIBILITY TO PROTECT (Ottawa: ICISS, 2001) [hereinafter "ICISS R2P"], *available at* http://responsibilitytoprotect.org/ICISS%20Report.

The requirements for UN sanctioned armed conflict are spelled out in Chapter VII of the UN Charter. This is noteworthy because it authorizes armed conflict outside of self-defense, thus transforming and legitimizing what would otherwise qualify as aggressive war, which is illegal. Chapter VII provides a checklist for the authorization of armed force. First, under Article 39, the Security Council must "determine the existence of any threat to the peace, breach of the peace or act of aggression..."[81] Second, it "shall make recommendations, or decide what measures shall be taken in accordance with Articles 41 and 42, to maintain or restore international peace and security."[82] Third it must consider measures available under Article 41, which provides for the imposition of non-military options, including sanctions and the disruption of the internal workings of the affected state.[83] Fourth, if the Security Council determines "that measures provided for in Article 41 would be inadequate or have proved to be inadequate" it may authorize military action under Article 42, including "demonstrations, blockade, and other operations by air, sea, or land forces" in order to "maintain or restore international peace and security."[84] Finally, under Article 43, Member States shall "undertake to make available to the Security Council, on its call and in accordance with a special agreement or agreements, armed forces, assistance, and facilities, including rights of passage, necessary for the purpose of maintaining international peace and security."[85]

The UN Charter was adopted in 1945 against the backdrop of World War II, in which an estimated 60 million people died, and just a generation after World War I resulted in the deaths of an estimated 37 million. The centrality of these wars was recognized in the Charter's Preamble, which declared the signatories' intent "to save succeeding generations from the scourge of war, which twice in our lifetime has brought untold sorrow to mankind."[86] Clearly, while sovereign inviolability was paramount, the

---

[81] Art. 39, UN Charter, *supra* note 14.

[82] *Id.*

[83] *Id.* at Art. 41. Article 41 provides that "The Security Council may decide what measures not involving the use of armed force are to be employed to give effect to its decisions, and it may call upon the Members of the United Nations to apply such measures. These may include complete or partial interruption of economic relations and of rail, sea, air, postal, telegraphic, radio, and other means of communication, and the severance of diplomatic relations."

[84] *Id.* at Art. 42.

[85] *Id.* at Art. 43.

[86] Preamble, UN Charter, *supra* note 14.

new international system desired a limited mechanism for intervention, which was codified in Chapter VII of the UN Charter.

Violations of the *jus ad bellum* were originally qualified as crimes against peace and later as aggression.[87] Article 6(a) of the London Charter of the International Military Tribunal (IMT) used the phrase "crime of aggression" to criminalize the "planning, preparation, initiation or waging of a war of aggression, or a war in violation of international treaties, agreements or assurances, or participation in a common plan or conspiracy for the accomplishment of any of the foregoing."[88] A similar provision was included in the Tokyo Charter of the International Military Tribunal for the Far East (IMTFE).[89] The IMT entered convictions for crimes against peace against several defendants, although during the Subsequent Nuremberg Trials several accused were acquitted due to the lack of evidence that they maintained effective control over the military and police forces under their command.[90]

Several years later, the General Assembly underscored the central importance of aggression, affirming that "whatever the weapons used, any aggression, whether committed openly, or by fomenting civil strife in the interest of a foreign power, or otherwise, is the gravest of all crimes against peace and security throughout the world."[91] In response to several calls by the General Assembly,[92] the International Law Commission (ILC) was tasked with creating a modern definition of aggression, which it was unable to do. Eventually the General Assembly adopted a definition of aggression in 1974 in Resolution 3314, which forms the basis for the modern definition of aggression that was adopted by the Assembly of States Parties at the Kampala Review Conference of the ICC in 2010. Resolution 3314 defines aggression as "the use of armed force by a State against the sovereignty, territorial integrity or political independence of another

---

[87] For a detailed survey of the history of the crime of aggression, *see* M. CHERIF BASSIOUNI, INTRODUCTION TO INTERNATIONAL CRIMINAL LAW, SECOND REVISED EDITION 632–42 (Leiden, The Netherlands: Martinus Nijhoff, 2d ed., 2013); M. Cherif Bassiouni & Benjamin Ferencz, *The Crime Against Peace, in* 1 INTERNATIONAL CRIMINAL LAW: CRIMES 167–97 (M. Cherif Bassiouni ed., 1986).

[88] London Agreement, *supra* note 70 at Art. 6(a).

[89] Article 5(a), Charter of the International Military Tribunal for the Far East, Jan. 19, 1946.

[90] *See e.g.*, the *I.G. Farben, Krupp* and *High Command* cases.

[91] GA Res. 380 (V), Nov. 7, 1950, UN Doc. A/RES/380 (V) at ¶ 1.

[92] GA Res. 177 (II), 21 Nov. 1947, UN Doc. A/RES/177 (II); GA Res. 378 B (V), Nov. 17, 1950, UN Doc. A/RES/378 B (V).

State, or in any other manner inconsistent with the Charter of the United Nations" and provides a non-exhaustive list of aggressive acts.[93]

In 1991, the ILC again took up the question of aggression and sought to formulate an adequate definition. Despite working on the issue for five years, the Commission was unable to generate consensus on the matter. Similar problems befell the drafters of the Rome Statute of the ICC, who could not agree on a definition, the conditions of exercising jurisdiction, the scope of the ICC's jurisdiction or the triggering mechanisms for jurisdiction.[94]

Ultimately a compromise was reached and aggression was listed in Article 5(1) of the Rome Statute among the four subject matter crimes over which the Court would have jurisdiction, in addition to genocide, crimes against humanity and war crimes.[95] Article 5(2), however, stipulated that aggression would only come under the competence of the Court after "defining the crime and setting out the conditions under which the Court shall exercise jurisdiction with respect to this crime."[96] In order to satisfy Article 5(2), the Assembly of States Parties formed a Special Working Group on the Crime of Aggression (SWGCA), which was tasked with addressing these unresolved issues. This was not achieved until June 2010, when States Parties assembled in Kampala to debate the matter on the basis of the text adopted by the SWGCA. The resulting amendment to the Rome Statute inserted the following definition as Article 8*bis*

1. For the purpose of this Statute, "crime of aggression" means the planning, preparation, initiation or execution, by a person in a position effectively to exercise control over or to direct the political or military action of a State, of an act of aggression which, by its character, gravity and scale, constitutes a manifest violation of the Charter of the United Nations.
2. For the purpose of paragraph 1, "act of aggression" means the use of armed force by a State against the sovereignty, territorial integrity or political independence of another State, or in any other manner inconsistent with the Charter of the United Nations. Any of the following acts, regardless of a declaration of war, shall, in accordance with United Nations General Assembly resolution 3314 (XXIX) of 14 December 1974, qualify as an act of aggression:

---

[93] GA Res. 3314 (XXIX) of Dec. 14, 1974, UN Doc. A/RES/3314 (XXIX) at ¶ 1.

[94] BASSIOUNI, INTRODUCTION TO INTERNATIONAL CRIMINAL LAW, *supra* note 87 at 634.

[95] Rome Statute of the International Criminal Court, July 17, 1998, 2187 U.N.T.S. 90 at Art. 5(1).

[96] Art. 5(2) was deleted in accordance with RC/Res.6, annex I, of June 11 2010.

(a) The invasion or attack by the armed forces of a State of the territory of another State, or any military occupation, however temporary, resulting from such invasion or attack, or any annexation by the use of force of the territory of another State or part thereof;

(b) Bombardment by the armed forces of a State against the territory of another State or the use of any weapons by a State against the territory of another State;

(c) The blockade of the ports or coasts of a State by the armed forces of another State;

(d) An attack by the armed forces of a State on the land, sea or air forces, or marine and air fleets of another State;

(e) The use of armed forces of one State which are within the territory of another State with the agreement of the receiving State, in contravention of the conditions provided for in the agreement or any extension of their presence in such territory beyond the termination of the agreement;

(f) The action of a State in allowing its territory, which it has placed at the disposal of another State, to be used by that other State for perpetrating an act of aggression against a third State;

(g) The sending by or on behalf of a State of armed bands, groups, irregulars or mercenaries, which carry out acts of armed force against another State of such gravity as to amount to the acts listed above, or its substantial involvement therein.[97]

It should be noted, however, that despite agreement on the text of Article 8*bis*, the ICC only gains jurisdiction over the crime of aggression one year after 30 States Parties have ratified the amendment, and after an affirmative vote of two thirds of States Parties after 1 January 2017.[98] As of May 2013, only five states have ratified the amendment.[99] Accordingly, the ICC did not enjoy jurisdiction over the crime of aggression at any point during the Libyan civil war despite having adopted a definition and trigger mechanism, described above. Moreover, beyond possible direct perpetration of aggression, Article 8*bis*(2)(f) would have given the court jurisdiction over states that "allow[ed] its territory, which it has placed at the disposal of another State, to be used by that other State for perpetrating an act of aggression against a third State."

---

[97] Res. RC/Res. 6, UN Doc. RC/Res. 6 (June 11 2010), annex I–II.

[98] *Id.* at Art. 15*bis*, ¶ 3.

[99] The states are: Estonia, Lichtenstein, Luxembourg, Samoa, and Trinidad and Tobago.

4. THE SECURITY COUNCIL'S PRACTICE UNDER CHAPTER VII
AND THE USE OF FORCE

In 1945, war was almost universally understood to be between sovereign states, as in WWI and WWII, and the practice of the Security Council reflected this. The war between North and South Korea remains a prime example of an international armed conflict in the Charter era. Although the resulting Security Council Resolutions did not invoke Chapter VII or specific articles by name, they did authorize military action under the "unified command under the United States of America."[100]

Throughout the course of the Cold War, and especially in the decades since its end, the nature of conflict has changed dramatically. International armed conflicts have lost their preeminence, and today armed conflicts of a non-international or purely internal character are most common. Consequently, the Security Council has adapted its practice to account for this change, finding that internal disputes pose a threat to international peace and security, although more recent examples of international armed conflict exist, as with the Iraqi invasion of Kuwait in 1990.[101]

One of the earliest examples of Security Council action on non-international armed conflicts arose in the context of South African Apartheid. For instance in Resolution 134, the Security Council determined that "the situation in the Union of South Africa is one that has led to international friction and if continued might endanger international peace and security."[102] Although the Council did not authorize military intervention under Article 42 "to maintain or restore international peace and security," it did request "the Secretary-General, in consultation with the Government of the Union of South Africa, to make such arrangements as would adequately help in upholding the purposes and principles of the Charter."[103]

Since the adoption of Resolution 134 in 1960, the Security Council has increasingly relied on Chapter VII to make a finding of a threat to international peace and security in internal conflicts. With the end of the Cold War it has developed this further to justify humanitarian intervention, including in Kuwait, where the Council found that internal repression was

---

[100] *See* SC Res. 84 (1950), July 7 1950, UN Doc. S/RES/84 (1950). *See also* SC Res. 82 (1950), June 27 1950, UN Doc. S/RES/83 (1950).

[101] SC Res. 678 (1990), Nov. 29 1990, UN Doc. S/RES/678 (1990).

[102] SC Res. 134 (1960), Apr. 1 1960, UN Doc. S/RES/134 (1960). Note, however, that Security Council Resolution 134 simply determined a threat to peace and security existed but did not make a special appeal to the use of force by Member States under Art. 42.

[103] *Id.*

causing refugee flows and a threat to international peace and security, which was interpreted as justifying a no-fly zone;[104] Somalia, where the Council found that the "heavy loss" of life and destruction of the country's material infrastructure constituted a threat to international peace and security, and authorized the "use [of] all necessary means to establish as soon as possible a secure environment for humanitarian relief operations in Somalia;"[105] the former Yugoslavia, where the Council determined that the heavy loss of life and the country's material destruction caused refugee flows that constituted a threat to international peace and security, and authorized the establishment of the United Nations Protection Force, which enabled military engagement in the former Yugoslavia;[106] and Rwanda, where the Council found that genocide and other IHL violations resulted in a "humanitarian crisis of enormous proportions" that constituted a threat to international peace and security, and therefore expanded the mandate of the United Nations Assistance Mission for Rwanda and authorized Member States to "us[e] all necessary means to achieve the humanitarian objectives" set out in the Resolution.[107]

While the Security Council has greatly expanded its interpretation of Chapter VII in order to account for humanitarian emergencies, no similar expansion has occurred for political emergencies. Not once in its history has the Security Council authorized or justified military intervention for the purpose of regime change or the promotion of a different governmental structure. Indeed, doing so would be a clear violation of Article 2(4) of the UN Charter, which protects the "territorial integrity" and "political integrity" of all states. In short, the only justification for military intervention into the internal affairs of a state are humanitarian grounds. Justifications for regime change have been made on the grounds of humanitarian needs, but government overthrow has never, and could never, form the sole or principal reason for Chapter VII action.[108]

---

[104] SC Res. 688 (1991), Apr. 5, 1991, UN Doc. S/RES/688 (1991). Note, however, that the Resolution did not explicitly reference military intervention.

[105] SC Res. 733 (1992), Jan. 23, 1992, UN Doc. S/RES/733 (1992); SC Res. 794 (1992), 3 Dec. 1992, UN Doc. S/RES/794 (1992).

[106] SC Res. 713 (1991), Sept. 25, 1991, UN Doc. S/RES/713 (1991); SC Res. 743 (1992), 21 Feb. 1992, UN Doc. S/RES/743 (1992).

[107] SC Res. 929 (1994), June 22, 1994, UN Doc. S/RES/929 (1994). *See also* SC Res. 918 (1994), 17 May 1994, UN Doc. S/RES/918 (1994).

[108] *See generally* Mehrdad Payandeh, *The United Nations, Military Intervention, And Regime Change In Libya*, 52 VA. J. INT'L L. 355, 369 (2012).

In those instances where Security Council action has authorized military intervention for explicitly political reasons, as in Haiti, it has been to restore a civilian government after a *coup d'état*, and with the support of the legitimate government of Jean-Bertrand Aristide.[109] The same is true of Sierra Leone, where the legitimate government of President Ahmad Tejan Kabbah was overthrown by the military, which renamed itself the Armed Forces Revolutionary Council and joined the rebel Revolutionary United Front, but was later ousted by the Economic Community of West African States (ECOWAS) and UN forces.[110]

As a matter of law, the UN Charter reserves to the Security Council the "primary responsibility" of maintaining international peace and security. This power is codified in Article 24 of the Charter, which provides that

1. In order to ensure prompt and effective action by the United Nations, its Members confer on the Security Council primary responsibility for the maintenance of international peace and security, and agree that in carrying out its duties under this responsibility the Security Council acts on their behalf.
2. In discharging these duties the Security Council shall act in accordance with the Purposes and Principles of the United Nations. The specific powers granted to the Security Council for the discharge of these duties are laid down in Chapters VI, VII, VIII, and XII.

It should be noted that Article 24(1) only extends the "primary responsibility" of preserving peace and security to the Security Council.[111] There

---

[109] SC Res. 940 (1994), July 31 1994, UN Doc. S/RES/940 (1994). Article 4 of the Resolution states:
> Acting under Chapter VII of the Charter of the United Nations, authorizes Member States to form a multinational force under unified command and control and, in this framework, to use all necessary means to facilitate the departure from Haiti of the military leadership, consistent with the Governors Island Agreement, the prompt return of the legitimately elected President and the restoration of the legitimate authorities of the Government of Haiti, and to establish and maintain a secure and stable environment that will permit implementation of the Governors Island Agreement, on the understanding that the cost of implementing this temporary operation will be borne by the participating Member States.

[110] *See* SC Res. 1313 (2000), Aug. 4 2000, UN Doc. S/RES/1313 (2000); SC Res. 1270 (1999), Oct. 22 1999, UN Doc. S/RES/1270 (1999); SC Res. 1132 (1997), Oct. 8 1997, UN Doc. S/RES/1132 (1997).

[111] The supplementary authority of the General Assembly in this respect has arisen in the context of its "Uniting for Peace" power. In General Assembly Resolution 377, the body recognized that primary authority of the Security Council for the maintenance of peace but recognized that the failure of the Security Council and the states to act "failure does not deprive the General Assembly of its rights or relieve it of its responsibilities under the

is nothing in the text of the Charter that prevents other organs or bodies from reviewing the findings of the Security Council, or even from making a finding that there has been a breach of international peace and security.

As a matter of practice, however, Security Council resolutions are not reviewable, irrespective of whether or not they are "in accordance with the Purposes and Principles of the United Nations" as required by Article 24(2) of the UN Charter. UN organs have historically refused to review the acts carried out by each other under the powers ascribed them by the Charter without a direct mandate to that effect. Organs of the United Nations are left to determine their own jurisdiction and procedures, a practice analogous to the power of certain courts to determine their own jurisdiction, which is alternatively known as the *competence de la competence* or *kompetenz-kompetenz*.[112] Under the *competence de la competence* theory, the Security Council has been invested with particular powers by the UN Charter and therefore has absolute power to determine the scope and content of its resolutions, which are outside the competence of any other body and therefore not reviewable.

The question of the Security Council's authority has been taken up on numerous occasions by judicial bodies who have been called upon to rule on attendant questions. In the *Certain Expenses of the United Nations* case

---

Charter in regard to the maintenance of international peace and security." On that basis, the Assembly:

> Resolved that if the Security Council, because of lack of unanimity of the permanent members, fails to exercise its primary responsibility for the maintenance of international peace and security in any case where there appears to be a threat to the peace, breach of the peace, or act of aggression, the General Assembly shall consider the matter immediately with a view to making appropriate recommendations to Members for collective measures, including in the case of a breach of the peace or act of aggression the use of armed force when necessary, to maintain or restore international peace and security. If not in session at the time, the General Assembly may meet in emergency special session within twenty-four hours of the request therefor. Such emergency special session shall be called if requested by the Security Council on the vote of any seven members, or by a majority of the Members of the United Nations;

GA Res. 377, ¶ 1, UN Doc. A/RES/377(V) A (Nov. 3, 1950).

112 *See* IBRAHIM SHIHATA, THE POWER OF THE INTERNATIONAL COURT TO DETERMINE ITS OWN JURISDICTION: COMPETENCE DE LA COMPETENCE (The Hague, The Netherlands: Martinus Nijhoff, 1965). *See also* HANS KÖCHLER, THE SECURITY COUNCIL AS ADMINISTER OF JUSTICE 27–29 (Vienna, Austria: International Progress Organization, 2011); YUSUF AKSAR, IMPLEMENTING INTERNATIONAL HUMANITARIAN LAW 37 (New York, USA: Routledge, 2004).

the International Court of Justice (ICJ) ruled on this very question, and held that

> In the legal systems of States, there is often some procedure for determining the validity of even a legislative or governmental act, but no analogous procedure is to be found in the structure of the United Nations. Proposals made during the drafting of the Charter to place the ultimate authority to interpret the Charter in the International Court of Justice were not accepted; the opinion which the Court is in course of rendering is an advisory opinion. As anticipated in 1945, therefore, *each organ must, in the first place at least, determine its own jurisdiction.*[113]

Similarly, in the *Namibia* case, the ICJ concluded that, "A resolution of a properly constituted organ of the United Nations which is passed in accordance with that organ's rules of procedure, and is declared by its President to have been so passed, must be presumed to have been validly adopted."[114]

The issue was raised again before the Appeals Chamber of the International Criminal Tribunal for the former Yugoslavia (ICTY). In the *Tadić Interlocutory Appeal on Jurisdiction*,[115] the majority upheld the supremacy of the Security Council's determination, although it adopted a slightly more nuanced approach

> *It is the Security Council that makes the determination that there exists one of the situations justifying the use of the "exceptional powers" of Chapter VII. And it is also the Security Council that chooses the reaction to such a situation*: it either makes recommendations (i.e., opts not to use the exceptional powers but to continue to operate under Chapter VI) or decides to use the exceptional powers by ordering measures to be taken in accordance with Articles

---

[113] Certain Expenses of the United Nations (Article 17, paragraph 2, of the Charter), Advisory Opinion, 1962 ICJ Reports 151, ¶ 168 (July 20) (emphasis added). *See also* Interpretation of the Greco-Turkish Agreement of December 1st, 1926 (Final Protocol, Article IV), Advisory Opinion, 1928 P.C.I.J. (ser. B) No. 16 (Aug. 28). In that case the Permanent Court of International Justice held that

> having regard amongst other things to the principle that, as a general rule, any body possessing jurisdictional powers has the right in the first place itself to determine the extent of its jurisdiction – that questions affecting the extent of the jurisdiction of the Mixed Commission must be settled by the Commission itself without action by any other body being necessary.

Interpretation of the Greco-Turkish Agreement of December 1st, *id.* at ¶ 48.

[114] Legal Consequences for States of the Continued Presence of South Africa in Namibia (South West Africa) Notwithstanding Security Council Resolution 276 (1970), Advisory Opinion, 1971 ICJ 16, ¶ 20 (June 21).

[115] *Prosecutor v. Tadić*, Case No. IT-94-1-I, Decision on the Defence Motion for Interlocutory Appeal on Jurisdiction (Int'l Crim. Trib. For the Former Yugoslavia, Oct. 2, 1995).

41 and 42 with a view to maintaining or restoring international peace and security.[116]

The majority continued that

> Once the Security Council determines that a particular situation poses a threat to the peace or that there exists a breach of the peace or an act of aggression, *it enjoys a wide margin of discretion in choosing the course of action*: as noted above ... it can either continue, in spite of its determination, to act via recommendations, i.e., as if it were still within Chapter VI (*"Pacific Settlement of Disputes"*) or it can exercise its exceptional powers under Chapter VII. In the words of Article 39, it would then "decide what measures shall be taken in accordance with Articles 41 and 42, to maintain or restore international peace and security." (United Nations Charter, art. 39.)[117]

The Appeals Chamber thus rejected Duško Tadić's jurisdictional appeal, but not without acknowledging that, "The determination that there exists such a threat [to peace] is not a totally unfettered discretion, as it has to remain, at the very least, within the limits of the Purposes and Principles of the Charter."[118] It did not, however, outline the logical corollary as to whether it had the jurisdiction to review acts not "within the limits of the Purposes and Principles of the Charter," leaving the matter slightly unsettled.

Several judges disagreed with the majority's reasons, however. Judge Li Haopei, in his Separate Opinion to the *Tadić Appeal Judgment*, disputed the Court's jurisdiction to even consider the question of the Council's competence, arguing that

> The Decision, relying on the doctrine of competence-competence, reviews the legality of the resolution of the Security Council on the establishment of this Tribunal. However, the said doctrine, properly understood, only allows the Tribunal to examine and determine its own jurisdiction, while here it has been improperly extended to the examination of the competence and appropriateness of the resolution of the Security Council on the establishment of this Tribunal. As Article 1 of the Statute of this Tribunal only grants this Tribunal "the power to prosecute persons responsible for serious violations of international humanitarian law committed in the territory of the former Yugoslavia since 1991 in accordance with the provisions of the present Statute", and as the Charter of the United Nations also has never given this Tribunal the power of reviewing the legality of the resolutions of

---

[116] *Id.* at ¶ 29 (emphasis added).
[117] *Id.* at ¶ 31 (emphasis added).
[118] *Id.* at ¶ 29.

the Security Council, it is crystal clear that this Tribunal has no such power. So this review is *ultra vires* and unlawful.[119]

The Separate Opinion of Judge Rustam Sohrabji Sidhwa,[120] while warning that the Charter did not permit the Security Council "to act according to its whims or purely on capricious considerations,"[121] concluded that "any attempt to limit the exercise of discretion in any form could destroy the very basis for which Article 39 has been created."[122] Ultimately,

> [T]he Security Council...with delegated authority from its Member States, acting within a much limited and sensitive field, has been given the power of taking important decisions. Thus, what follows is that each principal organ is competent to decide the scope of its authority, within the ambit of the Charter provisions, and to determine for itself the nature of the action it can take. Each organ respects the independence of the others and refrains from interfering in their working. Nowhere has any principal organ been given the power to judicially review the action of any other principal organ or of any sub-organ created by it.[123]

The authority of the Security Council in such matters is seemingly absolute to apply Chapter VII powers to any conflict, even ones that are completely internal such as in Somalia.[124]

5. THE SECURITY COUNCIL AND THE LIBYAN CONFLICT

The Security Council addressed the conflict in Libya on two occasions in 2011; first on 26 February when it adopted Resolution 1970, and again on 17 March when it adopted Resolution 1973. The former authorized non-military measures, while the latter authorized military engagement on humanitarian grounds, thus prompting engagement by NATO.

Resolution 1970 considered that "the widespread and systematic attacks currently taking place in the Libyan Arab Jamahiriya against the civilian population may amount to crimes against humanity" and expressed

---

[119] *Prosecutor v. Tadić*, Case No. IT-94-1-I, Separate Opinion of Judge Li on the Defence Motion for Interlocutory Appeal on Jurisdiction, ¶ 2 (Int'l Crim. Trib. For the Former Yugoslavia, Oct. 2, 1995).

[120] *Prosecutor v. Tadić*, Case No. IT-94-1-I, Separate Opinion of Judge Sidhwa on the Defence Motion for Interlocutory Appeal on Jurisdiction (Int'l Crim. Trib. For the Former Yugoslavia, Oct. 2, 1995).

[121] *Id.* at ¶ 21.

[122] *Id.* at ¶ 22.

[123] *Id.* at ¶ 26.

[124] ICISS R2P, *supra*, note 80 at ¶ 2.26.

concern over the plight of refugees.[125] It did not, however, find that the situation in Libya constituted a threat to international peace and security beyond identifying the Council's "primary responsibility for the maintenance of international peace and security under the Charter of the United Nations." Despite failing to make a finding that the situation constituted a threat to international peace and security, the Council invoked its Chapter VII powers. Using its powers under Article 41, the Council referred the situation in Libya to the ICC,[126] imposed an embargo on all arms and materiel,[127] banned the travel of senior government members,[128] and froze the assets of various senior government members and government entities.[129]

Several issues arise out of Resolution 1970. First, the arms embargo empowered individual states to conduct arms inspections of ships bound to and from Libya. While not in the nature of armed intervention, NATO forces deployed surveillance aircraft and naval ships which had the authority to stop and board vessels with military forces, for instance, to monitor the embargo. On 8 March, a week and a half after the adoption of Resolution 1970, "NATO stepped up its surveillance operations in the Mediterranean."[130]

Second, while the Resolution referred the situation to the ICC for investigation, it did create an exemption that

> [N]ationals, current or former officials or personnel from a State outside the Libyan Arab Jamahiriya which is not a party to the Rome Statute of the International Criminal Court shall be subject to the exclusive jurisdiction of that State for all alleged acts or omissions arising out of or related to operations in the Libyan Arab Jamahiriya established or authorized by the Council, unless such exclusive jurisdiction has been expressly waived by the State.[131]

When the Resolution was adopted there were no authorized foreign military operations in Libya other than the aforementioned arms inspections.

---

[125] SC Res. 1970 (2011), *supra* note 2.

[126] *Id.* at ¶¶ 4–8.

[127] *Id.* at ¶¶ 9–14.

[128] *Id.* at ¶¶ 15–16.

[129] *Id.* at ¶¶ 17–21.

[130] *NATO and Libya: Precursor to Operation Unified Protector*, NORTH ATLANTIC TREATY ORGANIZATION, Mar. 28, 2011, available at http://www.nato.int/cps/en/natolive/topics_71652.htm.

[131] SC Res. 1970 (2011), *supra* note 2 at ¶ 6.

The exemption perhaps foreshadowed future military engagement in Libya.

On 17 March, the Security Council revisited the burgeoning civil war in Libya, and adopted Resolution 1973.[132] The Resolution again expressed "grave concern at the deteriorating situation, the escalation of violence, and the heavy civilian casualties" and again expressed its concern over the plight of refugees, but did not make an explicit finding that the violence constituted a threat to international peace and security. The Council did, however, invoke Chapter VII of the Charter to authorize the use of force with "all necessary measures" by Member States in order to protect civilians under threat of attack from Qadhafi's government forces. It should be noted that despite making this authorization, the Security Council did not cite Article 42 of the Charter which serves as the basis for authorizing the use of force under Chapter VII when non-military measures (*e.g.*, sanctions) would be or had proven to be inadequate to restore peace.

Resolution 1973 also established a no-fly zone "in order to help protect civilians,"[133] renewed the arms embargo,[134] banned flights to and from Libya,[135] and renewed the asset freeze of Libyan holdings.[136]

Resolution 1973 is notable for its expansiveness. Its only limitation is the proscription on the deployment of "occupation forces," but it also failed to place any temporal or geographic limitations on military engagement, or define objectives or legitimate targets. The Security Council's limitation on occupation forces is curious and has caused some confusion due to the erroneous conclusion that this precluded the deployment of any soldiers to Libya. The Council deliberately did not use the broader limitation on "ground forces," focusing instead only on the prohibition of foreign occupation, which is qualitatively different.[137]

In formulating Resolution 1973 as it did, the Security Council granted Member States significant latitude to interpret its requirements and establish their own terms of engagement. Professor Mehrdad Payandeh has argued that

---

[132] SC Res. 1973 (2011), *supra* note 3.
[133] *Id.* at ¶¶ 6–12.
[134] *Id.* at ¶¶ 13–16.
[135] *Id.* at ¶¶ 17–18.
[136] *Id.* at ¶¶ 19–21.
[137] *See also* Payandeh, *The United Nations, Military Intervention, And Regime Change In Libya, supra* note 108.

Through the authorization of the use of force in the case of Libya, the Security Council, to a considerable degree, transferred its Chapter VII powers to the intervening states. It retained neither authority nor control over the intervention. Subsequent adjustments to the authorization or its complete retraction were subject to the "reverse veto" of the permanent members.[138]

Further, Payandeh argues

And while the authorization has a humanitarian mandate and is not explicitly aimed at regime change, the open-textured and wide objective of the resolution – the protection of civilians and civilian populated areas – allowed for military measures that facilitated and advanced the overthrowing of the Gadhafi regime while protecting human rights.[139]

It must be presumed that the Security Council acted with full understanding of the implications of the Resolution it adopted. In effect, it extended to Member States a *carte blanche* to do as they saw fit to protect the civilian population.

5.1. Compliance with the UN Charter and the Security Council Resolution Authorizing Use of Force

Given the unconstrained latitude afforded the Security Council by the UN Charter and juridical interpretations to make a determination under Article 39, or to decide on measures under Articles 41 and 42, Resolution 1973 must be taken at face value as justifying military intervention in Libya by NATO. What is not clear is whether all forms of intervention were legitimate.

As indicated above, the only limit contained in Resolution 1973 is on the deployment of occupation forces. Nowhere in the Resolution is there any reference to removing the existing Qadhafi government, as the Charter does not recognize the use of force for regime change. While the Resolution does call for a solution, which "responds to the legitimate demands of the Libyan people," it at most calls upon the Libyan government to honor its obligations under international human rights law.[140] It is not clear that these two demands of the Security Council were incompatible

---

[138] *Id.* at 399–400.

[139] *Id.* at 391.

[140] SC Res. 1973 (2011), *supra*, note 3. Paragraph 3 of the Resolution "Demands that the Libyan authorities comply with their obligations under international law, including international humanitarian law, human rights and refugee law and take all measures to protect civilians and meet their basic needs, and to ensure the rapid and unimpeded passage of humanitarian assistance."

with the continued rule of Qadhafi. As noted, while the Security Council has intervened in ostensibly internal political disputes to displace a *de facto* government, as in Haiti or Sierra Leone, it has done so to bolster the recognized *de jure* government, and never against it. It is therefore difficult to conclude, based on its practice, that Resolution 1973 positively endorsed regime change. Indeed, in the preambular text to the Resolution, the Security Council "Reaffirm[ed] its strong commitment to the sovereignty, independence, territorial integrity and national unity of the Libyan Arab Jamahiriya."[141] A plain meaning reading of that requirement is not consistent with current definitions of sovereignty, which include non-intervention in politics and not simply non-colonization.

Therefore, while not explicitly constrained in such a manner, by the Resolution NATO was obligated to refrain from political intervention, which would constitute a violation of Articles 2(4) and 2(7) of the UN Charter. While it is clear that regime change may follow as a natural consequence of humanitarian intervention, there is a distinction between military actions that are humanitarian in essence and those that are military in essence. Determining the boundary between the two requires a complex and fact specific analysis of each military action that is beyond the scope of this chapter. It is clear, however, that military actions aimed at regime change would fall outside the scope of the Security Council's authorization. Without such authorization, a military action would either have to be justified by the customary law permission for self-defense, as codified in Article 51 of the Charter, or would qualify as an act of aggression. Consequently, if the military action was aimed at regime change or failed to protect civilians or civilian objects, it would be *ultra vires* and accordingly a violation of international law. Neither NATO nor its constituent members justified their intervention in Libya on the basis of self-defense, and accordingly all military actions must have been grounded in Resolution 1973 in order to remain lawful.

For its part, NATO maintains that OUP was "based on three clear principles: a sound legal basis, strong regional support and a demonstrable need."[142] Execution of these principles had three components

---

[141] *Id.*

[142] *NATO and Libya: Commitment to protecting the Libyan people*, NORTH ATLANTIC TREATY ORGANIZATION, Mar. 28, 2012, *available at* http://www.nato.int/cps/en/natolive/topics_71652.htm. The additions of regional needs and demonstrable support have no legal bearing on the legitimacy of NATO's military action, as Resolution 1973 empowered any Member State or States to engage in military action in support of the Resolution.

1. "Enforcing an arms embargo in the Mediterranean Sea to prevent the transfer of arms, related materials and mercenaries to Libya;"
2. "Enforcing a no-fly zone to prevent aircraft from bombing civilian targets;" and
3. "Conducting air and naval strikes against military forces involved in attacks or threatening to attack Libyan civilians and civilian populated areas."[143]

First, it should be noted that nowhere in NATO's official sphere of foreseen activity is there a provision resembling sanctioned political intervention, nor for assisting militarily parties to the conflict. Further, the third aspect of NATO's involvement is problematic and the one most likely to run up against the limits of Resolution 1973, as it legitimizes military action in two circumstances. First, NATO allows strikes against forces that are *involved in* attacking civilians. This would include regime forces in Benghazi,[144] Zawiyya,[145] Ajdabiya,[146] or Misrata[147] that were actively attacking unarmed protesters and civilian populations. Upon first blush, such attacks comply with the requirements of Resolution 1973, subject to the *jus in bello* requirements outlined below.

The second form of strike outlined by NATO is for forces *threatening* to attack civilians. NATO's materials do not describe what such a threat comprises, and at what point a force stops being a threat to civilians and civilian populated areas. A plain meaning reading of this requirement would indicate deference to the imminence of attack. This is an elastic concept analogous to inchoate crimes in common law systems. Regime forces on their way to Ajdabiya from Brega could very likely qualify,[148] as could regime forces moving into the Nafusa Mountains region towards *thuwar* controlled villages.[149] Conversely, a barracked soldier in Sabha or on the border to the Sudan would very likely not pose a threat to civilians or civilian populated areas, and as such his targeting would fall afoul of Resolution 1973.

The most difficult assessments of military strikes are those of so called "command and control (C2)" sites outside of the theaters of military operations where civilians were at risk. This includes the 30 April 2011

---

[143] *Id.*
[144] *See* Ch. VI, Sec. 2.
[145] *See* Ch. XII, Sec. 2.
[146] *See* Ch. VII, Sec. 2.
[147] *See* Ch. IX, Sec. 2.
[148] *See* Ch. VII, Sec. 2.
[149] *See* X Sec. 2.

strikes in Tripoli on Qadhafi's residence, which reportedly resulted in the death of his son Saif al-'Arab and three grandchildren.[150] NATO denied targeting Qadhafi or civilians, arguing instead that it had targeted a regime military installation as part of its "strategy to disrupt and destroy the command and control of those forces which have been attacking civilians."[151] It was not apparent, however, that the residence was being used as a military installation to deploy and communicate with Qadhafi forces outside of the capital.[152] Moreover, it is unclear whether, given the date on which the strike occurred and its distance from combat zones, it could conceivably constitute a strike "against military forces involved in attacks or threatening to attack Libyan civilians and civilian populated areas" as required by NATO's "principles" for intervention based on their interpretation of Resolution 1973. The legitimization of the strike in the capital at this point in the conflict would require a finding that destroying a "command and control" center in Tripoli would have a bearing on the capacity of regime forces involved in or threatening attacks against civilians in conflict zones, such as in Cyrenaica, Zawiyya, Misrata, or the Nafusa Mountains region. Even this, however, would require an expansion of NATO's mandate to strike not simply forces engaged in combat or threatening to engage in combat, but also any forces that might have some relationship to active combat in which civilians and civilian populated areas are at risk.

Similarly, as the civil war entered its final days and Qadhafi was trapped in Sirte, the capacity of the remaining regime forces to inflict civilian casualties was drastically reduced and NATO involvement may be interpreted to have been simply to hasten his fall from power. Other questions arise regarding the airstrike that disabled Qadhafi's convoy as he attempted to flee Sirte on 20 October, and the capacity of such a convoy to attack or threaten civilians.[153] On their face, these attacks, and especially the latter,

---

[150] *See* Ch. XIII, Sec. 4. *See also* Tim Hill, *Muammar Gaddafi son killed by NATO air strike – Libyan government*, THE GUARDIAN, May 1, 2011, *available at* http://www.guardian.co.uk/world/2011/may/01/libya-muammar-gaddafi-son-nato.

[151] Press statement, *NATO strikes command and control facility in Tripoli*, NORTH ATLANTIC TREATY ORGANIZATION, May 1, 2011, *available at* http://www.nato.int/cps/en/SID-A29434A7-58904AE4/natolive/news_72972.htm.

[152] Julian Borger et al., *Gaddafi family deaths reinforce doubts about Nato's UN mandate*, THE GUARDIAN, May 1, 2011, *available at* http://www.guardian.co.uk/world/2011/may/01/gaddadi-family-deaths-reinforce-doubts.

[153] For more on the killing of Qadhafi *see* Ch. IV, Sec. 6.3. *See also* Thomas Harding, *Col Gaddafi killed: convoy bombed by drone flown by pilot in Las Vegas*, THE TELEGRAPH, Oct. 20, 2011, *available at* http://www.telegraph.co.uk/news/worldnews/africaandindianocean/

seems at best to have had an attenuated connection to protecting Libya's civilian population.

NATO strikes were not strictly aimed at protecting civilians and civilian populated areas, and in certain circumstances they were designed to weaken the military capacity of the Qadhafi regime. While if in the course of attacking regime forces who were attacking civilians, NATO had destroyed a substantial enough portion of the regime forces to cripple it against a *thuwar* counteroffensive on Tripoli, this would have clearly been within the bounds of Resolution 1973 and NATO's terms of engagement. It is not obvious, however, that NATO abided by these limitations and focused only on legitimate targets.

The comments of leaders of NATO states demanding the removal of Qadhafi and their recognition of the NTC provides collateral support for the proposition that military strikes might have had the primary objective of removing Qadhafi from power. On 29 March 2011, less than two weeks after the adoption of Resolution 1973, the foreign ministers of NATO states and delegates from the United Nations, the League of Arab States, the Organization of the Islamic Conference, the European Union and NATO convened to discuss the situation in Libya. At the conclusion of the conference William Hague, the British Foreign Secretary declared that they were "preparing for Libya's future." The participants

> agreed that it is not for any of the participants here today to choose the government of Libya: only the Libyan people can do that. Participants agreed that *Qadhafi and his regime have completely lost legitimacy* and will be held accountable for their actions. The Libyan people must be free to determine their own future. Participants recognised the need for all Libyans, including the Interim Transitional National Council, tribal leaders and others, to come together to begin an inclusive political process, consistent with the relevant UNSCRs, through which they can choose their own future.[154]

Hague continued

> This Conference has shown that we are united in our aims. We are united in seeking *a Libya that does not pose a threat to its own citizens, the region or*

---

libya/8839964/Col-Gaddafi-killed-convoy-bombed-by-drone-flown-by-pilot-in-Las-Vegas.html.

[154] *Chair's Statement by William Hague, London Conference on Libya* 2, NORTH ATLANTIC TREATY ORGANIZATION, Mar. 29, 2011, *available at* http://www.nato.int/nato_static/assets/pdf/pdf_2011_03/20110927_110329_-London-Conference-Libya.pdf (emphasis added).

more widely; and in working with the people of Libya as they choose their own way forward to a peaceful and stable future.[155]

It is noteworthy that while a paean was made to the self-determination of the Libyan people, Hague implicitly excluded Qadhafi from any place in the country's future dispensation. The statement clearly delegitimized the extant government, which by implication could only impede the NTC and the Libyan people from defining and building their new state.

Two months later, at the May 2011 G8 summit, French President Sarkozy stated in no uncertain terms that Qadhafi "must leave power."[156] Shortly thereafter the G8 released a communiqué in which they declared that, "Gaddafi and the Libyan government have failed to fulfill their responsibility to protect the Libyan population and have lost all legitimacy. He has no future in a free, democratic Libya. He must go."[157]

To be clear, these statements do not, in themselves, indicate that NATO's intervention was simply a mechanism for political change in the guise of humanitarian considerations. They do, however, provide collateral support for the proposition that NATO member countries wanted to remove Qadhafi and seized upon Resolution 1973 to do so. The problematic strikes identified below cast a similar shadow of doubt over the operation.

Contrary arguments can, of course, be made. Professor Payandeh has argued that the "all necessary measures" clause in Resolution 1973 requires "that the use of force...not be excessive and that it must bear a relation to the objectives of the resolution. It is not required that each single act is strictly necessary to avoid violations of human rights in the sense that no alternative, less intrusive means is available."[158] He later argues that, "In a civil war scenario in which human rights violations are carried out by the regime, no clear distinction between humanitarian intervention and intervention in order to overthrow the regime can be upheld."[159]

---

[155] *Id.*

[156] *G8 summit: Sarkozy offers Libya's Gaddafi 'options'*, BBC, May 26, 2011, *available at* http://www.bbc.co.uk/news/world-europe-13564999. Sarkozy's full quote was: "We are not saying that Gaddafi needs to be exiled. He must leave power and the quicker he does it, the greater his choice." He continued on to explain that the sooner his departure from power, the better and that thereupon "we'll look at what the name should be on the plane ticket and even what class he should travel." *Id.*

[157] Patrick Wintour & Kim Willsher, *G8 Summit: Gaddafi Isolated as Russia Joins Demand for Libyan Leader to Go*, THE GUARDIAN, May 27, 2011, *available at* http://www.guardian.co.uk/world/2011/may/27/g8-gaddafi-libya-russia.

[158] Payandeh, *The United Nations, Military Intervention, And Regime Change In Libya, supra* note 108.

[159] *Id.* at 397.

This interpretation is problematic as it effectively allows a legitimate humanitarian justification to freight in parallel illegitimate interests that patently violate the UN Charter, and nullify a core element of the text's object and purpose.[160] It is simply not the case that the outbreak of war permits all conduct and all ends; if anything the opposite obtains, as evidenced by the canons of IHL. It raises practical questions over selectivity and the misappropriation of legitimate humanitarian issues for cynical political ends, and potentially undermines the entire foundation of humanitarian intervention: if the entrenched regime cannot reform or withdraw once the Security Council gives its go-ahead, there is no incentive to do so. If the Security Council authorization for humanitarian intervention is a *fait accompli* for pursuing any end, repressive regimes will have every incentive to continue with their impermissible conduct.

The proposition that regime change can follow from a subsequently concluded humanitarian crisis also misapprehends the law insofar as it presumes that no distinction is possible within the context of a civil war, or indeed any complex circumstance in which difficult choices must be made. The object of IHL has been to bound and "humanize"[161] war, not to remove constraints through artificially importing improper and cynical methods under the guise of legitimate ends. While the law clearly provides wide latitude for belligerents and allows for regime change in the natural course of events, the proposition that all constraints are loosened or that there can be no distinction drawn or discernment made is incorrect. The law in itself is practiced in making these kinds of distinctions. For instance, with respect to necessity, duress or inchoate crimes, courts are consistently called upon to explore intent and make fine distinctions. It is not clear that the laws of war are any different, especially given the firm admonitions in Articles 2(4) and 2(7) against actions that pose a threat to self-determination and sovereignty.

Consider, for example, the following hypotheticals. After the adoption of Resolution 1973, the Libyan government voluntarily grounded its air force and

---

[160] Payandeh acknowledges the difficulties with this interpretation and that "the mixing of the two concepts makes the UN-mandated intervention vulnerable to the accusation that the reference to human rights violations and to the need to protect civilians is a mere pretext for military intervention to pursue other policy objectives." *Id.*

[161] M. Cherif Bassiouni, *Introduction, in* A MANUAL ON INTERNATIONAL HUMANITARIAN LAW AND ARMS CONTROL AGREEMENTS 1, 4 (M. Cherif Bassiouni ed., Ardsley, USA: Transnational Publishers, 2000).

1. barracked its forces;
2. withdrew its ground forces, and emplaced them around rebel controlled areas, but allowed supplies to enter; or
3. withdrew its forces, but responded when attacked by rebels.

In the hypotheticals identified above, the Libyan government would not have engaged in attacks against civilians or civilian controlled areas. In hypothetical (1) a NATO strike would have clearly been *ultra vires* as it would violate both Resolution 1973 and the NATO rules of engagement. In hypothetical (2) there would be no actual or impending attack, and although a threat might remain it is unclear that the mere presence of military personnel in the vicinity of civilians or civilian populated areas would constitute such a threat. In hypothetical (3) the civil war would continue, but on terms dictated by the opposition, in effect transforming them into the aggressors. In such a case, a plausible argument could be made that a hypothetical NATO airstrike would trigger the Libyan regime's right to self-defense against both the rebels and NATO. There is nothing in the *jus ad bellum* that can deprive a state of its right to self-defense, conditioned, of course, on compliance with the *jus in bello*.

The civil war in Libya did not proceed in line with any of the hypotheticals identified above. The regime did, however, ground its air force and later the war ceased to be characterized exclusively by regime forces attacking civilian populated areas controlled by the opposition forces. Rather, as the conflict escalated the nature of the war fueled the conditions where the opposition forces were themselves perpetrating violations against civilian populations. Any NATO support for the *thuwar* groups operating in areas where these violations were taking place, therefore, would result in a clear violation of Resolution 1973 and the NATO's stated intention to protect the civilian population.

5.2. Jus in Bello *and the Absolute Obligation to Comply with the Laws of War: The Rules of Distinction and Proportionality*

As stated above, the *jus in bello* is the set of rules that apply to the manner in which war itself is waged. These laws, solemnized by the 1907 Hague Convention as the "laws of humanity,"[162] generally attempt to humanize

---

[162] International Conferences (The Hague), *Hague Convention (IV) Respecting the Laws and Customs of War on Land and Its Annex: Regulations Concerning the Laws and Customs of War on Land*, Oct. 18, 1907 at Preamble.

war itself, insofar as this is possible.[163] The origins of the *jus in bello* date back at least five millennia, and "have either specifically prohibited or at least condemned unnecessary use of force and violence against certain categories of persons and against certain targets."[164] Starting in the middle of the 19th century, states began formalizing these laws, beginning with the Paris Declaration of 1856 and continuing through the more recent Land Mine Convention and Rome Statute of the ICC.[165]

These conventions largely reflect customary law and are binding at all times and in all situations. In particular the core requirements of IHL, namely the duties of discrimination and proportionality, are non-derogable and absolutely binding in all circumstances.

The Rule of Distinction demands that combatants distinguish between civilians and combatants, and that attacks can only ever be directed at combatants.[166] As the ICJ declared in the *Nuclear Weapons* Advisory Opinion

> It is undoubtedly because a great many rules of humanitarian law applicable in armed conflict are so fundamental to the respect of the human person and "elementary considerations of humanity" as the Court put it in its Judgment of 9 April 1949 in the *Corfu Channel* case (1. C. J. Reports 1949, p. 22), that the Hague and Geneva Conventions have enjoyed a broad accession. Further these fundamental rules are to be observed by all States whether or not they have ratified the conventions that contain them, because *they constitute intransgressible principles of international customary law.*[167]

The ICTY Appeals Chamber addressed the question of distinction on several occasions. In the *Blaškić* case the Chamber declared that, "there is an absolute prohibition on the targeting of civilians in customary international law."[168] The Appeals Chamber affirmed the principle in the *Kordić and Čerkez* case, holding that

---

[163] *Id.* at 4.

[164] M. Cherif Bassiouni, *Introduction, supra* note 161 at 5.

[165] For a full list of International Treaties relating to the laws of war, *see* M. CHERIF BASSIOUNI, INTRODUCTION TO INTERNATIONAL CRIMINAL LAW: SECOND REVISED EDITION, Ch. II (Leiden, The Netherlands: Martinus Nijhoff, 2d ed., 2013).

[166] CUSTOMARY INTERNATIONAL HUMANITARIAN LAW 3 (Jean-Marie Henckaerts and Louise Doswald-Beck eds., Cambridge, UK: Cambridge University Press, 2d ed. 2013).

[167] Legality of the Threat or Use of Nuclear Weapons, Advisory Opinion, 1996 ICJ 226 (July 8, 1996).

[168] *Prosecutor v. Blaškić*, Appeals Judgement, Case No.: IT-95-14-A, ¶ 109 (Int'l Crim. Trib. for the Former Yugoslavia, July 29, 2004).

The civilian population as such shall not be the object of attack. This
fundamental principle of international customary law is specified in
Articles 51(2), and 51(3) of Additional Protocol I. Article 50(1) of Additional
Protocol I states that

[a] civilian is any person who does not belong to one of the categories of
persons referred to in Article 4A(1), (2), (3) and (6) of the Third Geneva
Convention and in Article 43 of this Protocol... [169]

The Rule of Distinction is found in international treaties dating back to
the St. Petersburg Declaration of 1868, and was included in Article 8(b)
(i)–(ii) of the Rome Statute, which makes it a criminal act to

  (i) Intentionally direct[] attacks against the civilian population as such or
      against individual civilians not taking direct part in hostilities;
  (ii) Intentionally direct[] attacks against civilian objects, that is, objects
      which are not military objectives;

The Rule of Proportionality prohibits "[l]aunching an attack which may be
expected to cause incidental loss of civilian life, injury to civilians, damage
to civilian objects, or a combination thereof, which would be excessive in
relation to the concrete and direct military advantage anticipated."[170] In
other words, an act of military force is prohibited if the potential damage
it would cause to the civilian population or civilian objects outweighs the
projected military gain of such an act. It should be noted that the proportionality requirement does not, in itself, prohibit any attack in which a
civilian person or object may be harmed. Rather, such collateral damage
must be weighed against the legitimate military advantage to be gained
through the military strike. Where the collateral damage outweighs the
military advantage, it is impermissible. In other words, "where the military
advantage is outweighed by the damage or death to civilians and/or civilian objects, the attack is forbidden."[171]

In the *Kordić and Čerkez* case the ICTY Appeals Chamber also addressed
the proportionality requirement, holding that

It is...accepted that attacks aimed at military objectives, including objects
and combatants, may cause 'collateral civilian damage.' International customary law recognises that in the conduct of military operations during

---

[169] *Prosecutor v. Kordić and Čerkez*, Appeals Judgement, Case No.: IT-95-14/2-A, ¶ 72
(Int'l Crim. Trib. for the Former Yugoslavia, Dec. 17, 2004).

[170] CUSTOMARY INTERNATIONAL HUMANITARIAN LAW 46 (Jean-Marie Henckaerts and
Louise Doswald-Beck eds., Cambridge, UK: Cambridge University Press, 2d ed., 2013).

[171] Report of the International Commission of Inquiry (Mar. 2012), *supra* note 26 at
Annex I, ¶ 615.

armed conflicts a distinction must be drawn at all times between persons actively taking part in the hostilities and civilian population and provides that

- the civilian populations as such shall not be the object of military operations, and
- every effort be made to spare the civilian populations from the ravages of war, and
- all necessary precautions should be taken to avoid injury, loss or damage to the civilian population.

Nevertheless, international customary law recognises that this does not imply that collateral damage is unlawful per se.[172]

The Trial Chamber took up the question of proportionality in the *Galić* case, holding that

> The practical application of the principle of distinction requires that those who plan or launch an attack take all feasible precautions to verify that the objectives attacked are neither civilians nor civilian objects, so as to spare civilians as much as possible. Once the military character of a target has been ascertained, commanders must consider whether striking this target is 'expected to cause incidental loss of life, injury to civilians, damage to civilian objectives or a combination thereof, which would be excessive in relation to the concrete and direct military advantage anticipated.' If such casualties are expected to result, the attack should not be pursued. The basic obligation to spare civilians and civilian objects as much as possible must guide the attacking party when considering the proportionality of an attack. In determining whether an attack was proportionate it is necessary to examine whether a reasonably well-informed person in the circumstances of the actual perpetrator, making reasonable use of the information available to him or her, could have expected excessive civilian casualties to result from the attack.[173]

In Libya, while the CoI found, "The vast majority of NATO airstrikes did not result in civilian casualties or collateral damage to civilian objects,"[174] the question of military emplacements in civilian areas arose repeatedly under IHL. It is impermissible to place military objects in civilian locations. The NATO strikes on the Qadhafi residence in Tripoli or the airstrike on Major General Al-Khawayldi al-Hamadi's home in Zawiyya may

---

[172] *Prosecutor v. Kordic and Cerkez, supra* note 169 at ¶ 52. (italic added).

[173] *Prosecutor v. Galić,* Trial Judgement, Case No.: IT-98-29-T, ¶ 58 (Int'l Crim. Trib. for the Former Yugoslavia, Dec. 5, 2003).

[174] Report of the International Commission of Inquiry (Mar. 2012), *supra* note 26 at Annex I, ¶ 615.

have constituted such emplacements.[175] Yet, even if there were a military function to these locations, it is still incumbent upon the combatant to appreciate the dual use and consider the proportionality of the strike. The ICTY Trial Chamber addressed this question in the *Galić* case, holding that

> [T]he parties to a conflict are under an obligation to remove civilians, to the maximum extent feasible from the vicinity of military objectives and to avoid locating military objectives within or near densely populated areas. However, the failure of a party to abide by this obligation does not relieve the attacking side of its duty to abide by the principles of distinction and proportionality when launching an attack.

A determination of whether a particular NATO attack satisfied the requirements of the rules of distinction and proportionality is beyond the scope of this chapter. The incidents recorded below, however, show that in several instances there exist serious questions over NATO's actions and use of force, as described in the following section.

6. NATO AIRSTRIKES

The succeeding survey examines a sample of NATO airstrikes that can be generally categorized as either "deliberate strikes" or "dynamic strikes."[176] Deliberate strikes were planned in advance and targets selected before aircraft took off, based on intelligence collected by observers or aerial drones and vetted by the NATO command. Such strikes were conducted primarily against fixed targets, such as buildings, air-defense systems or immobile government assets.[177] Dynamic strikes were unplanned strikes against targets of opportunity that presented themselves once the fighter was in the air.[178] In dynamic strike sorties, fighter pilots reported back information and received instructions to engage a target. As the war progressed, OUP fighters flew fewer deliberate and more dynamic strike sorties. Chief of Allied Powers in Europe, Brigadier General Mark van Uhm, stated in late April 2011 that only ten percent of the daily sorties represented deliberate strikes, while the vast majority of the strikes by this time

---

[175] *See infra* Sec. 6.2.
[176] C.J. Chivers & Eric Schmitt, *In Strikes on Libya by NATO, an Unspoken Civilian Toll, supra* note 49.
[177] *Id.*
[178] *See* Report of the International Commission of Inquiry (Mar. 2012), *supra* note 26 at ¶ 604.

were dynamic in nature.[179] By the end of the conflict, sources estimated more than two thirds of all sorties were of the dynamic variety.[180]

Dynamic strikes involved aircraft remaining in the air longer in search of targets, and required more extensive intelligence, surveillance and reconnaissance (ISR) efforts.[181] The United States first introduced drones into the conflict in April, helping provide more actionable intelligence for both deliberate and dynamic strikes.[182] Other countries also provided surveillance technology, such as Italy, which supplied Tornado aircraft to conduct ISR missions.[183] France and the United Kingdom provided helicopters to gather intelligence and provide more precision targeting in difficult terrain, such as in the Nafusa Mountains region, where NATO increased strikes from June 2011 onwards.[184]

As the NATO campaign progressed, coalition forces appear to have acquired a better ability to gather real-time intelligence through enhanced surveillance and reconnaissance, thereby increasing the capacity of dynamic strike operations. As the Qadhafi forces switched to using make-shift bases and civilian infrastructure for protection, NATO increasingly employed dynamic targeting. Dynamic strikes were not immune from error, however, such as mistakes resulting from inaccurate intelligence from rebels or miscalculations of civilian presence. The 16 September 2011 strike on armed trucks in Sirte is an example of such a case, as NATO engaged military in real-time, but struck a large group of civilians in the area as well.[185]

6.1. *Phases of Operations*

The first combat operations began in the eastern part of Libya on 19 March 2011, with French aircraft engaging government armor in Benghazi in direct support of the rebels, and with U.S., UK and French strikes targeting Qadhafi air force defense systems.[186] On 23 March, Air Vice Marshall

---

[179] Anrig, *Allied Air Power over Libya, supra* note 37 at 99.

[180] C.J. Chivers & Eric Schmitt, *In Strikes on Libya by NATO, an Unspoken Civilian Toll, supra* note 49.

[181] Anrig, *Allied Air Power over Libya, supra* note 37 at 99.

[182] Cloud, *U.S. begins using Predator drones in Libya, supra* note 64.

[183] Anrig, *Allied Air Power over Libya, supra* note 37 at 93.

[184] Elizabeth Pineau & John Irish, *France provided weapons, food to Libya rebels, supra* note 204.

[185] *See* Ch. XV, Sec. 4.

[186] Anthony Bell & David Witter, Institute for the Study of War, 2 The Libyan Revolution: Escalation and Intervention 24 (Sept. 2011) [hereinafter "Escalation

Greg Bagwell stated, "Effectively, their air force no longer exists as a fighting force, and [Qadhafi's] integrated air defense system and command and control networks are severely degraded to the point that we can operate with near impunity across Libya."[187] Although OUP aircraft could operate unimpeded across Libya, the Libyan Air Force still had numerous mobile air defenses that NATO continued to target throughout the war.

During the initial phase of the conflict, coalition forces also carried out tactical strikes on military bases and targeted ground troops that were threatening *thuwar* held areas and attacking civilians.[188] United States officials reported on 28 March that coalition forces had struck the headquarters of the Khamis Katiba, a security unit that "remained at the forefront of operations against civilians."[189] On 23 March, NATO also began its intervention in Misrata, 187 kilometers (116 miles) to the east of Tripoli, focusing many of its strikes on breaking the siege on the strategically important city.[190] NATO's involvement helped alleviate the effects of the siege, but was not able to fully break Qadhafi's military hold on the city.[191]

United States AFRICOM Commander General Ham warned on 7 April 2011 that there was a risk the conflict was falling into a stalemate.[192] It became apparent that NATO airstrikes alone were not going to be sufficient to deter the advances of the Qadhafi forces. As the war progressed, conditions on the ground shifted, and rebel forces began using tanks and armored vehicles, while regime forces started using pick-up trucks and other civilian vehicles.[193] This changing nature of the conflict

---

AND INTERVENTION"], *available at* www.understandingwar.org/sites/default/files/Libya_Part2_o.pdf.

[187] *Libyan Air Forces Destroyed*, RT, Mar. 23, 2011, *available at* http://rt.com/news/air-destroyed-british-force; *Libyans Air Force 'no longer exists'* AL JAZEERA, Mar. 23 2011 *available at* http://www.aljazeera.com/news/africa/2011/03/201132316258646677.html.

[188] BLANCHARD, UNREST AND U.S. POLICY, *supra* note 22 at 7.

[189] *Id.* at 5. For more on the role of the Khamis 32nd Katiba in operations against civilians, *see also* Chs. IX, X, XII at XIII.

[190] Chris McGreal et al., *Libya: Allied air strikes secure Misrata for rebels*, THE GUARDIAN, Mar. 24 2011, *available at* http://www.guardian.co.uk/world/2011/mar/23/libya-allied-air-strikes-misrata.

[191] *See* Ch. IX, Sec. 4.

[192] BLANCHARD, UNREST AND U.S. POLICY, *supra* note 22 at 6.

[193] Kareem Fahim & David D. Kirkpatrick, *Rebel Advance Halted Outside Qaddafi Hometown*, N.Y. TIMES, Mar. 29, 2011, *available at* http://www.nytimes.com/2011/03/29/world/africa/29libya.html; *NATO 'careful' over airstrikes, vows to protect civilians*, AFP, Apr. 6, 2011, *available at* http://www.pelte.com/story.php?title=nato-careful-over-air-strikes-vows-to-protect-civilians-afp.

led to strikes that accidentally hit *thuwar* forces, such as those documented in the eastern region around Ajdabiya and Brega in early April.[194]

In order to avoid friendly fire strikes and improve coordination with the *thuwar* forces, NATO dispatched liaison officers to Libya to instruct the rebel fighters on airstrike policies. In several locations, including Ajdabiya and Misrata, *thuwar* forces were made aware of "red lines" – areas where unplanned, dynamic strikes would engage any suspicious target.[195] The enhanced communication between the rebel forces and NATO allowed for greater opportunities for dynamic strikes carried out according to the shifting nature of the conflict.

Through April and May 2011, NATO targeted Qadhafi forces in Misrata and Brega,[196] including deliberate strikes against command and control centers. NATO reported on 10 May that 30 military targets had been destroyed in the area, including command and control buildings, and military storage sites.[197] On 7–8 May, French and British navy ships engaged Qadhafi forces they had detected firing rocket launchers into Misrata.[198] The naval power provided support for air attacks, and contributed to lifting the siege on Misrata in mid-May.[199]

On 1 June, NATO announced that it would extend its mission in Libya for a further 90 days. The decision was made during a meeting of ambassadors from the 28 NATO member states plus ambassadors from the five non-NATO countries participating in the campaign – Jordan, Morocco, Qatar, Sweden and the UAE.[200]

On 3–4 June, French and British combat helicopters engaged ground targets for the first time, further restraining the regime forces' ground maneuvers.[201] These strikes concentrated on regions along the Gulf of Sidra, the most southern point of the Mediterranean Sea, to help break

---

[194] *See* Ch. VII, Sec 4.

[195] Chris Stephen & Nick Hopkins, *Libya rebels frustrated by NATO's safety-first strategy*, THE GUARDIAN, June 8, 2011, *available at* http://www.guardian.co.uk/world/2011/jun/07/libya-rebels-nato-strategy; ANTHONY BELL & DAVID WITTER, INSTITUTE FOR THE STUDY OF WAR, 3 THE LIBYAN REVOLUTION: STALEMATE & SIEGE 15 (Oct. 6, 2011) [hereinafter "STALEMATE & SIEGE"], *available at* http://www.understandingwar.org/sites/default/files/Libya_Part3_0.pdf.

[196] *See* Chs. VII & IX.

[197] Romero and Gabellini, Press Briefing on Libya, May 10, 2011, *supra* note 6.

[198] Anrig, *Allied Air Power over Libya*, *supra* note 37 at 98.

[199] *Id.*

[200] *NATO Extends Operation in Libya*, NEWS 24, June 1, 2011, *available at* http://www.news24.com/Africa/News/Nato-extends-operation-in-Libya-20110601.

[201] Anrig, *Allied Air Power over Libya*, *supra* note 37 at 100.

the deadlock between *thuwar* and Qadhafi forces in eastern Libya.[202] NATO's air campaign also increased in the west, with a series of airstrikes in the Nafusa Mountains region in May and June that weakened Qadhafi forces and aided *thuwar* offenses in the region.[203] From June onwards, NATO enhanced its involvement in the Nafusa Mountains region with an increased number of precision strikes as a result of French and British helicopters joining the operations.[204]

After a June incursion by *thuwar* forces in Zawiyya, NATO reported that it would continue to focus intelligence gathering on the region.[205] After Zawiyya fell to the *thuwar* on 15 August, NATO intensified its strikes to weaken regime forces in the area between Zawiyya and Tripoli and clear the way for rebel advances on the capital.[206] The strikes continued in Tripoli in August, and on 22 August, NATO reported destroying tanks and artillery, and striking the secret Baroni Intelligence Center.[207] NATO attacked Qadhafi's Bab al-'Aziziyya compound in the capital, and on 23 August, rebel forces took the compound and gained control of the capital.[208] The remaining Qadhafi forces moved to Sirte, where NATO carried out extensive attacks in September.[209] The ongoing fighting led NATO to announce on 21 September it would again extend its mission by 90 days as it had on 1 June.[210]

---

[202] *Id.*

[203] *See* Ch. X. *See also* ANTHONY BELL ET AL., INSTITUTE FOR THE STUDY OF WAR, 4 THE LIBYAN REVOLUTION: THE TIDE TURNS 14 (Nov. 2011) [hereinafter "THE TIDE TURNS"], *available at* http://www.understandingwar.org/sites/default/files/Libya_Part4.pdf.

[204] Elizabeth Pineau & John Irish, *France provided weapons, food to Libya rebels*, REUTERS, June 29, 2011, *available at* http://www.reuters.com/article/2011/06/29/us-libya-france-weapons-idUSTRE75S22P20110629.

[205] Oana Lungescu & Mike Bracken, *Press Briefing on Libya, June 14, 2011*, NORTH ATLANTIC TREATY ORGANIZATION, *available at* http://www.nato.int/cps/en/natolive/opinions_75403.htm.

[206] Kareem Fahim, *Libya Rebels Threaten a Supply Line to the Capital*, N.Y. TIMES, Aug. 15, 2011, *available at* http://www.nytimes.com/2011/08/15/world/africa/15libya.html.

[207] Sean Rayment, *How the Special Forces Helped Bring Qaddafi to His Knees*, THE TELEGRAPH, Aug. 28, 2011, *available at* http://www.telegraph.co.uk/news/worldnews/africaand indianocean/libya/8727076/How-the-special-forces-helped-bring-Gaddafi-to-his-knees .html.

[208] *Id.*

[209] *See* Ch. XV.

[210] *NATO extends Libya mission for another three months*, REUTERS, Sept. 21, 2011, *available at* http://www.reuters.com/article/2011/09/21/nato-libya-mission-idUSB5E7KD01U20110921.

On 20 October, a Predator drone and French aircraft engaged a convoy outside of the city of Sirte.[211] The convoy was hit while it was transporting Qadhafi out of the city in an attempt to reach Jarif. Qadhafi then fled his vehicle on foot and attempted to hide in a nearby concrete drain. *Thuwar* forces subsequently captured Qadhafi and he was killed while in their custody.[212]

Upon the capture of Sirte and the subsequent Declaration of Liberation, hostilities in Libya officially came to an end.[213] On 26 October, the NTC President, Mustafa 'Abd al-Jalil, requested that NATO extend its mission in Libya. However, the following day the UN Security Council, in a unanimous vote, decided to end the NATO mandate.[214] The Security Council lifted the no-fly zone over Libya on 27 October,[215] and four days later NATO concluded its operations.[216]

In May 2012, NATO released a statement in response to mounting reports of civilian casualties caused by NATO strikes, emphasizing that while conducting 9,700 strikes using 7,700 precision bombs, "No target was approved or struck if we [NATO] had any reason to believe that civilians would be at risk." The statement continued

> Whenever possible, we used the weapon with the smallest yield to avoid unnecessary harm or damage. In some cases, as many as 50 hours of airborne video observation was conducted and analysed before a strike was authorised. Hundreds of possible strikes were aborted at the last moment due to the perceived possibility of a civilian presence. Military forces and facilities were only struck if they were directly involved in directing, enabling or facilitating attacks on civilians. Troops that did not pose a threat to civilians were not targeted.[217]

---

[211] Ben Farmer, *Gaddafi's final hours: NATO and the SAS helped rebels drive hunted leader into endgame in a desert drain*, TELEGRAPH, Oct. 22, 2011, *available at* http://www.telegraph .co.uk/news/worldnews/africaandindianocean/libya/8843684/Gaddafis-final-hours-Nato-and-the-SAS-helped-rebels-drive-hunted-leader-into-endgame-in-a-desert-drain.html.

[212] *See* Ch. IV, Sec. 6.3. *See also Id.*

[213] *See* Report of the International Commission of Inquiry (Mar. 2012), *supra* note 26 at ¶ 98.

[214] *Libya*, MAX PLANCK INSTITUTE FOR COMPARATIVE PUBLIC LAW AND INTERNATIONAL LAW, *available at* http://www.mpil.de/ww/en/pub/research/details/know_transfer/consti tutional_reform_in_arab_/libyen.cfm.

[215] SC Res. 2016 (2011), Oct. 27 2011, UN Doc. S/RES/2016 (2011).

[216] Fact Sheet, Operation Unified Protector Final Mission Stats, *supra* note 53.

[217] *Statement by the NATO spokesperson on Human Rights Watch report*, NORTH ATLANTIC TREATY ORGANIZATION, May 14, 2012, *available at* http://www.nato.int/cps/en/SID-5040B041-666DF7DC/natolive/news_87171.htm?selectedLocale=en.

6.2. A Survey of Incidents

This section provides details about 25 NATO airstrikes conducted between March and October 2011 that resulted in the deaths of civilians and *thuwar* fighters, or destroyed facilities where a military presence was questionable. Information on the 25 incidents is culled from the CoI, independent investigative reports, media sources and NATO's daily operational updates and press briefings. Of these, the majority are deliberate strikes, in that they were apparently planned with the view of striking a specific target. A smaller proportion of the strikes can be considered dynamic. Dynamic strikes are distinguished from deliberate strikes, as discussed above, in that they struck targets of opportunity rather than pre-planned targets. Because of the nature of dynamic strikes, the amount of available information on these types of operations is limited compared to the amount of information on deliberate strikes. Therefore, the relatively small proportion of dynamic strikes featured in this survey is based on the availability of information, not on the number of overall strikes carried out during the NATO campaign. There were numerous dynamic strikes conducted during the conflict and those below are illustrative rather than exhaustive.

29 March 2011. Mizda (The Nafusa Mountains region, 80 kilometers/50 miles from Zintan). On 29 March, coalition airstrikes repeatedly hit an ammunition depot in Mizda, setting off huge secondary explosions. One missile flew several kilometers before hitting a home next to the local hospital,[218] wounding two civilians and setting fire to the home. One of the victims suffered a head wound and a severe injury to his left foot, while the other victim suffered a skull fracture. Both were left physically disabled as a result of injuries sustained during the bombings.[219] The explosions also reportedly caused the release of cluster munitions that were being stored in a facility used by Qadhafi forces in the region.[220]

30 March 2011. Surman (15 kilometers/9 miles west of Zawiyya).[221] On 30 March, a NATO airstrike hit warehouses at a former plastic factory

---

[218] Craig Allen et al., *Errant NATO Airstrikes in Libya: 13 Cases (Mizdah)*, N.Y. TIMES, Dec. 16, 2011, *available at* http://www.nytimes.com/interactive/2011/12/16/world/africa/nato-airstrikes-in-libya.html?_r=0#page/ammunition-depot.

[219] *Id.*

[220] Report of the International Commission of Inquiry (Mar. 2012), *supra* note 26 at Annex I ¶ 665.

[221] Craig Allen et al., Errant nato Airstrikes in Libya: 13 Cases (Mizdah), N.Y. Times, Dec. 16, 2011, available at http://www.nytimes.com/interactive/2011/12/16/world/africa/natoairstrikes-in-libya.html#page/warehouses.

in the town of Surman.[222] There were no casualties, but questions arose regarding the justification for targeting the warehouses. Residents in the neighborhood reported that the warehouses had been used as storage for ammunition in February 2011, but that the materiel had been moved, and that the facility was being used to stock canned tomatoes at the time of the strike. The attack on the warehouses constitutes an example of a bombing strike that potentially relied on poor and/or outdated intelligence.[223]

1 April 2011. Ajdabiya/Brega. A NATO airstrike between Ajdabiya and Brega struck a convoy of *thuwar* fighters that reportedly killed 13 individuals.[224] A NATO spokesperson responded to questions regarding the strike by saying it was "an unfortunate incident" and that opposition forces had already "stated it was their fault" for "giving some celebratory fire in the air, which attracted the reaction."[225] The spokesperson added that the opposition forces "learned their lesson" from the strike and "directed more experienced people to the front line" to ensure that "those celebratory fires should not be used anymore."[226] This was not the last friendly fire incident, however, as similar incidents continued to occur in the region leading to frustration and anger among the *thuwar* forces and local population.[227]

6 April 2011. Near Zaltan (between Sirte and Brega).[228] The Qadhafi regime claimed that an airstrike on the Sarir oil field killed three guards and injured several workers. The regime further claimed that the strike damaged a pipeline to the coast.[229] Both the *thuwar* fighters and the information manager at the Arabian Gulf Oil Company denied these claims, and attributed the attack to Qadhafi forces.[230] NATO's daily update

---

[222] Craig Allen et al., *Errant NATO Airstrikes in Libya: 13 Cases (Surman – warehouse)*, *supra* note 218.

[223] *Id.*

[224] *See* Ch. VII, Sec. 4. *See also Libyan rebels near Ajdabiya 'killed in NATO air strike'*, BBC, Apr. 7, 2011, *available at* http://www.bbc.co.uk/news/world-africa-12997181.

[225] Oana Lungescu & Mark van Uhm, *Press Briefing on Libya*, NORTH ATLANTIC TREATY ORGANIZATION, Apr. 5, 2011, *available at* http://www.nato.int/cps/en/natolive/opinions_72027.htm.

[226] *Id.*

[227] *Libyan rebels near Ajdabiya 'killed in NATO air strike'*, BBC, *see supra* note 224.

[228] The transliteration of this place name was adopted from the reference.

[229] *WRAPUP 2-Libya says NATO air strike hits major oil field*, REUTERS, Apr. 6, 2011, *available at* http://af.reuters.com/article/libyaNews/idAFLDE7352B620110406.

[230] *Rebels say Gaddafi, not British, attacked oilfield*, REUTERS, Apr. 7, 2011, *available at* http://af.reuters.com/article/topNews/idAFJOE7360AU20110407.

reports conducting 72 strikes on 6 April, but does not indicate the geographic region where the strikes took place.[231]

7 April 2011. Brega. In another friendly fire incident, a NATO airstrike hit a *thuwar* convoy of tanks and armed vehicles as they advanced towards Brega. The strikes reportedly killed as many as 13 people, and left many more injured.[232] The following day, a NATO spokesperson reported that, "It would appear that two of our strikes yesterday may have resulted in the deaths of a number of Transitional National Council, or, TNC forces who were operating main battle tanks."[233] The spokesperson made clear that NATO would not issue an apology, explaining that the situation on the ground was "extremely fluid" and that NATO had not been made aware that the TNC or the opposition forces were using tanks. The spokesperson further defended the decision to strike, remarking

> Tanks have been used in the past to directly target civilians, and indeed the other day we had questions and we were examining the case in Misrata where we've seen tanks right in the centre with population areas of people round about them.[234]

The *Thuwar* claimed they had informed NATO of their location and had marked their vehicles with paint to distinguish their equipment from that of the Qadhafi forces.[235] General 'Abd al-Fattah Yunis also told reporters that *thuwar* commanders had informed NATO its plans to move tanks into Ajdabiya, and that the tanks were marked with tri-color rebel flag.[236] In addition to causing further anger in the region, the incident raised concerns over NATO's sources of information, and its procedures used to vet targets before carrying out its strikes.

11 April 2011. Kikla (The Nafusa Mountains region). The Libyan government claimed that a NATO airstrike hit the village of Kikla on 11 April,

---

[231] *Operational Media Update for 6 April 2011*, NORTH ATLANTIC TREATY ORGANIZATION, Apr. 7, 2011, *available at* http://www.nato.int/nato_static/assets/pdf/pdf_2011_04/20110407_110407-oup-update.pdf.

[232] *See* Ch. VII, Sec. 4. *See also Libyan rebels near Ajdabiya 'killed in NATO air strike'*, BBC, *see supra* note 224; Craig Allen et al., *Errant NATO Airstrikes in Libya: 13 Cases (Brega)*, *supra* note 218.

[233] *NATO and Libya, Operational Media Update for 7 April 2011*, NORTH ATLANTIC TREATY ORGANIZATION, Apr. 8, 2011, *available at* http://www.nato.int/nato_static/assets/pdf/pdf_2011_04/20110408_110408-oup-update.pdf.

[234] *Id.*

[235] BELL ET AL., STALEMATE AND SIEGE, *supra* note 195 at 33.

[236] Leila Fadel and Simon Denyer, *Libyan rebels targeted in airstrike despite no-fly zone, rebels say*, THE WASHINGTON POST, Apr. 8, 2011, *available at* http://articles.washingtonpost.com/2011-04-07/world/35262954_1_ajdabiya-government-attacks-libyan-rebels.

killing several individuals.[237] NATO acknowledged airstrikes in the region on 11 April, but denied responsibility for any action in Kikla. Rather, NATO claimed in its daily update that its airstrike hit targets in Zintan, roughly 20 kilometers away.[238]

27 April 2011. Misrata. Two NATO airstrikes hit a column of trucks at a salt packing plant where *thuwar* forces had moved to recover weapons left behind by Qadhafi forces.[239] Twelve opposition fighters were killed and three others were wounded.[240] According to the New York Times, a NATO spokesperson stated that he had checked the "facts as best as possible" and that NATO could not "independently verify reports that these vehicles were operated by opposition forces." The spokesperson added, "there was no NATO attack on any building in or around Misurata."[241] NATO's operational media updates for 27 April, however, report that NATO engaged in a strike that targeted two rocket launchers, two artillery vehicle storage buildings, and one surface-to-air missile storage facility in the vicinity of Misrata.[242] Moreover, when reporters from the New York Times investigated the area, they found evidence of a NATO strike, including components from a GBU-12 bomb, such as fins, pieces of wing assemblies, internal parts and an external piece with writing that read, "For Use On MK 82," an American-made 500-pound (226-kilogram) bomb.[243]

30 April 2011. Tripoli. A NATO strike in Tripoli resulted in the killing of Qadhafi's son Saif al-'Arab, along with three of his grandchildren. Qadhafi had reportedly been in the residence of Saif al-'Arab when the strike hit on the evening of 30 April, but had escaped unharmed.[244] NATO released a statement on 1 May, reporting that Qadhafi regime military installations,

---

[237] Carmen Romero & Mark van Uhm, *Joint Press Briefing on Events Concerning Libya,* NORTH ATLANTIC TREATY ORGANIZATION, Apr. 12, 2011, *available at* http://www.nato.int/cps/en/natolive/opinions_72290.htm.

[238] *See* Ch. X, Sec. 4. *See also NATO and Libya, Operational Media Update for 27 April 2011,* NORTH ATLANTIC TREATY ORGANIZATION, Apr. 12, 2011, *available at* http://www.nato.int/nato_static/assets/pdf/pdf_2011_04/20110412_110412-oup-update.pdf.

[239] *See* Ch. IX, Sec. 4.

[240] Craig Allen et al., *Errant NATO Airstrikes in Libya: 13 Cases (Misurata), supra* note 218.

[241] *Id.*

[242] *NATO and Libya, Operational Media Update for 27 April 2011,* NORTH ATLANTIC TREATY ORGANIZATION, Apr. 28, 2011, *available at* http://www.nato.int/nato_static/assets/pdf/pdf_2011_04/20110428_110428-oup-update.pdf.

[243] Craig Allen et al., *Errant NATO Airstrikes in Libya: 13 Cases (Misurata), supra* note 218.

[244] Julian Borger et al., *Gaddafi family deaths reinforce doubts about Nato's UN mandate, supra* note 152.

including a "command and control building" in the Bab al-ʿAziziyya neighborhood, had been hit the day before. Lieutenant-General Charlie Bouchard (head of military operations) stated that he was "aware of unconfirmed media reports that some of Qadhafi's family members may have been killed," and that "We [NATO] regret all loss of life, especially the innocent civilians being harmed as a result of the ongoing conflict."[245]

The incident drew criticism over allegations that NATO was targeting individual leaders, and Chinese and Russian officials raised concerns that NATO's actions went beyond the UN Security Council mandate.[246] British Prime Minister David Cameron defended NATO's actions to reporters, stating that the UN mandate permitted attacks against Qadhafi's command and control sites in order to prevent further attacks against civilians.[247] General Bouchard added that in order to reduce potential danger to civilians in the future, "all civilians in Libya should distance themselves as much as possible from Qadhafi regime forces, equipment and known military infrastructure."[248]

13 May 2011. Brega. Reports indicate that a NATO airstrike hit a guesthouse in Brega on 13 May, where Muslim clerics were meeting for a religious ceremony. The strike caused 16 civilian casualties and 40 injuries. A NATO spokesperson, Squadron Leader Mike Bracken, provided no information for media outlets regarding the incident at the time.[249]

In January 2012, NATO's legal adviser Peter Olson provided information in response to the CoI's queries over the incident. Olson explained that on 12–13 May NATO carried out a deliberate strike on the Marsa El Brega Residence and Command Facility, which "served as the primary C2 [command and control] facility for forces fielded by the 32nd Brigade in and around Brega." Olson's letter further elaborated that the target was hit

---

[245] NORTH ATLANTIC TREATY ORGANIZATION, *NATO strikes command and control facility in Tripoli, supra* note 151.

[246] *Nato strike 'kills Saif al-Arab Gaddafi', Libya says,* BBC, May 1, 2011, *available at* http://www.bbc.co.uk/news/world-africa-13251570.

[247] Julian Borger et al., *Gaddafi family deaths reinforce doubts about Nato's UN mandate, supra* note 152.

[248] *NATO strikes command and control facility in Tripoli,* NORTH ATLANTIC TREATY ORGANIZATION, Press Briefing on Libya, May 1, 2011, *supra* note 151.

[249] *See* Ch. VII, Sec. 4. *See also UPDATE 1-NATO strike kills at least 16 in Brega-Libyan TV,* REUTERS, May 13, 2011, *available at* http://af.reuters.com/article/energyOilNews/idAFLDE 74C1GL20110513; Andrew Gilligan, *Libya: Nato air strike 'kills 11 imams',* TELEGRAPH, May 13, 2011, *available at* http://www.telegraph.co.uk/news/worldnews/africaandindianocean/libya/8513402/Libya-Nato-air-strike-kills-11-imams.html.

by four precision-guided munitions, and that battle damage assessment indicated no collateral damage.[250]

16 June 2011. Ajdabiya. In another friendly fire incident in the eastern region, a NATO airstrike hit a column belonging to *thuwar* forces, destroying six vehicles and wounding 16 rebel fighters.[251] On 21 June NATO confirmed that a strike took place in the area of Brega in which "NATO hit a column military vehicles which was observed in the area where Qadhafi forces had recently been operating."[252] As with the previous incidents in the region, NATO determined that the vehicles posed a threat to civilians, and an aircraft fired on the column. NATO subsequently confirmed the vehicles were part of an opposition patrol, and the spokesperson expressed regret on the part of NATO for any injuries caused by the "unfortunate incident."[253]

20 June 2011. Tripoli. At approximately 1:30 am, NATO airstrikes destroyed three homes in Suq al-Jumaʿ in Tripoli. NATO had identified the strike's target as a "military missile site."[254] Five people were killed, including two children, and eight were wounded.[255] On 21 June, NATO announced that a "weapons systems failure" caused a strike to miss the intended target, which may have led to civilian casualties. NATO reported that the intended target was a military missile site in Tripoli with a number of laser-guided bombs.[256] In January 2012, NATO's legal advisor provided further information about the incident to the CoI

> During the 19 June target engagement in question, the targeted structures were positively identified and two precision-guided weapons were dropped. The second of these weapons appears to have malfunctioned due to laser guidance problems, its impact was not observed and NATO was not able to determine where it in fact landed...After reviewing the case, it was

---

[250] Letter from Paul Olson to Philippe Kirsch, Chair of the International Commission of Inquiry (Jan. 23, 2012), in Report of the International Commission of Inquiry (Mar. 2012), *supra* note 26 at Annex II.

[251] *See* Ch. VII, Sec. 4. *See also NATO probes reported errant strike on Libya rebels*, REUTERS, June 17, 2011, *available at* http://af.reuters.com/article/topNews/idAFJOE75G0EZ20110617.

[252] Oana Lungescu & Mike Bracken, *Press Briefing on Libya*, NORTH ATLANTIC TREATY ORGANIZATION, June 21, 2011, *available at* http://www.nato.int/cps/en/natolive/opinions_75652.htm.

[253] *Id.*

[254] *See* Ch. XIII, Sec. 4. *See also* Report of the International Commission of Inquiry (Mar. 2012), *supra* note 26 at Annex I ¶ 626.

[255] *Id.* at ¶ 627.

[256] Lungescu & Bracken, NATO, *supra* note 252.

concluded that it was possible that the errant weapon had caused such casualties... This incident is under further assessment."[257]

Human Rights Watch (HRW) and the CoI found no evidence of military activity during their respective visits to the site.[258] There were no signs of weapon debris or military signatures found during a site visit in December 2011 to indicate the site had a military significance. Satellite imagery analysis from 10 June and after the strike similarly showed no evidence to suggest the site had a military utility.[259]

20 June 2011. Surman (west of Zawiyya). NATO targeted a farm in Surman belonging to a former member of Qadhafi's Revolutionary Council, Major General Al-Hamadi.[260] HRW reported that 13 persons were killed as a result of the strike, including four women and five children.[261] Sources reported that Al-Hamadi was not at the farm during the attack,[262] and his family claimed that the General was retired, and women, children and staff occupied the homes at the time of the strike.[263] Members of the opposition argued that the General and his son were commanders directing operations in western Libya, and that Qadhafi military officers had visited the compound for meetings with the General.[264]

NATO declared that Al-Hamadi's residence was a "legitimate military target, a command and control node" but denied specifically targeting Al-Hamadi.[265] NATO Commander General Charlie Bouchard also stated that the bombing had carefully avoided striking a mosque and hospital

---

[257] Letter from Paul Olson to Philippe Kirsch, Chair of the International Commission of Inquiry (Jan. 23, 2012), in Report of the International Commission of Inquiry (Mar. 2012), *supra* note 26 at Annex II.

[258] HUMAN RIGHTS WATCH, UNACKNOWLEDGED DEATHS, *supra* note 5 at image 5; Report of the International Commission of Inquiry (Mar. 2012), *supra* note 26 at Annex I ¶ 627.

[259] Report of the International Commission of Inquiry (Mar. 2012), *supra* note 26 at Annex I ¶ 627.

[260] *See* Ch. XII. *See also* Lungescu Bracken, NORTH ATLANTIC TREATY ORGANIZATION, Press Briefing on Libya, June 21, 2011, *supra* note 252.

[261] HUMAN RIGHTS WATCH, UNACKNOWLEDGED DEATHS, *supra* note 5 at 39–40.

[262] INTERNATIONAL LEGAL ASSISTANCE CONSORTIUM, PRE-ASSESSMENT MISSION, LIBYA 19 (Dec. 7, 2011) [hereinafter "PRE-ASSESSMENT MISSION, LIBYA], *available at* http://www.ilac .se/download/reports_documents/mission-reports_documents/LIBYA_FF_REPORT_111221 .pdf.

[263] Craig Allen et al., *Errant NATO Airstrikes in Libya: 13 Cases (Surman – warehouse),* *supra* note 218.

[264] *Id.*

[265] Lungescu Bracken, NORTH ATLANTIC TREATY ORGANIZATION, *supra* note 252.

nearby.[266] In its correspondence to the CoI, NATO reaffirmed its assessment that it was a military site, stating that they had, "No evidence of a
civilian presence and that all measures were taken to confirm that conclusion, and that the strike was executed in a manner designed to avoid
any risk to transient civilians."[267] Regarding the issue of civilian casualties,
NATO's legal adviser explained, "NATO did not have access to contemporaneous ground observation from reliable neutral observers and cannot make a definitive statement with respect to the reports of civilian
deaths."[268]

While NATO acknowledged allegations of civilian casualties, it stated
it could not independently verify these reports.[269] The CoI was unable
to determine whether the strike met NATO's objective to avoid civilian
casualties, or whether the organization satisfied its burden to avoid such
an outcome.[270] HRW and the CoI reported that they did not find any
evidence of military activity on the site and satellite imagery presented
by HRW from three weeks prior to the attack revealed no signs of military
activity.[271]

20 June 2011. Surman (near Zawiyya). Reports indicate that on 20 June
NATO airstrikes destroyed the post office neighboring a communications
tower in the town of Surman.[272] According to the reports, a residential
area next to the post office was also damaged by flying debris. Rebel forces
stated that the Qadhafi forces had used the two destroyed buildings as a
communications site connected to the command center at Al-Hamadi's
home. Although occupied by a family at the time, there were no casualties.

---

[266] Jonathan Beale, *Libya Conflict: NATO's man against Gaddafi*, BBC, June 26, 2011, *available at* http://www.bbc.co.uk/news/world-europe-13919380; AMNESTY INTERNATIONAL, THE
BATTLE FOR LIBYA: KILLINGS, DISAPPEARANCES AND TORTURE (Sept. 13, 2011), *available at*
http://www.amnesty.org/en/library/asset/MDE19/025/2011/en/8f2e1c49-8f43-46d3-917d-
383c17d36377/mde19025201en.pdf.

[267] Letter from Paul Olson to Philippe Kirsch, Chair of the International Commission of
Inquiry (Feb. 15, 2012), in Report of the International Commission of Inquiry (Mar. 2012),
supra note 26 at Annex II.

[268] *Id.*

[269] Lungescu & Bracken, NATO, *supra* note 252.

[270] Report of the International Commission of Inquiry (Mar. 2012), *supra* note 26 at
Annex I ¶ 639.

[271] HUMAN RIGHTS WATCH, UNACKNOWLEDGED DEATHS, *supra* note 5 at 40–2; Report
of the International Commission of Inquiry (Mar. 2012), *supra* note 26 at Annex I ¶ 637.

[272] *See* Ch. XII, Sec. 4.

The strike, although apparently hitting a legitimate military target, caused severe damage to adjacent civilian infrastructure.[273]

25 June 2011. Brega. Libya's state news agency reported that on 25 June a NATO airstrike on a bakery and a restaurant in Brega killed 15 civilians and injured 20 more.[274] NATO did not comment on the airstrike.[275] According to its daily update, NATO conducted several strikes in Brega, including destroying a command and control node, a military storage facility, 14 truck-mounted guns, a tank, two armored personnel carriers, three logistic trucks and seven military shelters.[276]

25 July 2011. Zlitan. NATO carried out a strike in the town of Zlitan on 25 July, reportedly hitting a medical clinic and food storage buildings in the area.[277] According to its daily update for 25 July, NATO made several strikes in the vicinity of Zlitan, destroying three command and control nodes, one military armored vehicle storage facility and two armed vehicles.[278] *Thuwar* fighters in the area reported that the site had no military use, and that after the attack no military equipment was found, questioning the reasons for NATO's attack on the facility. Residents said one body was discovered in the rubble after the attack. Doctors at the hospital said they could not verify deaths resulting from the strike, or any prior deaths in the region, due to hospital registry records having been confiscated by Qadhafi officials.[279]

4 August 2011. Zlitan. At around 6:00 am, a NATO bomb struck a house belonging to a family, killing one woman and two children, and severely injuring another woman.[280] The family's home stood next to a compound

---

[273] Craig Allen et al., *Errant NATO Airstrikes in Libya: 13 Cases (Surman – post office)*, *supra* note 218.

[274] *See* Ch. VII, Sec 4.

[275] *Libyan state media say NATO airstrike kills 15*, AP, June 26, 2011, *available at* http://www.usatoday.com/news/world/2011-06-25-Libya-NATO-airstrike_n.htm.

[276] *NATO and Libya, Operational Media Update for 25 June 2011*, NORTH ATLANTIC TREATY ORGANIZATION, June 25, 2011, *available at* http://www.nato.int/nato_static/assets/pdf/pdf_2011_06/20110626_110626-oup-update.pdf.

[277] *NATO raids clinic in Libya: 7 killed*, AFP, July 25, 2011, *available at* http://www.newstoday.com.bd/index.php?option=details&news_id=34314&date=2011-07-26.

[278] *NATO and Libya, Operational Media Update for 25 July 2011*, NORTH ATLANTIC TREATY ORGANIZATION, July 26, 2011, *available at* http://www.nato.int/nato_static/assets/pdf/pdf_2011_07/20110726_110726-oup-update.pdf.

[279] Craig Allen et al., *Errant NATO Airstrikes in Libya: 13 Cases (Surman – warehouse)*, *supra* note 218.

[280] HUMAN RIGHTS WATCH, UNACKNOWLEDGED DEATHS, *supra* note 5 at 32.

owned by 'Umran al-Shammam, a doctor and regime supporter whose residence served as a meeting place for Qadhafi military officers.[281]

Witnesses told HRW that Qadhafi military personnel used the house next door to the residence until 2 August. The family denied that their residence had housed any military equipment or personnel, and stated that they had moved from their home out of fear from attack. When the regime forces moved out, the family moved back on 2 August.[282]

HRW reported that on 3 August satellite imagery showed no signs of military activity, and the organization's inspection of the premises a few days later supported that finding.[283] In January 2012, NATO's legal adviser stated in a letter to the CoI that the site was a "regime senior commander's command and control node, located within a residential property," and that it was "used exclusively by senior regime commanders as an active command and control facility directing forces in the Zlitan area."[284] NATO claimed this strike was carried out on 4, not 3, August and denied accusations that the attack had missed its intended target and had determined that the strikes all hit "legitimate military targets."[285] The letter goes on, "This target would not have been struck if NATO had any evidence or other reason to believe that a strike would injure or kill civilians."[286]

HRW found that NATO's response failed to provide sufficient evidence that the al-Morabit[287] residence met the criteria for military engagement.[288] In the course of its investigation, the CoI interviewed survivors and witnesses, and similarly concluded that "those killed were civilians and the building served no military function."[289]

6 August 2011. Tripoli. NATO conducted a strike against a missile depot in Tripoli, hitting a warehouse that allegedly held a dozen missiles, boosters, warheads and toxic rocket-fuel containers.[290] The depot was in a civilian

---

[281] Craig Allen et al., *Errant NATO Airstrikes in Libya: 13 Cases (Ziltan – houses), supra* note 218.

[282] HUMAN RIGHTS WATCH, UNACKNOWLEDGED DEATHS, *supra* note 5 at 33.

[283] *Id.* at 34, image 3.

[284] Letter from Paul Olson to Philippe Kirsch, Chair of the International Commission of Inquiry (Feb. 15 2012), in Report of the International Commission of Inquiry (Mar. 2012), *supra* note 26 at Annex II.

[285] *Id.*

[286] *Id.*

[287] The transliteration of this name was adopted from the reference. HUMAN RIGHTS WATCH, UNACKNOWLEDGED DEATHS, *supra* note 5.

[288] *Id.* at 35-6.

[289] Report of the International Commission of Inquiry (Mar. 2012), *supra* note 26 at Annex I ¶ 634.

[290] *See* Ch. XIII, Sec. 4.

neighborhood and neighboring buildings were destroyed. Powerful secondary explosions sent debris flying and at least one missile landed in the surrounding neighborhood. Several businesses and apartment buildings were badly damaged, and residents were injured a result of the strike.[291]

8 August 2011. Majer (10 kilometers south of Zlitan). A NATO operation in the town of Majer on 8 August led to the deaths of an estimated 34 victims. At around 11:30 pm NATO aircraft began an operation that destroyed four houses in Majer. The first strike hit a two-story house owned by a family, which at the time held about 82 people who had fled the fighting in nearby areas. According to a report presented by the families occupying the house, 14 persons were killed and 17 were wounded. At least three of the persons killed were children, along with at least four women.[292]

A few moments later NATO carried out a second strike, often referred to as a "double tap," that hit two houses in a nearby compound belonging to a family. At least four people were killed, including three women and a baby. During this strike a bomb also hit outside the family's house, killing 18 men and wounding 15 others who had rushed to the scene to assist the victims from the first attack.[293] Doctors confirmed a total of 34 deaths, including women and children, and stated that the men were wearing civilian clothes.[294]

HRW first visited the homes the day following the attacks and observed the funeral of the victims. There were no signs of military activity or reports that suggested the houses were legitimate military targets.[295] During a subsequent visit in December 2011, HRW found remnants of bombs such as a GBU-12 laser guided bomb, which allows the pilot to guide the bombs to the target.[296] NATO's response confirmed the findings with regard to weaponry deployed and claimed that the homes had been legitimate military targets.[297]

---

[291] Craig Allen et al., *Errant NATO Airstrikes in Libya: 13 Cases (Tripoli – missiles), supra* note 218.

[292] Human Rights Watch, Unacknowledged Deaths, *supra* note 5 at 27. *See also* Report of the International Commission of Inquiry (Mar. 2012), *supra* note 26 at Annex I ¶ 619–625.

[293] *Id.*

[294] Craig Allen et al., *Errant NATO Airstrikes in Libya: 13 Cases (Majer), supra* note 218.

[295] Human Rights Watch, Unacknowledged Deaths, *supra* note 5 at 30–2.

[296] GBU-12 laser-guided bombs have an infrared system used by the pilot to guide the bomb to its target. This means that the pilots of the aircraft dropping the bombs in the strike would have had to observe the target throughout the strike. *See* Ch. II, Appendix: Glossary of the Weapons used During the Conflict.

[297] Human Rights Watch, Unacknowledged Deaths, *supra* note 5 at 31.

NATO's daily update for 8 August reported that airstrikes destroyed a military facility and a communications system in the vicinity of Zlitan.[298] NATO announced that the strike was based on solid intelligence demonstrating that it was a military target. NATO reported that the attack targeted two former farm buildings that Qadhafi forces had transformed into a field military complex, and that the premises were used as a staging point for regime forces to provide temporary accommodation, troop reinforcement and military equipment.[299]

The incident was the most serious of all reported NATO attacks causing civilian deaths, and raises a number of unanswered questions. The reasoning for the second strike, in particular, which occurred while civilians were looking for injured persons among the rubble caused by the first attack, is questionable. The use of GBU-12 laser-guided bombs suggests that the pilot chose to carry out the attack even though it was impossible to determine whether the persons at the site were legitimate military targets.[300] The strike also raises concerns regarding the use of expired equipment by NATO that potentially led to malfunctioning weapons. The CoI found remnants from the Majer strike that showed that the guidance system on at least one of the bombs used in this attack was dated October 2005, well past its warranty date. NATO responded to questions over the expired weapons stating, "The fact alone that an expiration date has been passed does not mean that a weapon is no longer reliable, and the period of time during which a guidance system or munition is considered appropriate for use is thus a matter for individual Nations rather than for NATO itself."[301] The issue of expired weapons is one that has not been sufficiently addressed by either NATO as a coalition or the member countries that participated in the 8 August strike in Majer.

NATO provided further information to the CoI concerning the Majer incident in a February 2012 letter to the CoI, stating, "At the time of these strikes, these buildings had been identified as being used as a staging area

---

[298] *NATO and Libya, Operational Media Update for 9 August 2011*, NORTH ATLANTIC TREATY ORGANIZATION, Aug. 9, 2011, *available at* http://www.nato.int/nato_static/assets/pdf/pdf_2011_08/20110809_110809-oup-update.pdf.

[299] Carmen Romero & Roland Lavoie, *Press Briefing on Libya*, NORTH ATLANTIC TREATY ORGANIZATION, Aug. 9, 2011, *available at* http://www.nato.int/cps/en/natolive/opinions_77137.htm; *Libya says Nato air strike kills dozens south of Zlitan*, BBC, Aug. 9, 2011, *available at* http://www.bbc.co.uk/news/world-africa-14464400.

[300] HUMAN RIGHTS WATCH, UNACKNOWLEDGED DEATHS, *supra* note 5 at 32.

[301] Report of the International Commission of Inquiry (Mar. 2012), *supra* note 26 at Annex I ¶ 622.

for regime forces actively engaged in attacks on civilians and civilian-populated areas." The letter goes on to add, "It should be noted that at this point in the campaign regime forces, as well as mercenaries augmenting those forces, often wore civilian clothing."[302] The CoI's investigation, however, did not find any material, testimonial or satellite evidence indicating that the site of the strike served a military purpose, and found that NATO failed to provide "an adequate explanation of the military value of the target, nor an explanation of the second strike." Further, it concluded that the casualties at the site were all civilian, which also led the CoI to conclude there was no military rationale for the initial attack or subsequent decision to launch the second strike.[303]

29/30 August 2011. Bani Walid. During the night on 29 August and early morning 30 August, NATO aircraft carried out attacks that hit two adjacent homes belonging to a family.[304] NATO reported that on 29 August it carried out a strike in the vicinity of Bani Walid, leading to the destruction of two command and control nodes, and one ammunition storage facility.[305] Five persons were reportedly killed during the attacks, including two women and a girl. Another girl was seriously wounded. HRW obtained copies of the medical reports for all five casualties, and it noted that the causes of death were documented as a variety of traumatic injuries that were consistent with strikes carried out by NATO.[306]

NATO informed the CoI that the site had been a "major command and control node, which was reliant on non-traditional/informal methods to carry out that function." NATO added, "The site was actively controlling regime forces which were attacking civilians in the area."[307] During its site examination on 22 January 2012, the CoI found evidence that the homes were struck by GBU-12 laser guided bombs. It found no sign of weapon debris or military signatures to suggest a military base or storage facility,

---

[302] Letter from Paul Olson to Philippe Kirsch, Chair of the International Commission of Inquiry (Feb. 15, 2012), in Report of the International Commission of Inquiry (Mar. 2012), *supra* note 26 at Annex II.

[303] Report of the International Commission of Inquiry (Mar. 2012), *supra* note 26 at Annex I, ¶ 625.

[304] *See* Ch. XIV, Sec. 4.

[305] *NATO and Libya, Operational Media Update for 29 August 2011*, NORTH ATLANTIC TREATY ORGANIZATION, Aug. 30, 2011, *available at* http://www.nato.int/nato_static/assets/pdf/pdf_2011_08/20110830_110830-oup-update.pdf.

[306] HUMAN RIGHTS WATCH, 13 UNACKNOWLEDGED DEATHS, *supra* note 5 at 43.

[307] Letter from Paul Olson to Philippe Kirsch, Chair of the International Commission of Inquiry (Feb. 15, 2012), in Report of the International Commission of Inquiry (Mar. 2012), *supra* note 26 at Annex II.

or other signs such as communications equipment that would suggest the building was a command and control node. A review of satellite imagery revealed military activity in the area in the months preceding the strike, but none within 125 meters of the site itself. The CoI noted that while military activity may have taken place at the site after the satellite images were viewed, based on its investigations there was no evidence of any military purpose for striking the compound.[308]

9 September 2011. Bani Walid. On 9 September, NATO bombed a medical school in Bani Walid consisting of more than 35 buildings.[309] NATO reported that it carried out a 9 September strike in the vicinity of Bani Walid, leading to the destruction of an armed vehicle.[310] During its investigations the CoI was unable to find any physical evidence suggesting that the buildings served a military purpose. Rather, it found evidence, including schoolbooks and medical equipment, supporting the testimony given by locals that the complex was a school.[311] NATO maintained that the complex was being used as a command and control facility, but failed to substantiate its claims with evidence.[312]

16 September 2011. Sirte. NATO aircraft carried out an attack that struck a large seven-story apartment complex called 'Imara al-Ta'min in central Sirte.[313] A pregnant woman was killed, as well as a young man. Several persons were injured; one was a four-year-old girl who suffered shrapnel wounds to several parts of her body. The area had been the scene of intense fighting prior to the strike. Qadhafi forces reportedly tried to occupy the building and position snipers on the roof of the complex, but it is not clear if they succeeded.[314]

HRW's investigation of the incident found remnants of military activity, which, if they had been present before the NATO airstrike, would make the building a valid military target. However, according to the laws of

---

[308] Report of the International Commission of Inquiry (Mar. 2012), *supra* note 26 at Annex I ¶ 634.

[309] *See* Ch. XIV, Sec. 4.

[310] *NATO and Libya, Operational Media Update for 9 September 2011*, NORTH ATLANTIC TREATY ORGANIZATION, Sept. 10, 2011, *available at* http://www.nato.int/nato_static/assets/pdf/pdf_2011_09/20110910_110910-oup-update.pdf.

[311] Report of the International Commission of Inquiry (Mar. 2012), *supra* note 26 at Annex I ¶ 641.

[312] *Id.* at Annex I ¶ 643.

[313] *See* Ch. XV, Sec. 4. *See also* HUMAN RIGHTS WATCH, UNACKNOWLEDGED DEATHS, *supra* note 5 at 47.

[314] HUMAN RIGHTS WATCH, UNACKNOWLEDGED DEATHS, *supra* note 5 at 50.

proportionality, the military gain of destroying the building would need to be weighed against the potential harm to civilians.[315]

16 September 2011. Sirte. On 16 September, two dynamic strikes led to the deaths of an estimated 58 individuals, of whom 47 were reportedly civilians.[316] In the first strike, two pick-up trucks belonging to Qadhafi forces were destroyed and 30 persons in the vicinity of the trucks were killed.[317] NATO maintained that the trucks had been firing into civilian areas and that the airstrikes had been authorized once the vehicles left civilian areas, stating, "The vehicles were not struck until they left the populated area where they had initially been observed, and had relocated to an area free of civilians and civilian structures." NATO added, "The two vehicles struck were sufficiently separated that a singe precision-guided weapon of the type employed would have been insufficient to destroy them both."[318] The CoI concluded, "Although the vehicles were a legal target they were engaged on the edge of Sirte within 30 meters of civilian structures."[319] Witnesses stated that shortly thereafter a second bomb hit the site, killing an additional 28 civilians, some of whom were children.[320] The CoI's investigation determined that

> [T]he weapons used were GBU-12 laser guided bombs based on bomb guidance fins recovered at the site. The Commission's investigation showed those killed were in fact most likely armed civilian volunteers. The Commission was unable to come to a conclusion on the presence of non-combatants, as witness information was contradictory.[321]

23 September 2011. Gurdabiyya (20 kilometers/12 miles east of Sirte). At about 4:00 pm, NATO struck a house on a farm east of Sirte, killing three persons – an elderly man and two young girls. HRW obtained copies of death certificates for all three people. The extended family had congregated

---

[315] *Id.*

[316] PRE-ASSESSMENT MISSION, LIBYA, *supra* note 262 at 45.

[317] *See* Ch. XV, Sec. 4. *See also* Report of the International Commission of Inquiry (Mar. 2012), *supra* note 26 at Annex I ¶ 647.

[318] Letter from Paul Olson to Philippe Kirsch, Chair of the International Commission of Inquiry (Feb. 15 2012), in Report of the International Commission of Inquiry (Mar. 2012), *supra* note 26 at Annex II.

[319] Report of the International Commission of Inquiry (Mar. 2012), *supra* note 26 at Annex I ¶ 647.

[320] *Id.* at Annex I ¶ 648.

[321] *Id.* at Annex I ¶ 648.

there after their homes in central Sirte had been shelled. Three children and a woman were also wounded.[322]

The strike damaged the northeast corner of the house but the building was still standing after the attack, and the strike produced a crater just outside the house. HRW inspected the premises on 6 February 2012 and found no evidence of military activity apart from a green uniform and two spent weapons cartridges. HRW reported that other materiel may have been removed prior to the visit, and found remnants of a GBU-12 laser guided bomb.[323] A neighbor said that the farm belonged to a colonel in the Libyan army who had not been present at the time of the attack. Another witness claimed that there had been fighting in the area at the time between Qadhafi and *thuwar* forces. The family members however, said there had not been any fighting on the day of the NATO strike.[324]

25 September 2011. Sirte. At around 4:30 am in the eastern part of central Sirte, NATO carried out two airstrikes on the home of Salam Diyab, the target presumably being the owner's brother, Brigadier General Musba Ahmad Diyab.[325] It has not been confirmed whether the General was present in the home at the time of the attack. Seven of his relatives, all women and children, were killed.[326] The reasons for the attack were not clear since NATO declined to comment or provide information regarding the intended target.[327] While General Diyab could be considered a legitimate military target due to his position in the Qadhafi military, the attack was not consistent with NATO's explicit policy of not targeting individuals. In addition, the loss of civilian lives in the attack appears disproportionate in relation to the military gain, unless proven otherwise by NATO.[328]

10 October 2011. Bani Walid. On 10 October, a NATO airstrike in Bani Walid destroyed a tile factory.[329] During its investigation, the CoI was unable to identify any physical or testimonial evidence that the building had served a military purpose, as there was no military debris or evidence of a secondary explosion from locally stored weapons.[330] Subsequent

---

[322] Human Rights Watch, Unacknowledged Deaths, *supra* note 5 at 53.
[323] *Id.* at 54.
[324] *Id.*
[325] *See* Ch. XV, Sec. 4.
[326] Human Rights Watch, Unacknowledged Deaths, *supra* note 5 at 47.
[327] Craig Allen et al., *Errant NATO Airstrikes in Libya: 13 Cases (Surt – general's home),* *supra* note 218.
[328] Human Rights Watch, Unacknowledged Deaths, *supra* note 5 at 50.
[329] *See* Ch. XIV, Sec. 4.
[330] Human Rights Watch, Unacknowledged Deaths, *supra* note 5 at 50.

analysis of satellite imagery failed to reveal any military activity at the site prior to the strike.[331]

NATO claimed that the site was "an industrial compound that had been taken over for military purposes and was being used at the time as a command and control node." NATO also found that "on the basis of its standard targeting methodology...it was concluded that no civilians were at this isolated facility."[332] The CoI found that this assertion was contradicted by testimonial evidence by locals and the absence of physical evidence linking the site to military activity.[333]

7. ASSESSING NATO OPERATIONS

7.1. *Direct Foreign Assistance for Opposition Forces*

The authorization for foreign intervention in Libya was based on Resolution 1973, which called on UN Member States to take "all necessary measures" to protect civilians under threat of attack from regime forces.[334] Third party states interpreted the Resolution as a mandate to use force to protect civilians and, in many instances, extended this to include direct support for rebels seeking to overthrow the Libyan government. NATO's direct support to one party in the conflict through the provision of weapons and training expands the scope of civilian protection under Resolution 1973. This support may also be viewed as an attempt on the part of NATO to effect regime change.[335] The expansion of the mission to include foreign support for regime change calls into question the legality of and justification for certain activities that may have transgressed the boundaries set by Resolution 1973, NATO's rules of engagement and Article 2(4) of the UN Charter. Additionally, the use of force when not sanctioned by Articles 2(4) and 2(7) of the Charter may constitute a crime of aggres-

---

[331] Report of the International Commission of Inquiry (Mar. 2012), *supra* note 26 at Annex I, ¶ 645.

[332] Letter from Paul Olson to Philippe Kirsch, Chair of the International Commission of Inquiry (Feb. 15 2012), *in* Report of the International Commission of Inquiry (Mar. 2012), *supra* note 26 at Annex II.

[333] Report of the International Commission of Inquiry (Mar. 2012), *supra* note 26 at Annex I ¶ 646.

[334] SC Res. 1973 (2011), *supra* note 3 at ¶ 4.

[335] Similarly the bombing of Qadhafi's home in Tripoli and the bombing of his convoy in Sirte shortly before his death do not appear to have any justification under the original rationale for intervention.

sion. This section addresses certain actions undertaken by foreign actors in Libya and the legal and policy implications of such actions.

NATO's role in Libya quickly shifted from carrying out selective air-strikes against Qadhafi's security installations and military forces to coordinating directly with rebel groups. NATO commanders sought better intelligence as Qadhafi forces shifted tactics and moved command and control centers and weapons installations around the country. The mission also appeared to shift from protecting civilians to effecting regime change, as NATO refused offers for a ceasefire that would have allowed for Qadhafi to stay in power.[336] Firsthand accounts and witness testimonies indicate that NATO adopted an offensive posture in support of rebel advances during the conflict.[337]

The U.S. State Department sent Christopher Stevens to Benghazi in April 2011 to serve as a liaison to the NTC,[338] establishing a direct line of communication with Libya's opposition movement.[339] On 14 April, UK and Qatari representatives organized the first Libya Contact Group meeting, involving the United Kingdom, Qatar, Italy, Kuwait, France and others who agreed to develop a mechanism for providing financial support to the NTC.[340] The Contact Group had been promoted by the UK Prime Minister and backed by the UN Secretary-General, as a way to broaden and strengthen Resolution 1973.[341] Members of the Contact Group, in particular France and Qatar, soon began supplying weapons to opposition forces.[342]

The United Kingdom, Italy and France acknowledged sending military advisers to Libya to work to improve opposition command and control arrangements and communications, in addition to their support for NATO

---

[336] *See* Ch. II, Sec. 3.2. *See also* Etzioni, *supra* note 45 at 49.

[337] PRE-ASSESSMENT MISSION, LIBYA, *supra* note 262 at 43.

[338] *See* Ch. VI, Sec. 2.

[339] *See* BLANCHARD, UNREST AND U.S. POLICY, *supra* note 22 at 11.

[340] *Id.* at *Summary.*

[341] Report of the High Commissioner under Human Rights Council resolution S-15/1, U.N. HRC 17th Sess., ¶ 15, U.N. Doc. A/HRC/17/45, advanced unedited version (June 7, 2011).

[342] BELL ET AL., STALEMATE AND SIEGE, *supra* note 195 at 15; U.N. Security Council, Final report of the Panel of Experts established pursuant to resolution 1973 (2011) concerning Libya, ¶ 62–72, U.N. S/2013/99 (Mar. 9, 2013); *France airdropped arms to the rebels*, BBC, June 29, 2011, *available at* http://www.bbc.co.uk/news/world-africa-13955751; *Qatari weapons reaching rebels in the Libyan Mountains*, REUTERS, Mar. 31, 2011, *available at* http://www.reuters.com/article/2011/05/31/us-libya-weapons-idUSTRE74U3C520110531.

operations.[343] On 19 April, Britain's Foreign Secretary, William Hague, announced the United Kingdom's diplomatic mission in Benghazi would expand to include an additional military liaison advisory team. The military advisers were sent to work with the NTC to improve their military organizational structures, communications and logistics.[344] Hague attested that the deployment was fully within the terms of Resolution 1973, and would not involve direct training or arming the rebel forces.[345]

The relationship between foreign actors and rebel forces deepened following the establishment of relations with the NTC and the creation of the Contact Group, providing support that included diplomatic exchanges, non-lethal equipment supplies, defensive weapons, logistical support and training for *thuwar* forces, in addition to intelligence sharing.[346]

On 26 April, the United States approved the provision of $25 million in "non-lethal" commodities, equipment and services for the NTC.[347] The commodities included, but were not limited to, "vehicles, fuel trucks, and fuel bladders, ambulances, medical equipment, protective vests, binoculars, and non-secure radios."[348] By the end of June, France conducted weapons airdrops that included machine guns, rocket-propelled grenades and anti-tank rockets, significantly strengthening the rebel capacity to battle the Qadhafi forces.[349] The French Defense Ministry spokesperson, Thierry Burkhard, claimed that these weapons transfers fell under the

---

[343] Alan Cowell, *France and Italy Will Also Send Advisers to Libya Rebels*, N.Y. TIMES, Apr. 20, 2011, *available at* http://www.nytimes.com/2011/04/21/world/africa/21libya.html.

[344] Press Release, *UK Ministry of Defense, UK military liaison advisory team to be sent to Libya*, MINISTRY OF DEFENCE, Apr. 19 2011, *available at* http://www.mod.uk/Defence Internet/DefenceNews/DefencePolicyAndBusiness/UkMilitaryLiaisonAdvisoryTeam ToBeSentToLibya.htm.

[345] *Id.*

[346] *See* Ch. II, Sec. 2.3.

[347] *Obama directs $25M to support Libyan rebels*, CBS NEWS, Apr. 26 2011, *available at* http://www.cbsnews.com/2100-250_162-20057689.html.

[348] BLANCHARD, UNREST AND U.S. POLICY, *supra* note 22 at 11.

[349] *See* Ch. II, Sec. 3.3. *See also* France gives Libya rebels arms but Britain balks, AFP, June 29, 2011, *available at* http://www.google.com/hostednews/afp/article/ALeqM5gst8wAKgJwnMv BWiTl9EQ1Zpylmg?docId=CNG.041943dc452c61a507ee986061b49f2d.1031; Louis Charbonneau & Hamuda Hassan, *France defends arms airlift to Libya rebels*, REUTERS, June 30, 2011, *available at* http://www.reuters.com/article/2011/06/29/us-libya-idUSTRE7270JP20110629; Michael Birnbaum, *France sent arms to Libyan rebels*, WASHINGTON TIMES, June 29, 2011, *available at* http://articles.washingtonpost.com/2011-06-29/world/35235276_1_nafusa-moun tains-hans-hillen-libyan-rebels; Nick Hopkins, *NATO reviews Libya campaign after France admits arming rebels*, THE GUARDIAN, June 29, 2011, *available at* http://www.guardian. co.uk/world/2011/jun/29/nato-review-libya-france-arming-rebels; INTERNATIONAL CRISIS GROUP, HOLDING LIBYA TOGETHER: SECURITY CHALLENGES AFTER QADHAFI (Dec. 14 2011), *available at* http://www.crisisgroup.org/~/media/Files/Middle%20East%20North%20

classification of humanitarian drops because, "The humanitarian situation was worsening and at one point it seemed the security situation was threatening civilians who could not defend themselves."[350]

The weapons drops reportedly came as a surprise to NATO command headquarters, which conducted a review of the legality of the provision of weapons in the conflict, and had difficulty finding a legal basis for the weapons transfers.[351] Russian officials called into question the legality of arming the rebels, claiming that the actions were outside the scope of the UN mandate. France's Foreign Affairs Minister Alain Juppe countered, stating, "We believe that within the frameworks of Resolutions 1970 and 1973 – and 1970 as a whole – it is clear that all means are legitimate for protecting peaceful civilians."[352]

By the time NATO took over official command of operations, reports of covert intelligence operations taking place in Libya began to surface. On 31 March 2011, the New York Times published a report quoting several U.S. and UK officials who confirmed, off the record, the CIA and MI6's involvement in operations in Libya.[353] These operations included meeting with rebels and gathering intelligence on Qadhafi's military installations.[354] While the U.S. administration would not comment publicly on U.S. intelligence involvement in Libya, in April 2011 the White House did not rule out the option of the United States providing direct security assistance to the Libyan opposition.[355]

Special forces from third party states played a particularly significant role in the 2011 conflict and capture of Tripoli.[356] Reports indicate that the first arrival of special forces occurred on 23–24 February 2011, when

---

Africa/North%20Africa/115%20Holding%20Libya%20Together%20--%20Security%20Chal lenges%20after%20Qadhafi.pdf.

[350] Pineau & Irish, *France provided weapons, food to Libya rebels, supra* note 204.

[351] Hopkins, *NATO reviews Libya campaign after France admits arming rebels, supra* note 195.

[352] Nicholas Rushworth, *France Under Fire for Arming Rebels*, FRANCE 24, July 3, 2011, *available at* http://www.france24.com/en/20110701-france-arms-libya-rebels-un-resolution-russia-juppe-diplomacy-military.

[353] Mark Mazzetti & Eric Schmitt, *C.I.A. Agents in Libya Aid Airstrikes and Meet Rebels*, N.Y. TIMES, Mar. 30, 2011, *available at* http://www.nytimes.com/2011/03/31/world/africa/31intel.html.

[354] *Id.*

[355] BLANCHARD, UNREST AND U.S. POLICY, *supra* note 22 at 11.

[356] *See* Ch. XIII, Sec. 4. *See also* Sean Rayment, *How the special forces helped bring Gaddafi to his knees*, TELEGRAPH, Aug. 28, 2011, *available at* http://www.telegraph.co.uk/news/worldnews/africaandindianocean/libya/8727076/How-the-special-forces-helped-bring-Gaddafi-to-his-knees.html.

foreign nations deployed soldiers to help evacuate their citizens.[357] At the same time, UK and French units reportedly entered Benghazi and Tobruq to begin establishing links with rebel groups.[358] The new supply of French weapons delivered in June gave rise to the need for weapons training. France and the United Kingdom each reportedly had 30–40 personnel in Misrata and Zintan by June 2011, and focused on tactical coordination with *thuwar* forces and intelligence units.[359] Further sources indicate that France and the United Kingdom's special forces served as spotters to provide intelligence for NATO pilots.[360]

NATO commanders openly discussed the importance of accurate on-the-ground intelligence to facilitate targeted strikes. After a June incursion by *thuwar* forces in the western city of Zawiyya, for example, NATO reported that it would continue to focus intelligence gathering on the region to build a better understanding of the events on the ground.[361] While the spokesperson did not give specifics on the intelligence gathering methods, he did report that NATO relied on "highly sophisticated intelligence reporting, and information analysis" to enable the United States and its allied forces to carry out their mission.[362] Due to the limits set by the Security Council Resolution, however, NATO continued to maintain that the coalition forces had no direct line communications with rebel units.[363]

Independent fact finding missions collected information, including testimony from rebel commanders, indicating that NATO personnel were on the ground in Libya during the fighting to provide logistical support and coordinate NATO airstrikes.[364] Numerous sources provided details about NATO missions, including the deployment of advisers to make contact with the rebels. According to rebel leaders, a NATO adviser was attached to every rebel unit or "front."[365]

---

[357] ROYAL UNITED SERVICES INSTITUTE, ACCIDENTAL HEROES, *supra* note 24 at 10.

[358] *Special forces swoop on Libya to pull Britons to safety*, DAILY TELEGRAPH, Feb. 26, 2011, *available at* http://www.telegraph.co.uk/news/worldnews/africaandindianocean/libya/8349896/Special-forces-swoop-on-Libya-to-pull-Britons-to-safety.html; Alan Cowell & Ravi Somaiya, *France and Italy will also send advisers to Libya rebels*, N.Y. TIMES, Apr. 20, 2011, *available at* http://www.nytimes.com/2011/04/21/world/africa/21libya.html.

[359] ROYAL UNITED SERVICES INSTITUTE, ACCIDENTAL HEROES, *supra* note 24 at 12.

[360] BELL ET AL., STALEMATE AND SIEGE, *supra* note 195 at 33, n. 34.

[361] Lungescu & Bracken, NATO, *supra* note 205.

[362] *Id.*

[363] Anrig, *Allied Air Power over Libya, supra* note 37 at 99.

[364] PRE-ASSESSMENT MISSION, LIBYA, *supra* note 262 at 43.

[365] *Id.*

Non-NATO countries also played a critical role in providing weapons, equipment and training for rebel forces. For example, Egyptian forces were involved from the start of the conflict, reportedly providing weapons and training in eastern Libya.[366] Qatar's involvement perhaps went further than that of any other country, providing significant amounts of weapons, aid, materiel and weapons training. Qatari officials openly reported having advisers on the ground, who also served as a link between NATO and the *thuwar* forces.[367] NATO officials, rebel commanders and the Qatari Prime Minister all pointed to the important role of the Gulf state in the conflict, and reported on shipments of weapons, such as shoulder-fired anti-tank weapons to the rebels.[368]

The provision of weapons and training for rebel fighters helped turn the tide of the civil war towards the *thuwar* forces.[369] The foreign support not only consisted of providing necessary equipment, but also the technology that made communication and coordination among rebel groups possible. As early as April 2011, reports indicated that Qatari weapons and training were enhancing rebel capacity in Cyrenaica.[370] In the Nafusa Mountains accounts from August 2011 indicated that special forces units from France, Qatar and Jordan were dramatically increasing the capacity of the rebel forces.[371] British, French and Qatari special forces also provided weapons, fuel, food and medicine to *thuwar* in Tripolitania, in preparation for the final assault on the capital.[372]

Some NATO and allied countries interpreted the UN mandate to justify direct support for Libya's rebel factions. Other Security Council members questioned the legitimacy of these actions, citing the Resolution 1973 stipulation that explicitly did not allow for "a foreign occupation force of

---

[366] ROYAL UNITED SERVICES INSTITUTE, ACCIDENTAL HEROES, *supra* note 24 at 11.

[367] Ian Black, *Qatar admits sending hundreds of troops to support Libya rebels*, GUARDIAN, Oct. 26, 2011, *available at* http://www.guardian.co.uk/world/2011/oct/26/qatar-troops-libya-rebels-support.

[368] BELL ET AL., THE TIDE TURNS, *supra* note 203 at 15.

[369] Michael Georgy, *Captured Libyan soldiers say army morale is low*, REUTERS, July 29, 2011, *available at* http://www.reuters.com/article/2011/07/29/us-libya-morale-idUSTRE76R4KD20110729.

[370] *See* Ch. II, Sec. 2.3. *See also* BELL ET AL., STALEMATE AND SIEGE, *supra* note 195 at 15.

[371] Margaret Coker, *Length of Libya's standoff hinges on leader's militia*, WALL STREET JOURNAL, Aug. 24, 2011, *available at* http://online.wsj.com/article/SB10001424053111903327904576526642369893206.html; *Battle for Tripoli: pivotal victory in the mountains helped big push*, GUARDIAN, Aug. 22 2011, *available at* http://www.guardian.co.uk/world/2011/aug/22/battle-for-tripoli-libya-gaddafi.

[372] *See* Ch. XIII, Sec. 4. *See also* BELL ET AL., THE TIDE TURNS, *supra* note 203 at 17.

any form on any part of Libyan territory."[373] Under these guidelines, it remains contested whether materiel and personnel support qualify as a foreign occupation force.

Some analysts have suggested the vagueness of the phrase, "all means necessary" to protect civilians is problematic, allowing for loose guidelines and restrictions on military intervention. NATO and other third party states' interpretation of the meaning of "all necessary measures" as justification for certain actions, such as the arming and training of rebel forces, continues to be subject to debate.[374] While it is virtually impossible to conclude that the provision of materiel to one party or another would fall afoul of the civilian protection mandate of Resolution 1973 the Security Council has yet to offer its guidance on the matter. Furthermore, there is extensive information indicating that *thuwar* forces were likewise committing violations against civilians in the form of reprisal violence in towns and villages where NATO operations were taking place.[375] The extent to which NATO's provision of materiel contributed to the occurrence of such violations should therefore be examined. In order to clarify the foregoing, it would be helpful for the United Nations to develop a set of policy guidelines to enhance its collaboration with military bodies such as NATO.[376] Laying out clear terms of what the UN resolutions permit and what they do not permit would help avoid the challenges that arise from third party direct intervention in sovereign states.

7.2. *Military Targets and Civilian Casualties*

As outlined above, the Geneva Conventions and customary IHL obligate parties to an armed conflict to determine that a target constitutes a valid military objective prior to the use of force and to take all possible precautions to minimize civilian casualties.[377] This rule requires that attackers distinguish between civilian and military targets, and that under no circumstances should civilian objects be directly targeted. International law requires that attackers "take all feasible precautions" to determine

---

[373] SC Res. 1973, *supra* note 3.

[374] Pre-Assessment Mission, Libya, *supra* note 262 at 43.

[375] *See* Chs. IX, X, XII, & XIII.

[376] Ademola Abass, *Assessing NATO's Involvement in Libya*, United Nations University, Oct. 27, 2011, *available at* http://unu.edu/publications/articles/assessing-nato-s-involvement-in-libya.html.

[377] Pre-Assessment Mission, Libya, *supra* note 262 at 44.

the legality of the strike and minimize harm to civilians and civilian objects.[378]

It is evident that NATO took measures to minimize civilian deaths in its air campaign; the number of civilian casualties from thousands of sorties was relatively low. Several independent investigations found, however, that NATO failed to adequately investigate a number of incidents.[379] The CoI recorded several incidents in which NATO airstrikes caused civilian deaths or damage to civilian objects. Among the 20 NATO airstrikes the CoI studied, five resulted in civilian casualties, including 60 dead and 55 injured. In two cases, the CoI could not identify a valid military target among the damaged civilian infrastructure.[380] The incidents outlined in the survey above call into question whether NATO was consistently diligent in distinguishing between civilian and military targets in accordance with the requirements of conventional and customary IHL. During the attack in Majer on 8 August, for example, the pilot could not have been able to determine whether civilians were in danger after the first strike, yet decided to carry out a second strike that led to more civilian casualties. The justification and reasoning for not aborting this mission should be further investigated.

In several instances documented above, NATO claimed that certain civilian structures constituted legitimate military targets because they were being used as command and control nodes. However, investigations based on witness testimony and on-the-ground forensic analysis documented cases where there were no signs of military activity at locations claimed to be command and control centers. Independent commissions that visited sites after strikes in many cases found no evidence of military weapons, munitions or communication equipment. These observers have called into question the reasoning for destroying structures where no military activity could be determined.[381]

Of the five cases where the CoI documented civilian casualties resulting from airstrikes, NATO claimed four of these were command and control

---

[378] Report of the International Commission of Inquiry (Mar. 2012), *supra* note 26 at Annex I ¶ 614.

[379] *See e.g.*, HUMAN RIGHTS WATCH, UNACKNOWLEDGED DEATHS, *supra* note 5 at 56–9.

[380] Report of the International Commission of Inquiry (Mar. 2012), *supra* note 26 at ¶ 86.

[381] PRE-ASSESSMENT MISSION, LIBYA, *supra* note 262 at 19.

nodes or troop staging areas.[382] The CoI's investigation into these sites, however, provided no corroboration for this claim, either from the physical evidence available or on the basis of witness statements. In response to the CoI's findings, NATO responded that, "The regime was using civilian rather than military structures in support of military action." The CoI expressed concern that if NATO based its strikes according to this assessment, civilian casualties would invariably occur.[383] The CoI also found evidence to suggest that in some instances NATO hit the wrong target or hit homes adjacent to military facilities. This was the case in Zlitan, where the CoI found evidence suggesting that NATO hit a civilian structure that served no military function, killing civilians.[384]

Human rights organizations also documented strikes where the presence of military activity was questionable. HRW investigated eight NATO airstrikes and reported they caused at least 72 civilian deaths, including 24 children and 20 women.[385] In five of the sites, there were possible signs of military presence. In two of the eight sites, HRW found no evidence of military activity.[386] The HRW report acknowledged the fact that military equipment might have been removed from the sites by the Qadhafi regime or residents in order to incriminate NATO. However, other evidence, such as witness statements and satellite imagery, supports the claim that the sites did not host military forces or equipment.[387]

During the conflict, human rights organizations began advocating for investigations into civilian casualties resulting from the NATO campaign. Groups such as Amnesty International called on NATO to take the necessary precautions to avoid civilian casualties during military operations, and in early August 2011 urged NATO to investigate reports of civilian harm.[388]

---

[382] The four cases were Tripoli (Suq al-Juma') Zlitan on Aug. 4, Majer on Aug. 8, Bani Walid on Aug. 29/30.

[383] Report of the International Commission of Inquiry (Mar. 2012), *supra* note 26 at ¶ 88.

[384] *Id.* at Annex I ¶ 632.

[385] The report included investigations of civilian casualties in eight locations; Zlitan on Aug. 4, Majer on Aug. 8, Tripoli (Suq al-Juma') on June 20, Surman on June 20, Bani Walid on Aug. 29/30, Sirte on Sep. 16, Gurdabiyya on Sep. 23 and Sirte on Sep. 25.

[386] These sights were Tripoli (Suq al-Juma') on June 20 and Zlitan on Aug. 4.

[387] HUMAN RIGHTS WATCH, UNACKNOWLEDGED DEATHS, *supra* note 5 at 36, 40 & 54.

[388] *NATO urged to investigate civilian deaths during Libya air strikes*, AMNESTY INTERNATIONAL, Aug. 10, 2011, *available at* http://www.amnesty.org/en/news-and-updates/nato-urged-investigate-civilian-deaths-during-libya-air-strikes-2011-08-10.

NATO denied the allegations that illegitimate military targets were attacked during its air campaign in Libya. NATO claimed that its efforts went beyond the requirements of international humanitarian law, stating that civilian casualties were avoided due to the organization's advanced methods and well-planned attacks. This included a targeting review process for preplanned and dynamic targets, the use of precision-guided weapons and delayed fusing of munitions. In addition, NATO reported that civilians were warned to avoid military targets with the help of leaflets dropped by aircraft and media broadcasts.[389]

When NATO's involvement in Libya came to an end on 31 October 2011, NATO Secretary-General Anders Fogh Rasmussen stated, "We have carried out this operation very carefully, without confirmed civilian casualties."[390] This statement contradicts NATO's own accounts during combat operations, as they did in fact acknowledge civilian casualties on several occasions. On 21 June 2011, for example, a NATO spokesperson acknowledged civilian casualties resulting from a "technical failure" in which one of NATO's weapons did not strike the intended military target the previous day in Tripoli, resulting in "a number of civilian casualties."[391] The NATO spokesperson stated

> Where NATO believes we have caused civilian casualties we will say so and we will do it as swiftly as we can establish the facts. The tragic accident in Tripoli is an exception. If you look at our track record after over 4,000 strike sorties you can see we have taken utmost care to avoid civilian casualties and will continue to do so.[392]

Media accounts reported that the strike killed up to nine civilians in their home, including two children.[393]

After the end of the Libyan civil war, a report by Campaign for Innocent Victims in Conflict and Refugees International claimed that despite credible reports of civilian casualties, NATO "failed to track, investigate, or

---

[389] HUMAN RIGHTS WATCH, UNACKNOWLEDGED DEATHS, *supra* note 5 at 24.

[390] C.J. Chivers & Eric Schmitt, *In Strikes on Libya by NATO, an Unspoken Civilian Toll, supra* note 49.

[391] Lungescu & Bracken, NATO, *supra* note 252.

[392] *Id.*

[393] Adam Schreck, *Libya says NATO airstrike killed 9 civilians*, AP, June 19, 2011, *available at* http://www.seattlepi.com/news/article/Libya-says-NATO-airstrike-killed-9-civilians-1429 866.php.

make amends to civilians unintentionally harmed by its military actions."[394] NATO did not regularly include figures or record information on civilian casualties in its otherwise very detailed summary fact sheet or daily briefings for OUP. The group also noted that NATO policy in Libya was different from its policy in Afghanistan where NATO officials apologized to victims and their families, explained what happened and offered reparations.[395]

When called on to investigate the civilian deaths that resulted from its strikes, NATO claimed that it had no mandate to conduct investigations in Libya after the conflict, but that it would "cooperate fully" with the Libyan authorities to review the incidents.[396] The new Libyan government took initial steps to investigate the incidents by forming an inter-ministerial task force. According to Libya's Ambassador to the United Nations, the government intended to establish "a mechanism to indemnify victims with financial and moral support once we have obtained the results of the investigations."[397] The results of the investigation were to be made public. However, due to the role played by NATO in the ousting of the Qadhafi regime, NGOs such as HRW surmised that the investigation was not likely to present any serious criticism of NATO's air campaign.[398]

In December 2011, investigative reporters from the New York Times published an extensive report on civilian casualties stemming from "errant" NATO airstrikes.[399] In the report, the journalists investigated 13 NATO strike sites in Libya and concluded that between 40 and 70 individuals had been killed.[400] After the publication of the New York Times article and continued pressure for investigations, NATO responded by acknowledging civilian casualties but defending actions taken during the campaign.

---

[394] CAMPAIGN FOR INNOCENT VICTIMS IN CONFLICT, LIBYA: PROTECT VULNERABLE MINORITIES & ASSIST CIVILIANS HARMED (Nov. 2011), *available at* http://www.civicworld wide.org/storage/documents/civic-ri%20libya%20report%202011%20final.pdf.

[395] *Id.*

[396] HUMAN RIGHTS WATCH, UNACKNOWLEDGED DEATHS, *supra* note 5 at 25.

[397] *Id.* at 22.

[398] Human Rights Watch reported that as of late April 2012, no such investigation was underway. *Id.* at 23.

[399] Craig Allen et al., *Errant NATO Airstrikes in Libya: 13 Cases (Surman – warehouse)*, *supra* note 218.

[400] The Times analysis included an investigation into three air strikes in Surman, a town outside Zawiyya; Mizda, a town south of Al-Gharyan in the country's far south; two in Tripoli; two in Zlitan, a city between Tripoli and Misrata; one in Majer, a village also located between Tripoli and Misrata; two in Sirte; and one in Brega in eastern Libya. *See also* C.J. Chivers & Eric Schmitt, *In Strikes on Libya by NATO, an Unspoken Civilian Toll*, *supra* note 49.

In NATO's January 2012 letter to Philippe Kirsch, the then Chair of the CoI, NATO's legal adviser Olson argued that NATO's methods were "as well-designed and as successfully implemented to avoid civilian casualties as was humanly and technically possible."[401] Similarly, NATO spokesperson Oana Lungescu said, "No target was approved or struck if we had any reason to believe that civilians would be at risk."[402] Lungescu also responded to the New York Times exposé stating, "From what you [the New York Times] have gathered on the ground, it appears that innocent civilians may have been killed or injured, despite all the care and precision...We deeply regret any loss of life."[403] NATO's Deputy Assistant Secretary General Richard Froh wrote to HRW in March 2012, conceding, "No complex campaign can exclude that civilians suffer harm during its course."[404]

NATO did provide information in response to inquiries regarding specific precautions taken to avoid civilian casualties. However, when it came to providing clarifying information on the legal justification for attacks on each of the intended targets, NATO was less forthcoming.[405] When asked to release gun camera video from the strikes, for example, NATO replied that, "Video footage is the property of individual nations and is classified in order to protect important information about platform capabilities."[406] NATO also provided details about the sites investigated by the CoI, but failed to provide information to support its claim that these targets were legitimate military targets. The CoI concluded that it was unable to draw conclusions on targets that showed no evidence of military activity, and recommended further investigations into these strikes.[407] The vague responses from NATO failed to present a clear picture of what had actually taken place during many of the incidents in question, and NATO continued to state that if any credible evidence was presented which suggested that NATO's actions were unlawful, this would be taken into account.[408]

---

[401] Letter from Paul Olson to Philippe Kirsch, Chair of the International Commission of Inquiry (Jan. 23 2012), in Report of the International Commission of Inquiry (Mar. 2012), *supra* note 26 at Annex II.

[402] HUMAN RIGHTS WATCH, UNACKNOWLEDGED DEATHS, *supra* note 5 at 23.

[403] C.J. Chivers & Eric Schmitt, *In Strikes on Libya by NATO, an Unspoken Civilian Toll*, *supra* note 49.

[404] HUMAN RIGHTS WATCH, UNACKNOWLEDGED DEATHS, *supra* note 5 at 24.

[405] *Id.*

[406] *Id.*

[407] Report of the International Commission of Inquiry (Mar. 2012), *supra* note 26 at ¶ 122.

[408] HUMAN RIGHTS WATCH, UNACKNOWLEDGED DEATHS, *supra* note 5 at 24.

It should be noted that NATO made investigations difficult, as they failed to specify which countries were involved in particular strikes, and claimed that individual nations were responsible for their own assessments of the alleged incidents.[409] However, seven out of eight countries involved in the strikes responded that the issue should be referred to NATO because "the operation was conducted under NATO command."[410] In May 2012, NATO stated that, as an organization, it had reviewed all the information it held and "confirmed that the specific targets struck by NATO were legitimate military targets," adding "individual allies are continuing to conduct further assessments into some of the alleged incidents." The statement, as others made by NATO, provides no further details as to which countries this referred to or in what capacity these investigations were being carried out.[411]

8. Conclusion

The legal authority conferred by the Security Council in Resolution 1973, whose purpose was the protection of civilians, did not give license for NATO or its member countries to support one side in the conflict against the other. Nor was it conferred without limitations on NATO's use of force, which was authorized within the boundaries of the immediate scope of protecting civilians. There is obviously a discretionary margin inherent in such a mandate that gave NATO the authority to decide when and where civilians may be endangered, and when and where to use force to minimize or remove that danger. Yet the UN Charter does not permit the use of force for regime change.

The use of military force by NATO to effect regime change was beyond the scope of protecting the civilian population as mandated in Resolution 1973. Forcible regime change constitutes a violation of the UN Charter and may even be deemed an act of aggression. As stated above, Article 2(4) of the Charter prohibits such intervention in the domestic affairs of a state, and there is nothing in Resolution 1973 that indicates that the authorization of the use of force was anything but for the protection of civilian

---

[409] *Id.* at 25.

[410] *Id.*

[411] *Statement by the NATO spokesperson on Human Rights Watch report*, NORTH ATLANTIC TREATY ORGANIZATION, May 14, 2012, *available at* http://www.nato.int/cps/en/SID-5040B041-666DF7DC/natolive/news_87171.htm?selectedLocale=en.

populations. Regime change by UN Member States, even in reliance upon legal authorization of the use of force as in the case of Resolution 1973, can also be deemed a violation of Article 1(1) of the International Covenant on Civil and Political Rights. The conclusion that NATO may have violated Resolution 1973, the UN Charter and customary international law is bolstered by the Qadhafi regime response to Resolution 1973, which was a declaration of full compliance with the non-use of air power against the civilian population and the grounding of his air force. Another factor was Qadhafi's offer of a ceasefire, which NATO rejected. These facts alone are not conclusive given the history of the Qadhafi regime and its lack of credibility, but these propositions nonetheless must be considered. The point made herein is that NATO had an obligation to account for its conduct and to describe the reasons as to why it acted in the manner in which it did. The Security Council should have demanded such accountability, but it failed to do so. This raises serious questions with regard to the Security Council's good faith discharge of its legal obligations under the charter.

The use of force, no matter the legal authority pursuant to which it may be used, is limited by the UN Charter and customary international law. Authorization by the Security Counsel is not a sanction to act with impunity. Throughout its history there does not appear to have been a similar granting of authority by the Security Council to its Member States to engage in what is in the nature of "humanitarian intervention," save for the case of Kosovo in 1999 (Resolution 1244). In the immediate case, as in Kosovo, the Security Council did not establish an accountability mechanism such as requiring Member States executing the Resolution to report back to the Council, including reporting back on any accountability measures they may have undertaken in cases of alleged IHL violations. The same applies to the Resolution on the First Gulf War (Resolution 678) concerning Iraq's invasion of Kuwait in 1990. For all practical purposes, these three Resolutions grant an almost unbridled authority to those states seeking to implement a resolution permitting the use of force. Of course, when military action is aimed at regime change or fails to protect civilians or civilian objects it constitutes actions *ultra vires* in violation of international law. As Member States in all three situations – the First Gulf War, Kosovo and Libya – carried out their military actions without any constraints or requirements placed on them by the Security Council to maintain records from which they would report back to the Council on their actions, the outcome in all these cases was that civilian targets were struck and non-combatants were injured or killed.

Indeed, as the "all necessary measures" clause in Resolution 1973 required "the use of force...not be excessive," the Resolution compelled NATO to abide by the IHL principles of distinction and proportionality. Yet, while NATO initially denied allegations that it had attacked illegitimate targets or that innocent civilians had been killed or injured, it simultaneously claimed that it was not required to investigate casualties in Libya after the end of the conflict. NATO went to great lengths to demonstrate that its strikes were carried out with precision and with the intent of protecting civilians from Qadhafi forces.[412] NATO was able to provide detailed information regarding successful strikes, but was not forthcoming with information when it came to strikes that led to civilian casualties or the destruction of civilian infrastructure. Only when media outlets such as the New York Times made public that civilian casualties had resulted from the actions of the coalition forces did NATO admit any possible wrongdoing. It is extremely problematic when NATO relies on a news outlet to account for and report on its own violations of IHL because it does not have a mandate or the disposition to do so. This problem can be attributed in part to the sweeping language of Resolution 1973; naturally, what followed from such language were rationalizations for NATO's actions, such as those of the French Foreign Affairs Minister, who noted "it is clear [from Resolutions 1970 and 1973] that all means are legitimate for protecting peaceful civilians." For its part, the Security Council has not developed accountability measures or policy guidelines to clarify the bounds of its resolutions passed pursuant to Chapter VII, in this case, effectively offering NATO *carte blanche* to employ the means it deems appropriate.

The Security Council has similarly failed to clarify whether individual nations were responsible for their own assessments of alleged IHL violations or whether NATO would possess sole authority over investigations, thus allowing the parties to point the finger at one another. The lack of specific guidelines for investigative responsibility for different Member States involved in the conflict poses additional challenges for victims seeking accountability from NATO countries. NATO has made it difficult to pursue accountability measures, and there is no compensation program for Libya as there is for Afghanistan. The Security Council and NATO must recognize victim redress as a basic humanitarian interest that they are

---

[412] For example, NATO press briefings involved showing videos to reported that demonstrated the accuracy and precision of NATO strikes. *See* Romero and Gabellini, NATO, *supra* note 6.

not serving. According to international law, if such an investigation were to find that coalition forces did not comply with their obligations, NATO would be required to provide compensation to families for civilian deaths, injuries and loss of property.[413]

It is noteworthy that the interested parties to the First Gulf War and the conflicts in Kosovo and Libya did not conduct investigations or hold anyone accountable for any potential violations of IHL. There can be no doubt that the Security Council must be held responsible for the extensive authority it has conceded to its Member States and for its failure to require reporting and accountability for IHL violations. In the case of Libya, civilian targets were hit and non-combatants were injured and killed. While the civilian casualties were low in number due to developments in ordnance technology, NATO has provided no reporting and no accounting for these incidents. NATO has, however, acted as if the authority conferred upon it by the Security Council exempts it from reporting and accountability on the assumption that its armed forces naturally act in conformity with IHL. This, however, does not satisfy the obligations of IHL whenever there are cases of attacks upon protected persons and targets and for which no reporting has been made by NATO and accountability measures have not been taken. Moreover, given the subsequent investigations finding that opposition forces committed violations of IHL during the conflict and after the retreat of Qadhafi forces, NATO's responsibility flowing from arming and supporting rebel forces must also be examined. The Security Council must bear the responsibility of requiring an investigation of these and similar incidents.

As this chapter has shown, the use of force by NATO militarily benefitted the *thuwar* against the regime – which goes beyond the Security Council's authority to limit action to humanitarian purposes. Moreover, neither NATO nor its member states sought to justify the intervention on the basis of self-defense, thus making the ambit of Resolution 1973 the appropriate legal regime. Yet, the facts show that a number of strikes were made against protected civilian targets that caused death and injury to non-combatant civilians. Both of these questions should be addressed by NATO and the UN Member States whose forces have been used, and also by the Security Council for its failure to carry out its implicit supervisory authority over the actions of those Member States relying on the Council for the legality of their use of force against other Member States.

---

[413] HUMAN RIGHTS WATCH, UNACKNOWLEDGED DEATHS, *supra* note 5 at 6.

NATO interpreted Resolution 1973 loosely, placing military trainers on the ground, which went against the intent of the Resolution not to interfere with the conflict on the ground. Reports of CIA and MI6 involvement in the operations, along with special forces from France, offer incidental support of direct assistance to the Libyan opposition by NATO member countries. Of gravest concern is that while nations work feverishly to stop weapons transfers from Qadhafi's stockpiles to other actors, more advanced weapons provided by the coalition to Libyan rebels have already spread to countries such as Mali and Syria.[414]

Concerning NATO's bombing and airstrikes, which resulted in the destruction of civilian property and the killing and injuring of civilian non-combatants, the question remains as to whether NATO violated IHL. In this case, the countries involved in these NATO operations, as well as those that provided support such as the United States, have an obligation to ensure accountability, namely to investigate each single event and if evidence of criminality is found, to prosecute those responsible whether they be the pilots, the military planners or commanding officers under the law of superior responsibility. Failure to do so also constitutes a violation of IHL for which superior responsibility exists. In addition, these countries have an obligation to provide for damages and other forms of compensation to the victims, as is evident from various sources of conventional and customary international law. These sources of international law have been combined in the United Nations Declaration of Basic Principles of Justice for Victims of Crime and Abuse of Power.[415] So far, none of the NATO countries involved or NATO as an organization have undertaken such an exercise. Whether Libya will take up this issue on behalf of its nationals remains an open question.

In the meantime however, the lack of accountability and the absence of transparency regarding NATO's conduct in connection with strikes that led to civilian casualties and civilian property damage raises legitimate legal concerns. Importantly, what military experts will no doubt ask is why NATO was able to carry out so many strikes with extraordinary accuracy while at the same time conducting a few significantly inaccurate strikes

---

[414] *See* Ch. V, Sec. 3. *See also* James Risen et al., *U.S. Approved Arms for Libya Rebels Fell Into Jihadis' Hands*, N.Y. TIMES, Dec. 5, 2012, *available at* http://www.nytimes.com/2012/12/06/world/africa/weapons-sent-to-libyan-rebels-with-us-approval-fell-into-islamist-hands.html.

[415] Declaration of Basic Principles of Justice for Victims of Crime and Abuse of Power, Nov. 29, 1985, G.A. Res. 40/34.

that produced civilian casualties and damage to civilian property. There are three possible explanations: (1) pilot error, which is unlikely in view of the training and expertise of the pilots and of their record throughout the air campaign; (2) faulty intelligence, which is probable but not likely in all of the cases in which civilian targets have been hit and casualties have occurred (the United States was the main source of intelligence information); and (3) malfunctioning of the ordnance guiding systems (most of the ordnance, if not all, was supplied by the United States).

This leads to speculation that the reason NATO did not conduct transparent investigations into strikes that caused civilian casualties and destruction of civilian property is that such investigations would have led to the source of intelligence in those cases in which faulty intelligence was the reason for the unlawful air strike. This would implicate the United States and more particularly those within the U.S. military and civilian intelligence sectors who provided the faulty intelligence to NATO command. Furthermore, if the unlawful strikes resulting in civilian casualties and destruction of civilian property was indeed shown to be the result of faulty guidance systems in the ordnances, the responsibility would fall upon the supplier of that ordnance, which would also be the United States. This responsibility would be greater if it was found that the ordnance supplied had guidance systems that had exceeded their expiration date. The CoI discovered one such incident, that of the 8 August 2011 strike on the town of Majer, in which the guidance system on at least one of the bombs used had an expiration date in 2005. NATO responded that the question of expired guidance systems or munitions was a matter "for individual Nations rather than for NATO itself."[416] This statement is demonstrative of the overall obfuscation of responsibility and the reluctance by NATO and all the actors involved in the Libyan conflict to properly investigate matters that are critical for transparency and legal accountability.

---

[416] Report of the International Commission of Inquiry (Mar. 2012), *supra* note 26 at Annex I ¶ 622.

APPENDIX – LETTERS FROM NATO's LEGAL ADVISER
REGARDING CONTROVERSIAL STRIKES

LEGAL ADVISER
LE CONSEILLER JURIDIQUE

OLA(2012)006
23 January 2012

Dear Judge Kirsch,

This letter responds, on behalf of the North Atlantic Treaty Organization (NATO), to the Commission's letters of 11 November and 15 December, 2011. Those letters posed a series of questions regarding the conduct of Operation Unified Protector (OUP), the military operation in Libya led by NATO. As the Commission's queries are almost entirely confined to airstrikes conducted in accordance with the "protect civilians" mandate contained in operative paragraph 4 of United Nations Security Council Resolution (UNSCR) 1973 (2011) and focus in particular on questions relating to possible harm to civilians, unless otherwise noted the comments below relate to those aspects of the overall operation.

After expressing grave concern at the "escalation of violence, and the heavy civilian casualties" and considering that the "widespread and systematic attacks ... against the civilian population may amount to crimes against humanity," the Security Council determined that the situation in Libya constituted a threat to international peace and security. UNSCR 1973 consequently authorized a series of actions to address the situation in Libya associated with the violent suppression of protests against the regime led by Col. Muammar Gaddafi. Building on the Security Council's earlier Resolution 1970 (2011), UNSCR 1973 provided for strengthened enforcement of an arms embargo, expanded an assets freeze, banned flights of Libyan aircraft outside Libya and authorized UN member States, acting nationally or through regional organizations or arrangements, to take "all necessary measures" in order to implement a No Fly Zone and to "protect civilians and civilian populated areas under threat of attack" in Libya.

The 28 UN member States making up the North Atlantic Alliance authorized the planning and execution of OUP as a contribution to implementing their mandate under UNSCR 1973. OUP was accordingly an operation established by the members of the Alliance in implementation of their responsibilities as UN member States.

In the discussion below, "OUP" and "NATO" are for convenience often treated as co-terminous, but it should be understood that the two are not, strictly speaking, co-extensive. While all NATO Allies participated in the approval and overall direction of OUP, not all played active operational roles. In addition, several

1

North Atlantic Treaty Organization - Organisation du Traité de l'Atlantique Nord
Boulevard Léopold III - B-1110 Bruxelles - Belgique
Tel. direct: +32 2 707 40 08 - Fax: +32 2 707 91 67 - Bureau/Office: OA 308 - E-mail: olson .peter@hq.nato.int

non-NATO Nations joined and participated in OUP which became, as a result, a NATO-led operation. NATO's supreme decision-making authority, the North Atlantic Council, exercised overall direction of OUP. The execution of that direction was the responsibility of the military chain of command consisting of the Supreme Headquarters, Allied Powers in Europe (SHAPE); its subordinates were Joint Force Command Naples which delegated the execution to Combined Joint Task Force Command OUP (in Naples), which in turn operationally commanded OUP and consequently commanded the tactical air operations headquarters at Poggio Renatico and the tactical maritime operations at Maritime Command Naples headquarters. Non-NATO partners participated in almost all meetings of the NAC relating to OUP as well as at the operational headquarters.

We agree with the Commission that international humanitarian law is the *lex specialis* applicable to armed conflict; that body of law is intended to minimize harm to civilians. It does so in large part through principles of distinction, proportionality and military necessity designed to ensure that the risk to civilians is not excessive in relation to the military advantage anticipated. Strict compliance with these requirements was of obvious importance in a case such as OUP, where a core purpose of the Security Council's mandate authorizing use of "all necessary measures" – and thus the essential military objective – was itself to protect civilians and civilian areas from attack or threat of attack, in particular by their own government. NATO believes that its attentiveness during the course of OUP to a rigorous implementation of the rules of that body of law – and, indeed, to a standard exceeding what was required under international humanitarian law – contributed significantly to an extraordinarily low incidence of harm to civilians and civilian property.

The conduct of Operation Unified Protector was highly successful, both overall in protecting the civilian population of Libya and in implementation of an operational approach which minimized harm to civilians. Although no complex campaign can exclude that civilians suffer harm during its course, NATO deeply regrets any such harm that may have been caused by those strikes.

Many of the Commission's questions are best addressed by a general description of the targeting policy and practices followed by NATO during OUP. Application of that policy in particular cases is further treated in several of the subsequent discussions of individual incidents.

OUP Targeting Policy. OUP targets were all affirmatively selected to advance the operation's military objectives, which in turn derived ultimately from UNSCR 1973. Targets struck included military forces attacking or threatening to attack civilians or civilian-populated areas, as well as the command and control, logistics and other systems directly involved in directing, enabling or facilitating those attacks. Facilities and resources that did not provide a definite military advantage in achieving the military objectives were not targeted.

The OUP targeting policy was designed and implemented with the Security Council mandate to "protect civilians and civilian-populated areas under threat of attack" firmly at its core. The overriding objective throughout the campaign was to avoid any harm to civilians. Not one of the targets struck, involving over

7700 weapons, was approved for attack, or in fact attacked, if either those designating and approving the target or the pilot executing it had any evidence or other reason to believe that civilians would be injured or killed by a strike. As explicitly directed in the Operation Plan for OUP as approved by the North Atlantic Council, no civilians, and no specific individual, civilian or military, were ever intentionally targeted in that operation.

Rigorous procedures were in all cases followed for approving both "deliberate" (i.e., pre-planned) and "dynamic" strikes (i.e., strikes on targets that presented themselves during the course of a mission) to ensure that there was a "zero expectation" of death or injury to civilians.

In determining which targets should and could be struck, intelligence from all available sources (including signals intelligence, imagery and other sources) was obtained and analyzed to ensure its continued accuracy and to confirm that civilians were not inadvertently put at risk. In appropriate cases, as much as fifty hours of airborne video observation was conducted and analyzed before a strike was authorized. The potential for harm to civilians was carefully assessed with respect to each proposed target, including before authorizing "re-strikes" of targets following an unsuccessful or partially unsuccessful attack or when regime forces were observed re-using a previously struck facility.

Whether deliberate or dynamic, no target was struck that had not been extensively considered in light of all available intelligence, assessed in light of the targeting standards approved by the North Atlantic Council, reviewed by legal officers for compliance with the requirements of the law of armed conflict and specifically approved by the overall OUP commander or deputy commander or, in some cases of dynamic targeting, the general officer in command of the Combat Air Operations Centre. All deliberate strikes, and the great majority of dynamic attacks, were made on the basis of multiple intelligence sources. Some two-thirds of sites seriously assessed as possible targets were for one or another reason, notably including concerns over potential harm to civilians, removed from consideration during the course of these reviews.

Equally rigorous procedures were followed with respect to strike execution. Through leaflets and other means, general and location-specific warnings to the civilian population were repeatedly made in order to advise them to avoid areas likely to be struck. The day of the week, time of day or night (notably during Ramadan), on occasion even the direction of attack were all carefully considered to minimize any risk of civilian casualties. In most cases information was available permitting an analysis of the construction materials and design of buildings, and munitions were selected and fused so as to contain the blast within the structure to the maximum extent possible. The great majority of munitions used delayed fusing for this reason. In preparing for individual missions, planners consistently employed the minimum-sized munitions necessary to accomplish the military objective; on numerous occasions multiple munitions with lower blast radii, rather than fewer munitions or even a single larger one, were employed to ensure that the blast and ejecta radius did not include civilian areas or other risk to civilians. All aerial munitions employed in OUP were precision-guided, and the type of precision guidance (e.g., GPS- or laser-guided) was selected to maximize accuracy in light of local conditions at the time. (A limited number of strikes involved use of direct-fire munitions, which are under the direct control of pilots and of comparable accuracy to precision-guided munitions.) In many cases special measures were taken to increase the ability of commanders and pilots to assess whether civilians were present up virtually to the moment of attack. For certain strikes near civilian areas, for example, essentially contemporaneous air-borne video observation was required before a target was struck. With respect to deliberate naval fires, all salvoes were fired under positive control, with the fall of shot observed by spotters embarked in aircraft. Many attacks were called off, including some at the last minute, in order to avoid striking those whom NATO was mandated to protect.

Battle damage assessment following attacks was conducted when possible to determine damage and otherwise evaluate the effects of the strike. NATO had no ground observers in Libya, and had no ability during the campaign to assess the effects of its strikes from the ground. It did, however, employ its extensive air and intelligence, surveillance and reconnaissance assets of all kinds, as well as video footage and other evidence acquired during the attack and open source and media reporting, to assess those effects. Although weather and atmospheric conditions on occasion precluded doing so, additional assessment was carried out where possible in instances where there was a claim of civilian casualties.

Targeting and execution practices were further enhanced during the course of OUP with the goal of avoiding any civilian loss. In keeping with standard practice, NATO is reviewing the conduct of OUP in order to identify any ways in which its planning and execution can be further improved as a result of experience gained during the campaign.

As a result of all the precautions taken, NATO is convinced – and considers that the record of OUP amply demonstrates – that the targeting and strike methods employed in OUP were as well-designed and as successfully implemented to avoid civilian casualties as was humanly and technically possible.

Conduct of the campaign. The North Atlantic Council mandated OUP on 31 March 2011, and the operation terminated seven months later, on 31 October. During the course of the campaign a total of 25,944 air sorties were made, of which 25,011 were by fixed-wing aircraft, 424 by rotary-wing aircraft and 509 by unmanned aerial vehicles (UAVs) conducting intelligence, surveillance or reconnaissance (ISR) missions. All sorties were armed, either defensively or offensively, with the exception of air-to-air refuelling flights, and some UAV electronic warfare and ISR flights. Of the 17,939 sorties (approximately 70%) that were armed, 17,314 were by fixed-wing aircraft, 375 by rotary-wing aircraft and 250 by UAVs conducting ISR missions.

A total of 7642 air-to-surface weapons, including 3644 laser-guided bombs (e.g., GBU-12, GBU-24), 2844 GPS-guided munitions (e.g., GBU-31, GBU-38), 1150 precision-guided direct fire weapons (e.g., AGM-114 Hellfire and HOT missiles), as well as four miscellaneous precision-guided munitions, were employed during

4

OUP. 6278 (82.2%) were 500-lb. or smaller in weight, 562 (7.4%) between 500 and 1000 lb., and 802 (10.5%) between 1000 and 2000 Ib

The scale of the use of precision-guided munitions during this campaign is unprecedented; due to their increased precision, such weapons dramatically reduce the risk of collateral damage, both because they require greatly reduced explosive effect to achieve their purpose and because they are less likely to cause unintended damage by hitting the wrong location.

The minimum-sized weapon required to achieve the military objective and consistent with the "zero expectation of civilian casualties" targeting criterion was used on all occasions. The great majority of weapons were fitted with delayed fusing, thereby further minimizing risk to civilians who might have been in the vicinity of the target We can confirm that no incendiary or obscuring (white phosphorus) munitions were used during OUP. Fewer than a hundred illuminating rounds were fired by NATO vessels as part of operations relating to coastal targets near Zlitan, Sirte, al Khums and Misrata. All such rounds are designed to initiate in the air and illuminate the ground under parachute from above; all are fused to burn to extinction before the parachute drifts to ground.

The munitions and guidance systems used by Nations in execution of actions during a NATO or NATO-led operation are provided by those Nations, and NATO does not have information on their expiration date. The fact alone that an expiration date has been passed does not mean that a weapon is no longer reliable, and the period of time during which a guidance system or munition is considered appropriate for use is thus a matter for individual Nations rather than for NATO itself. Multiple weapons systems checks, following national procedures, are standard when munitions are loaded onto the aircraft.

The Commission has as a rule not requested information from NATO regarding weapons use by regime forces, but in response to its specific query, NATO is aware of three SCUDs that were launched by regime forces during the course of OUP – one targeting Misrata on 14 August, and two targeting Brega on 23 August. None of these launches was intercepted.

Individual incidents. The following discussions of the individual incidents or groups of events referred to by the Commission in its two letters must be read in conjunction with the general information on targeting and strike execution provided above. Please note that it is longstanding NATO policy not to provide information as to which Nation may have conducted any particular military action during a NATO operation.

Please note as well that in certain cases the description provided was of such a general character that it was difficult or impossible to identify the specific strikes or incidents to which the Commission referred. In those cases, we have looked at information on strikes taking place at the same time and in the same area in an effort to respond to the Commission's inquiries.

The first six incidents are referenced in the Commission's 11 November letter, and the final three (numbers 7 through 9 below) in its letter of 15 December.

1.   20 June (Surman). The compound included a number of command and control buildings as well as an ammunition storage facility. Between 20 and 30 satellite communication dishes were observed in the compound and on the buildings, along with a lattice tower aerial immediately across the street. The compound was at an isolated location outside Tripoli and was guarded by check-points, guards and patrol vehicles forming several rings of security around the facility. Although a school and mosque were located in close proximity to the target, aerial video surveillance identified no civilians in the area. The target was struck at night to minimize any possibility of casualties to transient civilians; for similar reasons the ammunition dump and other military objects located on the site were also not struck.

2.   30 July (Libyan State Television). Transmission dishes belonging to Libyan State Television were deliberately targeted and destroyed to prevent their contin-ued use to incite regime supporters to violence against civilians. This transmis-sion station was a key element in broadcasting such incitement by regime leaders. Although the target had earlier been rejected because the rhetoric broadcast over it did not at that time reach the threshold of incitement to violence, speeches made in early July reached a new level of intensity and focus. It should also be noted that the crimes against humanity (including murder and persecution) for which the International Criminal Court (ICC) had in late June indicted Col. Gad-dafi and other senior regime members corresponded closely to the actions incited via the Libyan State Television transmission station.

The target was struck at night, on a particular heading, to mlmmlze any chance of injury to civilians. The dishes were targeted precisely and with low-intensity weapons both to minimize the risk of collateral damage and to avoid broader dis-ruption to the Libyan communications infrastructure. Battle damage assessment indicated that these precautions were fully successful in avoiding such injury or damage.

3.   1 May (Tripoli). This site was a key node for regime-associated forces in Tripoli, and served as an alternate command authority site for the Libyan leader-ship. The critical element of this facility was the command building. While sev-eral VIP buildings and satellite communication dishes were also located at this site, these were neither targeted nor struck. Destruction of the command building degraded the regime command authority's backup command and control capa-bilities and in turn its overall military effectiveness.

As noted above, civilians and specific individuals were at no point targeted during OUP. Full-motion video acquired by manned aircraft and UAVs at the time of the strike indicated that no civilians were in the target area. In addition, the strike was conducted at night to reduce the possibility that transient person-nel would be in the target area. Multiple smaller munitions were utilized on a single building to minimize collateral damage to surrounding buildings within the installation.

4.   23 April. NATO did not target health or water facilities, including those at military sites, at any time during OUP. On 23 April, there were strikes at five sepa-rate deliberate targets including command and control and ammunition bunkers.

No known health or water facilities were within the target or weapons effects areas, and post-strike battle damage assessment indicated no collateral damage. In addition, 14 dynamic targets (main battle tanks, missile and rocket launchers, tank carriers, other military vehicles and a military command post) were struck in the Misrata and central regions; assessment by the aircraft delivering the weapon immediately following these strikes gave no indication of collateral damage.

5.   9 May. No strikes took place in the Tripoli region on 9 May. A total of eight strikes took place in the Tripoli region on 8 and 10 May, including five on deliberate targets on known military installations including intelligence headquarters and communications facilities and a weapons storage and vehicle maintenance area, and three on dynamic targets, all positively identified as surface-to-air missile launchers. Battle damage assessment indicated no collateral damage.

6.   12–13 May (Brega). The Marsa El Brega Residence and Command Bunker Facility served as the primary C2 facility for forces fielded by the 32d Brigade in and around Brega. It was deliberately targeted and struck on 13 May. During engagement of the target, it was positively identified and four precision-guided munitions were dropped. The strike was highly effective, and decisively degraded command and control in the Brega area. Battle damage assessment indicated no collateral damage.

After this strike, an engineer who had been involved in design and construction of the command bunker facility publicly confirmed that it had been constructed for Col. Gaddafi and had been purpose-built for command and control functions.

7.   EI-Grarry residence (Mhalat El Fath). The Tarabulus SA-2 Support Facility was an active military storage and support site directly supporting regime forces in the region with military equipment as well as efforts to reconstitute air-defense capabilities throughout Libya. It was struck on three separate occasions, targeting at least ten separate buildings and bunkers. During the 19 June target engagement in question, the targeted structures were positively identified and two precision-guided weapons were dropped. The second of these two weapons appears to have malfunctioned due to laser guidance problems, its impact was not observed and NATO was not able to determine where it in fact landed.

After reviewing the case, it was concluded that it was possible that the errant weapon had caused such casualties. A public statement was made at the time by the OUP commander acknowledging this possibility and expressing regret for any casualties that may have resulted. This incident is under further assessment.

8.   Mustafa Najl residence (Zlitan). This target had been identified as a regime senior commander's command and control node, located within a residential property four miles west of Zlitan. At no time were civilians intentionally targeted. The target building and buildings immediately adjacent to it were used exclusively by senior regime commanders as an active command and control facility directing forces in the Zlitan area. The structure was positively identified and one precision-guided weapon was dropped on 4 August. Review of intelligence confirms that the correct and intended building was struck, and assessment

of the claimed civilian casualties at the time concluded that this was highly unlikely. This incident is under further assessment.

9. Majer. The four buildings addressed in the questions relating to Majer were deliberate targets, based on their functioning as a troop staging area. They were located within a farm compound in a rural area. On the basis of observation and other intelligence, it was assessed that no civilians were in the area, and none were observed at the time of the attack or of the subsequent re-strike of one of those buildings. If civilians had been identified, standard procedure was to abort the drop or, if noticed after time of release, to direct a laser-guided weapon away from the target area. This incident is under further assessment.

In the comments above, NATO has done its utmost to address the substantive points raised by the Commission with respect to NATO's conduct of OUP. As has been indicated in previous correspondence, some of the specific information sought by the Commission cannot be made public. Video footage in particular is the property of the individual Nations operating the video recording platforms and is classified in order to protect important information about platform capabilities. Where possible, however, information has been declassified in order to respond comprehensively to the Commission's questions.

Two other considerations, one relating to the scope of the Commission's inquiry and the second to the evidence supporting allegations of violation of international law, affect the character of our response. The Human Rights Council's Resolution S-15/1 mandated the Commission to look into "alleged violations of international human rights law" Although NATO has in this letter responded in detail to the Commission's request for information, it is for a variety of reasons not evident that many of the queries posed in the Commission's letters of 11 November and 15 December, including those relating to the law of armed conflict, fall within that mandate. NATO nonetheless trusts that its comments in this letter will address any concerns the Commission may have with respect to the lawfulness of NATO actions during OUP.

In several cases, the descriptions of the incidents referenced by the Commission appear to derive in whole or in part from allegations made by the former regime during the course of OUP. While we have discussed all incidents referenced by the Commission, in light of the fact that regime statements were repeatedly shown to be incomplete, inaccurate, or based upon fabricated or non-existent evidence, we assume the Commission agrees that uncorroborated regime assertions, are not credible evidence as to the actual facts. We note in this context the Commission's comments, in its 1 June Report to the Human Rights Council, that on the occasion of its visit to Libya in late April 2011 the "the [former] Libyan Government did not provide the details or show concrete evidence of alleged incidents, such as civilian objects which had been destroyed (e.g. schools)" and that "the Commission has not seen evidence to suggest that civilian areas have been intentionally targeted by NATO forces, nor that it has engaged in indiscriminate attacks on civilians" (paragraphs 233 and 235).

Throughout OUP, and to the present day, NATO has given consideration to every allegation of harm to civilians of which it has been made aware, and in each such case reviews its actions with care in order to assess whether there is merit to the allegation. That review involves, as appropriate to the individual case, assessment of all NATO's records from selection of the target through any data it possesses gathered following the attack.

As noted above, NATO did not have a presence on the ground in Libya during OUP; following conclusion of the operation on 31 October, the Organization has no mandate that would allow it to establish such a presence. While NATO therefore does not itself have the ability to gather evidence onsite with respect to strikes conducted during OUP, it appreciates that the Libyan authorities, officials of NATO Allies and other states, international organizations and bodies including the Commission, journalists and others will gather such evidence. If as a result serious questions arise with respect to NATO's conduct or understanding of the effects of its strikes, NATO is fully prepared to evaluate those questions and any new evidence that may be adduced.

I trust that the above comments address the Commission's concerns with regard to NATO's actions during the course of Operation Unified Protector.

Yours sincerely,

Peter Olson
Legal Adviser

Judge P. Kirsch, Q.C.
Chair
International Commission of Inquiry on Libya
United Nations
coilibyasecretariat@ohchr.org

LEGAL ADVISER
LE CONSEILLER JURIDIQUE

OLA(2012)0014
15 February 2012

Dear Judge Kirsch,

Thank you for your letter of 3 February, 2012, which inquired about five additional sites struck during the course of NATO's Operation Unified Protector (OUP), and presented further questions relating to three sites discussed in our letter of 23 January. Your letter also commented on several other matters addressed below.

As we discussed when we spoke by telephone on 2 February, gathering and reviewing information of the sort requested in your letter requires considerable coordination. While we are replying to you more quickly than we were able to in response to your 15 December request, it was not possible to complete that work by the requested date of last Friday, 10 February.

Before turning to the specific incidents about which you inquired, I would like to address certain points of a more general character.

As you are aware, we retain concerns about some aspects of the Commission's application of its mandate from the Human Rights Council (HRC), which was given in the specific context of gross repression and manifest human rights violations committed by and against Libyans in the context of political protests in that country. That mandate is to "investigate all alleged violations of international human rights law in Libya, to establish the facts and circumstances of such violations and of the crimes perpetrated" and to make recommendations "all with a view to ensuring that those individuals responsible are held accountable."

NATO is in no doubt that the former regime committed serious violations of international law during the course of the internal conflict in Libya which emerged from its repression. We are not, however, persuaded that examination of the conduct of parties to the Libyan internal conflict implies expansion of the Commission's work to include "investigation" of NATO's actions giving effect to the mandate contained in UN Security Council Resolution 1973.

1

North Atlantic Treaty Organization - Organisation du Traité de l'Atlantique Nord
Boulevard Léopold III - B-1110 Bruxelles - Belgique
Tel. direct: +32 2 707 40 08 - Fax: +32 2 707 91 67 - Bureau/Office: OA 308 - E-mail: olson
.peter@hq.nato.int

We understand that the Commission has been conducting a careful review of several incidents involving NATO about which it has had some concerns, and trust that the description of OUP policies and comments on specific incidents contained in our letter of 23 January have been of assistance to the Commission in that work. I was pleased the other evening to hear that, based on that review, the members of the Commission consider that NATO did not deliberately target civilians and did not commit war crimes in Libya. Such a view is of course fully consistent with our own firm belief as set forth in that letter which noted that not one of the targets struck was approved for attack, or was in fact attacked, if NATO had any evidence or other reason to believe that civilians would be injured or killed by a strike.

We would be concerned, however, if "NATO incidents" were included in the Commission's report as on a par with those which the Commission may ultimately conclude did violate law or constitute crimes. We note in this regard that the Commission's mandate is to discuss "the facts and circumstances of . . . violations [of law] and . . . crimes perpetrated."

We would accordingly request that, in the event the Commission elects to include a discussion of NATO actions in Libya, its report clearly state that NATO did not deliberately target civilians and did not commit war crimes in Libya.

We appreciate the preview of certain recommendations the Commission is considering including in its report, and we welcome the opportunity to offer comments on them.

As a general point, similar to the one just made, we doubt the appropriateness of including in the report recommendations relating to NATO. The Commission's mandate to make recommendations is made in the specific context of ensuring the accountability of those perpetrating crimes and violating international law – a category we believe it is clear does not include NATO.

With respect to the two specific recommendations anticipated in your 2 February letter, we would first recall the statement in NATO's letter of 23 January that OUP has been terminated and that NATO has no mandate to conduct any activities in Libya. As our letter acknowledged – and as since demonstrated by the Commission itself – a wide range of parties may and will gather information relating to strikes, and that information will in turn be given due consideration.

In addition, particularly as there have been very few claims for compensation associated with NATO actions during OUP, we see little rationale for a NATO-specific recommendation on compensation. There is no legal obligation to provide compensation for damage occurring in the course of lawfully-conducted military activities, nor is it the case that establishment of programs for compensation for such damage has become standard or expected practice. Any issues of compensation are accordingly questions of a political character. It is in fact our understanding that the Libyan representative recently informed the Security Council that a commission is being formed to consider questions of civilian casualties and that his government plans to establish a mechanism to indemnify victims following its investigations. NATO has made clear to the government of Libya its desire and intent to be supportive of this process.

Allow me, finally, to address two possible misapprehensions with respect to NATO activities in Afghanistan. First, neither NATO nor ISAF has in fact established or conducts a compensation program in that country. Secondly, while there is important sharing of information between ISAF and UNAMA, the context of that information-sharing is highly specific – both ISAF and UNAMA have large and long-term presences on the ground, a major purpose of sharing information is to assure the physical security of UNAMA, and any sharing of information is done on the basis of specific operational requirements for such sharing and of institutional relationships and understandings that have been developed over the course of a decade of collaboration. There is no information-sharing agreement applicable to the Commission that would permit NATO to share classified information with it.

Individual incidents. The Commission has asked for comment on five new incidents, and asked further questions with respect to three addressed in our letter of 23 January. These are discussed below in the order found in the Commission's letter of 3 February. As before, the discussion of these individual incidents must be read in conjunction with the general information on targeting and strike execution provided in that letter. In short, however, not one of the targets struck was approved for attack, or was in fact attacked, if NATO had any evidence or other reason to believe that civilians would be injured or killed by a strike. Please note that a number of the incidents below are the subject of further assessment, which will take into account the further information provided by the Commission in its 3 February letter.

It should also be noted that most of the strikes referenced in the Commission's 3 February letter occurred in the later stages of the campaign, and in particular after the fall of Tripoli. The campaign at this stage was highly fluid and for tactical reasons the regime was using civilian rather than military structures in support of military action. The regime's conventional command and control in particular had been severely degraded and it relied increasingly on non-traditional/informal methods. Such methods did not involve the kind of dedicated structures, wiring, equipment and other infrastructure that would identify a command and control node as "military" in character.

1.   29 August (Bani Walid). This was a major command and control node which was reliant on non-traditional/informal methods to carry out that function. The site was actively controlling regime forces which were attacking civilians in the area. The full targeting procedure described in our 23 January letter was applied in this case, including that no target was selected for attack, or in fact struck, if there was any reason to believe that civilian casualties would result.

3

2.   16 September (Sirte). This was a dynamic strike. OUP observed multiple military vehicles with substantial numbers of associated military personnel on the ground over an extended period. Those vehicles were engaging in continuing rocket fire against civilian areas, and authorization was granted to engage them once they were clear of civilians. The vehicles were not struck until they left the populated area where they had initially been observed, and had relocated to an area free of civilians and civilian structures. The two vehicles struck were sufficiently separated that a single precision-guided weapon of the type employed would have been insufficient to destroy them both.

3.   Undated (Bani Walid). The only strike at this location took place on 9 September. Two SCUD missiles, which are vehicle-mounted, were stored at this building, which was not a permanent or purpose-built SCUD storage facility. On the basis of its standard targeting methodology as previously described, it was concluded that no civilians were at this isolated facility. It is not known whether the SCUDs were destroyed in the attack.

4.   9 September (Bani Walid). The only strike on this location took place on 5 October. This facility was a confirmed military facility in a walled compound, and was being used at the time of the strike as a command and control facility. On the basis of its standard targeting methodology as previously described, it was concluded that no civilians were at this isolated facility.

5.   10 October (Bani Walid). This was a building in an industrial compound that had been taken over for military purposes and was being used at the time as a command and control node. On the basis of its standard targeting methodology as previously described, it was concluded that no civilians were at this isolated facility.

6.   20 June (Surman). NATO's principal concern with this site was its functioning as a military command and control node, and it was that function that was struck. We remain confident of our information that this was a military site, that there was no evidence of a civilian presence and that all measures were taken to confirm that conclusion, and that the strike was executed in a manner designed to avoid any risk to transient civilians. The weapons storage facility to which the Commission refers was known to NATO, but that target was not engaged on the basis of its proximity to a mosque and school. NATO did not have access to contemporaneous ground observation from reliable neutral observers and cannot make a definitive statement with respect to the reports of civilian deaths.

7.   3 August (Zlitan). NATO information, as indicated in our earlier letter, is that this site was struck on 4, not 3, August. As stated previously, NATO identified this site as a senior regime commander's command and control node located within a residential property. As noted in other contexts as well, this target would not have been struck if NATO had any evidence or other reason to believe that a strike would injure or kill civilians.

8.   8–9 August (Majer). At the time of these strikes, these buildings had been identified as being used as a staging area for regime forces actively engaged in attacks on civilians and civilian-populated areas. It should be noted that at this point in the campaign regime forces, as well as the mercenaries augmenting those forces, often wore civilian clothing.

Naval and other ordnance. The Commission has also requested information on use of naval weapons. It should be noted that no naval weapons were used in any of the 14 incidents with respect to which the Commission has posed questions. During the course of OUP, approximately 470 naval rounds were fired. No cluster munitions, including CBU-107 or other passive attack cluster munitions, were used during OUP.

Leaflets and warnings to civilians. The Commission's military advisor has separately requested information on leaflets used to warn civilians of possible attacks. Copies of representative leaflets are being provided separately by electronic means. NATO used both physical leafleting and broadcast media to provide warnings, as well as to generally advise both regime forces and civilians on how to act to minimize risk, on literally hundreds of occasions throughout the campaign.

Please be assured that NATO appreciates and values the work of the Commission, and trusts that these comments will assist it in preparing its final report.

Yours sincerely,

Peter Olson
Legal Adviser

Judge P Kirsch, Q.C.
Chair
International Commission of Inquiry on Libya
United Nations
coilibyasecretariat@ohchr.org

Source: Report of the International Commission of Inquiry on Libya, U.N. HRC. 19th Sess., Annex II, U.N. Doc. A/HRC/19/68, advance unedited version (Mar. 2, 2012).

CHAPTER FOUR

ACCOUNTABILITY ISSUES

1. INTRODUCTION

The modalities of post-conflict justice involve a number of interdisciplinary strategies, including "prosecutions; truth commissions; reparations; vetting, sanctions, and administrative measures; memorialization, education and archives; traditional, indigenous and religious approaches; and, institutional reform."[1] Among other goals, post-conflict justice measures aim to remedy the atrocities of war and build durable peace by, *inter alia*, holding to account those responsible for prohibited acts of conflict-related violence. Societies emerging from war almost always lack the political will needed to minimize impunity for all parties to the conflict, and enforce the rule of law fairly and impartially. Also, because their judicial systems are impaired by the general breakdown of state institutions, post-conflict justice is difficult to realize[2] without first implementing important legal reforms.[3] Finally, given the evolution of international justice mechanisms since the 1990s, there is an increasing interplay between domestic,

---

[1] M. CHERIF BASSIOUNI ET AL., THE CHICAGO PRINCIPLES ON POST-CONFLICT JUSTICE 23 (Chicago, USA: International Human Rights Law Institute, 2008) [hereinafter "THE CHICAGO PRINCIPLES"], *available at* http://www.law.depaul.edu/centers_institutes/ihrli/pdf/chicago_principles.pdf. *See generally*, ACCOUNTABILITY FOR ATROCITIES: NATIONAL AND INTERNATIONAL RESPONSES (Jane Stromseth ed., Ardsley, USA: Transnational Pub, 2003); POST-CONFLICT JUSTICE (M. Cherif Bassiouni ed., Ardsley, USA: Transnational Pub, 2002); 1–3 TRANSITIONAL JUSTICE: HOW EMERGING DEMOCRACIES RECKON WITH FORMER REGIMES (Neil Kritz ed., Washington, USA: United States Institute of Peace, 1995).

[2] *See e.g.*, 1–2 THE PURSUIT OF INTERNATIONAL CRIMINAL JUSTICE: A WORLD STUDY ON CONFLICTS, VICTIMIZATION, AND POST-CONFLICT JUSTICE (M. Cherif Bassiouni ed., Antwerp, Belgium: Intersentia, 2010); BASSIOUNI, POST-CONFLICT JUSTICE, *supra* note 1; STROMSETH, ACCOUNTABILITY FOR ATROCITIES: NATIONAL AND INTERNATIONAL RESPONSES, *supra* note 1.

[3] *See generally*, Louis Aucoin, *Building the Rule of Law and Establishing Accountability for Atrocities in the Aftermath of Conflict*, 8(1) WHITEHEAD J. DIPL. & INT'L REL. (Winter/Spring 2007), *available at* http://blogs.shu.edu/diplomacy/files/archives/04-Aucoin.pdf. In the case of Libya, crimes committed prior to the armed conflict for which no justice was ever served must also be addressed. *See Libya: Pursuing al-Gaddafi – the legal questions answered*, AMNESTY INTERNATIONAL, Aug. 25 2011, *available at* http://www.amnesty.org/en/news-and-updates/libya-pursuing-al-gaddafi-%E2%80%93-legal-questions-answered-2011-08-25.

international and mixed model approaches to post-conflict justice,[4] as well as attendant questions of jurisdictional priorities.[5]

Legal accountability in the aftermath of conflict is a vital part of the transitional process, which includes helping to recognize the suffering of victims, restore trust among the public and prevent the collapse of peace.[6] While every conflict is unique, and in this sense may be labeled *sui generis*, history has proven that, absent the inclusion of post-conflict justice in postwar governance, political stability and national reconciliation are negatively affected by the absence of post-conflict measures.[7] Furthermore, post-conflict justice is not only a question of good policy, but it is increasingly becoming a legal obligation, particularly for state parties to the Rome Statute of the International Criminal Court ("Rome Statute"),[8] and other international conventions such as the Geneva Conventions of 1949[9] and the UN Convention Against Torture ("CAT").[10]

---

[4] For more on the various international and mixed model forms of post-conflict justice, *see* M. CHERIF BASSIOUNI, INTRODUCTION TO INTERNATIONAL CRIMINAL LAW: SECOND REVISED EDITION 487–784 (Leiden, The Netherlands: Martinus Nijhoff, 2013) [hereinafter "INTERNATIONAL CRIMINAL LAW"].

[5] For more on the question of Jurisdictional priorities, *see* BASSIOUNI, INTRODUCTION TO INTERNATIONAL CRIMINAL LAW, *id.* at 81–84.

[6] BASSIOUNI ET AL., THE CHICAGO PRINCIPLES, *supra note* 1 at 5 & 56. *See also* Navanethem Pillay, *Establishing Effective Accountability Mechanisms for Human Rights Violations*, UN CHRONICLE, Dec. 31, 2012, *available at* http://www.un.org/wcm/content/site/chronicle/home/archive/issues2012/deliveringjustice/establishingeffectiveaccountability-mechanisms.

[7] *See e.g.*, Barbara F. Walter, *Does Conflict Beget Conflict? Explaining Recurring Civil War*, 41 J PEACE RES. 3, 384 (May 2004). Walter notes that "there is . . . a clear indication that true democracies are less likely to experience renewed civil war than semi-democracies" (internal citation omitted), *available at* http://www.uky.edu/~clthyn2/PS439G/readings/walter_2004.pdf. *See generally*, CHARLES T. CALL, WHY PEACE FAILS: THE CAUSES AND PREVENTION OF CIVIL WAR RECURRENCE (Washington, USA: Georgetown University Press, 2012).

[8] Rome Statute of the International Criminal Court, July 17, 1998, 2187 U.N.T.S. 90 [hereinafter "Rome Statute"].

[9] Geneva Convention for the Amelioration of the Condition of the Wounded and Sick in Armed Forces in the Field, Aug. 12, 1949, 6 U.S.T. 3114, 75 U.N.T.S. 31 [hereinafter "First Geneva Convention"]; Geneva Convention for the Amelioration of the Wounded, Sick and Shipwrecked Members of Armed Forces at Sea, Aug. 12, 1949, 6 U.S.T. 3217, 75 U.N.T.S. 85 [hereinafter "Second Geneva Convention"]; Geneva Convention Relative to the Treatment of Prisoners of War, Aug. 12, 1949, 6 U.S.T. 3316, 75 U.N.T.S. 135 [hereinafter "Third Geneva Convention"]; Geneva Convention Relative to the Protection of Civilian Persons in Time of War, Aug. 12, 1949, 6 U.S.T. 3516, 75 U.N.T.S. 287 [hereinafter "Fourth Geneva Convention"].

[10] Convention Against Torture, and Other Cruel, Inhuman or Degrading Treatment or Punishment, G.A. Res. 39/46, at 1, U.N. Doc. A/RES/39/46 (Dec. 10, 1984) [hereinafter "CAT"]. *See generally* Basic Principles and Guidelines on the Right to a Remedy and Reparation for Victims of Gross Violations of International Human Rights Law and Serious

Promoting post-conflict justice and attendant accountability in the case of Libya is complex. This is due in part to the effects of decades of Mu'ammar Qadhafi's authoritarian rule that undermined the judiciary, and in part due to Libya's diverse demography and regional factionalism.[11] During the four-plus decades under Qadhafi, Libyan citizens were never held accountable for violations of international legal norms under domestic law. Indeed, Libyan domestic law does not include core international crimes such as genocide, crimes against humanity, war crimes, and other international criminal law ("ICL") violations such as enforced disappearances or extrajudicial killings.[12] Enhancing the effectiveness of domestic legal institutions to address core international crimes and ICL violations will prove difficult, particularly given the absence of relevant norms in the Libyan criminal code, and a dearth of trained personnel. Moreover, the entire judicial system is in need of reform, because during the Qadhafi-era it was not much more than a tool used by a despotic ruler to control and suppress the population,[13] which caused Libyan society to develop an understandable distrust for the judiciary. When compounded by the post-conflict pace of reform, a new general reticence to the legal process has developed among the population.[14]

Another challenge arises due to the fact that many in post-conflict Libya hail the *thuwar* as heroes who were able to confront and defeat the Qadhafi regime, and the public supports their claim that they are not accountable for any crimes they may have committed during and after the conflict against those who fought for or supported the previous regime. Nevertheless, even revered members of the revolutionary forces must be held accountable for the violations whether committed during the conflict

Violations of International Humanitarian Law, G.A. Res. 60/147, U.N. Doc A/Res/60/147 (Dec. 16, 2005) [collectively hereinafter "Geneva Conventions"].

[11] As discussed throughout this book, cultures and values across Libya are deeply factionalized, thus contributing to the difficulties of post-conflict reconciliation.

[12] Report of the International Commission of Inquiry on Libya, U.N. HRC. 19th Sess., Annex I, ¶ 771. U.N. Doc. A/HRC/19/68, advance unedited version (Mar. 2, 2012). *See also* AMNESTY INTERNATIONAL, *Libya: Pursuing al-Gaddafi – the legal questions answered, supra* note 3.

[13] For a discussion of the Abu Salim and 'Ain Zara prisons in Tripoli which were used to house critics of the regime, *see* Ch. V, Sec. 2.3. *See also* Report of the International Commission of Inquiry, advance unedited version (Mar. 2, 2012), *supra* note 12 at Annex I, ¶ 41.

[14] INTERNATIONAL CRISIS GROUP, TRIAL BY ERROR: JUSTICE IN POST-QADHAFI LIBYA 35–36 (Apr. 17, 2013), *available at* http://www.crisisgroup.org/~/media/Files/Middle%20 East%20North%20Africa/North%20Africa/libya/140-trial-by-error-justice-in-post-qadhafi-libya.pdf. *See also* Report of the International Commission of Inquiry, advance unedited version (Mar. 2, 2012), *supra* note 12 at Annex I, ¶ 41.

or the post-conflict period through today.[15] So far, no former *thuwar* have been brought to justice.[16]

Accountability for the *thuwar* is further complicated by the factional-ized nature of the *thuwar* forces, who for the most part developed locally and independently of one another.[17] As regional armed groups, they acted in diverse territories and lacked a unified command and control struc-ture, as discussed in Chapter II and Part Two. This makes it difficult to ascertain accountability for the patterns of violations that occurred, not to mention the ability to enforce accountability mechanisms. Qadhafi forces also lacked a unified command and control structure, and lacked central-ized control over military operations, as discussed in Chapter II and Part Two, factors that also complicate the ascertainment of systemic patterns and superior responsibility. These contextual and factual characteristics of the conflict make it difficult to ascertain and establish criminal respon-sibility under international humanitarian law (IHL) and ICL, as enforced before an international forum such as the ICC, or national ones other than Libya that may seek to exert their criminal jurisdiction for international crimes under their national laws. The same difficulties are also likely to be encountered under Libyan criminal law.

Apart from their organizational structures, both the Qadhafi forces and the *thuwar* committed repeated violations of IHL and ICL during the conflict, and with respect to the *thuwar* after its end as described below in Chapter V, and in Part Two with respect to the different theaters of military operations. It is clear that certain acts of violence perpetrated by regime forces constitute crimes against humanity,[18] while other acts were war crimes.[19] Similarly, the *thuwar* committed war crimes by violating

---

[15] *See* Report of the International Commission of Inquiry, advance unedited version (Mar. 2, 2012), *supra* note 12 at Annex I, ¶ 44. Human Right Watch's description of the on-going violations, which include, *inter alia*, arbitrary detentions, reported acts of torture and resulting deaths of regime sympathizers currently held in custody. *See* HUMAN RIGHTS WATCH, WORLD REPORT 2013: LIBYA (Feb. 2013), *available at* http://www.hrw.org/world-report/2013/country-chapters/libya?page=1.

[16] *See infra* Sec. 6.

[17] *See* Part Two.

[18] *See generally* M. CHERIF BASSIOUNI, CRIMES AGAINST HUMANITY: HISTORICAL EVO-LUTION AND CONTEMPORARY APPLICATION (Cambridge, UK: Cambridge University Press, 2011) [hereinafter "CRIMES AGAINST HUMANITY"].

[19] For more on the legal regime of ICL, *see infra* Sec. 2.

customary and conventional international humanitarian law.[20] Both sides committed violations of ICL, particularly torture under the CAT.[21]

These and other issues are relevant to an assessment of legal accountability in the aftermath of the conflict, which includes three applicable legal regimes, namely: international human rights law (IHRL), IHL and ICL. Furthermore, only IHL, in part, and ICL contain norms establishing individual criminal responsibility.

Against the foregoing backdrop, this chapter addresses, for substantive purposes, twelve patterns of violations carried out by Qadhafi forces and the *thuwar* during the conflict. Specific violations include: i) the use of excessive force against protestors and demonstrators; ii) unlawful killings; iii) arbitrary detentions and enforced disappearances; iv) torture and other forms of ill-treatment; v) denial of access to medical treatment; vi) continued restrictions on the freedom of expression;[22] vii) attacks against civilians, civilian objects, protected persons and objects;[23] viii) the prohibited use of weapons; ix) the recruitment of mercenaries; x) violations against specific groups; xi) sexual violence; and xii) the use of children and their treatment in armed conflict. As described below, these categories are illustrative and not legal in nature due to the various requirements of each the various legal regimes that apply, depending in part on the phase of the conflict during which the violation occurred and the context in which it occurs.[24] The details of the violations themselves are recounted in Part Two. This chapter next discusses issues specific to post-conflict justice, including proceedings against former regime officials, extradition requests and domestic legislative measures, and issues relating to Libya's cooperation with the ICC and complementarity.

As indicated above, the two legal regimes that establish individual criminal responsibility are ICL and IHL, the latter including two sub-regimes for

---

[20] *See id.* For more on the legal regime of IHL, *see* Sec. 2.

[21] CAT, *supra* note 10.

[22] Reference is made above to "continued" restrictions on the freedom of expression as a conflict-specific violation because, under Qadhafi, freedom of expression in Libya was also regularly denied by law prior to the conflict. *See* Libyan domestic Law 75 of 1973, *infra* note 80.

[23] Attacks against civilians, civilian objects, protected persons and objects may include: Intentional or Indiscriminate Attacks on Civilians; Attacks on Cultural Objects and Places of Worship; Impeding Access to Humanitarian Relief and Attacks on Humanitarian Personnel; Attacks on Humanitarian Personnel and Transport; Attacks on Protected Medical Personnel, Transport and Facilities; and Misuse of the Emblem.

[24] For more on the categories, *see infra* Sec. 4. For more on the phases of the conflict, *see infra* Sec. 3. For more on the applicable law, *see infra* Sec. 2.

international armed conflicts (IAC) and non-international armed conflicts (NIAC).[25] In addition, the Rome Statute of the ICC constitutes a separate legal regime. With respect to IHL and ICL, their respective normative proscriptions will be applied by different national *fora*, and even though the legal sources of these normative proscriptions are respectively the same for all states, their application will differ depending upon the substantive and procedural norms of each separate national legal system.

Steps toward accountability for these and other violations in post-conflict Libya have thus far been almost nonexistent, and the proposals for conducting proceedings before special or military tribunals are unacceptable because of their potential for unfairness.[26] The lingering inaction on post-conflict questions in Libya has drawn the attention of the international community, human rights groups and Libyan civil society organizations, who together recognize and advocate for the prompt and effective implementation of accountability mechanisms for serious conflict-related violations[27] through an effective and impartial judiciary.[28] The lack of any significant progress on accountability measures has been a recurrent issue internationally, and on 14 March 2013, the Security Council itself addressed the issue, adopting Resolution 2095, which expressed in part the Council's "grave concern at continuing reports of reprisals, arbitrary detentions without access to due process, wrongful imprisonment, mistreatment, torture and extrajudicial executions in Libya" and called "upon the Libyan government to take all steps necessary to accelerate the judicial process..."[29] Ultimately, it is clear that a functional and indepen-

---

[25] *See also infra* Sec. 2. This chapter uses the abbreviations "NIAC" and "IAC" as used by, *e.g.*, a legal advisor in the Legal Division of the International Committee of the Red Cross, and numerous other relevant sources. *See* Jelena Pejic, *The protective scope of Common Article 3: more than meets the eye*, INTERNATIONAL COMMITTEE OF THE RED CROSS, *available at* http://www.icrc.org/fre/assets/files/review/2011/irrc-881-pejic.pdf. Along the same lines, this chapter adopts the abbreviation "CAC" for a coexisting armed conflict (*i.e.*, to describe the phenomenon when parallel conflicts of both a non-international and international character take place simultaneously within the same conflict and state).

[26] *See e.g.*, INTERNATIONAL CRISIS GROUP, TRIAL BY ERROR: JUSTICE IN POST-QADHAFI LIBYA, *supra* note 14.

[27] The term "violations" as used in this chapter references breaches of IHRL, IHL and ICL. For a detailed description of conflict-related violations that occurred in ten theaters of military operations, *see* Part Two.

[28] *See generally*, INTERNATIONAL CRISIS GROUP, TRIAL BY ERROR: JUSTICE IN POST-QADHAFI LIBYA, *supra* note 14.

[29] Security Council, S.C. Res. 2095, Mar. 14, 2013, U.N. Doc. S/RES/2095 (2013).

dent judicial system capable of carrying out criminal justice[30] for past and on-going international and domestic law violations is paramount to rebuilding Libya and ensuring it stability going forward.[31]

2. APPLICABLE LAW[32]

The three international legal regimes applicable to the situation in Libya during each of the stages of the conflict are IHRL, IHL and ICL. These three regimes share the same values, namely the protection of human and social interests. To a large extent, these regimes overlap. At the same time, however, they evidence ambiguities in their prescriptions and pro-scriptions, as well as gaps in their protective schemes.[33] In particular, differences exist between these regimes with respect to their structures, enforcement modalities and, more particularly, the contexts to which they apply. The most significant issue with respect to the applicability of these three legal regimes are their divergent legal contexts.

IHRL is the broadest of the three regimes, as it applies during both times of peace and conflict, although human rights treaties envisage and permit a number of derogations when permissible "states of emergency" are declared.[34] Libya did not seek to derogate from any of its obligations under the IHRL treaties to which it is a state party, thereby making the

---

[30] ICL sanctions certain violations of IHRL, including crimes against humanity and tor-ture. IHRL does not entail its own penal consequences.

[31] For more on issues relating to post-conflict justice, *see infra* Sec. 6.

[32] Section 2 on Applicable Law quotes or paraphrases in large part from two publica-tions authored by the Editor of this text. *See* M. Cherif Bassiouni, *"Terrorism": Reflections on Legitimacy and Policy Considerations, in* VALUES AND VIOLENCE: INTANGIBLE ASPECTS OF TERRORISM 233 (I.A. Karawan et al. eds., Dordrecht, The Netherlands: Springer, 2008). *See also* M. Cherif Bassiouni, *The New Wars and the Crisis of Compliance with the Law of Armed Conflict by Non-State Actors*, 98 J. CRIM. L. & CRIMINOLOGY 711 (2008).

[33] As evidenced by the International Court of Justice, in its decision on the Legal Consequences of the Construction of a Wall in the Occupied Palestinian Territory, 2004 I.C.J. 131 (July 9), in which it discusses the applicability of the IHRL and IHL regimes, but without indicating how these overlapping regimes apply simultaneously and in what way they cumulatively enhance the protection goal sought to be achieved. *See also* M. Cherif Bassiouni, *The Normative Framework on International Criminal Law: Overlaps, Gaps, and Ambiguities in Contemporary International Law, in* 1 INTERNATIONAL CRIMINAL LAW 469 (M. Cherif Bassiouni ed., Leiden, The Netherlands: Martinus Nijhoff, 3d ed. 2008).

[34] *See generally* Joan F. Hartman, *Derogation from Human Rights Treaties in Public Emergencies*, 22 HARVARD INT'L. L. J. 1 (1981). Under Art. 4(2) of the International Covenant on Civil and Political Rights, no derogation is permitted from Arts. 6, 7, 8 (¶¶ 1 and 2), 11, 15, 16 & 18. *See* International Covenant on Civil and Political Rights, G.A. Res. 2200A (XXI), U.N. Doc. A/6316 (1966), 999 U.N.T.S. 171 (Dec. 16, 1966) [hereinafter "ICCPR"].

rights as defined under these instruments applicable during the conflict.[35] Certain violations of IHRL are criminalized under ICL in both times of peace and war, such as crimes against humanity[36] and torture.[37] It should also be noted that while IHRL applies in times of war and peace,[38] it is a *lex generalis* while IHL[39] is considered the *lex specialis*, which has priority in its application during armed conflicts.[40]

---

[35] The relevant IHRL instruments and optional protocols to which the former Libyan Arab Jamahiriya was a party throughout the course of the conflict include: "The International Covenant on Civil and Political Rights and the International Covenant on Economic, Social and Cultural Rights, were both ratified by Libya on 15 May 1970. The Convention on the Elimination of All Forms of Racial Discrimination was ratified on 3 July 1968. The Convention on the Elimination of Discrimination Against Women, the Convention on the Prevention and Punishment of the Crime of Genocide, the Convention on the Non-Application of Statutory Limits to War Crimes and Crimes against Humanity, and the Convention Against Torture and other Cruel, Inhuman or Degrading Treatment and Punishment, were all ratified by Libya on 16 May 1989. The Convention on the Rights of Child was ratified on 15 April 1993. The International Convention on the Protection of the Rights of all Migrant Workers and Members of their Families was ratified by Libya on18 June 2004. Libya has ratified the Optional Protocol to the Convention on the Rights of Child on the involvement of children in armed conflict on 29 October 2004 with a binding declaration made under Article 3. At a regional level, Libya is a party to the African Charter on Human and Peoples' Rights which it joined on 19 July 1986, the African Charter on the Rights and Welfare of the Child, which it ratified on 23 September 2000, the Protocol to the African Charter on Human and Peoples' Rights on the Establishment of an African Court on Human and Peoples' Rights, which it ratified on 19 November 2003 and the Protocol on the Rights of Women in Africa which it ratified on 23 May 2004." Report of the International Commission of Inquiry, advance unedited version (Mar. 2, 2012), *supra* note 12 at ¶ 16, n. 23.

[36] *See generally*, BASSIOUNI, CRIMES AGAINST HUMANITY, *supra* note 18.

[37] *See* CAT, *supra* note 10.

[38] The ICJ has articulated the applicability of IHRL to armed conflicts, stating that "The Court observes that the protection of the International Covenant of Civil and Political Rights does not cease in times of war, except by operation of Article 4 of the Covenant whereby certain provisions may be derogated from in a time of national emergency." Advisory Opinion on the Legality of the Threat or Use of Nuclear Weapons, 1996 I.C.J. 226, ¶ 25. *See also supra* note 34, regarding certain provisions of the ICCPR which are non-derogable.

[39] The term IHL includes genocide, crimes against humanity and war crimes. *See* Bassiouni, *The Normative Framework on International Criminal Law: Overlaps, Gaps, and Ambiguities in Contemporary International Law, supra* note 33.

[40] The ICJ found that, while IHL and IHRL may both apply to a certain matter, "the Court will have to take into consideration both these branches of international law, namely human rights law and, as *lex specialis*, international humanitarian law. *See* ICJ, *Legal Consequences of the Construction of a Wall in the Occupied Palestinian Territory, supra* note 33 at ¶ 106. It should also be noted that transgressions of the norms of IHL in conflicts of an international character are "grave breaches". The four Geneva Conventions of August 12, 1949, apply to both types of conflict. *See* the Geneva Conventions, *supra* note 10. These conventions apply to "conflicts of a non-international character" as stated in Common Article 3, where the transgressions equivalent to "grave breaches" are referred to as "violations." *See also* Protocol I Additional to the Geneva Conventions of August 12, 1949,

IHL is the law that establishes, *inter alia*, norms for the conduct of war, protections for non-combatants and prohibitions on certain means and methods used to wage war during conflicts of an international and non-international character.[41] During conflicts, IHL promotes the humane treatment of combatants and non-combatants by protecting certain categories of persons from conflict-related harm. It also includes protections for certain places and for civilian property. The four Geneva Conventions, whose implementation is overseen by the ICRC,[42] and their three Additional Protocols serve as the foundation of conventional IHL.[43] The Geneva Conventions and their Additional Protocols apply to states in addition to customary international law, which begins with The Hague Conventions of 1899 and 1907, and is supplemented by the evolving practice of states.[44]

---

opened for signature Dec. 12, 1977, U.N. Doc. A/21/144 Annex I [hereinafter "Protocol I"]; Protocol II Additional to the Geneva Convention, *opened for signature Aug. 12, 1949*, U.N. Doc. No. 32/144 Annex 2 [hereinafter "Protocol II"].

[41] Even within the IHL regime there is a distinction between conventional and customary IHL, and there is also a distinction as to the legal norm applicable to conflicts of an international character and conflicts of a non-international character. IHL excludes purely domestic conflicts and internal hostility.

[42] CUSTOMARY INTERNATIONAL HUMANITARIAN LAW (Jean-Marie Henckaerts and Louise Doswald-Beck eds., Cambridge, UK: Cambridge University Press, 2d ed. 2013); Michael Ignatieff, *International Committee of the Red Cross (ICRC)*, CRIMES OF WAR, *available at* http://www.crimesofwar.org/a-z-guide/international-committee-of-the-red-cross-icrc.

[43] The body of law governing IHL also includes other instruments and customary international law. *See* CUSTOMARY INTERNATIONAL HUMANITARIAN LAW, *supra* note 42. *See also* Report of the International Commission of Inquiry, advance unedited version (Mar. 2, 2012), *supra* note 12 at Annex I, ¶ 19.

[44] For more on conventional and customary international humanitarian law, *see* A MANUAL ON INTERNATIONAL HUMANITARIAN LAW AND ARMS CONTROL AGREEMENTS 18 (M. Cherif Bassiouni ed., Ardsley, USA: Transnational Publishers, 2000); COMMENTARY ON THE ADDITIONAL PROTOCOLS OF 8 JUNE 1977 TO THE GENEVA CONVENTIONS OF 12 AUGUST 1949 (Y. Sandoz et al. eds., Dordrecht, The Netherlands: Martinus Nijhoff, 1987); GERALD I.A.D. DRAPER, THE RED CROSS CONVENTIONS OF 1949 (New York, USA: Praeger, 1958); Jean-Marie Henckaerts, *Study on Customary International Humanitarian Law: A Contribution to the Understanding and Respect for the Rule of Law in Armed Conflict*, 857 INT'L REV. RED CROSS (2005).

The Four Geneva Conventions of August 12, 1949, which, as of January 1, 2007, have been ratified by 194 states, are deemed to reflect customary international law. ICRC, International Humanitarian Law: Treaties and States Parties to Such Treaties, *available at* http://www.icrc.org/ihl.nsf?opendatabase. Also deemed customary international law are parts of Protocol I (1977), which deals with conflicts of an international character (ratified by 167 states), and Protocol II (ratified by 163 states). *Id.* In short, the Geneva Conventions embody customary international law and ultimately have become customary international law, while the two Additional Protocols (1977) embody, in part, customary international law, but have not, in their entirety, risen to the level of customary international law. CUSTOMARY INTERNATIONAL HUMANITARIAN LAW, *supra* note 43. The ICRC undertook a study published in 2005 on what has become customary international law, and in a sense it

In the context of conflicts of an international character, violations of IHL that are deemed "grave breaches" entail criminal consequence. They are considered war crimes under customary international law. If the conflict is deemed not of an international character, the "grave breaches" are labeled "violations" under Common Article 3 of the Geneva Conventions,[45] but they are deemed by customary IHL as equivalent to "grave breaches" and war crimes,[46] and therefore that they entail criminal consequence for individuals.

In summary, the sources of IHL norms are conventional and customary international law, commonly referred to as "the Law of Geneva" (for the conventional law of armed conflicts) and "the Law of The Hague" (for the customary law of armed conflicts).[47] The Law of The Hague is not, however, exclusively customary law since it is partially made of treaty law, and also because some treaty law has become part of customary law.[48] In turn, the Law of Geneva is not exclusively treaty law, because it reflects customary law and because it has become customary law.[49] Additionally, the treaty law that applies to weapons control derives from customary and conventional law, and some of its specific norms have become part of customary law subsequent to its drafting.[50]

---

represents the equivalent of the 1899 and 1907 Hague Conventions on the codification of the customary law of armed conflict. *Id.* While the ICRC's study may be deemed doctrinal, it nonetheless fills a gap left open by the political inability of states to update the 1907 Hague Convention codifying the customary international law of armed conflicts. *Id. See also* JEAN PICTET, 1–4 COMMENTARY ON THE GENEVA CONVENTIONS OF 12 AUGUST 1949 (Geneva, Switzerland: International Committee of the Red Cross, 1952); JEAN PICTET, DEVELOPMENT AND PRINCIPLES OF INTERNATIONAL HUMANITARIAN LAW (Dordrecht, The Netherlands: Martinus Nijhoff, 1985).

[45] *See* the Geneva Conventions, *supra* note 10.

[46] *See e.g.* Rome Statute, *supra* note 8 at art. 8.

[47] *See supra* note 43.

[48] BASSIOUNI, A MANUAL ON INTERNATIONAL HUMANITARIAN LAW *supra* note 47 at 18.

[49] *Id.* at 20.

[50] *Id.* at 18 & 20. With respect to the prohibition of certain weapons on the basis that they are "indiscriminate" or because they cause "unnecessary pain and suffering," the first international instrument was the 1868 St. Petersburg Declaration which prohibits the use of dum-dum and explosive bullets. St. Petersburg Declaration Renouncing the Use, in Time of War, of Explosive Projectiles Under 400 Grammes Weight, Nov. 29/Dec. 11, 1868, *reprinted in* 1 AM. J. INT'L L. SUPP. 95 (1907). It was followed by the 1925 Geneva Convention on Asphyxiating Gases. Protocol for the Prohibition of the Use in War of Asphyxiating, Poisonous, or other Gases and Bacteriological Methods of Warfare, June 17, 1925, 26 U.S.T. 571, 94 L.N.T.S. 65, *reprinted in* 25 AM. J. INT'L L. 94 (1931). *See also* Convention on the Prohibition of the Use, Stockpiling, Production and Transfer of Anti-Personnel Mines and on their Destruction, Sept. 18, 1997, 36 I.L.M. 1507; Convention on the Prohibition of the Development, Production, Stockpiling and Use of Chemical Weapons and on their Destruction, 13 Jan. 1993, S. Treaty Doc. No. 103–21, 1974 U.N.T.S. 45; Protocol on Prohibitions or Restrictions on the Use of Incendiary Weapons (Protocol III), Oct. 10, 1980, 1342

Thus, the traditional distinctions between conventional and customary law have been eroded.[51]

The two sources of IHL, namely customary and conventional international law, have established sub-regimes depending upon the legal characterization of the conflict as an IAC or NIAC. Thus, a person who would otherwise qualify as a lawful combatant in an IAC may become a common criminal in a NIAC or a purely internal conflict. This unfair imbalance is undoubtedly a factor that negatively affects voluntary compliance with IHL by non-state actors.[52] As noted above, ICL criminalizes serious violations of IHRL, including crimes against humanity[53] and torture,[54] and does so in times of war and peace. In this regard, IHRL is declarative or prescriptive, while ICL is proscriptive.

All three legal regimes are applicable to the conflict in Libya, from mid to late February 2011 until the cessation of active hostilities on or about 1 November, when Libya returned to a state of peace under IHL as discussed in Section 3.5. Subsequently, IHRL remained in effect, along with ICL and certain post-conflict IHL obligations, including towards detainees and displaced persons.[55] Further, no matter how the Libyan conflict is ultimately characterized under IHL – i.e. as international, non-international or purely internal – the three legal regimes discussed above apply.[56] Nevertheless, any judicial action will have to determine what substantive law is applicable depending upon the legal characterization of the

---

U.N.T.S. 171, 19 I.L.M. 1534 [hereinafter "Protocol III"]; Convention on the Prohibition of the Development, Production and Stockpiling of Bacteriological (Biological) and Toxin Weapons and on Their Destruction, Apr. 10, 1972, 26 U.S.T. 583 1015 U.N.T.S. 163. There are thirty-five Weapons Control conventions, but few specifically criminalize the use of these weapons. BASSIOUNI, INTRODUCTION TO INTERNATIONAL CRIMINAL LAW, *supra* note 4 at 142–44. Instead, their criminalization can be adduced from customary international law and from the writings of the most distinguished publicists. *See, e.g.*, Statute of the International Court of Justice, art. 38, June 26, 1945, 156 U.N.T.S. 77 (*citing* the sources of international law).

51 BASSIOUNI, A MANUAL ON INTERNATIONAL HUMANITARIAN LAW *supra* note 47 at 20.
52 For more on IHL compliance by non-state actors, *see supra* Sec. 2.
53 *See generally*, BASSIOUNI, CRIMES AGAINST HUMANITY, *supra* note 18.
54 *See* CAT, *supra* note 10.
55 Report of the International Commission of Inquiry, advance unedited version (Mar. 2, 2012), *supra* note 12 at ¶ 29 & n. 51. "For example, the Geneva Conventions require Contracting Parties to facilitate the return of civilian populations to their homes (*See* ICRC Study Rules 133 and 134). Customary IHL also provides that at the end of hostilities that the authorities in power must endeavour to grant the broadest possible amnesty to those who have not breached international criminal law (Rule 159), and to release from detention as soon as practicable anyone detained in relation to the conflict (Rule 128)."
56 *See Prosecutor v. Tadić*, Case No. IT-94-1-A, Appeal Judgement (Int'l Crim. Trib. for the Former Yugoslavia, July 15, 1999).

nature of the conflict, context and parties to the conflict. In Libya, the initial period of the conflict was purely internal, as it consisted of unrest (*i.e.* protests and demonstrations) and repression but not armed resistance, but the determination of precisely when that stage ended will have to be judicially determined. The following stage was a NIAC, and once again when it began and when it ended will have to be determined on the basis of the facts. The conflict became one of an international character beginning with NATO's involvement, but only as between NATO (and the states participating in Operation Unified Protector) and Libya government forces under the command of Qadhafi.[57] Finally, once the IAC and NIAC ended the conflict was purely internal in nature, and therefore only ICL and IHRL applied fully, with only certain residual provisions of IHL in effect, primarily concerning detainees and displaced persons.

2.1. *Non-State Actors*[58]

One of the primary distinctions between IHL, IHRL and ICL is that IHL and ICL do not differentiate between its violators, namely, between state and non-state actors. However, IHL has two legal regimes, one for IACs and the other for NIACs. Only state actors may be parties to an IAC, and therefore may be subject to ICL for "grave breaches."[59] Non-state actors who are included in this regime must operate under the control of a state, or for and on behalf of the interests of the state, or as state surrogates.[60]

As discussed below, the IHL provisions applicable during non-international armed conflicts are Common Article 3 and Additional Protocol II ["Protocol II"], both of which apply to non-state actors. In order to trigger their applicability, non-state actors must qualify as combatants. The Third Geneva Convention requires four conditions in order for non-state actors to benefit from the status of lawful combatants and therefore secure the

---

[57] An argument can also be made that NATO's intervention favored the *thuwar*, effectively making the entire conflict one of an international character, but evidence assembled by the CoI does not weigh in favor of this conclusion under IHL. For more on NATO's involvement in the conflict, including an analysis of the influence NATO had over the conflict's outcome, *see* Ch. III. *See also* Report of the International Commission of Inquiry to investigate all the alleged violations of international human rights law in the Libyan Arab Jamahiriya, U.N. HRC. 17th Sess., ¶ 56. U.N. Doc. A/HRC/17/44 (Jan. 12, 2012).

[58] The Section on Non-State Actors quotes or paraphrases in large part from a previous publication authored by the Editor of this text. *See* Bassiouni, *The New Wars and the Crisis of Compliance with the Law of Armed Conflict by Non-State Actors, supra* note 32.

[59] *See* Rome Statute, *supra* note 8 at Art. 8(2)(a).

[60] Military and Paramilitary Activities in and against Nicaragua (Nicar. v. U.S.), Merits, 1986 ICJ REP. 4 (June 27).

protections contained in Common Article 3. These conditions are: (1) "being commanded by a person responsible for his subordinates;" (2) "having a fixed distinctive sign recognizable at a distance;" (3) "carrying arms openly;" and (4) "conducting their operations in accordance with the laws and customs of war."[61] Protocol II refers to the following requirements for non-state actors engaged in conflicts of a NIAC, namely that (1) they must be an "organized armed group"; (2) which acts "under responsible command"; and (3) exercises "such control over a part of its territory as to enable them to carry out sustained and concerted military operations and to implement [the] Protocol."[62] If a non-state actor group does not fulfill the foregoing criteria, the Protocol will not apply, and the violence they perpetrated no longer benefits from the lawful combatant characterization, but becomes subject to domestic criminal law.[63]

Unlike ICL and IHL (under certain circumstances), IHRL treaties are not open to non-state actors such as the *thuwar*, and therefore its provisions do not apply. However as summarized by the CoI "it is increasingly accepted that where non-state groups exercise *de facto* control over territory, they must respect the fundamental human rights of persons in that territory."[64]

International law and IHL first recognized non-state actors in the era of de-colonization during the 1950s-1980s when these groups were engaged in what are called "wars of national liberation."[65] The limited recognition that they were given under public international law was based on the likely expectation that, after independence, these groups would become part of the legitimate government in their new state. Thus, in effect creating an exception for certain non-state actors based on future political expectations. This and other *de facto* exceptions, coupled with the post-

---

[61] Third Geneva Convention, *supra* note 10 at Art. 4(2).

[62] Protocol II, *supra* note 40.

[63] One effect of losing the combatant privilege is that killing an individual may constitute a criminal act, whereas it would not constitute murder when done in the course of conduct unless it violated some other specific provision of IHL.

[64] *See* UN Secretary-General, *Report of the Secretary-General's Panel of Experts on Accountability in Sri Lanka,* ¶ 188, Mar. 31, 2011, *available at*: http://www.un.org/News/dh/infocus/Sri_Lanka/POE_Report_Full.pdf. *See generally* ANDREW CLAPHAM, HUMAN RIGHTS OBLIGATIONS OF NON-STATE ACTORS (Oxford, UK: Oxford University Press 2006).

[65] Bassiouni, *"Terrorism": Reflections on Legitimacy and Policy Consideration, supra* note 32 at 222; Georges Abi-Saab, *Wars of National Liberation in the Geneva Conventions and Protocols,* 165 RECUEIL DES COURS 353 (1979); Gerald I.A.D. Draper, *Wars of National Liberation and War Criminality, in* RESTRAINTS ON WAR: STUDIES IN THE LIMITATION OF ARMED CONFLICT (Michael Howard ed., Oxford, UK: Oxford University Press, 1979).

conflict practices of impunity and amnesty addressed in Section 6, *infra*, have resulted in the unequal application of international law to different participants engaged in violent conflicts, often based on political rather than legal factors. This political dimension has undermined the value-oriented goals of international norms designed to minimize the harmful consequences of violent conflicts and interactions. In turn, this situation negatively affects individual and collective compliance with principles and norms designed to minimize harmful consequences to protected persons and targets in the course of armed conflict regardless of how the given conflict is legally characterized. The outcome has been an increase in harmful conduct, which paradoxically enhances political gains as non-state actors use their conduct to secure their position.[66] Thus, non-state actors who have the capacity to commit greater harm, even when violating IHL, are likely to receive greater political recognition, including the likelihood of impunity for their violations of IHL.

In some situations, non-state groups exercise dominion and control over a portion of a state's territory and may even manifest some of the characteristics of sovereignty or public authority over a given part of the national territory and over its inhabitants. This is the case of the Revolutionary Armed Forces of Colombia (FARC),[67] which controls significant portions of the southern part of the country, or Hamas in Gaza, which has broken from the Palestinian National Authority and is effective a non-state group that has come to power electorally.[68] In these cases, interna-

---

[66] This is evident in so many resolutions of the General Assembly and other specialized bodies of the United Nations, giving recognition to wars of national liberation and providing standing for these organizations. For example, the PLO was admitted as an observer to the United Nations in 1975. *See* G.A. Res. 3375, U.N. Doc. A/RES/3375 (Nov. 10, 1975). The recognition gave these groups some immediate legitimacy, and it gave some of their acts the legal status of a quasi-public entity. However, recognition was dependent upon certain political considerations. These political considerations were translated into legal elements, such as the extent of de facto territorial control exercised by these groups, their presumed level of representation of the indigenous population, the legitimacy of their ultimate goal, and the public law nature of their actions.

[67] The acronym "FARC" stems from the Spanish name of the non-state actor group, "Fuerzas Armadas Revolucionarias de Colombia." *See* JAIME GUARACA, COLOMBIA Y LAS FARC-EP: ORIGEN DE LA LUCHA GUERRILLERA (Nafarroa, Spain: Txalaparta 1999).

[68] The Hamas government is a *de facto* non-state armed group that falls within the meaning of Additional Protocol I, Article 1(4) or within the meaning of Common Article 3 and Additional Protocol II, depending upon political perspectives. *See* Abi-Saab, *Wars of National Liberation in the Geneva Conventions and Protocols, supra* note 65; Bassiouni, *"Terrorism": Reflections on Legitimacy and Policy Consideration, supra* note 32 at 220; Draper, *supra* note 65. *See also* 1–2 DOCUMENTS ON THE ARAB-ISRAELI CONFLICT: EMERGENCE OF CONFLICT IN PALESTINE AND THE ARAB-ISRAELI WARS AND PEACE PROCESS

tional law tends to give such groups enhanced recognition. This means that groups that do not exercise exclusive dominion and control over a more or less defined portion of a given territory (because they operate out of a narrow territorial base from which they carry out incursions in the same or different parts of the state's territory), do not enjoy full or quasi-political legitimacy.[69]

The difference between the *de facto* exercise of territorial dominion and control and its absence bears upon international law's recognition of the acts of such groups as quasi-public acts that carry or imply some internationally recognized legal consequences. However, it does not bear upon the lawfulness or unlawfulness of their conduct, which is regulated by IHL.[70] Additionally, as with the NTC in Libya, groups occasionally succeeded in their belligerency or insurgency, and were thus able to form a government to replace the ousted one, thereby acquiring full legitimacy and the corollary duty to ensure that their wartime depredations not go unpunished. Because of the political transformation and evolution of these groups, international law, reflecting the practices of states, grants them a measure of international legal recognition. While this political recognition should have no bearing on these groups' compliance or lack thereof with IHL norms, acquiring political legitimacy unfortunately seems to overshadow their previous violations of IHL. This situation tends to enhance non-compliance because of the expectations of later impunity, especially where the group is seen as virtuous or having deposed a particularly repugnant regime.[71]

(M. Cherif Bassiouni ed., Ardsley, USA: Transnational Publishers, 2005) [hereinafter "DOCUMENTS ON THE ARAB-ISRAELI CONFLICT"].

[69] Consider, for example, such contemporary conflicts as those in the Sudan, Uganda and the DRC. In these conflicts, guerrilla groups or insurgents moved from one area of the territory to another without remaining in established geographic areas. Nevertheless some of the groups may have fixed bases in some of the regions or provinces, thereby allowing their paramilitary units to go into other areas to operate from there. The purpose of this illustration is merely to indicate to the reader that the geographic positions of protagonists in these types of conflicts vary. As a whole, it is possible to distinguish between groups which have control over a certain territory and have an effective presence there and are capable of exercising some dominion and control over the population, while in other types of conflicts, the protagonists may be more nomadic in terms of their movement across the territory, region, or province.

[70] W. THOMAS MALLISON & SALLY MALLISON, THE PALESTINE PROBLEM IN INTERNATIONAL LAW AND WORLD ORDER (Essex, UK: Longman, 1983).

[71] Diane F. Orentlicher, *Settling Accounts: The Duty to Prosecute Human Rights Violations of a Prior Regime*, 100 YALE L.J. 2537 (1991). *See also* M. Cherif Bassiouni, *Combating Impunity for International Crimes*, 71 U. COLO. L. REV. 409 (2000); M. Cherif Bassiouni, *The*

Since governments only give belligerent and insurgent groups limited international legal recognition, the latter may seek to acquire such standing by declaring themselves to be bound by IHL.[72] By conforming their conduct to IHL, they may therefore seek partial recognition before the international community. These groups believe that by doing so they implicitly become legitimate groups with some semblance of equal status to the governments with which they are in conflict. Precisely in order to avert such public recognition, however, governments strongly oppose the back door legitimization of these groups irrespective of their declarations, which in turn removes the incentives for such groups to comply with IHL and in effect encourages them to continue to act outside the boundaries of the law.[73]

A few non-state actors have, at times, manifested their willingness to comply with IHL, presumably in exchange for the recognition of lawful combatant status and protections akin to those enjoyed by POWs, the preconditions of which are set forth above in this section.[74] However, governments have almost always rejected such offers from groups like the Irish Republican Army, the African National Congress, the Palestine Liberation Organization.[75]

Perennial Conflict between International Criminal Justice and Realpolitik, 22 GA. ST. U. L. REV. 541 (2006).

[72] *See* Churchill Ewumbue-Monono, *Respect for International Humanitarian Law by Armed Non-State Actors in Africa*, 864 INT'L REV. RED CROSS 905, 905–24 (2006). The ICTR, in deciding the applicability of Protocol II to Rwanda, noted that the Rwandan Patriotic Front had expressly considered itself bound by IHL. *Prosecutor v. Kayishema & Ruzindana*, Case No. ICTR-95-1-T, Trial Judgement, ¶ 156 (Int'l Crim. Trib. for Rwanda, May 21, 1999); *Prosecutor v. Akayesu*, Case No. ICTR-96-4-T, Judgement, ¶ 627, (Int'l Crim. Trib. for Rwanda, Sept. 2, 1998).

[73] Bassiouni, *"Terrorism": Reflections on Legitimacy and Policy Consideration, supra* note 32 at 223.

[74] *See* Ewumbue-Monono, *Respect for International Humanitarian Law by Armed Non-State Actors in Africa, supra* note 72.

[75] For example, the Provisional Revolutionary Government of Algeria attempted to formally adhere to IHL, but Switzerland and France challenged it. Switzerland also challenged an attempt by the Smith government in Souther Rhodesia (now Zimbabwe). The Kosovo Liberation Army expressed its desire to sign the Geneva Conventions, but was turned down. LIESBETH ZEGVELD, THE ACCOUNTABILITY OF ARMED OPPOSITION GROUPS IN INTERNATIONAL LAW 14 n.18 (Cambridge, UK: Cambridge University Press, 2002). These groups made offer to comply with IHL with the state with which they were in conflict; some of these declarations or offers were made in political communiqués, public speeches or statements. Established governments considered those as being merely propaganda. These were missed opportunities. The international organizations such as the UN and ICRC could have used these openings no matter how narrow they may have been, to push forward the agenda of compliance. Prior to Protocol I, these included the Provisional Government of the Algerian Republic (1958), the Provisional Government of Vietnam (1974), the Eritrean People's Liberation Front (1977), the African National Congress (1980),

Non-state actors who engage in conflicts may also commit violations of ICL, *inter alia* slavery, slave-related practices and trafficking in human beings, or drug trafficking.[76] These and other similar violations are governed by multilateral treaties for which individual criminal responsibility arises, and which are enforced under the national laws of state parties.

3. Phases of the Conflict

3.1. *Classification of Phases*

In order to conduct a legal analysis of the Libyan conflict, it must first be classified into its constituent phases, as the legal regimes that govern the violations that occurred vary depending upon the phase during which they were committed. The four relevant phases of the Libyan conflict were: (i) the pre-conflict, purely internal period; (ii) the NIAC period; (iii) the coexisting IAC period; and (iv) the post-conflict period, purely internal period.

The CoI found that the NTC possessed "*de facto* control over territory akin to that of a Governmental authority," and therefore IHRL violations committed by *thuwar* forces are also examined herein.[77] In late February 2011, the development from protests to a NIAC brought with it the applicability of Common Article 3 and Protocol II to the Geneva Conventions. Foreign intervention by NATO based on Resolution 1973 transformed the character of the conflict, as addressed below.

3.2. *Emergence of an Internal Conflict*

Libya was in a state of peace prior to the mid-February 2011 demonstrations in Benghazi.[78] Throughout Qadhafi's forty-two year rule Libyan citizens

---

União Nacional pela Independência Total de Angola (1980), South West Africa People's Organization (1981), and the Palestine Liberation Organization (1982). Such declarations are filed with the ICRC in Geneva. *See e.g.*, Ewumbue-Monono, *Respect for International Humanitarian Law by Armed Non-State Actors in Africa, supra* note 72. The ICTR, in deciding the applicability of Protocol II to Rwanda, noted that the Rwandan Patriotic Front had expressly considered itself bound by IHL. *See Prosecutor v. Kayishema & Ruzindana, supra* note 72 at ¶ 156; *Prosecutor v. Akayesu, supra* note 72 at ¶ 627.

[76] For a list of the 27 categories of ICL violations and 281 conventions applicable to individuals, irrespective of whether they are state of non-state actors (except for Torture under CAT), *see* Bassiouni, Introduction to International Criminal Law, *supra* note 4 at 143-146 and Ch. III.

[77] Report of the International Commission of Inquiry (Jan. 12, 2012), *supra* note 57 at ¶ 62.

[78] *Id.* at ¶ 51.

remained predominantly silent on matters relating to the oppression they faced, despite having endured several human rights violations and psycho-social trauma at the hands of the regime, as described in Chapter I.[79] Silence was due in large part to Qadhafi's intolerance for dissent – a policy rooted in law and brutally enforced through military means including the Libyan Revolutionary Guard Corps.[80] While political instability and isolated acts of unrest occurred throughout the 1990s, they were immediately quelled.[81] The same pattern did not manifest itself in early 2011, as the protests against the Qadhafi regime quickly spiraled into a NIAC. The precise date on which the early-2011 wave of protests and general unrest that began in Benghazi was transformed into a NIAC is difficult to determine exactly due to the nature of the facts and the threshold level of violence required under IHL, among other reasons set forth below.

3.3. *Emergence of a Conflict of a Non-International Character*

The protections afforded under IHL pertaining to NIACs are codified primarily in Common Article 3 of the four Geneva Conventions ("Common Article 3")[82] and Article 4 of Additional Protocol II of 1977 ("Protocol II").[83] At all times relevant to the conflict, the former Libyan Arab Jamahiriya

---

[79] *See* Ch. I, Sec. 11.

[80] Dissent was made illegal under Libya's domestic Law 75 of 1973, when the "Revolutionary Command Council issued a 'Law for the Protection of the Revolution,' making it a criminal offense to proselytize against the state, to arouse class hatred, to spread falsehood, or to participate in strikes and demonstrations." *See* GEOFF SIMONS, LIBYA: THE STRUGGLE FOR SURVIVAL 192–193 (New York, USA: St. Martin's Press, 1996).

[81] LUIS MARTÍNEZ, THE LIBYAN PARADOX (New York, USA: Columbia University Press, 2007).

[82] Referred to as "Common" Article 3 because its language appears identically in each of the four Geneva Conventions. *See* Geneva Conventions, *supra* note 10. The ICJ recognized that Common Article 3 is a part of customary IHL, applicable during both international and non-international armed conflicts. *See also Nicaragua, supra* note 60 at ¶¶ 118–120.

[83] Other relevant legal instruments governing NIACs include Article 19 of the: Convention for the Protection of Cultural Property in the Event of Armed Conflict, 249 U.N.T.S. 240 (May 14, 1954); Second Protocol to the Hague Convention for the Protection of Cultural Property in the Event of Armed Conflict, 2253 U.N.T.S. 212 (Mar. 26, 1999); Convention on the Prohibition of Military or Any Other Hostile Use of Environmental Modification Techniques, G.A. Res. 31/72, 1108 U.N.T.S. 151 (May 18, 1977); Protocol on Prohibitions or Restrictions on the Use of Mines, Booby-Traps and Other Devices as amended on 3 May 1996 (Protocol II), 1342 U.N.T.S. 168 (May 3, 1996); Chemical Weapons Convention, 1974 U.N.T.S. 137 (Jan. 13, 1993); Convention on the Prohibition of the Use, Stockpiling, Production and Transfer of Anti-Personnel Mines and on their Destruction, 2056 U.N.T.S. 211 (Sept. 18, 1997). Parties to an armed conflict must also obey the customary international humanitarian law. *See* CUSTOMARY INTERNATIONAL HUMANITARIAN LAW, *supra* note 42.

was a party to all four Geneva Conventions and its Additional Protocols I and II.[84] Common Article 3 seeks to protect persons not taking an active part in hostilities, including the wounded, sick and those rendered *hors de combat*, but who do not qualify for protections under the four Geneva Conventions due to the lack of an IAC.[85] Article 4 of Additional Protocol II[86] includes among other protections those designed for children and interned persons, and also encompasses the duties upon warring parties to distinguish between civilians and combatants, and between civilian objects necessary for survival (*e.g.*, crops) and valid military targets (*e.g.*, weapons installations).

An important distinction exists with respect to "intensity" as described under Common Article 3 and under Protocol II. While these provisions apply only to conflicts taking place on the territory of a state party, the requisite threshold of application under Protocol II is higher than it is under

---

[84] Rule of law in armed conflicts project RULAC, *Libya, Applicable International Law*, GENEVA ACADEMY OF INTERNATIONAL HUMANITARIAN LAW AND HUMAN RIGHTS, *available at* http://www.academy.ch/RULAC/applicable_international_law.php?id_state=128. Libya is a also "party to the Protocol for the Prohibition of the Use of Asphyxiating, Poisonous or other Gases, and of Bacteriological Methods of Warfare (ratified on 29 December 1971), the Convention for the Protection of Cultural Property in the Event of Armed Conflict, the Convention on the Prohibition of the Development, Production and Stockpiling of Bacteriological (Biological) and Toxin Weapons and on their Destruction (ratified on 19 January 1982), the Convention on the Prohibition on the Development, Production, Stockpiling and Use of Chemical Weapons and on their Destruction (ratified on 6 January 2004). Libya is also a party to the OAU Convention for the Elimination of Mercenarism in Africa and the International Convention against the Recruitment, Use, Financing and Training of Mercenaries. Both were ratified by Libya on 22 September 2000." *See* Report of the International Commission of Inquiry, advance unedited version (Mar. 2, 2012), *supra* note 12 at ¶ 19, n. 29.

[85] Protocol I to the Geneva Conventions defines a person *hors de combat* when: "(a) he is in the power of an adverse Party; (b) he clearly expresses an intention to surrender; or (c) he has been rendered unconscious or is otherwise incapacitated by wounds or sickness, and therefore is incapable of defending himself; provided that in any of these cases he abstains from any hostile act and does not attempt to escape..." *See* Protocol I, *supra* note 42.

[86] The relationship between Common Article 3 and Protocol II is explicitly provided for in Article 1(1) of Protocol II, namely that Protocol II "develops and supplements [Common Article 3] without modifying its existing conditions of application..." *See* Protocol II, *supra* note 42.

Common Article 3.[87] Along with its more restrictive scope of application,[88] Protocol II offers wider protection.[89] In other words, Common Article 3 provides fewer protections in a greater number of circumstances, while

---

[87] Common Article 3 of the Geneva Conventions provides that certain protections apply, namely

> In the case of armed conflict not of an international character occurring in the territory of one of the High Contracting Parties, each Party to the conflict shall be bound to apply, as a minimum, the following provisions:
> (1) Persons taking no active part in the hostilities, including members of armed forces who have laid down their arms and those placed ' hors de combat ' by sickness, wounds, detention, or any other cause, shall in all circumstances be treated humanely, without any adverse distinction founded on race, colour, religion or faith, sex, birth or wealth, or any other similar criteria.
> To this end, the following acts are and shall remain prohibited at any time and in any place whatsoever with respect to the above-mentioned persons:
> (a) violence to life and person, in particular murder of all kinds, mutilation, cruel treatment and torture;
> (b) taking of hostages;
> (c) outrages upon personal dignity, in particular humiliating and degrading treatment;
> (d) the passing of sentences and the carrying out of executions without previous judgment pronounced by a regularly constituted court, affording all the judicial guarantees which are recognized as indispensable by civilized peoples.
> (2) The wounded and sick shall be collected and cared for.

[88] Additional Protocol II only applies to conflicts

> 1. ... which take place in the territory of a High Contracting Party between its armed forces and dissident armed forces or other organized armed groups which, under responsible command, exercise such control over a part of its territory as to enable them to carry out sustained and concerted military operations and to implement this Protocol.
> 2. This Protocol shall not apply to situations of internal disturbances and tensions, such as riots, isolated and sporadic acts of violence and other acts of a similar nature, as not being armed conflicts.

[89] However, while the situations in which Additional Protocol II apply are more limited than under Common Article 3, Article 4 of Additional Protocol II on "Fundamental Guarantees," provides more robust protections, namely that

> 1. All persons who do not take a direct part or who have ceased to take part in hostilities, whether or not their liberty has been restricted, are entitled to respect for their person, honour and convictions and religious practices. They shall in all circumstances be treated humanely, without any adverse distinction. It is prohibited to order that there shall be no survivors.
> 2. Without prejudice to the generality of the foregoing, the following acts against the persons referred to in paragraph 1 are and shall remain prohibited at any time and in any place whatsoever
> (a) violence to the life, health and physical or mental well-being of persons, in particular murder as well as cruel treatment such as torture, mutilation or any form of corporal punishment;
> (b) collective punishments;
> (c) taking of hostages;
> (d) acts of terrorism;

Protocol II offers more expansive protections in fewer situations. This deficit has been used by states seeking to deny that protections apply to a given conflict taking place on their territory by maintaining that on-going violent clashes between state and non-state actors do not give rise to a NIAC because it does not rise to the level of legal and factual "intensity" required by Additional Protocol II and not Common Article 3.[90]

The International Criminal Tribunal for the former Yugoslavia (ICTY) has sought to clarify to the issue in a number of judgments, most notably the seminal *Tadić* case, in which the Appeals Chamber ruled that a NIAC exists where there is "protracted armed violence between governmental authorities and armed groups or between such groups within a State."[91] The Appeals Chamber echoed this in *Kordić and Čerkez*, holding that "The requirement of protracted fighting is significant in excluding

---

      (e) outrages upon personal dignity, in particular humiliating and degrading treatment, rape, enforced prostitution and any form of indecent assault;
      (f) slavery and the slave trade in all their forms;
      (g) pillage;
      (h) threats to commit any of the foregoing acts.
  3. Children shall be provided with the care and aid they require, and in particular:
      (a) they shall receive an education, including religious and moral education, in keeping with the wishes of their parents, or in the absence of parents, of those responsible for their care;
      (b) all appropriate steps shall be taken to facilitate the reunion of families temporarily separated;
      (c) children who have not attained the age of fifteen years shall neither be recruited in the armed forces or groups nor allowed to take part in hostilities;
      (d) the special protection provided by this Article to children who have not attained the age of fifteen years shall remain applicable to them if they take a direct part in hostilities despite the provisions of sub-paragraph (c) and are captured;
      (e) measures shall be taken, if necessary, and whenever possible with the consent of their parents or persons who by law or custom are primarily responsible for their care, to remove children temporarily from the area in which hostilities are taking place to a safer area within the country and ensure that they are accompanied by persons responsible for their safety and well-being.

   [90] Jed Odermatt, 'New Wars' and the International/Non-international Armed Conflict Dichotomy, INTERNATIONAL INSTITUTE FOR HIGHER STUDIES IN CRIMINAL SCIENCE, *available at* http://www.isisc.org/portal/images/stories/PDF/Paper%20Odermatt.pdf. ("The reluctance of governments to recognize the peculiarities of conflicts of a non-international character and to provide for compliance-inducing factors by non-state actors, while carving out exceptions for transgressions of IHL, contributes to non-compliance by both state and non-state actors.") *See also* Bassiouni, *The New Wars and the Crisis of Compliance with the Law of Armed Conflict by Non-State Actors, supra* note 32.

   [91] *Prosecutor v. Dusko Tadić*, Case No. IT-94-1, Decision on the Defence Motion for Interlocutory Appeal on Jurisdiction, ¶ 70 (In'tl Crim. Trib. Former Yugoslavia, Oct. 2, 1995).

mere cases of civil unrest or single acts of terrorism."[92] By use of the term protracted, the Chamber noted a temporal scope in the plain language of Common Article 3 before the triggering of its application. The *Haradinaj* Trial Chamber later elaborated on this by distinguishing NIACs from "banditry, riots, isolated acts of terrorism, or similar situations."[93]

The Trial Chamber in *Limaj* also included a discussion of the intensity of the conflict, noting that

> the determination of the existence of an armed conflict is based solely on two criteria: the intensity of the conflict and organisation of the parties, the purpose of the armed forces to engage in acts of violence or also achieve some further objective is, therefore, irrelevant.[94]

In *Haradinaj* the Trial chamber provided a more thorough exposition on the criteria for the intensity of the conflict, holding that the

> indicative factors relevant for assessing the "intensity" criterion, none of which are, in themselves, essential to establish that the criterion is satisfied. These indicative factors include the number, duration and intensity of individual confrontations; the type of weapons and other military equipment used; the number and calibre of munitions fired; the number of persons and type of forces partaking in the fighting; the number of casualties; the extent of material destruction; and the number of civilians fleeing combat zones. The involvement of the UN Security Council may also be a reflection of the intensity of a conflict.[95]

The Rome Statute mirrors the conclusions reached by the ICTY in its Article 8(f).[96]

Therefore, for purposes of IHL a NIAC under Common Article 3 began in Libya on or about 24 February 2011, when organized rebel forces took control of Tobruq and Misrata.[97] On 26 February, the Security Council affirmed this in Resolution 1970 where it welcomed the international community's disapproval of serious violations of IHRL and IHL taking

---

[92] *Prosecutor v. Kordić and Čerkez*, Case No. IT-95-14/2-A, Appeals Judgement, ¶ 341 (In'tl Crim. Trib. Former Yugoslavia, Dec. 17, 2004).

[93] *Id.* at ¶ 38 (internal citations omitted). *See also* Protocol II(2), stating that the Protocol does "not apply to situations of internal disturbances and tensions, such as riots, isolated and sporadic acts of violence and other acts of a similar nature, as not being armed conflicts." Protocol II, *supra* note 42.

[94] *Prosecutor v. Limaj*, Case No. IT-03-66-T, Trial Judgement ¶ 170 (In'tl Crim. Trib. Former Yugoslavia, Nov. 30, 2005).

[95] *Prosecutor v. Haradinaj*, Case No. IT-04-84-T, Trial Judgement ¶ 49 (In'tl Crim. Trib. Former Yugoslavia, Apr. 3, 2008).

[96] Rome Statute, *supra* note 8 at Art. 8(f).

[97] Report of the International Commission of Inquiry (Jan. 12, 2012), *supra* note 57 at ¶ 55.

place in Libya.[98] With regards to Protocol II protections and their higher requisite threshold, these protections may be said to have applied from about mid-2011 onwards, when the rebel forces achieved more territorial control and began to satisfy the requirements outlined above.[99] Foreign intervention in Libya, by virtue of UN Security Council Resolution 1973 and later NATO involvement, contributed to modifying the character of the conflict.

3.4. Coexistence of an International Armed Conflict

Conflicts of an international character are governed by Common Article 2 of the Geneva Conventions ("Common Article 2"), which applies to conflicts between two or more state parties, irrespective of the conflict's duration.[100] Common Article 2 notes the application each of the four Geneva Conventions to IACs.

It should be noted that the mere presence of the armed forces of one state in the territory of another state in which an armed conflict is taking place does not necessarily transform it into an IAC. For instance, when one state supports the government of another state engaged in a NIAC, the conflict remains a NIAC even if it involves the presence and activity of the other state's military. However, when a state supports rebel groups in another state where the conflict occurs, the conflict may qualify as international depending on the nature of the support.[101] The exact conditions under which foreign military support for rebels during a NIAC internationalizes the entire conflict or creates a parallel conflict – *i.e.*, one conflict between two states, and another between a state and one or more insurgent armed groups within its territory – is as yet unresolved under IHL.

---

[98] S.C. Res. 1970 (2011), Feb. 26 2011, U.N. Doc. S/RES/1970 (2011). Moreover, "[t]he involvement of the UN Security Council may also be a reflection of the intensity of a conflict." *Haradinaj, supra* note 95 at 49.

[99] Rule of law in armed conflicts project RULAC, *Libya, Applicable International Law, supra* note 84.

[100] *See* Art. 2 in each of the four Geneva Conventions. Geneva Conventions, *supra* note 10. *See also* PICTET, COMMENTARY ON THE GENEVA CONVENTIONS OF 12 AUGUST 1949, *supra* note 44 at 20–21.

[101] MICHAEL N. SCHMITT ET AL., THE MANUAL ON THE LAW OF NON-INTERNATIONAL ARMED CONFLICT WITH COMMENTARY, INTERNATIONAL INSTITUTE OF HUMANITARIAN LAW 2 (2006) *available at* http://www.iihl.org/iihl/Documents/The%20Manual%20on%20 the%20Law%20of%20NIA.pdf. *See also Rule of law in armed conflicts project RULAC, Qualification of armed conflicts*, GENEVA ACADEMY OF INTERNATIONAL HUMANITARIAN LAW AND HUMAN RIGHTS, *available at* http://www.geneva-academy.ch/RULAC/qualification_ of_armed_conflict.php.

Of particular importance is whether or not the foreign intervening state or states exercises "overall" or "effective" control over rebels.[102]

The coexistence of an AIC and a NIAC is also clear in the jurisprudence of the ICTY. In *Tadić*, the Appeals Chamber held that

> It is indisputable that an armed conflict is international if it takes place between two or more States. In addition, in case of an internal armed conflict breaking out on the territory of a State, it may become international (or, depending upon the circumstances, be international in character alongside an internal armed conflict) if (i) another State intervenes in that conflict through its troops, or alternatively if (ii) some of the participants in the internal armed conflict act on behalf of that other State.[103]

Quoting extensively from *Tadić*, the Trial Chamber in *Brđanin* explicitly declared that an "armed conflict can be international as well as internal in nature."[104]

The International Court of Justice also addressed this matter in the *Nicaragua v. United States* case, holding that

> The conflict between the contras' forces and those of the Government of Nicaragua is an armed conflict which is 'not of an international character.' The acts of the contras towards the Nicaraguan Government are therefore governed by the law applicable to conflicts of that character; whereas the actions of the United States in and against Nicaragua [during the same period] fall under the legal rules relating to international conflicts.[105]

This phenomenon is hereinafter referred to as a coexisting (or "internationalized") armed conflict ("CAC").[106]

The CoI found that Resolution 1973 and the subsequent NATO airstrikes that began on 19 March 2011 created an IAC between NATO member countries and Libya.[107] The CoI further concluded that NATO and other foreign States involved were not exercising control over the military actions of

---

[102] For the distinction, *compare* the *Tadić* case at the ICTY and the *Nicaragua* case at the ICJ, which were analyzed in Leo Van den Hole, *Towards a Test of the International Character of an Armed Conflict: Nicaragua And Tadic*, 32 Syracuse J. Int'l L. & Com. 269 (Spring 2005).

[103] *Tadić, supra* note 56 at ¶ 84.

[104] *Prosecutor v. Brđanin*, Case No. IT-99-36-T, Trial Judgement, ¶ 131 (In'tl Crim. Trib. Former Yugoslavia, Sept. 1, 2004).

[105] *Nicaragua, supra* note 60 at 114.

[106] *See supra* note 25.

[107] Report of the International Commission of Inquiry (Jan. 12, 2012), *supra* note 57 at ¶ 56. The CoI noted that NATO was not exercising control, but did not distinguish between the requisite *Tadić* and *Nicaragua* criteria outlined above. *See also supra* note 102.

either of the parties to the NIAC,[108] and therefore that a CAC began on or about 19 March by way of the first NATO airstrikes. Stated another way, the parallel conflict in Libya comprised, on the one hand, the *thuwar* as a non-state armed group against the Qadhafi regime (the "NIAC"), and, on the other, NATO along with other foreign States against the Qadhafi regime (the "IAC").[109] However, if the NATO action is deemed an authorized action is deemed an authorized action by the Security Council pursuant to Chapter VII of the United Nations Charter, the NATO action will be deemed lawful under the *jus ad bellum*, and violations limited to where there is a specific "grave breach," in which case the person or commander involved will be deemed responsible. This means that the NATO action is not likely to give rise to state responsibility for participating states in the conflict.[110]

3.5. *Post-Conflict*

Following the death of Qadhafi on 20 October 2011, and the declaration by the NTC on 23 October that Libya had been liberated, a major decrease in conflict intensity resulted. The last NATO sortie was flown on 31 October 2011.[111] Thereafter, by 1 November 2011, Libya returned to a state of peace for purposes of IHL, despite residual post-conflict tension and acts of violence in cities such as Bani Walid.[112] Applicability of the Geneva Conventions to NIACs ceases for the most part when the requisite

---

[108] *Id.*

[109] For more on NATO's involvement in the conflict, including an analysis of the influence NATO had over the conflict's outcome, *see* Ch. III.

[110] *See Responsibility of States for Internationally Wrongful Acts*, 2 YEARBOOK OF THE INTERNATIONAL LAW COMMISSION, 2011, U.N. Doc A/56/10 (2011). *Nicaragua, supra* note 60. It should also be noted that Resolution 1970, which referred the matter to the ICC, contained an explicit limitation that

> nationals, current or former officials or personnel from a State outside the Libyan Arab Jamahiriya which is not a party to the Rome Statute of the International Criminal Court shall be subject to the exclusive jurisdiction of that State for all alleged acts or omissions arising out of or related to operations in the Libyan Arab Jamahiriya established or authorized by the Council, unless such exclusive jurisdiction has been expressly waived by the State

See S.C. Res. 1970, *supra* note 98 at ¶ 6. This limitation effectively shields personnel from the United States or Qatar, for instance, from investigation by the ICC, although it does not shield individuals from prosecution under the domestic codes of their states.

[111] *NATO and Libya, Operation Unified Protector, Ending the Mission*, NORTH ATLANTIC TREATY ORGANIZATION, available at http://www.nato.int/cps/en/natolive/topics_71652.htm%E2%80%8E.

[112] Isolated or sporadic acts of violence do not give rise to the threshold level of an armed conflict under IHL. *See* Protocol II, *supra* note 42. *See also* Ch. XV.

"organization" and "intensity" thresholds discussed above no longer existed. More simply, the parallel IAC came to an end as soon as NATO ceased operations in Libya. However, important post-conflict issues remain under IHL in that displaced civilian populations must be returned to their homes,[113] and individuals detained in relation to the conflict must be released.[114] One illustration of this enduring post-conflict problem is that, currently, thousands of civilians await return to Tawergha after having been forcibly expelled, without the benefit of government-assisted facilitation.[115] Moreover, the CoI estimated in March 2012 that the *thuwar* held approximately 8,000 thousand prisoners,[116] roughly 3,000 of which have yet to be released.[117] Post-conflict issues remain under IHL, ICL and IHRL as well, for example with regards to the treatment of those prisoners who continue to be subject to detention-related torture and ill-treatment.[118]

4. VIOLATIONS

The categories of violations identified in this book are: i) the use of excessive force against protestors and demonstrators; ii) unlawful killings; iii) arbitrary detentions and enforced disappearances; iv) torture and other forms of ill-treatment; v) denial of access to medical treatment;

---

[113] *See* Henckaerts, *Study on Customary International Humanitarian Law, supra* note 44 at Rules 133 & 134.

[114] *See Id.* at Rule 128, regarding the Release and Return of Persons Deprived of Their Liberty, which provides

    A. Prisoners of war must be released and repatriated without delay after the cessation of active hostilities.

    B. Civilian internees must be released as soon as the reasons which necessitated internment no longer exist, but at the latest as soon as possible after the close of active hostilities.

    C. Persons deprived of their liberty in relation to a non-international armed conflict must be released as soon as the reasons for the deprivation of their liberty cease to exist.

The persons referred to may continue to be deprived of their liberty if penal proceedings are pending against them or if they are serving a sentence lawfully imposed.

[115] Hadi Fornaji, *Grand Mufti tells Tawerghans not to return home on Tuesday*, LIBYA HERALD, June 23, 2013, *available at* http://www.libyaherald.com/2013/06/23/grand-mufti-tells-tawerghans-not-to-return-home-on-tuesday.

[116] Report of the International Commission of Inquiry, advance unedited version (Mar. 2, 2012), *supra* note 12 at Annex I, ¶ 105.

[117] HUMAN RIGHTS WATCH, WORLD REPORT 2013, *supra* note 15. *See also* Ch. V.

[118] *Id. See also* Rome Statute, *supra* note 8 at art. 8(2)(c)(i); CAT, *supra* note 10.

vi) continued restrictions on the freedom of expression;[119] vii) attacks against civilians, civilian objects, protected persons and objects;[120] viii) the prohibited use of weapons; ix) the recruitment of mercenaries; x) violations against specific groups; xi) sexual violence; and xii) the use of children and their treatment in armed conflict.

These categories of violations are illustrative and not legal in nature. This is done for the essential reason that different legal regimes categorize the same conduct differently: there is no universal criminal code or regime that would allow for an absolute categorization of every type of illicit act. Accordingly, the same conduct may result in different legal characterizations based on whether the charges are based on the domestic laws of various states – which have often categorized these forms of conduct in different ways – or the statutes of the various international tribunals – which all have their own statutes and rules of procedure and evidence (although the caselaw of the ICTY and International Criminal Tribunal for Rwanda (ICTR) has been significantly harmonized due to their shared Appeals Chamber). The 12 characterizations employed by this book are therefore used to illustrate patterns of conduct that may be characterized subsequently as needed by the forum or entity addressing the issue, and should not be seen as an absolute affirmation or formal legal characterization in itself.

As described above, there are three applicable international regimes, namely IHL (and its sub-regimes for IACs and NIACs), ICL and IHRL, as well as various domestic legal characterizations, with further sub-divisions for countries that apply the Common law, Civilist/Romanist law, and *Sharī'a* law. To a significant extent, these regimes address the same conduct, but each does so in a different manner and provides different definitions of the act and different pre-requisites for that legal characterization. In order to remain neutral as to the ultimate characterization of the facts and not prejudice that determination, non-legal terms are used in this book.

---

[119] Reference is made above to "continued" restrictions on the freedom of expression as a conflict-specific violation because, under Qadhafi, freedom of expression in Libya was also regularly denied by law prior to the conflict. *See* Libyan domestic Law 75 of 1973, *infra* note 80.

[120] Attacks against civilians, civilian objects, protected persons and objects may include: Intentional or Indiscriminate Attacks on Civilians; Attacks on Cultural Objects and Places of Worship; Impeding Access to Humanitarian Relief and Attacks on Humanitarian Personnel; Attacks on Humanitarian Personnel and Transport; Attacks on Protected Medical Personnel, Transport and Facilities; and Misuse of the Emblem.

To illustrate these differences, consider the three international legal regimes. Of these, IHL requires as a predicate the existence of an armed conflict for the violation to qualify as a war crime, while ICL and IHRL contain no such requirement. Contrariwise, crimes against humanity, the most common form of ICL, requires that that the violation occurs in the context of a widespread or systematic attack against a civilian population, neither of which is required for the existence of a war crime. Therefore, the context in which the conduct occurs, and the separate prior legal qualification of the existence of an armed conflict, on the one hand, or a widespread or systematic attack on a civilian population, on the other, must be determined prior to the actual legal classification of the conduct, and then applies different names for the same conduct under each regime.

Therefore, the killing of a group of civilians during an armed conflict would qualify as a war crime for "willful killing", while it could also be charged as a crime against humanity for "extermination" if it is part of a widespread or systematic attack against a civilian population.[121] Furthermore, to add another wrinkle, the killing of those individuals could also qualify as genocide if the perpetrator possessed the requisite specific intent to destroy, in whole or in part, a protected group of which the killed were part.[122] Similarly, the act of arresting and detaining a civilian for his/her views might qualify as a war crime for "wilfully depriving a prisoner of war or a civilian of the rights of fair and regular trial" or "unlawful deportation or

---

[121] See Kordić and Čerkez, supra note 92 at ¶ 1037 (holding that "convictions under Articles 2 and 5 are also permissibly cumulative. While Article 5 ["Crimes against Humanity"] requires proof that the act occurred as part of a widespread or systematic attack against a civilian population, Article 2 [Grave breaches of the Geneva Conventions of 1949] requires proof of a nexus between the acts of the accused and the existence of an international armed conflict as well as the protected persons status of the victims under the Geneva Conventions." See also Prosecutor v. Jelesić, Case No. IT-95-10-A, ¶ 82 (Int'l Crim. Trib. For the Former Yugoslavia, July 5, 2001) (holding that "Article 3 [war crimes] requires a close link between the acts of the accused and the armed conflict; this element is not required by Article 5. On the other hand, Article 5 requires proof that the act occurred as part of a widespread or systematic attack against a civilian population; that element is not required by Article 3."

[122] See Prosecutor v. Musema, Case No. ICTR-96-13-A, Appeals Judgement, ¶¶ 366 & 370 (Int'l Crim. Trib. for Rwanda, Nov. 16, 2001) ("Genocide requires proof of an intent to destroy, in whole or in part, a national, ethnical, racial or religious group; this is not required by extermination as a crime against humanity. Extermination as a crime against humanity requires proof that the crime was committed as a part of a widespread or systematic attack against a civilian population, which proof is not required in the case of genocide.... [T]he Appeals Chamber holds that convictions for genocide and extermination as a crime against humanity, based on the same set of facts, are permissible. Musema's ground of appeal is thus dismissed.")

transfer or unlawful confinement of a civilian" if committed in the context of an armed conflict, but might be qualified as "imprisonment" as a crime against humanity, or as "persecution" as a crime against humanity if done with the specific intent to discriminate and suppress a protected right.

Thus, using the example of killing above, the same act could qualify as a) a violation either as a war crime (IHL), a crime against humanity (ICL) or genocide; b) a violation of all three regimes; or c) any combination of the three depending on the factual circumstances surrounding the commission of the act. As indicated above, small differences in context can result in profound differences on the classification of the conduct and the applicable nomenclature.[123]

At present there are two different jurisdictions with proceedings against Libyans for violations committed during the 2011 conflict. The first, and most publicized, is the case against Saif al-Islam Qadhafi and 'Abdullah al-Senussi before the International Criminal Court (ICC). The specifics of the proceedings before the ICC are detailed below in Section 6.2, and in particular whether the ICC's complementarity provision allows for the prosecution of the two in Libya under Libyan law, or demands that they be prosecuted in The Hague. These proceedings are subject to the provisions of the Rome Statute, which is the foundational document of the court, and which contains criminal provisions for murder and persecution as crimes against humanity, which is what the two were charged with.

Under the terms of Article 7(1) of the Rome Statute, a "'crime against humanity' means [the commission of one of the enumerated acts] when committed as part of a widespread or systematic attack directed against any civilian population, with knowledge of the attack."[124] Murder is codified under Article 7(1)(a), and persecution under Article 7(1)(h).

The ICC's Elements of Crimes provides that under the Rome Statute, murder consists of the following elements

1. The perpetrator killed one or more persons.

---

[123] To address the complexities of cumulative charging and cumulative convictions for the various international legal regimes, the ICTY has adopted the American *Blockburger* test. In the famous *Čelebići* case, the ICTY Appeals Chamber held that

> multiple criminal convictions entered under different statutory provisions but based on the same conduct are permissible only if each statutory provision involved has a materially distinct element not contained in the other. An element is materially distinct from another if it requires proof of a fact not required by the other.

Prosecutor v. Mucić et al., Case No. IT-96-21-A, Appeals Judgement, ¶ 412, (Int'l Crim. Trib. for the Former Yugoslavia, Feb. 20, 2001).

[124] Rome Statute, *supra* note 8 at art. 7.

2. The conduct was committed as part of a widespread or systematic attack directed against a civilian population.
3. The perpetrator knew that the conduct was part of or intended the conduct to be part of a widespread or systematic attack against a civilian population.[125]

Persecution as a crime against humanity consists of the following elements:

1. The perpetrator severely deprived, contrary to international law, one or more persons of fundamental rights.
2. The perpetrator targeted such person or persons by reason of the identity of a group or collectivity or targeted the group or collectivity as such.
3. Such targeting was based on political, racial, national, ethnic, cultural, religious, gender as defined in article 7, paragraph 3, of the Statute, or other grounds that are universally recognized as impermissible under international law.
4. The conduct was committed in connection with any act referred to in article 7, paragraph 1, of the Statute or any crime within the jurisdiction of the Court.
5. The conduct was committed as part of a widespread or systematic attack directed against a civilian population.
6. The perpetrator knew that the conduct was part of or intended the conduct to be part of a widespread or systematic attack directed against a civilian population.

As the CoI noted, Libyan criminal law does not contain specific provisions for IHL and ICL violations. Rather, Libyan criminal law encompasses "ordinary crimes" and *sharī'a* law provisions. These provisions are contained in the 1953 Libyan Penal Code,[126] which is based on the Italian Criminal Code of 1931 and the Egyptian Criminal Code of 1937. Since the Penal Code's promulgation on 29 November 1953, it has been amended 20 times. The most significant of these revisions was Law 48 of 1956, Law 148 of 1972, Law 7 of 1988, Law 6 of 2002 and Law 10 of 2013.[127] In particular, Law 148 provides for the punishment of *ḥudūd* crimes such as thievery and highway brigandry,[128] Law 7 of 1988 and Law 6 of 2002 provide for the

---

[125] ASSEMBLY OF STATES PARTIES, INTERNATIONAL CRIMINAL COURT, ELEMENTS OF CRIMES 5 (2011), *available at* http://www.legal-tools.org/doc/3c0e2d/.

[126] Libyan Penal Code of 1953 (Nov. 28 1953), *available at* http://archive.org/details/LibyanPenalCodeEnglish.

[127] For a list of amendments, *see* MINISTRY OF FOREIGN AFFAIRS, www.aladel.gov.ly/main/modules/sections/category.php?start=0&categoryid=17.

[128] The *ḥudūd* are a set of crimes that are explicitly proscribed by the *Qur'ān* and are thus accorded special status in Islamic law. Under Libyan law, the *ḥadd* crimes of thievery and brigandry entail punishment by the amputation of a hand and beheading, respectively.

provision of *diyya* for *qiṣāṣ* crimes,[129] and Law 10 of 2013 criminalizes torture and extra-judicial executions.

As indicated by Libya in its submissions to the ICC regarding the proposed domestic prosecution of Saif al-Islam, he will be prosecuted under the ordinary criminal law provisions contained in the 1953 Penal code, namely for intentional murder (article 368), torture, (article 435), incitement to civil war (article 293), misuse of authority against individuals (article 296), arresting people without just cause (article 431) and the unjustified deprivation of personal liberty (article 433).[130] The Libyan government also indicated that he may be prosecuted for insulting constitutional authorities (article 195), devastation, rapine and carnage (article 202), civil war (article 203), conspiracy (article 211), attacks upon the political rights of a Libyan (article 217), arson (article 297), spreading disease among plants and livestock (article 362), concealment of a corpse (article 294), aiding members of a criminal association (article 322), use of force to compel another (article 429) and search of persons (article 432).[131]

As noted above, the Libyan Penal Code and amendments do not contain specific provisions on IHL and ICL violations (outside the newly introduced legislation on torture and extrajudicial killing, which may not apply due to their *ex post facto* nature), it nevertheless contains provisions for ordinary crime and *sharī'a* principles that are directly applicable to conflict situations such as the 2011 conflict. While not traditionally considered in the context of post-conflict justice and accountability, the *sharī'a* effectively contains all of the proscriptions provided for in IHL and ICL, although with different terminologies and methodologies.[132]

The manner in which an act is criminalized and the language it employs is not important, however, as long as it effectively proscribes the underlying conduct. The object is not the absolute harmonization of terminologies, but rather the harmonization of provisions addressing the illicit conduct so that there are no gaps between them. To that end, the ICC

---

[129] *Diyya* is the act of a perpetrator compensating an inured person for a *qiṣāṣ* crime, and applies in lieu of punishment. *Qiṣāṣ* crimes entail an attack upon the life or the physical integrity of an individual.

[130] Situation in the Libyan Arab Jamahiriya, Case No. ICC-01/11-01/11, Decision on the admissibility of the case against Saif Al-Islam Gaddafi, ¶ 28 (Int't Crim. Ct., May 31, 2013).

[131] *Id.* at ¶ 38.

[132] *See generally* M. CHERIF BASSIOUNI, THE *SHARĪ'A* AND ISLAMIC PUBLIC LAW IN TIME OF PEACE AND WAR (Cambridge, UK: Cambridge University Press, forthcoming 2014); M. CHERIF BASSIOUNI, THE ISLAMIC CRIMINAL JUSTICE SYSTEM (Dobbs-Ferry, USA: Oceana Publications, 1982).

Pre-Trial Chamber ruled in its 31 May 2013 decision on the admissibility of
the case against Saif al-Islam that

> there is no requirement under the Statute that the investigation at the
> national level be aimed at the prosecution of "international" crimes as long
> as the investigation covers the same conduct.[133]

In other words, as long as the laws under which the accused is prosecuted addresses the same conduct, the nomenclature and terminology in
which they do so is irrelevant. There is a requirement, however, that the
domestic legislation provide for the effective investigation and prosecution of the same issues.[134] While the Pre-Trial Chamber found that there
were sufficient flaws in the Libyan investigation, the question of the legal
characterization of the underlying acts was not contentious, a finding
affirmed in this book: there is nothing in the Libyan Penal Code itself that
precludes Libyan judicial authorities from addressing these issues under
domestic law.

In other words, there are a number of different ways to look at the same
conduct. Under some legal regimes a particular act may be criminal, while
under others that same conduct may not, depending on very particular factual circumstances surrounding the commission of the act. In certain situations multiple regimes may apply. As indicated above, although conduct
is grouped together and described broadly, the terminology used by this
book to describe violations is illustrative and ultimately agnostic as to the
legal regime that should be applied. This illustrative framework allows
the reader to look at the facts and apply them as needed, whether under
the rubric of IHL (for both IACs and NIACs), IHRL, ICL or domestic law.

5. Other Legal Issues

5.1. *Superior Responsibility for IHL and ICL Violations*

The doctrine of superior responsibility, which is often referred to as command responsibility, is the mechanism by which military commanders and civilian leaders are held criminally accountable for the conduct
of their subordinates that violates IHL and ICL norms. Although some
forms of superior responsibility under IHL and ICL are well known and

---

[133] Decision on the admissibility of the case against Saif Al-Islam Gaddafi, *supra* note
130 at ¶ 108.
[134] *Id.*

regarded, the extent and scope of the doctrine is not as clear as it may appear to be. The lack of clarity is due to the fact that the doctrine evolved out of a number of cases – or as the US Supreme Court held in *Griswold v. Connecticut*, the "penumbras" and "emanations" of a number of cases – beginning with the controversial WWII case against General Tomoyuki Yamashita and a number of subsequent cases at ICTY and ICTR. While the doctrine has been included in the statutes of the ICTY, ICTR and the International Criminal Court (ICC), the extent and scope of its application has not been codified, allowing for its continual development and curtailment by the judges of the various international tribunals. In other words, while the principle of superior responsibility is well established, its particulars are in continual evolution.

As described above, the doctrine of superior responsibility is the mechanism by which the criminal conduct of the principal perpetrators in any given conflict situation is linked and imputed to their superiors, [135] including the highest levels of the belligerents' civilian government.[136]

---

[135] It should be noted that under the doctrine of superior responsibility, criminal liability can attach to multiple commanders, including for conduct by individuals several ranks below the commander. *See Prosecutor v. Strugar*, Case No. IT-01-42-T, Trial Judgement, ¶ 363 (Int'l Crim. Trib. For the Former Yugoslavia, Jan. 31, 2005) ("The Chamber holds that there is no legal requirement that the superior-subordinate relationship be a direct or immediate one for a superior to be found liable for a crime committed by a subordinate, provided that the former had effective control over the acts of the latter."); *Prosecutor v. Krnojelac*, IT-97-25-T, Trial Judgement ¶ 93 (Int'l Crim. Trib. For the Former Yugoslavia, Mar. 15, 2001) ("Two or more superiors may be held responsible for the same crime perpetrated by the same individual if it is established that the principal offender was under the command of both superiors at the relevant time.").

[136] *Prosecutor v. Delalic et al.*, IT-96-21-A, Appeals Judgment, ¶ 377 (Int'l Crim. Trib. For the Former Yugoslavia, Feb. 20, 2001) (holding that "a superior, whether military or civilian, may be held liable under the principle of superior responsibility on the basis of his de facto position of authority. . . ."). A number of civilian heads of state and ministers have been prosecuted under the doctrine of superior responsibility for the conduct of the military. The most well-known modern cases of prosecutions of civilians under the doctrine of superior responsibility include Slobodan Milošević and Radovan Karadžić at the ICTY, and Jean Kambanda and Pauline Nyiramasuhuko at the ICTR. The ICC has indicted a number of heads of state, including Mu'ammar Qadhafi of Libya, Laurent Gbagbo of Côte d'Ivoire, and Omar al-Bashir of the Sudan. The ICTR also extended the doctrine of superior responsibility to completely non-military circumstances in the *Nahimana* case, where a former university lecturer and director of the Rwandan Office of Information was convicted by the ICTR and sentenced to 30 years imprisonment on account of his superior position at Radio Télévision Libre des Mille Collines (RTML), a private radio station that Nahimana founded and directed. RTLM employees were found by the ICTR to have used the radio station as a platform for public and direct incitement to genocide and crimes against humanity directed against the Rwandan Tutsi population. *The Prosecutor v. Nahimana et al.*, Case No. ICTR-99-52–A, Appeals Judgment, ¶¶ 363 2 & 803–822 (Int'l Crim. Trib. For

Without a system of superior responsibility, military commanders and civilian leaders could avoid any form of accountability for their role in the commission of crimes, as they were not themselves directly involved, and thereby escape any accountability despite their clear involvement.[137] Superior responsibility – and its corollary nullification of the defense of superior orders for subordinates – is therefore the mechanism by which all individuals participating in a conflict are obligated to heed IHL and ICL norms, and also the mechanism by which those norms are enforced internally, as the commander is exposed to criminal sanction to enforce compliance for those under his/her command.

The rationale for superior responsibility, as with IHL and ICL generally, is the humanization war, for the reasons described above: to ensure that the norms apply to all and to incentivize enforcement throughout military structures by obligating commanders to enforce those norms. As the ICTY Trial Chamber explained in *Halilović*

> the purpose behind the concept of command responsibility is to ensure compliance with the laws and customs of war and international humanitarian law generally. The principle of command responsibility may be seen in part to arise from one of the basic principles of international humanitarian law aiming at ensuring protection for protected categories of persons and objects during armed conflicts. This protection is at the very heart of international humanitarian law. Ensuring this protection requires, in the first place, preventative measures which commanders are in a position to take, by virtue of the effective control which they have over their subordinates, thereby ensuring the enforcement of international humanitarian law in armed conflict. A commander who possesses effective control over the actions of his subordinates is duty bound to ensure that they act within the dictates of international humanitarian law and that the laws and customs of war are therefore respected.[138]

Rwanda, Nov. 28, 2007). *See also* Statute of the International Criminal Tribunal for Rwanda, S.C. Res. 955, U.N. Doc. S/RES/955, Nov. 8, 1994 [hereinafter "ICTR Statute"].

[137] This problem famously arose in the early trial of Peter von Hagenbach, who was tried in 1474 by member states of the Holy Roman Empire for crimes committed in Breisach, Germany. At the trial, Peter attempted to introduce written evidence that his lord, Charles the Duke of Burgundy, had instructed him to commit the crimes for which he was being tried, but the judges refused to entertain the idea that a nobleman could be prosecuted, thereby effectively limiting punishment to Peter. *See* BASSIOUNI, INTRODUCTION TO INTERNATIONAL CRIMINAL LAW, *supra* note 4 at 416.

[138] *Prosecutor v. Halilović*, Case No. IT-01-48, Trial Judgement, ¶ 39 (Int'l. Crim. Trib. For the Former Yugoslavia, Nov. 16, 2005).

As with many core doctrines of IHL and ICL, superior responsibility is a relatively recent doctrine, effectively dating back to the *Yamashita* case in the aftermath of WWII. Although a few antecedents existed for prosecuting superiors for issuing orders for the commission of crimes by subordinates – as with the famous *Llandovery Castle* case before the Leipzig Trials that followed WWI, in which a submarine commander was tried for ordering his subordinates to open fire on the survivors of a torpedoed ship[139] – the notion of criminal liability for acts of omission, or failing to prevent and punish crimes committed by subordinates, was novel until the controversial case *Yamashita* case, in which a Japanese General was prosecuted for the crimes of troops under his nominal command.[140] Despite the controversial manner in which the facts of the case were interpreted, the *Yamashita* case clearly established that a commander may be held individually criminally responsible for failing to act to prevent or punish crimes committed by subordinates, a principle that has since become

---

[139] *Llandovery Castle*, 16 Am. J. Int'l L. 708 (1922).

[140] In that case, Japanese General Tomoyuki Yamashita was prosecuted for war crimes committed by soldiers of the Imperial Japanese Navy during the war. In 1945, a U.S. military commission sitting in Manila convicted the general on account of his failure to prevent forces ostensibly under his command from committing massacres and other atrocities against civilians in the Philippines. BASSIOUNI, INTERNATIONAL ENFORCEMENT, *supra* note 152 at 290. Yamashita was charged with criminal negligence by "dereliction of duty" for "fail[ing] to provide effective control [over his] troops as was required by the circumstances." *See Trial of General Tomoyuki Yamashita*, Case No. 21 (United States Military Commission, Manila, Oct. 8–Dec. 7, 1945), *available at* http://lawofwar.org/Yamashita%20 Commission.htm. *See also* SHANE DARCY & JOSEPH POWDERLY, JUDICIAL CREATIVITY AT THE INTERNATIONAL CRIMINAL TRIBUNALS 171 (Oxford, UK: Oxford University Press, 2011). The Commission held that where "vengeful actions are widespread offences and there is no effective attempt by a commander to discover and control the criminal acts, such a commander may be held responsible, even criminally liable, for the lawless acts of his troops..." *Trial of General Tomoyuki Yamashita, Id.* The *Yamashita* ruling is contentious due the fact that a general was for the first time convicted, and subsequently executed by hanging, based on a negligence theory of superior responsibility. *See, e.g.,* Anne E. Mahle, *Justice & The Generals The Yamashita Standard*, PBS, *available at* http://www.pbs.org/ wnet/justice/world_issues_yam.html. More importantly, the question of whether a commander had constructive knowledge of crimes perpetrated by his subordinates in that he "must have known" about the existence of such crimes due to their widespread nature is of course a broad attribution of criminal responsibility, and one which has largely been rejected since *Yamashita*. Because the general was convicted irrespective of his ability to effectively control the actions of his troops at the time, the legal standard for superior responsibility applied in *Yamashita* is arguably more akin to one of strict liability, which is a form of "[l]iability that does not depend on actual negligence or intent to harm, but that is based on the breach of an absolute duty to make something safe." BLACK'S LAW DICTIONARY 996 (St. Paul, US: West, 9th ed. 2009). *See also* BASSIOUNI, INTERNATIONAL ENFORCEMENT, *supra* note 152 at 464.

firmly rooted in international law, albeit with a far less stringent standard than that applied in *Yamashita*.[141]

The notion of superior responsibility was subsequently codified in Additional Protocol I of the Geneva Conventions ("Protocol I"),[142] as well as in the Statutes of the ICTY, ICTR, ICC and the mixed-model tribunals,[143] and the military codes of a number of countries. These codifications have incorporated the doctrine with responsibility for acts of omission, although as indicated above the extent and scope of the doctrine is as yet unsettled.

(a) *The Application of the Doctrine of Superior Responsibility*

As indicated above, the doctrine of superior responsibility is a form of vicarious or imputed criminal liability whereby military commanders and civilian leaders are held accountable for criminal acts committed by their subordinates over whom they assert effective control. Criminal responsibility under the doctrine may arise pursuant to either acts of commission or omission on the part of the commander or civilian leader. There are three instances in which superior responsibility obtains, each independent of the commander's rank or the number of individuals in the chain of command between the commander and the subordinate principal perpetrator. The three forms of superior responsibility are:

---

[141] *See, e.g.*, Protocol I, *supra* note 42 at art. 86; ICTR Statute, *supra* note 136 at art 6(3); Statute of the International Criminal Tribunal for Yugoslavia, S.C. Res. 827, U.N. Doc. S/RES/827, art. 7(3), May 25, 1993 [hereinafter "ICTY Statute"]; Rome Statute, *supra* note 8 at art. 25; Statute of the Special Court for Sierra Leone Statute, S.C. Res. 1315, U.N. Doc. S/RES/1315, art. 6(3), Jan. 16, 2001 [hereinafter "Sierra Leone Statute"].

[142] For example, superior responsibility under Protocol I exists when superiors "knew, or had information which should have enabled them to conclude in the circumstances at the time, that [a subordinate] was committing or was going to commit such a breach and if they did not take all feasible measures within their power to prevent or repress the breach." Protocol I, *supra* note 85 at art. 86.

[143] The Mixed-Model Tribunals, also known as hybrid or internationalized tribunals, employ some mixture of international and domestic law, or exist not as an international tribunal, but formally speaking are domestic courts that apply international law. Examples of Mixed-Model tribunals include the Special Court for Sierra Leone, the Special Tribunal for Lebanon and the Extraordinary Chambers in the Courts of Cambodia. For more information, *see* BASSIOUNI, INTRODUCTION TO INTERNATIONAL CRIMINAL LAW, *supra* note 4 at 721–784.

a) *commission*, in which a commander explicitly orders subordinates to commit violations of IHL, ICL[144] or domestic criminal or military law;[145]

b) *omission* by failing to prevent the commission of a crime, in which a commander fails to take the necessary steps to prevent the commission of a crime by subordinates when that commander knew or had reasonable grounds to believe that a violation was going to occur or could reasonably be anticipated to occur;[146] or

c) *omission* by failing to punish the commission of a crime, in which a commander fails to investigate or punish an individual or individuals for violations when that commander acquires sufficient evidence or knowledge of a violation by a subordinate after the fact to warrant an investigation or punishment.[147]

As outlined by the Appeals chamber of the ICTY, criminal responsibility for the second and third forms of superior responsibility is contingent on a number of factors, namely

(i) the existence of a superior-subordinate relationship; (ii) the superior knew or had reason to know that the criminal act was about to be or had been committed; and (iii) the superior failed to take the necessary and reasonable measures to prevent the criminal act or punish the perpetrator thereof.[148]

In practice, the essential factors for establishing superior responsibility for the second and third forms are the existence of a superior-subordinate relationship[149] and the effective control by the commander over the

---

[144] As described above, during armed conflicts of a non-international character, war crimes as defined under Art. 8 of the Rome Statute constitute serious violations of Common Article 3 and Additional Protocol II of the Geneva Conventions, in addition to other serious violations customary IHL. During international armed conflicts, war crimes under ICL constitute "grave breaches" of the Geneva Conventions, among other serious violations of customary IHL. *See* Rome Statute, *supra* note 8 at art. 8.

[145] This form of liability is codified in article 7(1) of the ICTY Statute, and article 6(1) of the ICTR Statute, and article 25(b)(3) of the Rome Statute of the ICC.

[146] This form of liability is codified in article 7(3) of the ICTY Statute, and article 6(3) of the ICTR Statute, and article 28(a) of the Rome Statute of the ICC with respect to military commanders and 28(b) with respect to others.

[147] *Id.*

[148] *Kordić and Čerkez, supra* note 92 at ¶ 839.

[149] *Prosecutor v. Kordić and Čerkez, id.* at ¶ 840 ("The basis of the superior-subordinate relationship is the power of the superior to control the actions of his subordinates."); *Limaj, supra* note 94 at ¶ 521 ("The superior-subordinate relationship lies in the very heart of the doctrine of a commander's liability for the crimes committed by his subordinate. It is the position of command over and the power to control the acts of the perpetrator which forms the legal basis for the superior's duty to act, and for his corollary liability for a failure to do so."); *Halilović, supra* note 138 at ¶ 63 ("The main factor in determining a position of command is the 'actual possession or non-possession of powers of control over the actions of subordinates.'").

subordinate.[150] The assessment of these factors is invariably fact specific and requires a careful analysis of the facts in each case,[151] in particular whether or not the commander actually exercised effective control and was in a position to take corrective action.[152] This is the kind of assessment that was not performed in *Yamashita*, where the court effectively adopted a strict liability standard for any conduct committed by anyone under the superior's command, and which caused so much controversy over the ultimate verdict of the commission.

It should also be noted that under the second and third forms of superior responsibility outlined above, the crimes of the principal perpetrator is not imputed to the commander. Rather, under the doctrine the commander is found to be in dereliction of duty for having failed to properly supervise those under his/her command, either by failing to prevent their illicit conduct from occurring in the first place, or by failing to investigate and punish their prior transgressions. As the ICTY Appeals Chamber held in *Krnojelac*, "It cannot be overemphasised that, where superior responsibility is concerned, an accused is not charged with the crimes of his

---

[150] *Delalic et al., supra* note 136. In the *Delalic* case the Appeals Chamber determined that "In determining questions of responsibility it is necessary to look to effective exercise of power or control and not to formal titles." *Id.* at ¶ 197. In reaching its judgment, the Appeals Chamber analyzed the ICRC Commentary on Article 86 of Protocol I Additional to the Geneva Conventions of 1949, and noted that "effective control" over subordinates is required and satisfied when a superior has "the material ability to prevent and punish criminal conduct." *Id.* at ¶ 256. Not all situations satisfy this threshold, however, and "substantial influence" in itself does not satisfy the requirements of superior responsibility. *Id.* at 266.

[151] For more on the case-by-case factual assessment of superior responsibility, *see Prosecutor v. Blaškić*, Case No. IT-95-14-A, Appeals Judgement ¶ 69 (Int'l Crim. Trib. For the Former Yugoslavia, July 29, 2004) ("The indicators of effective control are more a matter of evidence than of substantive law...."); *Halilović, supra* note 138 at ¶ 63. *See also United States v. List* ("Hostage Case"), 11 TRIALS OF WAR CRIMINALS BEFORE THE NUERNBERG MILITARY TRIBUNALS UNDER CONTROL COUNCIL LAW No. 10, Nuernberg, Oct. 1946–Nov. 1949 (1951), *available at* http://www.loc.gov/rr/frd/Military_Law/pdf/NT_war-criminals_Vol-X .pdf; *United States v. Von Leeb* ("High Command Case").

[152] *See Delalic et al., supra* note 136 at ¶197 (holding that "the ability to exercise effective control is necessary for the establishment of de facto command or superior responsibility" and affirming the Trial Chamber holding that "it is necessary that the superior have effective control over the persons committing the underlying violations of international humanitarian law, in the sense of having the material ability to prevent and punish the commission of these offences"); *Blaškić, supra* note 151 at para 375 ("It is settled in the jurisprudence of the International Tribunal that the ability to exercise effective control is necessary for the establishment of superior responsibility"). *See also The Current Elements of Command Responsibility Under International Law, in* 3 INTERNATIONAL CRIMINAL LAW: INTERNATIONAL ENFORCEMENT 467 (M. Cherif Bassiouni ed., Leiden, The Netherlands: Martinus Nijhoff, 3d rev. ed., 2008) [hereinafter "INTERNATIONAL ENFORCEMENT"].

subordinates but with his failure to carry out his duty as a superior to exercise control."[153]

The same standards of criminal responsibility for a military commander also apply to the highest military or civil ranks, which may include a head of state if the civilian leader was able to exercise effective control over the military or police, or a given combatant group.[154] As the ICTY Trial Chamber held in *Delalic*, "a superior, *whether military or civilian*, may be held liable under the principle of superior responsibility on the basis of his *de facto* position of authority..."[155] The operative question for criminal liability for civilian leaders is not their *de jure* authority over the principal perpetrators, but rather their *de facto* authority, along with the requisite superior-subordinate relationship,[156] and the ability to exercise effective control.[157] This capacity is therefore not exclusive to military leadership and may encompass civilian actors, including heads of state.

A number of civilian leaders have been indicted or prosecuted by international and mixed-model tribunals, including most notably Slobodan Milošević and Radovan Karadžić at the ICTY; Jean Kambanda and Pauline Nyiramasuhuko at the ICTR; Charles Taylor at the Special Court for Sierra Leone; Nuon Chea and Ieng Sary at the Extraordinary Chambers in the Courts of Cambodia; and Muʿammar Qadhafi, Laurent Gbagbo, and Omar al-Bashir at the ICC. Civilian leaders have also been prosecuted before domestic courts. Most recently, the trials of the former Egyptian President Hosni Mubarak,[158] and former *de facto* Guatemalan President Efraín Ríos

---

[153] *Prosecutor v. Krnojelac*, Case No. IT-97-25-A, Appeals Judgement, ¶ 171 (Int'l Crim. Trib. For the Former Yugoslavia, Sept. 17, 2003).

[154] For more on effective control, *see supra* notes 140 & 152.

[155] *Prosecutor v. Delalic et al.*, Case No. IT-96-21-T, Trial Judgment, ¶ 377 (Int'l Crim. Trib. For the Former Yugoslavia, Nov. 16, 1998).

[156] *Brdanin, supra* note 194 at ¶ 281.

[157] *Id.*

[158] In Egypt, ex-President Hosni Mubarak was tried in a civilian court and sentenced to life imprisonment on June 2, 2012 on charges of complicity in the murder of protesters for failing to prevent the police forces from attacking and killing demonstrators during the events taking place in Egypt between Jan. 25–31, 2011. Mubarak was charged under Articles 40(2), 45, 230, 231, and 235 of Egyptian Penal Code. *See Egypt: The Trial of Hosni Mubarak, Questions and Answers,* HUMAN RIGHTS WATCH, May 2012, *available at* http://www.hrw.org/news/2012/05/28/egypt-qa-trial-hosni-mubarak. On Jan. 13, 2013, the court of appeals overturned Mubarak's life sentence and ordered a retrial on the grounds that such a standard of responsibility does not exist under the Egyptian Criminal Code, rather only under the military code. Importantly, the Egyptian Criminal Code likewise does not criminalize superior responsibility due to acts of omission, unless there exists proof of specific intent regarding the failure to act. Mubarak's retrial began in Mar. 2011, and is underway at the time of writing. *See Mubarak appears in fresh trial over protesters death,*

Montt,[159] are examples of heads of state facing prosecution for, respectively, complicity by failing to prevent security forces under their control from carrying out acts of violence against civilians, and actively planning and executing genocide against the indigenous population.

(b) *Superior Responsibility in Libya*

One of the persistent problems with the application of superior responsibility is the divergent standards used by different countries with respect to omission. As described above, there are two variants of superior responsibility for omission, namely the failure of the commander to prevent the commission of the crime by his/her subordinates, and the other the failure of the commander to adequately investigate and punish violations once he/she has learned of their commission or acquired a reasonable basis to believe a violation may have been committed.

Beginning with the *Yamashita* case, superior responsibility for omissions took on what is effectively a strict liability standard, in which the commander is exposed to prosecution for dereliction of duty for any act by any subordinate, irrespective of the circumstances in which the commander is operating, his/her knowledge of the situation or the effectiveness of the command structure at the time of the violation. The most common standards for assessing superior responsibility, however, are differences over the *mens rea* of the commander, namely whether he/she must possess specific of general intent.

AFP, May 11, 2013, *available at* http://www.nation.co.ke/News/africa/Mubarak-appears-in-fresh-trial-/-/1066/1849126/-/q57wv2z/-/index.html. *See also* M. Cherif Bassiouni, *17 Egypt Update: Chronicles Of The Egyptian Revolution Of 25 January 2011* (June 2012), *available at* http://t.co/WtpdQzo6.

[159] Former *de facto* President of Guatemala, *Efraín Ríos* Montt, was tried before a civilian court for crimes against humanity and genocide, stemming from massacres and other atrocities committed by military forces in the Mayan highlands in 1982. A three-judge tribunal ruled on May 10, 2013 that *Ríos* Montt had superior responsibility, and according to the presiding judge, had knowledge of the massacres and the authority to stop the crimes. The conviction was overturned, however, on May 20 after Guatemala's Constitutional Court ruled that the proceedings had to address appeal issues raised during earlier proceedings on Apr. 19. The outcome of the trial is uncertain at the time of writing. *See* Kate Doyle, *Guatemala's Genocide on Trial*, THE NATION, May 22, 2013, *available at* http:// www.thenation.com/article/174488/guatemalas-genocide-trial; Christina M. Fetterhoff, *Ríos Montt Genocide Trial Tests Durability of Domestic & International Legal Protections*, CENTER FOR HUMAN RIGHTS AND HUMANITARIAN LAW, Apr. 16, 2013, *available at* http:// hrbrief.org/2013/04/rios-montt-genocide-trial-tests-durability-of-domestic-international-legal-protections.

The two major legal systems of the world, the Common law and Civilist/ Romanist law, take very different approaches to superior responsibility for omission. Under the Common law, criminal responsibility obtains where the commander has the general intent not to prevent or punish, while under the Civilist / Romanist system the commander must have the specific intent not to prevent or punish the commission of crimes by subordinates.

In practical terms, under the Common law, the prosecutor must simply show that the superior was negligent or reckless in failing to address the problem. Under the Civilist/Romanist system, on the other hand, the prosecutor must show that the superior specifically intended for the crime not to be prevented or the perpetrators punished. A good example of the Civilist/Romanist approach was the prosecution of former Egyptian President Hosni Mubarak, who was acquitted on appeal of superior responsibility for the killing of protestors, as the court found that he did not have the requisite specific intent, as required under the Egyptian military code, to prevent or punish the principal perpetrators.

As described above, the 1953 Libyan Penal Code is based on the Egyptian criminal code and requires specific intent of the superior that the principal perpetrator not be prevented or punished. This distinction could have serious implications for the prosecution of senior leaders of the Qadhafi regime before Libyan courts. International criminal systems, however, have tended to follow the Common law approach and require only a heightened level of general intent, although the question is still unsettled and may be one of the reasons for the recent contraction of ICL before the ICTY, as discussed below. Should Libyans like Saif al-Islam Qadhafi and 'Abdullah al-Senussi be tried by the ICC, it is likely that it will employ the general intent requirement, thereby making a guilty verdict more likely for acts of omission.[160]

5.2. *The Contracting Scope of Vicarious Liability under International Criminal Law*

One of the significant innovations of IHL and ICL is the establishment of individual criminal responsibility for serious violations of human dignity and basic rights. Prior to the advent of IHL and ICL, and the notion of individual accountability, these violations were seen as regrettable

---

[160] It should be noted that this has no effect on the law of commission by superiors. All orders given by commanding officers are specific intent crimes.

but in many respects inevitable and certainly not an individual criminal offense. Over the last two hundred years, international law has witnessed a paradigm shift regarding such individual liability. When Napoleon was defeated in 1814, he was exiled to Elba and later Saint Helena since it was inconceivable that a head of state could be punished for the transgressions of his forces; just over 100 years later the victorious Allies in WWI attempted to prosecute Kaiser Wilhelm for various crimes against peace in order to placate their angry citizens, but drafted the charges in such a way as to facilitate his asylum in The Netherlands.[161] Today, one hundred years after Kaiser Wilhelm avoided accountability for his role in WWI, the notion that any individual, much less a head of state, could automatically escape sanction by mere fact of his/her position is inconceivable.[162]

Today the notion of individual criminal responsibility for international crimes is firmly enmeshed in conventional and customary international law. Nevertheless, the extent and scope of that liability, especially for vicarious or imputed responsibility, is still a matter of debate, largely because it is driven by the caselaw and the evolving interpretations of judges at international tribunals. This was the case with the doctrine of superior responsibility,[163] as well as other forms of liability for the acts of third parties, including Joint Criminal Enterprise (JCE)[164] and aiding and

---

[161] BASSIOUNI, INTRODUCTION TO INTERNATIONAL CRIMINAL LAW, *supra* note 4 at 1024.

[162] *See generally Id.* at Ch. XI–XII.

[163] *See supra* Sec. 5.1.

[164] JCE is a form of liability shared criminal liability between a number of individuals who have a joint or common purpose, wherein the direct acts of some are imputed to others based on their participation and contribution to the joint or common purpose. In this sense, it is similar to the common law notion of conspiracy. JCE was first enunciated by the ICTY Appeals Chamber in the famous *Tadić* case, where it held that

> all those who have engaged in serious violations of international humanitarian law, whatever the manner in which they may have perpetrated, or participated in the perpetration of those violations, must be brought to justice. If this is so, it is fair to conclude that the Statute does not confine itself to providing for jurisdiction over those persons who plan, instigate, order, physically perpetrate a crime or otherwise aid and abet in its planning, preparation or execution. The Statute does not stop there. It does not exclude those modes of participating in the commission of crimes which occur where several persons having a common purpose embark on criminal activity that is then carried out either jointly or by some members of this plurality of persons. Whoever contributes to the commission of crimes by the group of persons or some members of the group, in execution of a common criminal purpose, may be held to be criminally liable, subject to certain conditions...

Tadić, supra note 56 at ¶ 190. In particular, the Appeals Chamber explained that

> Most of the time these crimes do not result from the criminal propensity of single individuals but constitute manifestations of collective criminality: the crimes are often carried out by groups of individuals acting in pursuance of a common criminal

abetting, all of which were propounded or expounded over the last 20 years at the ICTY and ICTR.[165] However, the progressive development of these doctrines by judicial opinions has not resulted in the firm codification of these norms, and consequently its application is subject to being curtailed by the same judges and institutions, as has recently been the case at the ICTY, as discussed below.

In broad terms, these doctrines were interpreted expansively by the ICTY and ICTR during the 1990s and 2000s, when the notion of ICL was ascendant and vicarious liability mechanisms were seen as indispensible in order to ensure accountability for all participants to the conflicts, and especially in the former Yugoslavia where some of those most responsible for violations were located in Serbia and did not directly participate in the fighting or the direct commission of violations. The use of superior

---

design. Although only some members of the group may physically perpetrate the criminal act (murder, extermination, wanton destruction of cities, towns or villages, etc.), the participation and contribution of the other members of the group is often vital in facilitating the commission of the offence in question. It follows that the moral gravity of such participation is often no less – or indeed no different – from that of those actually carrying out the acts in question.

Id.

[165] In *Vasiljević*, the ICYY Appeals Chamber defined the actus reus and mens rea of aiding and abetting, holding that

(i) The aider and abettor carries out acts specifically directed to assist, encourage or lend moral support to the perpetration of a certain specific crime (murder, extermination, rape, torture, wanton destruction of civilian property, etc.), and this support has a substantial effect upon the perpetration of the crime. By contrast, it is sufficient for a participant in a joint criminal enterprise to perform acts that in some way are directed to the furtherance of the common design.

(ii) In the case of aiding and abetting, the requisite mental element is knowledge that the acts performed by the aider and abettor assist the commission of the specific crime of the principal. By contrast, in the case of participation in a joint criminal enterprise, i.e. as a co-perpetrator, the requisite mens rea is intent to pursue a common purpose.

Prosecutor v. Vasiljević, Case No. IT-98-32-A, Appeals Judgement, ¶ 102 (Int'l Crim. Trib. For the Former Yugoslavia, Feb. 25, 2004).

As with superior responsibility, aiding and abetting may arise either out of commission or omission. As the ICTY Appeals Chamber stated in *Blaškić*

the actus reus of aiding and abetting may be perpetrated through an omission, 'provided this failure to act had a decisive effect on the commission of the crime and that it was coupled with the requisite mens rea.' It considered:

In this respect, the mere presence at the crime scene of a person with superior authority, such as a military commander, is a probative indication for determining whether that person encouraged or supported the perpetrators of the crime.

The Appeals Chamber leaves open the possibility that in the circumstances of a given case, an omission may constitute the actus reus of aiding and abetting."

Prosecutor v. Blaškić, supra note 151 at ¶ 47.

responsibility, JCE, and aiding and abetting were thus seen as important means of ensuring accountability for all individuals, and especially those seen as being most responsible for the atrocities in the former Yugoslavia and Rwanda, whether military commanders like Ratko Mladić and Augustin Bizimungu, or civilian leaders like Radovan Karadžić and Jean Kambanda.

More recently, however, the judges of the ICTY have been ratcheting up the requirements to prove criminal liability under these doctrines, and in effect judges are contracting the effective scope of the doctrines. In practical terms, these recent decisions will make it much more difficult to prove criminal liability for military commanders and civilian leaders, especially where the link between the principal perpetrator and the accused is less direct.

Three recent ICTY judgments, delivered between late 2012 and mid 2013, resulted in the acquittal of a number of individuals for vicarious liability offenses, after the Appeals and Trial Chambers began applying a more stringent evidentiary standards in cases. These decisions gained notoriety and prompted allegations that the decisions were politically motivated and designed to limit the potential applicability of these doctrines to western military commanders.[166]

In *Gotovina and Markač*,[167] the first case, the Appeals Chamber reversed a Trial Chamber conviction and acquitted two Croatian military and police commanders accused of participating in a JCE to drive Serbs from the Krajina region. Although the Appeals Chamber accepted the Trial Chamber's findings regarding the existence of a JCE to clear the region, it rejected the Trial Chamber's findings regarding the underlying crime, namely the shelling of four towns. While the Trial Chamber concluded that the shelling by Croatian forces was too imprecise and was not directed at a lawful target, as evidenced by the fact that the shells fell more than 200 meters from the lawful targets based on an "impact analysis" of the attack, the Appeals Chamber determined that the impact analysis was itself too imprecise and reversed the Trial Chamber's verdict, albeit without enunciating a new standard or explaining what level of precision might be required to allow a factfinder to distinguish between

---

[166] *See generally* Marlise Simons, *Hague Judge Faults Acquittals of Serb and Croat Commanders*, N.Y. TIMES, June 14, 2013, *available at* http://www.nytimes.com/2013/06/14/world/europe/hague-judge-faults-acquittals-of-serb-and-croat-commanders.html.

[167] *Prosecutor v. Ante Gotovina and Mladen Markač*, Case No. IT-06-90-A, Appeals Judgement, (Int'l Crim. Trib. For the Former Yugoslavia, Nov. 16, 2012).

lawful and unlawful attacks. In the absence of an underlying criminal act, such as shelling civilian targets, the Appeals Chamber concluded that the JCE was void. The Appeals Chamber judgment, which was delivered over the strong dissents of two judges, is curious because it overturns the Trial Chamber's factual finding without providing an alternative standard for evaluating whether a shelling has a lawful military purpose, leading some to the conclusion that the finding was merely a pretense for acquitting the accused. One of the dissenting judges addressed the reasoning of the majority, suggesting it "grotesque".[168]

In *Perišić*, the second case, the ICTY Appeals Chamber reversed the conviction of the chief of the General Staff of the Yugoslav Army, who had been convicted of aiding and abetting the Army of Republika Srpska and the Army of Serbian Krajina, and for failing to prevent and punish the soldiers under his command that were seconded to those armies, in dereliction of his duties as a superior. The Appeals Chamber made several findings, determining *inter alia* that Perišić lacked effective command over the principal perpetrators, and that he only influenced them, despite the existence of evidence that he issued direct orders to the personnel seconded to Republika Srpska, had a role in the promotion and demotion of seconded personnel there, and participated in the disciplining of seconded soldiers.[169] With regard to aiding and abetting, the Appeals Chamber held that the prosecution had failed to lead evidence showing that Perišić had *specifically intended* the aid and materiel to be used for particular crimes. Absent the requisite "specific direction" for the commission of crimes, the Appeals Chamber held that the aid [for the] overall war effort," might have a legitimate purpose and was therefore not subject to criminal sanction.[170]

Finally, in *Stanišić and Simatović* the Trial Chamber acquitted the head of the State Security Service of the Serbian Ministry of Interior Affairs and one of his deputies of having participated in a JCE (along with various well known individuals including Milošević and Karadžić) and for superior responsibility for the conduct of soldiers in units that were alleged to have participated in the attempts to cleanse areas of Bosnia, including

---

[168] *See Id. Prosecutor v. Ante Gotovina and Mladen Markač*, Case No. IT-06-90-A, Dissenting Opinion of Judge Fausto Pocar, ¶ 26 (Int'l Crim. Trib. For the Former Yugoslavia, Nov. 16, 2012).

[169] *Prosecutor v. Momčilo Perišić*, Case No. IT-04-81-A, Appeals Judgement, ¶¶ 114–18 (Int'l Crim. Trib. For the Former Yugoslavia, Feb. 28, 2013).

[170] *Id.* at ¶ 60.

Vukovar, and Croatia of non-Serbs. Despite the participation of Stanišić in meetings at which the JCE was formed and despite his active role in organizing and training units engaged in such conduct, the Trial Chamber concluded that due to his "limited participation"

> The majority... allows for the reasonable possibility that Stanišić's intent in relation to the Unit's operations was limited to establishing and maintaining Serb control over large areas of Croatia and Bosnia-Herzegovina. The majority understands the evidence so as that it may have been reasonably foreseeable that crimes would be committed during the establishing and maintaining of Serb control but to be insufficient for the first form of JCE liability. Under these circumstances, the majority... does not consider the evidence of Stanišić's actions in relation to the Unit's operations, in itself or in light of the totality of the evidence regarding the Accused, sufficient to establish beyond a reasonable doubt that Stanišić shared the intent to further the alleged common criminal purpose through the commission of crimes.[171]

As with *Perišić* the Trial Chamber appears to be setting out a heightened standard in which the prosecution must establish a direct connection and a more clear showing of intent to establish responsibility for crimes. In other words, the Trial Chamber has significantly circumscribed superior responsibility and JCE, concluding that notwithstanding the participation of the accused in various meetings in which crimes were discussed and the establishment and training of various implicated units, the "reasonable possibility" of alternative explanations was sufficient to exculpate him of criminal responsibility.[172]

While the various judgments of the ICTY are not binding upon the ICC or any other court, the trajectory of the caselaw suggests a tightening of requirements and a heightened burden upon the prosecution to show the specific intent of the accused to commit crimes. It remains to be seen what effect these holdings will have upon the Appeals Judgment in the Taylor case before the Special Court for Sierra Leone or Ratko Mladić and Radovan Karadžić before the ICTY, but the general trend at international tribunals appears to be towards heightened scrutiny for vicarious liability crimes, and accordingly a more defense friendly standard. It also, perhaps more nefariously, suggests the resurgent nature of *realpolitik* at international tribunals, something that can be seen in the "penumbras" and

---

[171] *Prosecutor v. Jovica Stanišić and Franko Simatović*, Case No. IT-03-69-T, Trial Judgement, ¶ 2326 (Int'l Crim. Trib. For the Former Yugoslavia, May 30, 2013).
[172] *Id.*

"emanations" of these findings, to quote the U.S. Supreme Court Justice William Douglas.[173]

It should be noted, however, that the determinations by international tribunals are not biding on domestic courts, whether in Libya or any other country that would seek to prosecute individuals for IHL and ICL violations using their domestic laws and jurisdictional provisions.

6. The Peculiarities of Post-Conflict Justice in Libya

Libya's transitional authorities, namely the NTC and General National Congress ("GNC"), have faced enormous impediments in overcoming a legacy of impunity, establishing a modern judiciary, and achieving accountability in the post-Qadhafi and post-conflict era. The most significant challenges stem from the lack of a strong and independent judicial system that is committed to the rule of law, as the judiciary under Qadhafi functioned as a tool for internal repression.[174] During the Qadhafi era, many cases, in particular those that were deemed political, were routed through a "parallel judicial system" that lacked independence or credibility. The origins of this system can be drawn to 1971, when the Qadhafi regime established the "People's Court," an institution that conducted closed-door trials of regime opponents until it was abolished in 2005. Although Qadhafi abolished the system, a replacement, known as the "Special Security Court," was quickly established in 2007.[175] The Qadhafi regime also used special courts run by the Revolutionary Committees to try opposition figures, students, members of Islamist groups, or anyone considered a threat.[176] Finally, political opponents were targeted by extrajudicial means to ensure the regime's stability, a practice that was also tied to the country's judicial history.[177] The legacy of the Qadhafi era use of judicial means to repress individuals resulted in an understandable lack of trust in judicial and legal institutions that has persisted into the post-conflict era, specifically among victims seeking redress for past

---

[173] See *Griswold v. Connecticut*, 381 U.S. 479 (1965).

[174] Report of the International Commission of Inquiry, advance unedited version (Mar. 2, 2012), *supra* note 12 at Annex I, ¶ 41.

[175] *Id.* at ¶ 40.

[176] *See* Ch. I, Sec. 9. *See also* DIRK VANDEWALLE, A HISTORY OF MODERN LIBYA 68 (Cambridge, UK: Cambridge University Press, 2006).

[177] INTERNATIONAL CRISIS GROUP, TRIAL BY ERROR: JUSTICE IN POST-QADHAFI LIBYA, *supra* note 14 at 8.

crimes.[178] It is clear that neither the general public nor victims have much faith in the system, and moreover, that the country lacks the necessary judicial institutions and personnel to implement the necessary reforms to foster trust among those groups.

This section discusses Libya's challenges to building a fully functioning and fair judicial system with the capacity to carry out effective accountability measures for past and on-going violations of international and domestic law. The transitional authorities, and the leaders of the first elected legislature (the GNC) were faced with the task of establishing a judicial system capable of upholding the rule of law. In its report to the Human Rights Council, the CoI noted that many existing Libyan laws failed to conform to human rights standards and needed to be repealed or amended.[179] As indicated above, the judicial system not only lacks the judges and lawyers needed to effectively reform the system and implement accountability mechanism, but also the investigators, forensics experts, judicial police and other staff involved in the administration of justice. Moreover, the existing judicial officers are not trained in human rights standards, which is a prerequisite for any official tasked with dealing with sensitive legal proceedings dealing with political violence. It cannot be overstated that the lack of trained officials to manage a functioning court system remains a major impediment to holding perpetrators accountable for past and on-going crimes.[180]

The labyrinthine nature of the political and military structure during the Qadhafi era adds to the challenges facing investigators, lawyers, and judges attempting to hold former officials accountable for past violations. As described in previous chapters, the security apparatus consisted of multiple overlapping entities, with no clear command structures or lines of communication between the various agencies.[181] The political and military institutions were deliberately structured in a complicated manner in order to obfuscate responsibility and ensure impunity for state-sponsored crimes and repression. Moreover, members of the Qadhafi family carried out political, diplomatic, and security tasks with unclear roles within the state apparatus. For example, Qadhafi's cousin, Ahmad Qadhaf al-Dam,

---

[178] Report of the International Commission of Inquiry, advance unedited version (Mar. 2, 2012), *supra* note 12 at Annex I, ¶ 41.

[179] *Id.* at ¶ 40.

[180] Report of the International Commission of Inquiry, advance unedited version (Mar. 2, 2012), *supra* note 12 at Annex I, ¶ 781.

[181] *See* Ch. II, Secs. 2.1. & 2.2. *See also id.* at ¶ 50.

served as the special representative or "General Coordinator of Egyptian-Libyan Relations", and tasked with handling diplomatic affairs and certain intelligence matters with neighboring Egypt.[182] Similarly, Saif al-Islam did not carry an official position in the regime, but was responsible for the most sensitive international and domestic affairs with the powers typical of a "de facto Prime Minister."[183] The question of his role in the regime has proven a minor issue in the case before the ICC, as he is charged with *de facto* control over various security agencies and forces despite his civilian status.[184]

As a result of the convoluted political and security structures in Qadhafi's Libya, it is difficult to produce an exhaustive analysis of the organization of the military and police forces that operated under Qadhafi. It is possible, however, to examine the security units and known individuals within the government apparatus who were responsible for orchestrating security operations and implementing policies under Qadhafi. Moreover, it is possible to identify certain figures within the regime who, according to the doctrine of superior responsibility, could be responsible for the commission of crimes by security forces under their authority.[185] The armed forces under Mu'ammar Qadhafi, for example, included specialized and well-equipped brigades designed to protect the regime, such as the Khamis 32nd Katiba, which was commanded by his son, Khamis Qadhafi.[186] The Presidential Guard was another important regime protection unit, under the control of Colonel Khalifa Hanaysh.[187] The head of Qadhafi's personal security, 'Abd al-Qader Yusuf Dibri, reportedly directed violence

---

[182] *See supra* Sec. 6.4. *See also* Press Release of Dec. 2009, Egyptian Embassy, *available at* http://www.egyptembassy.se/press/23dec09.pdf; *Libya demands Extradition of Qaddafi exiles from Egypt*, Libya Herald, Feb. 12, 2012, *available at* http://www.libyaherald.com/2012/02/29/qaddafi-exiles-living-in-egypt-under-false-identities.

[183] *See supra* Sec. 2.3. *See also Situation in the Libyan Arab Jamahiriya*, Case No. ICC-01/11, Warrant of Arrest for Saif Al-Islam Gaddafi (June 27, 2011).

[184] *See infra* Sec. 6.3(b)(i).

[185] For more on the doctrine of superior responsibility, *see supra* Sec. 5.1.

[186] For more on Khamis Qadhafi, who is reported deceased by the Libyan authorities, *see infra* Sec. 6.3.

[187] *See* Ch. I, Sec. 9. *See also* Hanspeter Mattes, *Challenges to Security Sector Governance in the Middle East: The Libyan Case* 7–8 (Geneva Centre for the Democratic Control of Armed Forces conference paper presented 12–13 July 2004), *available at* http://www.dcaf.ch/Event-Attachement/Challenges-to-Security-Sector-Governance-in-the-Middle-East-the-Libyan-Case.

against the dissidents.[188] The Social People's Leadership Committees, an
important political body, was coordinated by Sayyid Muhammad Qadhaf
al-Dam,[189] who also allegedly involved in the regime's dissident assassination campaign as well as arms procurement.[190]

In addition to the regular armed forces, Qadhafi created separate irregular forces, such as the Revolutionary Guard, Popular Guard and Revolutionary Committees. These bodies functioned similarly to paramilitary
forces, operating to safeguard the regime and counterbalance any potential internal dissent within the regular armed forces.[191] Former senior
regime officials such as Matuq Mohammed Matuq have been accused of
orchestrating acts of violence by members of the Revolutionary Committees in order to suppress dissent.[192] Qadhafi entrusted his son Mu'tassim
to oversee the National Security Council (NSC), which served as a link
between the ministries, the armed forces and other security agencies.[193] In
addition, the Qadhafi regime relied upon intelligence agencies to ensure
its control over the country. The intelligence agencies were the Internal
Security Agency (ISA),[194] and the External Security Agency (ESA),[195] both
of which carried out investigative as well as security functions, and operated along with the Military Intelligence Service to monitor and detain
political opponents at home and abroad.[196] Due to the Qadhafi regime's
complete control of the judiciary, the entire security apparatus operated

---

[188] Security Council Committee Established Pursuant to Resolution 1970 (2011) Concerning Libya, *List of Individuals Subject to the Measures Imposed by Paragraph 15 of Resolution 1970 (2011) (the Travel Ban) and/or Paragraph 17 of Resolution 1970 (2011) or Paragraph
19 of Resolution 1973 (2011) (the Assets Freeze)*, UNITED NATIONS, Apr. 2, 2011 [hereinafter
"Resolution Measures"], *available at* http://www.un.org/sc/committees/1970/pdf/List%20
of%20Individuals%20and%20Entities.pdf.

[189] *See* Ch. I, Sec. 9. *See also* Mattes, *Challenges to Security Sector Governance in the
Middle East, supra* note 187.

[190] *See* Resolution Measures, *supra* note 188.

[191] *See* Ch. I, Sec. 9 & Ch. II, Sec. 2.2.

[192] Matuq Mohammed Matuq is subject to a travel ban, according to Security Coun-
cil Resolution 1970. Other officials who were reportedly involved with the Revolutionary
Committees and violence against demonstrators include Dr. Abdul Qader Mohammed Al-
Baghdadi, also subject to a travel ban in accordance with Security Council Resolution 1970.
See also Resolution Measures, *supra* note 188.

[193] *See* Ch. II, Sec. 2.2. *See also* U.S. Embassy in Tripoli, secret cable, *Libya's National
Security Council: Experiencing Growing Pains*, Dec. 23, 2007, *available at* http://www.tele-
graph.co.uk/news/wikileaks-files/libya-wikileaks/8294769/LIBYAS-NATIONAL-SECURITY-
COUNCIL-EXPERIENCING-GROWING-PAINS.html.

[194] 'Abdullah al-Senussi served as the head of the ISA. *See infra* Sec. 6.3(b)(ii).

[195] Musa Kusa was the head of the ESA until Abu Zayid Durda took over in 2009. *See
infra* Sec. 6.3(b)(iii) & 6.4.

[196] *See* Ch. I, Sec. 11.2 & Ch. II, Sec. 2.2.

in a culture of impunity, and was clearly not subject to conventional accountability mechanisms as one would expect from most military and civilian judicial systems in the world.[197]

During the 2011 conflict, the regime employed its informal and formal security forces in an attempt to intimidate protest organizers, neutralize the protest movement itself, carry out widespread arrests, secret detentions, acts of torture, besiege and assault cities, and attack *thuwar* forces. Since the end of the conflict, there have been investigations into a number of individuals who were in charge of regime security forces during the civil war, and in few case charged brought against individuals accused of acts of corruption and other past abuses.

This section includes information on these individuals, along with others who were known for their prominent role in shaping and carrying out policy in the Qadhafi regime. In addition to Qadhafi's inner circle and high-level officials, there are many other individuals in charge of the police and military units who have been implicated in the violations committed during the conflict. Thus far, the international and domestic investigations have tended to focus more on family members and close associates with the regime, along with political figureheads, including former ministers and diplomats, rather than the commanders who led the ground forces during the conflict. This is due in part to the difficultly in identifying the individuals at the command level who were responsible for carrying out the orders of the military high command and directing troops in battle.[198] While the role of some commanders is evident, such as that of Khamis Qadhafi, it is difficult to determine all the other regime commanders who received and gave orders to deploy their units in the field. While investigations have found that Qadhafi delivered orders to suppress the demonstrations, and that these orders were transmitted to police forces as an order to use live ammunition against protesters,[199] it is unclear how the information was translated and who served as the

---

[197] Report of the International Commission of Inquiry, advance unedited version (Mar. 2, 2012), *supra* note 12 at Annex I, ¶ 51.

[198] The CoI found that "In many instances, the Commission was able to obtain information on the commanders of specific military or security units allegedly involved in violations, and thereby to assign responsibility to senior military officers based on their command and control of those under their supervision. In other instances, victims and witnesses interviewed by the Commission were unable to identify either individuals or the entities allegedly responsible for the atrocities." *See* Report of the International Commission of Inquiry, advance unedited version (Mar. 2, 2012), *supra* note 12 at Annex I, ¶ 49.

[199] *See* Ch. II, Sec. 3.2.

intermediaries. Similarly, instructions were passed by the Khamis 32nd Katiba to ground commanders to fire on protesters in Misrata,[200] and orders were transmitted by Qadhafi to enforce a siege on the city,[201] but it is not unclear who implemented or transmitted the orders. While the information suggests that commanders relied on orders from higher up the command chain, it is not clear whether security forces acted independently at times, or whether commanders maintained effective control over their troops.[202]

Further investigations are required to determine command structures and military commands given during the conflict, as well as the individuals responsible for directing the military and police forces. It should be noted that the CoI reported that it produced a list of names of individuals linked to violations, either directly or through superior responsibility, to the UN High Commissioner for Human Rights.[203] This information could provide critically useful information for investigations into those responsible for violations committed during the conflict. It is unknown, however, whether this information has been shared with the Libyan national authorities, or it has been used in international venues to investigate those allegedly responsible for conflict-related violations. Domestic investigations could benefit significantly from this information, given the current challenges facing investigators in Libya. It is likely that important evidence related to past crimes is in security installations across the country, but accessing these facilities given the country's current security climate will prove difficult.[204]

With respect to the *thuwar* brigades that were involved in the 2011 conflict, the complex and often improvised composition of their forces and command structures poses similar challenges to accountability efforts. As discussed in other chapters, the *thuwar* groups formed regionally, were mostly autonomous of other rebel forces, and operated independently of any centralized authority.[205] For the most part, the *thuwar* operated with

---

[200] Report of the International Commission of Inquiry, advance unedited version (Mar. 2, 2012), *supra* note 12 at Annex I, ¶ 18.

[201] *See* Ch. II, Sec. 3.3.

[202] For more on effective control, *see supra* notes 140 & 152.

[203] Report of the International Commission of Inquiry, advance unedited version (Mar. 2, 2012), *supra* note 12 at Annex I, ¶ 797.

[204] Additionally, in the event that domestic prosecutors are able to gather enough evidence to prove responsibility at the commander level, Libya's domestic legal code still might not be able to prosecute for superior responsibility.

[205] *See* Ch. II, Sec. 2.3.

independent military structures and chains of command throughout the course of the conflict. While there were some commanders in Benghazi who attempted to organize the *thuwar* vertically, they were largely powerless and in some cases killed, as was the case with 'Abd al-Fattah Yunis.[206] The persistent problem with the diffuse organization and independent operations of the *thuwar* is evident in the on-going difficulties faced by the GNC in attempting to secure the transfer of Saif al-Islam from the Zintan brigade.[207] The horizontal organization of the *thuwar* and the lack of a hierarchical command structure makes proving superior responsibility highly difficult.[208]

It must be recalled that the politicization of legal institutions under Qadhafi increases the risk that the post-Qadhafi judicial system will become a mechanism for "victor's justice," particularly with regards to the violations committed by the *thuwar* leaders and members of their fighting forces.[209] This is clear in the findings of the CoI, which show that the interim government downplayed the seriousness of violations committed by *thuwar* during and after the conflict, and failed to publicly condemn on-going reprisals, including attacks against the targeted communities such as the Tawerghans and Mashashiyyans.[210]

The post-Qadhafi government has demonstrated a considerable lack of political will to prosecute those who fought to overthrow the former regime, as *thuwar* suspected of violations are often regarded as heroes, and accordingly shielded from investigations for past crimes.[211] One of the most egregious examples of this is the adoption of Law 38 of May 2011, which gave a blanket amnesty for those "military, security, or civil actions dictated by the February 17 Revolution that were performed by

---

[206] *See* Ch. II, Sec. 2.3.

[207] *See supra* Sec. 6.2.

[208] *See supra* Sec. 5.1.

[209] Human rights observers have noted the tendency towards victor's justice in Libya. HRW Director Kenneth Roth writes, "It is no surprise that a revolution's victors, long repressed by the old regime, do not want to hear about new restraints once they have final found their way to power...Frustrating as it can be, majority preferences in any democracy worthy of its name must be constrained by respect for the rights of individuals and the rule of law." *See* Kenneth Roth, *The Day After, in* HUMAN RIGHTS WATCH WORLD REPORT 2013 (Feb. 2013), *available at* https://www.hrw.org/sites/default/files/wr2013_web.pdf.

[210] Report of the International Commission of Inquiry, advance unedited version (Mar. 2, 2012), *supra* note 12 at Annex I, ¶ 44.

[211] INTERNATIONAL CRISIS GROUP, TRIAL BY ERROR: JUSTICE IN POST-QADHAFI LIBYA, *supra* note 14 at 28.

revolutionaries with the goal of promoting or protecting the revolution."[212]
The inability of the national authorities to hold *thuwar* groups to account
is also attributable to the un-governable security situation that pervades
the country, in which powerful armed brigades gave established dominance in the capital and throughout the country in order to preserve their
vested economic, political and social interests.[213] Attempts to investigate
former *thuwar* allegedly responsible for acts of torture and ill-treatment
have been impeded by retaliatory violence and threats that cultivate fear
among lawyers trying to bring cases forward.[214]

As the successor state to the Libyan Arab Jamahiriyya, the NTC inherited
its international human rights and humanitarian treaty law obligations.[215]
Irrespective of the non-compliance of the Qadhafi regime with many of
these obligations, they are binding on the GNC today and must be com-
plied with. Given these obligations, the interim authorities faced pressure
from various internal and international actors in the final stage of the
conflict and its aftermath to satisfy their duties and obligations, especially
after the NTC was recognized by the UN General Assembly as the legitimate representative of the Libyan people on 16 September 2011. There was
pressure from the ICC for the extradition of Saif al-Islam to stand trial in
The Hague, and NGOs were applying pressure and demanding accountability and the humane treatment of various groups in the aftermath of
the conflict. This external pressure had to be measured against evolving
internal dynamics and an on-going armed conflict. Domestic pressures
included the need to prosecute former Qadhafi officials, many whom had
fled Libya, for corruption, political repression, and crimes committed during the conflict; prisons full of thousands of prisoners held outside any
legal framework by the *thuwar* in unofficial detention centers;[216] rampant

---

[212] *Quoted in Libya: Amend New Special Procedures Law: Reject Impunity for Serious Crimes*, HUMAN RIGHTS WATCH, May 11, 2012, *available at* http://www.hrw.orgnews/2012/05/11/libya-amend-new-special-procedures-law.

[213] *See* Ch. V, Sec. 2. *See also* Report of the International Commission of Inquiry, advance unedited version (Mar. 2, 2012), *supra* note 12 at Annex I, ¶ 44.

[214] INTERNATIONAL CRISIS GROUP, TRIAL BY ERROR: JUSTICE IN POST-QADHAFI LIBYA, *supra* note 14 at 30.

[215] *See* Report of the International Commission of Inquiry, advance unedited version (Mar. 2, 2012), *supra* note 12 at Annex I, ¶ 30.

[216] *See* Ch. V, Sec. 2.3. *See* Report of the International Commission of Inquiry, advance unedited version (Mar. 2, 2012), *supra* note 12 at Annex I, ¶ 105; AMNESTY INTERNA-TIONAL, LIBYA RULE OF LAW OR RULE OF MILITIA 14 (July 5, 2012), *available at* http://www.amnesty.org/en/library/asset/MDE19/012/2012/en/f2d36090-5716-4ef1-81a7-f4b1ebd082fc/mde190122012en.pdf.

reprisal violence by *thuwar* militias who took the law into their own hands; and the absence of a functioning national police or judiciary.

The remainder of this chapter deals with specific issues of accountability. Section 6.1 deals with the legislative challenges facing the interim government, including not only the lack of effective legislation on international crimes but also the adoption of laws clearly designed to impede justice.

Section 6.2 details the involvement of the International Criminal Court (ICC) in the Libyan situation and the on-going wrangling over the treatment of Saif al-Islam and 'Abdullah al-Senussi, both of whom have been indicted by the Court.

Section 6.3(a) examines the death of Mu'ammar Qadhafi on 20 October 2011, which marked the official end to the 2011 war. The events related to the killing of Qadhafi and its aftermath provide strong evidence for the lack of accountability and overall impunity that existed in the wake of the conflict, both domestically and internationally, as it was a NATO strike on Qadhafi's convoy that precipitated his capture and killing.[217] The killing of Qadhafi has been investigated as a potential unlawful killing, and the act of displaying the bodies of Mu'ammar Qadhafi and his son Mu'tassim has also been considered a violation of international customary law.[218] The killing of Qadhafi in the context of the conflict and its aftermath is therefore not without controversy, and merits consideration with regards to accountability in the post-Qadhafi era.[219]

Section 6.3 analyzes the treatment of the Qadhafi regime's inner circle and his family after the end of the civil war, including most notably Mu'ammar Qadhafi's son Saif al-Islam, the head of intelligence 'Abdullah al-Senussi, and the former head of external security, Musa Kusa, as well as a series of others. These individuals, all of whom played a central role

---

[217] The use of drones to target Qadhafi's convoy is itself of dubious legality, as it has an only tenuous connection to the protection of civilians. *See* Ch. III, Sec. 5. *See also* Thomas Harding, *Col Gaddafi killed: convoy bombed by drone flown by pilot in Las Vegas*, THE TELEGRAPH, Oct. 20, 2011, *available at* http://www.telegraph.co.uk/news/worldnews/africaandindianocean/libya/8839964/Col-Gaddafi-killed-convoy-bombed-by-drone-flown-by-pilot-in-Las-Vegas.html.

[218] *See* CUSTOMARY INTERNATIONAL HUMANITARIAN LAW, *supra* note 42 at 414 (Rule 115 states "The dead must be disposed of in a respectful manner and their graves respected and properly maintained.")

[219] Additionally, the *thuwar* fighter believed responsible for killing Qadhafi, 'Umran Sha'ban, was later killed in an apparent revenge killing in Bani Walid, sparking further conflict in the region For more on the conflict in Bani Walid stemming from the killing of Sha'ban, *see* Ch. XIV, Sec. 2.4.

in the conflict, have not been treated the same, as some are in detention and facing criminal proceedings while others seem to have completely escaped justice and effectively granted amnesty.

Finally, Section 6.4 examines the transitional justice efforts against members of the former regime in Libya, in particular the various judicial proceedings, the legislative measures undertaken and the international support the country has received.

6.1. *Legislative Measures*

After the collapse of the Qadhafi government, Libya's transitional government was faced with a multitude of challenges ranging from exerting control over the various *thuwar* forces and securing internal security to rebuilding the institutions of state and economy. One of the most significant challenges was the inability to build a legal system and judicial institutions committed to the rule of law, when its only focus under Qadhafi had been repression.

In the aftermath of the conflict, NTC officials pledged to establish transitional justice initiatives and hold individuals accountable. For instance, the military spokesman for the NTC stated on 30 October 2011 that "every alleged crime that occurred in the course of the Libyan conflict will be investigated, regardless of past loyalties."[220] The interim authorities, and its successor the GNC,[221] initiated a number of mechanisms and passed several laws to facilitate this process. Many measures, although intended to contribute to accountability, were unable to achieve their stated goals as a result of political or security impediments. Other measures were by their nature incompatible with existing Libyan or international laws, and directly counteracted transitional justice efforts.

One of the first initiatives undertaken by the NTC was the establishment of the National Council for Civil Liberties and Human Rights (NCHR). Law No. 5, adopted on 28 December 2011, established the Council and appointed its first members, who were tasked with a number of important initiatives, including, "making proposals on human rights legislation, receiving complaints on violations of human rights, monitoring

[220] *NTC will investigate allegations of crimes against pro-Gadhafi forces, official says*, CNN, Oct. 30, 2011, available at http://edition.cnn.com/2011/10/30/world/africa/libya-militias.

[221] The GNC is the legislative authority that was created through national elections held on 7 July 2012. The GNC is composed of 200 members, and replaced the NTC as the country's national authority on 8 August 2011.

implementation of international human rights treaties and engaging in human rights education and public awareness authority."[222] The NCHR also had the authority to file complaints regarding decisions or laws of the NTC that it determined to be in violation of human rights norms.[223] Although the creation of the NCHR was seen as a positive for the interim government its attempts to create a system that respected human rights, it encountered a number of challenges that limited the scope of its work, most notably interference by militias and *thuwar* who saw the body as a threat to their continued operation. These problems were clearly identified by the U.S. State Department, which reported that threats from militia groups was a major hindrance to the ability of the NCHR to follow through on investigations into acts of abuse and corruption by the post-revolutionary police and security forces.[224] Others, including members of the human rights community, complained that the NCHR was not carrying out its intended goals, and accused it of intentionally turning a blind eye to on-going violations, and called for the GNC to dissolve and restructure the NCHR.[225]

Another important early development was the formation of the National Fact-finding and Reconciliation Commission (NFRC), which was established by Law 17 on Transitional Justice (known as the law "Laying a Foundation for National Reconciliation and Transitional Justice") and adopted in February 2012.[226] The NFRC was given a broad mandate and tasked with investigating incidents of human rights violations committed during the Qadhafi era, during the conflict, and in the post-Qadhafi era.[227] The mandate of the NFRC included producing reports on human rights violations and their perpetrators, and making recommendations and proposals on disarmament, demobilization and integration of non-state armed

---

[222] *See* Report of the International Commission of Inquiry, advance unedited version (Mar. 2, 2012), *supra* note 12 at Annex I, ¶ 788.

[223] *Id.*

[224] *Libya 2012 Country Report on Human Rights Practices*, UNITED STATES DEPARTMENT OF STATE, Apr. 19, 2013, *available at* http://www.state.gov/documents/organization/204585.pdf.

[225] Abdul-Wahab Ashraf, *Libyan Human Rights Network demands actions on murder victim*, THE LIBYAN HERALD, Mar. 15, 2011, *available at* http://www.libyaherald.com/2013/03/15/libyan-human-rights-network-demands-action-on-murder-victim/.

[226] *See* Report of the International Commission of Inquiry, advance unedited version (Mar. 2, 2012), *supra* note 12 at Annex I, ¶ 186; *Libya: State of the Transformation Process*, MAX PLANCK INSTITUTE FOR COMPARATIVE PUBLIC LAW AND INTERNATIONAL LAW, *available at* http://www.mpil.de/ww/en/pub/research/details/Know_transfer/libyen.cfm.

[227] *See* Report of the International Commission of Inquiry, advance unedited version (Mar. 2, 2012), *supra* note 12 at ¶ 108.

actors, namely the various *thuwar* forces.[228] The law also established a victims' compensation fund, but did not provide an avenue for victims seeking redress or legal accountability through courts.[229]

The NFRC and its establishing law were not without its critics. From the beginning Libyan lawyers and activists highlighted shortcomings in the Transitional Justice law, and indicated that the human rights community was not broadly consulted before the law was passed. The United Nations Support Mission in Libya (UNSMIL) also raised concerned that the NFRC was composed purely of senior judges, and that it followed a quasi-judicial process that may not allow for sufficient victim participation.[230] The CoI similarly noted that the Law lacked an independent and impartial appointment process, and that it did not disqualify persons responsible for past violations from appointment.[231] Concerns over the law led to the Minister of Justice, Salah el-Marghani, to submit a draft law making amendments that specified that the members of the NFRC could not be limited to judges, and that it could include individuals from other professions, including sociologists, archivists and psychologists.[232] The amended NFRC is still problematic, however, as it does not specify whether clashes and acts of violence carried out after the official end of hostilities are to be covered by the law and whether it will be a permanent body designed to deal with human rights violations.[233] Without an explicit mandate it is unlikely that the NFRC will investigate violations that took place after the fall of Qadhafi.

Despite the lofty proposals contained in the NFRC's mandate it has yet to commence operation nearly a year and a half after its creation, although this is partially due to the need to reform the law before it was even implemented.[234] The new proposal for the NFRC was introduced to the GNC in March 2013, and was subject to the deliberation by the body, where it remains.[235]

---

[228] *Id.*

[229] *Libya 2012 Country Report on Human Rights Practices, supra* note 224.

[230] UNITED NATIONS SUPPORT MISSION IN LIBYA (UNSMIL), TRANSITIONAL JUSTICE-FOUNDATION FOR A NEW LIBYA 2 (Sept, 17, 2012), *available at* http://unsmil.unmissions .org/LinkClick.aspx?fileticket=8XrRUO-sXBs%3D&tabid=3543&language=en-US.

[231] *See* Report of the International Commission of Inquiry, advance unedited version (Mar. 2, 2012), *supra* note 12 at ¶ 803.

[232] INTERNATIONAL CRISIS GROUP, TRIAL BY ERROR: JUSTICE IN POST-QADHAFI LIBYA, *supra* note 14 at 18.

[233] *Id.*

[234] *Id.*

[235] Tom Westcott, *Transitional Justice: perspectives from and for young Libyans*, LIBYA HERALD, Mar. 17, 2012, *available at* http://www.libyaherald.com/2013/03/17/transitional-justice-perspectives-from-and-for-young-libyans.

Beyond the ineffectual laws discussed above, the NTC adopted two laws on 2 May 2012 that significantly impeded transitional justice efforts, and sparked an immediate backlash from within Libya and in the international community. The first, Law 38 on Special Procedures for the Transitional Period, mandated that the Defense and Interior Ministries refer all detainees who had supported the Qadhafi regime to the judicial authorities for prosecution. Simultaneously, and more problematically, Law 38 granted a broad amnesty for violations committed during the conflict by members of the *thuwar* forces if they were carried out for the "success and protection" of the revolution. The law states there shall be no penalty for "military, security, or civil actions dictated by the February 17 Revolution that were performed by revolutionaries with the goal of promoting or protecting the revolution."[236]

Clearly the law seriously impeded the implementation of the rule of law in Libya as the victors were not subject to any accountability mechanism, and raised concerns that it would provide blanket immunity to former *thuwar* and armed militias responsible for on-going violations. In response to the adoption of Law 38, a broad coalition of Libyan civil society organizations came out in opposition to the law, and warned it would allow for the continuation of a culture of impunity that existed under Qadhafi, where acts of violence and repression were justified in the name of the 1969 Revolution.[237] Internationally, HRW called for the UN Security Council to condemn the attempts by the GNC to block accountability for serious and on-going crimes committed in Libya, and called the law an example of "victor's justice."[238] Amnesty International similarly condemned Law 38 and called for it to be amended, and for specific articles to be abolished, such as Article 2, which gives legal weight to information extracted through torture or under duress.[239] Other international organizations urged the GNC to amend Law 38 to clarify that perpetrators of

---

[236] *UN Security Council: Press Libya on Impunity*, HUMAN RIGHTS WATCH, May 16, 2012, *available at* http://www.hrw.org/news/2012/05/16/un-security-council-press-libya-impunity; *Libya: Amend New Special Procedures Law*, HUMAN RIGHTS WATCH, May 11, 2012, *available at* http://www.hrw.org/news/2012/05/11/libya-amend-new-special-procedures-law.

[237] *Open letter condemning Laws 37 and 38*, LAWYERS FOR JUSTICE IN LIBYA, May 9, 2012, *available at* http://www.libyanjustice.org/downloads/Letter%20re%20Laws%2037%20and%2038.pdf.

[238] HUMAN RIGHTS WATCH, *UN Security Council: Press Libya on Impunity, supra* note 236.

[239] *Libya: 10 Steps for Human Rights: Amnesty International's Human Rights Manifesto for Libya* AMNESTY INTERNATIONAL, Sept. 25, 2012, *available at* http://www.amnesty.org/en/library/asset/MDE19/017/2012/en/234877c1-0d9b-4917-af8f-82f3a9bdc730/mde190172012en.pdf.

crimes such as torture, murder and rape committed during and after the 2011 war will not be granted legal immunity.[240]

Law 37, also passed on 2 May 2012, placed specific restrictions on freedom of expression by criminalizing statements that offend the revolution, and impose a prison sentence for those who spread false or vicious news or "propaganda" that glorified Qadhafi, his regime, ideas or sons, with the aim of "terrorizing people," or weakening the morale of citizens.[241] The law also applied to any person who "insults Islam, or the prestige of the state or its institutions or judiciary, and every person who publicly insults the Libyan people, slogan or flag."[242] As HRW pointed out, one of the peculiarities of Law 37 is that its ban on any language damaging the February 17 revolution was apparently modeled on similar laws that were passed under the Qadhafi regime that banned any speech insulting to the revolution that brought Qadhafi to power in 1969.[243]

As with Law 38, this legislation came under significant criticism for being irreconcilable with IHRL. It is clear on its face that Law 37 is incompatible with Libya's Interim Constitutional Declaration,[244] as well as international conventions to which Libya is a party to, namely the International Covenant on Civil and Political Rights (ICCPR) and the African Charter on Human and Peoples' Rights (ACHPR).[245] Law 37 also came under domestic scrutiny, and was challenged in court by Lawyers for Justice in Libya (LFJL), a Libyan human rights organization. In response to the challenge by LFJL, on 14 June 2012 the Libyan Supreme Court ruled that Law 37

---

[240] INTERNATIONAL CRISIS GROUP, TRIAL BY ERROR: JUSTICE IN POST-QADHAFI LIBYA, *supra* note 14 at i.

[241] LAWYERS FOR JUSTICE IN LIBYA, *Open letter condemning Laws 37 and 38, supra* note 237.

[242] George Grant, *Supreme Court strikes down Law 37*, LIBYA HERALD, June 14, 2012, *available at* http://www.libyaherald.com/2012/06/14/supreme-court-strikes-down-law-37.

[243] *Libya: Revoke Draconian New Law*, HUMAN RIGHTS WATCH, May 5, 2012, *available at* http://www.hrw.org/news/2012/05/05/libya-revoke-draconian-new-law.

[244] Human Rights Watch reported that Article 6 of Libya's Interim Constitutional Declaration affords all Libyans "equal civil and political rights" and "the same opportunity" without distinction on grounds of "religion, belief, language, wealth, sex, kinship, political opinions or social status; or on tribal, regional or personal association." In addition, Libya is a state party to the International Covenant on Civil and Political Rights (ICCPR), and is required "to allow its citizens equal opportunity to participate in political life, without discrimination or 'unreasonable restrictions.'" The country has also ratified the African Charter on Human and Peoples' Rights, which requires states "to ensure that every citizen has the right to participate freely in the government of their country." *See Id.*

[245] International Covenant on Civil and Political Rights, G.A. Res. 2200A (XXI), U.N. Doc. A/6316 (1966), 999 U.N.T.S. 171 (Dec. 16, 1966); African Charter on Human and Peoples' Rights, 21 I.L.M. 58 (June 27, 1981).

constituted an unconstitutional restriction on free speech based on the Constitutional Declaration passed by the NTC on 3 August 2011.[246] Despite the unfortunate content of Law 37 itself, the case that saw it overturned was a landmark decision, as it was the first instance of judicial review in the transitional period and the first formal rebuke of a law adopted by the NTC on the grounds that it violated the Constitutional Declaration.[247]

It is clear that significant challenges to accountability and transitional justice measures remain. Notwithstanding these on-going problems, Libyans and the international community have continued to raise demands for stronger measures and the adoption of true transitional justice measures. Human rights groups, both inside and outside Libya, continue to urge the GNC to carry out legislative reforms and protect fundamental rights in the post-conflict era.[248] What is more, the dissatisfaction with the progress of transitional justice procedures, as well as the slow pace of reforms and delays over the drafting of the constitution, has led to a growing dissatisfaction among many Libyans over the work of the GNC and the limit progress it has achieved.

A serious problem is the sense by some that political leaders with ties to the former regime are responsible for the shortcomings of the transitional government. As such, a growing movement developed in support for the adoption of a law that would ban senior level officials from the Qadhafi regime from serving in the current government. However, it is clear that certain political actors who stood to benefit from the adoption of such a law have taken advantage of the growing sentiment not only for their political gain but also by pushing out capable officials who happened to serve in the former regime.[249] Given the hunger for reform among the general public and the genuine need for reform, these shortcomings have posed serious problems and will continue do so going forward unless they are properly addressed. Undoubtedly, without some reform the situation will continue to deteriorate. For instance, in the aftermath of the bombing

---

[246] Grant, *Supreme Court strikes down Law 37, supra* note 242.

[247] *Libya: Law Restricting Speech Ruled Unconstitutional,* HUMAN RIGHTS WATCH, June 14, 2012, *available at* http://www.hrw.org/news/2012/06/14/libya-law-restricting-speech-ruled-unconstitutional.

[248] *Libya: Slow pace of Reform Harms Rights,* HUMAN RIGHTS WATCH, Feb. 6, 2013, *available at* http://www.hrw.org/news/2013/02/06/libya-slow-pace-reform-harms-rights.

[249] Eric Knecht, *The Questionable Campaign Behind Libya's Political Isolation Law,* THE ATLANTIC COUNCIL, May 8, 2013; Anas El Gomati, *Why Libya's 'Isolation Law' Threatens Progress,* CARNAGIE ENDOWMENT, May 22, 2013, *available at* http://carnegieendowment.org/2013/05/21/why-libya-s-isolation-law-threatens-progress/g5g2.

of the French Embassy on 23 April 2013, armed groups, including those reportedly from the Supreme Security Committee (SSC), seized key ministries and demanded the removal of officials with previous ties to the Qadhafi regime.[250] It is likely that such acts will continue unless the situation is addressed.

Despite the dangers of a purge of Qadhafi era officials the GNC adopted a "political Isolation law" on 5 May, which bars individuals from serving in government if they held a senior government post in the Qadhafi regime, regardless of whether they had defected to join the opposition movement at any time of the uprising or during the Qadhafi era. The adoption of the law followed with the resignation of the President of the GNC, Muhammad al-Mugarayf, as he had served in the Qadhafi government before defecting in 1980 and becoming a prominent opposition figure abroad.[251] The law applies to several other high-level officials in the government, and poses a significant threat to the stability of the government of Prime Minister ʿAli Zaydan because it is over inclusive and implicates a number of qualified and needed government officials.

Despite these on-going concerns over the stability of the Libyan government, it has seen the emergence of civil society actors as key players in promoting accountability and transitional justice. NGOs have emerged as integral actors in organizing and advocating for transitional justice and reconciliation efforts, including LFJL, which challenged Law 37 as described above.[252] Libya's civil society groups have also joined with international organizations, such as the World Organisation Against Torture (OMCT), to carry out workshops and training sessions on transitional justice efforts. In April 2013, for example, a group of NGOs, including OMCT, organized a workshop to draft a memorandum for the Ministry

---

[250] Nihal Zaroug, *Justice Ministry seized by SSC; minister and staff ejected*, THE LIBYA HERALD, Mar. 31, 2013, available at http://www.libyaherald.com/2013/03/31/moj-building-sieged-by-armed-members-of-the-ssc; El Gomati, *Why Libya's 'Isolation Law' Threatens Progress, supra* note 249; Libya: Reject 'Political Isolation Law', HUMAN RIGHTS WATCH, May 4, 2013, *available at* http://www.hrw.org/news/2013/05/04/libya-reject-political-isolation-law.

[251] Mugarayf, once a member of the Muslim Brotherhood, helped create the National Front for the Salvation of Libya (NFSL) in 1981, which became one of the most prominent exile opposition groups. Mugarayf lived in the U.S. during most of his years in exile, where, for years, he organized political and militant opposition to the Qadhafi regime. See Ch. I, Sec. 9.2. See also Alison Pargeter, Qadhafi and Political Islam In Libya, in Dirk Vandewalle, *Libya's Revolution in Perspective, in* LIBYA SINCE 1969: QADHAFI'S REVOLUTION REVISITED 87 (Dirk Vandewalle ed., New York, USA: Palgrave McMillan 2011).

[252] Grant, *Supreme Court strikes down Law 37, supra* note 242.

of Justice and the GNC on the monitoring and improvement of the bill adopted on 9 April that criminalizes torture, enforced disappearances, and discrimination.[253] In May, civil society organizations held an event aimed at raising awareness of transitional justice issues in Sirte. The event included discussions on the conflict, potential transitional justice mechanisms, and measures to achieve reconciliation in Sirte and the country in general.[254] Civil society also teamed with international government bodies, including UNSMIL, which provided support for transitional justice in several different capacities, as discussed in the following section.

(a) *International Support Mechanisms*

International support for Libya's accountability measures has taken on many different forms, including capacity building and institutional capacity development. UNSMIL has been one of the principle actors involved in organizing these efforts, with a mandate to provide the Libyan authorities "[A]ssistance that improves institutional capacity, transparency and accountability…"[255] According to UNSMIL, transitional justice "comprises the full range of processes and mechanisms associated with a society's attempts to come to terms with a legacy of large-scale past abuses, in order to ensure accountability, serve justice and achieve reconciliation."[256]

On 12 and 13 December 2012 a conference was held in Tripoli on truth-seeking and reconciliation in Libya named Truth and Reconciliation in Libya: the Way Forward. The conference marked the increased interest of the new authorities in national reconciliation and the role of civil society in the process. The conference brought together Libyan officials, including Justice Minister Salah Marghani, the Deputy Head of the Fact-Finding and Reconciliation Commission, civil society activists and experts from around the world. The event was planned by the Fact-Finding and Rec-

---

[253] *Libyan public institutions and NGOs draft '10 Steps to End Torture'*, THE WORLD ORGANIZATION AGAINST TORTURE, Apr. 25, 2013, *available at* http://www.omct.org/events/libya/2013/04/d22233.

[254] International Criminal Justice Program, *Libya: NPWJ Raises Awareness about Transitional Justice and Reconciliation in Sirte*, NO PEACE WITHOUT JUSTICE, May 17, 2013, *available at* http://www.npwj.org/ICC/Libya-NPWJ-Raises-Awareness-about-Transitional-Justice-and-Reconciliation-Sirte.html.

[255] *UNSMIL Mandate*, UN SUPPORT MISSION IN LIBYA, *available at* http://unsmil.unmissions.org/Default.aspx?tabid=3544&language=en-US.

[256] *Secretary-General's Report on Transitional Justice and the Rule of Law in Conflict and Post-Conflict Societies*, Aug. 3, 2004, S/2004/616, *cited in Transitional Justice – Foundation for a new Libya*, *supra* note 230.

onciliation Commission and the Human Rights Committee of the GNC, in partnership with UNSMIL and the UN Development Programme (UNDP). The conference dealt with issues such as "challenges of truth-seeking, the role of victim groups as well as the legal and institutional framework required for truth-seeking." [257]

Among other things, the conference resulted in the adoption of recommendations to the Libyan government, including the requirement that the government should "Immediately resolve the issue of detainees currently held outside the scope of the law, screen them and release those against whom there is no sufficient evidence, and try those who bear the greatest responsibility for crimes committed by the former regime." Other recommendations to the government included that the government "Seek urgently to improve security and create the conditions for truth-seeking, including in due course through the demobilisation and disarmament of illegal brigades; Improve the role of the media, which has the potential for broadening social dialogue and should be encouraged to play a more positive role; Assist in developing the performance, capacity and independence of the judiciary." Finally, it was recommended that those who "committed violations in the past should be excluded from public life based on their conduct rather than affiliation".[258]

UNSMIL reported that besides implementing a transitional justice program addressing the signature violations of Qadhafi during his 42-year reign, the government also needed to incorporate the violations carried out by *thuwar*, declaring that

> Crimes committed during the conflict are fresh in memory, generating strong emotions among the communities that suffered the most. In some cases, perpetrators of past crimes became victims, while victims also became perpetrators. While the Libyan society honors those who selflessly fought against the brutality of the former regime, particularly those who lost life or limb, it is also faced with the difficult responsibility of holding accountable members of revolutionary forces for crimes committed during and after

---

[257] *UN representatives urges reconciliation in Libya*, INTERNATIONAL CENTER FOR TRANSITIONAL JUSTICE, Dec. 13, 2012, *available at* http://ictj.org/news/un-representative-urges-reconciliation-libya.

[258] *Truth and Reconciliation Conference Makes Recommendations on Way Forward for Libya*, THE TRIPOLI POST, Dec. 19, 2012, *available at* http://www.tripolipost.com/article detail.asp?i=9649&c=1; *Conference on Truth and Reconciliation in Libya Concludes with Recommendations on the Way Forward*, UN SUPPORT MISSION IN LIBYA, Feb. 8 2012, *available at* http://unsmil.unmissions.org/Default.aspx?tabid=3543&ctl=Details&mid=6187&ItemID=807743&language=en-US.

the Revolution, including torture of detainees and revenge attacks against communities perceived to be supporters of the former regime. Transitional justice will also have to deal with such violations.[259]

UNSMIL also reported on the problems facing Libyan authorities in processing the thousands of Qadhafi loyalists that are still held in Libyan detention centers across the country, and recommended that it should focus on only the most serious cases. To that end, it declared that

> Charges should go beyond the events of 2011 to cover historic crimes even if this requires additional investigation. As it will not be possible to try everyone who is currently suspected or detained, trials should focus on those who organized or masterminded crimes. This strategy will need to be communicated and explained not only to legal professionals, but also to the brigades, victims, and the general public. A strategic approach to prosecutions of the former regime, resulting in fair trials, will contribute to strengthening public confidence in the judiciary and the importance of rule of law in Libya.[260]

The Secretary-General's Special Representative and head of UNSMIL, Tarek Mitri, said in relation to the conference on reconciliation held in Tripoli in December 2012, that "seeking truth and reconciliation can restrain revenge and collective punishment tendencies"[261] but "that seeking truth and justice and moving down the path of reconciliation is not a call for amnesty for past crimes and does not morally equate between the aggressor and the victim." He called for "combating revenge and collective punishment tendencies that do not ensure the accountability of individuals for their acts, but punishes them for acts of others with whom they happen to share family, tribal, local or cultural ties and affiliations."[262] Such issues relates to the joint work between the Fact-Finding and Reconciliation Commission and that of tribal leaders in reconciliation.[263] According to Mirti, regional conflicts that flared up across Libya during

---

[259] *Transitional Justice- Foundation for a new Libya, supra* note 230 at 1-2.

[260] *Id.* at 4.

[261] *January 2013 Monthly Forecast*, SECURITY COUNCIL REPORT, Dec. 21, 2012, *available at* http://www.securitycouncilreport.org/monthly-forecast/2013-01/libya_2.php.

[262] *At conference, UN envoy highlights importance of reconciliation process in Libya*, UN NEWS CENTER, Dec. 12, 2012, *available at* http://www.un.org/apps/news/story.asp?News ID=43754#.URTP02cryAo.

[263] *UN representatives urges reconciliation in Libya*, INTERNATIONAL CENTER FOR TRANSITIONAL JUSTICE, Dec. 13, 2012, *available at* http://ictj.org/news/un-representative-urges-reconciliation-libya.

the post conflict period hindered reconciliation and transitional justice, stating that

> The eruption of local conflicts in many parts of Libya based on historical grievances shows the need for a comprehensive approach to addressing the past. Since October 2011, such conflicts have flared up in various parts of the country, including in Bani Walid; in Kufra, between Tabu and Zwaya; in Sabha; in Zawiya with the Warshafana tribe; in Zintan, with the Mashashiya tribe; in Zuwara, with al-Jumail and Regdalin; and in Ghadames, between Arab and Tuareg. These conflicts have cost many civilian lives. While different delegations were dispatched to try to achieve reconciliation on the local level, these initiatives stopped short of tackling historical root causes and injustices based on recognition of rights. Until now, there is no uniform process of national reconciliation in Libya.[264]

UNSMIL also addressed the issue of self-governing groups that refused to give up arms after the conflict and effectively took on the role of the state in their region, arguing that "Libya's legal institutions are still weak and rule of law remains a fundamental challenge."[265] UNSMIL called for the strengthening of the judiciary in order to execute accountability, stating

> A coherent overall strategy to prosecutions will require a policy directive and a centralized approach from the General Prosecutor's office. Trials should not simply be conducted in a haphazard way in local courts where high-level detainees are currently being held, but require a deliberate overall strategy.[266]

Finally, UNSMIL emphasized the need for "a victim-centered approach" to reparations, whether the for victims of the Qadhafi regime or *thuwar* forces, concluding that "... those who suffered reprisal violations deserve reparations and their displacement must end, or else it risks the festering of wounds that will give rise to future conflict." Furthermore, a transitional justice strategy that includes truth-seeking was argued to provide the necessary tools to resolve contentious issues and prevent "further conflict and cycles of revenge."[267]

Finally, it should be noted that the Ministry of Justice held meetings in December 2012 on state law, justice and the future respect for human rights. It is reported that participants at the meetings discussed plans to raise the level of performance of departments and to develop an independent judiciary in order to facilitate transitional justice and fair trials in accor-

---

[264] *Transitional Justice – Foundation for a new Libya, supra* note 230 at 2.
[265] *Id.* at 3.
[266] *Transitional Justice – Foundation for a new Libya, supra* note 230 at 4.
[267] *Id.* at 3.

dance with international standards.[268] As part of the meetings, the Ministry came up with a work plan to transfer prisoners and train security officials, and Justice Minister Saleh Marghani has expressed the desire to train thousands of new recruits to the judicial police to strengthen the police corps to control the judicial facilities that are taking control over facilities under militia control.[269]

6.2. *Post Conflict Justice before the International Criminal Court and National Courts*

(a) *Background*

The conflict in Libya resulted in the commission of numerous crimes under domestic and international law. Like many conflicts in recent years, the Libyan civil war resulted in massive international attention and eventually a criminal investigation by the ICC, which gained jurisdiction over the "situation" via a referral by the UN Security Council. The investigation resulted in the issuing of arrest warrants for Mu'ammar Qadhafi, Saif al-Islam Qadhafi and 'Abdullah al-Senussi. In the aftermath of the conflict, however, Libya also announced its plans to prosecute individuals for crimes committed during the conflict, which has led to a jurisdictional battle between the two sides that is still on-going in June 2013. This section reviews these proceedings and the underlying law, with particular reference to Saif al-Islam, who has proven to be a test case for the court.

On 26 February 2011, the UN Security Council referred the situation in Libya to the ICC under its Chapter VII powers respond to "threats to the peace, breaches of the peace, and acts of aggression."[270] In Security Council Resolution 1970, the Council empowered the ICC's Prosecutor to investigate suspected violations of international law committed by the Qadhafi government since 15 February 2011.[271] The ICC would eventually exercise jurisdiction over the situation in Libya under article 13(b) of the Rome Statute, which allows it to investigate and prosecute cases in states that have not ratified or acceded to the Rome Statute on the basis of a Security Council referral.

---

[268] وزير العدل يستعرض خطة عمل الوزارة في الفترة القادمة, Ministry of Justice, Dec. 4 2012, *available at* http://www.aladel.gov.ly/main/modules/news/article.php?storyid=490.

[269] *Statement by Justice Minister of Libya Saleh Marghani about Libya Chapter of HRW World Report 2013*, Human Rights Watch, Feb. 6, 2013, *available at* http://www.hrw.org/sites/default/files/related_material/2013_Libya_Worldreport.pdf.

[270] For more on the authority of the Security Council, *see* Ch. III, Sec. 4.

[271] S.C. Res. 1970 (2011), *supra* note 98.

On the basis of the Security Council referral, the then ICC Prosecutor, Luis Moreno Ocampo, announced that the Office of the Prosecutor (OTP) had opened an investigation into violations under the Rome Statute that were being committed in Libya. In particular, Moreno Ocampo identified Benghazi, Misrata, Al-Bayda, Darna, Zintan, Ajdabiya, Tripoli and Zawiyya as the locations in which the worst violations were being committed.[272] Six weeks later, on 16 May 2011, the OTP applied to the Pre-Trial Chamber (PTC) for arrest warrants for Mu'ammar Qadhafi, Saif al-Islam Qadhafi and 'Abdullah al-Senussi for murder and persecution as crimes against humanity.[273]

On the basis of these submissions, on 27 June 2011, the PTC issued a warrant for the arrest of Mu'ammar Qadhafi, Saif al-Islam Qadhafi and 'Abdullah al-Senussi as indirect co-perpetrators of murder and persecution as crimes against humanity under article 7 (a) and (h) of the Rome Statute.[274] As described above, Mu'ammar Qadhafi was killed by *thuwar* forces on 20 October 2011, while Saif al-Islam was captured on 20 November 2011 in the Nafusa Mountains and al-Senussi was detained in Mauritania on 16 March 2012. The killing of Mu'ammar Qadhafi resulted in the termination of the case against him on 22 November 2011.[275] The case against Saif al-Islam, however, took on central importance after the Libyan government challenged the admissibility of the case, and al-Senussi's is similarly winding its way through the admissibility process.

Saif al-Islam was captured by the Zintan Brigade on 19 November 2011, five months after the issuing of the ICC warrant. But instead of being surrendered to the Court he was detained in Zintan by the local militia, where he remains to this day outside of the control of the NTC and its successor GNC. Despite not having physical custody over Saif al-Islam or having rebuilt its judicial system, the Libyan government challenged the jurisdiction of the ICC on 1 May 2012, "on the grounds that its national

---

[272] *Id.*

[273] *Situation in the Libyan Arab Jamahiriya*, Case No. ICC-01/11, Prosecutor's Application Pursuant to Article 58 as to Muammar Mohammed Abu Minyar Gaddafi, Saif Al-Islam Gaddafi and Abdullah Al-Senussi (Int'l Crim. Ct., May 16, 2011).

[274] Warrant of Arrest for Saif Al-Islam Gaddafi, *supra* note 183.

[275] It should be noted that in December 2011, the OTP stated that it would not investigate the killing of Qadhafi subject to the adequate handline of the case by the Libyan government. Nic Roberts, *War crimes court leaves Gadhafi probe to Libya*, CNN, Dec. 20, 2011, *available at* http://articles.cnn.com/2011-12-20/africa/world_africa_libya-gadhafi-death_1_moammar-gadhafi-saif-al-islam-gadhafi-sirte. Although there is no evidence to date that the Libyan government has adequately investigated the matter, the ICC has yet to announce an investigation.

judicial system is actively investigating Mr. Gaddafi and Mr. Al-Senussi for their alleged criminal responsibility for multiple acts of murder and persecution, committed pursuant to or in furtherance of State policy, amounting to crimes against humanity."[276] By challenging the admissibility of the case before the ICC, the Libyan government asserted its right to take primary responsibility for the investigation and possible prosecution of Saif al-Islam, as is its right under the terms of the Rome Statute.

(b) The Legal Framework of the Admissibility of Cases before the ICC

The notion that states bear primary responsibility for the enforcement of international criminal law is firmly enmeshed in the Rome Stature. In the words of the preamble to the Rome Statute, "it is the duty of every State to exercise its criminal jurisdiction over those responsible for international crimes."[277] The corollary principle is that the ICC's jurisdiction is "complementary to national criminal jurisdictions".[278] In other words, under the complementarity principle the ICC only has jurisdiction where states prove unable or unwilling to address matters domestically, in effect by waiving their primacy in the process.[279] Thus, the complementarity provision of the Rome Statute ensures that the ICC cannot exert jurisdiction if a state is in the process of investigating or prosecuting a case, where it has previously investigated or prosecuted a case, or where it previously investigated a case and declined to prosecute, unless there is evidence that the state is "unwilling or unable genuinely to carry out the investigation or prosecution."[280] As summarized by the ICC's PTC, "The principle of complementarity expresses a preference for national investigations and prosecutions but does not relieve a State, in general, from substantiating all requirements set forth by the law when seeking to successfully challenge the admissibility of a case."[281] Where the ICC has exercised jurisdiction over the case, as in Libya after the Security Council referral, a state

---

[276] *Situation In Libya*, Case No. ICC-01/11-01/11, Application on behalf of the Government of Libya pursuant to Article 19 of the ICC Statute, ¶ 1 (Int'l Crim. Ct, 1 May 2012).

[277] Rome Statute *supra* note 8 at *preamble*.

[278] *See* Rome Statute, *supra* note 8 at art. 1. *See also* M. Cherif Bassiouni & Douglass Hansen, *The Inevitable Practice of the Office of the Prosecutor*, *in* HUMAN RIGHTS & INTERNATIONAL CRIMINAL LAW ONLINE FORUM (2013).

[279] Rome Statute *supra* note 8 at art. 17.

[280] *Id.* at Art. 17(1).

[281] Application on behalf of the Government of Libya pursuant to Article 19 of the ICC Statute, *supra* note 276.

may challenge the Court's jurisdiction under articles 17 and 19 of the Rome Statute, which is what Libya did with regard to Saif al-Islam.

As described above, under article 17(1)(a), the Court loses jurisdiction where "The case is being investigated or prosecuted by a State which has jurisdiction over it, unless the State is unwilling or unable genuinely to carry out the investigation or prosecution."[282] Article 17(2) clarifies this provision by further providing that

> 2. In order to determine unwillingness in a particular case, the Court shall consider, having regard to the principles of due process recognized by international law, whether one or more of the following exist, as applicable:
>   (a) The proceedings were or are being undertaken or the national decision was made for the purpose of shielding the person concerned from criminal responsibility for crimes within the jurisdiction of the Court referred to in article 5;
>   (b) There has been an unjustified delay in the proceedings which in the circumstances is inconsistent with an intent to bring the person concerned to justice;
>   (c) The proceedings were not or are not being conducted independently or impartially, and they were or are being conducted in a manner which, in the circumstances, is inconsistent with an intent to bring the person concerned to justice.

Finally, in a clause that would take on particular importance in the Saif al Islam case, Article 17(3) deals provides that

> 3. In order to determine inability in a particular case, the Court shall consider whether, due to *a total or substantial collapse or unavailability of its national judicial system*, the State is unable to obtain the accused or the necessary evidence and testimony or otherwise unable to carry out its proceedings.[283]

Complementarity at the ICC is therefore based on the presumption that states possess a judicial system that is not in collapse or unavailable. In other words, the state seeking to exert jurisdiction must show that it has the capacity to replace the functions and operations of the ICC, and therefore be able to investigate and prosecute individuals fairly and expeditiously. Capacity in this regard requires that states enact laws in order to gain subject matter jurisdiction over the crimes contained in the Rome Statute (although it does not require that the crimes be characterized using the same nomenclature and phrasing), and that states have a

---

[282] *See* Rome Statute, *supra* note 8 at art. 17(1)(a).
[283] *Id.* at art. 17(1)(a) (emphasis added).

cadre of trained judges, prosecutors, investigators and defense attorneys with knowledge of the substantive law involved, an effective system of evidence collection and analysis, a witness protection program, and trial procedures that ensure the rights of the accused, witnesses and victims.

(c) Libya's Admissibility Challenge in the Saif al-Islam Qadhafi Case

As indicated above, the Libyan government challenged the admissibility of the case against Saif al-Islam on 1 May 2012, and further requested the postponement of his surrender until the admissibility issue had been resolved.[284] One month later, on 1 June 2012, the PTC affirmed the postponement[285] to allow the parties to present oral and written arguments on question of admissibility. Over the coming months Libya, the OTP, the Defense, the Office of Public Counsel for Victims, and amici curiae filed submissions and made oral submissions in October 2012.

The admissibility case continued until 31 May 2013, when the PTC rejected Libya's admissibility challenge and determined that the case was admissible before the ICC.[286] It should not noted that although 'Abdullah al-Senussi was not considered in the same case, the facts are substantially the same and *mutatis mutandis* the Pre-Trial Chamber will for the same reasons reject Libya's admissibility challenge in the al-Senussi case. Libya formally challenged the admissibility of al-Sinuses' case on 23 April 2013, and the matter is still pending.[287]

In ruling the case against Saif al-Islam admissible, the PTC conducted an examination of each prong of the test articulated in article 17(1) of the Rome Statute, namely whether 1) Libya was conducting an investigation into the same facts investigated by the ICC's Prosecutor; and if so 2) whether Libya was willing and able to genuinely investigate and prosecute the case against Saif al-Islam.

In assessing the first prong, the PTC determined that although the investigation in Libya was not exactly the same as that of the ICC, the Chamber

---

[284] Application on behalf of the Government of Libya pursuant to Article 19 of the ICC Statute, *supra* note 276.

[285] *Situation in Libya*, Case No. ICC-01/11-01/11, Decision on the postponement of the execution of the request for surrender of Saif Al-Islam Gaddafi pursuant to article 95 of the Rome Statute (Int'l Crim. Ct., June 1, 2012).

[286] Decision on the admissibility of the case against Saif Al-Islam Gaddafi, *supra* note 130.

[287] *Situation in Libya*, Case No. ICC-01/11-01/11, Decision on the conduct of the proceedings following the "Application on behalf of the Government of Libya relating to Abdullah Al-Senussi pursuant to Article 19 of the ICC Statute" (Int'l Crim. Ct., Apr. 26, 2013).

allowed for some divergences, noting that "the Chamber considers that it would not be appropriate to expect Libya's investigation to cover exactly the same acts of murder and persecution ... as constituting instances of Mr Gaddafi's alleged course of conduct."[288] Ultimately, while the Chamber held that the cases need not parallel each other exactly, Libya had failed to provide thorough documentation showing that the scope of its investigation aligned in significant ways with that of the OTP. On the basis of the evidence presented, the Chamber concluded that the Libyan case is of an apparently smaller geographic scope than that of the OTP. In the view of the PTC, the more limited scope of the Libyan investigation negated the requisite overlap between the two cases, and necessarily nullified the admissibility challenge on the first prong.[289]

Irrespective of the merits of this argument over scope, it is noteworthy that the PTC ruled that the use of existing domestic "ordinary" crimes does not nullify the admissibility challenge. As the CoI noted, Libya's existing criminal code does not adequately define international crimes such as crimes against humanity and war crimes,[290] but under the PTC's ruling the use of ordinary criminal law provisions, as opposed to international crimes, does not automatically negate the capacity of the Libyan government to effectively prosecute the case, and that domestic crimes likely covers the same conduct.[291] This may prove especially important should further cases arise.

With respect to the second prong – whether Libya is willing and able to conduct an investigation and prosecution of Saif al-Islam – the PTC ultimately concluded that the Libyan government was unable to genuinely carry out the judicial proceedings against Safe al-Islam due to the "multiple challenges ... and substantial difficulties [Libya faces] ... in exercising its judicial powers".[292] Among these are 1) the fundamental inability of the government to gain custody over Saif al-Islam since 19 November 2011, and the subsequent "lack of concrete progress" towards that end;[293] 2) the government's inability to ensure the appearance of witnesses, including

---

[288] Application on behalf of the Government of Libya pursuant to Article 19 of the ICC Statute, *supra* note 276 at ¶ 89.

[289] *Id.* at ¶ 135.

[290] *See* Report of the International Commission of Inquiry, advance unedited version (Mar. 2, 2012), *supra* note 12 at ¶ 102.

[291] Application on behalf of the Government of Libya pursuant to Article 19 of the ICC Statute, *supra* note 276 at ¶¶ 108–113.

[292] *Id.* at ¶ 205.

[293] *Id.* at ¶¶ 206–208.

the inability to access witness detained in facilities outside the control of the central government and the lack of witness protection plans;[294] and, 3) the inability of the Libyan government to secure adequate representation for Saif al-Islam.[295] In the words of the Chamber

> although the authorities for the administration of justice may exist and function in Libya, a number of legal and factual issues result in the unavailability of the national judicial system for the purpose of the case against Mr Gaddafi. As a consequence, Libya is, in the view of the Chamber, unable to secure the transfer of Mr Gaddafi's custody from his place of detention under the Zintan militia into State authority and there is no concrete evidence that this problem may be resolved in the near future. Moreover, the Chamber is not persuaded that the Libyan authorities have the capacity to obtain the necessary testimony. Finally, the Chamber has noted a practical impediment to the progress of domestic proceedings against Mr Gaddafi as Libya has not shown whether and how it will overcome the existing difficulties in securing a lawyer for the suspect.[296]

Having ruled on the inability of the Libyan judiciary to satisfy the requirements of articles 17 and 19, the PTC did not inquire into the willingness of the Libyan state to carry out the proceedings, the second component of the second prong of the article 17 test.[297]

In sum, the Libyan admissibility challenge was rejected by the PTC and the jurisdiction of the ICC affirmed. As of early June, the Libyan government has indicated that it will appeal the decision to the Appeals Chamber, although in late June it appeared to concede that it would have to move the trial to Zintan as it could not secure the transfer of Saif al-Islam to Tripoli.[298]

(d) *Violations by* Thuwar *Forces*

While the jurisdictional struggle between the ICC and Libya over Saif al-Islam Qadhafi and al-Senussi continues to generate the majority of

---

[294] *Id.* at ¶¶ 209–211.

[295] *Id.* at ¶¶ 212–214.

[296] *Id.* at ¶ 215. For more on the status of the Libyan judiciary, which has been described as "in chaos", *see* Vivienne Walt, *Libya's Disaster of Justice: The Case of Saif al-Islam Gaddafi Reveals a Country in Chaos*, Time, June 28, 2013, *available at* http://world .time.com/2013/06/28/libyas-disaster-of-justice-the-case-of-saif-al-islam-gaddafi-reveals-a-country-in-chaos/#ixzz2YdNkb6oK.

[297] *Id.* at ¶ 216.

[298] *Situation in Libya*, Case No. ICC-01/11-01/11, Document in Support of the Government of Libya's Appeal against the "Decision on the admissibility of the case against Saif Al-Islam Gaddafi", ¶ 161 (Int'l Crim. Ct., June 24, 2013).

international attention concerning post-conflict justice in Libya, it should not overshadow the fact that Security Council Resolution 1970 also gives the ICC authority to investigate violations by members of the *thuwar* committed during the conflict. There is no limiting language in Security Council Resolution 1970, and the language of the Rome Statute refers to situations and not specific actors or sides, which implies that the Security Council referral is not limited to the conduct of the Qadhafi forces but includes those by *thuwar* forces.

It should be noted that Security Council Resolution 1970 does not indicate at what point the ICC's jurisdiction ceases. An important question therefore is therefore when the temporal limit on the referral for the purposes of investigating and prosecuting incidents expired. The limit could coincide with the effective fall of the Qadhafi regime in October 2011, which coincides with the conclusion of Operation Unified Defender, although it could also continue until all violations ended, which is a much more difficult determination. Given the inactivity of the OTP beyond the initial investigation, it appears that the jurisdictional limit coincided with the death of Qadhafi and the fall of the government. This determination would likely preclude the investigation and prosecution by the OTP of ongoing violations, such as the attacks on individuals in Bani Walid in 2012, or on-going acts against Tawerghans and other minority groups.

Nevertheless, as is clear from the evidence collected in this book, *thuwar* forces were responsible for numerous violations within the subject matter jurisdiction of the ICC during the conflict and within the more limited timeframe identified above. As the CoI concluded, acts of violence perpetrated by *thuwar* forces constituted war crimes and possibly crimes against humanity, both of which fall within the jurisdiction of the ICC.[299] As detailed above in Sec. 2, war crimes are violations of international humanitarian law and are binding proscriptions on acts committed during international armed conflicts and non-international armed conflicts.[300] Crimes against humanity, on the other hand, can be committed during war or peacetime, when certain acts – including *inter alia* murder, enslavement, torture or rape – are "committed as part of a widespread or systematic attack directed against any civilian population."[301] The former clearly came to an end with the end of the conflict, while the

---

[299] *See* Report of the International Commission of Inquiry, advance unedited version (Mar. 2, 2012), *supra* note 12 at Annex I, ¶ 63.

[300] *See* Rome Statute, *supra* note 8 at art. 8.

[301] *Id.* at art. 7.

latter survived its end, subject only to the reasonable culmination of the Security Council's referral.

While it is clear that *thuwar* forces committed violations of IHL and ICL norms during and after the conflict, Libya's senior government figures have failed to publicly condemn attacks carried out against entire communities, or hold accountable *thuwar* forces responsible for such violations.[302] Despite the rebuke by the CoI in March 2012, to date there have been no known charges brought against former rebel fighters. Moreover, it is unlikely that the Libyan government can or will prosecute individuals as NTC Law 38 of May 2012 provides full amnesties for "military, security, or civil actions dictated by the February 17 Revolution that were performed by revolutionaries with the goal of promoting or protecting the revolution."[303] In other words, through this blanket declaration, all *thuwar* forces were amnestied and exculpated for their violations of international humanitarian law and international criminal law.

It should be noted that blanket amnesties are highly questionable under international law, as they come into direct conflict with numerous positive obligations to prevent and punish crimes.[304] Such provisions are contained in various documents, including the Genocide Convention[305] and the Convention against Torture,[306] both of which require states parties to prevent and punish perpetrators of those crimes, or alternatively extradite suspects to states that will.

---

[302] *See* Report of the International Commission of Inquiry, advance unedited version (Mar. 2, 2012), *supra* note 12 at Annex I, ¶ 44.

[303] *Quoted in Libya: Amend New Special Procedures Law: Reject Impunity for Serious Crimes*, HUMAN RIGHTS WATCH, May 11, 2012, *available at* http://www.hrw.org/news/2012/05/11/libya-amend-new-special-procedures-law.

[304] *See also* M. CHERIF BASSIOUNI & EDWARD WISE, AUT DEDERE AUT JUDICARE: THE DUTY TO EXTRADITE OR PROSECUTE IN INTERNATIONAL LAW (Dordrecht, The Netherlands: Martinus Nijhoff Publishers, 1995).

[305] Convention on the Prevention and Punishment of the Crime of Genocide, Dec. 9, 1948, 78 U.N.T.S. 277. "The Contracting Parties confirm that genocide, whether committed in time of peace or in time of war, is a crime under international law which they undertake to prevent and to punish." *Id.* at Art. 1.

[306] Convention against Torture and Other Cruel, Inhuman or Degrading Treatment or Punishment, Dec. 10, 1984, G.A. res. 39/46, U.N. Doc. A/39/51. "1. Each State Party shall ensure that all acts of torture are offences under its criminal law. The same shall apply to an attempt to commit torture and to an act by any person which constitutes complicity or participation in torture. 2. Each State Party shall make these offences punishable by appropriate penalties which take into account their grave nature." *Id.* at art. 4. *See also* "The State Party in the territory under whose jurisdiction a person alleged to have committed any offence referred to in article 4 is found shall in the cases contemplated in article 5, if it does not extradite him, submit the case to its competent authorities for the purpose of prosecution." *Id.* at art 7(1).

Various regional human rights bodies have contemplated this question. In the famous *Velásquez-Rodríguez* case, the Inter-American Court of Human Rights stated that

> [T]he State has a legal duty to take reasonable steps to prevent human rights violations and to use the means at its disposal to carry out *a serious investigation of violations committed within its jurisdiction, to identify those responsible, to impose the appropriate punishment and to ensure the victim adequate compensation.*[307]

The African Commission on Human and People's Rights similarly stated that

> It is of the view [of the Commission] that an amnesty law adopted with the aim of nullifying suits or other actions seeking redress that may be filed by the victims or their beneficiaries, while having force within Mauritanian national territory, cannot shield that country from fulfilling its international obligations under the Charter.[308]

Beyond the evolving proscription on blanket amnesties for international crimes, it is clear that domestic Libyan procedures are not binding upon the ICC, and that adherence to Law 38 or other amnesty provisions would contradict the object and purpose of the Rome Statute and the Court itself. There is no limiting clause in the Rome Statute for amnesties – which only provides for a deferral in the limited circumstance in which the Security Council passes a resolution to that effect – and once the Court gains jurisdiction over a situation, whether by Security Council action, a state referral or the *proprio motu* act of the Prosecutor, the burden is upon the State to show why jurisdiction should be removed and the case declared inadmissible.[309] Ultimately, the amnesties created by Law 38 would undermine any admissibility challenge by Libya should the ICC attempt to investigate and prosecute *thuwar* forces for crimes committed during the conflict.

It must be recalled that the primary responsibility for criminal investigations and prosecutions rests with Libya. By the terms of the Rome

---

[307] *Velásquez-Rodríguez case*, Judgement of July 29, 1988, Inter-Am. Ct. H.R. (ser. C) No. 4, ¶ 174 (1988) (emphasis added).

[308] *Malawi African Association et al. v. Mauritania, quoted in* 13TH ANNUAL ACTIVITY REPORT OF THE AFRICAN COMMISSION ON HUMAN AND PEOPLES' RIGHTS, 1999–2000, AHG/222 (XXXVI) at annex V, ¶¶ 82–83.

[309] *Situation in the Republic of Kenya*, Case No. ICC-01/09-01/11-307, Decision on the Application by the Government of Kenya Challenging the Admissibility of the Case Pursuant to Article 19(2)(b) of the Statute, ¶ 62 (Int'l Crim. Ct., Aug. 30, 2011).

Statute, the ICC only has "jurisdiction over persons for the most serious crimes of international concern"[310] and therefore cannot exert jurisdiction over each and every Libyan who has committed a crime. Just as primary responsibility for the enforcement of the principles of the Rome Statute is reserved to states, so is the responsibility for prosecuting the vast majority of those who, by dint of their lower rank or more limited role, cannot be prosecuted by the ICC. While there is no explicit limitation in the Rome Statute other than the one identified above, judicial economy and prudence militate against the prosecution of individuals who are not senior leaders or those who are most responsible for particularly serious crimes. In the context of Libya, it is clear that Libya bears the primary responsibility for investigating and prosecuting individuals, including *thuwar* forces, especially for acts committed after the ICC presumably lost its temporal jurisdiction in late 2011 or early 2012.

Although the jurisdictional struggles between the ICC and Libya are particularly important, the international community should not forget or lose focus on the significant shortcomings in Libya's domestic judicial practice and the on-going impunity for violations of IHRL and ICL. In light of the serious shortcomings of the Libyan judiciary and the on-going inability of the government to pursue violations by *thuwar* forces for crimes within the jurisdiction of the ICC – in effect those committed before October 2011 – the situation should be investigated by the ICC, if only as a means of promoting domestic accountability measures. While international tribunals such as the ICC are ultimately courts of last resort and cannot replace the essential work of domestic courts, they should be selectively used in order to further the essential next phase of justice and accountability for Libya.

i. *Specific Issues of Accountability in the Post-Qadhafi Era*
The on-going inability of the Libyan government authorities to hold rebel groups accountable is perhaps most evident in the violations committed against the Tawerghan community by the Misrata *thuwar*.[311] There is significant evidence that the Tawerghan community has been targeted on the basis of its alleged allegiance to the Qadhafi regime and their skin color, and many remain refugees more than a year after they fled from

---

[310] *See* Rome Statute, *supra* note 8 at Preamble.
[311] Fore more on violations committed against the Tawerghan community in the town of Tawergha as well as in Internally Displaced Persons camps in other cities in Libya, *see* Ch. IX, Sec. 3, Ch. XIII, Sec. 3 & Ch. XV, Sec. 3.

their homes.[312] While some of these acts were committed after the likely end of the Security Council's referral, some are on-going crimes that began before October 2011. More broadly, these violations are emblematic of the kinds of violations that took place before the end of the conflict, which are further discussed in Part Two.

Due to on-going concerns, Human Rights Watch sent a letter to the leaders of the Misrata Local Council on 8 April 2012, expressing concern over acts committed by against members of the Tawerghan community, claiming that the abuses amounted to crimes against humanity.[313] The letter pointed out that international legal bodies, including the ICC, could hold senior officials criminally responsible for ordering these crimes, or for failing to prevent or punish individuals responsible. The letter presented a series of recommendations[314] on measures to be taken to end the on-going abuses and hold the responsible persons responsible.[315]

The Misrata Local Council replied on 11 April 2012, addressing the accusations put forward by HRW. In it, the Council claimed that any violations against the Tawerghan community were "no more than individual, and not systematic infractions." The Council also claimed that many violations were wrongly attributed to Misrata *thuwar*, such as those committed in Mansour on 6 February 2012.[316] Moreover, they argued that some of the accusations levied against the council were against brigades located outside the city of Misrata, and therefore not subject to the authority of the Misrata Local Council or its military council. Such brigades were claimed

---

[312] *See* Leila Fadel, *After The War, A Bitter Feud Remains In Two Libyan Towns*, NPR, May 29, 2013, *available at* http://www.npr.org/blogs/parallels/2013/05/29/186927435/after-the-war-a-bitter-feud-remains-in-two-libyan-towns?sc=tw&cc=share.

[313] *Libya: Letter to Misrata Councils*, HUMAN RIGHTS WATCH, Apr. 8, 2012, *available at* http://www.hrw.org/news/2012/04/08/libya-letter-misrata-councils.

[314] "End all abuse in detention facilities run by armed groups and militias under your effective control. Support and cooperate with investigations of abuse in detention facilities in Misrata and prosecutions by the competent state authorities of those suspected of wrongdoing; Transfer all detainees to the custody of competent state authorities; Remove individuals responsible for the physical and psychological maltreatment of detainees from their positions in detention facilities, and provide all evidence of such abuse to the competent state authorities; Issue immediate orders to armed groups under your command to stop killings, arbitrary arrests, looting and home destructions in Tawergha, as well as in Tomina and Kararim, and make clear that any such acts will be treated as a criminal offense; Support and cooperate with investigations of attacks on the Tawergha community by competent state authorities and prosecution of those suspected of wrongdoing; Ensure that all individuals who wish to do so can return to their homes in Tawergha, Tomina and Kararim." *See id.*

[315] *Id.*

[316] *Id.*

to not represent the city of Misrata or its *thuwar*.[317] However, the Misrata Local Council expressed its willingness to prosecute any person proven to have committed violations, and stressed their willingness to cooperate with all national and international rights organizations.[318] Despite this pledge by the Misrata Local Council and on-going evidence of violations, no such prosecutions or pending investigations have yet to be initiated. Further, as indicated above, these violations have continued into mid-2013 without any indication of abating.[319]

6.3. *The Major Cases*

(a) *The Death of Qadhafi*

United Nations Security Council Resolution 1970 of 26 February 2011 brought the situation in Libya into the international spotlight, insofar as the Council invoked its Chapter VII powers and forced the international community to engage with the situation. This entailed, *inter alia*, the referral of the case to the ICC, the imposition of sanctions on the Libyan government, the imposition of a travel ban and the seizure of certain assets. Less than a month later, on 17 March 2012, the Council adopted Resolution 1973, which empowered states to engage in military intervention in Libya. With the passage of Resolution 1973 attention shifted, and the main objective of the international forces turned to ensuring regime change opposed to apprehending and prosecuting the alleged perpetrators responsible for the violence.[320]

Similarly, as the conflict progressed, the implicit aim of the foreign intervention shifted from protecting civilians to ensuring Qadhafi's departure from power, dead or alive. To that end, NATO forces increasingly attacked targets with only minimal connections to the protection of civilians, including so called "command and control nodes" in Tripoli and the western part of the country, and even more explicit air strikes that appeared to be aimed at killing him and those close to him, such as a 30 April 2011 strike in Tripoli that reportedly killed his son Saif al-'Arab and

---

[317] *Id.*

[318] *Misrata Local Council Response to Human Rights Watch*, HUMAN RIGHTS WATCH, Apr. 11, 2012, *available at* http://www.hrw.org/news/2012/04/11/misrata-local-council-response-human-rights-watch.

[319] *See* Fadel, *After The War, A Bitter Feud Remains In Two Libyan Towns, supra* note 312.

[320] For a detailed discussion of the NATO intervention, *see* Ch. III.

three of his grandchildren.[321] For its part, NATO denied that it targeted individuals or Qadhafi himself, and claimed its strikes were intended to destroy military installations.[322] Nevertheless, airstrikes such as the one on 30 April drew criticism from some Security Council member states who accused NATO of targeting individual leaders and operating outside of their mandate to protect civilians.[323] Qadhafi's daughter 'A'isha also filed lawsuits in Paris and Brussels in June 2011 against NATO over the alleged death of Saif al-'Arab, claiming that the target of the strike was a private residence of the Qadhafi family and that NATO's actions constituted a war crime.[324]

In the midst of the conflict, the Prosecutor of the ICC continued to investigate violations and on 16 May 2011 applied to the PTC of the ICC for arrest warrants for Mu'ammar Qadhafi, Saif al-Islam Qadhafi and 'Abdullah al-Senussi, for crimes against humanity in relation to the February violence against protesters.[325] On 27 June, the PTC issued arrest warrants for the three, indicting them for being indirect co-perpetrators of crimes against humanity for overseeing a "state policy...designed at the highest level of the Libyan State machinery and aimed at deterring and quelling, by any means, including by the use of lethal force, the demonstrations of civilians against the regime."[326] As the leader of Libya, Qadhafi was considered to have had "ultimate and unquestioned control over the Libyan State apparatus of power, including the Security Forces,

---

[321] See Ch. III, Sec. 6 & Ch. XIII, Sec. 2. After the NATO strike there was also information that surfaced alleging that Saif al-Islam and Khamis Qadhafi played a role in the death of their brother Saif al-'Arab, and that the Qadhafi regime used the incident as propaganda to generate criticism against NATO.

[322] *NATO strikes command and control facility in Tripoli*, NORTH ATLANTIC TREATY ORGANIZATION, May 1, 2011, *available at* http://www.nato.int/cps/en/SID-A29434A7-58904AE4/natolive/news_72972.htm.

[323] See Ch. III, Sec. 6. *See also Nato strike 'kills Saif al-Arab Gaddafi', Libya says*, BBC, May 1, 2011, *available at* http://www.bbc.co.uk/news/world-africa-13251570.

[324] Luke Harding, *Gaddafi's daughter files "war crimes" lawsuit related to NATO air strike that killed relatives*, GLOBAL POST, June 8, 2011, *available at* http://www.globalpost.com/dispatch/news/regions/middle-east/110607/muammar-gaddafi-daughter-lawsuit-war-crimes-assassination-n; Kim Willsher, *Gaddafi's daughter sues over deadly Nato air strike*, THE GUARDIAN, June 7, 2011, *available at* http://www.guardian.co.uk/world/2011/jun/07/gaddafi-daughter-sues-nato-air-strike.

[325] Report of the International Commission of Inquiry (Jan. 12, 2012), *supra* note 57 at ¶ 35.

[326] *Situation In The Libyan Arab Jamahiriya*, Case No. ICC-01/11, Warrant of arrest Muammar Mohammed Abu Minyar Gaddafi (Int'l Crim. Ct., June 27, 2011); *Situation in the Libyan Arab Jamahiriya*, Case No. ICC-01/11, Warrant of Arrest for Abdullah Al-Senussi, (Int'l Crim. Ct., June 27, 2011).

and that, by virtue of that position and in coordination with his inner circle, including his son Saif al-Islam Gaddafi, he conceived and orchestrated a plan to deter and quell, by all means, the civilian demonstration against his regime."[327]

The three wanted individuals remained at large throughout the conflict, and by the time *thuwar* entered the Bab al-'Aziziyya compound in Tripoli in August 2011, Mu'ammar Qadhafi had already fled the capital. Having been forced out of the capital, he fled to his hometown of Sirte, which he called the "new capital" and took cover in the last remaining regime stronghold.[328]

As documented by the CoI, NATO airstrikes on Sirte intensified after Qadhafi established himself there, and the *thuwar* forces progressively encircled the city. Increasingly isolated and without options, Qadhafi attempted to flee the city on the morning of 20 October, setting off in a heavily armed convoy of approximately 50 vehicles. The convoy included Mu'ammar, his son Mu'tassim (who had been wounded previously), Defense Minister Abu Bakr Yunis, an unidentified high level military commander,[329] and approximately 200 armed men. There were also women and children reportedly in the convoy, along with wounded men from the prior fighting.[330]

The convoy quickly ran into a *thuwar* ambush as it headed east on the main road, and was forced to split up with some cars circling around to head in the other direction. At this point reports indicate that a car in front of the green Landcruiser carrying Mu'ammar Qadhafi was hit by a missile fired from a Predator drone.[331] Armed U.S. Predator and French drones had reportedly been staking out the center of Sirte for several weeks monitoring the battlefield in an attempt to track Qadhafi's movements.[332]

---

[327] *Warrant of arrest Muammar Mohammed Abu Minyar Gaddafi, supra* note 326.

[328] *Libya crisis: Col Gaddafi vows to fight a 'long war,'* BBC, Sept. 1, 2011, *available at* http://www.bbc.co.uk/news/world-africa-14753645.

[329] The military commander later spoke to the CoI and is identified by number [50] in the CoI reports in order to protect his identify.

[330] *See* Report of the International Commission of Inquiry, advance unedited version (Mar. 2, 2012), *supra* note 12 at Annex I, ¶ 237.

[331] Spencer Akerman, *Libya: The Real U.S. Drone War,* WIRED, Oct. 20, 2011, *available at* http://www.wired.com/dangerroom/2011/10/predator-libya/; Ian Black, *Muammar Gaddafi's 'trophy' body on show in Misrata meat store,* THE GUARDIAN, Oct. 22 2011, *available at* http://www.guardian.co.uk/world/2011/oct/21/muammar-gaddafi-body-misrata-meat-store.

[332] Thomas Harding, *Col Gaddafi killed: convoy bombed by drone flown by pilot in Las Vegas,* THE TELEGRAPH, Oct. 20, 2011, *available at* http://www.telegraph.co.uk/news/

After the strike Qadhafi switched cars and drove south towards a power facility when *thuwar* forces opened fire, again forcing him to abandon his car and take refuge in a nearby house.[333]

At this point another airstrike hit the vehicles, causing secondary explosions. Qadhafi and Mu'tassim fled the house and found refuge in nearby drainage pipes.[334] At that point, one of Qadhafi's men reportedly raised a white flag in surrender, and the Misrata katiba surrounded and captured Qadhafi.[335] The eyewitness accounts documented by the CoI end at this point, but videos of the incident show a wounded Qadhafi being beaten by members of the Misrata *thuwar* before being taken to an ambulance.[336] The details of what transpired next are unclear. Videos show Qadhafi bleeding from a head injury, and appear to suggest Qadhafi was killed by his captures.[337] What is clear is that Qadhafi was alive when he was taken into custody and that he was dead when the ambulance arrived in Misrata.[338] Reports further indicate that the Tiger Katiba was the *thuwar* group responsible for the detention and transfer of Qadhafi.[339]

The CoI visited the site of Qadhafi's capture, and found numerous burned vehicles and other remnants of the NATO airstrikes, including fragments of ammunition that had exploded during the strikes. The CoI determined that this corroborated testimony that the vehicles had been

---

worldnews/africaandindianocean/libya/8839964/Col-Gaddafi-killed-convoy-bombed-by-drone-flown-by-pilot-in-Las-Vegas.html.

[333] Report of the International Commission of Inquiry, advance unedited version (Mar. 2, 2012), *supra* note 12 at Annex I, ¶ 238.

[334] *Id.* at Annex I, ¶ 239.

[335] *Id.* at Annex I, ¶ 241.

[336] M Gee, *Blood & Guts Gaddafi Beaten To A Pulp as Part of Celebrations*, YouTube. com (Oct. 21, 2011), *available at* http://www.youtube.com/watch?v=1chIX37laso; Report of the International Commission of Inquiry, advance unedited version (Mar. 2, 2012), *supra* note 12 at Annex I, ¶ 242.

[337] Solane Pyne, *Video: Decoding Gaddafi's death*, GLOBALPOST (Oct. 21, 2011), *available at* http://www.globalpost.com/video/5678826.

[338] Report of the International Commission of Inquiry, advance unedited version (Mar. 2, 2012), *supra* note 12 at Annex I, ¶ 244.

[339] For Tiger Katiba, *see* Ch. II, Sec. 2.3. For more on the *thuwar* fighter 'Umran Sha'ban believed to have discovered and killed Qadhafi, who was later killed in Bani Walid, *see* Ch. XIV. *See also* Gert Van Langendonck, *In Qaddafi's hometown, signs of trouble for Libya*, THE CHRISTIAN SCIENCE MONITOR, Oct. 25, 2011, *available at* http://www.csmonitor.com/World/Middle-East/2011/1025/In-Qaddafi-s-hometown-signs-of-trouble-for-Libya; Alastair Macdonald & Oliver Holmes, *Special Report: Libya – divided it stands*, REUTERS, Dec. 16, 2011, *available at* http://www.reuters.com/article/2011/12/16/us-libya-future-idUSTRE7B-FoMG20111216; Gert Van Langendonck, *In Qaddafi's hometown, signs of trouble for Libya*, THE CHRISTIAN SCIENCE MONITOR, Oct. 25, 2011, *available at* http://www.csmonitor.com/World/Middle-East/2011/1025/In-Qaddafi-s-hometown-signs-of-trouble-for-Libya.

carrying weapons and ammunition. The CoI was unable to conclude whether the death of Qadhafi was an unlawful killing, and found that further investigation is required to conclusively determine what happened.[340] After securing evidence that confirmed the death of Qadhafi, the ICC officially closed it case against him on 22 November 2011.[341]

After their deaths, the bodies of Mu'ammar and Mu'tassim Qadhafi were placed on public display in a meat locker in Misrata for three days.[342] Along with Abu Bakr Yunis, they were reportedly buried at dawn on 25 October 2011 in a secret location, five days after their deaths.[343] The CoI found that the public display of the bodies of both Mu'ammar and Mu'tassim Qadhafi was a breach of customary international law.[344] The Second Additional Protocol to the Geneva Conventions provides that

> Whenever circumstances permit, and particularly after an engagement, all possible measure shall be taken, without delay, to search for and collect the wounded, sick and shipwrecked, to protect them against pillage and ill-treatment, to ensure their adequate care, and to search for the dead, prevent their being despoiled, and decently dispose of them.

The International Committee of the Red Cross identifies this as a customary rule of international humanitarian law, concluding that "The dead must be disposed of in a respectful manner and their graves respected and properly maintained."[345]

On 21 October 2011, the UN Office of the High Commissioner on Human Rights (OHCHR) called for a full investigation into the killing of Qadhafi. The spokesman for the High Commissioner for Human Rights, Navanethem Pillay told reporters that an investigation was needed to

---

[340] Report of the International Commission of Inquiry, advance unedited version (Mar. 2, 2012), *supra* note 12 at Annex I, ¶ 246.

[341] *ICC Weekly Update*, INTERNATIONAL CRIMINAL COURT, *available at* http://www.icc-cpi.int/NR/rdonlyres/9316F88E-EA95-4952-A619-3E56B6ED9CD3/284915/ED143_ENG.pdf.

[342] *Libyans line up to see Gaddafi's body on display; groups call for probe into death*, WASHINGTON POST, Oct. 21, 2011, *available at* http://www.washingtonpost.com/world/middle_east/libyans-delay-burial-of-gaddafi-pending-inquiries/2011/10/21/gIQAZkTQ3L_story .html; Report of the International Commission of Inquiry, advance unedited version (Mar. 2, 2012), *supra* note 12 at Annex I, ¶ 248.

[343] *Gaddafi buried in secret location*, THE GUARDIAN, Oct. 25, 2011, *available at* http://www.guardian.co.uk/world/2011/oct/25/muammar-gaddafi-buried-libya; *Gaddafi Funeral Video: Footage Claims To Show Secret Ceremony*, HUFFINGTON POST, Oct. 26, 2011, *available at* http://www.huffingtonpost.com/2011/10/26/gaddafi-funeral-video_n_1032728.html.

[344] Report of the International Commission of Inquiry, advance unedited version (Mar. 2, 2012), *supra* note 12 Annex I, ¶ 250.

[345] *See* CUSTOMARY INTERNATIONAL HUMANITARIAN LAW, *supra* note 42 at Rule 115 (Disposal of the Dead).

determine whether Qadhafi was killed during fighting or was executed.[346] In addition, the ICC encouraged the NTC to investigate the killing in the interests of justice and to set the correct precedent,[347] and Amnesty International and other human rights organizations also called for investigations into this matter and stated that the NTC must apply the same standards of accountability to everyone to ensure that justice is applied equally.[348]

In response to external pressure, the Libyan government announced that it would conduct investigations, but no details were given as to who would carry them out.[349] Mahmud Jibril, the head of the NTC, suggested that Qadhafi had been shot in the crossfire between loyalists and *thuwar* forces,[350] and NTC officials also maintained that most Libyans would have preferred to see Qadhafi stand trial, but it is believed that Jibril's followers wanted to prevent this at all costs as they feared being implicated in past crimes.[351]

For their part, the Qadhafi family issued a statement insisting that NATO's role in the death of Qadhafi should be the focus of an investigation. According to the lawyer representing the Qadhafi family, NATO was responsible for "willful killing" in contravention of the Geneva Convention.[352] The family further announced its intention to submit the case before the ICC.[353] In December 2011, the Office of the Prosecutor (OTP) of the ICC, announced that it would allow the Libyan transitional authorities to manage the investigations of Qadhafi's death, and that it would

---

[346] Sarah Posner, *UN rights office calls for investigation into Gaddafi killing*, JURIST, Oct. 21, 2011, available at http://jurist.org/paperchase/2011/10/un-rights-office-calls-for-investigation-into-gaddafi-killing.php.

[347] *Gaddafi's death may be war crime: ICC prosecutor*, REUTERS, Dec. 16, 2011, *available at* http://www.reuters.com/article/2011/12/16/us-libya-icc-idUSTRE7BF0882011216.

[348] *Libya urged to investigate whether al-Gaddafi death was a war crime*, AMNESTY INTERNATIONAL, Oct. 21, 2011, *available at* http://www.amnesty.org/en/news-and-updates/libya-urged-investigate-whether-al-gaddafi-death-was-war-crime-2011-10-21.

[349] *Libyan authorities announce Gaddafi death investigation*, BBC, Oct. 24, 2011, *available at* http://www.bbc.co.uk/news/world-africa-15435281.

[350] Vivienne Walt, *How Did Gaddafi Die? A Year Later, Unanswered Questions and Bad Blood*, TIME WORLD, Oct. 18, 2012, *available at* http://world.time.com/2012/10/18/how-did-gaddafi-die-a-year-later-unanswered-questions-and-bad-blood; *Libyan government orders probe into Gaddafi's death*, THE WASHINGTON POST, Oct. 25, 2011, *available at* http://www.washingtonpost.com/world/middle_east/libya-to-investigate-gaddafis-death/2011/10/24/gIQAjuQtCM_story.html.

[351] Roberts, *War crimes court leaves Gadhafi probe to Libya, supra* note 275.

[352] *Gaddafi Dead: Family May File War Crimes Complaint*, HUFFINGTON POST, Oct. 26, 2011, *available at* http://www.huffingtonpost.com/2011/10/26/gaddafi-dead-war-crimes-family_n_1033458.html.

[353] *Col. Gaddafi's family French lawyer to sue NATO through ICC*, DIGITAL JOURNAL, Oct. 29, 2011, *available at* http://digitaljournal.com/article/313579#ixzz27Ui0FkMa.

determine at a later time whether it would conduct its own investigation,[354] stating "The Office of the Prosecutor will review such activities and make its findings public in May 2012 during the prosecutor's second report to the United Nations Security Council."[355]

(b) Developments Related to Qadhafi's Family and Inner-Circle

This section examines the cases of three of the most identifiable senior members of the Qadhafi regime. The three individuals, Saif al-Islam Qadhafi, 'Abdullah al-Senussi and Musa Kusa, were all at the highest echelons of the Qadhafi government, the former as *de facto* prime minister, and the later two as senior intelligence and security officials. As such, they played a central role in shaping and carrying out Qadhafi's policies and bear significant responsibility for the regime's violations.[356] These three individuals have generated the most international attention as a result of the pending ICC cases against Saif al-Islam and Senussi, as well as the notoriety of Senussi and Musa Kusa stemming from their suspected roles in historical acts of international terrorism.

To be certain, there were other individuals who were highly influential in the regime, particularly Qadhafi's children, some of whom were killed during the conflict or fled after the toppling of the regime. In addition to Saif al-Islam, a number of Qadhafi's other sons held key military and political positions. As mentioned above, Khamis Qadhafi commanded the Khamis 32nd Katiba, an elite brigade that played a central role in the regime's response to the February 2011 protests and subsequent fighting during the conflict.[357] Reports of the death of Khamis surfaced on several separate occasions, including during fighting in Bani Walid in October 2012.[358] Mu'tassim served as national security advisor of the National Security Council (NSC), which functioned as a interlocutor between the

---

[354] Roberts, *War crimes court leaves Gadhafi probe to Libya, supra* note 275.

[355] *Id.*

[356] *See supra* Sec. 1.

[357] For information on Khamis, *see* Ch. I, Sec 9.1, 10.3 & 11.1; Ch. II, Sec. 2.1, 2.1, 3.2 & 3.3.

[358] Libya's national congress spokesman, Omar Hamdan, reported that Khamis was killed in battle in Bani Walid on Oct. 20, 2012, exactly a year after the death of Mu'ammar Qadhafi. *See Khamis Gaddafi 'killed during fighting in Bani Walid'*, THE GUARDIAN, Oct. 20, 2012, *available at* http://www.guardian.co.uk/world/2012/oct/20/khamis-gaddafi-killed-bani-walid-muammar. *See also Gaddafi family Tree*, BBC, Oct. 20, 2011, *available at* http://www.bbc.co.uk/news/world-africa-12531442.

political and military bodies.[359] Sa'adi commanded the regime's special forces' units that were deployed and involved in the repression of demonstrations during the 2011 conflict.[360] After Sa'adi fled Tripoli in September 2011, Interpol issued a red notice for his arrest in response to a request by the NTC.[361] Sa'adi eventually took shelter in Niger, where he has resided since, despite repeated extradition attempts by Libya.[362] Other family members include his sons Muhammed and Hannibal, who fled to Algeria along with their sister 'A'isha on 29 August 2011.[363] The three later moved to Oman, where they reside as of June 2013.[364]

In addition to the powerful Qadhafi family, a number of former regime officials were captured in the wake of the conflict or extradited from other countries and few have faced charges in Libya.[365]

i. Saif al-Islam Qadhafi

Saif was the second son of Mu'ammar Qadhafi, and was seen by many in Libya and by the international community as the likely successor. Although he had for years declared that he was not a member of government, Saif was a prominent figure in diplomatic matters and represented the Qadhafi regime in in diplomatic exchanges. Most notably, he engaged in negotiations with western governments over critically important matters such as the Lockerbie bombing settlement and agreements over Libya's WMD program. Having been educated in the west and comfortable in diplomatic circles, Saif proved to play a central role in ushering in

---

[359] Mu'tassim was killed along with his father in October 2011. *See supra* Sec. 6.3(a). For more on Mu'tassim and his role in the regime, *see* Ch. I, Sec. 10.3, 12, Ch. II, Sec. 2.2, Ch. IV, Sec. 6.3(b) & Ch. VII, Sec. 2.

[360] For more on Sa'adi, *see* Ch. II, Sec. 1. *See also* Resolution Measures, *supra* note 188.

[361] *INTERPOL issues Red Notice for Assaadi Gaddafi at Libya's request*, INTERPOL, Sept. 29, 2011, *available at* http://www.interpol.int/News-and-media/News-media-releases/2011/PR080.

[362] Sudarsan Raghavan, *Niger Resists Libyan demands for extradition of Moammar Gaddafi's playboy son*, THE WASHINGTON POST, July 3, 2012, *available at* http://articles.washingtonpost.com/2012-07-03/world/35489060_1_gaddafi-loyalists-saif-al-islam-gaddafi-moammar-gaddafi.

[363] Luke Harding, *Gaddafi's family escape Libya net to cross into Algeria*, THE GUARDIAN, Aug. 29, 2011, *available at* http://www.guardian.co.uk/world/2011/aug/29/gaddafi-family-escape-libya-algeria.

[364] Henry Samuel and Nabila Ramdan, *Gaddafi's daughter thrown out of Algeria after she 'set fire to presidential residence'*, THE TELEGRAPH, Apr. 2, 2013, *available at* http://www.telegraph.co.uk/news/worldnews/africaandindianocean/libya/9967203/Gaddafis-daughter-thrown-out-of-Algeria-after-she-set-fire-to-presidential-residence.html.

[365] For more on these cases, *see infra* Sec. 6.3.

the era of rapprochement with the West, during which time he engaged with western officials over security, political and diplomatic matters.[366]

The ICC warrant for the arrest of Saif al-Islam Qadhafi states that although Saif al-Islam did not have an official position in the regime, he was Mu'ammar Qadhafi's "unspoken successor and the most influential person within his inner circle and... exercised control over crucial parts of the State apparatus, including finances and logistics and had the powers of a de facto Prime Minister." The ICC investigations also found that, along with his father, Saif al-Islam "conceived and orchestrated a plan to deter and quell, by all means, the civilian demonstrations against Gaddafi's regime."[367]

Saif al-Islam went into hiding after the fall of Tripoli in August 2011, and was detained on 19 November by members from the Zintan Katiba near the southwestern desert town of 'Ubari, in the Fezzan region. The Zintan fighters reportedly were acting on a tip they received a month before and intercepted two cars carrying Saif al-Islam, who they believed was trying to secure passage into neighboring Niger.[368] After being captured, Saif al-Islam was taken to a nearby airbase and flown to the headquarters of the Zintan Katiba, in the Nafusa Mountains.[369] The capture of Saif al-Islam sparked enthusiastic reactions across Libya.[370] Since his capture, the case of Saif al-Islam has generated considerable attention and sparked discussion about whether Libya's legal system has the capacity to carry out fair legal proceedings against such a high-profile former leader of the Qadhafi regime.[371]

The Zintan Katiba took Saif al-Islam to an undisclosed location in Zintan, stating that it was for his own protection, and that the interim government was unable to protect him from *thuwar* groups eager to see him suffer the same fate of his father.[372] The Zintan fighters also told reporters

---

[366] For background on Saif al-Islam, *see* Ch. I, Secs. 10.3, 10.4, 11.2 & 12.

[367] *Warrant of Arrest for Saif Al-Islam Gaddafi, supra* note 183.

[368] *How Saif al-Islam was captured*, BBC, Nov. 20, 2011, *available at* http://www.bbc.co.uk/news/world-middle-east-15805583.

[369] *Timeline: Saif al-Islam detained, say officials*, REUTERS, Nov. 19, 2011, *available at* http://www.reuters.com/article/2011/11/19/us-libya-events-idUSTRE7AI0HV20111119.

[370] Francois Murphy, Janet Lawrence & Jon Boyle, *From east to west, Libyans cheer Gaddafi capture*, REUTERS, Nov. 19, 2011, *available at* http://www.reuters.com/article/2011/11/19/us-libya-saif-mood-idUSTRE7AI0QY20111119.

[371] For more on the legal proceedings against Saif al-Islam, *see* Sec. 6.3(b)(i).

[372] Oliver Holmes & Philippa Fletcher, *Zintan's hold on Saif al-Islam reflects Libya divisions*, REUTERS, Nov. 20, 2011, *available at* http://www.reuters.com/article/2011/11/21/us-libya-zintan-idUSTRE7AK0872011121.

that they were bound by a 200-year-old tribal agreement between the Zintan tribe and the Qadhadhfa tribe, to which Saif al-Islam belonged, to guarantee his protection as a prisoner of war. Zintan fighters also reported that Saif al-Islam had requested to be detained in Zintan.[373]

Photos taken after his capture reveal that Saif al-Islam had a bandaged hand when he was transferred to Zintan, an injury he said he had sustained in a NATO strike a month before his capture.[374] When a picture of his bandaged hand was released, rumors spread that his captors had cut-off his fingers as punishment for remarks he made on television threatening the rebels and made menacing hand gestures.[375] Notwithstanding these theories, a Ukrainian doctor in Zintan who treated Saif al-Islam reported that the injuries appeared to predate his captivity and that amputation was necessary because the wound had become infected.[376]

Saif al-Islam's continued custody by the Zintan Katiba caused significant consternation by the international community, who expressed concern over his treatment. In response to these concerns, then-Prime Minister 'Abd al-Rahman Keib stated in November 2011 that although Saif al-Islam was not in government custody he was receiving the best possible treatment.[377] A HRW delegation interviewed Saif al-Islam on 18 December 2011,[378] and Saif al-Islam told them that he was being treated in a fair manner, had not suffered abuse, and had been seen by a doctor on a weekly basis. He confirmed that he had had an operation on his hand, which he confirmed had been injured in a NATO strike in October near Bani Walid in which 26 members of his convoy had been killed.[379] Saif further indicated that the injury indirectly lead to his arrest because members of the *thuwar* forces received information that he was seeking

---

[373] *Id.*

[374] BBC, *How Saif al-Islam was captured, supra* note 368.

[375] *Gaddafi son needs surgery on gangrenous fingers: doctor*, REUTERS, Nov. 24, 2011, *available at* http://www.reuters.com/article/2011/11/24/us-libya-saif-health-idUSTRE7AN1VW 20111124; *Gaddafi's son had fingers 'cut off'*, THE AUSTRALIAN, Nov. 24, 2011, *available at* http://www.theaustralian.com.au/news/world/gaddafis-son-had-fingers-cut-off/story-e6frg6so-1226204095145.

[376] *Saif al-Islam's gangrenous fingers need amputating*, THE TELEGRAPH, Nov. 25, 2011, *available at* http://www.telegraph.co.uk/news/worldnews/africaandindianocean/libya/8916912/Saif-al-Islams-gangrenous-fingers-need-amputating.html; *Gaddafi son needs surgery on gangrenous fingers: doctor*, REUTERS, Nov. 24, 2011, *available at* http://www.reuters.com/article/2011/11/24/us-libya-saif-health-idUSTRE7AN1VW20111124.

[377] *ICC backs down on Saif Gadhafi trial demand*, CNN, Nov. 23, 2011, *available at* http://edition.cnn.com/2011/11/23/world/africa/libya-icc/index.html.

[378] *Libya: Ensure Gaddafi's Son Access to Lawyer*, HUMAN RIGHTS WATCH, Dec. 21, 2011, *available at* http://www.hrw.org/news/2011/12/21/libya-ensure-gaddafi-son-s-access-lawyer.

[379] *Id.*

medical treatment in Fezzan, and that he was intercepted on his way to the doctor.[380] Saif al-Islam did complain that he had been kept in isolation, denied access to family and friends, and that he needed help arranging legal representation.[381] HRW urged the interim authorities to provide Saif al-Islam with immediate access to a lawyer.[382] Despite these claims, then Interior Minister Fawzi 'Abd Al-'Al claimed in February 2012 that Saif al-Islam had not asked for a lawyer, and that if he requested one, he/she would be provided.[383]

His arrest prompted an on-going debate over the best means of holding Saif al-Islam accountable for his conduct during the conflict. At the time there was an arrest warrant pending from the ICC, and according to later filings by the Libyan government at the Court, Libyan investigators and prosecutors started working on the case immediately after his detention. International actors and human rights groups raised concerns over whether the Libyan justice system was capable of providing a fair trial that would satisfy the standards of international law,[384] and the ICC called for Saif al-Islam's transfer to The Hague.[385] Although Libya is not a party to the Rome Statute, international law requires the Libyan authorities to cooperate with the ICC according to the terms of UN Security Resolution 1970, which is binding on all states.[386] Despite this, NTC authorities repeatedly said they would not hand over Saif al-Islam and would instead ensure a fair trial in Libya,[387] although at the time they did not have physical custody over him, and to date they have been unable to secure his transfer from the control of the Zintan Katiba.

Libyan officials reported that they were gathering witnesses and documents to build a case against Saif al-Islam, and in April 2012, then Justice Minister 'Ali Ahmayda 'Ashur told reporters that the trial of Saif would

---

[380] *Id.*

[381] *Id.*

[382] *Id.*

[383] *Hand over Saif Gadhafi, court tells Libya*, CNN, Apr. 5, 2012, *available at* http://articles.cnn.com/2012-04-05/africa/world_africa_libya-saif-gadhafi_1_moammar-gadhafi-saif-al-islam-gadhafi-zintan.

[384] Marie-Louise Gumuchian, *Libya says building case against Gaddafi son: ICC prosecutor*, REUTERS, Apr. 21, 2012, *available at* http://www.reuters.com/article/2012/04/21/us-libya-icc-idUSBRE83K09J20120421.

[385] *UPDATE 2-Gaddafi's son will get fair trial – Libyan PM*, REUTERS, Nov. 19, 2011, *available at* http://www.reuters.com/article/2011/11/19/libya-saif-pm-idUSL5E7MJ1062011119.

[386] *Libya and the ICC: What Next?*, OPEN SOCIETY FOUNDATIONS, Nov. 21, 2011, *available at* http://www.opensocietyfoundations.org/voices/libya-and-icc-what-next.

[387] Francois Murphy, *Libya will try Gaddafi's son fairly: ICC prosecutor*, REUTERS, Nov. 24, 2011, *available at* http://www.reuters.com/article/2011/11/24/us-libya-icc-idUSTRE7ANoQY20111124.

be fair and transparent, and in accordance with international laws and standards.[388] The Minister further said that Saif al-Islam would be transferred from Zintan to Tripoli to stand trial in Tripoli, where he would be charged under Libyan law with wasting of public funds and violations of killing, torture, rape and incitement to such acts.[389] This has not happened through June 2013, and Saif remains in detention in Zintan under the control of the Zintan Katiba.

The Libyan government filed an appeal to the ICC on 30 April 2012, challenging the ICC's jurisdiction over the case.[390] Libya's "admissibility challenge" of the case before the ICC maintains that the Libyan judiciary is competent to satisfactorily prosecute Saif al-Islam, and that is has jurisdictional priority over the ICC under the terms of the complementarity principle.[391] The Libyan submission declared that the national proceedings were consistent with the Libyan government's commitment to post-conflict transitional justice and national reconciliation. The submission also emphasized the significance of the trial for the Libyan people, stating that "To deny the Libyan people this historic opportunity to eradicate the long-standing culture of impunity would be manifestly inconsistent with [the purpose of ICC principles] which accords primacy to national judicial systems."[392] In June 2012 the ICC ruled that Saif al-Islam could stay in detention in Libya while the court decided if it has the jurisdiction to try him.[393]

During the course of the jurisdictional struggle before the ICC, the Libyan authorities agreed to provide Saif al-Islam with access to ICC-appointed defense lawyers, and an ICC delegation from the Office of the Public Council for Defense (OPCD) met with him in detention on 3 March 2012.

---

[388] *Libya appeals ICC to secure Saif Al-Islam trial here*, LIBYA HERALD, Apr. 29, 2012, *available at* http://www.libyaherald.com/libya-appeals-icc-to-secure-saif-qaddafi-trial-here.

[389] *Id.* For more on the difficulties of obtaining custody over Saif al-Islam, *see* Vivienne Walt, *Libya's Disaster of Justice: The Case of Saif al-Islam Gaddafi Reveals a Country in Chaos*, Time, June 28, 2013, *available at* http://world.time.com/2013/06/28/libyas-disaster-of-justice-the-case-of-saif-al-islam-gaddafi-reveals-a-country-in-chaos/#ixzz2YdNkb6oK.

[390] Gumuchian, *Libya says building case against Gaddafi son: ICC prosecutor, supra* note 384.

[391] For more on this issue, *see infra* Sec. 6.2. *Libya appeals ICC to secure Saif Al-Islam trial here, supra* note 388.

[392] Owen Bowcott, *Saif Gaddafi should go on trial in Libya, war crimes tribunal told*, THE GUARDIAN, May 1, 2012, *available at* http://www.guardian.co.uk/world/2012/may/01/saif-gadaffi-trial-libya-icc.

[393] Ali Shuaib & Hadeel Al Shalchi, *ICC lawyer meeting Gaddafi son detained in Libya*, REUTERS, June 9, 2012, *available at* http://www.reuters.com/article/2012/06/09/us-libya-icc-idUSBRE8580FH20120609.

The delegation included ICC appointed defense counsel Melinda Taylor, and another undisclosed official. The OPCD submitted a document on 5 March to the PTC detailing observations from their meeting with Saif al-Islam. The document stated that Saif al-Islam was attacked by individuals from Misrata during the beginning of his detention, but that the Zintan Commander had intervened to protect him.[394] The Libyan government later denied reports of this attack.[395] Affirming the report from HRW, the OPCD report also stated that Saif al-Islam had asked for legal representation, but that the Libyan government said that it was impossible for a lawyer to come to Zintan.[396]

In June 2012, a delegation of the ICC defense team again travelled to Libya to meet with Saif al-Islam. The delegation again included Melinda Taylor, along with Alexander Khodakov, Esteban Peralta Losilla and translator Helene Assaf. During the visit Melinda Taylor was accused of carrying suspicious documents for Saif al-Islam, and the delegation was detained in Zintan and transferred to a prison on 10 June.[397] The detention, and the circumstances under which it took place, led to an international fiasco. The ICC and NATO, among other members of the international community, expressed concerns for the delegation's safety and called for their release, arguing that the four international civil servants had immunity when on an official ICC mission.[398] Libya's prosecutor-general in charge of the Saif al-Islam case, Milad 'Abd al-Nabi, rejected this, stating that the Taylor should have disclosed the materials to the prosecutor-general's office before taking them into the cell.[399]

In the face of outside criticism, Al Ajmi Ali Ahmed al Atiri,[400] the head of the Zintan Brigade, told reporters that the conduct of the ICC delegates warranted their detention, as they had been caught with "spying and recording" materials during a search. Al Atiri claimed that the ICC

---

[394] *Situation in Libya*, Case No. ICC-01/11-01/11, Public Redacted Addendum to the Urgent Report Concerning the Visit to Libya OPCD (Int'l Crim. Ct., Mar 5, 2012).

[395] Marie-Louise Gumuchian, *Wrangling hampers Libyan drive to try Gaddafi son*, REUTERS, Apr. 29, 2012, *available at* http://www.reuters.com/article/2012/04/29/us-libya-saif-idUSBRE83S06K20120429.

[396] *Public Redacted Addendum to the Urgent Report Concerning the Visit to Libya OPCD*, *supra* note 394.

[397] *ICC delegation visits colleagues held in Zintan, Libya*, BBC, June 12, 2012, *available at* http://www.bbc.co.uk/news/world-africa-18419756.

[398] Shuaib & Al Shalchi, *ICC lawyer meeting Gaddafi son detained in Libya*, *supra* note 393.

[399] *Id.*

[400] The transliteration of this name was adopted from the reference. *Id.*

delegates had a letter written in English that they wanted Saif al-Islam to sign requesting his transfer to the ICC. The Zintan Brigade also claimed that when they searched Taylor they found correspondence between Saif al-Islam and his assistant Muhammed Ismail.[401]

The ICC promised to investigate any claims of wrongdoing by its staff upon their release and to impose "appropriate sanctions" if necessary.[402] On 2 July 2012 the delegates were released, which prompted the President of the ICC to offer an apology to the Libyan authorities for the "difficulties" caused by the mission, thanked them agreeing to release the delegates and expressed his relief that the ICC staff members were well treated during their detention.[403]

On 16 August 2012 the Libyan justice minister, Ahmad al-Jahani, declared that Saif al-Islam would be tried in September 2012 in Zintan.[404] However, on 8 October 2012 the Libyan prosecutor-general's office declared that the trial of Saif al-Islam would be postponed by five months in order to take account of the testimony of 'Abdullah al-Senussi.[405]

Members of Qadhafi's immediate family challenged the national efforts to prosecute Saif al-Islam. In January 2012, Saif's sister 'A'isha applied to the PTC requesting the right to intervene as an *amicus curiae*.[406] In her application, 'A'isha claimed to be in possession of confidential information demonstrating that the Libyan government was unable to provide Saif al-Islam with a fair trial and effective legal representation.[407] On 2 February 2012, the PTC rejected the applications for leave to submit the *amicus curiae* observations by 'A'isha Qadhafi, as well as subsequent requests for leave to appeal the decision.[408]

The admissibility challenge before the ICC continued until 31 May 2013, when the PTC rejected Libya's admissibility challenge on the grounds that

---

[401] *Id.*

[402] *Libya ICC lawyer Melinda Taylor and colleagues fly out*, BBC, July 2, 2012, *available at* http://www.bbc.co.uk/news/world-africa-18683786.

[403] *Id.*

[404] *Libya*, MAX PLANCK INSTITUTE FOR COMPARATIVE PUBLIC LAW AND INTERNATIONAL LAW, *available at* http://www.mpil.de/ww/en/pub/research/details/know_transfer/consti tutional_reform_in_arab_/libyen.cfm.

[405] *Id.*

[406] *Situation in Libya*, Case No. ICC-01/11-01/11, Application on behalf of Aisha Gaddafi for leave to submit amicus curiae observations concerning her brother – Saif al-Islam Gaddafi (Int'l Crim. Ct., Jan. 31, 2012).

[407] *Id.*

[408] *Situation in Libya*, Case No. ICC-01/11-01/11, Decision on the Application of Mishana Hosseinioun and Aisha Gaddafi to submit Amicus Curiae observations to the Chamber, (Int'l Crim. Ct., Feb. 2, 2012).

the case it was pursuing against Saif al-Islam was not the same as the one before the ICC, and that Libya was unable to genuinely prosecute him for a number of reasons, including the government's inability to secure his custody, ensure the protection of defense witnesses and secure adequate legal representation.[409]

Shortly thereafter, on 17 June 2013, the Libyan prosecution authority announced that it would begin proceedings against Saif al-Islam in August, in clear contravention of the PTC decision.[410]

ii. 'Abdullah al-Senussi

'Abdullah al-Senussi is one of the most recognizable figures from the Qadhafi era. He is connected by marriage to the Qadhafi family, and was a close colleague of Mu'ammar Qadhafi going back to the 1970s.[411] He was known as Qadhafi's "right-hand man" and given the name the "executioner" for his role as head of the Internal Security Agency (ISA), which was responsible for internal intelligence and national security matters.[412] As a close confidant of Qadhafi, Senussi was integral to the operation of the regime's internal and external security affairs.[413]

Senussi was significantly responsible for organizing and operating the Qadhafi regime's machinery of internal repression. He has been accused of overseeing the internal security forces that were responsible for carrying out acts of torture and assassination of real and perceived political opponents of the Qadhafi regime, including the notorious Abu Salim Prison massacre.[414] Externally, he has been implicated in acts of international terrorism, including the 1988 Lockerbie bombing and 1989

---

[409] Decision on the admissibility of the case against Saif Al-Islam Gaddafi, *supra* note 130.

[410] *Saif al-Islam Gaddafi to be tried in Libya in August*, BBC, June 17, 2013, *available at* http://www.bbc.co.uk/news/world-africa-22945159.

[411] *See also* Mattes, *Challenges to Security Sector Governance in the Middle East, supra* note 187 at 15–16.

[412] *Prosecutor's Application Pursuant to Article 58 as to Muammar Mohammed Abu Minyar GADDAFI, Saif Al-Islam GADDAFI and Abdullah AL-SENUSSI, supra* note 273.

[413] Luke Harding, Ian Black, Severin Carrell & Chris Stephen, *Abdullah al Senussi: spy with secrets of Lockerbie bombing sent back to Libya*, THE GUARDIAN, Sept. 5, 2012, *available at* http://www.guardian.co.uk/world/2012/sep/05/abdullah-al-senussi-lockerbie-libya; *Libyan ex-spy chief Abdullah al-Senussi held in Tripoli*, BBC, Sept. 5, 2012, *available at* http://www.bbc.co.uk/news/world-africa-19497390; Ian Black, *Abdullah al-Senussi: a trial of strength between the ICC and Tripoli*, THE GUARDIAN, Sept. 5, 2012, *available at* http://www.guardian.co.uk/world/2012/sep/05/abdullah-senussi-trial-icc-tripoli.

[414] David D. Kirkpatrick, *Spy Chief for Qaddafi Is Extradited to Libya*, N.Y. TIMES, Sept. 5, 2012, *available at* http://www.nytimes.com/2012/09/06/world/africa/senussi-qaddafi-spy-chief-is-extradited-to-libya.html.

bombing of French UTA flight 772.[415] He was also increasingly important diplomatically as time passed, including being responsible for discussions and meetings with U.S. officials over regional security matters after the normalization of relations with the West.[416]

In his capacity as head of the ISA Senussi took a lead role in the Qadhafi regime's response to the demonstrations in February 2011.[417] Because of his conduct, the PTC of the ICC issued a warrant of arrest for Senussi on 27 June 2001, for his "alleged criminal responsibility for the commission of murder and persecution of civilians as crimes against humanity from 15 February 2011 onwards throughout Libya."[418] According to the ICC arrest warrant, Senussi was a key figure in the government campaign of violence and had exercised his authority to command Libya's forces to attack civilian demonstrators. In particular, it is alleged that Senussi was responsible for the acts of violence carried out in Benghazi, where he had been deployed before the uprising in an attempt to pressure organizers into cancelling the planned "Day of Rage" protests.[419] According to the ICC arrest warrant, Qadhafi met regularly with Senussi and Saif al-Islam to "plan the repression of the protests."[420] After receiving instructions from Qadhafi, Senussi transmitted orders and directed the coordination of the security forces in Benghazi, and "expressly ordered the shooting at civilians."[421] The ICC arrest warrant concludes that "murders constituting crimes against humanity were committed from 15 February 2011 until at least 20 February 2011 by Security Forces under the command of Abdullah Al-Senussi, as part of the attack against the civilian demonstrators or alleged dissidents to Gaddafi's regime."[422]

---

[415] *See* Ch. I, Sec. 11.2.

[416] This included meetings with United States Special Envoy Scott Gration over peace-process initiatives in the Sudan in 2009. *See* U.S. Embassy in Tripoli, Confidential Cable, *SE Gration's Meeting with Abdulla Sanussi on Rebel Unification Efforts*, Nov. 1, 2009, *available at* http://www.telegraph.co.uk/news/wikileaks-files/libya-wikileaks/8294672/SE-GRATIONS-MEETING-WITH-ABDULLA-SANUSSI-ON-REBEL-UNIFICATION-EFFORTS-TRIPOLI-00000873-001.2-OF-002.html.

[417] For history of Senussi, his role as head of the Internal Security Agency (ISA), *see* Ch. I, 9.1, 10.4, 11.2 & Ch. II, Sec. 2.2.

[418] *Warrant of Arrest for Abdullah Al-Senussi, supra* note 326.

[419] *See* Ch. II, Secs. 1. *See also* ALISON PARGETER, LIBYA: THE RISE AND FALL OF QADDAFI 219 (New Haven, USA: Yale University Press, 2012).

[420] *Prosecutor's Application Pursuant to Article 58 as to Muammar Mohammed Abu Minyar GADDAFI, Saif Al-Islam GADDAFI and Abdullah AL-SENUSSI, supra* note 273.

[421] *Id.*

[422] *Warrant of Arrest for Abdullah Al-Senussi, supra* note 326.

Senussi went into hiding in August 2011 and fled Tripoli while it was under a final assault by the *thuwar* forces. In mid-march 2012 he was apprehended in Mauritania, reportedly with the assistance of French intelligence services.[423] French authorities had sought Senussi since a French court tried and convicted Senussi *in absentia* in 1999 for his role in the French UTA airliner bombing that killed 170 people in 1989.[424] Because of his alleged role in the UTA incident, as well as the 1988 bombing of Pan Am Flight 103 over Lockerbie, several governments had on-going interest in questioning Senussi, and when he was flushed out of Libya they were able to track him down and facilitate his capture.[425]

At the time of his capture, Senussi was being sought by both Libya and the ICC, resulting in complicated wrangling over which had jurisdictional primacy, a process that took months to resolve. According to Senussi, he was questioned by government officials from the United States, Saudi Arabia, and Lebanon during his detention in Mauritania.[426] According to his reports to HRW, FBI agents questioned him on two occasions during his detention.[427] As indicated above, both the ICC and the Libyan government sought Senussi's surrender, and after many months Mauritanian officials determined that he should be extradited to Libya to face prosecution there.[428] On 5 September 2012, Senussi was deported from Mauritania to Libya and taken to a detention center in Tripoli where he awaits trial.[429]

After his extradition to Libya, Senussi was held in the Al-Habda detention center in Tripoli, along with a number of officials from the Qadhafi regime.[430] HRW representatives visited Senussi in detention in April 2013,

---

[423] Kirkpatrick, *Spy Chief for Qaddafi Is Extradited to Libya, supra* note 414.

[424] Paul Reynolds, *UTA 772: The Forgotten Flight*, BBC, Aug. 19, 2003, *available at* http://news.bbc.co.uk/2/hi/uk_news/3163621.stm.

[425] Severine Carrell & Chris Stephen, *Abdullah al Senussi extradition unites Lockerbie relatives*, THE GUARDIAN, Sept. 5, 2012, *available at* http://www.guardian.co.uk/uk/2012/sep/05/abdullah-senussi-extradition-lockerbie-relatives. For more on Senussi's alleged role in the French UTA airliner and Lockerbie bombings, *see* Ch. I, Sec. 11.2.

[426] *Libya: Ensure Abdallah Sanussi Access to Lawyer*, HUMAN RIGHTS WATCH, Apr. 17, 2013, *available at* http://www.hrw.org/news/2013/04/17/libya-ensure-abdallah-sanussi-access-lawyer.

[427] *Id.*

[428] Kirkpatrick, *Spy Chief for Qaddafi Is Extradited to Libya, supra* note 414.

[429] *Libyan ex-spy chief Abdullah al-Senussi held in Tripoli*, BBC, Sept. 5, 2012, *available at* http://www.bbc.co.uk/news/world-africa-19497390; Ian Black, *Abdullah al-Senussi: a trial of strength between the ICC and Tripoli*, THE GUARDIAN, Sept. 5, 2012, *available at* http://www.guardian.co.uk/world/2012/sep/05/abdullah-senussi-trial-icc-tripoli.

[430] HUMAN RIGHTS WATCH, *Libya: Ensure Abdallah Sanussi Access to Lawyer, supra* note 426.

and found that he had neither been given access to a lawyer, nor been formally notified of the charges against him.[431] When confronted with these statements, Libya's Justice Minister Salah Marghani told HRW that Senussi had the right to a lawyer of his choosing, and stated "Libya is committed to provid[ing] a fair trial."[432] As of May 2013, Senussi remains in detention in Al-Habda awaiting trial or surrender to the ICC.[433]

As indicated above, Senussi was one of three individuals for whom the ICC PTC issued an arrest warrant. Despite his six-month detention in Tripoli, the Libyan government refused to comply with the ICC arrest warrant, and on 6 February 2013, the PTC found that Libya was still under obligation to comply with the existing arrest warrant and surrender Senussi to the ICC, just as it was under the obligation to surrender Saif al-Islam Qadhafi.[434] Libya, however, has rejected the ICC's orders and has reiterated its intent to prosecute Senussi domestically. To that end, the Libyan government formally challenged the admissibility of the case before the ICC on 2 April 2013.[435] The question of domestic prosecutions is not merely academic, as many continue to demand justice for his alleged role in the 1996 Abu Salim prison massacre, at which time he oversaw the internal security of the country,[436] as well as his numerous alleged acts of political violence. Notwithstanding the difficulties posed by domestic prosecutions, the political will to see Senussi tried in Libya for past crimes is strong.

---

[431] *Id.* The CoI has also noted that according to the Libyan Code of Criminal Procedure, detainees can only be held for 48 hours before transfer to the General Prosecution who determines either to release detainees or to place them in pre-trial detention. For certain crimes, the period of detention before transfer to the General Prosecution can be extended to 7 days. Article 30 of the code apparently requires an arrest warrant in instances where a suspect is not detained *en flagranti*. According to Libyan law, suspects only have the right to see a lawyer once they are transferred to the General Prosecution. *See* Report of the International Commission of Inquiry, advance unedited version (Mar. 2, 2012), *supra* note 12 at ¶ 259.

[432] HUMAN RIGHTS WATCH, *Libya: Ensure Abdallah Sanussi Access to Lawyer, supra* note 426.

[433] *May 2013 Monthly Forecast*, UN SECURITY COUNCIL REPORT, May 2013, *available at* http://www.securitycouncilreport.org/monthly-forecast/2013-05/libya_4.php.

[434] *ICC: Libya's Bids to Try Gaddafi, Sanussi*, HUMAN RIGHTS WATCH, May 13, 2013, *available at* http://www.hrw.org/news/2013/05/13/qa-libya-and-international-criminal-court.

[435] HUMAN RIGHTS WATCH, *Libya: Ensure Abdallah Sanussi Access to Lawyer, supra* note 426.

[436] For history of Senussi, his role as head of the Internal Security Agency (ISA), and the Abu Salim affair, *see* Ch. I, Sec. 10.4 & 11.2, and Ch. II, Secs. 1 & 2.2. *See also Libya: Abu Salim Prison Massacre Remembered*, HUMAN RIGHTS WATCH, June 27, 2012, *available at* http://www.hrw.org/news/2012/06/27/libya-abu-salim-prison-massacre-remembered.

The politics of prosecuting Senussi are complicated, however. Due to his history and alleged involvement in international acts of terrorism, any trial of Senussi is incredibly sensitive. The prosecution of Senussi would inevitably result in the release of details about the inner-workings of Qadhafi's security apparatus and heretofore-unknown facts regarding past acts of terrorism.

iii. *Musa Kusa*

Musa Kusa was one of the most powerful and well known figures of the Qadhafi regime. A committed Qadhafi loyalist, Kusa was and career intelligence officer who directed The External Security Agency (ESA),[437] Libya's foreign security agency, from September 1994[438] until March 2009.[439] Officially part of the State's Jamahiriyya Security Organization (JSO), the ESA was best known for supporting terrorist groups and orchestrating state-sponsored acts of terrorism.[440] By the time Kusa was appointed Chief of the ESA in 1994, he already had developed a reputation for targeting dissidents abroad for assassination and was wanted for questioning for his role in Libyan acts of terrorism, including the 1989 bombing of the French airliner UTA 772 in Niger.[441]

During the thaw with the West that started after 2000, Kusa played an important role, along with Saif al-Islam Qadhafi, in negotiations with the West over Libya's WMD program. In the process, he developed close ties with western government officials.[442] As part of the so-called war on terror, Kusa collaborated with U.S. and UK intelligence officials in counter-terrorism activities, and fostered close relationships with MI6 and CIA officials.[443] After the start of the revolution in February 2011, Kusa remained

---

[437] The CoI refers to the foreign intelligence services as the External Security Agency (ESA), while other sources refer to it as the External Security Organization (ESO).

[438] U.S. Central Intelligence Agency, secret cable, *Terrorism Review*, COUNTERTER-RORIST CENTER, June 1995, *available at* http://www.foia.cia.gov/docs/DOC_0000918468/ DOC_0000918468.pdf.

[439] Report of the International Commission of Inquiry (Jan. 12, 2012), *supra* note 57 at ¶ 40.

[440] *Libya, Intelligence*, Haiat amn al Jamahiriya – *Jamahiriya Security Organization*, GLOBAL SECURITY.ORG, *available at* http://www.globalsecurity.org/intell/world/libya/jso.htm.

[441] U.S. Central Intelligence Agency, secret cable, *Terrorism Review*, Counterterrorist Center, June 1995, *available at* http://www.foia.cia.gov/docs/DOC_0000918468/ DOC_0000918468.pdf.

[442] CHRISTOPHER M. BLANCHARD, CONGRESSIONAL RESEARCH SERVICE, LIBYA: BACKGROUND AND U.S. RELATIONS 35 (Aug. 6, 2008), *available at* http://fpc.state.gov/documents/ organization/109510.pdf.

[443] *See* Ch. I, Sec. 10.1.

loyal to the Qadhafi regime, and only resigned from the Libyan government on 30 March, flying to London by way of Tunisia.[444] Upon his arrival in London, British Foreign Secretary William Hague announced he had been in contact with Musa Kusa over the previous weeks, and that Kusa was voluntarily talking with British officials in London.[445] Hague made a point of noting that the United Kingdom would not grant Kusa immunity from British or international justice.[446] British police and Scottish prosecutors reportedly had the opportunity to question Kusa concerning his knowledge about the 1988 Lockerbie bombing while he was in London.[447] On 4 April 2011, the U.S. Treasury Department announced it would lift sanctions against Kusa, claiming that the sanctions had worked as intended by incentivizing members of the Qadhafi's inner circle to defect from the regime.[448] Shortly after, in another controversial decision, the European Union lifted its sanctions against Kusa, giving him the ability to travel around Europe and eventually leave for Qatar, where he settled.[449] As of May 2013, Kusa is reported to be residing in Qatar, with no known charges pending against him for past crimes.

The story of Kusa did not end with his *de facto* asylum in Qatar. In September 2011, files were discovered in the ESA's offices in Tripoli that provided significant details about the close relationship maintained between Musa Kusa, the CIA, and MI6.[450] The documents reveal that the United States and United Kingdom worked with the Qadhafi government to capture Libyan dissidents abroad, interrogate them, and render them back to Libya where they faced torture by regime officials.[451] The joint rendition

---

[444] *Foreign Secretary on Musa Kusa's resignation*, UK FOREIGN AND COMMONWEALTH OFFICE, Mar. 31, 2012, *available at* http://www.fco.gov.uk/en/news/latest-news/?view=News&id=576566082.

[445] *Id.*

[446] *Id.*

[447] *Musa Kusa traced to Qatar Resort*, THE GUARDIAN, Oct. 23, 2011, *available at* http://www.guardian.co.uk/uk/feedarticle/9909309.

[448] Josh Rogin, *Musa Kusa gets his money back*, FOREIGN POLICY, Apr. 4, 2011, *available at* http://thecable.foreignpolicy.com/posts/2011/04/04/musa_kusa_gets_his_money_back.

[449] *'Astonishing' to end Musa Kusa sanctions*, THE INDEPENDENT, Apr. 14, 2011, *available at* http://www.independent.co.uk/news/world/politics/astonishing-to-end-musa-kusa-sanctions-2267796.html.

[450] *Secret Intelligence Documents Discovered in Libya*, HUMAN RIGHTS WATCH, Sept. 9, 2011, *available at* http://www.hrw.org/news/2011/09/08/secret-intelligence-documents-discovered-libya.

[451] HUMAN RIGHTS WATCH, DELIVERED INTO ENEMY HANDS: US-LED ABUSE AND RENDITION OF OPPONENTS TO GADDAFI'S LIBYA 15 (Sept. 2012), *available at* http://www.hrw.org/sites/default/files/reports/libya0912webwcover_1.pdf.

campaign led to the capture and transfers of former LIFG leaders such as 'Abd al-Hakim Balhaj and Sami Mustafa al-Sa'adi, both long-time opponents of the Qadhafi government. With the reported assistance of the CIA and MI6, Balhaj was detained in Malaysia and Sa'adi in Hong Kong, and transferred to Libya in 2004.[452] Human Rights Watch documented other similar cases of rendition and torture of Libyan dissidents.[453]

The so-called "Tripoli Documents" found in the ESA's offices provide an extensive collection of primary source evidence of past rendition operations, and have important historical and legal ramifications. The documents are particularly important for policymakers in the United States, as they show evidence that it collaborated closely with Libya despite the fact that the Libyan government was on the U.S. State Department's list of state sponsors of terrorism.[454] These documents support the proposition that critically important information related to illegal detention, torture, and forced disappearances carried out in the name of the war on terror exists in the intelligence records of other governments, including those in the West.

There is on-going pressure to bring Kusa to account. Libyans who were delivered to the Qadhafi government to face torture have sought accountability for those responsible for their extrajudicial detention, rendition and abuse. In July 2012, for instance, lawyers representing Balhaj and al-Sa'adi filed a civil suit in British courts against Jack Straw, the former foreign secretary, and Sir Mark Allen, the former head of counter-terrorism at MI6.[455] The civil complaint includes allegations of unlawful detention, conspiracy to injure, and negligence – reportedly the first time such charges have ever been levied against a former British foreign secretary.[456] The law firm representing Balhaj and al-Sa'adi noted that the Tripoli Documents discovered in September 2011 strengthen the case against

---

[452] *Id.* at 9.

[453] *See* Ch. I, Sec. 10.1, for more on the files discovered in Kusa's office, and his role in rendition and torture of LIFG members.

[454] The U.S. did not remove Libya from the state sponsors of terrorism list until June 2006. CHRISTOPHER M. BLANCHARD, CONGRESSIONAL RESEARCH SERVICE, LIBYA: BACKGROUND AND U.S. RELATIONS 7 (Aug. 6, 2008), *available at* http://fpc.state.gov/documents/organization/109510.pdf.

[455] *Libyan politician questioned by British police over rendition allegations*, LEIGH DAY & CO SOLICITORS, July 19, 2012, *available at* http://www.leighday.co.uk/News/2012/July-2012/Libyan-politician-questioned-by-British-police-ove.

[456] Richard Norton-Taylor, *Jack Straw accused of misleading MPs over torture of Libyan dissidents*, THE GUARDIAN, Oct. 10, 2012, *available at* http://www.guardian.co.uk/world/2012/oct/10/jack-straw-torture-libyan-dissidents.

Jack Straw and Mark Allen, most notably the records that "congratulate" Kusa on the arrival of Balhaj in Libya. One such document from 19 March 2004, implicates the United Kingdom in the rendition of Balhaj to Libya, stating "this was the least we could do for you and for Libya to demonstrate the remarkable relationship we have built over the years."[457]

The case has led to a deeper examination by some in the British parliament of UK policy during the years of rapprochement with the Qadhafi regime. The rendition of Balhaj took place two weeks before the historic visit of Tony Blair to Libya in March 2004, and al-Sa'adi was delivered just days later.[458] Given the complicity of at least Allen and potentially Straw in this illegal activity, it is plausible that Blair was aware of the renditions before his visit to Libya.[459] Should his knowledge be established it would of course greatly embarrass his legacy, and potentially raise questions of criminal liability for aiding and abetting torture. While these acts may fall under the British Justice and Security Bill, which protects ministries and government officials from public scrutiny over sensitive matters of government security affairs,[460] it cannot shield Blair, Straw and Allen from potential criminal sanction. As established by the House of Lords in the Pinochet case, torture cannot lawfully constitute a lawful act of state or a government official, and therefore immunity cannot obtain.[461] Ultimately, the apparent complicity of parts of the UK government and senior officials will test the United Kingdom's resolve to live up to its domestic laws and international obligations *vis-à-vis* international crimes, and the demands for full accountability for UK involvement in human rights violations committed against Libyan detainees at the hand of the Qadhafi regime. It is clear that a full accounting of these rendition operations is essential for

---

[457] LEIGH DAY & CO SOLICITORS, *Libyan politician questioned by British police over rendition allegations, supra* note 455.

[458] Ian Cobain, *Libyan dissidents launch action against UK government over rendition*, THE GUARDIAN, June 28, 2012, *available at* http://www.guardian.co.uk/world/2012/jun/28/libyan-dissidents-action-government-rendition.

[459] Norton-Taylor, *Jack Straw accused of misleading MPs over torture of Libyan dissidents, supra* note 456.

[460] Cobain, *Libyan dissidents launch action against UK government over rendition, supra* note 458.

[461] *See* Regina v. Bow Street Metropolitan Stipendiary Magistrate (No. 1), *ex parte* Pinochet Ugarte, [1998] 3 W.L.R. 1456 (H.L.), *reprinted in* 37 I.L.M. 1302 (1998); Regina v. Bow Street Metropolitan Stipendiary Magistrate, *ex parte* Pinochet Ugarte (No. 2), [1999] 2 W.L.R. 272 (H.L.), *reprinted in* 38 I.L.M. 430 (1999); Regina v. Bow Street Metropolitan Stipendiary Magistrate, *ex parte* Pinochet Ugarte (No. 3), [1999] 2 W.L.R. 827 (H.L.). *See* BASSIOUNI, INTRODUCTION TO INTERNATIONAL CRIMINAL LAW: SECOND REVISED EDITION, *supra* note 4 at 78–79.

the clarification of Libya's past, and that the Kusa case demands judicial accountability for past human rights violations.

6.4. *Other Domestic Investigations and Proceedings*

While the cases involving members of Qadhafi's family and his inner circle have generated the most international attention, no regime operates without multiple layers of officials and agents. In fact, international humanitarian law (IHL) and international criminal law (ICL) apply to all layers of a military or state hierarchy, from the most senior to the most junior.[462] Given the universal application of IHL, IHRL and ICL, it is clear that a significant number of individuals serving the Qadhafi regime bear criminal responsibility for violations stemming from their conduct over the four decades of Qadhafi's rule or commanding security units during the 2011 conflict. Their conduct requires attention as well.

The charges against former regime officials include a mixture of financial crimes stemming from the mismanagement of state funds, to acts of political repression, to violations of national and international law committed during the conflict. The assortment of charges levied by the current Libyan government against Qadhafi era officials demonstrates the connection between corruption and political repression, and the manner in which the Qadhafi regime acted as a kleptocracy that employed government officials, an entourage of family members and individuals in corrupt private enterprises. The diversity of corruption of these individuals is evident in the travel ban and assets freeze imposed by Security Council Resolution 1970. The list includes leaders of the security apparatus, ministers, diplomats, government advisers, as well as relatives and associates

---

[462] One of the clearest expositions of this principle is expressed in the first Nürnberg principle, which states that "Any person who commits an act which constitutes a crime under international law is responsible therefor and liable to punishment." Principles of International Law Recognized in the Charter of the Nuremberg Tribunal and in the Judgment of the Tribunal, *adopted by* the International Law Commission of the United Nations, 1950 at Principle I. The London Charter, which established the International Military Tribunal, expressly rejected the defense of superior orders, proclaiming that "The fact that the Defendant acted pursuant to order of his Government or of a superior shall not free him from responsibility, but may be considered in mitigation of punishment if the Tribunal determines that justice so requires." *Principles of International Law Recognized in the Charter of the Nürnberg Tribunal and in the Judgment of the Tribunal,* 2 YEARBOOK OF THE INTERNATIONAL LAW COMMISSION 97 (1950). Both of these principles have been recognized in the statute and judgments of the ICTY and ICTR, and have been codified in the Rome Statute of the Criminal Court. *See, e.g.,* Rome Statute, *supra* note 8 at arts. 25(1) and 33.

who all played a role in the Qadhafi government's four decade-long hold on power.[463]

The individuals described in this section and in the cases below are not exhaustive, as there are many more cases emerging. The Libyan authorities continue to seek the extradition of former officials and regime co-conspirators from various countries, and individuals who have been extradited await trial. As new cases emerge and new information surfaces, there is a cascading effect that has the potential to lead to new charges against former officials. This attention has not, however, been turned to the crimes committed by the *thuwar* groups, and the post-conflict justice mechanisms deployed in Libya have been drastically one-sided.[464] The legal accountability measures implemented in post-conflict Libya have focused exclusively on violations committed by former regime officials. The CoI reported that although it received reports of violations carried out by *thuwar* against members of the former regime and its perceived supports, it was not aware of a single member from a *thuwar* group who had been arrested or was facing charges for these crimes.[465] According to publicly available information, the only *thuwar* who have been indicted in the year and a half since the end of the conflict are those individuals implicated in the killing of General 'Abd al-Fattah Yunis. The overall lack of accountability for the former rebels is attributable in part to amnesty laws passed by the transitional authorities, discussed below, which essentially gave a blanket immunity to anyone who fought on the side of the opposition forces.[466]

This section provides a brief synopsis of the cases that have been initiated against officials from the Qadhafi regime. It includes cases related to former officials detained in Libya after the end of the conflict, as well as those extradited from other countries at the request of the post-Qadhafi government. Libya's national authorities have actively pursued individuals associated with the former regime who fled to neighboring countries, and have secured the extradition of several high-profile figures. In many cases the extraditions and national trials have helped to bolster the

---

[463] Resolution Measures, *supra* note 188.

[464] The CoI warned that the "Failure to apply criminal law to crimes committed by *thuwar* during and after the end of the conflict creates an environment of impunity and leaves the victims of *thuwar* violations without protection of the law, justice and redress." Report of the International Commission of Inquiry, advance unedited version (Mar. 2, 2012), *supra* note 12 at ¶ 799.

[465] *Id.* at ¶ 103.

[466] *See infra* Sec. 6.1.

popularity of the NTC and GNC, and served to emphasize the passing of the old guard. However, many ordinary citizens lacked confidence in the ability of judges from the former regime to carry out impartial trials in the high-profile cases. Additionally, the cases suffered from significant delays, procedural flaws, limited investigative capabilities, and structural short-comings.[467]

Case 1

On 10 September 2012, proceedings began against former Foreign Minister *'Abd al-'Ati al-'Ubaydi* and *Muhammad Al-Zway*, the former head of the legislative council.[468] Al-'Ubaydi served as foreign minister from 1982–84, and again after Musa Kusa fled Libya on 30 March 2011.[469] In addition to serving as head of the General People's Congress, Al-Zway was Justice Minister and Ambassador to the United Kingdom.[470] The two former officials have been charged with wasting public funds by facilitating compensation payments to the families of 1988 Lockerbie victims in exchange for the cancelling of UN sanctions and lifting of U.S. trade sanctions.[471]

   The trail faced delays resulting from procedural complications. Following the first proceedings the trial was adjourned after the interim Justice Minister, Mohammed al-Alagi, determined that the trials of the Qadhafi-era officials were invalid, because certain procedures had not been followed. In particular, according to al-Alagi, the prosecutor general's office had bypassed the Indictment Chamber, which was necessary in order to review the legality of detention of the individuals held in custody.[472] The second hearing of the case was held on 10 December 2012,[473] and the case is on-going as of May 2013.

---

[467] INTERNATIONAL CRISIS GROUP, TRIAL BY ERROR: JUSTICE IN POST-QADHAFI LIBYA, *supra* note 14 at 17.

[468] Ali Shuaib, *Gaddafi-era officials go on trial accused over Lockerbie case*, REUTERS, Sept. 10, 2012, *available at* http://uk.reuters.com/article/2012/09/10/uk-libya-trials-idUK BRE889oYK20120910.

[469] Ashraf Abdul-Wahab, *Two more Qaddafi figures set to go on trial on 10 September*, LIBYA HERALD, Sept. 6, 2012, *available at* http://www.libyaherald.com/2012/09/06/two-more-regime-figures-set-to-go-on-trial-on-10-september.

[470] *Id.*

[471] Shuaib, *Gaddafi-era officials go on trial accused over Lockerbie case*, *supra* note 468. For more on the Lockerbie settlement, *see* Ch. I, Sec. 11.2.

[472] Shuaib, *Gaddafi-era officials go on trial accused over Lockerbie case*, *supra* note 468.

[473] *Former Libyan officials stand trial in Tripoli*, XINHUANET, Dec. 11, 2012, *available at* http://news.xinhuanet.com/english/photo/2012-12/11/c_132033134_2.htm.

Case 2

Abu Zayid Durda served as head of the External Security Agency (ESA) after Musa Kusa was made foreign minister in 2009.[474] According to the CoI, Durda commanded the special operations unit of the ESA at the time of the February 2011 uprising.[475] Unlike other former officials, Durda did not flee Tripoli after the fall of the Qadhafi regime and was taken into custody on 10 September 2011.[476] After five months of detention, Durda had not been given access to a lawyer, been charged or brought before a judge.[477] In February 2012 HRW expressed concern over Durda's treatment during detention, and reported that he was in need of medial attention.[478] In July 2012 Durda again stated that that he had been denied access to a lawyer, and that he had been subjected to improper interrogations.[479]

The trial against Durda began its first proceedings on 5 June 2012, but the trial has been adjourned on four occasions on procedural grounds similar to the ones described above.[480] The charges that were finally brought against Durda charge him with crimes committed against protesters during the initial phase of the conflict, including conspiracy to kill and arming individuals to murder civilians, as well as abuse of authority and the mismanagement of public funds.[481] The prosecution has accused Durda specifically of "mobilising security forces to fire bullets at the heads and chests of civilians" and "preventing, through the use of force and intimidation, the staging of peaceful protests."[482]

---

[474] *Exclusive: At bay, captured Libyan spy chief defiant*, REUTERS, Sept. 11, 2011, *available at* http://www.reuters.com/article/2011/09/11/us-libya-spy-idUSTRE78A3PR20110911.

[475] Report of the International Commission of Inquiry (Jan. 12, 2012), *supra* note 57 at ¶ 40.

[476] *Exclusive: At bay, captured Libyan spy chief defiant*, REUTERS, Sept. 11, 2011, *available at* http://www.reuters.com/article/2011/09/11/us-libya-spy-idUSTRE78A3PR20110911.

[477] *Libya: Ex-Premier Needs Lawyer, Medical Care*, HUMAN RIGHTS WATCH, Feb. 14, 2012, *available at* http://www.hrw.org/news/2012/02/14/libya-ex-premier-needs-lawyer-medical-care.

[478] *Id.*

[479] Ashraf Abdul Wahab, *Trial of Qaddafi spy chief resumes – and is postponed – for third time*, LIBYA HERALD, July 11, 2012, *available at* http://www.libyaherald.com/2012/07/11/trial-of-qaddafi-spy-chief-resumes-and-is-postponed-for-third-time/.

[480] *Id. See also* Shuaib, *Gaddafi-era officials go on trial accused over Lockerbie case, supra* note 468.

[481] *Dorda trial opened and adjourned*, LIBYA HERALD, June 5, 2012, *available at* http://www.libyaherald.com/2012/06/05/dorda-trial-opened-and-adjounred.

[482] *Libyan ex-spy chief Dorda charged over protester deaths*, BBC, June 5, 2012, *available at* http://www.bbc.co.uk/news/world-africa-18330584.

Case 3

Al-Baghdadi ʿAli al-Mahmudi served as Prime Minister in the Qadhafi government, and was one of the most high-profile figures of the Qadhafi regime. Al-Mahmudi fled to Tunisia in mid-August 2011, where he was arrested on 21 September on charges of entering the country illegally.[483] After being detained in Tunisia he reportedly suffered abuse, was denied access to a lawyer and denied contact with his family.[484] In particular, he told HRW that he was threatened and beaten with sticks by Tunisian guards.[485] Despite international concerns, Al-Mahmudi was extradited on 24 June 2012 after Libya provided the Tunisian government with guarantees to respect the rights and physical integrity of Al-Mahmudi.[486] HRW, as well as Amnesty International, expressed concern following his extradition to Libya on 24 June 2012, stating that Libya had not yet established the necessary judicial institutions to deal with such high-profile cases.[487] The Tunisian Prime Minister responded to these concerns, however, stating that the decision was made after a Tunisian delegation had visited Tripoli and determined that the conditions required for a fair trial had been met.[488]

After his extradition, a Tunisian lawyer claimed that Al-Mahmudi was tortured in Libyan custody. According to the lawyer, the beating took place

---

[483] *Ex-Libya PM al-Baghdadi al-Mahmoudi 'jailed in Tunisia'*, BBC, Sept. 22, 2011, *available at* http://www.bbc.co.uk/news/world-middle-east-15022757.

[484] *Tunisia extradites Gaddafi's last PM to Libya*, AL JAZEERA, June 25, 2012, *available at* http://www.aljazeera.com/news/africa/2012/06/2012624135853340329.html; Hadi Fornaji, *Human Rights Watch demands fair treatment for Mahmoudi*, LIBYA HERALD, July 6, 2012, *available at* http://www.libyaherald.com/2012/07/06/human-rights-watch-demands-fair-treatment-for-mahmoudi.

[485] *Libya: Ensure Due Process for Detained Ex-Prime Minister*, HUMAN RIGHTS WATCH, July 6, 2012, *available at* http://www.hrw.org/news/2012/07/06/libya-ensure-due-process-detained-ex-prime-minister.

[486] *Tunisia: Extradition of former Libyan prime minister violates human rights*, AMNESTY INTERNATIONAL, June 25, 2012, *available at* http://www.amnesty.org/en/news/tunisia-extradition-former-libyan-pm-al-mahmoudi-condemned-2012-06-25.

[487] *Fugitive Baghdadi Mahmoudi "starving to death"*, LIBYA HERALD, Mar. 9, 2012, *available at* http://www.libyaherald.com/2012/03/09/fugitive-baghdadi-mahmoudi-starving-to-death; *Mahmoudi will not get fair trial in Libya claims Tunisian human rights president*, LIBYA HERALD, June 11, 2012, *available at* http://www.libyaherald.com/2012/06/11/mahmoudi-will-not-get-fair-trial-in-libya-claims-tunisian-human-rights-president; HUMAN RIGHTS WATCH, *Libya: Ensure Due Process for Detained Ex-Prime Minister, supra* note 485; AMNESTY INTERNATIONAL, *Tunisia: Extradition of former Libyan prime minister violates human rights, supra* note 486.

[488] George Grant & Ashraf Abdul Wahab, *Baghdadi Al-Mahmoudi refutes allegations of torture in TV interview*, LIBYA HERALD, July 1, 2012, *available at* http://www.libyaherald.com/2012/07/01/baghdadi-al-mahmoudi-refutes-allegations-of-mistreatment-in-tv-interview.

in a detention facility at Tripoli's Mitiga military airport.[489] Following reports of his ill-treatment, however, Al-Mahmudi told reporters that he had not been abused and had been treated well in detention.[490] On 3 July 2012 HRW representatives were allowed to conduct a confidential interview with Al-Mahmudi, in which he stated that although he felt generally safe in his detention facility, he feared suffering ill-treatment "by random people and militias."[491] He also told HRW that the chief of staff of the Libyan Army was on board the same plane, and that the chief of staff had also assured him that he would be treated well.[492] In response to continuing allegations or torture and ill-treatment, UNSMIL representatives later interviewed Al-Mahmudi in his place of detention in Tripoli in February 2013, at which time Al-Mahmudi told them in private conversations that he had not been mistreated. He also stated that he was being represented by a legal team consisting solely of Libyan lawyers.[493]

Al-Mahmudi has reportedly been charged with ordering the rape of women during the conflict in Zuwara, as well as ordering hospital officials to transfer dead bodies to buildings hit during NATO airstrikes in order to generate criticism of the NATO campaign.[494] Along with two co-defendants, Al-Mahmudi has also been charged with arranging the transfer of an estimated $25 million of public funds through Tunisia to support the Qadhafi regime's security forces during the conflict.[495] He has denied any wrongdoing.[496] The second hearing of his trial was held on 10 December 2012, and the trial was adjourned and set to resume in 2013.[497]

---

[489] Chris Stephen & Luke Harding, *Libya's former PM Mahmoudi 'tortured' on forced return to Tripoli*, THE GUARDIAN, June 27, 2012, *available at* http://www.guardian.co.uk/world/2012/jun/27/libya-mahmoudi-tortured-return-tripoli.

[490] Grant & Wahab, *Baghdadi Al-Mahmoudi refutes allegations of torture in TV interview, supra* note 488. *See also Id.* For video footage, *see* Webmaster MFM, *interview exclusive de Baghdadi Mahmoudi avec la chaine Zitouna TV*, YouTube (Jun 29, 2012), *available at* http://www.youtube.com/watch?v=RoS5HHW_IpM.

[491] Fornaji, *Human Rights Watch demands fair treatment for Mahmoudi, supra* note 484.

[492] HUMAN RIGHTS WATCH, *Libya: Ensure Due Process for Detained Ex-Prime Minister, supra* note 485.

[493] *Libya: Al-Mahmoudi Denies He was Tortured in Prison or Represented by Non-Libyan Lawyers*, THE TRIPOLI POST, Mar. 1, 2013, *available at* http://www.tripolipost.com/articledetail.asp?c=1&i=9954

[494] Grant & Wahab, *Baghdadi Al-Mahmoudi refutes allegations of torture in TV interview, supra* note 488.

[495] *Libya ex-PM al-Baghdadi al-Mahmoudi on trial in Tripoli*, BBC, Dec. 10, 2012, *available at* http://www.bbc.co.uk/news/world-africa-20668492.

[496] *Id.*

[497] *Id.*

Case 4

One of the most significant individual crimes that took place during the 2011 conflict was the killing of *'Abd al-Fattah Yunis*, which received considerable attention both inside and outside Libya. Yunis was an important and powerful official in the Qadhafi regime, who held the posts of Minister of Interior and Minister of Defense, as well as the rank of Major General in the Libyan armed forces. At the outbreak of violence in February 2011, Yunis was sent to Benghazi, where he promptly defected, joined the opposition movement and in short order became a prominent commander in the *thuwar* forces in eastern Libya.[498] In one of the hazier chapters of the conflict, Yunis was killed on 28 July after being called for a meeting with NTC officials.[499]

Charges were eventually brought against 17 individuals, mostly soldiers, accused of involvement in Yunis' murder. Only one of them, however, was taken into custody, a soldier named Salam al-'Ubayd.[500] In June 2012 investigations into the case were reopened after the main defendant in the case alleged that NTC officials were involved in the assassination.[501] On 31 October 2012, Mustafa 'Abd al-Jalil, the former chairman of the NTC, was called for questioning concerning the death of Yunis.[502]

Other individuals with links to the NTC were also charged in connection to the murder. The main suspect was 'Ali al-'Issawi, the NTC's interim deputy prime minister, who was accused of assisting in the abduction of Yunis.[503] Al-'Issawi reportedly signed the arrest warrant for Yunis that led to his abduction.[504] Mustafa 'Abd al-Jalil was summoned three times

---

[498] *Nations' Feedback on Libyan Uprising*, TRIPOLI POST, Feb. 23, 2011, *available at* http://www.tripolipost.com/articledetail.asp?c=1&i=5463; Kim Sengupta, *Top Libyan rebel commander shot dead*, THE INDEPENDENT, July 29, 2011, *available at* http://www.independent.co.uk/news/world/africa/top-libyan-rebel-commander-shot-dead-2328028.html.

[499] *Libya opposition arrests senior leader*, AL JAZEERA, July 28, 2011, *available at* http://www.aljazeera.com/news/africa/2011/07/2011728144624965299.html.

[500] *Court reopens investigation into Younis killing*, LIBYA HERALD, June 1, 2012, *available at* http://www.libyaherald.com/2012/06/01/court-reopens-investigation-into-younis-killing.

[501] *Id.*

[502] *Id.*

[503] *Id.*

[504] Mohamed Eljarh, *Jalil ordered not to leave country*, LIBYA HERALD, Dec. 12, 2012, *available at* http://www.libyaherald.com/2012/12/12/jalil-order-not-to-leave-country/.

testify during the trial of another individual charged in the case, Salam al-Mansuri,[505] but failed to appear each time.[506]

As of November 2012, there were still 11 individuals suspected for their connection to the murder.[507] Reports on the actual number of suspects and charges are contradictory. Besides Al-'Issawi, and Al-Mansuri, a number of officials have been named as suspects, including Ibrahim Barghati, a member of the preventive security forces, Fawzi Abu Kattif, former member of the 17 February brigade, Jalal 'Abd al-Gaili, defense minister in the NTC, and Salem Sheikhi, former minister of religious affairs.[508]

After appearing for questioning in December 2012, 'Abd al-Jalil was ordered by Benghazi's military prosecutor not to leave the country.[509] However, the head of the military prosecutor's office in Benghazi, Saleh Albishari,[510] later indicated that the prosecutor did not prevent 'Abd al-Jalil from traveling abroad, and instead simply requested that he inform the court of the date of his travel in order not to contrast with the date of the trial.[511]

Benghazi's military prosecutor has reportedly charged 'Abd Al-Jalil with political irresponsibility for the resulting murder of Yunis, and for abuse of authority as head of the transitional council.[512] A colleague of the military prosecutor investigating the case claimed in December 2012 that the trial would begin soon, and that 'Abd al-Jalil had been charged with two separate offences, namely Misuse of Powers and Committing Acts that

---

[505] Ghaith Shennib, *Libyan wartime leader Jalil faces questioning over killing*, AL JAZEERA, Nov. 2, 2012, *available at* http://af.reuters.com/article/worldNews/idAFBRE 8A61FP20121107.

[506] Maha Ellawati & Nihal Zaroug, *Younis murder judge orders Jalil to appear in Benghazi court*, LIBYA HERALD, Nov. 9, 2012, *available at* http://www.libyaherald.com/2012/11/10/younis-murder-judge-orders-jalil-to-appear-in-benghazi-court.

[507] *Libya: Jalil faces Abdel Fattah Younes questions*, BBC, Nov. 7, 2012, *available at* http://www.bbc.co.uk/news/world-africa-20241092.

[508] The transliteration of these names was adopted from the reference. Maha Ellawati & Nihal Zaroug, *Younis murder judge orders Jalil to appear in Benghazi court*, LIBYA HERALD, Nov. 9, 2012, *available at* http://www.libyaherald.com/2012/11/10/younis-murder-judge-orders-jalil-to-appear-in-benghazi-court/.

[509] Mohamed Eljarh, *Jalil ordered not to leave country*, LIBYA HERALD, Dec. 12, 2012, *available at* http://www.libyaherald.com/2012/12/12/jalil-order-not-to-leave-country.

[510] The transliteration of this name was adopted from the reference. Mohamed Bujaneh, et al., *Abdul Jalil will stand trial "very soon" in connection with Younis murder*, LIBYA HERALD, Dec. 16, 2012, *available at* http://www.libyaherald.com/2012/12/16/abdul-jalil-will-stand-trial-very-soon-in-connection-with-younis-murder.

[511] *Id.*

[512] Eljarh, *Jalil ordered not to leave country*, LIBYA HERALD, *supra* note 509.

Would Harm Libyan Unity.[513] At a hearing in December 2012, the prosecutor ordered Mahmud Jibril, the NTC's prime minister at the time of the killing, to be present for the next court session.[514]

Case 5

Libyan authorities continue to pursue former regime loyalists and seek their extradition from other countries to stand trial in national courts. The Libyan government has placed significant pressure on neighboring Egypt in particular, which has become a prominent destination for former regime officials to settle. The new Libyan government reportedly requested that Egypt arrest an estimated 40 suspects in Egypt in 2012, and made a second request for an additional 80 in March 2013.[515] This pressure has led to the arrests of high-profile Qadhafi regime figures including *Ali Mohammed Marya, Muhammad Ibrahim Mansour* and *Ahmad Qadhaf al-Dam* after Libya issued Interpol red notices requesting their arrest.[516] Ali Mohammed Marya had served as ambassador to Egypt, while Ibrahim Mansour is known as a private businessman who reportedly served as a finance officer for the Qadhafi regime, and is also the brother of former Qadhafi spokesperson Musa Ibrahim.[517]

Days after the three were arrested in Egypt, the Libyan government completed an agreement with Egypt to deposit $2 billion in the Egyptian central bank as part of an aid package to increase the country's reserves.[518] The timing of the agreement drew public suspicion that the aid package was part of an effort to secure the extradition of individuals wanted by the Libyan national authorities. A few days later, on 26 March, Egypt extradited Ali Mayra and Muhammad Ibrahim to Libya to stand trial on charges of corruption.[519] On 3 April, Egypt denied the extradition

---

[513] Bujaneh, et al., *Abdul Jalil will stand trial "very soon" in connection with Younis murder, supra* note 510

[514] Eljarh, *Jalil ordered not to leave country*, LIBYA HERALD, *supra* note 509.

[515] David D. Kirkpatrick, *Libya Putting $2 Billion into Egypt's Central Bank*, N.Y. TIMES, Mar. 24, 2013, *available at* http://www.nytimes.com/2013/03/25/world/middleeast/libya-putting-2-billion-into-egypts-central-bank.html.

[516] *Libya: Ensure due process for extradited Libyans*, HUMAN RIGHTS WATCH, Mar. 13, 2013, *available at* http://www.hrw.org/news/2013/03/30/libya-ensure-due-process-extradited-libyans.

[517] Farah Waleed, *Extradited Qaddafi regime figures flown into Tripoli*, LIBYA HERALD, Mar. 26, 2013, *available at* http://www.libyaherald.com/2013/03/26/extradited-qaddafi-regime-figures-flown-into-tripoli.

[518] Kirkpatrick, *Libya Putting $2 Billion into Egypt's Central Bank, supra* note 515.

[519] Hadi Fornaji, *Egyptian Court Blocks Qaddaf al-Dam Extradition*, LIBYA HERALD, Apr. 3, 2013, *available at* http://www.libyaherald.com/2013/04/03/egyptian-court-blocks-qaddaf-al-dam-extradition.

request for al-Dam, declaring he would remain in Egypt to face charges there.[520]

As a cousin of Mu'ammar Qadhafi, al-Dam was entrusted with handling sensitive bilateral matters as the special representative to Egypt.[521] One of Al-Dam's roles in the Qadhafi regime was conducting high-level negotiations with the Egyptian government, including President Hosni Mubarak and intelligence chief Oman Suleiman.[522] The Libyan authorities have alleged that Al-Dam took part in planning operations against Libya dissidents abroad,[523] and he has been accused of involvement in one of the most notable political crimes during the Qadhafi era, namely the abduction and disappearance of Mansur Rashid Kikhya.[524] Kikhya was a prominent opposition figure who was abducted in Cairo by Egyptian government agents in 1993.[525] After Al-Dam was arrested in Cairo, a Libyan politician named Ibrahim Amesh[526] stated that he was in possession of documents implicating Al-Dam in the Kikhya disappearance and that he would disclose them to Egyptian authorities.[527]

There has been speculation that Al-Dam's links to Egyptian intelligence and military officials has dissuaded Egyptian authorities from extraditing him to Libya.[528] Al-Dam, who also has Egyptian citizenship, remains in Egypt where he faces charges for reportedly shooting a police officer during his arrest.[529] After the aforementioned loan from Libya to Egypt, Al-Dam accused the Libyan authorities of attempting to buy his arrest and extradition.[530] As of May 2013, he is reportedly being held in the

---

[520] *Id.*

[521] *Libya: Ensure due process for extradited Libyans*, HUMAN RIGHTS WATCH, Mar. 13, 2013, *available at* http://www.hrw.org/news/2013/03/30/libya-ensure-due-process-extradited-libyans.

[522] For information on the role of Qadhaf al-Dam in discussions with Egyptian officials, *see* Ch. I, Sec. 11.2.

[523] Bradley Hope, *Qaddafi cousin: Egypt sold me out for aid*, THE NATIONAL, Mar. 15, 2013, *available at* http://www.thenational.ae/news/world/middle-east/qaddafi-cousin-egypt-sold-me-out-for-aid.

[524] Farah Waleed, *Qaddaf Al-Dam implicated in disappearance of Mansour El-Kikhia*, LIBYA HERALD, Mar. 28, 2013, *available at* http://www.libyaherald.com/2013/03/28/qaddaf-al-dam-implicated-in-disappearance-of-mansour-el-kikhia.

[525] For more on the case of Mansur Kikhya, and the discovery of his body in Libya in December 2012, *See* Ch. I, Sec. 11.2.

[526] The transliteration of this name is adopted from the source.

[527] Waleed, *Qaddaf Al-Dam implicated in disappearance of Mansour El-Kikhia, supra* note 524.

[528] Fornaji, *Egyptian Court Blocks Qaddaf al-Dam Extradition, supra* note 519.

[529] Hope, *Qaddafi cousin: Egypt sold me out for aid, supra* note 523.

[530] *Id.*

Tora Prison outside of Cairo, the same prison where Hosni Mubarak is imprisoned.[531]

On-going Investigations

In addition to the investigations relating to political figures from the Qadhafi regime, there are continuing efforts to investigate incidents of political violence in the post-conflict period that are linked to the country's overall transitional justice efforts. The investigations into the 11 September 2012 attack on the U.S. consulate in Benghazi are on-going, although to date there have been no reported arrests of individual suspects within Libya. In December 2012, Egyptian authorities reportedly detained Muhammed Jamal Abu Ahmad,[532] a former member of the Egyptian Islamic Jihad with alleged links to Al-Qa'ida.[533] Another suspect named Ali Harzi[534] was arrested in Turkey in October 2012 and deported to Tunisia, his home country, where he was questioned by U.S. authorities, before being released in January 2013.[535] In May 2013, it was reported that the FBI had identified five individuals believed responsible for the attack, but were waiting to determine how to go about apprehending the suspects in Libya.[536] Investigations within Libya have been virtually impossible due to the unstable security situation, where top police chiefs have been killed in Benghazi, hindering any potential arrests in the region.[537] Any potential suspects in the attack, in particular Ahmed Abu Khattala,[538] the reported leader of the Ansar al-Sharī'a armed group, have not been questioned due to fear of reprisals from extremist groups.[539]

---

[531] *Id.*

[532] The transliteration of this name was adopted from the reference.

[533] *Egyptians arrest suspected terror leader in connection with Benghazi consulate attack*, LIBYA HERALD, Dec. 8, 2012, *available at* http://www.libyaherald.com/2012/12/08/egyptians-arrest-suspected-terror-leader-in-connection-with-benghazi-consulate-attack.

[534] The transliteration of this name was adopted from the reference.

[535] David D. Kirkpatrick, *Lone Suspect Held in Benghazi Attack is Freed in Tunisia*, N.Y. TIMES, Jan. 8, 2013, *available at* http://www.nytimes.com/2013/01/09/world/africa/lone-suspect-held-in-benghazi-attack-is-freed-in-tunisia.html.

[536] Kimberly Dozier, *Benghazi Suspects Identified by FBI, But no Arrests Made Yet*, AP, May 21, 2013, *available at* http://www.huffingtonpost.com/2013/05/21/benghazi-suspects_n_3314153.html.

[537] *See* Ch. V, Sec. 2.4.

[538] The transliteration of this name was adopted from the reference. Vivienne Walt, *Benghazi's Real Scandal: Why is the Libyan Investigation Such a Mess?*, TIME WORLD, Nov. 15, 2012, *available at* http://world.time.com/2012/11/15/benghazis-real-scandal-why-is-the-libyan-investigation-such-a-mess.

[539] *Id.*

Investigations are also on-going related to incidents of violence perpetrated by security forces comprised of revolutionary brigades, such as the Libyan Shield Forces (LSF).[540] On 8 June 2013, clashes erupted in Benghazi after protesters gathered in front of the headquarters of one of the LSF brigades to demand the closure of the base and call for investigations into the militia members accused of abuses.[541] At least 32 people were killed during the clashes, and the incident led to the resignation of Army Chief of Staff General Yusuf al-Mangush, who had authority over the LSF. In addition to ordering the government to shut down the unlawful armed groups, the GNC ordered the general prosecutor to promptly investigate the incident those responsible for the killings.[542] The incident underscored the security challenges as well as the need to end impunity for on-going militia abuses.

7. Conclusion

As discussed in Chapter One, the history of Libya is not marked by a prominent role in its judiciary or prominence of the pursuit of justice. Moreover, there is no historical basis for a national concept of accountability in a society that has historically lacked a sense of nationhood.[543] That sense of nationhood is still being consolidated in Libya today, and its challenges are prominent in areas such as security, political stability, social cohesion and reconciliation. The challenges faced by the present government indicate that the different parts of Libya and its populations have not yet formed a cohesive national whole. While there is certainly an identifiable growing sense of Libyan nationalism in the wake of the overthrow of Qadhafi, it is yet to be determined if this will prevail over the deep social divides and larger influences that exist in Libya and the

---

[540] For a background on the formation and genesis of the Libyan Shield Forces, *see* Ch. V, Sec. 2.

[541] *Libya: No Impunity for 'Black Saturday' Benghazi Deaths*, Human Rights Watch, June 13, 2013, *available at* http://world.time.com/2012/11/15/benghazis-real-scandal-why-is-the-libyan-investigation-such-a-mess.

[542] *Id.*

[543] The term society is used advisedly, as discussed in Chapter I, there has always been regional distinctions that revolve around three different provinces; Cyrenaica, traditionally closer to Egypt in the east, Tripolitania, closer to Tunisia in the west, and Fezzan to the south, which has little inhabitants but significant territorial proportion that reaches in its confines to the Sudan, Chad, and Niger.

region as a whole.[544] All of these issues are important factors in determining prospects for accountability in Libya.

Accountability – meaning that individuals should be held accountable for violations of established legal norms, irrespective of who they are and the illegitimacy/legitimacy of their causes – has not traditionally been part of Libyan culture. For that matter, it is not part of Arab/Islamic culture in general. This does not mean that Islam does not place a high value on justice, but it does mean that the goals of justice differ. These goals are designed to influence reconciliation much more than they are designed to bring about retribution or deterrence (viewed as individual deterrence). Retribution occurs in this culture collectively and that in itself is believed to engender deterrence.

Moreover, accountability in its contemporary meaning of submitting all persons who commit violations of established legal norms to prosecution and punishment on an equal basis and with fairness to all irrespective of what the ultimate legitimate claim of the protagonist may be, has not been clearly established in the post-WWII history of Libya. Under Italian rule the colonialists dominated the legal institutions until giving way to the monarchy that adopted a legal system copied from the Egyptian system. This persisted after the rise of Qadhafi in 1969 and the establishment of the Libyan Arab Republic. The establishment of Socialist People's Libyan Arab Jamahiriyya 1977 brought with it sweeping "revolutionary" policies that in effect undermined the legal and judicial system of Libya, rendering it in time no more than a shell.[545] The legal structures continued to exist on paper, where persons were appointed judges and pursued their careers as such, and the courts continued to function mostly in connection with civil matters. When it came to criminal matters, however, the process was entirely politically directed and controlled, thus eliminating its integrity along with any judicial or prosecutorial independence. In addition there were a variety of alternative mechanisms and processes by which the regime imposed its will on the people under the name of "justice."[546] The extent to which the justice system functioned during the

---

[544] These include Islamist forces, external and internal, including some factions that are militant and others that political. *See* Ch. V, Sec. 5.

[545] *See* Ch. I, Secs. 8 & 9.

[546] These mechanisms included the establishment of "revolutionary courts" that acted at the behest of Qadhafi to carry out arbitrary arrests and secret trials of opponents. *See* Ch. I, Sec. 9.1. The regime also created prisons that operated outside of the Ministry of Justice (Justice Secretariat) to hold political prisoners, notably the Abu Salim and 'Ain Zara prisons in Tripoli. *See* Ch. V, Sec. 2.3.

decades of dictatorship, it did so to serve as a tool for carrying out a state policy of political repression. Thus there were no lawful or legitimate processes in most aspects of the criminal justice system's functions. Thus, for most Libyans the justice system became synonymous with injustice.

Against this general backdrop, and also in light of other political considerations relating to the post-conflict justice period, it is understandable why accountability as understood in the contemporary sense is unlikely to take place. The historical and cultural factors mentioned above and the impairment of the judicial system, including more specifically the prosecutorial system, would alone explain why accountability would face significant challenges. But the absence of a national law enforcement system, as described in Chapter Five, is in itself a factor significant enough to impair the pursuit of accountability anywhere.

In addition to these contemporary and historical factors, the social and political conditions that determined the evolution and outcome of the 2011 armed conflict are directly relevant to accountability in post-Qadhafi Libya. As described in Chapter Two, the conflict was regionalized with *thuwar* forces developing locally and operating largely independent of one another.[547] It is not by chance that the conflict occurred in different regions at different times and that no unified military operation emerged on either the side of the regime or that of the opposition. All of these factors evidence the existence of regional factionalism, which reflects local characteristics and the differing goals of the local groups that engaged in the conflict, and continue to challenge the government authority.

There is no clear indication of where these regional groups and their militias are headed for in terms of national unity and accountability. The government has been unable to exercise effective control over the entire territory of Libya. Non-state armed actors continue to operate above the law, controlling detention centers, and acting with impunity as they take on the role of the police, prosecutors, and judges.[548] It is therefore unlikely that in such a situation a legal system can function effectively and fairly let alone establish accountability for anyone who has committed a violation of international humanitarian law and the domestic criminal laws in existence.

---

[547] *See* Ch. II, Secs. 2.3 & 3.
[548] International Crisis Group, Trial by Error: Justice in Post-Qadhafi Libya, *supra* note 14 at i.

There are other important factors that will determine the future of accountability in the country, namely the uncertainty of what the country's final political and economic settlement will look like. There are two primary issues at stake, one being the distribution of oil resources. The other issue is in ensuring that accountability is equally and fairly applied to former regime figures, combatants and to the *thuwar* groups that carried out violations during and after the conduct.[549] The failure to have an equitable agreement on the allocation of oil resources necessarily leads to conflict whose goal is to maximize the claims of one group over another, and it is not likely in such a context that accountability can prevail with respect to all participants from the 2011 conflict and its aftermath.

Just as there exists the risk that the country's resources will be distributed unequally, there is also the risk that justice will be applied unevenly.[550] The revolutionary brigades, and the government that formed out of the winning forces of war, have already demonstrated a tendency towards "victor's justice," whereby the legitimacy of overthrowing Qadhafi trumps the legality of their actions. This is reflected in the actions of the *thuwar* during and in the wake of the conflict, which include reprisal violence against civilian populations that supported the Qadhafi regime. It appears the *thuwar* consider the crimes and misdeeds of the regime as justifying the illegal conduct of their own combatants during the course of and in the wake of the revolution.[551] In the post-conflict period, the protections of legality have been applied to those who fought against the regime, and denied for those considered to have operated without legitimacy. This uneven application of the law is apparent in the passage of certain laws by the NTC, most notably the Amnesty Law passed in May 2012, which protects from prosecution people who committed crimes if their

---

[549] These two issues have been evident in the situation in Iraq since the American occupation in 2003, and have been intertwined ever since. *See* Tariq Abdell, *Iraq's political sectarianism: National Reconciliation and the Oil Curse*, IRAQ BUSINESS NEWS, Oct. 10, 2010, *available at* http://www.iraq-businessnews.com/2010/10/01/iraqs-political-sectarianism-national-reconciliation-and-the-oil-curse. *See also* Nancy Bisdsall & Arvind Subramanian, *Saving Iraq from its Oil*, 83(4) FOREIGN AFFAIRS, July/Aug. 2004.

[550] The CoI noted in the wake of the conflict that the law had not been applied consistently or equally when it came to the alleged violations committed by the *thuwar*. *See* Report of the International Commission of Inquiry, advance unedited version (Mar. 2, 2012), *supra* note 12 at ¶ 103.

[551] Many of the *thuwar* forces did not consider themselves combatants and had little consideration for civilian versus combatant status. Ch. II, Sec. 2.3. The *thuwar* seemed to consider attacks on civilian populations that had been loyal to the regime as justified actions not only in the context of war, but well into the post-conflict period. *See* Ch. V, Sec. 2.

actions were aimed at "promoting or protecting the revolution," against the Qadhafi regime.[552]

The NTC did take steps towards significant accountability measures, such as the establishment of the National Council for Civil Liberties and Human Rights in December 2011, and the National Fact-Finding and Reconciliation Commission (NFRC) through the Transitional Justice Law in February 2012.[553] The CoI also obtained information, however, that some local reconciliation committees operated outside the framework of any existing law.[554] One of these unofficial commissions arose out of a law that was proposed in November 2011, but was never passed.[555] Without legal authorization, the commission began going into militia prisons and working to reconcile detained perpetrators and surviving victims, carrying with them the draft of the proposed law. It was apparent that the majority of the commission were Islamists and the "reconciliation" process appeared to an effort to gain goodwill towards the Islamists political movement in the country.[556] In a tribal society the release of from prison of a member of a given tribe is likely to generate appreciation by a large number of relatives and tribe members. Consequently this became a mechanism by which to reverse the negative effects of holding former regime officials in detention into a benefit when a prisoner would be released. Thus, the continued detention of former regime officials, combatants, and others was not only a source of income for the militias but also source of political power trade-off.[557]

Upon close examination, given the present state of internal division that exists in Libya, particularly with respect to areas of territorial control by different groups and considering the proliferation of weapons throughout the population, it is unlikely that any group or militia will submit its own in order to fulfill international or national accountability.[558] As discussed in Chapter Five, there are an estimated 3,000 persons held in detention

---

[552] *Libya: Amend New Special Procedures Law*, HUMAN RIGHTS WATCH, May 11, 2012, *available at* http://www.hrw.org/news/2012/05/11/libya-amend-new-special-procedures-law.

[553] Report of the International Commission of Inquiry, advance unedited version (Mar. 2, 2012), *supra* note 12 at ¶¶ 788–792.

[554] *Id.* at ¶ 796.

[555] A copy of this law is available in the files of the ISISC project.

[556] The rector of this project, in his capacity of Chairmen of the CoI, encountered this unofficial commission in one of the prison settings in Tripoli in December 2011 and had discussions with them regarding their activities.

[557] *See* Ch. V, Sec. 2.3.

[558] *See* Ch. V, Sec. 3.

centers outside of government control, mostly belonging to the previous regime, who have been held without any legal process or determination of any criminal responsibility on their part. Such detention is clearly in violation of Libyan criminal procedural law and it is also in violation of IHL and IHRL.[559] In a number of cases these persons are held for ransom in exchange for money or political favors.[560] In time, these prisoners have become a source of income to the respective militias holding them, and in the absence of any other source of funding the militias are not likely to release them without some *quid pro quo*. This environment is far from conducive to judicial accountability.

Moreover, the focus of the international community on the accountability of Saif al-Islam, as well as 'Abdullah al-Senussi, seems to have diverted attention not only from the former senior Qaddafi operatives, such as Musa Kusa, who appears to have completely escaped justice,[561] but also from the larger population of perpetrators from the Qadhafi regime and *thuwar* forces who have yet to be held to account for violations committed before, during, and in the wake of the conflict. As a result of over 40 years of dictatorship and repression, there are many more individuals who have committed numerous crimes in Libya and are not contemplated by any notions of accountability. It is likely that the militias will insist on submitting a number of persons in their detention to prosecution, but it is unlikely that any of the militias will agree to submit any of their own to face charges no matter what the criminal violation might have been, especially in light of the existing amnesty laws. As discussed above, however, it is important to note that the ICC continues to have jurisdiction over crimes against humanity and war crimes committed after February 2011.[562] The OTP is therefore in a position to open up investigations into alleged violations committed by *thuwar* forces. If the investigations lead

---

[559] The general treatment and conditions in these prisons are also in violation of the United Nations' Standard of Minimum Rules for the Treatment of Prisoners. *See* Standard Minimum Rules for the Treatment of Prisoners, E.S.C. Res. 663 C (XXIV) UN Doc. E/3048, July 31, 1957, *amended by* E.S.C. res. 2076, UN Doc. E/5988 (May 13, 1977).

[560] *See* Ch. V, Sec. 2.3. *See also* Report of the International Commission of Inquiry, advance unedited version (Mar. 2, 2012), *supra* note 12 at Annex I, ¶ 298. *See also* AMNESTY INTERNATIONAL, LIBYA RULE OF LAW OR RULE OF MILITIA 41 (July 2012), *available at* http://www.amnesty.org/en/library/asset/MDE19/012/2012/en/f2d36090-5716-4ef1-81a7-f4b1ebdo82fc/mde190122012en.pdf; *Libya: Cease Arbitrary Arrests, Abuse of Detainees*, HUMAN RIGHTS WATCH, Sept. 30, 2011, *available at* http://www.hrw.org/news/2011/09/30/libya-cease-arbitrary-arrests-abuse-detainees.

[561] *See supra* Sec. 6.3(b)(iii).

[562] *See supra* Sec. 6.2. *See also* Ch. III, Sec. 2.

to charges, the existence of the amnesties passed in May 2012 could help
the ICC argue that charges are admissible based on the apparent inability
inability/unwillingness on the part of the Libyan government to prosecute
in its own courts.

In sum, the obstacles to accountability are many. As stated above, they
include a system of justice where law enforcement and prosecution does
not have the capacity to carry out its responsibilities. The CoI noted that
few of the officials it met with demonstrated a real understanding of basic
legal and human rights standards, such as the right to a defense.[563] This
is one issue that can easily be remedied through effective human rights
training. Regrettably, however, the international community has not seen
fit to pressure the government and use whatever influence in could to
carry out an effective capacity-building in country. Instead, it has allowed
Qatar, a country that supported the *thuwar* with weapons during the conflict, to offer itself as a training ground for the legal system when that
country does not have the capacity to do so. As for law enforcement, Jordan had offered to do the training, but it has come to the realization that
the personnel sent by Libya was so undisciplined that it returned most of
them and is only focusing on a limited number. The Libyan government
has no effective law enforcement system, and its recruitment of militia
members into the system is hardly an effective means to recruit qualified
persons. The Justice Minister Saleh Marghani has expressed the desire to
train thousands of new recruits to the judicial police to strengthen the
police corps to manage the detention facilities that the Justice Ministry
is taking over from the militias.[564] The capacity and support provided by
the international community to carry out this training, however, remains
to be seen.

---

[563] Report of the International Commission of Inquiry, advance unedited version (Mar.
2, 2012), *supra* note 12 at Annex I, ¶ 40.
[564] *Statement by Justice Minister of Libya Saleh Marghani about Libya Chapter of HRW
World Report 2013, supra* note 269.

CHAPTER FIVE

THE POST-CONFLICT PERIOD

1. Introduction

To outside observers, the Libyan conflict appeared to have ended with the killing of Muʿammar Qadhafi on 20 October 2011. To the initiated observer, however, the conflict started coming to an end several months earlier when the balance of military power had shifted to the *thuwar* largely as a result of NATO. The latter had by then gone well beyond the original scope of its civilian protection mandate[1] and was heavily involved in neutralizing the military capabilities of the Qadhafi regime and aiding the *thuwar* advances.[2] As this process unfolded, both sides realized that the end was inevitable and that the regime would ultimately fall, except for a few on the regime side, the zeal of pro-regime supporters abated and the *thuwar* became more encouraged and emboldened. Many in the population who had not taken sides rallied to the prospective winners and the ranks of the *thuwar* grew significantly. This followed a familiar pattern in which a large number of the population flock to the side of the more clearly identified prospective winner. This process was significantly enhanced in Libya by the availability of large stockpile of weapons in the country, whereby the newcomers to the *thuwar* side were able to arm themselves effectively and acquire a new role in the conflict.[3]

The increase in individuals joining the *thuwar* in the latter days of the conflict was in part based on the expectation that they would benefit from the fruits of victory. Many expected jobs or other material rewards for their participation in the conflict. When these rewards were not forthcoming these *thuwar* held on to those who they had taken as prisoners as a way of securing ransoms and other financial benefits. These factors made it difficult for the government to screen out individual fighters with involvement

---

[1] For more on UN Security Council Resolution 1973 and the interpretation of the civilian protection mandate by NATO forces, *see* Ch. III.

[2] For information on the role of NATO within each theater of military operations, *see* Part Two.

[3] By comparison other conflicts such as the one in Syria, have not allowed this expansion due to the absence of weapons. *See infra* Sec. 3.

in past violations or criminal activity and select among the *thuwar* those who had effectively contributed to the war effort. The assumption was that those who had fought for longer periods and had clean backgrounds had the type of experience that could be incorporated into the armed forces and the police. With a large number of people who had simply joined the *thuwar* without having any such experience it became difficult to incorporate them into the security apparatus thus increasing the problems between the government and the various factions of the *thuwar* particularly those to which a large number of younger people had flocked to, and who because of their access to arms constituted a threat to security and stability in the country.

Another consequence of that situation was that various factions of the *thuwar* found it necessary or convenient to start selling weapons, particularly due to the large stockpiles they discovered during the war. This has had significant regional consequences, as UN experts have determined that an "outpouring" of arms and fighters from Libya has exacerbated neighboring conflicts, such as the one in Mali.[4] Fighters and weapons from Libya have reached the Syrian conflict as well, with the arms transfers organized by a range of actors in Libya, Syria, and neighboring countries.[5] The trafficking patterns have followed routs from Libya to the Sahel, as well as from eastern Libya to Egypt and through to the Gaza Strip.[6] The proliferation of arms was due in part to the failure of the interim authorities to guard the stockpiles of government-owned weapons after the fall of the Qadhafi regime, and the international community to regulate the flow of weapons across Libya's borders.[7]

The interim government's inability to stem the weapons flows and control the armed groups that dominated Libya's post-conflict environment stemmed from long-term political and structural deficiencies. The Qadhafi regime left behind a state that lacked functioning government institutions and was dominated by paramilitary and political structures that carried out systematic acts of state-sanctioned violence. Libya's entire pre-war security structure was very much a product of the erratic, if not psychotic, behavior of Qadhafi himself.[8] One of the defining characteristics

---

[4] U.N. Security Council, Final report of the Panel of Experts established pursuant to resolution 1973 (2011) concerning Libya, ¶ 19, U.N. S/2013/99 (Mar. 9, 2013).

[5] *Id.* at ¶ 158.

[6] *Id.* at ¶¶ 37–39.

[7] U.N. SC, ¶ 13, U.N. Doc 2/2012/178 (Mar. 26, 2012).

[8] For more on the Qadhafi's behavior and erratic policies, *see* Ch. I, Sec. 11. *See also* Ch. II, Sec. 2.2.

of the Qadhafi era was the pervasive influence of unofficial security organizations that operated as the enforcers of the regime's authoritarian policies.[9] The Revolutionary Guard, Popular Guard, Revolutionary Committees, and other paramilitary actors were part of an armed structure that operated parallel to the regular armed forces.[10] The policies enacted during Qadhafi's popular revolution served to dissolve government institutions and structures and left behind shadow administrative bodies with no substantive authority or mechanisms for accountability. Even the very minimal institutions that Qadhafi inherited from the previous monarchy, or that could be say to constitute a normal state, were stripped away, and for 42 years Libya was not run not by functioning institutions, but rather by Qadhafi's informal security bodies, members of his family and his trusted inner-circle.[11] This dysfunctional system provided Libyan society with a marginal foundation to build upon as the country transitioned in the post-dictatorship era.[12]

Due to this legacy of neglect and misuse, the interim government adopted a state without institutions capable of meeting the needs of society. The lack of trained officials to carry out basic public safety functions or provide social provisions allowed for non-state actors to assert their control, thereby making it difficult for the NTC and GNC to build a functional state. The Libyan government as well as the international community has been confronted with the fact that a large number of the members of the armed groups carried over from the war might not have any other trade or ability to be absorbed into society. Allowing these individuals to be marginalized and slip into unlawful activity poses a serious threat to domestic as well as regional security.

Many of Libya's post-conflict challenges are the direct consequence of the conflict or a result of its spillover effects. War brings about obvious

---

[9] Analysts have noted that repressive security structures built under authoritarian states are not easily transformed into democratic bodies, as it requires enormous efforts to disband and reform security organizations that are inextricably intertwined with past political repression. *See* JESSE FRANZBLAU, INFORMATION CONTROL AND HUMAN RIGHTS: TRANSFORMING GOVERNMENT ARCHIVES INTO TOOLS FOR CIVIL SOCIETY, 13 MICHIGAN JOURNAL OF PUBLIC AFFAIRS 4 (Spring 2012), *available at* http://www.mjpa.umich.edu/uploads/2012/franzblau.pdf.

[10] For information on irregular security organizations that operated under Qadhafi, *see* Ch. I, Sec. 9.

[11] For information on the Qadhafi security apparatus, *see* Ch. II, Sec. 2. For Qadhafi's family and inner-circle, *see* Ch. IV, Sec. 6.3.

[12] ALISON PARGETER, LIBYA: THE RISE AND FALL OF QADDAFI 117 (New Haven, USA: Yale University Press, 2012).

social and political strife that has a direct effect on the populations involved. The Libyan war involved extraordinary levels of violence that penetrated every segment of society and exacerbated divisions among the population by pitting groups and towns against each other for means of survival. As with all wars, the civilian population suffered drastically, as they were caught between opposing factions and suffered sieges, rocket fire, shelling, widespread arrests, and other abuses. The war, in addition to the legacy of four decades of repressive dictatorship, left behind deep wounds that caused social trauma at the personal and national level. While this chapter does not directly discuss the impact of the war on future generations, the lasting effects must be considered.[13]

There are other spillover effects that are related to the overthrow of Qadhafi that are addressed in this chapter. The spreading sphere of influence of Islamist groups, for example, is an issue of concern that is still unfolding and the extent of which is yet to be determined. The success of the Muslim Brotherhood in neighboring Egypt has inspired Libya's Islamist groups to organize and embrace the election process as a means for political and social influence. It is still unforeseen whether Libya's Islamists will follow the Egyptian model or that of Tunisia, which has been influenced by a liberal expatriate community that favors a more pluralistic system based on Islamist values. Libya, however, features unique characteristics in its history and evolution that distinguish it from both of these countries, notably the experience of the 2011 conflict. The militarization of society resulting from the proliferation of arms, many of which were supplied by foreign states during the 2011 conflict, has fueled the capacity of Islamist groups to form powerful armed forces calling for the imposition of Shar'ia law. This includes groups such as the Ansar al-Sharī'a militia – the group widely suspected for its involvement in the 11 September 2012 attack on the U.S. Consulate in Benghazi.[14]

The extent and the nature of the influence of political Islam in Libya remains to be seen. The attack in Benghazi was quickly followed by demonstrations with locals demanding the removal of the Ansar al-Sharī'a militia, voicing their objection to militarism and the imposition of Shar'ia law. These demonstrators could very well represent a strong majority of

---

[13] Tani Marilena Adams, Woodrow Wilson Center, Chronic Violence and its Reproduction: Perverse Trends in Social Relations, Citizenship, and Democracy in Latin America (Sept. 2011), *available at* http://www.wilsoncenter.org/sites/default/files/Chronic%20Violence%20and%20its%20Reproduction_1.pdf.

[14] *See infra* Sec. 4.

eastern Libya, and that the militant factions receive a disproportionate amount of attention due to the amplifying effect that sensational acts of terrorism tend to have.[15] This chapter examines the role of Libya's Islamists in the political, social and security landscape.

There is also a wide range of other factors, including regionalism, tribalism and ethnic divisions, that will make it difficult for any militia or single group to gain control over large areas of Libya. At the same time, however, this fractionalization could allow for an influential political party, such as the Muslim Brotherhood, to gain widespread control through the electoral process. There does not appear to be any unified force that can compete with an organized party such as the Muslim Brotherhood, which sustained an underground following for decades during the Qadhafi years and has a history of organizing and recruiting in eastern Libya.[16] Leaders of the Brotherhood attest that membership has doubled since the start of the uprising in February 2011, and the group has become increasingly influential in civil society and economic spheres.[17]

This chapter further highlights some of the unintended consequences that appear to have resulted from the 2011 foreign intervention in Libya. Overthrowing any regime by force brings with it certain consequences, many of which are unforeseen or ignored by the protagonists. In the Libyan context, the proliferation of non-state armed actors and weapons beyond Libya's borders after the end of the 2011 conflict has raised serious questions over the rationale for overthrowing Qadhafi while doing little to contain the weapons supplied to the opposition or control the domestic stockpiles acquired by the opposition.[18] Moreover, it is evident that the absence of a development plan for the post-Qadhafi era contributed to the country's ongoing turmoil, and it appears that the foreign actors did not fully consider the international impact of arming the Libyan insurgency that fostered the revolution.

---

[15] For more on terrorism and its amplified effects, *see* M. Cherif Bassiouni, *Legal Control of International Terrorism: A Policy-Oriented Assessment*, 43 HARV. INT'L L.J. 83 (2002).

[16] For more on the background on the Muslim Brotherhood, *see* Ch. I, Sec. 8.1.

[17] INTERNATIONAL CRISIS GROUP, HOLDING LIBYA TOGETHER: SECURITY CHALLENGES AFTER QADHAFI 10 (Dec. 14, 2011) [hereinafter "HOLDING LIBYA TOGETHER"], *available at* http://www.crisisgroup.org/~/media/Files/Middle%20East%20North%20Africa/North%20Africa/115%20Holding%20Libya%20Together%20--%20Security%20Challenges%20after%20Qadhafi.pdf.

[18] For more on materiel supplied by foreign actors during the 2011 conflict, *see* Ch. III, Sec. 7.1.

As the international community considers policy options with respect to interventions in other countries, the situation in Libya merits close attention. It is clear that there was little planning for a post-Qadhafi Libya in the lead-up to the February 2011 intervention, and no public discussion regarding the decision to arm and train the rebel forces on the ground. The current debate regarding Syria, similarly, is lacking serious deliberation with regards to the potential consequences of arming insurgents to fight the Assad regime. While the situations in the two countries are unique in their circumstances, they share commonalities – as is evidenced by the Libyan rebel fighters who are joining the fight in Syria – and this should be taken into account.[19] The on-going instability in Libya should be considered by policymakers as part of a wider examination of the potential consequences of foreign intervention in domestic conflicts, particularly in the MENA region.

2. The Security Landscape in the Post-Qadhafi Era

Libya's post-conflict security apparatus was comprised of a patchwork of *thuwar* forces and a mixture of militias that held power and control over particular areas, government facilities, and much of the country's prison system. As the transitional government worked to piece together a functioning police and military forces, it attempted to integrate the revolutionary brigades into the new armed forces by absorbing some groups and creating new forces under the control of government ministries. The result was a complex network of overlapping entities with un-defined chains of command and security organizations that operated with nominal government control or in parallel to official government forces.

Reports indicate that approximately 1,700 various armed groups emerged from the rebel forces that fought during the 2011 conflict.[20] Many of these groups were distrustful of the new government, and unwilling to give up the power and independence they fought hard to achieve. The various armed fronts around Libya had their own arguments that they claimed justified or legitimated them, whether they were the first to rebel in eastern Libya, played a role in liberating Tripoli (such as the Misrata and Zintan-based brigades), or had suffered most from Qadhafi's repression.

---

[19] For more on Libyan *thuwar* fighters who are now in Syria, *see infra* Sec. 3.

[20] *Disarming Libya's militias*, BBC, Sept. 28, 2012, *available at* http://www.bbc.co.uk/news/world-middle-east-19744533.

Regardless of their justifications, the armed actors were reluctant to relinquish their weapons and positions of influence in the post-conflict period.

The interests of the armed factions varied across the spectrum of groups, and were often difficult to define. The armed groups often had different loyalties, were varied in composition, and were defined by geographic boundaries and shifting political allegiances. During the war there was a sense of unity between the *thuwar* forces due to their desire to overthrow Qadhafi. As politics took center stage following the fall of regime, however, solidarity in a common struggle began to dissipate and the intentions of the militia groups became divided among competing interests and objectives.

The autonomous armed factions that operated in the post-conflict period were an outgrowth of Libya's long-standing social divisions based on regional affiliation, tribal allegiance, and in some cases religion. For example, some groups political Islamist groups had a history of militarily resisting the Qadhafi regime and who fought on the front lines and held influential positions among the *thuwar*, saw the National Transitional Council (NTC) as overly secular and far removed from ordinary Libyans.[21] Trying to reconcile these groups in the most-Qadhafi era has proved difficult. Adding to the complexities are the large numbers of people joined the ranks of the *thuwar* forces in the final phase of the conflict in order to ensure that they would be on the winning side. These individuals had no real allegiances or interests in contributing to a functioning state in the post-Qadhafi era, but they had weapons and held positions or power, which they used to secure their own economic and/or political interests.

All of these issues took center stages as the transitional government attempted to integrate the disparate armed actors that existed after the conflict into a unified security system. The following sections of this chapter trace the formation of the police and military forces during the transitional period, and the genesis of the non-state armed actors that came to hold unprecedented influence over the country's security and political affairs.

---

[21] For example, in early September 2011, Isma'il Sallabi, commander of the 17 February Katiba openly criticized the NTC leaders, referring to them as "secularists" and accusing them of having "their own private agenda." *See* HOLDING TOGETHER LIBYA, *supra* note 17 at 3 n. 3.

2.1. *Revolutionary Forces and the Interim-Government*

The history of repressive security forces, the nature of the 2011 war, and manner in which the conflict came to a close all factored into the challenges to creating a functioning and accountable security apparatus after the fall of Qadhafi. The power vacuum left behind in the wake of the war was quickly filled with an abundance of heavily armed *thuwar kata'ib* that held control over large spans of territory, the country's major cities and government installations. In an effort to stabilize the country, the NTC gave tacit or direct approval to military councils and armed groups to handle security detail and manage disputes within their area of control. *Thuwar* groups such as the Swihli Katiba, for example, which was formerly part of the Misrata Military Council, provided protection to government buildings in Tripoli after Qadhafi fled in August 2011. Led by Farah al-Swihli, the Swihli Katiba formed part of the state's auxiliary forces and operated with approval from the NTC but only answered to its own leadership.[22] Other powerful brigades carried out security functions in other cities, such as the 17 February Katiba, which provided security for government buildings in Benghazi, including the U.S. Special Mission.[23] The U.S. State Department Accountability Review Board report ("ARB report") described the 17 February Katiba as "a local umbrella organization of militias dominant in Benghazi (some of which were Islamist) an loosely affiliated with the Libyan government, but not under its control."[24]

In an attempt to gain control over the armed factions, in October 2011 the Ministry of Interior created the Supreme Security Committee (SSC) to incorporate the revolutionary brigades and bring them under the NTC's authority.[25] The creation of the SSC served its purpose by reducing the fragmentation of the brigades and providing a unified command and control structure. Additionally, the SSC provided the state with the auxiliary

---

[22] For more on the Misrata *kata'ib*, see Ch. II, Sec. 2.3. *See also* BBC, *Disarming Libya's militias, supra* note 20.

[23] For more on the attack on the 11 September 2012 U.S. consulate in Benghazi, *see infra* Sec. 4. *See also* Max Fisher, *Libyan militia's failed security at Benghazi*, THE WASHINGTON POST, Nov. 2, 2012, *available at* http://www.washingtonpost.com/blogs/worldviews/wp/2012/11/02/libyan-militias-failed-security-at-benghazi/.

[24] U.S. DEPARTMENT OF STATE OFFICE OF THE INSPECTOR GENERAL, ACCOUNTABILITY REVIEW BOARD (ARB) REPORT ON THE SEPTEMBER 11TH ATTACK IN BENGHAZI (Dec. 18, 2012) [hereinafter "U.S. DEPARTMENT OF STATE ARB REPORT"], *available at* http://www.state.gov/documents/organization/202446.pdf.

[25] HOLDING TOGETHER LIBYA, *supra* note 17 at 32.

forces urgently needed for dispatch whenever hostilities flared up.[26] Made up of recruits from former *thuwar* and disbanded security units, the SSC operated under the authority of the Ministry of Interior and was deployed across the country.[27] The SSC quickly became one of the most prominent security contingents in the country, numbering approximately 60,000 to 70,000 fighters in May 2012.[28] A few months later the SSC was estimated to include about 90,000 to 100,000 fighters.[29]

Despite the attempts by the Interior Ministry to integrate the security forces under its authority, the SSC often acted independently and answered largely to regional commanders outside of the central government's control.[30] In an attempt to assert control over the SSC and other armed actors, the NTC reserved leadership positions for individuals who held influence among the revolutionary fighters and militia forces. In November 2011, the NTC replaced several officials with those linked to local militias, apparently prioritizing regional affiliations and influence above political experience.[31] The appointments included former commanders of the Misrata and Zintan *kata'ib* to ministry positions.[32]

One of these officials included 'Usama al-Juwayli, a former leader of the Zintan Military Council, who was appointed as Minister of Defense.[33] The appointment of Al-Juwayli came days after the Zintan Katiba captured Saif al-Islam on 19 November, which raised the profile of al-Juwayli and his forces.[34] Under Al-Juwayli, the Defense Ministry took steps to

---

[26] Letter dated 23 March 2012 from the Chairman of the Security Council Committee established pursuant to resolution 1970 (2011) concerning Libya addressed to the President of the Security Council (S/2012/178), U.N. Doc. S/PV.6768 (May 10, 2012).

[27] Chris Stephen, *Libya sees claims of beatings and human rights abuses as elections near*, THE GUARDIAN, June 3, 2012, *available at* http://www.guardian.co.uk/world/2012/jun/03/libya-security-force-kidnapping-surgeon.

[28] Letter dated 23 March 2012 from the Chairman of the Security Council Committee, *supra* note 26.

[29] Frederic Wehrey, *Libya's Militia Menace*, FOREIGN AFFAIRS, July 12, 2012, *available at* http://www.foreignaffairs.com/articles/137776/frederic-wehrey/libyas-militia-menace.

[30] The U.S. ARB report described the SSC as "a coalition of militia elements loosely cobbled into a single forces to provide interim security." *See* U.S. DEPARTMENT OF STATE ARB REPORT, *supra* note 24 at 17.

[31] Francois Murphy & Ali Shuaib, *Libya's NTC unveils new government line-up*, REUTERS, Nov. 22, 2011, *available at* http://www.reuters.com/article/2011/11/22/us-libya-idUSTRE7AL0JM20111122.

[32] Amanda Kadlec, *Disarming Libya's Militias*, CARNEGIE ENDOWMENT, Feb. 16, 2012, *available at* http://carnegieendowment.org/sada/2012/02/16/disarming-libya-s-militias/9ofa.

[33] BBC, *Disarming Libya's militias*, *supra* note 20.

[34] Francois Murphy & Ali Shuaib, *Local commander made Libya Defense Minister: NTC source*, REUTERS, Nov. 21, 2011, *available at* http://www.reuters.com/article/2011/11/22/us-libya-idUSTRE7AI0G820111122. For more on the capture of Saif al-Islam, *see* Ch. IV, Sec. 6.

dissolve and integrate the armed factions by giving official accreditation to the military councils, revolutionary brigades and other armed groups across the country.[35] The measures involved little or no investigation into the composition or membership of the groups, however, and effectively entailed paying brigades to register with the army, a policy that embroiled the government in accusations of favoritism.[36] The policies did allow for the formation of another security force that became a prominent actor in the post-war security landscape, namely the Quwat Dira' Libya or Libyan Shield Forces (LSF).[37]

The LSF were created by a network of *thuwar kata'ib* that attempted to organize themselves under a single unified command. In contrast to the SSC, the LSF was created from the bottom up by established by the revolutionary brigades as opposed to an initiative by the government.[38] Eventually, the LSF became better armed than the state forces, and while technically answering to the army chief of staff it operated as a *de facto* army outside of official government control.[39]

The LSF were divided into regional divisions, based on the power bases of the revolutionary brigades, and were reportedly under the command of army General Yusuf al-Mangush, who was appointed chief of staff of the National Army on 2 January 2012.[40] Mangush had fought with the *thuwar* forces in Misrata as a field commander during the uprising, and his appointment was seen as part of the new government's ongoing attempts to appease the militias and encourage the disarmament process.[41] Following his appointment, however, Mangush was able to establish only nominal control over the revolutionary brigades, which accepted his authority but retained autonomy in their decision-making process.[42]

---

[35] *Divided We Stand: Libya's Enduring Conflict*, INTERNATIONAL CRISIS GROUP, Sept. 14, 2012, *available at* http://www.crisisgroup.org/~/media/Files/Middle%20East%20North%20Africa/North%20Africa/libya/130-divided-we-stand-libyas-enduring-conflicts.

[36] *Id.*

[37] BRIAN MCQUINN, SMALL ARMS SURVEY, ARMED GROUPS IN LIBYA: TYPOLOGY AND ROLES (June 2012), *available at* http://www.smallarmssurvey.org/fileadmin/docs/H-Research_Notes/SAS-Research-Note-18.pdf.

[38] Wehrey, *Libya's Militia Menace, supra* note 29.

[39] INTERNATIONAL CRISIS GROUP, *Divided We Stand: Libya's Enduring Conflict, supra* note 35.

[40] Joe Sterling, *Libya picks armed forces chief*, CNN, Jan. 5, 2012, *available at* http://edition.cnn.com/2012/01/04/world/africa/libya-army-chief/.

[41] *Id.*

[42] INTERNATIONAL CRISIS GROUP, *Divided We Stand: Libya's Enduring Conflict, supra* note 35 at 17.

As with the SSC, the LSF functioned as an auxiliary force that was used by the interim government to quell disputes and intervene in communal conflicts taking place in the western Nafusa Mountains region and the Saharan towns of Kufra and Sabha. The first LSF unit was established by Defense Minister 'Usama Juwayli in Kufra in March 2012 weeks after the outbreak of fighting in the region.[43] Shortly after its formation the unit was deployed to Kufra in an effort to manage the conflicts taking place there and in the nearby town of Sabha.[44] The deployment of the LSF inflamed tensions in the area, however, as its soldiers carried out indiscriminate shelling of Kufra and targeted the Tebu community for forceful displacement in April 2012.[45] Clashes between LSF soldiers and Tebu fighters in June led to the reported deaths of 15 people.[46] The LSF came to be seen as an uncontrollable force that carried out security tasks in an abusive manner, was involved in settling old scores, and was accused of favoritism based on its commanders' regional or tribal affiliations.[47]

There were also controversial incidents that drew attention to similar abuses being carried out by SSC forces. On May 17, 2012, for example, a prominent surgeon named Salim Furjani was arrested in Tripoli by members of the SSC. He was accused of having links to the former regime, and was held for five days and tortured before being released.[48] The incident highlighted the precarious security environment and raised international concerns over the ability of the Libyan authorities to control the country's security forces, particularly with the planned June 2012 national elections drawing near.[49] In response to the Furjani incident and numerous complaints over SSC actions, the UK reportedly dispatched a senior police officer to advise Libya's new interior ministry in Tripoli.[50] This advisory mission reportedly was to focus on promoting human rights and facilitating investigations of allegations of abuse, promoting the restoration of

---

[43] *Id.* at 18.

[44] *Report of the Secretary-General on the United Nations Support Mission in Libya,* UNITED NATIONS, U.N. Doc. S/2012/675 (August 30, 2012).

[45] Wehrey, *Libya's Militia Menace, supra* note 29.

[46] *More deaths in Kufra reported,* THE LIBYA HERALD, June 29, 2012, *available at* http://www.libyaherald.com/2012/06/29/more-deaths-in-kufra-reported/.

[47] Frederic Wehry, *Libya's Militia Menace, supra* note 29.

[48] *See* Ch. XIII. *See also* Chris Stephen, *Libya sees claims of beatings and human rights abuses as elections near,* THE GUARDIAN, June 3, 2012, *available at* http://www.guardian.co.uk/world/2012/jun/03/libya-security-force-kidnapping-surgeon.

[49] *See infra* Sec. 6.1.

[50] Stephen, *Libya sees claims of beatings and human rights abuses as elections near, supra* note 48.

security and reintegration of the militias in society.[51] Despite the efforts by the UK government and other international actors, the SSC and other armed groups remained largely outside government control.

Considering the legacy of repressive paramilitary security organizations in Libya, fears grew over the SSC and LSF becoming powerful, self-governing security forces.[52] These concerns were shared by international observers, such as Ian Martin, the UN Special Representative of the Secretary-General (SRSG) and the then head of the UN Support Mission in Libya (UNSMIL), who made statements about the challenges facing the interim government in May 2012 and noted that the SSC was designed to serve a temporary function and that the challenge remained for the Interior Ministry to integrate its forces into the government apparatus.[53] SRSG Martin emphasized the need for stronger coordination of plans for integration, demobilization, and control of weapons to keep the SSC from becoming a parallel security structure.[54]

While the objective for the various security forces identified above was to provide security during the transitional period, they essentially became forces unto themselves,[55] and were only under nominal authority of the government.[56] The LSF came to operate in parallel to the National Army, while the SSC forces operated in parallel to the police.[57] Both functioned as regular military forces, carrying out separate weapons and vehicle registration procedures, and had their own identification cards. They conducted investigations, issued warrants, and arrested and detained suspects without any mechanisms in place to ensure accountability.[58]

Measures taken on behalf of the national government to assert control by placing military officers in charge of the militia groups were tainted by questionable loyalties and overlapping roles the revolutionary forces served during the transitional period. On 24 September 2012, for example, Libya's military announced it would replace the chiefs of the Rafallah al-Sahati Katiba and the February 17 Katiba with government army

---

[51] *Id.*

[52] For more on Qadhafi's paramilitary organizations, *see* Ch. I, Sec. 9 & Ch. II. Sec. 2.

[53] Letter dated 23 March 2012 from the Chairman of the Security Council Committee, *supra* note 26.

[54] *Id.*

[55] Wehry, *Libya's Militia Menace, supra* note 29.

[56] INTERNATIONAL CRISIS GROUP, *Divided We Stand: Libya's Enduring Conflict, supra* note 35.

[57] *Id.*

[58] HOLDING TOGETHER LIBYA, *supra* note 17 at 4.

commanders. Isma'il Sallabi, former leader of the 17 February Katiba, and then-commander of the Raffallah al-Sahati Katiba, stated that he accepted the government's decision to put army officers in charge of the groups, noting that the colonel appointed – Colonel Salahaddin bin 'Umran – was already a member of his militia forces.[59]

2.2. *Disarming and Disbanding Non-State Armed Actors*

The disarmament, demobilization, and reintegration of the revolutionary brigades proved to be one of the most pressing challenges facing the interim authorities in the wake of the conflict. This was most prominent in Tripoli, where *thuwar* groups participated in the liberation of the capital and remained in control of much of the city and its government buildings afterwards.[60] Groups such as the Zintan Katiba from the Nafusa Mountains and the Swihli Katiba from Misrata steadfastly resisted surrendering their weapons and leaving the capital. The Zintan Katiba had played a defining role in the western rebellion, and stationed an estimated 1,000 men at the Tripoli International Airport after helping liberate the capital.[61] The Misrata *kata'ib*, which claimed to have sacrificed thousands during the battle for Tripoli, also maintained a strong presence in the capital.[62] The Tripoli Military Council, a powerful leadership and coordinating body that formed during the conflict, also "maintained its own procedures, detention facilities, weapons depots, and registration systems after the war."[63]

The revolutionary forces became the unofficial power brokers in the capital, occupying government buildings and checkpoints while answering to their own commanders and chain of command structures, disregarding

---

[59] Richard Spencer, *US consulate attack in Benghazi 'disrupted major intelligence operation'*, THE TELEGRAPH, Sept. 24, 2012, *available at* http://www.telegraph.co.uk/news/worldnews/africaandindianocean/libya/9563831/US-consulate-attack-in-Benghazi-disrupted-major-intelligence-operation.html.

[60] Joseph Logan, William Maclean & Barry Malone, *Tripoli armed group says arms spreading to regions*, REUTERS, Sept. 24, 2011, *available at* http://www.reuters.com/article/2011/09/24/libya-weapons-idUSL5E7KO0TQ20110924.

[61] Anthony Shadid, *Libya Struggles to Curb Militias as Chaos Grows*, N.Y. TIMES, Feb. 8, 2012, *available at* http://www.nytimes.com/2012/02/09/world/africa/libyas-new-government-unable-to-control-militias.html; Kadlec, *Disarming Libya's Militias, supra* note 32.

[62] Kadlec, *Disarming Libya's Militias, supra* note 32.

[63] *See* Ch. XIII, Sec. 2. *See also* Report of the International Commission of Inquiry on Libya, U.N. HRC. 19th Sess., Annex I, Par. 72. U.N. Doc. A/HRC/19/68 (Mar. 2, 2012).

the authority of the interim government.[64] The NTC took measures to disarm the militias and encourage them to return to their local cities and towns, ordering all heavy weapons to be removed from Tripoli after the official end to hostilities in October 2011.[65] The NTC also attempted to establish control over territory outside of the capital, including strategic points along the country's borders.[66] The dialogue over the disarmament of militias continued to escalate, and in March 2012, the Libyan authorities demanded the militias put down arms or face confrontation with the new national security forces.[67] The interim authorities were unable to back up the threats with credible action, however, as a result of the continued reliance on the SSC and LSF security bodies as the state's auxiliary forces.

In an effort to take control of the situation, the defense and interior ministries created weapons collection centers and pressured brigades to turnover their arms. By March 2012 the government authorities reported some progress, absorbing 25,000 men into the government forces[68] and registering weapons with the government authorities, sometimes on an individual basis.[69] In general, however, the effort was met with only very limited success as most armed groups did not respond to the initiatives. The efforts to reduce the amount of guns in circulation were also hindered by rumors of future government weapon buy-back programs, which inadvertently encouraged fighters and civilians to retain their weapons.[70]

At the same time, non-state armed groups took it upon themselves to register weapons, often without NTC approval or coordination. In Misrata, for example, unregulated armed groups continued to exercise control over large stockpiles of light weapons and other conventional weapons obtained or used during the war.[71] At these sites and elsewhere, brigades

---

[64] Ayman al-Sahli, *Libya interior minister calls time on rogue militias*, REUTERS, Mar. 10, 2012, *available at* http://www.reuters.com/article/2012/03/10/us-libya-militias-idUSBRE8290DA20120310.

[65] *Libya to disarm Tripoli by year end*, AL JAZEERA, Dec. 7, 2011, *available at* http://www.aljazeera.com/news/africa/2011/12/20111262350566641.html.

[66] Gabriel Gatehouse, *Battle of wills over control of Libya's border crossings*, BBC, Mar. 2, 2012, *available at* http://www.bbc.co.uk/news/world-africa-17233519.

[67] Al-Sahli, *Libya interior minister calls time on rogue militias, supra* note 64.

[68] *Id.*

[69] INTERNATIONAL CRISIS GROUP, *Divided We Stand: Libya's Enduring Conflict, supra* note 35.

[70] MCQUINN, ARMED GROUPS IN LIBYA: TYPOLOGY AND ROLES, *supra* note 37.

[71] *City's huge arsenal a test for new Libyan rulers*, REUTERS, Dec. 7, 2011, *available at* http://www.reuters.com/article/2011/12/07/libya-misrata-weapons-idUSL5E7N72IH20111207.

maintained their own security and implemented their own procedures for registering weapons.[72]

The reluctance by the armed groups to turn over their weapons stemmed in part from a lack of confidence in the transitional authorities or any central authority ruling from Tripoli. Many of the powerful militia forces around Libya in the wake of the war were distrustful of those within the NTC government, based on concerns over their legitimacy and lack of transparency over public affairs.[73] Further undermining the NTC's authority was the perception that it continued to favor Qadhafi-era loyalists. The appointment of Yusuf al-Mangush – a former colonel who had defected from the Qadhafi regime – as the army chief of staff, for example, placated some groups but was rejected by others who opposed anyone with a connection to the former regime.[74] Some of the *thuwar* were also displeased by the fact that their candidates for influential positions in government were dismissed in favor of individuals connected to other revolutionary forces.[75] Finally, many feared being out-maneuvered by politicians and returning exiles who had not participated in the fighting, but were gaining positions of influence in the post-Qadhafi government.[76]

While the interim government relied on some of the non-state armed actors for security purposes, it issued orders to others to disband and surrender their weapons, often conveying an uneven policy of favoritism. In the wake of the 11 September 2012 attack in Benghazi, for example, head of the General National Congress (GNC) and interim head of state Muhammad al-Mugarayf ordered "unauthorized" militias such as Ansar al-Sharī'a to disband and leave their military compounds.[77] Following these orders, however, Chief of Staff General Mangush warned that a number of Libya's militias were officially authorized, operating under the army's direction, and were still needed to control the country.[78] The incident demonstrated the contradictory policy where the interim government continued to rely

---

[72] McQuinn, Armed Groups in Libya: Typology and Roles, *supra* note 37.

[73] *Id.*

[74] Kadlec, *Disarming Libya's Militias, supra* note 32.

[75] *Id.*

[76] Ali Shuaib, *Anti-Gaddafi fighters demand role in the new Libya*, Reuters, Nov. 19, 2011, *available at* http://www.reuters.com/article/2011/11/19/us-libya-government-fighters-idUSTRE7AI0W320111119.

[77] David D. Kirkpatrick, *Government Issues Order to Disband Libya Forces*, N.Y. Times, Sept. 23, 2012, *available at* http://www.nytimes.com/2012/09/24/world/africa/libya-orders-unauthorized-militias-to-disband.html.

[78] *Id.*

on the militia groups as auxiliary forces for security matters while at the same time it attempted to reign in on their influence.

The policy of dismantling militias unfavorable to parts of the interim government also heightened the risk that armed brigades would splinter into uncontrollable factions that would become more deeply involved in illicit criminal activity and political violence. As a result of the swelling of the ranks of the *thuwar* forces near the end of the conflict, criminal elements were able to infiltrate or establish revolutionary military councils, including "gangs, criminal groups or local armed communities with their own specific agendas," while "others engaged in looting or were involved in criminal activities."[79] Dismantling the unauthorized armed structures, therefore, raised concerns that the policy could unintentionally drive some factions of these groups even further towards criminal activity. The aforementioned influential militia leader, Isma'il Sallabi, made reference to this issue when he warned that disbanding groups like the Ansar al-Sharī'a Katiba could force its members underground, "into the shadows" of Libyan society.[80]

The efforts to dismantle some militias and integrate others into the state forces without proper vetting procedures allowed for parallel powers to form and operate outside of official government control. The reigning influence of unaccountable armed militias also conjured up memories from the Qadhafi-era when paramilitary security organizations infiltrated state institutions for decades.[81] Without viable alternatives for employment and marginalized from the security forces, those with weapons have demonstrated their capacity to hold the government institutions hostage, making security sector and judicial reform that much more difficult.[82]

Libya's armed forces from the war posed difficult security and political challenges for the transitional government. The attempts to clear the capital from militias were largely unsuccessful and a long-term plan of disarmament and reintegration was clearly lacking. The entrenched power of

---

[79] INTERNATIONAL CRISIS GROUP, *Divided We Stand: Libya's Enduring Conflict, supra* note 35.

[80] Spencer, *US consulate attack in Benghazi 'disrupted major intelligence operation', supra* note 59.

[81] AMNESTY INTERNATIONAL, LIBYA: RULE OF LAW OR RULE OF MILITIAS (June 2012), *available at* http://www.amnesty.org/en/library/asset/MDE19/012/2012/en/f2d36090-5716-4ef1-81a7-f4b1ebdo82fc/mde190122012en.pdf.

[82] William Wheeler, *Libya's purge of former Gaddafi officials reveals growing power of militias*, GLOBAL POST, June 4, 2013, *available at* http://www.globalpost.com/dispatches/globalpost-blogs/groundtruth/libya-political-isolation-law-militias.

the revolutionary brigades and competing interest within Libya's government in transition exacerbated the challenge of establishing centralized control and stabilizing the country, particularly with regards to the country's detention facilities.

2.3. Detention Facilities

Many of the country's prison buildings and police stations were destroyed during the conflict, either by retreating Qadhafi forces or by *thuwar* who sought to destroy the symbols of repression of the Qadhafi regime.[83] Indeed, the prisons had been sites of systematic abuses during the Qadhafi era, particularly those used to hold political prisoners such as Abu Salim and 'Ain Zara in Tripoli. In these prisons those accused of crimes had been denied access to proper defense and lawyers were not allowed to visit, and were often subject to severe treatment.

During the fighting, and in the wake of the 2011 conflict, *thuwar* forces carried out sweeping arrests and took control of many of the country's detention facilities in the process, and also set up their own independent detention facilities. The establishment of new facilities by non-state armed groups, which had only an informal relationship with the state,[84] led to problems over the management and chain of authority over the prison system, with some facilities coming under NTC control and others under the control of *thuwar kata'ib* operating autonomous of the NTC. As the CoI pointed out, after the fall of the regime, "most detained Qadhafi soldiers and alleged loyalists were held in unofficial centres outside of the legal framework."[85]

The CoI reported that as of March 2012 there had been limited progress in the transfer of detainees and detention facilities from *thuwar* military councils and committees to the control of the government ministries, and that individual *thuwar* brigades continued to hold detainees outside the framework of the law.[86] UN SRSG Martin, reported in May 2012 that conflict-related detentions were ongoing, and that their transfer of custody

---

[83] Report of the International Commission of Inquiry (Mar. 2012) *supra* note 63 at Annex I, ¶ 40.

[84] *Libya: Diplomat Dies in Militia Custody*, HUMAN RIGHTS WATCH, Feb. 3, 2012, *available at* http://www.hrw.org/news/2012/02/02/libya-diplomat-dies-militia-custody.

[85] Report of the International Commission of Inquiry (Mar. 2012) *supra* note 63 at Annex I, ¶ 50.

[86] *Id.* at Annex I, ¶ 46.

to the Ministry of Justice was slow.[87] The Ministry of Justice stated at the time that it had taken control of 31 facilities, accounting for some 3,000 total detainees.[88] Amnesty International reported, however, that as of July 2012 it had a list of 11 of the prisons under the control of the Ministry of Justice: 'Ain Zara, Al-Jadayda, Open Prison (Maftu) and Tajura (known as Hofra)[89] in Tripoli and its suburbs; Dafniyya, Tumina and Al-Wahda in Misrata; Khums Prison; Zlitan Prison; and Jadayem Prison in Zawiyya.[90] The total number of prisoners under the custody of the Ministry of Justice was less that half the total number of prisoners held in Libya. The United Nations reported in May 2012 that of the approximately 7,000 detainees in the country, 3,000 were held in the government-run facilities, while around 4,000 prisoners remained under the custody of *thuwar*, either at known or secret detention facilities.[91] Human Rights Watch (HRW), however, has reported a higher numbers of detainees as of October 2012, concluding that the number of conflict-related detainees was stable at an estimated 8,000 in detention, of which 3,000 were outside the nominal control of government ministries or the military.[92]

In a practice reminiscent of the former regime, detainees at these facilities have not been provided with adequate access to legal representation or made aware or of their right to representation. In most instances, detainees have been granted access to lawyers only once their case has been transferred to court.[93] Detention officials told Amnesty International that lawyers were permitted to visit the prison only if they had permission from the General Prosecution.[94]

In this system, where detainees were denied access to justice and outside the protection of the government, they were vulnerable to ransom,

---

[87] Letter dated 23 March 2012 from the Chairman of the Security Council Committee, *supra* note 26 at 5.

[88] *Id.* at 5.

[89] The transliteration of this place was adopted from the reference. AMNESTY INTERNATIONAL, LIBYA: RULE OF LAW OR RULE OF MILITIAS *supra* note 81 at 14.

[90] *Id.*

[91] Letter dated 23 March 2012 from the Chairman of the Security Council Committee, *supra* note 26 at 5. *See also* Press Release, *High Expectations for Quick Progress in Libya Strain Political System, but Given 'Terrible Legacy', Transitional Team Should Be Praised*, Security Council Told, UNITED NATIONS, May 10, 2012, *available at* http://www.un.org/News/Press/docs/2012/sc10644.doc.htm.

[92] HUMAN RIGHTS WATCH, WORLD REPORT 2013: LIBYA (February 2013), *available at* http://www.hrw.org/world-report/2013/country-chapters/libya.

[93] AMNESTY INTERNATIONAL, LIBYA: RULE OF LAW OR RULE OF MILITIAS *supra* note 81 at 30.

[94] *Id.*

extortion and abuse, as detention center guards and militia members sought to benefit financially from the large number of detainees in their custody. As the conflict drew to a close, arrests by *thuwar* forces became more arbitrary, and detainees were able to buy their way out of jail, or were released through friends or relatives with the right connections.[95] In one example at the Bu Rashada detention center in the city of Al-Gharyan in the Nafusa Mountains region, officials forced non-Libyan nationals to pay fines to secure their release after being arrested.[96]

Amnesty International documented incidents of extortion, where perpetrators of the arrests contacted family members of the victims demanding payment in exchange for their release. If the demands were not met, the victims suffered abuse in detention, in some cases leading to death. One such case was documented at a detention center in Tripoli in October 2011.[97] Thus, prisoners were used as bargaining chips for financial gain as well as for political favors. In other prisons, detainees, notably migrant workers, were forced to perform hard labor for lucrative private ventures.[98]

In a troubling trend, the physical abuse of detainees has re-emerged in the post-conflict period. The CoI observed that the practice of abusing detainees, which was prevalent during the Qadhafi era, was common in the post-conflict period.[99] In the wake of the conflict, most of the country's prison facilities, official and unofficial, failed to meet the UN Standard Minimum Rules for the Treatment of Prisoners.[100] The unclear lines of authority and lack of accountability and oversight mechanisms allowed for rampant abuses to occur in detention facilities across the country, including

---

[95] *See* Report of the International Commission of Inquiry (Mar. 2012), *supra* note 75 at Annex I, ¶ 298.

[96] AMNESTY INTERNATIONAL, LIBYA: RULE OF LAW OR RULE OF MILITIAS, *supra* note 81 at 43.

[97] AMNESTY INTERNATIONAL, MILITIAS THREATEN HOPES FOR NEW LIBYA 27 (Feb. 16, 2012), *available at* http://www.amnesty.org/en/library/asset/MDE19/002/2012/en/dd7c1d69-e368-44de-8ee8-cc9365bd5eb3/mde190022012en.pdf.

[98] AMNESTY INTERNATIONAL, LIBYA: RULE OF LAW OR RULE OF MILITIAS, *supra* note 97 at 41; *Libya: Cease Arbitrary Arrests, Abuse of Detainees*, HUMAN RIGHTS WATCH, Sept. 30, 2011, *available at* http://www.hrw.org/news/2011/09/30/libya-cease-arbitrary-arrests-abuse-detainees.

[99] Report of the International Commission of Inquiry (Mar. 2012), *supra* note 63 at Annex I, ¶ 42.

[100] Standard Minimum Rules for the Treatment of Prisoners, E.S.C. Res. 663 C (XXIV) UN Doc. E/3048, July 31, 1957, *amended by* E.S.C. res. 2076, UN Doc. E/5988 (May 13, 1977); Report of the International Commission of Inquiry (Mar. 2012), *supra* note 63 at Annex I, ¶ 40.

acts of torture. At times, government authorities acknowledged the incidents of torture, but claimed they were unable to curtail the abuses.[101]

Amnesty International documented cases of torture taking place in the prisons after the conflict, such as in two interrogation centers in Misrata, which it visited in January 2012.[102] While the centers were reportedly under the control of government bodies, such as the SSC and military security, there were unclear lines of authority between the state officials and the non-state actors involved in the transfer and detention of prisoners in the facilities. Officials in charge of interrogations told Amnesty International that torture did not take place at the detention center, claiming that the individuals showing signs of torture had been delivered to the detention facility in that condition.[103] The detainees themselves, however, reported being tortured by both the armed groups that brought them to the detention facilities and by the guards at the detentions facilities themselves.[104] There are recorded incidents in which the judicial police or prosecutors ordered the release of detainees, but *thuwar* forces controlling the detention centers refused to implement the judicial release orders.[105] In some cases torture and mistreatment led to the deaths of detainees. In April 2012, SRSG Martin expressed particular concern over a deaths taking place in a detention center in Misrata.[106]

In order to address the ongoing problems with detention facilities, Justice Minister Salah Marghani issued a statement in February 2013 indicating that thousands of new judicial police recruits would be trained, and that efforts to take over all the country's detention centers in Libya and criminalize detentions outside the control of the Ministry of Justice were still underway.[107] In order to successfully implement these policies, however, the government authorities need to overcome serious challenges

---

[101] Shadid, *Libya Struggles to Curb Militias as Chaos Grows, supra* note 61.

[102] For more on documented abuses in the detention facilities in Misrata, *see* Ch. IX, Secs. 3.3. & 3.4.

[103] AMNESTY INTERNATIONAL, MILITIAS THREATEN HOPES FOR NEW LIBYA, supra note 97 at 14.

[104] *Id.*

[105] AMNESTY INTERNATIONAL, DETENTION ABUSES STAINING THE NEW LIBYA 18 (Oct. 2011), *available at* http://www.amnesty.org/en/library/asset/MDE19/036/2011/en/e1c30d0f-8ec3-4368-8537-03f1bb15a051/mde190362011en.pdf.

[106] Letter dated 23 March 2012 from the Chairman of the Security Council Committee, *supra* note 26 at 5.

[107] *Statement by Justice Minister of Libya Saleh Marghani about Libya Chapter of HRW World Report 2013*, HUMAN RIGHTS WATCH, Feb. 6, 2013, *available at* http://www.hrw.org/sites/default/files/related_material/2013_Libya_Worldreport.pdf.

remaining from the entrenched militia influence and unstable security environment.

2.4. *Continued Instability*

In addition to the challenges stemming from the lack of control over the country's prison system, the presence of non-state armed actors has led to ongoing clashes in several regions during the post-war period. The clashes that erupted in Tripoli and in other parts of Libya after the fall of Qadhafi reflected the inability of the interim government to assert effective control over the country's security institutions, which is essential in preventing such clashes in the future.[108] In Tripoli, the armed *kata'ib* competed for control of the capital, occupying strategic areas and government installations. The presence of groups from different regions led to conflicts with the Tripoli Military Council, headed by ʿAbd al-Hakim Balhaj.[109] While there have been some attempts by *kata'ib* to coordinate and work together, such as a meeting between local *kata'ib* in Misrata on 22 September 2011, which was reportedly attended Balhaj, tensions remain high between the various armed groups.[110] Clashes between the various militias have often involved the use of heavy weaponry and led to deaths and serious injuries in Tripoli.[111]

Outside of the capital, clashes have also continued into 2012 in Bani Walid, one of the last Qadhafi loyalist strongholds after the fall of the regime.[112] The kidnapping, torture, and death of ʿUmran Shaʿban – the *thuwar* fighter from Misrata who was credited with the capture of Qadhafi – prompted a string of violent clashes in the Bani Walid between *thuwar* and Qadhafi loyalists. The attack on Shaʿban on 24 September 2012 was seen as a revenge attack by Qadhafi loyalists, and led to the GNC authorizing the Defense Ministry to use force to apprehend the perpetrators.[113] This, in turn, led to heavy clashes in Bani Walid on 17 October 2012, which

---

[108] Mahmoud Habboush, *Battle between Tripoli, Misrata militias kills 4*, REUTERS, Jan. 3, 2012, *available at* http://www.reuters.com/article/2012/01/03/us-libya-rebels-clash-id USTRE8021FP20120103.

[109] The Tripoli Military Council was based at the Maʿatiga Military Airport.

[110] HOLDING TOGETHER LIBYA, *supra* note 17 at 29.

[111] *See* Ch. XIII, Sec. 2. *See also* Report of the International Commission of Inquiry (Mar. 2012) *supra* note 63 at Annex I, ¶ 73.

[112] *See* Ch. XIV, Sec. 2.

[113] Amir Ahmed, *Libyan rivals clash; at least 11 killed*, CNN, Oct. 18, 2012, *available at* http://edition.cnn.com/2012/10/17/world/meast/libya-violence/index.html.

prompted the deployment of Defense Ministry and LSF units,[114] which surrounded and began to shell the city. It is unclear, however, whether the government gave the authorization for the shelling or whether LSF units and their commanders acted on their own accord.[115]

The existence of conflict in Bani Walid and elsewhere demonstrated the inability of the interim government to ensure peace, security and stability in Libya. The use of heavy weapons to shell Bani Walid was also a troubling demonstration of force that mirrored attacks by Qadhafi forces during the war. Indeed, the violations that were carried out during the conflict did not cease with the fall of the regime, rather they continued and were widespread. *Thuwar* forces targeted Qadhafi loyalists and those perceived to have supported the regime. Pre-existing tensions also flared with attacks fuelled by the desire to collectively punish any persons or groups linked to the Qadhafi regime. These attacks occurred along ethnic lines, as dark-skinned communities, both Libyan and Sub-Saharan African, were particularly targeted.[116] Serious violations continued, such as unlawful killings, arbitrary arrests and detentions and attacks on civilians. The significant difference is that the violations in the post-conflict period were committed on an individual or unit level, rather than as a matter of state-sanctioned policy.[117] While there was no policy in place there was, however, clearly a lack of political will and/or capacity on the part of the government authorities to curb the violations taking place on the part of the non-state armed actors.

The growing influence of the non-state armed groups became increasingly evident in 2013, as militia factions showed a new capacity to hold institutions hostage and influence political and legislative developments. On 31 March armed groups from the SSC surrounded the Ministry of Justice, forcing Minister Salah Marghani and his staff out of the building.[118] Marghani later made statements indicating that the act was in protest against his ministry's efforts to take over the prisons from militia groups.[119]

---

[114] *Id.*

[115] *Confusion rife as Libyan army storms town of Bani Walid*, THE GUARDIAN, Oct. 19, 2012, *available at* http://www.guardian.co.uk/world/2012/oct/19/libyan-army-storms-bani-walild.

[116] Report of the International Commission of Inquiry (Mar. 2012) *supra* note 63 at Annex I, ¶ 81.

[117] For more on superior responsibility, *see* Ch. IV, Sec. 5.1. *See also* Report of the International Commission of Inquiry (Mar. 2012), *supra* note 63 at Annex I, ¶ 39.

[118] Nihal Zaroug, *Justice Ministry seized by SSC; minister and staff ejected*, THE LIBYA HERALD, Mar. 31, 2013, available at http://www.libyaherald.com/2013/03/31/moj-building-sieged-by-armed-members-of-the-ssc/.

[119] *Id.*

The militias reportedly demanded the passage of the Political Isolation Law, which had been proposed as a measure to prevent officials from the Qadhafi era from serving in government.[120] On 28 April militias besieged the Foreign Ministry, making similar demands for the ouster of diplomats affiliated with the old regime.[121] The GNC ultimately succumbed to the pressure, and on 5 May adopted the Political Isolation Law, barring individuals who held senior government post in the Qadhafi regime from serving in government, regardless of whether they had defected from the regime at any time.[122] The law took effect immediately, leading to the resignation of President of the GNC, Muhammad al-Mugarayf, and could lead to the removal of several other officials.[123]

In a show of frustration with the government's inability to reign in on the non-state armed actors, demonstrators gathered in Benghazi in front of an LSF headquarters in June 2103 to demand the closure of the Shield bases and call for investigations into abuses committed by members of the militia groups. The demonstrations turned violent on 8 June when clashes erupted between the demonstrators and the LSF, leading to the deaths of 32 people.[124] Sources indicate that rockets were fired rockets into the LSF base, as members of the army's special forces (Sa'iqa brigade) stormed the base[125] and LSF fighters fired upon the crowd with antiaircraft guns, grenades, and mortars.[126] The incident drew widespread condemnation and led to the immediate resignation of Chief of Staff, Major

---

[120] Tom Westcott, *"We won't use these weapons": militiamen at Justice Ministry siege*, Libya Herald, May 1, 2013, available at http://www.libyaherald.com/2013/05/01/we-wont-use-these-weapons-militiamen-at-justice-ministry-siege/.

[121] *Militia gunmen besiege Libyan Foreign Ministry, demand resignations*, RT, Apr. 28, 2013, available at *http://rt.com/news/libya-foreign-ministry-riot-532/*.

[122] *See* Ch. IV, Sec. 6. *See also Sami Zaptia, Political Isolation Law passed overwhelmingly*, Libya Herald, May 5, 2013, *available at* http://www.libyaherald.com/2013/05/05/political-isolation-law-passed-overwhelmingly/.

[123] Anas El Gomati, *Why Libya's 'Isolation Law' Threatens Progress*, Carnegie Endowment, May 22, 2013, available at http://carnegieendowment.org/2013/05/21/why-libya-s-isolation-law-threatens-progress/g5g2; *Libya: Reject 'Political Isolation Law'*, Human Rights Watch, May 4, 2013, *available at* http://www.hrw.org/news/2013/05/04/libya-reject-political-isolation-law.

[124] *Libya: No Impunity for 'Black Saturday' Benghazi Deaths*, Human Rights Watch, June 14, 2013, *available at* http://www.hrw.org/news/2013/06/13/libya-no-impunity-black-saturday-benghazi-deaths.

[125] *Libya's government and the militias: Is the tide turning?*, The Economist, June 15, 2013, *available at* http://www.economist.com/news/middle-east-and-africa/21579520-defeat-islamist-militia-raises-hope-law-and-order-may-return.

[126] David Kirkpatrick, *Libyan Violence Threatens to Undercut Power of Militias*, N.Y. Times, June 9, 2013, *available at* http://www.nytimes.com/2013/06/10/world/africa/libyan-violence-threatens-to-undercut-power-of-militias.html.

General Yousuf al-Mangush.[127] The day after the killings the GNC issued a decree ordering the government to take all means necessary to shut down the unlawful brigades and armed factions in Libya.[128] Two of the LSF brigades based in Benghazi reportedly handed over their bases and weapons to the national army after the GNC passed the 9 June decree, and another LSF brigade left its station in Kufra in response to the decree.[129] The decree also ordered Prime Minister 'Ali Zaydan to establish mechanism to demobilize and integrate the armed militias and to complete the process by the end of 2013.[130]

Locals in Benghazi expressed hope that the violence would lead to the government taking definitive measures to ensure the brigades submit to the central authorities.[131] The replacement chief of staff vowed to confront the armed groups, where Mangush had been accused of co-opting them, and many expected a purge of the Islamist factions entrenched in the militias.[132] Reporters in Benghazi noted that police officers and contingents of uniforms troops once again patrolled the streets, and that LSF militia leaders appeared to be in hiding.[133] The situation in Benghazi was still far from stable, however, and other reports noted that while LSF members had fled their base, they took their weapons with them.[134]

It remains to be seen whether the renewed attempts by the government authorities to establish control over the militia groups will prove successful. The reliance on the LSF and other unofficial armed factions as auxiliary forces since the end of the conflict has allowed the armed groups to become powerfully entrenched in the security apparatus posing serious risks to any renewed efforts to dismantle the brigades. As discussed above, disbanding the armed factions without curbing their ability to access weapons runs the risk that the brigades will slinter into smaller criminal factions more difficult to monitor and equally as destabilizing. Reports noted that while the LSF left their bases after the 8 June killings,

---

[127] *Libya Army Chief Resigns After Clash in Benghazi*, AP, June 9, 2013, *available at* http://www.npr.org/templates/story/story.php?storyId=190005204.

[128] *Libya: No Impunity for 'Black Saturday' Benghazi Deaths*, HUMAN RIGHTS WATCH, *supra* note 124.

[129] *Id.*

[130] *Id.*

[131] Kirkpatrick, *Libyan Violence Threatens to Undercut Power of Militias*, *supra* note 126.

[132] THE ECONOMIST, *Libya's government and the militias: Is the tide turning?*, *supra* note 125.

[133] Kirkpatrick, *Libyan Violence Threatens to Undercut Power of Militias*, *supra* note 126.

[134] THE ECONOMIST, *Libya's government and the militias: Is the tide turning?*, *supra* note 125.

armed Islamist groups still held bases near Benghazi, and that armed factions operating underground can be even more dangerous than those operating openly.[135]

Days after the GNC decree, there were incidents of violence that appeared to be retaliatory strikes by members of dismantled LSF brigades.[136] On 15 June armed gunmen reportedly from LSF units attacked an army base in Benghazi, leading to the deaths of 6 members of the Sa'iqa ("strike") special forces and injuries to five other soldiers.[137] The fighting between the Sa'iqa forces – which operated under Qadhafi to repress political Islamists in the LIFG – and the LSF was seen as reflective of deeper rivalries in the region.[138] The attack also highlighted the dangers of attempting to remove the militia factions, and the urgent need to curb the availability of weapons in order to ensure stability. In the face of recurring violence, there appears to be strong political will to dismantle Libya's non-state armed actors, but ability to reign in on the militias will be contingent on many factors, most notably, the ability to control the proliferation of weapons throughout the country.

3. THE PROLIFERATION OF WEAPONS

During the post-conflict phase, internal and international security concerns grew regarding the enormous weapons holdings in the possession of non-state armed actors in Libya. The availability of massive amounts of weapons in the country is in part a product of the policies implemented under Qadhafi, who purchased weapons in large quantities and stockpiled them without assuring their security.[139] In a self-defeating policy, Qadhafi also hid from his military commanders the locations of weapons stockpiles, and failed to provide adequate maintenance to military equipment,

---

[135] *Id.*

[136] Fred Abrams, *For Libya to end the violence, it needs to shut down the militias*, HUMAN RIGHTS WATCH, June 18, 2013, *available at* http://www.hrw.org/print/news/2013/06/18/libya-end-violence-it-needs-shut-down-militias.

[137] *Six killed in attacks on army in Benghazi*, LIBYA HERALD, June 15, 2013, *available at* http://www.libyaherald.com/2013/06/15/four-killed-in-attacks-on-army-in-benghazi/; Feras Bosalum, *Six Libyan soldiers killed in Benghazi violence*, REUTERS, June 15, 2013, *available at* http://www.reuters.com/article/2013/06/15/us-libya-attack-benghazi-idUSBRE95E04Y20130615.

[138] THE ECONOMIST, *Libya's government and the militias: Is the tide turning?*, supra note 125.

[139] For more on Qadhafi's weapons purchases and stockpiles, *see* Ch. II, Secs. 2.1. & 2.2.

particularly airplanes and tanks. It should be noted, however, that the majority of Libya's weapons stockpiles are legacy weapons dating back to the cold war.[140] While they were significant in size, and more than enough to arm an insurgency or provide explosives to a terrorist organization, they were not modern battlefield weapons. Although there is no accurate count of the number of Qadhafi's stockpiled weapons, it is estimated that they exceeded those in Saddam Hussein's stockpiles, which armed and fueled the Iraqi insurgency.[141]

The Qadhafi regime also pursued and acquired chemical weapons, and intended to develop biological and nuclear weapons. After extensive negotiations with the West, the Libyan government agreed to abandon its weapons of mass destruction (WMD) program in 2003 and destroy its unconventional weapons stockpiles. The deal did not address conventional weapons, however, but lifted sanctions and allowed the Qadhafi regime to spend billions on conventional weapons, the latest weapons technology, and upgrades for military equipment.[142]

The post-conflict fractionalization of Libyan society – with heavily armed regional, tribal, and communal groups pitted against each other – is in part a consequence of these policies. During the conflict, *thuwar* captured weapons and materiel from Qadhafi forces and poorly guarded government weapon depots, and distributed them to combatant forces composed of mostly civilians.[143] This resulted in the uncontrolled circulation of large quantities of military materiel during the war, as regional populations formed heavily armed militia groups acting largely autonomous of central authorities.[144] In mid-June 2011, for example, *thuwar* forces seized an arms depot 15 miles south of Zintan, which provided it with weapons and important military information such as the size of the regime's stockpile of shoulder-fired surface-to-air missiles (SAMs).[145] In Misrata, *thuwar* groups acquired weapons such as rifles, RPGs, and 106mm rockets, often sized from retreating Qadhafi forces.[146] Additionally, *thuwar*

---

[140] *See* Ch. II, Sec. 2.1.

[141] Adam Rawnsley, *Gadhafi's Loose Weapons Could Number a 'Thousand Times' Saddams*, WIRED, Aug. 25, 2011, *available at* http://www.wired.com/dangerroom/2011/08/gadhafis-loose-weapons-could-be-1000-times-worse-than-saddams/.

[142] *See* Ch. I, 10.3 & Sec. Ch. II, Sec. 2.1.

[143] For weapons seized from Qadhafi forces' stockpiles, *see* Chs. VI, VII, IX, X, & XII.

[144] U.N. SC, U.N. Doc. S/2012/178 (March 26, 2012).

[145] *See* Ch. X. *See also* ANTHONY BELL, SPENCER BUTTS & DAVID WITTER, INSTITUTE FOR THE STUDY OF WAR, 4 THE LIBYAN REVOLUTION: THE TIDE TURNS 15 (Nov. 2011), *available at* http://www.understandingwar.org/sites/default/files/Libya_Part4.pdf.

[146] *See* Ch. IX.

forces acquired an unknown amount of rifles, which had been leftover from a purchase of 130,000 Kalashnikovs in 2008.[147] After the fall of Tripoli in late September, a multitude of weapons were seized by fighters who took part in the capture of the capital, and transported to other parts of Libya, including the Nafusa Mountains and Misrata.[148]

International actors also contributed to Libya's weapons surplus, as countries including France and Qatar supplied arms to the rebel groups as part of the NATO-led intervention.[149] NATO and non-NATO members of the coalition that took part in Operation Unified Protector provided the rebels with modern weapons via air-drops, and sea and overland deliveries in an attempt to support the revolution. France was the first nation to admit to providing arms, ammunition and tanks to the Libyan rebels. France acknowledge that it had air-dropped over 40 tons of arms and munitions and smuggled tanks via Tunisia.[150] Qatar also admitted to providing weapons to Libya, including modern French-manufactured anti-tank missiles and weapons from Russia.[151] The United Arab Emirates also

---

[147] The rifles, which allegedly originated in Romania, were routed through the United Kingdom, where a UK company acted as an intermediary between a Libyan businessman and a Ukrainian seller. The UK government had denied export licenses to the company over concerns that the weapons would end up in the hands of rebel factions in Chad and the Sudan. Nevertheless, in the absence of UN regulations, the deal went forward. *See* U.S. Embassy, Secret cable, *UK Denies Licenses for Export of Kalashnikovs to Libya, GOL Potentially Seeking Alternative Sellers*, THE TELEGRAPH, Nov. 6, 2008, *available at* http://www.telegraph .co.uk/news/wikileaks-files/libya-wikileaks/8294874/U.K.-DENIES-LICENSE-FOR-EXPORT-OF-KALASHNIKOVS-TO-LIBYA-GOL-POTENTIALLY-SEEKING-ALTERNATIVE-SELLERS.html. Other sources indicate that Libya procured 100,000 Kalashnikovs from the Ukraine itself, although it is not clear whether the weapons identified in the US embassy cable are the same as the ones alleged to have come from the Ukraine. *See* Vivienne Walt, *Conflicting Priorities Imperil Effort to Gather Up Gaddafi's Discarded Arms*, TIME, Nov. 15, 2011, *available at* http://www.time.com/time/world/article/0,8599,2099549,00.html; Richard Norton-Taylor & Nick Hopkins, *Libya warned smugglers are looting Gaddafi's guns*, THE GUARDIAN, Sept. 2, 2011, *available at* http://www.guardian.co.uk/world/2011/sep/02/west-warns-smugglers-looting-libya-arms.

[148] Joseph Logan, William Maclean & Barry Malone, *Tripoli armed group says arms spreading to regions*, REUTERS, Sept. 24, 2011, *available at* http://www.reuters.com/ article/2011/09/24/libya-weapons-idUSL5E7KO0TQ20110924.

[149] For further details on role of international actors in providing weapons to Libya's rebel, *see* Ch. III, Sec. 7.1.

[150] *Libya Conflict: France air-dropped arms to rebels*, BBC, June 29, 2011 *available at* http://www.bbc.co.uk/news/world-africa-13955751.

[151] Ian Black, *Liyan rebels receiving anti-tank weapons from Qatar*, THE GUARDIAN, Apr. 14, 2011, *available at* http://www.guardian.co.uk/world/2011/apr/14/libya-rebels-weapons-qatar.

provided weapons to Libya.[152] Investigations conducted by the UN Panel of Experts (the "UN Panel") on Libya found that both Qatar and the UAE provided weapons and ammunition to the Libyan opposition in breach of the arms embargo established pursuant to UNSCR 1970.[153]

The United States reportedly approved many of the weapons shipments that were paid for and supplied by Qatar and the UAE.[154] United States officials later voiced concern, however, that the weapons, including French and Russian designed arms, were ending up in the hands of militant groups that were not representative of U.S. interests in the region.[155] The weapons were distributed to groups involved in the fight against the Qadhafi regime, without any vetting procedures to determine the composition of such groups. Some of the weapons ended up in the hands of local Islamist fundamentalist groups with suspected affiliation with Al-Qaʻida -linked organizations in the region, such as Al-Qaʻida in the Maghreb (AQIM).[156] The UN Panel also determined that "the deliveries of arms and ammunition during the uprising in Libya were completed without any control measures on the ground, resulting in the uncontrolled movement of materiel."[157]

The threat of arms proliferation in Libya quickly extended beyond its borders to the wider Middle East and Northern Africa region. According to the UN Panel, "Some 18 months after the end of the conflict, some of this materiel under the control of non-State actors within Libya has been found in seizures of military materiel being trafficked out of Libya."[158] Specifically, the UN Panel examined cases in which the illicit transfer of heavy and light weapons, including man-portable air defense systems (MANPADS), has involving more than 12 countries in the region.[159] The Syrian conflict, in particular, has been dramatically impacted as a result

---

[152] James Risen, Mark Mazzetti & Michael S. Schmidt, *U.S. Approved Arms for Libya Rebels Fell Into Jihadis' Hands*, N.Y. TIMES, Dec. 5, 2012, *available at* http://www.nytimes .com/2012/12/06/world/africa/weapons-sent-to-libyan-rebels-with-us-approval-fell-into-islamist-hands.html.

[153] Final report of the Panel of Experts, *supra* note 4 at ¶ 60.

[154] James Risen, Mark Mazzetti & Michael S. Schmidt, *Weapons sent to Libyan rebels with US approval fell into Islamist hands*, N.Y. TIMES, Dec. 5, 2012, *available at* http://www .nytimes.com/2012/12/06/world/africa/weapons-sent-to-libyan-rebels-with-us-approval-fell-into-islamist-hands.html.

[155] *Id.*

[156] *See infra* Sec. 5.

[157] Final report of the Panel of Experts, *supra* note 4 at ¶ 61.

[158] *Id.*

[159] *Id.*

of the Libyan conflict due to the influx of both rebel fighters and materiel from Libya.[160] Former Libyan rebel commanders, such as the Mahdi al-Harati, have given interviews to reporters from within Syria, where they are fighting with the Free Syrian Army.[161] Reports of Libyan weapons flowing to Syrian rebels started circulating as early as November 2011 with the approval of the NTC.[162] Syrian bound weapons reportedly are routed through Turkey and are said to include RPGs and man-portable SAMs that have assisted the rebels in targeting the Syrian Air Force.[163] The UN Panel found that these transfers "have been organized under the supervision, or with consent of a range of actors in Libya and the Syrian Arab Republic and in countries neighboring the Syrian Arab Republic."[164]

Beyond Syrian, Libyan weapons have increasingly ended up the hands of armed groups in the Sahel region.[165] The UN Panel reported that during the Libyan uprising, "a number of convoys of combatants and weapons moved from Libya to Mali through southern Algeria and northern Niger, sometimes alternating between the two."[166] The 2012 insurrection in Northern Mali was invigorated in large part by weapons from Libya

---

[160] *Id.* at ¶ 158. The *N.Y. Times* has reported that weapons are being shipped to Syria via boat and plane. In particular, the *N.Y. Times* has found that Qatari military transport planes have flown at least three shipments of weapons from Tripoli, thought to be bound for the Syrian conflict. Beyond finding credible evidence of distribution networks in Turkey and Syria, the *N.Y. Times* also found numerous crates of weapons in Syria containing markings that the weapons and materiel were originally sold to Libya by arms manufacturers from various countries, dating back as far as the 1980s. *See* C. J. Chivers, Eric Schmitt & Mark Mazzetti, *In Turnabout, Syria Rebels Get Libyan Weapons*, N.Y. TIMES, June 21, 2013, *available at* http://www.nytimes.com/2013/06/22/world/africa/in-a-turnabout-syria-rebels-get-libyan-weapons.html. Some have speculated that U.S. Ambassador Christopher Stevens was in Benghazi in September 2012 to coordinate the transfer of weapons and materiel from eastern Libya to Syria, although this is unsubstantiated as of this moment.

[161] Jomana Karadsheh, *Libyan rebels move into Syrian battlefield*, CNN, Jul. 28, 2012, *available at* http://www.cnn.com/2012/07/28/world/meast/syria-libya-fighters. For more on Mahdi al-Harati's role in the *thuwar* forces *see* Ch. II, Sec. 3.3.

[162] Adam Housley, *Arms shipments traveled from Libya to anti-Assad fighters, sources say*, FOX NEWS, Dec. 6, 2012, *available at* http://www.foxnews.com/politics/2012/12/06/arms-shipments-traveled-from-libya-to-anti-assad-fighters-sources-say/.

[163] Sheera Frankel, *Syrian rebels squabble over weapons as biggest shipload arrives in Libya*, THE TIMES, Sept. 14, 2012, *available at* http://www.thetimes.co.uk/tto/news/world/middleeast/article3537770.ece; Mary Fitzgerald, *The Syrian Rebels' Libyan Weapon*, FOREIGN POLICY, Aug. 9, 2012, *available at* http://www.foreignpolicy.com/articles/2012/08/09/the_syrian_rebels_libyan_weapon.

[164] Final report of the Panel of Experts, *supra* note 4 at ¶ 158.

[165] Sahel is the region of western and north-central Africa extending from Senegal eastward to The Sudan and is a transitional zone between the Sahara desert to the north and the savannas to the south. *See* U.N. SC, ¶¶ 40–43, U.N. Doc. S/2012/178 (Mar. 26, 2012).

[166] Final report of the Panel of Experts, *supra* note 4 at ¶ 144.

that reached armed groups fighting the central government in Bamako.[167] Reports also indicate that the Tuareg population displaced during the Libyan conflict returned to Mail, bringing with them an unknown quantity of weapons, including MANPADS.[168] Many of the weapons found in Mali, including M40 recoilless rifles, have been traced back to Libyan military stockpiles or that were used during the 2011 conflict.[169]

The vast stockpiles of MANPADS looted from Libya during the conflict has been one of the central concerns of the international community. In April 2011, General Carter Ham, Commander of the United States Africa Command, estimated Qadhafi had some 20,000 MANPADS.[170] As the conflict was underway, the U.S. government established a program to send teams of civilian specialists to Libya to work with NTC officials to locate MANPADS, and in September 2011 "these teams swept the country, scouring ammunition storage sites and more than 1,500 bunkers," eventually recovering and securing approximately 5,000 MANPADS and components by February 2012.[171] The program was funded in part by the $40 million pledged by the U.S. State Department to assist Libya's efforts to secure and recover its weapons stockpiles.[172]

Concern remain high over the lack of a serious arms control program within Libya, and for border security measures to control arms trafficked

---

[167] David Lewis & Adama Diarra, *Insight: Arms and men out of Libya fortify Mali rebellion*, REUTERS, Feb. 10, 2012, *available at* http://www.reuters.com/article/2012/02/10/us-mali-libya-idUSTRE81g0UX20120210.

[168] Morgan Lorraine Roach & Jessica Zuckerman, *MANPADS on the Loose: Countering Weapons Proliferation in North Africa and the Sahel*, THE HERITAGE FOUNDATION, Nov. 5, 2012, *available at* http://www.heritage.org/research/reports/2012/11/manpads-countering-weapons-proliferation-in-north-africa-and-the-sahel.

[169] The M40 recoilless rifles in Libya's stockpiles were provided to the army of King Idris by the United States in the 1950s-60s, and later to the Qadhafi regime by Belgian. *See* C.J. Chivers, *Looted Libyan Arms in Mali May Have Shifted Conflict's Path*, N.Y. TIMES, Feb. 7, 2013, *available at* http://www.nytimes.com/2013/02/08/world/africa/looted-libyan-arms-in-mali-may-have-shifted-conflicts-path.html. For more on assault rifles from the Libyan conflict, *see* Ch. II, Appendix: Glossary of Weapons used During the Conflict.

[170] Senate Armed Services Committee, *Hearing to receive testimony in U.S. Transportation command in review of the defense authorization request for fiscal year 2012 and the future years defense program*, Apr. 7, 2011, *available at* http://www.armed-services.senate.gov/Transcripts/2011/04%20April/11-26%20-%204-7-11.pdf.

[171] U.S. State Department, Remarks by Andrew J. Shapiro, *Addressing the Challenge of MANPADS proliferation*, Feb. 2, 2012, *available at* http://www.state.gov/t/pm/rls/rm/183097.htm.

[172] Kate Brannen, *U.S. Still Hunting for Missing Libyan MANPADS*, DEFENSE NEWS, Feb. 2, 2012, *available at* http://www.defensenews.com/article/20120202/DEFREG02/302020009/U-S-Still-Hunting-Missing-Libyan-MANPADS; Shapiro, *Addressing the Challenge of MANPADS proliferation, supra* note 171.

from the country that are fueling conflicts in other regions, such as those in the Sahel and Syria.[173] As of March 2013, the UN Security Council encouraged the UN Panel to "assist the Libyan authorities to counter illicit proliferation of all arms and related material of all types, in particular man-portable surface-to-air missiles, and to secure and manage Libya's borders, [and] to continue its investigations regarding sanctions non-compliance, including illicit transfers of arms and related materiel to and from Libya."[174] The proliferation of weapons stemming from Libya is clearly a pressing matter of critical importance for regional and international security, as demonstrated in the 11 September 2012 attacks on the U.S. Special Mission in Benghazi that involved heavy weaponry left over from the 2011 conflict.

4. The 11 September 2012 Attack in Benghazi

The 11 September 2012 attack on the U.S. Special Mission compound and annex building in Benghazi that lead to the death of the U.S. Ambassador and three other Americans, sparked renewed international concern over Libya's unstable security environment. Prior to the attack, there had been a series of incidents in Benghazi that highlighted the serious unrest and insecurity in eastern Libya. The United States had reportedly conducted surveillance missions using drones to monitor suspected jihadist camps in eastern Libya, particularly after a failed attack on the U.S. Mission compound in June.[175] In cable traffic with the U.S. State Department, Ambassador Christopher Stevens had warned in August that conditions in Benghazi were becoming unpredictable, volatile and violent.[176] The U.S. State Department ARB report indicated that at the time of the attack, Benghazi was a "lawless town nominally controlled by the Supreme Security Council (SSC)... but in reality run by a diverse group of local Islamist militias, each of whose strength ebbed and flowed depending on the ever-

---

[173] *May 2013 Monthly Forecast*, UN Security Council Report, May 2013, *available at* http://www.securitycouncilreport.org/monthly-forecast/2013-05/libya_4.php.

[174] Final report of the Panel of Experts, *supra* note 4 at ¶ 8.

[175] Nic Robertson, Paul Cruickshank & Jomana Karadsheh, *Libyan official: U.S. drones seeking jihadists in Libya*, CNN Security Blog, June 7, 2012, *available at* http://security.blogs.cnn.com/2012/06/07/senior-libyan-official-u-s-deploying-drones-as-concerns-rise-over-al-qaeda-in-eastern-libya/.

[176] Alex Sundby, *Ambassador Warned Libya was 'volatile and violent'*, CBS, Oct. 19, 2012, *available at* http://www.cbsnews.com/8301-250_162-57536446/ambassador-warned-libya-was-volatile-and-violent/.

shifting alliances and loyalties of various members."[177] The attacks brought to the forefront the seriousness of Libya's armed, organized, and influential militia forces, and their links to international terrorist activities.[178]

According to the State Department ARB report, the attacks began around 8pm in the evening of 11 September, and involved several phases of assaults on the Mission compound and the annex building. The attack started at the Mission compound, where arms assailants forced their way inside and set buildings and cars ablaze. The living quarters and adjacent vehicles of the 17 February Katiba members who were providing security detail for the U.S. Mission were burned, causing heavy smoke to pour into the villa of Ambassador Stevens.[179] A security team was then dispatched from the nearby annex building, which located the body of Sean Smith, an IT expert attached to the consulate, but was unable to locate the ambassador.[180] Shortly before midnight, the attack shifted to the annex targeting the building with RPGs. At around 5am in the morning of 12 September, the annex "came under mortar and RPG attack...Three rounds hit the roof of an Annex building, killing security officers Tyrone Woods and Glen Doherty."[181] At around 6:30am, all U.S. government personnel were evacuated with "support from a quasi-governmental Libyan militia."[182] The evacuation was overseen by an armed U.S. Department of Defense drone aircraft that had been deployed from the U.S. AFRICOM base in Germany.[183]

United States government officials initially refrained from characterizing the incident as an orchestrated attack, calling it a spontaneous, not premeditated, response to an anti-Islam film. The U.S. Ambassador to the UN, Susan Rice, attributed the attack to a demonstration that turned violent as a result of "some individual clusters of extremists who came with heavier weapons."[184] In the days and weeks that followed, however, more details emerged about the nature of the incident, as U.S. intelligence officials began to report that the incident was the result of a "deliberate

---

[177] *See* U.S. DEPARTMENT OF STATE ARB REPORT, *supra* note 24 at 17.
[178] For more details on the timeline of events in Benghazi, *see* Ch. III, Sec. 2.2.
[179] *See* U.S. DEPARTMENT OF STATE ARB REPORT, *supra* note 24 at 23–24.
[180] *Id.* at 24.
[181] *Id.* at 27.
[182] *Id.*
[183] *Id.*
[184] *Statements on the Attack in Benghazi*, N.Y. TIMES, Sept. 27, 2012, *available at* http://www.nytimes.com/interactive/2012/09/27/world/africa/administration-statements-on-the-attack-in-benghazi.html.

and organized attack carried out by extremists."[185] United States Defense Secretary Leon Panetta said it was a planned terrorist attack, but did not give any indication as to what terrorist group was believed responsible.[186] Investigators soon began focusing on the possible connections between the attack and Benghazi-based armed militias such as the Ansar al-Sharī'a brigade.[187] The FBI team dispatched to investigate the attack began looking into individuals connected to the Ansar al-Sharī'a group, who were reportedly recorded making calls to members AQIM.[188] Experts on Libya reported that the responsible militants likely came more specifically from a group called the Imprisoned Omar Abdul Rahman Brigades, which was also implicated in an attack on the International Red Cross office in Benghazi in May 2012.[189]

More details soon surfaced in the wake of the 11 September 2012 affair. Media accounts reported that the attack led to the evacuation from Libya of a large contingent of CIA officials who had been working in Benghazi. The New York Times quoted U.S. officials, off the record, who said the CIA had been monitoring militia groups in eastern Libya, such as Ansar al-Sharī'a, for their weapons and suspected links to AQIM.[190] The report stated that CIA officials had been present in Benghazi within months of the February 2011 uprising, after U.S. intelligence began establishing a relationship with the rebels in the region.[191] The CIA had moved quickly to analyze events on the ground in order to gather information on the capacity and composition of the nascent rebel groups, and was on the ground

---

[185] John Hudson, *U.S. Intelligence Takes the Blame for the Government's Mixed Messages on Libya*, THE ATLANTIC WIRE, Sept. 28, 2012, *available at* http://www.theatlanticwire.com/global/2012/09/us-intelligence-takes-blame-governments-mixed-messages-libya/57416/.

[186] *Panetta: Terrorist carried out consulate attack*, CBS, Sept. 28, 2012, *available at* http://www.cbsnews.com/8301-202_162-57522061/panetta-terrorists-carried-out-consulate-attack/.

[187] Eric Schmitt, Helene Cooper & Michael S. Schmidt, *Attack in Libya was Major Blow to CIA Efforts*, N.Y. TIMES, Sept. 23, 2012, *available at* http://www.nytimes.com/2012/09/24/world/africa/attack-in-libya-was-major-blow-to-cia-efforts.html.

[188] *FBI in Benghazi to investigate consulate killings as hunt for attackers narrows*, THE GUARDIAN, Oct. 4, 2012, *available at* http://www.guardian.co.uk/world/2012/oct/04/fbi-investigate-benghazi-consulte-attack.

[189] Nic Robertson, Paul Cruickshank & Tom Lister, *Pro-al Qaeda group seen behind deadly Benghazi attack*, CNN, Sept. 13, 2012, *available at* http://edition.cnn.com/2012/09/12/world/africa/libya-attack-jihadists/index.html.

[190] Eric Schmitt, Helene Cooper & Michael S. Schmidt, *Attack in Libya was Major Blow to CIA Efforts, supra* note 187.

[191] *Id.*

before the United States sent Christopher Stevens to establish diplomatic relations with the opposition movement in Benghazi in April 2011.

The CIA remained in Benghazi and established a significant base for monitoring terrorist activity on the ground. According to the Obama administration's talking points later released on the Benghazi attack, the CIA had "produced numerous pieces on the threat of extremists linked to al-Qa'ida in Benghazi and eastern Libya."[192] These noted that since April 2011, there had been "at least five other attacks against foreign interests in Benghazi by unidentified assailants, including the June attack against the British Ambassador's convoy."[193] The information regarding the CIA presence raised larger questions about the nature of the attack, suggesting that it was potentially motivated by larger forces with the intent of disrupting U.S. intelligence and counter-terrorism efforts in the region.

As a result of U.S. congressional investigations and regular reporting into the affair, more information came to light in the months following the Benghazi attack. United States intelligence officials told reporters, off the record, that CIA officials stationed in the security annex connected to the Mission building had provided support during the attack. There were reports that two of the men who died in the attack, former NAVY Seals Tyrone Woods and Glen Doherty, initially identified as State Department security contractors, were actually CIA contractors stationed there as part of a larger operation to collect intelligence and provide security in Benghazi.[194] Doherty had told reporters before his death that he was working with the State Department on an intelligence mission to track down and destroy MANPADs.[195] Doherty's mission would coincide with the State Department's efforts to locate and secure MANPAD stockpiles that had been underway since September 2011.[196] Allegations also surfaced that the CIA had been holding Libyan prisoners in holding cells in

---

[192] Jonathan Kar, *The Benghazi Emails: Talking Points Changed at State Dept.'s Request*, ABC, May 15, 2013, *available at* http://abcnews.go.com/Politics/benghazi-emails-talking-points-changed-state-depts-request/story?id=19187137#.Ub_QF-ioUdU.

[193] *Id.*

[194] Adam Entous, Siobhan Gorman & Margaret Coker, *CIA Takes Heat for Role in Libya*, THE WALL STREET JOURNAL, Nov. 1, 2012, *available at* http://online.wsj.com/article/SB1000 1424052970204712904578092853621061838.html.

[195] ABC news reported that Doherty had told ABC in August 2012 that he was in Libya as part of a State Department mission to find and destroy weapons. *See* Lee Ferran, *American Killed in Libya was on Intel Mission to Track Weapons*, ABC, Sept. 13, 2012, *available at* http://abcnews.go.com/Blotter/glen-doherty-navy-seal-killed-libya-intel-mission/story?id=17229037#.UMn536VpKfQ.

[196] *See supra* Sec. 3.

the annex, and that the attack was an effort to free the prisoners.[197] While the exact details remain unclear, all the information appeared to indicate that the U.S. mission in Benghazi was more than just a diplomatic mission, and that the annex building was used for significant intelligence operations in the region.

Months after the affair, investigations into the incident had failed to identify and arrest any suspects within Libya believed responsible for the attacks.[198] A string of violence against security officials in Benghazi, including the top security chief in November 2012, highlighted the continued insecurity in the country.[199] A former intelligence chief for the NTC told reporters in November 2012 that he believed some elements of Libya's law enforcement structures were themselves involved in the attack. Reports indicated that one of the suspects in the attack, Ahmed Abu Khattala,[200] the leader of the Ansar al-Sharī'a armed group, had not been arrested due to fear of reprisals from extremist groups.[201] The Interior Ministry official responsible for eastern Libya, Wanis al-Sharif, told reporters that extremist Islamist movements were behind the string of violence targeting top law enforcement officials in an effort to undermine security in the region.[202] Targeted attacks continued into 2013, including the killing of Judge Mohamed Naguib Huwaidi,[203] who was killed in a drive-by shooting in the city of Derna on 16 June.[204] The incident was the latest in a series of threats and assaults against the judiciary in Derna, where courts were temporarily shut down in protest against the unstable

---

[197] *Paula Broadwell claims about Benghazi attack dismissed as 'baseless' by CIA*, THE GUARDIAN, Nov. 12, 2012, *available at* http://www.guardian.co.uk/world/2012/nov/12/paula-broadwell-benghazi-cia-petraeus.

[198] For more on Benghazi investigations and arrests of suspects in Egypt and Turkey, *see* Ch. IV, Sec. 6.4.

[199] *Libyan security chief assassinated in Benghazi*, THE GUARDIAN, Nov. 12, 2012, *available at* http://www.guardian.co.uk/world/2012/nov/21/libya-security-chief-assassinated-benghazi.

[200] The transliteration of this name was adopted from the reference. Vivienne Walt, *Benghazi's Real Scandal: Why is the Libyan Investigation Such a Mess?*, TIME WORLD, Nov. 15, 2012, *available at* http://world.time.com/2012/11/15/benghazis-real-scandal-why-is-the-libyan-investigation-such-a-mess/.

[201] *Id.*

[202] Steven Sotloff, *Libya's New Crisis: A Wave of Assassinations Targeting its Top Cops*, TIME WORLD, Nov. 26, 2012, *available at* http://world.time.com/2012/11/26/libyas-new-crisis-a-wave-of-assassinations-targeting-its-top-cops/.

[203] The transliteration of this name was adopted from the reference.

[204] *The Assassination of judges in Libya undermines justice and threatens the foundation of the rule of law*, THE ARAB CENTER FOR THE INDEPENDENCE OF THE JUDICIARY AND THE LEGAL PROFESSION (ACIJLP), June 18, 2013.

security situation there.[205] The on-going targeted assassinations continue to raise serious concern over the ability Libya's militant Islamist groups to paralyze the judicial system from carrying out successful investigations into acts of political violence.

5. The Influence of Political Islam in Libya

It is important to consider how Libya's Islamist groups differ, based on composition, roots, ideology, goals and interests. Political Islamist groups played a prominent role among the revolutionary fighting forces during the war and are determined to play a role in Libya's post-Qadhafi political landscape. As is the case in Egypt, many of the groups are linked to the Muslim Brotherhood or their affiliates, and have been trying to garner support in an effort to gain political power. The important difference with the rise of the Muslim Brotherhood in Egypt, however, is that in Libya they face traditional resistance of a more tolerant, and relatively secular tribal society that makes it more difficult for the Islamists to achieve the same political critical mass. Their strength will vary from region to region, and from tribe to tribe. While it is impossible to make an accurate assessment of their political strength across the country, analysts estimate that they could marshal a third of the vote in an election.

There is a wide spectrum of actors that represent political Islam in Libya. On the far end of the spectrum there exist extreme hardline groups, such as Ansar al- Sharīʿa, that reject Libya's post-Qadhafi political process and the resulting elections in favor of the imposition of strict Islamist law. Additionally, within the militia structures, some of the more radical strains of political Islam are represented by Salafists who reportedly have international links to other militant groups in Pakistan, Afghanistan, Tunisia and elsewhere. Members of these groups had been residing abroad, and only returned to Libya during the 2011 uprising.[206] The city of Darna in the far east of the country, according to the U.S. Army, reportedly includes militants who fought with the insurgency in Iraq over the last decade.[207]

---

[205] *Derna judge murdered outside courthouse*, Libya Herald, June 16, 2013, *available at* http://www.libyaherald.com/2013/06/16/35028/.

[206] Frederic Wehrey, Carnegie Endowment for International Peace, The Struggle for Security in Eastern Libya (Sept. 2012), *available at* http://carnegieendowment.org/files/libya_security_2.pdf.

[207] Giorgio Cafiero, *Beyond Libya's election*, Foreign Policy in Focus, July 18, 2012, *available at* http://www.fpif.org/articles/beyond_libyas_election.

Darna is also home to a branch of the Ansar al-Sharīʿa militia that is reportedly composed of former members of the Abu Salim Martyrs' Katiba, and led by Sufyan bin Qumu.[208] Qumu was held in detention in Guantanamo Bay for six years before being transferred to Libya where he was imprisoned until 2010.[209] Qumu has been linked to other former militants, such as ʿAbd al-Hakim al-Hasadi, who are both former members of the Libyan Islamic Fighting Group (LIFG),[210] and part of a faction that never relinquished violence against Qadhafi.[211]

Some of Libya's Islamist leaders were radicalized as a result of policies that involved imprisonment, and in some cases, rendition and torture.[212] Abu Yahya al-Libi (a nom de guerre) was Al-Qaʿida's second in command before being killed by a U.S. drone strike in Pakistan in June 2012.[213] Al-Libi had reportedly been detained and held in a U.S. detention center in Afghanistan before he escaped and joined the ranks of Al-Qaʿida. According to Al-Libi's brother, ʿAbd al-Qaham Muhammad Qaʾid, al-Libi and other LIFG members had rejected Al-Qaʿida initially, but became radicalized after their imprisonment by U.S. forces in Afghanistan.[214] Other Libyans who led the revolutionary brigades in Libya had been captured by coalition forces in Afghanistan, and turned over to the Qadhafi regime by U.S. and UK intelligence.[215] They allegedly suffered waterboarding in U.S. detention centers, and other forms of torture and decades of abuse while imprisoned in Libya.[216]

Other LIFG veterans, however, have rejected anti-government policies and spoken out against militancy, and have encouraged Libya's Islamists

---

[208] WEHREY, THE STRUGGLE FOR SECURITY IN EASTERN LIBYA, *supra* note 206.

[209] David D. Kirkpatrick, *Libya Democracy Clashes With Fervor for Jihad*, N.Y. TIMES, June 23, 2012, *available at* http://www.nytimes.com/2012/06/24/world/africa/libya-jihadis-offer-2-paths-democracy-or-militancy.html.

[210] For more background on the formation of the LIFG and other anti-Qadhafi militant groups, *see* Ch. I, Sec. 9.2.

[211] WEHREY, THE STRUGGLE FOR SECURITY IN EASTERN LIBYA, *supra* note 206.

[212] For more information on the rendition and torture of Libyan dissidents overseas, *see* Ch. I, Sec. 10.1.

[213] *Abu Yahya al-Libi, al Qaeda deputy leader, killed in U.S. drone strike*, CBS News, June 5, 2011, *available at* http://www.cbsnews.com/8301-202_162-57447601/abu-yahya-al-libi-al-qaeda-deputy-leader-killed-in-u.s-drone-strike/.

[214] David D. Kirkpatrick, *Political Islam and the Fate of Two Libyan Brothers*, N.Y. TIMES, Oct. 6, 2012, *available at* http://www.nytimes.com/2012/10/07/world/africa/political-islam-and-the-fate-of-two-libyan-brothers.html.

[215] WEHREY, THE STRUGGLE FOR SECURITY IN EASTERN LIBYA, *supra* note 206.

[216] HUMAN RIGHTS WATCH, DELIVERED INTO ENEMY HANDS: US-LED ABUSE AND RENDITION OF OPPONENTS TO GADDAFI'S LIBYA (Sept. 2012), *available at* http://www.hrw.org/sites/default/files/reports/libya0912webwcover_1.pdf.

to take-part in the political process. Muhammad Qa'id, also a former LIFG anti-Qadhafi militant, is now a moderate member of Libya's new Parliament. 'Abd al-Hakim Balhaj, the most prominent ex-leader of the LIFG, has similarly renounced violence and co-founded the Al-Hizb al-Watan Party.[217] The Watan Party gained a seat in the National Congress in the July 2012 elections.[218] Members of the Watan Party have used their position in the new government to encourage groups such as Ansar al-Sharī'a to lay down their weapons and work within Libya's institutional framework. Qa'id and others share a vision of Libya's political system in line with that of Turkey and Tunisia – where certain precepts of Islamic law are adopted with tolerance and respect for pluralism.[219]

Other leaders in Libya's Islamist movement, such as 'Ali al-Sallabi, also point to moderate Islamist parties in Tunisia and Turkey as examples for Libya.[220] Al-Sallabi was also detained by the Qadhafi government and held in Abu Salim prison for eight years before leaving Libya and living in exile in Qatar. Al-Sallabi returned to fight in the uprising and, along with his brother Isma'il Sallabi, where he organized formidable fighting forces in eastern Libya. He is part of group of Islamists who received training abroad from countries such as Qatar and Morocco, and returned to fight in brigades, including several formed in Tripoli and Misrata. During the conflict, al-Sallabi's brigade reportedly received weapons and other aid from Qatar, a country that supported Islamist brigades without NTC authorization.[221] Al-Sallabi, however, has denied these allegations, while Qatari officials spoke openly to providing weapons and training to rebels during the conflict. As 'Ali al-Sallabi and others began forming political parties along Islamic lines, some NTC officials complained in November 2011 over Qatar's involvement, and criticized its influence in Libya.[222]

---

[217] *Libya's Political Parties*, AL JAZEERA, July 3, 2012, *available at* http://www.aljazeera .com/news/africa/2012/06/2012626224516206109.html .

[218] *Official Final Election Results in Libya Show Liberals got 62 percent of Votes*, THE TRIPOLI POST, July 17, 2012, *available at* http://www.tripolipost.com/articledetail.asp?c=1&i=8837.

[219] Kirkpatrick, *supra* note 214.

[220] Richard Spencer, *Libyan cleric announces new party on lines of 'moderate' Islamic democracy*, THE GUARDIAN, Nov. 10, 2011, *available at* http://www.telegraph.co.uk/news/ worldnews/africaandindianocean/libya/8879955/Libyan-cleric-announces-new-party-on-lines-of-moderate-Islamic-democracy.html.

[221] Rang Alaaldin, *Libya: Defining its Future*, LSE IDEAS!, *available at* http://www2.lse .ac.uk/IDEAS/publications/reports/pdf/SR011/FINAL_LSE_IDEAS__LibyaDefiningIts Future_Alaaldin.pdf.

[222] Spencer, *Libyan cleric announces new party on lines of 'moderate' Islamic democracy, supra* note 220. Sallabi rejected the allegations that Qatar influenced his militia or political party.

Recent events indicate that there is strong movement against the more radical strains of political Islam that desire to impose strict Shar'ia law in Libya. On 7 June 2011, as Ansar al-Sharī'a and other affiliated militias organized a large rally in support of imposing Islamic law, a large counterdemonstration took place, led by civil society, NGOs, and women's groups.[223] In another incident, thousands took to the streets in Benghazi on 21 September 2012 and seized control of several headquarters, including that of Ansar al-Sharī'a.[224] The demonstration, referred to as 'Rescue Benghazi Day,' was seen as an act of opposition to the armed militias, and a call for the government to disband the groups.[225] The storming of the militia bases in Benghazi in the wake of the U.S. consulate attacks also represent a rejection of the more militant elements political Islam in Libya's politics.[226]

Still, other events continued to highlight the threat posed by militant factions in Libya and the region. On 6 June 2012, for example, a bomb exploded outside a building used by the U.S. diplomatic mission in Benghazi – allegedly in response to the drone attack that killed Abu Yahya al-Libi in Pakistan two days prior.[227] After June 6th bombing, a Libyan official reported that the United States was flying surveillance missions using drones to monitor suspected jihadist training camps in eastern Libya.[228] On 11 September 2012, Al-Qa'ida leader Ayman al-Zawhiri released a video to coincide with the anniversary of 9/11/2001, confirming for the first time

---

[223] WEHREY, THE STRUGGLE FOR SECURITY IN EASTERN LIBYA, *supra* note 206.

[224] Suliman Ali Zway & Kareem Fahim, *Libyan Protesters Besiege Militant Group in Benghazi*, N.Y. TIMES, Sept. 21, 2012, *available at* http://www.nytimes.com/2012/09/22/world/africa/pro-american-libyans-besiege-militant-group-in-benghazi.html.

[225] Peter Graff & Suleiman Al Khalidi, *Benghazi Anti-Militia Protest: Libyan Protesters Drive Islamist Militia from Country's 2nd Largest City*, REUTERS, Sept. 22, 2011, *available at* http://www.huffingtonpost.com/2012/09/21/libya-militia-protests-benghazi_n_1905288.html.

[226] Maggie Michael, *Libyans storm militia in backlash of attack on US*, AP, Sept. 21, 2012, *available at* http://news.yahoo.com/libyans-storm-militia-backlash-attack-us-225317193.html.

[227] Mohammed Al-Tommy, *Bomb targets U.S. mission in Libya's Benghazi*, REUTERS, June 6, 2011, *available at* http://www.reuters.com/article/2012/06/06/us-libya-attack-us-idUSBRE8550GX20120606.

[228] Nic Robertson, Paul Cruickshank & Jomana Karadsheh, *Libyan official: U.S. drones seeking jihadists in Libya*, CNN, June 7, 2012, *available at* http://security.blogs.cnn.com/2012/06/07/senior-libyan-official-u-s-deploying-drones-as-concerns-rise-over-al-qaeda-in-eastern-libya/.

the death of Abu Yahya al-Libi.[229] The video drew immediate concerns that Al-Qa'ida was involved in the consulate attack in Benghazi. Shortly after the incident, security experts assessed that the attack appeared to have been orchestrated by AQIM, and carried out by local militias.[230] On 14 November 2012, the head of U.S. Africa Command, General Carter Ham, affirmed that the militants who carried out the attacks were likely linked to AQIM, and warned of the growing threat of the group. General Ham also said the U.S. military plan to dislodge AQIM from northern Mali was still in progress.[231]

Despite the efforts of the Libyan government and moderate Islamists, Islamist violence has increased significantly over 2012 and 2013 as local and regional problems have mounted. Internally, the Libyan government has been unable to secure the forces necessary to oust Islamist militias from cities in eastern Libya, and similarly it has been unable to put forward a persuasive political and legal system to undermine support for various groups in Cyrenaica. The policy thus far has been to use intelligence, including surveillance drones, coupled with military action to counter the resurgent Islamists, a policy that has not been without its critics. Bill Lawrence of the International Crisis Group has succinctly argued that "There's always bad guys who may blow up buildings – the question is what sea are they swimming in? The priority should be the support of a legitimate government that reflects the aspirations of all elements of Libyan society."[232] In the face of the inability of the Libyan government to assert its authority, Islamism has been filling the void, and increasingly through the expression of violent Islam.

Islamist violence was at first localized in the more conservative East, including Benghazi and Derna. These attacks have significantly focused on the foreigners, and particularly Westerners. The most notable of these was the attack on the U.S. Consulate in September 2012, which resulted

---

[229] *9/11 anniversary: Ayman al-Zawahiri confirms June death of Abu Yahya al-Libi*, THE TELEGRAPH, Sept. 11, 2012, *available at* http://www.telegraph.co.uk/news/worldnews/september-11-attacks/9534938/911-anniversary-Ayman-al-Zawahiri-confirms-June-death-of-Abu-Yahya-al-Libi.html.

[230] Walt, *The Motive and the Means: Did al-Qaeda Stage the Benghazi Attack?*, *supra* note 200.

[231] John Irish, *Qaeda links to militants in Libya envoy attack: U.S. general*, REUTERS, Nov. 16, 2012, *available at* http://articles.chicagotribune.com/2012-11-14/news/sns-rt-us-mali-usa-libyabre8ad13c-20121114_1_mali-crisis-qaeda-links-aqim.

[232] Chris Stephen & Afua Hirsch, *Libya Faces Growing Islamist Threat*, THE GUARDIAN, Apr. 28, 2013, *available at* http://www.guardian.co.uk/world/2013/apr/28/libya-mali-islamist-violence-tripoli.

in the death of Ambassador Christopher Stevens and two other staff.[233] In June of 2012 the Tunisian consulate in Benghazi was attacked,[234] and that same month the UK Ambassador to Libya was ambushed while visiting Benghazi.[235] More recently, in January 2013 the Italian consulate in Benghazi was closed after an ambush on the consul general.[236]

While these attacks have traditionally been localized in the East, it has spread to the more liberal West in recent months, culminating with an attack on the French Embassy in Tripoli in April 2013. The attack resulted in severe injuries to several French guards and Libyans visiting the building,[237] as well as the significant destruction of the facility itself.[238] The attack marked the first attack on foreign diplomatic facilities in Tripoli, and has sparked concerns over the increasing influence and impact of Islamic militancy in Libya.[239]

The internal problems confronting Libya have combined with regional issues, most notably the Malian civil war of 2012 and the subsequent French intervention in January 2013. After the fall of the Qadhafi government elements of the government forces, and in particular Tuaregs, fled South only to re-establish themselves in northern Mali, where they joined local forces in a fight against the Malian government in Bamako. The Malian insurgency resulted in the near collapse of that state as Islamist fighters took control of nearly two-thirds of the country. After the French and African Union intervention in January 2013 Islamist fighters, including the National Movement for the Liberation of Azawad (MNLA), fled North in Algeria and Fezzan. The Libyan government has been working to close its porous Southern border, including the construction of a 108-mile long trench and the creation of free fire zones.[240] It is clear, however, that some of these heavily armed forces are now establishing themselves in

---

[233] *See supra* Sec. 4.

[234] *Gunmen attack Tunisian consulate in Benghazi,* REUTERS, June 18, 2003, *available at* http://www.reuters.com/article/2012/06/18/us-libya-gunmen-tunisia-idUSBRE85H1V6 20120618.

[235] *UK diplomat's convoy attacked in Libya,* AL JAZEERA, June 11, 2012, *available at* http://www.aljazeera.com/news/middleeast/2012/06/201261152127356825.html.

[236] Elisabetta Povoledo, *Italy Closes Consulate in Benghazi After New Attack,* N.Y. TIMES, Oct. 15, 2012, *available at* http://www.nytimes.com/2013/01/16/world/africa/italy-closes-benghazi-consulate-after-ambush-attempt.html.

[237] Chris Stephen, *Libya bomb attack hits French embassy in Tripoli,* THE GUARDIAN, Apr. 23, 2013, *available at* http://www.guardian.co.uk/world/2013/apr/23/libya-bomb-attack-french-embassy.

[238] Stephen & Hirsch, *Libya Faces Growing Islamist Threat, supra* note 232.

[239] *Id.*

[240] *Id.*

Libya, and that attacks such as the one on the French Embassy are either being carried out in retaliation by those forces, or by Libyan forces in support of their comrades in Mali.

In short, the increasing influence of Islamists in Libya, as evidenced by the attack on the U.S. and Tunisian consulates and Italian and UK Ambassadors in Benghazi, as well as the attack on the French embassy in Tripoli, and the entry of fundamentalist elements from Mali into Libya are all adding to this new problem. While there is no conclusive evidence linking Islamist groups in Libya to their counter-parts in other North African states or the loosely knit al-Qaʿida network, some inferences can be drawn from the attacks outlined above and the increasing number of violent attacks by Islamists in Libya. Based on experience it is possible to conclude that foreign Islamists from across the Middle East and North Africa[241] who sympathize with Libyan Islamist groups, and who may had fought at one time or another in Afghanistan, Iraq, and elsewhere, may be drifting into Libya to continue their struggle, adding to the volatile internal mix and further threatening the fledgling Libyan state.

While continuing its investigation into the embassy attack, the U.S. government also began concerted steps to enhance its security presence in Libya. In September 2012, the U.S. State Department and Pentagon reportedly began planning to fund and train a special commando unit of Libyan soldiers to counter terrorist and violent extremist organizations.[242] The U.S. Congress reportedly approved $8 million to build an elite Libyan force of an estimated 500 soldiers over the following year.[243] The head of the Libyan Shield Forces (LSF) told reporters in early November 2012 that the CIA had led a U.S. embassy delegation to Benghazi to meet and recruit fighters from the group.[244]

The proposed securitization plans raise concerns that using purely military means to combat Islamic fundamentalism with lead to further marginalizing and targeting of moderate political Islamist groups, including those who have renounced violence and are using their positions in the

---

[241] There is also likelihood that some of these elements in Egypt, who has ceased functioning in a violent way, may have easily found their way into Libya.

[242] Eric Schmitt, *U.S. to Help Create Libyan Commando Force*, N.Y. TIMES, Oct. 15, 2012, *available at* http://www.nytimes.com/2012/10/16/world/africa/us-to-help-create-libyan-commando-force.html.

[243] *Id.*

[244] It was unclear if this training was part of the $8 million from the Pentagon funds. *See* Abigail Hauslohner, *US-backed force in Libya face challenges*, THE GUARDIAN, Nov. 13, 2012, *available at* http://www.guardian.co.uk/world/2012/nov/13/libya-middleeast.

GNC to encourage their former brethren to abandon violence. This raises the danger of repeating past policies of dealing with Islamists in a way that leads to further radicalization, and more violence. The more pragmatic approach would involve recognizing the various forms of moderate political Islam that exist in Libya today, now represented within political parties and in the legislature. Many former militants who NATO forces helped overthrow the Qadhafi regime, reject Al-Qaʻida and are playing a prominent role in shaping Libya's attempted transition to democracy. The success of this transition will be determined, to a large extent, by the willingness of Western governments to engage with leaders who reject violence and are committed to working within the boundaries of Libya's political system.

6. THE POLITICAL LANDSCAPE

6.1. *The 2012 Elections*

In the midst of ongoing conflicts and insecurity, Libya moved forward with plans for elections to be held across the country in July 2012. The 2012 national elections were seen as a fundamental component in the transition from dictatorship to representative government. Thus, the national and local authorities prepared the country for elections to elect a General National Congress (GNC), which would serve as a representative governing body and replace the existing NTC. Once elected, the GNC would be tasked with appointing a Prime Minister, who would then name a government cabinet within 30 days of the GNC's first meeting. The GNC was also tasked with selecting a Constituent Assembly, comprised of individuals outside of the GNC, to draft the official constitution that would replace the Interim Constitutional Declaration introduced by the NTC on 3 August 2011, and with organizing future elections as stipulated in the new constitution.[245] The constitution was to be drafted and adopted within 120 days of the GNC's first meeting, and then submitted to the public referendum before its adoption.[246]

---

[245] PROJECT ON MIDDLE EAST DEMOCRACY, POMED'S BACKGROUNDER: PREVIEWING LIBYA'S ELECTIONS 2 (July 5, 2012), *available at* http://pomed.org/wordpress/wp-content/uploads/2012/07/Previewing-Libyas-Elections.pdf.

[246] *Elections in Libya: 7 July General National Congress Elections – Frequently Asked Questions*, LIBYA HERALD, June 30, 2012, *available at* http://www.libyaherald.com/?p=10175.

For four decades under Qadhafi, political parties had been banned and public organizing was nonexistent. Thus, the NTC authorities were faced with the task of implementing certain measures to establish the basic foundation for the election process. The first measure came on 18 December 2011, when the NTC adopted Law 192 (2011) on Transparency and Honesty, regarding future candidates for the election of the GNC.[247] On 4 January 2012, the NTC adopted Law 2 (2012) legalizing political parties.[248] The NTC reportedly had attempted to receive general comments online from the public on the law making process, but the process still experienced backlash, particularly from those in eastern Libya, who felt marginalized from the political process in Tripoli.[249] In January 2012, the NTC's offices in Benghazi were attacked by protesters who called for greater transparency.[250]

Despite the protests, the NTC proceeded to adopt Law 3 (2012) on 18 January, establishing the High National Elections Commission (HNEC) to oversee the electoral process.[251] The HNEC worked in conjunction with the United States-based non-governmental organization the Carter Center, which was asked to monitor the election process.[252] On 28 January, the NTC issued Law 4 (2012) for the Election of the GNC, establishing the framework for planned elections, and setting the provisions for the election of 200 members to the GNC. 120 of its representatives were to be elected by majority and 80 by proportional representation.[253]

As the basic initiatives were passed in preparation for the elections, the NTC implemented other measures that had an impact on the election

---

[247] *Libya*, MAX PLANCK INSTITUTE FOR COMPARATIVE PUBLIC LAW AND INTERNATIONAL LAW, *available at* http://www.mpil.de/ww/en/pub/research/details/know_transfer/constitutional_reform_in_arab_/libyen.cfm.

[248] *Id. See also Draft Libyan Electoral Law 2012 – English Translation*, LIBYAN PROGRESS, *available at* http://www.libyanprogress.org/articles/draft-libyan-electoral-law-2012-english-translation/.

[249] *Libyans storm transitional government headquarters in Benghazi*, THE GUARDIAN, Jan. 21 2012, *available at* http://www.guardian.co.uk/world/2012/jan/21/libyans-transitional-government-headquarters-benghazi.

[250] *Id. See also* Ch. VI, Sec. 2.

[251] *Libya*, MAX PLANCK INSTITUTE FOR COMPARATIVE PUBLIC LAW AND INTERNATIONAL LAW, *supra* note 247; POMED, POMED'S BACKGROUNDER: PREVIEWING LIBYA'S ELECTIONS, *supra* note 245 at 3.

[252] *Monitoring Elections*, CARTER CENTER, *available at* http://www.cartercenter.org/countries/libya-peace.html.

[253] MAX PLANCK INSTITUTE FOR COMPARATIVE PUBLIC LAW AND INTERNATIONAL LAW, LAW N°04-2012 ON THE ELECTION OF THE NATIONAL GENERAL CONGRESS, *available at* http://www.mpil.de/shared/data/pdf/the_election_law_libya.pdf; *Libya*, MAX PLANCK INSTITUTE FOR COMPARATIVE PUBLIC LAW AND INTERNATIONAL LAW, *supra* note 247.

process. On 2 May, the NTC passed Law 38 (2012) on Special Procedures for the Transitional Period, providing a broad amnesty to those who fought on the side of the *thuwar* forces against the Qadhafi regime.[254] The same day, 2 May, the NTC also passed Law 37 (2012) restricting freedom of expression, including banning any language criticizing the 2011 revolution or insulting Islam. The laws were seen as at attempt to restrict criticism of those who took part in the revolution and shield former fighters involved in the political process from facing accusations of past violations. Both laws were heavily rebuked by the international community and domestic human rights groups, and in June Law 37 (2012) was declared unconstitutional Libya's Supreme Court as it violated the Interim Constitutional Declaration.[255] The NTC also created the Integrity and Patriotism Commission in April 2012 with the aim of investigating all "senior and government and security officials, members of congress, and the heads of trade unions, universities and other public institutions."[256] HRW found the law to be overly broad in scope, as appeared to be used for political purposes to ban individuals from various posts, including those who were elected to the GNC.[257]

Two days before the scheduled election, on 5 July, the NTC adopted Constitutional Amendment Number 3 (2012) which modified Amendment Number 1 (2012) so that members of the constitutional assembly could be elected, instead of appointed.[258] The same day, the NTC adopted Declaration Number 7 of 2012 recommending the GNC to consider Islam as the main source of legislation. It also suggests that the issue should be submitted to a referendum.[259]

As is well known, political activity was severely repressed under Qadhafi, leaving no space for public organizing in any form. Thus, the majority of the parties taking part in the 2012 elections were not well established

---

[254] *Libya: Amend New Special Procedures Law*, HUMAN RIGHTS WATCH, May 11, 2012, *available at* http://www.hrw.org/news/2012/05/11/libya-amend-new-special-procedures-law.

[255] *Libya: Law Restricting Speech Ruled Unconstitutional*, HUMAN RIGHTS WATCH, June 14, 2012, *available at* http://www.hrw.org/news/2012/06/14/libya-law-restricting-speech-ruled-unconstitutional.

[256] *Libya: Ensure 'Political Isolation Law' Respects Rights*, HUMAN RIGHTS WATCH, Jan. 22, 2013, *available at* http://www.hrw.org/news/2013/01/22/libya-ensure-political-isolation-law-respects-rights.

[257] *Id.*

[258] *Libya*, MAX PLANCK INSTITUTE FOR COMPARATIVE PUBLIC LAW AND INTERNATIONAL LAW, *supra* note 247.

[259] *Id.*

and poorly organized. However, there were a few exceptions such as National Front Party and Justice and Construction Party, which had roots in preexisting organizations that had operated underground or abroad.[260] The Muslim Brotherhood, which is affiliated with the Justice and Construction Party, had been banned and targeted by the Qadhafi regime but continued to organize clandestinely for decades.[261] The Brotherhood remains especially influential in eastern Libya, where the group remained connected to their Egyptian counterparts.[262]

As in neighboring Egypt, the first open elections in the country were held before a developed or organized political spectrum had had been established. The parties that emerged in the post-conflict period were mostly regional, and represented particular towns or neighborhoods.[263] While all parties expressed the intention to develop a strong and independent Libya, increase employment, improve schools and hospitals, disband the militias and restore public security, the specific means to achieve such goals were unclear. Specific strategies on measures dealing with issues such as healthcare, defense, foreign policy, education and the economy were seemingly absent from the campaign process.[264]

Libya's political parties have generally been characterized as divided into 4 broad camps: nationalists, liberals, Islamists, and secularists. The nationalists, said to be the largest camp, comprise nearly half of the political spectrum. They are non-ideological and seek to build a state based on Libyan culture and democracy. Liberals are said to comprise nearly a quarter of the Libya's political participants, and support an open democratic system with a free market economy. Islamists, are said to comprise around a fifth of the spectrum, and are further subdivided into salafists, the Muslim Brotherhood representatives, and jihadists. Secularists make up a small proportion, roughly 2–5 percent, and strive for a secular state where religion plays no role at all.[265]

In total 130 parties, or political entities, were represented in the national elections.[266] The parties included 1,207 candidates competing for the 80

---

[260] For more on the history of the Muslim Brotherhood in Libya, *see* Ch. I, Secs. 8 & 9.

[261] *Libya's political parties*, AL JAZEERA, July 3, 2012, *available at* http://www.aljazeera.com/news/africa/2012/06/2012626224516206109.html.

[262] *See supra* Sec. 5.

[263] AL JAZEERA, *Libya's political parties*, *supra* note 261.

[264] George Grant, *Elections Analysis: So who are they and what do they actually stand for?*, LIBYA HERALD, June 30 2011, *available at* http://www.libyaherald.com/?p=10156.

[265] *A guide to Libya's new political landscape*, THE GUARDIAN, Sept. 1, 2011, *available at* http://www.guardian.co.uk/commentisfree/2011/sep/01/libya-political-landscape.

[266] Grant, *Elections Analysis: So who are they and what do they actually stand for?*, *supra* note 264.

out of 200 GNC seats allotted for party representatives. Another 2,501 candidates stood as independents competing for the remaining 120 seats.[267] The six most prominent parties that emerged were the Justice and Construction Party (JCP), the Nation Party (NP), the Homeland Party (HP), the National Forces Alliance (NFA), the National Front Party (NFP) and the National Centrist Party (NCP).[268]

The Justice and Construction Party (Hizb al-'Adala wa-l-Bina) is believed to be the face of the Muslim Brotherhood. The party's establishment goes back as far as 1949, but it did not operate openly due to the repression of political parties during the Qadhafi period.[269] The party's leader is Muhammad Sawan[270] who was a political prisoner under Qadhafi.[271] Due to its long history the party was, similarly to the Egyptian Freedom and Justice party, believed to be the country's most organized political force[272] with well educated and influential members.[273] The party put forward 73 candidates during the election process.[274] With the Muslim Brotherhood's prominence in Egypt raising regional concerns, Sawan made public statements distancing the Justice and Construction Party from the Brotherhood, stating that his part was administratively, and financially independent from the group.[275]

The Nation Party (Hizb al-Watan) was supported by the aforementioned Islamist/Salafi cleric 'Ali al-Sallabi[276] and was also said to include the former head of the LIFG and leader of the Tripoli Military Council 'Abd al-Hakim Balhaj. As discussed elsewhere, both al-Sallabi and Balhaj have a long history of militant opposition, as well as political organizing, and both were imprisoned for several years under Qadhafi.[277]

---

[267] *Id.*

[268] POMED, POMED'S BACKGROUNDER: PREVIEWING LIBYA'S ELECTIONS, *supra* note 245 at 9.

[269] Grant, *Elections Analysis: So who are they and what do they actually stand for?*, *supra* note 264.

[270] The transliteration of this name was adopted from the reference.

[271] Grant, *Elections Analysis: So who are they and what do they actually stand for?*, *supra* note 264.

[272] AL JAZEERA, *Libya's political parties*, *supra* note 261.

[273] Grant, *Elections Analysis: So who are they and what do they actually stand for?*, *supra* note 264.

[274] *Id.*

[275] AL JAZEERA, *Libya's political parties*, *supra* note 261.

[276] *See supra* Sec. 5.

[277] For more on Balhaj, *see* Ch. I, Sec. 10 & Ch. II, Sec. 3.3. *See also* AL JAZEERA, *Libya's political parties*, *supra* note 261.

The Nation Party put forward 59 candidates and was said to be a favorite among former revolutionary fighters.[278] During the campaign the party emphasized security issues and the need to create a strong national army and protect the country's borders. The party advocates the decentralization of power, although it rejects federalism. The platform of the party calls for a "moderate" Islamic democracy with a constitution based on Sharī'a law.[279] The party has been characterized as a Salafi party.

The Union for Homeland (Hizb al-Ittihad min 'Ajl al-Watan) party was led by 'Abd al-Rahman al-Suwahli. Al-Suwahli was targeted by Qadhafi for his opposition organizing against the regime while in exile in London during the 1970s and 1980s.[280] His party put forward 60 candidates,[281] and came out in strong opposition to the participation of candidates who have served in the Qadhafi regime.[282]

The National Forces Alliance (Tahaluf al-Quwa al-Wataniyya) is a broad coalition of 58 political parties, forty political organizations, hundreds of NGOs and almost 300 independent figures.[283] The alliance called for the application of "moderate Islam" and "for the establishment of the foundations of a democratic civil state."[284] It was led by the interim Prime Minster Mahmud Jibril. Despite being a coalition, the NFA stood as one political entity with 70 candidates running for seats in the GNC. Known for its liberal political leanings it proved to be popular among international actors and Libyans living in the diaspora.[285]

The National Front Party (Hizb al-Jabha al-Wataniyya) was formed in May 2012 out of the dissolved National Front for the Salvation of Libya (NFSL). The NFSL was an armed opposition movement that was created during Qadhafi's rule.[286] It was established in 1981 by Muhammad Yusuf al-Magarayf, who had served as Qadhafi's ambassador to India before defecting and becoming a prominent opposition figure. Mugarayf lived

---

[278] Other sources say that the party fielded 57 candidates over 17 lists. *See* AL JAZEERA, *Libya's political parties, supra* note 261.

[279] *Id.*

[280] Michael Cousins, *Party Profile: Union for the Homeland,* LIBYA HERALD, July 4, 2012, *available at* http://www.libyaherald.com/?p=10516.

[281] Grant, *Elections Analysis: So who are they and what do they actually stand for?, supra* note 264.

[282] Cousins, *Party Profile: Union for the Homeland, supra* note 280.

[283] AL JAZEERA, *Libya's political parties, supra* note 261.

[284] *Id.*

[285] Grant, *Elections Analysis: So who are they and what do they actually stand for?, supra* note 264.

[286] For more on the history of the NFSL, *see* Ch. I, Sec. 9.2.

in the United States for years, where he organized political and militant opposition to the Qadhafi regime.[287] In 1984, after a failed coup against Qadhafi, many of the organization's members were arrested and some of its leaders publicly executed.[288] The organization continued to operate from outside of Libya.[289] Al-Magarayf emphasized the party's historic anti-Qadhafi stance in the run-up to the elections.[290] The party positioned itself as a liberal party and ran 45 candidates for the GNC seats.[291]

The National Centrist Party (Hizb al-Tayyar al-Watani al-Wasati) was founded by 'Ali Tarhuni, the former deputy prime minister in the NTC's interim cabinet. Like Jabril and other NTC officials, Tarhuni was not allowed to run directly as a candidate. The part was one of the ten parties that had support in several constituencies around Libya,[292] and put forward 43 candidates in the 2012 elections.[293]

6.2. Election Results

The election campaigning officially began on the 18 June 2012 and ended 24 hours before the commencement of voting on 7 July.[294] Disruptions at polling stations were limited and reported mostly in the east, where armed groups stopped people from voting in parts of Ra's Lanuf, Brega and Ajdabiya.[295] Across the country, the elections were carried out with a reported 94% of the voting stations operating mostly without incident.[296]

On 17 July, the results were announced, and the NFA was declared the majority winner, securing 39 of the 80 seats available for political parties.[297] The Justice and Construction party was the most successful after the NFA,

---

[287] Alison Pargeter, *Qadhafi and Political Islam In Libya*, *in* LIBYA SINCE 1969: QADHAFI'S REVOLUTION REVISITED 83, 87 (Dirk Vandewalle ed., New York, USA: Palgrave McMillan 2011).
[288] AL JAZEERA, *Libya's political parties*, *supra* note 261.
[289] Grant, *Elections Analysis: So who are they and what do they actually stand for?*, *supra* note 264.
[290] *Id.*
[291] *Id.*
[292] AL JAZEERA, *Libya's political parties*, *supra* note 261.
[293] Grant, *Elections Analysis: So who are they and what do they actually stand for?*, *supra* note 264.
[294] POMED, POMED'S BACKGROUNDER: PREVIEWING LIBYA'S ELECTIONS, *supra* note 245 at 8.
[295] *Libya Election: High Turnout in Historic Vote*, BBC, July 7, 2012, *available at* http://www.bbc.co.uk/news/world-africa-18749808.
[296] *Id.*
[297] *National Forces Alliance sweeps party lists as election results finally announced*, LIBYA HERALD, July 17, 2012, *available at* http://www.libyaherald.com/?p=11212.

winning 17 out of the 80 seats.[298] The National Centralist Party came in third with three seats and other parties gained one or two seats each. The 120 remaining seats were assigned to the independent candidates.[299]

The large gap between the NFA and the JCP came as a surprise to many observers who predicted the Islamist parties would gain more seats, and was touted as a victory by many who supported the more secular and liberal leaning political parties. Reports indicated that liberal parties had won the majority of the votes in 11 of Libya's 13 electoral districts.[300] The victory by the NFA, however, did not necessarily reflect the overall political influence of the Islamists in the country. Observers noted that the Islamist parties could still gain a majority block by recruiting individuals from the 120 independent seat holders in the GNC. Members of the Brotherhood also fielded a number of individual candidates who won seats, and experts predicted that along with the seats gained by the JCP, the Brotherhood and its allies could achieve anywhere from 40-80 seats in total.[301] The ability of the major parties to rule is therefore contingent on their ability to form alliances with independents and build a majority block.

Overall, the elections were viewed as a success and as a pivotal step in Libya's transitional process. Reports indicate that 2.8 million people registered to vote, with over 1.7 million casting their votes,[302] leading to a voter turnout of approximately 62 percent.[303] International observers from the Carter Center found that despite Libya's inexperience with elections, the vote had been a success.[304] While the results were deemed to be credible and accurate, the Center noted that improvements could be

---

[298] *Id.*

[299] *Libya*, Max Planck Institute for Comparative Public Law and International Law, *supra* note 247.

[300] *Libya's defeated Islamists*, Al Jazeera, Jul. 18 2012, *available at* http://www.aljazeera.com/indepth/opinion/2012/07/20127187155487377.html.

[301] Alison Pargeter, *Llibya and Islamism: the deeper story*, OpenDemocracy, Aug. 7, 2012, *available at* http://www.opendemocracy.net/alison-pargeter/libya-and-islamism-deeper-story.

[302] *Report of the Secretary General and Head of UN Mission to Libya* 3, United Nations, July 28, 2012, U.N Doc. S/PV.6807, *available at* http://unsmil.unmissions.org/Portals/unsmil/Documents/Briefing18July2012.pdf.

[303] *Libya*, Max Planck Institute for Comparative Public Law and International Law, *supra* note 247.

[304] *The Carter Center Finds Libya's Tabulation Process Credible*, Carter Center, July 18, 2012, *available at* http://www.cartercenter.org/news/pr/libya-071812.html?gclid=CMme_4zD2LICFYqV3godyWEAFw.

made in the future with regards to accuracy and adherence to international and national electoral standards.[305] SRSG Martin commended the Libyan people for holding successful election in his address to the Security Council and noted that campaigning was peaceful and the registration process largely successful.[306] He noted that the HNEC did everything in its power to making the election a success and that violence in the east had not derailed election outcome.[307]

On 9 August 2012 the NTC officially handed over power to the GNC.[308] On 10 August 2012, Mohammad al-Magarayf was elected President of the GNC, replacing Mustafa 'Abd al-Jalil as the head of state.[309] Al-Magarayf was to hold the position until the new constitution could be drafted.[310] The 200-member GNC also elected Mustafa Abu Shagur, as prime minister on 12 September 2012.[311]

Shagur was tasked with appointing a cabinet composed of 10 ministry positions, which became highly politicized and controversial act, resulting in demonstrations in cities such as Zawiyya.[312] Shagur failed to receive congressional approval for his cabinet nominees and was subsequently removed from his position after a vote of no confidence was passed on 7 October 2012, with 125 of 200 members voting for his removal.[313] He was

---

[305] *Id.*

[306] *Report of the Secretary General and Head of UN Mission to Libya* 2, UNITED NATIONS, July 28, 2012, U.N Doc. S/PV.6807 *available at* http://unsmil.unmissions.org/Portals/unsmil/Documents/Briefing18July2012.pdf.

[307] *Id.*

[308] *Libya*, MAX PLANCK INSTITUTE FOR COMPARATIVE PUBLIC LAW AND INTERNATIONAL LAW, *supra* note 247.

[309] Al-Magarayf had previously lived in exile where he led NFSL opposition group.

[310] *Mohammed el-Megarif elected as Libya's interim president*, THE GUARDIAN, Aug. 10, 2012, *available at* http://www.guardian.co.uk/world/2012/aug/10/mohammed-el-megarif-libya-president.

[311] Shagur was a notable opposition figure from the Qadhafi era who had spent 30 years in exile in the United States. *See Libya's congress gives new PM ultimatum to name government*, REUTERS, Sept. 26, 2012, *available at* http://www.reuters.com/article/2012/09/26/us-libya-government-idUSBRE88P1U320120926; *Libyan government in disarray after parliament sacks prime minister-elect*, THE GUARDIAN, Oct. 7, 2012, *available at* http://www.guardian.co.uk/world/2012/oct/07/libyan-government-disarray-mustafa-abushagur; *Libya's Prime Minister Is Dismissed*, N.Y. TIMES, Oct. 7, 2012, *available at* http://www.nytimes.com/2012/10/08/world/africa/libyas-prime-minister-is-dismissed.html.

[312] *Libyan assembly passes vote of no confidence dismissing prime minister*, REUTERS, Oct. 8, 2012, *available at* http://in.reuters.com/article/2012/10/08/libya-government-mustafa-abushagur-idINDEE89701B20121008.

[313] *Id.*

replaced by 'Ali Zaydan[314] on 14 October 2012, who won with 93 votes and a clear majority over the other candidates for the position.[315]

The political developments continued to trigger unrest and protests around the country. On 31 October 2012, militiamen occupied the Libyan parliament building in Tripoli in protest against the formation of the new government. The militiamen called for the removal of ministers who had links to the Qadhafi government.[316] Protests and continued agitation by militias led to the adoption of the Political Isolation Law on 5 May by the GNC, which barred any individual from holding office should he/she have held a senior position under Qadhafi, regardless of whether the person had defected before or during the 2011 conflict.[317] As indicated above, the adoption of the law came after increasing agitation by militias, including the occupation or besieging of various ministries.[318] The effect of the adoption of the Political Isolation Law was the removal of various senior politicians, most notably al-Magarayf, the President of the GNC.[319]

6.3. Demands for Representation

Large segments of the population protested the political process and feared exclusion from the reconstruction process or wealth distribution in the post-conflict period. In the lead up to the national elections, political groups in eastern Libya began calling for greater autonomy for

---

[314] 'Ali Zaydan was a diplomat under Qadhafi but he defected in the 1980s and joined Libya's NFSL opposition group from Geneva which is where he was based. *Libyan lawmakers elect ex-diplomat Ali Zidan as new prime minister*, NBC, Oct. 19, 2012, *available at* http://worldnews.nbcnews.com/_news/2012/10/14/14434669-libyan-lawmakers-elect-ex-diplomat-ali-zidan-as-new-prime-minister.

[315] *Id.*

[316] *Libya gunmen end occupation of parliament building*, BBC, Nov. 2, 2012, *available at* http://www.bbc.co.uk/news/world-africa-20178222.

[317] *See* Ch. IV, Sec. 6.1. *See also* Sami Zaptia, *Political Isolation Law passed overwhelmingly*, May 5, 2013, LIBYA HERALD, *available at* http://www.libyaherald.com/2013/05/05/political-isolation-law-passed-overwhelmingly/.

[318] *See supra* Sec. 2.4. *See also* Tom Westcott, *"We won't use these weapons": militiamen at Justice Ministry siege*, LIBYA HERALD, May 1, 2013, *available at* http://www.libyaherald.com/2013/05/01/we-wont-use-these-weapons-militiamen-at-justice-ministry-siege/; *Militia gunmen besiege Libyan Foreign Ministry, demand resignations*, RT, Apr. 28, 2013, *available at* http://rt.com/news/libya-foreign-ministry-riot-532/.

[319] Anas El Gomati, *Why Libya's 'Isolation Law' Threatens Progress*, CARNAGIE ENDOWMENT, May 22, 2013, *available at* http://carnegieendowment.org/2013/05/21/why-libya-s-isolation-law-threatens-progress/g5g2; *Libya: Reject 'Political Isolation Law'*, HUMAN RIGHTS WATCH, May 4, 2013, *available at* http://www.hrw.org/news/2013/05/04/libya-reject-political-isolation-law.

Cyrenaica, and a more federalist-leaning system,[320] raising issues that had befuddled Libya in the run-up to independence in 1951. On 6 March 2012, a 3,000-representative congress announced the formation of the Cyrenaica Transitional Council, with Ahmad al-Senussi, a descendant of King Idris al-Senussi, as its leader.[321] The Council declaration was seen as a direct challenge to the NTC, particularly with regards to the oil negotiations and production that was based in the east.

On 3 May 2012, the Cyrenaica Council called for the boycotting of national assembly elections.[322] In June, a blockade was set up in the east, closing off military and commercial traffic on the road to Tripoli.[323] The blockade was reportedly established in protest over the formula for the distribution of seats in the GNC, as it allocated 40 seats for southern Fezzan, 60 for the eastern Cyrenaica and 100 for northwestern Tripolitania.[324] The designation of seats was based on population rather than territory, and many in the east feared the unequal distribution of seats would leave Cyrenaica with little influence over the drafting of the Constitution and ultimately excluded from the seat of power in Tripoli. The fears stemmed from eastern Libya being historically marginalized and excluded under Qadhafi,[325] but also harkened to earlier questions of distribution during the Kingdom of Libya.

In an effort to placate the concerns emanating out of Cyrenaica, the NTC issued an amendment to the August 2011 Interim Constitutional Declaration, stating that the committee responsible for drafting the constitution would be equally represented by all three of the country's provinces, with 20 delegates from each province.[326] The amendment also stipulated that the Constitution must be ratified by a majority vote in a nationwide referendum, and required more than a two-thirds majority in the GNC to pass.[327] In spite of these efforts, tensions in eastern Libya remained high

---

[320] *See* Ch. VI, Sec. 2.

[321] Issam Fetouri, *Eastern Libya defies Tripoli to create autonomous council*, REUTERS, Mar. 6, 2012, *available at* http://www.reuters.com/article/2012/03/06/libya-east-federalism-idUSL5E8E64JK20120306.

[322] Christian Lowe, *Call for election boycott in Libya's turbulent east*, REUTERS, May 3, 2012, *available at* http://www.reuters.com/article/2012/05/03/libya-vote-boycott-idU-SL5E8G3I7Q20120503.

[323] Grant, *Elections Analysis: So who are they and what do they actually stand for?*, *supra* note 264.

[324] *Id.*

[325] *Id.*

[326] *Id.*

[327] *Id.*

and incidents of violence were reported in early July in the lead up to the elections.[328]

There were also election-related disturbances reported in the southern region of the country, which had also been neglected by the Qadhafi government, and suffered from a lack of infrastructural development, communal conflicts and discrimination against minority groups.[329] Tebu leaders threatened to boycott elections if the government did not withdraw its tanks and LSF soldiers from the region that had participated in heavy shelling and violent clashes in the Kufra district and the city of Sabha.[330] Leaders of the Tebu and Tuareg minority communities in the south that had been discriminated against under the former regime also demanded greater representation through the political process,[331] and voiced concern that their people lacked proper identification as a result of the exclusive policies of the former regime and were being excluded from the voter registration process and unable to run for political office.[332]

Similar demands were made in the western Nafusa Mountains region, where Amazigh communities demanded greater political representation and an enhanced Amazigh status under Libyan law. Amazigh had suffered Arabization policies under the Qadhafi regime, which had banned their language and prevented them from expressing cultural traditions and identity.[333] Amazigh communities had played a pivotal role in the uprising and the *thuwar* forces that took control of the Nafusa Mountains region, and had participated in the battle of Tripoli.[334] Amazigh leaders voiced their disapproval that the interim government cabinet included

---

[328] *Libya protesters storm Benghazi voting office*, AL JAZEERA, July 1, 2012, *available at* http://www.aljazeera.com/news/africa/2012/07/20127118412233197.html; Marie-Louise Gumuchian, *Protesters storm Libya election office in Benghazi*, REUTERS, July 1 2012, *available at* http://www.reuters.com/article/2012/07/01/us-libya-elections-idUSBRE8600H520120701.

[329] *Analysis: Libyan minority rights at a crossroads*, INTEGRATED REGIONAL INFORMATION NETWORKS, May 24, 2012, *available at* http://www.irinnews.org/report/95524/Analysis-Libyan-minority-rights-at-a-crossroads.

[330] *Libyan militia storm election office in Benghazi as violence spreads*, THE GUARDIAN, July 1, 2012, *available at* http://www.guardian.co.uk/world/2012/jul/01/libyan-militia-storm-election-office; *More deaths in Kufra reported*, THE LIBYA HERALD, June 29, 2012, *available at* http://www.libyaherald.com/2012/06/29/more-deaths-in-kufra-reported/.

[331] Grant, *Elections Analysis: So who are they and what do they actually stand for?*, *supra* note 264.

[332] *Analysis: Libyan minority rights at a crossroads*, INTEGRATED REGIONAL INFORMATION NETWORKS, *supra* note 329.

[333] ANTHONY BELL ET AL., THE TIDE TURNS, *supra* note 145 at 14.

[334] *The Berber Rising: The "Other Arab Spring"*, BROOKS FOREIGN POLICY REVIEW, Feb. 20, 2012 *available at* http://brooksreview.wordpress.com/2012/02/20/the-berber-rising-the-other-arab-spring.

no Amazigh representatives and demanded representation to ensure recognition of their language and culture.[335] In protest, the Libyan Amazigh
Congress subsequently suspended relations with the NTC, and five Amazigh NTC members boycotted the ceremony when the cabinet was inaugu-
rated in November 2011.[336] Amazigh leaders complained that the draft of
the Constitution did not specifically recognize the Amazigh and worried
the political trends calling for an "Islamic and Arab country," would once
again lead to the discrimination of the non-Arab population.[337]

6.4. *Drafting the Constitution*

The process of drafting a new constitution poses a challenge of incorporating and satisfying the demands of all of the various groups that had been
traditionally marginalized under the former regime. The Interim Constitutional Declaration, finalized by the NTC on 3 August 2011,[338] was to remain
in place until a permanent constitution was drafted. The declaration drew
immediate concerns by members of civil society who claimed that it was
drafted without popular consultation,[339] and it faced significant delays to
its implementation as a result of various political challenges.

The creation of a new constitution encompassed all of the most pressing issues facing the new Libya, including as the role of human rights, the
relationship between state and religion, the balance between national and
regional authority, and the distribution of political and economic power
within the country. Those tasked with its drafting faced the challenge of
producing a constitution that encouraged political participation and civil
society organizing, as well as helped the country overcome the country's
historically deep social and ethnic divides.[340] The constitution needed to
incorporate specific language protecting the human rights of all of Libya's
citizens. Women's rights groups, in particular, have maintained active

---

335 *Excluded from cabinet, Libya's Berbers fear isolation,* AL ARABIYA NEWS, Nov. 28, 2011,
available at http://english.alarabiya.net/articles/2011/11/25/179187.html.
336 *Id.*
337 *Libya's Berbers feel rejected by transitional government,* DEUTSCHE WELLE, Nov. 8,
2011, *available at* http://www.dw.de/libyas-berbers-feel-rejected-by-transitional-government/
a-15515687-1.
338 *Libya Constitutional Declaration,* WIPO RESOURCES, available at http://www.wipo
.int/wipolex/en/details.jsp?id=11248.
339 *Constitution Building and Legal Reform,* LAWYERS FOR JUSTICE IN LIBYA, *available at*
http://www.libyanjustice.org/our-programmes/constitution-building-and-legal-reform.
340 Duncan Pickard, *Libya's constitution controversy,* FOREIGN POLICY, Sept. 5, 2012,
available at http://mideast.foreignpolicy.com/posts/2012/09/05/libyas_constitution_
controversy.

pressure to ensure that the constitution includes clauses to safeguard certain rights, such as equal inheritance, equal-protection, and the right to pass citizenship to their children. Additionally, ethnic and linguistic minority groups, which were often suppressed during Qadhafi's rule, have sought to obtain the rights previously denied them including access to citizenship, recognition of their languages, and the right of return for internally displaced persons.[341]

According to the interim declaration, the constitution was to be drafted within 60 days after the first meeting of the GNC, and followed by a national referendum 30 days thereafter.[342] Many saw the timeframe as unrealistically optimistic, however, and on 13 March 2012, the NTC passed an amendment to the Constitutional Declaration, extending the timeframe and giving the drafters 120 days from the date of Congress' first meeting in July 2012.[343] The drafting of the constitution was to be followed by a 30-day period for a referendum to be held, and if the constitutional draft was rejected, the drafters would have another 30 days to re-submit a draft to the public.[344] The amendment also established a 60-person committee that was responsible for the drafting, with 20 representatives from each of the three provinces.[345] It was not determined, however, whether the committee was to be appointed by the GNC or elected on a regional basis.[346]

Civil society groups complained that the initially proposed timeframe did not allow for sufficient public input and participation and lobbied for an extension. The argument used to justify the short timeline was that the 1951 constitution would work as a solid base for the new constitution.[347] Those who proposed the extension, however, argued that the

---

[341] *Id.*

[342] *Id.*

[343] Lorianne Updike Toler, *Libya's shortened constitutional timeline and why it should be extended*, LIBYA HERALD, Oct. 9, *available at* http://www.libyaherald.com/2012/10/09/libyas-shortened-constitutional-timeline-and-why-it-should-be-extended/; *Libyan Constitution Deadline Extended*, PROJECT ON THE MIDDLE EAST DEMOCRACY, June 28, 2012, *available at* http://pomed.org/blog/2012/06/libyan-constitution-deadline-extended.html/#. UIVgAoavrU4.

[344] Toler, *Libya's shortened constitutional timeline and why it should be extended, supra* note 343.

[345] *Libya*, MAX PLANCK INSTITUTE FOR COMPARATIVE PUBLIC LAW AND INTERNATIONAL LAW, *supra* note 247; PROJECT ON THE MIDDLE EAST DEMOCRACY, *Libyan Constitution Deadline Extended, supra* note 247.

[346] *January 2013 Monthly Forecast*, SECURITY COUNCIL REPORT, Dec. 21, 2012, *available at* http://www.securitycouncilreport.org/monthly-forecast/2013-01/libya_2.php.

[347] While the 1951 constitution established a federal system with three sub-national governments the 1963 amendments abandoned the federal model. *See* Ch. I, Sec. 7.2.

drafting of the new constitution needed time to ensure that it reflected the fundamental political, social and economic changes to Libya over the past 60 years, and that the new constitution needed to resolve the ever present question of the distribution of Libya's wealth.[348] Libya's resources have traditionally been unequally distributed between the country's three provinces. While the eastern region holds the majority of the country's oil, the northwest Tripolitania region holds the majority of the population. Fezzan, the southern province, is the least populated and poorest region in Libya. In effect, a constitution that distributes benefits according to population size benefits Tripolitania, while a dispensation that decentralizes benefits to the regions benefits Cyrenaica to the exclusion of Tripolitania and Fezzan. In order to quell conflicts between the regions, the constitution will need to address the critical resource issue, and determine how the oil revenue will be distributed and invested into the population through education and social programs. Post-conflict peace is largely contingent on the political settlement of this issue.

On 10 April 2013, the GNC issued another constitutional amendment declaring that Libya's constitutional-drafting committee would be elected directly, opposed to being appointed by the GNC. The committee was given 45-days to draft the law, which then was to be passed to the GNC's Legislative and Constitutional Committee. As of April 2013, the constitutional drafting process was still underway.[349]

7. CONCLUSION

While the official end of hostilities was declared with the death of Qadhafi, the conflict in Libya did not end there. The interim government, and indeed, the international community continued to face challenges that went well beyond Libya's borders. The international community, however, largely left post-conflict reconstruction up to the Libyans, particularly with regards to building a security sector and judicial system capable of carrying out basic law and order functions.

The security landscape has been defined by unregulated armed factions that were born in the war and who still wield widespread control. As the

---

[348] Pickard, *Libya's constitution controversy, supra* note 340.

[349] Karim Mezran and Duncan Pickard, *Libya's Constitutional Process: Moving Forward?*, THE ATLANTIC COUNCIL, Apr. 22, 2013, *available at* http://www.acus.org/viewpoint/libya's-constitutional-process-moving-forward.

revolutionary brigades provided security and filled the power vacuum left after the fall of the Qadhafi regime, and consolidated control over the country's security installations and detention facilities, they became inextricably intertwined with the state security apparatus. On many occasions, the NTC gave tacit or direct approval to these groups to carry out security functions, and there were overlapping and complicated lines of authority with the new security bodies such as the LSF and the SSC. International observers raised concerns that these new security structures were acting as parallel security bodies with little civilian oversight or accountability, and that they resembled the irregular paramilitary security organizations that were common under Qadhafi.

The armed forces that make up these structures pose a significant challenge to Libya's post-conflict security sector and judicial reform efforts. The accreditation process for the integration of the revolutionary fighters into the state security forces has thus far lacked the type of vetting procedures needed to ensure the origins and objectives of the various armed actors. The attempted policy of disarmament, demobilization, and reintegration has similarly proven ineffective in curbing the influence of these armed actors. The Libyan authorities will need to combine security measures along with social intervention programs that provide alternative opportunities as incentives for militia members to lay down their weapons. Additionally, any future efforts to consolidate Libya's armed groups will need to live up to standards of transparency and legal accountability for past violations.

In addition to the non-state armed actors, the proliferation of weapons posses one of the most pressing security challenge to security in the MENA region. The failure of the international community to stem Libya's acquisition of conventional weapons during the years of normalization with western governments allowed for the Qadhafi regime to replenish and upgrade its stockpile of military equipment and small arms. In addition to these weapons, those provided by NATO and non-NATO states to the *thuwar* groups during the 2011 war have spread to regional conflicts such as those in Mali and Syria.[350]

---

[350] United States officials foresaw this tragic outcome in the midst of the conflict; as a U.S. Navy officer predicted as the fighting was underway that, regardless of the outcome, "the weapons they [rebel fighters] have broken out of Libyan military stockpiles will be proliferated around the region and popping up in conflicts from North Africa to Yemen for years to come." *See* Varun Vira, Anthony H Cordesman & Arleigh A. Burke, Center for Strategic and International Studies, The Libyan Uprising: An Uncertain Trajectory 46 (June 20, 2011), *available at* http://csis.org/files/publication/110620_libya.pdf.

Examination of the post-conflict environment illuminates the connection between the weapons shipments delivered to the revolutionary
forces during the conflict, trans-regional security threats, and the post-war
power structure dominated by non-state armed groups. The brigades that
received weapons and training from international actors, notably from
Qatar and France, with approval from the U.S., later engaged in reprisal
violence against specific communities, and perceived Qadhafi loyalists.
The fighting in the cities of Kufra between the LSF and the local Tebu
fighters[351] and clashes involving the Tuaregs in Ghademes reflects the
danger of the weapons left behind from war.[352]

The spreading influence of political Islam after the fall of Qadhafi has
also been a cause for concern for regional security. The foreign intervention led, deliberately or inadvertently, to weapons ending up in the hands
of Islamist militants with the will and the means of carry out acts of violence and disrupt the political process. The attacks on the U.S. consulate in Benghazi, and the targeted violence aimed at thwarting investigative efforts in the aftermath of the attack, demonstrate the danger of this
threat. Empowered by their role in the fighting forces, some elements of
political Islam took advantage of the security vacuum to establish militant camps and expand terrorist links to regional militant factions, such
as AQIM. The militia factions, some with links to criminal activities and
terrorist violence were absorbed into the armed factions that made-up
the patchwork of armed-alliances in the post-Qadhafi era. This phenomenon poses a major challenge to Libya's new government, and raises the
threat of criminal networks infiltrating Libya's security, judicial and political institutions.

When considering the terrorist threat, it is essential to consider the
differences across the spectrum of groups that represent political Islam
in Libya. There exist militant factions along this spectrum, as well as
reformers, such as former LIFG militants who years past struck a blow to
international Jihadist by rejecting its principles. These former militants,
such as 'Abd al-Hakim Balhaj, were influential leaders who helped overthrow Qadhafi, and now promote peaceful actions through the legitimate
political process. It is critically important to consider the nuances of
these factions, which will be essential for the international community to

---

[351] *More deaths in Kufra reported*, THE LIBYA HERALD, June 29, 2012, *available at* http://
www.libyaherald.com/2012/06/29/more-deaths-in-kufra-reported/.
[352] *Deadly clashes in Libyan border town*, AL JAZEERA, May 16, 2012, *available at* http://
www.aljazeera.com/news/africa/2012/05/201251620515544315.html.

establish relations with these groups based on their principles and actions. The damaging counter-terror policies enacted after 11 September 2011 that involved confronting all political Islamist groups in a sweeping security-based approach should be avoided in future relations with Libya.[353]

The international community should not underestimate the tolerant secularist trend that exists among Libya's population, which transcends regions and tribes. In order to satisfy the demands of the population, however, the government will need to implement a national plan to distribute oil resources throughout the country that satisfies all of the parties. While the majority of Libya's population lives in the western province of Tripolitania, most of the oil is in the eastern province of Cyrenaica. Additionally, the province of Fezzan and much of the south is sparsely populated and has traditionally lacked access to the national resources. This un-even division makes compromise and consensus an ongoing challenge for the Libyan government. The allocation of resources entails strategic planning on the part of the Libyan government, as well as by the international community.

The lack of any planning for Libya's post-conflict development was a dramatic strategic failure on the part of the United States and the NATO allies. The policymakers in Washington, London and Paris in particular, planned for the overthrow of Qadhafi apparently without any policy in place for how to unify a dysfunctional post-war state. The goal of using Libya's abundant oil resources to create a democratic and prosperous state was untenable in the absence of any unified or systematic plan or preparation. As soon as the regime fell it became clear that the major powers would pursue their own security and economic interests in the form of oil contracts or public work projects, without regard for Libya's need for institutional development. The international community runs the risk of making the same mistakes it did in Iraq, where the post-Saddam government failed to allocate oil resources, which allowed for Sunni, Shi'a, and Kurdish conflicts that are unresolved to this day.

In addition to overcoming socio-economic cleavages, understanding the communal, racial, tribal and regional divisions is also integral to future reconciliation and social recovery efforts in Libya. The post-conflict government has been unable to respond to the demand for social reconciliation

---

[353] This includes the detention and rendition of 'Abd al-Hakim Balhaj as discussed in Ch. I, Sec. 10.1. The legal action resulting from rendition cases is also discussed in Ch. IV, Sec. 6.3(b)(iii).

efforts, and has fallen short on assisting targeted communities that were perceived as being loyal to Qadhafi during the war 2011, such as the Tawerghans and the Mashashiyya. In the light of the egregious continuing violations being perpetrated against the Tawerghan and other targeted communities now scattered across Libya, the Libyan government will need to take considerable measures to end the culture of impunity that fueled these attacks.[354]

Libya's political and social future will be determined in large part by the population's ability to overcome decades of repression, and re-build the country's legislative framework, judicial and national institutions. Accountability measures for the perpetrators of past violations committed during the war and under the former regime are essential for Libya's social recovery efforts.[355] The control over the country's judicial system and prison by non-state armed actors remains a major obstacle that continues to hinder these accountability efforts. The strength of the judicial institutions to hold those accountable for past and ongoing violations is integral to the country's stability.

---

[354] Report of the International Commission of Inquiry (Mar. 2012) *supra* note 63 at Annex I, ¶ 495.

[355] *See* Ch. IV, Sec. 6.4.

ADDENDUM AS OF SEPTEMBER 15, 2013

The research and drafting of this book formally concluded in June 2013, and the chapters of this book are current through that date. A number of developments occurred between June and September that require additional coverage, and are therefore consolidated in this addendum, in particular the ongoing problem with political killings, kidnappings and the ongoing problem

September 2013 effectively marks the end of the second year since the fall of the Qadhafi regime, as the Security Council recognized the NTC on 16 September 2011 and Mu'ammar Qadhafi was forced to flee Tripoli for his last stronghold in Sirte. Since the fall of the Qadhafi regime and the rise of the NTC the country has conducted elections and initiated reforms of its military and police forces, as well as its economy, as discussed throughout this chapter.

Despite some promising developments, including what might be the first democratic government in the country's history, Libya remains a turbulent place. As described in Chapter One, Libya is a state without a nation in the conventional sense, a problem that is only compounded by the frailty of central authorities. In the aftermath of the fall of the Qadhafi regime and his death in Sirte in October 2011, Libya has failed to build a strong central government capable of reigning in some *thuwar*, in particular the most powerful *kata'ib* in Zintan, Misrata and Benghazi. In general terms Libyans have failed to coalesce around the NTC or its successor GNC, and the country remains as Balkanized as ever. In many respects the situation is devolving, an issue in dire need of remedy by Libya and the international community.

The period after the fall of the Qadhafi regime saw the emergence of political parties and political leaders, as described above, as well as a vibrant civil society that advocated for a number of issues. The July 2012 elections marked the highpoint of Libyan efforts towards a democratic and inclusive form of government. Since then the situation has deteriorated, however. Beyond the occupation of governmental and ministerial buildings by various *kata'ib*, as discussed in this chapter, and the lack of stability at the highest levels of government, including through the resignation of Ashour Shuail in May and Mohammed Khalifa al-Sheikh in

August 2013 from the position of Minister of Interior,[1] there has been a recent spate of political executions across the country as individuals have been targeted for elimination in the ongoing struggle for control of the government and control of the public sphere. The ongoing situation is particularly serious in the Cyrenaican cities of Benghazi and Derna, where political killings peaked in July 2013.[2]

The most recent spate of political killings began with the killing of Abdulasalam Elmessmary on 26 July 2013. According to Human Rights Watch, Elmessmary's killing was the first of a political activist since the fall of the Qadhafi regime, and precipitated a "wave of political assassinations" that has taken the lives of at least 51 individuals. Of those, 44 were members of the security forces, most of whom had previously served under Qadhafi and at least six of whom had held high ranking positions. In addition, judges and an activist have been targeted for killing. While only confirming the killing of 51 individuals during the recent spree in mid-2013, HRW estimates that the true number is larger.[3]

The police and judiciary have not investigated these problems,[4] and it appears that it either lacks the capacity or the will to enforce its laws or protect civilians, perhaps most notably with respect to the former the April 2013 laws criminalizing torture and kidnapping.[5] In many cases, the police has been unable to defend itself or its officers[6] at all levels of the hierarchy, including the Chief of Police, Faraj al-Deirsy, who was shot

---

[1] *Libyan interior minister resigns*, AL JAZEERA, Aug. 18, 2013, *available at* http://www.aljazeera.com/news/africa/2013/08/2013818140684416.html.

[2] *Libya: Wave of Political Assassinations*, HUMAN RIGHTS WATCH, Aug. 8, 2013, *available at* http://www.hrw.org/news/2013/08/08/libya-wave-political-assassinations.

[3] *Id.*

[4] *Id.*

[5] *Libyan Parliament Criminalises Torture and Kidnapping*, REUTERS, Apr. 9, 2013, *available at* http://uk.reuters.com/article/2013/04/09/uk-libya-law-idUKBRE9380WU20130409; Laura Klein Mullen, *Libya National Assembly Criminalizes Torture, Kidnapping*, JURIST, Apr. 10, 2013, *available at* http://jurist.org/paperchase/2013/04/libya-national-assembly-criminalizes-torture-kidnapping.php; *Libyan PM's Chief of Staff, Mohamed Ali Ghatous, Vanishes Amid Abduction Fears*, ASSOCIATED PRESS, Apr. 1, 2013, *available at* http://www.telegraph.co.uk/news/worldnews/africaandindianocean/libya/9965259/Libyan-PMs-chief-of-staff-Mohamed-Ali-Ghatous-vanishes-amid-abduction-fears.html. *See also* Abigail Hauslohner, *In the New Libya, former Prisoners Guard their Onetime Captors*, WASHINGTON POST, Mar. 3, 2013, *available at* http://articles.washingtonpost.com/2013-03-03/world/37418071_1_saif-al-islam-gaddafi-senussi-libyan-rebels.

[6] *See generally Car Bomb Kills Policeman in Benghazi as Violence Escalates*, REUTERS, Jan. 16, 2013, *available at* http://www.reuters.com/article/2013/01/16/us-libya-benghazi-bomb-idUSBRE90F0OB20130116.

to death in November 2012.[7] In that case, the powerlessness of the police was amplified by the kidnapping of the chief investigator in Benghazi who was working on the case,[8] and who has yet to be released or found.[9] More recently, on 23 August 2013, Mustafa Agela Almurgbi, a senior bomb expert, was killed in Benghazi, apparently in retaliation for diffusing bombs throughout the city and region.[10] Less than a week later, on 29 August 2013, Yousef al-Assayfer, the chief military prosecutor in Benghazi, was killed by a remote car bomb.[11]

HRW's investigation into the mid 2013 "wave" of killings in Benghazi and Derna determined that the police failed to "conduct comprehensive investigations", including crime scene examinations and interviewing witnesses.[12] These determinations were confirmed by Libyan officials, who argued that they lacked the capacity to conduct thorough investigations.[13] To that end, Izzedin Abdelfafith el-Ghwelli, the acting head of the Criminal Investigation Department in Benghazi, told HRW that

> In the absence of functioning state institutions, amid a proliferation of arms and of various active armed groups, we cannot work according to our usual procedures. The main issue we face with witnesses is that they are scared and often do not show up even if they are summoned. All of these assassination cases remain unresolved. We do not know who our enemies are anymore—there are too many of them.[14]

As described in this chapter, Libya remains awash with armed non-state actors who act with complete disregard of the government and the law. Attempts to curtail these holdover *kata'ib* have generally failed, and Libya is no more unified today than it was in 2011. If anything, the country is

---

[7] *Police Chief Killed in Libya's Benghazi*, ALJAZEERA, Nov. 21, 2012, *available at* http://www.aljazeera.com/news/africa/2012/11/2012112173121714516.html; *Libya: Benghazi Police Chief Assassinated*, BBC, Nov. 21, 2013, *available at* http://www.bbc.co.uk/news/world-africa-20424432.

[8] *Libyan Police Captain Abducted in Benghazi*, REUTERS, Jan. 3, 2013, *available at* http://www.nytimes.com/2013/02/04/world/middleeast/police-captain-in-benghazi-is-abducted.html.

[9] HRW, *supra* note 1.

[10] *Benghazi Bomb Disposal Officer Murdered*, LIBYA HERALD, Aug. 23, 2013, *available at* http://www.libyaherald.com/2013/08/23/benghazi-bomb-disposal-officer-murdered/#axzz2f3SoVMoo.

[11] *Military Prosecutor in Benghazi Killed in Car Bomb Attack*, LIBYA HERALD, Aug. 29, 2013, *available at* http://www.libyaherald.com/2013/08/29/military-prosecutor-in-benghazi-killed-in-car-bomb-attack/.

[12] *Id.*

[13] *Id.*

[14] *Id.*

hardening into various autonomous regions that have little to say to each other.

Violence has been commonplace throughout Libya since the fall of the Qadhafi regime in 2011,[15] but the most recent spate of violence strikes a very different tone. In particular, the recent upsurge in violence is not simply retributive or vestigial of the 2011 conflict, but increasingly political in nature.[16] In other words, violence is being perpetuated not out of revenge or to eliminate regime holdovers or loyalists, but for personal gain or in order to destabilize the country itself.

One of the most significant recent challenges to the authority of the Libyan state has been the growth of the separatist movement in Cyrenaica. Separatists in the east, who agitate for a weak central state and only a very loose confederacy, refer to this new state not as Cyrenaica, but as Barqa. There have been recent attempts to create a semi-autonomous state in the past, most recently in early 2012 when regional leaders broached the idea under the auspices of the Cyrenaica Transitional Council (CTC), but which were ultimately unsuccessful,[17] and more recently in June and July 2013 under the leadership of Ahmed Zubair al-Senussi of the CTC.[18] On 1 June 2013, more than 3,000 CTC members gathered in Cyrenaica to declare the province a self-governing region under the 1951 Constitution.[19] By August 2013, the CTC's demands became more ardent, and on the 17th the Council declared in Ra's Lanuf that unless its proposals for federalism were accepted—under their manifesto absolute autonomy within the

---

[15] *See for instance* a June 2013 battle between Arab and African Libyans in Fezzan, in which opposing belligerents fired weapons and RPGs at each other. *Libya: 5 dead in tribal clashes in southern town*, AL ARABIYA, June 3, 2013, *available at* http://english.alarabiya.net/en/News/africa/2013/06/03/Libya-5-dead-in-tribal-clashes-in-southern-town.html.

[16] *Military Prosecutor in Benghazi Killed in Car Bomb Attack*, LIBYA HERALD, Aug. 29, 2013, *available at* http://www.libyaherald.com/2013/08/29/military-prosecutor-in-benghazi-killed-in-car-bomb-attack/.

[17] *Libyan Tribal Leaders Declare Semi-Autonomous Eastern State*, ASSOCIATED PRESS, Mar. 6, 2012, *available at* http://www.theguardian.com/world/2012/mar/06/libya-benghazi-state-of-barqa.

[18] Ahmed Zubair al-Senussi was a member of the NTC and is a relative of King Idris. *Regional Group Declares Self-Government for East Libya*, AL ARABIYA, June 2, 2013, *available at* http://english.alarabiya.net/en/News/africa/2013/06/02/Regional-group-declares-self-government-for-east-Libya.html.

[19] Ahmed Ruhayam, *Cyrenaica Federalists Declare Self-Government on 64th Anniversary of Cyrenaica Independence*, LIBYA HERALD, June 1, 2013, *available at* http://www.libyaherald.com/2013/06/01/cyrenaica-federalists-declare-self-government-on-64th-anniversary-of-emirate-of-cyrenaica-independence/; *Regional Group Declares Self-Government for East Libya*, AL ARABIYA, June 2, 2013, *available at* http://english.alarabiya.net/en/News/africa/2013/06/02/Regional-group-declares-self-government-for-east-Libya.html.

context of the unity of the Libyan state—it would disrupt oil production,[20] a proposition that can only be rejected by the GNC in Tripoli as any turbulence in the oil sector would effectively cost the central government the majority of its revenues and seriously threaten its ability to consolidate control and build the country's institutions.

On 17 August 2013 the leadership of the CTC also called for a turn-over in leadership and the transitioning of authority from tribal elders to youth leaders.[21] This change in leadership may be apparent in the late August 2013 declarations of the newly formed Barqa Youth Movement, which has also declared the autonomy for Cyrenaica, with its capital in Benghazi and Ibrahim Saeed Jizran as its president.[22] According to media sources, the Barqa Youth Movement has powerful backers from various non-state armed groups and leaders in the region, including Al-Saddiq al-Ghaithi, a former member of the Libyan Islamic Fighting Group and ally of ʿAbd al-Hakim Balhaj.[23] Allegedly the Barqa Youth Movement is already contacting foreign oil firms concerning oil sales independent of the central government.[24]

Even before these most recent problems it was quite common for regional groups and non-state actors to occupy various oil fields—which has caused at least a 30 percent drop off in oil exports from 2012—and the concerted efforts by separatists to consolidate control in Cyrenaica could pose even more substantial problems for the central government.[25] Since the ramping up of separatist agitation the problem has only grown. Due to the occupation of most major oil fields by members of the Petroleum Facilities Guards—the military unit charged with defending oil fields— by early September 2013 oil production in Libya fell from 1.5 million barrels a day to 100,000 barrels, or approximately $130 million a day in lost

---

[20] Nigel Ash & Maha Elawi, *Cyrenaica Federalists Threaten more Oil Disruption*, LIBYA HERALD, Aug. 17, 2013, *available at* http://www.libyaherald.com/2013/08/17/cyrenaica-federalists-threaten-more-oil-disruption/#axzz2f3SoVMoo.

[21] *Id.*

[22] *Libya's Government Losing Control of Oil Fields to Jihadist Groups*, EL-KHABAR, Aug. 20, 2013, *available at* http://www.elkhabar.com/ar/monde/350474.html (*Translation available at* http://www.al-monitor.com/pulse/security/2013/08/libya-loses-control-oil-fields-east-emirate.html).

[23] *Id.*

[24] *Id.*

[25] William Wheeler, *Libyan Militias' New Strategy: Occupy Oil Field*, GLOBAL POST, Aug. 28, 2013, *available at* http://www.globalpost.com/dispatches/globalpost-blogs/groundtruth/militias-new-strategy-libya-occupy-oil-field.

revenue.[26] During mid-2013 many facilities were blocked by members of the Petroleum Facilities Guards over corruption and pay issues,[27] but it is unclear whether these oil-field occupations have been sparked by separatist feelings and the impetus provided by the Barqa Youth Movement.[28] It is nevertheless clear that many Libyans, especially youths in Cyrenaica, feel disillusioned with the 2011 revolution and the fact that their lives have not improved since the ouster of Qadhafi.[29]

As is clear from the assassination epidemic in Cyrenaica and the increasing political destabilization that has gone with it, the Libyan government's ability to enforce the law and protect its citizens is marginal in good portions of the country. In some cases, government forces themselves perpetrate crimes, as was the case with the kidnapping of Anoud al-Senussi, the daughter of ʿAbdullah al-Senussi.[30] In that case, Anoud al-Senussi was being taken from the prison holding her father to the airport by members of the judicial police, but was apparently kidnapped by members of the Supreme Security Committee.[31]

The Kidnapping of Anoud al-Senussi was unique only in that is was committed by one of the elite units of the post-Qadhafi era. Throughout Libya various Katiba are engaging in kidnapping and other criminal activities in order to bankroll their operations and secure their power regionally.[32] In some instances, as with the kidnapping of Mohamed Ali Ghatous, the

---

[26] Rana Jawad, *Why Gunmen have Turned Off Libya's Oil Taps*, BBC, Sept. 11, 2013, *available at* http://www.bbc.co.uk/news/world-africa-24051371.

[27] *Id.* Note, however, that Petroleum Facilities Guards had already clashed with other military units in June 2013. *See* Nihal Zaroug, *Petroleum Facilities Guards Clash in Triploi's Salahaddin Area*, LIBYA HERALD, June 25, 2013, *available at* http://www.libyaherald.com/2013/06/25/petroleum-facilities-guards-clash-in-tripolis-salahaddin-area/#axzz2f3SoVM00.

[28] Reuters identified one of the strike leaders as threatening to sell oil directly from one facility on in mid-August 2013, at roughly the same time as a press report claimed that a Barqa Youth Movement leader was trying to sell oil directly. It is not clear if the two offers are the same. *See End to Libya oil strikes in sight despite exports move*, REUTERS, Aug. 19, 2013, *available at* http://www.ft.com/intl/cms/s/0/35246678-08e4-11e3-ad07-00144feabdc0.html.

[29] *Id.*

[30] Chris Stephen, *Libyan Police Unit Admits Kidnapping ex-Spy Chief's Daughter*, GUARDIAN, Sept. 5, 2013, *available at* http://www.theguardian.com/world/2013/sep/05/libyan-police-kidnap-senussi-daughter.

[31] *Id.*

[32] *See generally* Mustafa Fetouri, *Libya's Kidnappings for Ransom Show a State Mired in Chaos*, THE NATIONAL, Apr. 27, 2013, *available at* http://www.thenational.ae/thenational conversation/comment/libyas-kidnappings-for-ransom-show-a-state-mired-in-chaos.

chief of staff to the Libyan Prime Minister Ali Zeidan, in March 2013,[33] the purpose appears political in nature and designed to further destabilize the country. In other cases, as with the kidnapping of journalists, which has become an increasingly serious problem in 2013, the intent appears to be the control of the dissemination of information throughout the country and internationally.[34]

All of this shows a deep inability of the Libyan state to assert itself and carry out its basic mandates. Beyond the inability of the police and security forces to do their work, the judiciary seems equally unable or unwilling to carry out its duties. To date, the post-Qadhafi government has only shown interest in prosecuting former regime members. The headlining cases are those of Saif al-Islam Qadhafi and 'Abdullah al-Senussi. In addition, there have been reports of trials and convictions in a few places, including the conviction of former Minister of Education Ahmad Ibrahim in Misrata in July and the apparent trial of 40 Qadhafi regime members in Zawiyya in April.[35]

At present, there is only apparent judicial action with respect to Saif al-Islam Qadhafi and 'Abdullah al-Senussi, who are both poised to stand trial in mid September 2013. At present, however, Saif al-Islam is still being held in Zintan and has not been surrendered to central authorities in Tripoli, and according to statements by his captors he will not. In late August 2013 a senior member of the Zintan Katiba stated that: "It us impossible to hand him [Saif al-Islam] over to Tripoli. And you can put three red lines under the word 'impossible'."[36] At present sources indicate that the trials of Saif al-Islam Qadhafi and 'Abdullah al-Senussi will begin on 19 September

---

[33] *Libyan PM's Chief of Staff, Mohamed Ali Ghatous, Vanishes Amid Abduction Fears*, AP, Apr. 1, 2013, *available at* http://www.telegraph.co.uk/news/worldnews/africaandindian ocean/libya/9965259/Libyan-PMs-chief-of-staff-Mohamed-Ali-Ghatous-vanishes-amid-abduction-fears.html.

[34] *Multiple Kidnappings of Media Workers*, REPORTERS WITHOUT BORDERS, Apr. 29, 2013, *available at* http://en.rsf.org/libya-multiple-kidnappings-of-media-29-04-2013,44459 .html. *See also Six kidnapped in armed assault on private Libyan TV station*, RT, Mar. 8, 2013, *available at* http://rt.com/news/gunmen-kidnapped-libya-tv-979/.

[35] *Trial of 40 Gaddafi-era officials opens in Libya*, XINHUA, Mar. 7, 2013, *available at* http://news.xinhuanet.com/english/world/2013-03/07/c_132216810.htm; *Libya: al-Gaddafi loyalists at risk of 'revenge' death sentences*, AMNESTY INTERNATIONAL, Aug. 2, 2013, *available at* http:// www.amnesty.org/en/news/libya-al-gaddafi-loyalists-risk-revenge-death-sentences-2013-08-02.

[36] Michael Cousins & Ahmed Elumani, *"We Will Not Hand Over Saif Al-Islam" says Zintan*, LIBYA HERALD, Aug. 30, 2013, *available at* http://www.libyaherald.com/2013/08/30/ we-will-not-hand-over-saif-al-islam-says-zintan/#axzz2f3S0VM00.

after numerous delays and extensions to the start of the trial.[37] Important questions have yet to be resolved, however, including how the trial will proceed against Saif al-Islam Qadhafi in Zintan and where he will be imprisoned should he be convicted. It is also possible that the Zintan Katiba will make an arrangement with Saif al-Islam to release him or provide him with a comfortable detention on the condition that he surrenders to it the various funds Muʿammar Qadhafi is believed to have smuggled out of the country and which is still accessible to various family members. It is also unclear how the trial against ʿAbdullah al-Senussi will proceed, especially in light of the kidnapping of al-Senussi's daughter and the chilling effect this will have on potential witnesses. In general, it is unclear how either Saif al-Islam or ʿAbdullah al-Senussi will be able to secure a fair trial in light of the 31 May 2013 decision of the Pre-Trial Chamber of the ICC, which found that the Libyan judiciary was in collapse.[38] In that decision the Pre-Trial Chamber determined that it was difficult to see how the defense in either case could secure the presence of witnesses or the proffer of evidence given the general climate in the country and the inability of the government to provide adequate assurances.

With respect to the ongoing case before the ICC, it appears at present that notwithstanding the rejection of the Libyan government's admissibility challenge the case against Saif al-Islam will go forward and that neither the International community nor the UN Security Council, which made the referral to the ICC in the first place, will enforce the Court's decision and demand his surrender.

Beyond the questions of accountability, little progress has been made in the recovery of private assets that Muʿammar Qadhafi stashed in other countries. In June 2013, South Africa agreed to the repatriation of an estimated $1 billion of Qadhafi's money that had been positively traced to that country.[39] Other Qadhafi assets, which are estimated in the billions, are yet to be identified definitively and returned to the Libyan state.

---

[37] *Gaddafi's Son to Stand Trial Next Month*, AL JAZEERA, Aug. 27, 2013, *available at* http://www.aljazeera.com/news/africa/2013/08/2013827164926837916.html; *Libya 'sets September trial' for Saif al-Islam Gaddafi*, BBC, Aug. 23, 2012, *available at* http://www.bbc.co.uk/news/world-africa-19358595.

[38] *See also Libya: 'Anoud al-Senussi's Abduction Exposes Country's Inability to Try Saif Gaddafi and Others*, AMNESTY INTERNATIONAL, Sept. 3, 2013, *available at* http://www.amnesty.org.uk/news_details.asp?NewsID=20946.

[39] Ntsakisi Maswanganyi, *Gaddafi's billions to be repatriated to Libya*, BUSINESS DAY, June 14, 2013, *available at* http://www.bdlive.co.za/national/2013/06/14/gaddafis-billions-to-be-repatriated-to-libya.

PART TWO

THEATERS OF MILITARY OPERATIONS

INTRODUCTION TO PART TWO

Part Two of this book provides detailed accounts of specific cities or regions affected by the 2011 conflict in Libya. Unlike Part One, which deals with the conflict on a national level, Part Two examines it from a local perspective. Accordingly, Part Two is divided into ten different "theaters" and provides an overview, factual review and analysis of violations in each. It therefore expands on the overview of the conflict contained in Chapter Two of Part One, as well as the post-conflict issues raised in Chapter Five.

As indicated above, each of the ten chapters in Part Two examines the same events as discussed in Part One, but instead of taking a national perspective, it examines the conflict within the context of each region, how it developed, how it was fought and the violations that were particular to each. As highlighted in Chapter One, Libya is a complex patchwork of groups with sometimes convergent and sometimes divergent interests and needs, and these had an impact on the development of the conflict across the country, making it impossible to extrapolate larger principles from any particular incident in any particular area. Moreover, as highlighted in Chapter Two, the conflict affected different cities and regions to varying degrees during the conflict, with the situation in each determined significantly by geography, the social, cultural, tribal and socio-economic divisions within each, and the nature of the Qadhafi regime's intervention and NATO's response.

Focusing on each theater independently allows for a more thorough examination of the international humanitarian law (IHL), international human rights law (IHRL) and international criminal law (ICL) violations in the specific context of each region. Each chapter in Part Two contains five sub-sections: an introduction providing basic information about the city or region in question, and anything else the reader might need to understand the events in question; a summary of events in the location; illustrations of the violations that took place in the region by violation; the role of NATO in each theater; and a conclusion. The third section, which illustrates the violations in each theater, is sub-divided into sections focusing on: the excessive use of force; unlawful killings; arbitrary detention and enforced disappearances, torture and other forms of ill-treatment; the denial of access to medical treatment; limitations on freedom of expression; attacks on civilians, civilian objects and protected persons, and in particular deliberate and indiscriminate attacks on civilians and civilian objects, attacks on cultural objects and places of worship, the destruction of objects indispensible to the survival of the civilian population, impeding access to humanitarian relief and attacks on humanitarian personnel, attacks on protected medical personal, transport and facilities, and the misuse of the red cross/red crescent emblem; the use of prohibited weapons; the deployment of mercenaries; the targeting of specific groups; sexual violence; and the use of children in armed conflict. It should be noted that not all of the forgoing violations occurred in each theater, and therefore each chapter contains a different structure, although each follows the order listed above.

While the 2011 war affected the entire country, fighting was not spread evenly throughout. The ten theaters examined in Part Two were selected on the basis that they experienced the most extensive fighting and highest levels of violence or violations, or that they have a persistent importance in the post-conflict period. Most of the chapters are based on specific cities, namely Benghazi, Khums, Bani Walid and Sirte. Other chapters include the specific cities and surrounding areas, such as the Tripoli chapter that includes information on the capital's suburbs, the Misrata chapter that includes the nearby town of Tawergha, and Zawiyya that includes Surman. The chapter focusing on the Nafusa Mountains covers events in several cities and villages intertwined in the same military campaign in western Libya, and the chapters on Ajdabiya & Brega along with Ra's Lanuf & Bin Jawad each cover two cities that were connected by the fighting taking place on the frontlines in eastern Libya. While other locations were witness to conflict and violations, they are not treated individually here due to the comparatively limited number of violations committed in each, their more limited importance to the outcome of the conflict or the post-conflict situation. Where important incidents occurred in those locations, both during and after the conflict, they are discussed in Part One.

Originally the geographic scope of this book overlapped with the locations identified by the February 2012 ISISC report to the Commission of Inquiry (CoI), which covered the most important locations at that time.[1] The scope of this book was expanded, however, due to ongoing issues in other locations that demanded further examination and ultimate

---

[1] *See* the General Introduction to this book for more on the production of the ISISC report submitted to the UN CoI in February 2012.

inclusion. Most notably, Bani Walid was expanded into a separate chapter because it was one of the last strongholds for regime loyalists. While comparatively few human rights abuses were reported in Bani Walid during the 2011 war, the city remained a conflict area after the fall of the regime in October 2011, and presented a serious challenge to Libya's post-Qadhafi government, as well as being the site of ongoing reprisal attacks. Similarly, the chapter on Ra's Lanuf & Bin Jawad was added due to its link to the Ajdabiya & Brega conflict region, and its importance to Libya's oil production. In other circumstances, such as Khums, information only became available after the end of the conflict as the city was inaccessible to the media and NGOs until the *thuwar* forces took control on 21 August 2011. It was only in the aftermath of the conflict that the seriousness and extent of the human rights violations committed in Khums was fully understood.[2]

The structure of Part Two is intended to highlight the manner in which the uprising and subsequent fighting progressed but also to highlight the differences between each theater, and the very localized effects of the conflict in each, something that largely results from the absence of an overarching strategy on the part of the regime or the *thuwar*. The absence of a larger strategic plan, or even basic coordination, is apparent in the different military operations in each theater. As discussed in Chapter II, local military councils took control of and responsibility for the prosecution of the war effort in the absence of an effective national coordination body. This dynamic led to the formation of *thuwar* groups that did not communicate with each other and lacked a centralized command structure, both of which were necessary to design or implement a strategic plan. This also exacerbated the situation in the post-conflict period, whereby various non-state armed actors controlled different parts of the country, and even different parts of Tripoli, thereby hampering the centralization and consolidation of the post-Qadhafi government.[3]

NATO was the only party to the conflict that appeared to have a larger strategy for the conflict itself, which at first entailed protecting civilians but quickly evolved into enhancing the capabilities of the *thuwar* and

---

[2] A full accounting of what happened at Khums has yet to be made, perhaps because of the decreased media and NGO attention after the end of the conflict. As a result of the still limited information available regarding the military operations that took place in Khums, the chapter focuses mostly on the violations carried out in the detention facilities within the city.

[3] For more on the role of the non-state armed actors in the post-conflict period, *see* Ch. V, Sec. 2.

ensuring the fall of the Qadhafi regime, as discussed in Chapter Three. As a general rule, the opposing belligerents largely fought each other to a stalemate initially, with the tide turning in favor of the *thuwar* forces only after NATO strikes were carried out on the Qadhafi regime's forces, equipment, supplies, supply routes, command and control centers, and other targets.[4] Nevertheless, like the *thuwar*, NATO and allied states made absolutely no provisions for the country after the fall of Libya, at best naively presuming that the situation would resolve itself and that the opposition would congeal and stabilize long-term in the crucible of conflict. Again, while the goal of both the *thuwar* forces and NATO was regime change, from a military perspective, only NATO had a coordinated and tactical strategy, or the effective ability to swing the balance in favor of the opposition. The *thuwar* forces' military actions were improvised, and the groups held together only by a shared determination to see the end of Qadhafi, but this appears in itself to have been insufficient to achieve that end.

The counterinsurgency campaign of the Qadhafi regime also varied by region in terms of tactics and methods used, and similarly lacked an overall strategy. The level of fighting was also shaped by the amounts of weapons the *thuwar* seized from stockpiles[5] or received from third-party states,[6] as well as by their ability to organize resistance against the more powerful government troops.[7] Consequently, the nature and intensity of the IHL, IHRL and ICL violations differed across the country. The Qadhafi regime, for example, employed siege tactics to starve and terrorize the populations of various cities into submission, most extensively in Misrata, but also to varying degrees in cities such as Zawiyya, Ajdabiya, and Zintan, Nalut and Yafran in the Nafusa Mountains region. These cities, in addition to Ra's Lanuf in the east, also experienced indiscriminate shelling leading to large-scale civilian casualties. The practice of arbitrary arrest and forced disappearance was used early on in Benghazi and other cities in Cyrenaica to target organizers of the initial protests, and then used extensively in the Nafusa Mountains region and in Misrata in an attempt to quell the growing rebel movement in Tripolitania. The evidence suggests that Tripoli witnessed the greatest degree of torture and other types of ill-treatment of detainees at the hands of Qadhafi forces. Extrajudicial killings of detainees

---

[4] *See* Ch. III, Secs. 6 & 7.

[5] For weapons seized from Qadhafi forces' stockpiles, *see* Chs. VI, VII, IX, X, & XII.

[6] For weapons and training provided by 3rd party states, *see* Chs. VI, IX & X. *See also* Ch. III, Sec. 7.1.

[7] For superior weaponry of the Qadhafi forces, *see* Chs. VIII, X, XII & XIII.

were reported in several detention centers in the capital and the nearby city of Khums in August when Qadhafi forces retreated.

The level and intensity of violations committed by *thuwar* forces also varied based on the regional context. After the Qadhafi forces were defeated in Misrata, for example, the city's environs witnesses some of the worst violations committed by the *thuwar* forces, as they targeted specific groups, including the Tawerghan community, in a campaign of vengeance that involved widespread arrests, torture and indiscriminate killings. The city of Sirte, where Qadhafi made his last stand, also experienced a wave of reprisal violence after the death of the former ruler in October 2011. In the Nafusa Mountains region, the powerful Zintan Katiba targeted the towns and communities, such as the Mashashiyya, who they accused of having aided regime forces. *Thuwar* groups also carried out widespread arrests and held prisoners in different cities across the country, and continue to do so at the time of writing.[8] As discussed further in Chapter Four, accountability for these violations has been severely lacking, particularly when it comes to the violations committed by the *thuwar* forces.[9]

Part Two of this book provides a unique view of these violations from within each geographic region where the conflict unfolded. Understanding the geographic distinctions and unique circumstances that led to the differing patterns of IHL, IHRL and ICL violations in each respective area is imperative to addressing the post-conflict challenges to successfully implementing justice and accountability measures in Libya. Part Two also contributes to an understanding of political imbalances in the state as a whole following the fall of Qadhafi, and why national governance in Libya continues to prove a complex and difficult proposition.

---

[8] *See* Ch. V, Sec. 2.3.
[9] *See* Ch. IV, Sec. 2.

CHAPTER SIX

BENGHAZI

1. INTRODUCTION

The city of Benghazi is located on the Mediterranean Sea facing west on the Gulf of Sidra, and is the capital of Libya's eastern province of Cyrenaica.[1] With an urban population of approximately 700,000 inhabitants, and over 1 million if the surrounding residential areas are included, it is Libya's second largest city.[2] Benghazi's inception as a city goes back to the classical Greek period when it was a polis, and over the centuries the city has been one of Libya's major regional urban centers and trading hubs.[3]

Benghazi began seeing infrastructural developments and population growth during the Italian colonial period, when it emerged as a major colonial administrative and commercial hub, and grew to become a relatively modern city. At the start of the 19th century Benghazi was already the major coastal town of Cyrenaica, with an estimated population of 5,000 people, mostly comprising Tripolitanian, Tunisian, Cretan and other European settlers, half of which were Jewish.[4] Towards the end of the century the city had grown to approximately 30,000 inhabitants.[5] While the Benghazi economy was dominated by sponge fishing, the town's economic significance lay in the fact that it was also the terminus of the great

---

[1] Cyrenaica is composed of all of the eastern part of Libya, an administrative division dating from Italian Libya. DAVIDE RODONGO, FASCISM'S EUROPEAN EMPIRE: ITALIAN OCCUPATION DURING THE SECOND WORLD WAR 61 (Cambridge, UK: Cambridge University Press, 2006).

[2] *Benghazi*, WOLFRAMALPHA, *available at* http://www.wolframalpha.com/input/?i= Benghazi. *See also* Mike Elkton, *In Benghazi, brutal memories fuel opposition*, USA TODAY, Mar. 3, 2011, *available at* http://usatoday30.usatoday.com/news/world/2011-03-03-libya-unrest_N.htm.

[3] ALI ABDULLATIF AHMIDA, THE MAKING OF MODERN LIBYA: STATE FORMATION, COLONIZATION, AND RESISTANCE 20 (Albany, USA: SUNY Press, 2d ed., 2009) [hereinafter "THE MAKING OF MODERN LIBYA"].

[4] *Id.* at 75–76.

[5] DIRK VANDEWALLE, A HISTORY OF MODERN LIBYA 15 (Cambridge, UK: Cambridge University Press, 2006).

trans-Saharan trade routes originating in the Wadai Empire of modern day Chad.[6]

Italian forces invaded Benghazi in October 1911, and began developing the city and its infrastructure extensively. By the start of World War II there were nearly 40,000 Italians in Cyrenaica, mainly in Benghazi and its surrounding farmland. Italian forces maintained control over the city until World War II, when it was the site of extensive fighting between Axis and Allied forces and the target of more than 1,000 Allied air raids that significantly destroyed the Italian-built infrastructure.[7]

Benghazi has played an integral role in Libya's modern history: the nation's first constitution was adopted in Benghazi in October 1951, and King Idris proclaimed independence there a few months later on 24 December from the Al-Manar Palace.[8] After Libyan independence, Benghazi served as one of the two officially recognized capitals of the Kingdom of Libya, a political compromise reached between Cyrenaican and Tripolitanian leaders in the months leading up to independence. Most of King Idris's years in power were spent in Cyrenaica and many of the important federal institutions of the kingdom were based in Benghazi.[9] The city again played a pivotal role in Libyan history in 2011 when the National Transitional Council (NTC) was established there, serving as the political base of the uprising against Qadhafi.[10]

Benghazi was rebuilt after World War II, and particularly after 1960 when Libya started exporting oil in commercial quantities.[11] The city of Benghazi radiates outward in concentric circles from its port on the Gulf of Sidra. Its growth inland includes five circular ring roads that circumscribe various neighborhoods in the city. Directly to the east of the city lies Banina International Airport, some 20 kilometers (12.4 miles) from the city center. To the north lies the suburb of Kuwafiyya, which is home to the Benghazi Central Prison. The major Libyan Coastal Highway runs north-south through Benghazi. Al-Bayda is the nearest city to the north

---

[6] AHMIDA, THE MAKING OF MODERN LIBYA, *supra* note 3 at 20.

[7] VANDEWALLE, A HISTORY OF MODERN LIBYA, *supra* note 5 at 34–36.

[8] GEOFF SIMONS, LIBYA: THE STRUGGLE FOR SURVIVAL 154 (New York, USA: St. Martin's Press, 1996).

[9] AHMIDA, THE MAKING OF MODERN LIBYA, *supra* note 3 at 154.

[10] *Libya's ex-justice minister forms interim government in Benghazi,* HAARETZ, Jan. 25, 2013, *available at* http://www.haaretz.com/news/world/libya-s-ex-justice-minister-forms-interim-government-in-benghazi-1.345892. For more on the formation of the NTC, *see* Ch. II, Sec. 2.3.

[11] AHMIDA, THE MAKING OF MODERN LIBYA, *supra* note 3 at 156.

of Benghazi, around 160 kilometers (100 miles) away, and Ajdabiya is the nearest city to the south of Benghazi, around 150 kilometers (93 miles) away.[12]

Benghazi plays a central role in the Cyrenaican economy and as home to the second largest port in Libya after Tripoli is a major economic hub for the entire country.[13] Due to Libya's arid climate and lack of industrial development the country imports much of its foodstuffs and manufactured goods. Benghazi is a major port of entry for these goods, and serves as a gateway for the export of oil products. As in other areas of the country where oil is concentrated, the oil industry drives the city's economy, and several large companies have sizeable operations in Benghazi including the Brega Petroleum Marketing Company and the Arabian Gulf Oil Company.[14]

Benghazi, like other cities in Libya, is home to a diverse Libyan population and foreign residents with different backgrounds. The population in eastern Libya is largely of Arab-Berber ethnicity, divided into tribal subgroups. Additionally, there has been a recent increase of migration from Egypt and other parts of Africa to the region. There are a number of tribes that are indigenous to Cyrenaica, the most prominent of which are the Al-Awagir, Al-Abaydat,[15] Drasa, Al-Barasa, Al-Fawakir, Al-Zuwaiyya, Al-Majabra, 'Ubayda, Kargala, Tawajir and Ramla.[16] Due to economic migration to the region over the past fifty years, several western Libyan tribes have also assimilated into Cyrenaica, including the Warfalla, the Misrata and the Tarhuna. The Warfalla is the largest tribe in Libya and the Misrata the largest tribe in eastern Libya, with a significant base in Benghazi.[17] The Awlad Ali is the largest border tribe in eastern Libya, with half of its

---

[12] WOLFRAMALPHA, *Benghazi, supra* note 2.

[13] *Id.*

[14] Andrew England & Javier Blas, *Libya rebels fight to keep oil lifeline open*, FINANCIAL TIMES, Apr. 7, 2011, *available at* http://www.ft.com/intl/cms/s/0/711c6cd6-6146-11e0-ab25-00144feab49a.html#axzz2MmfaFCq7.

[15] The transliteration of this term was adopted from the reference. Abdulsattar Hatitah, *Libyan Tribal Map: Network of loyalties that will determine Gaddafi's fate*, ASHARQ ALWASAT, Feb. 22, 2011, *available at* http://www.asharq-e.com/news.asp?section=3&id=24257. *See also, e.g., Libyan People*, TEMEHU, *available at* http://www.temehu.com/Libyan-People.htm.

[16] Hatitah, *Libyan Tribal Map, supra* note 15. *See also, e.g.*, TEMEHU, *Libyan People, supra* note 15.

[17] Peter Apps, *Factbox: Libya's key cultural, tribal divisions*, REUTERS, Feb. 22, 2011, *available at* http://us.mobile.reuters.com/article/topNews/idUSTRE7294TD20110310; Hatitah, *Libyan Tribal Map, supra* note 15; *Two Benghazi tribes support Gaddafi-Libyan TV*, REUTERS, Mar. 16, 2011, *available at* http://www.reuters.com/article/2011/03/16/libya-tribes-tv-id USLDE72F1YA20110316. For more on Libya's tribes, *see* Basic Facts about Libya.

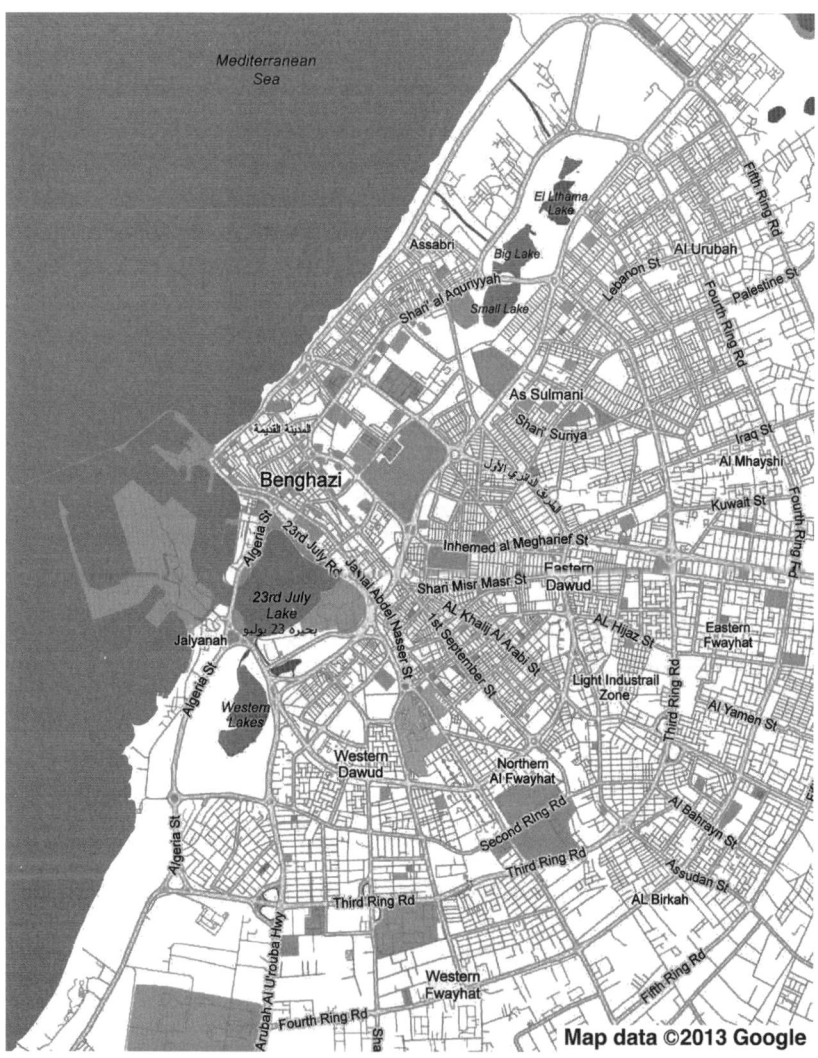

Map 3: Map of Benghazi (Map data © 2013 Google).

members inhabiting eastern Libya and the other half western Egypt, after having migrated to Egypt in the late-17th century.[18] The political affiliations of these tribes and smaller sub-groups varied during throughout the course of the 2011 conflict.

Benghazi was the first city in Libya that saw anti-regime protests in February 2011, and soon developed into the most strategically important *thuwar* stronghold in Cyrenaica. The history of Benghazi created the social conditions that allowed the city to become the political epicenter of the uprising and the location of the transitional government. Many Libyans in Cyrenaica had felt that the Qadhafi regime provided little for the people of eastern Libya, despite the province being the source of the majority of the country's oil wealth. Cyrenaicans contended that Qadhafi focused resources disproportionately on Sirte, the home of his own tribe, and areas surrounding Tripoli, while depriving Cyrenaica equitable investment in infrastructure. This resulted in high poverty and unemployment in the region, fuelling widespread dissatisfaction.[19] Benghazi also has a history of political activism and the protests there were sparked by a group of lawyers and activists who represented the families of victims of the 1996 Abu Salim Prison massacre.[20] The dissatisfaction exploded into social unrest in the midst of the uprisings taking place in neighboring countries and fueled demonstrations that led to end of the Qadhafi regime.

2. SUMMARY OF EVENTS

In February 2011, demonstrations erupted in Benghazi with protesters initially calling for democratic political and social reforms and later for the fall of the Qadhafi regime. The regime responded quickly, warning on state media outlets that if the unrest continued, the military would

---

[18] Farrag Ismail, *Egypt border tribes declare support to Libya revolt*, AL ARABIYA, Feb. 24, 2011, *available at* http://www.alarabiya.net/articles/2011/02/24/139018.html.

[19] *The liberated east – Building a new Libya – Around Benghazi, Muammar Qaddafi's enemies have triumphed*, THE ECONOMIST, Feb. 24, 2011, *available at* http://www.economist .com/node/18239900. For more on historical divisions between Tripolitania and Cyrenaica, *see* Ch. I.

[20] HOLDING LIBYA TOGETHER: SECURITY CHALLENGES AFTER QADHAFI, INTERNATIONAL CRISIS GROUP, Dec. 14, 2011 [hereinafter "HOLDING LIBYA TOGETHER"], *available at* http:// www.crisisgroup.org/~/media/Files/Middle%20East%20North%20Africa/North%20 Africa/115%20Holding%20Libya%20Together%20--%20Security%20Challenges%20 after%20Qadhafi.pdf.

quell demonstrations with force.[21] This precipitated a rapid escalation in violence that by late February became civil war.[22]

The unrest began on 15 February when Fathi Terbil, a lawyer and human rights defender was arrested by Internal Security Agency (ISA) forces. Terbil, who had himself lost family members in the 1996 Abu Salim Prison massacre, represented families calling for accountability.[23] Terbil, along with other lawyers and activists, had been organizing demonstrations on 17 February dubbing it the "Day of Rage," on a date that coincided with the killing of 14 peaceful protesters in Benghazi by security forces five years earlier.[24] The regime had taken preemptive measures in an attempt to stop the planned demonstrations, such as sending the chief of the ISA, 'Abdullah al-Senussi, to question Terbil and pressure him to call off the event, but this only led to further mobilization.[25] While the planned Day of Rage demonstrations were not initially intended as a call for regime change, the incident became the catalyst for the Libyan revolution.

On 15–16 February, Libyan security forces from the ISA arrested an estimated 14 people for their role in organizing the demonstrations planned for 17 February, with no other apparent charges brought against them.[26] The crowds grew as more people gathered in front of the general security directorate in Benghazi to demand the release of Terbil and the other detainees.[27] Protesters reportedly attacked and burned government buildings and police stations.[28] Monuments associated with the regime were

---

[21] *Libya protests: 84 killed in growing unrest, says HRW,* BBC, Feb. 19, 2011, *available at* http://www.bbc.co.uk/news/world-africa-12512536.

[22] Report of the International Commission of Inquiry to investigate all the alleged violations of international human rights law in the Libyan Arab Jamahiriya, U.N. HRC. 17th Sess., ¶ 26. U.N. Doc. A/HRC/17/44 (Jan. 12, 2012).

[23] For more information about the Abu Salim prison and the 1996 killings, *see* Ch. I, Sec. 10.4.

[24] ALLISON PARGETER, LIBYA: THE RISE AND FALL OF QADDAFI 214 (New Haven, USA: Yale University Press, 2012); Report of the International Commission of Inquiry (Jan. 12, 2012), *supra* note 22 at ¶ 27.

[25] PARGETER, LIBYA: THE RISE AND FALL OF QADDAFI, *supra* note 24 at 219.

[26] *Libya: Arrests, Assaults in Advance of Planned Protests,* HUMAN RIGHTS WATCH, Feb. 17, 2011, *available at* http://www.hrw.org/news/2011/02/16/libya-arrests-assaults-advance-planned-protests. For more on the arrests leading up to the protests, *see* Ch. II, Secs. 1 & 3.2.

[27] PARGETER, LIBYA: THE RISE AND FALL OF QADDAFI, *supra* note 24 at 219.

[28] *Libya protests: massacres reported as Gaddafi imposes news blackout,* THE GUARDIAN, Feb. 18, 2011, *available at* http://www.guardian.co.uk/world/2011/feb/18/libya-protests-massacres-reported.

likewise destroyed.[29] Demonstrators gathered outside the buildings that were symbols of Qadhafi's rule, such as the Revolutionary Committee offices and the Green Book Studies Center.[30]

On the evening of 15 February, uniformed and plainclothes officers used teargas and batons to disperse protesters, reportedly killing one and injuring 14.[31] The Qadhafi regime denied using live ammunition on 15 February, but acknowledged the use of tear gas, maintaining that the use of force was necessary to deter the violence of the demonstrators and their attacks on police stations.[32]

Demonstrations took place outside the courthouse in Benghazi on 17 February, prompting the beginning of mass protests in the east that spread across the country.[33] Libyan authorities responded by trying to suppress the protests and prevent further mass gatherings by blocking websites such as Facebook and Al Jazeera Arabic, and arresting opposition leaders and protest organizers.[34] Witnesses stated that Qadhafi forces fired live ammunition and heavy artillery directly at protesters, who were largely unarmed in the early days of the demonstrations. On 18 February, the Qadhafi regime sent reinforcements to Benghazi, including elite military forces, plainclothes police and militias to quell the unrest. Violent clashes erupted as demonstrators took control of substantial parts of the city.[35]

The clashes intensified during a funeral procession on 18 February when thousands of mourners passed the Al-Fadil bin 'Umar military barracks, which was a symbol of regime power both because it was a notorious military facility and the place where Qadhafi stayed when he visited the city.

---

[29] *Bloodshed as tensions rise in Libya*, BBC, Feb. 19, 2011, *available at* http://www.bbc.co.uk/news/world-middle-east-12513941; *20 reported dead Friday in Libya as thousands take to streets*, CNN, Feb. 19, 2011, *available at* http://edition.cnn.com/2011/WORLD/africa/02/18/libya.protests/index.html.

[30] PARGETER, LIBYA: THE RISE AND FALL OF QADDAFI, *supra* note 24 at 220.

[31] HUMAN RIGHTS WATCH, *Libya: Arrests, Assaults in Advance of Planned Protests*, *supra* note 26.

[32] Report of the International Commission of Inquiry (Jan. 12, 2012), *supra* note 22 at ¶ 72.

[33] *Libya protests leave 24 dead, says rights group*, BBC, Feb. 18, 2011, *available at* http://www.bbc.co.uk/news/world-africa-12502657; Report of the International Commission of Inquiry (Jan. 12, 2012), *supra* note 22 at ¶ 27.

[34] *Libya: Security Forces Kill 84 Over Three Days*, HUMAN RIGHTS WATCH, Feb. 19, 2011, *available at* http://www.hrw.org/en/news/2011/02/18/libya-security-forces-kill-84-over-three-days; BBC, *Libya protests: 84 killed in growing unrest, says HRW*, *supra* note 21; Report of the International Commission of Inquiry (Jan. 12, 2012), *supra* note 22 at ¶¶ 27 & 132.

[35] BBC, *Bloodshed as tensions rise in Libya*, *supra* note 29; HUMAN RIGHTS WATCH, *Libya: Security Forces Kill 84 Over Three Days*, *supra* note 34.

As the first mourners passed the military barracks in the city center, they threw rocks at soldiers who then opened fire on the marchers.[36] As the protesters moved towards the main square, they were met with gunfire from Revolutionary Guard forces. A witness reported that the chief of the Revolutionary Guard stood in front of the Islamic Da'wah building as his forces shot at demonstrators from inside the offices.[37]

Hospital staff on duty on 18 February recorded numerous casualties and hundreds of injuries.[38] Doctors from several hospitals reported overcrowding and complained that the number of injuries and casualties went beyond their capacity, and medical supplies began to dwindle.[39] One official at Al-Jala' Hospital, the main medical facility in Benghazi, reported that 24 dead bodies and hundreds of wounded had been brought to the hospital.[40] Other reports stated that 15 dead bodies had been brought to Al-Jala', including a 13–year-old boy.[41] A doctor at the hospital told journalists that the patients were civilians aged 13 to 35, and did not include any police or military personnel. All the gunshot victims had bullet wounds to the head, chest and/or abdomen from guns with high muzzle velocities.[42] Other doctors further noted that the victims' chest wounds were concentrated around the heart.[43]

On 19 February, mourners passed by the Al-Fadil bin 'Umar military barracks to bury the dead from the previous day, and violence again erupted between the protesters and soldiers.[44] Thousands of mourners gathered outside a Revolutionary Guard building on their way back from the cemetery and chanted anti-Qadhafi slogans, describing the Revolutionary

---

[36] Paul Schemm, *Battle at army base broke Gadhafi hold in Benghazi*, THE WASHINGTON POST, Feb. 25, 2011, *available at* http://www.washingtonpost.com/wp-dyn/content/article/2011/02/25/AR2011022505021.html; Report of the International Commission of Inquiry on Libya, U.N. HRC. 19th Sess., Annex I, ¶ 115. U.N. Doc. A/HRC/19/68, advance unedited version (Mar. 2, 2012).

[37] *Id.* at Annex I, ¶ 114.

[38] BBC, *Libya protests leave 24 dead, says rights group HRW, supra* note 33.

[39] Schemm, *Battle at army base broke Gadhafi hold in Benghazi, supra* note 36.
Libyan leader must end spiralling killings, AMNESTY INTERNATIONAL, Feb. 20, 2011, *available at* http://www.amnesty.org/en/for-media/press-releases/libyan-leader-must-end-spiralling-killings-2011-02-20. *See also infra* Secs. 2.3.1 & 2.3.2.

[40] Schemm, *Battle at army base broke Gadhafi hold in Benghazi, supra* note 36.

[41] BBC, *Libya protests leave 24 dead, says rights group HRW, supra* note 33; HUMAN RIGHTS WATCH, *Libya: Security Forces Kill 84 Over Three Days, supra* note 34.

[42] *Libya forces 'open fire' at funeral*, AL JAZEERA, Feb. 19, 2011, *available at* http://www.aljazeera.com/news/africa/2011/02/2011219811665897.html.

[43] Schemm, *Battle at army base broke Gadhafi hold in Benghazi, supra* note 36.

[44] *Id.*

Guard as killers.[45] The protesters threw stones and crude bombs made of tin cans stuffed with gunpowder, and drove bulldozers into the walls. The security forces responded with live ammunition, including machine guns.[46] Protesters were also killed the same day when security forces opened fire on hundreds of people holding a sit-in in front of Benghazi's North Court.[47] Lawyers, doctors and members of the Abu Salim families organizing committee were involved in the sit-in.[48]

Reports of the killings began to come out of Benghazi and reach international audiences, sparking widespread condemnation from human rights groups. Officials at Al-Jala' Hospital's morgue told journalists that they had documented 30 deaths as a result of the 19 February fighting.[49] HRW spoke with senior medical officials from the hospital who said they had received 23 bodies on 19 February, and by the morning of 20 February, the number had reached 70.[50] Other media accounts reported 35 casualties in one Benghazi hospital on 19 February.[51]

On 20 February, 10,000 protesters took to the streets of Benghazi.[52] Thousands gathered at a funeral and were subsequently joined by more protesters in a procession from the Benghazi courthouse to the Hawari cemetery, a route that brought demonstrators by Al-Fadil bin 'Umar military barracks for the third consecutive day.[53] There are conflicting accounts as to the details of the incidents that then transpired in front of the barracks. Some reports indicate that a protester drove a car rigged with makeshift explosives into the gates of the barracks and a battle ensued between security forces and armed protesters from Benghazi, Darna and Al-Bayda.[54] Other reports suggest that regime forces opened fire with machine-guns, large-caliber weapons and snipers on protesters

---

[45] Amnesty International, *Libyan leader must end spiralling killings, supra* note 39.

[46] Schemm, *Battle at army base broke Gadhafi hold in Benghazi, supra* note 36.

[47] Amnesty International, *Libyan leader must end spiralling killings, supra* note 39.

[48] *Id.*

[49] Schemm, *Battle at army base broke Gadhafi hold in Benghazi, supra* note 36.

[50] *Libya: Governments Should Demand End to Unlawful Killings*, Human Rights Watch, Feb. 20, 2011, *available at* http://www.hrw.org/news/2011/02/20/libya-governments-should-demand-end-unlawful-killings; Schemm, *Battle at army base broke Gadhafi hold in Benghazi, supra* note 36.

[51] *See, e.g.*, Kenneth Ang, *84 protesters killed in Libya*, Allvoices, Feb. 19, 2011, *available at* http://www.allvoices.com/contributed-news/8240740-deaths-in-libya-protest-rise-to-84.

[52] Human Rights Watch, *Libya: Governments Should Demand End to Unlawful Killings, supra* note 50.

[53] *Id. See also* BBC, *Libya protests leave 24 dead, says rights group HRW, supra* note 33; Al Jazeera, *Libya forces 'open fire' at funeral, supra* note 42.

[54] Schemm, *Battle at army base broke Gadhafi hold in Benghazi, supra* note 36.

from within the barracks compound, and that the crowd responded, confronting soldiers on the ground.[55]

The conflicting accounts do agree, however, that 20 February was the bloodiest of the three days of conflict at Al-Fadil bin 'Umar military barracks. Reports of casualties from the barracks arriving at Al-Jala' Hospital ranged from 45 to 70.[56] Medical staff at Hawari Hospital recorded that 14 dead bodies were brought to the hospital morgue.[57] There were also reports that soldiers at the barracks who refused to participate in the 19 February attacks on demonstrators were also killed.[58]

On the afternoon of 20 February, Al-Fadil bin 'Umar military barracks came under *thuwar* control when 'Abd al-Fattah Yunis entered the city with elite units and seized the building in support of the opposition. Yunis had been charged by Qadhafi to relieve the besieged barracks, but instead announced his defection and promised the soldiers safe passage on the condition that they leave eastern Libya.[59]

As defections increased and the regime soldiers were forced out of the city, after 20 February, the only substantive resistance to the opposition in Benghazi came from rogue groups of Qadhafi loyalists.[60] Some of the defecting soldiers established a *thuwar* unit known as the Thunderbolt Squad, which defended demonstrators and reportedly brought the injured to Al-Jala' Hospital.[61] The defecting soldiers also provided the *thuwar* groups with guns and training, as they began to organize and formed a determined insurgent force.[62]

The opposition groups did not fall under a unified command, however, and there were no accountability measures put in place for those that took up arms against the regime. Many groups acted on their own accord, and carried out a wave of reprisal violence as they took control over large

---

[55] *Benghazi witness: They are firing on civilians*, BBC, Feb. 20, 2011, *available at* http://www.bbc.co.uk/news/world-middle-east-12517229.

[56] Schemm, *Battle at army base broke Gadhafi hold in Benghazi, supra* note 36; HUMAN RIGHTS WATCH, *Libya: Governments Should Demand End to Unlawful Killings, supra* note 50; *Libya revolt spreads to Tripoli*, AL JAZEERA, Feb. 21, 2011, *available at* http://www.aljazeera.com/news/africa/2011/02/20112213439291589.htmls.

[57] HUMAN RIGHTS WATCH, *Libya: Governments Should Demand End to Unlawful Killings, supra* note 50.

[58] Schemm, *Battle at army base broke Gadhafi hold in Benghazi, supra* note 36. *See also infra* Sec. 3.2(a).

[59] Schemm, *Battle at army base broke Gadhafi hold in Benghazi, supra* note 36.

[60] AL JAZEERA, *Libya revolt spreads to Tripoli, supra* note 56.

[61] *Id.*

[62] *Id.*

areas of Cyrenaica. The newly formed *thuwar* groups targeted Qadhafi security officials, suspected regime loyalists as well as Sub-Saharan African nationals and dark-skinned Libyan nationals. The Commission of Inquiry (CoI) reported that in late February, armed men from the *thuwar* forces killed a number of individuals from Chad by gunfire or burning.[63] Other NGOs, such as Amnesty International, also found that in the early days of the uprising groups of protesters in Al-Bayda, Benghazi and Darna had killed suspected mercenaries and soldiers who had been detained, "[s]ome were beaten to death, at least three were hanged, and others were shot dead after they had been captured or had surrendered."[64] The security vacuum and unguarded weapons depots in the wake of the retreat of the Qadhafi forces provided the conditions that allowed for these killings to take place.[65]

Militarily, one of the most important consequences of the capture of Benghazi was that it provided the *thuwar* with a secure and protected area to regroup and organize.[66] In the days after the capture of Al-Fadil bin 'Umar military barracks, protesters rapidly took control of the rest of the city.[67] By 24 February Benghazi was completely under the authority of the rebels, who began establishing committees in various government buildings in the center of the city.[68] The city came under the control of the Benghazi Council, and became the headquarters for the National Transitional Council (NTC) on 27 February.[69] The NTC, led by former Minister of Justice Mustafa 'Abd al-Jalil, held its first meeting in Benghazi and issued

---

[63] Report of the International Commission of Inquiry, advance unedited version (Mar. 2, 2012), *supra* note 36 at Annex I, ¶ 211. *See infra* Sec. 3.2(a).

[64] Amnesty International, Battle for Libya: Killings, Disappearances and Torture 17 (Sept. 2011) [hereinafter "Battle for Libya"], *available at* http://www.amnesty.org/en/library/asset/MDE19/025/2011/en/8f2e1c49-8f43-46d3-917d-383c17d36377/mde19025201ien.pdf; Report of the International Commission of Inquiry, advance unedited version (Mar. 2, 2012), *supra* note 36 at Annex I, ¶ 211.

[65] Report of the International Commission of Inquiry, advance unedited version (Mar. 2, 2012), *supra* note 36 at Annex I, ¶ 213.

[66] International Crisis Group, Holding Libya together, *supra* note 20.

[67] Al Jazeera, *Libya revolt spreads to Tripoli*, *supra* note 56; *Libya: Anti-Gaddafi protests spread to Tripoli*, bbc, Feb. 20, 2011, *available at* http://www.bbc.co.uk/news/world-africa-12520366.

[68] *Libya protests: Benghazi 'returning to normal'*, bbc, Feb. 25, 2011, *available at* http://www.bbc.co.uk/news/world-africa-12575784; *Benghazi opts for township government*, bbc, Feb. 26, 2011, *available at* http://news.bbc.co.uk/today/hi/today/newsid_9408000/9408121.stm; *'Vehemence to violence' in Benghazi*, bbc, Feb. 24, 2011, *available at* http://news.bbc.co.uk/today/hi/today/newsid_9406000/9406270.stm.

[69] *Libya opposition launches council*, Al Jazeera, Feb. 27, 2011, *available at* http://www.aljazeera.com/news/africa/2011/02/2011227175955221853.html; *The Interim National Council*, Temehu, *available at* http://www.temehu.com/ntc.htm.

a statement on 5 March, declaring itself the country's sole representative authority.[70] The NTC maintained its headquarters in Benghazi, a reliable base for anti-regime activity that also provided army defectors relative security.

After seizing control of Benghazi, the *thuwar* organized militarily to advance on other cities, recruiting soldiers and sending armed units to various parts of the country.[71] The rebel military forces in Benghazi were composed of dozens of security units established in eastern Libya in February 2011. Terbil, the NTC's security liaison, identified 11 independent security forces operating in Benghazi alone, some with multiple bases. Jamal Bannur, the justice coordinator of the Benghazi Council, put the number of volunteer security forces at over 40.[72] The National Army of the NTC would later be headquartered in Benghazi, but was never able to consolidate central authority over rebel forces in Cyrenaica, much less across the rest of the country.[73]

In mid-March, Qadhafi forces began a concerted campaign to retake Benghazi. On 19 March, Qadhafi forces began shelling the city including civilian neighborhoods. Libyan jets bombed the road leading from the city center to the airport to the east and the city's outskirts. NTC officials reported that Qadhafi military units had entered the city and were attempting to flank *thuwar* forces.[74] A jet plane reportedly belonging to the *thuwar* forces was shot down over Benghazi.[75] During the fighting, NTC leader 'Abd al-Jalil pleaded for international action, warning that there would be "a catastrophe if the international community does not implement the resolutions of the UN Security Council."[76]

The international community interpreted the actions of the Qadhafi regime as a direct violation of UN Security Council Resolution 1973, passed

---

[70] Report of the International Commission of Inquiry, advance unedited version (Mar. 2, 2012), *supra* note 36 at Annex I, ¶ 82.

[71] BBC, *Libya protests: Benghazi 'returning to normal'*, *supra* note 68.

[72] *Libya: Opposition Arbitrarily Detaining Suspected Gaddafi Loyalists*, HUMAN RIGHTS WATCH, June 5, 2011, *available at* http://www.hrw.org/news/2011/06/05/libya-opposition-arbitrarily-detaining-suspected-gaddafi-loyalists.

[73] INTERNATIONAL CRISIS GROUP, HOLDING LIBYA TOGETHER, *supra* note 20.

[74] David Batty & Warren Murray, *Libya military action*, THE GUARDIAN, Mar. 19, 2011, *available at* http://www.guardian.co.uk/world/blog/2011/mar/19/libya-live-blog-ceasefire-nofly.

[75] *See* AlJazeeraEnglish, *Battle for Libya, Opposition Fighter Jet Shot Down*, YOUTUBE .COM (Mar. 19, 2011), *available at* http://www.youtube.com/watch?v=-nUrxp74Hgg.

[76] *Libya: Gaddafi forces attacking rebel-held Benghazi*, BBC, Mar. 19, 2011, *available at* http://www.bbc.co.uk/news/world-africa-12793919.

on 17 March.[77] On 19 March, NATO launched its first airstrikes on Qadhafi targets, concentrating on the regime's air force defense systems and military forces in the Benghazi region.[78] NATO destroyed tanks and artillery on the open desert road near Benghazi, halting the Qadhafi forces' advance on the city.[79] NATO later reported that the NTC and opposition units had been outgunned and were "running" from regime forces.[80] According to NATO, the targeted strikes relieved pressure on the NTC, which gave it time to build its military command and control structures and allowed humanitarian assistance to flow in and out of Benghazi by air and sea.[81] The no-fly zone was later eased around Benghazi to allow humanitarian flights to use the city's airport.[82]

French, UK and U.S. forces took the initial lead in the foreign intervention while NATO members deliberated over the management of the Libyan campaign. The flying missions were conducted with little return fire from the Qadhafi military. On 22 March, however, an American fighter jet on a bombing mission crashed after experiencing equipment failure. The pilot and weapons officer ejected and were recovered by a U.S. rescue team. During the rescue mission, the U.S. team reportedly shot and injured six civilians who rushed to the scene.[83] The incident demonstrated the unorganized nature of the early operations, and the need for better coordination between foreign forces, *thuwar* forces, the NTC, and the local population.

The U.S. government deployed a senior diplomat to Benghazi to serve as a liaison to the NTC. The U.S. State Department reported in April 2011

---

[77] For more on the interpretation of UN Security Council Resolution 1973 and the foreign intervention, *see* Ch. III, Sec. 5.

[78] Christian F. Anrig, *Allied Air Power over Libya*, 91 AIR AND SPACE POWER JOURNAL 89 (Winter 2011), *available at* http://www.airpower.au.af.mil/digital/pdf/articles/winter2011/11-VA-Anrig.pdf.

[79] Chris McGreal et al., *Libya: Allied air strikes secure Misrata for rebels*, THE GUARDIAN, Mar. 24, 2011, *available at* http://www.guardian.co.uk/world/2011/mar/23/libya-allied-air-strikes-misrata.

[80] *Press briefing on Libya*, NORTH ATLANTIC TREATY ORGANIZATION, May 27, 2011, *available at* http://www.nato.int/cps/en/natolive/opinions_74826.htm.

[81] *Id.*

[82] *Press briefing on Libya*, NORTH ATLANTIC TREATY ORGANIZATION, Oct. 18, 2011, *available at* http://www.nato.int/cps/en/natolive/opinions_79613.htm. For more on initial phase of the coalition airstrikes in and around Benghazi, *see* Ch. IV, Secs. 2 & 6.

[83] Mark Landler & Steven Erlanger, *Obama Seeks to Unify Allies as More Airstrikes Rock Tripoli*, N.Y. TIMES, Mar. 22, 2011, *available at* http://www.nytimes.com/2011/03/23/world/africa/23libya.html; Ewen MacAskill et al., *Libya: Six injured as US team botches rescue of downed airmen*, THE GUARDIAN, Mar. 22, 2011, *available at* http://www.guardian.co.uk/world/2011/mar/22/libya-downed-airmen-rescue.

that they were getting a better sense of the opposition and the NTC's vision for Libya's future as a result of meetings.[84] The diplomat assigned to serve as the Special Representative to the NTC was Christopher Stevens, who after the conflict became U.S. Ambassador to Libya, and was later killed in Benghazi on 11 September 2012.[85]

The NTC leaders became the political representatives of the revolution, establishing relations with foreign governments in preparation for a post-Qadhafi Libya. The military operations of the NTC were under the command of General Yunis, and the opposition leadership attempted to create a Libyan National Army under his authority. For various reasons the National Army was a failed cause from the onset, which were compounded by the fact that Yunis' previous role in the Qadhafi regime led many in the rebel factions to question his credibility.[86] After Yunis' assassination on 28 July 2011, the possibility of unifying a national rebel army became even more remote. The circumstances and reasons for the killing of Yunis were unclear at the time, with some reports indicating that he was killed by his own soldiers.[87] Those loyal to Yunis, such as members of his 'Ubaydi tribe, vowed to arrest those believed to be responsible for his killing, and accused senior members of the opposition of not fully investigating the crime.[88] As Interior Minister, Yunis had been involved in the campaign of violent repression against Islamic groups in the Benghazi region, and his killing was believed by some to be revenge for his previous role as part of the Qadhafi regime.[89] Other sources indicated that he was murdered over accusations of sabotaging the eastern military campaign

---

[84] CHRISTOPHER M. BLANCHARD, CONGRESSIONAL RESEARCH SERVICE, LIBYA: UNREST AND U.S. POLICY 11, Apr. 25, 2011, [hereinafter "UNREST AND U.S. POLICY"], *available at* http://www.hsdl.org/?view&did=5616.

[85] Alastair Jamieson, *US Ambassador Chris Stevens was 'courageous and exemplary',* *Obama says,* ABC NEWS, Sept. 12, 2012, *available at* http://worldnews.nbcnews.com/_news/2012/09/12/13826542-us-ambassador-chris-stevens-was-courageous-and-exemplary-obama-says. For more on the 11 September 2012 attacks in Benghazi, *see* Ch. V, Sec. 4.

[86] Report of the International Commission of Inquiry, advance unedited version (Mar. 2, 2012), *supra* note 36 at ¶ 64. For more on efforts to create a national rebel army, *see* Ch. II, Sec. 2.3.

[87] Members of Yunis's tribe 'Ubaydi vowed to avenge the murder. *See e.g.,* Rob Crilly, *Libya: tribe pledges to arrest rebels it believes were behind murder of opposition military commander,* THE TELEGRAPH, Aug. 26, 2011, *available at* http://www.telegraph.co.uk/news/worldnews/africaandindianocean/libya/8725413/Libya-tribe-pledges-to-arrest-rebels-it-believes-were-behind-murder-of-opposition-military-commander.html.

[88] Gamal Nkrumah, *Yearning for Younis,* AL AHRAM, Aug. 4–10, 2011, *available at* http://weekly.ahram.org.eg/2011/1059/re8.htm.

[89] ANTHONY BELL ET AL., INSTITUTE FOR THE STUDY OF WAR, THE LIBYAN REVOLUTION: STALEMATE & SIEGE 34, n. 49 (Oct. 2011) [hereinafter "STALEMATE & SIEGE"], *available at*

by failing to provide adequate intelligence about opposition movements to NATO.[90]

The day after Yunis' killing, *thuwar* and Qadhafi forces clashed in Benghazi when Qadhafi loyalists freed approximately 300 soldiers from detention.[91] The *thuwar* were able to subdue the Qadhafi forces, but the incident was a sign of challenges ahead. The killing of Yunis and the ensuing fighting renewed fears both among the NTC and the public that regime loyalist forces had infiltrated the area and were undermining confidence in the NTC's capacity to ensure public safety and maintain unity.[92]

The NTC did succeed in establishing training camps in eastern Libya in an effort to prepare rebel forces from other parts of the country before going into battle.[93] The training camps in Benghazi began hosting *thuwar* from other cities in February, including fighters from the capital who had formed the Tripoli Katiba. Initially comprising no more than a few hundred men, the Tripoli Katiba was commanded predominantly by expatriate Libyans. By mid-August, however, it had grown to roughly 1,200 fighters, and began operating in the Nafusa Mountains region. The Benghazi camp operated with the support of several foreign governments including Qatar, which sent representatives to Benghazi and maintained a strong presence in the region.[94]

Following the fall of Tripoli, the NTC declared its intention to move its political base from Benghazi to the capital. On 10 September 2011, 'Abd al-Jalil together with several other council members arrived in Tripoli, announcing that the NTC was now headquartered in the capital and had

---

http://www.understandingwar.org/sites/default/files/Libya_Part3_0.pdf. For more on the background of General Yunis and his role in the Qadhafi regime, *see* Ch. II, Sec. 2.2.

[90] Craig Allen et al., *Errant NATO Airstrikes in Libya: 13 Cases (Brega)*, N.Y. TIMES, Dec. 16, 2011, *available at* http://www.nytimes.com/interactive/2011/12/16/world/africa/nato-air-strikes-in-libya.html?ref=africa&_r=0#page/rebel-convoy. For more on the killing of General Yunis, *see* Ch. II, Sec. 2.3.

[91] Rania El Gamal, *Rebels clash with Gaddafi loyalists in rebel-held east*, REUTERS, July 31, 2011, *available at* http://www.reuters.com/article/2011/07/31/us-libya-idUSTRE 76Q76620110731.

[92] Peter Apps, *Analysis: Libya rebel killing takes shine off opposition gains*, REUTERS, July 29, 2011, *available at* http://www.reuters.com/article/2011/07/29/us-libya-killing-idUS-TRE76S46W20110729.

[93] Report of the International Commission of Inquiry, advance unedited version (Mar. 2, 2012), *supra* note 36 at ¶ 65. For more on the composition of the *thuwar* groups and rebel training in eastern Libya, *see* Ch. II, Secs. 2.3 & 3.3.

[94] INTERNATIONAL CRISIS GROUP, HOLDING LIBYA TOGETHER, *supra* note 20. For more on the role of Qatar and other 3rd party states in the Libyan conflict, *see* Ch. IV, Sec. 7.1.

left a branch of the council to operate in Benghazi.[95] Several weeks later, on 23 October, the NTC issued a declaration of liberation from Benghazi, signaling the end of armed hostilities in the country. 'Abd al-Jalil spoke to a crowd in Benghazi, announcing the end of the conflict and the start of a new era.[96]

The NTC faced immediate challenges in a post-Qadhafi period. Following its move to Tripoli, Benghazi residents voiced widespread dissatisfaction over the transfer of political authority from the eastern part of the country. Those angered by the decision ranged from local tribes to political Islamist groups and local political leaders who worried that Cyrenaica would again be marginalized and treated unfairly by a government based in Tripolitania. The dissatisfaction quickly spread to the streets. On 23 November, 150 people held a protest in front of NTC offices to voice their objection to the composition of the new government, carrying banners that read, "No to a government of outsiders!" The demonstrators objected to those they saw as outsiders – in many cases Libyans exiles returning to the country – filling high-level positions in the post-Qadhafi administration. The Benghazi-based Maghariba and Awagi tribes led the protests, expressing frustration over being poorly represented and denied key positions in the new government.[97]

The protests grew, and by early December reports indicated that 20,000–30,000 had gathered in the central Shajara Square in Benghazi to protest the NTC, and demonstrations continued on for days at a time.[98] The dissatisfaction stemmed from the growing perception that the NTC was disconnected from the population in the east and was conducting affairs in an opaque manner. The political process of the NTC raised questions of legitimacy, particularly because many saw the NTC as being affiliated with officials or collaborators from the Qadhafi era.[99]

---

[95] *Libya's NTC Chairmen arrives in Tripoli*, XINHUA NEWS, Sept. 10, 2011, *available at* http://news.xinhuanet.com/english2010/world/2011–09/11/c_131132048.htm.

[96] Ian Black, *Benghazi's moment of joy as Libya's tyranny ends*, THE GUARDIAN, Oct. 23, 2011, *available at* http://www.guardian.co.uk/world/2011/oct/23/benghazi-joy-end-libya-tyranny.

[97] Christian Lowe & Francois Murphy, *Libyan tribes protest at new government line-up*, REUTERS, Nov. 23, 2011, *available at* http://www.reuters.com/article/2011/11/23/us-libya-idUSTRE7AL0JM20111123.

[98] Matt Robinson, *New Libyan leaders juggle demands, grievances*, REUTERS, Dec. 23, 2011, *available at* http://www.reuters.com/article/2011/12/23/libya-mood-idUSL6E7NN1X920111223.

[99] *Id.* See also *Libya: Make Urgent Justice System Reforms*, HUMAN RIGHTS WATCH, Dec. 22, 2011, *available at* http://www.hrw.org/news/2011/12/22/libya-make-urgent-justice-system-reforms.

Instability spread in Benghazi as national authorities were unable to satisfy the demands of the local population. The transitional government also faced serious challenges from local groups in the east and across the country that remained militarized after the end of the conflict and targeted suspected Qadhafi loyalists with impunity. Amnesty International documented several incidents of reprisal violence by former *thuwar* groups in Cyrenaica. In one emblematic incident, a man who had defected from Qadhafi forces was approached and questioned on 15 December 2011 by *thuwar* at the 17 February Katiba camp.[100] He was detained and accused of participating in the February shootings of protesters by the Qadhafi forces, before being transferred to a military police prison in Buhdima where he was badly beaten.[101] Amnesty International reported that the 17 February Katiba held and interrogated hundreds of prisoners in Benghazi before turning them over to the military police.[102]

The NTC authorities began taking measures to control the local armed factions and ease the tensions in Benghazi. On 20 December, 'Abd al-Jalil held a meeting with local council leaders and protesters. In an effort to satisfy local demands, he suspended the NTC Benghazi representatives and issued a proposal to elect new representatives.[103]

Benghazi continued to experience instability as a result of unresolved issues stemming from the war. On 5 January 2012, Libyan soldiers and military police held a protest demanding payment for wages in arrears. They expressed their desire to go back to work, but demanded overdue compensation in order to do so.[104] The soldiers complained that the revolutionary *kata'ib*, who had taken the form of militia groups, were receiving compensation from the NTC. They warned that the militias were taking over the official bases and acting outside of any national authority.[105]

Various groups in Benghazi demonstrated publicly in an effort to ensure their voices would be heard in the post-Qadhafi era. Political Islamist groups, in particular, emerged as influential actors in the wake of the war, most notably in Cyrenaica, where there was a long history of

---

[100] AMNESTY INTERNATIONAL, LIBYA RULE OF LAW OR RULE OF MILITIAS? 31 (July 2012), *available at* http://www.amnesty.org/en/library/asset/MDE19/012/2012/en/f2d36090-5716-4ef1-81a7-f4b1ebd082fc/mde190122012en.pdf.

[101] *Id.*

[102] *Id.*

[103] Robinson, *New Libyan leaders juggle demands, grievances, supra* note 98.

[104] *Libyan soldiers demand salaries, complain about militias*, THE WASHINGTON POST, Jan. 6, 2012, *available at* http://www.washingtonpost.com/world/libyan-soldiers-demand-salaries-complain-about-militias/2012/01/05/gIQAQj5mdP_story.html.

[105] *Id.*

political Islamist activism. Many of these groups were eager to assert their influence and assure a position in Libya's post-war political landscape. On 20 January, Islamist groups held public protests demanding that Libya's new legislation be based on Islamic Sharī'a Law.[106] The demonstrators reportedly included members of the Muslim Brotherhood as well as other groups, and the protests demonstrated the type of contestations and tensions that would arise between secularists, Islamist factions and political parties in the coming period.[107]

Further incidents highlighted the unpopularity of the NTC in Benghazi, and the tenuous control of the national government in the region. On 21 January, protesters stormed a government building where 'Abd al-Jalil was working, breaking windows and destroying the metal gate as they entered.[108] Some reports indicated that the protesters were armed with machine guns and bayonets,[109] while other suggested they carried stones, iron bars, and homemade bombs.[110] 'Abd al-Jalil attempted to address the crowd but retreated from the building before teargas was fired at the protesters.[111] Benghazi's mayor, Saleh al-Ghazal, resigned as a result of the incident and 'Abd al-Jalil announced that elections would take place for his replacement.[112] The protests were also followed by the resignation of NTC vice-president 'Abd al-Hafiz Ghuga who had been an official in the Qadhafi government and was seen as a regime hold over.[113] The week before his resignation he had to be rescued from an angry crowd of university students who had surrounded him during a visit to Benghazi.[114]

---

[106] Mahmoud Habboush, *Libyan Islamists rally to demand sharia-based law*, REUTERS, Jan. 20, 2012, *available at* http://www.reuters.com/article/2012/01/20/us-libya-sharia-rallies-idUSTRE80J23G20120120.

[107] *Id. See also* Ch. V, Sec. 5.

[108] Oliver Holmes, *Enraged Benghazi residents feel ignored, forgotten*, REUTERS, Jan. 22, 2011, *available at* http://www.reuters.com/article/2012/01/22/libya-benghazi-anger-idUSL5E8CM0DK20120122.

[109] *Id.*

[110] *Libya: NTC deputy chief Abdel Hafiz Ghoga resigns*, BBC, Jan. 22, 2012, *available at* http://www.bbc.co.uk/news/world-africa-16671590.

[111] Mohammad Al Tommy, *Protesters storm Libyan government HQ in Benghazi*, REUTERS, Jan. 21, 2011, *available at* http://www.reuters.com/article/2012/01/22/us-libya-ntc-benghazi-idUSTRE80K0OC20120122.

[112] *Libya could fall into "bottomless pit" – NTC Chief*, REUTERS, Jan. 22, 2012, *available at* http://www.reuters.com/article/2012/01/22/libya-benghazi-protests-idUSL5E8CM06F20120122.

[113] BBC, *Libya: NTC deputy chief Abdel Hafiz Ghoga resigns, supra* note 110; Holmes, *Enraged Benghazi residents feel ignored, forgotten, supra* note 108.

[114] Holmes, *Enraged Benghazi residents feel ignored, forgotten, supra* note 108.

In addition to the religious and political tensions, Benghazi's citizens had to deal with the physical remnants of war. The use of landmines during the war had been documented in Benghazi, as well as in other cities in March 2011. The government began taking measures to destroy landmines in March 2012. International actors encouraged the new Libyan government to ensure that all local authorities and armed groups hand over landmines for destruction.[115] The UN-led Joint Mine Action Coordination Team reported that by the end of March 2012 it had destroyed 1,399 anti-tank and anti-personnel mines in 44 separate demolitions in Benghazi.[116] The presence of mines and the remnants of other weapons continued to be a great cause of concern in post-conflict Libya.

Local officials in Benghazi also faced immediate challenges when dealing with those accused of crimes of war. To process the perpetrators of crimes committed during the 2011 conflict proved difficult, and in many instances the cases were characterized by a lack of fair procedures or due process, and defense lawyers complained of abuses in the detention facilities. The CoI reported on the difficulties of the penal proceedings, highlighting cases such as one that began on 5 February 2012 in Benghazi for 41 men accused of having committed crimes during the conflict. The CoI reported that

> The accused were being prosecuted under the Military Code before a military court that was presided over by two military judges and one civilian judge. The 41 defendants, who are currently in detention, have been charged with three offences: using excessive violence against the national force, using light and medium weapons against prison guards of Quefia prison on 28 July 2011, and committing crimes with the intention to vandalize property and kill people at random with the intention of undermining state security.[117]

The case was subsequently transferred to an appropriate civilian court, but continued to face challenges. Defense lawyers of the accused complained that they were denied access to their clients for the first two months of detention, and that their clients were tortured while in detention.[118]

---

[115] *Libya's Government Destroys Landmines*, HUMAN RIGHTS WATCH, Mar. 29, 2012, *available at* http://www.hrw.org/news/2012/03/29/libya-s-government-destroys-landmines. *See also infra* Sec. 3.8.

[116] *Libya Weekly Report 2 April, 2012*, JOINT MINE ACTION COORDINATION TEAM, Apr. 2, 2012, *available at* http://reliefweb.int/report/libya/joint-mine-action-coordination-team-%E2%80%93-libya-weekly-report-2-april-2012.

[117] Report of the International Commission of Inquiry, advance unedited version (Mar. 2, 2012), *supra* note 36 at Annex I, ¶ 785.

[118] *Id. at* Annex I, ¶ 786.

The case represented the challenges that Benghazi's judicial system would continue to face during the post-conflict period. Allegations of torture and lack of due process came to be common in Benghazi as well as other parts of the country. Further complicating matters, the former rebels continued to hold thousands of detainees, and transfer to state authorities was a slow and arduous process.

On 17 February 2012, city officials in Benghazi held events and processions, marking a year since the start of the uprising that led to the fall of Qadhafi.[119] One year on from beginning of the revolution, security analysts and human rights groups raised concerns over the proliferation of armed groups beyond central control. Amnesty International released a report documenting the abuses committed by armed militias, raising concerns that these groups were hindering efforts to rebuild state institutions.[120]

Cyrenaican local leaders decided to create an autonomous administrative council to manage Benghazi's political affairs.[121] On 6 March 2012, a 3,000-member delegate congress met to establish the Cyrenaica Transitional Council, also known as the Barqa Council. Ahmad al-Senussi, a relative of King Idris al-Senussi and political prisoner under Qadhafi, was appointed head of the new council.[122] While it was initially unclear whether the council would coordinate with or challenge the national government, the NTC clearly saw it as a threat to its authority. International oil companies worried over the prospect of having to negotiate contracts with the new council in addition to national authorities.[123] Additionally, the council reportedly maintained an armed wing, headed by former army commander Hamid al-Hasi, who had defected and become an influential leader of the rebel forces.[124]

---

[119] *Libya celebrates first anniversary of uprising against Gaddafi*, THE TELEGRAPH, Feb. 17, 2012, *available at* http://www.telegraph.co.uk/news/worldnews/africaandindianocean/libya/9088010/Libya-celebrates-first-anniversary-of-uprising-against-Gaddafi.html.

[120] *Libya: 'Out of control' militias commit widespread abuses, a year on from uprising*, AMNESTY INTERNATIONAL, Feb. 15, 2012, *available at* http://www.amnesty.org/en/news/libya-out-control-militias-commit-widespread-abuses-year-uprising-2012-02-15. For more on the proliferation of militia groups in the post-conflict period, *see* Ch. V, Sec. 2.

[121] Issam Fetouri, *Eastern Libya defies Tripoli to create autonomous council*, REUTERS, Mar. 6, 2012, *available at* http://www.reuters.com/article/2012/03/06/libya-east-federalism-idUSL5E8E64JK20120306.

[122] *Id.*

[123] *Id.*

[124] FREDERIC WEHREY, CARNEGIE ENDOWMENT FOR INTERNATIONAL PEACE, THE STRUGGLE FOR SECURITY IN EASTERN LIBYA 6 (Sept. 2012), *available at* http://carnegieendowment.org/files/libya_security_2.pdf.

In response to the declaration of the Cyrenaica Council, on 7 March, 'Abd al-Jalil publicly stated that he would use force if necessary to maintain Libya's unity.[125] The moves towards increasing political autonomy underscored the internal divisions of Benghazi's population, as those who opposed local autonomy held public demonstrations. In a display of support for a unified Libya, on 9 March thousands gathered in Tahrir Square to renounce the proposition of an autonomous east.[126] Clashes between opposing armed factions broke out, lasting for several days, and leading to five injuries.[127]

In a move that further heightened tensions between local and national authorities, on 27 March local leaders in Benghazi threatened to stop supplying oil to Tripoli. Bubaker Buera, a founder of the Cyrenaican congress, said this was in response to the eastern province receiving only 60 out of 200 seats in the national assembly, calling for more proportionate representation and demanding at least one third of the seats.[128]

The power and influence of non-state armed actors remained a prominent issue of concern in Benghazi, and local residents voiced frustrations over the government's inability to disarm the former *thuwar* groups. On 6 April, hundreds of protesters, including policemen and soldiers gathered to call for the militia forces to surrender their weapons or join the national army.[129] The failure of the national authorities to rein in the armed groups fueled insecurity and unrest in the region. Days after the protest, on 10 April, armed men targeted a UN envoy carrying the Special Representative of the Secretary-General (SRSG) and head of the UN Mission in Libya,

---

[125] Chris Stephen, *Libyan leader vows to keep nation together by force*, THE GUARDIAN, Mar. 7, 2012, *available at* http://www.guardian.co.uk/world/2012/mar/07/libya-vows-nation-together-force.

[126] Christian Lowe, *Thousands rally in Libya against autonomy for east*, REUTERS, Mar. 9, 2012, *available at* http://www.reuters.com/article/2012/03/09/libya-east-autonomy-idUSL5E9AWK20120309.

[127] Ibrahim Majbari, *Armed clashes erupt after federalist rally in Libya*, AFP, Mar. 6, 2012, *available at* http://reliefweb.int/report/libya/armed-clashes-erupt-after-federalist-rally-libya.

[128] Hadeel Al-Shalchi, *East Libyans threaten to stop oil to press govt*, REUTERS, Mar. 27, 2012, *available at* http://www.reuters.com/article/2012/03/27/libya-east-oil-idUSL6E8ER9WR20120327. For more on the 2012 elections, *see* Ch. V, Sec. 6.

[129] Mohammed al Tommy, *Hundreds rally in Benghazi against militia*, REUTERS, Apr. 7, 2012, *available at* http://in.reuters.com/article/2012/04/06/libya-protest-idINDEE8350DZ20120406.

Ian Martin.[130] In another incident in late April, a bomb exploded in a Benghazi courthouse, injuring one person.[131]

There was also concern in Benghazi that the economic policies of the Qadhafi era would continue, whereby Cyrenaica would generate oil profits for the state without receiving a fair portion of the economic benefits in turn. On 23 April, around 50 demonstrators blocked the entrance of the Arabian Gulf Oil Company (Agoco), one of the biggest oil companies in Benghazi, protesting the government's lack of transparency in its dealing with the nation's oil assets.[132] The protests lasted for two weeks and severely disrupted business.[133] The police responded by arresting 30 people to put an end to the protests.[134]

Tensions came to a head as the elections planned for 7 July to elect a national assembly grew near. On 3 May, the Council of Cyrenaica called for a boycott of the elections, announcing they would participate in the election process only when the NTC guaranteed fair representation for all of Libya's provinces. The Council had no legal power to declare a boycott, however, and it was not clear whether the local population supported the call.[135]

Despite the tense situation, on 19 May local elections were held in Benghazi to choose a city council – the first elections of any kind to be held in the city since 1960.[136] Election results were announced a few days later after 138,312 people voted. 41 candidates were chosen from the 400 who ran for office, with 11 electoral districts represented by the candidate with the most votes. The election was also historical in the sense that a

---

[130] Ian Martin was also the UN Special Representative of the Secretary General. *See UN convoy targeted in explosion in east Libya-source*, REUTERS, Apr. 10, 2011, *available at* http://www.reuters.com/article/2012/04/10/libya-explosion-idUSL6E8FA3SS20120410.

[131] Mohammed al Tommy, *Courthouse bomb in Libya's Benghazi injures one*, REUTERS, Apr. 27, 2012, *available at* http://www.reuters.com/article/2012/04/27/us-libya-explosion-idUSBRE83Q0EU20120427.

[132] Mohammed al Tommy, *Protesters shut Libya's Agoco office for day*, REUTERS, Apr. 23, 2012, *available at* http://www.reuters.com/article/2012/04/23/libya-oil-protest-idUSL5E8F-NBHI20120423.

[133] Mohammed al Tommy, *UPDATE 1 – Libya police put end to protest at oil firm Agoco*, REUTERS, May 9, 2012, *available at* http://www.reuters.com/article/2012/05/09/libya-agoco-idUSL5E8G92XU20120509.

[134] *Id.*

[135] Lowe, *Thousands rally in Libya against autonomy for east, supra* note 126.

[136] Hadeel Al-Shalchi, *Vote in Libya's Benghazi tests support for autonomy*, REUTERS, May 19, 2012, *available at* http://www.reuters.com/article/2012/05/19/libya-benghazi-council-idUSL5E8GJ1BJ20120519.

woman candidate, Najat Rashid Mansur al-Kikhya, became the Benghazi representative in the NTC.[137]

Notwithstanding the political advancements, the security situation in Benghazi continued to deteriorate, and non-state armed groups continued to commit acts of violence. This included incidents of extrajudicial arrests and abuses against those suspected of supporting the Qadhafi forces during the war, with individuals being taken to bases run by former *thuwar* and/or militia groups.[138] Amnesty International documented dozens of cases, such as an incident where two Tebu men driving from Benghazi to Kufra were arrested and tortured by armed militia on 20 May.[139] In another incident, a former Qadhafi military officer was detained on 29 May after being caught in possession of prohibited material and severely beaten in a *thuwar* prison.[140]

The transitional authorities did begin making progress in bringing prisons and detention facilities under governmental control. In Benghazi a military prison holding some 380 individuals was transferred to the authority of the Ministry of Defense in early June.[141] The process was slow, however, and the dividing lines between the militia groups and the sanctioned government security forces were unclear. Unofficial armed groups carried out official duties, such as weapons registration, investigations and arrest, and security operations.[142] Armed groups, such as the 17 February Katiba, provided security services for government installations, including the U.S. consulate building in the city.[143] Due to the unclear divisions of authority, the attempts by the national authorities to reign in the militia factions were often met with resistance. For instance, on 4 June violence erupted between armed groups and the military after a young militia

---

[137] George Grant, *Benghazi local election results announced – woman candidate wins most votes UPDATE*, Libya Herald, May 21, 2012, *available at* http://www.libyaherald.com/benghazi-local-election-results-announced-2.

[138] Amnesty International, Libya Rule of Law or Rule of Militias?, *supra* note 100 at 16.

[139] Amnesty International, Libya Rule of law or Rule of Militias?, *supra* note 100 at 55. *See infra* Sec. 3.4.

[140] Amnesty International, Libya Rule of Law or Rule of Militias?, *supra* note 100 at 19. *See infra* Sec. 3.4.

[141] Amnesty International, Libya Rule of Law or Rule of Militias?, *supra* note 100 at 6.

[142] International Crisis Group, Holding Libya Together, *supra* note 20. For more on non-state armed actors in the post-conflict period, *see* Ch. V, Sec. 2.

[143] Max Fisher, *Libyan militia's failed security at Benghazi*, The Washington Post, Worldview, Nov. 2, 2012, *available at* http://www.washingtonpost.com/blogs/worldviews/wp/2012/11/02/libyan-militias-failed-security-at-benghazi.

member was killed at a checkpoint near Al-Gawarsha. Militia members responded to the killing by attacking a military police installation in in the Abu Dima district.[144] The incident was indicative of the ability of the non-state armed actors to directly challenge official government authority.

The lawless environment led to a series of attacks on government installations in early 2012, signaling serious concern over the deteriorating security situation and foreshadowing tragic events to come. On 22 May, a rocket propelled grenade hit offices in an International Committee of the Red Cross building, causing damage to the building but no casualties.[145] Less than a month later, on 6 June, a bomb exploded outside a building used by the U.S. Diplomatic Mission.[146] Initial reports indicated that the bombing was a response to the killing of Abu Yahya al-Libi, a Libyan-born cleric and senior Al-Qaʿida member who was killed two days prior in a U.S. drone strike in Pakistan. U.S. officials had announced al-Libi's death on 6 June, just hours before the bombing took place in Benghazi, but they quickly rejected allegations that the attack in Libya was connected to the U.S. drone operation. International security analysts disagreed, however, and considered it likely that the attack was carried out in response to al-Libi's killing.[147]

Other incidents of political violence continued to take place in Benghazi, and on 11 June two British bodyguards were wounded when attackers fired at a convoy meters away from the British consulate carrying the British Ambassador Dominic Asquith.[148] Later the same month, on 22 June, the high-profile military prosecutor, Jumaʿ ʿUbaydi al-Jazawi was shot and of killed as he left a mosque. Al-Jazawi had signed an order for the arrest of Yunis, leading to his abduction and killing after he was separated from

---

[144] *Libyan police clash with armed group in Benghazi*, AFP, June 5, 2012, *available at* http://www.moroccoworldnews.com/2012/06/43035/libyan-police-clash-with-armed-group-in-benghazi.

[145] Hadeel Al-Shalchi & Rosalind Russell, *Rocket damages Red Cross office in Libya's Benghazi*, REUTERS, May 22, 2012, *available at* http://www.reuters.com/article/2012/05/22/us-libya-redcross-bomb-idUSBRE84L0OB20120522.

[146] Mohammed al Tommy, *Bomb targets U.S. mission in Libya's Benghazi*, REUTERS, June 6, 2012, *available at* http://www.reuters.com/article/2012/06/06/us-libya-attack-us-idUSBRE8550GX20120606.

[147] *Id.* For more background on Abu Yahya al-Libi, *see* Ch. I, Sec. 10.1. & Ch. V, Sec. 5.

[148] Mohammed al Tommy, *British envoy's convoy ambushed in Libya, two wounded*, REUTERS, July 11, 2012, *available at* http://www.reuters.com/article/2012/06/11/us-libya-attack-britain-idUSBRE85A0TV20120611.

his bodyguards in Benghazi. Al-Jazawi had been suspected of collaborating in Yunis' killing because of his role in signing the arrest order.[149]

In addition to the ongoing attacks and assassinations, tensions continued to grow over the national elections scheduled for 7 July 2012. On 1 July, 300 armed protesters stormed the national election commission building and destroyed ballot boxes and computers. The protesters, reportedly favoring greater autonomy for the east, chanted pro-federalism slogans as they destroyed election material.[150] The day before the elections were scheduled to take place, two rockets hit Benghazi Medical Center.[151] A worker was also killed when a helicopter transferring election material was shot down just south of Benghazi.[152] On 7 July, more anti-election protesters took to the streets, storming polling stations and burning ballot papers in the public square.

Despite the unrest, voting continued in 94% of the national voting centers (1,453 out of 1,554).[153] On 12 July, it was reported that the National Forces Alliance (NFA) candidate, Prime Minister Mahmud Jibril, was leading the election race by a clear majority in Benghazi and Tripoli.[154] Election officials then carried out a recount in parts of Benghazi and reviewed

---

[149] Chris Stephen, *Libyan military prosecutor shot dead in Benghazi*, THE GUARDIAN, June 22, 2012, *available at* http://www.guardian.co.uk/world/2012/jun/22/libyan-military-prosecutor-shot-benghazi.

[150] *Libya protesters storm Benghazi voting office*, AL JAZEERA, July 1, 2012, *available at* http://www.aljazeera.com/news/africa/2012/07/20127118412233o197.html; Marie-Louise Gumuchian, *Protesters storm Libya election office in Benghazi*, REUTERS, July 1, 2012, *available at* http://www.reuters.com/article/2012/07/01/us-libya-elections-idUSBRE8600H520120701.

[151] Jay Deshmukh, *Violence mars eve of key Libya election*, AFP, July 6, 2012, *available at* http://reliefweb.int/report/libya/violence-mars-eve-key-libya-election; *Libya's Elections under Threat*, AFP, July 3, 2012, *available at* http://reliefweb.int/report/libya/libyas-elections-under-threat-enar.

[152] *Libya election helicopter 'shot near Benghazi'*, BBC, July 6, 2012, *available at* http://www.bbc.co.uk/news/world-africa-18740803.

[153] Luke Harding, *Libya elections: polling station raids mar first vote since Gaddafi's death*, THE GUARDIAN, June 7, 2012, *available at* http://www.guardian.co.uk/world/2012/jul/07/libya-elections-polling-raids-vote; Dominique Soguel, *Libyans in historic vote amid tensions in east*, AFP, July 8 2012, *available at* http://reliefweb.int/report/libya/libyans-historic-vote-amid-tensions-east; Hadeel Al Shalchi, *Discontent Rules in cradle of Libya Revolution*, REUTERS, July 7, 2012, *available at* http://www.reuters.com/article/2012/07/07/us-libya-elections-cradle-idUSBRE866oDS20120707; Mark John & Diana Abdallah, *Anti-poll protesters burn Libyan ballots in Benghazi*, REUTERS, July 7 , 2012 *available at* http://www.reuters.com/article/2012/07/07/us-libya-elections-protest-idUSBRE86604920120707.

[154] Mark John & Andrew Roche, *UPDATE 3 – Libya's Jibril in election landslide over Islamists*, REUTERS, July 12, 2012, *available at* http://www.reuters.com/article/2012/07/12/libya-elections-idUSL6E8ICDCU20120712.

appeals by candidates in the city before announcing the final results.[155] Official results were released on 17 July, declaring Mahmud Jibril's National Forces Alliance as the victorious party. The results were seen by some as a victory for secularists, as Jibril's party took more than double the number of seats of the Muslim Brotherhood's party.[156] The elections did not resolve the ongoing political disputes, however, and the security situation in Benghazi continued to deteriorate.

Targeted assassinations continued to take place in Benghazi, as the atmosphere of impunity allowed for old scores to be settled through violent means. On 28 July, Colonel Sulayman Buzraydah – a former Qadhafi military intelligence chief who had joined the rebels – was assassinated.[157] The following day, unidentified assailants attempted to assassinate the Commander of the Libyan ground forces, General Khalifa Haftar. The bomb was found in the basement of a popular hotel frequented by government officials, and defused before it exploded.[158] On 10 August, General Muhammad Hadya al-Fayturi, the Defense Ministry official responsible for arms and ammunition under Qadhafi, was shot and killed. He was one of the first generals to abandon the Qadhafi regime and support the revolution during its early stages.[159]

Poor security in the detention centers also allowed for high-profile prison escapes, such as the escape of Salam al-ʿUbaydi, accused of killing Yunis, on 1 August when armed men invaded the prison.[160] The same day, unknown assailants targeted the military intelligence headquarters in Benghazi, seriously damaging the building.[161]

The event that received the most international attention and scrutiny was the 11 September attack on the U.S. consulate in Benghazi that led

---

[155] *Benghazi votes to be recounted*, IRISH EXAMINER, July 15, 2012, *available at* http://www.irishexaminer.com/breakingnews/world/benghazi-votes-to-be-recounted-559185.html.

[156] Mary Casey & Jennifer Parker, Middle East Daily Brief, *Jibril's centrist party wins Libya's elections*, FOREIGN POLICY, July 18, 2012, *available at* http://mideast.foreignpolicy.com/posts/2012/07/18/jibril_s_centrist_party_takes_libya_s_elections. For more on elections in the post-conflict period, *see* Ch. V, Sec. 6.

[157] *Libyan Army General Escapes Assassination Attempt in Benghazi*, TRIPOLI POST, July 30, 2012, *available at* http://www.tripolipost.com/articledetail.asp?c=1&i=8911.

[158] *Id.*

[159] *Libyan General Haida killed in Benghazi shooting*, BBC, Aug. 10, 2012, *available at* http://www.bbc.co.uk/news/world-africa-19220027.

[160] *Alleged Killer of Abdel-Fattah Younis Escapes Jail and Blast Damages Military Building in Benghazi*, TRIPOLI POST, Aug. 1, 2012, *available at* http://www.tripolipost.com/articledetail.asp?c=1&i=8927.

[161] *Id.*

to the deaths of U.S. Ambassador to Libya Christopher Stevens and three other American officials. The details of the incident were initially unclear, and U.S. officials refrained from characterizing it as an organized terrorist attack. On 14 September, White House press secretary Jay Carney reported "we have no information to suggest that it was a pre-planned attack."[162]

However, more information emerged in the days and weeks following the incident indicating that it was indeed a planned terrorist operation. U.S. investigators and intelligence officials soon began focusing on the possible connection to Al-Qaʿida in the Islamic Maghreb (AQIM), and their potential links to the Benghazi-based Ansar al-Sharīʿa militia.[163] Survivors of the attack reported that it was well orchestrated and entailed multiple assaults. The assailants first focused on the main diplomatic facility, where Ambassador Stevens and computer technician Sean Smith reportedly died from smoke asphyxiation. They then proceeded to attack the compound half a mile away that was reportedly an annex to the main U.S. facility.[164]

The event sparked international alarm and renewed attention on the security situation in Libya. It also led to widespread condemnation and a backlash from local residents who rejected the presence of militia forces believed to be responsible for the attack. On 21 September, thousands of Libyans took to the streets in Benghazi calling for the disarmament of militia groups and seized control of several militia headquarters, including that of the Ansar al-Sharīʿa militia.[165] The demonstrators forced members of the militia to flee, as they set fires and pillaged weapons from the buildings.[166] The demonstrations, dubbed "Rescue Benghazi Day," were seen as a show of opposition to the armed militias and a call for the government to disband the groups.[167]

---

[162] *Were The Libya Attacks A Failure of the Obama Administration?*, ABC NEWS, Sept. 14, 2012, *available at* http://abcnews.go.com/Politics/video/libya-attacks-failure-obama-administration-17238467.

[163] Eric Schmitt et al., *Attack in Libya was Major Blow to CIA Efforts*, N.Y. TIMES, Sept. 23, 2012, *available at* http://www.nytimes.com/2012/09/24/world/africa/attack-in-libya-was-major-blow-to-cia-efforts.html?pagewanted=all.

[164] *Id.*

[165] Suliman Ali Zway & Kareem Fahim, *Libyan Protesters Besiege Militant Group in Benghazi*, N.Y. TIMES, Sept. 21, 2012, *available at* http://www.nytimes.com/2012/09/22/world/africa/pro-american-libyans-besiege-militant-group-in-benghazi.html.

[166] *Id.*

[167] Peter Graff & Suleiman Al Khalidi, *Benghazi Anti-Militia Protest: Libyan Protesters Drive Islamist Militia from Country's 2nd Largest City*, REUTERS, Sept. 22, 2011, *available at* http://www.huffingtonpost.com/2012/09/21/libya-militia-protests-benghazi_n_1905288.html.

In response to the attack on the U.S. consulate, Libya's interim government ordered the militias to disband and took further measures to assert control over the armed groups.[168] On 24 September, the military announced it would replace the chiefs of the Rafallah al-Sahati Katiba and the 17 February Katiba with official army commanders. Isma'il Sallabi, former leader of the 17 February Katiba and then-commander of the Raffallah al-Sahati militia, reported that he was in negotiations with the army about authority over his militia. Sallabi stated his agreement to the government's decision to put army officers in charge of the militias and tie them more closely to the official military.[169]

The new Libyan government also took steps to investigate past acts of violence and high-profile killings. On 31 October 2012, 'Abd al-Jalil was called for questioning over the killing of Yunis. Other individuals with links to the NTC were also charged in connection to the murder; the main suspects were 'Ali al-'Issawi, the NTC's interim deputy prime minister, who was accused of assisting in the abduction of Yunis, and Salam al-Mansuri, who was charged with carrying out the killing.[170]

Benghazi continued to experience instability in the face of major security challenges. Investigations into the attack on the U.S. consulate stalled as the judicial institutions remained paralyzed by the influence of non-state armed actors. There was a string of killings targeting police officials in Benghazi in October-November 2012 carried out in an apparent effort to disrupt investigative efforts in the region.[171] The ongoing violence raised concerns over the capacity of Benghazi's institutions, as well as the political will of local leaders to carry out basic security functions and effective justice measures in the post-conflict period.

---

[168] For more on the Benghazi attack and subsequent investigations into the incident, see Ch. V, Sec. 4.

[169] Richard Spencer, *US consulate attack in Benghazi 'disrupted major intelligence operation'*, THE TELEGRAPH, Sept. 24, 2012, *available at* http://www.telegraph.co.uk/news/worldnews/africaandindianocean/libya/9563831/US-consulate-attack-in-Benghazi-disrupted-major-intelligence-operation.html. *See also* Ch. V, Sec. 2.

[170] Ghaith Shennib, *Libyan wartime leader Jalil faces questioning over killing*, AL JAZEERA, Nov. 2, 2012, *available at* http://af.reuters.com/article/worldNews/idAFBRE8A61FP20121107.

[171] Steven Sotloff, *Libya's New Crisis: A Wave of Assassinations Targeting its Top Cops*, TIME WORLD, Nov. 26, 2012, *available at* http://world.time.com/2012/11/26/libyas-new-crisis-a-wave-of-assassinations-targeting-its-top-cops.

3. Illustrations of the Violations

3.1. *Excessive Use of Force*

(a) *Qadhafi Forces*

Evidence indicates that the security forces belonging to the Qadhafi regime engaged in excessive use of force against civilian protesters in Benghazi. Between 17 to 20 February, incidents of excessive use of force against protesters by regime forces were reported near the Juliana Bridge[172] and the al-Fadil bin ʿUmar military barracks.[173] Hundreds of protesters suffered injuries,[174] and the CoI reported at least 100 killings.[175] Protesters were shot at with live ammunition including possibly high-velocity rifles and RPGs.[176]

Based on testimony from on duty medical personnel, along with medical records and photographs, the CoI confirmed that the killings and injuries sustained by protesters demonstrate that the Qadhafi regime used excessive force in an effort to put an end to the demonstrations. Additionally, the ICC found that "a State policy was designed at the highest level of the Libyan State machinery and aimed at deterring and quelling, by any means, including by the use of lethal force, the demonstrations of civilians against the regime."[177]

According to evidence reviewed by the CoI, including testimonies from senior military officers, the regime's initial response was to "crush" the demonstrators through the use of heavy force.[178] A high-level military commander in the Qadhafi regime provided testimony that Qadhafi had given orders to suppress the protests using "all means necessary." The

---

[172] Report of the International Commission of Inquiry, advanced unedited version (Mar. 2, 2012), *supra* note 36 at ¶ 17.

[173] *Battle at army base broke Gadhafi hold in Benghazi*, THE WASHINGTON POST, Feb. 25, 2011, *available at* http://www.washingtonpost.com/wp-dyn/content/article/2011/02/25/AR2011022505021.html.

[174] Report of the International Commission of Inquiry, advanced unedited version (Mar. 2, 2012), *supra* note 36 at Annex I, ¶ 112.

[175] Report of the International Commission of Inquiry (Jan. 12, 2012), *supra* note 22 at ¶ 76.

[176] *Libya forces 'open fire' at funeral*, AL JAZEERA, Feb. 19, 2011, *available at* http://www.aljazeera.com/news/africa/2011/02/201121981665897.html.

[177] *Situation in the Libyan Arab Jamahiriya*, Case No. ICC-01/11, Warrant of Arrest for Abdullah Al-Senussi, (Int'l Crim. Ct., June 27, 2011) [hereinafter "ICC, Al-Senussi Arrest Warrant"].

[178] Report of the International Commission of Inquiry, advance unedited version (Mar. 2, 2012), *supra* note 36 at Annex I, ¶ 110.

same official stated that in the early days of the uprising, commanders were ordered to keep protesters from reaching the military camps, and only began using living ammunition after the protesters acquired arms. This version of events was disputed by the CoI, however, which found that based on the death tolls and injuries logged by hospitals in Benghazi, the use of live ammunition began before protesters took up arms.[179]

The CoI gathered substantial accounts from security officials, medical personnel and witnesses indicating that Qadhafi forces used excessive force against civilian demonstrators. A former soldier told the CoI that he was among a contingent of 250 soldiers deployed by the regime to "contain demonstrators" in Benghazi on 17 February 2011. In addition to witness statements, the CoI also reviewed interrogation records provided by the Benghazi General Prosecutor's Office, which confirm that superior officers commanded members of the security forces to use force against protesters.[180]

Medical personnel provided information on the injuries sustained by demonstrators, which showed they were the result of extreme acts of violence perpetrated by the Qadhafi security forces. The numbers themselves indicate disproportionate use of force. A doctor from Hawari Hospital confirmed that he counted 64 wounded brought to the hospital on 18 February, and 89 people the following day.[181] The CoI reviewed medical records confirming the number of injuries reportedly treated by medics after the 17 February protests.[182]

In addition to the numbers of injuries and casualties, the types of injuries sustained by protesters indicate the regime used weaponry unnecessarily against unarmed protesters. The same doctor from Hawari Hospital provided photographs showing bodies that had "literally been blown in two, consistent with the use of higher caliber weapons."[183] Medical officials gave public statements confirming that between 17 and 21 February, injured civilians were brought to various facilities with injuries to the head, chest and abdomen from bullet injuries from high-velocity rifles and rocket propelled grenades.[184] The injuries to protesters

---

[179] *Id.* at Annex I, ¶ 111.

[180] Report of the International Commission of Inquiry (Jan. 12, 2012), *supra* note 22 at ¶ 87.

[181] Report of the International Commission of Inquiry, advance unedited version (Mar. 2, 2012), *supra* note 36 at Annex I, ¶ 112.

[182] *Id.* at Annex I, ¶ 113.

[183] *Id.* at Annex I, ¶ 112 (internal citations omitted).

[184] AL JAZEERA, *Libya forces 'open fire' at funeral, supra* note 42.

showed a pattern of gunshot wounds to the head, neck and shoulders of the deceased and survivors.[185] Moreover, the fact that many of these injuries and deaths occurred on 17 and 18 February, indicates that the Qadhafi security forces used excessive force against civilians before protesters attempted to break into the Al-Fadil bin 'Umar military barracks.[186]

3.2. *Unlawful Killing*

(a) *Qadhafi Forces*

Sufficient documentation exists providing evidence of unlawful killings of protesters carried out by Qadhafi forces in Benghazi in February 2011. The first such death was reported on 15 February, when Qadhafi security forces killed a protester as they attempted to disperse a peaceful crowd using tear gas and batons.[187] Over the following days, the actions of the Qadhafi forces led to a number of casualties. Human rights organizations documented 20 protesters killed in Benghazi on 17 February, another 20 on 19 February, and 60 more on 20 February.[188] Hospital records of those either wounded or killed reveal that there were "77 victims from Al-Jalac' Hospital in Benghazi; 43 death certificates issued by the department of forensic pathology in Benghazi, and lists and death certificates of 58 in Bayda."[189]

The ICC determined that while the Qadhafi regime's efforts to cover-up evidence made it difficult to ascertain the exact number of casualties, it found "reasonable grounds to believe that, as of 15 February 2011 and within a period of less than two weeks in February 2011, the Security Forces killed and injured as well as arrested and imprisoned hundreds of civilians."[190]

---

[185] Human Rights Watch, *Libya: Governments Should Demand End to Unlawful Killings, supra* note 50.

[186] Protesters had returned with a bulldozer to Al-Fadil bin 'Umar military barracks on Feb. 19, following clashes between them and Qadhafi forces at the barracks the previous day. During the Feb. 18 clashes, protesters had used rocks but were met with gunfire. *See* Report of the International Commission of Inquiry, advance unedited version (Mar. 2, 2012), *supra* note 36 at Annex I, ¶ 115.

[187] Human Rights Watch, *Libya: Arrests, Assaults in Advance of Planned Protests, supra* note 26.

[188] Human Rights Watch, *Libya: Security Forces Kill 84 Over Three Days, supra* note 34; Amnesty International, *Libyan leader must end spiralling killings, supra* note 39; Human Rights Watch, *Libya: Governments Should Demand End to Unlawful Killings, supra* note 50.

[189] Report of the International Commission of Inquiry, advance unedited version (Mar. 2, 2012), *supra* note 36 at Annex I, ¶ 112, n. 128.

[190] ICC, *Al-Senussi Arrest Warrant, supra* note 177.

Information also strongly suggests that the Qadhafi forces killed soldiers who refused to fire on protesters in the early days of the demonstrations. Upon entering the Al-Fadil bin 'Umar barracks, protesters described finding burned bodies of people who had been killed. Severely burnt bodies from the barracks subsequently arrived at Al-Jala' morgue, several of which were believed to be those of soldiers who refused to kill protesters.[191] A doctor told the CoI that on 21 February he had visited the Al-Fadil bin 'Umar barracks, where nine burnt bodies had been found in an underground cell. He noted that their wrists had been cuffed behind their backs and they had gunshot wounds to the head. He believed that they had been burnt postmortem.[192] Other reports corroborate these findings, including accounts indicating that at least 11 soldiers were killed for refusing to fire on protesters.[193] Some of the soldiers' bodies were later found severely mutilated.[194]

The Benghazi Medical Center noted that 90 percent of the casualties it received were a result of gunshot wounds to the upper body, particularly to the head and chest.[195] The CoI found that the nature of injuries recorded in Benghazi indicated a "clear intention to kill" and that the level of violence suggested a "central policy of violent repression."[196]

The indiscriminate use of live ammunition against protesters, combined with the intention to kill and the resulting deaths of dozens of protesters, indicates that Qadhafi forces were responsible for unlawful killing in Benghazi during the protest phase of the 2011 war.

(b) Thuwar *Forces*

Evidence indicates that members of the *thuwar* forces carried out unlawful killings in Benghazi of individuals suspected of belonging to the Qadhafi forces as well as perceived regime loyalists. Amnesty International

---

[191] Schemm, *Battle at army base broke Gadhafi hold in Benghazi, supra* note 36.

[192] Report of the International Commission of Inquiry, advance unedited version (Mar. 2, 2012), *supra* note 36 at Annex I, ¶ 112.

[193] Jon Leyne, *Libya protests: Gaddafi regime shaken by unrest,* BBC, Feb. 21, 2011, *available at* http://www.bbc.co.uk/news/world-middle-east-12523669.

[194] Mark Tran et al., *Libya uprising – live updates,* THE GUARDIAN, Feb. 21, 2011, *available at* http://www.guardian.co.uk/world/blog/2011/feb/21/arab-and-middle-east-protests-middleeast.

[195] Report of the International Commission of Inquiry (Jan. 12, 2012), *supra* note 22 at ¶ 76.

[196] Report of the International Commission of Inquiry, advance unedited version (Mar. 2, 2012), *supra* note 36 at Annex I, ¶ 130.

found that between April and July 2011, at least 12 killings of suspected Qadhafi loyalists or members of the regime forces were carried out by opposition supporters.[197] In one case a former member of the ISA who had defected was found dead with his hands and feet bound. He had been shot in the head and a note was found next his body that read, "A dog among Gaddafi's dogs has been eliminated."[198] Another body of a former ISA member was found in a similar condition. He had been shot twice in the head and appeared to have been kneeling when he was shot.[199] A third body was found, also of a former ISA member, after he had been abducted. His body was found with a bullet wound to the head and other injuries to his head and hands.[200]

i. *Sub-Saharan Africans*
Thuwar forces and opposition supporters also targeted Sub-Saharan Africans, including migrant workers, based on their perceived support for the Qadhafi regime. The CoI, media and NGOs documented unlawful killings of foreign workers and residents of Benghazi.

In some instances men were accused of serving as mercenaries based on their race and foreign origin. Amnesty International reported several cases where, according to medical records, some were beaten to death, others were shot and killed after surrendering, while at least three were hanged.[201] Two bodies of Sub-Saharan African men were found near Benghazi on 23 and 24 of April. One had his throat slit and his ankles bound with rope, while the other had been shot in the head and had multiple contusions indicating that he had been beaten.[202]

Health workers in the town of Al-Sallum discussed an incident of four Chadian nationals with gunshot wounds who reported they were accused of being mercenaries and attacked in Benghazi.[203] Health workers also relayed an incident in which another Chadian migrant reported that

---

[197] Amnesty International, Battle for Libya, *supra* note 64 at 17.

[198] Donatella Rovera, Live Wire, *Revenge killings and reckless firing in opposition-held eastern Libya*, Amnesty International, May 11, 2011, *available at* http://livewire.amnesty .org/2011/05/13/revenge-killings-and-reckless-firing-in-opposition-held-eastern-libya.

[199] *Id.*

[200] *Id.*

[201] Amnesty International, Battle for Libya, *supra* note 64 at 17. *See infra* Sec. 3.10.

[202] *See also* Amnesty International, Battle for Libya, *supra* note 64 at 71. This incident also constitutes torture. *See infra* Sec. 3.4.

[203] Report of the International Commission of Inquiry (Jan. 12, 2012), *supra* note 22 at ¶ 197.

armed civilians detained his brother and two colleagues by force, before "slaughter[ing]" them.[204] In another case, five Chadian nationals, reportedly detained due to their nationality, were brought to the military barracks in Benghazi where, on 21 February, they were killed by burning. Dozens of armed men in military uniform as well as civilian clothing used kerosene to ignite the bodies.[205]

3.3. *Arbitrary Detentions and Enforced Disappearances*

(a) *Qadhafi Forces*

Activists, protesters and writers were detained based solely on their political activities or for their involvement preparing for the "Day of Rage" on 17 February 2011. The ISA arrested at least 14 people as protests began.[206] Anti-Qadhafi protesters and youths reportedly went missing on the evening of 20 February, during the clashes around Al-Fadil bin 'Umar military barracks. Amnesty International documented the cases of nine men disappeared, including four teenagers under 18. The missing persons were believed to have been arrested by members of the Katiba unit from the military barracks or by members of other security units.[207] The Libyan Red Crescent Society in Benghazi recorded 370 cases of missing persons from Al-Bayda and Benghazi.[208]

Amnesty International reported that as regime forces retreated from Benghazi, they targeted individuals for forced disappearance on the basis of their anti-regime views.[209] Qadhafi forces also targeted medical personnel, at least 14 of whom were disappeared from hospitals in Benghazi, Tripoli and Zawiyya.[210]

---

[204] *Id.*

[205] Report of the International Commission of Inquiry (Jan. 12, 2012), *supra* note 22 at ¶ 196.

[206] Human Rights Watch, *Libya: Arrests, Assaults in Advance of Planned Protests*, *supra* note 26.

[207] *Libya: detainees, disappeared and missing*, Amnesty International, Mar. 29, 2011, *available at* http://www.amnesty.org/en/library/asset/MDE19/011/2011/en/5a97c7df-aee8-4830-9f2b-d54f805d2dc1/mde190112011en.html.

[208] Report of the International Commission of Inquiry (Jan. 12, 2012), *supra* note 22 at ¶ 99. *See also Libya: At Least 370 Missing From Country's East: Fate of Libyans in Government Custody Unknown*, Human Rights Watch, Mar. 30, 2011, *available at* http://www.hrw.org/en/news/2011/03/30/libya-least-370-missing-countrys-east.

[209] Amnesty International, Battle for Libya, *supra* note 64 at 58. For more on arbitrary arrests and enforced disappearances, *see* Ch. IV, Sec. 2.

[210] Report of the International Commission of Inquiry (Jan. 12, 2012), *supra* note 22 at ¶ 106.

According to the Missing Persons Office in Benghazi, those missing from Benghazi totaled 1,300 individuals. Some of those taken by the Qadhafi forces were released after *thuwar* groups took over other cities and detention facilities. For example, in August 2011, 354 persons who had been detained returned to Benghazi after Qadhafi forces left Tripoli.[211] The CoI estimated that the number of those from Benghazi who remained missing was still 946 individuals.[212]

(b) Thuwar *Forces*

In the wake of the retreat of Qadhafi troops from Benghazi, the *thuwar* forces carried out dozens of arrests of civilians suspected of supporting the regime. HRW found that as of 28 May 2011, rebel forces had detained roughly 330 civilians and combatants, of which 118 were detained in Benghazi. Not all of the detainees were from Benghazi, but rather were captured in other towns in eastern Libya and transferred to Benghazi after interrogation. Several of the detainees reported physical abuse after being captured and none were provided access to a lawyer or the opportunity to challenge their detention before an independent judicial authority.[213]

The NTC allowed for volunteer security forces to arrest criminal suspects in eastern Libya, sometimes using excessive force, and delivering them to detention facilities run by opposition authorities. Armed non-state groups proliferated after the retreat of Qadhafi's forces and the dissolution of police forces in the east.[214] Several of the facilities were created after the NTC took control of Benghazi in February 2011 and many held prisoners for months without trial. Furthermore, the investigations and hearings were led by local committees and individuals, some of whom had little or no legal expertise or knowledge of human rights law and judicial standards.[215]

Arbitrary detentions continued to be a problem into the post-conflict period. Persons were taken to unofficial detention centers in Benghazi

---

[211] Report of the International Commission of Inquiry, advance unedited version (Mar. 2, 2012), *supra* note 36 at Annex I, ¶ 278.

[212] *Id.* at Annex I, ¶ 273.

[213] HUMAN RIGHTS WATCH, *Libya: Opposition Arbitrarily Detaining Suspected Gaddafi Loyalists, supra* note 72.

[214] *Id.*

[215] AMNESTY INTERNATIONAL, DETENTION ABUSES STAINING THE NEW LIBYA (Oct. 2011), *available at* http://www.amnesty.org/en/library/asset/MDE19/036/2011/en/e1c30d0f-8ec3-4368-8537-03f1bb15a051/mde19036201en.pdf.

where they were held for extended periods without charge.[216] In one illustrative incident in April 2012, armed men in civilian and army clothing arrested a man, beat him with rifle butts, punched him in the ear and detained him at their base.[217] In May and June 2012, Amnesty International visited four detention facilities including the Ganfuda detention center in Benghazi.[218] It was reported at the time that these facilities were holding around 1,680 people in total.[219]

i. *Sub-Saharan Africans*

On 23 March 2011, journalists and NGO representatives visited a detention facility in Benghazi where Sub-Saharan Africans were lined up for reporters while the guard explained that they were captured mercenaries. During the presentation, one of the detainees exclaimed his innocence, stating that he was a foreign worker, not a fighter. He stated that he had been taken from his home, arbitrarily detained, and that his wife had been raped. An opposition official produced two Gambian passports and indicated that the passports proved the man was guilty of fighting for the Qadhafi regime.[220]

At Ganfuda detention center, Amnesty International spoke to a 20-year-old Somali national. He stated that he had been robbed and taken to a militia-controlled detention center in Kufra in January 2012. He was beaten with rifle butts, metal sticks and water pipes. He was fed only once a day and had no access to medical care. The man was later transferred to Ganfuda detention center in Benghazi where this harsh treatment continued. The man stated that he was targeted due to his foreign origin and that other Somalis and Sub-Saharans were enduring the same harsh treatment.[221]

---

[216] Report of the International Commission of Inquiry, advance unedited version (Mar. 2, 2012), *supra* note 36 at Annex I, ¶ 106 (internal citations omitted).

[217] AMNESTY INTERNATIONAL, LIBYA RULE OF LAW OR RULE OF MILITIAS?, *supra* note 100 at 16.

[218] Other facilities included Tawaysha (Tripoli), Bu Rashada (Al-Gharyan), and Kufra detention center. Amnesty International could not determine the number of people who were detained for migration related violations because there seemed to be frequent arrests, transfers and deportations. *See* AMNESTY INTERNATIONAL, LIBYA RULE OF LAW OR RULE OF MILITIAS?, *supra* note 100 at 36.

[219] *See Id.*

[220] Luis Sinco, *Journalists visit prisoners held by rebels in Libya*, L.A. TIMES, Mar. 23, 2011, *available at* http://framework.latimes.com/2011/03/23/journalists-visit-prisoners-held-by-rebels-in-libya/#/0; David Zucchino, *Libyan rebels appear to take leaf from Kadafi's playbook*, L.A. TIMES, Mar. 24, 2011, *available at* http://articles.latimes.com/2011/mar/24/world/la-fg-libya-prisoners-20110324.

[221] In the same Amnesty International Report, they explain that an official from the Ganfuda prison told them that they generally try to find work for those they perceive to

Other foreign nationals detained at Ganfuda included Eritreans who were not given a chance to apply for asylum or the opportunity to challenge the legality of their detention.[222] Amnesty International also reported that the detention of migrants was becoming a business, according to a high level official who was interviewed in Benghazi, as many detainees were performing manual labor tasks for their jailers.[223]

3.4. *Torture and Other Forms of Ill-treatment*

(a) *Qadhafi Forces*

In the early days of the uprising, the Qadhafi forces tortured prisoners in an effort to deter the growing opposition movement. In one demonstrative case of torture in Benghazi, a man told the CoI that members of the ISA and other security bodies had detained him in Benghazi on 17 February 2011. The CoI described one such incident as follows:

> At that point, he and the other 26 persons arrested were all beaten by security personnel [who used clubs and rifles]. About 15 minutes after the beating finished, the group [was] transported to ISA premises in Sidi Jaber, in central Benghazi, where they were tortured with electricity shocks on their sexual organs. The man also reported seeing ISA forcibly removing the nails and teeth of another detainee.[224]

(b) Thuwar *Forces*

After the opposition authorities took control of the detention centers in and around Benghazi, reports surfaced of torture carried out by rebel forces against captured prisoners. The CoI found that a number of individuals were tortured and abused by members of the *thuwar* in Benghazi.[225]

Thuwar forces specifically targeted suspected Qadhafi loyalists and former members of the most notoriously repressive security forces. This took place most notably between April and early July 2011, when the rebel groups were consolidating their control over the security apparatus in the east of

---

be "good Somali Muslims" provided they have a valid passport, do not have any contagious diseases and their embassies can vouch for them. AMNESTY INTERNATIONAL, LIBYA RULE OF LAW OR RULE OF MILITIAS?, *supra* note 100 at 44.

[222] *Id.*

[223] *Id.* at 41.

[224] Report of the International Commission of Inquiry (Jan. 12, 2012), *supra* note 22 at ¶ 114. For more on the practice of torture and ill-treatment, *see* Ch. IV, Sec. 2.

[225] Report of the International Commission of Inquiry, advance unedited version (Mar. 2, 2012), *supra* note 36 at Annex I, ¶ 348.

the country.[226] In one case, a former Qadhafi military officer was detained by *thuwar* groups on 29 May 2012, beaten and subsequently held in solitary confinement for 30 days.[227] Amnesty International further reported on another detainee in solitary confinement with scars on his face who refused to talk out of fear of further beatings.[228] Detainees were interrogated at the 17 February Katiba camp in Benghazi, some held incommunicado and forced to sign false confessions after being tortured.[229]

i. *Sub-Saharan Africans*

Several cases of torture of migrants were reported in Benghazi including cases of public lynching that took place in February 2011.[230] Other incidents involved persons being subjected to attacks and abuse in their homes. In a statement to Amnesty International, one migrant recalled that *thuwar* forces came to his home and beat him before taking him to a courthouse located in Benghazi. His testimony relates that

> There were 40 to 50 people in the court's hall, mostly from Chad, Sudan and Nigeria. People would beat us all over the body with the end and the butt of their guns. They would take one person after another inside the rooms. I could hear the screaming of the people inside and I could see marks on their body after they came out; I believe they were being tortured. A Chadian national was shot in the shoulder; he was bleeding and had no medical help. The people around me would tell me to forget about my life, that we were dead. After six or seven hours my employer came to the court to confirm that I was not a mercenary. I was released.[231]

In another case, a Darfuri refugee in Benghazi stated that opposition forces specifically targeted black men, and that neighbors brought him and his family food because he feared leaving his home. He related that on 17 March 2011, three or four armed opposition soldiers entered his house and hit him on the face with the end of their guns, took his money, passport and mobile phone.[232]

---

[226] Amnesty International, Battle for Libya, *supra* note 64 at 58–59.
[227] Amnesty International, Libya Rule of Law or Rule of Militias?, *supra* note 100 at 19.
[228] *Id.*
[229] *Id.* at 31.
[230] *See supra* Sec. 3.2.
[231] Amnesty International, Europe: Now it is Your Time to Act 5 (Sept. 2011), *available at* http://www.amnesty.org/en/library/asset/MDE03/002/2011/en/dc59ca51-da8a-4c37-a30a-56daaf33f57f/mde030022011en.pdf.
[232] *Id.*

Video footage of torture and executions of Sub-Saharan migrants was uploaded to the Internet and disseminated to media outlets. The videos show interrogations and the beheadings of blindfolded detainees in Benghazi, including in hospitals. In July 2011, further videos were posted online showing the lynching of a young black man in Benghazi while being tortured by a second man with a blade. The video showed that the man's feet were bound and that he was hanging from bars in an exposed position before the second man started cutting the victim and stabbing him in the neck.[233]

ii. *The Tebu*

Two Tebu men were detained on 20 May 2012 while driving from Benghazi to Kufra. Their hands were tied with a plastic strip and they were blindfolded. At the military base they were beaten with sticks and metal bars. After hours of torture, the plastic strip was removed and they were bound with metal handcuffs. They were left tied-up with no food or water and were not permitted to go to the toilet. The next morning they were beaten on their backs with electric cables.[234]

iii. *The Tawerghans*

A Tawerghan man provided testimony of his account of being forced to sign a confession that he fought alongside the Qadhafi forces in Misrata. He was detained in March 2011, beaten with belts and threatened with death before he signed the false confession.[235]

3.5. *Denial of Access to Medical Treatment*

(a) *Qadhafi Forces*

The Qadhafi forces engaged in deliberate acts that were designed to prevent injured protesters from receiving medical treatment. A witness from Benghazi who had been shot on 17 February 2011, reported hearing military officials argue over delivering medical care to prisoners. The witness stated:

> I could hear the crowd around me say this one is still alive, I heard another reply don't touch anyone. Someone said to put me in the dumpster. I could

---

[233] *Lynching in Bengasi*, HUMAN RIGHTS INVESTIGATIONS, July 17, 2011, *available at* http://www.humanrightsinvestigations.org/2011/07/17/lynching-in-benghazi.

[234] AMNESTY INTERNATIONAL, LIBYA RULE OF LAW OR RULE OF MILITIAS?, *supra* note 100 at 55.

[235] *Id.* at 29.

hear a quarrel among them. One said: one is still alive, another said I will take him for medical help in the ambulance, another replied no, another replied I will take him in my personal car so the one who said no told them to disarm and take off their military uniform. They put me in the back seat and took me out of the military camp from the back gate and handed me to the Benghazi Medical Centre.[236]

There were several reports of attacks carried out by Qadhafi forces on wounded persons and of abductions from hospitals. In one incident, a witness from Benghazi reported that in the early days of the protests, a worker at Al-Jala' Hospital let armed men through the back door, allowing them to take away injured demonstrators. At another hospital, a nurse reported armed men in "military or police" uniform entered the hospital on 17 February and took away three patients who had been injured during the protests earlier that day.[237]

3.6. *Freedom of Expression*

(a) *Qadhafi Forces*

In early February 2011, Qadhafi forces and loyalists were accused of targeting journalists in Benghazi in order to subdue the opposition. Throughout the 2011 conflict a number of journalists were killed. The first documented killing of a journalist during the war took place on 12 March 2011, when a cameraman working for Al-Jazeera named Ali Hassan al-Jaber was shot and killed during an ambush on the outskirts of Benghazi.[238] Al-Jaber, who along with his colleague had been conducting interviews with demonstrators, was hit by three bullets, one of which passed through his heart. He was rushed to hospital, but did not survive. Al Jazeera's director-general, Wadah Khanfar, claimed that the ambush directly followed "an unprecedented campaign" against the network by Qadhafi.[239]

On 8 March 2011, three BBC employees were detained overnight before being released the next day.[240] In another case, five Libyan journalists who

---

[236] Report of the International Commission of Inquiry (Jan. 12, 2012), *supra* note 22 at ¶ 123.

[237] *Id.* at ¶ 126 (internal citations omitted).

[238] *Id.* at ¶ 138.

[239] *Al Jazeera staffer killed in Libya*, AL JAZEERA, Mar. 12, 2011, *available at* http://www .aljazeera.com/news/africa/2011/03/2011312192359523376.html.

[240] *Journalists under attack in Libya: The tally*, COMMITTEE TO PROTECT JOURNALISTS, May 20, 2011, *available at* http://www.cpj.org/blog/2011/05/journalists-under-attack-in-libya.php.

had been arrested in mid-February 2011 were reported missing in early March. The journalists had been critical of the Qadhafi regime and were detained in Benghazi during the protests.[241] One of the missing reporters, 'Atif al-Atrash, disappeared after speaking to Al Jazeera on air on 17 February. The following journalists also went missing: Muhammad al-Sahim, a blogger and political writer who published an article criticizing the regime shortly before 17 February; Muhammad al-Amin, a cartoonist; blogger Jalal al-Kawafi; and Idris al-Mismar, a writer and the former editor-in-chief of *Arajin*, a monthly culture magazine.[242]

3.7. *Attacks on Civilians, Civilian Objects, Protected Persons and Objects*

(a) *Qadhafi Forces*

Significant evidence indicates that Qadhafi regime forces systematically targeted civilians in Benghazi. As indicated above, regime units and plainclothes police officers targeted demonstrators on 15 and 16 February, using live ammunition to disperse crowds. Security forces again used live ammunition and artillery on 17 February in response to the growing protests. Hundreds of civilians were killed between 18 and 20 February when violent clashes broke out between protesters and security forces outside Al-Fadil bin 'Umar military barracks.[243] The executions of government soldiers by commanding officers for refusing to follow orders also exhibits unwarranted violence by Qadhafi forces against individuals' right to life.

(b) Thuwar *Forces*

The cases of opposition forces targeting suspected civilian loyalists for reprisal violence constituted attacks against protected persons.[244] There is also evidence of opposition supporters targeting civilians and civilian objects. As noted above, in the early days of the conflict in Benghazi, demonstrators attacked various government buildings and symbols of the regime. After taking control of Benghazi, the opposition forces attacked

---

[241] *Libya: Free Detained Journalists*, HUMAN RIGHTS WATCH, Mar. 24, 2011, *available at* http://www.hrw.org/news/2011/03/23/libya-free-detained-journalists.

[242] COMMITTEE TO PROTECT JOURNALISTS, *Journalists under attack in Libya: The tally*, *supra* note 240.

[243] For details on the killing of soldiers for insubordination, *see supra* Sec. 2.3.2.

[244] *See id. See also* AMNESTY INTERNATIONAL, BATTLE FOR LIBYA, *supra* note 64 at 9.

migrant workers, killing, detaining and torturing several in reprisal for their alleged collaboration with the Qadhafi government.[245]

3.8. *Prohibited Weapons*

(a) *Qadhafi Forces*

Substantial reports detailed the use of weapons prohibited under international law by Qadhafi forces in and around Benghazi. Doctors in Benghazi reported treating wounds "whose cause my be consistent with the use of 'expanding' bullets."[246] There were also documented cases of the use of landmines by the Qadhafi forces. The CoI noted that international law requires particular care be taken to reduce the indiscriminate effects of landmines to a minimum.[247] Evidence suggests, however, that this care was not taken by the Qadhafi regime. Multiple sources indicate that anti-tank mines that had been acquired by the Qadhafi regime were made largely out of hard-to-detect plastic.[248] Human Rights Watch reported that during the retreat of Qadhafi forces from Benghazi on 19 March 2011, anti-vehicle mines of this type were left behind in the area around Ghar Yunis University in Benghazi. At this time a United Nations de-mining expert reported the discovery of 12 warehouses storing tens of thousands of anti-vehicle mines.[249] A UN Mine Action Service investigator also documented similar discoveries at the Hight Ramza depot in Benghazi, including plastic anti-vehicle mines, napalm, anti-aircraft guns and plastic explosives.[250]

3.9. *Mercenaries*

(a) *Qadhafi Forces*

The CoI received reports of foreigners providing support for the Qadhafi forces in eastern Libya that

---

[245] For more the law of attacks on civilians, civilian objects, protected persons and objects carried out during the conflict, *see* Ch. IV, Sec. 2.

[246] Report of the International Commission of Inquiry (Jan. 12, 2012), *supra* note 22 at ¶ 174 (internal citations omitted).

[247] *Id.* at n. 144.

[248] *Id.* at ¶ 176.

[249] *Id.*

[250] *Libya: Abandoned Weapons, Landmines Endanger Civilians*, HUMAN RIGHTS WATCH, Apr. 5, 2011, *available at* http://www.hrw.org/news/2011/04/05/libya-abandoned-weapons-landmines-endanger-civilians-0.

In Benghazi, the Commission was provided documents by the Office of the Prosecutor containing some transcripts of interrogations of alleged mercenaries who had not yet been brought to trial. According to the transcripts of interviews with one individual of Libyan nationality, 'mercenaries' were used as snipers firing at demonstrators on 17 February. The transcript of another individual, a Nigerian-born Libyan disclosed that he was a member of Khamis Katiba, and was transported on 2 March to Ras Lanuf military base. He stated that a military officer provided him with a military uniform as well as a rocket-propelled grenade weapon. Documents collected by the Prosecutor's Office from those questioned concerning involvement in events included some 24 photocopies of passports from four sub-Saharan countries.[251]

There were numerous media accounts in February 2011 of mercenaries being used by the Qadhafi regime in Benghazi to intimidate and attack protesters. Many of the black Africans who had been detained by opposition forces, however, maintained that they had been brought to Libya under false pretenses, and some stated that they were in fact there merely to demonstrate in support of the regime and not to fight against the opposition.[252]

3.10. *Targeting Specific Groups*

(b) Thuwar *Forces*

i. *Sub-Saharan Africans*

After the opposition took control of Benghazi on 19 February 2011, foreigners, especially dark-skinned Africans, were targeted for their perceived support of the Qadhafi regime. Many were accused on the basis of their race or foreign origin of being mercenaries and subject to torture, and in extreme cases, public hangings.[253] There were numerous accounts of attacks and unlawful killings of foreign workers and Sub-Saharan Africans in Benghazi.[254] In some cases, merely presenting the "wrong" passport

---

[251] Report of the International Commission of Inquiry (Jan. 12, 2012), *supra* note 22 at ¶ 174.

[252] Nick Meo, *African mercenaries in Libya nervously await their fate*, THE TELEGRAPH, Feb. 27, 2011, *available at* http://www.telegraph.co.uk/news/worldnews/africaandindian-ocean/libya/8349414/African-mercenaries-in-Libya-nervously-await-their-fate.html.

[253] AMNESTY INTERNATIONAL, BATTLE FOR LIBYA, *supra* note 64 at 71.

[254] *See supra* Secs. 2.3.2, 2.3.3 & 2.3.4.

resulted in incarceration.[255] Migrants reported being robbed by *thuwar*,[256] while others suffered from ill-treatment in detention.[257]

ii. *The Tawerghans*

Tawerghans in Internally Displaced Persons (IDP) camps in Benghazi were vulnerable to attack by *thuwar* groups from Misrata.[258] After *thuwar* from Misrata pursued Tawerghans for attack in the Al-Jufra district, however, *thuwar* leaders from Benghazi intervened and moved the Tawerghan community to camps in Benghazi, namely to Al-Halis and Sidi Faraj, providing safeguard along the way.[259] The Tawerghan Council reported that as of January 2012, there were an estimated 12,000 Tawerghans displaced to Benghazi, along with 4,000 Tawerghans displaced to Al-Bayda, Ajdabiya, Sabha and Tobruq in the east.[260] The Tawerghan Council also reported that the *thuwar* in Benghazi had intervened numerous times to stop attacks by the Misrata *thuwar* on IDP camps in both Benghazi and Ajdabiya.[261]

iii. *The Tebu*

The opposition forces continued to target other groups in Benghazi when they splintered into non-state armed militias after the fall of the Qadhafi regime. Amnesty International documented an exemplary incident occurring on 20 May 2012, in which two Tebu men were arrested and tortured by armed militia.[262]

---

[255] Sinco, *Journalists visit prisoners held by rebels in Libya*, supra note 220. *See also* Zucchino, *Libyan rebels appear to take leaf from Kadafi's playbook*, supra note 220.

[256] AMNESTY INTERNATIONAL, EUROPE, NOW IT IS YOUR TIME TO ACT, supra note 231 at 5.

[257] AMNESTY INTERNATIONAL, LIBYA RULE OF LAW OR RULE OF MILITIAS?, supra note 100 at 42.

[258] For more on targeting of Tawerghans by *thuwar* from Misrata in IDP camps during the post-conflict period, *see infra*, Secs. 5 & 9.

[259] Report of the International Commission of Inquiry, advance unedited version (Mar. 2, 2012), *supra* note 36 at Annex I, ¶ 439.

[260] *Id.* at Annex I, ¶ 440.

[261] *Id.* at Annex I, ¶ 441.

[262] AMNESTY INTERNATIONAL, LIBYA RULE OF LAW OR RULE OF MILITIAS?, supra note 100 at 55.

3.11. *Sexual Violence*[263]

(a) *Qadhafi Forces*

The CoI noted reports made by displaced Sudanese of minors suffering sexual abuse in IDP camps, but was not able to confirm these reports.[264]

(b) Thuwar *Forces*

The CoI received information regarding a Syrian woman in the Benghazi area who was allegedly raped by armed *thuwar* forces in the latter part of February 2011, but no confirmation was obtained.[265]

4. THE ROLE OF NATO

The foreign military intervention in the Libyan war that began in Benghazi was not initially a NATO-led operation but rather a series of operations carried out by France, the United Kingdom and the United States.[266] France initially implemented a no-fly zone over the city before engaging armor on the ground, destroying four Libyan tanks in Benghazi on 19 March.[267] The UK and U.S. focused on air defenses, communications,

---

[263] The following terms are defined in accordance with the jurisprudence of the ICTY and ICTR, and other mixed-model tribunals.

    1. "Rape" is the penetration, however slight, of any part of the body of another person irrespective of gender (namely, the vagina, anus, or mouth) by means of the perpetrator's sexual organ or any object used by the perpetrator when accompanied by force or threat of force against the person or a third party which the victim believes is real.

    2. "Sexual violence" is defined as any physical act of a sexual nature which is committed on a person under circumstances which are coercive or threatening to the person or to any other person, which includes physical touching, groping, fondling, removal of a person's clothing to display intimate parts of the person's body whether in the presence of one or more persons, or any other act of a demeaning sexual nature.

    3. "Sexual harassment" is any threat of "rape" or "sexual violence," as defined above, against a person or any other person for purposes of demeaning, intimidating, or punishing the person in question.

[264] Report of the International Commission of Inquiry (Jan. 12, 2012), *supra* note 22 at n. 181.

[265] *Id.* at ¶ 207.

[266] Press Release, *Libye: point de situation opération Harmattan n°1*, FRENCH MINISTRY OF DEFENSE, Mar. 25, 2011, *available at* http://www.defense.gouv.fr/operations/autres-operations/operation-harmattan-libye/actualites/libye-point-de-situation-operation-harmattan-n-1.

[267] Colin Freeman & Sean Rayment, *Libya: British Forces Fire Missiles at Gaddafi*, THE TELEGRAPH, Mar. 19, 2011, *available at* http://www.telegraph.co.uk/news/worldnews/africa andindianocean/libya/8393128/Libya-British-forces-fire-missiles-at-Gaddafi.html.

and the Libyan Air Force with an intense Tomahawk missile attack fired from ships at sea. The U.S. continued to conduct strikes in and around Benghazi that focused on air defenses and armored forces.[268] The intervention likely saved the city and the nascent rebellion as Qadhafi ground forces had entered the city forcing the population to begin to flee. Foreign involvement allowed for the opposition to organize and establish a critical political base in the east.

The foreign intervention also led to controversial strikes and civilian casualties. The first civilian casualties caused by NATO occurred in Benghazi during a rescue mission for the crew of a crashed American F-15E ground attack aircraft. The United States launched a Tactical Recovery of Aircraft and Personnel (TRAP) to rescue the two American crewmen on the ground as Libyan locals rushed to the aid of the men. Two U.S. Marine Harrier jets then dropped two 500–pound (226-kilogram) bombs on the locals fearing they would harm the Americans, severely injuring six Libyan civilians.[269] The incident raised concerns regarding the distinction of civilian populations, as the locals should have been assumed to be noncombatants. This was the first of several cases of foreign forces conducting strikes that put civilians at risk in a way that was disproportionate relative to the intended military objective.

5. Conclusion

The Benghazi-based demonstrations of February 2011 provided the spark that fueled the revolution and led to civil war and the eventual fall of the Qadhafi regime. Benghazi was the scene of intense fighting between regime and opposition forces in mid-February 2011, mostly concentrated around the Al-Fadil bin 'Umar military barracks, where soldiers responded to provocations from funeral marchers and protesters with force that exacerbated the situation and led to numerous casualties. The Qadhafi regime responded swiftly to the demonstrations in Benghazi, deploying elite security forces to quell the protests with extreme force, including

---

[268] Tom Vanden Brook, *Gadhafi promises 'long war' after allies strike Libya*, USA TODAY, Mar. 20, 2011, *available at* http://usatoday30.usatoday.com/news/world/2011-03-19-libya_N .htm.
[269] Luis Martinez et al., *Inside the Rescue Mission: U.S. Air Force Pilots Eject from Malfunctioning F-15E Jet*, ABC NEWS, Mar. 22, 2011, *available at* http://abcnews.go.com/ International/us-fighter-jet-crashes-benghazi/story?id=13191505.

the use of RPGs, automatic rifles and snipers. After days of clashes and several high-level defections by military officials, the opposition was able to take control of the city and establish a critically important political and strategic base for the burgeoning revolution. The Benghazi-based demonstrations that began in mid-February 2011 fueled the revolution that led to civil war and the eventual fall of the Qadhafi regime.

There is substantial documentation of widespread violations by both Qadhafi and *thuwar* forces during the fighting in Benghazi. The evidence shows that regime forces were responsible for violations against protesters and suspected opposition forces in the early phase of the uprising. Evidence indicates that the Qadhafi forces had a "shoot to kill" policy, and that they deliberately targeted civilians using live ammunition, in particular during the incidents at the Al-Fadil bin 'Umar military barracks. Evidence similarly suggests that individuals were injured by artillery shells when regime forces attempted to retake the city in March 2011.

Beyond armed attacks, Qadhafi forces engaged in a targeted campaign of arbitrarily arresting and detaining activists who had organized the early protests, with arrests made by agents from the ISA and other security units. Many of these detainees were held for extended periods without due process. Human rights organizations, the CoI and media outlets provided evidence to reasonably conclude that the Qadhafi forces arbitrarily detained and disappeared numerous civilians and rebel combatants. The evidence also indicates that Qadhafi forces tortured and ill-treated rebel fighters, as well as suspected *thuwar* supporters, during their detention. There are documented cases of regime forces torturing individuals to specifically punish them for demonstrating against the regime or supporting the opposition.

There is also documentation showing violations by *thuwar* forces, who carried out reprisal attacks against regime security personnel, suspected Qadhafi loyalists and Sub-Saharan Africans after taking control of Benghazi. In particular, the evidence shows that *thuwar* forces carried out unlawful killings of suspected mercenaries, many of whom were Sub-Saharan African migrant workers targeted on the basis of their skin color and foreign origin. There is substantial evidence that *thuwar* forces targeted Qadhafi security officials and suspected regime supporters for arrest and detention without legal justification or the provision of due process. The evidence shows that while in detention, individuals were tortured and ill-treated by *thuwar* forces on the suspicion that they were Qadhafi supporters or mercenaries. In addition, the *thuwar* forces robbed, physically abused, and tortured or ill-treated individuals, particularly migrant workers. In a number of documented cases, migrant workers were subjected to extrajudicial killing and public lynching.

Beyond the above-mentioned violations directly harming individuals, there is substantial evidence of violations by Qadhafi forces due to their use of prohibited means and methods of waging war, and other violations against internationally protected rights. With regard to the former, there are documented cases of Qadhafi forces laying plastic mines and abandoning a large number in stockpiles around the country, including in the Benghazi region. International law requires that particular care be taken in military conflicts to reduce the indiscriminate effects of landmines. The use of plastic mines by the Qadhafi regime, which are particularly difficult to detect, indicates that this care was not taken. Evidence also indicates that foreign fighters constituted part of the Qadhafi forces in Benghazi, and that at least some of these foreigners engaged in combat for material compensation. Some of the foreigners claimed they were induced to participate under false pretenses, believing that they would only be required to demonstrate in support of the regime, while others claimed outright coercion on the part of the Government. On the basis of the available documentation, it can be concluded that Qadhafi forces included non-Libyan fighters.[270] With respect to the latter, the Qadhafi regime attempted to silence journalists and impede the flow of information between individuals in Benghazi. Reports indicate that a number of journalists were killed by regime forces. A number of domestic and foreign journalists were also detained by the regime and held for extended periods of time, apparently in order to silence media criticism. Furthermore, sources indicate that the Qadhafi government attempted to shut down the internet in the country in order to prevent communication between Benghazi and other areas in eastern Libya. The government's treatment of journalists amounts to infringement of the right to freedom of expression.

Ultimately, Benghazi was the tinderbox from which the Libyan revolution exploded. With Benghazi as their base, the NTC was able to establish diplomatic relations with foreign states, particularly those that eventually intervened in the conflict. Moreover, the violations committed by Qadhafi forces in their attempts to suppress the burgeoning revolution in Benghazi

---

[270] For more on the law on mercenaries, *see* International Convention against the Recruitment, Use, Financing and Training of Mercenaries, G.A. Res. 44/34, U.N. Doc. A/RES/44/34, 2163 UNTS 96 (Dec. 4, 1989).

galvanized large segments of the Libyan population and rallied international support to aid and assist the opposition to the Qadhafi regime. The
international community, and in particular the United States and NATO,
was swept up in the fervor of the revolution, and rallied support to the
rebel cause without an understanding of the myriad of groups and ideolo-
gies at work in Libya or a coherent strategy for dealing with these groups
and building the post-conflict Libyan state that they effectively helped
create.[271] This policy, or lack thereof, helped secure the overthrow of the
Qadhafi government, but also resulted in the ascent of Islamist groups,
most notably Ansar al-Sharīʿa, who entrenched themselves in the political
and security vacuum left after Qadhafi's fall. [272]

The lack of understanding or planning on the part of western governments, including the United States, became particularly apparent in the
rise and increasing power of non-state armed actors in Libya and beyond,
as well as in the increasing social unrest, political instability and Islamic
militancy in Benghazi and Cyrenaica after Qadhafi's fall. The lack of
advanced planning has allowed various groups to establish training and
logistical bases in Cyrenaica that are active throughout Libya and northern Africa.

Moreover, western policymakers shifted their focus away from Libya
after the fall of Qadhafi, which was a critical period in the country's
transition, and then lacked the necessary intelligence to respond effectively to the growing influence of militia forces with links to terrorist groups in the region, such as AQIM. The glaring security threats
could be seen in the deterioration of the security situation in Benghazi,
where westerners, international humanitarian institutions and foreign
diplomats were increasingly targeted in 2012. These events were largely
ignored until the killing of U.S. Ambassador Christopher Stevens in September, which was the most notable act of the resurgent Islamic militancy.
A number of consulates and diplomats were attacked before and after, and
the city has become nearly ungovernable, as not even the Libyan police
or armed forces can protect themselves. The failure of western states, and

---

[271] The naiveté of these states and their hubris recalls the earlier invasion of Iraq, and
to a lesser extent Afghanistan, where no thought was given to the long term ramifications
of ousting an authoritarian and repressive state and facilitating the transition to a stable
and decent state.

[272] For more on the spectrum of political Islamist groups active during the post-conflict
period, *see* Ch. V, Sec. 5.

in particular the United States and NATO, to consider the threats arising from a heavily-militarized post-war Libya and prepare for the ascendency of Islamists in Benghazi and Cyrenaica has had tragic consequences that cast an unfortunate shadow over the city and the prospects for stability in the region. Their continuing failure to do so, even in the aftermath of attacks on diplomats, has only compounded the problem.

CHAPTER SEVEN

AJDABIYA & BREGA

1. Introduction

Ajdabiya is a city of approximately 134,300 people, located in the eastern Libyan province of Cyrenaica near the Mediterranean Sea. The city lies approximately 6.4 kilometers (4 miles) from the eastern end of the Gulf of Sidra, where the gulf turns westward towards Tripolitania. Ajdabiya lies in an important geostrategic region of the country, with Tripoli 850 kilometers (528 miles) to the west, and Benghazi 150 kilometers (93 miles) to the northeast.[1] Brega, with a population of approximately 13,700, is located 72 kilometers (45 miles) southwest of Ajdabiya, and 196 kilometers (122 miles) southwest of Benghazi, directly on the Mediterranean Sea, at the bottom part of the Gulf of Sidra. The Marsa Brega Airport lies to the southeast of the town.[2]

Ajdabiya is the capital of the Al-Wahat District of Cyrenaica. The city itself is composed of three boroughs,[3] North Ajdabiya, West Ajdabiya and East Ajdabiya. The Libyan Coastal Highway bisects the city, with smaller roads leading west to the Gulf of Sidra and southeast into the Cyrenaican interior. Another road leads east to Tubruq on the Egyptian border.

Brega lies to the west of Ajdabiya, towards Sirte and Tripoli. Prior to World War II, the town was a small fishing village but with the discovery of oil in the Sirte Basin, Brega grew into a major oil production and shipping center.[4] The city of Brega is composed of a number of smaller towns and industrial facilities and is home to the fifth largest Libyan oil, natural gas and petrochemical refineries.[5]

---

[1] *Ajdabiya*, WolframAlpha, *available at* http://www.wolframalpha.com/input/?i=adjabiya.

[2] *Brega*, WolframAlpha, *available at* http://www.wolframalpha.com/input/?i=brega%2C+libya.

[3] These "boroughs" were in effect the "Basic People's Congresses" that constituted the basic governmental building blocks of Libyan society during the Qadhafi era.

[4] *Port Marsa El Brega*, World Port Source, *available at* http://www.worldportsource.com/ports/LBY_Port_Marsa_El_Brega_665.php.

[5] Anthony Bell & David Witter, Institute for the Study of War, 2 The Libyan Revolution: Escalation & Intervention 10 (Sept. 2011), *available at* http://www

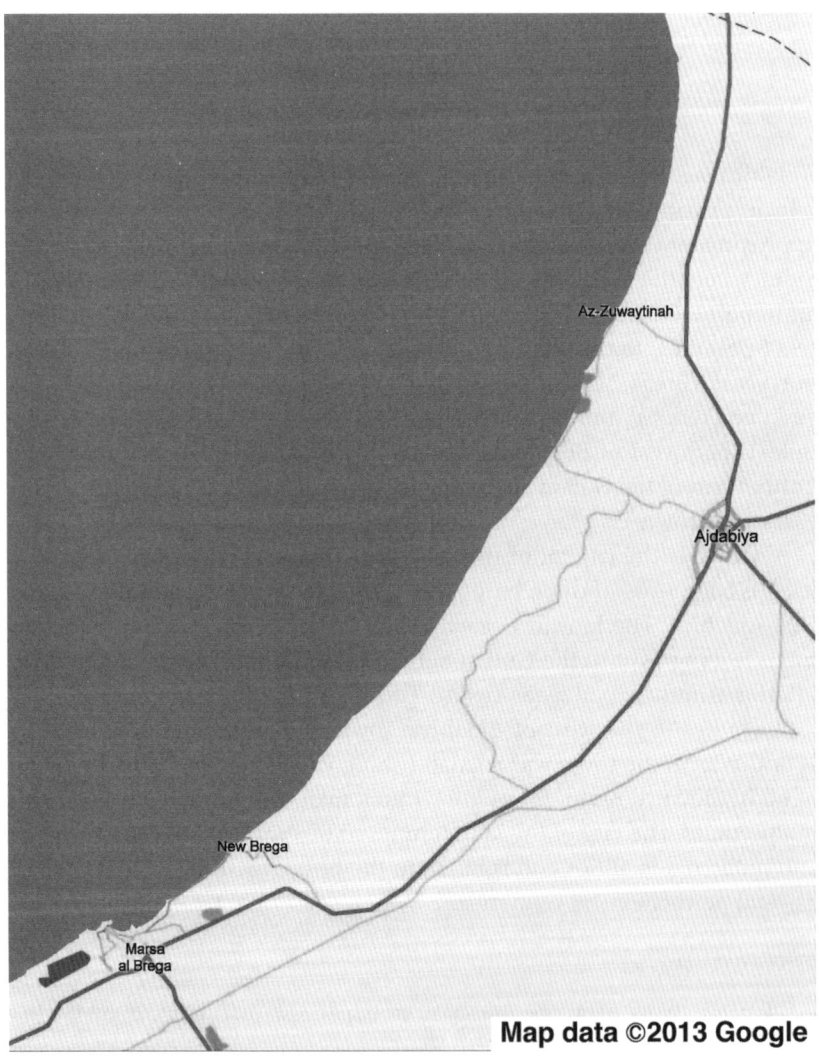

Map 4: Regional map of Ajdabiya and Brega (Map data © 2013 Google).

Ajdabiya and Brega were the scene of significant fighting during the Libyan civil war in 2011 and both towns, as well as the highway in between, were heavily contested by Qadhafi and *thuwar* forces, changing hands several times. Qadhafi and *thuwar* forces engaged in a back and forth battle along the highway between the cities until Qadhafi forces finally withdrew from Brega on 17 August.[6]

2. SUMMARY OF EVENTS

The first protests in Ajdabiya broke out on 18 February 2011 when demonstrators quickly organized themselves in the city.[7] As the protests grew, Qadhafi soldiers and police officers in the region began to defect and join the *thuwar*.[8] Qadhafi forces stepped up efforts to regain the vital region in March, and in an attempt to quell the growing opposition in Ajdabiya, Qadhafi forces began to directly assault the city with artillery shelling and mortar fire. This prompted a large part of the civilian population to flee the city for Benghazi, while some members of the *thuwar* left for Brega and confronted the Qadhafi forces there.[9]

On 3 March, Qadhafi forces moved in to Brega to take control of the city. The battle began early in the morning when Qadhafi forces attacked the outskirts of Brega and entered the city in 60–70 Toyota trucks. Qadhafi forces had started their advance during the night, setting up position in the industrial area on the edge of the city.[10] The Qadhafi forces' movement into Brega was well organized, as they took control of the town's university, airport, wharf and several factories. Most importantly, Qadhafi forces seized a vital power station that supplied Benghazi, as well as an oil refinery and the Sirte Oil Company, where more than 300 foreign nationals

---

.understandingwar.org/sites/default/files/Libya_Part2_0.pdf [hereinafter "ESCALATION & INTERVENTION"].

[6] *Id.*

[7] Richard Adams, *Libya's turmoil – Friday 25 February*, THE GUARDIAN, Feb. 25, 2011, *available at* http://www.guardian.co.uk/world/blog/2011/feb/25/gaddafi-libya-live-blog.

[8] *Id.*

[9] Martin Chulov, *Battle for Brega could mark start of real war in Libya*, THE GUARDIAN, Mar. 3, 2011, *available at* http://www.guardian.co.uk/world/2011/mar/02/libya-civil-war-bregga.

[10] *Id.*

were employed. In taking Brega, Qadhafi forces moved significantly closer to Benghazi where the opposition movement's leadership was based.[11]

On 14 March, Ajdabiya's *thuwar* defenses were overrun by regime forces. As Qadhafi forces advanced on the city, hundreds of *thuwar* and residents fled in cars, trucks and minibuses up the Libyan Coastal Highway towards Benghazi. Some of the vehicles were civilian, while a number of trucks bore rudimentary markings indicating that they belonged to *thuwar*. Within a few hours, Qadhafi forces had encircled Ajdabiya and fighting was taking place in the streets.[12]

On 17 March, the Qadhafi regime announced that it had advanced through Ajdabiya and had captured the oil town of Zuetina and made significant progress towards Benghazi. The Qadhafi government's assertion was disputed by the National Transitional Council (NTC), which denied the regime was that close to Benghazi.[13] At this time, U.S. President Barrack Obama publicly demanded that Qadhafi abide by Security Council Resolution 1973, halt his advance towards Benghazi and pull back from Ajdabiya. President Obama's warning was followed shortly thereafter by the start of the foreign intervention on 19 March, with U.S., UK, and French forces carrying out airstrikes against the Qadhafi forces in eastern Libya.[14]

On 19 March, Qadhafi forces continued their advance from Ajdabiya towards Benghazi along the Libyan Coastal Highway [15] Correspondingly, *thuwar* advanced from Benghazi in an attempt to retake Ajdabiya.[16] Beginning on 20 March, *thuwar* forces engaged Qadhafi forces in a six-day battle for the control of Ajdabiya. They were slowed by fire from Qadhafi tanks and rocket launchers from within the town, however, and were not able to enter the city until 23 March.[17]

---

[11] *Id.*

[12] Abigail Hauslohner, *Rumors from an Encircled Town: The Fate of Ajdabiyah*, TIME WORLD, Mar. 15, 2011, *available at* http://www.time.com/time/world/article/0,8599,2059229,00.html.

[13] *Rebels deny Gaddafi troops on Benghazi outskirts*, REUTERS, Mar. 17, 2011, *available at* http://af.reuters.com/article/libyaNews/idAFWEA926720110317.

[14] BELL & WITTER, ESCALATION & INTERVENTION, *supra* note 5 at 23. For more on the lead-up to the March 2011 NATO intervention into Libya, *see* Ch. III, Sec. 2.

[15] *Id.*

[16] Chris McGreal, *Coalition attacks wreak havoc on ground troops*, THE GUARDIAN, Mar. 20, 2011, *available at* http://www.guardian.co.uk/world/2011/mar/20/libya-air-strikes-rain-down.

[17] Dan Murphy, *Libya test for NATO starts at Ajdabiya*, CHRISTIAN SCIENCE MONITOR, Mar. 25, 2011, *available at* http://www.csmonitor.com/World/Middle-East/2011/0325/Libya-test-for-NATO-starts-at-Ajdabiya; Borzou Daragahi & David Zucchino, *Libyan rebels show*

By 26 March, NATO airstrikes had significantly weakened the Qadhafi forces in the east, most notably the regime's air defenses. The strikes both hampered Qadhafi's supply lines to Sirte and impeded the regime's firepower in Ajdabiya by destroying at least four T-72 tanks and an artillery piece.[18] The NATO intervention in eastern Libya, particularly the air support from U.S. warplanes, the A-10 Thunderbolt and AC-130 gunship significantly aided the *thuwar* advance and capture of Ajdabiya.[19] During the battle for Ajdabiya, *thuwar* forces were still untrained and only minimally prepared for significant battle. The opening up of Ajdabiya in the face of strong military pressure from the Qadhafi regime was made possible by the coalition airstrikes.[20] The haste with which Qadhafi forces withdrew suggested an increasing fear over facing further coalition airstrikes.[21]

Qadhafi forces realized their tenuous position and tried to negotiate a strategic withdrawal from the city.[22] By 26 March, however, *thuwar* had taken control of the city and reinforced their positions with rocket launchers and other weapons from Benghazi.[23] Having lost control over Ajdabiya, Qadhafi forces were forced to retreat along the Coastal Highway towards Brega, with some forces continuing to Sirte.[24] In the wake of defeat, Qadhafi forces left behind heavy weapons and armor, including

---

signs of life, L.A. TIMES, Mar. 24, 2011, *available at* http://articles.latimes.com/2011/mar/24/world/la-fg-libya-fighting-20110325.

[18] *Id.* For more on the fighting in March 2011 and NATO strikes during this period, *see* Ch. II, Sec. 4.

[19] While the coalition members did not publicize the use of these airplanes, evidence strongly supports their presence, particularly their use in the destruction of government armor. *See* ANTHONY BELL & DAVID WITTER, INSTITUTE FOR THE STUDY OF WAR, 3 THE LIBYAN REVOLUTION: STALEMATE & SIEGE 13 (Oct. 6, 2011) [hereinafter "STALEMATE & SIEGE"], *available at* http://www.understandingwar.org/sites/default/files/Libya_Part3_0.pdf; Greg Jaffe & Karen DeYoung, *U.S. deploys low-flying attack planes in Libya*, THE WASHINGTON POST, Mar. 28, 2011, *available at* http://www.washingtonpost.com/world/us-deploys-low-flying-attack-planes-in-libya/2011/03/26/AF9grPqB_story.html.

[20] *See* Ch. II, Sec. 3.2. *See also* Chris McGreal, *Libyan rebels rejoice in Ajdabiya as air strikes drive Gaddafi loyalists out*, THE GUARDIAN, Mar. 26, 2011, *available at* http://www.guardian.co.uk/world/2011/mar/26/libya-rebels-ajdabiya-gaddafi-loyalists.

[21] For more on NATO strikes, *see infra* Sec. 4.

[22] BELL & WITTER, STALEMATE & SIEGE, *supra* note 19 at 13; *Libyan rebel forces fight to retake Ajdabiya*, AFP, Mar. 24, 2011, *available at* http://english.ahram.org.eg/News/8523.aspx.

[23] McGreal, *Libyan rebels rejoice in Ajdabiya as air strikes drive Gaddafi loyalists out*, *supra* note 20.

[24] BELL & WITTER, STALEMATE & SIEGE, *supra* note 19 at 13; Kareem Fahim & David D. Kirkpatrick, *Airstrikes Clear Way for Libyan Rebels' First Major Advance*, N.Y. TIMES, Mar. 26, 2011, *available at* http://www.nytimes.com/2011/03/27/world/africa/27libya.html.

RPGs and missiles, which were seized by *thuwar* for use in subsequent battles.[25]

In the aftermath of the *thuwar* victory on 26 March, the two sides started fighting along the Coastal Highway west of Ajdabiya.[26] By 27 March, *thuwar* captured Brega and advanced a further 170 kilometers (106 miles) with little resistance, taking the small towns of Ra's Lanuf and Bin Jawad.[27] By 28 March, *thuwar* had reached Harawa, a small town just 80 kilometers (50 miles) to the east of Sirte. Qadhafi forces had prepared for the advance, however, and mined the roads along the way. Having resupplied in Sirte, the Qadhafi military ambushed the *thuwar*, forcing them back to Bin Jawad.[28] Two days later, Qadhafi forces pushed the *thuwar* forces all the way to Ajdabiya, allowing them to retake Brega.[29]

---

[25] McGreal, *Libyan rebels rejoice in Ajdabiya as air strikes drive Gaddafi loyalists out*, *supra* note 20. For more on weapons seized and used by *thuwar* forces during the conflict, *see* Ch. II, Sec. 2.3.

[26] *Id.*

[27] BELL & WITTER, STALEMATE & SIEGE, *supra* note 19 at 13; Kareem Fahim & David D. Kirkpatrick, *Rebels Retake Libyan City As Airstrikes Clear a Way*, N.Y. TIMES, Mar. 27, 2011, *available at* http://www.nytimes.com/2011/03/27/world/africa/27libya.html; AFP, *Kadhafi forces flee rebels sweeping west to Sirte*, YOUTUBE (Mar. 27, 2011), *available at* http://www.youtube.com/watch?v=KPNd5UIDO1s, Marc Burleigh, *Libyan rebels push towards Tripoli, promise new oil exports*, AFP, Mar. 27, 2011, *available at* http://www.thejakartaglobe.com/afp/libyan-rebels-push-towards-tripoli-promise-new-oil-exports/431978.

[28] *Libyan rebel advance halted, Sirte blasted by NATO jets*, AFP, Mar. 28, 2011, *available at* http://www.heraldsun.com.au/news/victoria/libyan-rebel-advance-halted-sirte-blasted-by-nato-jets/story-e6frf7lf-1226029688023; Ryan Lucas, *Libyan rebels close on key Gadhafi stronghold*, AP, Mar. 28, 2011, *available at* http://www.aolnews.com/2011/03/28/libyan-rebels-close-on-key-gadhafi-stronghold-of-sirte; Kareem Fahim & David D. Kirkpatrick, *Rebel Advance Halted Outside Qaddafi Hometown*, N.Y. TIMES, Mar. 29, 2011, *available at* http://www.nytimes.com/2011/03/29/world/africa/29libya.html.

[29] AFP, *Libyan rebel advance halted, Sirte blasted by NATO jets*, *supra* note 28; Tara Bahrampour & Greg Jaffe, *Libyan rebels push toward Gaddafi's home town*, THE WASHINGTON POST, Mar. 29, 2011, *available at* http://www.washingtonpost.com/world/libyan-rebels-push-toward-sirte-gaddafi-sends-reinforcements/2011/03/28/AFedisoB_story.html; Scott Peterson, *Qaddafi likens Western airstrikes to 'Hitler's campaigns'*, CHRISTIAN SCIENCE MONITOR, Mar. 29, 2011, *available at* http://www.csmonitor.com/World/Middle-East/2011/0329/Qaddafi-likens-Western-airstrikes-to-Hitler-s-campaigns; Ryan Lucas, *Libyan rebels retreating after Gadhafi onslaught*, AP, Mar. 29, 2011, *available at* http://www.washingtontimes.com/news/2011/mar/29/libyan-rebels-retreat-after-gadhafi-onslaught/; David D. Kirkpatrick & Kareem Fahim, *Allies count on defiant streak in Libya to Drive Out Qaddafi*, N.Y. TIMES, Mar. 30, 2011, *available at* http://www.nytimes.com/2011/03/30/world/africa/30libya.html; David Zucchino, *Kadafi's troops defending Surt force rebels to retreat 100 miles*, L.A. TIMES, Mar. 30, 2011, *available at* http://articles.latimes.com/2011/mar/30/world/la-fg-libya-counter-attack-20110330; Syed Murtaza Gheblehzadeh, *Air strikes resume as outgunned Libyan rebels scatter*, AFP, Mar. 30, 2011, *available at* http://www.brecorder.com/top-news/1-front-top-news/9443-air-strikes-resume-as-outgunned-libyan-rebels-scatter.html.

It is noteworthy that during the Qadhafi offensive in the final days of March 2011, only one NATO airstrike was reported.[30] The absence of air support was attributed to bad weather and logistical difficulties stemming from the transfer of the air campaign from U.S. command to a coalition-led NATO mission.[31] The inability of the *thuwar* to stall the Qadhafi forces' advance without foreign air support is demonstrative of their reliance on outside forces for successes during the war.[32]

After retreating to Ajdabiya, the *thuwar* stabilized and regrouped, holding their ground and marking the lines of the rebel eastern front. Brega became the focus of Qadhafi forces in eastern Libya from which they blocked the Coastal Highway and thwarted numerous attempts by *thuwar* to take the town and advance towards Sirte.[33] With Qadhafi forces occupying Brega and the rebels positioned in Ajdabiya, a stalemate developed between the two towns lasting until the end of July 2011.[34] The opposition's Libyan National Army was created in the east and attempted to orchestrate a nationally-unified rebel force, but was unable to coordinate or lead the military struggle against the regime. Rather, throughout the conflict it was largely confined to the eastern frontline around Brega.[35]

---

[30] Gheblehzadeh, *Air strikes resume as outgunned Libyan rebels scatter, supra* note 29.

[31] Zainab Fattah &Tamara Walid, *Libya rebels seek ceasefire as US vows to withdraw jets,* BLOOMBERG BUSINESSWEEK, Apr. 1, 2011, *available at* http://www.bloomberg.com/news/2011-04-01/libya-rebels-seek-cease-fire-after-u-s-vows-to-withdraw-its-fighter-jets.html.

[32] BELL & WITTER, STALEMATE & SIEGE, *supra* note 19 at 14.

[33] McGreal, *Libyan rebels rejoice in Ajdabiya as air strikes drive Gaddafi loyalists out, supra* note 20; *Gaddafi's forces battle rebels for Brega,* AL JAZEERA, Apr. 1, 2011, *available at* http://www.aljazeera.com/news/africa/2011/03/20113311420519843 58.html; Alexander Dziadosz, *East Libya rebels organize, head towards oil town,* REUTERS, Apr. 1, 2011, *available at* http://www.reuters.com/article/2011/04/01/us-libya-east-idUSTRE7301AG20110401; Marc Burleigh, *Battle for Brega rages after Kadhafi forces ambush,* AFP, Apr. 3, 2011, *available at* http://news.smh.com.au/breaking-news-world/battle-for-brega-rages-after-ambush-20110403-1ctek.html; Alexander Dziadosz, *Rebels flee east Libya oil town under rocket fire,* REUTERS, Apr. 5 2011, *available at* http://www.reuters.com/article/2011/04/05/us-libya-east-idUSTRE7342AJ20110405; Joby Warrick & Liz Sly, *U.S. envoy Chris Stevens arrives in Libya to help opposition fighters,* THE WASHINGTON POST, Apr. 6, 2011, *available at* http://www.washingtonpost.com/world/us-envoy-arrives-in-libya-to-help-opposition-fighters/2011/04/05/AFTIV6lC_story.html; Alexander Dziadosz, *Libya rebels push towards oil port,* REUTERS, Apr. 6, 2011, *available at* http://www.reuters.com/article/2011/04/06/us-libya-east-idUSTRE7351SU20110406.

[34] BELL & WITTER, STALEMATE & SIEGE, *supra* note 19 at 6. For more on the stalemate and fighting during this period *see* Ch. II, Sec. 3.3.

[35] Report of the International Commission of Inquiry on Libya, U.N. HRC. 19th Sess., Annex I, ¶ 66. U.N. Doc. A/HRC/19/68, advance unedited version (Mar. 2, 2012).

During the stalemate there were fierce battles along the Coastal Highway, with "fluid" changes during the clashes characterized by quick successes and hasty retreats in which neither side was able to gain the upper hand.[36] The situation bogged down between Ajdabiya and Brega for several reasons. First, the Qadhafi forces shifted to non-conventional tactics prompting a rise in friendly fire airstrikes by NATO forces. Second, NATO's clear demarcation of zones into which Qadhafi forces could not venture without reprisal prompted the regime forces to avoid open confrontations. Finally, political infighting between *thuwar* leaders led to a fracture in their command, leaving the rebel forces splintered and left to their own defenses based on regional capabilities.[37]

As indicated earlier, NATO airstrikes played a vital role in *thuwar* successes against Qadhafi forces on the Coastal Highway between Benghazi and Ajdabiya, and again during the *thuwar* push towards Sirte. The notable lack of NATO airstrikes similarly played an important role in allowing for the advancement of Qadhafi advances back to Brega. By the start of April, NATO turned its attention to Ajdabiya, making it a primary region of focus due to the ongoing battles taking place in the city between the Qadhafi and *thuwar* forces. NATO conducted airstrikes in the area targeting forces that were allegedly attacking civilian areas, destroying equipment, ammunition bunkers, and supply and communications lines.[38]

As the conflict moved into April when the Qadhafi regime changed tactics, it became more difficult for NATO to distinguish between rebels and regime ground forces. NATO reported that "Libyan Qaddafi forces have increasingly shifted to non-conventional tactics, blending in with road traffic and using civilian life as a shield for their advance."[39] The shift led to NATO strikes causing civilian and *thuwar* casualties on a number of occasions. On 1 April, 13 *thuwar* fighters were killed by a coalition air strike that attacked a convoy travelling between Brega and Ajdabiya. The attack reportedly took place after the *thuwar* fired an anti-aircraft gun.[40]

---

[36] *Libyan rebels near Ajdabiya 'killed in Nato air strike'*, BBC, Apr. 7, 2011, *available at* http://www.bbc.co.uk/news/world-africa-12997181; Alexander Dziadosz, *Libyan rebels fear fresh attack on Ajdabiyah*, REUTERS, Apr. 18, 2011, *available at* http://uk.reuters.com/article/2011/04/17/uk-libya-idUKLDE71Q0MP20110417.

[37] For more on the *thuwar* forces and political infighting, *see* Ch. II, Secs. 2.3.

[38] *Press briefing on Libya*, NORTH ATLANTIC TREATY ORGANIZATION, Apr. 12, 2011, *available at* http://www.nato.int/cps/en/natolive/opinions_72290.htm.

[39] *NATO 'careful' over airstrikes, vows to protect civilians*, AFP, Apr. 6, 2011, *available at* http://dawn.com/2011/04/07/nato-careful-over-air-strikes-rebel-oil-leaves-tobruk.

[40] BBC, *Libyan rebels near Ajdabiya 'killed in Nato air strike'*, *supra* note 36.

Another incident was reported to have taken place a few days later, when five civilians were killed and 25 injured by a NATO strike targeting a Qadhafi forces convoy near Brega.[41] A third incident took place on 7 April 2011, when two NATO airstrikes hit a *thuwar* convoy as they advanced on Brega for a surprise attack. After the initial strike, a number of local herders ran to help the wounded and a second missile struck the convoy, killing as many as 13 and injuring more.[42]

NATO adopted a strategy of creating "redlines" – demarcated areas where Qadhafi forces would be targeted. These areas subsequently became regions *thuwar* forces avoided out of fear of accidental strikes. This strategy limited the number of direct confrontations between Qadhafi and *thuwar* forces, contributing to the stalemate of the Ajdabiya/Brega front.[43] The political infighting within the opposition also limited the capacity of the rebels to organize a unified front against Qadhafi forces in this theater of operations. The tensions between General 'Abd al-Fattah Yunis, then NTC-commander 'Umar Hariri and General Khalifa Haftar, severely disrupted the rebels' attempts to take Brega and Sirte.[44]

On 16 April, the *thuwar* forces again amassed for an assault on Brega. While advancing on the city, they came under rocket fire, and although some made it through to the eastern outskirts along the Coastal Highway, they were quickly beaten back.[45] The Qadhafi forces launched a counter

---

[41] *Id.*

[42] Craig Allen et al., *Errant NATO Airstrikes in Libya: 13 Cases (Brega)*, N.Y. TIMES, Dec. 16, 2011, *available at* http://www.nytimes.com/interactive/2011/12/16/world/africa/nato-airstrikes-in-libya.html?ref=africa#page/rebel-convoy; BBC, *Libyan rebels near Ajdabiya 'killed in Nato air strike'*, *supra* note 36. *See also* Ch. III, Sec. 6.2.

[43] BELL & WITTER, STALEMATE & SIEGE, *supra* note 19 at 15.

[44] For more on political disagreements within the *thuwar* forces, *see* Ch. II, Sec. 3.1. *See also* Kareem Fahim, *Rebel leadership in Libya shows strain*, N.Y. TIMES, Apr. 1, 2011, *available at* http://www.nytimes.com/2011/04/04/world/africa/04rebels.html; Tara Bahrampour, *Libyan rebels struggle to explain rift*, THE WASHINGTON POST, Apr. 2, 2011, *available at* http://articles.washingtonpost.com/2011-04-02/world/35231483_1_khalifa-haftar-haftar-and-younis-abdul-fattah-younis; Charles Levinson, *Rebel Leadership Casts a Wide Net*, WALL STREET JOURNAL, Mar. 10, 2011, *available at* http://online.wsj.com/article/SB10001424052748704629104576190720901643258.html; Alan Greenblatt, *Leaders Of The Libyan Opposition Emerge*, NPR, Mar. 14, 2011, *available at* http://www.npr.org/2011/03/15/134452475/leaders-of-the-libyan-opposition-emerge; Derek Henry Flood, *Taking charge of Libya's rebels: an in-depth portrait of Colonel Khalifa Haftar*, 2 MILITANT LEADERSHIP MONITOR 3, Mar. 2011, *available at* http://mlm.jamestown.org/single/?tx_ttnews%5Btt_news%5D=37724&tx_ttnews%5BbackPid%5D=567&no_cache=1; Kareem Fahim, *Libyan rebels show division after setbacks*, N.Y. TIMES, Apr. 4, 2011, *available at* http://query.nytimes.com/gst/fullpage.html?res=9C06EEDF1639F937A35757C0A9679D8B63.

[45] Dziadosz, *Libyan rebels fear fresh attack on Ajdabiyah*, *supra* note 36.

attack the following day and began to advance towards Ajdabiya.[46] Qad-hafi and *thuwar* opposing forces met along the Coastal Highway between the two cities, and an estimated dozen rockets were fired at the west-ern entrance to Ajdabiya. Many of the remaining civilians fled east again along the Coastal Highway toward Benghazi. By the afternoon of 17 April, the *thuwar* had blocked the road to Ajdabiya with concrete blocks, tree branches and any other obstructive material they could find.[47]

In early May, *thuwar* forces were ordered by NATO to withdraw from their positions around Brega in advance of planned airstrikes on the city.[48] By mid-May Qadhafi forces in the vicinity of Brega were struggling to keep their supply lines open, as NATO airstrikes and *thuwar* actions blocked the flow of weapons, fuel and supplies into Brega. Without supplies Qad-hafi forces were unable to sustain any further attempts at advances on Ajdabiya, which by now was under complete *thuwar* control. They were equally unable to continue their artillery attacks on Ajdabiya.[49] With the fighting coming to an end in Ajdabiya and the cessation of artillery attacks, the humanitarian situation improved and by the end of June most of the civilian population was able to return to the city.[50]

With Ajdabiya firmly under rebel control, the *thuwar* prepared for a major offensive on Brega in mid-July. By this time the coordination between NATO and the rebels had improved, and NATO assisted the advance by launching multiple airstrikes on 13 and 14 July, destroying tanks, armored vehicles and other material in Brega.[51] On 14 July, *thu-war* began advancing on Brega but were repelled by heavy rocket fire and suffered serious injuries from landmines, stalling the attack and leading to an estimated 20 casualties and 180 injured.[52] The rebel forces kept up

---

[46] Xan Rice, *Libyan families flee Gaddafi forces in Ajdabiya as civilian death toll rise*, THE GUARDIAN, Apr. 17, 2011, *available at* http://www.guardian.co.uk/world/2011/apr/17/libya-attacks-ajdabiya-misrata-brega.

[47] Dziadosz, *Libyan rebels fear fresh attack on Ajdabiyah*, *supra* note 36.

[48] C.J. Chivers, *With Help From NATO, Libyan Rebels Gain Ground*, N.Y. TIMES, May 9, 2011, *available at* http://www.nytimes.com/2011/05/10/world/africa/10libya.html.

[49] *Press briefing on Libya*, NORTH ATLANTIC TREATY ORGANIZATION, May 20, 2011, *available at* http://www.nato.int/cps/en/natolive/opinions_74542.htm.

[50] Adams, *Libya's turmoil – Friday 25 February*, *supra* note 7.

[51] *Operational Media Update for 13, 14 June*, Operation Unified Protector, NORTH ATLAN-TIC TREATY ORGANIZATION, June 13–14, 2011. For more on coordination between NATO and *thuwar* forces, *see* Ch. III, Sec. 7.1.

[52] *Libyan rebels fall back after failed advance on eastern oil town*, AP, July 15, 2011, *available at* http://www.globaltvbc.com/libyan+rebels+fall+back+after+failed+advance+on+eastern+oil+town/305737/story.html; *Medical official: 10 Libyan rebels killed in push for east-*

the advancement, and on 17 July fought their way into the northern area of New Brega less than 20 kilometers (12.4 miles) from the town center, while Qadhafi forces held their ground around a petrochemical facility in the southwestern neighborhood of Old Brega.[53] NATO support was close at hand, as reports indicate that coalition forces provided boats for the *thuwar* forces to enter Brega by sea, allowing them to maneuver around the Qadhafi forces' positions.[54]

After three days of intense street fighting, Qadhafi soldiers retreated west to Ra's Lanuf, although a rearguard stayed behind in Old Brega.[55] Mu'tassim Qadhafi reportedly commanded the Qadhafi forces in Brega and oversaw the retreat[56] during which they flew rebel flags and lit fires to hide their movements from NATO jets.[57] Fighting continued in Brega between the remaining Qadhafi forces in the southwest of the town and

---

ern oil town, AP, July 16, 2011, *available at* http://feb17.info/news/medical-official-10-libyan-rebels-killed-in-push-for-eastern-oil-town; Peter Graff, *Heavy casualties reported in Libya fighting*, REUTERS, July 16, 2011, *available at* http://www.reuters.com/article/2011/07/16/us-libya-idUSTRE76E0M720110716; Chris Stephen, *Libyan rebels push towards Brega backed by Nato air strikes*, THE GUARDIAN, July 18, 2011, *available at* http://www.guardian.co.uk/world/2011/jul/18/libya-rebels-brega-nato.

[53] *Libya stages back-to-back rallies in face of world condemnation*, AP, July 17, 2011, *available at* http://www.news889.com/news/world/article/255217--libya-stages-back-to-back-rallies-in-face-of-world-condemnation.

[54] BELL & WITTER, STALEMATE & SIEGE, *supra* note 19 at 16; *"Operational Media Update for 15, 16, 17 June,"* Operation Unified Protector, NORTH ATLANTIC TREATY ORGANIZATION, June 15–17, 2011; Ariel Zirulnick, *Libya's rebels stage bold offensive in oil town of Brega*, CHRISTIAN SCIENCE MONITOR, July 18, 2011, *available at* http://www.csmonitor.com/World/terrorism-security/2011/0718/Libya-s-rebels-stage-bold-offensive-on-oil-town-of-Brega; David Zucchino, *In Libya, rebel casualties tell the story behind fight for key city*, L.A. TIMES, July 19, 2011, *available at* http://articles.latimes.com/2011/jul/19/world/la-fg-libya-rebels-wounded-20110719.

[55] *Libyan rebels claim victory in battle for Brega*, BBC, July 18, 2011, *available at* http://www.bbc.co.uk/news/world-africa-14180293; *Libyan rebels claim victory in fight for Brega*, AL JAZEERA, July 18, 2011, *available at* http://www.aljazeera.com/news/africa/2011/07/201171 8131010939797.html; Charles Levinson & Muneef Halawa, *Libya rebels battle for key oil town*, WALL STREET JOURNAL, July 19, 2011, *available at* http://online.wsj.com/article/SB10001424 052702304567604576454294028527696.html; David Zucchino, *Libya forces, rebels locked in battle for Port Brega*, L.A. TIMES, July 20, 2011, *available at* http://articles.latimes.com/2011/jul/20/world/la-fg-libya-fighting-20110720.

[56] Christian Fraser, *Libya conflict: US officials met Gaddafi envoys*, BBC, July 19, 2011, *available at* http://www.bbc.co.uk/news/world-africa-14195476.

[57] BELL & WITTER, STALEMATE & SIEGE, *supra* note 19 at 16; Zirulnick, *Libya's rebels stage bold offensive in oil town of Brega*, *supra* note 54; *Rebels clear landmines, advance on Brega*, UPI, July 18, 2011, *available at* http://www.upi.com/Top_News/World-News/2011/07/18/Rebels-clear-land-mines-advance-on-Brega/UPI-80801310987369; *Libyan troops shell rebels near eastern oil town, killing 8 rebels, hospital officials says*, AP, July 19, 2011, *available at* http://www.cbc.ca/news/world/story/2011/07/20/libya-rebels-killed.html.

thuwar in the east. By mid-August, however, the remaining regime forces were routed and retreated towards Sirte.[58]

Given the importance of oil to the region and the nation as a whole, oil supplies became a matter of critical concern as production levels began to drop dramatically. On 30 August, it was reported that a damaged oil tank caught fire in Brega, adding to mounting concerns.[59] At the same time, the National Oil Corporation (NOC) chairperson for the NTC reported that Libyan oil production was preparing to start back up again, but warned that landmines that had been laid by Qadhafi forces in Brega had to be cleared before production could resume.[60] On 31 August, concerns with regard to oil were somewhat allayed by the announcement that the EU oil embargo on six oil ports, including Brega, would be lifted.[61]

As Ajdabiya and Brega entered the post-Qadhafi era, new challenges emerged, similar to those in other parts of the country, particularly cities in Cyrenaica. The March 2012 creation of the Cyrenaica Transitional Council, which was well represented and influential in Ajdabiya, caused heightened tension with the national government trying to assert its authority in the region.[62] Likewise, the influence of local armed groups acting beyond government authority became a cause for concern, notably Islamic militants with suspected links to Al-Qaʿida in eastern cities, including Brega.[63]

---

[58] *Pro-Gaddafi forces use more civilian facilities*, ANTAR NEWS, July 27, 2011, *available at* http://www.antaranews.com/en/news/74160/pro-gaddafi-forces-use-more-civilian-facilities.

[59] Alexander Dziadosz, *Tank burns at Libya's biggest oil terminal*, REUTERS, Aug. 30, 2011, *available at* http://www.reuters.com/article/2011/08/30/us-libya-oil-tanks-idUSTRE77T1JZ20110830.

[60] Emma Farge, *Libya sees oil output at pre-war levels in 15 months*, REUTERS, Aug. 30, 2011, *available at* http://www.reuters.com/article/2011/08/30/us-libya-oil-noc-idUSTRE77T3DM20110830.

[61] *UPDATE 1 – EU sanctions on Libyan ports seen lifted on Friday*, REUTERS, Aug. 31, 2011, *available at* http://www.reuters.com/article/2011/08/31/libya-eu-sanctions-idUSLDE77U0EH20110831.

[62] FREDERIC WEHREY, CARNEGIE ENDOWMENT FOR INTERNATIONAL PEACE, THE STRUGGLE FOR SECURITY IN EASTERN LIBYA 6 (Sept. 2012), *available at* http://carnegieendowment.org/files/libya_security_2.pdf. For more on the creation of the Cyrenaica Transitional Council, *see supra* Sec. 2.

[63] Nic Robertson, *Concern grows over jihadist numbers in eastern Libya*, CNN, May 15, 2012, *available at* http://edition.cnn.com/2012/05/15/world/africa/libya-militants/index.html. For more on the influence of political Islam in eastern Libya in the post-conflict period, *see* Ch. V, Sec. 5.

In the lead up to national elections scheduled for 7 July 2012, unrest and demonstrations broke out, impacting the local and national economy.[64] On 6 July, a strike in Brega led to the temporary shutting down of the city's port.[65] Similar stoppages in Brega and other eastern cities led to Libya's oil exporting capacity being cut to half of what it was before the war.[66] The instability continued as the elections drew nearer. As in Benghazi, Ajdabiya experienced protests by those who supported the Cyrenaica Council and a more autonomous eastern Libya.[67] On election day, 7 July, one man was killed and two injured when anti-election gunmen attacked polling stations in Ajdabiya.[68] In Brega, several election booths were unable to open due to violent confrontations.[69] The head of the electoral commission, Nuri al-Abbar, reported that acts of sabotage prevented 101 polling stations from opening, mostly in the east. Despite the difficulties, the voting continued with 98 percent of the polling stations in Ajdabiya working normally.[70]

3. Illustrations of the Violations

3.1. *Excessive Use of Force*

(a) *Qadhafi Forces*

As the protests spread to Ajdabiya in mid-February 2011, Qadhafi forces used excessive force in an attempt to quell the demonstrations. The violent reaction of the regime, including the use of live ammunition to

---

[64] Jay Deshmukh, *Violence mars eve of key Libya election*, AFP, July 6, 2012, *available at* http://reliefweb.int/report/libya/violence-mars-eve-key-libya-election.

[65] Jessica Donati et al., *UPDATE 1 – Oil shipments delayed as strikes shut Libyan ports*, REUTERS, July 6, 2011, *available at* http://www.reuters.com/article/2012/07/06/libya-strikes-ports-idUSL6E8I67ZD20120706.

[66] Marie-Louise Gumuchian, *UPDATE 2 – Protest-hit Libyan oil terminals reopen – NOC*, REUTERS, July 8, 2012, *available at* http://www.reuters.com/article/2012/07/08/libya-elections-oil-idUSL6E8I82O20120708.

[67] For more on the unrest leading up to the July 2012 elections, *see* Ch. V, Sec. 6.

[68] *One killed at polling station in Libya*, SBS, July 8, 2012, *available at*, http://www.sbs.com.au/news/article/1667040/One-killed-at-polling-station-in-Libya; *Gunman attacks Libyan polling station, one dead*, THE AUSTRALIAN, July 8, 2012, *available at* http://www.theaustralian.com.au/news/breaking-news/gunman-attacks-libyan-polling-station-one-dead/story-fn3dxix6-1226420111171.

[69] *Election in Libya Proceeds as Federalist Protesters in the East Try to Disrupt Voting*, TRIPOLI POST, July 7, 2012, *available at* http://www.tripolipost.com/articledetail.asp?c=1&i=8760.

[70] SBS, *One killed at polling station in Libya*, supra note 68.

break up and disperse crowds, led to a number of civilian deaths and injuries.[71]

3.2. *Unlawful Killing*

(a) *Qadhafi Forces*

The actions of the Qadhafi forces entailed the unlawful killing of civilians in the cities of Ajdabiya and Brega. The use of indiscriminate weapons and the shelling of buildings in Ajdabiya resulted in civilian casualties. Human rights groups also documented evidence of extrajudicial killings. On 10 April 2011, Amnesty International delegates viewed the corpses of two opposition fighters found between Ajdabiya and Brega, who had been shot in the back of the head with their hands bound behind their backs with a metal wire.[72] The body of another victim, reportedly killed during the assault by Qadhafi forces on the eastern entry into Ajdabiya, was seen at the hospital with his hands and feet bound in a similar fashion.[73] Amnesty International received credible reports of four other cases of extrajudicial killings in the region carried out by Qadhafi forces.[74]

3.3. *Arbitrary Detentions and Enforced Disappearances*

(a) *Qadhafi Forces*

The practice of detention and enforced disappearance by the Qadhafi forces was prevalent in the eastern cities, including Ajdabiya. In the early days of the protests hundreds of people were arrested without charge, and abductions continued as the conflict unfolded. In some cases, Qadhafi forces threatened communities with abduction if they supported the opposition movement.[75] After Qadhafi forces recaptured Ajdabiya in mid-March 2011 there were further accounts of Qadhafi forces targeting *thuwar*

---

[71] See *Libya: Security Forces Fire on 'Day of Anger' Demonstrations*, HUMAN RIGHTS WATCH, Feb. 18, 2011, *available at* http://www.hrw.org/news/2011/02/17/libya-security-forces-fire-day-anger-demonstrations.

[72] AMNESTY INTERNATIONAL, THE BATTLE FOR LIBYA: KILLINGS, DISAPPEARANCES AND TORTURE 52 (Sept. 2011), *available at* http://www.amnesty.org/en/library/asset/MDE19/025/2011/en/8f2e1c49-8f43-46d3-917d-383c17d36377/mde1902520111en.pdf.

[73] *Id.*

[74] *Id.*

[75] Report of the International Commission of Inquiry to investigate all the alleged violations of international human rights law in the Libyan Arab Jamahiriya, U.N. HRC. 17th Sess., ¶ 98. U.N. Doc. A/HRC/17/44 (Jan. 12, 2012).

fighters and suspected supporters, and arresting them without providing information regarding their whereabouts.[76]

3.4. *Torture and Other Forms of Ill-treatment*

(a) *Qadhafi Forces*

Cases of torture and other forms of ill-treatment carried out by the Qadhafi forces were documented in Ajdabiya. Physicians for Human Rights (PHR) documented a number of cases, such as that of a prisoner detained in Ajdabiya, who gave testimony that he, along with other prisoners, suffered abuses that amounted to torture. The witness was beaten with rifle butts, kicked, spat on, and yelled at, and told PHR about the torture and ill-treatment faced by others in Ajdabiya, including prisoners who were stabbed in the buttocks and anus with bayonets.[77] The nature of the abuse and the context in which the arrests took place indicate that the victims were being punished for their opposition to the Qadhafi regime.

3.5. *Freedom of Expression*

(a) *Qadhafi Forces*

There were many recorded instances of Qadhafi forces targeting journalists with the aim of curbing the spread of information about the violent crackdown on the protests and opposition movement. The Committee to Protect Journalists recorded instances of the detention of more than 50 reporters who were stopped in combat zones in Libya, many of whom were detained in Ajdabiya and Brega.[78]

During fighting in Ajdabiya in March 2011, a number of journalists from various news outlets were detained. On 15 March, four journalists working for *The New York Times* were detained by Qadhafi soldiers in Ajdabiya and held until 21 March. During their six-day detention the journalists were threatened with death, beaten, slapped and punched; the female member of the team was sexually assaulted. Their driver, who was also detained,

---

[76] *See* McGreal, *Libyan rebels rejoice in Ajdabiya as air strikes drive Gaddafi loyalists out*, *supra* note 20.

[77] Physicians for Human Rights, Witness to War Crimes: Evidence from Misrata, Libya 13 (Aug. 2011), *available at* https://s3.amazonaws.com/PHR_Reports/Libya-WitnesstoWarCrimes-Aug2011.pdf.

[78] *See* Amnesty International, The Battle for Libya: Killings, disappearances and torture, *supra* note 72.

was killed.[79] On 19 March, a group of journalists from Agence France-Presse and Getty Images were arrested outside Ajdabiya and released on 23 March.[80] On 6 April, a Libyan cameraman and several colleagues working for the Middle East Broadcasting Corporation (MBC) were arrested by Qadhafi forces while driving from Ajdabiya to Brega. The Libyan cameraman's whereabouts remained unknown months after the incident.[81]

On 5 April, Anton Hammerl, a photojournalist, was shot and killed while covering the conflict on the outskirts of Brega. Hammerl's colleague, James Foley, witnessed two armored Libyan military trucks carrying Qadhafi troops who were firing AK-47s over their heads: "It all happened in a split second. We thought we were in the crossfire. But eventually, we realized they were shooting at us. You could see and hear the bullets hitting the ground near us."[82] Hammerl was with three other journalists; Foley, an American journalist with the Global Post; Manuel Varela de Seijas Brabo, a Spanish photographer and Morgana Gillis, an American journalist with the Christian Science Monitor. After Hammerl was shot, soldiers arrested the other journalists and confiscated their equipment. They were detained for more than six weeks before being released in Tripoli on 18 May 2011.[83]

3.6. *Attacks on Civilians, Civilian Objects, Protected Persons and Objects*

3.6.1. *Deliberate and Indiscriminate Attacks on Civilians and Civilian Objects*

(a) *Qadhafi Forces*
In Ajdabiya, Qadhafi forces reportedly used artillery and RPGs on civilian areas. A witness told the CoI about three individuals who were killed

---

[79] Jeremy Peters, *Freed Times Journalists Give Account of Captivity*, N.Y. TIMES, Mar. 21, 2011, *available at* http://www.nytimes.com/2011/03/22/world/africa/22times.html; *Libya: Free Detained Journalists*, HUMAN RIGHTS WATCH, Mar. 24, 2011, *available at* http://www.hrw.org/news/2011/03/23/libya-free-detained-journalists; *6 Journalists killed in Libya since 1992*, COMMITTEE TO PROTECT JOURNALISTS, *available at* https://cpj.org/killed/mideast/libya.

[80] *Journalists under attack in Libya: The tally*, COMMITTEE TO PROTECT JOURNALISTS, *available at* http://www.cpj.org/blog/2011/05/journalists-under-attack-in-libya.php.

[81] AMNESTY INTERNATIONAL, THE BATTLE FOR LIBYA: KILLINGS, DISAPPEARANCES AND TORTURE, *supra* note 72.

[82] Jon Jensen, *Reporter release tempered by news of colleagues death*, THE GLOBAL POST ONLINE, May 19, 2011, *available at* http://www.globalpost.com/dispatch/news/regions/africa/110519/libya-journalist-death-anton-hammerl-james-foley-clare-gillis; Report of the International Commission of Inquiry (Jan. 12, 2012), *supra* note 75 at ¶ 140.

[83] *Anton Hammerl*, COMMITTEE TO PROTECT JOURNALISTS, Apr. 5, 2011, *available at* https://cpj.org/killed/2011/anton-hammerl.php.

by rocket fire as they drove in their car with their family while fleeing Ajdabiya. A doctor from Ajdabiya corroborated that the type of injuries they saw at the hospital indicated the use of high caliber weapons and missiles.[84]

Human rights organizations documented the intentional targeting of civilians in the *thuwar* controlled residential areas of Cyrenaica. Qadhafi forces fired rockets, mortars and artillery shells indiscriminately into civilian neighborhoods, killing and injuring residents. Amnesty International further documented how Qadhafi forces fired live ammunition or heavy weapons, including tank shells and RPGs, at residents who were fleeing the fighting in Ajdabiya.[85]

There are also reports of Qadhafi forces using civilians as human shields on the outskirts of Brega in early March. As Qadhafi forces re-established control over cities which they had earlier evacuated, they moved tanks and military vehicles and equipment into residential areas, including Brega.[86] This charge was also made by NATO.[87]

In mid-March, when Qadhafi forces recaptured Ajdabiya, snipers were positioned in tall buildings in order to target the city's residents. These snipers targeted civilians and civilian objects and forced the evacuation of much of the population.[88] NGO reports indicate that many civilians were targeted and killed fleeing the city towards Benghazi, with cars being hit by rockets and artillery shells.[89]

3.6.2. *Impeding Access to Humanitarian Relief and Attacks on Humanitarian Personnel*

(a) *Qadhafi Forces*
Ajdabiya was briefly placed under siege by Qadhafi forces, involving blockades that obstructed the flow of food supplies and cut power and water supplies.[90] Media reports indicate that the greatest difficulty in Ajdabiya during the city's occupation by Qadhafi forces was the lack of

---

[84] Report of the International Commission of Inquiry (Jan. 12, 2012), *supra* note 75 at ¶ 153.

[85] AMNESTY INTERNATIONAL, THE BATTLE FOR LIBYA: KILLINGS, DISAPPEARANCES AND TORTURE, *supra* note 72 at 34.

[86] Chulov, *Battle for Brega could mark start of real war in Libya, supra* note 9.

[87] AFP, *NATO 'careful' over airstrikes, vows to protect civilians, supra* note 39.

[88] AMNESTY INTERNATIONAL, THE BATTLE FOR LIBYA: KILLINGS, DISAPPEARANCES AND TORTURE, *supra* note 72 at 48.

[89] *Id.* at 50–51.

[90] Report of the International Commission of Inquiry (Jan. 12, 2012), *supra* note 75 at ¶ 161.

access to basic supplies and the lack of access to healthcare due to the conflict and the fears of hospital staff. After the occupation of the city by Qadhafi forces the local hospital closed since most of its staff had fled out of fear that they would become targets after some doctors had publicly sided with the *thuwar*.[91]

3.6.3. *Attacks on Protected Medical Personnel, Transport and Facilities*

(a) *Qadhafi Forces*

There were instances of ambulances in Ajdabiya being shot at by Qadhafi forces. A fighter with the NTC reported an incident in Ajdabiya where he rode with other injured fighters in an ambulance that was shot at while on the way to the hospital.[92] PHR documented a case in which Qadhafi forces stopped and detained a volunteer ambulance driver on 17 March 2011. The individual was transporting a number of wounded individuals to the hospital in eastern Ajdabiya. On his return from the hospital, he was beaten and detained by Qadhafi forces.[93]

3.7. *Prohibited Weapons*

(a) *Qadhafi Forces*

Reports indicate that antipersonnel and anti-vehicle landmines were utilized by Qadhafi forces near Ajdabiya.[94] Human Rights Watch reported 24 anti-vehicle mines and approximately three dozen antipersonnel mines discovered on the eastern outskirts of Ajdabiya, in an area that Qadhafi forces controlled from 17 and 27 March 2011. Due to their location, the mines posed a direct threat to the civilian population.[95]

---

[91] McGreal, *Libyan rebels rejoice in Ajdabiya as air strikes drive Gaddafi loyalists out*, *supra* note 20.

[92] Report of the International Commission of Inquiry (Jan. 12, 2012), *supra* note 75 at ¶ 166.

[93] Physicians for Human Rights, Witness to War Crimes: Evidence from Misrata, Libya, *supra* note 77 at 12–13.

[94] Donatella Rovera, *Mines pose new danger as Libya battles rage on*, Amensty International, Apr. 6, 2011, *available at* http://livewire.amnesty.org/2011/04/06/mines-pose-new-danger-as-libya-battles-rage-on. For more on the use of prohibited weapons in Ajdabiya and the region, *see* Ch. VII, Sec. 7.

[95] Report of the International Commission of Inquiry (Jan. 12, 2012), *supra* note 75 at ¶ 177.

There was also evidence that Qadhafi forces laid mines along the Coastal Highway on the approach from Ajdabiya to Brega. The mines formed an integral part of the Qadhafi forces' defense of the town and helped thwart the advance of opposition forces in July 2011.[96] On 28 March 2011 two anti-personnel mines exploded less than a mile from Ajdabiya. A civil-defense group stated that they disarmed 24 anti-vehicle mines and more than 30 plastic antipersonnel mines in a clearance operation after the incident.[97]

After the cessation of hostilities, the Mines Advisory Group reported in June 2011 that, in conjunction with the International Committee of the Red Cross, they had destroyed more than 400 deadly items of unexploded ordnance from the Ajdabiya region, including bounding fragmentation mines.[98] 6,000 explosives were also reportedly found on Brega beach and, according to the NTC, 40,000 mines had been planted around Brega during the fighting.[99]

3.8. Mercenaries

(a) Qadhafi Forces

Leaders of the opposition alleged that mercenaries from Serbia had fought for the Qadhafi forces in Ajdabiya in March 2011. According to the opposition, these Serbs offered surrender in return for safe passage to Serbia.[100] There were reports of Qadhafi fighters in Brega, including young children, who had been flown in from Niger and were given weapons and promised money to fight.[101] In another case, witnesses reported being robbed

---

[96] AP, *Libyan rebels fall back after failed advance on eastern oil town*, *supra* note 52; AP, *Medical official: 10 Libyan rebels killed in push for eastern oil town*, *supra* note 52; Graff, *Heavy casualties reported in Libya fighting*, *supra* note 52; Stephan, *Libyan rebels push towards Brega backed by Nato air strikes*, *supra* note 52.

[97] Report of the International Commission of Inquiry (Jan. 12, 2012), *supra* note 75 at n. 151.

[98] *Hundreds of unexploded devices destroyed in Ajdabiya*, MINES ADVISORY GROUP, June 9, 2011, *available at* http://reliefweb.int/node/419314.

[99] Emma Farge, *Libya oil flows, foreign workers wait*, REUTERS, Sept. 23, 2011, *available at* http://www.reuters.com/article/2011/09/23/us-libya-oil-idUSTRE78M1TW20110923.

[100] McGreal, *Libyan rebels rejoice in Ajdabiya as air strikes drive Gaddafi loyalists out*, *supra* note 20.

[101] Korva Koleman, *Gadhafi Using Foreign Children As Mercenaries In Libya*, NPR, Mar. 3, 2011, *available at* http://www.npr.org/blogs/thetwo-way/2011/03/03/134223827/gadhafi-using-foreign-children-as-mercenaries-in-libya.

by mercenaries from Chad and Niger who were stationed at checkpoints outside of Ajdabiya.[102]

3.9. *Sexual Violence*[103]

(a) *Qadhafi Forces*

There were reports acts of sexual violence committed by Qadhafi forces in Ajdabiya. In one case involving a foreign journalist, a female photographer working for the New York Times, Lindsey Addario, was arrested by Qadhafi forces on 15 March at a checkpoint near Ajdabiya and detained for six days. During her detention she reported having suffered sexual harassment at the hands of several soldiers in the detention center.[104]

In another instance, a woman reported being raped in front of her family by Qadhafi soldiers who had come to detain her brothers.[105] The CoI also received allegations that minors, aged 7–10, were subjected to sexual assaults by Qadhafi soldiers in Ajdabiya.[106] The CoI could not confirm these alleged reports.

---

[102] PHYSICIANS FOR HUMAN RIGHTS, WITNESS TO WAR CRIMES: EVIDENCE FROM MISRATA, LIBYA, *supra* note 77 at 12–13. For more on the use of mercenaries, *see supra* Sec. 3.8.

[103] The following terms are defined in accordance with the jurisprudence of the ICTY and ICTR, and other mixed-model tribunals.

   1. "Rape" is the penetration, however slight, of any part of the body of another person irrespective of gender (namely, the vagina, anus, or mouth) by means of the perpetrator's sexual organ or any object used by the perpetrator when accompanied by force or threat of force against the person or a third party which the victim believes is real.

   2. "Sexual violence" is defined as any physical act of a sexual nature which is committed on a person under circumstances which are coercive or threatening to the person or to any other person, which includes physical touching, groping, fondling, removal of a person's clothing to display intimate parts of the person's body whether in the presence of one or more persons, or any other act of a demeaning sexual nature.

   3. "Sexual harassment" is any threat of "rape" or "sexual violence," as defined above, against a person or any other person for purposes of demeaning, intimidating, or punishing the person in question.

[104] Report of the International Commission of Inquiry (Jan. 12, 2012), *supra* note 75 at ¶ 141.

[105] *Id.* at ¶ 205.

[106] *Id. See also id.* at n. 181.

In March 2011, Al Jazeera reported that Viagra and condoms had been found on the bodies of dead Qadhafi soldiers in Ajdabiya.[107] Various stories subsequently circulated claiming that Viagra had been utilized to promote rape. However, the National Institute of Searching for Missing Persons in Misrata and Ajdabiya, which photographed and documented the bodies of dead Qadhafi soldiers, did not discover Viagra on their persons nor among their belongings.[108] The Viagra story was largely circulated throughout Libya, but never confirmed. It is more likely to be a hoax.

(b) Thuwar *Forces*

There were reports of armed opposition members committing rape during house raids in the areas of Ajdabiya and Al-Marj. One such report was by an Iraqi woman and a Libyan woman who respectively stated they had been raped by armed *thuwar* in their homes on Al-Tulatat Street in Ajdabiya in early March 2011.[109] No confirmation.

3.10. *The Use of Children and their Treatment in Armed Conflict*

(a) *Qadhafi Forces*

Media reports indicated that a number of Qadhafi soldiers in Al-Brega were mercenaries from Niger, at least one of whom was 13 but all of whom appeared to be children.[110]

4. THE ROLE OF NATO

During the first months of the armed conflict, NATO's air campaign was focused heavily on the areas around Ajdabiya and Brega. An important shift took place during this period as Qadhafi forces transitioned from the use of modern armor to using civilian vehicles. With the regime's

---

[107] Lakomtube, *Viagra and Condoms with Soldiers in Ajdabiya*, YOUTUBE (Mar. 27, 2011), *available at* http://www.youtube.com/watch?v=tYmdyy1kRoo.

[108] Report of the International Commission of Inquiry, advance unedited version (Mar. 2, 2012), *supra* note 35 at Annex I, ¶ 518.

[109] Report of the International Commission of Inquiry (Jan. 12, 2012), *supra* note 75 at ¶ 207.

[110] *Gadhafi Using Foreign Children As Mercenaries In Libya*, NPR, Mar. 3 2011, *available at* http://www.npr.org/blogs/thetwo-way/2011/03/03/134223827/gadhafi-using-foreign-children-as-mercenaries-in-libya.

air defenses essentially neutralized, the Qadhafi forces were forced to engage in ground warfare, and in doing so adopted some of the means and methods of the *thuwar*.[111] NATO pilots were thus unable to distinguish opposition from government vehicles, and strikes were accidentally carried out on opposition convoys in Ajdabiya and Brega, leading to the deaths of rebel fighters as well as civilians.[112]

Three airstrikes in early April that led to both *thuwar* and civilian deaths caused anger among the civilian population and rebel forces.[113] On 1 April 2011, 13 *thuwar* fighters were reported killed between Ajdabiya and Brega.[114] NATO maintained afterwards that the airstrike was prompted by celebratory fire from *thuwar* fighters.[115] Another reported incident a few days later involving a Qadhafi forces convoy near Brega resulted in five civilian casualties and 25 injuries.[116] A third incident took place on 7 April when NATO airstrikes hit a *thuwar* forces convoy on its way to Brega.[117] The airstrike was particularly damaging for the rebel forces as it destroyed tanks that had just been refurbished and were the first pieces of armor in their arsenal, significantly setting back their operational capacity in the Ajdabiya area.[118]

---

[111] Fahim & Kirkpatrick, *Rebel Advance Halted Outside Qaddafi Hometown*, *supra* note 28; AFP, *NATO 'careful' over airstrikes, vows to protect civilians*, *supra* note 39.

[112] Ben Hubbard & Ryan Lucas, *Libyan rebels say airstrike killed 13 of their own*, AP, Apr. 2, 2011, *available at* http://usatoday30.usatoday.com/money/topstories/2011-04-01-2450814691_x.htm; Bahrampour, *Libyan rebels struggle to explain rift*, *supra* note 44; Sebastian Abbot, *Libyan rebels: NATO airstrikes hit our forces*, AP, Apr. 7, 2011, *available at* http://www.navytimes.com/news/2011/04/ap-libyan-rebels-nato-airstrikes-hit-our-forces-040711w; Leila Fadel & Simon Denyer, *Libyan rebels targeted in airstrikes despite no-fly zone, rebels say*, THE WASHINGTON POST, Apr. 7, 2011, *available at* http://articles.washingtonpost.com/2011-04-07/world/35262954_1_ajdabiya-government-attacks-libyan-rebels; *Libyan rebels on run, NATO strike kills 2 fighters*, AFP, Apr. 7, 2011, *available at* http://173.254.58.56/~islamtri/2011/04/07/libyan-rebels-on-run-nato-strike-kills-2-fighters.html.

[113] Michael Georgy, *Rebels blame Libya air strike on mistake by NATO*, REUTERS, Apr. 7, 2011, *available at* http://www.reuters.com/article/2011/04/07/us-libya-east-strike-idUSTRE73625W20110407; BBC, *Libyan rebels near Ajdabiya 'killed in Nato air strike'*, *supra* note 36.

[114] *Id. See* Ch. VII, Sec. 2.

[115] Oana Lungescu & Mark van Uhm, *Press Briefing on Libya*, NORTH ATLANTIC TREATY ORGANIZATION, Apr. 5, 2011, *available at* http://www.nato.int/cps/en/natolive/opinions_72027.htm.

[116] BBC, *Libyan rebels near Ajdabiya 'killed in Nato air strike'*, *supra* note 36.

[117] *Id. See also* Allen et al., *Errant NATO Airstrikes in Libya: 13 Cases (Brega)*, *supra* note 42.

[118] Allen et al., *Errant NATO Airstrikes in Libya: 13 Cases (Brega)*, *supra* note 42; Oana Lungescu & Russell Harding, *Press Briefing on events concerning Libya*, NORTH ATLANTIC TREATY ORGANIZATION, Apr. 8, 2011, *available at* http://www.nato.int/cps/en/natolive/opinions_72150.htm. *See also* Ch. VII, Sec. 4.

Thuwar forces claimed that they had informed NATO of their location and that their vehicles had been clearly marked as friendly forces. NATO, however, denied that they had been informed and initially refused to apologize.[119] NATO described the military front between Brega and Ajdabiya as a "very fluid situation" where troops moved back and forth, making it difficult for NATO to carry out accurate airstrikes.[120] The issue over the lack of communication between *thuwar* and NATO forces was raised during a press conference on 8 April, in response to a question regarding whether opposition leader General Yunis had alerted NATO that *thuwar* forces were using tanks in the region.[121] The question of Yunis' loyalty became an issue of controversy with some members of the *thuwar* blaming the former military commander for providing misleading intelligence in order to sabotage the opposition's military in the east. The contestation over the issue was cited as a possible reason for Yunis' assassination in July 2011.[122]

After the incidents in April, NATO began to reconsider its strike tactics. The 7 April bombing, as with other operations around this period, involved two strikes, an initial assault and a follow-on bombing. This approach was highly criticized for endangering civilians. Following these incidents, a NATO spokesperson announced that the alliance would reconsider its tactics "as part of its internal campaign review."[123]

On 13 May 2011, a NATO airstrike hit a guesthouse in Brega, killing 16 civilians and wounding 40. Media outlets reported that a NATO spokesperson, Squadron Leader Mike Bracken, provided no information about the incident.[124] Libya's state television reported that the strike took place

---

[119] BELL & WITTER, STALEMATE & SIEGE, *supra* note 19 at 33.

[120] Lungescu & Harding, *Press Briefing on events concerning Libya, supra* note 118. *See also* Ch. VII.

[121] Press Release, *Operational Media Update for 7 April 2011*, NORTH ATLANTIC TREATY ORGANIZATION, Apr. 7, 2011, *available at* http://www.nato.int/nato_static/assets/pdf/pdf_2011_04/20110402_110402-oup-update.pdf; Press Release, *Operational Media Update for 8 April 2011*, NORTH ATLANTIC TREATY ORGANIZATION, Apr. 8, 2011, *available at* http://www.nato.int/cps/en/natolive/opinions_72150.htm.

[122] Allen et al., *Errant NATO Airstrikes in Libya: 13 Cases (Brega), supra* note 42. For more on the killing of General Yunis, *see supra* Ch. VI, Sec. 2.2. & Ch. II, Sec. 2.3.

[123] *Id. See also* Ch. III, Sec. 6.2.

[124] Sami Aboudi, *UPDATE 1 – NATO strike kills at least 16 in Brega -Libyan TV*, REUTERS, May 13, 2011, *available at* http://af.reuters.com/article/energyOilNews/idAFLDE74C1GL 20110513; Andrew Gilligan, *Libya: Nato air strike 'kills 11 imams'*, THE TELEGRAPH, May 13, 2011, *available at* http://www.telegraph.co.uk/news/worldnews/africaandindianocean/libya/8513402/Libya-Nato-air-strike-kills-11-imams.html. *See also* Ch. III. Sec. 6.2.

at dawn and hit a religious ceremony leading to the deaths of many clerics.[125]

On 16 June 2011, a NATO airstrike hit a *thuwar* forces column near Brega, destroying six vehicles and wounding 16 persons.[126] NATO daily updates confirmed carrying out strikes near Brega that hit seven truck-mounted guns and three tanks.[127] NATO again blamed the incident on the confusion caused by a "fluid battle scenario."[128] Just over a week later, on 25 June, Libya's state news agency, Jana, reported that a NATO airstrike near Brega killed 15 civilians and wounded 20 close to a restaurant and a bakery.[129] According to NATO daily updates, NATO made several strikes in Brega that day, destroying two tanks, one logistic truck, six technical vehicles, three military shelters, four military compounds and one antenna.[130]

5. CONCLUSION

The Ajdabiya and Brega theater of military operations experienced pivotal battles that helped determine the outcome of the conflict. One of the prominent characteristics of this theater was the long stalemate between Qadhafi and *thuwar* forces. It was the entrenched nature of the fighting in and around Ajdabiya and Brega that led to this region becoming the critical front for the rebels that kept the Qadhafi forces from advancing further into eastern Cyrenaica. The rebel forces on this front played a critical role in preventing the regime troops from reaching the NTC headquarters – the political base of the revolution – in Benghazi.

---

[125] Report of the International Commission of Inquiry (Jan. 12, 2012), *supra* note 75 at ¶ 224.

[126] *NATO probes reported errant strike on Libya rebels*, REUTERS, June 17, 2011, *available at* http://af.reuters.com/article/topNews/idAFJOE75G0EZ20110617. *See also* Ch. III, Sec. 6.2.

[127] Press Release, *Operational Media Update for 16 June 2011*, NORTH ATLANTIC TREATY ORGANIZATION, June 16, 2011, *available at* http://www.nato.int/nato_static/assets/pdf/pdf_2011_06/20110617_110617-oup-update.pdf.

[128] Oana Lungescu & Mike Bracken, *Press Briefing on events concerning Libya*, NORTH ATLANTIC TREATY ORGANIZATION, June 21, 2011, *available at* http://www.nato.int/cps/en/natolive/opinions_75652.htm.

[129] *Libyan state media say NATO airstrike kills 15*, AP, June 26, 2011, *available at* http://www.usatoday.com/news/world/2011-06-25-Libya-NATO-airstrike_n.htm. *See also* Ch. III, Sec. 6.2.

[130] *Operational Media Update for 25 June*, NORTH ATLANTIC TREATY ORGANIZATION, *available at* http://www.nato.int/nato_static/assets/pdf/pdf_2011_06/20110626_110626-oup-update.pdf.

NATO's intervention played an important role in Ajdabiya and Brega during the war, significantly aiding the *thuwar* successes in the region. The NATO strikes against Qadhafi forces helped shield the opposition from attack, aiding their advances and easing their retreats. By neutralizing the Qadhafi forces' air defenses, NATO transformed the conflict to a theater of ground operations. On the ground, Qadhafi forces then engaged in tactics similar to the rebels, using civilian vehicles for transport. As the regime forces adopted new tactics, however, targeted bombings became more difficult and NATO conducted strikes that led to the killings of friendly forces as well as civilians.

The nature of the conflict in Ajdabiya and Brega also created an environment that fueled violations against civilians and armed combatants alike. In February 2011, during the early days of the uprising, Qadhafi forces were deployed to crush the demonstrations with excessive force, involving the use of live ammunition to disperse gatherings. Evidence indicates that the Qadhafi forces failed to employ or attempt to employ standard policing methods to control the crowds. Further evidence indicates that the violence targeted unarmed civilian protesters before the opposition armed itself.

The use of indiscriminate weapons and excessive force by the Qadhafi regime resulted in the unlawful killing of civilians. In addition to this, Qadhafi forces also carried out extrajudicial killings of rebel fighters who had surrendered and were no longer armed. The available information indicates that Qadhafi forces perpetrated acts that constitute unlawful killings.

Evidence exists to conclude that the Qadhafi forces detained and disappeared protesters and members of the opposition in February 2011 when the first protests broke out, as well as in March 2011 when Qadhafi forces briefly retook Ajdabiya, and again in May 2011. In a number of these cases the individuals were held for extended periods without contact with their families and friends, and in some cases remain disappeared. During detention, *thuwar* fighters or suspected supporters of the opposition suffered abuses of torture and ill-treatment. Information suggests that the violent acts were meant to punish individuals for demonstrating publicly against the regime and for supporting the opposition movement.

There were several incidents reported in which Qadhafi forces targeted medical personnel and equipment, including ambulances and their drivers. Where the individuals were identifiable as medical providers and were in clearly marked vehicles, such targeting would constitute a violation of the protections afforded these individuals and objects. The targeting of clearly marked ambulances by Qadhafi forces in Ajdabiya would therefore constitute a violation of the protections afforded under international humanitarian law.

Reports indicate that Qadhafi forces detained journalists after capturing Ajdabiya in mid-March 2011. It appears that the affected reporters were detained in the area west of the city and along the road towards Brega. The cases of detention and abuses against journalists amounts to the limiting the freedom of expression and opinion during the fight for Ajdabiya and Brega.

There is substantial information indicating that the Qadhafi forces intentionally targeted and attacked civilians. Indiscriminate attacks against the civilian population in Ajdabiya were most prominent during the initial protests in mid-February 2011 and again in March 2011. These attacks involved placing snipers in buildings in western Ajdabiya, as well as using artillery, cluster bombs, rockets and mortars on civilian neighborhoods. Reports also indicate that the Qadhafi regime placed troops in civilian neighborhoods to avoid engagement from NATO jets and used civilians as human shields during their advances. The siege implemented by Qadhafi forces also caused the hospitals in Ajdabiya to run out of supplies during the conflict.

Information indicates that Qadhafi and *thuwar* forces committed acts of sexual violence against women in Ajdabiya, including rape and other forms of sexual abuse. On the basis of the available reports, it can be reasonably concluded that both Qadhafi and *thuwar* forces targeted women for sexual violence.

There were documented cases of the use of landmines by Qadhafi forces in Ajdabiya and Brega , and some evidence of the use of cluster munitions in Ajdabiya. Reports also indicate the presence of foreign fighters in Ajdabiya and Brega, including a contingent of young soldiers from Niger and the presence of Qadhafi forces reportedly of Chadian and Nigerian origin.[131]

---

[131] It is not determined if the suspected foreign fighters met the legal requirements to be classified as mercenaries. Media sources frequently reported the presence of mercenaries however doubt exists as to whether they were indeed mercenaries in the legal sense.

CHAPTER EIGHT

RA'S LANUF & BIN JAWAD

1. Introduction

Ra's Lanuf is a coastal town that lies 100 kilometers (62 miles) west of Brega[1] and 200 kilometers (126 miles) southeast of Sirte.[2] With a shipping harbor and an airport, it serves as an important center for Libya's petrochemical industry.[3] Ra's Lanuf is also a major oil exporting center and houses Libya's largest oil refinery, the Ra's Lanuf Refinery, which accounts for about 60 percent (220 out of 378 thousand barrels per day) of Libya's total oil refining capacity.[4] The town is also home to the Ra's Lanuf petrochemical complex and various oil pipelines.[5]

During the war, fighting erupted in Ra's Lanuf. The city was captured by *thuwar* forces in early March 2011 who pushed the frontline westwards towards Bin Jawad, a city situated approximately 30 kilometers (19 miles) west of Ra's Lanuf along the coast.[6] Qadhafi forces then pushed the frontline back eastwards towards Ajdabiya and Brega, and Ra's Lanuf remained under the control of the Qadhafi regime until August 2011.[7]

---

[1] Tom Pfeiffer, *UPDATE 1 – Libya rebels say Gaddafi forces retreat in east*, Reuters, July 18, 2011, *available at* http://www.reuters.com/article/2011/07/18/libya-east-idUSLDE-76H0MR20110718.

[2] Anthony Bell & David Witter, Institute for the Study of War, 2 The Libyan Revolution: The Roots of Rebellion 24 (Sept. 2011) [hereinafter "The Roots of Rebellion"], *available at* www.understandingwar.org/sites/default/files/Libya_Part2_0.pdf.

[3] *Ras Lanuf – Harbour*, Tracks 4 Africa, *available at* http://tracks4africa.co.za/listings/item/w185925; *RAS LANUF OIL Airport Private Jet Charter Flights and Air Charter Service*, Stratos Jet Charter Services, *available at* http://www.stratosjets.com/jet-charter-airports/Libya/RAS-LANUF-OIL.

[4] Bell & Witter, The Roots of Rebellion, *supra* note 2 at 26; Varun Vira & anthony H. Cordesman, The Libyan Uprising: An Uncertain Trajectory, Center for Strategic and International Studies 14 (June 20, 2011) [hereinafter "The Libyan Uprising"], *available at* http://csis.org/files/publication/110620_libya.pdf.

[5] *North Africa Pipelines map – Crude Oil (petroleum) pipelines – Natural Gas pipelines – Products pipelines*, Countries of the world, May 6, 2008, *available at* http://theodora.com/pipelines/north_africa_oil_gas_products_pipelines_map.html.

[6] *Libya: at least a dozen killed in Bin Jawad clashes*, The Telegraph, Mar. 7, 2011, *available at* http://www.telegraph.co.uk/news/worldnews/africaandindianocean/libya/8365811/Libya-at-least-a-dozen-killed-in-Bin-Jawad-clashes.html.

[7] Robert Birsel, *Clashes as Libyan rebels try to press Gaddafi stronghold*, Reuters, Aug. 25, 2011, *available at* www.jpost.com/Headlines/Article.aspx?id=235376.

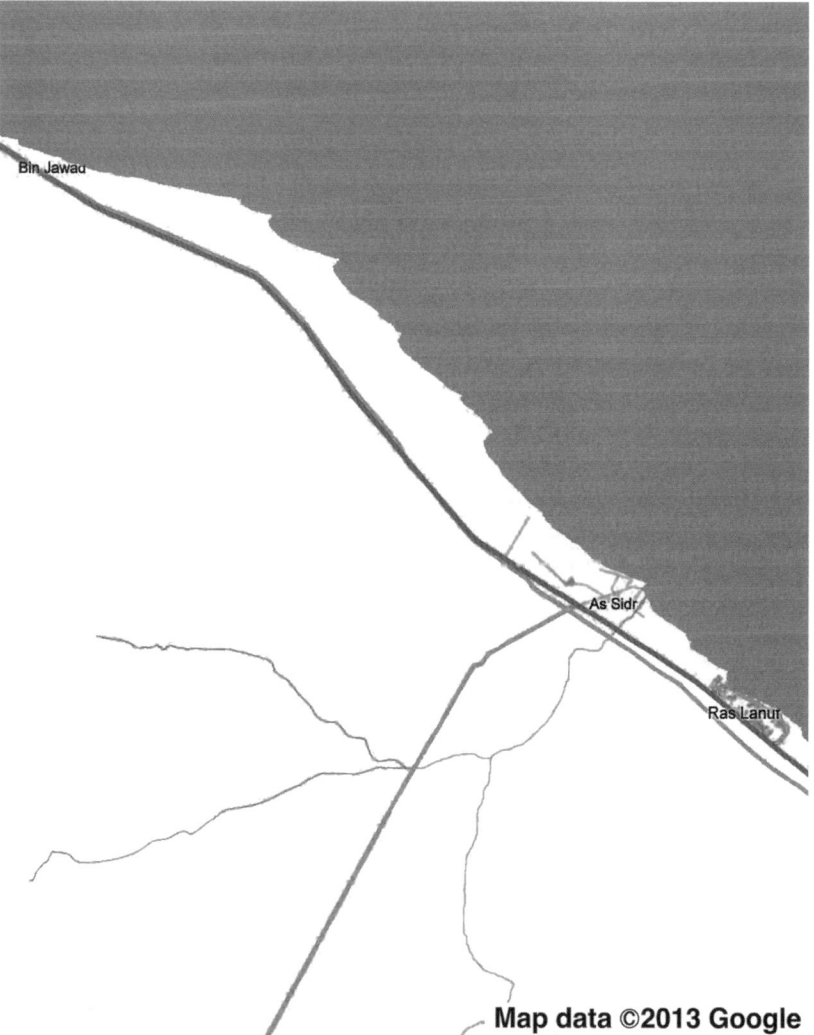

Map 5: Regional map of Ra's Lanuf and Bin Jawad (Map data © 2013 Google).

2. Summary of Events

Thuwar forces began to operate outside their stronghold in Benghazi and advanced westwards in late February-early March 2011.[8] On 4 March, their capture of Brega paved the way for an advance 112 kilometers (70 miles) further west into Ra's Lanuf, continuing westwards towards Bin Jawad.[9] Sources estimated that 7,000 fighters had deployed west from Benghazi towards the front in Ra's Lanuf and Bin Jawad.[10] Media accounts reported that fighting took place ten kilometers (6.2 miles) east of Ra's Lanuf,[11] and that Qadhafi aircraft were circling over both Ra's Lanuf and Bin Jawad to combat the sizeable *thuwar* troop deployments.[12]

As clashes over Ra's Lanuf ensued, one witness stated that he saw four people killed by Grad rockets fired by Qadhafi forces and that *thuwar* were retreating in the face of superior weaponry. A doctor reported from a hospital in Ra's Lanuf that there were "many dead and wounded" due to a rocket fired by Qadhafi forces.[13] Local hospitals reported ten casualties and 20 wounded. Opposition sources reported that 16 *thuwar* and 25 government fighters died during the clashes.[14]

The battle for Ra's Lanuf was brief, and the same day, on 4 March, *thuwar* sources reported that the city and its airport were under rebel

---

[8] Morgan Strong, *News Summary from the US/International Press on the Libyan Crisis*, The Tripoli Post, Mar. 8, 2011, *available at* http://tripolipost.com/articledetail .asp?c=1&i=5544; *Libyan warplanes strike rebels at oil port*, AP, Mar. 8, 2011, *available at* http://dawn.com/2011/03/08/libyan-warplanes-strike-rebels-at-oil-port.

[9] Leila Fadel & Steve Hendrix, *Libya's rebels hold back Gaddafi's forces*, The Washington Post, Mar. 3, 2011, *available at* http://www.washingtonpost.com/wp-dyn/content/ article/2011/03/02/AR2011030207023.html; Dan Murphy, *Battles erupt in key cities, moving Libya close to civil war*, Christian Science Monitor, Mar. 4, 2011, *available at* http:// www.csmonitor.com/World/Middle-East/2011/0304/Battles-erupt-in-key-cities-moving-Libya-closer-to-civil-war; Dan Murphy, *In disorganized surge, Libya's rebels push west along shifting front line*, Christian Science Monitor, Mar. 5, 2011, *available at* http:// www.csmonitor.com/World/Middle-East/2011/0305/In-disorganized-surge-Libya-s-rebels-push-west-along-shifting-front-line.

[10] *Gaddafi forces accused of 'massacre' as battles rage*, AFP, Mar. 6, 2011, *available at* http://www.timesofmalta.com/articles/view/20110305/local/gaddafi-forces-accused-of-massacre-as-battles-rage.353261.

[11] *Gaddafi forces hit rebels east and west*, The Australian, Mar. 5, 2011, *available at* http://www.theaustralian.com.au/news/world/gaddafi-forces-hit-rebels-east-and-west/ story-e6frg6so-1226016290063.

[12] AFP, *Gaddafi forces accused of 'massacre' as battles rage, supra* note 10. For more on the March 2011 fighting and *thuwar* advances, *see* Ch. II, Sec. 3.3.

[13] The Australian, *Gaddafi forces hit rebels east and west, supra* note 11.

[14] AFP, *Gaddafi forces accused of 'massacre' as battles rage, supra* note 10.

control.[15] Media outlets described how *thuwar* managed to shoot down government aircraft near Ra's Lanuf the following day, killing one pilot.[16] Similarly, on 10 March, *thuwar* stated that a government aircraft piloted by men of Syrian and Serbian origin had been shot down.[17]

Human Rights Watch also confirmed the use of Grad rocket launchers by *thuwar* forces around the town of Ra's Lanuf.[18] With such weaponry, the *thuwar* seized the city on 5 March,[19] and continued to Bin Jawad, 25 miles northwest of Ra's Lanuf. They then took control of Bin Jawad, but failed to establish a defensive position.[20] Many fighters returned to Ra's Lanuf overnight in preparation to move westwards towards Sirte the following day.[21]

Qadhafi forces returned the following day, attacking the city of Bin Jawad in the morning and halting a *thuwar* advance towards Sirte and

---

[15] Peter Millership, *UPDATE 1 – Libyan rebels take oil town of Ras Lanuf- rebels*, REUTERS, Mar. 4, 2011, *available at* http://www.reuters.com/article/2011/03/04/libya-port-idUSLDE72320420110304.

[16] Philip Sherwell, *Gaddafi and rebel forces in heavy clashes in town of Zawiya*, THE TELE-GRAPH, Mar. 5, 2011, *available at* http://www.telegraph.co.uk/news/worldnews/africaand-indianocean/libya/8363927/Gaddafi-and-rebel-forces-in-heavy-clashes-in-town-of-Zawiya.html; AFP, *Gaddafi forces accused of 'massacre' as battles rage, supra* note 10.

[17] Amy Chew, *Oil-rich town of Ras Lanuf a major battleground*, THE STAR ONLINE, Mar. 10, 2011, *available at* http://thestar.com.my/news/story.asp?file=/2011/3/10/nation/8224848&sec=nation.

[18] *Libya: Abandoned Weapons, Landmines Endanger Civilians*, HUMAN RIGHTS WATCH, Apr. 5, 2011, *available at* http://www.hrw.org/news/2011/04/05/libya-abandoned-weapons-landmines-endanger-civilians-0.

[19] *Libya rebels gain ground in east as council meets*, AFP, Mar. 5, 2011, *available at* http://www.timesofmalta.com/articles/view/20110305/local/libyan-rebels-gain-ground-in-east-as-council-meets.353258; Mariam Fam et al., *Gaddafi strikes rebels in west as battles rage in oil ports*, THE WASHINGTON POST, Mar. 4, 2011, *available at* http://www.washingtonpost.com/wp-dyn/content/article/2011/03/04/AR2011030402184.html; *Up to 10 killed in Libyan clashes at Ras Lanuf: doctor*, IPOT NEWS, Mar. 5, 2011, *available at* http://www.ipotnews.com/index.php?jdl=Up_to_10_killed_in_Libyan_clashes_at_Ras_Lanuf__doctor&level2=&level3=&level4=international&news_id=437294&group_news=ALLNEWS&taging_subtype=BANKING&popular=&search=y&q=.

[20] Dan Murphy, *Qaddafi strikes back at Libya rebels' western advance*, CHRISTIAN SCI-ENCE MONITOR, Mar. 6, 2011, *available at* http://www.csmonitor.com/World/Middle-East/2011/0306/Qaddafi-strikes-back-at-Libya-rebels-western-advance.

[21] *Rebels come under heavy fire in push to Gaddafi's heartland*, THE INDEPENDENT, Mar. 7, 2011, *available at* http://www.independent.co.uk/news/world/africa/regime-hits-back-as-rebels-push-on-to-gaddafis-heartland-2234232.html; CHRISTIAN SCIENCE MONITOR, *Qaddafi strikes back at Libya rebels' western advance, supra* note 20; David Zucchino, *Mistakes costing Libyan rebels: untrained fighters miss opportunities and waste ammunition*, L.A. TIMES, Mar. 8, 2011, *available at* http://articles.latimes.com/2011/mar/08/world/la-fg-libya-rebels-20110308. *See also* Ch. II, Sec. 3.3.

Tripoli.[22] While *thuwar* forces had returned to Ra's Lanuf, Qadhafi forces had taken up positions in Bin Jawad overnight, occupying houses and residential areas, and ambushed the *thuwar* as they re-entered the city.[23] International media reported that the local population of Bin Jawad remained loyal to Qadhafi and supported regime forces in their attacks against the *thuwar*.[24] Indeed, Qadhafi's soldiers were allowed to fire from residential homes and some residents assisted by taking up arms against the rebels. Opposition fighters reported that Qadhafi forces had ambushed them with machine guns and rocket-propelled grenades (RPGs) and were firing mortars.[25] Attack helicopters and warplanes were first used against *thuwar* in Bin Jawad, but had a limited impact.[26]

By the evening of 6 March, Bin Jawad was under Qadhafi's control and *thuwar* continued to retreat towards Ra's Lanuf. In Ra's Lanuf they were targeted with artillery and aerial bombardment over the next three days.[27] Qadhafi forces shelled the *thuwar* forces with artillery and mortar, continuing to push them eastwards, deterring several attempts to retake

---

[22] *Libyan rebels regroup and advance on Bin Jawad*, REUTERS, Mar. 6, 2011, *available at* http://af.reuters.com/article/topNews/idAFJOE7250D920110306.

[23] BELL & WITTER, THE ROOTS OF REBELLION, *supra* note 2 at 26; THE INDEPENDENT, *Rebels come under heavy fire in push to Gaddafi's heartland*, *supra* note 21; *Clashes as rebels deny Libyan counter-offensive claim*, Mar. 6, 2011, AFP, *available at* http://www.timesofmalta.com/articles/view/20110306/local/clashes-as-rebels-deny-libyan-counter-offensive-claim.353429; Lourdes Garcia Navarro, *Libya fight rages as Gadhafi strikes back*, NPR, Mar. 6, 2011, *available at* http://www.npr.org/2011/03/06/134314541/Libya-Fight-Rages-As-Gadhafi-Strikes-Back.

[24] BELL & WITTER, THE ROOTS OF REBELLION, *supra* note 2 at 26; NPR, *Libya fight rages as Gadhafi strikes back*, *supra* note 23.

[25] REUTERS, *Libyan rebels regroup and advance on Bin Jawad*, *supra* note 22.

[26] BELL & WITTER, THE ROOTS OF REBELLION, *supra* note 2 at 26; CHRISTIAN SCIENCE MONITOR, *Qaddafi strikes back at Libya rebels' western advance*, *supra* note 21; Navarro, *Libya fight rages as Gadhafi strikes back*, *supra* note 23.

[27] BELL & WITTER, THE ROOTS OF REBELLION, *supra* note 2 at 27; Kareem Fahim & David D. Kirkpatrick, *Libyan government presses assault on oil refinery in east and city in west*, N.Y. TIMES, Mar. 8, 2011, http://www.nytimes.com/2011/03/08/world/africa/08libya.html; *Kadhafi uses air strikes, artillery on rebel-held town*, AFP, Mar. 8, 2011, *available at* http://www.timesofmalta.com/articles/view/20110309/world/gaddafi-uses-air-strikes-and-artillery-on-rebel-held-town.353842; Dan Murphy, *Qaddafi air strikes intensify, unnerving Libya rebels*, CHRISTIAN SCIENCE MONITOR, Mar. 8, 2011, *available at* http://www.csmonitor.com/World/Middle-East/2011/0308/Qaddafi-air-strikes-intensify-unnerving-Libya-rebels; David Zucchino, *Air attacks put Libya town on edge*, L.A. TIMES, Mar. 9, 2011, *available at* http://articles.latimes.com/2011/mar/09/world/la-fg-libya-ras-lanuf-20110309; *Libyan rebels under intense artillery fire in east*, AL AHRAM, Mar. 9, 2011, *available at* http://english.ahram.org.eg/NewsContent/2/8/7346/World/Region/Libyan-rebels-under-intense-artillery-fire-in-east.aspx.

the town.[28] As previously mentioned, Qadhafi forces used helicopters and warplanes against *thuwar*, yet these attacks resulted in a small number of casualties.[29] Some analysts have argued that the ineffectiveness of the airstrikes shows a reluctance on the part of the pilots to kill rather than technical incompetence. However, the attacks succeeded in that they forced the *thuwar* groups to disperse and deterred their attempts to counterattack. By the 10–11 March, *thuwar* retreated towards Brega.[30]

Qadhafi forces continued to carry out airstrikes on Ra's Lanuf. A warplane attacked a small military base in the city with rockets and artillery, destroying three hangars and a small building. Ambulances rushed towards the town and *thuwar* forces moved trucks and four multiple-rocket launchers to the frontlines. Four people were killed in the fighting, and hospital officials reported that a French journalist with France 24 TV was wounded.[31] While Qadhafi forces fired rockets and artillery from the edge of Bin Jawad, about 50 *thuwar* fighters were trapped inside a mosque. Some of the fighters who had retreated earlier to the edge of Bin Jawad sent 20 pick-up trucks through the shelling to try to rescue them, and at least one of the trucks was hit.[32]

On 7 March, Libyan state television claimed that Qadhafi forces had gained control of Ra's Lanuf, while other media outlets reported that the town was still under heavy bombardment by Qadhafi forces.[33] One airstrike hit about 5 kilometers (3 miles) southeast of Ra's Lanuf. Planes flew over the area, and *thuwar* fired anti-aircraft guns in their direction. A later

---

[28] BELL & WITTER, THE ROOTS OF REBELLION, *supra* note 2 at 26; Kareem Fahim & David D. Kirkpatrick, *Attacks by government forces in Libya deal setback to rebel advance*, N.Y. TIMES, Mar. 7, 2011, *available at* http://www.nytimes.com/2011/03/08/world/africa/08libya .html.

[29] BELL & WITTER, THE ROOTS OF REBELLION, *supra* note 2 at 27.

[30] Kareem Fahim & David D. Kirkpatrick, *In Libya, fierce fight near site of refinery*, N.Y. TIMES, Mar. 10, 2011, *available at* http://query.nytimes.com/gst/fullpage.html?res=9503E4D 71F3FF933A25750C0A9679D8B63&pagewanted=all; Samer al-Atrush, *Kadhafi's forces have rebels in retreat*, AFP, Mar. 10, 2011, *available at* http://news.smh.com.au/breaking-news-world/kadhafis-forces-have-rebels-in-retreat-20110310-1bpvw.html; *Rebels retreat from Libyan oil port amid barrage*, AP, Mar. 11, 2011, *available at* http://www.aolnews.com/2011/03/11/ rebels-retreat-from-libyan-oil-port-amid-barrage; Jeffrey Fleishman, *Battered Libyan fighters try to keep spirits up*, L.A. TIMES, Mar. 12, 2011, *available at* http://articles.latimes.com/ 2011/mar/11/world/la-fg-libya-east-20110312.

[31] *Rebels make further advances*, GULF NEWS, Mar. 7, 2011, *available at* http://gulfnews .com/news/region/libya/rebels-make-further-advances-1.772651.

[32] *Id.*

[33] Strong, *News Summary from the US/International Press on the Libyan Crisis*, *supra* note 8.

airstrike targeted the main road heading into Ra's Lanuf. Some families fled the city to escape the bombing.[34]

On 9 March, government forces attacked the *thuwar* groups stationed on the outskirts of Ra's Lanuf, firing missiles and RPGs, in what was then reported as being the fiercest engagement yet between Qadhafi and *thuwar* forces. Although the *thuwar* forces managed to gain some ground by pushing westward, the initiative resulted in a stalemate as Qadhafi forces fired mortars and heavy artillery. The *thuwar* were forced to retreat and five opposition fighters were killed as a result of the operation.[35]

Regime forces used planes and heavy artillery to retake the city. A witness in Ra's Lanuf reported seeing warplanes circling the refinery in the early afternoon of 9 March, followed by an explosion and black smoke. The explosion did not seem to come from the heart of the facility, but from a nearby area where several large tanks were stored. Qadhafi forces also hit a pipeline in the nearby city of Sirte carrying crude oil to the refinery. The Qadhafi government claimed that *thuwar* forces connected to Al-Qaʿida were responsible for the blast.[36]

Qadhafi forces continued their intense artillery bombardment on the western edge of Ra's Lanuf, with at least 20 *thuwar* fighters reportedly killed in airstrikes between 6 and 10 March.[37] In that time wounded fighters took positions in parts of the town that suffered from a lack of water. Ambulances lined up in front of the emergency ward at Ra's Lanuf's main hospital to drop off the wounded.[38] In the face of the Qadhafi offensive hundreds of *thuwar* reportedly fled Ra's Lanuf.[39] Most of those injured in Bin Jawad were taken to the hospital in Ajdabiya, which reported seven dead and 52 wounded. According to the hospital, most casualties were

---

[34] *Id. See also* GULF NEWS, *Rebels make further advances, supra* note 31.

[35] Morgan Strong, *News Summary from the US/International Press on the Libyan Crisis*, THE TRIPOLI POST, Mar. 10, 2011, *available at* http://tripolipost.com/articledetail.asp?c=1&i=5558.

[36] *Id. See also UPDATE 2 – Rebels, Gaddafi forces skirmish over "ghost town"*, REUTERS, Mar. 11, 2011, *available at* http://af.reuters.com/article/commoditiesNews/idAFLDE72A1WR20110311.

[37] Chew, *Oil-rich town of Ras Lanuf a major battleground, supra* note 17.

[38] Strong, *News Summary from the US/International Press on the Libyan Crisis, supra* note 8.

[39] *Libyan rebels flee oil port battle*, THE INDEPENDENT, Mar. 9, 2011, *available at* http://www.independent.ie/breaking-news/world-news/libyan-rebels-flee-oil-port-battle-2573356.html.

fighters from Benghazi. Five corpses were transferred from Bin Jawad to Al-Jala' Hospital in Benghazi.[40]

Qadhafi forces proceeded to attack Bin Jawad on 9 March, with witnesses providing accounts of the use of gunboats (naval vessels carrying guns) and warplanes to bomb oil facilities.[41] On 10 March, Qadhafi forces attacked Ra's Lanuf with bombs and missiles that landed a few kilometers from Ra's Lanuf Refinery and close to another building belonging to the Libyan Emirates Oil Refinery Company. A witness told Reuters that the bombardment came from the direction of the sea.[42]

On 11 March, Qadhafi forces launched a large-scale offensive on Ra's Lanuf, attacking by sea, air and land. The offensive began with airstrikes in the early morning on the site of a key oil installation before reinforcements were brought by boats each carrying 40 to 50 men disembarking near the city's Fadil Hotel.[43] Fighting occurred at the western entrance to Ra's Lanuf, with Qadhafi forces attacking the opposition using warplanes.[44] *Thuwar* forces in Ra's Lanuf lost control of the residential parts of the town and began to retreat, before regaining control of the strategically important oil refineries in the town's port.[45] The *thuwar* forces then withdrew, moving their frontline forces eastwards.[46] Other sources indicate that the *thuwar* regrouped outside Ra's Lanuf and returned to counterattack, freeing the residential areas from government fighters and pushing them westwards.[47]

---

[40] THE TELEGRAPH, *Libya: at least a dozen killed in Bin Jawad clashes, supra* note 6.

[41] Strong, *News Summary from the US/International Press on the Libyan Crisis, supra* note 8.

[42] Richard Adams et al., *Libya uprising – Thursday 10 March*, THE GUARDIAN, Mar. 10, 2011, *available at* http://www.guardian.co.uk/world/blog/2011/mar/10/libya-uprising-gaddafi-live.

[43] *Pro-Government Forces Launch Large-Scale Offensive in Bid to Regain More Positions*, THE TRIPOLI POST, Mar. 11, 2011, *available at* http://tripolipost.com/articledetail .asp?c=1&i=5574; *Libyan troops enter Ras Lanuf*, THE GUARDIAN, Mar. 11, 2011, *available at* http://www.guardian.co.uk/world/2011/mar/11/libyan-troops-enter-ras-lanuf; Zeina Karam et al., *Gaddafi Showers Strategic Oil Port With Rockets*, THE HUFFINGTON POST, Mar. 11, 2011, *available at* http://www.huffingtonpost.com/2011/03/10/libya-drives-rebels-out-ras-lanuf_n_834055.html; REUTERS, *UPDATE 2 – Rebels, Gaddafi forces skirmish over "ghost town", supra* note 36.

[44] Zeina Karam et al., *Gaddafi Showers Strategic Oil Port With Rockets, supra* note 43.

[45] Strong, *News Summary from the US/International Press on the Libyan Crisis, supra* note 8.

[46] REUTERS, *UPDATE 2 – Rebels, Gaddafi forces skirmish over "ghost town", supra* note 36.

[47] Michael Georgy & Maria Golovnina, *Rebels repel Gaddafi assault on Libya oil port*, THE STAR ONLINE, Mar. 11, 2011, *available at* http://thestar.com.my/news/story.asp? file=/2011/3/12/worldupdates/2011-03-11T220327Z_01_NOOTR_RTRMDNC_0_-554981-4& sec=Worldupdates.

For the second time that week, Qadhafi forces launched attacks against the site of a major oil terminal, carrying out airstrikes on the storage tanks of a state-owned refinery.[48] During the assault, the main hospital in Ra's Lanuf was hit by either artillery shelling or an airstrike. The *thuwar* moved the staff from the hospital and evacuated patients to Ajdabiya and Brega.[49] The opposition forces began to withdraw from Ra's Lanuf towards Brega, in cars and pick-up trucks to escape the rockets and tank shells.[50] *Thuwar* forces prepared for a full-scale attack from Qadhafi forces, and were reinforced by the Sa'iqa 36 Katiba, which was composed of defector soldiers previously based in Benghazi.[51]

Ultimately, Qadhafi forces were able to turn back the *thuwar* advance and force them to retreat due to their superior firepower.[52] *Thuwar* forces' arsenal included outdated hand-cranked anti-aircraft guns, heavy machine guns, recoilless rifles, rockets, grenade launchers and assault rifles, while Qadhafi forces could attack from a distance using airpower, artillery, tanks and gunboats.[53]

On 11 March, Libyan state television declared that Ra's Lanuf had been freed from gangs, and showed people fleeing the city and Qadhafi forces searching houses for weapons. The report added that Qadhafi forces were advancing on Benghazi.[54] Libyan media outlets also reported that "[f]oreign journalists did not manage to get any information out of Ra's Lanuf" during the most intense days of the conflict.[55] In a final push to clear Ra's Lanuf, Qadhafi forces launched a large air offensive and

---

[48] REUTERS, *UPDATE 2 – Rebels, Gaddafi forces skirmish over "ghost town"*, supra note 36.

[49] Zeina Karam et al., *Gaddafi Showers Strategic Oil Port With Rockets*, supra note 43.

[50] Fahim & Kirkpatrick, *In Libya, fierce fight near site of refinery*, supra note 30; Samer al-Atrush, *Kadhafi's forces have rebels in retreat*, supra note 30; AP, *Rebels retreat from Libyan oil port amid barrage*, supra note 30; AP, *Libya rebels hold out in part of key oil facility*, supra note 30; Fleishman, *Battered Libyan fighters try to keep spirits up*, supra note 30; Zeina Karam et al., *Gaddafi Showers Strategic Oil Port With Rockets*, supra note 43.

[51] Zeina Karam et al., *Gaddafi Showers Strategic Oil Port With Rockets*, supra note 43.

[52] THE INDEPENDENT, *Libyan rebels flee oil port battles*, supra note 39; REUTERS, *UPDATE 2 – Rebels, Gaddafi forces skirmish over "ghost town"*, supra note 36.

[53] Morgan Strong, *News Summary from the US/International Press on the Libyan Crisis*, THE TRIPOLI POST, Mar. 13, 2011, *available at* http://tripolipost.com/articledetail .asp?c=1&i=5587; David Zucchino, *Libyan rebels' ragtag army left in disarray*, L.A. TIMES, Mar. 13, 2011, *available at* http://articles.latimes.com/2011/mar/13/world/la-fg-libya-rebels-20110313. For more on weapons used by Qadhafi and *thuwar* forces, *see* Ch. II, Appendix: Glossary of the Weapons used During the Conflict.

[54] *Pro-Gvernment [sic] Forces Launch Large-Scale Offensive in Bid to Regain More Positions*, THE TRIPOLI POST, Mar. 11, 2011, *available at* http://www.tripolipost.com/articledetail .asp?c=1&i=5574.

[55] *Id.*

thuwar were forced to withdraw as they lost control of the town's residential areas.[56] Qadhafi forces took control of the oil refinery and *thuwar* forces were pushed eastwards, 20 kilometers (12 miles) from the outskirts of the town.[57] Qadhafi forces continued to advance eastwards and *thuwar* withdrew to 'Uqayla.[58] It was later reported that Qadhafi forces blocked ambulances from entering Ra's Lanuf.[59] By 10–11 March, *thuwar* had fully retreated from Ra's Lanuf towards Brega.

On 12 March, three airstrikes on retreating opposition forces were reported at rebel checkpoints about 40 kilometers (25 miles) east of Ra's Lanuf. Reinforcements and ambulances drove to the western *thuwar* frontline, which was now between Brega Port and Benghazi. Large lines began to form at gas stations along the Libyan Coastal Highway as the fighting blocked access to many oil refineries in the region, causing a fuel shortage in the rebel-held east.[60]

During this time *thuwar* forces began implementing measures to control media coverage, requiring journalists to obtain permission to report on the battles of the eastern front. Prior to the Ra's Lanuf battle, opposition leaders had welcomed reporters, but the change in policy arose over concerns that some of the media coverage had disclosed *thuwar* positions and endangered their campaign.[61] Some *thuwar* also stopped journalists from photographing gun emplacements.[62]

After the *thuwar* forces recaptured Ajdabiya in mid-March, they attempted another advance west towards Sirte and Tripoli. *Thuwar* forces were able to retake the towns of Brega, Ra's Lanuf and Bin Jawad without heavy resistance, and on 28 March reached the village of Harawa, 80 kilometers (50 miles) outside of Sirte.[63] As they advanced, the rebels reported look-

---

[56] *Gaddafi loyalists launch offensive*, AL JAZEERA, Mar. 11, 2011, *available at* http://www.aljazeera.com/news/africa/2011/03/201131041228856242.html.

[57] *Libya: Gaddafi troops take rebel oil port of Ras Lanuf*, BBC, Mar. 12, 2011, *available at* http://www.bbc.co.uk/news/world-africa-12721908.

[58] Mohammed Abbas, *UPDATE 1 – Gaddafi pushes rebels east, more fighters ready*, REUTERS, Mar. 12, 2011, *available at* http://www.reuters.com/article/2011/03/12/libya-east-idUSLDE72B06120110312.

[59] AL JAZEERA, *Gaddafi loyalists launch offensive*, *supra* note 56.

[60] Strong, *News Summary from the US/International Press on the Libyan Crisis*, *supra* note 53; Zucchino, *Libyan rebels' ragtag army left in disarray*, *supra* note 53.

[61] REUTERS, *UPDATE 2 – Rebels, Gaddafi forces skirmish over "ghost town"*, *supra* note 36.

[62] Strong, *News Summary from the US/International Press on the Libyan Crisis*, *supra* note 53; Zucchino, *Libyan rebels' ragtag army left in disarray*, *supra* note 53.

[63] Kareem Fahim & David D. Kirkpatrick, *Rebels Retake Libyan City As Airstrikes Clear a Way*, N.Y. TIMES, Mar. 27, 2011, *available at* http://www.nytimes.com/2011/03/27/world/africa/27libya.html; *Gaddafi forces flee rebels sweeping west to Sirte*, AFP, Mar. 27, 2011,

ing for Qadhafi loyalists in the region.[64] Sirte was a loyalist stronghold, and the regime was able to repel the *thuwar* advance with heavy attacks that forced the rebels to withdraw to Bin Jawad. Qadhafi forces lacked the resupplies needed to pursue the opposition beyond Sirte, and remained in the city.[65] The decision to hold out in Sirte was reportedly ordered by Mu'tassim Qadhafi, Qadhafi's son and national security advisor.[66]

After the regime regrouped in Sirte, the *thuwar* reported that Qadhafi forces began pushing eastward with rocket attacks on 30 March, forcing the rebels out of Ra's Lanuf again. The retreat from Ra's Lanuf, home to several major oil refineries, was a major strategic loss to the *thuwar* because it decreased the volume of oil they could potentially export, leaving them with only a small port at Tobruq. At this point in the conflict, the *thuwar* were mostly armed with light weapons and mounted guns on four-by-four pick-up trucks, and were overwhelmed by the superior weaponry of the Qadhafi forces.[67] The rapid advance of the regime forces demonstrated the rebels' inferior weaponry and equipment. By the end of March, the *thuwar* advances had been reversed and the rebels withdrew to a position 150 miles east of Ajdabiya. The retreat enabled Qadhafi forces to re-occupy Brega and a stalemate developed that lasted until July, when

---

available at http://www.timesofmalta.com/articles/view/20110327/local/gaddafi-forces-flee-rebels-sweeping-west-to-sirte.356923; *Libyan rebels push towards Tripoli, promise new oil exports*, AFP, Mar. 27, 2011, *available at* http://www.channelnewsasia.com/stories/afp_world/view/1119188/1/.html; *Libyan rebel sharpshooters take aim at Kadhafi*, AFP, Mar. 27, 2011, *available at* http://www.cumhuriyet.com/?im=yhs&hn=228608.

  [64] Edmund Blair, *Gaddafi troops retreating westwards – Libyan rebels*, REUTERS, Mar. 27, 2011, *available at* http://www.reuters.com/article/2011/03/27/libya-east-westwards-idUSLDE72Q07F20110327.

  [65] *Libyan rebel advance halted, Sirte blasted by NATO jets*, AFP, Mar. 28, 2011, *available at* http://www.timesofmalta.com/articles/view/20110328/local/libyan-rebel-advance-halted-sirte-blasted-by-nato-jets.357079; *Libyan rebels close on key Gadhafi stronghold*, AP, Mar. 28, 2011, *available at* http://www.independent.co.uk/news/world/africa/libyan-rebels-close-on-key-gaddafi-stronghold-2255180.html; *Libyan rebels brought up short, vow to put Kadhafi on trial*, SAKAPFET, *available at* http://headlines.sakapfetstore.com/item/world_news/english/mar282011/libyan_rebels_brought_up_short_vow_to_put_kadhafi_on_trial.jsp; Kareem Fahim & David D. Kirkpatrick, *Rebel Advance Halted Outside Qaddafi Hometown*, N.Y. TIMES, Mar. 29, 2011, *available at* http://www.nytimes.com/2011/03/29/world/africa/29libya.html.

  [66] *Libya conflict: US officials met Gaddafi envoys*, BBC, July 19, 2011, *available at* http://www.bbc.co.uk/news/world-africa-14195476.

  [67] Alexander Dziadosz & Edmund Blair, *Aircraft, blasts heard in direction of Libya town*, REUTERS, Mar. 30, 2011, *available at* http://af.reuters.com/article/libyaNews/idAFWEA16692011030330; *Gaddafi forces move east, bombard rebels with rockets*, REUTERS, Mar. 30, 2011, *available at* http://www.reuters.com/article/2011/03/30/libya-east-advance-idUSWEA16462011030330.

the *thuwar* forces once again broke the stalemate and the Qadhafi forces fell back towards Ra's Lanuf.[68]

NATO attacked the Qadhafi forces in the region in April in order to aid the retreating *thuwar*.[69] In particular, NATO strikes targeted the regime's T-72 tanks, armored personnel carriers, rocket launchers, surface-to-air missiles and ammunition dumps. In early April, NATO announced that it was attacking ground forces and military targets that directly threatened civilians and civilian population areas. NATO also destroyed ammunition dumps that they connected with attacks on civilians along the coast in Ra's Lanuf, and attacked air defense sites in the region in order to enforce the no-fly zone.[70]

Even as the NATO campaign aided the opposition, Qadhafi forces continued to gain ground, reaching the city of Brega, which was the cornerstone of the eastern campaign, in July. NATO reported carrying out airstrikes in the region in order to protect the civilian population and help facilitate the safe delivery of humanitarian assistance from Benghazi to coastal towns such as Ra's Lanuf, which remained under Qadhafi control.[71] At the same time, *thuwar* forces prepared to advance westwards and soon gained strategic ground in Brega. The Qadhafi forces fell back towards Ra's Lanuf on 18 July and *thuwar* forces moved towards Bishr and 'Uqayla.[72]

In early July, NATO attacked oil facilities in Brega and Ra's Lanuf in order to deprive Qadhafi forces of critical fuel supplies. While NATO had previously insisted that it avoided attacks on infrastructure, these attacks were aimed at limiting fuel supplies for the Qadhafi forces and hindering them from carrying out attacks and advancing west. This marked a

---

[68] Anthony Bell et al., Institute For the Study of War, 3 The Libyan Revolution: Stalemate & Siege 6 (Oct. 2011) [hereinafter "Stalemate & Siege"], *available at* http://www.understandingwar.org/sites/default/files/Libya_Part3_0.pdf. *See also* Ch. II, Sec. 3.3.

[69] James Meikle, *Gaddafi troops retake key oil port of Ras Lanouf*, The Guardian, Mar. 30, 2011, *available at* http://www.guardian.co.uk/world/2011/mar/30/gaddafi-troops-retake-ras-lanouf.

[70] *Press briefing on Libya*, North Atlantic Treaty Organization, Apr. 8, 2011, *available at* http://www.nato.int/cps/en/natolive/opinions_72150.htm?selectedLocale=en. For more on NATO strikes in the region, *see* Ch. III, Sec. 6.2.

[71] *Press briefing on Libya*, North Atlantic Treaty Organization, July 7, 2011, *available at* http://www.nato.int/cps/en/natolive/opinions_76163.htm?selectedLocale=en. For NATO strikes in Benghazi, *see supra* Secs. 2.2. & 2.4.

[72] *UPDATE 1 – Libya rebels say Gaddafi forces retreat in east*, Reuters, July 18, 2011, *available at* http://206.132.6.105/article/libyaNews/idAFLDE76H0MR20110718.

change, as since early March, all actors in the conflict had avoided attacking oil facilities.[73]

After continued fighting and NATO strikes, *thuwar* forces advanced and captured Ra's Lanuf on 23 August, arriving in Bin Jawad the following day.[74] The advance was halted by a surprise attack by Qadhafi forces, however, which prevented the rebels from entering Bin Jawad.[75] The opposition forces again claimed that the local residents were aiding government forces, and accused them of supporting Qadhafi based on tribal allegiances.[76] The *thuwar* thus were unable to continue their advancement towards Sirte as planned.[77] NATO continued its strikes in the region, and hit two multiple rocket launchers used by government forces on 26 August in the vicinity of Ra's Lanuf.[78] The *thuwar* sustained their advance and were in full control of Bin Jawad by 27 August.

In August and September, several oil refineries in eastern Libya were damaged or destroyed. The Al-Sider oil terminal was bombed in late August, causing fire and damage. Witnesses reported the refinery was hit during fighting between Qadhafi and *thuwar* forces in the area. The incident was a setback for the NTC, which was struggling to revive the oil- and gas-based economy.[79] In September several oil-producing facilities were

---

[73] *Nato strikes at Libya's oil in bid to oust Gaddafi*, THE INDEPENDENT, July 8, 2011, *available at* http://www.independent.co.uk/news/world/africa/nato-strikes-at-libyas-oil-in-bid-to-oust-gaddafi-2308962.html; Emma Farge, *Libyan oil refinery attack 'isolated incident': NOC*, REUTERS, Sept. 15, 2011, *available at* http://www.reuters.com/article/2011/09/15/us-libya-oil-noc-interview-idUSTRE78E32E20110915.

[74] BELL & WITTER, THE ROOTS OF REBELLION, *supra* note 2 at 27; ANTHONY BELL ET AL., INSTITUTE FOR THE STUDY OF WAR, 4 THE LIBYAN REVOLUTION: THE TIDE TURNS 11 (Nov. 2011) [hereinafter "THE TIDE TURNS"], *available at* http://www.understandingwar .org/sites/default/files/Libya_Part4.pdf; *Evidence of 'mass execution' in Tripoli*, AL JAZEERA, Aug. 25, 2011, *available at* http://www.aljazeera.com/news/africa/2011/08/201182512484919 0250.html.

[75] Robert Birsel, *Clashes as Libyan rebels try to press Gaddafi stronghold*, REUTERS, Aug. 25, 2011, *available at* www.jpost.com/Headlines/Article.aspx?id=235376.

[76] *Id. See also* Dan Murphy, *Qaddafi strikes back at Libya rebels' western advance, supra* note 20; Navarro, *Libya fight rages as Gadhafi strikes back, supra* note 23; Paul Farhi, *Libyan rebel advance traps journalists inside hotel*, THE WASHINGTON POST, Aug. 22, 2011, *available at* http://www.washingtonpost.com/lifestyle/style/libyan-rebel-advance-traps-journalists-inside-hotel/2011/08/22/gIQAX91VXJ_story.html.

[77] *Rebels stuck at Bin Jawad on way to Gaddafi hometown*, AL AHRAM, Aug. 24, 2011, *available at* http://english.ahram.org.eg/NewsContent/2/8/19649/World/Region/Rebels-stuck-at-Bin-Jawad-on-way-to-Gaddafi-hometo.aspx.

[78] *Factbox: Latest developments in the Libyan conflict*, REUTERS, Aug. 27, 2011, *available at* http://www.reuters.com/article/2011/08/27/us-libya-nato-idUSTRE77Q0T720110827.

[79] Alexander Dziadosz, *Tank burns at Libya's biggest oil terminal*, REUTERS, Aug. 30, 2011, *available at* http://www.reuters.com/article/2011/08/30/us-libya-oil-tanks-idUSTRE77 T1JZ20110830.

attacked by Qadhafi forces, causing extensive damage.[80] Seventeen guards were killed in an attack on an oil facility in Ra's Lanuf on 12 September when it was attacked from several miles away by anti-aircraft weapons.[81] The incident was disregarded by the NTC as an isolated incident that did not constitute a threat to the oil and gas industry.[82] NATO reported that it did not represent a significant shift in the positions controlled by the Qadhafi forces.[83]

Despite another attack on 15 September, the British Government updated its travel advice and made note that travel to Ra's Lanuf was possible.[84] This announcement coincided with the visits of French President Nicolas Sarkozy and British Prime Minister David Cameron, in an apparent indication of increasing stability in Libya.[85] The lifting of EU sanctions in September on 28 Libyan oil entities, including one in Ra's Lanuf, was also a positive sign for the economic situation in the east.[86]

The effect of the fighting on the civilian population could be seen as the hostilities came to a close, with the International Committee of the Red Cross (ICRC) reporting on 15 September that about 1,300 people from Bin Jawad and nearby coastal towns west of Ra's Lanuf had fled their homes and were living in difficult conditions in the desert.[87] A mass grave in Bin Jawad was in March 2012, when 170 bodies were removed and buried

---

[80] Jessica Donati, *Libya's Waha Oil faces tough task to fix war damage*, REUTERS, Oct. 2, 2011, *available at* http://www.reuters.com/article/2011/10/02/us-libya-oil-waha-idUSTRE79117S20111002; Benoit Faucon, *Libya's Zueitina Oil Co Restarts Production – NOC Head*, DOW JONES NEWSWIRES, Oct. 18, 2011, *available at* http://english.capital.gr/News.asp?id=1306932.

[81] Annie Benard, *Libyan Transitional Leader Urges Reconciliation, Using Symbolism of Tripoli Site*, N.Y. TIMES, Sept. 12, 2011, *available at* http://www.nytimes.com/2011/09/13/world/africa/13libya.html.

[82] Media reports first reported fifteen casualties but it was later confirmed that there had been seventeen casualties. *See Gaddafi forces attack Libyan oil facility*, AL JAZEERA, Sept. 12, 2011, *available at* http://www.aljazeera.com/news/africa/2011/09/201912814553514 13.html; Farge, *Libya oil refinery attack 'isolated incident': NOC, supra* note 73.

[83] *Press briefing on Libya*, NORTH ATLANTIC TREATLY ORGANIZATION, Sept. 13, 2011, *available at* http://www.nato.int/cps/en/natolive/opinions_77984.htm?selectedLocale=en.

[84] *UK to update Libya travel advice*, REUTERS, Sept. 15, 2011, *available at* http://www.reuters.com/article/2011/09/15/libya-britain-travel-idUSL5E7KF2A220110915.

[85] *UK eases travel recommendations for Libya*, REUTERS, Sept. 15, 2011, *available at* http://www.reuters.com/article/2011/09/15/us-libya-britain-travel-idUSTRE78E3T320110915.

[86] *Post-war Tripoli port back in business, airport ready*, REUTERS, Sept. 2, 2011, *available at* http://www.reuters.com/article/2011/09/18/us-libya-port-idUSTRE78H1UU20110918.

[87] *Libya: Concerns for IDPs and migrants rise as fighting continues*, RELIEF WEB, Sept. 23, 2011, *available at* http://reliefweb.int/report/somalia/idp-news-alert-23-september-2011.

appropriately.[88] Forensic specialists determined that the cause of death in most of these cases was fatal gunshot wounds, including indications of executions. Some bodies were severely disfigured from rocket attacks.[89] The mass grave was discovered in December, but there had been several delays that prevented its excavation.[90] The delay in the excavation process was demonstrative of the persisting challenges the population faced in the wake of the war.[91]

Following the fall of the Qadhafi regime, the Libyan people were able to participate in the first democratic elections in the new Libya. As with other cities in the east, however, some of the local population opposed the election process and, on election day, 7 July 2012, armed men disrupted the voting in Ra's Lanuf.[92] Despite the local disruptions, the elections symbolized a new era of opportunity for political participation for many Libyans. The economy also began to record drastic improvement as Libya's largest oil refinery in Ra's Lanuf resumed production on 4 September 2012.[93] The refinery, which had been out of action since February 2011, had been expected to be up and running earlier, but disputes between Libya's National Oil Company and its United Arab Emirates partner caused delays.[94] The refinery accounts for almost two thirds of Libya's refining capacity producing 220,000 barrels per day.[95] The functioning of the refinery is therefore critical to Libya's development and the stability of the region in the post-Qadhafi era.

---

[88] *Libya Mass Grave Near Bin Jawwad Unearths 170 Bodies From Gaddafi Conflict*, HUFF-INGTON POST, Mar. 5, 2011, *available at* http://www.huffingtonpost.com/2012/03/05/libya-mass-grave-bin-jawwad_n_1322187.html.

[89] *Id.*

[90] *Id.*

[91] Human rights experts noted that the lack of forensic experts in post-conflict Libya complicated the excavation and identification process. *See* HUMAN RIGHTS WATCH, WORLD REPORT 2013: LIBYA (Feb. 2013), *available at* http://www.hrw.org/world-report/2013/country-chapters/libya.

[92] *Libya election: High turnout in historic vote*, BBC, July 7, 2012, *available at* http://www.bbc.co.uk/news/world-africa-18749808. For election violence in other cities in the east, *see supra* Secs. 2.2. & 2.3.

[93] April Yee, *Production resumes at Libya's largest refinery*, THE NATIONAL, Sept. 4, 2012, *available at* http://www.thenational.ae/business/energy/production-resumes-at-libyas-largest-refinery.

[94] *Id.*

[95] *Id.*

3. Illustrations of the Violations

3.1. *Excessive Use of Force*

(a) *Qadhafi Forces*

The CoI collected information about the use of force by the Qadhafi regime against demonstrators in Ra's Lanuf and Bin Jawad. According to information received by the Benghazi General Prosecutor's Office, the regime gave orders to shoot at demonstrators on 17 February 2011 in Ra's Lanuf and Qadhafi forces used anti-aircraft weaponry to carry out the orders.[96] Moreover, the CoI concluded that in the early days of the revolution protesters were likely to be unarmed and carrying out peaceful protests. The decision to use force against them by the regime in the form of live ammunition can, therefore, be considered excessive.[97]

3.2. *Unlawful Killing*

(a) *Qadhafi Forces*

The reports of violence, and the later discovery of mass graves in the region, provide evidence of unlawful killings carried out by Qadhafi forces in Ra's Lanuf and Bin Jawad. The deaths of civilians that resulted from the excessive use of force by Qadhafi forces against protesters also constitutes unlawful killing. The use of anti-aircraft weaponry against demonstrators on 17 February 2011 resulted in severe casualties.[98]

Witnesses also provided individual accounts to media outlets of killings by regime forces. In one case, a man told reporters that his brother had been executed by Qadhafi forces in Bin Jawad and subsequently buried in a mass grave that was unearthed in March 2012.[99] In another incident, a university student reported that Qadhafi soldiers answered his uncle's mobile phone after he called, and told him to listen as his uncle was being murdered.[100]

---

[96] Report of the International Commission of Inquiry to investigate all the alleged violations of international human rights law in the Libyan Arab Jamahiriya, U.N. HRC. 17th Sess., ¶ 87. U.N. Doc. A/HRC/17/44 (Jan. 12, 2012).

[97] *Id.* at ¶ 87–88.

[98] *Id.* at ¶ 87.

[99] Huffington Post, *Libya Mass Grave Near Bin Jawwad Unearths 170 Bodies From Gaddafi Conflict*, *supra* note 88.

[100] *Id.*

3.3. *Arbitrary Detentions and Enforced Disappearances*

(a) *Qadhafi Forces*

Arbitrary detentions and enforced disappearances took place across eastern Libya during both the protest stage and the armed conflict, including in the cities of Ra's Lanuf and Bin Jawad.[101] Media outlets reported that Qadhafi forces were responsible for the killings of at least 50 members of the opposition in early March 2011, and 700 men were reported missing.[102]

Amnesty International documented a number of cases of individuals, both civilians and combatants, missing in or near the frontline town of Bin Jawad. In one of the cases Amnesty International reported that a man was taken prisoner by Qadhafi forces early on 6 March 2011 in Bin Jawad as he was being transported with a dozen other persons towards the Al-Sa'idi Katiba military compound in Sirte. Later a brother of the detainee received phone calls from members of the Qadhafi forces using the detainee's mobile phone, issuing threats such as "We will burn you along with your family, your mother and siblings."[103]

In another case, an Egyptian physician reported the disappearance of his Libyan colleague along with an Egyptian practitioner at the beginning of March 2011 in Ra's Lanuf. The witness later saw his colleague wearing a military uniform and confessing his affiliation to Al-Qa'ida on Al-Libya state television. This case was mentioned by other sources and appeared to model a pattern of physician abductions during the war.[104]

The relative of another victim, Faraj Khamis Ibrahim, told Human Rights Watch that his brother, 'Umar Khamis Ibrahim, disappeared in Ra's Lanuf on 8 March 2011. He called his brother's mobile phone the same day, and a man answered telling him that he had been shot in the leg and that he could "come and get him." On 15 March, 'Umar Khamis Ibrahim appeared on state television with marks on his face.[105]

---

[101] Report of the International Commission of Inquiry (Jan. 12, 2012), *supra* note 96 at ¶ 98.

[102] Chew, *Oil-rich town of Ras Lanuf a major battleground, supra* note 17.

[103] *Libya: Campaign of enforced disappearances must end*, AMNESTY INTERNATIONAL, Mar. 29, 2011, *available at* http://www.amnesty.org/en/news-and-updates/report/libya-campaign-enforced-disappearances-must-end-2011-03-29.

[104] Report of the International Commission of Inquiry (Jan. 12, 2012), *supra* note 96 at ¶ 106.

[105] *Libya: At Least 370 Missing From Country's East*, HUMAN RIGHTS WATCH, Mar. 30, 2011, *available at* http://www.hrw.org/news/2011/03/30/libya-least-370-missing-countrys-east.

In another case, two brothers reportedly went missing on 11 March 2011 after they armed themselves and left Benghazi to join the *thuwar* in Bin Jawad. Another brother similarly disappeared the following day when he went to look for his brothers. The family called one of the brothers' mobile phones on 13 March, and a person with a western Libyan accent answered, saying he was an officer from the Al-Nasr army barracks in Tripoli and that the person who owned the phone was dead. They were told that they could collect his body in Tripoli.[106]

Media outlets relayed stories of a growing number of disappearances in March 2011. One father of a rebel fighter told reporters his son went missing after leaving to fight at the frontline in Ra's Lanuf against the Qadhafi regime.[107]

3.4. *Torture and Other Forms of Ill-treatment*

(a) *Qadhafi Forces*

There is little information relating to acts of torture in the Ra's Lanuf and Bin Jawad theater of military operations. One witness stated that while volunteering to wash bodies received at a hospital, he saw many bodies that had been mutilated. Some had their ears, nails or lips cut off. He reported that the bodies were *thuwar* who had been tortured by the Qadhafi forces.[108]

3.5. *Attacks on Civilians, Civilian Objects, Protected Persons and Objects*

(a) *Qadhafi Forces*

Ra's Lanuf experienced some of the most severe fighting during the conflict, leading to extensive attacks that forced civilians to leave their homes.[109] As part of the Qadhafi regime's attempt to retake Ra's Lanuf from the *thuwar* in the beginning of March 2011, they attacked the town indiscriminately by land, air and sea. Accounts of the attacks were often based on witness statements given by phone from civilians or rebel fight-

---

[106] *Id.*

[107] Chris McGreal, *'If he is dead, I hope not this way': a Libyan father's prayer for his rebel son*, THE GUARDIAN, Mar. 31, 2011, *available at* http://www.guardian.co.uk/world/2011/mar/31/libya-father-searches-rebel-son.

[108] *Id.*

[109] Report of the International Commission of Inquiry (Jan. 12, 2012), *supra* note 96 at n. 16.

ers since journalists did not have access to the area during the days of intense fighting.[110] Organizations such as Medicine Sans Frontiers (MSF) reported in April that, when leaving Benghazi in order to bring supplies and help persons at the frontline in the Ra's Lanuf area, their delegates had to return twice because of the Qadhafi forces' bombardment.[111]

NATO reported that Qadhafi forces carried out indiscriminate attacks in urban areas in Ra's Lanuf.[112] In Bin Jawad the use of mortars was reported on 6 March 2011 as regime forces ambushed *thuwar* positions with machine guns and RPGs.[113] There were several reports concerning the Qadhafi forces' use of mortars in Ra's Lanuf between 6 and 9 March.[114]

Civilians fled Ra's Lanuf and Bin Jawad due to the heavy attacks by Qadhafi forces. There were improvised camps set up by the local population in Nufliyya[115] – a town 32 kilometers (20 miles) east of Bin Jawad.[116] Hundreds of families fled from coastal towns west of Ra's Lanuf, in particular from Bin Jawad, and set up tents in the desert, some 150 kilometers (93 miles) south of the coastal town of Nufliyya. The ICRC delivered aid and reported that the living conditions were inadequate, and that at least 1,300 people were displaced in the desert.[117]

Displaced migrants and refugees from Ra's Lanuf and other cities took shelter in Tobruq, Darna and Al-Bayda where the United Nations High Commissioner for Refugees (UNHCR) sent humanitarian aid and assistance.[118] Thousands of Egyptian and African migrant workers fled to

---

[110] REUTERS, *UPDATE 2 – Rebels, Gaddafi forces skirmish over "ghost town"*, supra note 36.
Benghazi hospitals struggle to treat war-wounded, INTEGRATED REGIONAL INFORMATION NETWORKS, Apr. 13, 2011, *available at* http://reliefweb.int/node/396013.

[111] *Id.*

[112] *Press briefing on Libya*, NORTH ATLANTIC TREATY ORGANIZATION, Apr. 8, 2011, *available at* http://www.nato.int/cps/en/natolive/opinions_72150.htm?selectedLocale=en.

[113] *Id.*

[114] THE GUARDIAN, *Libya uprising – Thursday 10 March, supra* note 42.

[115] The transliteration of this term was adopted from the reference. Internal Displacement Monitoring Center, *Increasing reports of internal displacement*, RELIEF WEB, Apr. 21, 2011, *available at* reliefweb.int/node/397844.

[116] *Id.*

[117] *Libya: supporting medical services in disputed areas*, INTERNATIONAL COMMITTEE OF THE RED CROSS, Sept. 15, 2011, *available at* http://www.icrc.org/eng/resources/documents/update/2011/libya-update-2011-09-15.htm.

[118] *Update No. 22 on the humanitarian situation in Libya and the neighbouring countries*, UNHCR, Apr. 28, 2011, *available at* http://www.unhcr.org/cgi-bin/texis/vtx/home/opendoc PDFViewer.html?docid=4dba71b612b&query=lanuf.

Egypt during the regime's advances in the east in mid-March 2011.[119] Many of those who fled to Egypt also sought medical treatment. One witness arrived with gunshot wounds and another stated that after being shot while fighting in Ra's Lanuf, he had to leave for treatment because the hospital in Benghazi was over-capacity.[120]

3.6. *Mercenaries*

(a) *Qadhafi Forces*

Among the documents provided to the CoI by the General Prosecutor's Office in Benghazi were transcribed interrogations of men accused of being mercenaries. These documents included a transcript of a Nigerian-born Libyan man who reported being a member of the Khamis Katiba before being transported to the military base in Ra's Lanuf on 2 March 2011. The man said he was provided with a military uniform and RPG by a military officer.[121]

4. THE ROLE OF NATO

NATO airstrikes greatly assisted the *thuwar* forces in the battle for Ra's Lanuf.[122] The NATO intervention caused the Qadhafi forces to change tactics in order to avert airstrikes by using vehicles with opposition flags and lighting oil-filled trenches to draw the pilots' attention away from troop movements.[123] The intervention gave the rebels the support needed to counter the regime's advances, but the opposition complained

---

[119] *Libyan refugee numbers jump as Gaddafi pushes east*, REUTERS, Mar. 17, 2011, *available at* http://www.reuters.com/article/2011/03/17/us-libya-east-border-idUSTRE72G6YK20110317.

[120] *UNHCR warns of increased risk of mass displacement in Libya*, UNHCR, Mar. 18, 2011, *available at* http://reliefweb.int/node/392568.

[121] Report of the International Commission of Inquiry (Jan. 12, 2012), *supra* note 96 at ¶ 185.

[122] Chris McGreal, *Libyan rebels take back oil towns of Brega and Ras Lanuf in westward push*, THE GUARDIAN, Mar. 27, 2011, *available at* http://www.guardian.co.uk/world/2011/mar/27/libya-gaddafi-rebel-forces-take-brega.

[123] BELL & WITTER, STALEMATE & SIEGE, *supra* note 68 at 22; *Rebels clear landmines, advance on Brega*, UPI, July 18, 2011, *available at* http://www.upi.com/Top_News/World-News/2011/07/18/Rebels-clear-land-mines-advance-on-Brega/UPI-80801310987369; *Libyan troops shell rebels near eastern oil town, killing 8 rebels, hospital officials says*, AP, July 19, 2011, *available at* http://www.cbc.ca/news/world/story/2011/07/20/libya-rebels-killed.html. For more on Qadhafi forces shifting tactics, *see also* Ch. III, Sec. 6.1.

that there were not enough strikes in the Ra's Lanuf and Bin Jawad theater of military operations. When NATO took over from the coalition on 31 March 2011, opposition forces in the region contended that NATO strikes were insufficient and infrequent. *Thuwar* claimed that cities like Ra's Lanuf, Bin Jawad and Brega were being destroyed because NATO was not doing enough to deter the Qadhafi forces' assaults.[124] NATO defended its actions and asserted its support for the rebel cause. Admiral Russell Harding, NATO's deputy commander of operations, stated that "Libya must be 800 miles wide and in all that air space we are dominating, so perhaps, and I am not criticizing anyone, in one or two areas, if they don't hear us or see us, I can understand how that might lead to a lack of confidence."[125]

At the beginning of April 2011, NATO expanded its mandate and announced that it would attack targets that directly threatened civilians. NATO continued to bombard Qadhafi forces throughout the month of April, aiding *thuwar* forces who had been forced to retreat.[126] NATO successfully targeted T-72 tanks, Armored Personnel Carriers (APCs), rocket launchers, Surface to Air Missiles (SAMs) and ammunition dumps, reportedly those that were directly connected with attacks on civilians perpetrated by Qadhafi forces. NATO also attacked air defense sites in the region, enforcing the no-fly zone.[127]

NATO's airstrikes in the region were commensurate with the stated mission of protecting civilians and allowing for the delivery of humanitarian aid from Benghazi to Ra's Lanuf and other coastal towns.[128] Despite NATO stating that they avoided destroying infrastructure, however, they did target oil refueling facilities in Brega and Ra's Lanuf in July to deprive Qadhafi forces of fuel.[129]

---

[124] Alexander Dziadosz, *Libyan rebels regain ground near oil port*, REUTERS, Apr. 6, 2011, *available at* http://uk.reuters.com/article/2011/04/06/uk-libya-east-idUKTRE7351ZO20110406. For more on strikes in Brega, *see* Ch. VII Sec. 4.

[125] *Id.*

[126] Meikle, *Gaddafi troops retake key oil port of Ras Lanouf, supra* note 69.

[127] Strong, *News Summary from the US/International Press on the Libyan Crisis, supra* note 35. *See also* Ch. III, Sec. 6.1.

[128] *Press briefing on Libya,* NORTH ATLANTIC TREATY ORGANIZATION, July 7, 2011, *available at* http://www.nato.int/cps/en/natolive/opinions_76163.htm?selectedLocale=en. For more discussion on NATO and the civilian protection mandate, *see* Ch. III, Sec. 5.

[129] THE INDEPENDENT, *Nato strikes at Libya's oil in bid to oust Gaddafi, supra* note 73.

5. CONCLUSION

The eastern theater of military operations connecting Ra's Lanuf and Bin Jawad was a critically strategic battleground and heavily contested region during the war. *Thuwar* forces gained control of this theater in February 2011, but met heavy resistance from Qadhafi forces as they moved westwards from this position in early March. Qadhafi's strongholds in Sirte and Tripoli were threatened by *thuwar* advances, and could not survive losing this region. Qadhafi forces pushed back in March and April, carrying out heavy artillery and aerial attacks on Ra's Lanuf and Bin Jawad, thereby halting the *thuwar* forces' advance and forcing them to retreat. The Ra's Lanuf and Bin Jawad front became the last line of defense for the opposition base in Cyrenaica.

The superior weaponry of the Qadhafi government initially made *thuwar* advances impossible.[130] The opposition forces were mostly disorganized volunteers and army defectors armed with outdated weapons.[131] As a result, the rebels pleaded for external military assistance and called on the international community to enforce a no-fly zone to neutralize the Qadhafi regime's air forces.[132]

The recapture of Ra's Lanuf in early March 2011 was a major victory for the Qadhafi regime. By halting the opposition's advance westward, Qadhafi's forces managed to re-establish control over a vital oil facility and push the *thuwar* back along the main coastal road, while securing its two major strongholds of Tripoli and Sirte.[133]

The region saw some of the most intense fighting during the conflict, with the cities changing hands between the Qadhafi and *thuwar* forces several times. The civilian population in Ra's Lanuf and Bin Jawad suffered as a result of the regime's assaults and from the escalation of fighting between Qadhafi and *thuwar* forces from 6–10 March 2011. Civilians fled in large numbers, taking refuge in camps or crossing the border into Egypt. During this period. The violations reported were almost all carried out by the Qadhafi regime, with no documentation of violations committed by

---

[130] THE INDEPENDENT, *Libyan rebels flee oil port battles, supra* note 39; REUTERS, *UPDATE 2 – Rebels, Gaddafi forces skirmish over "ghost town", supra* note 36; Strong, *News Summary from the US/International Press on the Libyan Crisis, supra* note 53; Zucchino, *Libyan rebels' ragtag army left in disarray, supra* note 53.

[131] Strong, *News Summary from the US/International Press on the Libyan Crisis, supra* note 53; Zucchino, *Libyan rebels' ragtag army left in disarray, supra* note 53.

[132] THE INDEPENDENT, *Libyan rebels flee oil port battles, supra* note 39.

[133] *Id.*

rebel forces. It is important to note, however, that during the most intense period of conflict, reporters had limited access to the Ra's Lanuf and Bin Jawad region, hindering the documentation of any such violations.

The actions of the Qadhafi forces amounted to serious violations against demonstrators and civilian populations. The use of anti-aircraft weaponry against protesters in Ra's Lanuf constituted excessive use of force, and there is no indication that Qadhafi forces attempted to employ less extreme measures against protesters. Additionally, the largest mass grave discovered in the wake of the conflict was in Bin Jawad, and serves as an indication of how many lives were lost. 170 bodies were unearthed, with the most common cause of death coming from shelling and gunshot wounds. The use of mass graves to bury executed civilians alongside combatants killed in battle strongly suggests the commission of unlawful killings on the part of Qadhafi forces. Death by execution and the excessive use of force against protesters provide additional evidence to reasonably conclude that Qadhafi forces carried out acts of unlawful killings.

As the Qadhafi forces took control over the cities in the east, cases of arbitrary detention and enforced disappearances took place during the demonstrations and subsequent fighting. Human rights organizations, the CoI and media outlets provided evidence to reasonably conclude that the Qadhafi forces engaged in arbitrary detentions and were responsible for the disappearance of numerous civilians and rebel combatants. Reports also exist of torture and ill-treatment in detention centers under the control of the Qadhafi forces. However, due to insufficient documentation of violations in the region, there is limited information available with regards to specific acts of torture.

CHAPTER NINE

MISRATA

1. INTRODUCTION

Misrata is the third largest city in Libya, with a population of approximately 517,000 inhabitants before the conflict.[1] It is a port city located on the far western edge of the Gulf of Sidra along the Mediterranean Coast, 187 kilometers (116 miles) east of Tripoli and 825 kilometers (512 miles) west of Benghazi.[2] The city center lies just off the coast, with the seaport to the east and the airport to the south. The center is connected by a number of major roads, including Tripoli Street, the main commercial boulevard in downtown Misrata that connects to the Libyan Coastal Highway. A number of suburbs, including Al-Ghayran and Al-Shawati, extend out from the city center.[3]

Misrata is traditionally regarded as the country's business capital, serving as a central locale for the exchange of commodities and materials with other cities. The city's steel mill industry is one of its principal sources of income and employment, and the industry has been able to expand throughout the years with its owners holding considerable influence in the city. Misrata is one of the country's most modern cities, with infrastructure that includes new roads, electricity and communication centers,

---

[1] UNITED NATIONS INTER-AGENCY MISSION, MISRATA: 10 TO 14 JULY 2011, UN OFFICE FOR THE COORDINATION OF HUMANITARIAN AFFAIRS 4 (2011), *available at* http://reliefweb .int/sites/reliefweb.int/files/resources/Full_report_157.pdf. Other estimates put Misrata's population closer to 380,000 people before the conflict. *See Misratah*, WOLFRAMALPHA, *available at* http://www.wolframalpha.com/input/?i=Misratah&lk=1&a=ClashPrefs_*City .*Misratah.Misratah.Libya--. *See also* Aidan Lewis, *Misrata: City under siege*, BBC, May 10, 2011, *available at* http://www.bbc.co.uk/news/world-africa-13118724.

[2] PHYSICIANS FOR HUMAN RIGHTS, WITNESS TO WAR CRIMES: EVIDENCE FROM MISRATA, LIBYA (Aug. 2011) [hereinafter "WITNESS TO WAR CRIMES"], *available at* https:// s3.amazonaws.com/PHR_Reports/Libya-WitnesstoWarCrimes-Aug2011.pdf.

[3] *Misrata Factsheet*, UN OFFICE FOR THE COORDINATION OF HUMANITARIAN AFFAIRS, Apr. 24, 2011, *available at* http://ochanet.unocha.org/p/Documents/Misrata%20Factsheet %20-%2024%20April%202011_FINAL.pdf.

modern buildings, as well as large iron, steel, carpet and textile factories, and private companies and trade centers.[4]

During the 2011 war, the Misrata theater was the most strategically important location of military operations in the Tripolitania region, as it was caught between the two major Qadhafi strongholds of Sirte and Tripoli. Given its position along the Libyan coast, its large, modern port was vital to the *thuwar* forces' resupply efforts. Misrata was under siege by Qadhafi forces from February to May 2011, and arguably saw the bloodiest and most traumatic events of the civil war. Qadhafi forces shelled the city relentlessly between mid-March and mid-May 2011, and resumed shelling again in June. The fighting continued until early August, when Qadhafi forces retreated from the region.[5]

As the only major *thuwar* held city in Tripolitania during the war, Misrata was the subject of attacks by Qadhafi forces from Tripoli and Sirte.[6] Misrata was surrounded by cities held by the Qadhafi forces: Zlitan to the west, Tawergha to the southeast and Bani Walid to the south. The city was subjected to constant shelling and attack, as the rebels in Misrata put up stiff resistance, incurring a heavy death toll.[7] The Qadhafi regime was never able to regain control of the city during the war, and the Misrata *thuwar* prevented the regime from dividing the western part of the country from the *thuwar* controlled areas in the eastern region.[8]

Certain areas in the vicinity of Misrata were particularly affected during the conflict, such as the towns of Kararim, Tumina and Karzaz, located to the south of the city.[9] The town of Tawergha, located 38 kilometers (23 miles) southeast of Misrata along the road to Sirte, experienced the most dramatic effects from the war and its aftermath. Tawergha was home to an estimated 30,000 residents, before the entire community was

---

[4] Rob Young, *Libya's commercial hub recovers slowly*, BBC, *available at* http://www.bbc .co.uk/news/business-16366285. For more information *see Misrata*, WIKIPEDIA, *available at* http://en.wikipedia.org/wiki/Misrata.

[5] Report of the International Commission of Inquiry on Libya, U.N. HRC. 19th Sess., Annex I, ¶ 392. U.N. Doc. A/HRC/19/68, advance unedited version (Mar. 2, 2012).

[6] INTERNATIONAL CRISIS GROUP, HOLDING LIBYA TOGETHER: SECURITY CHALLENGES AFTER QADHAFI 7 (Dec. 14, 2011) [hereinafter "HOLDING LIBYA TOGETHER"], *available at* http://www.crisisgroup.org/~/media/Files/Middle%20East%20North%20Africa/North %20Africa/115%20Holding%20Libya%20Together%20--%20Security%20Challenges%20 after%20Qadhafi.pdf.

[7] *Id.*

[8] *Id. See also* Ch. II, Sec. 3.3.

[9] *See generally*, PHYSICIANS FOR HUMAN RIGHTS, WITNESS TO WAR CRIMES, *supra* note 2.

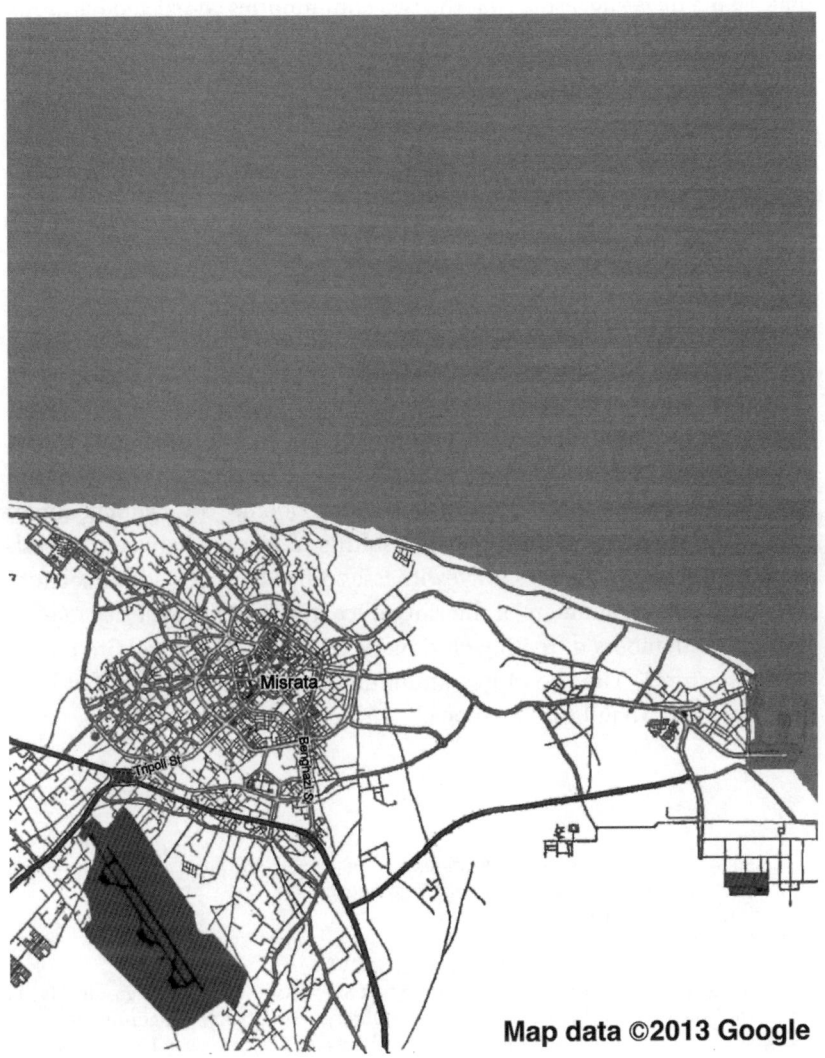

Map 6: Map of Misrata (Map data © 2013 Google).

displaced out fear of direct attacks by *thuwar* forces.[10] The relationship
between the people of Tawergha and Misrata reached levels of extreme
violence during the conflict. The CoI reported that opinions differ as to
the relationship between the communities prior to the conflict, finding
that, "some have suggested that the two communities co-existed harmoni-
ously, while others have stated that underlying tensions over land ownership and racism have always bubbled under the surface."[11] The historical
friction between the cities was said to be the result of socio-economic disparity and racial discrimination. Tawerghans are black Libyans, and were
relatively less prosperous economically, in contrast to Misrata, which consisted of relatively wealthier Arab communities.[12]

2. SUMMARY OF EVENTS

On 17 February 2011, dozens of protesters gathered in the streets of Misrata
in a show of support for the demonstrations in Benghazi.[13] In response,
Qadhafi forces carried out arrests that incited even larger demonstrations
in support of the detained protesters. On 19 February, protesters again
took to the streets after hearing reports of violence by Qadhafi forces
against demonstrators in Benghazi, resulting in clashes between protesters and local security forces.[14] Eyewitnesses reported that Qadhafi security
forces, including members of the riot police, the Internal Security Agency
(ISA), and members of the Revolutionary Committees opened fire on the
demonstrators.[15] The use of live ammunition led to the death of at least
one protester, Khalid Abu Shama'a.[16]

---

[10] Report of the International Commission of Inquiry, advance unedited version
(Mar. 2, 2012), *supra* note 5 at Annex I at ¶¶ 397–404.

[11] *Id.* at Annex I, ¶ 390.

[12] *Id.* at Annex I, ¶ 391.

[13] For more on the protests in Benghazi, *see* Ch. VI, Sec. 2.

[14] AMNESTY INTERNATIONAL, MISRATAH UNDER SIEGE AND UNDER FIRE 25–26 (May 6,
2011), *available at* http://www.amnesty.org/en/library/asset/MDE19/019/2011/en/4efa1e19-
06c1-4609-9477-fe0f2f4e2b2a/mde190192011en.pdf. *See also Clampdown in Libyan capital as
protests close in*, AP, Feb. 23, 2011, *available at* http://www.washingtontimes.com/news/2011/
feb/23/libyan-protesters-defiant-after-gadhafi-speech/.

[15] AMNESTY INTERNATIONAL, MISRATAH UNDER SIEGE AND UNDER FIRE, *supra* note 14
at 25–26. *See also* Ch. II, Sec. 3.2.

[16] Report of the International Commission of Inquiry to investigate all the alleged violations of international human rights law in the Libyan Arab Jamahiriya, U.N. HRC. 17th Sess.,
¶ 85. U.N. Doc. A/HRC/17/44 (Jan. 12, 2012).

On 20 February, Qadhafi forces occupied the city and hundreds of pro-testers were injured as a result of clashes.[17] Following a funeral procession for Abu Shama'a, Qadhafi forces again used live ammunition against dem-onstrators who had gathered on Misrata's Tripoli Street. The CoI received information that the Qadhafi forces and armed gangs used AK-47s and anti-aircraft weapons against the demonstrators.[18] Over the next two days, demonstrators attacked Revolutionary Committee offices, police stations and military barracks, and began arming themselves with weapons from these installations.[19]

On 21 February, protesters marched from 'Abd al-'Aziz Street to the People's Guard offices on Tripoli Street. Witnesses reported that Qadhafi forces opened fire with heavy weapons, including machine guns, rocket-propelled grenades (RPGs) and anti-aircraft guns. Snipers were spotted on top of buildings shooting at protesters along Tripoli Street.[20] According to hospital records and witness testimonies gathered by Amnesty Interna-tional, there were an estimated 20 deaths and over 120 injuries sustained from live ammunition and mortar shrapnel.[21]

Within the span of a few days, 70 people were reportedly killed by Qadhafi security forces in Misrata. Protesters continued to organize and resist, and Qadhafi's forces initially retreated, but returned two weeks later with heavier equipment, including tanks and armored vehicles. *Thuwar katiba*, armed with small weapons, created roadblocks to stop the advance of the tanks, and engaged in urban insurgency tactics to counter the Qadhafi forces. *Thuwar* also used the weapons from defeated Qadhafi military units to enhance their own arsenal.[22] The fighting continued as Qadhafi forces were pushed to the outskirts of the city in a matter of days, and by 24 February media reports indicated that the *thuwar* were officially in control of the city.[23]

---

[17] Physicians for Human Rights, Witness to War Crimes, *supra* note 2 at 8.

[18] *See infra* Sec. 3.1. *See also* Report of the International Commission of Inquiry (Jan. 12, 2012), *supra* note 16 at ¶ 85.

[19] *Id.*

[20] Amnesty International, Misratah Under Siege and Under Fire, *supra* note 14 at 25–26.

[21] *Id. See also infra* Sec. 3.2.

[22] Xan Rice, *Libyan rebels pay a heavy price for resisting Gaddafi in Misrata*, The Guard-ian, Apr. 21, 2011, *available at* http://www.guardian.co.uk/world/2011/apr/21/libyan-rebels-heavy-price-misrata. For more on the composition of *thuwar* forces in Misrata, *see* Ch. II, Sec. 2.3.

[23] *Gaddafi loses more Libyan cities*, Al Jazeera, Feb. 24, 2011, *available at* http://www.aljazeera.com/news/africa/2011/02/2011223125256699145.html.

Qadhafi forces did not give up on retaking Misrata, and continued to fight to regain control over the city due to its strategic importance between Tripoli and Sirte. The violent clashes resulted in hundreds of casualties and thousands of injuries. As Qadhafi forces advanced on the city they pushed *thuwar* towards the city center and coastline, and targeted the port in an attempt to cut the city's only remaining escape route and outlet for humanitarian supplies.[24] Entire suburbs near the frontlines were emptied, and families crammed into parts of the city under *thuwar* control.[25] Qadhafi forces conducted extensive shelling of the city and placed snipers that shot at both *thuwar* fighters and civilians. Medical staff reported over a thousand casualties, most of whom were killed by indiscriminate shelling or sniper fire.[26]

The *thuwar* groups in Misrata organized in neighborhoods and operated in cells without any central leadership structure. Despite lacking supplies and experience, they managed to keep Qadhafi forces on the outskirts of the city. However, the *thuwar* were not able to fight their way out or enable civilians to leave the city to safety. This scenario continued for months, with the front between Qadhafi and *thuwar* forces moving back and forth continuously. This took place at the expense of the city's civilian population, who were trapped in the midst of the crossfire, unable to escape the violence.[27] The battle for Misrata was distinct in that its residents were blocked from fleeing the city and had no choice but to endure the fighting, which makes their situation unique among the civilian victims of the 2011 conflict.[28]

As described above, Misratans faced some of the most aggressive and brutal attacks of the conflict from Qadhafi forces arriving from Tripoli and Sirte. The siege on the city was also the longest of the war, with *thuwar* managing to keep control of the core of the city against the better-armed Qadhafi forces. Misrata's rebellion gave rise to a distinct identity and military character that persisted in the aftermath of the war. Misratans felt their uprising was their own, disconnected from the National Transitional

---

[24] AMNESTY INTERNATIONAL, THE BATTLE FOR LIBYA: KILLINGS, DISAPPEARANCES AND TORTURE (Sept. 2011) [hereinafter "THE BATTLE FOR LIBYA"], *available at* http://www.amnesty.org/en/library/asset/MDE19/025/2011/en/8f2e1c49-8f43-46d3-917d-383c17d36377/mde19025201en.pdf.

[25] Rice, *Libyan rebels pay a heavy price for resisting Gaddafi in Misrata, supra* note 22.

[26] *Id.*

[27] *Id.*

[28] THE BATTLE FOR LIBYA, AMNESTY INTERNATIONAL, *supra* note 24. Amnesty estimates that there were hundreds of thousands of displaced persons in the 2011 conflict.

Council (NTC) political leadership in eastern Libya. Local Misrata *thuwar* leaders accused the NTC of providing little support, and even of charging for weapons.[29]

Local leaders created the Misrata Council under the command of Khalifa Zway, which incorporated representatives from the city's Military Council and Security Committee.[30] Reportedly, the Misrata Military Council evolved out of the city's youth movement and the *kata'ib* comprised civilians with no prior training. As described above, Misratan *kata'ib* were not organized through a centralized command structure, but instead formed loose coalitions. Katiba commanders improvised command-and-control structures as they led volunteer fighters into the battles for Tripoli and Sirte.[31]

As the Misrata *thuwar* became more organized and the Qadhafi regime conducted its campaign to retake the city, the violence intensified. Qadhafi forces placed Misrata under siege, cutting the city off from access by land or sea.[32] Using tanks and heavy artillery, Qadhafi troops launched an organized attack in March 2011.[33] Misrata was subject to an air, road and naval blockade that prevented food and medical supplies from reaching its residents. Farmers outside Misrata were unwilling to deliver their products to the city out of fear of shelling and snipers.[34]

On 6 March, Qadhafi forces attacked the city center using seven tanks and 25 pick-up trucks with mounted anti-aircraft machine guns (known as "technicals").[35] However, rebels were able to trap and destroy them inside the city, leading the Qadhafi forces to change tactics. Qadhafi troops instead established checkpoints around the city's perimeter, and on 14 March shelled the city using heavy artillery, disregarding any distinction between

---

[29] INTERNATIONAL CRISIS GROUP, HOLDING LIBYA TOGETHER, *supra* note 6 at 7, 27.

[30] Report of the International Commission of Inquiry, advance unedited version (Mar. 2, 2012), *supra* note 5 at Annex I, ¶ 68. *See also* Ch. II, Sec. 2.3.

[31] INTERNATIONAL CRISIS GROUP, HOLDING LIBYA TOGETHER, *supra* note 6 at 27.

[32] PHYSICIANS FOR HUMAN RIGHTS, WITNESS TO WAR CRIMES, *supra* note 2.

[33] Peter Beaumont, *Libya Rebels and Government Sources Locked in Battle for Bin Jawad*, THE GUARDIAN, Mar. 6, 2011, *available at* http://www.guardian.co.uk/world/2011/mar/06/libya-rebels-government-battle-bin-jawad.

[34] Morgan Strong, *News Summary from the US/International Press on the Libyan Crisis*, THE TRIPOLI POST, Mar. 17, 2011, *available at* http://tripolipost.com/articledetail.asp?c=1&i=5618.

[35] Beaumont, *Libya rebels and government forces locked in battle for Bin-Jawad*, *supra* note 33; *Libya Revolt as it happened: Monday*, BBC, Mar. 6, 2011, *available at* http://news.bbc.co.uk/2/hi/africa/9417359.stm.

combatants and civilians.[36] They then moved tanks and heavy military vehicles into Misrata's residential areas and positioned snipers on buildings at strategic locations throughout the city center. From these positions Qadhafi forces continued to launch relentless and indiscriminate attacks that hit residential neighborhoods.[37]

Around 15–16 March, Qadhafi forces entered the Zawiyyat al-Mahjub area and positioned themselves along the Sahili Road, the highway connecting Misrata to Tripoli.[38] On 17 March, the *thuwar* reported that Qadhafi forces were positioned on the southern, eastern and western edges of the city.[39] Fighting erupted, after which the *thuwar* reported that they had destroyed 16 tanks and captured 20 members of the Khamis Katiba.[40] The same day, doctors from Misrata's central hospital reported at least 60 people had been killed and 570 hospitalized in the fighting, many of whom were civilians. The *thuwar* reported that four rebel fighters were killed, as well as two civilians.[41] Reports also indicated that Qadhafi forces disconnected cell phones and landlines, and cut off electricity in areas of Misrata.[42]

Residents resorted to erecting homemade barricades to prevent Qadhafi forces from advancing deeper into the city. *Thuwar* fighters initially fought with light weapons left behind by Qadhafi forces or smuggled into Misrata by boat from Benghazi. As the fighting continued, the *thuwar* began to acquire additional weapons such as rifles, RPGs and 106mm

---

[36] Strong, *News Summary from the US/International Press on the Libyan Crisis*, *supra* note 34; Tarek Amara & Mariam Karouny, *Gaddafi Forces Shell West Libya's Misrata, 25 Dead*, REUTERS, Mar. 18, 2011, *available at* http://uk.reuters.com/article/2011/03/18/us-libya-misrata-bombard-idUKTRE72H4L520110318.

[37] AMNESTY INTERNATIONAL, MISRATAH UNDER SIEGE AND UNDER FIRE, *supra* note 14 at 10. *See also infra* Sec. 3.7.

[38] Live Wire, *Pain and loss hits every family in Misratah*, AMNESTY INTERNATIONAL, May 25, 2011, *available at* http://livewire.amnesty.org/2011/05/25/pain-and-loss-hits-every-family-in-misratah.

[39] Strong, *News Summary from the US/International Press on the Libyan Crisis*, *supra* note 34.

[40] Ian Black, *Libyan forces predict fall of rebel-held Benghazi 'within 48 hours'*, THE GUARDIAN, Mar. 17, 2011, *available at* http://www.guardian.co.uk/world/2011/mar/16/libya-benghazi-gaddafi-48-hours.

[41] Strong, *News Summary from the US/International Press on the Libyan Crisis*, *supra* note 34; Amara & Karouny, *Gaddafi Forces Shell West Libya's Misrata, 25 Dead*, *supra* note 36.

[42] Strong, *News Summary from the US/International Press on the Libyan Crisis*, *supra* note 34; *Assaults on Misurata, Ajdabijah and Zintan*, THE TRIPOLI POST, Mar. 23, 2011, *available at* http://www.tripolipost.com/articledetail.asp?c=1&i=5664.

rockets seized from retreating Qadhafi forces.[43] Misratans also manufactured their own makeshift weapons and vehicles.[44]

Qadhafi forces positioned themselves in neighboring cities – Zlitan in the west, Bani Walid in the south and Tawergha in the east. As the regime conducted attacks from their bases in these cities, the violence worsened, and the international community responded by passing UN Security Council Resolution 1973.[45] On 19 March, two days after the resolution was passed, 40 people were reportedly killed in the ongoing fighting. The next day, a doctor at the central Misrata hospital said that 13 were killed, bringing the total casualty count to 90 over the previous nine days. Four children were reported among the casualties.[46]

NATO began its intervention in Misrata on 23 March.[47] By 24 March, NATO airstrikes had destroyed tanks and artillery, easing the siege on the city and compelling a large number of Qadhafi forces to retreat.[48] A few hours later, however, Qadhafi forces returned and began shelling the area near the city's university hospital. Qadhafi forces surrounded the hospital with tanks, blocking the entrance and preventing injured residents from receiving treatment.[49] Snipers firing on the hospital entrance also put anyone trying to leave or enter the hospital at great risk.[50] A *thuwar* spokesperson reported that approximately 1,000 people were being treated in the hospital, most of them in critical condition, and that the hospital had lost power.[51] Another *thuwar* fighter reported that the

---

[43] AMNESTY INTERNATIONAL, MISRATAH UNDER SIEGE AND UNDER FIRE, *supra* note 14.

[44] Nick Carey, *Libya rebels boost firepower with homemade weapons*, REUTERS, July 12, 2011, *available at* http://www.reuters.com/article/2011/07/12/us-libya-misrata-weapons-idUSTRE76A38N20110712. *See also* Ch. II, Sec. 2.3.

[45] SC Res. 1973 (2011), Mar. 17 2011, UN Doc. S/RES/1973 (2011).

[46] Strong, *News Summary from the US/International Press on the Libyan Crisis*, THE TRIPOLI POST, Mar. 23, 2011, *available at* http://www.tripolipost.com/articledetail.asp?c=1&i=5661.

[47] *See* Ch. III, Sec. 6.1.

[48] *See infra* Sec. 4.

[49] *Libya crisis: Thursday 24 March*, THE GUARDIAN, Mar. 24, 2011, *available at* http://www.guardian.co.uk/world/blog/2011/mar/24/libya-crisis-live-updates.

[50] *Libyan Rebels Form 'Interim Government'*, AL JAZEERA, Mar. 22, 2011, *available at* http://english.aljazeera.net/news/africa/2011/03/201132219394862310.html; PHYSICIANS FOR HUMAN RIGHTS, WITNESS TO WAR CRIMES, *supra* note 2.

[51] Hamid Ould Ahmed, *Rebels say 16 dead in Misrata, hospital attacked*, REUTERS, Mar. 23, 2011, *available at* http://www.reuters.com/article/2011/03/23/us-libya-misrata-strikes-idUSTRE72M8BY20110323.

hospital was emptied of its patients, who had been moved to the city's other hospital.[52]

The assault continued on 24 March, as Qadhafi forces shelled Zibla Street, leading to civilian injuries.[53] Residents reported on the indiscriminate attacks in urban areas, and the presence of snipers shooting at both *thuwar* and civilians.[54] Medical staff also reported that snipers were targeting civilians, killing entire families. Misrata's hospitals were overwhelmed and medical personnel had to send patients without life threatening injuries home before they had time to recover in order to make room for newly admitted patients. Medical staff estimated the total injured at more than 1,300, of which approximately 115 were seriously injured.[55]

Qadhafi forces continued to target Misrata, shelling its city center continuously and attacking residential areas with mortars and tanks.[56] The assaults continued into April, leading to further civilian casualties and injuries. On 14 April, sustained rocket attacks on the Qasr Ahmad neighborhood began and lasted for two days, leading to the death of a dozen residents.[57] Attacks continued throughout April, and medical staff found themselves overwhelmed due to the lack of personnel, equipment and medicine. At Al-Hikma Hospital, staff reported receiving the bodies of ten persons killed, and admitting 50 wounded on 23 April.[58]

Misrata's seaport was closed on a few occasions in March and April due to repeated shelling by regime forces and fighting in the area.[59] *Thuwar* expressed fear that Qadhafi forces would attempt to seize the harbor in order to strangle the city's supply line.[60] In late April, Qadhafi forces laid

---

[52] *See infra* Sec. 3.7.4(a). *See also* THE GUARDIAN, *Libya crisis: Thursday 24 March, supra* note 49.

[53] AMNESTY INTERNATIONAL, MISRATAH UNDER SIEGE AND UNDER FIRE, *supra* note 14.

[54] *NATO air strikes target Misurata*, AL JAZEERA, Apr. 9, 2011, *available at* http://www .aljazeera.com/news/africa/2011/04/20114913167462559.html.

[55] Chris McGreal et al., *Libya: Allied air strikes secure Misrata for rebels*, THE GUARDIAN, Mar. 24, 2011, *available at* http://www.guardian.co.uk/world/2011/mar/23/libya-allied-air-strikes-misrata.

[56] Adam Tanner & Souhail Karam, *Six Killed in Libyan Town Shelling: Rebel*, REUTERS, Mar. 25, 2011, *available at* http://www.reuters.com/article/2011/03/25/us-libya-misrata-fighting-idUSTRE72O63720110325.

[57] *See infra* Sec. 3.2. *See also* AMNESTY INTERNATIONAL, MISRATAH UNDER SIEGE AND UNDER FIRE, *supra* note 14 at 11.

[58] *Libya rebels claim 'Misurata is free'*, AL JAZEERA, Apr. 23, 2011, *available at* http://www .aljazeera.com/news/africa/2011/04/20114231251998645.html.

[59] *Press briefing on Libya*, NORTH ATLANTIC TREATY ORGANIZATION, Apr. 19, 2011, *available at*http://www.nato.int/cps/en/natolive/opinions_72825.htm.

[60] C.J. Chivers, *Land Mines Descend on Misurata's Port, Endangering Libyan City's Supply Route*, N.Y. TIMES, May 6, 2011, *available at* http://www.nytimes.com/2011/05/07/world/africa/07libya.html.

mines in the approaches to Misrata's port in order to block shipping and thwart the delivery of humanitarian aid to the city. The Libyan Foreign Minister 'Abd al-'Ati al-'Ubaydi said that Qadhafi forces would sink any ship approaching Misrata, threatening NATO patrols and humanitarian aid vessels bringing in food and medical supplies to aid refugees and the wounded. NATO reported working to clear the mines from the port to maintain the safety of ships entering and leaving the port.[61]

NATO operations also led to accidental or friendly attacks. On 27 April, NATO carried out an attack east of Misrata that hit *thuwar* trucks, killing 12 *thuwar* fighters and wounding three.[62] NATO aircraft had struck a column of regime trucks the day before, halting their advance on rebel forces, causing soldiers to abandon their material. When *thuwar* returned to the scene to collect weapons and ammunition, they were hit by a NATO airstrike and three trucks were destroyed, along with half of a small building. A NATO spokesperson refuted that its airstrikes had killed *thuwar* fighters, saying they could not verify the attack.[63]

Overall, NATO airstrikes greatly aided the *thuwar* efforts in Misrata, as they weakened the Qadhafi regime's capabilities by destroying equipment and control centers.[64] By early May, NATO reported it had hit 30 military targets in the area, destroying large amounts of equipment, including tanks and artillery.[65] The strikes hindered the movement of Qadhafi forces and allowed the *thuwar* to gain control over the city.

By mid-May 2011, the combined assaults of the *thuwar* and NATO drove Qadhafi forces to retreat towards various rear positions, including into the town of Tawergha. The CoI received reports that the Qadhafi forces established checkpoints around the town, preventing civilians from leaving. A number of Tawerghan men, some of them already soldiers in the Libyan

---

[61] *Press briefing on Libya*, NORTH ATLANTIC TREATY ORGANIZATION, July 12, 2011, *available at* http://www.nato.int/cps/en/natolive/opinions_76355.htm; Chivers, *Land Mines Descend on Misurata's Port, Endangering Libyan City's Supply Route, supra* note 60.

[62] *See* Ch. III, Sec. 6.2. *See also* Craig Allen et al., *Errant NATO Airstrikes in Libya: 13 Cases (Misurata)*, N.Y. TIMES, Dec. 16, 2011, *available at* http://www.nytimes.com/interactive/2011/12/16/world/africa/nato-airstrikes-in-libya.html?ref=africa&_r=0#page/rebel-trucks.

[63] Allen et al., *Errant NATO Airstrikes in Libya: 13 Cases (Misurata), supra* note 62.

[64] *See infra* Sec. 4. *See also* Andrew Gilligan, *Libya: rebels celebrate seizing Misurata airport*, THE TELEGRAPH, May 11, 2011, *available at* http://www.telegraph.co.uk/news/worldnews/africaandindianocean/libya/8508488/Libya-rebels-celebrate-seizing-Misurata-airport.html.

[65] *Press briefing on Libya*, NORTH ATLANTIC TREATY ORGANIZATION, May 10, 2011, *available at* http://www.nato.int/cps/en/natolive/opinions_73660.htm.

army and some new volunteers, formed part of Qadhafi forces.[66] According to *thuwar* groups and civilians from Misrata, Tawerghans actively supported the regime in the assaults on Misrata and engaged in atrocities including theft, murder and rape against Misratans.[67]

By the end of May, *thuwar* were able to retake the Misrata airfield and establish positions in the south and west of the city.[68] NATO continued its airstrikes, cutting Qadhafi forces off from supplies and blocking their advances. NATO reported on 20 May that the city was no longer under siege. The shelling of the port and city center ended, with humanitarian aid flowing freely into the port.[69] Some of the victims who had fled the violence started to return, and electricity was restored to parts of the city.[70] Qadhafi forces sustained their attempts to retake Misrata, however, and continued shelling residential areas with long-range missiles.[71]

NATO reported conducting several strikes in the vicinity of Misrata on 29 June, destroying a multiple rocket launcher, five battle tanks, two artillery pieces, and three military vehicles.[72] NATO also carried out airstrikes on Qadhafi forces in Tawergha, and on 10 July targeted a former farm complex where it reported Qadhafi troops were storing long-range rocket systems. NATO reported that Qadhafi forces had used the facility to launch rockets indiscriminately in areas around Misrata, the city and the port.[73]

In August, after months of a military stalemate, *thuwar* made rapid advances that were fueled by Qatari weapons and ammunition that reached Misrata by air on 6 August. The supplies were destined for the western front and helped the *thuwar* forces to break through Zlitan

---

[66] Report of the International Commission of Inquiry, advance unedited version (Mar. 2, 2012), *supra* note 5 at Annex I, ¶ 393.

[67] INTERNATIONAL CRISIS GROUP, HOLDING LIBYA TOGETHER, *supra* note 6 at 7.

[68] *Press briefing on Libya*, NORTH ATLANTIC TREATY ORGANIZATION, May 27, 2011, *available at* http://www.nato.int/cps/en/natolive/opinions_74826.htm.

[69] *Press briefing on Libya*, NORTH ATLANTIC TREATY ORGANIZATION, May 20, 2011, *available at* http://www.nato.int/cps/en/natolive/opinions_74542.htm.

[70] PHYSICIANS FOR HUMAN RIGHTS, WITNESS TO WAR CRIMES, *supra* note 2.

[71] Ruth Sherlock & Damien McElroy, *Nato lacks firepower to ensure collapse of Gaddafi regime, experts claim*, THE TELEGRAPH, June 24, 2011, *available at* http://www.telegraph.co.uk/news/worldnews/africaandindianocean/libya/8597107/Natolacks-firepower-to-ensure-collapse-of-Gaddafi-regime-experts-claim.html; William Booth, *In war-torn Libya, no pause for Ramadan*, THE WASHINGTON POST, Aug. 1, 2011, *available at* http://www.washingtonpost.com/world/middle-east/in-war-tornlibya-no-pause-for-ramadan/2011/08/01/gIQA82pNoI_story.html.

[72] *NATO and Libya: Operational Media Update*, NORTH ATLANTIC TREATY ORGANIZATION, June 29, 2011, *available at* http://www.nato.int/nato_static/assets/pdf/pdf_2011_06/20110630_110630-oup-update.pdf.

[73] NORTH ATLANTIC TREATY ORGANIZATION, *Press briefing on Libya*, *supra* note 61.

towards Tripoli.[74] In mid-August, *thuwar* forces advanced on Tripoli from the port of Misrata.[75] NATO reported that *thuwar* freed nearby areas from regime forces, which was expected to reduce the intermittent and indiscriminate shelling by Qadhafi forces and eliminate the threat to the flow of humanitarian aid in the region.[76]

After driving the Qadhafi forces out of the region, the Misratan *thuwar* began an assault of Tawergha. From 10–12 August, *thuwar* groups fired unguided Grad and S5 rockets into the town.[77] After the shelling, the *thuwar* advanced on the town and took full control on 14 August, forcing the remaining population to flee.[78] *Thuwar* fighters carried out a campaign of reprisal violence, ransacking and burning houses.[79] The town of Tawergha, which had a population of 30,000, was completely emptied of its inhabitants as a result of the reprisal violence by Misrata *thuwar* forces.[80]

The day after the declaration of Libya's liberation from the Qadhafi regime was made on 23 October 2011, the Supreme Security Committee (SCC) supervised a ceremony during which a number of katiba from Misrata handed over 500 light arms to the Ministry of the Interior. The ceremony was intended to symbolize the transfer of power from the revolutionary forces to the interim government authorities.[81] Many of the Misratan *thuwar* groups remained heavily armed, however, and held control over important areas and government installations in the region and in Tripoli.[82]

In another symbolic gesture of a new era, the Misratan *thuwar* transferred the bodies of Qadhafi and his son Mu'tassim to Misrata for display

---

[74] *See* Ch. II, Sec. 2.3 & Ch. III, Sec. 7.1. *See also* Mussab al-Khairalla, *Qatari plane supplies ammunition to Libya rebels*, REUTERS, Aug. 6, 2011, *available at* http://www.reuters.com/article/2011/08/06/libya-rebels-ammunition-idAFLDE77505S20110806.

[75] Kareem Fahim & Mark Mazzetti, *Rebels' Assault on Tripoli Began With Careful Work Inside*, N.Y. TIMES, Aug. 22, 2011, *available at* http://www.nytimes.com/2011/08/23/world/africa/23reconstruct.html.

[76] *Press briefing on Libya*, NORTH ATLANTIC TREATY ORGANIZATION, Aug. 16, 2011, *available at* http://www.nato.int/cps/en/natolive/opinions_77212.htm.

[77] Report of the International Commission of Inquiry, advance unedited version (Mar. 2, 2012), *supra* note 5 at Annex I, ¶¶ 393–394.

[78] *See infra* Sec. 3.10. *See also* Report of the International Commission of Inquiry, advance unedited version (Mar. 2, 2012), *supra* note 5 at Annex I, ¶ 395.

[79] *Score-settling after Libya's war casts shadow*, AP, Oct. 29, 2011, *available at* http://www.guardian.co.uk/world/feedarticle/9920407.

[80] *See* Report of the International Commission of Inquiry, advance unedited version (Mar. 2, 2012), *supra* note 5 at Annex I, ¶ 397. *See also* Ch. IV, Sec. 2.

[81] *Report of the Secretary-General on the United Nations Support Mission in Libya*, UN Security Council, U.N. Doc. S/2011/727 (Nov. 22, 2011) at 2.

[82] *See* Ch. V, Sec. 2.

lasting three days, during which "[t]housands of Misratans visited the bodies in…a meat locker." At dawn on 25 October, Qadhafi, Mu'tassim and army commander Abu Bakr Yunis were buried.[83] They were given Muslim burials and interred in a secret location in order to avoid their graves becoming shrines.[84]

In November, the NTC announced that it was releasing hundreds of prisoners, many of whom were suspected of being Qadhafi loyalists, from cities including Misrata.[85] 200 detainees were released from one detention center alone. The NTC maintained, however, that African nationals accused of being mercenaries for the Qadhafi regime would remain in detention until their cases could be processed.[86]

The weapons in Misrata remaining from the war presented a major problem for central authorities, as *thuwar* groups refused to give up control of their armaments.[87] In December 2011, journalists visited Misratan warehouses where *thuwar* groups were storing tanks, rockets and small arms. Reports stated that the Misrata *thuwar* included six *kata'ib* with more than 200 units, all of which maintained weapons. This was said to tally 38 tanks, nine self-propelled guns, 16 field guns, 536 Russian-made Grad rockets and 13 truck-mounted Grad launchers, 2,480 mortar rounds and 202 artillery shells.[88] While the Misratan *thuwar* professed their loyalty to the interim leaders of the NTC, the abundance of weapons allowed them to assert their influence and convert it into political power.[89]

In the months following the end of the conflict, Misrata became a semi-independent city.[90] Residents of Misrata grew impatient with the lack

---

[83] Report of the International Commission of Inquiry, advance unedited version (Mar. 2, 2012), *supra* note 5 at Annex I, ¶ 250.

[84] Ian Black, *Gaddafi buried in secret desert location*, THE GUARDIAN, Oct. 25, 2011, *available at* http://www.guardian.co.uk/world/2011/oct/25/gaddafi-buried-libya-desert; Rania El Gamal, *Libya ends public showing of Gaddafi's body*, REUTERS, Oct. 25, 2011 *available at* http://www.reuters.com/article/2011/10/25/us-libya-gaddafi-body-idUSTRE79N2HW20111025.

[85] Similar releases were made in the Nafusa Mountains region and Tripoli. *See infra* Secs. 6 & 9. *See also* Ban Ki-Moon, *Report of the Secretary-General on the United Nations Support Mission in Libya*, U.N. Doc. S/2011/727, ¶ 22, Nov. 22, 2011.

[86] Karen Allen, *Hundreds of Libyan prisoners freed*, BBC, Nov. 5, 2011, *available at* http://www.bbc.co.uk/news/world-africa-15604542.

[87] *See* Ch. V, Sec. 2.2.

[88] *City's huge arsenal a test for new Libyan rulers*, REUTERS, Dec. 7, 2011, *available at* http://www.reuters.com/article/2011/12/07/libya-misrata-weapons-idUSL5E7N72IH20111207.

[89] *See* Ch. V, Sec. 2.2.

[90] Ranj Alaaldin, *Libya should embrace federalism*, THE GUARDIAN, Mar. 28, 2012, *available at* http://www.guardian.co.uk/commentisfree/2012/mar/28/libya-federalism-regions-revolution.

of guidance from the interim government, which was unable to control regional factions during the transitional period.[91] The interim government was widely perceived as ineffective and unaccountable.[92] Misrata maintained its own prisons and justice system run independently from the central authorities.[93] The Misrata *kata'ib*, along with those from Zintan, remained some of the most powerful non-state armed actors in the country. The NTC was forced to recognize the *kata'ib* from these cities and reserved leadership positions in the ministries of the Interior and Defense for their commanders.[94]

The *thuwar* also resisted the self-appointed city council that came to power in Misrata early in the uprising of corruption. After a sit-in outside the council building its members resigned, and on 20 February 2012, elections were held to put a new council in its place.[95] While Misrata acted independently from Tripoli in some of its political affairs, it did not form an independent council, unlike cities such as those in Cyrenaica.[96]

After a meeting held in Tripoli in December 2011, elders from Tawergha decided that the approximately 30,000 Tawerghans scattered in camps and other makeshift accommodations across Libya would return on 20 December, and urged the authorities to facilitate such a return. However, officials from Misrata refused, stating that it was too early and that the situation was not safe for the residents. Tawerghans were urged to wait until the NTC organized the community's return as part of a program of national reconciliation. NGOs in the area supported the recommendation to postpone the return to Tawergha.[97]

---

[91] *Libya Free Elections In Misrata First Since Fall Of Gaddafi*, AP, Feb. 20, 2012, *available at* http://www.huffingtonpost.com/2012/02/20/libya-free-elections-misrata_n_1289156.html.

[92] Gabriel Gatehouse, *Misrata votes for brighter Libyan future*, BBC, Feb. 20, 2012, *available at* http://www.bbc.co.uk/news/world-africa-17107048.

[93] *See* Ch. V, Sec. 2.3. *See also Libya: job done?*, THE GUARDIAN, Feb. 17, 2012, *available at* www.guardian.co.uk/commentisfree/2012/feb/17/libya-torture-human-rights-abuses.

[94] *See* Ch. V, Sec. 2. *See also* Amanda Kadlec, *Disarming Libya's Militias*, CARNEGIE ENDOWMENT FOR INTERNATIONAL PEACE (Feb. 16, 2012), *available at* http://carnegieendowment.org/sada/2012/02/16/disarming-libya-s-militias/90fa.

[95] AP, *Libya Free Elections In Misrata First Since Fall Of Gaddafi*, *supra* note 91.

[96] *See* Gabriel Gatehouse, *Benghazi's bid for Cyrenaica autonomy divides Libyans*, BBC, Mar. 10, 2012, *available at* http://www.bbc.co.uk/news/world-africa-17316264.

[97] Ali Shuaib, *UPDATE 1-Refugees of Libya revenge attacks plan to go home*, REUTERS, Dec. 14, 2011, *available at* http://www.reuters.com/article/2011/12/14/libya-tawargha-return-idUSL6E7NE4W620111214.

3. Illustrations of the Violations

3.1. *Excessive Use of Force*

(a) *Qadhafi Forces*

There were documented cases of Qadhafi troops' excessive use of force against unarmed protesters in February 2011, and against civilian populations trying to flee the fighting in Misrata.[98] The CoI documented cases of riot-control police using live ammunition against demonstrators that led to the death of at least one person, Abu Shama'a, on 19 February. The next day, following the funeral of Abu Shama'a, Qadhafi forces again used live ammunition on protesters gathered on Tripoli Street. The CoI documented the use of indiscriminate weapons, including AK-47s and anti-aircraft weapons.[99] A senior military figure reported that the Khamis Katiba passed instructions to ground commanders to shoot civilians.[100]

Consistent testimonies from witnesses and victims in Misrata point to a pattern of unwarranted and excessive use of lethal force against demonstrators. The Qadhafi regime reacted to the initial protests in February with extreme measures, and continued to use excessive force against demonstrators in the following weeks. Amnesty International reported an incident on 21 March 2011 in which RPGs, anti-aircraft machine guns and snipers were used by the Qadhafi forces. According to hospital records and testimonies, some 20 other people were killed by live ammunition and shrapnel from tank and mortar shells and more than 120 were injured during the 21 March incident.[101]

---

[98] Amnesty International, Misratah Under Siege and Under Fire, *supra* note 14 at 26.

[99] Report of the International Commission of Inquiry (Jan. 12, 2012), *supra* note 16 at ¶ 85.

[100] Report of the International Commission of Inquiry, advance unedited version (Mar. 2, 2012), *supra* note 5 at ¶ 18.

[101] Amnesty International, Misratah Under Siege and Under Fire, *supra* note 14 at 25–26.

3.2. *Unlawful Killing*

(a) *Qadhafi Forces*

Misrata was the scene of the most sustained fighting of the civil war, and the city's population experienced consistent indiscriminate attacks from Qadhafi forces resulting in numerous casualties.[102] On 11 April, the regional director of the United Nations Children's Fund (UNICEF) in the MENA region was able to "verif[y] at least 20 deaths and many more injuries due to shrapnel from mortars and tanks and bullet wounds."[103] Moreover, a medical doctor and administrator of the main Misrata hospital stated that "as of 18 April, about 1,000 people had been killed and 3,000 injured, with some 80 per cent of the deaths being civilian."[104] Likewise, between 21 and 22 May, the World Health Organization (WHO) conducted an inter-agency assessment mission and was able to conclude that an average of 70 people sustained injuries and 12 were killed each day of the conflict.[105]

The CoI noted that circumstances surrounding such deaths were often difficult to ascertain, including "whether the attacks were intentional, indiscriminate and/or disproportionate."[106] At the same time, there were numerous documented cases of Qadhafi forces launching indiscriminate attacks on residential neighborhoods from their positions around the city.[107] These attacks involved the use of heavy artillery weapons, which failed to distinguish between *thuwar* fighters and civilians. Medical staff provided information corroborating these findings, reporting over a thousand casualties, most of whom were killed by indiscriminate shelling or sniper fire. On 20 March, for example, doctors from Misrata's central hospital reported that many of their patients were civilians, and that children had been killed as a result of the attacks.[108]

---

[102] *See supra* Sec. 2. *See also* Report of the International Commission of Inquiry, advance unedited version (Mar. 2, 2012), *supra* note 5 at Annex I, ¶¶ 546–555.

[103] Report of the International Commission of Inquiry (Jan. 12, 2012), *supra* note 16 at ¶ 156.

[104] *Id.*

[105] *Id. Statement by UNICEF Executive Director Anthony Lake on situation of children in the Middle East and North Africa*, UNICEF, Apr. 20, 2011, *available at* http://www.unicef.org/media/media_58332.html.

[106] Report of the International Commission of Inquiry (Jan. 12, 2012), *supra* note 16 at ¶ 156; UNICEF, *Statement by UNICEF Executive Director Anthony Lake on situation of children in the Middle East and North Africa*, *supra* note 105 (internal citation omitted).

[107] AMNESTY INTERNATIONAL, MISRATAH UNDER SIEGE AND UNDER FIRE, *supra* note 14 at 10.

[108] Rice, *Libyan rebels pay a heavy price for resisting Gaddafi in Misrata*, *supra* note 22; Strong, *News Summary from the US/International Press on the Libyan Crisis*, *supra* note 34; Amara & Karouny, *Gaddafi Forces Shell West Libya's Misrata, 25 Dead*, *supra* note 36.

Amnesty International reported on civilian casualties resulting from shelling attacks on various neighborhoods in Misrata. On 16 March 2011, an elderly woman was fatally wounded by shelling in Zawiyyat al-Mahjub in western Misrata.[109] On 21 March, four children were killed by a projectile fired from Qadhafi soldiers in the center of Misrata.[110] Rocket fire also reached the residents of Ra's 'Ammar neighborhood and led to civilian deaths in the area on 30 March.[111]

Qadhafi forces carried out shelling attacks in the Qasr Ahmad neighborhood near the port of Misrata between 14 and 16 April, resulting in the deaths of several civilians.[112] Additionally, a dozen residents in the neighborhood were killed in attacks while standing in line at a bakery.[113] A week later in the same neighborhood, a 72-year-old man was killed in the early afternoon when a rocket exploded next to the house where he was staying.[114]

There were also reports of the use of snipers by Qadhafi forces at strategic positions in Misrata's city center to shoot at civilians. This was especially prevalent near the Bu Minyar building,[115] and the Ta'min (Insurance) Building[116] on Tripoli Street.[117] The attacks were effective in intimidating residents and hindering their movement in areas under *thuwar* control. A spokesperson for the *thuwar* reported that Qadhafi snipers killed at least 16 people on 23 March 2011.[118]

In an effort to maintain the siege and control the movement of persons, Qadhafi forces maintained checkpoints around Misrata, and shootings at these checkpoints led to civilian deaths.[119] Amnesty International documented several such incidents. On 11 March 2011, a man was killed on the road to the airport in Misrata. One of his family mem-

---

[109] AMNESTY INTERNATIONAL, *Pain and loss hits every family in Misratah, supra* note 38.

[110] AMNESTY INTERNATIONAL, MISRATAH UNDER SIEGE AND UNDER FIRE, *supra* note 14 at 24.

[111] AMNESTY INTERNATIONAL, *Pain and loss hits every family in Misratah, supra* note 38.

[112] AMNESTY INTERNATIONAL, MISRATAH UNDER SIEGE AND UNDER FIRE, *supra* note 14 at 11.

[113] *Id.* at 12.

[114] *Id.* at 13.

[115] Report of the International Commission of Inquiry (Jan. 12, 2012), *supra* note 16 at ¶ 156.

[116] The transliteration of this word was adopted from the reference. AMNESTY INTERNATIONAL, MISRATAH UNDER SIEGE AND UNDER FIRE, *supra* note 14 at 10.

[117] *Id.* at 10.

[118] Ahmed, *Rebels say 16 dead in Misrata, hospital attacked, supra* note 51.

[119] Report of the International Commission of Inquiry (Jan. 12, 2012), *supra* note 16 at ¶ 156.

bers told Amnesty International that members of Qadhafi Katiba were responsible.[120] Another incident on 5 April involved a man killed in the Al-Ghayran neighborhood.[121] On 11 April, a man was shot driving from his home in Tumina to Misrata city center. The man's son stated that Qadhafi snipers stationed on top of the Science College building were responsible for the shooting.[122]

Amnesty found that based on the information they received, snipers employed by Qadhafi forces were responsible for several of the documented deaths in Misrata during this period.[123]

(b) Thuwar *Forces*

There were documented cases of unlawful killings carried out by *thuwar* forces in Misrata. Human Rights Watch (HRW) reported that after the fall of Tripoli in August 2011 armed groups from Misrata were operating outside of any official military or civilian command, carrying out arbitrary detention, coerced confessions, torture and shootings of detainees.[124]

In some incidents, the torture in detention facilities controlled by *thuwar* led to deaths in custody. The head of United Nations Support Mission in Libya (UNSMIL), Ian Martin, reported on three deaths that occurred on 13 April 2012 at a detention center in Misrata controlled by the Supreme Security Committee (SSC), under the supposed authority of the Ministry of the Interior.[125] UNSMIL received credible information that the deaths were a direct result of torture. Martin put pressure on both the Prime Minister and the Interior Minister to investigate the incidents, and the SSC of Misrata publicly condemned the acts and announced its support for investigations.[126]

i. *The Tawerghans*

The CoI found that *thuwar* forces predominantly from Misrata carried out unlawful killings specifically aimed at the Tawerghan community.[127]

---

[120] AMNESTY INTERNATIONAL, *Pain and loss hits every family in Misratah, supra* note 38.

[121] *Id.*

[122] *Id.*

[123] AMNESTY INTERNATIONAL, MISRATAH UNDER SIEGE AND UNDER FIRE, *supra* note 14 at 20.

[124] Daniel Williams, *The Murder Brigades of Misrata*, HUMAN RIGHTS WATCH, Oct. 28, 2011, *available at* http://www.hrw.org/news/2011/10/28/murder-brigades-misrata.

[125] For more on the formation of the Supreme Security Committee, *see* Ch. IV, Sec. 2.

[126] U.N. SC, 67th year, 6768 mtg, U.N. Doc. S/PV.6768 (May 10, 2012) at 5.

[127] Report of the International Commission of Inquiry, advance unedited version (Mar. 2, 2012), *supra* note 5 at Annex I, ¶ 218.

The Misrata *kata'ib* were accused of several shootings of unarmed Tawerghans around the city and of those in detention. Three witnesses reported to HRW that a member of a Misrata katiba executed an unarmed man from Tawergha in late September 2011. They said that the man, a nurse at a Tawergha hospital, was shot once in the back and once in the leg at a military rest house in Hun, a facility being used as a camp for nearly 1,800 displaced Tawerghans. In two other cases, Misrata katiba members shot Tawerghans in their custody and left them on the side of a deserted road.[128]

A Tawerghan man, arrested in Shawarif and taken to Misrata, reportedly died in *thuwar* custody. Following an investigation by his family, it was discovered that the man had died and his body taken to the Sabiyya hospital. According to the CoI, the official autopsy report listed the cause of death as resulting from a fractured skull.[129]

3.3. *Arbitrary Detentions and Enforced Disappearances*

(a) *Qadhafi Forces*

From early to mid-March 2011, as Qadhafi forces attempted to retake control of Misrata, they carried out reprisal attacks against residents suspected of supporting the *thuwar*. The campaign of violence was conducted with the intent of intimidating the population into submission, as people were taken into custody and many subsequently disappeared. People were taken from their homes in a wave of sweeping arrests and family members of the victims were not informed as to their whereabouts.[130] Others were taken into custody on roads or other public places as Qadhafi forces advanced into *thuwar* controlled regions of the city.[131] Media outlets reported that more than 1,170 people were missing in the city by

---

[128] *Libya: Militias Terrorizing Residents of 'Loyalist' Town*, Human Rights Watch, Oct. 30, 2011, *available at* http://www.hrw.org/news/2011/10/30/libya-militias-terrorizing-residents-loyalist-town.

[129] Report of the International Commission of Inquiry, advance unedited version (Mar. 2, 2012), *supra* note 5 at Annex I, ¶ 436.

[130] Amnesty International, Misratah Under Siege and Under Fire, *supra* note 14 at 27.

[131] The Battle for Libya, Amnesty International, *supra* note 24 at 58.

June 2011.[132] The CoI documented 317 known persons reported as missing in Misrata.[133]

NGOs reported on hundreds of disappearances in Misrata. Most of these were men, arrested in the streets by Qadhafi forces, while others were taken from their homes or from mosques.[134] Amnesty International documented numerous cases of detention and enforced disappearances. A man from Misrata who participated in the fighting reported that Qadhafi forces forcibly entered his grandfather's home in the area of Kharuba in late March in search of him. Since he was not present, they took his uncle, who was not heard from after his abduction.[135] Another witness from Al-Ghayran stated that 25 members of a *kata'ib* from the Qadhafi forces jumped over the wall of his house on 17 March 2011 and handcuffed his five sons and ten nephews. The soldiers took away the sons, and their father had not heard from them since.[136] Another witness, a father of nine, stated that on 18 March 2011, Qadhafi forces came to his house in Al-Ghayran neighborhood and took his seven sons, his brother and two of his nephews. The man stated that the Qadhafi forces put them in a pick-up truck and took them away. In May 2011, the whereabouts of his children and relatives were still unknown.[137]

Physicians for Human Rights (PHR) documented similar cases of detentions and disappearances during the same period. A 21-year-old man who had fought on the side of the *thuwar* reported that on 16 March 2011 approximately 15 members of the Qadhafi forces, believed to be from Tawergha, entered his home. The soldiers forced the father of the witness into one of their white Toyota trucks and left, and his whereabouts remained unknown.[138]

---

[132] Portia Walker, *More than 1,000 Libyans Missing from Misurata*, THE WASHINGTON POST, June 4, 2011, *available at* http://www.washingtonpost.com/world/middle-east/more-than-1000-libyans-missing-from-misurata/2011/05/30/AGmuw2IH_story.html.

[133] Report of the International Commission of Inquiry, advance unedited version (Mar. 2, 2012), *supra* note 5 at Annex I, ¶ 273.

[134] Live Wire, *Families rent asunder by deaths and disappearances in Misratah*, AMNESTY INTERNATIONAL, May 21, 2011, *available at* http://livewire.amnesty.org/2011/05/21/families-rent-asunder-by-deaths-and-disappearances-in-misratah.

[135] AMNESTY INTERNATIONAL, MISRATAH UNDER SIEGE AND UNDER FIRE, *supra* note 14 at 29.

[136] *Id.* at 28.

[137] *Id.*

[138] PHYSICIANS FOR HUMAN RIGHTS, WITNESS TO WAR CRIMES, *supra* note 2 at 22.

i. *Residents of Tumina and Karzaz*

Many of the violations carried out by Qadhafi forces were in areas to the south and east of Misrata, which were taken by Qadhafi forces during the early stages of the conflict, such as Tumina, Kararim, Nusur al-Jaw, Karzaz and east of Qasr Ahmad. Several cases of arbitrary and brutal arrests and enforced disappearances by Qadhafi forces were reported in Karzaz and Tumina.[139]

Several cases of enforced disappearances in the Karzaz district took place in mid-March 2011, as Qadhafi forces attempted to capture parts of Misrata. Amnesty International documented numerous cases, including that of a 19-year-old man disappeared in mid-March in the area of Karzaz.[140] A witness who had fled from Karzaz with his family reported that soldiers had entered his home searching for weapons on 19 March, and abducted his brothers.[141] Local residents from Karzaz reported that on 19 March, Qadhafi forces also demolished a home for the elderly and abducted its 36 residents in military vehicles at gunpoint.[142] The violations continued into April as the fighting ensued in the area. A witness reported that Qadhafi forces abducted eight men from his neighborhood in Karzaz on 21 April.[143]

Several cases of enforced disappearances were also reported in the area of Tumina, located to the southeast of Misrata. It was reported that several residents of the area disappeared after Qadhafi forces abducted them from their homes or the streets. A man reported that his sons went missing on the morning on 7 April 2011 after leaving their house in Tumina to get provisions.[144] The wife of a 42-year-old man reported that her husband was abducted when visiting his brother's house in the neighborhood of Burwaiyya on 7 April. As in many other cases of arbitrary arrest in Misrata, all the men present at the house were detained.[145] Another witness from Tumina stated that on 20 March Qadhafi forces arrested the witness' son, and his whereabouts remained unknown in May 2011.[146]

---

[139] AMNESTY INTERNATIONAL, *Families rent asunder by deaths and disappearances in Misratah, supra* note 134.

[140] *Id.*

[141] *Id.*

[142] PHYSICIANS FOR HUMAN RIGHTS, WITNESS TO WAR CRIMES, *supra* note 2 at 22.

[143] *Id.* at 27.

[144] AMNESTY INTERNATIONAL, *Pain and loss hits every family in Misratah, supra* note 38.

[145] AMNESTY INTERNATIONAL, *Families rent asunder by deaths and disappearances in Misratah, supra* note 134.

[146] AMNESTY INTERNATIONAL, MISRATAH UNDER SIEGE AND UNDER FIRE, *supra* note 14 at 20.

According to NTC census data, 190 were reported missing and 34 killed in Karzaz and Tumina in June 2011. PHR reported that another 19 civilians, mainly men, were abducted by Qadhafi forces and in August 2011 were considered missing.[147]

(b) Thuwar *Forces*

i. *The Tawerghans*

The CoI documented widespread incidents of the targeting of members of the Tawerghan community for arbitrary arrest and detention by *thuwar* forces from Misrata. Misratan *thuwar* conducted house searches in the city of Tawergha in August 2011, carrying out sweeping arrests and taking victims to unofficial detention centers.[148] Amnesty International similarly documented cases of Tawerghans suffering targeted abuses such as arbitrary arrest at the hands of *thuwar* forces from Misrata.[149]

The CoI documented numerous cases of Misrata *thuwar* targeting Tawerghans in the months following the fall of Qadhafi.[150] These attacks involved abductions from IDP camps and towns to which Tawerghans had fled. The CoI documented abductions in the town of Al-Haysha, some 65 kilometers (40 miles) from Tawergha:

> Many of the Tawerghans stopped briefly in Al Hisha before heading either west towards Tripoli or south to the various towns in the Al Jufrah district. A few families settled there.... [S]ome brigades from the Misrata *thuwar* arrived on the outskirts of Al Hisha on 13 August 2011 and began to shell the town. Many Tawerghans fled before the *thuwar* entered the town.... [T]hose who remained in Al Hisha were attacked periodically by Misrata *thuwar*. On or about 20 September 2011, Misrata *thuwar* entered Al Hisha and arrested nine Tawerghan men who were then taken to Misrata. No grounds were given for their arrest or detention. [151]

---

[147] PHYSICIANS FOR HUMAN RIGHTS, WITNESS TO WAR CRIMES, *supra* note 2 at 23.

[148] Report of the International Commission of Inquiry, advance unedited version (Mar. 2, 2012), *supra* note 5 at Annex I, ¶ 398.

[149] AMNESTY INTERNATIONAL, LIBYA RULE OF LAW OR RULE OF MILITIAS? 15 (July 2012), *available at* http://www.amnesty.org/en/library/asset/MDE19/012/2012/en/f2d36090-5716-4ef1-81a7-f4b1ebd082fc/mde190122012en.pdf.

[150] For more information on Misrata *thuwar* targeting Tawerghans in the capital, *see infra* Sec. 3.10. *See also* Report of the International Commission of Inquiry, advance unedited version (Mar. 2, 2012), *supra* note 5 at ¶ 57.

[151] Report of the International Commission of Inquiry, advance unedited version (Mar. 2, 2012), *supra* note 5 at Annex I, ¶ 405 (internal citations omitted).

3.4. *Torture and Other Forms of Ill-treatment*

(a) *Qadhafi Forces*

There are documented incidents of torture and ill-treatment of captured *thuwar* or suspected supporters carried out by Qadhafi forces in Misrata.[152] This abuse and torture was found to have been carried out with the purpose of obtaining information about the *thuwar* activities and its members. PHR documented such cases, such as that of a witness who reported that he and his eight relatives (all *thuwar* fighters) were violently arrested in Misrata and beaten by Qadhafi forces with rifles on 18 March 2011. The witness was tortured and interrogated for two days as the guards attempted to obtain information about *thuwar* movements in the region.[153] There were also incidents of verbal abuse and degrading treatment of victims in detention facilities held by Qadhafi forces. A female detainee reported that for nearly three weeks she endured verbal harassment, threats and degrading treatment by guards in a detention facility in Misrata.[154]

(b) Thuwar *Forces*

During its investigations, the CoI found compelling evidence of torture and ill-treatment carried out by *thuwar* forces in Misrata.[155] The incidents of torture became most widespread after the fall of Qadhafi in August 2011, as over 100 *thuwar* from Misrata were reportedly operating outside of any official military or civilian command.[156] Amnesty International documented cases of torture taking place in Misrata's detention centers, where victims provided accounts of being suspended in contorted stress positions and physically abused for hours with a variety of tools and weapons.[157] Most of the detainees interviewed by Amnesty International in January and February 2012 were arrested on suspicion of being Qadhafi loyalists

---

[152] PHYSICIANS FOR HUMAN RIGHTS, WITNESS TO WAR CRIMES, *supra* note 2; Nick Carey, *Gaddafi war crimes in Misrata widespread: report*, REUTERS, Aug. 30, 2011, *available at* http://www.reuters.com/article/2011/08/30/us-libya-misrata-warcrimes-idUSTRE77T0J520110830.

[153] PHYSICIANS FOR HUMAN RIGHTS, WITNESS TO WAR CRIMES, *supra* note 2 at 17.

[154] *Id.*

[155] Report of the International Commission of Inquiry, advance unedited version (Mar. 2, 2012), *supra* note 5 at ¶ 49. Incidents also included torture in the form of sexual abuse, *see infra* Sec. 3.11.

[156] Williams, *The Murder Brigades of Misrata*, *supra* note 124.

[157] AMNESTY INTERNATIONAL, MILITIAS THREATEN HOPES FOR NEW LIBYA 6 (Feb. 16, 2012), *available at* http://www.amnesty.org/en/library/asset/MDE19/002/2012/en/dd7c1d69-e368-44de-8ee8-cc9365bd5eb3/mde190022012en.pdf.

who had fought for the regime. The pattern of abuse involved detainees being tortured immediately after being seized by militias as well as during interrogation. There were unclear dividing lines between the armed katiba and state security, and the interrogations at times took place at official detention centers.[158]

Amnesty International documented the case of a 23-year-old fighter who was detained in Tripoli in early September 2011 and transferred to Misrata where he was coerced to "confess" to having committed rape during the war.[159] Another case involved a 28-year-old soldier who was detained by a militia in mid-September 2011 in Tripoli and was subjected to torture for nearly three weeks. He was subsequently taken to Misrata where the torture continued.[160]

The international medical humanitarian organization Médecins Sans Frontières (MSF) similarly reported that detainees in Misrata suffered from torture at the hands of *thuwar* forces. MSF began working in Misrata's detention centers in August 2011, and were confronted with patients who suffered injuries caused by torture during interrogation sessions conducted by *thuwar*. The interrogations at times took place outside of detention centers. MSF stated that it treated 115 people who had injuries related to torture and reported these cases to the relevant authorities in Misrata.[161] MSF documented a case on 3 January 2012 when MSF officials treated a group of 14 detainees who displayed signs of torture on return from an interrogation center.

On 9 January, MSF sent an official letter to the Misrata Military Council, the Misrata Security Committee, the National Army Security Service, and the Misrata Local Civil Council, again demanding an immediate end to any form of ill-treatment of detainees. After noting that the torture did not subside, MSF ceased its activities at the detention centers.[162] UNSMIL reported in May 2012 that Misrata was of particular concern in terms of the ill-treatment and torture of detainees in Libya.[163]

---

[158] Amnesty International did report on some rare cases in eastern Libya where detainees were observed to have been provided with proper judicial council. *Id.*

[159] *Id.* at 12–13.

[160] *Id.* at 13.

[161] *Libya: Detainees tortured and denied medical care*, MEDICINS SANS FRONTIERS, Jan. 27, 2012, *available at* http://www.msf.org/msf/articles/2012/01/libya-detainees-tortured-and-denied-medical-care.cfm.

[162] *Id.*

[163] U.N. SC, U.N. Doc. S/PV.6768 (May 10, 2012), *supra* note 126 at 5; Michelle Nichols, *U.N. says three Libya prisoners likely tortured to death*, REUTERS, May 10, 2012, *available at* http://www.reuters.com/article/2012/05/10/us-libya-un-idUSBRE8491LK20120510.

i. *The Tawerghans*

The CoI identified a pattern of mistreatment against Tawerghans, reporting that they were tortured and subjected to other forms of ill-treatment
while detained, especially by Misratan *thuwar*. Acts of torture were
inflicted upon Tawerghan detainees who were imprisoned in various locations throughout Misrata, and the CoI examined injuries of victims substantiating these claims.[164] Examinations by the CoI involved interviews
with 50 Tawerghan witnesses and victims. Witnesses reported that most
of the beatings and/or torture of Tawerghan men took place on arrest,
and sometimes lasted until detention.[165] The beatings and/or torture
"consisted of being hit with hands, wooden sticks, metal sticks, rifle butts
and being kicked."[166] Female relatives who tried to intervene also claimed
to have been beaten.[167] The CoI also spoke to family members of Tawerghans deceased in detention as a result of torture[168] and was able to
obtain corroboration via medical records and death certificates.[169]

Tawerghans being held in Misrata were either detained in the city or
brought there from other locations around Libya. A few of the men interviewed by the CoI reported to having been held in "unacknowledged centers, such as houses or offices in Tripoli, Al Khums and elsewhere, in most
cases before being taken on to Misrata."[170] A few cases were also reported
where Tawerghan men were taken to Tripoli and Khums.[171]

The CoI reported several incidents where persons were arrested in other
cities before being transferred to Misrata where they were subjected to ill-
treatment.[172] Tawerghans were particularly targeted by Misratan *thuwar*
who accused them of rape. The CoI stated

> [A] pattern of severe torture [was] perpetrated in particular against Tawer-
> ghans by Misratan *thuwar*, who accuse[d] them of committing rapes and
> other crimes in Misrata. Detainees told the Commission that they confessed

---

[164] Report of the International Commission of Inquiry, advance unedited version
(Mar. 2, 2012), *supra* note 5 at ¶ 57 & Annex I, ¶ 361.

[165] *Id.* at Annex I, ¶ 363.

[166] *Id.* at Annex I, ¶ 364.

[167] *Id.*

[168] *See supra* Sec. 3.4.

[169] Report of the International Commission of Inquiry, advance unedited version
(Mar. 2, 2012), *supra* note 5 at Annex I, ¶ 363.

[170] *See infra* Secs. 9.3. & 11.3. *See also id.* at Annex I, ¶ 365.

[171] Report of the International Commission of Inquiry, advance unedited version
(Mar. 2, 2012), *supra* note 5 at Annex I, ¶ 365.

[172] *Id.* at Annex I, ¶ 369.

to serious crimes including rape – that they denied committing – after they could no longer withstand the torture.[173]

In late September 2011, HRW interviewed 50 prisoners who were being held in four Misrata prisons, including 22 Tawerghans and ten non-Libyans, and found evidence of mistreatment in three of the four facilities. Tawerghans were found in all four detention centers, and made up the majority of detainees in two of the facilities. Most of the Tawerghan detainees reported beatings at the time of their capture, both in Tripoli and Misrata.[174]

Several Tawerghans reported being mistreated at the Sikt detention facility near Misrata. One detainee, a Tawerghan man, stated that in August, members of the Murdaz Katiba forced him and other detainees to confess to raping civilians. He stated that most Tawerghans had been forced to make similar confessions, and that guards electrocuted him on his back and stomach and beat the soles of his feet. He stated that many people took part in inflicting the abuse, including persons dressed in civilian clothing. The man showed HRW investigators scars on his body consistent with his account.[175] HRW representatives also witnessed the abuse of detainees at the Al-Wahda detention facility in Misrata on 25 September 2011.[176]

Several people from Tawergha who were arrested by *thuwar* in Tripoli in September 2011 were transferred to Misrata, where they were questioned and suffered abuse. Amnesty International reported that those detained were beaten upon arrest and in the first days of detention, and documented the death of at least one detainee.[177]

Amnesty International observed that the number of Tawerghans among the detainees at the detention centers visited was disproportionately high. Most of the Tawerghans reported that they had been mistreated or tortured.[178] Individuals in charge of the detention centers were often

---

[173] Report of the International Commission of Inquiry, advance unedited version (Mar. 2, 2012), *supra* note 5 at ¶ 51.

[174] HUMAN RIGHTS WATCH, *Libya: Militias Terrorizing Residents of 'Loyalist' Town, supra* note 128.

[175] *Id.*

[176] *Id.*

[177] AMNESTY INTERNATIONAL, DETENTION ABUSES STAINING THE NEW LIBYA 13 (Oct. 13, 2011), *available at* http://www.amnesty.org/en/library/asset/MDE19/036/2011/en/e1c30dof-8ec3-4368-8537-03f1bb15a051/mde1903620011en.pdf.

[178] AMNESTY INTERNATIONAL, MILITIAS THREATEN HOPES FOR NEW LIBYA, *supra* note 157 at 19.

unable or unwilling to stop the attacks. During a visit to the Al-Wahda detention center in Misrata in January 2012, Amnesty International noted that prison guards refused to release Tawerghan detainees, and noted the unclear lines of authority between state and non-state actors in control of the prison facilities.[179]

A 26-year-old soldier from Tawergha reported being detained on 26 September 2011 on his way to Al-Jufra and transferred to a detention center run by military police in Misrata. He was abused at the facility, including by beatings with a plastic cable. In early January 2012, he was transferred to a detention center that Amnesty International reported belonged to the national military security section in Misrata, where he was interrogated and abused. He was questioned about his role in the conflict, and suspended from his wrists for an hour while he suffered further beatings.[180]

3.5. *Denial of Access to Medical Treatment*

(a) *Qadhafi Forces*

Amnesty International documented cases of Qadhafi forces denying civilians access to medical care in Misrata. A female medical student from Al-Ghayran stated that on 16 March 2011, Qadhafi forces came to her neighborhood with tanks, and were shelling and shooting in the area. The witness stated that in the evening of 18 March, they searched her house and informed her and her family that they would have to remain indoors. The family requested permission from the Qadhafi forces to take the witness' aunt for her required dialysis treatment three times per week. The Qadhafi forces refused and would not permit anyone to leave the house. On 20 March, five Qadhafi soldiers entered the witness' home and arrested her father. The witness stated that days later she smuggled her aunt out of the home to take her to the hospital.[181]

---

[179] *See Id.* at 14 For more on the authority over the detention centers in the post-conflict period, *see* Ch. V, Sec. 2.3.

[180] AMNESTY INTERNATIONAL, MILITIAS THREATEN HOPES FOR NEW LIBYA, *supra* note 157 at 19.

[181] AMNESTY INTERNATIONAL, MISRATAH UNDER SIEGE AND UNDER FIRE, *supra* note 14 at 28.

(b) Thuwar *Forces*

MSF reported that from September 2011 onwards, detainees in Misrata were tortured and denied urgent medical treatment by the *thuwar*.[182] Detainees were reportedly removed from detention centers and subjected to torture, including beatings and whipping with electric cables. MSF reported that after treating patients for injuries sustained during torture, they were subsequently taken back to interrogation and tortured again. In some cases, patients were brought to hospitals in the middle of questioning, to be treated so they could be interrogated further.[183]

3.6. *Freedom of Expression*

(a) *Qadhafi Forces*

On 20 April, a mortar attack resulted in the killing of photojournalist and filmmaker Tim Hetherington and photographer Chris Hondros, and injuries to two co-workers. Hetherington and Hondros were among a number of journalists reporting from Tripoli Street in Misrata when the incident took place.[184]

3.7. *Attacks on Civilians, Civilian Objects, Protected Persons and Objects*

3.7.1. *Deliberate and Indiscriminate Attacks on Civilians and Civilian Objects*

(a) *Qadhafi Forces*

Qadhafi forces carried out various types of intentional attacks on civilians in residential areas, such as attacks on civilians at checkpoints, extrajudicial executions and the intentional destruction and deprivation of property and food supplies.

Some of those civilians who managed to flee Misrata were able to return to their homes after Qadhafi forces retreated from their neighborhoods in late April 2011. Many of these families found their homes damaged or ransacked. In Al-Ghayran, a family reported that Qadhafi forces had used

---

[182] *MSF: Libya torture 'completely unacceptable'*, BBC, Jan. 26, 2012, *available at* http://www.bbc.co.uk/news/health-16751785.

[183] Mark Urban, *Libya: Is a breakdown in order forcing NGOs out?*, BBC, Jan. 27, 2012, *available at* http://www.bbc.co.uk/news/world-16761200.

[184] *Libya: Journalist Killed in Misrata*, HUMAN RIGHTS WATCH, Apr. 20, 2011, *available at* http://www.hrw.org/news/2011/04/20/libya-journalists-killed-misrata.

their home as a military base.[185] In other cases, Qadhafi forces targeted the family members and homes of soldiers who defected. One witness reported that his brother was an officer who had defected from the Libyan Air Force and was fighting with the *thuwar*. In March 2011, Qadhafi forces attacked the man's family home. The witness reported that when he and six other men from his village approached his home, they saw it in flames and witnessed soldiers exiting the property. The soldiers then shot and killed two of the men and injured the witness, whose home was nearly completely destroyed by fire and pillaging.[186]

The indiscriminate attacks on civilians in Misrata include the shelling of neighborhoods and the use of snipers to target civilians. The shelling by Qadhafi forces targeted the port area and eastern neighborhoods, as well as areas in the west and south of Misrata. In these areas, frequent rocket fire and mortar attacks caused damage and destruction to homes, schools, medical facilities and places of worship.[187] When Qadhafi forces returned to retake control of Misrata in mid-March, they carried out reprisals against the civilian population.[188] The CoI reported that Misrata experienced particularly intense shelling between mid-March and mid-May 2011, and again in June continuing sporadically until early August 2011.[189] Amnesty International recorded several incidents where civilian homes were destroyed and residents killed from the indiscriminate use of Grad rockets, mortars and artillery shells.[190]

The conflict prevented many from leaving their homes to get food or medicine and in several cases, civilians were trapped as a result of the indiscriminate shelling and sniper fire.[191] Information also exists demonstrating the intent to punish the civilian population through siege tactics. Reports indicate that Qadhafi forces received official military orders in

---

[185] AMNESTY INTERNATIONAL, MISRATAH UNDER SIEGE AND UNDER FIRE, *supra* note 14 at 30.
[186] PHYSICIANS FOR HUMAN RIGHTS, WITNESS TO WAR CRIMES, *supra* note 2 at 28.
[187] AMNESTY INTERNATIONAL, MISRATAH UNDER SIEGE AND UNDER FIRE, *supra* note 14 at 14.
[188] *Id.* at 27.
[189] Report of the International Commission of Inquiry, advance unedited version (Mar. 2, 2012), *supra* note 5 at Annex I, ¶ 87.
[190] AMNESTY INTERNATIONAL, MISRATAH UNDER SIEGE AND UNDER FIRE, *supra* note 14 at 10.
[191] *More civilians flee Libya's Western Mountains, new aid reaches the east*, UNHCR, Apr. 26, 2011, *available at* http://www.unhcr.org/cgi-bin/texis/vtx/search?page=search&docid=4db6dcf29&query=ajdabiya.

early March 2011 to starve Misrata's inhabitants.[192] Troops pillaged and burned civilian food supplies, farms, livestock and food stores. Qadhafi forces also restricted or blocked opposition-populated areas from receiving supplies and destroyed ships attempting to bring humanitarian aid into Misrata.[193]

PHR also received written testimony from residents in Misrata who reported that Qadhafi forces attacked them in their homes with explosive weapons. One civilian in Misrata reported that Qadhafi forces launched explosive weapons into Al-Bari neighborhood, where the witness lived. He stated that explosive devices hit his neighbor's home, where a family of ten with eight children lived.[194] Another civilian reported that his mother was killed from a falling explosive that landed 20 meters from where she stood outside of her home. The witness' father was also injured in the explosion, and underwent treatment for shrapnel injuries.[195]

Amnesty International documented other similar incidents. A witness reported that on 16 March 2011, Qadhafi forces came to Al-Ghayran and shelled the area, and a mortar explosion in the courtyard of his family home killed a relative.[196] During the night of 23 April 2011, several artillery shells hit the Ra's 'Ammar neighborhood of Misrata, killing at least six residents.[197] Another civilian reported that on 21 June 2011, Qadhafi troops launched an explosive device into the yard of his house, killing a child and injuring the witness' wife.[198]

There are numerous reports of Qadhafi forces using snipers to target civilians. A group of nurses told Amnesty International that they were trapped for weeks in areas near the frontline not far from Tripoli Street, unable to leave out of fear of being shot at by snipers.[199] Another victim

---

[192] Physicians for Human Rights was provided such documents by the Hikma Hospital on June 24, 2011. *See* PHYSICIANS FOR HUMAN RIGHTS, WITNESS TO WAR CRIMES, *supra* note 2 at 24. *See also* Chris Stephen, *Qaddafi Files Show Evidence of Murderous Intent*, THE GUARDIAN, June 18, 2011, *available at* http://www.guardian.co.uk/world/2011/jun/18/gaddafi-misrata-war-crime-documents.

[193] *Libya: UN official voices concern as fighting blocks aid delivery in West*, UN NEWS CENTRE, May 12, 2011, *available at* http://www.un.org/apps/news/story.asp?NewsID=38352&Cr=Libya&Crl; PHYSICIANS FOR HUMAN RIGHTS, WITNESS TO WAR CRIMES, *supra* note 2 at 24.

[194] PHYSICIANS FOR HUMAN RIGHTS, WITNESS TO WAR CRIMES, *supra* note 2 at 29.

[195] *Id.* at 28.

[196] AMNESTY INTERNATIONAL, MISRATAH UNDER SIEGE AND UNDER FIRE, *supra* note 14 at 28.

[197] *Id.* at 15.

[198] *Id.* at 29.

[199] *Id.* at 19.

stated he was shot on 9 April 2011 while on the street outside his house, and that the shot was fired from the direction of the buildings where Qadhafi forces were positioned.[200] Another witness stated that on 13 April, he was shot while in his vehicle in the Kharuba area of Misrata. The shot came from snipers in a building a few hundred meters to the south, and the bullet hole in the witness' vehicle indicated a downward trajectory, consistent with reports that the shot had been fired from a higher position.[201]

i. *Residents of Tumina, Kararim and Karzaz*

Qadhafi forces were reportedly present in Tumina and Kararim during the siege of Misrata in April and May 2011.[202] According to HRW and Amnesty International, displaced residents from Tumina and Kararim stated that Qadhafi forces ordered the civilian residents to evacuate their homes on 12 May 2011.[203] The residents were only given a few hours to leave the city, and most fled their homes with just a few of their belongings, leaving behind livestock and other important possessions.[204]

PHR also recorded incidents of Qadhafi forces using Grad rockets and mortars on civilian populations in Misrata's surrounding villages of Tumina, Kararim and Karzaz. A 23-year-old resident of Karzaz reported that on 19 April 2011 his home was destroyed by mortar fire that also seriously injured two young children.[205] Two days later, a 55 year-old widow reported that two explosive weapons directly hit and partially destroyed her family's home in Karzaz.[206]

There were also documented cases of Qadhafi forces using civilians as human shields in these areas. Qadhafi forces stationed troops and stored weaponry in civilian areas, using mosques, markets and schools in this way.[207] Witnesses reported that Qadhafi forces placed munitions and military vehicles next to a mosque in Karzaz[208] and destroyed an elementary school in Tumina, subsequently using the demolished interior as a storage facility to hold military equipment and stolen medical supplies.

---

[200] *Id.* at 18.

[201] *Id.* at 20.

[202] *Libya: Displaced People Barred from Homes*, HUMAN RIGHTS WATCH, Feb. 21, 2012, *available at* http://www.hrw.org/news/2012/02/21/libya-displaced-people-barred-homes.

[203] *Id.*

[204] *Id.*

[205] PHYSICIANS FOR HUMAN RIGHTS, WITNESS TO WAR CRIMES, *supra* note 2 at 28.

[206] *Id.* at 26.

[207] *Id.* at 23.

[208] *Id.* at 24.

In another incident on 26 April, a teacher reported that Qadhafi forces attacked her school and then used it as a military base.[209]

Actions of the Qadhafi forces compelled civilians to flee their homes in Tumina and Kararim. Witnesses described leaving Tumina to escape the violence in April.[210] In Kararim, a witness was forced to leave their farm in May by Qadhafi forces. The farm was looted and the man was stopped at checkpoints surrounding Misrata as he attempted to return with his family.[211]

(b) Thuwar *Forces*
There are documented cases of *thuwar* forces carrying out intentional attacks against civilians who they suspected of collaborating with or supporting Qadhafi forces.[212]

i. *The Tawerghans*
As discussed above, the town of Tawergha was targeted for attack by the *thuwar* after the retreat of Qadhafi forces.[213] The CoI received reports that civilians were killed and injured in Tawergha when the city was shelled by unguided Grad and S5 rockets from 10 to 12 August 2011.[214] Many Tawerghans were forced to flee during the assault, "leaving behind their possessions including clothes, passports and family photographs." Moreover, Misrata *thuwar* shot at Tawerghans as they were leaving the town, resulting in casualties.[215]

The Tawerghans who remained were ordered to leave the city if they did not wish to suffer reprisal violence or imprisonment,[216] and reported attacks on their homes and property.[217] Those civilians who remained stated to the CoI that "they were either arrested and taken to Misrata, or

---

[209] *Id.*

[210] HUMAN RIGHTS WATCH, *Libya: Displaced People Barred from Homes, supra* note 202.

[211] *Id.*

[212] AMNESTY INTERNATIONAL, MILITIAS THREATEN HOPES FOR NEW LIBYA, *supra* note 157 at 36.

[213] *See infra* Sec. 2.

[214] Report of the International Commission of Inquiry, advance unedited version (Mar. 2, 2012), *supra* note 5 at Annex I, ¶ 394 (internal citations omitted).

[215] *Id.* at Annex I, ¶¶ 394–395.

[216] Andrew Gilligan, *Gaddafi's ghost town after the loyalists retreat*, THE TELEGRAPH, Sept. 11, 2011, *available at* http://www.telegraph.co.uk/news/worldnews/africaandindianocean/libya/8754375/Gaddafis-ghost-town-after-the-loyalists-retreat.html.

[217] AMNESTY INTERNATIONAL, MILITIAS THREATEN HOPES FOR NEW LIBYA, *supra* note 157 at 31.

were beaten (or threatened with violence) and made to leave."[218] HRW reported an estimated 100 civilians stayed in Tawergha when the Misratan *thuwar* closed in on the city in mid-August 2011 before armed groups forced them out, threatening them never to return.[219] Soon after, Tawergha became deserted,[220] and the city's homes and buildings were "looted, shot at, and burnt by the Misratan *thuwar*."[221] The CoI heard from Tawerghans who stated that Tawergha was pillaged by Misrata *thuwar* as they took control of the city.[222]

On 21 January 2012, the CoI first visited the area and found all roads heading towards the town obstructed by sand masses. Misrata *thuwar* admitted that the town's buildings "were being used for target practice." CoI investigators also witnessed houses being set on fire. Moreover, all of Tawergha's buildings appeared as if they had been assailed by weapons, while some may have been intentionally bulldozed.[223] "Tawergha" was removed from the city's signs and sometimes substituted with the words "New Misrata." In addition, the word "slave" was written on the city's school, hospital, and other public structures.[224]

According to the United Nations High Commissioner for Refugees (UNHCR), approximately 35,000 people from Tawergha were displaced to different locations across Libya. Tawerghan community leaders reported that after the displacements, 16,000 were located in eastern Libya and 12,000 in the west, mostly in Tripoli, where they were more exposed to attacks.[225] Most Tawerghans took refuge in towns and IDP camps around

---

[218] Report of the International Commission of Inquiry, advance unedited version (Mar. 2, 2012), *supra* note 5 at Annex I, ¶ 396.

[219] *Libya: Tawergha Residents Terrorized by Militias*, HUMAN RIGHTS WATCH, Oct. 27, 2011, *available at* http://www.hrw.org/features/libya-tawergha-residents-terrorized-militias.

[220] Report of the International Commission of Inquiry, advance unedited version (Mar. 2, 2012), *supra* note 5 at Annex I, ¶ 397.

[221] The CoI reported that "According to an analysis of UNOSAT satellite imagery, 49 structures were destroyed or damaged in Tawergha between 12 June 2011 and 20 August 2011, including multiple buildings that were destroyed and showing indications of fire. Between 20 August 2011 and 24 November 2011, while the town was empty, an additional 27 buildings were destroyed or damaged, all likely residential and commercial structures. On 24 November 2011 imagery, a relatively large smoke plume from a fire is visible in central Tawergha." *Id.* at Annex I, ¶ 400.

[222] *Id.* at Annex I, ¶ 753.

[223] *Id.* at Annex I, ¶ 401.

[224] *Id.* at Annex I, ¶ 403.

[225] *Libya: Bolster Security at Tawergha Camps*, HUMAN RIGHTS WATCH, Mar. 5, 2012, *available at* http://www.hrw.org/news/2012/03/05/libya-bolster-security-tawergha-camps.

Tripoli, in Sirte, Benghazi, Al-Jufra and Al-Haysha.[226] In these camps, Tawerghans were subject to attacks involving widespread arrests, abductions and killings of civilians.[227] In the town of Al-Haysha, for instance, where Tawerghans had fled, Misrata *thuwar* arrived on 13 August 2011 and began to shell. The Tawerghans who remained in the town after the shelling were targeted by the *thuwar*, and some of the men were detained and taken to Misrata with no grounds given for their detention.[228]

3.7.2. *Attacks on Cultural Objects and Places of Worship*

(a) *Qadhafi Forces*

On 17 April 2011, rocket and mortar attacks from Qadhafi forces were reported to have caused extensive damage to the Umar 'Abd al-'Aziz al-Senussi Mosque.[229] Misratans also reported that the Qadhafi forces targeted mosques in the city and used them as locations from which to target civilians. Another reported incident took place in late July 2011, when Qadhafi forces targeted a mosque on Misrata's western front in the town of Dafniyya.[230]

i. *Residents of Tumina, Kararim and Karzaz*

PHR inspected three mosques in the towns of Karzaz and Tumina that were destroyed by shelling from Qadhafi forces. A shaykh from Karzaz reported that on 18 March 2011 he saw smoke in front of his home and rubble surrounding the minaret of the mosque that had collapsed from direct shelling. The shaykh stated that he had heard from his fellow worshippers that Qadhafi forces used some mosques to launch attacks against civilians.[231]

---

[226] HUMAN RIGHTS WATCH, *Libya: Tawergha Residents Terrorized by Militias, supra* note 219.

[227] For more on *thuwar* attacks on Tawerghan IDP camps near Tripoli, *see* Ch. XIII, Sec. 3. *See also* Report of the International Commission of Inquiry, advance unedited version (Mar. 2, 2012), *supra* note 5 at Annex I, ¶¶ 397 & 405; HUMAN RIGHTS WATCH, *Libya: Displaced People Barred from Homes, supra* note 202.

[228] Report of the International Commission of Inquiry, advance unedited version (Mar. 2, 2012), *supra* note 5 at Annex I, ¶ 405.

[229] Report of the International Commission of Inquiry (Jan. 12, 2012), *supra* note 16 at ¶ 157.

[230] Nick Carey, *Gaddafi war crimes in Misrata widespread: report*, REUTERS, Aug. 30, 2011, *available at* http://www.reuters.com/article/2011/08/30/us-libya-misrata-warcrimes-idUSTRE77T0J520110830.

[231] PHYSICIANS FOR HUMAN RIGHTS, WITNESS TO WAR CRIMES, *supra* note 2 at 28.

3.7.3. *Impeding Access to Humanitarian Relief and Attacks on Humanitarian Personnel*

(a) *Qadhafi Forces*

Qadhafi forces imposed a long-term siege on Misrata, preventing the transport of food and other essential supplies for humanitarian relief.[232] The CoI reported that "The Secretary-General of the United Nations and the Executive Director of the World Food Programme called on 11 and 12 May respectively for a ceasefire to allow humanitarian access to Misrata and the western area," but these calls were not "heeded by the Government."[233] Qadhafi forces also shelled the port of Misrata, severely hindering access to humanitarian aid and relief, and blocking the only evacuation route for the wounded.[234]

The CoI reported that Qadhafi forces attacked humanitarian personnel as they attempted to bring supplies into Misrata, noting

> In Misrata, one boat on which humanitarian activities were being conducted was shelled by Government forces. A number of humanitarian organizations conducting resupply (food and non-food items, medical supplies and equipment) and evacuation missions by boat to Misrata have been endangered by actions of Government forces. There have been reports of fire coming from the mainland on 25 April, anti-vehicle mines being dropped from shells over the port on 29 April and 5 May and sea mines being placed without notice.[235]

3.7.4. *Attacks on Protected Medical Personnel, Transport and Facilities*

(a) *Qadhafi Forces*

Reports indicate that Qadhafi forces intentionally targeted medical personnel who were carrying out their work in Misrata. Two medics from the Libyan Red Crescent were injured in a convoy including two ambulances as they travelled from Misrata. The medics were injured by shots that came from the installation occupied by the Hamza Katiba, a military

---

[232] *Libya: UN Secretary-General urges immediate end to attacks against civilians,* UN NEWS CENTRE, May 11, 2011, *available at* http://www.un.org/apps/news/story.asp?NewsID=38348&Cr=libya&Cr1=; UN NEWS CENTRE, *Libya: UN official voices concern as fighting blocks aid delivery in west, supra* note 193.

[233] Report of the International Commission of Inquiry (Jan. 12, 2012), *supra* note 16 at ¶ 161.

[234] Report of the International Commission of Inquiry, advance unedited version (Mar. 2, 2012), *supra* note 5 at Annex I, ¶ 87.

[235] Report of the International Commission of Inquiry (Jan. 12, 2012), *supra* note 16 at ¶ 162 (internal citations omitted).

force loyal to Qadhafi. The medics were wearing full uniforms at the time and arrived in two clearly marked Red Crescent ambulances, thus indicating that the attacks were deliberate.[236]

There were also several documented incidents of Qadhafi forces attacking ambulances carrying injured combatants.[237] PHR documented the partial destruction of two ambulances, both of which showed evidence of shelling. A medical student working at the western front field hospital witnessed one of the ambulance attacks. Another medical student reported that on 29 May 2011, he was wounded by shrapnel while driving in an ambulance toward the front.[238]

Libyan doctors gave public statements claiming that Qadhafi forces deliberately targeted them and other health workers who were treating injured combatants.[239] The conflict, and in particular attacks on hospitals, caused the exodus of foreign medical workers from Libya, including in Misrata. The CoI reported that, "A witness from Al Hikma Clinic in Misrata told the Commission that it had been targeted twice by Government forces but was still functioning." A Misratan doctor also "told media that the Misrata hospital had been targeted by Government tanks."[240]

On 23 March 2011, Reuters reported that Qadhafi forces bombarded the main hospital in Misrata as doctors were trying to move the wounded. A Misrata resident told Reuters by telephone that, "The snipers are shooting at the hospital and its two entrances are under heavy attack. No one can get in or out."[241] Amnesty International reported that that on 16 April 2011 rocket shells rained down around a clinic and eyewitnesses were wounded in the attack.[242] A number of witnesses also provided the CoI with information indicating that hospital supplies and medications were

---

[236] *Libyan paramedics targeted by pro-Gaddafi forces*, AMNESTY INTERNATIONAL, Mar. 4, 2011, *available at* http://www.amnesty.org/en/news-and-updates/libyan-paramedics-targeted-pro-gaddafi-forces-2011-03-04; *News Summary from the US/International Press on the Libyan Crisis*, THE TRIPOLI POST, Mar. 5, 2011, *available at* http://tripolipost.com/article detail.asp?c=1&i=5523.

[237] *Doctors operating without anesthesia in Misrata hospital*, CNN, Mar. 24, 2011, *available at* http://edition.cnn.com/2011/WORLD/africa/03/24/libya.hospital.scene/index.html.

[238] PHYSICIANS FOR HUMAN RIGHTS, WITNESS TO WAR CRIMES, *supra* note 2 at 28.

[239] Mary Fitzgerald, *Frontline surgeon says morale of anti-Gadafy forces high*, IRISH TIMES, June 7, 2011, *available at* http://www.irishtimes.com/newspaper/world/2011/0607/1224298498069.html.

[240] Report of the International Commission of Inquiry (Jan. 12, 2012), *supra* note 16 at ¶ 167.

[241] Ahmed, *Rebels say 16 dead in Misrata, hospital attacked, supra* note 51.

[242] AMNESTY INTERNATIONAL, MISRATAH UNDER SIEGE AND UNDER FIRE, *supra* note 14 at 14.

destroyed.[243] The indiscriminate attacks by Qadhafi forces on hospitals reportedly involved tanks and artillery that caused severe damage to medical facilities.[244] Indiscriminate rockets and mortars were also used to target hospitals and clinics.[245]

A doctor from Misrata's central hospital stated that on 23 March 2011 Qadhafi forces attacked the hospital in Misrata. The doctor stated that he witnessed snipers shooting at medical staff, patients and other civilians leaving the hospital, and that ambulances were also targeted. An estimated 100 patients had to be evacuated to another clinic. In early June 2011, the facility was deserted as patients and staff had been relocated to other facilities. PHR investigators witnessed destruction caused by shelling and gunshots during their visit to the facility in June 2011.[246]

Qadhafi forces reportedly occupied Misrata's university hospital beginning on 13 March 2011. The facility's physical structures exhibited evidence of damage from shelling and gunfire.[247]

(b) Thuwar *Forces*

The CoI received a report that *thuwar* from Misrata fired at an ambulance which led to the evacuation of injured and deceased persons from Tawergha on 11 August 2011.[248]

3.7.5. *Misuse of the Red Cross/Red Crescent Emblem*

(a) *Qadhafi Forces*

The CoI documented several incidents of Qadhafi forces misusing the Red Cross/Red Crescent emblem. There were also reports of helicopters dropping mines over Misrata on 8 May 2011 that carried either the Red Cross or the Red Crescent logo. In a statement issued on 9 May, the International

---

[243] Report of the International Commission of Inquiry (Jan. 12, 2012), *supra* note 16 at ¶ 167.

[244] *Libyan hospitals struggle amid heavy fighting*, BBC, Mar. 7, 2011, *available at* http:// www.bbc.co.uk/worldservice/news/2011/03/110307_libya_doctor_wt.shtml; *Libya: Misurata hospital damaged in fighting*, THE TELEGRAPH, Mar. 24, 2011, *available at* http://www .telegraph.co.uk/news/worldnews/africaandindianocean/libya/8405273/Libya-Misurata-hospital-damaged-in-fighting.html.

[245] AMNESTY INTERNATIONAL, MISRATAH UNDER SIEGE AND UNDER FIRE, *supra* note 14 at 14.

[246] PHYSICIANS FOR HUMAN RIGHTS, WITNESS TO WAR CRIMES, *supra* note 2 at 36.

[247] *Id.* at 32.

[248] Report of the International Commission of Inquiry, advance unedited version (Mar. 2, 2012), *supra* note 5 at Annex I, ¶ 395.

Committee of the Red Cross expressed its concern at what it described as "recent allegations of the red cross or red crescent emblem being used for military purposes in Libya" and added that "the alleged practices, if true, represent a serious misuse of the emblem."[249]

3.8. Prohibited Weapons

(a) Qadhafi Forces

There is considerable evidence that Qadhafi forces employed prohibited weapons during the fighting in Misrata.[250] The CoI confirmed widespread use of cluster munitions in Misrata, noting that

> [It] is aware of reports of the use of cluster munitions by pro-Government forces in their attempt to regain control of the besieged city of Misrata. On 15 April 2011, Human Rights Watch reported that Government forces had fired cluster munitions in residential neighbourhoods of Misrata further specifying that the cluster munitions were the Spanish-produced MAT-120mm mortar projectile, which open in mid-air and release 21 submunitions over a wide area.[251]

The CoI found evidence of the use of cluster munitions both within the city and its port, and witnesses reported the use of munitions against civilian areas.[252] NATO also contended that Qadhafi forces used banned cluster munitions in Misrata.[253] As quoted above, cluster munitions open in the air and disperse dozens to hundreds of small explosive devices over a large area, and thus cannot hit specific targets. They therefore lead to indiscriminate harm to civilian populations.[254]

---

[249] *Libya: much-needed humanitarian aid reaches Misrata*, INTERNATIONAL COMMITTEE FOR THE RED CROSS, May 9, 2011, *available at* http://www.icrc.org/eng/resources/documents/news-release/2011/libya-news-2011-05-09.htm.232; *Libya: Red Crescent volunteers and medical personnel in danger*, Operational Update No 05/11, INTERNATIONAL COMMITTEE FOR THE RED CROSS, May 17, 2011, *available at* http://www.icrc.org/eng/resources/documents/update/2011/libya-update-2011-05-17.htm.

[250] *Libya: Cluster Munitions Target Misrata*, HUMAN RIGHTS WATCH, Apr. 15, 2011, *available at* http://www.hrw.org/en/news/2011/04/15/libya-cluster-munitions-strike-misrata.

[251] Report of the International Commission of Inquiry (Jan. 12, 2012), *supra* note 16 at ¶ 175.

[252] Report of the International Commission of Inquiry, advance unedited version (Mar. 2, 2012), *supra* note 5 at Annex I, ¶ 664.

[253] *Press briefing on Libya*, NORTH ATLANTIC TREATY ORGANIZATION, May 3, 2011, *available at* http://www.nato.int/cps/en/natolive/opinions_72998.htm.

[254] PHYSICIANS FOR HUMAN RIGHTS, WITNESS TO WAR CRIMES, *supra* note 2 at 29.

There were also numerous reports of the use of mines in Misrata.[255] Qadhafi forces reportedly placed floating anti-ship mines outside Misrata's harbor in late April 2011 in order to block shipping and disrupt the delivery of humanitarian aid to the people in the besieged city.[256] Amnesty International reported that Qadhafi forces placed anti-personnel mines in residential areas of Misrata, posing serious risk to the civilian population.[257] More than 20 highly explosive anti-personnel mines were discovered in a residential neighborhood southeast of the city center. Two were accidentally set off by a passing car, which was reported to be the second incident involving the use of anti-personnel mines by Qadhafi forces in or close to population centers.[258] Anti-vehicle landmines meant to destroy tanks were also used to prevent the transport of humanitarian aid in Misrata, and *thuwar* fighters reported injuries resulting from such mines.[259]

3.9. *Mercenaries*

(a) *Qadhafi Forces*

The CoI received reports that the Qadhafi government set up voluntary recruitment offices in Sirte. Potential soldiers were offered daily payments of 250 dinars, and Libyan citizenship if they were foreign. The new recruits were deployed to fight on the frontlines where there was intense fighting,

---

[255] Rebecca Fordham, *Libyan Kids Maimed by War Remnants*, AL JAZEERA, June 7, 2011, *available at* http://english.aljazeera.net/indepth/features/2011/06/20116674436348565html; *Libya rebels take casualties in Zliten advance*, AFP, July 10, 2011, *available at* http://www.google.com/hostednews/afp/article/ALeqM5i9jbd5tDAHv4Zfe_9ADI_jFShTYw?docId=CNG.a51e0ccb6c8ecb11fbc3a0a97df80911.361; Chivers, *Land Mines Descend on Misurata's Port, Endangering Libyan City's Supply Route, supra* note 60.

[256] *Press briefing on Libya*, NORTH ATLANTIC TREATY ORGANIZATION, May 3, 2011, *supra* note 253; *Press briefing on Libya*, NORTH ATLANTIC TREATY ORGANIZATION, July 12, 2011, *available at* http://www.nato.int/cps/en/natolive/opinions_76355.htm?selectedLocale=en; Chivers, *Land Mines Descend on Misurata's Port, Endangering Libyan City's Supply Route, supra* note 60.

[257] *Libya: Civilians at Risk Amid New Mine Threat*, AMNESTY INTERNATIONAL, May 25, 2011, *available at* http://www.amnesty.org/en/news-and-updates/libya-civilians-risk-amid-new-mine-threat-2011-05-25; *Al-Qaddafi's Forces Carry Out Indiscriminate Attacks in Misratah*, AMNESTY INTERNATIONAL, May 8, 2011, *available at* http://www.amnesty.org/en/for-media/press-releases/al-Qaddafi%E2%80%99s-forces-carry-out-indiscriminate-attacksmisratah-2011-05-08.

[258] *Libya: Civilians at risk amid new mine threat*, AMNESTY INTERNATIONAL, May 25, 2011, *available at* http://www.amnesty.org/en/news-and-updates/libya-civilians-risk-amid-new-mine-threat-2011-05-25.

[259] Ernesto Londono, *In Libya, rebels gaining in the west*, THE WASHINGTON POST, July 6, 2011, *available at* http://www.washingtonpost.com/world/middle-east/in-libya-rebels-gaining-in-the-west/2011/07/06/gIQAmNvA1H_story.html.

including in Misrata.[260] According to media outlets, mercenaries were in Misrata in February 2011 when Qadhafi forces attempted to take over the Misrata airport. Two mercenaries were seized by *thuwar* and confessed to being paid $200 a day to carry out attacks against civilians.[261]

3.10. *Targeting Specific Groups*

(a) Thuwar *Forces*

i. *The Tawerghans*

The CoI found that *thuwar* from Misrata carried out targeted attacks against the Tawerghan community, and were responsible for acts of murder, torture and cruel treatment, and pillaging of homes.[262] The motivation behind the attacks was in part a campaign of reprisal violence against those perceived to have supported the Qadhafi regime during the fighting in Misrata. There were other elements that fueled the attacks, however, including widespread discrimination and xenophobia against dark-skinned Libyans from Tawergha.[263]

The CoI reported that the nature of the relationship between the residents of Misrata and Tawergha prior to the 2011 conflict was a source of contention.[264] Before the conflict, members of the Tawerghan community had reportedly been discriminated against, subjected to racial harassment and relegated to menial jobs because of their race.[265] The CoI noted "indications of racism in individual interactions between some Misratan *thuwar* and Tawerghans,"[266] supporting the presumption that pre-existing racism was also a factor in the violence.

---

[260] Report of the International Commission of Inquiry (Jan. 12, 2012), *supra* note 16 at ¶ 189.

[261] Duraid Al Baik, *Tension running high as Tripoli braces for attacks*, GULF NEWS, Feb. 17, 2011, *available at* http://gulfnews.com/news/region/libya/tension-running-high-as-tripoli-braces-for-attacks-1.768282.

[262] *See infra* Secs. 5.3.2, 5.3.4 & 5.3.7. *See also* Report of the International Commission of Inquiry, advance unedited version (Mar. 2, 2012), *supra* note 5 at Annex I, n. 335.

[263] AMNESTY INTERNATIONAL, MILITIAS THREATEN HOPES FOR NEW LIBYA, *supra* note 157 at 31.

[264] Report of the International Commission of Inquiry, advance unedited version (Mar. 2, 2012), *supra* note 5 at Annex I, ¶ 390.

[265] Kareem Fahim, *Accused of Fighting for Qaddafi, a Libyan Town's Residents Face Reprisals*, N.Y. TIMES, Sept. 23, 2011, *available* at http://www.nytimes.com/2011/09/24/world/africa/accused-of-fighting-for-qaddafi-tawerga-residents-face-reprisals.html.

[266] Report of the International Commission of Inquiry, advance unedited version (Mar. 2, 2012), *supra* note 5 at Annex I, ¶ 391.

Thus, the conflicts between the population of Misrata and Tawergha appear to be rooted in historical, cultural and political conditions. The CoI reported that

> While many Misratans believe that Tawerghans received preferential treatment under the Qadhafi Government, this has been rejected by a number of Tawerghans interviewed by the Commission. Several officials and residents of Misrata informed the Commission that Tawerghans relied heavily on Misrata in terms of employment, procurement of basic necessities, and higher education.[267]

The feelings of resentment and tension between the residents of Misrata and Tawergha were exacerbated by the nature of the fighting during the 2011 war. Qadhafi forces occupied the town of Tawergha, and some residents of the town either volunteered or were forced to participate in the assault on Misrata. Civilian volunteers from Tawergha were reportedly among Qadhafi forces who ransacked dozens of houses in Misrata in March 2011, carrying out widespread violations against its inhabitants.[268] Qadhafi forces stationed in Tawergha deployed to various regions in and around Misrata, and occupied towns such as Karzaz, Kararim and Tumina, where serious violations took place. This created a widespread perception that Tawerghans were participating in acts of violence. The level of involvement of Tawerghans in these violations is questionable, however. The CoI reported

> [T]he Misrata *thuwar*'s targeting of the Tawerghans was founded on a belief that Tawerghans supported the Qadhafi forces during the attacks on Misrata and that their men were responsible for the rape of Misratan women during the conflict.... The Commission, however, received no substantiated information indicating that individual Tawerghans or organised groups of Tawerghan men raped women in Misrata or elsewhere.[269]

In the wake of the retreat of Qadhafi forces, Misrata *thuwar* carried out a targeted campaign of violence against the city of Tawergha. Residents of the town were forced to leave, as *thuwar* groups looted, vandalized and burned down their homes and properties, making it impossible to return. Amnesty International delegates documented an increase in the destruction of the town during its visits in September 2011 and February

---

[267] *Id.* at Annex I, ¶ 404 (internal citations omitted).

[268] Gilligan, *Gaddafi's ghost town after the loyalists retreat, supra* note 216. *See also supra* Sec. 3.7.

[269] Report of the International Commission of Inquiry, advance unedited version (Mar. 2, 2012), *supra* note 5 at Annex I, ¶ 404 (internal citations omitted).

2012.[270] The CoI report concluded that the destruction of Tawergha made it uninhabitable.[271] HRW observers reported that upon their visits to Tawergha between September 2011 and January 2012, they saw Misrata militia members burning and destroying homes.[272] The wave of attacks went beyond the town of Tawergha, as *thuwar* groups from Misrata pursued residents who fled the city and went to IDP camps elsewhere. HRW found that Tawerghans were "harassed, attacked, arrested and killed by mainly Misrata militias, sometimes leading to deaths in detention."[273] Amnesty International similarly reported that militias from Misrata attacked and hunted displaced Tawerghans across Libya.[274]

Members of the *thuwar* groups, local authorities, as well as many residents, accused members of the Tawergha community of having taken part in the violations against Misrata while fighting alongside Qadhafi forces. Given that none of those detained in relation to the conflict were brought before a court or tribunal, however, it is impossible to determine if the allegations are true.[275] All Tawerghans interviewed by Amnesty International denied the accusations of murder and rape, and several detained Tawerghans testified to having confessed to such offences under torture.[276]

Tawergha was completely deserted, with most of its inhabitants having fled during the fighting and before the arrival of the Misrata *thuwar*.[277] The local and national authorities in the interim government were reluctant to link the desertion of the town with the actions of the *thuwar*, and suggested that the inhabitants left instead "out of fear, due to the crimes they committed."[278] The CoI presented evidence that

---

[270] AMNESTY INTERNATIONAL, MILITIAS THREATEN HOPES FOR NEW LIBYA, *supra* note 157 at 31.

[271] Report of the International Commission of Inquiry, advance unedited version (Mar. 2, 2012), *supra* note 5 at ¶ 63.

[272] HUMAN RIGHTS WATCH, *Libya: Displaced People Barred from Homes, supra* note 202.

[273] Report of the International Commission of Inquiry, advance unedited version (Mar. 2, 2012), *supra* note 5 at ¶ 63; HUMAN RIGHTS WATCH, *Libya: Displaced People Barred from Homes, supra* note 202.

[274] AMNESTY INTERNATIONAL, MILITIAS THREATEN HOPES FOR NEW LIBYA, *supra* note 157 at 33. For more on targeting of Tawerghans by *thuwar* from Misrata in IDP camps during the post-conflict period, *see supra* Sec. 2, and Chs. VI, XI, XIII & XV.

[275] *Id.*

[276] *Id. See supra* Sec. 3.4.

[277] Report of the International Commission of Inquiry, advance unedited version (Mar. 2, 2012), *supra* note 5 at Annex I, ¶ 89.

[278] *Id.* at Annex I, ¶ 399 (internal citations omitted).

suggests otherwise, noting the discriminatory attitudes towards the Tawerghans, and racially-motivated nature of the attacks. The CoI noted

> the Misratan *thuwar* have been open about their views of the Tawerghans. One fighter told the Commission he thought that Tawerghans deserved 'to be wiped off the face of the planet'. The language reportedly used by the Misratans during the arrests was often of a racist and derogatory nature, for example calling them 'slaves', 'blacks', and 'animals'. Some have been told that they cannot ever return.[279]

Some argue that race was a motivating factor in Misratans singling out the Tawerghan community for attack, while they ignored other Qadhafi loyalists. Racist graffiti such as "Misrata's slaves" found painted in the abandoned city of Tawergha supports the claim that the violence was racially motivated.[280] HRW also documented the racist graffiti sprayed on buildings in Tawergha, and reported that a militia commander interviewed by the organization had said that Tawerghans would never be allowed to return because they were African, and should "return to Africa."[281]

On 8 April 2012, HRW sent a letter to the leaders of the Misrata Council expressing concern regarding the crimes committed by armed groups from Misrata against members of the Tawerghan community.[282] In its response, the council claimed that the people of Misrata and the *thuwar* were not responsible for the forced displacement of the people of Tawergha, and that they had fled before the arrival of the *thuwar* forces. The letter claims that no attacks were made on the properties of the Tawerghans, stating that any violations that did take place were individual acts.[283] The issue of the Tawerghan community returning to their homes was also addressed in the Council's letter

> Although no one has prevented the people of Tawergha from returning to their homes, we know that the people of Tawergha depend entirely on the city of Misrata for their livelihood, as it provides them with jobs and food. This means their return without the provision of jobs in their area is virtually impossible because they will be like refugees in their homes.[284]

---

[279] *Id.* at ¶ 59.

[280] Fahim, *Accused of Fighting for Qaddafi, a Libyan Town's Residents Face Reprisals, supra* note 265.

[281] HUMAN RIGHTS WATCH, *Libya: Displaced People Barred from Homes, supra* note 202.

[282] *Misrata Local Council Response to Human Rights Watch,* HUMAN RIGHTS WATCH, Apr. 11, 2012, *available at* http://www.hrw.org/news/2012/04/11/misrata-local-council-response-human-rights-watch.

[283] *Id.*

[284] *Id.*

The issue of accountability for violations against the Tawerghans and the re-settlement of the Tawerghan community remains unresolved. As of February 2013, HRW reported there were an estimated 1,300 people from Tawergha who had been killed, detained or were still missing.[285] Meanwhile, the Tawerghan community continues to be denied the right to return to their town. The commonly held view in Misrata appears to be that the town of Tawergha no longer exists.[286] Officials in Misrata have continued to accuse the Tawerghans of committing war and honor crimes, and some argue that banishment is a proper punishment under the region's tribal laws. While the Libyan authorities have taken steps to deal with the issue of the thousands of displaced persons from the conflict, they have done little to address the re-settlement of the Tawerghan community.

ii. *Sub-Saharan Africans*

Dark-skinned Africans were also sought out for attack by *thuwar* forces. Amnesty International documented incidents of abuse against Sub-Saharans in detention centers in the wake of the conflict.[287] A 25-year-Ethiopian reported being detained in November 2012 while travelling by bus to Tripoli, along with ten Somali men. They were all questioned and received discriminatory threats. The men were subsequently taken to a detention center near Misrata where they were further abused. After several days they were released from detention.[288]

The man's 19-year-old brother gave an account of his own abuse after being detained along with another man from Eritrea by armed men in Sirte in October 2011 on their way to Tripoli from Benghazi. The men were accused of being mercenaries and taken to Misrata, where they suffered abuse included beatings with ropes to their backs, electric shocks to various parts of the body, and being tied to a chair and forced to bend over while beaten with a stick on the back. After a week, the men were released.[289]

---

[285] *Libya: Slow Pace of Reform Harms Rights*, HUMAN RIGHTS WATCH, Feb. 26, 2013, available at http://www.hrw.org/news/2013/02/06/libya-slow-pace-reform-harms-rights.

[286] Fahim, *Accused of Fighting for Qaddafi, a Libyan Town's Residents Face Reprisals*, *supra* note 265.

[287] AMNESTY INTERNATIONAL, MILITIAS THREATEN HOPES FOR NEW LIBYA, *supra* note 157 at 6.

[288] *Id.* at 23.

[289] *Id.* at 24.

3.11. Sexual Violence[290]

(a) Qadhafi Forces

There were reported cases of sexual violence committed by Qadhafi forces in detention centers in Misrata. A man from Tawergha gave an account to media sources of sexual abuse in December 2011 against 20 men in detention, where security forces used a stick to sodomize the victims.[291] Other media sources reported cases of rape and abduction at the hands of Qadhafi forces.[292] The CoI reported that witnesses consistently reported rape by Qadhafi forces. Misratans who had fled to Tunisia reported to the CoI that "the main reason for fleeing was to safeguard family members from rape."[293] These types of abuses carry a certain plausibility in light of prior practices reportedly committed by the regime's authorities against political detainees.

Several cases of sexual violence in Misrata involved victims being attacked in their homes.[294] The CoI heard from the father of a 30-year-old woman in Benghazi that

---

[290] The following terms are defined in accordance with the jurisprudence of the ICTY and ICTR, and other mixed-model tribunals.

  1. "Rape" is the penetration, however slight, of any part of the body of another person irrespective of gender (namely, the vagina, anus, or mouth) by means of the perpetrator's sexual organ or any object used by the perpetrator when accompanied by force or threat of force against the person or a third party which the victim believes is real.

  2. "Sexual violence" is defined as any physical act of a sexual nature which is committed on a person under circumstances which are coercive or threatening to the person or to any other person, which includes physical touching, groping, fondling, removal of a person's clothing to display intimate parts of the person's body whether in the presence of one or more persons, or any other act of a demeaning sexual nature.

  3. "Sexual harassment" is any threat of "rape" or "sexual violence," as defined above, against a person or any other person for purposes of demeaning, intimidating, or punishing the person in question.

[291] Tarik Kafala, *'Cleansed' Libyan town spills its terrible secrets*, BBC, Dec. 12, 2011, *available at* http://www.bbc.co.uk/news/magazine-16051349.

[292] *Q&A: Rebel spokesman Abdelbaset Abumzirig*, AL JAZEERA, Apr. 24, 2011, *available at* http://www.aljazeera.com/news/africa/2011/04/20114240556575343.html; Rania El Gamal, *In Gaddafi's hometown, residents accused NTC fighters of revenge*, REUTERS, Oct. 16, 2011, *available at* http://www.reuters.com/article/2011/10/16/us-libya-sirte-looting-idUSTRE79F2DL20111016.

[293] Report of the International Commission of Inquiry (Jan. 12, 2012), *supra* note 16 at ¶ 206.

[294] *Id.* at ¶ 204.

[H]is daughter was detained in her house in Misrata for two days and raped by Government forces. She had returned to check on the safety and whereabouts of her brother when Government forces "came and restrained them for two days, keeping them in separated rooms. They were raping her, while trying to extract information from my son about the 'rebels'.[295]

The CoI also received information from Misratans claiming that armed fighters and volunteers from the Khamis Katiba entered houses at night and abducted men, women and children. They said they knew of "women and girls who were raped, either in their homes or taken elsewhere and raped." These incidents were especially prevalent in the towns of Tumina, Dafniyya and Karamin.[296]

The CoI received information from a local organization that interviewed perpetrators of rape, who provided evidence of "five different rapes over five nights committed in Misrata by [a] perpetrator and his colleagues."[297] Amnesty International also reported several accounts of rape and sexual abuse in Misrata. One case involved a young woman in her twenties who was forced at gunpoint into a bedroom by a soldier. The soldier began to sexually assault the woman before her screams attracted enough attention and the assault stopped. The woman's relatives discouraged her from revealing the abuse in order to "preserve her honor and reputation."[298]

PHR received reports concerning rape in Tumina. A 20-year-old resident of Tumina reported that in April 2011 Qadhafi forces from Tawergha turned an elementary school into a detention center where women and young girls were raped. Another witness stated that tanks and other military vehicles were seen at the school in April and that he could hear screaming from women inside who were forcibly detained and gang raped.[299]

The BBC interviewed a young Qadhafi loyalist in a detention center who confessed to raping civilians. He stated that he and other soldiers broke into a house in Misrata and raped four girls. The officers in charge told the soldiers that they would pay them 10 dinars if they did so. In total, more than 20 men raped the four girls. The witness said that he thought rapes were a common practice on the part of Qadhafi forces and

---

[295] *Id.*

[296] Report of the International Commission of Inquiry, advance unedited version (Mar. 2, 2012), *supra* note 5 at Annex I, ¶ 517.

[297] *Id.* at ¶ 68.

[298] AMNESTY INTERNATIONAL, *Families rent asunder by deaths and disappearances in Misratah, supra* note 134.

[299] PHYSICIANS FOR HUMAN RIGHTS, WITNESS TO WAR CRIMES, *supra* note 2 at 19.

estimated there were about 50 families in Misrata that experienced such violations.[300]

The CoI received additional information indicating that minors were subjected to sexual assault in Misrata, reporting that "Several sources, for instance, spoke about a 10 year old girl raped in Misrata by Qaddafi forces who was later treated at Al-Jamahiryya Hospital in Benghazi."[301] Media outlets reported that Libyan children as young as eight suffered sexual violence, including rape. Other allegations of minors in Misrata being subjected to sexual violence emerged from refugees in camps in Benghazi.[302]

Libya is a conservative society and many regard rape as a matter of profound shame. For this reason, it is possible that other, unreported cases of rape occurred in Misrata.[303] Isma'il Fortya, an obstetrician living in Misrata, reported to media outlets that the final figures probably run into the hundreds. "I think this is a big problem – much bigger than we think. People [in Misrata] feel deep pain, and depression. This has affected us much more than anything else during the fighting."[304] Another obstetrician/gynecologist stated to PHR that Libyan women "won't go to the gynecologist," saying rape is a "difficult crime for female Libyan ladies." Another interviewee stated, "when Qaddafi rapes a woman, the whole community is destroyed forever. He knows this, and so rape is his best weapon."[305]

(b) *Thuwar Forces*

Amnesty International conducted interviews with 48 women and one girl detained by *thuwar* groups from Zawiyya, Tripoli and Misrata. The women stated that they had been physically and sexually abused by armed *thuwar*

---

[300] *Libya: Forced to rape in Misrata*, BBC, May 23, 2011, *available at* http://www.bbc.co.uk/news/world-africa-13502715.

[301] Report of the International Commission of Inquiry (Jan. 12, 2012), *supra* note 16 at ¶ 205.

[302] David Batty, *Libyan children suffering rape, aid agency reports*, THE GUARDIAN, Apr. 23, 2011, *available at* http://www.guardian.co.uk/world/2011/apr/23/libyan-children-suffering-rape.

[303] U.N. Special Representative of the Secretary-General Margot Wallström stated "The problem is very few women will actually come forward to report that they have been raped because it carries serious risks for them personally." *See* PHYSICIANS FOR HUMAN RIGHTS, WITNESS TO WAR CRIMES, *supra* note 2 at 16, n. 103.

[304] BBC, *Libya: forced to rape, supra* note 300.

[305] PHYSICIANS FOR HUMAN RIGHTS, WITNESS TO WAR CRIMES, *supra* note 2 at 19.

and endured verbal harassment. Two of the women said that before they were detained they had been raped by unidentified men.[306]

There were also reports of sexual abuse against men in detention facilities under *thuwar* control. Amnesty International documented a case of torture of a Sub-Saharan African man by *thuwar* forces that included beatings to the genitals.[307]

3.12. *The Use of Children and Their Treatment in Armed Conflict*

(a) *Qadhafi Forces*

Children were among the civilian population affected by the actions of the Qadhafi forces, such as the indiscriminate shelling and siege of Misrata. The CoI reported that

> The Commission received numerous accounts of children being killed and injured in the ongoing fighting in Libya, particularly in the context of attacks committed by Government forces. The situation for children, in the besieged Misrata, during the reporting period has been particularly dire, with children featured amongst the civilian victims of heavy shelling and bombardment, snipers and attacks on hospitals.[308]

Media outlets and NGO reports documented numerous cases of child casualties resulting from the indiscriminate shelling by Qadhafi forces during the siege of Misrata, particularly in the months of April and May 2011. On 5 April, in Zawiyya al-Mahjub, on the western outskirts of Misrata, a ten-year-old girl was killed in the courtyard of her home.[309] A three-year-old was killed on 11 April caught with her family in crossfire as they fled their farm in Dafniyya on the western outskirts of Misrata.[310] On 23–24 April, Qadhafi forces shelled the Ra's 'Ammar neighborhood of Misrata, killing at least six residents, among them a four-year-old girl and an eight-year-old boy.[311] On 26 April in Misrata, a nine-year-old boy was killed

---

[306] AMNESTY INTERNATIONAL, DETENTION ABUSES STAINING THE NEW LIBYA, *supra* note 177 at 17.

[307] AMNESTY INTERNATIONAL, MILITIAS THREATEN HOPES FOR NEW LIBYA, *supra* note 157 at 23.

[308] Report of the International Commission of Inquiry (Jan. 12, 2012), *supra* note 16 at ¶ 215.

[309] AMNESTY INTERNATIONAL, MISRATAH UNDER SIEGE AND UNDER FIRE, *supra* note 14 at 14.

[310] AMNESTY INTERNATIONAL, *Families rent asunder by deaths and disappearances in Misratah, supra note* 134.

[311] AMNESTY INTERNATIONAL, MISRATAH UNDER SIEGE AND UNDER FIRE, *supra* note 14 at 15.

while playing on his rooftop when a mortar exploded nearby.[312] Amnesty International reported the death of two teenagers in Zarug in May due to indiscriminate shelling.[313] In late May, two children, aged one and three years old, were reported killed when a rocket crashed through the ceiling of their house.[314]

Many children were also wounded by rocket fire from the Qadhafi forces. A 15-year-old was seriously wounded when a rocket exploded near his home. On 5 April two young children, both two years old, were injured in their home by shrapnel fired from a nearby rocket. One of them suffered a broken right arm and the other a fractured left femur. On the afternoon of 14 April, a six-year-old girl sustained serious shrapnel injuries to her neck and abdomen when a rocket or mortar struck her home.[315]

4. The Role of NATO

NATO began its intervention in Misrata on 23 March 2011, focusing a significant amount of operational focus on the region due to the nature of the siege on Misrata and the immediate threat to civilians.[316] The NATO intervention played an important role in easing the siege on the city, as well as aiding *thuwar* advances.[317] However, NATO's involvement was not sufficient to break the stranglehold of Qadhafi forces on the area surrounding the city, and the battle for Misrata became the longest and bloodiest in the war.[318] After NATO strikes were carried out Qadhafi forces were able to return to their positions on the perimeter.[319]

NATO maintained that without its support and strikes against Qadhafi forces in Misrata *thuwar* would have struggled to maintain their control

---

[312] James Elder, *Libya: Nine-year-old boy, injured in Misrata fighting, reflects risks facing Libyan children*, Relief Web, Apr. 25, 2011, *available at* http://reliefweb.int/node/398930.

[313] Amnesty International, *Families rent asunder by deaths and disappearances in Misratah, supra note* 134.

[314] Patrick Wells, *In the city of Misrata, children bear the brunt of the ongoing Libyan conflict*, unicef, June 6, 2011, *available at* http://www.unicef.org/infobycountry/laj_58763.html.

[315] Amnesty International, Misratah Under Siege and Under Fire, *supra note* 14 at 14. For more on the use of children in the conflict, *See* Ch. V, 2.12.

[316] *See* Ch. III, Sec. 6.1. *See also* Chris McGreal et al., *Libya: Allied air strikes secure Misrata for rebels, supra note* 55.

[317] Andrew Gilligan, *Libya: rebels celebrate seizing Misurata airport, supra note* 64.

[318] *See* Ch. II, Sec. 3.3. *See also NATO air strikes target Misurata*, Al Jazeera, Apr. 9, 2011, *available at* http://www.aljazeera.com/news/africa/2011/04/20114913167462559.html.

[319] The Guardian, *Libya crisis: Thursday 24 March, supra note* 49.

over the city center. In addition, NATO's engagement in the port of Misrata during April 2011 was an important factor in alleviating the siege on the city. NATO's navy forces worked to maintain the safety of ships entering and leaving the port, which continued to be the city's main lifeline.[320]

NATO operations were complicated, however, because Qadhafi forces positioning themselves in residential areas in order to avoid being targeted on the open roads.[321] Qadhafi forces also used human shields, as soldiers, tanks and weaponry were dispersed and hidden in residential areas in order to prevent NATO from being able to identify and target them.[322] This situation complicated NATO operations and made it more challenging to strike military targets in and around population centers like Misrata while avoiding civilian casualties.[323] However, in March 2011, residents of Misrata claimed that coalition forces managed to destroy the government's armor without any known civilian casualties.[324] NATO announced that Misrata was its main priority because of the dire situation in the city. Yet, during the height of the siege in April 2011, *thuwar* in Misrata reportedly called on NATO to step up its airstrikes on Qadhafi positions around the city in order to end the devastating siege and to protect the civilian population.[325]

On 27 April 2011, a NATO airstrike killed 12 *thuwar* fighters and wounded three east of Misrata in what became the most controversial incident in relation to NATO's involvement in and around Misrata. NATO initially denied responsibility for the incident and claimed that it could not "independently verify reports that these vehicles were operated by opposition forces." In an extensive investigative report published in December 2011, however, The New York Times found that NATO appeared to have made false statements and that evidence found at the site suggested that NATO bore responsibility for the attacks. When the area of the strikes was

---

[320] *See* Ch. III, Sec. 6.1. *See also* Press briefing on Libya, NORTH ATLANTIC TREATY ORGANIZATION, July 12, 2011, *available at* http://www.nato.int/cps/en/natolive/opinions_76355.htm?selectedLocale=en; Chivers, *Land Mines Descend on Misurata's Port, Endangering Libyan City's Supply Route, supra* note 60.

[321] McGreal et al., *Libya: Allied air strikes secure Misrata for rebels, supra* note 55.

[322] *Press briefing on Libya*, NORTH ATLANTIC TREATY ORGANIZATION, Apr. 5, 2011, *available at* http://www.nato.int/cps/en/natolive/opinions_72027.htm.

[323] *Press briefing on Libya*, NORTH ATLANTIC TREATY ORGANIZATION, May 10, 2011, *available at* http://www.nato.int/cps/en/natolive/opinions_73660.htm.

[324] McGreal et al., *Libya: Allied air strikes secure Misrata for rebels, supra* note 55.

[325] Harriet Sherwood, *Nato must send in troops to save Misrata, say rebels*, THE GUARDIAN, Apr. 16, 2011, *available at* http://www.guardian.co.uk/world/2011/apr/16/libya-muammar-gaddafi.

investigated, signature components from NATO weaponry were found, including remnants of an American-made 500-pound bomb.[326]

In mid-May 2011, the *thuwar* began to make serious advances in the Misrata region, gaining more ground against the Qadhafi forces. After the *thuwar* overran the front Qadhafi forces retreated and scattered into residential areas, making it increasingly difficult for NATO to identify military targets.[327] This trend continued in June 2011, with NATO strikes cutting Qadhafi forces off from resupplies of ammunition, forcing them to retreat again.[328] One of the fall back positions for Qadhafi forces was Tawergha, which was subsequently targeted by NATO air strikes during the final part of June.[329] NATO strikes continued into July, clearing the road to Tripoli for *thuwar* from Misrata to make their way into the capital in August.[330]

5. Conclusion

Misrata was a key theater of military operations during the Libyan civil war. The Misratan resistance tied down some of Qadhafi's most effective forces for months, keeping them from supporting operations in the east, from Brega to Benghazi. Furthermore, once the rebels completely took the city it was only a matter of time before Tripoli fell. After the battle for Misrata was won, hundreds of the most experienced and equipped *thuwar* were free to attack Tripoli.

Because of the city's strategic location, Misrata experienced the most drawn out battles and bloodiest fighting of the Libyan conflict. The city's port on the Mediterranean, and its location between the Qadhafi strongholds of Sirte and Tripoli, made it particularly important for the Qadhafi regime to retake control of the city. Qadhafi forces fought intensely to capture Misrata, but were unable to do so after it came under *thuwar*

---

[326] *See* Ch. III, Sec. 6.2. *See also* Allen et al., *Errant NATO Airstrikes in Libya: 13 Cases (Misurata)*, *supra* note 62.

[327] *Press briefing on Libya*, NORTH ATLANTIC TREATY ORGANIZATION, May 3, 2011, *available at* http://www.nato.int/cps/en/natolive/opinions_72998.htm.

[328] *Press briefing on Libya*, NORTH ATLANTIC TREATY ORGANIZATION, Oct. 24, 2011, *available at* http://www.nato.int/cps/en/natolive/opinions_79851.htm; PHYSICIANS FOR HUMAN RIGHTS, WITNESS TO WAR CRIMES, *supra* note 2 at 19.

[329] *See* Ch. III, Sec. 6.2. *See also Press briefing on Libya*, NORTH ATLANTIC TREATY ORGANIZATION, July 12, 2011, *available at* http://www.nato.int/cps/en/natolive/opinions_76355.htm.

[330] *See* Ch. II, Sec. 3.3.

control in early March 2011 and it remained under *thuwar* control until the end of the war. The *thuwar* received significant help from NATO in drawn out battles with Qadhafi forces to maintain control of the city.

Qadhafi forces used a hit and run tactic in Misrata, launching attacks that at times penetrated deep into the city. However, they did not follow up their attacks, thus losing tactical momentum. Qadhafi's forces gave the *thuwar* time to reorganize, rearm and prepare the battleground for defensive operations. The *thuwar* were also fighting on familiar ground and used this greatly to their advantage, allowing Qadhafi forces to enter certain areas before cutting them off and ambushing them. Failing to exploit their advances with follow-up attacks, Qadhafi forces resorted to bombardment with artillery, rockets, mortars and cluster munitions. These weapons had a terrorizing effect on the population but were not tactically significant. While a Grad rocket could damage a building, it could not be aimed precisely enough to hit rebel forces, especially given that the rebel fighters were often on the move in their own territory.

Qadhafi forces suffered from not being able to operate at night. This greatly decreased their fighting effectiveness. Daytime gains were often erased when they retreated to their nighttime defensive positions. NATO also degraded Qadhafi forces' ability to maneuver. Qadhafi forces could bring tanks into the city, but they could not move freely for fear of NATO airstrikes on the outskirts of the city, thereby hampering reinforcement and resupply. Qadhafi forces responded by using civilian vehicles, yet these vehicles had limited tactical applications without armor, and operating in urban settings, they became vulnerable to rebel attacks from high buildings and rear positions. Finally, without airpower Qadhafi's forces lost the main advantage they would have had against the rebels. Early fighting in Benghazi showed that Qadhafi's forces could depend on airpower to make up for their deficiencies on the ground.[331] NATO's ability to neutralize what would have been advantages for the Qadhafi regime helped turn the tide in the battle.

In the midst of the fighting in Misrata, Qadhafi forces carried out serious violations against the civilian population. Investigative reports, on-site visits, human rights reporting and media accounts provide evidence of systematic violations during the fight for Misrata and its aftermath. Qadhafi forces initially responded to the Misratan protests with brute

---

[331] *See* Ch. VI, Sec. 2.

force, arresting individuals and firing live ammunition at demonstrators. Evidence shows that Qadhafi forces used machine guns, RPGs and anti-aircraft guns against demonstrators. Protesters were unarmed and did not take up arms until after Qadhafi forces used live ammunition.

Reports indicate that Qadhafi forces engaged in a policy of arbitrary arrests and enforced disappearances of *thuwar* supporters. The detentions were conducted without legal sanction or evidence of actual crimes. In a number of cases, the Qadhafi forces did not provide information to the families regarding the victims' status or whereabouts.

There are documented incidents of Qadhafi forces targeting supporters or suspected supporters of the *thuwar* for torture and ill-treatment. *Thuwar* supporters were detained and tortured for information. There are also documented cases of Qadhafi forces using snipers to fire on civilians and medics inside or in the vicinity of hospitals, resulting in the death or serious injury of a number of civilians. Similarly, there is evidence to indicate that Qadhafi forces targeted medics in ambulances, including Red Crescent and Red Cross ambulances in order to prevent medics from aiding injured persons.

Qadhafi forces engaged in indiscriminate attacks that included the use of unguided weapons, firing artillery, mortars and Grad rockets into the city over prolonged periods, leading to deaths and injuries of civilians. Qadhafi forces also used civilians as human shields by stationing military units in or staging attacks from residential areas. There is also evidence suggesting that Qadhafi forces compelled civilians to accompany them in areas exposed to NATO strikes.

Qadhafi forces imposed a lengthy siege on the city of Misrata. In doing so, they prevented civilians from fleeing, and prevented the flow of humanitarian aid, particularly food and medicine, to the city. Evidence indicates that Qadhafi forces attempted to punish the civilian population as part of their fight to retake control of Misrata. Qadhafi forces intentionally targeted the city's infrastructure, including hospitals and sewage lines, placing the civilian population at considerable risk. Over the course of the siege and as part of the Qadhafi regime's assault on the city, its forces looted and destroyed civilian property. Reports indicate that Qadhafi forces used cluster bombs and mines in Misrata. These are weapons that place civilian populations at considerable risk and are banned by international law.

There were documented incidents of acts of sexual violence, including rape, against women in Misrata by Qadhafi forces throughout the campaign to retake the city. Reports also indicate that *thuwar* committed sexual violence against Qadhafi supporters or suspected supporters in the aftermath of the conflict.

Thuwar forces carried out a wide range of violations in Misrata, particularly targeting suspected Qadhafi loyalists. Such violations include unlawful killing, arbitrary arrests and enforced disappearances, torture and other forms of ill-treatment, denial of access to medical care, indiscriminate attacks on civilians and civilian objects and sexual violence. Reports indicate that one of the groups specifically targeted by the *thuwar* forces was Sub-Saharan Africans, singled out on the basis of race on suspicion that Qadhafi forces included mercenaries from Sub-Saharan countries.

Thuwar forces singled out Tawerghans extensively on the suspicion that they were Qadhafi supporters for retributive punishment or to coerce confessions to crimes against the Misratan population. *Thuwar* allegedly beat, electrocuted and whipped victims, and there were a number of deaths and serious injuries at the hands of *thuwar*. There are also reports indicating that *thuwar* prevented thousands of Tawerghan refugees from returning to their homes and targeted them in IDP camps and detention facilities. The attacks on Tawerghan camps indicate that the interim government lacked the capacity or political will to ensure the security of internally displaced and vulnerable communities, and failed to facilitate the return of the Tawerghan community to their homes.

The Misratan *thuwar* and the local authorities demonstrated an unwillingness to seek reconciliation with the displaced Tawerghan population or allow their return. Preventing entire communities from returning to their homes on the premise of the violations committed by certain individuals amounts to unlawful and arbitrary collective punishment.[332] Not only are the Tawerghans being punished collectively for the actions of individuals, but they are also being held indirectly responsible for the crimes of the former regime.[333] The reprisal violence after the fall of the Qadhafi regime was carried out by *thuwar* groups from Misrata and elsewhere demonstrates that the interim government lacked the capacity and resources to manage the challenges that faced the country in the wake of war.

---

[332] HUMAN RIGHTS WATCH, *Libya: Displaced People Barred from Homes, supra* note 202.
[333] Kafala, *'Cleansed' Libyan town spills its terrible secrets, supra* note 291.

CHAPTER TEN

THE NAFUSA MOUNTAINS

1. INTRODUCTION

The Nafusa Mountains lie to the southwest of Tripoli, extending parallel to the Mediterranean Sea from Libya's capital to the Tunisian border.[1] The Nafusa Mountains, also referred to as the Nafusa Highlands, mark the end of the Coastal Plain and beginning of the Tripolitania Plateau, which extends south into the Libyan interior and serves as a natural divider between the north and the south of the country.[2] The mountains rise to heights nearing 1,000 meters before plateauing and ending abruptly with 350-meter high bluffs on the north side facing the Mediterranean Sea.[3] The plateau and the mountains can be accessed from the north by a number of valleys that extend from the coastal plain. The region stretches from the city of Al-Gharyan[4] on the eastern edge of the mountains to the town of Wazin on the Tunisian border, with a road connecting the two cities.[5]

The Nafusa Mountains includes cities such as Al-Gharyan, Zintan, Yafran, Nalut and Jadu as well as dozens of villages. Most of the populated cities and towns are located on the ridgeline, providing a natural security barrier that historically functioned to ward off attackers. There are two main roads that run east to west through the Nafusa Mountains, the low

---

[1] ANTHONY BELL ET AL., THE LIBYAN REVOLUTION: THE TIDE TURNS, 4 INSTITUTE FOR THE STUDY OF WAR 13 (Nov. 2011), *available at* http://www.understandingwar.org/sites/default/files/Libya_Part4.pdf.

[2] *Battle for Tripoli: pivotal victory in the mountains helped big push*, THE GUARDIAN, Aug. 22, 2011, *available at* http://www.guardian.co.uk/world/2011/aug/22/battle-for-tripoli-libya-gaddafi.

[3] J.M. Asketell & S.M. Ghellali, *A palaeogeologic map of the pre-Tertiary surface in the region of the Jifarah Plain: its implication to the structural history of Northern Libya* [hereinafter "*A palaeogeologic map*"], *in* 6 THE GEOLOGY OF LIBYA. 4–7 THIRD SYMPOSIUM ON THE GEOLOGY OF LIBYA, HELD AT TRIPOLI 2381 (M.J. Salime et al. ed., Amsterdam, The Netherlands: Elsivier, 1991); Mohamed Megerisi & V.D. Mamgain, *The Upper Cretaceous-Tertiary formations of northern Libya*, *in* 1 THE GEOLOGY OF LIBYA: SYMPOSIUM ON THE GEOLOGY OF LIBYA 67 (M.J. Salem & M.T. Busrewil ed., New York, USA: Academic Press, 1980).

[4] Not to be confused with Ghayran in the outskirts of Misrata.

[5] Asketell & Ghellali, *A palaeogeologic map, supra* note 3. *See also* Megerisi & Mamgain, *The Upper Cretaceous-Tertiary formations of northern Libya, supra* note 3.

road and high road. The low road runs across the ridgeline linking the small settlements at the foot of the mountains, while the high road runs on the plateau connecting the southern mountain towns.[6]

The Nafusa Mountains are densely populated relative to the rest of Libya.[7] The mountain area is home to the indigenous Berber population (also called the Amazigh), with Arabs making up a minority of the area's residents.[8] While much of the Libyan Berber population are mixed with the Arab Bani Hilal and Bani Sulaym, the Berber language and practices remained strongest in the Nafusa Mountains region. The Berber communities of the region live primarily in the cities of Yafran, Kabaw, Jadu and Nalut as well as smaller mountain villages and communities. The main Arab tribes of the Nafusa Mountains are the Mashashiyya, Awlad Busayf, Nawayl, Rayaniyya, Al-Rujban, and the Zintan (one of the most prominent, and composed of both Arab and Berber sub-tribes). During the Qadhafi era, the Arab tribes generally enjoyed privilege relative to their Berber neighbors.[9]

The Berber communities' political relationship with the rest of the region is a long and complicated one, dating back to the Italian occupation when they chose not to side with the local Tripolitanian leadership. The Berbers of the Nafusa Mountains region generally supported King Idris and his strongly federalist policy, and opposed the Qadhafi regime. After 1969, Berbers were subjected to Arabization policies, including a prohibition on speaking their languages or giving children Berber names.[10] The relationship between the Nafusa Mountains Berbers and the Libyan state is therefore fused with a history of resistance and struggle for cultural survival.[11] At the start of the protest movement in February 2011, many Berber tribes – including the Yafran, Jadu, Fassatu, Kabaw and Haraba – joined the *thuwar*.[12]

The resentment accrued from historical marginalization of the Berber under the Qadhafi regime ended up contributing to the success of the

---

[6] BELL ET AL., THE TIDE TURNS, *supra* note 1 at 13.

[7] *Id.*

[8] *Id.* at 14.

[9] *Id.* at 11. For more background on tribes in Libya, *see* the Basic Facts about Libya.

[10] Scott Sayare, *Berber Rebels in Libya's West Face Long Odds Against Qaddafi*, N.Y. TIMES, Apr. 24, 2011, *available at* http://www.theglobeandmail.com/subscribe.jsp?art=1995361.

[11] AMNESTY INTERNATIONAL, LIBYA – DISAPPEARANCES IN THE BESIEGED NAFUSA MOUNTAIN AS THOUSANDS SEEK SAFETY IN TUNISIA, 5 (May, 2011), *available at* http://www.amnesty.org/en/library/asset/MDE19/020/2011/en/aed13a1a-07b4-434b-bb28-0c0aa1d53069/mde190202011en.pdf.

[12] BELL ET AL., THE TIDE TURNS, *supra* note 1 at 11.

thuwar in the Nafusa Mountains region.[13] While the Berber tribes dominate the region numerically, particularly in the western part of the mountains, many of the *thuwar* fighters in the eastern part of the Nafusa Mountains region were local Arabs.[14] The politics of the Nafusa Mountains Arab tribes and their relationship with the Qadhafi regime is even more complex than that of the Berbers. Some groups, such as the Zintan, generally rejected the Qadhafi regime, and Zintan military officers had taken part in several attempts to assassinate Qadhafi.[15] Several members of the Zintan tribe also participated in the failed 1993 coup.[16]

During the 2011 conflict, the population of the Nafusa Mountains region was more divided than other parts of eastern Libya over whether to support Qadhafi. Some groups in the north and east of the Nafusa Mountains region with ties to the Qadhadhfa tribe maintained their allegiance to the government, and opposed *thuwar* efforts in the region.[17] Some Arab tribes in the Nafusa Mountains region continued to support the Qadhafi regime throughout the conflict, including the Mashashiyya.

The split in attitude towards the Qadhafi regime in the Nafusa Mountains region did not fall solely along the lines of Arab or Berber divides, and there is a long history of alliances across tribal lines. The longstanding tensions between the Berber and Arab communities, however, certainly contributed to the multidimensional nature of the conflict in the region.[18]

Notwithstanding the fact that there were those who supported the regime during the war, most towns in the Nafusa Mountains region supported the *thuwar*, and some cities became powerful rebel strongholds in western Libya. *Thuwar* kata'ib were formed around regional centers in Zintan, Nalut, Yafran and other cities, reporting to local civilian and military councils as well as local security committees.[19] The most powerful

---

[13] Mathieu von Rohr, *Settling Old Scores – Tribal Rivalries Complicate Libyan War*, SPIEGEL ONLINE INTERNATIONAL, July 26, 2011, *available at* http://www.biyokulule.com/view_content.php?articleid=3695.

[14] *Id.*

[15] *Anti-government protests, clashes, spread to Libya*, AP, Feb. 16, 2011, *available at* http://abclocal.go.com/wpvi/story?section=news/national_world&id=7961876.

[16] *Libya: Zintan withdrawal rare success for rebels*, 3 NEWS, Mar. 24, 2011, *available at* http://www.3news.co.nz/Libya-Zintan-withdrawal-rare-success-for-rebels/tabid/417/articleID/203851/Default.aspx.

[17] *Libya: Rocket Attacks on Western Mountain Towns*, HUMAN RIGHTS WATCH, May 27, 2011, *available at* http://www.hrw.org/news/2011/05/27/libya-rocket-attacks-western-mountain-towns.

[18] BELL ET AL., THE TIDE TURNS, *supra* note 1 at 14.

[19] Report of the International Commission of Inquiry on Libya, U.N. HRC. 19th Sess., Annex I, ¶ 67. U.N. Doc. A/HRC/19/68, advance unedited version (Mar. 2, 2012).

katiba formed in Zintan, which became home to the western regional *thuwar* command center.[20] *Thuwar* in Zintan played a vital role in encouraging opposition groups in other cities in the Nafusa Mountains region to join the armed insurrection.[21] Zintan's strategic location led to its becoming a gateway for supplies entering into Libya from Tunisia. The city thus became the center of the opposition against Qadhafi in the west, and provided a training ground for *thuwar* from other cities, such as Zawiyya.[22] Former Qadhafi officers and army defectors led the war efforts from Zintan, organizing and supplying recruits and army defectors, and directing the *thuwar* in surrounding cities and villages.[23] By July 2011, the *thuwar* in the area controlled a territory extending 200 kilometers (124 miles) eastward from the Tunisian border. The Nafusa Mountains region operated like a loosely organized state, publishing its own newspapers, broadcasting a radio station and establishing a makeshift airfield.[24]

The Nafusa Mountains region witnessed some of the most intense fighting of the civil war as Qadhafi forces sought to control the region directly adjoining Tripoli and cut off routes to Tunisia. Qadhafi forces besieged several cities including Zintan, Yafran and Nalut, cutting off supplies and attacking towns and cities with tanks and artillery barrages. The challenging terrain, along with the complex social demographics made it difficult, however, to take control of the entire region.[25]

At the same time, the formidable mountains that deterred the Qadhafi forces also hampered the delivery of food and humanitarian supplies, exposing the population to the effects of a crippling military siege. NATO intervention in the region enabled *thuwar* forces to maintain most of the region under its control throughout the conflict. In July and August 2011, *thuwar* ended the regime siege with NATO support and subsequently advanced on Zawiyya and Tripoli.

---

[20] *See* Ch. II, Sec. 2.3. *See also* BELL ET AL., THE TIDE TURNS, *supra* note 1 at 15; von Rohr, *Settling Old Scores – Tribal Rivalries Complicate Libyan War*, *supra* note 13.

[21] INTERNATIONAL CRISIS GROUP, HOLDING LIBYA TOGETHER: SECURITY CHALLENGES AFTER QADHAFI 13 (Dec. 14, 2011) [hereinafter "HOLDING LIBYA TOGETHER"], *available at* http:/www.crisisgroup.org/~/media/Files/Middle%20East%20North%20Africa/North%20Africa/115%20Holding%20Libya%20Together%20-%20Security%20Challenges%20after%20Qadhafi.pdf.

[22] Report of the International Commission of Inquiry, advance unedited version (Mar. 2, 2012), *supra* note 19 at Annex I, ¶ 71.

[23] INTERNATIONAL CRISIS GROUP, HOLDING LIBYA TOGETHER, *supra* note 21 at 8.

[24] von Rohr, *Settling Old Scores – Tribal Rivalries Complicate Libyan War*, *supra* note 13.

[25] BELL ET AL., THE TIDE TURNS, *supra* note 1 at 14.

Many cities and villages in the Nafusa Mountains region were directly affected by the war, notably, from west to east, Wazin, Nalut, Tiji, Badr, Zintan, Awaniyya, Shayga, Zawiyyat al-Bajul, Yafran, Al-Qala', Qawalish, Kikla, Bir al-Ghanam and Al-Gharyan. The area between the Libyan town of Wazin and the Tunisian border-town of Dhehiba became a critical supply line during the war.[26] The city of Nalut, situated approximately 280 kilometers (175 miles) from Tripoli and 60 kilometers (37 miles) from the Tunisian border, served as a major smuggling and supply center for the *thuwar*.[27]

The towns of Tiji and Badr are situated in close proximity to one other in the western part of the Nafusa Mountains region near Nalut. Made up of mostly Arab communities, the residents of these towns were perceived as being loyal to the regime during the war. They were accused of staging attacks against *thuwar* in the area due to the fact that Qadhafi forces were stationed in Tiji and used the town as a base to launch attacks on other *thuwar* controlled cities in the area. Later, there was reprisal violence against the Tiji population.[28]

Zintan, with a population of approximately 25,000 residents,[29] is located at the base of the Nafusa Mountains, extending into the hills to the north and into the Tripolitanian plateau towards the south.[30] The city is also located along a major highway connecting Tripoli with the Nafusa Mountains region and the Fezzani interior, and has a small road running from Zintan into the mountains. The regional hubs in Yafran and Al-Gharyan are located 45 kilometers (28 miles) and 90 kilometers (56 miles), respectively, to the east of Zintan.[31]

The Nafusa Mountains military council served as the nominal leadership of the *thuwar* in the west from its headquarters in Zintan. Well armed

---

[26] *Gaddafi deploys forces as world raises Libya pressure*, ASHARQ ALAWSAT, Mar. 1, 2011, *available at* http://asharq-e.com/news.asp?section=1&id=24331.

[27] Report of the International Commission of Inquiry, advance unedited version (Mar. 2, 2012), *supra* note 19 at Annex I, ¶ 564.

[28] *Id.* at Annex I, ¶ 462.

[29] Sources vary in the estimation of Zintan's population with some reports estimating up to 40,000 residents. *See* Oliver Holmes & Philippa Fletcher, *Zintan's hold on Saif al-Islam reflects Libya divisions*, REUTERS, Nov. 20, 2011, *available at* http://www.reuters.com/article/2011/11/21/us-libya-zintan-idUSTRE7AK0872011121; von Rohr, *Settling Old Scores – Tribal Rivalries Complicate Libyan War*, *supra* note 13.

[30] 3 NEWS, *Libya: Zintan withdrawal rare success for rebels*, Mar. 24, 2011, *supra* note 16.

[31] *List of Libyan Ports*, TEMEHU, *available at* http://www.temehu.com/Libyan-ports .htm. *See also Benghazi*, WOLFRAMALPHA, *available at* http://www.wolframalpha.com/input/?i=Benghazi.

and with a long history of combat, the Zintan fighters composed one of the most powerful of the kata'ib in Libya that asserted its independence from the NTC immediately after the ouster of Qadhafi, and often refused to act in accordance with the interim government's directives.[32]

The towns of Awaniyya, Shayga and Zawiyyat al-Bajul, mainly inhabited by people from the Mashashiyya tribe, were reportedly Qadhafi strongholds. Awaniyya and Zawiyyat al-Bajul are only 5 kilometers apart,[33] while Shayga is situated southeast of Zintan near Mizda.[34]

Yafran, a city of approximately 15,000[35] is located 100 kilometers (60 miles) southwest of Tripoli and 100 kilometers (60 miles) from an important coastal road connected to the capital.[36] The town is situated on a hill, which left it exposed to assault as Qadhafi forces took control of the area below the town when besieged.[37] Yafran was an important city during the war due to its proximity to the Qadhafi stronghold of Al-Gharyan, a city just 80 kilometers (50 miles) south of Tripoli.[38] The town of Al-Qala' is situated east of Yafran, about 120 kilometers (193 miles) southwest of Tripoli.[39] The CoI reported a history of repression against the Amazigh Berber people in Al-Qala' and suppression of their culture and language, and noted that the local people quickly joined the uprising against Qadhafi.[40]

The town of Qawalish is located near the outskirts of Al-Gharyan, consisting mostly of a few dozen houses and a mosque, roughly 100 kilometers (60 miles) south of Tripoli. It is situated near an important highway

---

[32] von Rohr, *Settling Old Scores – Tribal Rivalries Complicate Libyan War, supra* note 13.

[33] Report of the International Commission of Inquiry, advance unedited version (Mar. 2, 2012), *supra* note 19 at Annex I, ¶ 745.

[34] *Libya Response Situation Report No. 68 18 December 2011,* U.N. OCHA, *available at* http://northafrica.humanitarianresponse.info/sites/default/files/20111218_Situation Report68.pdf.

[35] TEMEHU, *List of Libyan Ports, supra* note 31. *See also* WOLFRAMALPHA, *Benghazi, supra* note 31.

[36] Peter Graff & Mussab Al-Khairalla, *Anticipation in Tripoli as net tightens on Gaddafi,* REUTERS, June 8, 2011, *available at* http://www.reuters.com/article/2011/06/08/us-libya-tripoli-idUSTRE7573F720110608.

[37] Youssef Boudlal & Peter Graff, *Explosions in Tripoli, rebels seize Libyan town,* REUTERS, June 6, 2011, *available at* http://www.reuters.com/article/2011/06/06/us-libya-idUSTRE 7270JP20110606.

[38] BELL ET AL., THE TIDE TURNS, *supra* note 1 at 14.

[39] Maria Golovnina, *WRAPUP 2-Libya fighters amass near pro-Gaddafi town,* REUTERS, Sept. 7, 2011, *available at* http://www.reuters.com/article/2011/09/08/libya-idUSL5E7K74 ST20110908.

[40] Report of the International Commission of Inquiry, advance unedited version (Mar. 2, 2012), *supra* note 19 at Annex I, ¶ 161.

connecting the capital, Al-Gharyan, and Sabha to the south.[41] For the Qadhafi regime, the highway served as the key supply route to Tripoli during the conflict.[42] Besides allowing direct access to Al-Gharyan, Qawalish is home to the Mashashiyya tribe, the most prominent of the Nafusa Mountains tribes to support the regime during the war.[43] After gaining control of the village in July 2011, Qawalish played an important role in the *thuwar* advance on Tripoli.[44]

East of Yafran and Zintan is the town of Kikla, 150 kilometers (240 miles) southwest of Tripoli.[45] North of Yafran, on the northern edge of the mountains, lies Bir al-Ghanam, about 80 kilometers (50 miles) south of Tripoli.[46] Bir al-Ghanam is connected to a highway that leads north to the Mediterranean Coast and on to Tripoli.[47] The furthest city in the east of the Nafusa Mountains region is Al-Gharyan, 80 kilometers (50 miles) south of Tripoli.[48] Al-Gharyan also lies on the strategic highway connecting the capital to the south of Libya.[49]

2. Summary of Events

2.1. *Wazin*

In early March 2011, Qadhafi forces began a concerted campaign to take the Nafusa Mountains region from thuwar forces that had established control over much of the area. On 2 March, Qadhafi forces took control of the Tunisian border crossing at Wazin, with the aim of cutting *thuwar* supply lines.[50] Fighting ensued over the important border crossing area, and on 18 March, *thuwar* sources reported that their forces had attacked

---

[41] BELL ET AL., THE TIDE TURNS, *supra* note 1 at 16.
[42] Peter Graff et al., *Libya rebels say they retake western village*, REUTERS, July 13, 2011, *available at* http://www.reuters.com/article/2011/07/13/libya-village-idUSLDE76C1IG20110713.
[43] BELL ET AL., THE TIDE TURNS, *supra* note 1 at 16.
[44] *Id.*
[45] *Gaddafi's forces withdraw from Kikla, 150 km SW of Tripoli*, XINHUANET, June 15, 2011, *available at* http://news.xinhuanet.com/english2010/video/2011-06/15/c_13931305.htm.
[46] von Rohr, *Settling Old Scores – Tribal Rivalries Complicate Libyan War, supra* note 13.
[47] Michael Georgy, *Libya rebels say they hold gains south of capital*, REUTERS, Aug. 7, 2011, *available at* http://uk.reuters.com/article/2011/08/07/uk-libya-idUKTRE76Q30I20110807.
[48] *NATO tackles threat of attacks in western Libya*, NORTH ATLANTIC TREATY ORGANIZATION, June 1, 2011, *available at* http://www.nato.int/cps/en/natolive/news_75942 .htm.
[49] *Libya rebels take Garyan, south of Tripoli-witness*, REUTERS, Aug. 18, 2011, *available at* http://af.reuters.com/article/libyaNews/idAFLDE77H09I20110818.
[50] BELL ET AL., THE TIDE TURNS, *supra* note 1 at 15.

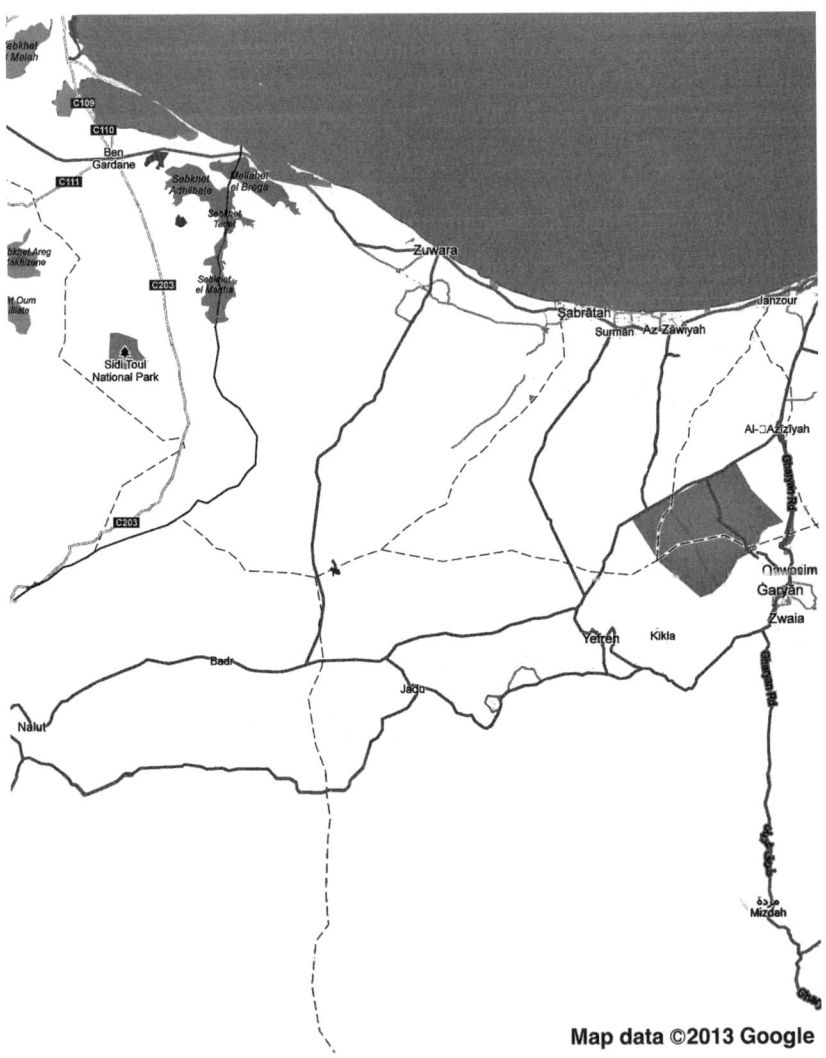

Map 7: Regional map of the Nafusa Mountains (Map data © 2013 Google).

Qadhafi positions close to the Tunisian border, leading to the deaths of one *thuwar* and four Qadhafi fighters.[51]

Qadhafi forces held positions along the lower road, shelling towns controlled by *thuwar* throughout April. The towns experienced shortages of food, medicine, electricity and fuel after the Wazin-Dhehiba border crossing was closed.[52] Qadhafi forces moved along the road to cut off towns such as Zintan and Yafran from the border. The critical border crossing changed hands several times by the end of April 2011.[53]

Thuwar took control of Wazin on 21 April, allowing for the transfer of essential supplies.[54] Heavy fire was exchanged, however, as Qadhafi forces deployed reinforcements to the border crossing. At the same time, there were reported regime defections in the area. Thirteen officers and soldiers, including a general, reportedly defected from the regime and handed themselves over to the Tunisian military at the border.[55]

Qadhafi forces launched another offensive to retake the town on 28 April, pushing *thuwar* into Tunisia, and continuing the fight on Tunisian ground.[56] *Thuwar* were able to repel the attack, eventually retaking control of the border and pushing Qadhafi forces out of Wazin.[57] At the end of April and beginning of May, Qadhafi forces reportedly fired artillery shells on the Tunisian town of Dhehiba. The shelling caused serious alarm among local officials, as the Tunisian authorities stationed troops in the area to prevent Qadhafi forces from entering.[58]

---

[51] Mariam Karouny, *Gaddafi's forces shell west Libya's Misrata*, REUTERS, Mar. 18, 2011, *available at* http://www.reuters.com/article/2011/03/18/us-libya-misrata-bombard-idUS-TRE72H27Y20110318.

[52] Tarek Amara, *Libyan refugees tell of border fight, fear revenge*, REUTERS, May 1, 2011, *available at* http://www.reuters.com/article/2011/05/01/us-libya-tunisia-border-idUS-TRE7402PH20110501.

[53] *See* Ch. II, Sec. 3.3. *See also* BELL ET AL., THE TIDE TURNS, *supra* note 1 at 15.

[54] BELL ET AL., THE TIDE TURNS, *supra* note 1 at 15.

[55] Tarek Amara, *Rebels seize Libya-Tunisia border crossing: witnesses*, REUTERS, Apr. 21, 2011, *available at* http://www.reuters.com/article/2011/04/21/us-libya-tunisia-border-id USTRE73K32K20110421; *Explosions, planes heard in Tripoli; rebels seize border crossing*, CNN, Apr. 21, 2011, *available at* http://articles.cnn.com/2011-04-21/world/libya.fighting_1_nato-commander-nato-military-official-moammar-gadhafi?_s=PM:WORLD.

[56] AMNESTY INTERNATIONAL, LIBYA – DISAPPEARANCES IN THE BESIEGED NAFUSA MOUNTAIN AS THOUSANDS SEEK SAFETY IN TUNISIA, *supra* note 11 at 7; *Gaddafi forces still at Tunisia border –witness*, REUTERS, Apr. 28, 2011, *available at* http://af.reuters.com/article/libyaNews/idAFLDE73R2C820110428. ISW reported that the opposition took control of the border on Apr. 21. *See* BELL ET AL., THE TIDE TURNS, *supra* note 1 at 15.

[57] Tarek Amara, *Libyan mountain town facing starvation: residents*, REUTERS, May 2, 2011, *available at* http://af.reuters.com/article/libyaNews/idAFLDE7411M020110502.

[58] Amara, *Libyan refugees tell of border fight, fear revenge*, *supra* note 52.

Qadhafi forces launched repeated assaults on Wazin throughout May.[59] On 14 and 17 May, Qadhafi forces reportedly fired rockets into a mountain pass leading from Libya into Tunisia, near Dhehiba.[60] Thousands of Libyans fleeing the Nafusa Mountains region began arriving at Dhehiba, as refugee camps were established in the area.[61]

2.2. *Nalut*

On 19 February, residents of Nalut became the second city in the region, after Zintan, to protest against the Qadhafi regime.[62] The following day locals reported hearing gunshots fired overnight. In response to these early signs of local resistance, Qadhafi forces moved towards Nalut, Zintan and Yafran, stationing troops in nearby towns.[63]

On 3 March, Qadhafi forces started shelling Nalut, Zintan and Yafran, while advancing on the cities with tanks, armored cars and anti-aircraft guns.[64] The three towns faced weeks of artillery bombardment.[65] As Qadhafi forces laid siege to the area in mid-March, supplies to Nalut and other towns were blocked from reaching the civilian population.[66]

On 16 March, Qadhafi forces reportedly used Grad rockets on Nalut, Zintan and Yafran, also destroying surrounding villages.[67] Civilians began fleeing in large numbers from Nalut and Yafran to Tunisia in April, bringing reports of attacks by Qadhafi forces to media outlets and NGO Investigators. The United Nations High Commissioner for Refugees (UNHCR)

---

[59] *See also* BELL ET AL., THE TIDE TURNS, *supra* note 1 at 15.

[60] HUMAN RIGHTS WATCH, *Libya: Rocket Attacks on Western Mountain Towns, supra* note 17.

[61] Amara, *Rebels seize Libya-Tunisia border crossing: witnesses, supra* note 55; *Libya and Middle East uprising- live updates*, THE GUARDIAN, Apr. 12, 2011, *available at* http://www .guardian.co.uk/world/blog/2011/apr/12/libya-middle-east-uprising-live-updates.

[62] BELL ET AL., THE TIDE TURNS, *supra* note 1 at 14.

[63] Report of the International Commission of Inquiry, advance unedited version (Mar. 2, 2012), *supra* note 19 at Annex I, ¶ 563.

[64] AMNESTY INTERNATIONAL, LIBYA – DISAPPEARANCES IN THE BESIEGED NAFUSA MOUNTAIN AS THOUSANDS SEEK SAFETY IN TUNISIA, *supra* note 11; BELL ET AL., THE TIDE TURNS, *supra* note 1.

[65] Peter Graff, *Divisions hamper Libyan rebel fighters' advance*, REUTERS, July 14, 2011, *available at* http://www.reuters.com/article/2011/07/14/libya-rebels-weakness-idUSLDE 76D16920110714.

[66] Report of the International Commission of Inquiry, advance unedited version (Mar. 2, 2012), *supra* note 19 at Annex I, ¶¶ 563–564; Ashish Kumar Sen, *Gadhafi lays siege to west mountain towns*, THE WASHINGTON TIMES, Apr. 16, 2011, *available at* http://www .washingtontimes.com/news/2011/apr/17/gadhafi-lays-siege-libyan-mountain-towns/.

[67] AMNESTY INTERNATIONAL, LIBYA – DISAPPEARANCES IN THE BESIEGED NAFUSA MOUNTAIN AS THOUSANDS SEEK SAFETY IN TUNISIA, *supra* note 11 at 7, 8 & 18.

reported that refugees from Libya first entered Tunisia through the Dhe-hiba crossing on 7 April, with over 18,000 crossing the border over the following two weeks.[68] The UNHCR reported that another 24,000 refu-gees entered Tunisia through the Dhehiba crossing between April 22 and May 4.[69]

By mid-April, Qadhafi forces occupied the towns below Nalut, includ-ing Al-Ghazaya, 6 kilometers (4 miles) from Dhehiba. Under a new com-mander, Qadhafi forces placed Nalut under a tight siege,[70] and reportedly shelled the town on 18 April, as clashes ensued on its outskirts.[71]

On 20 April, *thuwar* fighters reported clashes in Nalut and the use of Grad rockets by Qadhafi forces. The *thuwar* fighters in the Nafusa Moun-tains region were far less equipped than the Qadhafi forces at this time, both in terms of weaponry and military training.[72] On 25 April, *thuwar* reported suffering at least two casualties and several injuries during the fighting. They also reported capturing dozens of vehicles from Qadhafi forces in fighting not far from the town of Nalut.[73]

Throughout April and into May, Qadhafi forces continued to shell Nalut.[74] The attacks intensified in June, and *thuwar* fighters reported that Qadhafi forces shelled Nalut and Zintan on 4 June, injuring at least ten people in Nalut.[75] On 15 June, Qadhafi forces again shelled Nalut and the

---

[68] *Libya: End Indiscriminate Attacks in Western Mountain Towns*, HUMAN RIGHTS WATCH, May 9, 2011, *available at* http://www.hrw.org/en/news/2011/05/09/libya-end-indiscriminate-attacks-western-mountain-towns.

[69] *Id.*

[70] Report of the International Commission of Inquiry, advance unedited version (Mar. 2, 2012), *supra* note 19 at Annex I, ¶ 564.

[71] *See also* Ch. II, Sec. 3.3. *See also Thousands of Libyans flee remote western area: report*, REUTERS, Apr. 18, 2011, *available at* http://www.reuters.com/article/2011/04/18/us-libya-mountains-clashes-idUSTRE73H6WL20110418.

[72] Amara, *Rebels seize Libya-Tunisia border crossing: witnesses*, *supra* note 55; Michael Georgy, *Captured Libyan soldiers say army morale is low*, REUTERS, July 29, 2011, *available at* http://www.reuters.com/article/2011/07/29/us-libya-morale-idUSTRE76R4KD20110729.

[73] Tarek Amara, *Libyan mountain refugees tell of fearsome assault*, REUTERS, Apr. 26, 2011, *available at* http://www.reuters.com/article/2011/04/26/us-libya-mountains-idUSTRE73O33E20110426.

[74] *See* Report of the International Commission of Inquiry, advance unedited version (Mar. 2, 2012), *supra* note 19 at Annex I, ¶ 568.

[75] Peter Graff, *NATO helicopters ratchet up pressure on Gaddafi*, REUTERS, June 4, 2011, *available at* http://www.reuters.com/article/2011/06/04/us-libya-idUSTRE7270JP20110604.

nearby border crossing into Tunisia.[76] Despite the attacks, *thuwar* continued to advance and capture territory throughout the region.[77]

On 17 June, fighting continued around Nalut, as Qadhafi forces reportedly used Grad missiles and tanks to shell *thuwar* positions. *Thuwar* reported that NATO strikes in the region aided the rebel advances, but they complained that it was not enough to end the stalemate in the region.[78] On 18 June, eight *thuwar* fighters were reportedly killed and 13 wounded in fighting near Nalut during an advance from the western region.[79] Clashes also took place in the village of Takut, just outside Nalut, where the *thuwar* reported destroying six armored vehicles and killing more than 45 Qadhafi fighters.[80]

As a result of the increased fighting in the region, NATO stepped up its involvement in the area in June. On 21 June, NATO launched four air strikes against Qadhafi forces outside of Nalut.[81] On 4 July, NATO conducted 145 sorties, one of which hit a military camp in the vicinity of Nalut.[82] On 27 July, NATO conducted 133 air sorties, one of which hit a multiple rocket launcher near Nalut.[83]

Towards the end of July, *thuwar* enjoyed more successes, capturing Al-Ghazaya and Takut, thereby dominating the western end of the Nafusa Mountains region and gaining control of the road from Nalut to Wazin.[84] On 27–28 July, *thuwar* reinforced their positions around Nalut in prepara-

---

[76] Nick Carey, *WRAPUP 1 – Libyan rebels take new villges* [*sic*] *in Western Mountains*, REUTERS, June 15, 2011, *available at* http://www.reuters.com/article/2011/06/15/libya-idUSLDE75E29K20110615.

[77] Nick Carey, *WRAPUP 1 – Rebels dismiss election offer, NATO pounds Tripoli*, REUTERS, June 16, 2011, *available at* http://www.reuters.com/article/2011/06/16/libya-idUSLDE75F25S20110616.

[78] *See infra* Sec. 4. *See also* Matt Robinson, *Heavy fighting as Libyan rebels try to push out*, REUTERS, June 17, 2011, *available at* http://www.reuters.com/article/2011/06/17/us-libya-idUSTRE7270JP20110617.

[79] *CORRECTED – Gun battles in Libya's Nalut kill 8-rebes*, REUTERS, June 18, 2011, *available at* http://www.reuters.com/article/2011/06/18/libya-violence-idUSLDE75H04B20110618.

[80] Maria Golovnina, *Libyan rebels blame West for lack of cash*, REUTERS, June 18, 2011, *available at* http://www.reuters.com/article/2011/06/18/us-libya-idUSTRE7270JP20110618.

[81] Matt Robinson, *WRAPUP 1 – Gaddafi rockets dent sense of security in Misrata*, REUTERS, June 21, 2011, *available at* http://www.reuters.com/article/2011/06/22/libya-idUSLDE75K23920110622.

[82] *Factbox: Latest developments in Libyan conflict*, REUTERS, July 5, 2011, *available at* http://www.reuters.com/article/2011/07/05/us-libya-nato-idUSTRE7641V320110705.

[83] *NATO and Libya Operational Media Update for 27 July*, NORTH ATLANTIC TREATY ORGANIZATION, July 28, 2011, *available at* http://www.nato.int/nato_static/assets/pdf/pdf_2011_07/20110728_110728-oup-update.pdf.

[84] Chris Stephen, *Libyan rebels launch major offensive to capture key towns*, THE GUARDIAN, July 28, 2011, *available at* http://www.guardian.co.uk/world/2011/jul/28/libyan-rebels-

tion for a major offensive on the strategic town of Al-Ghazaya.[85] Media accounts reported that at least 20 heavily armed trucks were moving in the direction of Nalut, close to the border, and a group of around 30 camouflaged pick-up trucks were spotted further east preparing to join the assault.[86] By late afternoon, *thuwar* sources announced that Al-Ghazaya was under rebel control and that regime fighters were fleeing over the border to Tunisia.[87]

Nalut became the base for the Tripoli Katiba made up of Tripolitanian volunteers and expatriates who reportedly received training from foreign governments such as Qatar. It was led by Irish-Libyan Mahdi al-Harati and incorporated an estimated 1,200 fighters by mid-August when it took part in the *thuwar* advance on Tripoli.[88]

2.3. *Tiji and Badr*

Qadhafi forces stationed troops in Tiji from 25 March to 15 August 2011, using the town as a base from which to attack cities held by *thuwar* forces,[89] and according to satellite images operated from a military base on the outskirts of Tiji.[90] By the end of July, Tiji was the last pro-Qadhafi stronghold in the western part of the Nafusa Mountains region. *Thuwar* forces attempted to take Tiji, firing on the approximately 500 Qadhafi troops stationed in the city.[91]

---

launch-major-offensive; *Libya rebels launch offensive on strategic town of Ghezaia*, REUTERS, July 28, 2011, *available at* http://af.reuters.com/article/libyaNews/idAFL6E7IS0BL20110728.

[85] Georgy, *Captured Libyan soldiers say army morale is low*, *supra* note 72.

[86] *Libya rebels say plan attack on western mountain town*, REUTERS, July 27, 2011, *available at* http://www.reuters.com/article/2011/07/27/libya-ghezaia-idUSLDE76Q1OK20110727; *Libya rebels 'capture key supply route town of Ghazaya'*, BBC, July 28, 2011, *available at* http://www.bbc.co.uk/news/world-africa-14321751; Michael Georgy, *WRAPUP 1 – New pressure on Gaddafi on foreign, rebel fronts*, REUTERS, July 27, 2011, *available at* http://www.reuters.com/article/2011/07/27/libya-idUSLDE76Q1QJ20110727.

[87] *Libyan rebels say capture western mountain town*, REUTERS, July 28, 2011, *available at* http://www.reuters.com/article/2011/07/28/libya-ghezaia-capture-idUSLDE76R1KV 20110728.

[88] *See* Ch. II, Sec. 3.3. *See also* INTERNATIONAL CRISIS GROUP, HOLDING LIBYA TOGETHER, *supra* note 21 at 8.

[89] Report of the International Commission of Inquiry, advance unedited version (Mar. 2, 2012), *supra* note 19 at Annex I, ¶ 462.

[90] *NATO strikes destroy Libyan helicopters: rebels*, REUTERS, May 5, 2011, *available at* http://www.reuters.com/article/2011/05/05/us-libya-zintan-helicopters-idUSTRE7443RT20110505.

[91] Michael Georgy, *Rebels attack last Gaddafi Western Mountain stronghold*, REUTERS, July 30, 2011, *available at* http://www.reuters.com/article/2011/07/30/us-libya-western-mountains-idUSTRE76T0XB20110730; *WRAPUP 4 – Libyan rebel commander killed by allied militia*, REUTERS, July 31, 2011, *available at* http://www.reuters.com/article/2011/07/30/

On 15 August, *thuwar* from Nalut took control of Tiji as Qadhafi forces retreated.[92] *Thuwar* then reportedly carried out attacks on Tiji residents, including looting and vandalizing the town.[93] On 16 August, Badr fell to *thuwar* forces from Tripoli. The following day, *thuwar* forced the remaining residents leave the town.[94]

2.4. *Zintan*

The uprising in Zintan started shortly after the protests began in eastern Libya.[95] Zintan was the first town in the Nafusa Mountains region to join the resistance and align with the NTC, and became home to the western regional *thuwar* command center.[96] In the days following the start of the uprising in Zintan, several other cities and towns in the region also broke with the regime and joined the resistence.[97]

On 16 February, demonstrations erupted in Zintan, when 600 protesters gathered at the city center. As the crowd grew, some demonstrators set fire to buildings belonging to local Revolutionary Committees, the Internal Security Agency (ISA) and the main police station. The demonstrators returned to the city center, where the police used tear gas and sticks to disperse them. The protesters retaliated by throwing stones, and were able to force the police to retreat.[98]

The Qadhafi regime responded quickly, surrounding the town and installing checkpoints to prevent people and food from entering the city center where protesters had set up an encampment.[99] On 17 February, a local Revolutionary Committee unit arrived at the city center in armored

---

libya-idUSLDE76S1K320110730; Missy Ryan & Rania El Gamal, *Libyans start Ramadan fast amid conflict, divisions*, Reuters, Aug. 1, 2011, *available at* http://www.reuters.com/article/2011/08/01/us-libya-idUSTRE76Q7662011080.

[92] Report of the International Commission of Inquiry, advance unedited version (Mar. 2, 2012), *supra* note 19 at ¶ 61.

[93] *See Id.* at Annex I, ¶ 463. *See also* Ch. II, Sec. 3.3.

[94] *Id.*

[95] *Id.* at Annex I, ¶ 128.

[96] Amnesty International, Libya – Disappearances in the besieged Nafusa Mountain as thousands seek safety in Tunisia, *supra* note 11 at 5, 7 & 12.

[97] Bell et al., The Tide Turns, *supra* note 1 at 14.

[98] Amnesty International, Libya – Disappearances in the besieged Nafusa Mountain as thousands seek safety in Tunisia, *supra* note 11 at 12.

[99] Report of the International Commission of Inquiry, advance unedited version (Mar. 2, 2012), *supra* note 19 at ¶ 128.

cars and arrested 16 protestors. There were daily protests over the coming days demanding the release of the detained protesters.[100]

The Qadhafi regime sent reinforcements to positions in Al-Gharyan, Nalut, Kikla and Sabrata. Qadhafi officials also visited Zintan and other cities in an attempt to pay protesters to stop the demonstrations.[101] Throughout the region, Qadhafi forces deployed troops, set up check-points and started arresting those suspected of bringing in supplies.[102]

The *thuwar* forces quickly became armed and organized in Zintan, as groups raided the nearby town of Garaya[103] on 20 February, and looted ammunition from a regime compound. On 28 February, Qadhafi forces attacked Zintan, but the *thuwar* were able to repel the assault and capture more equipment from the Qadhafi troops, including anti-aircraft guns.[104] As the violence continued, the rebel forces grew stronger, and Zintan developed into a strategic gateway into the region for goods entering from Tunisia that were then flown to other cities, including Benghazi.[105]

By 25 February, Qadhafi forces stationed in Zintan either withdrew or defected.[106] Many of the defectors then organized *thuwar* troops and led the war effort from the city.[107] During this period, *thuwar* in the Nafusa Mountains numbered only a few hundred fighters, but within a few weeks they grew in size as defectors from local regiments and from as far away as Tripoli joined the rebels in the mountains.

By late February, *thuwar* were staging attacks in the Nafusa Mountains region, including assaults targeting local ISA and Revolutionary Committee facilities as well as the military barracks in Al-Kashaf, roughly 7 kilometers (4.3 miles) northeast of Zintan. Through these attacks, the *thuwar* forces were able to obtain more weapons.[108] On 3 March, Qadhafi forces started shelling Zintan, Nalut and Yafran, while troops advanced on the

---

[100] Amnesty International, Libya – Disappearances in the besieged Nafusa Mountain as thousands seek safety in Tunisia, *supra* note 11 at 12.

[101] Bell et al., The Tide Turns, *supra* note 1 at 14.

[102] *See infra* Sec. 3.3. *See also* Amnesty International, Libya – Disappearances in the besieged Nafusa Mountain as thousands seek safety in Tunisia, *supra* note 11 at 14.

[103] The transliteration of this place name was adopted from the reference. Human Rights Watch, *Libya: Rocket Attacks on Western Mountain Towns*, *supra* note 17.

[104] *Id.*

[105] International Crisis Group, Holding Libya Together, *supra* note 21 at 8.

[106] Report of the International Commission of Inquiry, advance unedited version (Mar. 2, 2012), *supra* note 19 at Annex I, ¶ 81.

[107] International Crisis Group, Holding Libya Together, *supra* note 21 at 8.

[108] Amnesty International, Libya – Disappearances in the besieged Nafusa Mountain as thousands seek safety in Tunisia, *supra* note 11 at 7.

cities with tanks, armored cars and anti-aircraft guns.[109] By 19 March, Qadhafi forces had encircled Zintan completely and were only kilometers away from the city center.[110] The *thuwar* managed to hold their positions over a three-day battle,[111] and the Qadhafi forces resorted to cutting electricity and besieging the city, causing serious food shortages.[112]

On 27 March, NATO started launching airstrikes on Qadhafi forces in the Nafusa Mountains region after *thuwar* had repelled the military attacks on Zintan, Nalut and Yafran.[113] Despite NATO airstrikes, Qadhafi forces made significant advances in April.[114] After capturing the village of Kikla on 4 April, Qadhafi forces were 60 kilometers (37.3 miles) from Zintan.[115] This advance allowed the military to tighten its control over the region and intensify the siege preventing the entry of supplies.[116]

Most of Zintan's residents fled to Tunisia or took refuge in the mountains as a result of the continued shelling. This was particularly the case at the end of April and early May when the shelling was particularly intense.[117] The siege continued into May, along with regular attacks using Grad rockets.[118] In mid-May, Qadhafi forces continued to launch extensive artillery attacks on Zintan, with the apparent aim of deterring civilians from fleeing the town. By 18 May, with the city severely damaged, Zintan's *thuwar* leadership called for outside assistance to help break the siege.[119]

---

[109] *See* Ch. II, Sec. 3.3. *See also Id.*; BELL ET AL., THE TIDE TURNS, *supra* note 1 at 15.

[110] BELL ET AL., THE TIDE TURNS, *supra* note 1 at 15.

[111] HUMAN RIGHTS WATCH, *Libya: Rocket Attacks on Western Mountain Towns, supra* note 17.

[112] *See infra* Sec. 3.7. *See also* BELL ET AL., THE TIDE TURNS, *supra* note 1 at 6.

[113] *Id.* at 15.

[114] Sen, *Gadhafi lays siege to west mountain in towns, supra* note 66.

[115] AMNESTY INTERNATIONAL, LIBYA – DISAPPEARANCES IN THE BESIEGED NAFUSA MOUNTAIN AS THOUSANDS SEEK SAFETY IN TUNISIA, *supra* note 11 at 18.

[116] BELL ET AL., THE TIDE TURNS, *supra* note 1 at 15; Lin Noueihed & Tarek Amara, *Libya angers Tunisia as war briefly crosses border*, REUTERS, Apr. 28, 2011, *available at* http://www .reuters.com/article/2011/04/28/us-libya-idUSTRE7270JP20110428; Tarek Amara, *Pro-Gaddafi forces clash with Tunisian military*, REUTERS, Apr. 29, 2011, *available at* http://af.reuters .com/article/topNews/idAFJOE73S00320110429?pageNumber=1&virtualBrandChannel=0.

[117] HUMAN RIGHTS WATCH, *Libya: Rocket Attacks on Western Mountain Towns, supra* note 17.

[118] *Id.*

[119] *Rebel forces in Libya's western mountains issue call for help*, CNN, May 18, 2011, *available at* http://edition.cnn.com/2011/WORLD/africa/05/17/libya.war; Nic Robertson, *Rebels battle Gadhafi forces in Libyan mountains*, CNN, May 21, 2011, *available at* http://edition .cnn.com/2011/WORLD/africa/05/21/libya.zintan.

Despite an increase in NATO airstrikes, Qadhafi forces were able to maintain pressure on Zintan.[120] On 19 May, Qadhafi forces attacked the nearby town of Rayaniyya, bringing troops just ten miles north of Zintan and caused panic within the city. A large number of residents fled Zintan for the east, fearing that regime forces would invade the town from the north.[121]

By early June, the situation on the ground started to change. Reports surfaced that *thuwar* were receiving assistance from special forces units that had arrived from France, Qatar and Jordan, dramatically improving the capacities of the *thuwar* in the region.[122] Additionally, France made weapons airdrops,[123] which reportedly included machine guns, rocket-propelled grenades (RPGs) and anti-tank missiles.[124] The series of NATO airstrikes that began after 20 May also started weakening Qadhafi forces. With regime forces weakened and improved weaponry at their disposal, the *thuwar* were able to launch increasingly successful attacks on regime positions.[125]

On 2 June, the rebels were able to break the siege of Zintan.[126] Despite ongoing shelling by regime forces, by mid-June *thuwar* and humanitarian organizations were able to distribute essential supplies to the people of the region, including food, water and medicine, as well as provide basic

---

[120] *Press briefing on Libya*, NORTH ATLANTIC TREATY ORGANIZATION, May 20, 2011, *available at* http://www.nato.int/cps/en/natolive/opinions_74542.htm; BELL ET AL., THE TIDE TURNS, *supra* note 1 at 16.

[121] HUMAN RIGHTS WATCH, *Libya: Rocket Attacks on Western Mountain Towns*, *supra* note 17.

[122] For more on military training and equipment provided to *thuwar* forces by 3rd party states, *see* Ch. II, Sec. 2.3. *See also* Margaret Coker, *Length of Libya's standoff hinges on leader's militia*, THE WALL STREET JOURNAL, Aug. 24, 2011, *available at* http://online.wsj .com/article/SB10001424053111903327904576526642369893206.html; THE GUARDIAN, *Battle for Tripoli: pivotal victory in the mountains helped big push*, *supra* note 2.

[123] *France gives Libya rebels arms but Britain balks*, AFP, June 29, 2011; Louis Charbonneau & Hamuda Hassan, *France defends arms airlift to Libya rebels*, REUTERS, June 30, 2011; Michael Birnbaum, *France sent arms to Libyan rebels*, THE WASHINGTON TIMES, June 29, 2011; Nick Hopkins, *Nato reviews Libya campaign after France admits arming rebels*, THE GUARDIAN, June 29, 2011, *available at* http://www.guardian.co.uk/world/2011/jun/29/ nato-review-libya-france-arming-rebels; INTERNATIONAL CRISIS GROUP, HOLDING LIBYA TOGETHER, *supra* note 21 at 8.

[124] *See* Ch. III, Sec. 7.1. *See also* Hopkins, *Nato reviews Libya campaign after France admits arming rebels*, *supra* note 123.

[125] BELL ET AL., THE TIDE TURNS, *supra* note 1 at 14.

[126] ANTHONY BELL ET AL., INSTITUTE FOR THE STUDY OF WAR, 3 THE LIBYAN REVOLUTION: STALEMATE & SIEGE (Oct. 2011) [hereinafter "STALEMATE & SIEGE"], *available at* http://www.understandingwar.org/sites/default/files/Libya_Part3_0.pdf.

shelter.[127] Through to mid-June, *thuwar* continued to press Qadhafi's troops, capturing villages and towns across the Nafusa Mountains region.[128] In the west, *thuwar* captured all of the small towns and villages between Zintan and Wazin along the Tunisian border.[129] In mid-June 2011, *thuwar* seized an arms depot 15 miles south of Zintan in the town of Gha'a.[130] The *thuwar* gained not only weapons, but also important military information, such as the size of the regime's stockpile of shoulder-fired surface-to-air missiles (SAMs).[131]

In July, *thuwar* continued to gain in strength, not only through continued training and armament, but also because of a steady influx of defectors from the Qadhafi military throughout western Libya, especially from Tripoli and Zawiyya.[132] In mid-July, 'Umar Hariri, the military coordinator of the NTC, went to Zintan to discuss military strategy with the local *thuwar* leadership. The meeting was the first indication to Hariri and the NTC that a unified national plan for the opposition movement was not possible, as many fighters from Zintan refused to take direct orders from the NTC authorities. Their interests were regionalized, and their allegiances remained primarily with local commanders.[133]

NATO airstrikes aided the significant gains made by *thuwar* forces in July and August.[134] During these months, *thuwar* forces stayed out of strategically marked "red line" areas where NATO strikes took out Qadhafi targets.[135] In early August, *thuwar* continued to press Qadhafi forces, pushing them out of the northern end of the Nafusa Mountains towards the Mediterranean Coast. *Thuwar* were able to fight their way through to

---

[127] *Press briefing on Libya*, NORTH ATLANTIC TREATY ORGANIZATION, June 21, 2011, *available at* http://www.nato.int/cps/en/natolive/opinions_75652.htm.

[128] BELL ET AL., STALEMATE & SIEGE, *supra* note 126.

[129] Xan Rice, *Muammar Gaddafi's forces come under fire from the west*, THE GUARDIAN, June 12, 2011, *available at* http://www.guardian.co.uk/world/2011/jun/12/muammar-gaddafis-forces-under-fire.

[130] The transliteration of this place name was adopted from the reference. BELL ET AL., THE TIDE TURNS, *supra* note 1 at 15.

[131] *Id.*

[132] Chris Stephen, *Misrata rebel forces seize arms after routing pro-Gaddafi troops*, THE GUARDIAN, July 31, 2011, *available at* http://www.guardian.co.uk/world/2011/jul/31/misrata-rebels-seize-gaddafi-arms; *Press briefing on Libya*, NORTH ATLANTIC TREATY ORGANIZATION, Aug. 2, 2011, *available at* http://www.nato.int/cps/en/natolive/opinions_76803.htm.

[133] von Rohr, *Settling Old Scores – Tribal Rivalries Complicate Libyan War*, *supra* note 13.

[134] *See infa* Sec. 4. *See also* INTERNATIONAL CRISIS GROUP, HOLDING LIBYA TOGETHER, *supra* note 21 at 30.

[135] *See* Ch. III, Sec. 6.1.

Bir al-Ghanam, a major approach to Zawiyya and Tripoli.[136] In a major breakthrough, *thuwar* captured a key section of the Libyan Coastal Highway, cutting off the Qadhafi regime's supply routes from Tunisia.[137]

On 19 August, media outlets reported that 'Abd al-Salam Jallud, Qadhafi's former deputy and prime minister, defected to the Nafusa Mountains region.[138] Jallud's defection was a major blow to the regime, because as a former minister and close associate of Qadhafi he could provide valuable information to the *thuwar* forces.[139]

By the middle of August, the area under the control of Qadhafi forces had diminished greatly. *Thuwar* forces controlled the western part of the Nafusa Mountains and continued to advance towards Al-Gharyan and Zawiyya where Qadhafi forces were stationed.[140] With the capture of Al-Gharyan and Zawiyya, *thuwar* forces were in full control of the western and southern approaches to Tripoli and had encircled the capital.[141] By 20 August, *thuwar* had almost completely secured the Nafusa Mountains region, capturing Zawiyya along the way. Joining with forces from Misrata and defectors from Tripoli, the *thuwar* made their advance on the capital.[142] *Thuwar* from the Nafusa Mountains played a major role in the final battle for Tripoli, and maintained a strong presence in the capital after the official end to hostilities.[143]

After the fall of Tripoli in late September, a multitude of weapons were seized from sites in the capital. The fighters who took part in the capture of Tripoli transported these weapons to other parts of Libya, including Zintan, in order to strengthen their regional control and authority.[144] At this time the interim government began to raise concerns that former

---

[136] *Press briefing on Libya*, NORTH ATLANTIC TREATY ORGANIZATION, Aug. 10, 2011, *available at* http://www.nato.int/cps/en/natolive/opinions_77137.htm.

[137] Stephen, *Misrata rebel forces seize arms after routing pro-Gaddafi troops, supra* note 132; NORTH ATLANTIC TREATY ORGANIZATION, *Press briefing on Libya, supra* note 132.

[138] Ulf Laessing et al., *Gaddafi's former No. 2 defects -Libya rebels*, REUTERS, Aug. 19, 2011, *available at* http://www.reuters.com/article/2011/08/19/libya-defection-jalloud-idU-SL5E7JJ3V820110819.

[139] *Libya rebels close in on Gadhafi*, MSNBC, Aug. 20, 2011, *available at* http://www.msnbc.msn.com/id/44202953/ns/world_news-mideast_n_africa#.T_FRsPW5koI.

[140] THE GUARDIAN, *Battle for Tripoli: pivotal victory in the mountains helped big push, supra* note 2; REUTERS, *Libya rebels take Garyan, south of Tripoli-witness, supra* note 49.

[141] INTERNATIONAL CRISIS GROUP, HOLDING LIBYA TOGETHER, *supra* note 21 at 9.

[142] BELL ET AL., THE TIDE TURNS, *supra* note 1 at 19.

[143] For more on the battle for Tripoli and the aftermath, *see* Ch. XIII, Sec. 2.

[144] Joseph Logan et al., *Tripoli armed group says arms spreading to regions*, REUTERS, Sept. 24, 2011, *available at* http://www.reuters.com/article/2011/09/24/libya-weapons-idU-SL5E7KOoTQ20110924.

thuwar groups were splintering into militias that would challenge efforts
to unify the country as weapons increasingly spread.[145]

On 19 November, members from the Zintan Katiba detained Qadhafi's
son Saif al-Islam near the town of Obari. Saif al-Islam was not wounded
during his capture and was taken to Zintan by plane.[146] The Zintan Katiba
took Saif al-Islam to an undisclosed location and reported they would
hold him there for his own safety, citing the inability of the interim government to protect him against reprisal violence.[147] The International
Criminal Court (ICC) called for Saif al-Islam's transfer to face trial in The
Hague, and on 31 May 2013 rejected Libya's admissibility challenge to the
case.[148] The interim government insisted that he would be tried in Libya,
a position maintained by the General National Congress.[149]

On 11 June 2012, fighting broke out in the Nafusa Mountains region
between *thuwar* groups around Zintan and members of the Mashashiyya
tribe. Clashes lasted for a week in the towns of Zintan, Mizda and Shayga.
Thuwar from Zintan received support from another tribe known as the
Guntrara from Mizda, and clashed with armed members of the Mashashiyya tribe based in Shayga.[150] The tensions reportedly related to issues of
land expropriation during the Qadhafi-era. Resentment between the two
groups led to fighting in December 2011, and erupted again in June 2012.
The killing of a man from Zintan in June 2012, which the Zintan Katiba
blamed on the Mashashiyya tribe, reportedly triggered the violence. Members of the Mashashiyya tribe claimed that they had acted in self-defense
after being attacked and shelled by fighters from Zintan.[151] On 18 June, the
NTC called for a ceasefire and sent in troops to restore calm.[152] Government spokesperson Nasir al-Mani', announced that 105 people had been

---

[145] *See* Ch. VI, Secs. 2 & 3. *See also id.*

[146] *Timeline: Saif al-Islam detained, say officials*, REUTERS, Nov. 19, 2011, *available at*
http://www.reuters.com/article/2011/11/19/us-libya-events-idUSTRE7AI0HV20111119.

[147] Holmes & Fletcher, *Zintan's hold on Saif al-Islam reflects Libya divisions, supra* note 29.

[148] *UPDATE 2 – Gaddafi's son will get fair trial – Libyan PM*, REUTERS, Nov. 19, 2011, *available at* http://www.reuters.com/article/2011/11/19/libya-saif-pm-idUSL5E7MJ106201119. *See
also* Ch. IV, Sec. 6.

[149] For more on Saif al-Islam and the ICC case, *see* Ch. IV, Sec. 6.2. *See also* Francois
Murphy, *Libya will try Gaddafi's son fairly: ICC prosecutor*, REUTERS, Nov. 24, 2011, *available
at* http://www.reuters.com/article/2011/11/24/us-libya-icc-idUSTRE7AN0QY20111124.

[150] *Libya's tribal clashes leave 105 dead*, BBC, June 20, 2012, *available at* http://www.bbc
.co.uk/news/world-africa-18529139.

[151] *Troops sent to quell clashes in western Libya*, BBC, June 17, 2012, *available at* http://
www.bbc.co.uk/news/world-africa-18474834.

[152] *Id.*

killed and 500 injured in the week of fighting, and medical personnel reported the use of both heavy and light weapons during the clashes.[153]

2.5. *Zawiyyat al-Bajul, Awaniyya and Shayga*

As the *thuwar* from Zintan took control of more towns in the region, they moved into Zawiyyat al-Bajul (located 5 kilometers, 3.1 miles, from Awaniyya) arriving in trucks with mounted machine guns on 7 May 2011. The CoI received witness accounts that after the *thuwar* entered the town, houses were looted and vandalized, and residents attacked and killed.[154]

On 19 May, Qadhafi forces still stationed in Zawiyyat al-Bajul reportedly launched an attack on the town of Rayaniyya, driving rebel forces into Zintan.[155] The Zintan *thuwar* entered Awaniyya in July, but many of the families had anticipated *thuwar* attacks and had already fled to Tripoli or Shayga. The residents who stayed suffered reprisal violence.[156] On 11 and 12 December, fighting reportedly took place in and around the town of Shayga. *Thuwar* from Zintan entered the town, demanding that residents expel the remaining Qadhafi loyalists. They reportedly shelled the town, which led to civilian casualties.[157]

2.6. *Yafran*

Qadhafi forces surrounded Yafran in March 2011, and enforced a siege on the town for several weeks before taking full control in late April.[158] Qadhafi troops repeatedly attacked Yafran and nearby towns with tanks and other armored vehicles in an attempt to block transport and movement in the Nafusa Mountains region.[159] In mid-March, Qadhafi's troops pressed their advantage and launched offensives against both Yafran and Zintan.[160] Qadhafi forces then retreated from Yafran and Zintan between

---

[153] Ali Shuaib et al., *More than 100 killed in west Libya clashes in a week*, REUTERS, June 20, 2012, *available at* http://www.reuters.com/article/2012/06/20/us-libya-clashes-toll-idUS-BRE85J1F620120620.

[154] *See infra* Sec. 3.7. *See also* Report of the International Commission of Inquiry, advance unedited version (Mar. 2, 2012), *supra* note 19 at Annex I, ¶ 745.

[155] *Id.*

[156] *Id.* at Annex I, ¶ 454.

[157] *Id.* at Annex I, ¶ 458.

[158] *See infra* Sec. 3.7. *See also Id.* at Annex I, ¶ 570.

[159] BELL ET AL., THE TIDE TURNS, *supra* note 1 at 15.

[160] *Id.*

22–27 March.[161] Qadhafi forces clashed with *thuwar*, and as they retreated, cut supply lines and fired artillery shells into the cities.[162]

Qadhafi forces carried out attacks on Yafran throughout April, resulting in thousands of residents fleeing the city, the majority of whom crossed the border into Tunisia.[163] *Thuwar* forces were not able to break through Qadhafi lines holding the cities, and Yafran remained subject to a regime siege with military forces surrounding vital infrastructure, including the hospital at the city's edge.[164]

In early April, Qadhafi forces regrouped and again advanced, gaining new territory in the region.[165] Qadhafi forces shelled Yafran, still under siege.[166] Regime troops captured Yafran, moving tanks into the city.[167] The troops then occupied the Yafran hospital on 19 April, remaining there until early June.[168] Testimony from hospital staff indicated that a paramilitary unit known as the Popular Guard (Al-Haras al-Sha'bi) initially occupied the hospital building.[169] The occupation placed around 30 staff and three patients at risk by preventing their departure and using weapons on the hospital grounds.[170]

On 25 May, media outlets reported that NATO strikes hit artillery positions around Yafran, forcing Qadhafi forces to retreat. Qadhafi forces were reinforced shortly thereafter, and continued to besiege Yafran from a distance.[171] Major General John Lorimer reported that British warplanes

---

[161] *Id.*

[162] Amnesty International, Libya – Disappearances in the besieged Nafusa Mountain as thousands seek safety in Tunisia, *supra* note 11 at 7; *Press briefing on Libya*, North Atlantic Treaty Organization, May 27, 2011, *available at* http://www .nato.int/cps/en/natolive/opinions_74826.htm.

[163] *Libyans flee violence in remote western areas*, Reuters, Apr. 17, 2011, *available at* http://www.reuters.com/article/2011/04/17/us-libya-tunisia-refugees-idUSTRE73G1IJ20110417.

[164] *Rebels Repel Assaults By Loyalists in Libya*, N.Y. Times, Apr. 28, 2011, *available at* http://www.nytimes.com/2011/04/29/world/africa/29libya.html.

[165] Amnesty International, Libya – Disappearances in the besieged Nafusa Mountain as thousands seek safety in Tunisia, *supra* note 11 at 7.

[166] *Syria, Libya and Middle East unrest*, The Guardian, May 18, 2011, *available at* http://www.guardian.co.uk/world/middle-east-live/2011/may/18/libya-syria-middle-east-unrest.

[167] North Atlantic Treaty Organization, *Press briefing on Libya, supra* note 132.

[168] *Libya: Gaddafi Forces Occupy Hospital, Terrify Patients and Staff*, Human Rights Watch, June 29, 2011, *available at* http://www.hrw.org/en/news/2011/06/29/libya-gaddafi-forces-occupy-hospital-terrify-patients-and-staff.

[169] Report of the International Commission of Inquiry, advance unedited version (Mar. 2, 2012), *supra* note 19 at Annex I, ¶¶ 88 & 583.

[170] Human Rights Watch, *Libya: Gaddafi Forces Occupy Hospital, Terrify Patients and Staff, supra* note 168.

[171] Matt Robinson, *NATO war-lite means Libyan rebels must improvise*, Reuters, May 25, 2011, *available at* http://www.reuters.com/article/2011/05/25/us-libya-westernmountains-idUSTRE74O2T920110525.

had destroyed two tanks and two armored personnel carriers in Yafran in a NATO strike on 2 June.[172]

A *thuwar* spokesperson reported that their forces were engaged in fighting with Qadhafi forces in Trumeet[173] to the south of Yafran and in Bir 'Ayyad.[174] *Thuwar* also reported having taken over Bir 'Ayyad, a road junction that controls access to Yafran from the north.[175]

The four-month stalemate in the Nafusa Mountains region ended in June when the *thuwar* won several battles, including in Yafran.[176] Qadhafi and *thuwar* forces continued to battle along the road between Yafran and Al-Gharyan, although by then the *thuwar* had gained firm control over the Nafusa Mountains region west of Yafran.[177]

The NATO air campaign in the Nafusa Mountains region in May and June 2011 focused on Yafran, Nalut, Al-Gharyan and Zintan.[178] With NATO airstrikes supporting *thuwar* offensives, Qadhafi forces were driven further from Zintan and Yafran.[179] NATO continued to carry out strikes in the area, and on 29 July NATO conducted 124 air sorties, one hitting an anti-aircraft gun in the vicinity of Yafran.[180]

2.7. Al-Qala'

The Amazigh of Al-Qala' had suffered from repression under Qadhafi, and the town's residents quickly joined the uprising against the regime.[181] Clashes erupted in Al-Qala' in mid-March 2011, as Qadhafi forces arrived with heavy artillery, tanks, armored personnel carriers and Grad rockets. Qadhafi forces attempted to enter Al-Qala' on 10 April, and shortly thereafter set up checkpoints to block the town from receiving fuel, food and water supplies.[182] The Qadhafi regime deployed the Khamis Katiba to Al-Qala' on 1 May, and shelled the town from Safiyyat, northwest of Al-Qala',

---

[172] Peter Graff, *China meets Libya rebels in latest blow to Gaddafi*, REUTERS, June 3, 2011, *available at* http://www.reuters.com/article/2011/06/03/us-libya-idUSTRE7270JP20110603.

[173] The transliteration of this place name was adopted from the reference. *Id.*

[174] *Id.*

[175] *Id.*

[176] BELL ET AL., THE TIDE TURNS, *supra* note 1 at 15.

[177] *Press briefing on Libya*, NORTH ATLANTIC TREATY ORGANIZATION, June 10, 2011, *available at* http://www.nato.int/cps/en/natolive/opinions_75263.htm.

[178] *See* Ch. III, Sec. 6.1. *See also* BELL ET AL., THE TIDE TURNS, *supra* note 1 at 15.

[179] BELL ET AL., THE TIDE TURNS, *supra* note 1 at 15.

[180] *Factbox: Latest developments in Libyan conflict*, REUTERS, July 30, 2011, *available at* http://www.reuters.com/article/2011/07/30/us-libya-nato-fb-idUSTRE76T17M20110730.

[181] *See also* Report of the International Commission of Inquiry, advance unedited version (Mar. 2, 2012), *supra* note 19 at Annex I, ¶ 160.

[182] *See* Ch. II, Sec. 3.3. *See also id.*

for four days. On 5 June, Qadhafi forces retreated towards Al-Mil'ab forest, where they used a Boy Scout camp on the edge of Al-Qala' as a military base. There they could hide tanks and rockets from NATO's view. The *thuwar* also reported the use of landmines, antipersonnel and anti-tank mines on roads leading to Al-Qala', which caused civilian casualties.[183] Qadhafi forces reportedly retreated from the area in July.[184]

2.8. *Qawalish*

Qawalish changed hands three times in July 2011. *Thuwar* took control of the town on 6 July from Qadhafi forces who had entered the town earlier that day.[185] The *thuwar* then began to return to their own villages, leaving the town unprotected, and Qadhafi forces easily regained control of the town on 20 July. As *thuwar* moved back to Qawalish from Zintan, Jadu and Kikla, they fought to regain control. Eight persons died as a result of the fighting on 20 July.[186]

Thuwar forces carried out acts of reprisal violence when they entered Qawalish on 6 July. The Mashashiyya tribe's perceived support for the Qadhafi regime incited animosity and revenge attacks from *thuwar* groups.[187] *Thuwar* forces, including members of the Zintan Katiba, pillaged Qawalish and its surrounding villages after pushing out the Qadhafi forces.[188] *Thuwar* beat suspected loyalists and burned their homes.[189]

Fighting continued throughout the conflict and into the post-conflict period. In December 2011, clashes erupted in Wamis near Qawalish (around 150 kilometers/93.3 miles southwest of Tripoli) between the Zintan Katiba

---

[183] *See also* Report of the International Commission of Inquiry, advance unedited version (Mar. 2, 2012), *supra* note 19 at Annex I, ¶ 160.

[184] *Id.* at Annex I, ¶ 161.

[185] BELL ET AL., THE TIDE TURNS, *supra* note 1 at 16.

[186] von Rohr, *Settling Old Scores – Tribal Rivalries Complicate Libyan War*, *supra* note 13; Nick Carey, *WRAPUP 1 – Italy calls for political solution in Libya*, REUTERS, July 11, 2011, *available at* http://www.reuters.com/article/2011/07/11/libya-idUSLDE76A1NC20110711.

[187] BELL ET AL., THE TIDE TURNS, *supra* note 1 at 16.

[188] *Id.*

[189] *See infra* Sec. 3.7. *See also* C.J. Chivers, *Libyan Rebels Accused of Pillage and Beatings*, THE N.Y. TIMES, July 13, 2011, *available at* http://www.nytimes.com/2011/07/13/world/africa/13libya.html; *Libya: Opposition Forces Should Protect Civilians and Hospitals*, HUMAN RIGHTS WATCH, July 13, 2011, *available at* http://www.hrw.org/news/2011/07/13/libya-opposition-forces-should-protect-civilians-and-hospitals.

and members of the Mashashiyya tribe, resulting in four casualties. The exchange involved heavy gunfire and lasted for three days.[190]

The incident prompted former *thuwar* fighters to set up a checkpoint in the area and arrest 20 Mashashiyyans for allegedly having supported Qadhafi. The former *thuwar* fighters from Zintan also tried to disarm the Mashashiyya tribe, which led to the killing of a member of the tribe in Zintan. During another clash with the Mashashiyya in December 2011, former *thuwar* allegedly fired Grad rockets, causing four casualties and 12 injuries.[191]

2.9. Kikla

After Qadhafi forces recaptured Al-Gharyan in early March, Kikla became the frontline of the conflict in the Nafusa Mountains region. On 4 April 2011, Qadhafi forces occupied the village of Kikla, coming within 25 kilometers (15.5 miles) of Yafran and 60 kilometers (37.3 miles) of Zintan.[192] This advance allowed the Qadhafi forces to tighten their control over the region and strengthen the siege effort, cutting the remaining cities off from essential food, medical supplies and electricity.[193] Throughout this period, the residents and rebels of the Nafusa Mountains region relied on rough-terrain mountain crossings to bring in food and medicine supplies from Tunisia. While some supplies were able to pass through these mountain routes, the quantities were insufficient.[194]

2.10. Bir al-Ghanam

On 26 June 2011, *thuwar* forces advanced to the outskirts of Bir al-Ghanam, and on 30 June were reported surveying the strategic town in preparation for an attack. *Thuwar* fighters told reporters that they were waiting for NATO airstrikes to aid their advance.[195] On 6 August, a *thuwar*

---

190 *Yearender: Uncertainties haunt Middle East, North Africa after sweeping unrest*, NEWS XINHUANET, Dec 18, 2011, *available at* http://news.xinhuanet.com/english/world/2011-12/18/c_131313145_2.htm.

191 *4 dead as anti-Gadhafi forces, tribesmen clash*, INQUIRER NEWS, Dec. 13, 2011, *available at* http://newsinfo.inquirer.net/110103/4-dead-as-anti-gadhafi-forces-tribesmen-clash.

192 AMNESTY INTERNATIONAL, LIBYA – DISAPPEARANCES IN THE BESIEGED NAFUSA MOUNTAIN AS THOUSANDS SEEK SAFETY IN TUNISIA, *supra* note 11 at 18.

193 BELL ET AL., THE TIDE TURNS, *supra* note 1 at 16.

194 Lin Noueihed and Tarek Amara, *Libya angers Tunisia as war briefly crosses border*, *supra* note 116; Amara, *Pro-Gaddafi forces clash with Tunisian military*, *supra* note 116.

195 Lutfi Abu-Aun, *Russia: arming Libya rebels is "crude violation"*, REUTERS, June 30, 2011, *available at* http://www.reuters.com/article/2011/06/30/us-libya-idUSTRE7270JP20110630.

spokesperson said Bir al-Ghanam was under rebel control after a clash with Qadhafi forces earlier that day, in which four *thuwar* fighters were killed. *Thuwar* searched the area for regime supporters before moving towards Zawiyya.[196]

Sources provide conflicting accounts of the battle for Bir al-Ghanam, as the Qadhafi regime claimed to drive out rebel forces, and *thuwar* forces claimed to still be in control of the town. According to the *thuwar* they had pushed Qadhafi forces about 10 kilometers (6 miles) northeast of Bir al-Ghanam and were planning to push them further towards the road leading to Zawiyya.[197] By 7 August, this was the closest the *thuwar* had come to Tripoli.[198] Making small gains and capturing small towns near the capital, such as Bir al-Ghanam, was vital for the *thuwar* in ending the stalemate in the Nafusa Mountains region and bringing about an end to the conflict.[199]

2.11. *Al-Gharyan*

In mid- February 2011, protesters and *thuwar* took control of Al-Gharyan, a town that commanded an important location at the edge of the Nafusa Mountains region on the road towards Tripoli. On 25 February, however, Qadhafi forces reclaimed the city, forcing *thuwar* fighters back towards Yafran.[200]

In mid-June, Al-Gharyan was still under the control of Qadhafi forces. *Thuwar* were unable to advance on Al-Gharyan, where regime forces held their ground and launched artillery fire towards *thuwar* controlled cities to the west.[201] Residents reported that fighting took place during the night.[202]

NATO conducted numerous sorties in the area in an effort to aid *thuwar* advances, and on 5 July destroyed two armed vehicles and four

---

[196] *WRAPUP 3 – Libya rebels say they are advancing on Brega*, REUTERS, Aug. 6, 2011, *available at* http://www.reuters.com/article/2011/08/06/libya-idUSLDE77504220110806.

[197] Georgy, *Libya rebels say they hold gains south of capital, supra* note 47.

[198] *Id.*

[199] *Id.*

[200] BELL ET AL., THE TIDE TURNS, *supra* note 1 at 6.

[201] Stephen, *Misrata rebel forces seize arms after routing pro-Gaddafi troops, supra* note 132; BBC, *Libya rebels 'capture key supply route town of Ghazaya', supra* note 86; *Press briefing on Libya*, NORTH ATLANTIC TREATY ORGANIZATION, July 12, 2011, *available at* http://www .nato.int/cps/en/natolive/opinions_76355.htm?selectedLocale=en; BELL ET AL., THE TIDE TURNS, *supra* note 1 at 15.

[202] Carey, *WRAPUP 1 – Libyan rebels take new villges* [sic] *in Western Mountains, supra* note 76.

tanks in the Al-Gharyan area.[203] On 6 July, NATO reported carrying out 140 air sorties, one of which hit an anti-aircraft gun in the vicinity of Al-Gharyan.[204] On 20 August, NATO said it conducted 105 air sorties, one of which targeted the vicinity of Al-Gharyan, hitting an armed vehicle and an anti-aircraft gun.[205]

In mid-August, the *thuwar* fighters launched a direct attack on Al-Gharyan and were able to defeat Qadhafi forces by 15 August.[206] Red, green and black flags were seen in the central square along with a T-34 tank and anti-aircraft gun. Qadhafi forces withdrew from the city towards Al-'Aziziyya.[207] Capturing Al-Gharyan gave the *thuwar* total control of the important corridor between Wazin and Al-Gharyan. It also cut off the regime's major supply lines into southern Libya and prevented any reinforcements moving in from Sabha, one of the few remaining regime strongholds.[208]

After the fall of Tripoli, conflicts between the residents of Al-Gharyan and of the nearby town of Asabiyya became violent. The Al-Gharyan *thuwar* accused Asabiyya fighters of supporting Qadhafi.[209] Al-Gharyan *thuwar* claimed they had been subjected to attacks by Qadhafi forces from Asabiyya during the conflict. In January 2012, a spokesperson for the Al-Gharyan local council, Isma'il al-Ayab, demanded the arrest of the 70 alleged perpetrators of the violations, declaring that if the NTC refused to enforce the arrests, Al-Gharyan *thuwar* would enter Asabiyya.[210]

The clashes between residents of Al-Gharyan and Asabiyya erupted on 14 January 2012.[211] Armed groups from the two towns reportedly used artillery and rockets in ensuring battles. Media accounts reported that *thuwar* used armored personnel carriers and pickup trucks with mounted anti-aircraft

---

[203] *NATO and Libya Operational Media Update for 5 July*, NORTH ATLANTIC TREATY ORGANIZATION, July 6, 2011, *available at* http://www.nato.int/nato_static/assets/pdf/pdf_2011_07/20110706_110706-oup-update.pdf.

[204] *NATO and Libya Operational Media Update for 6 July*, NORTH ATLANTIC TREATY ORGANIZATION, July 7, 2011, *available at* http://www.nato.int/nato_static/assets/pdf/pdf_2011_07/20110707_110707-oup-update.pdf.

[205] *NATO and Libya Operational Media Update for 20 August*, NORTH ATLANTIC TREATY ORGANIZATION, Aug. 21, 2011, *available at* http://www.nato.int/nato_static/assets/pdf/pdf_2011_08/20110821_110821-oup-update.pdf.

[206] REUTERS, *Libya rebels take Garyan, south of Tripoli-witness*, *supra* note 49.

[207] *Id.*

[208] THE GUARDIAN, *Battle for Tripoli: pivotal victory in the mountains helped big push*, *supra* note 2; BELL ET AL., STALEMATE & SIEGE, *supra* note 126 at 28.

[209] Mahmoud Habboush, *Two killed and 36 hurt in Libyan clashes*, REUTERS, Jan. 25, 2012, *available at* http://in.reuters.com/article/2012/01/15/libya-militia-idINDEE80E01020120115.

[210] *Id.*

[211] *Id.*

guns. Media accounts reported that the clashes killed 12 people and caused an estimated 100 injuries.[212]

3. Illustrations of the Violations

3.1. *Excessive Use of Force*

(a) *Qadhafi Forces*

Protests erupted in Zintan, Nalut and Yafran on 16 February, and reports indicate that anti-riot police initially tried to disperse the crowds with tear gas and sticks.[213] According to the CoI, as the protests grew in strength, Qadhafi forces shot and beat civilian protesters at the main Square in central Zintan.[214]

3.2. *Unlawful Killing*

(a) *Qadhafi Forces*

The actions of the Qadhafi forces entailed acts of unlawful killing in the Nafusa Mountains region. Many of the killings were connected to the arbitrary arrest and detention of persons, whose bodies were later found showing signs of summary executions.[215]

The CoI gathered witness testimony and evidence documenting the case of 37 individuals arbitrarily detained in the Nafusa Mountains region and executed by retreating Qadhafi forces at the Boy Scout camp in Al-Qalaʻ.[216] The bodies of 34 men and boys were later exhumed from the site. Their bodies were found blindfolded with their hands tied behind their backs. There were three other bodies lying nearby[217] according to a witness who helped carry out the exhumation process from 20 August to 1 September 2011 and helped family members identify the victims.[218]

---

[212] *Libyan defence minister in restive Bani Walid for talks*, REUTERS, Jan. 25, 2012, *available at* http://www.bbc.co.uk/news/world-africa-16725653.

[213] AMNESTY INTERNATIONAL, LIBYA – DISAPPEARANCES IN THE BESIEGED NAFUSA MOUNTAIN AS THOUSANDS SEEK SAFETY IN TUNISIA, *supra* note 11 at 12.

[214] *See also* Report of the International Commission of Inquiry, advance unedited version (Mar. 2, 2012), *supra* note 19 at Annex I, ¶ 128.

[215] *Id.* at *supra* note 19 at Annex I, ¶ 282.

[216] *See infra* Sec. 3.2 & 3.4. *See also Id.* at Annex I, ¶ 282.

[217] Report of the International Commission of Inquiry, advance unedited version (Mar. 2, 2012), *supra* note 19 at Annex I, ¶ 162.

[218] *Id.*

While witnesses provided some details regarding the officials in command at the site, they were unable to specify to the CoI which military or intelligence units were in charge of the military base at the Boy Scout camp. Witnesses told Human Rights Watch (HRW) during their site visit in September 2011 that most of the soldiers involved belonged to the Popular Guard[219] (Al-Haras al-Sha'bi).[220] Other witnesses who had been detained reported that Military Intelligence officers were present, including members of the External Security Agency (ESA) who had lists of people suspected of being in contact with anti-Qadhafi elements in Tunisia.[221]

In addition to extrajudicial killings, the use of heavy artillery and indiscriminate shelling carried out by Qadhafi forces in the Nafusa Mountains region also led to civilian casualties. There were 55 casualties, including women and children, reported in Zintan during the siege and shelling of the city. The CoI viewed a number of hospital records that listed the cause of death listed as "Grad rocket shrapnel."[222]

Amnesty International reported that Grad rockets were fired into Nalut, Zintan and Yafran, and the surrounding villages of Al-Qala', Al-Rujban, Jadu, Kikla and Takut. Several houses were destroyed killing civilians inside.[223] Similarly, the CoI reported that in the beginning of April 2011 the region suffered heavy shelling with little distinction being made between civilian and military targets. One witness recounted a bombardment in Kikla that resulted in at least 11 civilian casualties, including women and children.[224]

The CoI also received reports that towards the end of April 2011 an ambulance that was on its way to evacuate wounded persons was shot at by an 14.5mm anti-aircraft gun, killing one of the medical staff on board.[225]

---

[219] This unit is also referred to as the "Civil Guard." *See* Ch. II, Sec. 2.2.

[220] *Libya: Mass Grave Yields 34 Bodies*, HUMAN RIGHTS WATCH, Sept. 14, 2011, *available at* http://www.hrw.org/news/2011/09/14/libya-mass-grave-yields-34-bodies.

[221] *Id.*

[222] Report of the International Commission of Inquiry, advance unedited version (Mar. 2, 2012), *supra* note 19 at Annex I, ¶ 569.

[223] AMNESTY INTERNATIONAL, LIBYA – DISAPPEARANCES IN THE BESIEGED NAFUSA MOUNTAIN AS THOUSANDS SEEK SAFETY IN TUNISIA, *supra* note 11 at 7–8.

[224] Report of the International Commission of Inquiry to investigate all the alleged violations of international human rights law in the Libyan Arab Jamahiriya, U.N. HRC. 17th Sess., ¶ 154. U.N. Doc. A/HRC/17/44 (Jan. 12, 2012).

[225] Report of the International Commission of Inquiry, advance unedited version (Mar. 2, 2012), *supra* note 19 at Annex I, ¶ 595.

(b) Thuwar *Forces*

The CoI documented incidents of *thuwar* forces carrying out killings, including executions, against perceived regime loyalists, Sub-Saharan Africans suspected of being mercenaries and captured Qadhafi soldiers. Many documented cases occurred in the period directly after the *thuwar* took control of a city or territory.[226]

A mass grave was found in a water tank between Zintan and Qawalish in mid- July 2011. Media reports from 13 July indicate that evidence surrounding the grave suggested a rushed operation to dispose of the victims. The corpses showed signs of mistreatment; one had been decapitated, another had his trousers pulled down to his ankles and some had their arms or legs bound. The corpses bore the green uniforms worn by Qadhafi fighters. Several pistol and rifle cartridges were found close by.[227]

At the time of the discovery, *thuwar* commanders claimed that Qadhafi soldiers were responsible for the killings. The identities of the men were never discovered, however, and media accounts reported that *thuwar* authorities in the area obstructed attempts to identify the victims. The area was reportedly bulldozed and the bodies disappeared. Allegations surfaced that locals were ordered by *thuwar* not to take journalists to the site.[228]

The CoI documented other incidents of the deaths of detainees resulting from abuse or shootings. These deaths occurred in detention facilities under the control of various kata'ib, along with local *thuwar* councils and committees in a number of cities, including Zintan.[229] The CoI spoke with a witness who had been detained at the Zintan post office, which had been converted into a detention center. His cellmate had been shot and killed in detention by a *thuwar* fighter who was allegedly seeking revenge against detainees suspected of being Qadhafi loyalists.[230]

---

[226] *Id.* at 204.

[227] Chivers, *Libyan Rebels Accused of Pillage and Beatings, supra* note 189; Ruth Sherlock, *The headless corpse, the mass grave and worrying questions about Libya's rebel army,* THE TELEGRAPH, July 20, 2011, *available at* http://www.telegraph.co.uk/news/worldnews/africaandindianocean/libya/8650436/The-headless-corpse-the-mass-grave-and-worrying-questions-about-Libyas-rebel-army.html.

[228] *Id.*

[229] Report of the International Commission of Inquiry, advance unedited version (Mar. 2, 2012), *supra* note 19 at Annex I, ¶ 205.

[230] *Id.* at Annex I, ¶ 233.

Amnesty International also documented cases of extrajudicial killings by *thuwar*, including deaths in custody well into the post-conflict period.[231] On 14 January 2012, a former army colonel was detained by armed men based in Al-Gharyan, and was reported dead the next day. The forensic examination indicated that he had been tortured and that he died from his injuries; among the signs of torture was the removal of his fingernails.[232] Another incident took place on 14 April near Al-Gharyan when a man was arrested along with his three cousins and detained at Al-Thamna detention center where they were reportedly subjected to abuse and torture. On 27 May, the man's body turned up at the morgue with a gunshot wound to the head.[233]

i. *Residents of Tiji and Badr*

The CoI documented extrajudicial killings in Badr after *thuwar* took over the town in August 2011. On 17 August, *thuwar* from Nalut reportedly killed three brothers in Badr.[234] Civilian casualties were also reported in Tiji as a result of Grad rockets fired by *thuwar* groups from Nalut in October 2011.[235] A Tiji resident stated that shelling took place on 1 October, killing his sister-in-law and injuring other family members.[236] In another incident, a shell struck a house and led to the death of two women and injured three others in the house, including a nine-year-old boy.[237] The CoI documented evidence of the attacks, and observed that burning from the rocket fire was still visible in the town after the assaults.[238]

ii. *The Mashashiyyans*

Reports indicate that *thuwar* targeted members of the Mashashiyya community after gaining control of different cities, resulting in civilian casualties. *Thuwar* from Zintan reportedly targeted residents as they entered Zawiyyat al-Bajul in May 2011 and Awaniyya in July 2011, leading to killings

---

[231] AMNESTY INTERNATIONAL, MILITIAS THREATEN HOPES FOR NEW LIBYA (Feb. 16, 2012), *available at* http://www.amnesty.org/en/library/asset/MDE19/002/2012/en/dd7c1d69-e368-44de-8ee8-cc9365bd5eb3/mde19002012en.pdf.

[232] *Id.* at 28.

[233] AMNESTY INTERNATIONAL, LIBYA: RULE OF LAW OR RULE OF MILITIAS? 25 (July 2012), *available at* http://www.amnesty.org/en/library/asset/MDE19/012/2012/en/f2d36090-5716-4ef1-81a7-f4b1ebdo82fc/mde190122012en.pdf.

[234] Report of the International Commission of Inquiry, advance unedited version (Mar. 2, 2012), *supra* note 19 at Annex I, ¶ 463.

[235] *Id.* at ¶ 61.

[236] *Id.* at Annex I, ¶ 740.

[237] *Id.* at Annex I, ¶ 465.

[238] *Id.* at ¶ 61.

in these towns. On 7 May, an 82 year-old Mashashiyyan man from Zawi-yyat al-Bajul was shot dead in his home, reportedly by *thuwar* from Zintan. Witnesses told the CoI that two Mashashiyyan brothers were shot at close range after being captured by Zintan *thuwar*.[239] Mashashiyyan leaders provided the names of 20 people killed from their community. The CoI, however, was unable to confirm the circumstances of all the deaths.[240]

3.3. *Arbitrary Detentions and Enforced Disappearances*

(a) *Qadhafi Forces*

There is extensive documentation of arbitrary detention and enforced disappearances carried out by the Qadhafi forces in the Nafusa Mountains region. Witnesses reported the Qadhafi forces used the practice as a form of intimidation, using the threat of abduction as a warning to residents against aligning with the *thuwar* in the region. Witnesses reported that the use of checkpoints by Qadhafi forces was the most common method used to detain civilians in the area.[241] Detentions took place at checkpoints surrounding Zintan, for example.[242]

Amnesty International also reported on the use of checkpoints by Qadhafi forces to arrest civilians on suspicion of having participated in early protests.[243] Amnesty International documented the arrest of civilians who left *thuwar* controlled cities and villages to buy food or basic necessities. Some were arrested on their way to Tripoli, and the relatives of these victims believed they were taken to detention facilities in the capital, such as 'Ain Zara Prison. Some of these individuals subsequently appeared on Libyan state television making confessions.[244]

Abductions were carried out on the basis of perceived support for the rebel movement. The CoI interviewed a man whose cousin was abducted by Qadhafi forces from Nalut on 18 March 2011. He said that his cousin had

---

[239] *Id.* at Annex I, ¶ 221.

[240] Report of the International Commission of Inquiry, advance unedited version (Mar. 2, 2012), *supra* note 19 at Annex I, ¶ 454.

[241] Report of the International Commission of Inquiry (Jan. 12, 2012), *supra* note 224 at ¶ 98.

[242] Report of the International Commission of Inquiry, advance unedited version (Mar. 2, 2012), *supra* note 19 at Annex I, ¶ 129.

[243] AMNESTY INTERNATIONAL, LIBYA – DISAPPEARANCES IN THE BESIEGED NAFUSA MOUNTAIN AS THOUSANDS SEEK SAFETY IN TUNISIA, *supra* note 11 at 12.

[244] *Id.* at 14.

been arrested for expressing pro-*thuwar* views, but had not participated in the hostilities.[245]

Due to the nature of the practice of abductions and secret detentions, it is difficult to determine the exact number of people who disappeared during the conflict. The CoI received a list of 110 disappeared persons who were detained in the Nafusa Mountains region.[246] The CoI carried out over 50 interviews in refugee camps in Tunisia with eyewitnesses and family members of victims. They reported that a large number of persons had been disappeared since mid-February 2011.[247] As the CoI reported

> One interviewee told the Commission that hundreds of residents of the Nafusa Mountain area have disappeared as of mid-February throughout March and April 2011. He stated that his cousin from Yafran District and his friend from Jado District disappeared in March 2011. None of them had been [carrying] weapons.[248]

Witnesses also told the CoI that Qadhafi forces entered hospitals in Zintan and detained people who had been injured during the protests and early fighting.[249]

(b) Thuwar *Forces*

After the retreat of the Qadhafi forces, the *thuwar* carried out detentions on a large-scale in cities and towns throughout the Nafusa Mountains region. Amnesty International documented several cases of arbitrary arrest in Al-Gharyan during the final months of fighting and into the post-conflict period. On 13 October 2011, a man was stopped in his car at a checkpoint near Al-Gharyan and detained for three months by two different armed militias.[250] On 13 January 2012, armed men arrested a university student along with his brother at a checkpoint near Al-Gharyan. The two men were taken to the base of a local armed group in Al-Thamna, and released three days later without charge.[251]

---

245 Report of the International Commission of Inquiry (Jan. 12, 2012), *supra* note 224 at ¶ 103.

246 *Id.* at ¶ 99.

247 *Id.* at ¶¶ 90 & 100.

248 *Id.* at ¶ 103.

249 Report of the International Commission of Inquiry, advance unedited version (Mar. 2, 2012), *supra* note 19 at Annex I, ¶¶ 21 & 128.

250 Amnesty International, Libya: Rule of Law or Rule of Militias?, *supra* note 233 at 20.

251 *Id.*

The CoI visited local detention facilities in Zintan in January 2012 that were under the control of *thuwar* and local officials, and documented numerous cases of detainees held without proper cause.[252] A former Qadhafi soldier reported that he had been arrested along with 30 others in Tripoli, and sent to Zintan's Al-Barid prison for interrogation. There was no evidence against him, but his time in detention was extended due to his previous service in the Qadhafi military.[253]

i. *Residents of Tiji and Badr*

In the aftermath of the fall of the Qadhafi regime, *thuwar* forces detained individuals and members of tribes they accused of having aligned with the Qadhafi regime.[254]

In a practice that resembled that of the Qadhafi forces, *thuwar* from Nalut established checkpoints around the town of Tiji in October 2011, detaining civilians and taking them to the "Criminal Investigations building in Nalut."[255] Witnesses provided accounts of *thuwar* from Nalut attacking Tiji and Badr on 1 October 2011 carrying out widespread arrests in the towns.[256] The victims reported to the CoI that they were held for two to five days and suffered abuse in detention.[257] The Tiji local council compiled a list of 41 men detained on 1 October.[258]

ii. *The Mashashiyyans*

Thuwar from Zintan reportedly entered Zawiyyat al-Bajul in May 2011 and Awaniyya in July 2011, arresting local men, and targeting in particular members of the Mashashiyya community. One interviewee told the CoI he was detained by Zintan *thuwar* as he was driving with four others. They were then taken to a former police station where he was subjected to torture.[259] Mashashiyyan leaders gave the CoI lists of names of 13 people injured or beaten and of 26 people who remained in detention in Zintan.[260]

---

[252] Report of the International Commission of Inquiry, advance unedited version (Mar. 2, 2012), *supra* note 19 at Annex I, ¶ 308.

[253] *Id.* at Annex I, ¶ 309.

[254] AMNESTY INTERNATIONAL, MILITIAS THREATEN HOPES FOR NEW LIBYA, *supra* note 231 at 34.

[255] Report of the International Commission of Inquiry, advance unedited version (Mar. 2, 2012), *supra* note 19 at Annex I, ¶ 466.

[256] The Commission does not specify in which town the arrests took place. Report of the International Commission of Inquiry, advance unedited version (Mar. 2, 2012), *supra* note 19 at Annex I, ¶ 739.

[257] *Id.* at Annex I, ¶ 311.

[258] *Id.* at Annex I, ¶ 466.

[259] *Id.* at Annex I, ¶ 310.

[260] *Id.* at Annex I, ¶ 454.

3.4. *Torture and Other Forms of Ill-treatment*

(a) *Qadhafi Forces*

The CoI, Amnesty International and HRW documented cases of torture and other forms of ill-treatment at the Boy Scout camp located near Al-Qala' and Qawalish. A number of detainees were tortured at the base by Qadhafi forces. A nurse interviewed by the CoI said he was arrested at a hospital at Yafran and taken to the Boy Scouts base, where he was blindfolded, beaten and electrocuted.[261]

The CoI spoke to former detainees at the Boy Scout base who provided information on their detention, and reported that

> One told the Commission that he and three others had been arrested on 25 May 2011, while out searching for food in empty houses to bring back to the town. Four soldiers had arrested them and beat them with wooden sticks, military belts and the butts of their rifles. Their hands were tied behind their backs and they were blindfolded, before being taken to the scouts' base. After further interrogation, they were put in a room with 13 others...The detained said that those he was arrested with and those he was detained with were all amongst those later executed.[262]

HRW also documented cases of torture and ill-treatment at the Boy Scout base. One of the detainees stated that he observed two brothers being severely beaten, one whose leg was broken in order to coerce a confession from their father. One man was tied up and beaten with a heavy wooden stick on his leg while his brother was abused at the same time in the next room. According to the witness accounts, their bodies were later found among those buried at the Boy Scouts camp.[263]

Medical staff were also subject to detention and torture by Qadhafi forces. A nurse who worked in a hospital in Yafran reported to the CoI that he was detained in May 2011 by Qadhafi forces for having treated injured *thuwar*. He was taken to a local base outside of Yafran, where he was beaten before being transferred along with others to another military camp.[264]

---

[261] *Id.* at Annex I, ¶ 592.

[262] Report of the International Commission of Inquiry, advance unedited version (Mar. 2, 2012), *supra* note 19 at Annex I, ¶ 164 (internal citations omitted).

[263] HUMAN RIGHTS WATCH, *Libya: Mass Grave Yields 34 Bodies, supra* note 220.

[264] Report of the International Commission of Inquiry, advance unedited version (Mar. 2, 2012), *supra* note 19 at Annex I, ¶ 283.

(b) Thuwar *Forces*

The CoI visited the local prison in Zintan and the Manara detention
facility, and documented incidents of abuses carried out by *thuwar*
forces.[265] Amnesty International also reported widespread torture by *thuwar*. Amnesty International visited detention centers in in Al-Gharyan in
January–February and May–June 2012.[266] The facilities included official
prisons and detention centers run by *thuwar* and semi-official security
and military installations.[267] Amnesty International found evidence that
some of the detainees died in detention as a result of torture.[268]

Amnesty International reported that in Al-Gharyan at least nine men
were subjected to torture. Eight had to seek medical treatment for serious injuries. One victim stated that he had been made to kneel facing
the wall with his hands cuffed behind his back, and repeatedly hit by
different people with a metal chain, plastic hose, electric cables and a
metal bar. He said other detainees had been beaten more severely than
he was, and that at least one of them had had some of his fingernails
pulled out.[269]

Amnesty International interviewed eight victims from Asabiyya who
had been detained in Al-Gharyan. They described being beaten for prolonged periods with various instruments, including belts, water pipes and
electric cables, being suspended from metal bars, and receiving electric
shocks.[270] One of the victims from Asabiyya reported being detained on
13 October 2011 at a checkpoint near Al-Gharyan. He was abused, given
electric shocks with live wires, and denied food and water. His abuse continued into November.[271]

---

[265] *Id.* at Annex I, ¶¶ 308–311.
[266] The first visit included detention centers in Tripoli, Zawiyya, Misrata, and Sirte. The
second visit included detention centers in Zawiyya, Benghazi, Kufra, Tripoli and surrounding areas, and Sabha.
[267] AMNESTY INTERNATIONAL, LIBYA: RULE OF LAW OR RULE OF MILITIAS?, *supra* note
233 at 12.
[268] *Document – Libya: Militias threaten hopes for new Libya*, AMNESTY INTERNATIONAL,
available at http://www.amnesty.org/en/library/asset/MDE19/002/2012/en/608ac5a8-95d0-
4a3b-89de-b4a1b585feee/_Toc317144515.
[269] AMNESTY INTERNATIONAL, MILITIAS THREATEN HOPES FOR NEW LIBYA, *supra* note
231 at 28.
[270] AMNESTY INTERNATIONAL, LIBYA: RULE OF LAW OR RULE OF MILITIAS?, *supra* note
233 at 20.
[271] *Id.*

In February 2012, the Libyan government acknowledged that torture was taking place in detention centers throughout Libya but that the central authorities were not yet capable of stopping it.[272]

i. *Sub-Saharan Africans*

On 10 May, the United Nations special envoy for Libya, Ian Martin, presented his findings to the United Nations Security Council and voiced concern that *thuwar* were torturing detainees, many of whom were Sub-Saharan Africans suspected of having fought alongside Qadhafi forces. While Misrata was the main city of concern, Martin also noted that torture was taking place in detention centers in Zintan.[273]

Amnesty International found that most of the detainees interviewed in detention centers around Al-Gharyan were suspected of having fought for Qadhafi during the war. The detentions centers held hundreds of foreign nationals, mostly Sub-Saharan Africans, some of whom claimed to have been tortured.[274] A man from Mali reported being detained in March 2012 by armed men and taken to a militia base near Al-Gharyan that held other foreign nationals. The man suffered abuse, including the use of electric wires, and was accused of being a mercenary. He was later moved to the Bu Rashada holding center in Al-Gharyan.[275]

ii. *Residents of Tiji and Badr*

Witnesses stated that when *thuwar* from Nalut attacked Tiji and Badr on 1 October 2011, 41 residents were detained, several of whom were subjected to torture and ill-treatment.[276] The CoI stated that

> The Commission has received reports of men from Tiji being beaten with rifle butts and kicked while in detention there. According to the testimony received, the Nalut *thuwar* beat him about the face and told the five men that they were 'Arab dogs' and that 'this is not your land'. One

---

[272] Anthony Shadid, *Libya Struggles to Curb Militias as Chaos Grows*, N.Y. TIMES, Feb. 8, 2012, *available at* http://www.nytimes.com/2012/02/09/world/africa/libyas-new-govern ment-unable-to-control-militias.html.

[273] *See* Ch. V, Sec. 2.3. *See also* U.N. SC, 67th year, 6768 mtg, U.N. Doc. S/PV.6768 (May 10, 2012) at 5; Michelle Nichols, *U.N. says three Libya prisoners likely tortured to death*, REUTERS, May 10, 2012, *available at* http://www.reuters.com/article/2012/05/10/us-libya-un idUSBRE8491LK20120510.

[274] AMNESTY INTERNATIONAL, *Document – Libya: Militias threaten hopes for new Libya*, *supra* note 268.

[275] AMNESTY INTERNATIONAL, LIBYA: RULE OF LAW OR RULE OF MILITIAS?, *supra* note 233 at 38.

[276] Report of the International Commission of Inquiry, advance unedited version (Mar. 2, 2012), *supra* note 19 at Annex I, ¶ 739.

interviewee told the Commission that he was beaten with electric batons while being told that he and his community should leave Tiji.[277]

iii. *The Mashashiyyans*

The CoI documented cases of torture carried out against Mashashiyyan detainees in detention facilities controlled by Zintan *thuwar*, reporting that

> One Mashashiyan, a former member of the Qadhafi forces, was arrested and taken to a detention centre in Zintan. There, according to his testimony to the Commission he was beaten by hand, plastic hoses, metal bars and wooden sticks all over his body and head. At some point he was suspended by his tied hands to the door. The same interviewee indicated he knew of other Mashashiyans who had been tortured while held in the detention centre in Zintan.[278]

Another interviewee told the CoI that he was arrested by Zintan *thuwar* while driving with four other individuals and brought to the former police station where he and the others were subjected to beatings, insults and electric shocks.[279]

Amnesty International also provided reports corroborating that *thuwar*, and in particular from the Zintan Katiba, tortured Mashashiyyans while in detention.[280]

3.5. *Denial of Access to Medical Treatment*

(a) *Qadhafi Forces*

The occupation of the hospital in Yafran is the most prominent case of Qadhafi forces denying access to medical treatment during the military campaign in the Nafusa Mountains region. After entering the hospital in late April 2011, Qadhafi forces remained until early June. During the occupation, Qadhafi forces set up its headquarters and caused extensive damage to the facility. One of the military units present, the Popular

---

[277] *Id.* at Annex I, ¶ 467.

[278] *Id.* at Annex I, ¶ 455.

[279] *Id.* at Annex I, ¶ 310.

[280] For more on the torture of Mashashiyya by the Zintan *thuwar* in the capital *see infra* Sec. 3.3 & 3.4. *See also* MILITIAS THREATEN HOPES FOR NEW LIBYA, AMNESTY INTERNATIONAL, *supra* note 231 at 34; AMNESTY INTERNATIONAL, *Document – Libya: Militias threaten hopes for new Libya*, *supra* note 268. For more on the practice of torture and ill-treatment in other cities, *see* Ch. V, Sec. 2.4.

Guard, reportedly beat a man in intensive care, and stationed military vehicles on hospital grounds.[281]

There were also reports of Qadhafi forces blocking access to medical treatment in the early days of the uprising. An interviewee from Zintan stated that on the night of 21 February 2011, Qadhafi forces invaded hospitals, abducted patients and killed others.[282] A doctor from Zintan further noted that the wounded persons who were treated at his hospital were not registered out of fear that the Qadhafi forces would regain control and detain the injured.[283]

3.6. *Freedom of Expression*

(a) *Qadhafi Forces*

During a visit to Al-Jadayda detention center, the CoI interviewed a Tunisian-Canadian journalist and correspondent for a Canadian newspaper who had been arrested on 17 March 2011 after crossing into Libya through the Wazin-Dhehiba crossing, southeast of Tunisia. He was released on 19 May, having spent over 60 days in prison.[284]

Four Al Jazeera journalists were also arrested in early March 2011 in Zintan as they tried to leave Libya en route to Tunisia. They were Ahmad Fal Wald al-Din, a correspondent from Mauritania, Lutfi al-Massudi, a correspondent from Tunisia, 'Ammar al-Hamdan, a cameraman from Norway, and 'Ammar al-Tallu, a cameraman from the United Kingdom.[285]

3.7. *Attacks on Civilians, Civilian Objects, Protected Persons and Objects*

3.7.1. *Deliberate and Indiscriminate Attacks on Civilians and Civilian Objects*

(a) *Qadhafi Forces*

The military tactics of the Qadhafi forces in the Nafusa Mountains region involved assaults on civilian areas that resulted in significant harm to the civilian populations. The attacks were carried out through

---

[281] Report of the International Commission of Inquiry, advance unedited version (Mar. 2, 2012), *supra* note 19 at Annex I, ¶¶ 584–585.

[282] Report of the International Commission of Inquiry (Jan. 12, 2012), *supra* note 224 at ¶ 127.

[283] *Id.* at ¶ 168.

[284] *Id.* at ¶ 136.

[285] *Libya: Free Detained Journalists*, HUMAN RIGHTS WATCH, Mar. 24, 2011, *available at* http://www.hrw.org/news/2011/03/23/libya-free-detained-journalists.

the use of indiscriminate weapons and heavy artillery, as well as through siege tactics that blocked essential supplies from reaching civilian populations.

Towns in the Nafusa Mountains region under the control of the *thuwar* sustained heavy artillery shelling from Qadhafi forces. The most extensive damage was observed in Yafran, which was occupied by Qadhafi forces between 18 April and the first week of June 2011.[286] The CoI reported that

> There were reportedly 200–250 *thuwar* in Yafran, although not all were participating in the hostilities...The Commission also observed heavy damage to the secondary school. Members of the *thuwar* at the time told the Commission that they used the upper floor of the school as an observation point at night and that this attracted fire from the Qadhafi forces stationed opposite. The Commission was provided with a list of 312 houses shelled. No civilians died during the bombardment as most families had evacuated. The shelling finally ceased once Qadhafi forces retreated to Bir-al-Ghanem in July, by which time Yafran was out of range.[287]

Much of the population had already fled Yafran. As *thuwar* used schools and other civilian buildings in Yafran and Nalut to hold positions, these buildings could be considered to be military in character, and thus their targeting would not necessarily violate international law.[288] However, the nature of the weaponry used by the Qadhafi forces, particularly from long distances, makes it impossible to hit specific targets without large scale collateral damage. Due to the lack of any guidance system the Grad rocket is inherently indiscriminate. The CoI noted that the attacks had a disproportionate effect on the civilian population in the region.[289]

In May 2011, Qadhafi forces fired Grad rockets and mortars at the cities of Wazin and Zintan, then under *thuwar* control. The long distance attacks hit residential neighborhoods, causing significant damage to civilian objects, including homes, mosques, a school and severe damage to a hospital.[290] The attacks also led to civilian deaths and injuries, and

---

[286] Report of the International Commission of Inquiry, advance unedited version (Mar. 2, 2012), *supra* note 19 at ¶ 76.

[287] *Id.* at Annex I, ¶ 572 (internal citations omitted).

[288] *Id.* at Annex I, ¶ 574.

[289] Report of the International Commission of Inquiry (Jan. 12, 2012), *supra* note 224 at ¶ 152.

[290] *Syria, Libya and Middle East unrest*, THE GUARDIAN, May 9, 2011, *available at* http://www.guardian.co.uk/world/middle-east-live/2011/may/09/syria-libya-middle-east-unrest-live.

Qadhafi forces reportedly employed snipers in civilian areas in Zintan.[291] In general, as the conflict progressed and Qadhafi forces retreated to Al-Gharyan these attacks against cities in the Nafusa Mountains region were launched from greater distances with less precision, turning potentially targeted attacks into indiscriminate ones. Both Amnesty International and HRW made statements about long distance shelling and the use of inherently indiscriminate weapons such as Grad rockets and mortars.[292] After observing the three towns of Nalut, Yafran and Zintan, the CoI noted that

> The damage was consistent with sustained bombardment over a period of weeks by a mixture of Grad rockets, tank fire and artillery. The rockets were unguided, and thus – when used in a built-up area amongst civilian houses and other buildings – would be difficult to aim only at military targets…[293]

Amnesty International also reported that Qadhafi forces fired Grad rockets into Nalut, Zintan and Yafran, as well as the surrounding villages of Al-Qala', Al-Rujban, Jadu, Kikla, Nalut and Takut.[294] HRW reported after visiting Zintan that the town was severely damaged from Grad rocket attacks by Qadhafi forces. HRW investigators documented damage to private homes, a mosque, a school and other parts of the town. HRW also noted that their observers did not witness any valid military targets in the area.[295]

In addition to the heavy shelling, the sieges enforced on the cities in the Nafusa Mountains region led to suffering among the civilian population. The Qadhafi forces set up checkpoints that prevented essential food supplies and medicine from reaching residents.[296] Inhabitants of the region were blocked from accessing essential supplies from March to May 2011, causing a humanitarian crisis.[297] Without being able to access goods from

---

[291] *Libya: MSF Forced To Evacuate from Zintan*, MÉDECINS SANS FRONTIERS, May 27, 2011, *available at* http://www.doctorswithoutborders.org/press/release.cfm?id=5287.

[292] AMNESTY INTERNATIONAL, LIBYA – DISAPPEARANCES IN THE BESIEGED NAFUSA MOUNTAIN AS THOUSANDS SEEK SAFETY IN TUNISIA, *supra* note 11 at 7–8; HUMAN RIGHTS WATCH, *Libya: End Indiscriminate Attacks in Western Mountain Towns, supra* note 68.

[293] Report of the International Commission of Inquiry, advance unedited version (Mar. 2, 2012), *supra* note 19 at Annex I, ¶ 573.

[294] AMNESTY INTERNATIONAL, LIBYA – DISAPPEARANCES IN THE BESIEGED NAFUSA MOUNTAIN AS THOUSANDS SEEK SAFETY IN TUNISIA, *supra* note 11 at 14.

[295] HUMAN RIGHTS WATCH, *Libya: Rocket Attacks on Western Mountain Towns, supra* note 17.

[296] Report of the International Commission of Inquiry, advance unedited version (Mar. 2, 2012), *supra* note 19 at Annex I, ¶ 563.

[297] Sen, *Gadhafi lays siege to west mountain town, supra* note 66.

the outside, civilians in *thuwar* areas were subject to a policy of attrition and collective punishment.[298]

During the first half of April 2011, most media attention was focused on Misrata and Ajdabiya, leaving most of the incidents in the Nafusa Mountains region at the time unreported. The witness accounts from refugees in Tunisia, however, provide extensive documentation of the shelling attacks by Qadhafi forces in the region.[299] The estimated number of displaced persons from the Nafusa Mountains region varies. The United Nations reported that it registered an estimated 40,000 refugees fleeing the Nafusa Mountains region into Tunisia. HRW reported that according to the *thuwar* in the region, 30,000 people fled to Tunisia during the conflict.[300] In late April 2011, the UNHCR reported that 30,000 people had fled the Nafusa Mountains region for Tunisia during the three previous weeks, leaving the towns of Nalut and Wazin almost deserted.[301]

(b) Thuwar *Forces*

The use of civilian objects by *thuwar* in some instances may have encouraged further attacks by Qadhafi forces against civilian objects. For example, the decision by *thuwar* forces to use schools and mosques in Yafran and Zintan to take refuge and fire on Qadhafi troops, could have led to retaliatory actions from the regime forces.[302]

i. *Sub-Saharan Africans*

The CoI reported that in February 2011, after taking control of Zintan, *thuwar* forced carried out reprisal attacks against captured Qadhafi fighters. Sub-Saharan migrant workers, suspected of serving as mercenaries in the Qadhafi forces, were particularly targeted for beatings and ill-treatment.[303]

ii. *Residents of Tiji and Badr*

On 15 August 2011, *thuwar* from Nalut gained control over Tiji, as Qadhafi forces withdrew back from the town. According to witness and victim accounts, many Tiji residents fled before the arrival of the *thuwar* from Nalut, while men who still remained within the town were reportedly

---

[298] CNN, *Rebel forces in Libya's western mountains issue call for help, supra* note 119.

[299] REUTERS, *Thousands of Libyans flee remote western area: report, supra* note 71.

[300] HUMAN RIGHTS WATCH, *Libya: Rocket Attacks on Western Mountain Towns, supra* note 17.

[301] *WRAPUP 1-Deadlock in Libya exposes international rifts*, REUTERS, Apr. 26, 2011, *available at* http://www.reuters.com/article/2011/04/26/libya-idUSLDE73P20220110426.

[302] Report of the International Commission of Inquiry, advance unedited version (Mar. 2, 2012), *supra* note 19 at Annex I, ¶ 564.

[303] *Id.* at Annex I, ¶ 81.

beaten. *Thuwar* forces carried out acts of pillaging and vandalizing of houses and public buildings.[304] Witnesses also reported that *thuwar* from Nalut attacked Tiji and Badr on 1 October 2011, looted the town, and set properties on fire.[305] The Tiji local council made a complaint to the NTC and listed 323 persons who had reported their cars as stolen or destroyed.[306]

iii. *The Mashashiyyans*

Thuwar from the Nafusa Mountains region attacked members of the Mashashiyya tribe in retaliation for their support of the Qadhafi regime both during and after the conflict.[307] The incidents of abuse involved attacking civilians by looting and burning the towns and villages of tribes that remained loyal to the regime during the war. In particular, *thuwar* from Zuwara (described as anti-Qadhafi militias by HRW) allegedly looted property as compensation for damage they suffered during the war.[308] The CoI was able to confirm reports that Mashashiyyan towns were looted and their property burnt. Mashashiyyans who attempted to return to their homes, either to collect belongings or in an effort to return permanently, were reportedly beaten and/or denied passage at checkpoints managed by Zintan *thuwar*.[309]

Media outlets provided similar stories of how Awaniyya was looted and burned, describing shops and houses empty and ransacked, and some completely burned down.[310] Zawiyyat al-Bajul was similarly pillaged, with public and private properties ransacked and burned in May and July 2011.[311]

---

[304] *Id.* at Annex I, ¶ 463.

[305] *Id.* at Annex I, ¶ 739.

[306] *Id.* at Annex I, ¶ 469.

[307] AMNESTY INTERNATIONAL, MILITIAS THREATEN HOPES FOR NEW LIBYA, Doc., *supra* note 231; *Libyan militias accused of torturing detainees*, THE GUARDIAN, Feb. 16, 2012, *available at* http://www.guardian.co.uk/world/2012/feb/16/libyan-militias-detainee-torture-amnesty-international.

[308] Daniel Williams, *The Murder Brigades of Misrata*, HUMAN RIGHTS WATCH, Oct. 28, 2011, *available at* http://www.hrw.org/news/2011/10/28/murder-brigades-misrata.

[309] Report of the International Commission of Inquiry, advance unedited version (Mar. 2, 2012), *supra* note 19 at Annex I, ¶ 457.

[310] von Rohr, *Settling Old Scores – Tribal Rivalries Complicate Libyan War*, *supra* note 13.

[311] Report of the International Commission of Inquiry, advance unedited version (Mar. 2, 2012), *supra* note 19 at Annex I, ¶ 456; *Libya: Contact Group Should Press Rebels to Protect Civilians*, HUMAN RIGHTS WATCH, July 15, 2011, *available at* http://www.hrw.org/news/2011/07/15/libya-contact-group-should-press-rebels-protect-civilians.

Amnesty International reported that members of the Mashashiyya and Qawalish tribes where targeted by armed groups, particularly from Zintan, because of their suspected support for Qadhafi forces during the conflict.[312] HRW also reported that *thuwar* ransacked and pillaged Qawalish, Awaniyya, Rayaniyya and Zawiyyat al-Bajul in July 2011. During visits to these towns in early July, HRW found that *thuwar* had vandalized medical clinics and local hospitals, and taken medical equipment from the facilities. However, according to Colonel El-Muktar Firnana, a rebel military commander in the Nafusa Mountains region, these attacks violated orders issued to the *thuwar* forces not to attack civilians or damage civilian property.[313]

HRW urged the NTC authorities to put an end to the attacks, especially in the villages of Umm al-Jirsan and Qawalish, which had been particularly targeted by *thuwar*.[314] Qawalish and Awaniyya were left deserted and witnessed the looting and ransacking of shops, schools and homes.[315] HRW reported that Colonel Firnana stated that the attacks were reprisals for the victims' alleged support for Qadhafi forces. He also claimed the actions were not sanctioned, and that some of the perpetrators had been punished.[316]

3.7.2. *Attacks on Cultural Objects and Places of Worship*

(a) *Qadhafi Forces*

There were documented incidents of Qadhafi forces destroying buildings of cultural or religious importance. The CoI reported that the Ben Niran Palace, a place of cultural significance for the Amazigh community, was destroyed in early April 2011.[317]

Media accounts reported that Qadhafi forces hit a Zintan mosque with artillery fire in May 2011.[318] In Yafran, the CoI noted damage from fire to

---

[312] For a witness statement collected by Amnesty International reporting arbitrary arrest and torture, *see infra* Sec. 3.4. *See also* AMNESTY INTERNATIONAL, *Document – Libya: Militias threaten hopes for new Libya*, *supra* note 268.

[313] HUMAN RIGHTS WATCH, *Libya: Opposition Forces Should Protect Civilians and Hospitals*, *supra* note 189.

[314] Chivers, *Libyan Rebels Accused of Pillage and Beatings*, *supra* note 189.

[315] HUMAN RIGHTS WATCH, *Libya: Opposition Forces Should Protect Civilians and Hospitals*, *supra* note 189.

[316] Chivers, *Libyan Rebels Accused of Pillage and Beatings*, *supra* note 189.

[317] Report of the International Commission of Inquiry (Jan. 12, 2012), *supra* note 224 at ¶ 158.

[318] THE GUARDIAN, *Syria, Libya and Middle East unrest*, *supra* note 290.

a mosque in the hills above the town. The damage was reportedly caused by Qadhafi forces firing tracer rounds through the windows.[319] Amnesty International reported that Grad rockets were fired into Nalut, Zintan and Yafran as well as the surrounding villages of Al-Qalaʿ, Al-Rujban, Jadu, Kikla, Nalut and Takut. According to witnesses civilian objects, including mosques in these villages, were shelled and partly destroyed, but amnesty International could not independently confirm these reports.[320]

3.7.3. Destruction of Objects Indispensable to the Survival of the Civilian Population

(a) Qadhafi Forces

There were documented incidents of Qadhafi forces causing destruction to objects that are essential for the survival of the civilian population. Amnesty International reported that Qadhafi forces deliberately damaged and destroyed water wells used by civilians.[321] Various sources reported that Qadhafi forces cut electricity and water throughout the region.[322] Other media outlets carried similar accounts. Residents fleeing the Nafusa Mountains region reported upon their arrival in Tunisia that Qadhafi forces were shelling homes and poisoning wells.[323] The CoI reported on the alleged poisoning of the water system in Yafran, finding that

> The town was recaptured by thuwar in the first week of June 2011. The Commission received reports that retreating Qadhafi forces had poisoned the water system. This belief appeared to be based on the fact that chemical containers were found in the vicinity of the wells. The Commission examined the materials found at the site; some were empty canisters of insecticide, others were nerve agent antidote. As the water had been drained, it was not possible to determine whether it had been contaminated, although a Human Rights Watch representative told the Commission that they had tested it at the time and found no issues.[324]

---

[319] Report of the International Commission of Inquiry, advance unedited version (Mar. 2, 2012), *supra* note 19 at Annex I, ¶ 572.

[320] AMNESTY INTERNATIONAL, LIBYA – DISAPPEARANCES IN THE BESIEGED NAFUSA MOUNTAIN AS THOUSANDS SEEK SAFETY IN TUNISIA, *supra* note 11 at 14.

[321] *Id.* at 11.

[322] BELL ET AL., THE TIDE TURNS, *supra* note 1 at 15; AMNESTY INTERNATIONAL, LIBYA – DISAPPEARANCES IN THE BESIEGED NAFUSA MOUNTAIN AS THOUSANDS SEEK SAFETY IN TUNISIA, *supra* note 11 at 12.

[323] REUTERS, *Libyans flee violence in remote western areas, supra* note 163.

[324] Report of the International Commission of Inquiry, advance unedited version (Mar. 2, 2012), *supra* note 19 at Annex I, ¶ 571 (internal citations omitted).

3.7.4. *Impeding Access to Humanitarian Relief and Attacks on Humanitarian personnel*

(a) *Qadhafi Forces*

Qadhafi forces besieged cities and towns in the Nafusa Mountains region for long periods of time. Interviewees told the CoI that these sieges caused a shortage of food and other vital supplies for humanitarian relief.[325]

Throughout the Nafusa Mountains region campaign inhabitants had difficulty acquiring basic necessities. In April 2011, Nalut residents reported that hospital supplies were dwindling.[326] Similar reports emerged from displaced residents from Yafran and other towns. Witnesses fleeing Yafran told reporters that if the siege was not lifted, thousands of children would be at risk.[327]

The attacks on Zintan reached such intense levels that on 27 May 2011 the medical NGO Médecins Sans Frontières (MSF) announced it was withdrawing from Zintan, where its staff had been working for over a month. MSF cited the intensity of the fighting and the significant danger posed by ongoing shelling, including near hits of the hospital, as the reason for withdrawal.[328]

3.7.5. *Attacks on Protected Medical Personnel, Transport and Facilities*

(a) *Qadhafi Forces*

The CoI reported on attacks on medical personnel, vehicles and facilities by the Qadhafi forces.

An interviewee from Zintan told the CoI that on the night of 21 February 2011 regime forces invaded hospitals in the city, and killed and abducted both patients and medical personnel.[329] There were attacks on ambulances in Zintan documented as well, and the CoI found that

---

[325] This right is enshrined in Article 11 of the International Covenant on Economic, Social and Cultural Rights. Report of the International Commission of Inquiry (Jan. 12, 2012), *supra* note 224 at ¶ 161.

[326] REUTERS, *Thousands of Libyans flee remote western area: report, supra* note 71.

[327] Lin Noueihed, *Fighting rages in Libya's Western Mountains*, REUTERS, May 2, 2011, *available at* http://www.reuters.com/article/2011/05/02/us-libya-idUSTRE7270JP20110502.

[328] MEDECINS SANS FRONTIERS, *Libya: MSF Forced To Evacuate from Zintan, supra* note 291.

[329] Report of the International Commission of Inquiry (Jan. 12, 2012), *supra* note 224 at ¶ 127. In the Report, this paragraph is in the "Denial of medical treatment" section.

In Zintan, the Commission interviewed two witnesses who were shot at while in an ambulance heading towards Al Qawalish. The first was a nurse who was injured in the shooting. The second witness was in an ambulance when bullets fired by Qadhafi forces hit the ambulance. The driver had to turn back to Zintan. After doing so, another bullet hit the ambulance from the rear. The Commission received reports on similar incidents in Zintan.[330]

Qadhafi forces attacked the hospital in Zintan on several occasions. On 28 April, three Grad rockets damaged some of the cars and ambulances parked outside the hospital.[331] HRW reported that Grad rockets exploded about 100 meters from the Zintan hospital on 23 May.[332] Upon visiting the Zintan hospital, HRW observed two holes in the parking lot that appeared to have been caused by Grad rockets, as well as another hole on the street by the front gate.[333]

Some of the most notable attacks took place in Yafran, where Qadhafi forces occupied the main hospital for nearly two months, causing extensive damage to the facilities and assaulting wounded victims.[334] A nurse from the hospital in Yafran was arrested in May for treating *thuwar* and was then taken to the local Boy Scout camp military base, where he was beaten and tortured. He was then transferred along with others to Military Camp 77.[335]

(b) Thuwar *Forces*

On 7 May 2011, when Zintan *thuwar* entered Zawiyyat al-Bajul, they looted medical clinics, taking supplies and causing severe damage to the facilities.[336] During visits to Qawalish, Awaniyya Rayaniyya, and Zawiyyat al-Bajul in July 2011, HRW found evidence that *thuwar* had vandalized medical clinics and hospitals.[337]

---

[330] Report of the International Commission of Inquiry, advance unedited version (Mar. 2, 2012), *supra* note 19 at Annex I, ¶ 595.

[331] *Id.* at Annex I, ¶ 569.

[332] HUMAN RIGHTS WATCH, *Libya: Rocket Attacks on Western Mountain Towns, supra* note 17.

[333] *Id.*

[334] Report of the International Commission of Inquiry, advance unedited version (Mar. 2, 2012), *supra* note 19 at Annex I, ¶ 595 (internal citations omitted).

[335] *Id.* at Annex I, ¶ 283.

[336] HUMAN RIGHTS WATCH, *Libya: Opposition Forces Should Protect Civilians and Hospitals, supra* note 189.

[337] *Id.*

3.7.6. *Misuse of the Red Cross/Red Crescent Emblem*

(a) *Qadhafi Forces*

The CoI gathered evidence of several incidents of misuse of the Red Cross/
Red Crescent emblem. For instance, a witness in Nalut in the Nafusa
Mountains region told the CoI about ambulances being deployed "as a
trick, to enter towns carrying soldiers," who then proceeded to "shoot at
civilians in the street." Such accounts also raise the issue of perfidy. Similar reports came from Yafran.[338]

3.8. *Prohibited Weapons*

(a) *Qadhafi Forces*

The CoI reported the use of prohibited weapons by Qadhafi forces in the
Nafusa Mountains region. In particular, the CoI declared that

> The Commission saw mined areas in the Nafusa Mountains, as well as mines
> removed from areas around Misrata including Brazilian TAB-1 AP mines,
> Belgian M3 AT mines, and Chinese Type 72 AT mines. The Commission also
> notes reports of the use of Belgian NR413 stake mines and NR442 bounding
> mines, Yugoslav TMA-5 AT mines, and Czech PT-Ma-Ba-III AT mines.[339]

Amnesty International similarly reported the use of landmines in the
region.[340] HRW also confirmed that Qadhafi forces laid a large number
of anti-personnel mines north of Zintan in order to prevent *thuwar* offensives. HRW inspected disassembled mines discovered in June by *thuwar*
in Zintan.[341]

Media accounts from February 2012 reported on the discovery of Dual
Purpose Improved Conventional Munitions (DPICM) cluster submunitions in the town of Mizda in the Nafusa Mountains region.[342] DPICM

---

[338] Report of the International Commission of Inquiry (Jan. 12, 2012), *supra* note 224
at ¶ 169.

[339] Report of the International Commission of Inquiry, advance unedited version
(Mar. 2, 2012), *supra* note 19 at Annex I, ¶ 666 (internal citations omitted).

[340] Amnesty International, Libya – Disappearances in the besieged Nafusa
Mountain as thousands seek safety in Tunisia, *supra* note 11 at 16.

[341] *Libya: Government Using Landmines in Nafusa Mountains*, Human Rights Watch,
June 21, 2011, *available at* http://www.hrw.org/news/2011/06/21/libya-government-using-
landmines-nafusa-mountains.

[342] C.J. Chivers, *Can you Name this Cluster Bomb?*, N.Y. Times, Feb. 1, 2012, *available at*
http://atwar.blogs.nytimes.com/2012/02/01/can-you-name-this-cluster-bomb/.

and their spent cargo rockets utilized by the Qadhafi forces were also discovered near Jadu and Zintan.[343]

3.9. *Targeting Specific Groups*

(a) Thuwar *Forces*

i. *Sub-Saharan Africans*

Reports indicate that Sub-Saharan migrant workers were targeted by *thuwar* for arbitrary arrest and torture. The United Nations Special Envoy for Libya, Ian Martin, also reported findings of torture in Zintan of Sub-Saharan Africans suspected of being Qadhafi fighters.[344]

Amnesty International visited the Bu Rashada detention center in Al-Gharyan, holding immigrants in May and June 2012, reporting arbitrary arrests, detentions and torture of migrants by *thuwar* groups.[345]

Amnesty International also reported that the practices of the detention center at Bu Rashada were highly problematic. Somali and Eritrean nationals, for example, were forced to pay 1,000 dinars (approximately $795) to be released if they were released and brought back to Bu Rashada. If they could not pay the fine, they were subjected to indefinite detention. Amnesty International met three victims of this policy including an Eritrean and two Somali women who had left the detention center and tried to reach Europe by boat. All three had failed to do so and had been detained and brought back to Bu Rashada. Since they could not pay the fine, they were detained indefinitely.[346]

ii. *Residents of Tiji and Badr*

Residents of Tiji and Badr, towns with a majority Arab population, were targeted by *thuwar* for reprisal attacks on suspicion that residents fought for or supported Qadhafi forces during the conflict.[347] Several UN bodies, NGOs and media outlets reported on repeated acts of reprisal violence against the residents of Tiji and Badr, including unlawful killing, arbitrary arrest, torture and intentional attacks on persons and private property.

---

[343] Report of the International Commission of Inquiry, advance unedited version (Mar. 2, 2012), *supra* note 19 at Annex I, ¶ 665.

[344] U.N. SC, U.N. Doc. S/PV.6768 (May 10, 2012), *supra* note 273 at 5.

[345] *See infra* Sec. 3.4. *See also* AMNESTY INTERNATIONAL, LIBYA: RULE OF LAW OR RULE OF MILITIAS?, *supra* note 233 at 36 & 38.

[346] *Id.* at 43.

[347] *See also* Report of the International Commission of Inquiry, advance unedited version (Mar. 2, 2012), *supra* note 19 at Annex I, ¶ 462.

Nalut *thuwar* entered Tiji and Badr in August 2011, and again in October, carrying out reprisal acts and demanding that residents leave the area.[348] The CoI also reported on the deaths and injuries of civilians from the shelling of Tiji by *thuwar* forces from Nalut in October 2011 with Grad rockets and mortars.[349]

In the aftermath of the fall of Qadhafi regime, former *thuwar* forces detained individuals and members of tribes they suspected of having supported the regime.[350] According to the CoI, adult men were arrested without a warrant or explanation. They were then taken to the Criminal Investigations building in Nalut. The families were not informed of the men's whereabouts.[351] Many former detainees reported that they were ill-treated while in detention.[352]

iii. *The Mashashiyyans*

The CoI received multiple reports of abuses of Mashashiyyans. *Thuwar* from Zintan are reported to have carried out reprisal violence against the Mashashiyya[353] in towns such as Awaniyya, Zawiyyat al-Bajul, Qawalish, Shayga and Oumer. The Mashashiyya tribe benefited from privileges under the Qadhafi's regime, while tribes further west were discriminated against and marginalized. There was also animosity in relation to longstanding conflicts over land ownership between the Mashashiyya and the Zintan.[354] The Zintan did acknowledge, however, that the Qadhafi regime deliberately encouraged discord between the tribes in order to foment conflict and safeguard its own power.[355]

Other sources indicate that the Mashashiyya attempted to remain neutral during the 2011 conflict but were unable to do so. Qadhafi forces used Awaniyya as a base for their tanks, firing Grad rockets from there towards the civilian population of Zintan and the surrounding villages.[356] Zintan

---

[348] *Id.* at Annex I, ¶ 740.

[349] *See infra* Sec. 3.7(b)(ii). *See also* Report of the International Commission of Inquiry, advance unedited version (Mar. 2, 2012), *supra* note 19 at Annex I, ¶¶ 61, 465 & 740.

[350] *See also* MILITIAS THREATEN HOPES FOR NEW LIBYA, AMNESTY INTERNATIONAL, *supra* note 231 at 34.

[351] *See infra* Sec. 3.3. *See also* Report of the International Commission of Inquiry, advance unedited version (Mar. 2, 2012), *supra* note 19 at Annex I, ¶ 466.

[352] *See infra* Sec. 3.4. *See also Id.* at Annex I, ¶ 311.

[353] BELL ET AL., THE TIDE TURNS, *supra* note 1 at 11.

[354] *Id.* at 16 & 26.

[355] von Rohr, *Settling Old Scores – Tribal Rivalries Complicate Libyan War, supra* note 13.

[356] *Id.*

elders reportedly made an attempt to negotiate with the Mashashiyya prior to the July 2011 offensive but the efforts failed.[357]

Members of the Mashashiyya tribe interviewed by journalists denied fighting with the Qadhafi forces, claiming instead that many members of their tribe were detained and imprisoned by rebel forces solely because of their tribal affiliation.[358] The CoI reported that

> The Commission was able to confirm reports that Mashashiya detainees have been tortured, towns looted, and property burnt. Mashashiyans who have attempted to return to their homes have reportedly been beaten. In December 2011, Zintani *thuwar* reportedly shelled a town containing Mashashiya IDPs. The Military Council twice refused to allow the Commission to enter one of the towns.[359]

When *thuwar* from Zintan entered Zawiyyat al-Bajul in May 2011 and Awaniyya in July 2011, they vandalized, pillaged both towns, ransacking and burning public and private properties.[360]

Amnesty International reported that thousands of Mashashiyyans were forced to leave the Nafusa Mountains region, moving to camps near Tripoli. These communities remained displaced in makeshift camps around the country; the interim government, however, failed to take suitable action against the perpetrators or assist these communities to return home.[361]

In June – July 2011, after *thuwar* fighters from nearby areas took control of the area, the entire population of the village of Awaniyya was forced to leave their homes by militias from Zintan. Many were reportedly displaced in Tripoli or other parts of the Nafusa Mountains region.[362] Awaniyya was home to 15,000 people prior to the conflict.[363] In January 2012, Amnesty International interviewed several families that had been displaced after being forced to leave Awaniyya, and reported that the Mashashiyya families were hopeful that a reconciliation initiative sponsored by tribal

---

[357] BELL ET AL., THE TIDE TURNS, *supra* note 1 at 16 & 26.

[358] von Rohr, *Settling Old Scores – Tribal Rivalries Complicate Libyan War, supra* note 13.

[359] Report of the International Commission of Inquiry, advance unedited version (Mar. 2, 2012), *supra* note 19 at ¶ 60.

[360] *See infra* Sec. 3.7. *See also Id.* at Annex I, ¶ 456.

[361] *Amnesty International Says "Out of Control" Libyan Militias Are Committing Widespread Abuses Against Suspected Al-Gaddafi Loyalists, Including Torture and Killings,* AMNESTY INTERNATIONAL, Feb. 16, 2012, *available at* http://www.amnestyusa.org/news/news-item/amnesty-international-says-out-of-control-libyan-militias-are-commiting-widespread-abuses-against-su.

[362] AMNESTY INTERNATIONAL, *Document – Libya: Militias threaten hopes for new Libya, supra* note 268.

[363] von Rohr, *Settling Old Scores – Tribal Rivalries Complicate Libyan War, supra* note 13.

leaders and elders from different parts of Libya would allow them to return to their homes. By mid-February 2012, however, no resolution had been reached.[364]

3.10. *Sexual Violence*[365]

(a) *Qadhafi Forces*

The CoI took testimony from a female nurse who reported that she was detained for opposing the Qadhafi regime and subjected to torture and sexual abuse, but not rape.[366] The CoI also reported that at least one witness from Nalut stated that on 18 February 2011 Qadhafi forces patrolling the streets delivered threats to residents of the district that if they did not align themselves with the regime they would face serious consequences, including rape.[367]

Refugees fleeing government attacks in the Nafusa Mountains region reported to Reuters upon their arrival in Tunisia that Qadhafi forces had threatened to rape women across the area.[368]

---

[364] AMNESTY INTERNATIONAL, *Document – Libya: Militias threaten hopes for new Libya,* *supra* note 268.

[365] The following terms are defined in accordance with the jurisprudence of the ICTY and ICTR, and other mixed-model tribunals.
  1. "Rape" is the penetration, however slight, of any part of the body of another person irrespective of gender (namely, the vagina, anus, or mouth) by means of the perpetrator's sexual organ or any object used by the perpetrator when accompanied by force or threat of force against the person or a third party which the victim believes is real.
  2. "Sexual violence" is defined as any physical act of a sexual nature which is committed on a person under circumstances which are coercive or threatening to the person or to any other person, which includes physical touching, groping, fondling, removal of a person's clothing to display intimate parts of the person's body whether in the presence of one or more persons, or any other act of a demeaning sexual nature.
  3. "Sexual harassment" is any threat of "rape" or "sexual violence," as defined above, against a person or any other person for purposes of demeaning, intimidating, or punishing the person in question.

[366] Report of the International Commission of Inquiry, advance unedited version (Mar. 2, 2012), *supra* note 19 at Annex I, ¶ 592.

[367] Report of the International Commission of Inquiry (Jan. 12, 2012), *supra* note 224 at ¶ 206.

[368] REUTERS, *Libyans flee violence in remote western areas, supra* note 163.

3.11. *The Use of Children and Their Treatment in Armed Conflict*

(a) *Qadhafi Forces*

The indiscriminate shelling and bombardment by Qadhafi forces reportedly led to casualties of children in April 2011 in Zintan[369] and Kikla.[370]

(b) Thuwar *Forces*

The CoI reported that *thuwar* forces in the Nafusa Mountains region included children. The CoI gathered testimony of children taking part in the conflict and reported that

> One interviewee showed the Commission a photograph of his 11 year old brother sitting on the back of a pick-up truck which had anti-aircraft guns mounted on it. The interviewee indicated that the same brother had been actively participating in fighting and that he had witnessed 14 and 15 year olds fighting with the *thuwar*.[371]

In other interviews, several former *thuwar* indicated that minors had fought in the Nafusa Mountains region. The CoI noted that it was clear that "to fight with the *thuwar* was a source of pride both for fighters of any age and reportedly the parents of the younger fighters."[372]

4. THE ROLE OF NATO

NATO's intervention in the Nafusa Mountains region contributed to the *thuwar* advances in the area. The success of the June 2011 *thuwar* offensive was due largely to increased military support from NATO and its allies. The NATO air campaign in the Nafusa Mountains region in May and June 2011 hit targets mainly in the towns of Yafran, Nalut, Al-Gharyan, Zintan, Mizda and Badr,[373] thereby hindering the ability of Qadhafi forces to use

---

[369] Report of the International Commission of Inquiry, advance unedited version (Mar. 2, 2012), *supra* note 19 at Annex I, ¶ 569.

[370] Report of the International Commission of Inquiry (Jan. 12, 2012), *supra* note 224 at ¶ 154.

[371] Report of the International Commission of Inquiry, advance unedited version (Mar. 2, 2012), *supra* note 19 at Annex I, ¶ 707.

[372] *Id.* at Annex I, ¶ 708. For more on the use of children in the conflict, *see* Ch. V, 2.12.

[373] *Factbox: Latest developments in Libyan conflict*, REUTERS, *supra* note 82; *WRAPUP 5 – Gaddafi govt says in talks, rebels say he must go*, REUTERS, July 4, 2011, *available at* http://www.reuters.com/article/2011/07/04/libya-idUSL6E7I404020110704; BELL ET AL., THE TIDE TURNS, *supra* note 1 at 15.

tanks, artillery pieces and rocket launchers to strike *thuwar* positions effectively.[374]

Sources, including media outlets that relied on information from *thuwar* fighters, reported a complex picture of NATO's involvement in the region. NATO flew sorties over the Nafusa Mountains region starting in March 2011, but were limited in number as the coalition focused its attention on eastern Libya.[375] Initially these airstrikes appear to have done little to affect the outcome of the conflict in the west.[376] Strikes during the early period were reportedly irregular and focused entirely on Qadhafi forces around Zintan and Mizda.[377] *Thuwar* stated that the strikes did not assist them significantly in their fight against regime forces in Zintan or Yafran.[378]

Although NATO stepped up its intervention in the region in June 2011,[379] it was not enough to end the stalemate in the region,[380] and *thuwar* fighters were reportedly dissatisfied with NATO's involvement. *Thuwar* urged foreign actors to support their advance towards Tripoli as they were running out of equipment, claiming that they required assistance to end the stalemate.

Meanwhile, cracks were appearing in the NATO alliance, with some allies showing mission fatigue and the United States accusing some European allies of failing to contribute their share to the mission. The damage to the energy infrastructure in the eastern territory knocked out oil production and supplies were scarce in the western part of the country. *Thuwar* leaders thus struggled to pay for military operations. As a result, the European Union and the United States promised more aid and financial assistance to the rebel forces in the Nafusa Mountains region.[381] NATO was compelled to directly assist *thuwar* in the area in order to end the stalemate.

NATO also played an active role in aiding *thuwar* in the Nafusa Mountains region by supplying weapons and training fighters, though this has

---

[374] BELL ET AL., THE TIDE TURNS, *supra* note 1 at 15.
[375] THE GUARDIAN, *Battle for Tripoli: pivotal victory in the mountains helped big push*, *supra* note 2.
[376] Sen, *Gadhafi lays siege to west mountain in towns*, *supra* note 66.
[377] BELL ET AL., THE TIDE TURNS, *supra* note 1 at 15.
[378] *Id.*
[379] Robinson, *WRAPUP 1 – Gaddafi rockets dent sense of security in Misrata*, *supra* note 81.
[380] Robinson, *Heavy fighting as Libyan rebels try to push out*, *supra* note 78.
[381] Golovnina, *Libyan rebels blame West for lack of cash*, *supra* note 80.

not been officially acknowledged or denied by NATO.[382] Reports indicate that France, Qatar and Jordan deployed special forces to the region to provide training to *thuwar* forces.[383] France provided weapons, munitions and food to *thuwar* forces in the Nafusa Mountains region.[384] The airdrops included machine guns, RPGs and anti-tank rockets.[385] The *thuwar* fighters in the Nafusa Mountains region lacked in military training, coordination and weaponry compared to Qadhafi forces, and so relied rely heavily on NATO, both in terms of airstrikes and provision of weaponry.[386]

The French Defense Ministry spokesperson Thierry Burkhard stated that there were supply drops because "the humanitarian situation was worsening and at one point it seemed the security situation was threatening civilians who could not defend themselves."[387] He argued that the weapons were dropped in order to help the *thuwar* to defend themselves; the drops also included medicine and food. Prior to the French drops, *thuwar* had mainly received weapons from Qatar that came through the *thuwar* stronghold of Benghazi.[388]

On 30 June 2011, media outlets reported that Russia accused France of violating UN Security Council Resolution 1970 and the weapons embargo the Resolution mandated by arming Libyan *thuwar*. France responded by stating that it had not violated the United Nations embargo because the weapons it gave the *thuwar* were necessary to protect civilians from an

---

[382] *See* Ch. III, Sec. 7.1. *See also* Coker, *Length of Libya's standoff hinges on leader's militia, supra* note 122.

[383] Coker, *Length of Libya's standoff hinges on leader's militia, supra* note 122; *France gives Libya rebels arms but Britain balks,* AFP, June 29, 2011, *available at* http://www.google.com/hostednews/afp/article/ALeqM5gst8wAKgJwnMvBWiTl9EQ1Zpylmg?docId=CNG.o41943dc452c61a507ee986061b49f2d.1031; Louis Charbonneau & Hamuda Hassan, *France defends arms airlift to Libya rebels,* REUTERS, June 30, 2011, *available at* http://www.reuters.com/article/2011/06/29/us-libya-idUSTRE7270JP20110629; Michael Birnbaum, *France sent arms to Libyan rebels,* THE WASHINGTON TIMES, June 29, 2011, *available at* http://articles.washingtonpost.com/2011-06-29/world/35235276_1_nafusa-mountains-hans-hillen-libyan-rebels; Hopkins, *Nato reviews Libya campaign after France admits arming rebels, supra* note 123; INTERNATIONAL CRISIS GROUP, HOLDING LIBYA TOGETHER, *supra* note 21 at 8.

[384] Elizabeth Pineau & John Irish, *France provided weapons, food to Libya rebels,* REUTERS, June 29, 2011, *available at* http://www.reuters.com/article/2011/06/29/us-libya-france-weapons-idUSTRE75S22P20110629.

[385] Hopkins, *Nato reviews Libya campaign after France admits arming rebels, supra* note 123.

[386] *See* Ch. II, Sec. 2.3. *See also* Georgy, *Captured Libyan soldiers say army morale is low, supra* note 72.

[387] Pineau & Irish, *France provided weapons, food to Libya rebels, supra* note 384.

[388] *Id.*

imminent attack, which it said was allowed under UN Security Council Resolution 1973.[389]

At the time of the *thuwar* advance on the capital in early August 2011, NATO stepped up its efforts. Media outlets reported that it conducted several sorties in the area around Al-Gharyan in order to aid *thuwar* advances from the Nafusa Mountains region.[390]

The Qadhafi regime accused NATO of killing civilians in the Nafusa Mountains region a number of times. Incidents took place in Kikla on 11 April 2011,[391] in Yafran on 7 May 2011[392] and in Nalut on 3 July 2011.[393] NATO refuted the incident in Kikla, while no records are found of NATO addressing the incidents in Yafran or Nalut.

5. CONCLUSION

The Nafusa Mountains region often appeared as a sideshow to the civil war while attention focused on eastern Libya, or on Misrata and Tripoli. In addition, journalists had little access to the region, making it difficult to independently verify accounts of events in the area.[394] Despite this, the Nafusa Mountains campaign was one of the most significant advances for the *thuwar* in Libya and played a central role in the conflict, as it occupied Qadhafi forces in an area directly adjoining the capital.[395] It also provided a critical supply line to the rebels that helped them retake Zawiyya, thereby opening the way to Tripoli.

The complex social structures of the Nafusa Mountains region were a microcosm of pre-existing divides in Libya that were exacerbated by war. The loyalties of the region's population were split between the Qadhafi regime and the regional *thuwar* forces. Some communities in the region, both Arabs and Berber, had a long-standing history of opposing the

---

[389] *See* Ch. III, Sec. 7.1. *See also* Abu-Aun, *Russia: arming Libya rebels is "crude violation"*, *supra* note 195.

[390] *Factbox: Latest developments in Libyan conflict*, REUTERS, July 7, 2011, *available at* http://www.reuters.com/article/2011/07/07/us-libya-nato-idUSTRE7661QZ20110707.

[391] *See* Ch. III, Sec. 6.2. *See also Joint press briefing on events concerning Libya*, NORTH ATLANTIC TREATY ORGANIZATION, Apr. 12, 2011, *available at* http://www.nato.int/cps/en/natolive/opinions_72290.htm.

[392] *NATO hits several areas in Libya – state TV*, REUTERS, May 7, 2011, *available at* http://www.reuters.com/article/2011/05/07/libya-nato-idUSLDE7460A220110507.

[393] REUTERS, *WRAPUP 5 – Gaddafi govt says in talks, rebels say he must go*, *supra* note 373.

[394] Amara, *Rebels seize Libya-Tunisia border crossing: witnesses*, *supra* note 55.

[395] REUTERS, *Libyans flee violence in remote western areas*, *supra* note 163.

Qadhafi regime, while others were historically loyal. The Nafusa Mountains region therefore featured widespread opposition to the Qadhafi regime, in addition to remaining support in some towns throughout the region.[396]

The complex ethnic and tribal structures in the Nafusa Mountains region certainly made the patterns of violations in the region more complex and played a role in defining the nature of these violations. Without disputing the relevance of tribalism, which played an important role in Libya's governance, given the absence of state institutions during Qadhafi's rule,[397] the type of violations in the region depended largely on pre-existing disputes that went beyond tribal affiliations. The factors that determined allegiance in the Nafusa Mountains region often depended on the history of the area, involving land disputes and patronage policies from the Qadhafi era. Observers have pointed out that deep animosities repressed under Qadhafi's autocratic system have resurfaced since the end of his rule.[398]

Apart from tribal and regime loyalties, another important aspect to the nature of the conflict included regional factors. *Thuwar* fighters in the region developed autonomously and had stronger allegiances at the local than national level. As a result of this dynamic, most battles in the Nafusa Mountains region centered on individual towns without a vision of the larger civil war.[399] It was not until the end of the conflict, and the final push for Tripoli, that *thuwar* from the Nafusa Mountains region joined the national fight to carve out their stronghold in the capital and ensure that their own interests would be met in the post-Qadhafi era.

Some *thuwar* lacked military experience and weaponry, contributing to the long stalemate in the region. The battles went back and forth, with *thuwar* gaining and losing ground within short periods of time. Another factor was the small number of fighters on both sides relative to the expanse of the region, making it difficult to capture and hold large territories for extended periods of time. Finally, the heat during the summer months considerably slowed the pace of the fighting in the Nafusa Mountains region.[400]

---

[396] von Rohr, *Settling Old Scores – Tribal Rivalries Complicate Libyan War, supra* note 13.

[397] *Id.*

[398] BBC, *Troops sent to quell clashes in western Libya, supra* note 151.

[399] BELL ET AL., THE TIDE TURNS, *supra* note 1 at 16.

[400] von Rohr, *Settling Old Scores – Tribal Rivalries Complicate Libyan War, supra* note 13.

The NATO campaign targeted Qadhafi forces in the Nafusa Mountains region, although on a smaller scale than in eastern Libya. NATO airstrikes played a particularly significant role later in the conflict when *thuwar* started to advance on Al-Gharyan and into the coastal plain. As in the other theaters of military operations, however, the strikes led to the destruction of civilian property, and in some case civilian casualties. NATO was accused of targeting civilians on at least three occasions.

There are reports that NATO and non-NATO states played an even more significant role in supporting the *thuwar* ground operations in the Nafusa Mountains than other parts of the country. The weapons reportedly provided by France and Qatar, and training provided by other countries, significantly enhanced the *thuwar* forces' military capability in the region. While NATO claims that all of its actions during the conflict were in accordance with the mandate to protect civilians, the direct support for one side of the war is outside of the bounds of NATO's own rules of engagement as well as Security Council Resolution 1973. The violations committed by *thuwar* groups that benefited from this support also calls into question the role of NATO in the conflict and its aftermath.[401]

During the final phase of the war after the fall of Qadhafi, residents in the region accused other communities and tribes of loyalty to the Qadhafi regime during the war, fueling attacks by the still-armed and influential *thuwar* forces. The NTC struggled to maintain security and stability over a country with an abundance of weapons left over from the conflict, and acknowledged that there were problems, including with some of its own security forces.[402] Some *thuwar* groups rejected the calls made by the interim authorities to hand over their weapons, demonstrating a general distrust and lack of allegiance to the country's new government.[403] The Zintan *thuwar*, in particular, acted autonomously and holds formidable influence in the post-conflict security landscape.[404]

The continued clashes in the Nafusa Mountains region, such as in Al-Gharyan in January 2012 and in Zintan in June 2012, along with the reluctance of local militias to adhere to the mandates of the interim government, demonstrated the lack of centralized control over the region. A prime example of this was the refusal of the Zintan Brigade to hand over

---

[401] *See* Ch. III, Sec. 5.

[402] Sherlock, *The headless corpse, the mass grave and worrying questions about Libya's rebel army, supra* note 227.

[403] Habboush, *Two killed and 36 hurt in Libyan clashes, supra* note 209.

[404] *See* Ch. V, Sec. 2. *See also* Holmes & Fletcher, *Zintan's hold on Saif al-Islam reflects Libya divisions, supra* note 29.

Saif al-Islam to the central government to stand trial (which was part of Libya's claims before the ICC), taking him instead to a secret location, reflected a wider problem of powerful local militia and a weak central government. Saif al-Islam's capture enhanced the status of the Zintan Katiba considerably. They were distrustful of other militias and keen to assert their authority and independence.[405] Similarly, the reluctance of the Zintan Katiba to hand over control of the Tripoli International Airport to the government, even well into 2012, was another visible indicator of their desire for independence and influence.[406]

The Nafusa Mountains region saw serious fighting along with a number of human rights violations carried out by Qadhafi forces, including arbitrary detention, enforced disappearances, acts of unlawful killings, torture and ill-treatment, and attacks on civilians and the destruction of objects indispensable to the survival of the civilian population.

There is a significant amount of evidence collected by the CoI, NGOs and media outlets showing that in order to suppress the *thuwar* Qadhafi forces in the Nafusa Mountains region set up checkpoints to detain *thuwar* fighters and suspected supporters, and in a number of cases disappeared individuals. While some detainees were released, others did not return to their homes after the end of the conflict.

There is also evidence that Qadhafi forces engaged in acts of torture and ill-treatment against *thuwar* fighters and suspected combatants. Some bore marks of beatings and reported suffering ill-treatment based on their opposition to the regime. The documented cases indicate that the torture was carried out both to extract information and to punish suspected opponents. There is substantial evidence of Qadhafi forces carrying out acts of torture and extrajudicial executions at the Boy Scouts camp converted into a military base.

The CoI, NGOs and media outlets documented cases of intentional and indiscriminate attacks in the Nafusa Mountains region by Qadhafi forces. Civilian areas in cities, towns and villages across the Nafusa Mountains region were subject to continuous attacks by artillery shelling, mortar fire and rockets. Many of these attacks directly hit civilian area; at times Qadhafi forces engaged in night-time shelling to prevent civilians from

---

[405] Ali Shuaib, *Anti-Gaddafi fighters demand role in the new Libya*, REUTERS, Nov. 19, 2011, *available at* http://www.reuters.com/article/2011/11/19/us-libya-government-fighters-idUSTRE7AI0W320111119.

[406] *See* Ch. II, Sec. 2. *See also* Hadi Fornaji, *Tripoli International Airport still held by Zintan Brigade*, LIBYA HERALD, Mar. 25, 2012, *available at* http://www.libyaherald.com/2012/03/25/tripoli-international-airport-still-held-by-zintan-brigade.

fleeing the combat zone. In some instances, however, *thuwar* positioned forces in certain locations that may have justified military engagement on otherwise civilian infrastructure. This was the case in Yafran, for example, where *thuwar* forces established a position in a school, prompting fire from the Qadhafi forces. Nevertheless, the indiscriminate nature of the shelling carried out by the regime forces led to attacks on surrounding civilian populations that appeared to be disproportionate to the military objective. These attacks became increasingly indiscriminate as *thuwar* pushed back regime troops, leading to longer distance firing that was less precise. Zintan, in particular, suffered nearly continuous attacks by Qadhafi forces.

As a result of the shelling, cultural objects, including mosques, were damaged by Qadhafi forces during the conflict in the Nafusa Mountains region. The CoI presented evidence that these mosques were intentionally targeted. There is also evidence that a non-religious Berber cultural center was targeted and destroyed during the conflict.

There is evidence from the CoI and other sources that Qadhafi forces deliberately targeted livestock belonging to the towns supporting the *thuwar*, destroyed water wells and cut electricity to the region during the conflict. In doing so, Qadhafi forces destroyed the livelihood and the means of survival of many civilians with the knowledge that they were largely unable to bring in food from the outside due to the ongoing siege and the partial blockage of the border with Tunisia. Evidence shows that Qadhafi forces placed Zintan, Nalut and Yafran under siege and cut supply lines to the cities and towns, leaving civilians without electricity, water, food, medicine and other essential supplies.

CoI and media sources indicate that the Qadhafi forces directly targeted the provision of health care to the *thuwar* during the conflict. There is evidence that in Zintan and Yafran Qadhafi forces attacked hospitals, medical personnel and ambulances. In April 2011, the hospital in Yafran was occupied by Qadhafi forces, during which some patients were attacked and others were denied access to medical care. The medical personnel treating *thuwar* patients were also targeted, and medical staff were subject to arbitrary arrests and detentions, accompanied by torture, ill-treatment and harassment.

As the tide turned and the *thuwar* took control of towns with the retreat of Qadhafi forces, they carried out widespread violations. There is evidence that *thuwar* detained suspected Qadhafi supporters in the wake of the regime's collapse, and carried out reprisals in the process.[407] Such reprisals included acts of unlawful killing, arbitrary arrest, torture and other forms of ill-treatment, and attacks on civilians and private and public property.

Thuwar groups targeted particular groups in the Nafusa Mountains region. The Zintan Katiba targeted the Mashashiyya tribe in Awaniyya, Zawiyyat al-Bajul, Qawalish, Shayga and Oumer, while the Nalut Katiba targeted the residents of Tiji and Badr. To a lesser extent, residents of Asabiyya also suffered targeted attacks. The members of these communities, which were suspected of having aided Qadhafi forces during the war, were subject to unlawful killing, arbitrary arrest, and torture and other forms of ill-treatment. The towns were also looted, pillaged and vandalized, and property was destroyed. The residents were expelled from their homes and towns, and the interim-government authorities demonstrated an unwillingness to allow members of the communities to return to their homes.[408]

---

[407] Report of the International Commission of Inquiry, advance unedited version (Mar. 2, 2012), *supra* note 19 at Annex I, ¶ 221.

[408] *Id.* at Annex I, ¶ 489.

CHAPTER ELEVEN

KHUMS

1. Introduction

Khums[1] is located in the Murqub District of northwestern Libya, and has an estimated population of around 202,000 inhabitants.[2] It is a port city that lies along the Mediterranean Coast approximately 84 kilometers (52 miles) northwest of Misrata and 97 kilometers (60 miles) southeast of Tripoli.[3]

The city's economy revolves around tuna processing, esparto pressing, soap manufacture and the distribution of dates and regionally produced olive oil.[4] The UN World Heritage site of Leptis Magna – one of Libya's most important archaeological sites – is located just outside of Khums. These ancient Roman ruins, located along the Coastal Highway that connects Tripoli and Benghazi,[5] were reportedly used by Qadhafi forces to hide weapons during the conflict.[6]

The proximity of Khums to Tripoli made the city strategically important during the war. The city was particularly significant for its detention centers that held captured rebel fighters and suspected supporters. Qadhafi forces and regime loyalists brought prisoners from all over the country to Khums for detention, interrogation and, in many cases, extrajudicial killings. The city experienced some of the worst cases of mass killings during war.

---

[1] Otherwise known as Homs or Khoms.

[2] *Khums*, WOLFRAMALPHA, *available at* http://www.wolframalpha.com/input/?i=al+Hums%2C+Libya.

[3] *Id.*

[4] *Al-Khums*, ENCYCLOPEDIA BRITANNICA ONLINE, *available at* http://www.britannica.com/EBchecked/topic/317074/Al-Khums.

[5] *Id.*

[6] Ernesto Londono, *Fear for Libya's Roman Ruins*, THE WASHINGTON POST, June 15, 2011, *available at* http://articles.washingtonpost.com/2011-06-15/world/35236134_1_misrata-khums-rebel-spokesman; Ishaan Tharoor, *With Roman Ruins Under Threat, Libya's Ancient Past Presses Against Its Present*, TIME WORLD, June 14, 2011, *available at* http://world.time.com/2011/06/14/with-roman-ruins-under-threat-libyas-ancient-past-presses-against-its-present.

Map 8: Map of Khums (Map data © 2013 Google).

Events in Khums were not well documented, as the city was inaccessible to media and NGOs until 21 August 2011 when it came under *thuwar* control.[7] It is therefore difficult to produce a detailed description of all of the incidents that took place in the city during the conflict. The following uses the available information to highlight the important events that took place in and around the city of Khums during the 2011 war.

2. SUMMARY OF EVENTS

As the war continued into its third month, international actors developed new measures with the aim of hastening the fall of the Qadhafi regime. This included the NATO strategy that began on 19 May 2011 to attack Qadhafi's naval forces by targeting ports in Khums and other locations.[8] Another measure included the imposition of EU sanctions in June 2011 on the Libyan government, blocking shipments from entering several ports along the coast, including Khums. This was done with the intention of preventing refined fuel from reaching the Qadhafi forces.[9] Despite international efforts, the humanitarian situation rapidly deteriorated and, on 3 June 2011, the United Nations High Commissioner for Refugees (UNHCR) reported that some 49,000 internally displaced Libyans from Misrata were living in Khums in substandard conditions and in need of humanitarian aid.[10]

Khums also became a strategic location for holding prisoners detained by the Qadhafi regime. By May 2011, Qadhafi forces had created an *ad hoc* detention facility in Khums that consisted of two metal containers with bullet holes in the sides to allow air for the prisoners.[11] Evidence of the most large-scale violation recorded in Khums is provided by survivors,

---

[7] *Libya: Detainees left to suffocate in crowded metal containers*, AMNESTY INTERNATIONAL, Sept. 1, 2011, *available at* http://www.amnesty.org/en/news-and-updates/libya-detainees-left-suffocate-crowded-metal-containers-2011-09-01-1.

[8] VARUN VIRA & ANTHONY H. CORDESMAN, CENTER FOR STRATEGIC AND INTERNATIONAL STUDIES, THE LIBYAN UPRISING: AN UNCERTAIN TRAJECTORY 18 (June 20, 2011) [hereinafter "THE LIBYAN UPRISING"], *available at* http://csis.org/files/publication/110620_libya.pdf.

[9] *Id.* at 14.

[10] UNHCR REPORT UPDATE 27, HUMANITARIAN SITUATION IN LIBYA AND NEIGHBOURING COUNTRIES 1, June 3, 2011, *available at* http://reliefweb.int/sites/reliefweb.int/files/resources/Full_Report_1059.pdf.

[11] Report of the International Commission of Inquiry on Libya, U.N. HRC. 19th Sess., Annex I, ¶ 147. U.N. Doc. A/HRC/19/68, advance unedited version (Mar. 2, 2012). There is some confusion over the nationality of the company. Witnesses described it variously as a French company, a Turkish company and a Chinese company. *See e.g., Libya: 19 Suffocated*

who described how Qadhafi forces imprisoned and tortured them in these small cargo containers.[12] Human rights organizations and the CoI documented the violations that took place in this makeshift facility. The CoI documented that on 6 June 2011, 18 detainees died in Khums from suffocation due to the poor ventilation in the metal containers. 17 of the victims died trapped inside the containers, while one detainee later died in the hospital. The CoI received testimony from one of the guards who was at the facility at the time of the incident, as well as several of the survivors of the affair. Physical evidence gathered corroborates the information provided in witness accounts.[13]

3. Illustrations of the Violations

3.1. *Unlawful Killing*

(a) *Qadhafi Forces*

The deaths of the individuals held in the metal containers in Khums constitute acts of unlawful killing. After being severely tortured and beaten the victims were left to suffocate in poorly ventilated containers. The victims reportedly yelled for help and were denied sufficient food or water. One of the bodies revealed a bullet wound to the head, indicating the victim was executed by Qadhafi forces.[14] The CoI gathered testimony from officials and survivors held in the containers, and reported in detail on the incident. One previous senior intelligence official stated to the CoI that a Military Intelligence officer controlled the site housing the makeshift detention facility, and that the Search and Interrogation Office of Military Intelligence (Maktab al-Taharyyat wa-l-Bahith) reported to the head of Military Intelligence. Another officer from the Military Intelligence branch in Tripoli acted as second-in-command and was requested by the officer in charge to "create a 'dirty operation' brigade".[15]

---

in *Gaddafi Detention*, Human Rights Watch, Sept. 9, 2011, *available at* http://www.hrw.org/news/2011/09/09/libya-19-suffocated-gaddafi-detention.

[12] Syracuse Institute for National Security and Counter Terrorism, Syracuse University, Libya in Conflict Appendix C (2012), *available at* http://insct.syr.edu/uploaded Files/insct/publications/Mapping%20the%20Libyan%20Conflict%20-%20INSCT.pdf.

[13] *See infra* Sec. 3.1. *See also* Report of the International Commission of Inquiry, advance unedited version (Mar. 2, 2012), *supra* note 11 at Annex I, ¶ 24.

[14] Report of the International Commission of Inquiry, advance unedited version (Mar. 2, 2012), *supra* note 11 at Annex I, ¶ 157.

[15] *Id.* at Annex I, ¶ 148 (internal citations omitted).

The CoI also described witness testimonies provided by four survivors who were detained in the containers. The witnesses related their detention, during which they all suffered repeated beatings before being taken to the shipping containers in Khums.[16] The CoI recorded the details provided in testimonies about the conditions of the containers and the treatment of the detainees, and reported that

> They were sealed inside the containers, with inadequate ventilation, very little water and no regular access to latrines...They were beaten both during interrogation in the offices and inside the containers. They were also subject to electric shocks...Afterwards, fearing that he was going to die, the officer brought the other survivor interviewed by the Commission, a medical doctor, to treat him. The soldiers brought an intra-venous (IV) drip, which the doctor administered.[17]

The doctor described to the CoI being abused and was able to name the men responsible for his interrogation and torture. One of the men he identified as one of his interrogators was the second-in-command officer from the Tripoli branch of Military Intelligence.[18] The witnesses described to the CoI the events that transpired on 6 June 2011, the day the other detainees died, and the CoI concluded that

> As the sun heated the metal walls of the container, the temperature inside rose gradually...The detainees banged on the walls of container and called out for help...The guards ignored their cries for help. One by one, detainees appear to have lost consciousness. Finally, the guards opened the door...The guards took one of the survivors interviewed by the Commission, who was a doctor, to the second red container...Only two of the nine people there were still alive...[19] In the smaller container, eight of the 10 detainees were dead, while one died later in hospital. In the larger white container there were 18 detainees. Nine died and nine survived.[20]

The CoI verified most accounts recalled by survivors as "consistent with the treatment alleged" and interviewed one soldier from Military Intelligence in Tripoli who told the CoI that he had beaten detainees "with electric rods and sticks during interrogation by orders".[21]

---

[16] *Id.* at Annex I, ¶ 149–150, 336–7 (internal citations omitted).

[17] *Id.* at Annex I, ¶ 151 (internal citations omitted).

[18] *Id.* at Annex I, ¶ 152–153 (internal citations omitted).

[19] "Note the number of survivors counted by the doctor differs slightly from some other published accounts." *Id.* at Annex I, ¶ 155 (internal citations omitted).

[20] Report of the International Commission of Inquiry, advance unedited version (Mar. 2, 2012), *supra* note 11 at Annex I, ¶ 156.

[21] *Id.* at Annex I, ¶ 158 (internal citations omitted).

Amnesty International documented the same incident and examined the containers where the prisoners had been held.[22] The Amnesty International report corroborated the findings of the CoI, noting that 19 people were left to suffocate in locked metal containers in June 2011, and that Qadhafi forces ignored the detainees as they called for help.[23] The containers had no windows and the only ventilation was through the bullet holes in the walls.[24] The smaller container measured two by six meters. Only one of the ten people held in this container survived.[25] The other slightly larger container held 19 people, ten of whom survived.

The survivors indicated that some of the men had been in the containers as early as 20 May 2011.[26] One of the survivors stated that he was arrested in his home in Khums after participating in an anti-Qadhafi protest. After his arrest, he was subject to electrocutions and beatings with metal wires before being placed in the container.[27]

Another survivor told Amnesty International that the guards only opened the container door after he screamed and told them he was the only one left alive. After opening the door, the guards made him drag the other bodies out by their feet.[28] On 8 September 2011, a captured Qadhafi soldier led the military council of Khums to the grave where the bodies were buried in Wadi Dufan, between Bani Walid and Al-ʿUrban.[29] Human Rights Watch reported that the bodies were at an advanced stage of decomposition when they were discovered.[30] 18 bodies were exhumed and taken to the Tripoli Medical Center and identified as the men who died in the containers.[31] Human Rights Watch also received a video that was allegedly recorded by a Qadhafi soldier showing the detainees being beaten and whipped inside the container.[32]

---

[22] AMNESTY INTERNATIONAL, *Libya: Detainees left to suffocate in crowded metal containers, supra* note 7.

[23] *Id.*

[24] *Id.*

[25] *Id.*

[26] *Id.*

[27] *Id.*

[28] AMNESTY INTERNATIONAL, *Libya: Detainees left to suffocate in crowded metal containers, supra* note 7.

[29] *Deadline for Libyan towns' surrender passes*, CNN, Sept. 10, 2011, *available at* http://www.cnn.com/2011/WORLD/africa/09/09/libya.war/index.html.

[30] *Libya: 19 Suffocated in Gaddafi Detention*, HUMAN RIGHTS WATCH, Sept. 9, 2011, *available at* http://www.hrw.org/news/2011/09/09/libya-19-suffocated-gaddafi-detention.

[31] *Id.*

[32] CNN, *Deadline for Libyan towns' surrender passes, supra* note 29; *Libya: Detention and Torture in al-Khoms*, HUMAN RIGHTS WATCH, Sept. 9, 2011, *available at* http://www.hrw.org/video/2011/09/09/libya-detention-and-torture-al-khoms.

BBC documented a separate account of three men who were held in different containers in Khums. They were engineers who worked at the port in Khums, and had been instructed by Qadhafi forces to fix an old sea vessel so that it could be used to launch missiles into Misrata. Instead they sabotaged the vessel and fled to the home of a relative in Khums. They were tracked down, beaten, tortured and kept in shipping containers with other detainees.[33]

3.2. *Arbitrary Detentions and Enforced Disappearances*

(a) *Qadhafi Forces*

The men held in containers were detained arbitrarily. As detailed above, many of them were arrested and held without charge and received no information as to why they were detained. After several detainees died in captivity, soldiers were ordered to burn the bodies, and did so in a remote area south of Khums. The fate and remains of these victims remained unknown until the bodies were exhumed in September 2011 from a mass grave near Gharyan.

(b) Thuwar *Forces*

i. *The Tawerghans*

After the fall of Qadhafi, *thuwar* groups from Misrata detained and arrested Tawerghans in Khums without due process or evidence of alleged crimes. The CoI reported that by mid-September 2011 *thuwar* from Misrata had entered Khums, and concluded that

> [T]he armed men identified themselves as being from the Misratan *thuwar* and arrested five men and took them away. No reasons were given for the arrest and the families were not informed of where they were taken. Those that were eventually released informed the families of those still detained that the men were being held in Misrata by the *Shuhada* brigade.[34]

---

[33] Rana Jawad, *Libyans celebrate their freedom as they mourn the dead*, BBC, Sept. 1 2011, *available at* http://www.bbc.co.uk/news/world-africa-14752785.

[34] "Interview 0050 also details a separate incident in mid-September 2011 when a group of men from Misrata came to Al Khums and arrested all the Tawerghan men that they could find." *See* Report of the International Commission of Inquiry, advance unedited version (Mar. 2, 2012), *supra* note 11 at Annex I, ¶ 424 (internal citations omitted).

3.3. *Torture and Other Forms of Ill-treatment*

(a) *Qadhafi Forces*

The Qadhafi forces carried out widespread acts of torture and abuses against detainees in detention centers in Khums. Victims of the makeshift detention facilities in Khums provided testimony and evidence, mostly verified by the CoI, of torture in the form of severe beatings and the use of electric shocks while in captivity. Prisoners were subject to deplorable conditions, denied access to toilet facilities, and subject to extreme heat and severe overcrowding. These conditions constitute ill-treatment of detainees.[35]

The arrest and detention of men in containers as described above constitutes torture and ill-treatment. One survivor arrested by Qadhafi forces on 19 May 2011 provided testimony that he was electrocuted, beaten, slapped, kicked, punched and trampled on. He also indicated that he had been suspended upside down and tortured during interrogation.[36] Human Rights Watch was given a video, available online, that shows men being tortured in containers in the same manner as described by the victims.[37]

Moreover, the role of Military Intelligence officials in the detention, torture and interrogation of the prisoners in the containers indicates that a systematic government policy of torture was implemented by the highest authorities of the Qadhafi regime.[38]

(b) Thuwar *Forces*

i. *The Tawerghans*

After the *thuwar* took over the prison system in Khums, members of the Tawerghan community were severely beaten and tortured upon arrest and in detention in the city. *Thuwar* used rubber hoses, whips, cables and wooden sticks to beat their victims. The CoI documented the case of one interviewee who was held "along with nine others in a clinic in Al Khums where he said he was beaten all over his body with cables, rubber hoses, whips and wooden sticks. He was reportedly told that if he was killed, no one would be held to account."[39]

---

[35] *Id.* at ¶ 47.

[36] Human Rights Watch, *Libya: 19 Suffocated in Gaddafi Detention*, *supra* note 30.

[37] *Id.*

[38] *See* Ch. IV, Sec. 6.3.

[39] Report of the International Commission of Inquiry, advance unedited version (Mar. 2, 2012), *supra* note 11 at Annex I, ¶ 367 (internal citations omitted).

3.4. *Targeting Specific Groups*

(b) Thuwar *Forces*

i. *The Tawerghans*

Tawerghans left the town of Tawergha for camps for Internally Displaced Persons (IDPs) around Libya, including those that were located in Khums.[40] Some Tawerghan families also arrived in Khums fleeing attacks taking place in the capital.[41] *Thuwar* groups from Misrata pursued Tawerghans in cities across Libya, including in Khums.[42] Tawerghans in Khums were subsequently beaten, tortured, and held in unidentified centers including houses or offices in the city. In the majority of cases they were transferred to detention centers in other cities, mostly to Misrata.[43]

3.5. *Prohibited Weapons*

(a) *Qadhafi Forces*

Senior military officers told the CoI that Qadhafi troops sailed from Khums, as well as from Zlitan and Sirte, using inflatable boats in an attempt to lay mines in the Misrata harbor.[44]

4. THE ROLE OF NATO

Throughout the war, Khums was an important city for the Qadhafi regime and served as a staging ground for attacks on Misrata, but the NATO campaign carried out very few airstrikes on the city.[45] Early in the war, UK forces carried out strikes on the regime's naval base located in Khums as part of the campaign to neutralize the regime's air defenses.[46] Later in the conflict, NATO concentrated airpower on Qadhafi forces in Khums that were trying to defend Tripoli from *thuwar* advances along the Coastal

---

[40] *Id.* at Annex I, ¶ 397. *See also* Ch. XI.

[41] *Id.* at Annex I, ¶ 423.

[42] *Id.* at Annex I, ¶ 486.

[43] *Id.* at Annex I, ¶ 365.

[44] *Id.* at Annex I, ¶ 549.

[45] THE WASHINGTON POST, *Fear for Libya's Roman ruins, supra* note 6.

[46] *NATO targets Libyan Navy in Tripoli, Al Khums, and Sirte*, NORTH ATLANTIC TREATY ORGANIZATION, May 20, 2011, *available at* http://www.nato.int/cps/en/natolive/news_74524 .htm.

Highway.[47] The NATO campaign in the city remained limited, however, allowing the Qadhafi forces to hold Khums and control its detention centers until the last days of the war.[48]

5. Conclusion

Due to the fact that Khums was inaccessible for a large part of the conflict, there is limited information available upon which to confirm alleged violations. However, horrific human rights violations were documented after the fall of the Qadhafi regime. One of the most well documented violations that took place in Khums was committed by Qadhafi soldiers who detained, tortured and killed men held captive in shipping containers used as detention facilities. The suffocation and ultimate death of these men was preceded by grave acts of torture and degrading treatment. After the fall of the Qadhafi regime, *thuwar* groups, mostly from Misrata, also targeted the Tawerghan community in Khums for arbitrary arrest, torture and ill-treatment.

The substantial documentation of the deaths of the prisoners held in poorly ventilated detention containers provides evidence that acts of unlawful killing were carried out by Qadhafi forces in Khums. The CoI documented a number of cases of execution and death resulting from torture carried out by Qadhafi forces in the aforementioned detention centers.[49] The Qadhafi forces also held suspected *thuwar* fighters and supporters in detention centers in Khums without providing legal justification for their detention or information regarding their whereabouts. These actions constitute acts of arbitrary detention and enforced disappearances. Qadhafi forces also carried out acts of torture and other forms of ill-treatment against detainees held in detention centers in the city of Khums during the conflict.

After the fall of the Qadhafi regime, *thuwar* forces carried out arrests and held prisoners in detention centers in Khums without due process. The extrajudicial detention and imprisonment committed by *thuwar*

---

[47] *New video showing NATO airstrike on Gadhaffi regime (Khums, Libya)*, LIVELEAK, Aug. 2011, *available at* http://www.liveleak.com/view?i=123_1323777411. *See also* Chris Stephen et al., *Tripoli facing three-sided advance by Libyan rebels*, THE GUARDIAN, Aug. 19, 2011, *available at* http://www.guardian.co.uk/world/2011/aug/19/tripoli-facing-advance-libya-rebels.

[48] For more on the NATO campaign, *see* Ch. IV.

[49] Report of the International Commission of Inquiry, advance unedited version (Mar. 2, 2012), *supra* note 11 at ¶ 35.

groups constitute acts of arbitrary detention and deprivation of liberty. There are documented instances of *thuwar* forces also carrying out acts of torture and other forms of ill-treatment against detainees in the detention centers in Khums in the wake of the fall of the regime. *Thuwar* from Misrata specifically targeted the Tawerghan community in Khums. Torture, ill-treatment, arbitrary detentions and forced displacement were perpetrated against Tawerghans. These attacks were part of a wave of racially-motivated violence carried out by Misrata katiba that pursued Tawerghans for reprisal violence in the wake of the conflict.

CHAPTER TWELVE

ZAWIYYA

1. INTRODUCTION

Zawiyya is Libya's fourth largest city with an estimated population of 200,000 people.[1] Situated along the Mediterranean Sea on the western Libyan Coastal Plain, the city lies some 50 kilometers (31 miles) to the west of Tripoli and 130 kilometers (81 miles) east of the Tunisian border.[2]

Zawiyya is home to the second largest oil refinery in Libya, and processes oil from the city of Fezzan and other nearby oilfields.[3] The refinery and port are located on the outskirts of the city, along the coast to the northwest.[4] With the only oil refinery in western Libya, Zawiyya serves as the primary source of oil for Tripoli.[5] Due to Zawiyya's location between Tripoli and the Tunisian border, its proximity to Tripoli, its port facilities and the refinery, Zawiyya is a strategically important city and became a major theater of military operations during the conflict.

The Libyan Coastal Highway, running along the entirety of the Libyan coast, bisects the city into a northern and southern section. South of the city, a road extends into the interior towards Yafran in the Nafusa Mountains region. To the west of Zawiyya, along the Libyan Coastal Highway lies Surman, about 16 kilometers (10 miles) west of Zawiyya.[6] From Surman, a major road extends into the Nafusa Mountains region, joining the southern road from Zawiyya just outside Yafran.

---

[1] Anthony Bell & David Witter, Institute for the Study of War, 1 The Libyan Revolution: The Roots of Rebellion 33 (Sept. 2011) [hereinafter "The Roots of Rebellion"], *available at* www.understandingwar.org/sites/default/files/Libya_Part1_0 .pdf.

[2] *Id.* at 11.

[3] *Id.* at 11 & 34.

[4] Martin Chulov, *Libya: the importance of Zawiya to the rebels*, The Guardian, Aug. 18, 2011, *available at* http://www.guardian.co.uk/world/2011/aug/18/libya-rebels-zawiya-tripoli-assault.

[5] *Libya conflict: Rebels fight for Zawiya oil refinery*, BBC, Aug. 17, 2011, *available at* http://www.bbc.co.uk/news/world-africa-14561904.

[6] Karin Laub, *Rebels poised to cut off Tripoli*, AP, Aug. 16, 2011, *available at* http://www.boston.com/news/world/africa/articles/2011/08/16/rebels_poised_to_cut_off_tripoli.

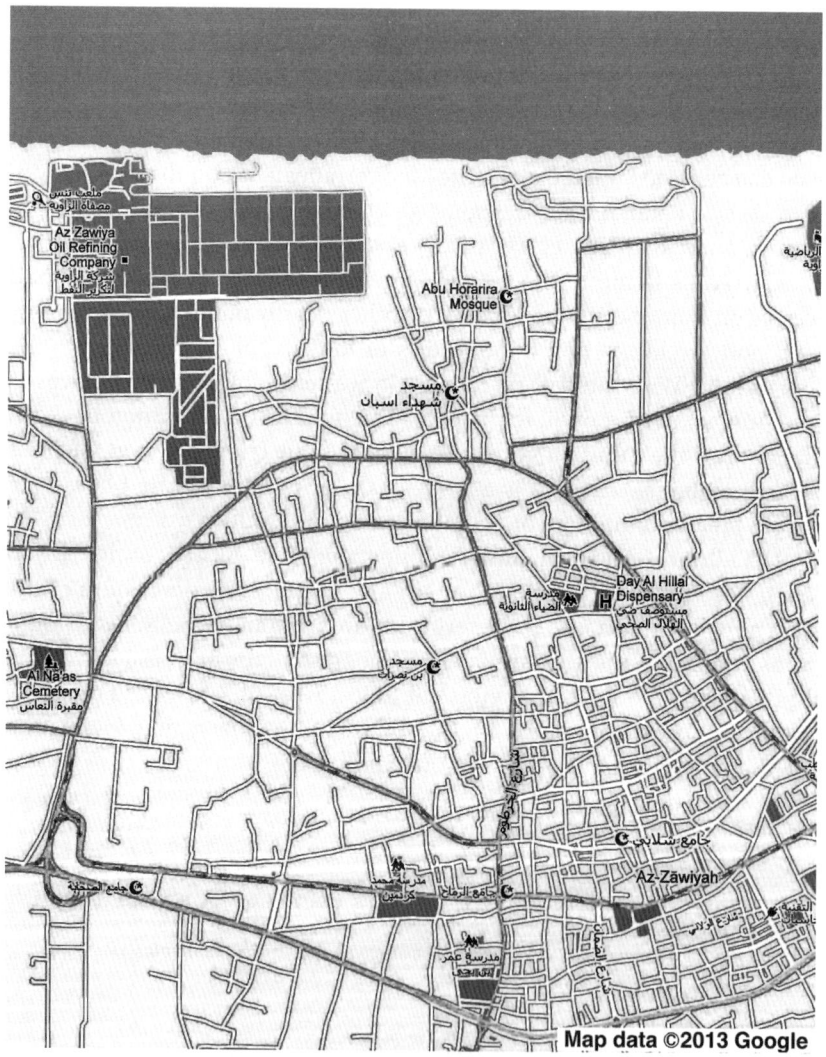

Map 9: Map of Zawiyya (Map data © 2013 Google).

The city hosts one of Libya's largest migrant detention centers for Sub-Saharan migrants returned from Europe.[7] After the retreat of the Qadhafi forces from Zawiyya, this detention facility was used by the local *thuwar* groups and the National Transitional Council (NTC) to hold foreigners suspected of fighting alongside the Qadhafi forces as mercenaries.[8]

Zawiyya was one of the first cities in western Libya to organize large opposition protests against the Qadhafi regime in February 2011 and became a fierce battleground when Qadhafi forces entered the city attacking civilians on 23 February. After an intense assault on the city in early March 2011, Qadhafi's forces controlled Zawiyya until near the end of the conflict when *thuwar* forces came from the Nafusa Mountains region and took the city with NATO support in August.[9]

2. SUMMARY OF EVENTS

Protests broke out in Zawiyya on 18–19 February 2011 when thousands gathered in the city's central square to express opposition to the Qadhafi regime's violent crackdown that was underway in Benghazi.[10] According to witness testimony to the CoI, protests began on the evening of 19 February when young men gathered in the central square in Zawiyya (later renamed Martyrs' Square). The protest resembled a sit-in and several of those interviewed by the CoI said that the police in Zawiyya refrained from attacking the protesters.[11]

The situation turned violent when military units from the Khamis Katiba arrived on 23 February, attempting to disperse the demonstrators and gain full control over Zawiyya.[12] Members of the brigade invaded the central square and fired on the protesters, who were still reportedly unarmed

---

[7] HUMAN RIGHTS WATCH, PUSHED BACK, PUSHED AROUND: ITALY'S FORCED RETURN OF BOAT MIGRANTS AND ASYLUM SEEKERS, LIBYA'S MISTREATMENT OF MIGRANTS AND ASYLUM SEEKERS 82 (Sept. 19, 2009), *available at* http://www.hrw.org/sites/default/files/reports/italy0909webwcover_0.pdf.

[8] AMNESTY INTERNATIONAL, DETENTION ABUSES STAINING THE NEW LIBYA 6 (Oct. 13, 2011), *available at* http://www.amnesty.org/sites/impact.amnesty.org/files/PUBLIC/mde1903 62011en.pdf.

[9] *Libya conflict: Rebels take two key coastal cities*, BBC, Aug. 20, 2011, *available at* http://www.bbc.co.uk/news/world-africa-14599156.

[10] *18 killed in Benghazi demos Friday*, NOW LEBANON, Feb. 19, 2011, *available at* http://www.nowlebanon.com/NewsArchiveDetails.aspx?ID=242231.

[11] Report of the International Commission of Inquiry on Libya, U.N. HRC. 19th Sess., Annex I, ¶ 125. U.N. Doc. A/HRC/19/68, advance unedited version (Mar. 2, 2012).

[12] *See* Ch. II, Sec. 3.2. *See also Id.* at Annex I, ¶ 126.

at this time.[13] Around this point a transfer of responsibility for operations in Zawiyya took place, and it is unclear if the Qadhafi forces were under local command in Zawiyya, or operating under the command of Khamis Qadhafi.[14]

The Qadhafi forces moved into the city center with 20-30 military vehicles and 200 armed soldiers, firing live ammunition as they entered. Seven male protesters were killed during the incursion.[15] The Qadhafi military units used heavy artillery, at one point firing an anti-aircraft gun that hit the central mosque where protesters had been camped out, destroying a minaret.[16] Migrant workers fleeing the violence reported to Human Rights Watch (HRW) officials that Qadhafi forces had fired on protesters gathering in Zawiyya's main square after Friday prayers on 25 February.[17] Casualty estimates range from 10 to 123.[18] Doctors from a field hospital in Zawiyya reported that 17 people were killed and 150 wounded during the first day of the clashes.[19]

As a reaction to the violence, the protesters began to take up arms and clash with Qadhafi forces. *Thuwar* in Zawiyya were made up of soldiers and police who defected from the Qadhafi regime as well as civilians armed with weapons captured in the early days of the fighting. The rebels organized a council of defected army officers, the Zawiyya Military Council, under the command of Colonel Hussayn Darbuk, to orchestrate

---

[13] *See infra* Sec. 3.1.

[14] Two interviewees, both soldiers, told the CoI that "Khamis Qadhafi had the assistance of the head of Qaddafi forces in Zawiya during this time." Report of the International Commission of Inquiry, advance unedited version (Mar. 2, 2012), *supra* note 11 at Annex I, ¶ 126.

[15] *Id.* at Annex I, ¶ 127. *See also infra* Secs. 3.1. & 3.2.

[16] *Gaddafi forces hit back at revolt*, INDEPENDENT IE, Feb. 24, 2011, *available at* http://www.independent.ie/breaking-news/world-news/gaddafi-forces-hit-back-at-revolt-2554397.html.

[17] *Libya: Security Forces Fire on Protesters in Western City*, HUMAN RIGHTS WATCH, Feb. 26, 2011, *available at* http://www.hrw.org/en/news/2011/02/26/libya-security-forces-fire-protesters-western-city.

[18] Paul Schemm & Bassem Mroue, *Protesters Hit by Hail of Gunfire in Libya March*, AP, Feb. 25, 2011, *available at* http://abclocal.go.com/wpvi/story?section=news/national_world&id=7979856; Maria Golovnina, *Rebels control Libya town of Zawiyah*, REUTERS, Feb. 27, 2011, *available at* http://www.reuters.com/article/2011/02/27/us-libya-protests-zawiyah-idUSTRE71Q10Q20110227; Ian Black, *Heavy fighting in former stronghold as Gaddafi's forces stage counterattacks*, THE GUARDIAN, Feb. 24, 2011, *available at* http://www.guardian.co.uk/world/2011/feb/24/muammar-gaddafi-libya-offensive; INDEPENDENT IE, *Gaddafi forces hit back at revolt, supra* note 16.

[19] *Doctors report 17 dead in Libyan city of Zawiya*, CNN, Feb. 25, 2011, *available at* http://www.cnn.com/2011/WORLD/africa/02/24/libya.protests/index.html.

the city's resistance.[20] The *thuwar* were able to repel the initial regime incursion, and quickly set up defenses throughout the city, concentrating in the area around the central square.[21]

After retreating from the city at the end of February, Qadhafi forces set up checkpoints along the entrances to Zawiyya, effectively trapping *thuwar* fighters inside the city and preventing the delivery of supplies.[22] Qadhafi officials also cut off all telephone and Internet connections.[23] The siege imposed by the Qadhafi regime led to a shortage of medical supplies, drastically hindering the ability of doctors and nurses to treat the wounded.[24] While doctors in Zawiyya pleaded with the international community for supplies, the medical crisis worsened as foreign nurses began to flee Libya.[25] The United Nations World Food Program (WFP) attempted to relieve the siege, but the security situation forced WFP vessels to turn back at the port of Benghazi.[26]

At the same time Qadhafi forces started to gather along the eastern and southern edges of the city in advance of a planned attack.[27] Zawiyyans began to suffer daily assaults in early March 2011 as Qadhafi forces attempted to move back into Zawiyya to claim the city from the *thuwar*.[28] Reports indicate that Brigadier General Mahdi al-ʿArabi, Deputy Chief of Staff of the Armed Forces and resident of Zawiyya, commanded a deterrent battalion into the city at this time.[29]

---

[20] BELL & WITTER, THE ROOTS OF REBELLION, *supra* note 1 at 31.

[21] *Conflict Analysis: Zawiya, Libya (as of 08 March 2011)*, UNITED NATIONS INSTITUTE FOR TRAINING AND RESEARCH, Mar. 23, 2011, *available at* http://reliefweb.int/sites/reliefweb.int/files/resources/7308EDFFF4FDA0478525785D00702BF7-map.pdf.

[22] HUMAN RIGHTS WATCH, *Libya: Security Forces Fire on Protesters in Western City, supra* note 17.

[23] Vivienne Walt, *Gaddafi Gets His Revenge: The Price of Rebellion*, TIME WORLD, Mar. 17, 2011, *available at* http://www.time.com/time/world/article/0,8599,2059596,00.html.

[24] *See infra* Sec. 3.7. *See also Libyan rebel-held city on guard, fear for supplies*, REUTERS, Mar. 3, 2011, *available at* http://www.reuters.com/article/2011/03/04/us-libya-zawiyah-idUS TRE72308920110304.

[25] *Conditions in Libya deteriorating*, AL JAZEERA, Mar. 4, 2011, *available at* http://www.aljazeera.com/indepth/spotlight/libya/2011/03/20113416274271330.html.

[26] *Libyans Need Food, WFP says*, UNITED INTERNATIONAL PRESS, Mar. 7, 2011, *available at* http://tripolipost.com/articledetail.asp?c=1&i=5532.

[27] REUTERS, *Libyan rebel-held city on guard, fear for supplies, supra* note 24.

[28] Mariam Karouny, *Zawiyah becomes ghost town as army ring tightens*, REUTERS, Mar. 10, 2011, *available at* http://www.reuters.com/article/2011/03/10/us-libya-zawiyah-city-idUSTRE7296P420110310.

[29] *See* Ch. II, Sec. 3.3. *See also* BELL & WITTER, THE ROOTS OF REBELLION, *supra* note 1 at 33.

On 4 March, Qadhafi forces moved into Zawiyya, launching extensive artillery, rocket and anti-aircraft barrages, and using snipers to target *thuwar* fighters.[30] Another battalion-sized force from the Khamis Katiba arrived with reinforcements from Tripoli with around 500 troops, tanks and armored vehicles.[31] Media reports also confirm that troops from the Khamis Katiba led the assault, and were later supported by another regime brigade.[32] In the face of overwhelming firepower, the *thuwar* withdrew to the central square.[33] By the end of the day, Qadhafi forces had captured most of Zawiyya outside the city center.[34] Death tolls on 4 March ranged from 18 to 50.[35] Witnesses from Zawiyya's main hospital indicated that 18 people were killed and 120 wounded in the fighting.[36]

According to witness statements provided to the CoI, Qadhafi forces targeted mainly unarmed protesters during the incursion, using rocket-propelled grenades (RPGs) and heavy machine guns.[37] The CoI was told by a former senior security official that during the fighting Qadhafi forces fired Grad rockets and mortars into the city from the outskirts of the town. Another former senior official stated that it was commonly understood within the military that the Grad rockets were indiscriminate and would lead to civilian casualties.[38]

Thuwar forces suffered a critical loss on 4 March when Coronel Darbuk and more than 40 rebels were killed, and 50 wounded after *thuwar* forces attempted a raid on a Qadhafi base in Harsha, 12 miles west of Zawiyya.

---

[30] *37 dead as Gaddafi regime hits back*, PRESS ASSOCIATION, Mar. 4, 2011, *available at* http://www.independent.ie/breaking-news/world-news/37-dead-as-gaddafi-regime-hits-back-2565656.html.

[31] BELL & WITTER, THE ROOTS OF REBELLION, *supra* note 1 at 33.

[32] Martin Chulov et al., *Libya: Fierce day of raids and clashes signals shift towards civil war*, THE GUARDIAN, Mar. 4, 2011, *available at* http://www.guardian.co.uk/world/2011/mar/04/libya-rebels-civil-war-gaddafi; PRESS ASSOCIATION, *37 dead as Gaddafi regime hits back, supra* note 30.

[33] PRESS ASSOCIATION, *37 dead as Gaddafi regime hits back, supra* note 30.

[34] *Libya unrest: Deadly clashes in battle for Zawiya*, BBC, Mar. 4, 2011, *available at* http://www.bbc.co.uk/news/world-africa-12652613; *Obama ups pressure, Interpol issues global alert on Gaddafi*, AFP, Mar. 5, 2011, *available at* http://www.thedailystar.net/newDesign/news-details.php?nid=176475; *Battle for Libya: Gaddafi troops engage Zawiya rebels*, BBC, Mar. 5, 2011, *available at* http://www.bbc.co.uk/news/world-africa-12654670.

[35] Chulov et al., *Libya: Fierce day of raids and clashes signals shift towards civil war, supra* note 34; BBC, *Libya unrest: Deadly clashes in battle for Zawiya*, 34.

[36] *See infra* Sec. 3.2. *See also* PRESS ASSOCIATION, *37 dead as Gaddafi regime hits back, supra* note 30.

[37] Report of the International Commission of Inquiry, advance unedited version (Mar. 2, 2012), *supra* note 11 at Annex I, ¶ 558.

[38] *See infra* Sec. 3.7; Report of the International Commission of Inquiry, advance unedited version (Mar. 2, 2012), *supra* note 11 at Annex I, ¶ 557.

After this failed raid, and with the military siege diminishing rebel supplies, regime control over Zawiyya was imminent.[39]

On 5 March, Qadhafi forces assaulted the city again using tanks and artillery fire to cover their advance. Military artillery shells hit residential neighborhoods, and local doctors reported that as many as 30 were killed in the fighting.[40] Over the following days, *thuwar* and Qadhafi forces engaged in fierce street battles, with *thuwar* fighting to hold control of Zawiyya's city center.[41] A rebel fighter told reporters that *thuwar* forces seized weapons during the fighting, and that *thuwar* fighters had taken hostage and killed at least ten Qadhafi soldiers in a hotel in the central square.[42]

Qadhafi forces reached the central square on 6 March, pushing *thuwar* fighters to the outskirts. The two sides fought again the following day for control over the square, heavily damaging a mosque in the process.[43] By 9 March, Qadhafi forces had fully pushed their way into the central square as the *thuwar* retreated.[44] The rest of the city was described as a "ghost town" with empty streets and buildings showing significant destruction.[45] The CoI gathered testimony relating to the fighting that had taken place in Zawiyya at the Suq Mosque in the central square. When the *thuwar* were losing ground, they reportedly retreated into the mosque and fired on Qadhafi forces from positions inside. Multiple testimonies indicated that the *thuwar* had used the mosque to store weapons, and as a field hospital, with mostly combatants stationed inside. Shortly after Qadhafi forces gained control of Zawiyya, they completely demolished the mosque, which had become a symbol of *thuwar* resistance.[46] The military assault

[39] BELL & WITTER, THE ROOTS OF REBELLION, *supra* note 1 at 33.

[40] BBC, *Battle for Libya: Gaddafi troops engage Zawiya rebels, supra* note 34.

[41] Karouny, *Zawiyah becomes ghost town as army ring tightens, supra* note 28.

[42] *See infra* Sec. 3.7. *See also Libya forces try to halt rebel move toward capital,* SUN STAR, Mar. 7, 2011, *available at* http://www.sunstar.com.ph/breaking-news/2011/03/07/libya-forces-try-halt-rebel-move-toward-capital-143492.

[43] *Libya revolt as it happened: Monday,* BBC, Mar. 22, 2011, *available at* http://news.bbc.co.uk/2/hi/africa/9432055.stm; Paul Schemm, *Libyan warplanes strike rebels at oil port,* AP, Mar. 7, 2011, *available at* http://www.staradvertiser.com/news/breaking/117515113.html; BBC, *Battle for Libya: Gaddafi troops engage Zawiya rebels, supra* note 34.

[44] *See* Ch. II, Sec. 3.3. *See also* Report of the International Commission of Inquiry, advance unedited version (Mar. 2, 2012), *supra* note 11 at Annex I, ¶ 560.

[45] Karouny, *Zawiyah becomes ghost town as army ring tightens, supra* note 28.

[46] Report of the International Commission of Inquiry, advance unedited version (Mar. 2, 2012), *supra* note 11 at Annex I, ¶ 560.

led to significant destruction in Zawiyya, leaving buildings leveled and residential structures heavily damaged.[47]

Due to the ability of the Qadhafi forces to quickly deploy elite military units from Tripoli, they were able to overwhelm the *thuwar* movement in Zawiyya. Despite the efforts of the several hundred *thuwar* fighters, largely composed of civilian recruits without military training, the *thuwar* were unable to effectively resist the overwhelming force of the Qadhafi military.[48] By 10 March, *thuwar* forces were surrounded and almost completely out of ammunition.[49] Many *thuwar* escaped or went underground, and 300–400 fighters fled into the surrounding areas or made their way to join the growing rebellion in the Nafusa Mountains region to the south, where they formed the Zawiyya Katiba.[50]

On 11 March, Qadhafi supporters rallied in the center of Zawiyya, marking the victory of Qadhafi forces over the city.[51] During the two weeks of battle there were accounts that over 200 *thuwar* fighters and civilians were killed and hundreds more wounded.[52] Doctors at the Zawiyya teaching hospital estimated that up to 100 people had died during the battles between Qadhafi and *thuwar* forces.[53] Other medical staff told reporters that they counted 175 people killed in battle.[54] The exact number of casualties is difficult to determine, however, as reports also indicate that bodies were promptly buried throughout the city and graves bulldozed to cover up evidence of the violence.[55]

---

[47] Donald MacIntyre, *Gaddafi's men try to obliterate traces of massacre in Zawiya*, THE INDEPENDENT, Apr. 6, 2011, *available at* http://www.independent.co.uk/news/world/africa/gaddafis-men-try-to-obliterate-traces-of-massacre-in-zawiya-2263670.html; BELL & WITTER, THE ROOTS OF REBELLION, *supra* note 1 at 34.

[48] INTERNATIONAL CRISIS GROUP, HOLDING LIBYA TOGETHER: SECURITY CHALLENGES AFTER QADHAFI 7 (Dec. 14, 2011) [hereinafter "HOLDING LIBYA TOGETHER"], *available at* http://www.crisisgroup.org/~/media/Files/Middle%20East%20North%20Africa/North%20Africa/115%20Holding%20Libya%20Together%20--%20Security%20Challenges%20after%20Qadhafi.pdf.

[49] *Libya: Gaddafi loyalists mount onslaught*, BBC, Mar. 11, 2011, *available at* http://www.bbc.co.uk/news/world-africa-12708687; Anthony Shadid, *Qaddafi Forces Bear Down on Strategic Town as Rebels Flee*, N.Y. TIMES, Mar. 10, 2011, *available at* http://www.nytimes.com/2011/03/11/world/africa/11libya.html.

[50] BELL & WITTER, THE ROOTS OF REBELLION, *supra* note 1 at 33.

[51] Michael Georgy & Maria Golovnina, *Rebels repel Gaddafi assault on Libya oil port*, REUTERS, Mar. 11, 2011, *available at* http://in.reuters.com/article/2011/03/11/idINIndia-55498020110311.

[52] BELL & WITTER, THE ROOTS OF REBELLION, *supra* note 1 at 33.

[53] Donald MacIntyre, *Gaddafi's men try to obliterate traces of massacre in Zawiya*, *supra* note 47.

[54] Walt, *Gaddafi Gets His Revenge: The Price of Rebellion*, *supra* note 23.

[55] *Id.*

In the wake of the assault, Qadhafi forces searched the city looking for *thuwar* holdouts, going from door to door and taking anyone suspected of participating in the uprising. Reports consistently confirm the role of units from the Khamis Katiba in the attack on Zawiyya and its aftermath.[56] Witnesses told reporters that the Khamis Katiba carried out "clean-up" operations after the battles subsided, sweeping through the city and detaining young men suspected of *thuwar* involvement.[57] Other accounts report that Qadhafi forces took injured *thuwar* from hospitals for questioning.[58]

After mid-March, opposition in Zawiyya that had gone underground continued to organize and carry out irregular guerrilla attacks against Qadhafi troops.[59] The *thuwar* were not able to engage in sustained battle due to insufficient supplies, but did connect with rebels in the Nafusa Mountains region who attempted to smuggle weapons into Zawiyya and spark another uprising.[60]

On 18 March, President Obama delivered public remarks demanding the Qadhafi regime abide by UN Security Council Resolution 1973 by halting the advance on Benghazi, and pulling back from Ajdabiya, Misrata and Zawiyya. Obama warned that failure to comply would lead to military action.[61] The United States, United Kingdom and France began their military intervention in Libya on March 19, focusing strikes in the Benghazi region, and launching attacks intended to cripple Qadhafi's air defenses.[62]

---

[56] *Libya unrest: Entering Zawiya*, BBC, Mar. 11, 2011, *available at* http://www.bbc.co.uk/news/world-africa-12720968.

[57] *See infra* Sec. 3.3. Bill Neely, *Zawiya town center devastated and almost deserted*, THE GUARDIAN, Mar. 10, 2011, *available at* http://www.guardian.co.uk/world/2011/mar/10/zawiya-town-itv-regime-battle.

[58] MacIntyre, *Gaddafi's men try to obliterate traces of massacre in Zawiya, supra* note 47.

[59] BELL & WITTER, THE ROOTS OF REBELLION, *supra* note 1 at 34; *'Many casualties' as Libyan rebels batter Zawiyah*, AHRAM ONLINE, Aug. 14, 2011, *available at* http://english.ahram.org.eg/NewsContent/2/8/18827/World/Region/Many-casualties-as-Libyan-rebels-batter-Zawiyah.aspx.

[60] BELL & WITTER, THE ROOTS OF REBELLION, *supra* note 1 at 11; Julian Borger et al., *Battle for Tripoli: pivotal victory in the mountains helped big push*, THE GUARDIAN, Aug. 22, 2011, *available at* http://www.guardian.co.uk/world/2011/aug/22/battle-for-tripoli-libya-gaddafi.

[61] *See* Ch. III, Sec. 2. *See also* BELL & WITTER, THE ROOTS OF REBELLION, *supra* note 1 at 34.

[62] *See* Ch. IV, 6.1. *See also* ANTHONY BELL & DAVID WITTER, INSTITUTE FOR THE STUDY OF WAR, 2 THE LIBYAN REVOLUTION: THE ROOTS OF REBELLION 24 (Sept. 2011), *available at* www.understandingwar.org/sites/default/files/Libya_Part2_0.pdf.

The NATO intervention would not turn its attention to Zawiyya until June, when fighting again broke out in and around the city.[63] On 11 June, *thuwar* re-entered the city from the Nafusa Mountains region, launching a significant attack on Qadhafi forces with heavy weapons. The *thuwar* offensive forced the closure of a section of the Libyan Coastal Highway east of the city. They also occupied the western part of Zawiyya, requiring the Qadhafi regime to commit more troops to the city's defense. Fighting continued and escalated on 12 June, with the two sides engaged in intense street battles. While Qadhafi forces were able to reclaim Zawiyya and reopen the Coastal Highway by the end of the day, the attack cut off Tripoli's critical supply lines from Tunisia.[64]

After the June incursion by *thuwar*, NATO reported that it was focusing intelligence gathering on the Zawiyya region to build a better understanding of the events on the ground.[65] On 20 June, NATO launched a strike on a compound suspected of being a Qadhafi command post in the town of Surman, situated west of Zawiyya.[66] Major General Al-Khawayldi al-Hamadi, a former member of Qadhafi's Revolutionary Council, was reportedly present in the compound.[67] The home of Khalid al-Hamadi, son of Al-Khawayldi, was hit in the attack, and 19 people reportedly killed, including eight children.[68] *Thuwar* fighters in the area stated that Qadhafi forces had used the buildings as a communications site connected to a command center at the Al-Hamadi residence.[69]

Despite NATO involvement and the June incursion from the Nafusa Mountains region, Qadhafi forces maintained firm control over the Zawiyya

---

[63] *See infra* Sec. 4.

[64] *See* Ch. II, Sec. 3.3.

[65] *Press briefing on Libya*, North Atlantic Treaty Organization, June 14, 2011, *available at* http://www.nato.int/cps/en/natolive/opinions_75403.htm.

[66] *See infra* Sec. 4. *See also Press briefing on Libya*, North Atlantic Treaty Organization, June 21, 2011, *available at* http://www.nato.int/cps/en/natolive/opinions_75652.htm.

[67] Report of the International Commission of Inquiry, advance unedited version (Mar. 2, 2012), *supra* note 11 at Annex I, ¶ 636; *Press briefing on Libya*, North Atlantic Treaty Organization, *supra* note 66; International Legal Assistance Consortium, Report of The Independent Civil Society Fact-Finding Mission to Libya 17 (Jan. 9, 2012), *available at* http://www.ilac.se/download/reports_documents/mission-reports_documents/LIBYA_FF_REPORT_111221.pdf.

[68] *See* Ch. III, Sec. 6.2. *See also* International Legal Assistance Consortium, Report of The Independent Civil Society Fact-Finding Mission to Libya, *supra* note 67 at 17.

[69] *Errant NATO strikes in Libya*, N.Y. Times, Dec. 16, 2011, *available at* http://www.nytimes.com/interactive/2011/12/16/world/africa/nato-airstrikes-in-libya.html?ref=africa#page/warehouses.

region, and continued to suppress the local population.[70] By the start of August, Zawiyya constituted a critical part of the regime's shrinking territory of control, standing as a barrier to a *thuwar* advance on Tripoli from the Nafusa Mountains region. It was also the last remaining source of fuel to Tripoli and a key stronghold on the road to Tunisia, Qadhafi's only remaining major source of supplies.[71]

On 13 August, *thuwar* forces made a rapid advance from the Nafusa Mountains region, taking the Coastal Highway junction at Surman and attacking key points on the Jafara Plain.[72] Many of the returning rebels were Zawiyyans who had fled and formed the Zawiyya Katiba with other fighters in the Nafusa Mountains region.[73] Later that day, *thuwar* entered Zawiyya from the south and west, initially engaging in light confrontation before encountering stronger resistance from Qadhafi troops stationed along the eastern edge of the city.[74] *Thuwar* forces fought through sniper and artillery fire and were able to enter the central square.[75] Their control of the square remained tenuous, however, as Qadhafi forces continued to attack.[76]

Sources in Zawiyya told reporters that *thuwar* advances were aided significantly by NATO airstrikes that hit Qadhafi targets around Zawiyya,

---

[70] *Press briefing on Libya*, NORTH ATLANTIC TREATY ORGANIZATION, July 12, 2011, *available at* http://www.nato.int/cps/en/natolive/opinions_76355.htm.

[71] Ghaith Abdul-Ahad, *Fuel smuggler's paradise: a day on the border between Libya and Tunisia*, THE GUARDIAN, Aug. 10, 2011, *available at* http://www.guardian.co.uk/world/2011/aug/10/fuel-smugglers-border-libya-tunisia; Damien McElroy, *Libyan rebels battle for Zawiya*, THE TELEGRAPH, Aug. 13, 2011, *available at* http://www.telegraph.co.uk/news/worldnews/africaandindianocean/libya/8700198/Libyan-rebels-battle-for-Zawiya.html.

[72] Michael Georgy, *Libyan rebels fly flag over key town near Tripoli*, REUTERS, Aug. 14, 2011, *available at* http://www.reuters.com/article/2011/08/14/us-libya-idUSTRE77A2Y920110814.

[73] *See* Ch. II, Sec. 3.3. *See also Id.*; Eman El-Shenawi, *Tripoli quick to deny rebel capture of strategic port town as fighters claim victory*, AL ARABIYA, Aug. 13, 2011, *available at* http://english.alarabiya.net/articles/2011/08/13/162174.html; VIRA VARUN ET AL., CENTER FOR STRATEGIC AND INTERNATIONAL STUDIES, THE LIBYAN UPRISING: AN UNCERTAIN TRAJECTORY 41 (June 20, 2011), *available at* http://csis.org/files/publication/110620_libya.pdf; *Armed battles in Libya city streets*, PRESS ASSOCIATION, Aug. 13, 2011, *available at* http://www.independent.ie/breaking-news/world-news/armed-battles-in-libya-city-streets-2847757.html.

[74] McElroy, *Libyan rebels battle for Zawiya*, *supra* note 71; AHRAM ONLINE, '*Many casualties' as Libyan rebels batter Zawiyah*, *supra* note 59; *Gunfire heard in Libyan town of Zawiyah*, REUTERS, Aug. 13, 2011, *available at* http://af.reuters.com/article/libyaNews/idAFL6E7JD07B20110813; PRESS ASSOCIATION, *Armed battles in Libya city streets*, *supra* note 73.

[75] *Libya blog*, AL JAZEERA, Aug. 13, 2011, *available at* http://blogs.aljazeera.net/liveblog/libya-aug-13-2011-2118; El-Shenawi, *Tripoli quick to deny rebel capture of strategic port town as fighters claim victory*, *supra* note 73.

[76] PRESS ASSOCIATION, *Armed battles in Libya city streets*, *supra* note 73.

including Nattafa to the south of the city.[77] As with other theaters of operation, however, a number of NATO strikes led to the accidental killings of friendly forces.[78] On 13 August, NATO planes reportedly destroyed a tank captured from Qadhafi forces, killing four *thuwar*.[79]

Fighting continued on 14 August, as *thuwar* forces took control of the Coastal Highway connecting Tunisia and Tripoli in the southern part of the city.[80] The city center remained contested as Qadhafi forces used snipers to repel the *thuwar* advance.[81] Qadhafi forces also continued to hold the critically important oil facilities on the northern edge of the town.[82] Clashes continued on 15 August as Qadhafi forces fought to re-claim Zawiyya's city center.[83] As the day progressed, Qadhafi forces continued to fire mortars and Grad rockets into *thuwar* controlled areas.[84]

By 16 August, *thuwar* forces had continued to consolidate control over Zawiyya as Qadhafi forces from the east shelled the city with artillery fire, wounding civilians.[85] Qadhafi forces held onto the vital refinery in the northwest and the hospital in the east of the city. From the start of the battle, Zawiyya's hospital was a strategic center for Qadhafi forces who used it as a base for snipers to control *thuwar* advances.[86]

On 16 and 17 August, *thuwar* engaged Qadhafi forces at the Zawiyya oil refinery. By the end of 16 August, *thuwar* were able to cut off outgoing oil and gas supplies to Tripoli despite stiff resistance and sniper fire from forces guarding the complex.[87] On 18 August, *thuwar* forces made

---

[77] Martin Veal & Missy Ryan, *Gaddafi forces, rebels fight over Zawiyah*, REUTERS, Aug. 13, 2011, *available at* http://uk.reuters.com/article/2011/08/13/libya-idUKLDE77C01F20110813.

[78] For other incidents involving accidental strikes and civilian casualties, *see* Ch. III, Sec. 6.2.

[79] AHRAM ONLINE, *'Many casualties' as Libyan rebels batter Zawiyah, supra* note 59.

[80] *Libya blog*, AL JAZEERA, Aug. 14, 2011, *available at* http://blogs.aljazeera.net/liveblog/libya-aug-14-2011-1615; AHRAM ONLINE, *'Many casualties' as Libyan rebels batter Zawiyah, supra* note 59.

[81] *Id.*

[82] Michael Georgy, *Libya's Zawiyah on edge after rebel capture*, REUTERS, Aug. 15, 2011, *available at* http://www.reuters.com/article/2011/08/15/us-libya-zawiyah-scene-idUSTRE77E3R020110815.

[83] Karin Laub, *Gadhafi forces try to block Libyan rebel advance*, AP, Aug. 15, 2011, *available at* http://www.katu.com/news/national/127736888.html.

[84] Georgy, *Libya's Zawiya on edge after rebel capture, supra* note 82.

[85] *Libyan rebels tighten grip around Tripoli*, AL JAZEERA, Aug. 17, 2011, *available at* http://www.aljazeera.com/news/africa/2011/08/20118171715442761275.html.

[86] *See infra* Sec. 3.7. *See also* Karin Laub, *Gadhafi's troops use hospital as base, doctors say*, AP, Aug. 16, 2011, *available at* http://www.msnbc.msn.com/id/44164314/ns/world_news-mideast_n_africa/#.Tz4acLEkKf5.

[87] *Libya conflict: Rebels fight for Zawiya oil refinery*, BBC, Aug. 17, 2011, *available at* http://www.bbc.co.uk/news/world-africa-14561904; Damien McElroy, *Libya: fierce battle under-*

major advances throughout Zawiyya, capturing the oil refinery and hospital where Qadhafi forces had gathered.[88] The next day, Qadhafi forces continued to barrage the city with rocket and artillery fire, while NATO airstrikes impeded their attempt to re-take the city.[89]

On 20 August, *thuwar* forces continued to push Qadhafi forces out of the town while rockets fell on the city from Qadhafi positions to the east.[90] Qadhafi's last holdouts around the central square were defeated and the city fell under complete *thuwar* control.[91] As *thuwar* forces captured Zawiyya, along with the strategic cities of Sabrata, Tarhuna and Al-Gharyan, Tripoli was surrounded as the war neared its end. With NATO carrying out raids on Qadhafi targets, *thuwar* forces from Zawiyya moved into Tripoli and took the headquarters of the Khamis Katiba.[92]

Human rights observers reported on violations committed by both Qadhafi and *thuwar* forces during the period of heavy fighting and after the retreat of Qadhafi forces in Zawiyya.[93] After gaining full control over Zawiyya, *thuwar* targeted suspected Qadhafi supporters. The CoI talked to residents in Zawiyya, who provided evidence of *thuwar* violations, including detentions, house raids, pillaging and destruction of property.[94] Media reports contain consistent accounts of *thuwar* targeting Qadhafi officials. On 12 September, NTC sources reported that 'Abd al-Hafid Zulaytini, a former Central Bank governor and finance minister during the Qadhafi era,

---

way for crucial Zawiyah oil refinery, THE TELEGRAPH, Aug. 17, 2011, *available at* http://www .telegraph.co.uk/news/worldnews/africaandindianocean/libya/8707413/Libya-fierce-battle-underway-for-crucial-Zawiyah-oil-refinery.html.

[88] Florent Marcie, *Libya rebels claim capture of two strategic towns*, AFP, Aug. 18, 2011, *available at* http://www.google.com/hostednews/afp/article/ALeqM5hCMHc1FtvRm5H_ ES2E0Sc43UAPaw?docId=CNG.de226b3f8ca77186559071adc6e480e0.161; *Libya rebels take control of Zawiyah oil refinery*, REUTERS, Aug. 18, 2011, *available at* http://www.trust.org/ alertnet/news/libya-rebels-take-control-of-zawiyah-oil-refinery; *Libyan Rebel Chief: 'The End is Near for Gaddafi'*, SKY NEWS, Aug. 20, 2011, *available at* http://news.sky.com/home/ world-news/article/16053368.

[89] *Libya Blog*, AL JAZEERA, Aug. 19, 2011, *available at* http://blogs.aljazeera.net/liveblog/ libya-aug-19-2011-2230.

[90] *Libya Blog*, AL JAZEERA, Aug. 21, 2011, *available at* http://blogs.aljazeera.net/liveblog/ libya-aug-21-2011-0017.

[91] SKY NEWS, *Libyan Rebel Chief: 'The End is Near for Gaddafi, supra* note 88.

[92] ALISON PARGETER, LIBYA: THE RISE AND FALL OF QADDAFI 240 (New Haven, USA: Yale University Press, 2012).

[93] *Both sides in Libya conflict must protect detainees from torture*, AMNESTY INTERNATIONAL, Aug. 25, 2011, *available at* http://www.amnesty.org/en/news-and-updates/both-sides-libya-conflict-must-protect-detainees-torture-2011-08-25.

[94] *See infra* Sec. 3.7. *See also* Report of the International Commission of Inquiry, advance unedited version (Mar. 2, 2012), *supra* note 11 at Annex I, ¶¶ 720–721.

was captured in Zawiyya.[95] The CoI reported that in late October, a Qadhafi soldier who was recovering in a Zawiyyan hospital was stabbed to death by a *thuwar*.[96]

As *thuwar* groups carried out violations against suspected Qadhafi loyalists, there were also clashes between the armed factions from various cities. Seven people were reportedly killed after violence erupted on 14 November between two armed groups (rival factions from Zawiyya and nearby Warshifana).[97] The violence lasted for several days and witnesses reported hearing gunfire and RPGs.[98] Medics in the Warshifana region put the death toll at 13; four of the dead were from Zawiyya and nine from Warshifana.[99] The clashes between *thuwar* groups also led to incidents of arbitrary arrest of persons associated with rival kata'ib.[100]

Human rights groups reported incidents of torture and other abuses in detention facilities under control of *thuwar* groups in the wake of the fall of the Qadhafi regime.[101] The violations included reprisal attacks against those suspected of supporting the Qadhafi regime, including the targeting

---

[95] *Libya: Bani Walid residents given two days to leave before onslaught*, THE TELEGRAPH, Sept. 14, 2011, *available at* http://www.telegraph.co.uk/news/worldnews/africaandin dianocean/libya/8761667/Libya-Bani-Walid-residents-given-two-days-to-leave-before-on slaught.html.

[96] SUN STAR, *Libya forces try to halt rebel move toward capital, supra* note 42.

[97] Karen Allen, *Libyan factions in deadly clashes near Zawiya*, BBC, Nov. 14, 2011, *available at* http://www.bbc.co.uk/news/world-africa-15726099; Rami Al-Shaheibi, *Rival Libyan militia clash near military base*, AP, Nov. 13, 2011, *available at* http://www.usatoday.com/news/world/story/2011-11-13/libya-militias/51184224/1; *Rival Military Militia clash near military base*, MSNBC, Nov. 13, 2011, *available at* http://www.msnbc.msn.com/id/45276784/ns/world_news-mideast_n_africa; *Clashes between Libyan Militia kills 2*, SEATTLE TIMES, Nov. 13, 2011, *available at* http://seattletimes.nwsource.com/html/nationworld/2016749284_apmllibya.html; *Libyan militias engage in battle*, BELFAST TELEGRAPH, Nov. 13, 2011, *available at* http://www.belfasttelegraph.co.uk/news/world-news/libyan-militias-engage-in-battle-16076585.html.

[98] Allen, *Libyan factions in deadly clashes near Zawiya, supra* note 97.

[99] *See infra* Sec. 3.7. *See also* Allen, *Libyan factions in deadly clashes near Zawiya, supra* note 97; *At Least Six Are Killed as Libyan Militias Clash on Coastal Highway Near Tripoli*, N.Y. TIMES, Nov. 14, 2011, *available at* http://www.nytimes.com/2011/11/14/world/africa/six-dead-as-libyan-militias-clash-near-tripoli.html; *Deadly faction clashes erupt in Libya*, AL JAZEERA, Nov. 13, 2011, *available at* http://www.aljazeera.com/news/africa/2011/11/20111 11341559598501.html; Ariel Zirulnick, *Libya militias clash in longest sustained fighting since Qaddafi's fall*, CHRISTIAN SCIENCE MONITOR, Nov. 14, 2011, *available at* http://www.csmonitor.com/World/terrorism-security/2011/1114/Libya-militias-clash-in-longest-sustained-fight ing-since-Qaddafi-s-fall?utm_source=feedburner&utm_medium=feed&utm_campaign=Fe ed%3A+feeds%2Fcsm+%28Christian+Science+Monitor+%7C+All+Stories%29.

[100] *See infra* Sec. 3.3.

[101] *See infra* Sec. 3.4. *See also 4,000 Gaddafi supporters in Libya prisons*, THE VOICE OF RUSSIA, May 11, 2012, *available at* http://english.ruvr.ru/2012_05_11/74362355. *See infra* Sec. 3.9.

of dark-skinned Libyans and foreigners.[102] There were also attacks against professors, doctors and members of Qadhafi forces.[103] On 11 May 2012, the United Nations Special Representative of the Secretary-General and Head of the United Nations Support Mission in Libya (UNSMIL), Ian Martin, reported that around 4,000 supporters of the Qadhafi regime were being held in secret prisons, and voiced concern over reports of widespread torture in detention facilities in Misrata, Tripoli, Zintan and Zawiyya.[104]

3. Illustrations of the Violations

3.1. *Excessive Use of Force*

(a) *Qadhafi Forces*

There is extensive evidence of the excessive use of force by the Qadhafi forces to subdue civilian protests that began in Zawiyya on 18 February 2011. While local police initially handled the demonstrations with restraint, Qadhafi forces entered the city in full force on 23 February. Over the following days, the Qadhafi regime deployed hundreds of soldiers from Tripoli who used anti-aircraft guns, RPGs and machine guns to disperse the crowds.[105] Roaming officers also reportedly fired at houses to scare residents from leaving their homes.[106] The actions of the Qadhafi forces were disproportionate and excessive in the face of demonstrators who were initially unarmed.

3.2. *Unlawful Killing*

(a) *Qadhafi Forces*

The use of excessive force by Qadhafi forces against protesters in Zawiyya resulted in the unlawful killing of civilians. On 24 February 2011, Qadhafi forces targeted a mosque using an anti-aircraft gun that killed civilians.

---

[102] *Id.*

[103] Amnesty International, Libya: Rule of Law or Rule of Militias? 20 (July 2012), *available at* http://www.amnesty.org/en/library/asset/MDE19/012/2012/en/f2d36090-5716-4ef1-81a7-f4b1ebd082fc/mde190122012en.pdf.

[104] *See* Ch. V, Sec. 2. *See also* The Voice of Russia, *4,000 Gaddafi supporters in Libya prisons, supra* note 101.

[105] Report of the International Commission of Inquiry, advance unedited version (Mar. 2, 2012), *supra* note 11 at Annex I, ¶ 127.

[106] Human Rights Watch, *Libya: Security Forces Fire on Protesters in Western City, supra* note 17.

Doctors from a field hospital in Zawiyya reported 17 civilian deaths resulted from these regime attacks.[107] Other witness accounts from hospitals and morgues put the death toll of protesters as high as 123.[108]

The CoI reported an incident on 3 March, when Qadhafi forces shot a father and son as they walked near the central square.[109] On 5 March, the indiscriminate shelling of residential areas by Qadhafi troops resulted in the death of 30 civilians.[110] By 11 March, reports estimate that more than 200 rebels and civilians were killed during the two-week battle for Zawiyya. It was also reported that Khamis Qadhafi had 135 soldiers executed because they refused to open fire on protesters.[111] Due to the use of heavy artillery weapons, and covering up of burial grounds, the precise number of deaths is difficult to determine.[112] Based on extensive reports, the evidence indicates that Qadhafi forces engaged in acts of unlawful killing against civilians and *thuwar* combatants alike.

(b) Thuwar *Forces*

The CoI gathered testimonies and evidence indicating that after Qadhafi forces retreated from the city *thuwar* committed violations against Qadhafi regime officials and suspected supporters. Two men detained by a local *thuwar* group on 17 September 2011 died on 9 October, according to the CoI's forensic pathologist reports. One of the men died in the Jadayem detention center, and another in a Zawiyya hospital. Pictures and autopsy reports of both men showed signs of torture.[113] The CoI documented another incident in late October, when *thuwar* reportedly stabbed a former Qadhafi soldier to death as he was recovering in a Zawiyya hospital.[114] Amnesty International also documented cases of deaths in detention centers under *thuwar* control, such as a case in February 2012, when a

---

[107] CNN, *Doctors report 17 dead in Libyan city of Zawiya, supra* note 19.

[108] Black, *Heavy fighting in former stronghold as Gaddafi's forces stage counterattacks, supra* note 18; Schemm & Mroue, *Protesters Hit by Hail of Gunfire in Libya March, supra* note 18.

[109] Report of the International Commission of Inquiry, advance unedited version (Mar. 2, 2012), *supra* note 11 at Annex I, ¶ 559.

[110] BBC, *Battle for Libya: Gaddafi troops engage Zawiya rebels, supra* note 34.

[111] *The Khamis Al Qaddafi Brigade killed 135 soldiers who refused to shoot protestors*, AL ARABIYA, Feb. 24, 2011, *available at* http://www.alarabiya.net/articles/2011/02/24/138976 .html.

[112] Walt, *Gaddafi Gets His Revenge: The Price of Rebellion, supra* note 23.

[113] Report of the International Commission of Inquiry, advance unedited version (Mar. 2, 2012), *supra* note 11 at Annex I, ¶ 226.

[114] *Id.* at Annex I, ¶ 374.

man detained in the Jadayem detention center was beaten to death after guards allowed a group of men into his cell.[115]

3.3. *Arbitrary Detentions and Enforced Disappearances*

(a) *Qadhafi Forces*

After the Qadhafi forces regained control over Zawiyya in early March 2011, there were numerous documented cases of arbitrary arrests, detentions and enforced disappearances.[116] During this period, the detention of suspected *thuwar* and opposition supporters at checkpoints established by Qadhafi forces around the city was widespread. A former Qadhafi official told the CoI that

> ...he helped establish 10 checkpoints in and around Al-Zawiyah on 17 March 2011 and the task of his unit was to search whoever passes through the checkpoint. They were provided with a list of people to be arrested as well as told to search passengers if they found anything that indicates that the person is supporting the *thuwar*... 'Or if we suspected that he might be thuwar we were to arrest him and send him to camp 77 or hand him over to the Military Intelligence (*Istikhbarat*).'[117]

Suspected *thuwar* supporters were systematically detained and disappeared by Qadhafi forces in a campaign of reprisals after re-taking control over the city. Amnesty International documented several incidents of Qadhafi forces abducting males during house raids in areas that had supported the *thuwar*.[118] Witness accounts reported that the Khamis Katiba carried out sweeping operations through the city after the fighting subsided to detain young men suspected of involvement with the *thuwar*.[119] Sources in Zawiyya reported that as many as 1,000 locals were arrested in the aftermath of the March fighting.[120] Reports indicate that Qadhafi

---

[115] AMNESTY INTERNATIONAL, LIBYA: RULE OF LAW OR RULE OF MILITIAS? *supra* note 103 at 26.

[116] Report of the International Commission of Inquiry, advance unedited version (Mar. 2, 2012), *supra* note 11 at Annex I, ¶ 84.

[117] *Id.* at Annex I, ¶ 270.

[118] AMNESTY INTERNATIONAL, THE BATTLE FOR LIBYA: KILLINGS, DISAPPEARANCES AND TORTURE (Sept. 2011) [hereinafter "THE BATTLE FOR LIBYA"], *available at* http://www.amnesty.org/en/library/asset/MDE19/025/2011/en/8f2e1c49-8f43-46d3-917d-383c17d36377/mde19025201en.pdf.

[119] Neely, *Zawiya town center devastated and almost deserted, supra* note 57.

[120] Walt, *Gaddafi Gets His Revenge: The Price of Rebellion, supra* note 23.

forces also searched homes and abducted *thuwar* supporters when fighting broke out again in August.[121]

Doctors provided testimony to the CoI of cases where four surgeons were detained and disappeared in Zawiyya between February and March 2011.[122] Media reports corroborate the findings of the CoI that from March onwards Qadhafi agents detained doctors and nurses suspected of sympathizing with the *thuwar* from hospitals. Many of the doctors and nurses were still missing in August 2011.[123] The detention of doctors and nurses appeared to be part of a larger systematic campaign carried out by Qadhafi forces to arrest and disappear suspected opponents, including *thuwar* fighters from hospitals.[124]

(b) Thuwar *Forces*

After taking control of Zawiyya in August 2011, *thuwar* forces targeted and arbitrarily detained Qadhafi officials and suspected supporters.[125] Amnesty International reported on *thuwar* forces carrying out house raids to detain alleged Qadhafi loyalists based on lists compiled by *thuwar* supporters.[126] Witnesses gave accounts to the CoI of their arbitrary arrest at the hands of *thuwar* during the month of August[127] A former member of Libya's intelligence service told Amnesty International that he was detained by *thuwar* in September 2011, then rearrested on 10 May 2012, and held for six days. His captors reportedly identified him by name.[128]

In some incidents, the judicial police or prosecutors ordered the release of detainees, but *thuwar* controlling the detention centers refused to implement judicial release orders.[129] Amnesty International estimated

---

[121] Laub, *Gadhafi's troops use hospital as base, doctors say, supra* note 86.

[122] Report of the International Commission of Inquiry to investigate all the alleged violations of international human rights law in the Libyan Arab Jamahiriya, U.N. HRC. 17th Sess., ¶ 106. U.N. Doc. A/HRC/17/44 (Jan. 12, 2012).

[123] Laub, *Gadhafi's troops use hospital as base, doctors say, supra* note 86.

[124] Neely, *Zawiya town center devastated and almost deserted, supra* note 57.

[125] Laub, *Gadhafi's troops use hospital as base, doctors say, supra* note 86.

[126] AMNESTY INTERNATIONAL, DETENTION ABUSES STAINING THE NEW LIBYA, *supra* note 8 at 7-8.

[127] Report of the International Commission of Inquiry, advance unedited version (Mar. 2, 2012), *supra* note 11 at Annex I, ¶¶ 303–304.

[128] AMNESTY INTERNATIONAL, LIBYA: RULE OF LAW OR RULE OF MILITIAS? *supra* note 103 at 17.

[129] *See* Ch. V, Sec. 2. *See also* AMNESTY INTERNATIONAL, DETENTION ABUSES STAINING THE NEW LIBYA, *supra* note 8 at 18.

that in Tripoli and Zawiyya alone, roughly 2,500 individuals were detained from August-September 2011 by *thuwar* forces.[130]

The *thuwar* from Zawiyya were also involved in cases of arbitrary detention of members of *thuwar* groups from nearby towns. The CoI interviewed a member of a Warshifana katiba who was arrested on 11 November and held with 64 other persons from Zawiyya. The two rival groups fought over territory and detained members of one another's forces. With the intervention and mediation of members of the NTC, detainees were exchanged between the rival kata'ib.[131] *Thuwar* forces are presumed responsible for kidnapping between 150 and 164 Tunisian workers from local oil refineries in April 2012. This occurred on more than one occasion as the zone between Zawiyya and the Tunisian border increasingly became plagued by arms trafficking, illicit trade and fuel smuggling.[132]

i. *Sub-Saharan Africans*

Amnesty International documented the cases of Sub-Saharan Africans, many of whom were migrant workers, subjected to racially motivated attacks that included arbitrary arrest based on perceptions that they fought on the side of the Qadhafi forces. Amnesty International documented that a third of the 400 detainees in the main detention facility in Zawiyya were Sub-Saharan Africans.[133]

Incidents continued into July, such as the detention of Somali women arbitrarily arrested in Zawiyya and transferred to Bu Rashada detention center in Gharyan[134] where they were told to pay 1,000 dinars ($795) to secure their release, a price they could not afford.[135]

---

[130] *Id.* at 6.

[131] Report of the International Commission of Inquiry, advance unedited version (Mar. 2, 2012), *supra* note 11 at Annex I, ¶ 312.

[132] Houda Mzioudet, *Five Tunisians Abducted by a Libyan Armed Group*, TUNISIA LIVE, Apr. 7, 2012, *available at* http://www.tunisia-live.net/2012/04/07/37967; *Tunisia accuses armed Libyans of kidnapping 80 nationals*, AFP, Apr. 17, 2011, *available at* http://english.alarabiya.net/articles/2012/04/17/208438.html.

[133] AMNESTY INTERNATIONAL, DETENTION ABUSES STAINING THE NEW LIBYA, *supra* note 8 at 8.

[134] For more on the Bu Rashada detention center in Gharyan, in the Nafusa Mountains region, *see supra* Ch. X, Sec. 3.3.

[135] AMNESTY INTERNATIONAL, LIBYA: RULE OF LAW OR RULE OF MILITIAS? *supra* note 103 at 43.

3.4. *Torture and Other Forms of Ill-treatment*

(a) *Qadhafi Forces*

On 7 March 2011, as a BBC news team attempted to reach Zawiyya to cover the battle, they were detained by Qadhafi forces. They were subsequently insulted, repeatedly beaten and subjected to a mock execution.[136]

(b) Thuwar *Forces*

On 10 November 2011, head of the UNSMIL, Martin, visited Zawiyya and documented accounts of torture committed by *thuwar* forces.[137] He reported his findings to the United Nations Security Council on 10 May 2012, concluding that incidents of torture were taking place on a regular basis in detention centers under *thuwar* control.[138]

Amnesty International similarly documented incidents of torture in detention centers under *thuwar* control in Zawiyya. Lines of authority between the central authorities and local *thuwar* groups running the facilities were unclear. For example, despite having written authorization, Amnesty International was not allowed to speak with detainees in private in Jadayem detention center, which was nominally under the control of the Directorate of the Judicial Police.[139] At another detention center in Zawiyya, prisoners said that two detainees bearing visible torture scars were removed just before the arrival of Amnesty International.[140] The human rights organization documented the case of a former Qadhafi soldier who was arrested by *thuwar* at the end of September 2011 and transferred to Jadayem detention center. In February 2012, his family was informed through unofficial channels that he had been killed. The Jadayem guards were charged with opening his cell to armed men who took him away and beat him to death.[141] Another victim – a schoolteacher accused of having ties to the former regime – told Amnesty International that armed militia detained him in Zawiyya for 17 days. He reported that eight men had beaten him four times using water pipes. The man still

---

[136] *Libya: Gaddafi forces detain and beat BBC Arabic team*, BBC, Mar. 10, 2011, *available at* http://www.bbc.co.uk/news/world-africa-12695077.

[137] Randa Jamal, *Libya Head of the United Nations in Libya, Ian Martin, visits Al-Zawiya*, RELIEF WEB, Nov. 17, 2011, *available at* http://reliefweb.int/node/459924.

[138] U.N. SC, 67th year, 6768 mtg, U.N. Doc. S/PV.6768 (May 10, 2012) at 5.

[139] AMNESTY INTERNATIONAL, LIBYA: RULE OF LAW OR RULE OF MILITIAS? *supra* note 103 at 12.

[140] *Id.* at 18.

[141] *Id.* at 26.

showed signed of injuries when Amnesty International interviewed him five days after his release in April 2012.[142]

A judicial officer investigating torture and unlawful killings in Zawiyya told Amnesty International he received verbal warnings not to carry out his work in the city.[143] In late May 2012, armed men from Sabrata detained a judicial police officer who was working at the Jadayem detention center in Zawiyya. Amnesty International examined pictures of his body, which showed scars, abrasions and signs of burns.[144] The forensic pathologist report stated he died of acute kidney injuries.[145]

3.5. *Denial of Access to Medical Treatment*

(a) *Qadhafi Forces*

The CoI recorded interviews with medical professionals who witnessed Qadhafi forces blocking entrances and exits to hospitals to prevent people from receiving treatment. A doctor in Tripoli reported that his colleagues working at the Abu Salim accident center in Zawiyya experienced Qadhafi forces blocking the exit and entry of the center.[146] In August 2011, Qadhafi snipers reportedly used Zawiyya's main hospital to fire at *thuwar* and positioned an anti-aircraft gun at its entrance.[147] These actions by Qadhafi regime forces prevented the treatment of injuries of both combatants and unarmed civilians.

3.6. *Freedom of Expression*

(a) *Qadhafi Forces*

During and following the conflict, journalists and media personnel reporting on the conflict were subject to arbitrary detention and harassment by the Qadhafi regime. Foreign journalists were monitored by Qadhafi officials and routinely detained by soldiers. Several of these documented incidents occurred in March 2011. On 2 March, journalists for The Guardian's Ghayth 'Abd al-Ahad and Andrei Netto were arrested in Sabrata near

---

[142] *Id.* at 18.

[143] *Id.* at 33.

[144] *Id.* at 25.

[145] AMNESTY INTERNATIONAL, LIBYA: RULE OF LAW OR RULE OF MILITIAS? *supra* note 103 at 25.

[146] Report of the International Commission of Inquiry (Jan. 12, 2012), *supra* note 122 at ¶ 124.

[147] Laub, *Gadhafi's troops use hospital as base, doctors say, supra* note 86.

Zawiyya while covering the conflict.[148] Qadhafi forces released Netto on 10 March, while 'Abd al-Ahad was released on 16 March.[149] Another incident took place on 5 March, when Qadhafi forces detained staff members from eight news outlets outside Zawiyya and held them for nearly seven hours.[150] Two days later, a BBC news team was detained and prevented from proceeding to Zawiyya, and they subsequently left the country.[151]

On 23 August 2011, four Italian journalists – Elisabetta Rosaspina, Giuseppe Sarcina of Corriere della Sera, Domenico Quirico of La Stampa, and Claudio Monici of Avvenire – were kidnapped as they drove from Zawiyya to Tripoli.[152] Armed men blocked their path, killed the driver, and robbed and detained the journalists, before handing them over to Qadhafi forces. Two of the journalists, Avvenire's Monici and Quirico of La Stampa, were allowed to make telephone calls and they reported that they were given food and water at the end of the Ramadan fast.[153] The journalists were released on 25 August.[154] The incidents demonstrate a pattern of

---

[148] Shadid, *Qaddafi Forces Bear Down on Strategic Town as Rebels Flee, supra* note 49; *Guardian journalist held in Libya,* PRESS ASSOCIATION, Mar. 10, 2011, *available at* http://www.independent.ie/breaking-news/world-news/guardian-journalist-held in libya-2575277.html.

[149] Sam Jones, *Guardian journalist freed at captivity in Libya,* THE GUARDIAN, Mar. 16, 2011, *available at* http://www.guardian.co.uk/media/2011/mar/16/guardian-journalist-freed-captivity-libya.

[150] Report of the International Commission of Inquiry (Jan. 12, 2012), *supra* note 122 at ¶ 136.

[151] *See infra,* Sec. 3.4. *See also* BBC, *Libya: Gaddafi forces detain and beat BBC Arabic team, supra* note 136.

[152] *Four Italian Journalists held by Qaddafi loyalists,* CORRIERE DELLA SERA, Aug. 25, 2011, *available at* http://www.corriere.it/english/11_agosto_25/italian-journalists-held-libia_c8f40a5a-cf04-11e0-9639-95c553466c70.shtml; Hada Messia, *Four Italian journalists kidnapped in Libya, official in Rome confirms,* CNN, Aug. 24, 2011, *available at* http://articles.cnn.com/2011-08-24/world/libya.italian.journalists_1_journalists-zawiya-war-reporters; Tom Kington, *Italian Journalists kidnapped in Libya,* THE GUARDIAN, Aug. 25, 2011, *available at* http://www.guardian.co.uk/world/2011/aug/25/italian-journalists-kidnapped-libya; *Four Italian Journalists abducted in Libya,* FOX NEWS, Aug. 24, 2011, *available at* http://www.foxnews.com/world/2011/08/24/italy-4-italian-journalists-abducted-in-libya; *Kidnapped Italians freed as rebels seek to consolidate hold,* IBT, Aug. 25, 2011, *available at* http://www.ibtimes.com/articles/203712/20110825/kidnapped-italians-freed-as-rebels-consolidate-hold-on-tripoli.htm.

[153] CORRIERE DELLA SERA, *Four Italian Journalists held by Qaddafi loyalists, supra* note 152.

[154] *Libya conflict: Kidnapped Italian journalists free,* BBC, Aug. 25, 2011, *available at* http://www.bbc.co.uk/news/world-africa-14662780; *Kidnapped Italian Journalists freed in Libya,* VOA, Aug. 24, 2011, *available at* http://www.voanews.com/content/article-4-kidnapped-italian-journalists-freed-in-libya-128375738/144287.html.

denying journalists the right to freedom of speech and expression in their reporting on the conflict.

3.7. *Attacks on Civilians, Civilian Objects, Protected Persons and Objects*

3.7.1. *Deliberate and Indiscriminate Attacks on Civilians*

(a) *Qadhafi Forces*
The CoI found that Qadhafi forces used weaponry that can only be used in an indiscriminate manner. The weapons included Grad rockets, mortars, tanks, rocket launchers and 14.5mm anti-aircraft guns and were deployed against civilian populations, causing casualties and harm to civilian infrastructure.[155] Witness accounts indicate that members of the Qadhafi forces used the weapons with the full understanding that the indiscriminate nature of these weapons would likely lead to civilian casualties.[156]

An abundance of media sources corroborate the findings that during protests in February 2011, Qadhafi forces attacked civilians with automatic weapons and heavy artillery, including RPGs and anti-aircraft guns.[157] Multiple reports also indicate that regime forces deployed tanks in central Zawiyya.[158]

The attacks escalated in March, as Qadhafi forces fired anti-aircraft guns, RPGs and artillery shells into Zawiyya's city center from their position on the eastern edge of the town.[159] Given the imprecision of these weapons and the high population density of the city, shells and rockets invariably hit civilians. Reporters who entered the city after the fighting noted the extensive damage to civilian objects, including the central mosque that was later destroyed.[160] A doctor in Zawiyya reported an estimated 60 civilians

---

[155] Report of the International Commission of Inquiry, advance unedited version (Mar. 2, 2012), *supra* note 11 at Annex I, ¶¶ 72 & 75.

[156] *Id.* at Annex I, ¶ 557.

[157] Golovnina, *Rebels control Libya town of Zawiyah, supra* note 18; Black, *Heavy fighting in former stronghold as Gaddafi's forces stage counterattacks, supra* note 18.

[158] BELL & WITTER, THE ROOTS OF REBELLION, *supra* note 1 at 33; *WRAPUP 10 – Gaddafi forces step up attack on western rebel town*, REUTERS, Mar. 5, 2011, *available at* http://www .reuters.com/article/2011/03/05/libya-idUSLDE72400F20110305.

[159] Chulov et al., *Libya: Fierce day of raids and clashes signals shift towards civil war, supra* note 34.

[160] It had lost its protected status. MacIntyre, *Gaddafi's men try to obliterate traces of massacre in Zawiya, supra* note 47; Walt, *Gaddafi Gets His Revenge: The Price of Rebellion, supra* note 23; BBC, *Libya revolt as it happened: Monday, supra* note 43; Schemm, *Libyan warplanes strike rebels at oil port, supra* note 43; BBC, *Battle for Libya: Gaddafi troops engage Zawiya rebels, supra* note 34.

had been killed on 4 and 5 March,[161] with 30 of these deaths a result of Qadhafi shelling of civilian neighborhoods on 5 March 2011.[162] Other estimates ranged up to 50 deaths on 4 March.[163]

During the August battle between Qadhafi forces and *thuwar*, Qadhafi forces again used heavy weapons, including artillery, Grad rockets and mortar shells. On 13 and 14 August, Qadhafi forces shelled the city and set up snipers to repel *thuwar* forces.[164] Qadhafi forces continued to use Grad rockets and mortars through 15 August and on 19 August fired from positions outside of the city.[165]

(b) Thuwar *Forces*

Reports indicate that *thuwar* fighters executed ten Qadhafi soldiers at a hotel in the central square during the March 2011 fighting.[166] Although they were not civilians, as *hors de combat* soldiers, they were entitled to protection under international law. This incident also constitutes an act of unlawful killing.

3.7.2. *Impeding Access to Humanitarian Relief and Attacks on Humanitarian Personnel*

(a) *Qadhafi Forces*

The siege on Zawiyya by Qadhafi forces led to the prevention of food and other vital supplies from reaching the civilian population. NGO reports confirm the CoI findings that after losing control over the city in late February 2011, Qadhafi forces set up checkpoints around Zawiyya to prevent the entry of vital goods into the city.[167] Media accounts also provided information on the situation in Zawiyya, detailing that supplies of medicine were soon low, hindering the ability of medical personnel to treat the wounded until the siege was lifted on 11 March.[168]

---

[161] REUTERS, *WRAPUP 10 – Gaddafi forces step up attack on western rebel town*, supra note 158.

[162] *Id.*; BBC, *Battle for Libya: Gaddafi troops engage Zawiya rebels*, supra note 34.

[163] Chulov et al., *Libya: Fierce day of raids and clashes signals shift towards civil war*, supra note 34; BBC, *Libya unrest: Deadly clashes in battle for Zawiya*, 34.

[164] Georgy, *Libya's Zawiya on edge after rebel capture*, supra note 82.

[165] *Libya Blog*, AL JAZEERA, supra note 89.

[166] SUN STAR, *Libya forces try to halt rebel move toward capital*, supra note 42.

[167] HUMAN RIGHTS WATCH, *Libya: Security Forces Fire on Protesters in Western City*, supra note 17.

[168] *Libya rebel-held city on guard, fears for supplies*, REUTERS, Mar. 3, 2011, *available at* http://www.reuters.com/article/2011/03/04/us-libya-zawiyah-idUSTRE72308920110304.

3.7.3. *Attacks on Protected Medical Personnel, Transport and Facilities*

(a) *Qadhafi Forces*

During the military campaign in Zawiyya, Qadhafi forces targeted medical personnel and facilities for attack. A doctor who had been treating wounded *thuwar* in Zawiyya told the CoI that he was detained by Qadhafi forces and tortured in a makeshift detention container in Khums.[169] The CoI received multiple reports that Qadhafi forces entered Zawiyya hospital and arrested doctors who treated victims of gunshots wounds. These patients were assumed to be *thuwar* fighters because of the nature of their injuries.[170] One doctor stated that he went into hiding after Qadhafi forces came looking for him, and that he knew at least three doctors who had been detained.[171] Qadhafi forces also fired on ambulances, shelled hospitals, restricted the delivery of medical supplies into Zawiyya and misused ambulances to transport armed soldiers into battle.[172] One incident took place on 6 March 2011, when Qadhafi forces opened fire on the front of a hospital in Zawiyya where the injured were being treated.[173]

3.7.4. *Attacks on Cultural Objects and Places of Worship*

(a) *Qadhafi Forces*

During the March 2011 battle for Zawiyya, Qadhafi forces inflicted extensive damage to civilian buildings in the city, most notably to the Suq Mosque in the city center's main square. The mosque was hit on several occasions, the first time during the initial assault on 24 February.[174] Reports indicate that *thuwar* fighters retreated into the mosque as they were losing ground in the square, and fired on Qadhafi forces from inside.[175] Qadhafi forces demolished the mosque after taking control of Zawiyya in

---

[169] For details about the doctors and other victims held in the containers turned into detention facilities in Khums, *see* Ch. XI.

[170] Report of the International Commission of Inquiry, advance unedited version (Mar. 2, 2012), *supra* note 11 at Annex I, ¶ 592.

[171] *Id.* at Annex I, ¶ 596.

[172] *Id.* at Annex I, ¶ 77.

[173] Report of the International Commission of Inquiry (Jan. 12, 2012), *supra* note 122 at ¶ 167.

[174] Jeffrey Kofman et al., *Gadhafi Compares Himself to Queen Elizabeth, Says Libya's Youth are on Hallucinogens*, ABC, Feb. 24, 2011, *available at* http://abcnews.go.com/Politics/moammar-gadhafi-speech-blames-libya-uprising-al-qaeda/story?id=12987097#.TzolarEkKf4.

[175] Report of the International Commission of Inquiry, advance unedited version (Mar. 2, 2012), *supra* note 11 at Annex I, ¶ 560.

March 2011.[176] The CoI concluded after examining reports of the attack on the Suq Mosque and other civilian locations, that in some cases the *thuwar* inappropriately misused civilian buildings, including mosques, for military purposes.[177] The use of the Suq Mosque for military purposes could therefore have led to the Qadhafi forces considering it a legitimate military target.

3.8. *Mercenaries*

(a) *Qadhafi Forces*

Media reports indicate that Qadhafi forces included foreign fighters during the battles for Zawiyya in March[178] and August 2011.[179] The CoI concluded that the Qadhafi regime did indeed bring in several hundred soldiers from Sudan between June and July 2011 to support the regime forces, but it could not establish if these individuals fell within the category of "mercenaries" under the United Nations Convention on Mercenaries or under the Organization of African Unity's Convention for the Elimination of Mercenarism in Africa.[180]

3.9. *Targeting Specific Groups*

(a) *Qadhafi Forces*

i. *Migrant Workers*
HRW reported that Qadhafi forces attacked Egyptian migrant workers in Zawiyya. Migrants described how their homes were attacked by Qadhafi forces and how they were threatened and attacked by men armed with knives and clubs following the speech given by Saif al-Islam Qadhafi on February 21, in which he blamed the Libyan uprising on foreigners. An Egyptian worker showed HRW bruises on his face from an attack following Saif al-Islam's speech.[181]

---

[176] MacIntyre, *Gaddafi's men try to obliterate traces of massacre in Zawiya, supra* note 47.

[177] Report of the International Commission of Inquiry, advance unedited version (Mar. 2, 2012), *supra* note 11 at ¶ 78.

[178] *Libya revolt as it happened: Monday,* BBC, Mar. 21, 2011, *available at* http://news.bbc .co.uk/2/hi/africa/9417359.stm.

[179] *Id. See also* Laub, *Gadhafi's troops use hospital as base, doctors say, supra* note 86.

[180] Report of the International Commission of Inquiry, advance unedited version (Mar. 2, 2012), *supra* note 11 at ¶ 689.

[181] HUMAN RIGHTS WATCH, *Libya: Security Forces Fire on Protesters in Western City, supra* note 17.

(b) Thuwar *Forces*

i. *Sub-Saharan Africans*

As discussed above, after taking full control of Zawiyya in August 2011, *thuwar* forces targeted Sub-Saharan Africans, including many migrant workers, for widespread detention.[182] Amnesty International documented over 100 Sub-Saharan Africans detained in one facility in Zawiyya.[183]

ii. *The Tawerghans*

The CoI reported that a Tawerghan man was arrested and beaten in Zawiyya so that he would sign a false confession of having committed rape. He stated that he had repeatedly been beaten with metal bars, wooden bars and whips. He reported that after the last beating he was left unconscious. The CoI noted marks on his body consistent with his testimony.[184]

3.10. *Sexual Violence*[185]

(a) *Qadhafi Forces*

Interviewees indicated to the CoI that the threat of rape from Qadhafi forces was a pervasive rumor during the conflict. Libyans interviewed in Tunisia reported that their relatives in Zawiyya gave accounts of collective rapes by Qadhafi forces, as well as by alleged mercenaries and unidentified

---

[182] *See infra* Sec. 3.3. *See also* Georgy, *Libya's Zawiya on edge after rebel capture, supra* note 82.

[183] AMNESTY INTERNATIONAL, DETENTION ABUSES STAINING THE NEW LIBYA, *supra* note 8 at 5.

[184] Report of the International Commission of Inquiry, advance unedited version (Mar. 2, 2012), *supra* note 11 at Annex I, ¶ 366.

[185] The following terms are defined in accordance with the jurisprudence of the ICTY and ICTR, and other mixed-model tribunals.

    1. "Rape" is the penetration, however slight, of any part of the body of another person irrespective of gender (namely, the vagina, anus, or mouth) by means of the perpetrator's sexual organ or any object used by the perpetrator when accompanied by force or threat of force against the person or a third party which the victim believes is real.

    2. "Sexual violence" is defined as any physical act of a sexual nature which is committed on a person under circumstances which are coercive or threatening to the person or to any other person, which includes physical touching, groping, fondling, removal of a person's clothing to display intimate parts of the person's body whether in the presence of one or more persons, or any other act of a demeaning sexual nature.

    3. "Sexual harassment" is any threat of "rape" or "sexual violence," as defined above, against a person or any other person for purposes of demeaning, intimidating, or punishing the person in question.

armed men.[186] The CoI spoke to a local doctor in Zawiyya, who confirmed 29 cases of rape based on medical check-ups, but there was no other independent confirmation.[187]

(b) Thuwar *Forces*

Amnesty International documented cases of female detainees in Zawiyya being sexually assaulted by *thuwar* forces in the post-conflict period. Two women gave evidence to Amnesty International of rape when detained by *thuwar* forces.[188]

4. THE ROLE OF NATO

The NATO campaign initially focused on Benghazi and the eastern region as it began on 19 March 2011, and did not provide support to cities such as Zawiyya. In some instances, however, the strikes in March did weaken Qadhafi's key military units and hindered their ability to deploy further forces to the region. On 28 March, for example, coalition forces struck the Khamis 32nd Katiba headquarters, damaging its deployment capabilities.[189] The Khamis Katiba had played a central role in the assault on Zawiyya, particularly during the months of February and March. In spite of the strikes on key military units, the Qadhafi forces continued to occupy the city. Moreover, not all of the NATO strikes were successful, as there were incidents that led to the destruction of buildings where military activity was questionable, in some cases suggesting reliance on outdated intelligence. This occurred in the city of Surman, west of Zawiyya, where NATO hit a warehouse that had previously been used as an ammunition storage facility.[190]

When fighting flared up again in Zawiyya in June, NATO forces turned their attention to the region. After the June clashes, NATO announced it

---

[186] Report of the International Commission of Inquiry (Jan. 12, 2012), *supra* note 122 at ¶ 206.

[187] Report of the International Commission of Inquiry, advance unedited version (Mar. 2, 2012), *supra* note 11 at Annex I, ¶ 514.

[188] AMNESTY INTERNATIONAL, DETENTION ABUSES STAINING THE NEW LIBYA, *supra* note 8 at 17.

[189] CHRISTOPHER M. BLANCHARD, CONGRESSIONAL RESEARCH SERVICE, LIBYA: UNREST AND U.S. POLICY 5 (Sept. 29, 2011) [hereinafter "UNREST AND U.S. POLICY"], *available at* http://fpc.state.gov/documents/organization/175868.pdf.

[190] *See* Ch. III, Sec. 6.2. *See also* N.Y. TIMES, *Errant NATO strikes in Libya, supra* note 69.

was gathering intelligence on the area around Zawiyya in order to gain a better understanding of the situation on the ground.[191] The intelligence likely showed the importance of the city given its pivotal location as a strategic conflict region that stood between the powerful *thuwar* of the Nafusa Mountains region and the final battle for Tripoli. NATO subsequently focused its efforts on aiding the *thuwar* in their campaign to take the city.

During the month of August, the NATO campaign conducted an intense assault of constant bombardment in and around Zawiyya. NATO launched daily missions during the height of the fighting between 13 and 19 August, destroying ten tanks, one anti-aircraft gun, five armed vehicles, one artillery piece, one military vehicle, one command center, one transloader and an armed boat.[192] The precision of the NATO strikes were reportedly aided by information received from *thuwar* on the ground as Qadhafi forces increasingly moved into civilian areas to avoid NATO attack.[193]

The *thuwar* success in Zawiyya during this period was greatly facilitated by NATO's air support. NATO conducted strikes that weakened Qadhafi targets around the city and prevented reinforcements from entering from the east.[194] As with the other theaters of military operations, however, the strikes also involved attacks on targets with questionable justification that led to civilian casualties. The 20 June strike in Surman on the compound of Major General All-Hamadi is one such incident.[195] HRW reported that

---

[191] *Press briefing on Libya*, NORTH ATLANTIC TREATY ORGANIZATION, *supra* note 65.

[192] *NATO and Libya: Operational Media Update*, NORTH ATLANTIC TREATY ORGANIZATION, Aug. 13, 2011, *available at* http://www.nato.int/nato_static/assets/pdf/pdf_2011_08/20110814_110814-oup-update.pdf; *NATO and Libya: Operational Media Update*, NORTH ATLANTIC TREATY ORGANIZATION, Aug. 14, 2011, *available at* http://www.nato.int/nato_static/assets/pdf/pdf_2011_08/20110815_110815-oup-update.pdf; *NATO and Libya: Operational Media Update,* NORTH ATLANTIC TREATY ORGANIZATION, Aug. 15, 2011, *available at* http://www.nato.int/nato_static/assets/pdf/pdf_2011_08/20110816_110816-oup-update.pdf; *NATO and Libya: Operational Media Update*, NORTH ATLANTIC TREATY ORGANIZATION, Aug. 17, 2011, *available at* http://www.nato.int/nato_static/assets/pdf/pdf_2011_08/20110818_110818-oup-update.pdf; *NATO and Libya: Operational Media Update*, NORTH ATLANTIC TREATY ORGANIZATION, Aug. 18, 2011, *available at* http://www.nato.int/nato_static/assets/pdf/pdf_2011_08/20110819_110819-oup-update.pdf; *NATO and Libya: Operational Media Update*, NORTH ATLANTIC TREATY ORGANIZATION, Aug. 19, 2011, *available at* http://www.nato.int/nato_static/assets/pdf/pdf_2011_08/20110820_110820-oup-update.pdf.

[193] Borger et al., *Battle for Tripoli: pivotal victory in the mountains helped big push, supra* note 60.

[194] *Libyan rebels fight for Zawiya, take Zlitan*, AP, Aug. 19, 2011, *available at* http://www.cbc.ca/news/world/story/2011/08/19/libya-rebels-zawiya.html.

[195] *See* Ch. III, Sec. 6.2. INTERNATIONAL LEGAL ASSISTANCE CONSORTIUM, REPORT OF THE INDEPENDENT CIVIL SOCIETY FACT-FINDING MISSION TO LIBYA, *supra* note 67 at 17.

13 were killed in this strike, including eight family members and five staff members.[196] NATO declared that Al-Hamadi's residence was a "legitimate military target, a command-and-control node," and defended the operation as a justified strike.[197] The CoI was unable to determine, however, whether the strike was "consistent with NATO's objective to avoid civilian casualties entirely, or whether NATO took all necessary precautions to that effect."[198]

Thus, while NATO played an important role in aiding the *thuwar*, there are lingering questions regarding its operations and decision-making processes during the Libya campaign. NATO's operations appeared to be most effective when provided with on-the-spot intelligence from overhead drones as well as communication from *thuwar* forces. This information from forces on the ground was not always reliable, however, as the conflict shifted to a more insurgent-like conflict, with both *thuwar* and Qadhafi forces using civilian vehicles and civilian objects to mask their movements. Although civilian casualties from NATO airstrikes were low relative to the number of bombing missions it carried out, those incidents where civilians were killed or civilian infrastructure was destroyed can be seen as arising from difficulties stemming from the fluid nature of the battlefield. The CoI noted potential problems NATO would have faced had it taken all feasible precautions to protect civilians, but without further information from NATO, the extent of those problems remains unknown.[199]

5. CONCLUSION

Zawiyya's geographic location and its early anti-Qadhafi activism made it a strategically important city during Libya's civil war. During the first phase of the conflict, Qadhafi forces deployed to Zawiyya to quell the demonstrations and remove protesters from the city square, launching a bloody assault in February 2011 that left as many as 600 dead. Many of the initial casualties were unarmed civilians. In March, the Qadhafi forces returned to the city with reinforced military detachments and conducted an indiscriminate assault and siege campaign on the city. During the final

---

[196] *Id.* at 17.

[197] *Press briefing on Libya*, NORTH ATLANTIC TREATY ORGANIZATION, June 21, 2011, *supra* note 66.

[198] Report of the International Commission of Inquiry, advance unedited version (Mar. 2, 2012), *supra* note 11 at Annex I, ¶ 639.

[199] *See* Ch. IV, Secs. 5, 7 & 8.

phase in August 2011, the Qadhafi and *thuwar* forces again fought for control of the city, this time with NATO targeting Qadhafi forces and thereby shifting the balance of power in favor of the *thuwar*. After the rebel victory in Zawiyya, Tripoli was effectively encircled by *thuwar* forces in neighboring cities, opening the way for the advance on the capital.

Extensive on-site investigations, media reports, forensic documents and witness accounts from victims and perpetrators indicate that violations were committed by both Qadhafi and *thuwar* forces in Zawiyya. Reports indicate that after 18 February 2011, Qadhafi forces used light and heavy weaponry against unarmed protesters in the city center in order to subdue the growing demonstrations, and firing at homes at night to deter residents from joining the protests. The available information suggests that Qadhafi forces engaged in the excessive use of force against civilian protesters.

Reports indicate that Qadhafi forces carried out acts of unlawful killing against armed *thuwar* as well as unarmed civilians during the initial fighting and throughout the prolonged battle for Zawiyya. The indiscriminate use of heavy weaponry and the shelling of civilian buildings resulted in unnecessary casualties. Members of the *thuwar* forces also engaged in acts of unlawful killing, particularly in detention centers where suspected Qadhafi supporters were held, and many cases of deaths as a result of torture were documented.

Reports indicate that Qadhafi forces systematically detained suspected *thuwar* supporters, including doctors and nurses, after taking control of Zawiyya in early March 2011. Qadhafi forces conducted door-to-door searches and house raids, and reports indicate that as many as 1,000 individuals were detained. Victims were targeted under suspicion of supporting the rebels, and many were detained and disappeared. This pattern of detentions and disappearances occurred again in August when fighting resumed in Zawiyya.

Reports also indicate that *thuwar* engaged in searches and roundups of suspected Qadhafi supporters after taking control of Zawiyya in August 2011. Sub-Saharan African migrant workers suspected of being mercenaries were specifically targeted en masse on the basis of their race or national origin. In detention centers under the nominal authority of the NTC in Zawiyya, local guards reportedly ignored judicial orders to release prisoners, indicating a lack of government control over the city's detention facilities.

There are documented cases indicating that *thuwar* targeted and tortured suspected supporters of the Qadhafi regime and non-Libyan nationals.

Based on its on-site investigations, along with forensic autopsy reports and witness testimony, Amnesty International documented multiple incidents of torture and other abuses committed in detention centers under *thuwar* control.

Reports indicate that Qadhafi forces at various times actively denied individuals access to medical treatment in Zawiyya. Qadhafi forces reportedly used the city's main hospital to position snipers, placed an anti-aircraft gun outside its front entrance, and blocked injured *thuwar* combatants from entering the building for treatment.

Qadhafi forces also severely restricted freedom of expression, as journalists were detained and abused by Qadhafi forces and regime loyalists. Several incidents demonstrate that members of the media were monitored and their movement restricted by the Qadhafi regime. While not all members of the media were ill-treated by Qadhafi forces in Zawiyya, reports show that the press did not enjoy freedom of movement and were harassed.

Evidence indicates that Qadhafi forces launched intentional attacks to crush demonstrations in February 2011, injuring civilians as they entered the city center. This was repeated in March, when Qadhafi forces used heavy artillery weapons against civilian homes and buildings. Various unguided weapons with limited targeting capability, including mortar shells and Grad rockets, were used against residential neighborhoods, resulting in hundreds of civilian casualties. These actions amounted to deliberate attacks on civilians on a large-scale.

Reports indicate that Qadhafi forces also laid siege to Zawiyya starting in late February and continuing into early March. Over a two and a half week period, Qadhafi forces blocked essential supplies from reaching the city, including food and medicine. By the end of the conflict, the siege had caused significant suffering, exacerbated by the active combat between Qadhafi and *thuwar* forces. While sieges that achieve a military objective are permitted in war, sieges that block essential supplies to the civilian population are a violation of International Humanitarian Law.[200]

Reports indicate that Qadhafi forces committed acts of sexual assault and rape in Zawiyya. Amnesty International also gathered witness accounts from females detained by the *thuwar* who were sexually abused and, in two incidents, raped by their guards and captors.

---

[200] Report of the International Commission of Inquiry, advance unedited version (Mar. 2, 2012), *supra* note 11 at Annex I, ¶ 542.

CHAPTER THIRTEEN

TRIPOLI

1. INTRODUCTION

Tripoli is the capital of Libya and largest city in the country. It is located in the Libyan Coastal Plain in the western part of the country, in the province of Tripolitania. The city itself lies on a large outcropping on the Mediterranean Coast. With an estimated urban population of more than one million and another million living in its suburbs, greater Tripoli is home to roughly one third of the Libyan population.[1]

The area of Tripoli has an ancient history dating back to at least the classical period when Phoenician merchants established a trading post there, which grew in size and importance. By the second century BCE, the Romans had incorporated three Phoenician cities into a single administrative unit, known as Tripoli.[2] It subsequently came under the control of Arab, Norman, Ottoman and Italian conquerors, providing Tripoli with a cosmopolitan nature that is somewhat unique in Libyan history, thereby distinguishing the city from the rest of the country. During the 18th century, Tripoli was the capital of the Qaramanli dynasty. In 1918, the city's local leaders founded the Tripolitanian Republic, the first republic in the Arab world.[3]

After Libyan independence, the capital of the United Kingdom of Libya was shared between Tripoli and Benghazi, as part of a political compromise between the leadership of Tripolitania and Cyrenaica.[4] While King Idris ruled from Benghazi and spent most of his time in Cyrenaica, Tripoli retained its pre-eminence as Libya's administrative and economic center. After the Free Unionist Officers coup, led by Mu'ammar Qadhafi in

---

[1] *The World Factbook: Libya*, CENTRAL INTELLIGENCE AGENCY, *available at* https://www.cia.gov/library/publications/the-world-factbook/geos/ly.html; *Tripoli*, WOLFRAMALPHA, *available at* http://www.wolframalpha.com/input/?i=tripoli.

[2] GEOFF SIMONS, LIBYA: THE STRUGGLE FOR SURVIVAL 93 (New York, USA: St. Martin's Press, 1996).

[3] DIRK VANDEWALLE, A HISTORY OF MODERN LIBYA 29 (Cambridge, USA: Cambridge University Press, 2006).

[4] *See* Ch. I, Sec. 7. *See also* SIMONS, LIBYA: THE STRUGGLE FOR SURVIVAL, *supra* note 2 at 153.

September 1969, Tripoli became the sole capital of the country. During the 1960s, the city grew significantly as the discovery of oil ushered in a large windfall, boosting urban development in the capital. Between 1973 and 1984, the city's population doubled in size.[5]

Tripoli has traditionally been a major economic hub for the country and the region. Throughout its history it served as the final destination of two of the major trans-Saharan caravan routes, and lies in one of the primary agricultural areas of the country.[6] The city is home to a broad mix of people and tribes, with the largest and most significant tribes in the capital and the region being the Farjan, Maraariha, Maslata, Masrata,[7] Qadhadhfa (Qadhafi's own tribe that is based in Sirte), Warfalla and Zawiyya.[8]

Tripoli spreads out along the Mediterranean Coast, with the major port based near the city center, and Tripoli International Airport roughly 20 kilometers (12 miles) to the south. The Libyan Coastal Highway cuts through the city, connecting it with Khums, Zlitan and Misrata in the east, and Zawiyya in the west. Major highways lead south from the city, one to Bani Walid, and the other through Al-Gharyan at the base of the Nafusa Mountains region all the way to Sabha in the southwestern province of Fezzan.

The southern suburbs of Tripoli were home to the Bab al-'Aziziyya barracks, which housed Qadhafi's family compound. Three concrete walls, each four meters high and one meter thick, surrounded the compound, with openings for weapons to point outwards. The interior walls were lower and surrounded with guards and metal detectors.[9] Inside the compound was Qadhafi's private residence as well as a number of military barracks for troops under the command of Qadhafi's inner circle and family members.[10] Other facilities at the barracks included a communications

---

[5] John L. Wright, *Tripoli*, Encyclopedia of the Modern Middle East and North Africa (2004), *available at* http://www.encyclopedia.com/topic/Tripoli.aspx.

[6] *Id.*

[7] The transliterations of these four tribe names were adopted from the reference. *Libyan Tribes – alphabetical list and by East West*, World View from Off the Strip, Feb. 26, 2011, *available at* http://www.sandraoffthestrip.com/2011/02/26/libyan-tribes-in-alphabetical-order-and-by-east-or-west.

[8] *Id.*

[9] Kathryn Westcott, *Muammar Gaddafi's presidential bolt-hole*, BBC, May 1, 2011, *available at* http://www.bbc.co.uk/news/world-africa-12831594.

[10] Abeer Tayel, *Libya rebels capture Qaddafi's Tripoli compound, hoist flag & smash statue*, Al Arabiya, Aug. 23, 2011, *available at* http://english.alarabiya.net/articles/2011/08/23/163724.html.

center and other administrative headquarters.[11] Qadhafi reportedly lived on the grounds in an air-conditioned tent. The compound itself was linked to various neighborhoods in the city via underground tunnels.[12]

During the war, Qadhafi commanded his forces from Tripoli, and the city remained a regime stronghold until August 2011. The demonstrations that took place in Tripoli were quickly subdued, and the opposition movement in the capital was mostly limited to underground organizing. After months of battle, in late August 2011, *thuwar* forces from the Nafusa Mountains region overran Zawiyya and Al-Gharyan and advanced on Tripoli with the aid of NATO airstrikes. Major clashes began in Tripoli on 20 August and one week later the city was under rebel control. The loss of Tripoli to the *thuwar* forces effectively signaled the end of the Qadhafi regime and the beginning of a new government.[13] The National Transitional Council moved its headquarters from Benghazi to Tripoli in September 2011 to govern from the capital.[14]

Surrounding areas such as Janzur, situated about 17 kilometers (10 miles) west of Tripoli and the city of Tarhuna, situated about 66 kilometers (40 miles) southeast of the city were also affected by the conflict. The events and violations carried out in these surrounding areas are also discussed in this chapter.[15]

2. SUMMARY OF EVENTS

Anti-Qadhafi protests in Tripoli erupted in Green Square (Sahat al-Khadra, later renamed Al-Shuhada' Square) beginning on 17 February 2011.[16]

---

[11] Westcott, *Muammar Gaddafi's presidential bolt-hole, supra* note 9.

[12] David A. Graham, *Inside Gaddafi's Compound*, THE DAILY BEAST, Aug. 23, 2011, *available at* http://www.thedailybeast.com/articles/2011/08/23/gaddafi-s-compound-inside-bab-al-azizya.html.

[13] Julian Borger et al., *Battle for Tripoli: pivotal victory in the mountains helped big push*, THE GUARDIAN, Aug. 22, 2011, *available at* http://www.guardian.co.uk/world/2011/aug/22/battle-for-tripoli-libya-gaddafi.

[14] *See* Ch. VI Sec. 2. *See also* Rod Nordland, *Libyan Transitional Council Prepares to Move Its Capital to Tripoli*, N.Y. TIMES, Sept. 8, 2011, *available at* http://www.nytimes.com/2011/09/09/world/africa/09libya.html.

[15] Christian Lowe & Taha Zargoun, *Rival militias wage turf war near Libyan capital*, REUTERS, Dec. 3, 2011, *available at* http://www.reuters.com/article/2011/12/03/us-libya-militias-idUSTRE7B20L620111203.

[16] *Libya follows deadly crackdown with mass arrests*, AFP, Apr. 19, 2011, *available at* http://www.google.com/hostednews/afp/article/ALeqM5i9oXPftOIEQ29EuNroc-jJkjxoXg?docId=CNG.30a7eb6de98a36de2dbb441ffee98187.

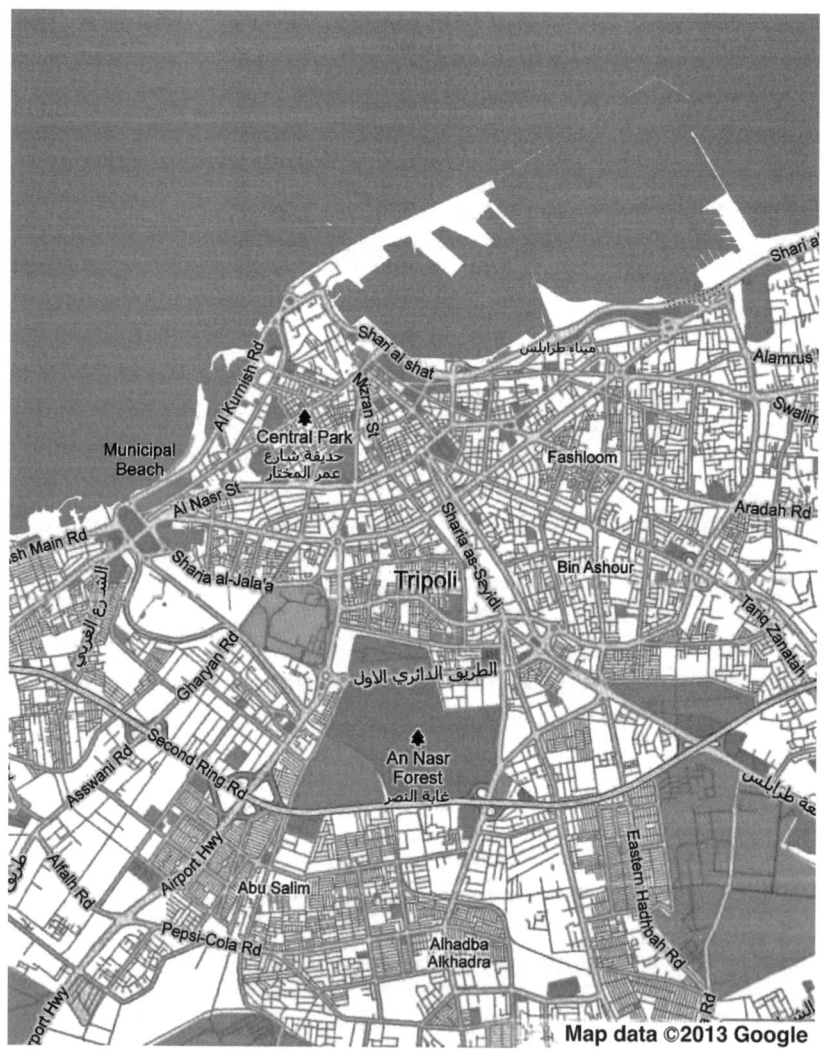

Map 10: Map of Tripoli (Map data © 2013 Google).

Pro-regime demonstrations took place in response, also in Green Square, with demonstrators shouting slogans in support of Qadhafi.[17] The protests became violent as Libyans again took to the streets in central Tripoli on 20 February, with Qadhafi forces firing live ammunition and protesters attacking government buildings.[18] Clashes ensued between anti- and pro-regime demonstrators. Protests continued in many locations around the capital, with the largest taking place in Green Square and the suburbs of Tajura and Fashlum.[19]

On 21 February, there were reports of *thuwar* demonstrators setting fire to police stations and the People's Congress building.[20] Qadhafi forces continued to fire live ammunition at demonstrators in the capital in an attempt to suppress the uprising. Protests and clashes continued, and on 25 February Qadhafi forces opened fire on marchers near the Suq al-Juma' and Fashlum districts. The shootings led to multiple deaths of protesters as large masses poured out of weekly mosque prayers and marched across the Libyan capital. Qadhafi forces reportedly killed 17 people outside the Tajura mosque, and opened fire on people exiting another mosque in Fashlum.[21] Later that day, Qadhafi made a public appearance in Green Square in front of 1,000 supporters, calling on them to "defend the nation."[22] The following week, on 4 March, Qadhafi forces fired tear gas and used live ammunition on hundreds of demonstrators who had gathered in Tajura after Friday prayers.[23] Government officials actively

---

[17] *Libya protests: Death in al-Bayda as unrest spreads*, BBC, Feb. 17, 2011, *available at* http://www.bbc.co.uk/news/world-middle-east-12500476.

[18] *See* Ch. XIII, Sec. 3.1. *See also Libya Revolt Spreads to Tripoli*, AL JAZEERA, Feb. 21, 2011, *available at* http://www.aljazeera.com/news/africa/2011/02/20112213143929189.html; Report of the International Commission of Inquiry on Libya, U.N. HRC. 19th Sess., Annex I, ¶ 78. U.N. Doc. A/HRC/19/68, advance unedited version (Mar. 2, 2012).

[19] Report of the International Commission of Inquiry, advance unedited version (Mar. 2, 2012), *supra* note 18 at Annex I, ¶ 119.

[20] *Libyan People's Hall on fire as protesters riot*, RIA NOVOSTI, Feb. 21, 2011, *available at* http://en.rian.ru/world/20110221/162699766.html. *See also* Christian Lowe, *UPDATE 1 – Government building on fire in Libyan capital*, REUTERS, Feb. 21, 2011, *available at* http://af.reuters.com/article/commoditiesNews/idAFLDE71K0OP20110221.

[21] Report of the International Commission of Inquiry, advance unedited version (Mar. 2, 2012), *supra* note 18 at Annex I, ¶ 120.

[22] *Gunfire hits protesters in Libya*, INDEPENDENT IE, Feb. 25, 2011, *available at* http://www.independent.ie/breaking-news/world-news/gunfire-hits-protesters-in-libya-2556477.html.

[23] *Journalists under attack in Libya: The tally*, COMMITTEE TO PROTECT JOURNALISTS, *available at* http://www.cpj.org/blog/2011/05/journalists-under-attack-in-libya.php; Peter Beaumont & Mark Tran, *Libya protests break out after Friday prayers*, THE GUARDIAN, Mar. 4, 2011, *available at* http://www.guardian.co.uk/world/2011/mar/04/libya-protests-gaddafi-tripoli.

prevented reporters from covering the demonstrations, forcing approximately 130 foreign journalists to remain at the Rixos Hotel, unless they agreed to a government escort.[24]

On 26 March, a woman named Iman al-ʿUbaydi entered the Rixos Hotel and began telling journalists that she had been raped and beaten by Qadhafi forces. A commotion ensued, as hotel employees restrained her and tried to prevent journalists from obtaining her story. Qadhafi forces physically abused journalists who attempted to protect her, destroying a CNN video camera and seizing a recorder used by a journalist from the Financial Times in the process. The woman was forcibly removed from the hotel by Qadhafi forces after nearly an hour of struggle.[25]

Thuwar forces took control of the city of Zawiyya in late February, just 50 kilometers (31 miles) to the west of Tripoli, posing a threat to the regime's hold on the capital. Qadhafi responded by deploying his best-equipped and most elite military units westward in early March to attack the rebels and re-take Zawiyya on 11 March.[26] As the war escalated across the country, the foreign military intervention began to target the Qadhafi forces, aiding the efforts of the rebel movement.

NATO began its airstrikes on the capital in March, and by early May it had destroyed command-and-control structures as well as ammunition and weapons supplies. A NATO strike hit one of Qadhafi's residential compounds in the Gargur neighborhood of Tripoli on 30 April, reportedly killing his youngest son, Saif al-ʿArab, and three of his grandchildren.[27] The compound reportedly housed a command bunker from where Qadhafi forces had been directing operations.[28] On 13 May, NATO announced that it had attacked an important C2 bunker that was being used as a command-and-control facility to coordinate attacks against civilians.[29] On

---

[24] COMMITTEE TO PROTECT JOURNALISTS, *Journalists under attack in Libya: The tally*, supra note 23.

[25] *See* Ch. XIII, Sec. 3.7. *See also* David D. Kirkpatrick, *Libyan Woman Struggles to Tell Media of Her Rape*, N.Y. TIMES, Mar. 27, 2011, *available at* http://www.nytimes.com/2011/03/27/world/middleeast/27tripoli.html.

[26] *See* Ch. XII, Sec. 2. *See also* Michael Georgy & Maria Golovnina, *Rebels repel Gaddafi assault on Libya oil port*, REUTERS, Mar. 11, 2011, *available at* http://in.reuters.com/article/2011/03/11/idINIndia-55498020110311.

[27] *See* Ch. XIII, Sec. 4. *See also* Tim Hill, *Muammar Gaddafi son killed by NATO air strike – Libyan government*, THE GUARDIAN, Apr. 30, 2011, *available at* http://www.guardian.co.uk/world/2011/may/01/libya-muammar-gaddafi-son-nato.

[28] This statement is based on information provided to the ISISC Project by the consultant.

[29] *Press briefing on Libya*, NORTH ATLANTIC TREATY ORGANIZATION, May 13, 2011, *available at* http://www.nato.int/cps/en/natolive/opinions_74038.htm.

17 May, coalition forces targeted military training facilities, surface-to-air missile launchers, ammunition storage facilities, armored vehicles, rocket launchers, tanks and anti-aircraft guns in and around Tripoli.[30] On 19 and 20 May, NATO conducted strikes against Qadhafi maritime forces in the ports of Tripoli, Khums and Sirte, attacking eight warships.[31] The Bab al-'Aziziyya barracks and surrounding areas were targeted repeatedly by NATO forces. On 24 May, NATO increased its airstrikes in what was reported to be one of the heaviest nights of NATO attacks on the capital. More than 20 strikes were carried out during the early hours of the morning and a vehicle storage facility adjacent to Bab al-'Aziziyya was hit.[32]

Tripoli remained the base of regime control over the war efforts, and the foreign intervention continued to concentrate on the capital. On 10 June, NATO reported it was targeting command-and-control centers, military equipment, intelligence structures and other military facilities in the city. The coalition forces explained that their activities were intended to increase pressure on the Qadhafi regime, and stressed that its operations were conducted with great care in order to avoid civilian casualties.[33] Nevertheless, the NATO strikes led to civilian casualties, as a result of malfunctioning equipment, poor intelligence and other operational errors. On 20 June, a NATO laser-guided bomb malfunctioned and hit a three-story house in the Suq al-Juma' neighborhood in Tripoli. Reports stated that nine civilians were killed, including two children.[34]

On 19 July, NATO announced that it had targeted a key antenna communication system located at Tripoli's International Airport, claiming the antenna was being used for military purposes. NATO reported that the information obtained from the antenna was being used to coordinate tactical operations NATO air assents and Libyan civilians. A NATO

---

[30] *Press briefing on Libya*, NORTH ATLANTIC TREATY ORGANIZATION, May 17, 2011, *available at* http://www.nato.int/cps/en/natolive/opinions_74411.htm.

[31] *Press briefing on Libya*, NORTH ATLANTIC TREATY ORGANIZATION, May 20, 2011, *available at* http://www.nato.int/cps/en/natolive/opinions_74542.htm; *Press briefing on Libya*, NORTH ATLANTIC TREATY ORGANIZATION, July 12, 2011, *available at* http://www.nato.int/cps/en/natolive/opinions_76355.htm.

[32] *See* Ch. II, Sec. 3.3. *See also Tripoli hit by NATO airstrikes in heaviest bombing yet*, NDTV, May 24, 2011, *available at* http://www.ndtv.com/article/world/tripoli-hit-by-nato-airstrikes-in-heaviest-bombing-yet-107799.

[33] *Press briefing on Libya*, NORTH ATLANTIC TREATY ORGANIZATION, June 20, 2011, *available at* http://www.nato.int/cps/en/natolive/opinions_75263.htm.

[34] *See* Ch. III, Sec. 6.2. *See also* Adam Schreck, *Libya says NATO airstrike killed 9 civilians*, AP, June 19, 2011, *available at* http://www.seattlepi.com/news/article/Libya-says-NATO-air-strike-killed-9-civilians-1429866.php.

spokesperson stated that maintaining full control over Libyan air space was necessary for it to carry out its mandate of enforcing a no-fly zone, while at the same time ensuring the safe movement of all legitimate humanitarian and diplomatic flights entering Libya.[35]

The NATO-led intervention extended beyond its original objective of enforcing the no-fly zone, however, as foreign actors increased their involvement by providing direct support to the *thuwar* forces. This involvement included British, French and Qatari special forces that reportedly provided weapons, fuel, food and medicine to *thuwar* forces in Tripolitania to help them prepare for the final battle for the capital.[36] NATO airstrikes intensified in August, with the *thuwar* forces closing in on Tripoli from all directions. On 6 August, NATO attacked a missile depot in a neighborhood where the government had stationed an SA-2 anti-aircraft missile storage complex. Residential buildings and businesses were severely damaged and residents were wounded as a result of the strike.[37] The following day, on 7 August, NATO aircraft conducted several precision strikes on a ship on the military side of the port of Tripoli, destroying weapons and ammunition. The strikes were carried out based on intelligence that Qadhafi forces were removing weaponry and ammunition from the warship.[38]

On 16 August, NATO announced that it would increase its pressure on Tripoli in order to assist the *thuwar* advance on the city. *Thuwar* had been able to encircle the capital by taking control of Bir al-Ghanam, Zawiyya, Sabrata, Surman, Al-Gharyan and Tarhuna.[39] Eventually Zlitan fell under *thuwar* control on 19 August, resulting in the opposition controlling the main coastal road in western Libya, and increasing pressure on the Qadhafi regime from both sides of the capital.[40]

---

[35] *Press briefing on Libya*, NORTH ATLANTIC TREATY ORGANIZATION, July 19, 2011, *available at* http://www.nato.int/cps/en/natolive/opinions_76568.htm.

[36] *See* Ch. III, Sec. 7.1. *See also* ANTHONY BELL ET AL., INSTITUTE FOR THE STUDY OF WAR, 4 THE LIBYAN REVOLUTION: THE TIDE TURNS 17 (Nov. 2011) [hereinafter "THE TIDE TURNS"], *available at* http://www.understandingwar.org/sites/default/files/Libya_Part4.pdf.

[37] *See* Ch. III, Sec. 6.2. *See also Errant NATO Airstrikes in Libya: 13 Cases*, N.Y. TIMES, Dec. 16, 2011, *available at* http://www.nytimes.com/interactive/2011/12/16/world/africa/nato-airstrikes-in-libya.html?ref=africa#page/missile-depot.

[38] *Press briefing on Libya*, NORTH ATLANTIC TREATY ORGANIZATION, Aug. 19, 2011, *available at* http://www.nato.int/cps/en/natolive/opinions_77137.htm.

[39] *Press briefing on Libya*, NORTH ATLANTIC TREATY ORGANIZATION, Aug. 16, 2011, *available at* http://www.nato.int/cps/en/natolive/opinions_77212.htm.

[40] *See* Ch. II, Sec. 3.3. *See also* Chris Stephen et al., *Tripoli facing three-sided advance by Libyan rebels*, THE GUARDIAN, Aug. 19, 2011, *available at* http://www.guardian.co.uk/world/2011/aug/19/tripoli-facing-advance-libya-rebels.

On 20 August, with the help of NATO, the *thuwar* forces embarked on Operation Mermaid.[41] Rebel kata'ib from Zintan (part of the western mountain command), and the Tripoli Katiba led the operation.[42] While NATO explained that it was acting in accordance with its mandate to protect civilians, its involvement in the operation was criticized for exceeding the United Nations Security Council mandate by directly assisting *thuwar* in achieving their military and political goals.[43]

The *thuwar* were aided by local residents who, quickly joined the battle. On 20 August 2011, calls went out from mosque megaphones at evening prayers for residents to join the uprising.[44] By now, the fighting had reached most of the suburbs in Tripoli, including Tajura, Suq al-Juma' and Fashlum. *Thuwar* in Tripoli received reinforcements from kata'ib advancing from Misrata, Benghazi, Zawiyya and Zintan. They entered Green Square with little resistance on 21 August.[45]

Thuwar arrived from Misrata by sea and engaged in fighting in the neighborhood of Tajura.[46] The rebel forces from Tajura had coordinated with the Misratan *kata'ib* in the lead-up to the 20 August advance, providing weapons and supplies by boat.[47] Meanwhile, fighting between the *thuwar* and Qadhafi forces ensued in Suq al-Juma', Armada[48] and the Ma'atiga Airport.[49]

Thuwar forces suffered a setback on 21 August in a clash 35 kilometers (22 miles) west of Tripoli, when Qadhafi forces pushed them back with

---

[41] Dario Lopez, *Heavy gunfire in Tripoli as rebels close in*, 3 NEWS, Aug. 21, 2011, *available at* http://www.3news.co.nz/Heavy-gunfire-in-Tripoli-as-rebels-close-in/tabid/417/articleID/222904/Default.aspx.

[42] INTERNATIONAL CRISIS GROUP, HOLDING LIBYA TOGETHER: SECURITY CHALLENGES AFTER QADHAFI 14 (Dec. 14, 2011) [hereinafter "HOLDING LIBYA TOGETHER"], *available at* http://www.crisisgroup.org/~/media/Files/Middle%20East%20North%20Africa/North%20Africa/115%20Holding%20Libya%20Together%20--%20Security%20Challenges%20after%20Qadhafi.pdf.

[43] *See* Ch. III, Sec. 7.1. *See also Libya conflict: Rebels take base on push to Tripoli*, BBC, Aug. 21, 2011, *available at* http://www.bbc.co.uk/news/world-africa-14606618.

[44] INTERNATIONAL CRISIS GROUP, HOLDING LIBYA TOGETHER, *supra* note 42 at 4.

[45] Report of the International Commission of Inquiry, advance unedited version (Mar. 2, 2012), *supra* note 18 at Annex I, ¶ 91.

[46] BBC, *Libya conflict: Rebels take base on push to Tripoli, supra* note 43; *UPDATE 1 – Libyan rebels fight for Tripoli airbase-activist*, REUTERS, Aug. 20, 2011, *available at* http://af.reuters.com/article/libyaNews/idAFLDE77J06920110820.

[47] INTERNATIONAL CRISIS GROUP, HOLDING LIBYA TOGETHER, *supra* note 42 at 30. *See also* Ch. II, Sec. 3.3.

[48] The transliteration of this place was adopted from the reference. REUTERS, *UPDATE 1 – Libyan rebels fight for Tripoli airbase-activist, supra* note 46.

[49] *Id.*

artillery attacks, forcing them to establish a new frontline outside of the town. After the retreat, however, NATO launched airstrikes in the area, allowing *thuwar* to capture the Khamis Katiba base, home of the most elite brigade, located 22 kilometers (13 miles) west of Tripoli.[50]

By 21 August, *thuwar* forces had taken control of the Tajura, Suq al-Juma', Arada[51] and al-Sabaa[52] neighborhoods, while heavy fighting was still reported in Qadah Zawiyya al-Dahmaniyya, Fashlum and Bin 'Ashur.[53] *Thuwar* sought to take over Qadhafi's Bab al-'Aziziyya compound, which was the last stronghold and remaining symbol of the regime.[54] Much of the fighting on 21 August reportedly involved Tripoli residents confronting the Qadhafi forces without the aid of *thuwar* from outside of the capital.[55] Residents of Tripoli had been developing their own network of opposition supporters since the beginning of the uprising in February 2011, and they fought on the frontlines in the battle for Tripoli. Some residents of Tripoli contested that it was the local rebels who took the lead in the final battle for the capital, with the *thuwar* from outside playing a smaller role.[56]

NATO carried out several large strikes on Tripoli during the final fight for the capital, and on 22 August reported destroying tanks, artillery, and striking the secret Baroni Intelligence Center.[57] NATO continued to attack Qadhafi's Bab al-'Aziziyya compound, and on 23 August, *thuwar* took the compound and officially announced control of the capital.[58] Securing Bab al 'Aziziyya was a major challenge, however, as Qadhafi forces sent tanks and carried out missile attacks in the city.[59] The confrontations continued

---

[50] BBC, *Libya conflict: Rebels take base on push to Tripoli, supra* note 43.

[51] The transliteration of this place was adopted from the reference. *Battle for Tripoli,* THE WASHINGTON POST, Aug. 21, 2011, *available at* http://www.washingtonpost.com/world/battle-for-tripoli/2011/08/21/gIQA3CG9UJ_graphic.html?tid=sm_twitter_washingtonpost.

[52] The transliteration of this place was adopted from the reference. *Id.*

[53] *Gadhafi defiant as rebels claim to take 'revolution' inside Tripoli,* CNN, Aug. 21, 2011, *available at* http://edition.cnn.com/2011/WORLD/africa/08/20/libya.war; *Libya Live Blog,* AL JAZEERA, Aug. 21, 2011, *available at* http://blogs.aljazeera.net/liveblog/libya-aug-21-2011-1407; *Battle for Tripoli,* THE WASHINGTON POST, *supra* note 51.

[54] CNN, *Gadhafi defiant as rebels claim to take 'revolution' inside Tripoli, supra* note 53.

[55] BBC, *Libya conflict: Rebels take base on push to Tripoli, supra* note 50.

[56] INTERNATIONAL CRISIS GROUP, HOLDING LIBYA TOGETHER, *supra* note 42 at 9.

[57] Sean Rayment, *How the Special Forces Helped Bring Qaddafi to His Knees,* THE TELEGRAPH, Aug. 28, 2011, *available at* http://www.telegraph.co.uk/news/worldnews/africaand-indianocean/libya/8727076/How-the-special-forces-helped-bring-Gaddafi-to-his-knees.html.

[58] *Id. See also* Ch. III, Sec. 6.1.

[59] *Press briefing on Libya,* NORTH ATLANTIC TREATY ORGANIZATION, August 23, 2011, *available at* http://www.nato.int/cps/en/natolive/opinions_77362.htm.

around the compound for six hours until *thuwar* fighters were able to enter the complex. The compound was subsequently looted and vandalized, but Qadhafi and his family had left the grounds well before the capital fell.[60]

During the month of August 2011, and the height of fighting and NATO strikes in Tripoli, foreign journalists were forced to remain at the Rixos Hotel by Qadhafi forces.[61] Libya's minister of information held regular news conferences at the hotel, and some foreign journalists believed they were being used as human shields.[62] On 22 August, Saif al-Islam held a press conference at the hotel denying rumors that he had been captured. On 24 August, the foreign journalists were permitted to leave after having their movements restricted by armed Qadhafi gunmen for five days.[63]

Clashes continued after the opposition forces took the Bab al-ʿAziziyya compound, concentrated mostly in the southwest of Tripoli, in the areas of Hadba and Abu Salim.[64] *Thuwar* released hundreds of political prisoners after securing the Abu Salim Prison and an intelligence building in the district on 24 August.[65] Detainees also reportedly escaped or were released from detention facilities in ʿAin Zara, Al-Jadayda, Tajura, Khilit al-Firjan and Qasr Bin Ghashir.[66] The CoI reported that thousands of detainees held in custody by Qadhafi forces in Al-Jadayda, ʿAin Zara and Abu Salim prisons in Tripoli were freed by *thuwar* between 20 and 24 August 2011.[67] As *thuwar* took control of government buildings, evidence of atrocities carried out in detention centers in the capital surfaced, such as the discovery of bodies of persons reportedly executed by Qadhafi forces before abandoning the city.[68]

---

[60] BELL ET AL., THE TIDE TURNS, *supra* note 36 at 19.

[61] *BBC journalist describes release from Rixos hotel*, BBC, Aug. 24, 2011, *available at* http://www.bbc.co.uk/news/world-africa-14654958.

[62] *See* Ch. XIII, Sec. 3.6. *See also Journalists Trapped Inside Tripoli Hotel*, 9NEWS WORLD, Aug. 22, 2011, *available at* http://news.ninemsn.com.au/world/8288763/journalists-trapped-inside-tripoli-hotel.

[63] BBC, *BBC journalist describes release from Rixos hotel, supra* note 61.

[64] BELL ET AL., THE TIDE TURNS, *supra* note 36 at 19; *Libya rebels storm Tripoli's Abu Salim district*, REUTERS, Aug. 25, 2011, *available at* http://af.reuters.com/article/commoditiesNews/idAFLDE77O0SH20110825.

[65] BELL ET AL., THE TIDE TURNS, *supra* note 36 at 20.

[66] AMNESTY INTERNATIONAL, THE BATTLE FOR LIBYA: KILLINGS, DISAPPEARANCES AND TORTURE 58 (Sept. 2011), *available at* http://www.amnesty.org/en/library/asset/MDE19/025/2011/en/8f2e1c49-8f43-46d3-917d-383c17d36377/mde1902520¹¹en.pdf.

[67] Report of the International Commission of Inquiry, advance unedited version (Mar. 2, 2012), *supra* note 18 at Annex I, ¶ 92.

[68] *See* Ch. XIII, Sec. 3.2. *See also Evidence of 'mass execution' in Tripoli*, AL JAZEERA, Aug. 25, 2011, *available at* http://www.aljazeera.com/news/africa/2011/08/2011825124849190250.html.

On 25 August, the head of the Tripoli Military Council (TMC), 'Abd al-Hakim Balhaj, publicly announced the council's existence. The TMC had played a central role in organizing the uprising and final battle in the capital, and quickly established control over key strategic locations in the capital. The Council consisted of *thuwar* leaders from Tripoli representing the different geographic divisions of the capital, each with its own headquarters. The TMC oversaw 11 different Tripoli-based *thuwar kata'ib* operating in the city, and managed the political affairs with the NTC and other *kata'ib* in the city.[69] The Council held control over much of the strategic infrastructure and took on administrative authority in different capacities. It worked with the NTC in some instances, but acted on its own authority without necessarily seeking approval from the governing authorities. By bringing some of the Tripoli *kata'ib* under central control, the Council did help stabilize the situation in Tripoli, and restore some order in the city. By the end of August, commercial traffic and humanitarian shipments were freely entering and leaving the port of Tripoli, and NATO ships continued to provide a security presence in the area. The war was still not over, however, as *thuwar* forces prepared for their next operation, which would be conducted in Sirte–Qadhafi's hometown and remaining regime holdout.

On 28 August, *thuwar* captured the remaining areas in Tripoli still under Qadhafi control.[70] There were reportedly scenes of jubilation around the city as symbols of Qadhafi's rule were defaced or destroyed.[71] Foreign leaders visited the capital as a sign of support for the transitional process. In September, in the first visit by a senior western leader since the start of the uprising, French President Nicolas Sarkozy and British Prime Minister David Cameron arrived in Tripoli to meet with the transitional authorities.[72] Hillary Clinton followed shortly after, visiting Tripoli on 18 October to show U.S. support for the interim government. Clinton was the first high-ranking U.S. official to visit Libya after the uprising.[73]

---

[69] INTERNATIONAL CRISIS GROUP, HOLDING LIBYA TOGETHER, *supra* note 42 at 20.

[70] BELL ET AL., THE TIDE TURNS, *supra* note 36 at 11.

[71] *Libya: the fall of Tripoli – Wednesday 24 August 2011*, THE GUARDIAN, Aug. 24, 2011, *available at* http://www.guardian.co.uk/world/middle-east-live/2011/aug/24/libya-rebels-take-gaddafi-compound-live-updates.

[72] *Libya: Cameron and Sarkozy visit Tripoli – video*, THE GUARDIAN, Sept. 15, 2011, *available at* http://www.guardian.co.uk/world/video/2011/sep/15/libya-david-cameron-nicolas-sarkozy-tripoli.

[73] *Clinton holds talks in Tripoli with Libya's interim authority*, BBC, Oct. 18, 2011, *available at* http://www.bbc.co.uk/news/world-africa-15360308.

On 14–16 October 2011, following Qadhafi's appearance on television calling for his supporters to continue fighting, the first incidents of serious fighting were reported in the capital between *thuwar* and Qadhafi forces since the *thuwar* secured Bab al-ʿAziziyya compound. A gun battle and clashes erupted when Qadhafi loyalists marched with weapons and chanted pro-Qadhafi songs in the Abu Salim area. They attempted to raise a green flag (Qadhafi-era flag that the NTC had replaced with the pre-1969 tri-color flag) on Abu Salim Street before *thuwar* arrived on the scene and a gun battle erupted. The fighting spread to other parts of Tripoli, and *thuwar* forces continued to carry out arrests of suspected Qadhafi loyalists in the Abu Salim area.[74] On 16 October, bulldozers demolished what remained of Bab al-ʿAziziyya.[75]

After *thuwar* forces established firm control of the capital they began carrying out regular security functions and asserted significant influence over the city. The TMC, for example, "possessed its own procedures, detention facilities, weapons depots, and registration systems." Other smaller military councils were also established, and assumed control over local areas and neighborhoods. The CoI estimated that there were at least 132 military councils operating in Tripoli in the immediate wake of the war.[76]

Thuwar kataʾib from other parts of the country, most notably from Misrata and Zintan, remained in the capital after the fall of the Qadhafi regime and in several instances competed for control with other armed actors. The armed groups fought over contested installations in Tripoli, such as the Tripoli International Airport, which initially came under the control of the Zintan Brigade from the Nafusa Mountains.[77] On 18 November, the head of the TMC, Balhaj, was prevented from boarding a plane by Zintan fighters at the airport. Members of the Zintan Katiba attempted

---

[74] *See* Ch. XIII, Sec. 3.3. *See also Libya: Tight security after Tripoli unrest*, BBC, Oct. 16, 2011, *available at* http://www.bbc.co.uk/news/world-africa-15325186; *'Gaddafi loyalists' and Libya NTC Tripoli battle ends*, BBC, Oct. 15, 2011, *available at* http://www.bbc.co.uk/news/world-africa-15319952; *Libyan NTC troops and Gaddafi loyalists clash in Tripoli*, BBC, Oct. 14, 2011, *available at* http://www.bbc.co.uk/news/world-africa-15314365.

[75] *Libya: Bulldozers demolish Gaddafi compound*, BBC, Oct. 16, 2011, *available at* http://www.bbc.co.uk/news/world-africa-15330050.

[76] *See* Ch. V, Sec. 2. *See also* Report of the International Commission of Inquiry, advance unedited version (Mar. 2, 2012), *supra* note 18 at Annex I, ¶ 72.

[77] *Militia hands over Tripoli airport to government*, REUTERS, Oct. 10, 2011, *available at* http://www.reuters.com/article/2011/10/10/libya-tripoli-airport-idUSL5E7LA3QV20111010.

to deflect attention from the affair, however, responding that Balhaj was only briefly detained because his passport was out of date.[78]

There were a series of incidents where Tripoli-based militias used force to assert their authority over armed actors from other cities in the capital.[79] Following the end of the conflict in October 2011, numerous clashes resulted in casualties and serious injuries. Some of the clashes involved the use of anti-aircraft machine guns in residential areas.[80] On 10 November, territorial disputes turned into fighting between armed groups along a highway in Tripoli, and two casualties were reported the following day. Clashes on 11 November involved the use of mortars, rocket-propelled grenades (RPGs) and Soviet-built Grad missiles, and led to a dozen casualties.[81] Another clash was reported on 22 November 2011, when 20 heavily-armed men opened fire near a complex of luxury villas on the outskirts of the capital.[82]

The fighting between the armed groups in the capital intensified in December. On 2 December, violence erupted just outside of the capital in the town of Janzur, resulting in the death of one local official and the destruction of the Zintan Katiba headquarters.[83] Two days later a group of armed men belonging to the Al-Rujban Katiba attempted to assist a *thuwar* fighter who had been accused of murder escape from prison. They rushed to Tripoli's main courthouse and the office of the Attorney General, 'Abd al 'Aziz al-Hasadi, and demanded that the accused fighter be released.[84] Another gunfight took place when an armed group attacked

---

[78] *Rival militia briefly holds Libya Islamist chief*, REUTERS, Nov. 24, 2011, *available at* http://www.reuters.com/article/2011/11/24/libya-belhadj-airport-idUSL5E7MO46X20111124.

[79] Marie-Louise Gumuchian, *Shootout erupts at Tripoli foreign worker compound*, REUTERS, Nov. 22, 2011, *available at* http://www.reuters.com/article/2011/11/22/us-libya-shooting-idUSTRE7AL1MR20111122.

[80] Report of the International Commission of Inquiry, advance unedited version (Mar. 2, 2012), *supra* note 18 at Annex I, ¶ 73.

[81] Alastair Macdonald & Oliver Holmes, *Special Report: Libya – divided it stands*, REUTERS, Dec. 16, 2011, *available at* http://www.reuters.com/article/2011/12/16/us-libya-future-idUSTRE7BF0MG20111216.

[82] Marie-Louise Gumuchian, *Shootout erupts at Tripoli foreign worker compound*, *supra* note 79.

[83] Christian Lowe & Taha Zargoun, *Rival militias wage turf war near Libyan capital*, REUTERS, Dec. 3, 2011, *available at* http://www.reuters.com/article/2011/12/03/us-libya-militias-idUSTRE7B20L620111203.

[84] *Libya to disarm Tripoli by year end*, AL JAZEERA, Dec. 7, 2011, *available at* http://www.aljazeera.com/news/africa/2011/12/20111262350566641.html.

a convoy carrying a senior military official, Khalifa Haftar, near Tripoli's International Airport.[85]

The central authorities made several attempts to disarm the militias and consolidate control, ordering some groups to leave Tripoli and attempting to integrate others into the government security forces. The interim government ordered all heavy weapons to be removed from the capital on 5 October.[86] Other attempts followed on 7 December, when the interim government and the Tripoli council gave militias a two-week deadline to leave the capital. Officials at the Tripoli Military Council, such as the President 'Abd al-Razaq Abu Hajar, publically urged the militias to leave Tripoli to allow for the restoration of peace. He emphasized that while the non-Tripoli based militias had been important actors in the liberation of Tripoli, they were urged to return to their hometowns and cities. The local authorities announced they would respond with force if the militias failed to meet the deadline.[87]

Some of the most powerful armed groups rejected these government directives. Misratan *thuwar* operating in Tripoli held vast weapon supplies that were said to include tanks, rockets and guns. The armed groups maintained that they would not abandon their bases in Tripoli until the central government put adequate security forces in place.[88] The NTC authorities dismantled checkpoints around the capital in an effort to diminish the militias' presence in the capital.[89] The NTC also attempted to absorb militia fighters into the state's security apparatus by allowing them to sign up at the Interior Ministry's main recruitment center in Tripoli. The measures were met with limited success, however, and most armed groups refused to join the government apparatus.[90]

Despite attempts to remove the non-state armed groups from the capital, the violence continued. On 3 January 2012, a gun battle erupted on Tripoli's Zawiya Road, one of the busiest streets in Tripoli, killing four fighters. The battle was reportedly between *thuwar* from Tripoli and

---

[85] Ali Shuaib, *Armed groups clash in turf war near Tripoli airport*, REUTERS, Dec. 11, 2011, *available at* http://af.reuters.com/article/topNews/idAFJOE7BA02P20111211.

[86] AL JAZEERA, *Libya to disarm Tripoli by year end, supra* note 84.

[87] *Id.*

[88] Mahmoud Habboush, *Battle between Tripoli, Misrata militias kills 4*, REUTERS, Jan. 3, 2012, *available at* http://www.reuters.com/article/2012/01/03/us-libya-rebels-clash-id USTRE8021FP20120103.

[89] *See* Ch. V, Sec. 2.

[90] Ali Shuaib, *Libya militia hands Tripoli airport control to govt*, REUTERS, Apr. 20, 2012, *available at* http://www.reuters.com/article/2012/04/20/libya-airport-idUSL6E8FKF0P 20120420.

Misrata over a group of detainees.[91] On 1 February, gunfights erupted in the center of Tripoli between Misratan and Zintan *thuwar*. The exchanges involved both heavy and light weapons in the beach area of Al-Sa'adi.[92]

Conflicts also ensued over compensation for the fighters who had fought with the *thuwar* forces. The NTC announced a program in early 2012 to pay fighters 500 dinars ($380), but the payment was halted due to allegations of fraud. On 8 May, armed men from the Nafusa Mountains region stormed and occupied the Tripoli office of the interim prime minister, 'Abd al-Rahman Keib, demanding compensation. At least one person was killed but Keib was not in the building at the time.[93] The Zintan fighters held Tripoli International Airport for leverage in an effort to get the interim government to provide salaries for former *thuwar*, until finally handing over the airport on 20 April. The main commander of the Zintan Katiba, Mukhtar al-Akhdar, declared that the government was not doing enough to provide jobs and security for the fighters who helped topple the Qadhafi regime.[94]

In an attempt to establish control over Libya's non-state armed factions, the interim government's Ministry of Interior created the Supreme Security Committee (SSC) forces to integrate the former rebels under central authority.[95] Security challenges in the capital persisted, however, as the SSC forces lacked accountability and often acted outside of official channels. There were several incidents involving SSC forces, including the controversial arrest on 17 May of a prominent heart surgeon, Salam Furjani, at the largest medical center in Tripoli.[96] The incident triggered criticism of the SSC and the failure of the central government to control armed groups nominally under its control.[97]

In early June, the Deputy Minister of Interior 'Umar al-Khadrawi stated that the ministry had dismantled four "lawless" armed militias in Tripoli,

---

[91] Habboush, *Battle between Tripoli, Misrata militias kills 4, supra* note 88.

[92] *Rival Libya militias fight gunbattle in capital*, REUTERS, Feb. 1, 2012, *available at* www .reuters.com/article/2012/02/01/libya-tripoli-battle-idUSL5E8D14QS20120201.

[93] Chris Stephen, *Libyan rebels storm prime minister's office*, THE GUARDIAN, May 8, 2012, *available at* http://www.guardian.co.uk/world/2012/may/08/libyan-rebels-storm-prime-minister-office.

[94] Shuaib, *Libya militia hands Tripoli airport control to govt, supra* note 90.

[95] *See* Chapter V, Sec. 2.1.

[96] *See infra* Sec. 3.4.

[97] Chris Stephen, *Libya sees claims of beatings and human rights abuses as elections near*, THE GUARDIAN, June 3, 2012, *available at* http://www.guardian.co.uk/world/2012/jun/03/libya-security-force-kidnapping-surgeon.

and that efforts were being made to bring militias under official bodies.[98] The interim authorities continued to face challenges from the various armed factions, however. On 4 June, the government lost control of the Tripoli International Airport to armed *thuwar* from Tarhuna belonging to the Al-ʿAwfiyya Katiba.[99]

Violent clashes continued in Tripoli into August 2012. The large amounts of weapons that remained from the war made it difficult for the new government to rein in the non-state armed factions.[100] On 19 August, two people died and up to five were injured in twin car bombings in Tripoli. One bomb was close to the former military academy for women on ʿUmar al-Mukhtar Avenue and the other near the Interior Ministry. The attacks coincided with the one-year anniversary of the battle for Tripoli and with mass morning prayers during the Muslim celebration ʿEid al-Fitr.[101]

There were isolated incidents of protests that continued into October, and on 31 October armed men briefly occupied the Libyan parliament building to protest the formation of the new government. Gunmen broke through security and at least a dozen trucks mounted with anti-aircraft guns lined the main road to the parliament the following day. Reports indicated that the armed groups were from the capital and, wearing both military and civilian clothes. The militiamen called for the removal of ministers who they claimed had links to the Qadhafi government.[102] In another incident, on 4 November, at least five people were wounded when militias clashed over the detention of one of their members. The militias were reportedly part of the SCC.[103]

---

[98] AMNESTY INTERNATIONAL, LIBYA RULE OF LAW OR RULE OF MILITIAS? 6 (July 2012), *available at* http://www.amnesty.org/en/library/asset/MDE19/012/2012/en/f2d36090-5716-4ef1-81a7-f4b1ebd082fc/mde190122012en.pdf.

[99] *Libya: Flights resume at Tripoli airport after seizure*, BBC, June 5, 2012, *available at* http://www.bbc.co.uk/news/world-africa-18335015.

[100] *See* Ch. V, Sec. 2. *See also Libya seizes tanks from pro-Gaddafi militia*, BBC, Aug. 24, 2012, *available at* http://www.bbc.co.uk/news/world-africa-19364536.

[101] Eid al Fitr is one of the most important Muslim holidays celebrating the end of Ramadan. *See* BBC, *Libya seizes tanks from pro-Gaddafi militia*, *supra* note 100; *Libya holds 32 'Gaddafi loyalists' over Tripoli attack*, BBC, Aug. 20, 2012, *available at* http://www.bbc .co.uk/news/world-africa-19314714.

[102] *Libya gunmen end occupation of parliament building*, BBC, Nov. 2, 2012, *available at* http://www.bbc.co.uk/news/world-africa-20178222.

[103] For more on the Supreme Security Committee and post-conflict security challenges, *see* Ch. V, Sec. 2. *See also* Kareem Fahim, *Clashes and Car Bombing Highlight Insecurity Across Libya*, N.Y. TIMES, Nov. 4, 2012, *available at* http://www.nytimes.com/2012/11/05/world/africa/clashes-car-bombing-highlight-insecurity-in-libya.html; *Libya: Rival militia spray bullets and grenades in Tripoli*, BBC, Nov. 5, 2012, *available at* http://www.bbc.co.uk/news/world-africa-20202065.

3. Illustrations of the Violations

3.1. *Excessive Use of Force*

(a) *Qadhafi Forces*

In the early days of the protests, the Qadhafi forces responded to protests in the capital with excessive use of force against demonstrators. Witnesses provided testimony of the regime forces using force to disperse demonstrators in response to the protest that began on 17 February 2011. As the demonstrations spread, protesters stormed government installations, including police stations and other buildings on 21 February. While a government response was justified in these circumstances, the Qadhafi forces responded with an indiscriminate use of force that led to unwarranted civilian casualties.[104] There were numerous injuries and casualties documented as a result of the use of live ammunition against demonstrators from 20–25 February 2011. HRW reported that at least "62 corpses were brought to the morgues in Tripoli between 20 and 22 February after protestors had been fired at randomly by Libyan forces."[105]

3.2. *Unlawful Killing*

(a) *Qadhafi Forces*

In addition to the violence that took place in February 2011, unlawful killings were carried out in detention centers under the control of Qadhafi forces. The Qadhafi regime created detention centers after the February 2011 demonstrations began, with the purpose of holding *thuwar* and suspected supporters of the opposition movement. Before withdrawing from Tripoli there were large-scale executions carried out by Qadhafi forces in several detention facilities, including Khilit al-Firjan in Yarmuk and Gargur in Tripoli.[106]

---

[104] *See infra* Sec. 2. *See also* Report of the International Commission of Inquiry to investigate all the alleged violations of international human rights law in the Libyan Arab Jamahiriya, U.N. HRC. 17th Sess., ¶ 77. U.N. Doc. A/HRC/17/44, final version (Jan. 12, 2012).

[105] *Id.* at ¶ 78. *See also Libya: Commanders Should Face Justice for Killings*, HUMAN RIGHTS WATCH, Feb. 22, 2011, *available at* www.hrw.org/en/news/2011/02/22/libya-commanders-should-face-justice-killings.

[106] Report of the International Commission of Inquiry, advance unedited version (Mar. 2, 2012), *supra* note 18 at Annex I, ¶¶ 26-27 & 92.

A detention center was established in a warehouse adjacent to the Khamis Katiba base at Yarmuk.[107] The Qadhafi regime began bringing prisoners to the warehouse after the demonstrations began, and it was operational by early March 2011. Witnesses who survived detention in Yarmuk reported that up to 50 prisoners were brought to the facility in June 2011, some from outside of Tripoli. By early August, an estimated 90 detainees were being held there.[108] While some of the prisoners were released during the conflict, at the time of the massacre there were reportedly 153 detainees.[109]

The CoI reported that in the last weeks of August, guards in charge of the prison facility were given grenades and ordered to kill the prisoners before giving up control. One of the guards who left before the killings took place stated that he had been threatened by superior officials for refusing to take the grenades.[110] On 23 August, guards threw grenades into the warehouse, blasting the doors open and began firing on the tightly-packed prisoners inside.[111] 106 people were believed to have died in the attack.[112] The guards proceeded to burn the bodies on 25 August.[113]

Evidence of the massacre was also obtained by independent sources, and corroborates the findings of the CoI. Physicians for Human Rights (PHR) found that the prison had been established at an agricultural compound following a NATO strike on the Khamis Katiba's Yarmuk military base, and that Qadhafi forces began holding suspected opposition supporters by early March 2011. PHR also reported that at least 53 charred human skeletons were discovered inside the warehouse three days following the massacre, and concluded that the Khamis Katiba soldiers tried to incinerate the remains of the executed detainees.[114]

---

[107] *Id.* at Annex I, ¶ 169.

[108] *Id.* at Annex I, ¶ 170.

[109] PHYSICIANS FOR HUMAN RIGHTS, 32ND BRIGADE MASSACRE: EVIDENCE OF WAR CRIMES AND THE NEED TO ENSURE JUSTICE AND ACCOUNTABILITY IN LIBYA 15 (Dec. 2011) [hereinafter "32ND BRIGADE MASSACRE"], *available at* https://s3.amazonaws.com/PHR_Reports/Libya-32nd-Brigade-Massacre.pdf. For more on the Yarmuk detention center, and violations of torture that took place at the facility, *see infra* Sec. 3.4.

[110] Report of the International Commission of Inquiry, advance unedited version (Mar. 2, 2012), *supra* note 18 at Annex I, ¶ 175.

[111] *Id.* at Annex I, ¶ 176.

[112] *Id.* at Annex I, ¶ 179.

[113] *Id.* at Annex I, ¶ 178.

[114] PHYSICIANS FOR HUMAN RIGHTS, 32ND BRIGADE MASSACRE, *supra* note 109 at 15.

A few hundred meters from the agricultural compound, there was another warehouse facility also used as a makeshift detention center. The warehouse, which had belonged to a Brazilian company, was under control of some of the same officials controlling the agricultural compound at Yarmuk, and in some cases, detainees were transferred from Yarmuk to the Brazilian facility.[115] By the beginning of August, 26–30 people were being held in the Brazilian warehouse,[116] and when Tripoli began to fall to the *thuwar*, orders were reportedly given to execute the prisoners.[117] On 22 August one of the guards, along with a soldier from the Khamis Katiba, took six detainees outside and witnesses heard gunshots. After hearing the gunshots, the witnesses left their cell to find three of the six detainees dead and the other three injured.[118] A former guard later told the CoI that the guards from the Brazilian warehouse showed up at Yarmuk shortly after the shooting and reported having "performed the assignment."[119]

A third ad hoc detention center was located in Gargur, south of the Bab al-ʿAziziyya compound, in a building that had reportedly belonged to the Internal Security Agency (ISA).[120] The building was known at the time as the Green Security Building and was under the command of an official who reported to the head of Military Intelligence.[121] Victims told the CoI they were brought to the detention facility on 18–19 August 2011, and identified the perpetrators of their arrest as being members of the Popular Guard and Revolutionary Guard.[122] Other witnesses reported the involvement of the Khamis Katiba in their detention and transfer to the prison in Gargur[123] Shooting at the facility began on 23 August, leading to numerous injuries and the deaths of an estimated 21 prisoners.[124]

---

[115] *Id.* at 32.

[116] Report of the International Commission of Inquiry, advance unedited version (Mar. 2, 2012), *supra* note 18 at Annex I, ¶ 183.

[117] *Id.* at Annex I, ¶ 184.

[118] *Id.* at Annex I, ¶ 185.

[119] *Id.*

[120] Human Rights Watch refers to the building as formerly under control of the Internal Security service. *See Libya: Gaddafi Forces Suspected Of Executing Detainees*, HUMAN RIGHTS WATCH, Aug. 28, 2011, *available at* http://www.hrw.org/news/2011/08/28/libya-gaddafi-forces-suspected-executing-detainees.

[121] Report of the International Commission of Inquiry, advance unedited version (Mar. 2, 2012), *supra* note 18 at Annex I, ¶¶ 187 & 684.

[122] *Id.* at Annex I, ¶ 188. The CoI uses the number 008 to identify the Head of Military Intelligence, and does not provide the name of the official.

[123] Human Rights Watch refers to the building as formerly under control of the Internal Security service. *See* HUMAN RIGHTS WATCH, *Libya: Gaddafi Forces Suspected Of Executing Detainees, supra* note 120.

[124] Report of the International Commission of Inquiry, advance unedited version (Mar. 2, 2012), *supra* note 18 at Annex I, ¶ 189.

Bodies were later discovered in a dry riverbed between the Gargur prison and the Bab al-'Aziziyya compound, showing signs of execution.[125] Witnesses reported that the victims had been executed by Qadhafi forces prior to 25 August 2011, as *thuwar* were closing in on the Qadhafi compound in the capital. HRW observed the victims and noted that two of the men had their hands tied behind their backs and wore medical staff clothing.[126] Witnesses supported HRW's observations by providing the CoI with photos that showed bodies in the dry riverbed, in some cases with hands tied behind their backs. The photos showed "[t]wo of the bodies... wearing medical scrubs, suggesting they were doctors or medical staff."[127] Witnesses told reporters that the soldiers from the Khamis Katiba were responsible for the killings.[128]

Other cases of arbitrary killing were documented by Amnesty International, which reported that on 24 August 2011 guards shot and killed five detainees in the Qasr Bin Ghashir military camp.[129] Witnesses stated they heard guards open five cells and fire gunshots. Some detainees panicked and broke out of their cells to avoid execution. The guards responsible reportedly fled the scene.[130]

(b) Thuwar *Forces*

In the wake of the fall of Tripoli, there were reports of *thuwar* and other opponents of Qadhafi killing perceived regime loyalists, captured soldiers, and non-Libyan nationals. Deaths occurred in detention centers under control of various *thuwar kata'ib*, local civilian and military councils, and local security committees in Tripoli.[131] Many of the unlawful killings

---

[125] *Id.* at Annex I, ¶ 193.

[126] HUMAN RIGHTS WATCH, *Libya: Gaddafi Forces Suspected Of Executing Detainees, supra* note 120.

[127] Report of the International Commission of Inquiry, advance unedited version (Mar. 2, 2012), *supra* note 18 at Annex I, ¶ 198.

[128] Richard Spencer, *Libya: last act of bloody vengeance by Khamis Brigade*, THE TELEGRAPH, Aug. 28, 2011, *available at* http://www.telegraph.co.uk/news/worldnews/africaand indianocean/libya/ 8728597/Libya-last-act-of-bloody-vengeance-by-Khamis-Brigade.html.

[129] They included three men from Zlitan, and two doctors, one of which is believed to be a man from Misrata, who was taken prisoner near the eastern frontline in July and had not been heard from since. *Libya: Detainees killed by al-Gaddafi loyalists*, AMNESTY INTERNATIONAL, Aug. 26, 2011, *available at* http://www.amnesty.org/en/news-and-updates/ libya-detainees-killed-al-gaddafi-loyalists-2011-08-26.

[130] *Id.*

[131] Report of the International Commission of Inquiry, advance unedited version (Mar. 2, 2012), *supra* note 18 at Annex I, ¶ 205.

documented in Tripoli from late August 2011 onwards differed in some
respects from previously documented targeted revenge killings of perceived Qadhafi loyalists in that they appeared to be "driven by financial
gain and facilitated by the breakdown of law and order."[132]

The CoI documented deaths resulting from torture in Tripoli detention
centers. From late August to 5 December 2011, ten bodies were delivered
to one hospital in Tripoli, bearing signs of severe torture.[133] The CoI documented cases of deaths in detention centers where victims fell into two
broad categories, namely

> . . . agents of Qadhafi's security apparatus and perceived associates of promi-
> nent former government figures, and the Tawerghan community. The for-
> mer have been arrested and detained by *thuwar* from different parts of Libya
> including Al Zawiyah, Garabulli, Misrata, Tajoura and Tripoli. Tawerghans
> have been arrested and detained, in almost all instances, by the Misrata *thu-
> war*. The recorded deaths took place between 12 September and 31 December
> 2011.[134]

After September 2011, Amnesty International documented cases of detainees dying in custody or in hospitals after interrogation in the capital. In
one case, a 26-year-old man was seized by a group of militia on 5 October
2011 as he walked towards the mosque near his home. He was tortured,
along with his brother, in a cell in the militia headquarters. The man died,
and the forensic report concluded that his death was caused by injuries
sustained from beatings.[135] Less than two weeks later, a man was detained
in his home on 16 October, and died in hospital after being delivered by
armed men. Forensic examinations found signs of beatings, and concluded
his death was the result of this abuse.[136] In another case, on 11 September
2011 a man was detained near Tripoli by a militia from Misrata, handed
over to a local council and subsequently to the Sidi Khalifa Military Council. He was held in the former Internal Security Agency (ISA) building in
downtown Tripoli,[137] where he was severely beaten, and died shortly after
as a result of grave injuries.[138]

---

[132] *Id.* at Annex I, ¶ 206.
[133] *Id.* at Annex I, ¶ 223 (internal citations omitted).
[134] *Id.* at Annex I, ¶ 224.
[135] Amnesty International, Militias threaten hopes for New Libya 26 (Feb. 16,
2012), *available at* http://www.amnesty.org/en/library/asset/MDE19/002/2012/en/dd7c1d69-
e368-44de-8ee8-cc9365bd5eb3/mde190022012en.pdf.
[136] *Id.*
[137] *Jamahiriya* Street, now 17 February Street.
[138] Amnesty International, Militias threaten hopes for New Libya, *supra* note
135 at 26.

Many of those unlawfully killed in Tripoli in the period following the fall of the Qadhafi regime appeared to be targeted for their perceived wealth and belongings, in addition to their political affiliations. The CoI documented several of these cases in December 2011, finding that

> ... a member of a Tripoli brigade was fatally shot on 14 December 2011 in central Tripoli by *thuwar* from Misrata. According to an eyewitness and relatives of the victim, a group of *thuwar* from Misrata wanted to confiscate a female relative's car under the pretext that it was government property (the vehicle belonged to a woman whose spouse worked in Qadhafi's security apparatus)... As he was trying to evade the Misrata *thuwar*, they opened fire fatally injuring him in the heart and kidney.[139]

Another killing took place two days later, when a group of armed men stopped a car and tried to confiscate it in downtown Tripoli. The driver refused, and attackers opened fire, killing one passenger.[140]

Amnesty International documented similar cases of fatal attacks at the hands of non-state armed groups that involved looting and extortion. A 31-year-old police officer was detained in his home in a suburb of Tripoli on 17 October 2011 by dozens of armed men in vehicles marked with different militia insignia. They ransacked the house, stole money and phones, and took the man and his brothers to a detention center in Tajura. The assailants called the victim's family and demanded his car in exchange for his release. The man was severely abused in detention, and died after being taken to Abu Salim's hospital.[141]

i. *The Tawerghans*

The CoI gathered extensive amounts of information regarding the deaths of Tawerghans in *thuwar* custody in Tripoli.[142] The *thuwar* groups from Misrata, in particular, targeted the Tawerghan community for arrest and abuse in detention centers. The documented deaths of Tawerghans in custody took place between September and December 2011.[143] A Tawerghan woman recounted how her son-in law was arrested at a checkpoint in Tripoli on 12 September 2011 by Misratan *thuwar* and killed while in

---

[139] Report of the International Commission of Inquiry, advance unedited version (Mar. 2, 2012), *supra* note 18 at Annex I, ¶ 205 (internal citations omitted).

[140] *Id.* at Annex I, ¶ 235.

[141] AMNESTY INTERNATIONAL, MILITIAS THREATEN HOPES FOR NEW LIBYA, *supra* note 135 at 27. *See also* Ch. V Sec. 2.3.

[142] Report of the International Commission of Inquiry, advance unedited version (Mar. 2, 2012), *supra* note 18 at Annex I, ¶ 229.

[143] *Id.* at Annex I, ¶ 224. For more on attacks on Tawerghans by Misrata *thuwar, see* Ch. IX, Sec. 3.

detention.[144] Amnesty International produced similar findings, documenting the case of a Tawerghan factory worker who died in custody after being
detained on 12 September 2011 in Tripoli by a militia from Misrata.[145]

There were also cases of extrajudicial killing of Tawerghans carried out
in IDP camps around Tripoli. One of the most publicized and well documented incident took place on 6 February 2012 at an IDP camp holding
over 2,000 Tawerghans at the Janzur Naval Academy in Tripoli. 13 people
were injured, and seven were killed during the attack, including an elderly
woman and three children.[146] The CoI reported that

> According to multiple interviews of survivors conducted by the Commission,
> armed men arrived in 25 vehicles, including pick-up trucks with mounted
> anti-aircraft guns, their weapons outmatching those of the guards protecting
> the camp. According to eyewitness accounts, the *thuwar* included brigades
> from Misrata (*Shuhada* Misrata and *Soukour* Misrata). The Commission was
> also informed that at least one of the vehicles had a "National Army" plate,
> suggesting that Ministry of Defence personnel were involved...[147] Eyewit-
> nesses and relatives of those killed told the Commission that the *thuwar* did
> not provide any reasons for the raids and began to search houses and fired
> at random. Two Tawerghans, an old man and a woman, were killed. Fol-
> lowing these shooting deaths, Tawerghans from the camp began to march
> towards Palm City, where the United Nations is based...[148] During this
> march the Tawerghans came under fire, allegedly from *thuwar* from Misrata
> and from Janzour, resulting in the deaths of a further five people, including
> two boys and a girl, all minors. According to eye-witnesses there was no
> warning issued before the shooting started.[149]

---

[144] *See infra* Sec. 3.3. *See also* Report of the International Commission of Inquiry,
advance unedited version (Mar. 2, 2012), *supra* note 18 at Annex I, ¶ 231.

[145] AMNESTY INTERNATIONAL, MILITIAS THREATEN HOPES FOR NEW LIBYA, *supra* note
135 at 25.

[146] Report of the International Commission of Inquiry, advance unedited version
(Mar. 2, 2012), *supra* note 18 at ¶ 56; AMNESTY INTERNATIONAL, MILITIAS THREATEN HOPES
FOR NEW LIBYA, *supra* note 135 at 31. Media outlets differ somewhat in their reporting
of the incident on Feb. 6, 2012 in Janzour. *See* Oliver Holmes & Taha Zargoun, *Gunmen
kill five in Libyan refugee camp: hospital staff*, REUTERS, Feb. 6, 2012, *available at* http://
www.reuters.com/article/2012/02/06/us-libya-violence-idUSTRE81526T20120206; *Journalists kidnapped by Misrata brigade were reporting on the racist lynchings of Tawerghans*,
GLOBAL CIVILIANS FOR PEACE, Mar. 7, 2012, *available at* http://globalciviliansforpeace
.com/2012/03/07/journalists-kidnapped-by-misrata-brigade-were-reporting-on-the-racist-
lynchings-of-tawerghans.

[147] Report of the International Commission of Inquiry, advance unedited version
(Mar. 2, 2012), *supra* note 18 at ¶ 419 (internal citations omitted).

[148] *Id.* at Annex I, ¶ 420 (internal citations omitted).

[149] *Id.* at Annex I, ¶ 421 (internal citations omitted).

Witnesses told Amnesty International that some of those carrying out the assault were recognized from previous raids by Misrata militias. Others corroborated accounts that the Ministry of Defense provided support in the attack.[150] The men's vehicles were mounted with 14.5mm guns and 23mm artillery pieces and the assailants were armed with AK-47s. Some of the vehicles had the marking of the militias from Misrata.[151] The armed men had claimed to be looking for weapons as they entered the camp, which HRW noted was poorly guarded upon a staff visit following the attack.[152] Witnesses also described how the boys killed during the incident were pursued and shot as they ran for safety. According to forensic examinations, one boy was shot three times in the back and once in the right arm, and the other was shot once in the chest and once in the knee.[153]

Following the incident in Janzur, the United Nations mission in Libya called on the interim government to increase protection for the displaced people of Tawergha and to investigate the attack. According to findings from HRW, the interim government had made no progress in the investigation into the deaths in Janzur.[154] In response to the claims that insignia of Misrata groups were written on the vehicles of the armed men who entered the camp, the Misrata Military Council denied any involvement in the affair.[155]

3.3. Arbitrary Detentions and Enforced Disappearances

(a) Qadhafi Forces

The Qadhafi regime detained individuals they believed were involved in organizing demonstrations both before and after the demonstrations began in the capital.[156] The CoI reported that

> Arbitrary arrests were conducted on a large scale in Tripoli, especially following demonstrations. In one typical example, the Commission met with

---

[150] AMNESTY INTERNATIONAL, MILITIAS THREATEN HOPES FOR NEW LIBYA, *supra* note 135 at 33.

[151] *Libya: Bolster Security at Tawergha Camps*, HUMAN RIGHTS WATCH, Mar. 5, 2012, *available at* http://www.hrw.org/news/2012/03/05/libya-bolster-security-tawergha-camps.

[152] *Id.*

[153] AMNESTY INTERNATIONAL, MILITIAS THREATEN HOPES FOR NEW LIBYA, *supra* note 135 at 33.

[154] HUMAN RIGHTS WATCH, *Libya: Bolster Security at Tawergha Camps, supra* note 151.

[155] Holmes & Zargoun, *Gunmen kill five in Libyan refugee camp: hospital staff, supra* note 146.

[156] *Libya: detainees, disappeared and missing*, AMNESTY INTERNATIONAL, Mar. 29, 2011, *available at* http://www.amnesty.org/en/library/asset/MDE19/011/2011/en/5a97c7df-aee8-4830-9f2b-d54f805d2dc1/mde190112011en.html.

one former detainee who stated that, in February 2011, he and his father had been organizing the collection of information on the revolution and sending it to the international media. On 26 February 2011, when the two were in their house in Al Falah area in Tripoli, six four wheel drive pickups carrying a group of about 25 armed men in civilian clothes and carrying AK-47s and other guns arrived. They said that they were from the Popular Guard, although the interviewee later learned that others in the group were from Military Intelligence... The men covered the son's eyes using his T-shirt and tied his hands, put him in the vehicle and took him to the criminal investigation department (CID) in the Salahadeen military camp in Tripoli. There, he was reportedly beaten and locked in a cell with eight other persons. He was interrogated some time later.[157]

The CoI also documented high-profiles arrests in Tripoli of prominent activists who had called for public demonstrations. This included the arrest of Jamal al-Haji on 1 February 2011, who had written articles calling for democratic reforms in Libya. A group of activist brothers were also arrested on 16 February 2011; Faraj, Al-Mahdi, Sadiq and Ali Hmeid.[158]

The Qadhafi forces were responsible for arbitrary arrests of individuals at checkpoints in different parts of the country and prison transfers to Tripoli for detention. The CoI report stated that

> Consistent testimonies received by the Commission indicate that Government forces stopped civilians at checkpoints or in the streets, regularly verified identity cards of travellers, arrested and detained persons according to their place of origin or residence, each being used as proxies to indicate that persons were supporters of the opposition. While some were released after being questioned, others were taken by authorities and are suspected to be held in detention facilities or prisons in Tripoli, or transferred to Ianzana, Al-Jdaydah and Abu Salim detention facilities.[159]

There is evidence of unlawful detentions in Tripoli, where prisoners were held in unofficial or secret sites and denied due process.[160] In most cases, no information was provided to the detainees' families regarding their whereabouts, amounting to enforced disappearance. Qadhafi forces also

---

[157] *See infra* Sec. 3.10. *See also* Report of the International Commission of Inquiry, advance unedited version (Mar. 2, 2012), *supra* note 18 at ¶ 274.

[158] Report of the International Commission of Inquiry (Jan. 12, 2012), *supra* note 104 at n. 9; PALESTINIAN CENTRE FOR HUMAN RIGHTS (PCHR), ARAB ORGANIZATION FOR HUMAN RIGHTS (AOHR) & INTERNATIONAL LEGAL ASSISTANCE CONSORTIUM, REPORT OF THE INDEPENDENT CIVIL SOCIETY FACT-FINDING MISSION TO LIBYA 10, n. 5 (Jan. 2012), *available at* http://www.pchrgaza.org/files/2012/FFM_Libya-Report.pdf.

[159] Report of the International Commission of Inquiry (Jan. 12, 2012), *supra* note 104 at ¶ 97.

[160] Report of the International Commission of Inquiry, advance unedited version (Mar. 2, 2012), *supra* note 18 at ¶ 39.

entered hospitals and abducted medical personnel in Tripoli. In one case, a physician from Misrata was detained with his four children in Tripoli, and his whereabouts were unknown.[161]

i. *Migrant Workers*

Migrants were arbitrarily arrested in and around Tripoli in raids conducted by Qadhafi forces during the conflict. Foreign nationals provided testimony to the CoI of arrests and disappearances, which concluded that

> Interviewees in refugee camps in Tunisia noted that migrant workers had disappeared since the uprising had begun, mainly in raids conducted by Government forces in migrants' camps in Tripoli. Their whereabouts are still unknown. Several interviewees mentioned that Saif al-Islam Qadhafi's *Katiba* had entered workers' compounds, ill-treated residents, robbed them of their belongings and had taken people away. They also told the Commission that migrants had been abducted in the streets, taken from their homes, ill-treated and/or blackmailed against their release. While some had succeeded in finding a way out by paying ransoms, others remain in custody.[162]

The CoI noted that it was difficult to determine whether the attacks by the Qadhafi forces against non-Libyan nationals during the war were motivated by race or by perceived political affiliation with the opposition forces.[163]

(b) Thuwar *Forces*

Thuwar forces carried out arbitrary arrests on a large scale in Tripoli after the fall of Qadhafi in August 2011. Local brigades, militias and other security groups aligned with the NTC carried out sweeping arrests and held prisoners without proper legal review. These armed groups operated without effective oversight or accountability mechanisms, and military brigades and neighborhood militias operating in Tripoli made arbitrary arrests. The perpetrators often did not provide information to the relatives of the victims as to their whereabouts or regarding the reason for their arrests.[164] A former Qadhafi security official told the CoI of his arrest at his parents' home outside of Tripoli

---

[161] Report of the International Commission of Inquiry (Jan. 12, 2012), *supra* note 104 at ¶ 108.

[162] *Id.*

[163] *Id.* at ¶ 198.

[164] For more on detention facilities controlled by non-state armed militia factions, *see* Ch. V, Sec. 2.3. *See also Libya: Cease Arbitrary Arrests, Abuse of Detainees,* HUMAN RIGHTS

> ... in October, 2011, the former policeman and several members of his family saw approximately 90 armed men in 30 cars, mostly pick-ups and Land Cruisers, arrive at the house early in the morning. The men reportedly did not present an arrest or search warrant. They stayed at the house for about two hours and the interviewee told the Commissioner they stole some 22,000 dinars, televisions, telephones and gold jewellery. The men arrested the former policeman and several other males at the house...[165] The Commission recorded 12 cases of a similar nature in Tripoli alone.[166]

It was common for the *thuwar* forces to detain a family member of the individual they were seeking if that person was not at home.[167] In another case

> ... the Commission interviewed a man who stated how, in late November 2011, a group of *thuwar* from Misrata (*Katiba Al-Shahid Khaled Qarkas*) came to his house in Tripoli in the early afternoon. They came in about five to six cars that had anti-aircraft weapons mounted on them, with the men inside carrying Kalashnikovs. The man was home with his wife and two children at the time. The *thuwar* said they were looking for the man's brother-in-law who had served in Qadhafi's administration, although they presented no arrest warrant. The man said they took three cars from the family home as well as several thousand dinars, and other valuables. When two of the man's brothers arrived to help, all three were arrested, blindfolded, put in cars, and questioned about the location of the brother-in-law.[168]

Local officials in Janzur, a town 12 kilometers west of Tripoli, told Amnesty International that arrests were carried out on the basis of neighborhood lists compiled without any investigative process or legal basis for detention.[169] While some armed groups, such as the Al-Saraya al-Hamra' Katiba in Tariq Swanee[170] produced their own version of arrest warrants, most

---

WATCH, Sept. 30, 2011, *available at* http://www.hrw.org/news/2011/09/30/libya-cease-arbitrary-arrests-abuse-detainees.

[165] Report of the International Commission of Inquiry, advance unedited version (Mar. 2, 2012), *supra* note 18 at Annex I, ¶ 293 (internal citations omitted).

[166] *Id.* at Annex I, ¶ 294 (internal citations omitted).

[167] HUMAN RIGHTS WATCH, *Libya: Cease Arbitrary Arrests, Abuse of Detainees, supra* note 164.

[168] Report of the International Commission of Inquiry, advance unedited version (Mar. 2, 2012), *supra* note 18 at Annex I, ¶ 295 (internal citations omitted).

[169] AMNESTY INTERNATIONAL, DETENTION ABUSES STAINING THE NEW LIBYA 8 (2011), *available at* http://www.amnesty.org/en/library/asset/MDE19/036/2011/en/e1c30d0f-8ec3-4368-8537-03f1bb15a051/mde1903620 en.pdf.

[170] The transliteration of this place was adopted from the reference. *See infra* note 171.

detainees reported being arrested without a warrant, on mere suspicion that they had been Qadhafi loyalists or supporters.[171]

Amnesty International documented cases of detentions carried out by the Tripoli based Suq al-Juma' Katiba in January 2012.[172] In some cases, individuals were arrested, released and re-arrested by another armed militia group. One military officer from Benghazi was initially arrested on 18 September 2011 in Tripoli by *thuwar* from Tajura. After being abused and moved to Benghazi he received a release order dated 11 March 2012 and signed by "the head of the military prosecution of the region." However, on 11 April 2012 he was re-arrested, without being informed of the reasons.[173] On 26 April 2012, another man was arrested without a warrant at his brother's home by armed men in pick-up trucks with anti-aircraft machine-guns mounted on the back, and taken to a makeshift detention center in the neighborhood. He had previously been held by another Tripoli militia for three months and released without charge.[174]

Amnesty International also reported several incidents where persons were arrested, taken to undisclosed locations and subsequently disappeared. A 24-year-old man was arrested when *thuwar* swept into Tripoli in late August 2011. The man's family told Amnesty International that they had no information about his whereabouts after searching several prisons in Tripoli and Zawiyya. Another enforced disappearance took place on 13 March 2012, when the former Inspector General of Industry and Minerals was arrested in the Mizran area by men from Suq al-Juma' in Tripoli. Months after his arrest, his family was unable to obtain any information regarding his whereabouts.[175]

i. The Tawerghans
Thuwar groups from Misrata targeted members of the Tawerghan community for arbitrary arrest and detention in and around Tripoli. As the CoI reported

> The Commission received multiple reports that, in the months which followed the capture of Tripoli, there were arbitrary arrests of Tawerghans by

---

[171] HUMAN RIGHTS WATCH, *Libya: Cease Arbitrary Arrests, Abuse of Detainees, supra* note 164.

[172] AMNESTY INTERNATIONAL, MILITIAS THREATEN HOPES FOR NEW LIBYA, *supra* note 135 at 15.

[173] AMNESTY INTERNATIONAL, LIBYA RULE OF LAW OR RULE OF MILITIAS? *supra* note 98 at 31.

[174] *Id.* at 16.

[175] *Id.* at 28.

Misratan *thuwar* on the streets of Tripoli. Their whereabouts often remain unknown. Those who have been released report being beaten…[176] Most victims were arrested at checkpoints or taken from their temporary homes or IDP camps, where they found shelter after fleeing Tawergha. They were all apprehended by Misrata *thuwar*, who either transported them from the location of their arrest back to Misrata or detained them at their own brigades' bases in Tripoli.[177]

In one case, on 10 September 2011, approximately 85 men from the town of Tawergha were arrested by a brigade from Misrata from an IDP camp in the Abu Salim neighborhood.[178] Witnesses reported that eight armed men entered the camp in eight black pick-up trucks – the style favored by the Misrata brigades – and took the men away. Relatives of the abducted men stated they had not heard from them since the abductions.[179]

The CoI received information about the arbitrary arrests of Tawerghans at the Salahadin camp, reporting that

The Commission has conducted multiple interviews which indicated that on 10 and/or 11 September 2011, there were a number of distinct attacks on Tawerghans in Tripoli. The Misratan *thuwar* re-entered Salahadeen camp and arrested between 40–50 Tawerghan men. The men were reportedly beaten during the arrest in view of their families and the women were told to leave the camp. According to testimonies received, the *thuwar* presented no arrest warrants and the families were not told of the reasons for the arrest nor where their male relatives were being taken. The Commission was informed that some of the men reached their relatives by telephone and informed them that they are being held in Misrata.[180]

After taking control of the capital, the *thuwar* adopted the Qadhafi regime's practice of arresting people at checkpoints, which particularly affected Tawerghans in Tripoli. According to the CoI report

The Commission received two separate reports of arrests and beatings occurring at a checkpoint in Ghout-al-Ruman where Tawerghan men were

---

[176] Report of the International Commission of Inquiry, advance unedited version (Mar. 2, 2012), *supra* note 18 at ¶ 57.

[177] *Id.* at Annex I, ¶ 229.

[178] This incident was reported by the New York Times and Human Rights Watch. It is the same incident as reported by the Commission on September 10 and 11 in the Salahadeen IDP camp.

[179] Kareem Fahim, *Accused of Fighting for Qaddafi, a Libyan Town's Residents Face Reprisals*, N.Y. TIMES, Sept. 23, 2011, *available at* http://www.nytimes.com/2011/09/24/world/africa/accused-of-fighting-for-qaddafi-tawerga-residents-face-reprisals.html.

[180] Report of the International Commission of Inquiry, advance unedited version (Mar. 2, 2012), *supra* note 18 at Annex I, ¶ 414 (internal citations omitted).

removed from vehicles and arrested. In one interview, a man who was detained at the checkpoint in October 2011 and then released, his third arrest and detention since August 2011, said he and some 35-40 others were arrested at the checkpoint by the "*Shuhuda Tajoura* Misrata brigade" and taken to a house in Tajoura where they were held for between 8 and 20 days.[181]

There were several other accounts of *thuwar* groups from Misrata entering IDP camps in Tripoli in search of Tawerghans who had fled their homes seeking safety in the capital. Residents of the Mashru' IDP camp stated that *thuwar* came to their camp between late August and early September 2011, fired weapons in the air, and gathered the men of the camp and arrested them. Approximately 70 men, some as young as 16 years old, were arrested and the 130 families residing in the camp subsequently fled.[182] A Tawerghan camp on Airport Road in Tripoli, housing about 300 people, was raided twice in February 2012. Three men were abducted during the raids.[183]

Amnesty International reported that four men from Tawergha were arrested at Tripoli International Airport on 6 May 2012 upon their arrival from Benghazi. The men were singled out and asked for their identity cards, then arrested under the pretext that they would be subjected to a quick investigation. The four men disappeared and several days later one of them called and informed their families that they were being held in Misrata.[184]

Thuwar groups from Misrata also pursued Tawerghans in their homes in and around Tripoli for arbitrary arrest and detention.[185] The CoI reported several instances of Tawerghans being detained in their homes, such as the following

> In late August 2011, armed fighters from a brigade of the Misratan *thuwar* reportedly entered the house of a Tawerghan family in the Tajoura area of Tripoli where they arrested 27 males, including two minors ... [T]he family

---

[181] *See infra* Sec. 3.4. *See also* Report of the International Commission of Inquiry, advance unedited version (Mar. 2, 2012), *supra* note 18 at Annex I, ¶ 411 (internal citations omitted).

[182] Amnesty International, Detention Abuses Staining the New Libya, *supra* note 169 at 13.

[183] Human Rights Watch, *Libya: Bolster Security at Tawergha Camps*, *supra* note 151.

[184] Amnesty International, Libya Rule of Law or Rule of Militias?, *supra* note 98 at 16.

[185] *See* Ch. IX.

has learned from other Tawerghans who have been released from detention that the men are being held in Misrata.[186]

In early September 2011, a Tawerghan man was reportedly arrested in his house in Tripoli by a Misrata brigade and taken to an unoffocial [sic] detention centre at Matiga airport where he saw other Tawerghan men who been tortured.[187]

In October 2011, a Tawerghan man and his brother were reportedly taken from their house in the Abu Salim area of Tripoli by uniformed armed men who took them to Misrata where they were held in a shipping container for 17 days where they were badly tortured.[188]

Amnesty International similarly documented dozens of cases where people from Tawergha were arrested in their homes, at checkpoints or in hospitals. In one case, a 45-year-old man from Tawergha told Amnesty International that on 28 August 2011 he and a relative were stopped in the Al-Firnaj area of Tripoli by four armed men and taken to the Ma'atiga Airport detention facility.[189] Another victim reported fleeing Tawergha with 11 relatives in mid-August 2011, and being arrested by *thuwar* forces in Tripoli.[190]

ii. *Sub-Saharan Africans*

The CoI received reports of *thuwar* forces targeting Sub-Saharan Africans, some of whom were long-term residents of Libya, for arbitrary arrests and detention in Tripoli.[191] Many of those arbitrarily arrested were dark-skinned Libyans or Sub Saharan African migrant workers accused of fighting for Qadhafi as loyalists or mercenaries.[192]

In September 2011, Qadhafi forces in neighborhoods around the capital conducted mass arrests of migrant workers from Chad, Sudan, Niger and Mali. The migrants were detained in makeshift detention facilities, including a school and a soccer club. The majority of African detainees interviewed in detention claimed to be migrant workers detained because of their nationality and denied serving as mercenaries for the Qadhafi regime.

---

[186] *See infra* Sec. 3.11. *See also* Report of the International Commission of Inquiry, advance unedited version (Mar. 2, 2012), *supra* note 18 at Annex I, ¶ 410 (internal citations omitted).

[187] Report of the International Commission of Inquiry, advance unedited version (Mar. 2, 2012), *supra* note 18 at Annex I, ¶ 412 (internal citations omitted).

[188] *Id.* at Annex I, ¶ 417.

[189] AMNESTY INTERNATIONAL, DETENTION ABUSES STAINING THE NEW LIBYA, *supra* note 169 at 11.

[190] *Id.* at 12.

[191] Report of the International Commission of Inquiry, advance unedited version (Mar. 2, 2012), *supra* note 18 at Annex I, ¶ 481.

[192] *See infra* Sec. 3.9. *See also* HUMAN RIGHTS WATCH, *Libya: Cease Arbitrary Arrests, Abuse of Detainees, supra* note 164.

Officials at the Bab al-Bahr facility reported that local security forces had arrested between 200 and 300 men over a few days in September, all allegedly foreign fighters. The widespread arrests seemed to be decentralized with no oversight, regulation or control by the NTC.[193]

HRW visited 300 detainees on 1 September 2011 in Tripoli, about 50 of whom were Libyan while the rest were Sub-Saharan Africans. Most of the Sub-Saharan African detainees stated that armed men had picked them up for no reason after *thuwar* took control of Tripoli.[194] At a detention facility at a school in the Intisar neighborhood next to Bab al-'Aziziyya compound, the local council held 76 detainees, about half of whom appeared to be Sub-Saharan Africans.[195]

Amnesty International further recorded numerous accounts of Sub-Saharan Africans who fell victim to arbitrary arrest and abuse in detention centers. A Mali man was arrested on 21 August 2011 from his house, brought to a mosque in the Bin 'Ashur neighborhood, and held with approximately 200 other Sub-Saharan migrants.[196] Another group of Mali nationals reported being arrested the same day, and taken by truck to an unknown location where they were stripped and beaten.[197] Days later, on 26 August 2011, in the Al-Madina al-Qadima neighborhood of Tripoli, *thuwar* entered a building and searched people's homes looking for weapons and money. They arrested 26 persons in the building, including a dozen dark-skinned Libyans and Sub-Saharan African nationals from Chad, Mali, Niger and Sudan.[198] On 4 September 2011, *thuwar* in the Salahadin neighborhood detained 36 Nigerians, including 19 women. On 5 September, a *thuwar* katiba in the Abu Salim neighborhood arrested more than 90 Nigerians and Ghanaians, 30 of whom were women.[199]

Amnesty International visited detention facilities known as "holding centers" for undocumented migrants in May and June 2012.[200] They

---

[193] *Libya: Stop Arbitrary Arrests of Black Africans*, HUMAN RIGHTS WATCH, Sept. 4, 2011, *available at* http://www.hrw.org/news/2011/09/04/libya-stop-arbitrary-arrests-black-africans.

[194] *Id.*

[195] *Id.*

[196] *Id.*

[197] AMNESTY INTERNATIONAL, DETENTION ABUSES STAINING THE NEW LIBYA, *supra* note 169 at 9.

[198] *Id.*

[199] HUMAN RIGHTS WATCH, *Libya: Cease Arbitrary Arrests, Abuse of Detainees*, *supra* note 164.

[200] AMNESTY INTERNATIONAL, LIBYA RULE OF LAW OR RULE OF MILITIAS?, *supra* note 98 at 40.

included nationals from Burkina Faso, Cameroon, Chad, Egypt, Eritrea, Ethiopia, Ghana, Niger, Nigeria, Somalia and Sudan.[201] Detainees in several of the holding facilities, including 'Ain Zara Prison, were accused of serving as mercenaries. At the time, the holding centers were controlled by armed militias beyond the oversight of local or central government authorities. The government authorities did little to prevent the targeted detentions or ensure due process. The Minister of Justice stated, for example, that foreign nationals found to have breached Libyan law regulating their entry and stay ought to be deported after serving their sentences.[202]

3.4. *Torture and Other Forms of Ill-treatment*

(a) *Qadhafi Forces*

Detainees in Tripoli were subjected to torture and other forms of ill-treatment at the hands of the Qadhafi forces. During the war, the Qadhafi forces engaged in long-established and well-documented patterns of torture and other ill-treatment against perceived opponents or critics of the regime. This abuse was particularly prevalent in the Abu Salim and 'Ain Zara prisons in Tripoli. Methods of torture included electric shocks, beatings, *falaqa* (beatings on the soles of the feet), sleep deprivation, prolonged contortion of the body in stress positions and solitary confinement for long periods.[203] The COI reported that

> When the Commission visited Al-Jdaydah detention centre in Tripoli, two detainees of the five interviewed, told the Commission that they had been subjected to severe beating during the first days of their detention.[204] There were at least five locations in the Tripoli region where the Qadhafi forces detained and interrogated suspected *thuwar* and their supporters. Among them were prisons in Ein Zara, Abu Salim, Maftouh, Jdeida, as well as the locations of the former Internal Security Agency (*Jihaz Al-Amn Al-Dakhli*), External Security Agency (*Jihaz Al-Amn Al-Kharaji*), and Military Intelligence headquarters (*Jihaz Al-Amn Al-Askari* or *Istikhbarat*). The security agencies had detention facilities at their headquarters, but also within both

---

[201] *Id.* at 36.

[202] *Id.* at 37. For more on arbitrary arrests and enforced disappearances carried out during the conflict, *see* Ch. V, Sec. 2.3.

[203] AMNESTY INTERNATIONAL, THE BATTLE FOR LIBYA: KILLINGS, DISAPPEARANCES AND TORTURE, *supra* note 66 at 65.

[204] Report of the International Commission of Inquiry (Jan. 12, 2012), *supra* note 104 at ¶ 114.

Ein Zara and Abu Salim. The Commission gathered convincing evidence that torture had taken place in these locations.²⁰⁵

The detention center in Yarmuk, detailed above in the Unlawful Killing section, was also the site of torture and other forms of ill-treatment, with the COI reported that

> Inmates there reported severe beatings being meted out during interrogations together with electrical shocks from a cable in the wall. The Commission visited the site and found evidence corroborating the torture allegations. The Commission noted the presence of the cross bar on which one witness stated that detainees were suspended. It found ropes described by a survivor as a means for hanging and torturing detainees and wire manacles... Separately, the Commission interviewed a survivor who showed scars on the back of his hand and on the inner surface of the victim's right leg, which he said were caused by the application of electrical wire connected to a wall outlet. ²⁰⁶

The CoI reported on an incident in Tripoli when media personnel were tortured, concluding that

> A three-person BBC news team was detained on 7 March at an army road-block and taken to a military barrack in Tripoli. They reported that they were blindfolded, beaten with fists, knees and rifles, hooded and subjected to mock executions by members of the Libyan army and secret police. One of the three, Chris Cobb Smith was quoted saying that the situation inside the detention centre was horrendous, with people being handcuffed with swelling hands and broken ribs. He stated that at one point a guy in plainclothes with a small sub-machine gun, walked up to him, putting his gun next to his neck and pulling the trigger twice. The bullet whisked past his ear. The soldier just laughed. The second member of the team, Feras Killani, a correspondent of Palestinian descent, was particularly singled out for repeated beatings and was accused of being a spy. At some point, they were all convinced they were going to die.²⁰⁷

One doctor in Tripoli reported witnessing 90 deaths as a result of torture perpetrated by regime forces during the course of the conflict.²⁰⁸

---

²⁰⁵ Report of the International Commission of Inquiry, advance unedited version (Mar. 2, 2012), *supra* note 18 at Annex I, ¶ 332 (internal citations omitted).

²⁰⁶ *Id.* at Annex I, ¶ 334 (internal citations omitted).

²⁰⁷ Report of the International Commission of Inquiry (Jan. 12, 2012), *supra* note 104 at ¶ 142 (internal citations omitted).

²⁰⁸ Report of the International Commission of Inquiry, advanced unedited version (Mar. 2, 2012), *supra* note 18 at ¶ 328.

Amnesty International recorded the testimony of two women who were verbally and physically abused by Qadhafi forces while in detention. One of the victims was arrested, blindfolded and taken to an unknown location where she was interrogated and beaten. The witness stated that during the beatings, she was asked about colleagues who may have been sympathetic to the rebels and was threatened with rape if she did not confess to collaborating with the *thuwar*. The victim also reported having been electrocuted on her arms, back and nipples. Throughout her detention, she was not allowed to contact her family. The witness was released after Tripoli came under the control of *thuwar* on 24 August 2011.[209]

Another female detainee provided testimony that she was arrested from her home on 31 July 2011 by a group of armed men in plainclothes. The witness believes she was arrested for attempting to deliver audio-visual material to contacts in Tunisia that implicated the Qadhafi forces in war crimes. The witness stated she was interrogated about her activities and links with the *thuwar* and was subjected to physical abuse while in detention. The witness was also released on 24 August 2011 after *thuwar* took control of Tripoli. The woman added that she witnessed male detainees being beaten, electrocuted and insulted at the Sabri detention facility.[210]

(b) Thuwar *Forces*

Upon taking control of Tripoli and its surrounding suburbs in August 2011, *thuwar* captured and detained former members of the regime, targeting them for physical abuse.[211] The CoI found that

> The fall of Tripoli in late August 2011 saw the surrender of the Qadhafi forces on a large scale. The *thuwar* subjected a significant number of them to serious maltreatment, including torture. Kicks and blows with fists and with rifle butts were dealt out upon their arrest. Detainees were generally held in a temporary facility before being transferred to a prison or to another location. Lower and middle ranks tended to receive the brunt of the maltreatment. Although many higher ranking members of the former Qadhafi Government were also mistreated, they appeared not to suffer at the same level.[212]

---

[209] Diana Eltahawy, *Women who defied al-Gaddafi regime not spared from brutal jails*, AMNESTY INTERNATIONAL, Sept. 5, 2011, *available at* http://livewire.amnesty.org/2011/09/05/women-who-defied-al-gaddafi-regime-not-spared-from-brutal-jails.

[210] *Id.*

[211] AMNESTY INTERNATIONAL, DETENTION ABUSES STAINING THE NEW LIBYA, *supra* note 169 at 13; HUMAN RIGHTS WATCH, *Libya: Cease Arbitrary Arrests, Abuse of Detainees*, *supra* note 164.

[212] Report of the International Commission of Inquiry, advance unedited version (Mar. 2, 2012), *supra* note 18 at Annex I, ¶ 350 (internal citations omitted).

After the fall of Qadhafi, captured individuals were transferred to make-shift detention centers where torture and other forms of ill-treatment took place.[213] An unknown number of militias from outside the capital established bases in Tripoli. At times, these militia operated in loose collaboration, carrying out the seizure, detention, transfer, and interrogation of persons. Ill-treatment and torture often occurred in more than one location, either at detention centers or houses of Qadhafi supporters.[214] Militias also held detainees at detention centers that were under the control of the judicial authorities; in Tripoli these included Jadayda, Maftuh and 'Ain Zara prisons.[215] There is compelling evidence that abuse and torture occurred at these detention centers. As described by the CoI

> Most frequently used methods [of torture] included beating with objects such as electric wires, rubber hoses, wooden sticks; electric shocks; falaqa; and suspension in contorted positions. The purpose of torture appeared to be the extraction of information or confessions, and\or punishment for alleged crimes.[216]
>
> The Commission interviewed a young soldier who had been recruited into the 32nd (Khamis) Brigade just before the fall of Tripoli. He described how most of his group surrendered when Tripoli fell. The interviewee said that, upon arrest, the *thuwar* checked the cartridges in the magazines of the weapons to determine who had fired shots against them. Those who had missing rounds in their weapons were severely beaten... He said that the group was taken to a makeshift prison in a school in Marawna district in Tajoura, kept there for eight days and subjected to sporadic beatings.[217]

The CoI reported cases of forced confessions obtained through torture in Tripoli, including

> The Commission interviewed a detainee who fought with the Revolutionary Guard. He told the Commission that when Tripoli fell in August 2011, soldiers allegedly from the *Souk al-Juma'a* Brigade found and arrested him. He described how he was beaten severely upon arrest and taken to another location... He stated that two ribs had been broken during the torture sessions and that he had been forced to sign a statement confessing to have raped two girls. The interrogations allegedly continued even around the

---

[213] AMNESTY INTERNATIONAL, MILITIAS THREATEN HOPES FOR NEW LIBYA, *supra* note 135 at 15.

[214] *Id.* at 13.

[215] *Id.* at 15.

[216] Report of the International Commission of Inquiry, advance unedited version (Mar. 2, 2012), *supra* note 18 at ¶ 49.

[217] *Id.* at Annex I, ¶ 351 (internal citations omitted).

time of the Commission's visit. He informed the Commission that he did not kill or rape anyone.[218]

Detention centers in Tripoli were either officially recognized security installations or run by militias operating without legal authority.[219] Amnesty International visited 'Ain Zara Prison, Al-Jadayda Prison, the detention center in Ma'atiga Airport and the Noflin[220] National Army detention facility in Tripoli in August and September 2011. Amnesty International also visited other facilities around Tripoli such as the General Security Offices in Janzur suburb (used to hold detainees until their transfer in early September to other detention centers) and the Al-Hufra detention center in Tajura suburb.[221] During the visit, two guards openly admitted that they had beaten detainees because they would not "confess."[222] A resident of Tripoli provided testimony that he had been seized and beaten by a group of armed *thuwar* because he was suspected of being a Qadhafi loyalist. Another detainee reported that he had been arrested by *thuwar* on 25 August 2011 because he had been suspected of killing an anti-Qadhafi protester.[223]

Acts of torture continued to be documented in February 2012 in Tripoli's Al-Jadayda, Maftuh and 'Ain Zara prisons in Tripoli.[224] Detainees reported that they had been suspended in contorted positions, beaten for hours with whips, cables, plastic hoses, metal chains, bars and wooden sticks, and given electric shocks with live wires and Taser-like electro-shock weapons. Forensic and medical reports from some of the deceased confirmed the use of these torture methods.[225]

A number of individuals raised complaints at police stations or investigative offices, but were met with obstruction or little action. One woman who was abducted from her home in Tripoli and tortured in detention in October 2011 lodged a complaint with the Supreme Security Committee, the General Prosecutor, the Tripoli General Prosecutor, and the Tripoli

---

[218] *Id.* at Annex I, ¶ 359 (internal citations omitted).

[219] AMNESTY INTERNATIONAL, MILITIAS THREATEN HOPES FOR NEW LIBYA, *supra* note 135 at 11.

[220] The transliteration of this place was adopted from the reference. *See infra* note 221.

[221] AMNESTY INTERNATIONAL, DETENTION ABUSES STAINING THE NEW LIBYA, *supra* note 169 at 6.

[222] *Id.* at 15.

[223] *Id.* at 16.

[224] This included detention centers in Tripoli, Zawiyya, Al-Gharyan, Misrata and Sirte.

[225] AMNESTY INTERNATIONAL, MILITIAS THREATEN HOPES FOR NEW LIBYA, *supra* note 135 at 6.

Military Council. The woman was subsequently threatened and in March 2012 her home was targeted and hit with gunfire. In mid-June 2012, the perpetrators of her detention called her and she received threats warning her to withdraw her complaint.[226]

Between August 31 and September 29 2011, HRW inspected eight prisons in Tripoli and 12 smaller detention facilities, among them two private homes where local security forces were holding detainees. The detainees reported mistreatment in six facilities, including beatings and the use of electric shocks, with some showing scars supporting their claims. None of the detainees had been brought before a judge nor been allowed to speak with a lawyer.[227] HRW interviewed 53 detainees, 37 of whom were Libyan and 16 Sub-Saharan African. Interviewees included 16 women, four children, and five people considered "high value" because of their positions in the government.[228]

On 20 January 2012, Libyan diplomat 'Umar Brebesh died after less than 24 hours in custody in a detention facility in Tripoli under control of a militia from Zintan. The victim's family indicated that Brebesh had voluntarily submitted himself to questioning by the Al-Shuhada' 'Ashur militia in Tripoli.[229] He was detained on 19 January and reported dead the following day. An autopsy report stated that the cause of death was multiple bodily injuries and fractured ribs. Photos of the body showed welts, cuts, the apparent removal of toenails, extensive bruising on the abdomen, lacerations on both legs, and a large wound on the sole of the left foot. A report by the judicial police in Tripoli stated that Brebesh had died from torture and that an unnamed suspect had confessed to his killing.[230]

The Swihli Katiba from Tripoli had established a base in the Girls' Military College in Tripoli by October 2011. The base allegedly held 60 detainees at the time, who were beaten during interrogations.[231] Militias from outside the capital continued to control various installations in Tripoli

---

[226] AMNESTY INTERNATIONAL, LIBYA RULE OF LAW OR RULE OF MILITIAS?, *supra* note 98 at 24.

[227] HUMAN RIGHTS WATCH, *Libya: Cease Arbitrary Arrests, Abuse of Detainees, supra* note 164.

[228] Id.

[229] Report of the International Commission of Inquiry, advance unedited version (Mar. 2, 2012), *supra* note 18 at Annex I, ¶ 355.

[230] *Libya: Diplomat Dies in Militia Custody*, HUMAN RIGHTS WATCH, Feb. 3, 2012, *available at* http://www.hrw.org/news/2012/02/02/libya-diplomat-dies-militia-custody.

[231] *Libya: Militia Should Transfer Journalists to State*, HUMAN RIGHTS WATCH, Feb. 27, 2012, *available at* http://www.hrw.org/news/2012/02/27/libya-militia-should-transfer-jour nalists-state-0.

where torture took place. As late as May 2012, the Swihli Katiba alone controlled 12 different detention centers.[232]

i. *The Tawerghans*

The Tawerghan community suffered abuse and torture at the hands of *thuwar* from Misrata in Tripoli.[233] A Tawerghan man gave testimony of his abuse, after being grabbed on the street and thrown into a car by a group of armed men on 25 August 2011 in the Abu Salim area. He said he was subjected to a mock execution and was taken to the Ma'atiga Airport detention facility, where he was beaten with rifle butts and whipped. He was later taken to another detention facility.[234] Another Tawerghan man, a former army officer, was taken from his home and abused in a detention facility in Tripoli under militia control. The man was arrested and tortured, after his colleague informed the militia he was of Tawerghan origin.[235]

ii. *The Mashashiyyans*

Members of the Mashashiyya tribe were also targeted by *thuwar* groups in Tripoli, in particular by groups from Zintan.[236] In one typical case, armed men from the Zintan Katiba detained a 20-year-old fighter from the Mashashiyya region in Tripoli on 16 January 2011. He was taken to a farm, tied to a post, and severely beaten before his family collected him from a detention center near Tripoli International Airport.[237]

iii. *Sub-Saharan Africans*

Sub-Saharan Africans were subjected to torture and other forms of ill-treatment in Tripoli. The CoI documented cases in October 2011, such as that of a Sudanese man detained and abused at a military camp in Tripoli

---

[232] Amnesty International, Libya Rule of Law or Rule of Militias?, *supra* note 98 at 15.

[233] *See supra* Sec. 3.3.

[234] Amnesty International, Detention Abuses Staining the New Libya, *supra* note 169 at 12.

[235] Amnesty International, Militias threaten hopes for New Libya, *supra* note 135 at 19.

[236] The Mashashiyya are a group that inhabits the Nafusa Mountains region. They were perceived as supporting the Qadhafi regime during the conflict, and suffered extensive reprisal violence at the hands of *thuwar* groups from Zintan. *See* Ch. X.

[237] Amnesty International, Militias threaten hopes for New Libya, *supra* note 135 at 21.

In or around October 2011, a Sudanese man, a long-term resident in Libya, was reportedly arrested, without the benefit of a warrant, by one of the Tripoli *thuwar*, the *Dagshi* brigade. He was taken to the brigade's military camp where he was held for 3 days and beaten after which he was then transferred to one of the official detention centres in Tripoli.[238]

A similar incident took place in November 2011, where a Chadian man, who had also been a long-term resident of Libya, was arrested without a warrant

> ...and taken to the Ghirarat Military Council building by the *thuwar*. According to testimony received, he was hung from a door and beaten with rubber hoses before being made to sit on the ground and beaten on the soles of his feet... The man was reportedly then transferred to Ein Zara, an official detention centre, where he was again beaten. In the interview with the Commission, the man displayed severe scarring on his back and his head and had difficulty walking.[239]

Sub-Saharan Africans were abused and forced to sign confessions of aiding the Qadhafi forces during the conflict. A man from Niger who was detained in Tripoli said he had falsely confessed to receiving payment to fight for the Qadhafi regime after he was beaten repeatedly for two days.[240] A 17-year-old boy from Chad was accused of rape and serving as a mercenary after he was arrested from his home in August 2011. The armed men who arrested him were looking for a relative, a dual Libyan-Chadian national, whom they accused of recruiting mercenaries for the Qadhafi forces. The boy was arrested and held in a makeshift facility, where he was punched and beaten with sticks, belts, rifles and rubber cables, mostly on the head, face and back. The beatings were so severe that he confessed to anything that the guards wanted to hear.[241]

There were numerous cases of torture documented in Tripoli displaying a pattern of violations that involved the targeting of Sub-Saharan Africans. A 36-year-old Sudanese man was arrested, along with his friend, and taken to 'Ain Zara Prison, where they were beaten by eight to ten guards who used sticks and a water hose. The victim stated that in 'Ain Zara Prison, there was a special section for foreigners and that in his cell he was placed

---

[238] Report of the International Commission of Inquiry, advance unedited version (Mar. 2, 2012), *supra* note 18 at Annex I, ¶ 482 (internal citations omitted).

[239] *Id.* at Annex I, ¶ 483 (internal citations omitted).

[240] AMNESTY INTERNATIONAL, DETENTION ABUSES STAINING THE NEW LIBYA, *supra* note 169 at 15.

[241] *Id.*

with another Sudanese person and four other foreigners.[242] A 24-year-old Ghanaian man was arrested in February 2011, along with three other Sub-Saharan Africans, by armed men at a checkpoint on his way from Sabha to Tripoli because they lacked papers. The man was beaten in detention, and showed scars that corroborated his account. Another detainee at the same facility, a Chadian man, similarly showed torture scars. The man had been suspended from his hands tied behind his back and beaten for an hour by seven or eight men with sticks.[243]

Cases of women migrants being subjected to torture were also reported. A 22-year-old Nigerian woman was arrested in her home in Tripoli with a group of other Nigerians in late March 2012. Before being transferred to Bu Rashada detention center in Al-Gharyan, she was held by armed men for six days in an abandoned military camp. During the detention she was abused and beaten with a stick all over her body, including her head.[244] On 18 April 2012, two Nigerian women in their 20s were arrested from their home in the area of Qasr Bin Ghashir. The women described to Amnesty International how they were taken to a base and then to another detention facility, where they were humiliated and abused by armed men.[245]

iv. *Supreme Security Committee*

On 17 May 2012, Salam Furjani was seized at the largest medical center in Tripoli. A prominent heart surgeon, Furjani had been appointed director of the hospital prior to his detention. Furjani was arrested by forces from the SSC and dragged through the hospital while the perpetrators beat him unconscious. He was taken to a base at Naklia,[246] a suburb of Tripoli, where he was beaten and kicked in the groin, leaving him with a ruptured testicle. Furjani was kept incommunicado for five days, until he was moved to Tripoli's Ma'atiga Airport. The SSC released him without charging him with any crime or providing a reason for his arrest.[247]

It later emerged that Furjani's arrest and detention were the result of rumors that linked him to the Qadhafi regime. Furjani was known, however, as a human rights activist who had chaired investigations into

---

[242] AMNESTY INTERNATIONAL, MILITIAS THREATEN HOPES FOR NEW LIBYA, *supra* note 135 at 22.

[243] AMNESTY INTERNATIONAL, LIBYA RULE OF LAW OR RULE OF MILITIAS?, *supra* note 98 at 39.

[244] *Id.* at 40.

[245] *Id.* at 39.

[246] The transliteration of this place was adopted from the reference. *See infra* note 247.

[247] *See* Ch. V, Sec. 2. *See also* Chris Stephen, *Libya sees claims of beatings and human rights abuses as elections near*, THE GUARDIAN, June 3, 2012, *available at* http://www.guardian.co.uk/world/2012/jun/03/libya-security-force-kidnapping-surgeon.

abuses committed by the Qadhafi regime, including the Abu Salim Prison massacre. The failure of the interim government to fully investigate and address the Furjani incident led to concern that the government's security actors, such as the SSC, were acting with limited oversight or accountability.[248]

3.5. *Denial of Access to Medical Treatment*

(a) *Qadhafi Forces*

Qadhafi forces took measures to block medical treatment of injured protesters in the capital. Medical professionals loyal to the Qadhafi regime also refused to treat individuals for injuries sustained during the demonstrations. The CoI reported that

> ... [S]enior hospital staff sympathetic to the Qadhafi Government gave orders that no protesters were to be treated in the hospital, but some doctors treated them secretly. Another doctor stated that injured demonstrators were being admitted in other hospitals, but that Qadhafi forces had priority. One doctor stated that Qadhafi forces were removing injured demonstrators from their hospitals, confirming the earlier findings of the Commission.[249]

A doctor working in Tripoli's Medical Center witnessed members of the Qadhafi forces abducting the wounded from the hospital. These abductions had a "chilling" effect on medical staff treating demonstrators.[250] The CoI reported that

> Security forces were also said to have raided hospitals to remove injured persons. It was also reported to the Commission that a number of wounded were denied access to hospitals, while others did not seek medical treatment for fear of being detained by the security forces.[251]

There were documented cases of Qadhafi soldiers denying medical access by seizing ambulances and arresting those inside them and using the vehicles for security patrols.[252] A doctor reported witnessing an incident in late February 2011 of Qadhafi forces seizing ambulances in front of the hospital where he worked, and saw soldiers on board two ambulances

---

[248] *Id.*

[249] Report of the International Commission of Inquiry, advance unedited version (Mar. 2, 2012), *supra* note 18 at Annex I, ¶ 123 (internal citations omitted).

[250] Report of the International Commission of Inquiry (Jan. 12, 2012), *supra* note 104 at ¶ 128.

[251] *Id.*

[252] Report of the International Commission of Inquiry, advance unedited version (Mar. 2, 2012), *supra* note 18 at ¶ 19.

on 20 February 2011 "heading towards Saha-al-Khadra Square where protests were on-going."[253] In April 2011, members of the Revolutionary Guard seized four ambulances from the Tripoli Medical Center in the Suq al-Juma' district.[254]

(b) Thuwar *Forces*

i. *The Tawerghans*

Documented instances indicate that *thuwar* groups entered hospitals in Tripoli to apprehend and remove Tawerghan men. Amnesty International reported that on 29 August 2011 a Tawerghan patient at the Tripoli Central Hospital was taken to Misrata by three men, one of whom was armed. There were cases of at least two other Tawerghan men who disappeared after being taken for questioning from Tripoli hospitals.[255]

3.6. *Freedom of Expression*

(a) *Qadhafi Forces*

The Qadhafi forces took deliberate action to limit the flow of information in the capital, and its treatment of journalists constitutes violations of freedom of expression. Restricted by authorities and Qadhafi forces, journalists could not move freely in the capital and were refused access to certain areas. Most were confined to the Rixos Hotel and several journalists were arrested by Qadhafi forces. Authorities welcomed international journalists into Tripoli to report about the events based on information provided by government officials. Journalists who attempted to report independently were often expelled, detained or assaulted.[256] As reported by the CoI

> Media activists based in Tripoli reported restrictions on means of communication and reported remaining under persistent Government surveillance. Some foreign journalists faced expulsion. Several received warnings from the authorities to leave the country.[257]

---

[253] *Id.* at Annex I, ¶ 122.

[254] *Id.* at Annex I, ¶ 597.

[255] Andrew Gilligan, *Gaddafi's ghost town after the loyalists retreat*, THE TELEGRAPH, Sept. 11, 2011, *available at* http://www.telegraph.co.uk/news/worldnews/africaandindian ocean/libya/8754375/Gaddafis-ghost-town-after-the-loyalists-retreat.html.

[256] AMNESTY INTERNATIONAL, THE BATTLE FOR LIBYA: KILLINGS, DISAPPEARANCES AND TORTURE, *supra* note 66 at 20.

[257] Report of the International Commission of Inquiry (Jan. 12, 2012), *supra* note 104 at ¶ 134 (internal citations omitted).

International journalists were prevented from reporting on specific incidents of regime violence, such as the crackdown against demonstrators on 4 March 2011.[258] The Committee to Protect Journalists reported

> A group of foreign journalists was prevented from covering protesters who had gathered in a mosque in the Tajoura district of Tripoli ... The journalists were approached by men in uniforms, told they must leave, and then driven back to their hotel. Another reporter who tried to reach Tajoura by taxi was stopped by police and barred from traveling there.[259]

The incident involving Al-'Ubaydi at the Rixos Hotel in Tripoli highlighted the extensive efforts undertaken to block information about violations carried out by the Qadhafi regime from leaving Tripoli. During the incident, security guards forcibly blocked Al-'Ubaydi from speaking with journalists and assaulted foreign reporters who tried to protect her after she entered the Rixos Hotel.[260]

On 8 March 2011, The Guardian journalist Peter Beaumont reported that journalists were not able to operate freely in Tripoli, "despite repeated promises from individuals including [Qaddafi's] son, Saif al-Islam, and the deputy foreign minister, Khalid Khayem."[261] Beaumont was detained by security forces twice while covering the conflict in Libya, once in Zawiyya and once in Tripoli. Three other journalists were detained with him in Tripoli.[262]

There were numerous other documented cases of the arrest and detention of journalists in Tripoli. A Syrian journalist named Rana al-Aqbani and her brother Hani al-Aqbani[263] were arrested on 28 March 2011 from their home in Tripoli, and held incommunicado after being accused of "communicating with enemy bodies during war time."[264] In April 2011,

---

[258] *Id.* at ¶ 144.

[259] COMMITTEE TO PROTECT JOURNALISTS, *Journalists under attack in Libya: The tally*, *supra note* 23.

[260] *See infra* Sec. 3.10. *See also* Report of the International Commission of Inquiry (Jan. 12, 2012), *supra note* 104 at ¶ 145 (internal citations omitted).

[261] COMMITTEE TO PROTECT JOURNALISTS, *Journalists under attack in Libya: The tally*, *supra note* 23.

[262] *Id.*

[263] The transliterations of these names were adopted from the reference. *See infra* note 264.

[264] *Take Action! Libya: Syrian journalist and her brother detained and at risk of torture*, AMNESTY INTERNATIONAL CONCORDIA, Apr. 6, 2011, *available at* http://amnestyconcordia .wordpress.com/2011/04/06/take-action-libya-syrian-journalist-and-her-brother-detained-and-at-risk-of-torture.

two Tripoli-based journalists, Salma al-Shaab,[265] head of the Libyan Journalists Syndicate, and Suad al-Turabouls,[266] a correspondent for the pro-government Al-Jamahiriyya, were detained and subsequently went missing.[267]

Foreign journalists faced expulsion or received warnings from the authorities to leave the country. A Reuters correspondent named Michael Georgy, who was among a group of foreign journalists allowed to report from Tripoli under government restrictions, was expelled by Libyan authorities in March 2011.[268] Authorities in the Qadhafi government also ordered Damien McElroy, a correspondent for London's Daily Telegraph newspaper, to leave Tripoli, without providing any explanation for the decision.[269]

In an effort to hinder citizens' ability to disseminate information, the Qadhafi forces also arrested individuals caught speaking with journalists. On 16 February 2011, regime forces arrested and took away four individuals as they were being interviewed by a foreign journalist.[270] In other instances, the Qadhafi forces targeted citizens attempting to document the violations taking place in response to demonstrations in the capital. As described by the CoI

> Persons who were using mobile phones to take photograph [sic] or to film the demonstrations were allegedly arrested and had their phones seized by security forces. One man interviewed by the Commission reported that persons were prevented from filming injured persons in Tajurah on 25 February by security forces. The Commission also received information suggesting that the Government forces continued to confiscate electronic equipment, including mobile phones, cameras, computer and memory sticks, from persons leaving Libya in order to prevent the transmission of information outside the country.[271]

---

[265] The transliteration of this name was adopted from the reference. COMMITTEE TO PROTECT JOURNALISTS, *Journalists under attack in Libya: The tally, supra* note 23.

[266] The transliteration of this name was adopted from the reference. *See infra* note 267.

[267] COMMITTEE TO PROTECT JOURNALISTS, *Journalists under attack in Libya: The tally, supra* note 23.

[268] *See Libyan Government expels Reuters Correspondent*, REUTERS, Mar. 30, 2011, *available at* www.reuters.com/article/2011/03/30/us-libya-reuters-idUSTRE72T3XH20110330; COMMITTEE TO PROTECT JOURNALISTS, *Journalists under attack in Libya: The tally, supra* note 23.

[269] COMMITTEE TO PROTECT JOURNALISTS, *Journalists under attack in Libya: The tally, supra* note 23.

[270] Report of the International Commission of Inquiry (Jan. 12, 2012), *supra* note 104 at ¶ 135.

[271] Report of the International Commission of Inquiry (Jan. 12, 2012), *supra* note 104 at ¶ 133 (internal citations omitted).

The Qadhafi regime took measures to deter Libyan citizens from following Al Jazeera news coverage of the conflict. The country's leading cell phone provider sent residents of Tripoli text messages in February 2011 telling them "a local cleric issued a fatwa against watching television channels 'like Al Jazeera,' that incite bloodshed."[272]

(b) Thuwar *Forces*

After the fall of the Qadhafi regime, members of the *thuwar* groups targeted journalists in the capital covering Libya's post-conflict environment. On 22 February 2012, two journalists from the United Kingdom working for the Iranian news outlet Press TV, Gareth Montgomery-Johnson and Nicholas Davies-Jones, were detained in Tripoli by the Swihli Katiba from Misrata. The two journalists were detained at the militia base at the Girls' Training Military College in Tripoli, and later accused of not possessing the proper immigration papers to be in Libya.[273] On 14 March 2012, the journalists were handed over to the Interior Ministry after a public apology.[274]

In another incident, on 20 June 2012, media professional Sulayman Dugha was arrested by the Sa'dun Sahili Katiba in Tripoli. He was handed over to a Misratan militia in Tripoli and taken to Misrata where he was detained and abused. Dugha was accused of being a Qadhafi loyalist and spreading lies about Misrata. Due to a public outcry he was released later the same day.[275]

3.7. *Attacks on Civilians, Civilian Objects, Protected Persons and Objects*

3.7.1. *Deliberate and Indiscriminate Attacks on Civilians and Civilian Objects*

(a) *Qadhafi Forces*
Qadhafi forces carried out attacks against demonstrators and individuals perceived as supporting the opposition movement in Tripoli. The attacks

---

[272] COMMITTEE TO PROTECT JOURNALISTS, *Journalists under attack in Libya: The tally,* *supra* note 23.

[273] HUMAN RIGHTS WATCH, *Libya: Militia Should Transfer Journalists to State, supra* note 231.

[274] *UK journalists held in Libya after Welsh mistaken for Hebrew,* BBC, Mar. 20, 2012, *available at* http://www.bbc.co.uk/news/uk-wales-17444890.

[275] AMNESTY INTERNATIONAL, LIBYA RULE OF LAW OR RULE OF MILITIAS?, *supra* note 98 at 17.

involved the indiscriminate use of live weapons against civilian protesters, as well as detentions and extrajudicial executions of prisoners in detention facilities. As detailed above, Qadhafi forces perpetrated numerous acts of extrajudicial killing in August 2011 during their retreat from the capital. These cases were thoroughly documented after the fall of Tripoli when bodies were discovered in the capital showing signs of execution.[276] These acts constitute violations against civilians and protected persons.

i. *Migrant Workers.* Migrants, notably Sub-Saharan Africans, were victims of attacks by Qadhafi forces in Tripoli. Armed men from a katiba reportedly under the authority of Saif al-Islam attacked Sudanese men after entering a camp housing Sudanese and Egyptian workers in Tripoli.[277] The CoI documented two cases involving attacks by Qadhafi forces against Sub-Saharan Africans

> In the first incident, the victim reported that he was stabbed in the right leg when he was walking in the streets of Tripoli on 25 February 2011. In the second case, the victim alleged being beaten on 22 February 2011 by the *Katiba* of Saif al-Islam when they entered the camp of Sudanese and Egyptian workers in Tripoli.[278]

Foreign nationals were also vulnerable to attacks involving theft by Qadhafi forces, particularly as they attempted to escape the violence and flee the country. For instance

> ...the Commission was informed of a Sudanese resident who witnessed large number [sic] of security checkpoints between Tripoli and Ras-Ajdir crossing point. He noted that the Qadhafi security forces carried out extensive searches of travellers and confiscated electronic products and other valuable items. An Eritrean refugee interviewed by the Commission in April 2011 in a refugee camp at the borders said protests in Tripoli were followed by a confrontation which left many dead and injured. Armed groups loyal to Qadhafi were involved in looting as well as other crimes. People were sporadically attacked and robbed. In checkpoints on the way to Tunisia Qadhafi forces were looting money and electronic goods from passengers.[279]

---

[276] HUMAN RIGHTS WATCH, *Libya: Gaddafi Forces Suspected Of Executing Detainees,* *supra* note 120.

[277] Report of the International Commission of Inquiry (Jan. 12, 2012), *supra* note 104 at ¶ 198.

[278] *Id.* at ¶ 198, n. 174.

[279] Report of the International Commission of Inquiry, advance unedited version (Mar. 2, 2012), *supra* note 18 at Annex I, ¶ 716 (internal citations omitted).

Amnesty International documented several instances of Qadhafi forces entering civilian homes, in some cases the homes of migrants. An Eritrean national told Amnesty International that on 26 February 2011, about eight men in plainclothes, two of them armed with Kalashnikov rifles, broke down the door of his home and raided the premises. When they did not find any weapons, they urged the victim and other Eritreans living there to join the pro-Qadhafi demonstrations. The victim left Tripoli for Tunisia shortly after the incident.[280]

(b) Thuwar *Forces*

Thuwar groups carried out attacks on civilians and civilian property as the Qadhafi forces retreated from the capital. Members of different *thuwar* groups raided and looted the homes of suspected Qadhafi loyalists. The CoI documented a case in which

> A relative of a senior Qadhafi military officer told the Commission that his family's home was raided around 21 August 2011. Flammable matter was thrown inside, and the house was fired upon. Armed men – allegedly from *Kataeb Fashloum* and *Kataeb al-Qous* of Tripoli – stormed in to find three workers, from sub-Saharan Africa. They were reportedly beaten and their money and phones taken. Money, gold jewellry, mobiles, a computer, and guns had been taken. The family farm in Salahadeen was also raided and pillaged.[281]

Thuwar groups from outside Tripoli, such as armed groups belonging to the Misrata-based *kata'ib*, also carried out thefts on civilian property. The CoI

> Visited a house where allegedly in mid-November 2011 a group of *thuwar*, identifying themselves as the Free Misrata Brigade (*Misrata al-Hurra*) searched the house and took documents, clothes, watches, money, two laptops, a desktop, and six cars.[282]

Armed men from the Zintan Brigade similarly carried out thefts of civilian property in Tripoli. As documented by the CoI

> The Commission received reports in December 2011 that a group of armed men from the Zintan Brigade used the house of relatives of a Qadhafi Government official as their base for about a week. When the Commission visited the house in late December 2011, they saw signs of forced entry into doors and drawers; empty spaces on TV stands; and impact on inside walls

---

[280] Amnesty International, The Battle for Libya: Killings, disappearances and torture, *supra* note 66 at 80.

[281] Report of the International Commission of Inquiry, advance unedited version (Mar. 2, 2012), *supra* note 18 at Annex I, ¶ 722 (internal citations omitted).

[282] *Id.* at Annex I, ¶ 723.

from fired bullets ... Another man told the Commission that a *thuwar* group searching for his brother-in-law, who worked for the Qadhafi Government, took three cars, 38,000 dinars and 300 USD, two playstations, two iPhones, and mobile phones from his house.[283]

Amnesty International met with a number of individuals who raised complaints at police stations and prosecutor's offices concerning attacks by armed groups. A 54-year-old café owner in Tripoli reported that on 24 February 2012, seven *thuwar* from Misrata entered his café and attacked him. He was saved by men from the Suq al-Juma' Katiba. The Misratan *thuwar* then fired a RPG at his café, destroying it. He filed a police report in Tripoli, and travelled to Misrata in March 2012 to file a complaint, but no action was taken.[284] The incident exemplifies the lack of control exercised by central authorities over armed groups in the capital in the post-conflict period.

3.7.2. *Attacks on Protected Medical Personnel, Transport and Facilities*

(a) *Qadhafi Forces*

Qadhafi forces were responsible for carrying out attacks on medical personnel during the course of the conflict, including instances of arrest, detention, harassment and intimidation. There were reports of 18 medical personnel arrested by Qadhafi forces in Tripoli[285] and of three medical staff executed in an ambulance in the Gargur district of the capital.[286]

3.8. *Mercenaries*

(a) *Qadhafi Forces*

Qadhafi forces reportedly recruited and used African mercenaries from Chad, Sudan and other countries to fight in Tripoli. HRW documented the existence of a large base used by hundreds of mercenaries from other African countries. The mercenaries were reportedly recruited and commanded by the Khamis Katiba.[287]

---

[283] *Id.* at Annex I, ¶ 724 (internal citations omitted).

[284] AMNESTY INTERNATIONAL, LIBYA RULE OF LAW OR RULE OF MILITIAS? *supra* note 98 at 22.

[285] Report of the International Commission of Inquiry, advance unedited version (Mar. 2, 2012), *supra* note 18 at Annex I, ¶ 590.

[286] *Id.* at Annex I, ¶ 588.

[287] HUMAN RIGHTS WATCH, *Libya: Stop Arbitrary Arrests of Black Africans*, *supra* note 193.

3.9. *Targeting Specific Groups*

(a) Thuwar *Forces*

As described above, *thuwar* groups from different parts of the country targeted specific communities for violations in Tripoli, and these communities suffered a disproportionate level of violence during and in the aftermath of the war.

i. *The Tawerghans*

Misratan *thuwar* groups specifically targeted the Tawergha community for violations in Tripoli.[288] In the immediate aftermath of the conflict, Tawerghans were detained on the streets of Tripoli, at checkpoints and in their homes.[289] There were several documented cases where Tawerghans were attacked and arrested from IDP camps in and around the capital, including the Salahadin camp, Janzur Naval Academy, a camp by the Tripoli Airport Road and a camp in the Abu Salim neighborhood.[290] The perpetrators were members of *thuwar* groups from Misrata, who either transported the victims to Misrata or detained them at their own bases located in Tripoli.[291] Detained Tawerghans suffered abuse and torture.[292]

ii. *Sub-Saharan Africans*

After *thuwar* gained control of Tripoli in August 2011, violence against Sub-Saharan migrants in the capital escalated. Many were attacked, arrested and detained on suspicion of involvement in the conflict, without any evidence.[293] Sub-Saharan migrants were largely subjected to arbitrary arrest, torture and other forms of ill-treatment.[294]

Sub-Saharan Africans comprised a disproportionate number of the detainees held in Tripoli detention centers in the aftermath of the war. An estimated half of the detainees in Tripoli's three largest detention facilities – Al-Jadayda Prison, 'Ain Zara Prison and the Ma'atiga Airport

---

[288] For more information regarding attacks against Tawerghans by Misrata-based *thuwar*, *see* Ch. IX.

[289] Report of the International Commission of Inquiry, advance unedited version (Mar. 2, 2012), *supra* note 18 at Annex I, ¶ 410.

[290] *See supra* Sec. 3.3.

[291] Report of the International Commission of Inquiry, advance unedited version (Mar. 2, 2012), *supra* note 18 at Annex I, ¶ 229.

[292] *See supra* Sec. 3.4.

[293] AMNESTY INTERNATIONAL, THE BATTLE FOR LIBYA: KILLINGS, DISAPPEARANCES AND TORTURE, *supra* note 66 at 9.

[294] *See supra* Sec. 3.4.

detention facility – were foreign nationals.[295] The port at Janzur, located between Tripoli and Zawiyya, held more than 1,000 people from Nigeria, Ghana, Senegal, Gambia, Mali, Niger and other African countries. The conditions in these camps were poor and security was severely lacking.[296] Sub-Saharan Africans attempted to flee en masse as the *thuwar* consolidated control over Tripoli. The International Organization of Migration reported that it had evacuated over 1,500 foreign nationals from Tripoli by boat in August 2011, to escape the fighting and the intensified attacks taking place against Sub-Saharan Africans.[297] In some cases, migrants were prevented from leaving the country and detained. Amnesty International reported that around 20 Somali women were detained on 29 March 2012 after having been stopped at sea by two ships. They were taken to a detention center in Tajura, along with 80 other migrants, and then transferred to the Tawaysha detention center.[298]

iii. *Dark-skinned Libyans*

Similar to Sub-Saharan Africans, dark-skinned Libyan nationals were also vulnerable to violations such as house raids, arbitrary detention and violent attacks based on their skin color and the perception that they were mercenaries.[299] HRW gathered testimony from dark-skinned Libyan men who reported having been detained and tortured in an attempt by *thuwar* forces to coerce confessions. One man reported being detained and interrogated in a large prison in Tripoli, where guards used cables to beat him every day. He also stated that he was repeatedly electrocuted on his side, thighs, shoulders and back and reported that guards forced him to stand, electrocuting him if he fell to the floor.[300]

Amnesty International interviewed several dark-skinned Libyans in detention centers in Tripoli who reported being subjected to torture and other forms of ill-treatment. One man was captured by a group of armed

---

[295] Amnesty International, Detention Abuses Staining the New Libya, *supra* note 169 at 8.

[296] Human Rights Watch, *Libya: Stop Arbitrary Arrests of Black Africans, supra* note 193.

[297] Amnesty International, The Battle for Libya: Killings, disappearances and torture, *supra* note 66 at 87.

[298] Amnesty International, Libya Rule of Law or Rule of Militias?, *supra* note 98 at 42.

[299] Report of the International Commission of Inquiry, advance unedited version (Mar. 2, 2012), *supra* note 18 at Annex I, ¶ 211.

[300] Human Rights Watch, *Libya: Cease Arbitrary Arrests, Abuse of Detainees, supra* note 164.

men from the Misrata *kata'ib* near a mosque in the Abu Salim area of Tripoli on 21 August 2011 and detained in three different facilities in western Libya. He stated that when he was arrested, militia men put plastic handcuffs on his wrists, beat, threatened and insulted him with racial epithets.[301] Three days later, on 24 August 2011, armed men entered a home in the Abu Salim district, detained two men, and took them to 'Ali Ureit School – which was being used as a detention facility in the Abu Mashmasha area of Tripoli. The men stated they were beaten with rifles and whipped and then transferred to the Ma'atiga Airport detention facility, where they were forced to walk on their knees during beatings, insulted and accused of being mercenaries.[302]

3.10. Sexual Violence[303]

(a) *Qadhafi Forces*

Numerous cases of sexual violence committed by Qadhafi forces in Tripoli were documented. The case of one 26-year-old woman, Iman Al-'Ubaydi, is the most well known, having received the most international attention. After Al-'Ubaydi burst into the Rixos Hotel on 16 March 2011, she showed journalists bruises, scratches and marks that appeared to have come from binding around her hands and feet. Al-'Ubaydi revealed how she had been raped by 15 regime members after they had drank whiskey. The young woman recalled how she and her brother were stopped at a checkpoint and, after reviewing her identity card and seeing she was from

---

[301] AMNESTY INTERNATIONAL, DETENTION ABUSES STAINING THE NEW LIBYA, *supra* note 169 at 10.

[302] *Id.*

[303] The following terms are defined in accordance with the jurisprudence of the ICTY and ICTR, and other mixed-model tribunals.

1. "Rape" is the penetration, however slight, of any part of the body of another person irrespective of gender (namely, the vagina, anus, or mouth) by means of the perpetrator's sexual organ or any object used by the perpetrator when accompanied by force or threat of force against the person or a third party which the victim believes is real.

2. "Sexual violence" is defined as any physical act of a sexual nature which is committed on a person under circumstances which are coercive or threatening to the person or to any other person, which includes physical touching, groping, fondling, removal of a person's clothing to display intimate parts of the person's body whether in the presence of one or more persons, or any other act of a demeaning sexual nature.

3. "Sexual harassment" is any threat of "rape" or "sexual violence," as defined above, against a person or any other person for purposes of demeaning, intimidating, or punishing the person in question.

Tobruk, regime members had detained her. In addition to her allegations concerning rape, Al-'Ubaydi recounted appalling details, including regime members urinating and defecating on her. One government official at the time, Moussa Ibrahim, discounted her stories, referring to her as "a prostitute."[304]

The CoI reported other cases of sexual violence against women in Tripoli, including

> ... The Commission met with one woman who had been arrested in June 2011 near her university... She was transferred to Ein Zara prison where 80 other anti-Qadhafi women were held. She was stripped naked as were the other women. She said the women were regularly raped and she said she had been raped twenty-four times over two months. She was also electrocuted on her genitals and burned by cigarettes... The Commission was unable to find other victims of the 80 to corroborate this account.[305]

The CoI also reported that acts of sexual violence were carried out against male detainees. One detainee in Abu Salim reported that "rape was rampant in prisons."[306] There were multiple accounts of men suffering electric shocks and burnings to different parts of their body, including their genitals, while detained Tripoli.[307] Acts of sexual violence perpetrated by the Qadhafi forces upon those detained followed a pattern of targeting individuals involved with the *thuwar* or perceived as supporting them. One man told the CoI that he was coordinating with *thuwar* groups in February 2011 when he was detained and held in a detention center in Tripoli. He was interrogated, beaten, sodomized and threatened with death.[308] In another case that took place on 26 February 2011, a man was detained by Qadhafi forces, then interrogated for information about the *thuwar* and raped in prison.[309] In another case, a man who had been

---

[304] Steven Sotloff, *The Rape of Iman al-Obeidi: The Libyan Regime's Other Crisis,* TIME WORLD, Mar. 29, 2011, *available at* hhttp://www.time.com/time/world/article/0,8599, 2062007,00.html. *See also* Kirkpatrick, *Libyan Woman Struggles to Tell Media of Her Rape, supra* note 25.

[305] Report of the International Commission of Inquiry, advance unedited version (Mar. 2, 2012), *supra* note 18 at Annex I, ¶ 527 (internal citations omitted).

[306] *See* citation in *Id.* at Annex I, ¶ 532.

[307] *Id.* at Annex I, ¶ 343; AMNESTY INTERNATIONAL, MILITIAS THREATEN HOPES FOR NEW LIBYA, *supra* note 135 at 26.

[308] Report of the International Commission of Inquiry, advance unedited version (Mar. 2, 2012), *supra* note 18 at Annex I, ¶ 528.

[309] *See supra* Sec. 3.3 for the case of the man detained on Feb. 26, 2011 and questioned about his father's involvement with the *thuwar*. *See also* Report of the International Commission of Inquiry, advance unedited version (Mar. 2, 2012), *supra* note 18 at Annex I, ¶ 274.

participating in anti-Qadhafi demonstrations was detained by Qadhafi forces in early March 2011 and taken to Abu Salim Prison. There, he was beaten and raped, and his genitals burned. He remained in prison until the fall of the Qadhafi regime in August 2011.[310]

Another man described the sexual assaults he suffered during his detention in June 2011 by members of the External Security Agency (ESA) in Tripoli, which the CoI reported as follows

> He had been smuggling arms to the *thuwar*. For five days he was tortured. He was suspended from a beam by his wrists; forced to stand in a bucket of water while his genitals were electrocuted with live wires; and beaten with a rubber hose. The guards attempted to force him to rape a female prisoner, but he refused and was then sodomized by six men as punishment. He said he continued to be sexually tortured until Tripoli was liberated in August. He said he has since suffered severe psychological trauma from the torture.[311]

Amnesty International reported a similar case involving the sexual abuse of a male detainee by Qadhafi forces. The man reported being arrested on suspicion of supporting the *thuwar* and suffered abuse in detention, including being raped twice with a hose and a wooden stick.[312]

(b) Thuwar *Forces*

Thuwar groups used the threat of rape in order to force detainees to cooperate. A female detained by armed men in October 2011 gave testimony to Amnesty International that she was threatened that her mother would be raped if she did not provide information about her relationship to individuals in the Qadhafi regime.[313]

i. *Sub-Saharan Africans*

Amnesty International interviewed Sub-Saharan women in detention centers in Tripoli, including in Tajura, who reported having been fondled by prison guards or by *thuwar* groups during transfers between facilities.[314]

---

[310] Report of the International Commission of Inquiry, advance unedited version (Mar. 2, 2012), *supra* note 18 at Annex I, ¶ 343.

[311] *Id.* at Annex I, ¶ 530 (internal citations omitted).

[312] *Diana Eltahawy, Women who defied al-Gaddafi regime not spared from brutal jails, supra* note 209.

[313] Amnesty International, Libya Rule of Law or Rule of Militias?, *supra* note 98 at 24.

[314] Amnesty International, Detention Abuses Staining the New Libya, *supra* note 169 at 17.

In the Tawaysha and Bu Rashada holding centers, Amnesty International described how women were held without female guards present and most West African women said they had been strip-searched by men upon arrival.[315] A group of 15 young Nigerian women reported they had been arrested at a Tripoli market on 25 March 2012 by armed men in civilian clothing. They were taken to a base and moved to another militia base where their money, passports and mobile phones were confiscated. Upon their arrival at the detention center they were strip-searched by men and sexually molested.[316]

3.11. *The Use of Children and Their Treatment in Armed Conflict*

(a) *Qadhafi Forces*

According to witness accounts documented by the CoI, the Qadhafi regime forced children to take direct part in hostilities. The regime also used child soldiers at checkpoints throughout the country. Witnesses who fled the country reported that the Qadhafi forces distributed a large number of weapons during the conflict to a wide range of civilians, including children.[317] A 16-year-old wounded soldier told reporters that about 90 young boys between the ages of 15 and 19 were called to military barracks in Tripoli "for training" as soon as the revolution began. Another young soldier captured by *thuwar* forces told reporters, "we were kept locked in the camp and trained a little and then they took us to the battalion."[318]

The CoI noted with concern that the Qadhafi regime paid families to allow their children to participate in pro-government demonstrations in Tripoli.[319] Witnesses also described how they were recruited by the Qadhafi forces near the end of the conflict. The CoI interviewed three 17-year-olds in detention, who had been recruited during the first week of August 2011. The minors had seen a series of advertisements in which the Qadhafi regime promised money to those who volunteered to fight with the

---

[315] AMNESTY INTERNATIONAL, LIBYA RULE OF LAW OR RULE OF MILITIAS? *supra* note 98 at 40.

[316] *Id.* at 39.

[317] Report of the International Commission of Inquiry (Jan. 12, 2012), *supra* note 104 at ¶ 223.

[318] *Child soldiers sent by Gaddafi to fight Libyan*, CHANNEL 4 NEWS, Apr. 23, 2011, *available at* http://www.channel4.com/news/child-soldiers-sent-by-gaddafi-to-fight-libyan-rebels.

[319] Report of the International Commission of Inquiry (Jan. 12, 2012), *supra* note 104 at ¶ 226.

Khamis Katiba in Tripoli.[320] They went to a training camp for the Khamis Katiba where they received AK-47s and were then assigned checkpoints to defend in Tajura on 19 August. They were arrested shortly afterwards, on 22 August, by *thuwar* from Misrata.[321]

Media outlets corroborated accounts of the use of child soldiers by Qadhafi forces. A 16-year-old boy told reporters he was recruited by the Qadhafi regime as a soldier, trained in Tripoli in the use of 14.55mm anti-aircraft weapons and bussed to Misrata to fight with another 90 boys aged 16 to 17 around 3 April 2011. The boy was injured the first day of fighting and taken to Al-Hikma Hospital where his leg was amputated.[322]

(b) Thuwar *Forces*

There were documented instances of *thuwar* forces violating the rights of children in armed conflict in Tripoli. The CoI reported two cases of the arrest of minors in Tripoli, both involving Tawerghans. One case entailed the mass arrest of Tawerghans from a residence in Tripoli, in which a 12-year-old boy was detained.[323] The other case involved the arrest of two minors during a broader arrest of Tawerghans in the Tajura area of Tripoli. In detention, the minors suffered abuse, and their bodies showed signs of bruising and swelling.[324]

NGO reports also documented the detention of children held with adults, such as in Tajura and Al-Jadayda Prison in Tripoli. HRW interviewed three boys and one girl under 17 years old who were held with adults.[325] Amnesty International similarly found unaccompanied minors held together with adults in Tawaysha holding center.[326]

---

[320] Report of the International Commission of Inquiry, advance unedited version (Mar. 2, 2012), *supra* note 18 at Annex I, ¶ 702.

[321] *Id.* at 703.

[322] *Gaddafi's New Forces: The Teenagers and Women Keeping Libya's Rebels from Taking Tripoli*, TIME, July 8, 2011, *available at* http://www.time.com/time/world/article/0,8599,2081970,00.html.

[323] *See supra* Sec. 3.3. *See also* Report of the International Commission of Inquiry, advance unedited version (Mar. 2, 2012), *supra* note 18 at Annex I, ¶ 416 (internal citations omitted).

[324] *See supra* Sec. 3.3. *See also* Report of the International Commission of Inquiry, advance unedited version (Mar. 2, 2012), *supra* note 18 at Annex I, ¶ 410 (internal citations omitted).

[325] HUMAN RIGHTS WATCH, *Libya: Cease Arbitrary Arrests, Abuse of Detainees*, *supra* note 164.

[326] AMNESTY INTERNATIONAL, LIBYA RULE OF LAW OR RULE OF MILITIAS?, *supra* note 98 at 36. For more on the use of children in the conflict, *see* Ch. V, 2.12.

4. The Role of NATO

The role of NATO in Tripoli was perhaps the most prominent of any theater of military operations. NATO began its airstrikes in Tripoli in March 2011 and by early May 2011 it had targeted command-and-control structures, military training facilities as well as ammunition and weapons supplies. NATO also targeted maritime forces in Tripoli's port.[327] NATO dropped leaflets in and around Tripoli requesting Qadhafi forces leave the area and halt their violence.[328] In an effort to disrupt the military communication to the field, NATO targeted communications installations, such as a key antenna system at Tripoli's International Airport.[329]

Since Tripoli was the base of the Qadhafi regime's military operations, NATO focused a significant number of its airstrikes on the command-and-control centers, military equipment facilities and intelligence structures located in the capital.[330] The attacks were intended to put pressure on the Qadhafi regime and to dismantle its ability to effectively coordinate attacks and manoeuver its forces. The NATO attacks also destroyed ammunition bunkers and facilities, hindering the supply of munitions from reaching the frontlines in other theaters of military operations.[331]

Qadhafi coordinated operations from the Bab al-'Aziziyya compound and a command bunker in nearby Gargur and was reportedly using facilities once used for civilian purposes as military installations. NATO argued that this deprived the once-civilian facilities of protected status and made them valid military targets for coalition forces.[332] In July 2011, British, French and Qatari forces provided weapons, fuel, food and medicine to *thuwar* forces in Tripolitania.[333] The U.S. also removed all intelligence-sharing restrictions with *thuwar* forces, thus allowing NATO forces to

---

[327] *Press briefing on Libya*, NORTH ATLANTIC TREATY ORGANIZATION, May 20, 2011, *available at* http://www.nato.int/cps/en/natolive/opinions_74542.htm; *Press briefing on Libya*, NORTH ATLANTIC TREATY ORGANIZATION, July 12, 2011, *available at* http://www.nato.int/cps/en/natolive/opinions_76355.htm.

[328] *Press briefing on Libya*, NORTH ATLANTIC TREATY ORGANIZATION, May 27, 2011, *available at* http://www.nato.int/cps/en/natolive/opinions_74826.htm.

[329] *Press briefing on Libya*, NORTH ATLANTIC TREATY ORGANIZATION, July 19, 2011, *available at* http://www.nato.int/cps/en/natolive/opinions_76568.htm.

[330] *Press briefing on Libya*, NORTH ATLANTIC TREATY ORGANIZATION, June 20, 2011, *available at* http://www.nato.int/cps/en/natolive/opinions_75263.htm.

[331] *Press briefing on Libya*, NORTH ATLANTIC TREATY ORGANIZATION, July 14, 2011, *available at* http://www.nato.int/cps/en/natolive/opinions_75403.htm.

[332] *Press briefing on Libya*, NORTH ATLANTIC TREATY ORGANIZATION, July 26, 2011, *available at* http://www.nato.int/cps/en/natolive/opinions_76680.htm.

[333] *See* Ch. III, Sec. 7.1.

supply the rebels with satellite intelligence in order to help coordinate their assault.[334]

During the *thuwar* advance on the capital around mid-August 2011, NATO announced it would focus its operations on Tripoli.[335] On 20 August 2011, *thuwar* embarked on Operation Mermaid with the help of NATO forces.[336] The operation was led by the western mountain command, and coordinated by *thuwar* from Zintan and the Tripoli *kata'ib*.[337] Although NATO explained that it was acting in accordance with its remit to protect civilians, its involvement in the operation was criticized for exceeding the United Nations mandate by assisting *thuwar* in pursuing their military and political agendas.[338]

NATO's actions in and around Tripoli significantly aided the efforts of the *thuwar* forces during the advances on the capital. *Thuwar* forces had suffered a setback on 21 August 2011 in Al-Maya, 35 kilometers (21 miles) west of Tripoli, when Qadhafi forces pushed them back with artillery attacks. The setback threatened to stall the *thuwar* advance on the capital until NATO launched airstrikes in the area, allowing the *thuwar* to capture the Khamis Katiba base, home of the elite brigade loyal to Qadhafi, located 22 kilometers (13 miles) west of Tripoli.[339]

NATO's operations were not without controversy, however, as there were documented instances where strikes led to civilian casualties and the destruction of civilian infrastructure. On 30 April 2011, for example, it was reported that a NATO airstrike on a bunker in Tripoli resulted in the killing of Saif al-'Arab, along with Qadhafi's youngest son, his wife and three grandsons.[340]

In one of the most notable cases, on 21 June 2011, NATO reported that a "weapons systems failure" caused a strike to miss its intended target the day before, and acknowledged that civilian casualties may have occurred.[341] A NATO spokesperson reported that the strike was intended for a military missile site in Tripoli holding a number of laser-guided bombs,

---

[334] BELL ET AL., THE TIDE TURNS, *supra* note 36.

[335] *Press briefing on Libya*, NORTH ATLANTIC TREATY ORGANIZATION, Aug. 16, 2011, *available at* http://www.nato.int/cps/en/natolive/opinions_77212.htm.

[336] Lopez, *Heavy gunfire in Tripoli as rebels close in, supra* note 41.

[337] INTERNATIONAL CRISIS GROUP, HOLDING LIBYA TOGETHER, *supra* note 42 at 14.

[338] *See* Ch. IV, 7.1. *See also* BBC, *Libya conflict: Rebels take base on push to Tripoli, supra* note 50.

[339] *Id.*

[340] Report of the International Commission of Inquiry (Jan. 12, 2012), *supra* note 104 at ¶ 224.

[341] *See* Ch. III, Sec. 6.2.

but a weapon system failure caused the weapon to miss its intended target.[342] HRW reported that the NATO strike had hit a three-story house on 20 June in Suq al-Juma‘, leading to five casualties and eight injuries.[343]

HRW visited the site two months after the attack and found no evidence of military activity in the area to indicate the building was a legitimate military target.[344] The CoI also visited the site on 2 December 2011, and investigations uncovered no evidence of weapons or military equipment among the debris. Interviews and official records likewise produced no evidence of a military connection to the intended target.[345] Ultimately, the CoI concluded that "no obvious signs of military activity before the strike were observed in the satellite imagery on 10 June 2011, nor was anything visible after the strike which might suggest the houses had a military utility."[346]

NATO acknowledged that a malfunctioning weapon could have been the cause of the civilian casualties in Suq al-Juma‘.[347] A NATO spokesperson confirmed in December 2011 that a weapon had not hit its target and that "It [was] very likely that those casualties may have been caused by this weapon's malfunction."[348] NATO claimed that it was the first such malfunction after three months of operations.[349]

In another controversial incident, on 6 August 2011, NATO attacked a a Qadhafi missile depot on at least two occasions. Located in a residential neighborhood, the depot housed an SA-2 anti-aircraft missile storage complex with a dozen missiles and their boosters, warheads and toxic rocket-fuel containers. Residential buildings and businesses were located within about 36.5 meters (40 yards) of the nearest bunkers. One strike hit the top of an empty bunker directly across the street from businesses, which were destroyed. Another strike caused a powerful secondary explo-

---

[342] *Press briefing on Libya*, NORTH ATLANTIC TREATY ORGANIZATION, June 21, 2011, *available at* http://www.nato.int/cps/en/natolive/opinions_75652.htm.

[343] HUMAN RIGHTS WATCH, UNACKNOWLEDGED DEATHS: CIVILIAN CASUALTIES IN NATO'S AIR CAMPAIGN IN LIBYA 37 Image 5 (May 2012) [hereinafter "UNACKNOWLEDGED DEATHS"], *available at* http://www.hrw.org/sites/default/files/reports/libya0512webwcover .pdf; N.Y. TIMES, *Errant NATO Airstrikes in Libya: 13 Cases, supra* note 10.

[344] HUMAN RIGHTS WATCH, UNACKNOWLEDGED DEATHS, *supra* note 343 at 37, Image 5.

[345] Report of the International Commission of Inquiry, advance unedited version (Mar. 2, 2012), *supra* note 18 at Annex I, ¶ 627.

[346] *Id.*

[347] HUMAN RIGHTS WATCH, UNACKNOWLEDGED DEATHS, *supra* note 343.

[348] N.Y. TIMES, *Errant NATO Airstrikes in Libya: 13 Cases, supra* note 10.

[349] *Press briefing on Libya*, NORTH ATLANTIC TREATY ORGANIZATION, June 21, 2011, *available at* http://www.nato.int/cps/en/natolive/opinions_75652.htm.

sion. Many missiles and components were thrown around and debris, including at least one missile and another booster, landed in residential neighborhoods. Several businesses and apartments were severely damaged, and residents wounded.[350]

Thus, while the NATO campaign enabled the *thuwar* forces to advance on the capital and take control of the Bab al-ʿAziziyya compound, there were components of NATO's operations that raised concerns. By actively supporting the *thuwar* forces, the alliance may have transgressed the boundaries set by UNSCR 1973 and NATO's own rules of engagement.[351] The strikes that led to civilian casualties and damage of civilian infrastructure call into question the legitimacy of the military targets. The foregoing aspects of NATO's role in the Tripoli theater of military operations are vital to understanding the nature of the foreign intervention, along with the factors that determined the outcome of the Libyan conflict.

5. CONCLUSION

Tripoli became the launching pad for various battles during the civil war, including in the military theaters of Zawiyya and Misrata. Various *thuwar* groups from different theaters of war took part in the advance on Tripoli in August 2011 that led to the capture of the Bab al-ʿAziziyya compound, and ouster of the Qadhafi regime. The clashes erupting in Tripoli after the fall of Qadhafi between *thuwar kataʾib*, particularly the powerful armed groups from Zintan, Misrata and Tripoli, reflected the interim government's struggle to control the different factions that would define the post-conflict security landscape. The militias had regional allegiances elsewhere, particularly in Zintan and Misrata, but still retained power and carved up Tripoli into competing domains. The power of the militias was based on their involvement in the "liberation" of Tripoli and the uncontrolled flow of weapons available to the armed groups in the capital.[352]

The incident on 18 November 2011 at Tripoli International Airport involving Balhaj, the head of Tripoli's military council, reflected the tension between the various armed factions that controlled the capital. The post-conflict tension and problems faced by the interim government were

---

[350] N.Y. TIMES, *Errant NATO Airstrikes in Libya: 13 Cases, supra* note 10.

[351] *See* Ch. III, Sec. 5.

[352] *See* Ch. V, Sec. 2. *See also* Habboush, *Battle between Tripoli, Misrata militias kills 4, supra* note 88.

compounded by the violations committed during the war, as perpetrators remained at large and justice was elusive.[353]

The protests that began in February 2011 in Tripoli were met with a swift and aggressive response from the Qadhafi regime, quelling the uprising before it could gain strength in the capital. Qadhafi forces suppressed the protests by engaging in indiscriminate attacks against unarmed demonstrators with the unwarranted use of live ammunition, leading to injuries and civilian casualties in the capital. The nature of the injuries indicates that the Qadhafi forces responded to the demonstrators with either an utter disregard for life and security, or a clear intention to kill.[354] Information indicates that the protesters were unarmed, and that Qadhafi forces engaged in the excessive use of force against civilians.

The factual record contains substantial evidence indicating that both Qadhafi forces and *thuwar* committed acts amounting to unlawful killing in Tripoli. The CoI, along with human rights organizations, compiled extensive documentation of Qadhafi forces executing detainees and civilians in Tripoli prior to the *thuwar* takeover in late August 2011. Bodies were found in Yarmuk in a detention center controlled by the Khamis Katiba in the Khilit al-Firjan area,[355] in Gargur in the ad hoc detention center formerly known as the Green Security Building[356] and around the Bab al-ʿAziziyya compound.[357] As the *thuwar* took control of Tripoli, their forces carried out killings motivated by revenge, prejudice and financial gain.

Ample evidence exists to indicate that both Qadhafi forces and *thuwar* arbitrarily arrested individuals, often without due process – by not informing them of the reasons for their detention, not permitting them to contact their family nor providing any legal recourse. Indeed, the Qadhafi regime established detention centers after the demonstrations began with the sole purpose of confining *thuwar* and those suspected of supporting them. Reports also indicate that after *thuwar* gained control of Tripoli, they took over these detention facilities and some makeshift detention centers were further set up by militias, armed groups and *kataʾib* mainly from Tripoli, Zintan and Misrata.

---

[353] *See* Ch. V.
[354] *See also* Report of the International Commission of Inquiry, advance unedited version (Mar. 2, 2012), *supra* note 18 at Annex I, ¶ 130.
[355] *Id.* at Annex I, ¶ 169.
[356] *Id.* at Annex I, ¶ 187.
[357] *Id.* at Annex I, ¶ 193.

Testimonial evidence, bolstered by the findings of the CoI and human rights organizations, indicates that both Qadhafi forces and *thuwar* committed torture and other forms of cruel, inhuman or degrading treatment against individuals who were arrested or detained. Detainees often reported being severely beaten with fists, knees, rifles or rubber hoses, as well as being subjected to whippings with electrical wires, electrocution, mock executions, and in some cases were raped or threatened with rape. Other mistreatment involved the practice of *falaqa* (beatings on the soles of the feet). This ill-treatment was often conducted for the purpose of obtaining information or coercing a confession from the detainee.

Media reports indicate Qadhafi forces conducted raids on hospitals in which they removed injured persons believed to have been involved with the *thuwar*. Qadhafi forces further seized ambulances in Tripoli for regime use. The documented cases suggest that Qadhafi forces engaged in a campaign to deny access to medical treatment to *thuwar* fighters and suspected supporters.

Reports indicate that the Qadhafi regime prevented international journalists from reporting on the violence against protesters by restricting their movement and prohibiting them from reaching areas where demonstrations were occurring. Qadhafi forces also seized and destroyed the recording equipment of journalists who attempted to record the story of Al-ʿUbaydi. In some cases, international journalists reported that they were detained and physically abused by Qadhafi forces. Reports also indicate that the Qadhafi regime arrested individuals believed to have been involved in planning demonstrations, had otherwise showed support for the *thuwar* or had criticized the regime. These incidents amount to the active restriction of freedom of opinion and expression on the part of the Qadhafi forces.

Reports indicate that Qadhafi forces intentionally targeted civilians in late August 2011 and engaged in acts of extrajudicial killing. HRW conducted interviews with several witnesses who reported seeing Qadhafi forces, believed to be members of the Khamis Katiba, detain individuals at checkpoints, shoot them, and then dump their bodies in a dried-up riverbed nearby. Other cases of extrajudicial killing by Qadhafi forces were also reported throughout Tripoli.

Reports indicate that Qadhafi forces carried out acts of sexual violence against both men and women, subjecting detainees to rape and other forms of sexual abuse. Reports also indicate that *thuwar* sexually abused individuals during arrest or detention. Sexual violence and the threat of rape were used in detention centers controlled by *thuwar*.

Reports indicate that boys as young as 15 years old were conscripted by Qadhafi forces to take a direct part in hostilities. Qadhafi forces trained, armed and sent children to the battlefield. On the basis of the available reports, it can reasonably be concluded that Qadhafi forces included child soldiers who actively participated in hostilities. Reports also indicate that children were detained by *thuwar* in Tajura, Al-Jadayda prison and Taway-sha holding center, and were not separated from adults.

Reports indicate that as *thuwar* gained control of Tripoli, they targeted migrant workers, Sub-Saharan Africans, and dark-skinned Libyans because they believed these groups had been loyal to the Qadhafi regime. The suspected Qadhafi loyalists were attacked, arbitrarily detained, killed, tortured and ill-treated, had their property attacked and were forced to sign false confessions. Reports indicate that Sub-Saharan African women were sexually assaulted and in some cases raped by *thuwar* upon their arrest and in detention centers in Tripoli, including Tawaysha holding center.

The targeted attacks included Tawerghans living in and around Tripoli in IDP camps. Reports also indicate that the NTC was unable to prevent or adequately address these human rights violations because of the decentralized structure of the *thuwar*. The failure to prevent and investigate attacks on vulnerable groups became especially clear following the 6 February attack on Tawerghans in the IDP camp in Janzur in 2012.

Reports indicate that a number of Tawerghans died as a result of torture while in *thuwar* custody. Cases of extrajudicial killing of Tawerghans by Misratan *thuwar* were reported in IDP camps around the capital. Most noteworthy was the incident on 6 February 2012 in Janzur Naval Academy, when seven civilians were shot and killed. Reports also indicate that when *thuwar* forces did not unlawfully kill Tawerghans, they often abused them by taking them to detention facilities where they were tortured and subjected to other forms of ill-treatment.

CHAPTER FOURTEEN

BANI WALID

1. Introduction

Bani Walid is located in the Tripolitania region, approximately 170 kilometers (105.6 miles) southeast of the capital, with an estimated population of 50,000 people.[1] The center of the town is densely populated, with sparsely populated pockets in the surrounding hills and valleys.[2] There are 52 villages in the region.[3]

Bani Walid was a strategically important city during the uprising and in the post-conflict period due in part to the longstanding tribal links in the area to the Qadhafi regime.[4] The region is home to the Warfalla, considered the largest and most influential tribe in Libya, and making up roughly 15 percent of the population.[5] Along with the Qadhadhfa and Magarha tribes, the Warfalla were generally strong supporters of the Qadhafi regime.[6] The Qadhafi regime traditionally provided financial support and employment for the young men of Bani Walid, relying on economic incentives and informal agreements to ensure strong social support in the

---

[1] *Libya conflict: Where could Muammar Gaddafi be hiding?*, BBC, Oct. 3, 2011, *available at* http://www.bbc.co.uk/news/world-africa-14751660; *Muammar Gaddafi loyalists on the road to dusty death*, THE AUSTRALIAN, Sept. 3, 2011, *available at* http://www.theaustralian.com.au/news/world/muammar-gaddafi-loyalists-on-the-road-to-dusty-death/story-e6frg6so-1226128426097.

[2] Maria Golovnina, *Libyan veteran prepares assault on pro-Gaddafi bastion*, REUTERS, Sept. 14, 2011, *available at* http://www.reuters.com/article/2011/09/14/us-libya-bastion-idUSTRE78D3PK20110914.

[3] Shiv Malik & Lizzy Davies, *Gaddafi issues defiant message from hiding*, THE GUARDIAN, Sept. 8, 2011, *available at* http://www.guardian.co.uk/world/2011/sep/08/gaddafi-defiant-message-hiding.

[4] *Gaddafi stronghold Bani Walid falls*, THE GUARDIAN, Oct. 17, 2011, *available at* http://www.guardian.co.uk/world/2011/oct/17/libyan-rebels-capture-bani-walid.

[5] *Id.*

[6] *Former Libya rebels attack Bani Walid, Sirte on day before surrender deadline*, AP, Sept. 10, 2011, available at http://www.haaretz.com/news/middle-east/former-libya-rebels-attack-bani-walid-sirte-on-day-before-surrender-deadline-1.383572; ANTHONY BELL & DAVID WITTER, INSTITUTE FOR THE STUDY OF WAR, 1 THE LIBYAN REVOLUTION: THE ROOTS OF REBELLION 33 (Sept. 2011) [hereinafter "THE ROOTS OF REBELLION"], *available at* www.understandingwar.org/sites/default/files/Libya_Part1_0.pdf.

tribal region.[7] The strategy was part of the Qadhafi regime's reliance on a patronage system on which the country's political power structure was based.[8] Due to the historical connections to the regime, Bani Walid was one of Qadhafi's last bastions of support and experienced continued violence after the fall of the regime.[9]

The Warfalla are roughly divided into three large clans – the Watiyun, the Fawqiyun and the Wadtiyun – spread all over Libya but concentrated mostly in the Bani Walid region.[10] The Warfalla traditionally supported Qadhafi's tribe, the Qadhadhfa, due to tribal kinship and a history of joining together against rival forces and foreign occupiers. Qadhafi appointed members of the Warfalla to high-ranking military positions, solidifying the close allegiance and support from the tribe.[11] During the 2011 uprising, however, Warfalla loyalty to the Qadhafi regime wavered, with some small factions supporting the rebellion. The most prominent Warfalla leader, Mansur Khalaf, initially aligned with Qadhafi, but in May 2011 refused to send Warfalla members to fight on the side of the regime.[12] Qadhafi continued to send money to the tribe in a bid to maintain support, at the same time as intimidating them by deploying a large number of soldiers in Bani Walid.

Bani Walid became a heavily contested battleground between Qadhafi and *thuwar* forces, with NATO airstrikes targeting the region after the fall of Tripoli with heavy bombing from 24 August through 17 October 2011. When the rebels finally brought the town under NTC control on 17 August, *thuwar* forces proceeded to commit violations against local residents in a wave of reprisal violence.[13]

2. Summary of Events

While events in February and March 2011 in Bani Walid were not immediately documented, details later emerged of the early protests and response

---

[7] Golovnina, *Libyan veteran prepares assault on pro-Gaddafi bastion, supra* note 2.

[8] *See* Ch. I, Sec. 9. *See also* Alison Pargeter, *Libya: Reforming the Impossible?*, 33 Rev. of Afr. Pol. Econ. 225 (2006).

[9] *See* Ch. V, Sec. 2.

[10] Bell & Witter, The Roots of Rebellion, *supra* note 6 at 18.

[11] *Id.*

[12] Sam Dagher *Key Tribe Wavers as Gadhafi Ally*, Wall Street Journal, Apr. 30, 2011, *available at* http://online.wsj.com/article/SB1000142405274870365540457629312404438557 8.html.

[13] Pargeter, Libya: The Rise and Fall of Qaddafi 243 (New Haven, USA: Yale University Press, 2012).

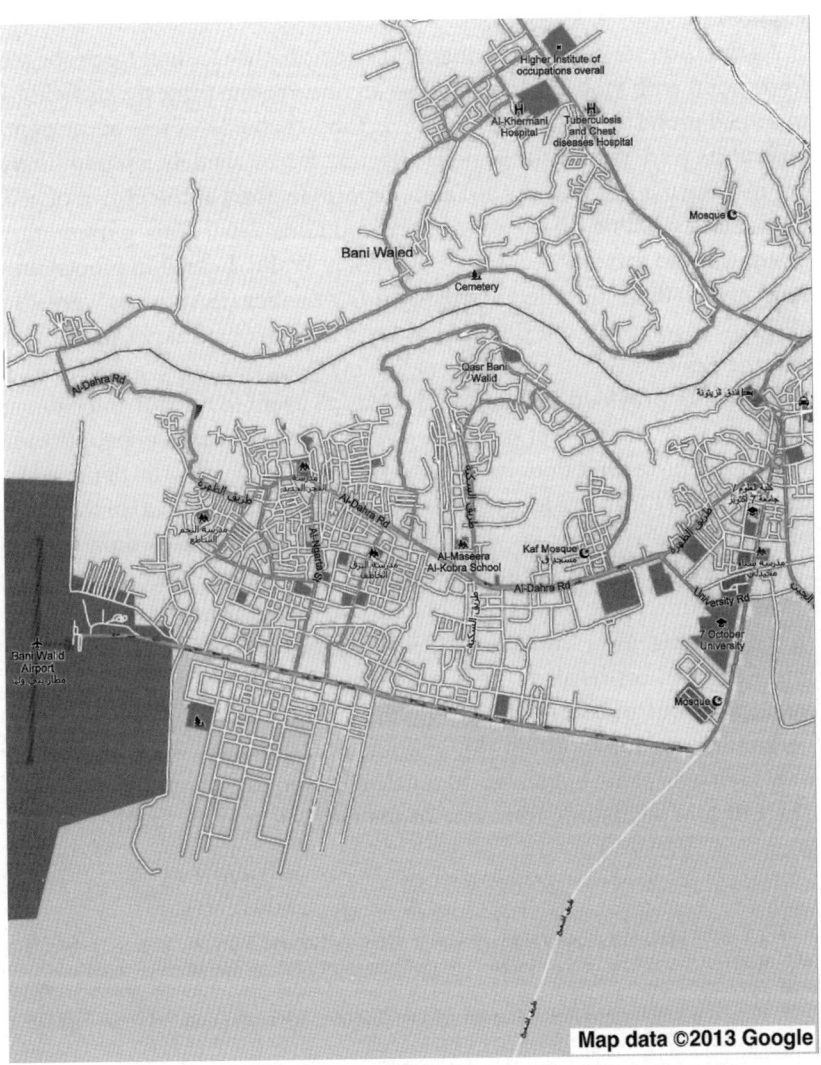

Map 11: Map of Bani Walid (Map data © 2013 Google).

of the Qadhafi regime. On 20 February, demonstrators gathered for the first anti-government protests in Bani Walid, with Qadhafi forces responding by firing into the air to scatter a crowd of approximately 800 civilians.[14] The second anti-regime protest occurred on 3 March and passed without incident.

As the protests grew in number and strength, the Qadhafi forces began to respond with violence. On 28 May, an anti-regime protest was held by unarmed protesters in front of the Sa'di Tabuli School.[15] A few of the demonstrators were reportedly armed.[16] Regime forces, namely a paramilitary group known as Jafal Nusur al-Fatah, reportedly fired at the crowd of 300, immediately killing at least two and wounding ten.[17] This paramilitary group was the primary security force in Bani Walid dressed in official uniform and civilian clothing. Internal Security Agency (ISA) forces were also allegedly involved in the shooting as were the Revolutionary Committees and the Popular Guard (Al-Haras al-Sha'bi).[18]

Witnesses provided accounts of the May 28 event to the CoI and Human Rights Watch, stating that protesters were gunned down as 13 people took shelter on the second floor in a nearby trade building after the demonstration.[19] One of the men hiding in this building believed that two of the other protesters hiding with him were carrying guns. The witness then left the building and observed events from the other side of the street. According to his account, while there he received a call from one of the men trapped in the building. After three hours inside, the men surrendered their weapons – the witness recalled there were three guns at most. He said that a man came out of the building holding the rifles and quickly after, the paramilitary group stormed the building and gunshots were heard. The only men who came out alive and unharmed were the paramilitary men.[20] The CoI took testimony from one of the Qadhafi soldiers involved in the

---

[14] *Libya: 10 protestors apparently executed,* HUMAN RIGHTS WATCH, Aug. 18, 2011, *available at* http://www.hrw.org/news/2011/08/18/libya-10-protesters-apparently-executed.

[15] *Id.*

[16] Report of the International Commission of Inquiry, advance unedited version (Mar. 2, 2012), at Annex I, ¶ 199.

[17] *See infra* Sec. 3.1. *See also* HUMAN RIGHTS WATCH, *Libya: 10 protestors apparently executed, supra* note 14.

[18] *Id.*

[19] Report of the International Commission of Inquiry, advance unedited version (Mar. 2, 2012), *supra* note 16 at Annex I, ¶ 200; HUMAN RIGHTS WATCH, *Libya: 10 protestors apparently executed, supra* note 14.

[20] HUMAN RIGHTS WATCH, *Libya: 10 protestors apparently executed, supra* note 14.

shooting who confirmed that the protesters had rifles but no ammunition and that they were shot by his fellow soldiers. The corpses were taken to a local hospital and then sent to Tripoli.[21]

Bani Walid did not experience any substantial fighting after the initial protest phase, until the end of the conflict when the area became one of the last strongholds for the Qadhafi forces. After the fall of Tripoli to the *thuwar* forces, Bani Walid became a primary target for NATO operations. On 24 August, the first NATO strike on the town took place, hitting an anti-tank rifle.[22] Three days later, on 27 August, NATO hit a military supply storage in the vicinity of Bani Walid.[23]

While the strikes served to target and destroy the remaining armament of the Qadhafi forces, the flurry of strikes led to civilian casualties along with the destruction of civilian infrastructure.[24] On 29 August, one ammunition storage facility and two command-and-control nodes were destroyed in a strike in the vicinity of Bani Walid.[25] According to HRW, a NATO strike carried out during early morning of 30 August in Bani Walid hit two adjacent civilian houses, causing the deaths of five civilians, including a woman and child.[26]

On 30 August, NATO announced that its main area of attention was the corridor between Bani Walid and the eastern edge of Sirte where, according to NATO, Qadhafi forces still maintained a presence in several coastal cities.[27] The same day, NATO reported destroying an ammunition storage facility, and a military tank and multiple rocket launcher storage area in

---

[21] *See infra* Sec. 3.2. *See also* Report of the International Commission of Inquiry, advance unedited version (Mar. 2, 2012), *supra* note 16 at Annex I, ¶ 200.

[22] *NATO and Libya Operational Media Update for 24 August 2011*, NORTH ATLANTIC TREATY ORGANIZATION, Aug. 25, 2011, *available at* http://www.nato.int/nato_static/assets/pdf/pdf_2011_08/20110825_110825-oup-update.pdf.

[23] *NATO and Libya Operational Media Update for 27 August 2011*, NORTH ATLANTIC TREATY ORGANIZATION, Aug. 28, 2011, *available at* http://www.nato.int/nato_static/assets/pdf/pdf_2011_08/20110825_110825-oup-update.pdf.

[24] *See infra* Sec. 4.

[25] *NATO and Libya Operational Media Update for 29 August 2011*, NORTH ATLANTIC TREATY ORGANIZATION, Aug. 30 2011, *available at* http://www.nato.int/nato_static/assets/pdf/pdf_2011_08/20110830_110830-oup-update.pdf.

[26] *See* Ch. III, Sec. 6.2. *See also* HUMAN RIGHTS WATCH, UNACKNOWLEDGED DEATHS CIVILIAN CASUALTIES IN NATO'S AIR CAMPAIGN IN LIBYA 43 (May 2012) [hereinafter "UNACKNOWLEDGED DEATHS"], *available at* http://www.hrw.org/sites/default/files/reports/libya0512webwcover.pdf.

[27] *Press briefing on Libya*, NORTH ATLANTIC TREATY ORGANIZATION, Aug. 30, 2011, *available at* http://www.nato.int/cps/en/natolive/opinions_77480.htm.

the vicinity of Bani Walid.[28] The next day, on 31 August, NATO destroyed one ammunition storage facility and one command-and-control node.[29] The strikes continued on a daily basis into September, with a strike carried out on 1 September where one ammunition storage facility and one armed vehicle were destroyed.[30] The next day, NATO destroyed one military vehicle storage facility,[31] followed by attacks on 3 September which led to the destruction of one ammunition storage facility.[32]

As the NATO strikes continued, the NTC authorities attempted to negotiate with the tribal leaders in Bani Walid so that the Qadhafi forces would surrender the town. On 3 September, negotiations between the NTC and the tribal leaders and elders of Bani Walid stalled, and *thuwar* forces began to move towards Bani Walid from Tripoli and Misrata.[33] On 4 September, it was reported that the *thuwar* forces were 60 kilometers (37.3 miles) from Bani Walid and steadily advancing.[34] On 5 September, Bani Walid elders met again at a *thuwar* controlled checkpoint just outside of Bani Walid in a last attempt to try to resolve the situation and put an end to the fighting.[35] The elders explained that 90 percent of the villages supported the *thuwar,* although many in Bani Walid believed the rumors about *thuwar* looting and pillaging villages after the retreat of Qadhafi forces.[36] NTC leader Mahmud Jibril intervened by making a phone call

---

[28] *NATO and Libya Operational Media Update for 30 August 2011*, NORTH ATLANTIC TREATY ORGANIZATION, Aug. 31 2011, *available at* http://www.nato.int/nato_static/assets/pdf/pdf_2011_08/20110831_110831-oup-update.pdf.

[29] *NATO and Libya Operational Media Update for 31 August 2011*, NORTH ATLANTIC TREATY ORGANIZATION, Sept. 1, 2011, *available at* http://www.nato.int/nato_static/assets/pdf/pdf_2011_09/20110901_110901-oup-update.pdf.

[30] *NATO and Libya Operational Media Update for 1 September 2011*, NORTH ATLANTIC TREATY ORGANIZATION, Sept. 2, 2011, *available at* http://www.nato.int/nato_static/assets/pdf/pdf_2011_09/20110902_110902-oup-update.pdf.

[31] *NATO and Libya Operational Media Update for 2 September 2011*, NORTH ATLANTIC TREATY ORGANIZATION, Sept. 3, 2011, *available at* http://www.nato.int/nato_static/assets/pdf/pdf_2011_09/20110903_110903-oup-update.pdf.

[32] *NATO and Libya Operational Media Update for 3 September 2011*, NORTH ATLANTIC TREATY ORGANIZATION, Sept. 4, 2011, *available at* http://www.nato.int/nato_static/assets/pdf/pdf_2011_09/20110904_110904-oup-update.pdf.

[33] Simon Denyer, *Libyan fighters prepare for assault on Gaddafi desert bastion*, THE WASHINGTON POST, Sept. 5, 2011, *available at* http://www.washingtonpost.com/world/middle-east/libyan-fighters-prepare-for-assault-on-gaddafi-desert-bastion/2011/09/04/gIQA4awT2J_story.html.

[34] Noora Faraj, *NTC fighters advance to Bani Walid*, AL ARABIYA, Sept. 5, 2011, *available at* http://www.alarabiya.net/articles/2011/09/04/165394.html.

[35] Rod Norland, *Near a Libyan Holdout Town, a Waiting Game*, N.Y. TIMES, Sept. 6, 2011, *available at* http://www.nytimes.com/2011/09/07/world/africa/07rebels.html.

[36] *Id.*

to leaders in Bani Walid, promising that the transitional leaders would deliver food, and provide water and electricity.[37] The Bani Walid representatives stated they wanted a peaceful resolution and agreed to consult with other leaders in the town.[38]

Qadhafi forces were still well-armed with heavy artillery, including Grad rockets.[39] *Thuwar* commanders estimated that the Qadhafi forces had less than 300 soldiers left in Bani Walid and could be quickly overcome.[40] Qadhafi was still at large, however, providing hope for loyalists that the regime could still survive. In a broadcast message, Qadhafi claimed that tribes in Bani Walid would fight for him until the bitter end, and urged loyalists to continue fighting.[41] Reports also began to surface indicating that members of Qadhafi's inner circle were hiding in Bani Walid.[42] By early September 2011, there were reports that Saif al-Islam Qadhafi was taking refuge in Bani Walid, and was reportedly spotted in the city on 6 September.[43] Later reports also indicated that Saif did in fact end up in Bani Walid, where he received protection from local members of the Warfalla tribe.[44]

Fighting erupted on 8 September, when Qadhafi forces carried out an attack injuring 20 *thuwar*, who in turn retaliated by taking out Qadhafi snipers.[45] NTC authorities stated that they had intended to wait to carry out a coordinated operation to take the city, but reported that Bani Walid

---

[37] *Id.*

[38] *Id.*

[39] Andrew Harding, *Battle for Bani Walid begins*, BBC, Sept. 10, 2011, *available at* http://www.bbc.co.uk/news/world-africa-14865736; *Libyan fighters forced to retreat*, INDEPENDENT IE, Sept. 16, 2011, *available at* http://www.independent.ie/breaking-news/world-news/libyan-fighters-forced-to-retreat-2879319.html.

[40] THE AUSTRALIAN, *Muammar Gaddafi loyalists on the road to dusty death*, *supra* note 1.

[41] Broadcast on Syria's Arrai TV Station. Malik & Davies, *Gaddafi issues defiant message from hiding*, *supra* note 3.

[42] THE AUSTRALIAN, *Muammar Gaddafi loyalists on the road to dusty death*, *supra* note 1; *Libya media: Gaddafi mouthpieces fall silent*, BBC, Sept. 2, 2011, *available at* http://www.bbc.co.uk/news/world-africa-14766907; Peter Biles, *Libya conflict: NTC forces attack Sirte and Bani Walid*, BBC, Sept. 16, 2011, *available at* http://www.bbc.co.uk/news/world-africa-14946777; Samia Nakhoul et al., *Gaddafi believed to be in Bani Walid; NTC commander*, REUTERS, Sept. 1, 2011, *available at* http://www.reuters.com/article/2011/09/01/us-libya-gaddafi-idUSTRE7801EZ20110901.

[43] Malik & Davies, *Gaddafi issues defiant message from hiding*, *supra* note 3.

[44] PARGETER, LIBYA: THE RISE AND FALL OF QADDAFI, *supra* note 13 at 242.

[45] Harding, *Battle for Bani Walid begins*, *supra* note 39; INDEPENDENT IE, *Libyan fighters forced to retreat*, *supra* note 39; *Libya conflict: Rockets fired from Bani Walid*, BBC, Sept. 8, 2011, *available at* http://www.bbc.co.uk/news/world-africa-14841901.

thuwar fighters wanted to liberate their city without external help.[46] Disputes surfaced between the *thuwar* over plans to take Bani Walid, raising concerns over the level of coordination between fighters on the ground and the NTC.[47]

NATO continued to concentrate on the Bani Walid region in order to hasten the surrender of the Qadhafi forces, destroying a surface-to-air missile storage facility on 8 September.[48] Again, there were reports of the destruction of civilian infrastructure, and concerns over the targets hit in the NATO campaign. NATO reported destroying an armed vehicle in the vicinity of Bani Walid on 9 September.[49] This strike reportedly led to the destruction of a medical school consisting of a number of buildings.[50]

At the same time, the Qadhafi forces were maintaining their ground, and the *thuwar* fighters were forced to retreat after coming under heavy fire.[51] The NTC reported withdrawing from the city to wait for further NATO air support. Reports emerged estimating the number of Qadhafi soldiers still fighting was close to 1,000 fighters, a figure much higher than previous estimates.[52] NATO strikes continued to target Qadhafi forces in the region. Media accounts reported five NATO airstrikes in Bani Walid on 10 September.[53] NATO operational updates confirm that they carried out strikes in the Bani Walid vicinity, destroying a tank, a multiple rocket launcher and two armed vehicles.[54] *Thuwar* forces launched a renewed

---

[46] *Battle for Bani Walid rages in Libya*, VOA, Sept. 11, 2011, *available at* http://blogs.voanews.com/breaking-news/2011/09/11/battle-for-bani-walid-rages-in-libya-2.

[47] *See* Ch. V, Sec. 2. *See also Libya's interim leader promises to build 'a state of law'*, CNN, Sept. 12, 2011, *available at* http://articles.cnn.com/2011-09-12/world/libya.war_1_libyan-leader-moammar-gadhafi-libyan-people-national-transitional-council; Sue Turton, *Fighters breach Bani Walid*, AL JAZEERA, Sept. 10, 2011 *available at* http://blogs.aljazeera.net/topic/libya/libya-sep-10-2011-1405.

[48] *NATO and Libya Operational Media Update for 8 September 2011*, NORTH ATLANTIC TREATY ORGANIZATION, Sept. 9, 2011, *available at* http://www.nato.int/nato_static/assets/pdf/pdf_2011_09/20110909_110909-oup-update.pdf.

[49] *NATO and Libya Operational Media Update for 9 September 2011*, NORTH ATLANTIC TREATY ORGANIZATION, Sept. 10, 2011, *available at* http://www.nato.int/nato_static/assets/pdf/pdf_2011_09/20110910_110910-oup-update.pdf.

[50] *See infra* Sec. 4. *See also* Ch. III, Sec. 6.2.

[51] Marina Golovnina, *WRAPUP 5-Libya fighters assault Gaddafi-held Bani Walid*, REUTERS, Sept. 10, 2011, *available at* http://www.reuters.com/article/2011/09/10/libya-idUSL5E7KA00820110910.

[52] *Id.*

[53] *NATO strikes pro-Gaddafi town: Reuters witness*, REUTERS, Sept. 10, 2011, *available at* http://www.reuters.com/article/2011/09/10/us-libya-nato-strikes-idUSTRE7891AR20110910.

[54] *NATO and Libya Operational Media Update for 10 September 2011*, NORTH ATLANTIC TREATY ORGANIZATION, Sept. 11, 2011. *available at* http://www.nato.int/nato_static/assets/pdf/pdf_2011_09/20110911_110911-oup-update.pdf.

attack, prompting Qadhafi loyalists to seek reinforcements, reportedly coming from Qadhafi's secret police, Legion Thuriyya and the Khamis Katiba.[55]

With these reinforcements, the Qadhafi forces still faced heavy NATO bombardment and a steady ground assault. On 11 September, *thuwar* forces made advances, and towards the end of the day they captured most of the city, Qadhafi forces slowly retreating. An NTC spokesperson reported Qadhafi fighters were using civilians as human shields and placing missile and mortar launchers on the rooftops of civilian homes, making it more difficult for the rebels or NATO planes to strike.[56]

On 14 September, residents of Bani Walid were urged to evacuate and given two days to leave before a renewed assault on the city would begin.[57] Residents were in need of food and began fleeing to Tripoli.[58] There were reports of *thuwar* and the NTC assisting evacuation by providing fuel for the journey to travel to Tripoli.[59] Reports indicated that many residents were still trapped and that roughly a quarter had managed to escape.[60] The United Nations Office for the Coordination of Humanitarian Affairs (OCHA) estimated that by October, 80,000 people had fled from Bani Walid and Sirte.[61] In the midst of the fighting and as civilians fled the city, NATO continued its strikes, destroying two armed vehicles in the region on 14 September.[62]

On 16 September, *thuwar* forces coordinated an advance on Bani Walid from different locations with roughly 1,000 men. *Thuwar* fighters told reporters they would not use heavy artillery to avoid harming civilians.[63]

---

[55] Chris Stephen et al., *Gaddafi's diehard secret police dig in as Nato jets blast desert stronghold*, THE GUARDIAN, Sept. 10, 2011, *available at* http://www.guardian.co.uk/world/2011/sep/10/gaddafi-beni-walid-rebels-nato.

[56] Alistair Lyan, *Civilians in peril; Gaddafi son flees to Niger*, REUTERS, Sept. 11, 2011, *available at* http://www.reuters.com/article/2011/09/11/us-libya-idUSTRE7810I820110911.

[57] *Libya: Bani Walid residents given two days to leave before onslaught*, THE TELEGRAPH, Sept. 14, 2011, *available at* http://www.telegraph.co.uk/news/worldnews/africaandindian ocean/libya/8761667/Libya-Bani-Walid-residents-given-two-days-to-leave-before-on-slaught.html.

[58] *Id.*

[59] *Id.*

[60] Golovnina, *Libyan veteran prepares assault on pro-Gaddafi bastion, supra* note 2.

[61] Report of the International Commission of Inquiry, advance unedited version (Mar. 2, 2012), *supra* note 16 at ¶ 102.

[62] *NATO and Libya Operational Media Update for 14 September*, NORTH ATLANTIC TREATY ORGANIZATION, Sept. 15, 2011, *available at* http://www.nato.int/nato_static/assets/pdf/pdf_2011_09/20110915_110915-oup-update.pdf.

[63] Phillipa Fletcher & Slyvia Westall, *Anti-Gaddafi forces speed towards Bani Walid,* REUTERS, Sept. 16, 2011, *available at* http://www.reuters.com/article/2011/09/16/us-libya-baniwalid-idUSTRE78F0YW20110916.

After hours of fierce fighting, the *thuwar* withdrew, citing a lack of ammunition and the need to reorganize their soldiers.[64]

The CoI documented several incidents of violations committed by Qadhafi forces during this period. One victim told the CoI that on 17 September he was detained at a false *thuwar* checkpoint set up by Qadhafi forces and taken to a detention center. He was beaten and insulted, along with 13 other prisoners in the facility. The witness was released along with two others, but he reported that eight of the men were shot and killed by the Qadhafi forces.[65] Another witness described how Qadhafi soldiers arrested him when he returned to his home in Bani Walid, which he had fled to avoid the shelling.[66] In other cases, witnesses reported that Qadhafi forces detained and executed men suspected of fighting with the *thuwar* forces.[67]

The battle for Bani Walid continued, with the *thuwar* forces retreating yet again on 18 September.[68] *Thuwar* fighters from different tribes blamed each other for the retreat and the need for a more organized approach became increasingly apparent.[69] Such problems and mis-communication arose, for example, when trucks loaded with foot soldiers were sent by the NTC, while fighters on the ground were expecting anti-aircraft guns and rocket launchers.[70] There were also reports of *thuwar* fighters mishandling their weapons. In one reported incident, a soldier killed himself and his fellow fighter while mishandling a rocket-propelled grenade.[71] The fighting intensified when Qadhafi reinforcements arrived from Sirte and the NTC sent more men from Tripoli to assist the *thuwar* fighters in Bani Walid.[72] The Red Cross warned that the remaining residents in Bani Walid

---

[64] Barry Malone, *Libyan NTC forces retreat from Bani Walid-Reuters witness*, Reuters, Sept. 16, 2011, *available at* http://www.reuters.com/article/2011/09/16/libya-bani-walid-idUSL5E7KG2T120110916.

[65] *See infra* Sec. 3.2. *See also* Report of the International Commission of Inquiry, advance unedited version (Mar. 2, 2012), *supra* note 16 at Annex I, ¶ 202.

[66] *Id.* at Annex I, ¶ 203.

[67] *Id.* at Annex I, ¶ 202.

[68] *Libyan forces battle to loosen grip on Gaddafi towns*, Reuters, Sept. 18, 2011, *available at* http://in.reuters.com/article/2011/09/18/idINIndia-59404220110918.

[69] Bell & Witter, The Roots of Rebellion, *supra* note 6 at 7.

[70] *WRAPUP 5 – Libyan forces retreat again as Gaddafi bastions hold*, Reuters, Sept. 18, 2011, *available at* http://af.reuters.com/article/libyaNews/idAFL5E7KH0PV20110918.

[71] Alexander Dziadosz & Maria Golovnina, *WRAPUP 2 – Libya rulers say they seize Gaddafi desert outposts*, Reuters, Sept. 22, 2011, *available at* http://www.reuters.com/article/2011/09/22/libya-idUSL5E7KL86N20110922.

[72] Reuters, *Libyan forces battle to loosen grip on Gaddafi towns*, *supra* note 68.

were in need of humanitarian aid as food, water and electricity supplies became limited.[73] On 19 September, a Turkish military cargo plane (C-130) was hit as it attempted to drop humanitarian aid over Bani Walid.[74]

On the same day, NATO airstrikes hit a command-and-control node.[75] The battle continued unabated, and the fighting led to a number of casualties. By 24 September, the NTC reported 30 of their fighters had been killed in Bani Walid and another 50 severely injured.[76] NATO continued its campaign of strikes in the region, and on 26 September, destroyed two bunkers, command-and-control nodes as well as one firing point.[77]

On 28 September, *thuwar* suffered losses as Qadhafi forces gained ground in Bani Walid.[78] In a major setback, senior NTC commander and leading figure in the fight for Bani Walid, Daou al-Salhine al-Jadak,[79] was killed by a rocket that struck his car.[80] The next day, NATO destroyed an ammunition storage facility and one multiple rocket launcher.[81]

On 1 October, it was reported that fighting in Bani Walid was at its most intense[82] and by 9 October *thuwar* forces had taken control of the villages

---

[73] *Libya conflict: Nato hits Gaddafi stronghold of Sirte*, BBC, Sept. 28, 2011, *available at* http://www.bbc.co.uk/news/world-africa-15095594.

[74] *Libya Live blog*, AL JAZEERA, Sept. 19, 2011, *available at* http://blogs.aljazeera.net/topic/libya/libya-sep-19-2011-1041.

[75] *NATO and Libya Operational Media Update for 19 September*, NORTH ATLANTIC TREATY ORGANIZATION, Sept. 20, 2011, *available at* http://www.nato.int/nato_static/assets/pdf/pdf_2011_09/20110920_110920-oup-update.pdf.

[76] *Libya: 30 government fighters killed in battle for Bani Walid*, VANGUARD, Sept. 24, 2011, *available at* http://www.vanguardngr.com/2011/09/libya-30-govt-fighters-killed-in-battle-for-bani-walid.

[77] *NATO and Libya Operational Media Update for 26 September*, NORTH ATLANTIC TREATY ORGANIZATION, Sept. 27, 2011, *available at* http://www.nato.int/nato_static/assets/pdf/pdf_2011_09/20110927_110927-oup-update.pdf.

[78] Jay Deshmukh, *Anti-Gaddafi forces suffer heavy losses*, SYDNEY MORNING HERALD, Sept. 28, 2011 *available at* http://news.smh.com.au/breaking-news-world/antigaddafi-forces-suffer-heavy-losses-20110928-1kvrv.html.

[79] The transliteration of this name was adopted from the reference. *Rebels urge more NATO strikes after heavy losses in Qaddafi's hometown*, AL ARABIYA, Sept. 28, 2011, *available at* http://www.alarabiya.net/articles/2011/09/29/169230.html.

[80] *Id.*

[81] *NATO and Libya Operational Media Update for 29 September*, NORTH ATLANTIC TREATY ORGANIZATION, September 30, 2011, *available at* http://www.nato.int/nato_static/assets/pdf/pdf_2011_09/20110930_110930-oup-update.pdf.

[82] Jay Deshmukh & Rory Mulholland, *Snipers halt NTC fight for Kadhafi hometown*, JAKARTA GLOBE, Oct. 1, 2011, *available at* http://www.thejakartaglobe.com/afp/snipers-halt-ntc-fight-for-kadhafi-hometown/468894.

of Teninai[83] and Shuwaykh as well as the airport.[84] A NATO airstrike destroyed one multiple rocket launcher firing point and one ammunition storage facility.[85] NATO reported its next successful strike on 4 October when it destroyed a command-and-control node.[86] On 5 October, NATO had many successful hits, destroying one military installation, six command-and-control nodes and one military staging location.[87] The next day, NATO destroyed a tank,[88] and three days later, on 9 October, destroyed three armed vehicles.[89]

Despite the daily airstrikes, Qadhafi fighters managed to take control of the airport and killed 17 *thuwar* fighters in the process.[90] *Thuwar* reinforcements coming from Tripoli and the Nafusa Mountains region were expected to arrive in order to coordinate a renewed attack on the Qadhafi forces.[91] As the battle continued into October, NATO's strikes continued on a regular basis. On 11 October, NATO attacked and destroyed six military vehicles.[92] On 12 October, NATO destroyed one military vehicle,[93]

---

[83] The transliteration of this place was adopted from the reference. *Libya fighters in 'final stages' to take Gadhafi hometown, they say*, CNN, Oct. 9, 2011, *available at* http://articles.cnn.com/2011-10-09/africa/world_africa_libya-war_1_libya-fighters-gadhafi-hometown-pro-gadhafi.

[84] *Id.*

[85] *NATO and Libya Operational Media Update for 1 October*, NORTH ATLANTIC TREATY ORGANIZATION, Oct. 2, 2011, *available at* http://www.nato.int/nato_static/assets/pdf/pdf_2011_10/20111002_111002-oup-update.pdf.

[86] *NATO and Libya Operational Media Update on 4 October*, NORTH ATLANTIC TREATY ORGANIZATION, Oct. 4, 2011, *available at* http://www.nato.int/nato_static/assets/pdf/pdf_2011_10/20111005_111005-oup-update.pdf.

[87] *NATO and Libya Operational Media Update for 5 October*, NORTH ATLANTIC TREATY ORGANIZATION, Oct. 6, 2011, *available at* http://www.nato.int/nato_static/assets/pdf/pdf_2011_10/20111006_111006-oup-update.pdf.

[88] *NATO and Libya Operational Media Update for 6 October*, NORTH ATLANTIC TREATY ORGANIZATION, Oct. 7, 2011, *available at* http://www.nato.int/nato_static/assets/pdf/pdf_2011_10/20111007_111007-oup-update.pdf.

[89] *NATO and Libya Operational Media Update for 9 October*, NORTH ATLANTIC TREATY ORGANIZATION, Oct. 10, 2011, *available at* http://www.nato.int/nato_static/assets/pdf/pdf_2011_10/20111010_111010-oup-update.pdf.

[90] *17 NTC fighters killed in Libya's Bani Walid*, AHRAM, Oct. 10, 2011, *available at* http://english.ahram.org.eg/NewsContent/2/8/23753/World/Region/-NTC-fighters-killed-in-Libyas-Bani-Walid.aspx.

[91] *17 NTC fighters killed in Libyan city of Bani Walid*, AL ARABIYA, Oct. 10, 2011, *available at* http://www.alarabiya.net/articles/2011/10/10/171105.html.

[92] *NATO and Libya Operational Media Update for 11 October*, NORTH ATLANTIC TREATY ORGANIZATION, Oct. 12, 2011, *available at* http://www.nato.int/nato_static/assets/pdf/pdf_2011_10/20111012_111012-oup-update.pdf.

[93] *NATO and Libya Operational Media Update for 12 October*, NORTH ATLANTIC TREATY ORGANIZATION, Oct. 13, 2011, *available at* http://www.nato.int/nato_static/assets/pdf/pdf_2011_10/20111013_111013-oup-update.pdf.

and on the following day four military vehicles and one multiple rocket launcher.[94] On 14 October, NATO struck another military vehicle.[95]

15 October, saw a renewed *thuwar* assault when they managed to gain ground and take over the eastern part of the city. Local NTC leaders reported that Qadhafi forces were running out of ammunition and other supplies.[96] The media committee of the local council of Bani Walid told reporters that the *thuwar* had managed to free most of the city, including a hospital and an important industrial district.[97] Only parts of the market area remained under the control of Qadhafi forces.[98]

As the battle continued, conflicting reports on the status of the progress of the *thuwar* emerged. On 16 October, it was reported that the *thuwar* had control over the city center and the northern parts of the city.[99] Twenty Qadhafi supporters were allegedly arrested and the remaining supporters were confined to the Dahra region in Bani Walid.[100] Other reports indicated that Bani Walid was entirely under *thuwar* control and that the Tricolor flag[101] had been raised, although no official statements by the NTC about liberation had been made.[102] A spokesperson for the southern frontline, Mahmud Tawfiq, said that *thuwar* fighters were approaching from three different sides and would converge in the town center.[103] On

---

[94] *NATO and Libya Operational Media Update for 13 October*, NORTH ATLANTIC TREATY ORGANIZATION, Oct. 14, 2011, *available at* http://www.nato.int/nato_static/assets/pdf/pdf_2011_10/20111014_111014-oup-update.pdf.

[95] *NATO and Libya Operational Media Update for 14 October*, NORTH ATLANTIC TREATY ORGANIZATION, Oct. 15, 2011, *available at* http://www.nato.int/nato_static/assets/pdf/pdf_2011_10/20111015_111015-oup-update.pdf.

[96] *Libyan NTC slows down in Sirte, advances in Bani Walid*, XINHUANET, Oct. 16, 2011, *available at* http://news.xinhuanet.com/english2010/world/2011-10/16/c_131193592.htm.

[97] *Id.*

[98] *Id.*

[99] *Libyan leaders claim new areas in Bani Walid*, CNN, Oct. 16, 2011, *available at* http://edition.cnn.com/2011/10/16/world/africa/libya-war/index.html; BELL & WITTER, THE ROOTS OF REBELLION, *supra* note 6 at 7.

[100] CNN, *Libyan leaders claim new areas in Bani Walid*, Oct. 16, 2011, *available at* http://edition.cnn.com/2011/10/16/world/africa/libya-war/index.html.

[101] The Tricolor flag was the flag of Libya under the Kingdom of Idris Al Senussi, but was not used after the 1969 coup, when the plain green flag was adopted during the Qadhafi era. The Tricolor flag was adopted by the *thuwar* and the NTC and reclaimed as the national flag with the interim Constitutional Declaration of Aug. 3, 2011.

[102] *Libya's Bani Walid "liberated:" official*, XINHUANET, Oct. 16, 2011, *available at* http://news.xinhuanet.com/english2010/world/2011-10/17/c_131194884.htm; Barry Malone, *Libyan forces say raised flag in Bani Walid*, REUTERS, Oct. 16, 2011, *available at* http://af.reuters.com/article/libyaNews/idAFL5E7LG0NH20111016; *Libya conflict: NTC forces claim Bani Walid victory*, BBC, Oct. 16, 2011, *available at* http://www.bbc.co.uk/news/world-africa-15330551.

[103] XINHUANET, *Libya's Bani Walid "liberated:" official*, *supra* note 102.

17 October, numerous reports indicated that Bani Walid was finally under *thuwar* control and the new flag could be seen everywhere.[104] Sources said that senior leaders of the Warfalla tribe agreed to accept NTC leadership in a bid to prevent further bloodshed.[105] On 19 October, Saif al-Islam was reportedly seen leaving Bani Walid with his motorcade.[106] Reports later surfaced indicating that Qadhafi had been hiding in Bani Walid for a month during the fighting before fleeing.[107]

Despite the official end to hostilities in Bani Walid, unrest continued, and on 26 October there were reports that the Warfalla people were raising concerns over the looting conducted by *thuwar* fighters. Reports indicate that the local people were ready to expel the NTC presence by means of an insurgency.[108] There were also reports of daily shots exchanged between NTC soldiers and Qadhafi supporters on the outskirts of Bani Walid. In Tamalat neighborhood, freshly sprayed graffiti in support of Qadhafi was seen on the walls of buildings and reports about *thuwar* raids and the destruction they wrought increased.[109]

On 20 January 2012, the May 28 Katiba reportedly arrested a man from Bani Walid, prompting a protest. The man was released but it was evident that he had been tortured by his captors.[110] An argument ensued, which reportedly triggered further violence on 23 January.[111] Forces carrying the green flag of the former regime attacked the May 28 Katiba base in Bani

---

[104] BBC, *Libya conflict: NTC forces claim Bani Walid victory, supra* note 102; *Libyan fighters claim capture of Bani Walid*, AL JAZEERA, Oct. 18, 2011, *available at* http://www.aljazeera.com/news/africa/2011/10/20111017134373519111.html; Joseph Nasr, *WRAPUP 4 – NTC forces celebrate capture of Gaddafi bastion Bani Walid*, REUTERS, Oct. 17, 2011, *available at* http://af.reuters.com/article/libyaNews/idAFL5E7LH3NI20111017.

[105] *Gaddafi stronghold Bani Walid falls*, THE GUARDIAN, Oct. 17, 2011, *available at* http://www.guardian.co.uk/world/2011/oct/17/libyan-rebels-capture-bani-walid.

[106] *Muammar Gaddafi's son Saif al-Islam tells International Criminal Court he is innocent*, NATIONAL POST, Oct. 19, 2011, *available at* http://news.nationalpost.com/2011/10/29/muammar-gaddafis-son-saif-al-islam-tells-international-criminal-court-he-is-innocent.

[107] *UPDATE 2 – Libyan government concedes to restive town's demands*, REUTERS, Jan. 25, 2012, *available at* http://af.reuters.com/article/libyaNews/idAFL5E8CP2IG20120125; *A Deceptive Calm*, QANTARA.DE, Apr. 21, 2012, *available at* http://en.qantara.de/A-Deceptive-Calm/18997c19927i0p.

[108] Maria Golovnina, *FEATURE – Gaddafi loyalists fight on as Libya tries to unite*, REUTERS, Oct. 2, 2011, *available at* http://af.reuters.com/article/libyaNews/idAFL5E7LQ31N20111026.

[109] *Id.*

[110] Alistair Macdonald, *UPDATE 1 – Anger, chaos but no revolt after Libya violence*, REUTERS, Jan. 24, 2012, *available at* http://af.reuters.com/article/libyaNews/idAFL5E8CO2HB20120124?pageNumber=2&virtualBrandChannel=0&sp=true.

[111] *Id.*

Walid, killing four *thuwar* and wounding 20.[112] Other reports said five were killed and 30 injured.[113] This was the first major outburst of violence in the country since the fall of the Qadhafi regime. During the attack, several former Qadhafi administration officials who had been arrested for war crimes escaped with the assistance of the attackers.[114] The attack was carried out by an estimated 150 men who were reportedly carrying heavy artillery.[115] The May 28 Katiba had suspected that an attack was imminent and requested assistance from the NTC, but their requests were not answered.[116] Other reports indicated that this attack was not conducted by resurgent Qadhafi groups, but by Bani Walid locals taking revenge on the May 28 Katiba who were reportedly harassing the locals, raiding and looting homes.[117]

The May 28 Katiba were also accused of carrying out arbitrary arrests and detentions, and there were claims of enforced disappearances.[118] There were reports of an increase in the number of torture cases, especially the torture of suspected Qadhafi supporters at the hands of the *thuwar*.[119] The NTC government in Tripoli announced that it would not intervene until it was clear what had transpired. A government official who spoke on condition of anonymity told journalists that there would be no move against Bani Walid, as he suspected it was a matter of a localized dispute and not a counter revolutionary attack.[120]

---

[112] *'Pro-Kadhafi' attack kills four in Libya*, AFP, Jan. 23, 2011, *available at* http://www.google.com/hostednews/afp/article/ALeqM5gen8BhzM9lp1R5N_zm2yUUMniuig?docId=CNG.019fba2fc3e3a19df21e46d42102fda8.8c1; *Fighting erupts in Libya's Bani Walid*, AL JAZEERA, Jan. 24, 2011, *available at* http://www.aljazeera.com/news/africa/2012/01/2012123182559826642.html.

[113] *Libya Kadhafi diehards seize former regime bastion*, AFP, Jan. 23, 2012, *available at* http://reliefweb.int/node/472042.

[114] Chris Stephen, *Libya militias prepare to retake Bani Walid from Gaddafi loyalists*, THE GUARDIAN, Jan. 24, 2011, *available at* http://www.guardian.co.uk/world/2012/jan/26/libya-militias-bani-walid-gaddafi-loyalists.

[115] AFP, *'Pro-Kadhafi' attack kills four in Libya*, *supra* note 112.

[116] *Id.*

[117] Reports released in April 2012 stated that 4,000 cars were stolen. 300 houses were robbed and destroyed. Only the houses that allegedly belonged to pro Qadhafi supporters were attacked. *See* QANTARA.DE, *A Deceptive Calm*, *supra* note 107; Macdonald, *UPDATE 1 – Anger, chaos but no revolt after Libya violence*, *supra* note 110.

[118] *See infra* Sec. 3.3. *See also* Macdonald, *UPDATE 1 – Anger, chaos but no revolt after Libya violence*, *supra* note 110.

[119] *See infra* Sec. 3.4. *See also* Nick Meo & Hassan Morajea, *Militia chaos in Bani Walid raises danger of civil war in post-Gaddafi Libya*, THE TELEGRAPH, Jan. 28, 2011, *available at* http://www.telegraph.co.uk/news/worldnews/africaandindianocean/libya/9046372/Militia-chaos-in-Bani-Walid-raises-danger-of-civil-war-in-post-Gaddafi-Libya.html.

[120] Macdonald, *UPDATE 1 – Anger, chaos but no revolt after Libya violence*, *supra* note 110.

Bani Walid elders urged the NTC not to get involved, making it clear that they would not accept NTC interference.[121] By 24 January 2012, a sense of calm returned and according to Colonel Salem al-Ouaer,[122] a tribal leader from Bani Walid, part of the frustration stemmed from demands for compensation for those who had been injured or affected in other ways by the war.[123] Ouaer said that representatives from the local tribes were meeting to assess the situation, along with delegations from Zintan and Sabrata.[124] This meeting was held just outside Bani Walid, while other local shaykhs held a meeting in a mosque in Bani Walid.[125] Ouaer said he had kept Mustafa 'Abd al-Jalil, head of the ruling NTC, and 'Usama al-Juwayli, Minister of Defense, informed about the situation. He also made it clear that the conflict was indeed local and not an uprising by Qadhafi-loyalist forces.[126]

By midday on 24 January, it was reported that the shaykhs and the elders had decided to abolish the NTC-appointed military council and appoint their own local council.[127] The elders maintained that they did not want to be obstacles to progress, but that they would not be dictated to by the NTC.[128] Reports indicated that the *thuwar* were preparing to take back Bani Walid.[129] The contention stemmed in part from the fact that Qadhafi-loyalists who had been accused of war crimes were being sheltered by locals. *Thuwar* requested permission from the elders to round up the 300 men who were accused of the crimes. They issued an ultimatum, warning that if the elders refused, a full assault would be launched, but if they handed over the suspects, there would be no bloodshed.[130]

On 25 January, Minister of Defense Al-Juwayli drove to Bani Walid and held discussions with the concerned parties. He reported that the situa-

---

[121] *Id.*

[122] The transliteration of this name is adopted from the reference. *Pro-Gaddafi fighters take back Bani Walid*, AL JAZEERA, Jan. 25, 2012, *available at* http://www.aljazeera.com/news/middleeast/2012/01/2012124133415649500.html.

[123] *Id.*

[124] *Id.*

[125] *Id.*

[126] *Id.*

[127] *Former Gaddafi stronghold revolts against Tripoli*, REUTERS, Jan. 24, 2012, *available at* http://af.reuters.com/article/libyaNews/idAFL5E8CO1LY20120124.

[128] *Id.*

[129] Stephen, *Libya militias prepare to retake Bani Walid from Gaddafi loyalists*, *supra* note 114.

[130] *Id.*

tion was calm and under control.[131] He also accepted the newly appointed local council.[132] By 27 January, it was reported that the *thuwar* – in particular the ousted May 28 Katiba – were ready to retake Bani Walid but were waiting for the green light from the Prime Minister.[133] The military leader of the May 28 Katiba declared that it was their right to re-enter Bani Walid.[134] The families of members of the May 28 Katiba were also reportedly forced to leave and flee to Tripoli.[135] The elders announced that the May 28 Katiba would be welcome back to Bani Walid, but on condition that they return without their weapons.[136] On 25 February, head of the NTC Al-Jalil said that the situation in Bani Walid was being carefully monitored and that they hoped discussions with the elders would result in the handing over of pro-Qadhafi men, warning that failure to do so would result in force being used to apprehend them.[137]

On 11 May, the new government announced that soldiers belonging to the Libya National Shield Forces[138] (LSF) – military forces composed of *thuwar kata'ib* and aligned with the Defense Ministry – had been sent to the area between Bani Walid and Tarhuna.[139] The transitional government authorities stated it was not their intention to invade Bani Walid, but to monitor illegal immigration and illicit arms dealing. Violence erupted just outside Bani Walid on 12 May between *thuwar* fighters and local fighters

---

[131] Meo & Morajea, *Militia chaos in Bani Walid raises danger of civil war in post-Gaddafi Libya, supra* note 119.

[132] REUTERS, *UPDATE 2 – Libyan government concedes to restive town's demands, supra* note 107; *Libya Government yields to Tribe*, N.Y. TIMES, Jan. 25, 2011, *available at* http://www.nytimes.com/2012/01/26/world/africa/libya-government-yields-to-tribe-in-bani-walid.html.

[133] *INTERVIEW-Libyan commander says will retake Bani Walid*, REUTERS, Jan. 27, 2012, *available at* http://af.reuters.com/article/libyaNews/idAFL5E8CR41Y20120127.

[134] *Libyan Commander says will retake Bani Walid*, DAILY STAR, Jan. 28, 2011, *available at* http://www.dailystar.com.lb/News/Middle-East/2012/Jan-28/161395-libyan-commander-says-will-retake-bani-walid.ashx#axzz1zetEF3ZC.

[135] *Libyan city's fate in the balance*, AL JAZEERA, Feb. 28, 2011, *available at* http://www.aljazeera.com/video/africa/2012/02/201222818102884959.html.

[136] *Qadhafi 'lives on in our hearts': Bani Walid residents*, DAWN.COM, Jan. 27, 2012, *available at* http://dawn.com/2012/01/27/kadhafi-lives-on-in-our-hearts-bani-walid-residents.

[137] *Libya: NTC Chairman Denies Khamis Capture, Warns Neighbouring Countries over Harbouring Pro-Gaddafi Criminals*, TRIPOLI POST, Feb. 25, 2011, *available at* http://www.tripolipost.com/articledetail.asp?c=1&i=7946.

[138] At times, the interim government used the National Shield as a proxy army to quell disputes in conflict areas. *See* Ch. V, Sec. 2. *See also Libya: Residents of Bani Walid at Risk*, HUMAN RIGHTS WATCH, Oct. 24, 2012, *available at* http://www.hrw.org/news/2012/10/24/libya-residents-bani-walid-risk.

[139] *Fighting outside Bani Walid*, LIBYA HERALD, May 12, 2012, *available at* http://www.libyaherald.com/fighting-outside-bani-walid.

opposed to the NTC.[140] Two members of the Libya Shield Forces were killed during the clashes.[141] The ongoing fighting fueled widespread discontent among the population, which manifested itself in public outcry against the actions of the NTC. Around 14 May, Bani Walid residents held a demonstration protesting the presence of government troops.[142]

Despite the death of Qadhafi and the NTC declaration that Libya had been liberated, violence in Bani Walid continued. 'Umran Sha'ban, a *thuwar* fighter who was made into a hero for discovering Qadhafi hiding in drain pipes in Sirte, was kidnapped, beaten and shot in Bani Walid by suspected Qadhafi loyalists. He died from his wounds on 24 September.[143] The General National Congress stated that it would not hesitate to use force to apprehend the perpetrators.[144]

On 2 October, Libya Shield Forces clashed with militia from Bani Walid, resulting in the death of one person.[145] The resistance of Bani Walid's locals and their general disapproval of the interim government added to the multitude of problems facing the new Libya. The government issued an ultimatum for Bani Walid to hand over Sha'ban's attackers, and subsequently sent forces to shell Bani Walid. Reports indicate that at least three people were killed.[146]

Bani Walid militias remained heavily armed with RPGs, automatic weapons and artillery. Reports indicated that residents of the town still displayed Qadhafi's picture during weddings and that young children listened to his speeches. Teachers reportedly refused to sing the new national anthem or teach the new curriculum.[147]

---

[140] *Id.*

[141] *Id.*

[142] *Bani Walid negotiator hospitalised after clashes with NTC troops*, LIBYA HERALD, May 21, 2012, *available at* http://www.libyaherald.com/bani-walid-negotiator-hospitalised-after-clashes-with-ntc-guards.

[143] Amir Ahmed, *Libyan rivals clash; at least 11 killed*, CNN, Oct. 18, 2012, *available at* http://edition.cnn.com/2012/10/17/world/meast/libya-violence/index.html.

[144] *Libya's Misrata tense after Kadhafi catcher's death*, AFP, Sept. 26, 2012, *available at* http://www.google.com/hostednews/afp/article/ALeqM5ivxwGflYsiaoLuwyNq9YauVtPEQ?docId=CNG.aab6b66c9c0a82a2e9c935cbcc9c0635.211.

[145] *Libya: Deadly Clashes Reported Near Bani Walid*, ALL AFRICA, Oct. 3, 2012, *available at* http://allafrica.com/stories/201210041421.html.

[146] Ramadan Al-Fatash, *Troops shell besieged Libyan town*, IOL NEWS, Oct. 11, 2012, *available at* http://www.iol.co.za/news/africa/troops-shell-besieged-libyan-town-1.1401153#.UIfNJMVvCS0.

[147] *Omran Shaaban who captured Libya's Muammar Gaddafi dies after being shot and kidnapped by supporters of old regime*, THE TELEGRAPH, Sept. 26, 2012, *available at* http://www.dailytelegraph.com.au/news/world/omran-shaaban-who-captured-libyas-muammar-gaddafi-dies-after-being-shot-and-kidnapped-by-supporters-of-old-regime/story-fnddckzi-1226481760151.

Violence continued and on 17 October it was reported that 11 people died in clashes between armed forces aligned with the Defense Ministry and Qadhafi loyalists.[148] The NTC-backed forces shelled the city and Qadhafi loyalists responded with mortar fire[149] in clashes that injured 100.[150] Confusion was rife and it remained unclear as to whether the government ordered the shelling or whether senior commanders were acting on their own accord.[151] In the wake of the heavy fighting, *de facto* President Muhammad Yusuf al-Magarayf stated that, "The campaign to liberate the country has not been fully completed," claiming that Bani Walid had become the home of "outlaws, anti-revolutionaries and mercenaries."[152] On 20 October, it was reported that Khamis Qadhafi was killed in the attack on Bani Walid.[153] The following day, 200 people stormed the Libyan parliament in Tripoli demanding an end to the violence in Bani Walid.[154]

The ongoing fighting raised concerns over the lack of stability and governance in post-Qadhafi Libya. On 22 October, United Nations Secretary-General Ban Ki-moon urged the Libyan government to find a peaceful solution to the situation in Bani Walid.[155] Civilians fled the town as it was no longer safe and the living conditions had deteriorated.[156] Demonstrations increased, and on 24 October protesters gathered in objection to the violence, blocking a vital road in Benghazi.[157]

---

[148] *11 Libyans Killed In Attack on Bani Walid*, TRIPOLI POST, Oct. 18, 2012, *available at* http://www.tripolipost.com/articledetail.asp?c=1&i=9332.

[149] Ahmed, *Libyan rivals clash, at least 11 killed, supra* note 143.

[150] *Id.*

[151] *Confusion rife as Libyan army storms town of Bani Walid*, THE GUARDIAN, Oct. 19, 2012, *available at* http://www.guardian.co.uk/world/2012/oct/19/libyan-army-storms-bani-walild.

[152] *Libya leader says country not fully liberated*, AL JAZEERA, Oct. 20, 2012, *available at* http://www.aljazeera.com/news/africa/2012/10/2012102010122783919.html.

[153] *Youngest son of Colonel Gaddafi dead after Bani Walid siege – Libya deputy PM*, RT, Oct. 20, 2011, *available at* http://rt.com/news/khamis-gaddafi-libya-captured-874.

[154] *See Protesters storm parliament grounds over Bani Walid violence*, REUTERS, Oct. 21, 2012, *available at* http://www.reuters.com/article/2012/10/21/libya-clashes-tripoli-idUSL5E8LL2CX20121021.

[155] *Bani Walid standoff should be settled peacefully – Ban Ki-moon*, VOICE OF RUSSIA, Oct. 22, 2012, *available at* http://english.ruvr.ru/2012_10_22/Bani-Walid-standoff-should-be-settled-peacefully-Ban-Ki-moon.

[156] George Grant, *Bani Walid residents say military in control of surrounding districts as tens of thousands flee*, LIBYA HERALD, Oct. 23, 2012, *available at* http://www.libyaherald.com/2012/10/23/bani-walid-residents-say-military-in-control-of-surrounding-districts-as-tens-of-thousands-flee.

[157] *Protesters from the Bani Walid tribe shut down a vital road in Benghazi*, REUTERS ALERT NET, Oct. 24, 2012, *available at* http://www.trust.org/alertnet/multimedia/pictures/detail.dot?mediaInode=b6f84ca3-0632-4407-a3f7-6c7ff866ea56.

The fighting continued, and NGOs reported that the humanitarian situation was deteriorating. HRW reported that more government and government-aligned military forces had entered Bani Walid and that the civilians were in dire need of food, water and humanitarian aid.[158] HRW also reported that the reason those in Bani Walid refused to hand over the Qadhafi-loyalists accused of war crimes was their lack of confidence in the country's post-conflict justice system. Bani Walid elders also noted that Misratans were trying to invade Bani Walid and exact acts of revenge, which was consistent with allegations of torture of Bani Walid residents being held in Misrata.[159] The cycle of violence continued, as conflict between the populations of Misrata and Bani Walid ensued. *Thuwar* fighters from Misrata joined the Libya Shield Forces and were accused of indiscriminately shelling the city.[160]

3. ILLUSTRATIONS OF THE VIOLATIONS

3.1. *Excessive Use of Force*

(a) *Qadhafi Forces*

Media sources and NGOs report that excessive force was used against protesters in Bani Walid in particular on 28 May 2011, when Qadhafi forces fired at the protesting crowd, immediately killing two and wounding ten.[161]

3.2. *Unlawful Killing*

(a) *Qadhafi Forces*

The CoI found that large-scale killings took place in Bani Walid.[162] The execution of the 28 May 2011 protesters who had sought refuge in a building constitutes as an act of unlawful killing. Witness statements, including statements from perpetrators, indicate that the victims had surrendered and had no ammunition in their rifles when they were shot.[163]

---

[158] HUMAN RIGHTS WATCH, *Libya: Residents of Bani Walid at Risk, supra* note 138.

[159] *Id.*

[160] *See infra* Sec. 3.7. *See also Libyan Town Under Siege Is a Center of Resistance to the New Government,* N.Y. TIMES, Oct. 21, 2012, *available at* http://www.nytimes.com/2012/10/22/world/africa/libyan-town-under-siege-is-a-center-of-resistance.html.

[161] HUMAN RIGHTS WATCH, *Libya: 10 protestors apparently executed, supra* note 14. For more on the excessive use of force against protesters, *see* Ch. IV, Sec. 2.1.

[162] Report of the International Commission of Inquiry, advance unedited version (Mar. 2, 2012), *supra* note 16 at ¶ 29.

[163] *Id.* at Annex I, ¶ 200.

In another incident of unlawful killing, the CoI documented the detention of two men on 17 September 2011, at a false *thuwar* checkpoint that was controlled by Qadhafi soldiers. The two victims were detained and beaten, and reported that eight others who had been captured and held in the same room were shot and unlawfully killed.[164] In another case on the same day, 11 men were arrested, shot and killed.[165]

3.3. *Arbitrary Detentions and Enforced Disappearances*

(a) *Qadhafi Forces*

There were several documented incidents of arbitrary arrests and enforced disappearances carried out by Qadhafi forces. After the 28 May 2011 protest, Qadhafi forces arrested a man from a hospital where he was seeking medical care after being shot in the knees by Qadhafi forces.[166] The case involving the man who was apprehended on 17 September 2011 at a false *thuwar* checkpoint by Qadhafi soldiers also constitutes an act of arbitrary detention. Another witness was subjected to the same treatment on the same day.[167] Another man told the CoI that he was arrested and detained by Qadhafi forces on his way home.[168] A father told the CoI that his son and three nephews had been detained and arrested by Qadhafi soldiers.[169]

(b) Thuwar *Forces*

There are several documented cases of arbitrary detention and enforced disappearances of suspected Qadhafi supporters at the hands of *thuwar* forces. On 17 September 2011, a man was arrested by the *thuwar* in front of his relatives and detained, then found a few days later in the hospital. The *thuwar* also arrested a man in Bani Walid without providing justification on 20 January 2012.[170] Amnesty International reported that people in Bani Walid specifically were victims of arbitrary arrest and detention due to the fact that it was one of Qadhafi's strongholds.[171] The May 28

---

[164] *Id.* at Annex I, ¶ 202.

[165] *Id.*

[166] HUMAN RIGHTS WATCH, *Libya: 10 protestors apparently executed, supra* note 14.

[167] Report of the International Commission of Inquiry, advance unedited version (Mar. 2, 2012), *supra* note 16 at Annex I, ¶ 202.

[168] *Id.* at Annex I, ¶ 203.

[169] *Id.* at Annex I, ¶ 202.

[170] Macdonald, *UPDATE 1 – Anger, chaos but no revolt after Libya violence, supra* note 110.

[171] AMNESTY INTERNATIONAL, MILITIAS THREATEN HOPES FOR NEW LIBYA 8 (Feb. 16, 2012), *available at* http://www.amnesty.org/en/library/asset/MDE19/002/2012/en/dd7c1d69-e368-44de-8ee8-cc9365bd5eb3/mde190022012en.pdf.

Katiba were also been accused of arbitrary arrests and illegally detaining people.[172]

3.4. *Torture and Other Forms of Ill-treatment*

(a) *Qadhafi Forces*

All the men arrested and detained by Qadhafi forces on 17 September 2011 were tortured. They were beaten, handcuffed with their hands behind their backs, and insulted.[173] One survivor explained that he was beaten so severely with rifles that he fainted.[174]

(b) Thuwar *Forces*

According to reports, the May 28 Katiba tortured a man whom they arrested on 20 January 2012.[175] No specific details regarding the nature of the torture were given. Other reports indicated that this kind of behavior was typical of the May 28 Katiba, and that many detainees under their control were tortured or suffered ill-treatment.[176]

3.5. *Denial of Access to Medical Treatment*

(a) *Qadhafi Forces*

After the May 28 2011 protest, a man who had been shot in the knees by Qadhafi forces was taken to the hospital by his friend, but before receiving treatment he was arrested by Qadhafi's forces. He was denied medical treatment and taken to Tripoli.[177]

3.6. *Freedom of Expression*

(b) Thuwar *Forces*

On 9 July 2012, two journalists from Misrata were detained in Bani Walid.[178] Reporter-cameraman ʿAbd al-Qadir Fassuq and cameraman Yusuf Badiʿ

---

[172] Macdonald, *UPDATE 1 – Anger, chaos but no revolt after Libya violence, supra* note 110.
[173] Report of the International Commission of Inquiry, advance unedited version (Mar. 2, 2012), *supra* note 16 at Annex I, ¶ 202.
[174] *Id.* at Annex I, ¶ 203.
[175] Macdonald, *UPDATE 1 – Anger, chaos but no revolt after Libya violence, supra* note 110.
[176] *Id.*
[177] Human Rights Watch, *Libya: 10 protestors apparently executed, supra* note 14.
[178] Luke Harding & Chris Stephen, *Libyan elections: moderate Mahmoud Jibril poised for victory*, The Guardian, July 9, 2012, *available at* http://www.guardian.co.uk/world/2012/jul/09/libyan-elections-moderate-mahmoud-jibril.

who worked for Misrata based Tobacts television station were covering elections in Mizda, and were detained as they were making their way back to Misrata. They were released on 15 July, after negotiations.[179]

3.7. *Attacks on Civilians, Civilian Objects, Protected Persons and Objects*

(a) *Qadhafi Forces*

Qadhafi forces reportedly used civilians as human shields and placed weapons on the roofs of houses with the aim of preventing NATO from targeting them.[180] The use of civilians as human shields and the placement of weapons on rooftops placed civilians in the way of unwarranted harm during the conflict.[181] Qadhafi forces also carried out assaults using Grad rockets and mortar launchers against civilian protesters and against armed *thuwar* in civilian areas.[182]

(b) Thuwar *Forces*

The CoI documented incidents where the *thuwar* used Grad rockets seized in battle.[183] The May 28 Katiba were reportedly responsible for looting and pillaging villages in Bani Walid. Reports indicate that they vandalized civilian property and attacked civilian objects.[184] One witness who had fought with the *thuwar* in the battle for Bani Walid testified that such acts took place, and told the CoI he was disappointed with the behavior of his companions who took part in the looting.[185]

---

[179] Ali Shuaib, *Libya journalists freed from ex-Gaddafi stronghold*, REUTERS, July 15, 2012, *available at* http://www.reuters.com/article/2012/07/15/libya-elections-journalists-idUSL6E8IF2NA20120715.

[180] Lyan, *Civilians in peril; Gaddafi son flees to Niger, supra* note 56; Golovnina, *Libyan veteran prepares assault on pro-Gaddafi bastion, supra* note 2.

[181] "'Attacks' means acts of violence against the adversary, whether in offense or in defense." International Committee of the Red Cross (ICRC), *Protocol Additional to the Geneva Conventions of 12 August 1949, and relating to the Protection of Victims of International Armed Conflicts (Protocol I)*, 8 June 1977, 1125 UNTS 3 at Part IV, Sec. 1, Ch. 1, Art. 48.

[182] Lyan, *Civilians in peril; Gaddafi son flees to Niger, supra* note 56.

[183] Report of the International Commission of Inquiry, advance unedited version (Mar. 2, 2012), *supra* note 16 at Annex I, ¶ 69.

[184] Rod Norland, *Near a Libyan Holdout Town, a Waiting Game, supra* note 35.

[185] Report of the International Commission of Inquiry, advance unedited version (Mar. 2, 2012), *supra* note 16 at Annex I, ¶ 748.

4. The Role of NATO

NATO's airstrikes that began in the late stages of the conflict greatly aided the *thuwar* forces in the fight for Bani Walid. It started carrying out regular airstrikes in the region on 24 August 2011 and completed operations on 17 October 2011. NATO's operational reports document the intense campaign of bombings conducted by coalition forces during this period, carrying out strikes on a near-daily basis on weapons stockpiles and military equipment. Some of the strikes were questionable as legitimate military targets, however, as they led to civilian casualties and the destruction of civilian property. According to HRW, a NATO aircraft struck two adjacent homes and killed five people (two men, two women and one girl) on 29 August 2011.[186] NATO reported that the site "was a major command-and-control node...actively controlling Government forces which were attacking civilians in the area."[187] The surviving victims who were interviewed, however, reported that there had been no military activity in the area or any presence of Qadhafi forces.[188]

The CoI investigated two other airstrikes that led to the destruction of civilian infrastructure. The nature of these strikes calls into question the military necessity of the attacks. In a strike carried out on 9 September 2011, NATO hit a building complex in Bani Walid consisting of over 35 buildings.[189] According to NATO, "this facility was a confirmed military facility in a walled compound, and was being used at the time as a command-and-control facility."[190] The site, which was reported to be a medical school, did not show any sign of military use and satellite imagery revealed no indication that the school had been used for any military purpose.[191]

Another strike just over a month later, on 10 October, destroyed two buildings in Bani Walid housing a tile factory.[192] The owner of the factory and other witnesses reported that the site was not used for any military

---

[186] *See* Ch. III, Sec. 6.2. *See also* Human Rights Watch, Unacknowledged Deaths, *supra* note 26 at 43.

[187] *Letter from Paul Olson to Philippe Kirsch, Chair of the International Commission of Inquiry (Feb. 15, 2012), in* Report of the International Commission of Inquiry (Mar. 2012), *supra* note 16 at Annex II.

[188] Human Rights Watch, Unacknowledged Deaths, *supra* note 26 at 43.

[189] *See* Ch. III, Sec. 6.2.

[190] Report of the International Commission of Inquiry, advance unedited version (Mar. 2, 2012), *supra* note 16 at Annex I, ¶ 643.

[191] *Id.* at Annex I, ¶ 642.

[192] *See* Ch. III, Sec. 6.2.

purpose. The CoI did not find any evidence to indicate that the building was being used for ammunition or weapon storage, or any other visible indications as to why the factory may have been targeted.[193]

NATO suggested that the conflict had a fluid character, and the strikes in the Bani Walid region were complicated by Qadhafi forces using civilian facilities. It cannot be ruled out that Qadhafi forces took shelter in the facilities or used them for purposes that would not leave behind evidence of military activity.[194] The attacks that led to civilian deaths and destroyed civilian infrastructure demonstrate the challenges that NATO perhaps faced in distinguishing targets with limited intelligence. It is likely that the intelligence could not keep up with the aggressive campaign of strikes conducted during the final phase of the conflict in Bani Walid.

NATO operations assisted *thuwar* forces, but also caused a great deal of controversy as a result of civilian casualties and destruction of civilian infrastructure. At the end of the conflict, many of NATO's airstrikes were no longer necessary militarily, as a *thuwar* victory was inevitable at that point. Additionally, the NATO strikes were taking place at a time when the *thuwar* forces were firing indiscriminately into civilian areas of Bani Walid with Grad rockets. It can be argued, therefore, that NATO was not only failing to protect the civilian population, but was aiding forces committing violations against civilians.

5. CONCLUSION

Bani Walid was one of Qadhafi's strongholds and went on to resist the NTC government after the fall of Qadhafi. In Bani Walid, the importance of tribal allegiances was evident. As historic Qadhafi supporters, the Warfalla tribe had significant influence in the early phase of the uprising, but as the conflict progressed they were harshly treated because of their history of support for Qadhafi. The lingering conflict and tension in Bani Walid continued into the post-conflict period, and contributed to the crisis of governance of the NTC authorities.

Reports indicate that human rights violations were committed by both the *thuwar* and Qadhafi forces in Bani Walid. In the early days of the protests, Qadhafi forces used excessive force against demonstrators, notably in response to the protests of 28 May 2011. This included the use of live

---

[193] *Id.* at Annex I, ¶ 644.
[194] *Id.* at Annex I, ¶ 640.

ammunition that resulted in the death of two protesters and the wounding of ten. Reports indicate a few members of the crowd were armed, but it is uncertain whether they used their weapons against the Qadhafi forces.[195]

Reports show that many people were unlawfully killed. The CoI reported summary executions committed by Qadhafi forces in Bani Walid, as well as the execution of protesters who sought refuge on 28 May 2011. Witnesses spoke to the CoI about unlawful killings of family members and fellow detainees. The *thuwar* forces also carried out acts of unlawful killing during their assault on Bani Walid that involved the use of heavy weaponry.

Reports indicated many cases of arbitrary detentions and enforced disappearances. There are documented cases of Qadhafi forces detaining suspected members of the *thuwar* who were subsequently disappeared. The *thuwar* similarly engaged in this practice, particularly in Bani Walid where they targeted suspected Qadhafi supporters. This practice continued after the conflict was officially declared over and Qadhafi was no longer in power.

Torture and other forms of ill-treatment took place in Bani Walid. Qadhafi forces and the *thuwar* used torture to exact revenge against their political opponents as well as against the civilian population. Qadhafi forces beat people with rifles, handcuffed their hands behind their backs and insulted them. The *thuwar* also engaged in acts of torture and other forms of ill-treatment against suspected Qadhafi loyalists in the wake of the fall of the Qadhafi regime.

Reports show that freedom of expression was restricted in Bani Walid. The detention of journalists from Misrata on 9 July 2012 by *thuwar* constitutes an act of limitation of the right to freedom of expression.

Reports indicate that Qadhafi forces used civilians as human shields by placing weapons on the rooftops of civilian homes. These tactics constitute an attack against civilians as it intentionally places civilian lives in danger. The *thuwar* were widely accused of looting and pillaging villages in Bani Walid. The May 28 Katiba, in particular, was one of the worst offenders as they vandalized property and raided homes.

During interviews the CoI was consistently told about how Bani Walid was placed under siege by the *thuwar*. While it was clear that areas of

---

[195] *Id.* at Annex I, ¶ 199; HUMAN RIGHTS WATCH, *Libya: 10 protestors apparently executed, supra* note 14.

the city had been struck by direct and indirect fire from weapons such as recoilless rifles and Grad rockets, the damage observed was not extensive. Bani Walid was not destroyed as Sirte and Misrata were during the war. The local population was more enflamed by what they described as continued pillaging by *thuwar* groups. The conflict in Bani Walid after the fall of the regime demonstrated the continued tensions that were a result of Qadhafi's patronage system and divisive policies. The lack of coordination between the NTC and *thuwar* forces was evident during the final fight for Bani Walid, indicating the challenges that would face the post-Qadhafi government. The experience in Bani Walid is important for understanding the enduring challenges to reconciliation and social cohesion in post-conflict Libya.

CHAPTER FIFTEEN

SIRTE

1. Introduction

Sirte is a major Libyan city lying on the western edge of the Gulf of Sidra. With approximately 100,000 residents, it is one of the largest cities in the country and an important center of the Libyan oil industry.[1]

The city of Sirte lies directly on the Mediterranean Coast. The nearest cities are Misrata, roughly 200 kilometers (125 miles) to the northwest, and Ra's Lanuf, roughly 150 kilometers (95 miles) to the southeast.[2] Sirte sits on the eastern edge of the Tripolitania province, near the dividing line between eastern and western Libya. The city of Sirte grew along with the oil industry after 1960, becoming the first major city to the west of the oil fields in the Sirte Basin.[3]

As the birthplace of Qadhafi, Sirte benefitted greatly during his time in power.[4] Qadhafi built up the city considerably and used it as a luxurious spot to host foreign dignitaries and other important guests. It was also the place where the Sirte Declaration was signed in 1999 that laid the foundation for the establishment of the African Union.[5]

Throughout Qadhafi's rule, some tribes were favored and offered more opportunities for advancement and employment than others. The three largest among these privileged tribes were the Qadhadhfa – the tribe to which Qadhafi belonged – the Magarha and the Warfalla. The Qadhadhfa tribe was particularly dominant in Sirte and while small in comparison to other tribes, its members took on a prominent political role under

---

[1] *Profile: Sirte*, BBC, Sept. 18, 2011, *available at* http://www.bbc.co.uk/news/world-africa-12885322.

[2] *Sirte*, WOLFRAMALPHA, *available at* http://www.wolframalpha.com/input/?i=sirte; Rob Crilly, *Libya: the battle for control of Sirte*, THE TELEGRAPH, Aug. 25, 2011, *available at* http://www.telegraph.co.uk/news/worldnews/africaandindianocean/libya/8723027/Libya-the-battle-for-control-of-Sirte.html.

[3] BBC, *Profile: Sirte*, *supra* note 1.

[4] Nicholas Pelham, *The Battle for Libya*, N.Y. REVIEW OF BOOKS, Apr. 7, 2011 *available at* http://www.nybooks.com/articles/archives/2011/apr/07/battle-libya.

[5] BBC, *Profile: Sirte*, *supra* note 1.

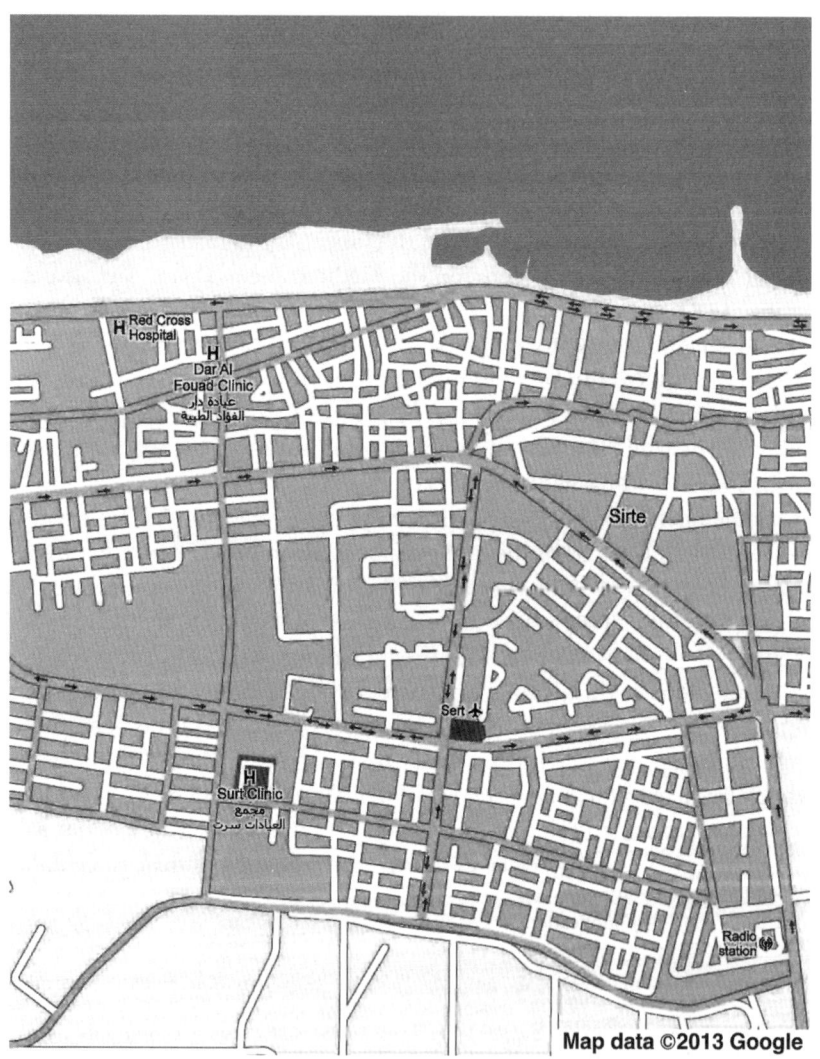

Map 12: Map of Sirte (Map data © 2013 Google).

Qadhafi and held key positions in the government and security apparatus.[6] Because of the longstanding loyalty to Qadhafi in the city, it was difficult for the *thuwar* to make any advancements on the city during the conflict.[7]

Sirte was of strategic importance for the Qadhafi forces during the civil war, particularly because it came to be the only city with a port on the Mediterranean Sea under regime control. The city was also home to a large number of troops throughout the Qadhafi era.[8] For this reason, the city became home to many regime loyalists and was the last regime stronghold during the civil war. It was also where Qadhafi made his last stand, and was killed on 20 October 2011.[9]

2. SUMMARY OF EVENTS

Unlike many other cities across Libya, Sirte did not witness mass uprisings in February 2011. Consequently, the city was spared intense fighting between Qadhafi and *thuwar* forces during the first months of the civil war. *Thuwar* did attempt to advance on the city in early March from Ra's Lanuf,[10] but were unable to take control and were met with thousands of Qadhafi troops who demonstrated their allegiance in the streets of Sirte.[11] While there was not much fighting in the city, during March the region experienced a heavy concentration of NATO strikes that sought to weaken the regime's military capacity around the Qadhafi stronghold.

---

[6] ANTHONY BELL ET AL., INSTITUTE FOR THE STUDY OF WAR, 4 THE LIBYAN REVOLUTION: THE TIDE TURNS 11, 26 (Nov. 2011), *available at* http://www.understandingwar.org/sites/default/files/Libya_Part4.pdf; *Uprising in Libya: Survival Hinges on Tribal Solidarity*, SPIEGEL ONLINE, Feb. 23, 2011, *available at* http://www.spiegel.de/international/world/0,1518,747234,00.html.

[7] Pelham, *The Battle for Libya, supra* note 4; VARUN VIRA & ANTHONY H. CORDESMAN, CENTER FOR STRATEGIC AND INTERNATIONAL STUDIES, THE LIBYAN UPRISING: AN UNCERTAIN TRAJECTORY 66 (June 20, 2011) [hereinafter "THE LIBYAN UPRISING"], *available at* http://csis.org/files/publication/110620_libya.pdf.

[8] *Id.* at 12.

[9] Ben Farmer, *Gaddafi's final stronghold falls: Libyan forces conquer Sirte*, THE TELEGRAPH, Oct. 20, 2011, *available at* http://www.telegraph.co.uk/news/worldnews/africaand-indianocean/libya/8838122/Gaddafis-final-stronghold-falls-Libyan-forces-conquer-Sirte.html.

[10] *See infra* Sec. 4. *See also* Dan Murphy, *In disorganized surge, Libya's rebels push west along shifting front line*, CHRISTIAN SCIENCE MONITOR, Mar. 5, 2011, *available at* http://www.csmonitor.com/World/Middle-East/2011/0305/In-disorganized-surge-Libya-s-rebels-push-west-along-shifting-front-line; *Gaddafi loyalists launch offensive*, AL JAZEERA, Mar. 11, 2011, *available at* http://www.aljazeera.com/news/africa/2011/03/201131041228856242.html.

[11] Evan Hill, *Rebel push stalls outside of Ras Lanuf*, AL JAZEERA, Mar. 10, 2011, *available at* http://www.aljazeera.com/indepth/spotlight/libya/2011/03/2011310131427537949.html.

NATO forces targeted the Libyan Air Force, including installations around Sirte, with strikes against important bases such as the Ma'atiga air base in Tripoli and the Gurdabiyya air base near Sirte during the initial phase of the NATO campaign.[12]

By mid-June, Qadhafi was faced with advances by *thuwar* forces on several fronts and the regime stronghold of Sirte played an important part in slowing the advance of the *thuwar* from the east.[13] Qadhafi stationed a large contingent of soldiers in Sirte to ensure the city remained under regime control. Throughout the month of June 2011, the regime faced incursions from *thuwar*.[14]

Qadhafi forces also used the city as a point of deployment to send reinforcements to other military theaters of operation. Throughout August, Qadhafi forces in Sirte launched attacks on Misrata and Brega. When *thuwar* attempted to advance on Sirte again the same month, Qadhafi forces from surrounding cities such as Brega, Al-Jufra, Sabha and Bani Walid were able to prevent *thuwar* from reaching the city. The National Transitional Council (NTC) reported that Qadhafi had issued a communiqué in which he had called on the population to fight the *thuwar* to the death.[15] The NTC expressed concerned that Sirte was being used to launch missiles toward Misrata.[16]

By late August 2011, the tide of the war had turned and the *thuwar* were rapidly taking control of several parts of the country. After the fall of Tripoli, *thuwar* began advancing toward Sirte in full force on 24 August. *Thuwar*, having already taken control of Brega and Ra's Lanuf, were moving in from the east. As *thuwar* from Misrata approached from the west, Qadhafi forces reportedly continued to deploy SCUD-B ballistic missiles towards Misrata.[17] In all, *thuwar* brigades from Darna, Al-Bayda, Ajdabiya, Brega and Misrata participated in the offensive against Sirte.[18]

---

[12] *See* Ch. III, Sec. 6.1. *See also* VIRA &. CORDESMAN, THE LIBYAN UPRISING, *supra* note 7 at 30.

[13] VIRA &. CORDESMAN, THE LIBYAN UPRISING, *supra* note 7 at 12.

[14] *Id.* at 7–11.

[15] Christopher Stephen, *Libyan rebels advance on Gaddafi's home town*, THE GUARDIAN, Aug. 24, 2011, *available at* http://www.guardian.co.uk/world/2011/aug/24/libya-rebels-advance-gaddafi-home-town.

[16] *Id.*

[17] *Id.*

[18] INTERNATIONAL CRISIS GROUP, HOLDING LIBYA TOGETHER: SECURITY CHALLENGES AFTER QADHAFI 25 (Dec. 14, 2011) [hereinafter "HOLDING LIBYA TOGETHER"], *available at* http://www.crisisgroup.org/~/media/Files/Middle%20East%20North%20Africa/

With Tripoli firmly in the hands of the *thuwar* by late August, the city of Sirte became the major focus of attention of both the *thuwar* and NATO forces. On 30 August, Mustafa ʿAbd al-Jalil of the NTC issued an ultimatum to the Qadhafi forces to surrender or face military action by the interim government forces.[19] On 1 September, Qaddafi declared Sirte the new Libyan capital, indicating that the city would be the site of the impending final battle of the war.[20] On 6 September, the NTC forces and *thuwar* brigades marched on Sirte, but Qadhafi forces were able to fight off their attempts to take control of the city. As the fighting continued, humanitarian conditions deteriorated, and food and water supplies in the city began to run low.[21]

NATO forces concentrated their operations on the city and, in addition to weakening the Qadhafi forces, the strikes led to civilian casualties, injuries and destruction of civilian infrastructure. On 16 September, a strike hit a large seven-story apartment complex called ʿImara al-Taʾmin in downtown Sirte.[22] The area had been the scene of intense fighting prior to the strike. Qadhafi forces allegedly had tried to occupy the building and position snipers on the roof of the complex, but it is not clear if they were able to do so.[23] A week later, on 25 September, a strike hit the home of Salam Diyab, the brother of a general in the Qadhafi military, also leading to civilian casualties.[24]

As the NATO campaign intensified, *thuwar* from Misrata and Benghazi encircled Sirte, meeting with heavy resistance from Qadhafi forces on

North%20Africa/115%20Holding%20Libya%20Together%20--%20Security%20Challenges%20after%20Qadhafi.pdf.

[19] *Libyan rebels give 4–day ultimatum to Gadhafi forces*, VOICE OF AMERICA, Aug. 30, 2011, *available at* http://blogs.voanews.com/breaking-news/2011/08/30/libyas-rebels-give-4-day-ultimatum-to-gadhafi-forces.

[20] *From voice said to be Gadhafi, a defiant message to his foes*, CNN, Sept. 1, 2011, *available at* http://articles.cnn.com/2011-09-01/world/libya.war_1_moammar-gadhafi-national-transitional-council-libyan-people.

[21] *Libya's Surt Short of Food, Water as Anti-Qaddafi Fighters Pursue Siege*, BLOOMBERG, Sept. 14 2011, *available at* http://www.bloomberg.com/news/2011-09-14/libya-s-Surt-lacking-food-water-as-anti-qaddafi-fighters-pursue-siege.html.

[22] *See infra* Sec. 4.

[23] *See* Ch. III, Sec. 6.2. *See also Errant NATO strikes in Libya: 13 Cases*, N.Y. TIMES, Dec. 16, 2011, *available at* http://www.nytimes.com/interactive/2011/12/16/world/africa/nato-air-strikes-in-libya.html?ref=africa#page/apartment-building.

[24] *See infra* Sec. 4. *See also* HUMAN RIGHTS WATCH, UNACKNOWLEDGED DEATHS: CIVILIAN CASUALTIES IN NATO's AIR CAMPAIGN IN LIBYA (May 2012) [hereinafter "UNACKNOWLEDGED DEATHS"], *available at* http://www.hrw.org/sites/default/files/reports/libya0512webwcover.pdf.

15–16 September.[25] *Thuwar* from Misrata entered the city but were forced back by Qadhafi's elite military units and snipers.[26] Over the coming days, Qadhafi and *thuwar* forces engaged in continuous street fighting.[27] During this time reports emerged that Qadhafi forces were hiding in urban areas and using civilians as human shields against *thuwar* and NATO forces.[28] The ground pressure and the air assault wore away at the Qadhafi defenses, and on 23 September, *thuwar* arrived from the east and entered the city without significant opposition.[29] In October, however, reports emerged of a disagreement between *thuwar* from Misrata and those from Benghazi and other parts of the east. The *thuwar* from the east complained that fighters from Misrata were misfiring shells and mortars that resulted in friendly-fire deaths.[30] The in-fighting between the *thuwar* groups made it difficult to sustain a coordinated attack against the remaining Qadhafi holdouts in the city.

The *thuwar* resorted to siege tactics, cutting off supplies from entering the city. By October, Qadhafi forces were running low on supplies and materials, and soldiers increasingly used whatever weapons they could find.[31] On 4 October, the *thuwar* began a major new offensive against the city. The battle was desperate and for the first time in the war there were reports that Qadhafi forces used a suicide bomber.[32] On October 7, the *thuwar* launched what they anticipated would be the final assault on Sirte. For the first time, the *thuwar* were able to launch a coordinated attack on three sides with hundreds of Grad rockets hitting the city.[33]

---

[25] Report of the International Commission of Inquiry on Libya, U.N. HRC. 19th Sess., Annex I, ¶ 95. U.N. Doc. A/HRC/19/68, advance unedited version (Mar. 2, 2012).

[26] *Libya conflict: NTC fighters meet Surt resistance,* BBC, Sept. 16, 2011, *available at* http://www.bbc.co.uk/news/world-africa-14941326.

[27] *After a day of intense fighting, anti-Gadhafi forces pull back,* CNN, Sept. 16, 2011, *available at* http://articles.cnn.com/2011-09-16/world/libya.war_1_anti-gadhafi-moammar-gadhafi-Surt.

[28] Rob Crilly, *Libya: Gaddafi loyalists 'using prisoners as human shields to protect Sirte',* THE TELEGRAPH, Sept. 11, 2011, *available at* http://www.telegraph.co.uk/news/worldnews/africaandindianocean/libya/8755935/Libya-Gaddafi-loyalists-using-prisoners-as-human-shields-to-protect-Sirte.html.

[29] *Libyan fighters ready for final Surt assault,* AL JAZEERA, Sept. 24, 2011, *available at* http://www.aljazeera.com/news/africa/2011/09/201192444319839381.html.

[30] Peter Beaumont, *In the chaos of Surt, anti-Gaddafi fighters are killing each other,* THE GUARDIAN, Oct. 14, 2011, *available at* http://www.guardian.co.uk/world/2011/oct/14/Surt-fighters-shoot-own-side.

[31] *Id.*

[32] *Gaddafi uses, for the first time, a suicide bomber against combatants,* ENNAHAR ONLINE, Oct. 6, 2011, *available at* http://www.ennaharonline.com/en/international/7404.html.

[33] *See infra* 11.3.4. *See also* Ruth Sherlock, *Libyan rebels launch the final push for Surt and their crowning victory,* THE TELEGRAPH, Oct. 7, 2011, *available at* http://www.telegraph

The month of October saw intense fighting in Sirte, with reports of substantial looting and ransacking.[34] Residents described the city as unrecognizable after weeks of the siege and heavy shelling. After a 13-day bombardment by *thuwar*, on 20 October *thuwar* defeated the last Qadhafi forces in Sirte.[35] During the chaotic final days, reports emerged of serious violations committed by both Qadhafi and *thuwar* forces. Qadhafi soldiers were accused of removing their uniforms and shooting at civilians.[36] *Thuwar* were accused of retribution killings and widespread looting.[37] Reports indicate that on 20 October, *thuwar* stopped several cars carrying Qadhafi soldiers attempting to flee the city and executed those inside.[38] Throughout the day *thuwar* pursued Qadhafi soldiers, who in turn were removing their uniforms.[39] *Thuwar* also appear to have engaged in widespread looting of homes of regime supporters. Reports indicated that the *thuwar* from Misrata committed these violations more often than other *thuwar* groups.[40]

On 20 October 20, Qadhafi was killed, marking the very final battle for Sirte. The details of his capture and killing remain unclear.[41] It appears that Qadhafi was leaving the city in a convoy which was attacked by French warplanes and a U.S. predator drone.[42] The CoI concluded that Qadhafi and his son Mu'tassim had been captured alive, but died in unclear circumstances.[43] It is reported that Qadhafi was captured and killed by members of the Misrata Katiba.[44] On 23 October, NTC leaders

---

.co.uk/news/worldnews/africaandindianocean/libya/8813811/Libyas-rebels-launch-the-final-push-for-Surt-and-their-crowning-victory.html.

[34] Hadeel Al-Shalchi, *Libya: Anti-Gaddafi Fighters Loot, Burn Homes In Sirte*, AP, Oct. 5, 2011, *available at* http://www.huffingtonpost.com/2011/10/05/libya-gaddafi-fighters-looting_n_997154.html.

[35] *Muammar Gaddafi killed as Surt falls*, AL JAZEERA, Oct. 21, 2011, *available at* http://www.aljazeera.com/news/africa/2011/10/2011102011520869621.html.

[36] *See infra* Sec. 3.4. *See also* Farmer, *Gaddafi's final stronghold falls: Libyan forces conquer Surt, supra* note 9.

[37] *See infra* 11.3.4.

[38] AL JAZEERA, *Muammar Gaddafi killed as Surt falls, supra* note 35.

[39] Farmer, *Gaddafi's final stronghold falls: Libyan forces conquer Surt, supra* note 9.

[40] *Surt fighter indignant at level of city's destruction*, THE DAILY STAR LEBANON, Oct. 20, 2011, *available at* http://www.dailystar.com.lb/News/Middle-East/2011/Oct-20/151711-Surt-fighter-indignant-at--level-of-citys-destruction.ashx#axzz1bKo54RwM.

[41] *See* Ch. IV, Sec. 6.3(a).

[42] Ian Black, *Muammar Gaddafi's 'trophy' body on show in Misrata meat store*, THE GUARDIAN, Oct. 22, 2011, *available at* http://www.guardian.co.uk/world/2011/oct/21/muammar-gaddafi-body-misrata-meat-store.

[43] Report of the International Commission of Inquiry, advance unedited version (Mar. 2, 2012), *supra* note 25 at Annex I, ¶ 96.

[44] For more on the *thuwar* fighter 'Umran Sha'ban believed to have discovered Qadhafi, who was later killed in Bani Walid, *see* Ch. V, Sec. 2.4 & Ch. XIV.

announced from Benghazi the official Declaration of Liberation and conclusion of hostilities following the death of Qadhafi and the surrender of
Sirte.[45] The United Nations then lifted the no-fly zone, and on 31 October
2011, NATO ceased its military operations.[46]

There were still many unresolved issues and a great deal of tension in
Sirte in the wake of Qadhafi's death. There was lingering resentment on
the side of Qadhafi loyalists, who viewed the abuses of the *thuwar* forces
and the actions of the NTC as retributive and collective punishment. The
city's residents saw support going to other cities that had shown support
for the *thuwar* during the conflict.[47] On 20 December, protesters in Sirte
gathered in a show of discontent with the transitional government, criticizing it for neglecting the city and punishing its citizens for past loyalties
to the former regime.[48]

Adding to these problems was the danger posed by weapons from the
war. Qadhafi had left behind an abundance of stockpiles of weapons,
many of which had been used in battle by the *thuwar,* and some of
which remained unused. Human Rights Watch (HRW) reported on vast
amounts of unsecured explosive weapons in the area of Sirte in October
2011, highlighting the deficiencies of the NTC in securing weapons in the
post-conflict period. Two unguarded sites near Sirte were examined by
HRW on 22 October, where they discovered surface-to-air missiles, tank
and mortar rounds, munitions and thousands of guided and unguided
aerial weapons.[49]

Armed *thuwar* groups continued to carry out violations in Sirte. The
beginning of 2012 saw the emergence of more reports regarding widespread arrests and incidents of torture and ill-treatment in *thuwar*

Ch. IX. Alastair Macdonald & Oliver Holmes, *Special Report: Libya – divided it stands,*
REUTERS, Dec. 16, 2011, *available at* http://www.reuters.com/article/2011/12/16/us-libya-
future-idUSTRE7BF0MG20111216.

[45] *Libya's new rulers declare country liberated,* BBC, Oct. 23, 2011, *available at* http://
www.bbc.co.uk/news/world-africa-15422262.

[46] Report of the International Commission of Inquiry, advance unedited version (Mar.
2, 2012), *supra* note 25 at Annex I, ¶ 98.

[47] *Shattered Gaddafi town says forgotten in new Libya,* REUTERS, Feb. 29, 2012, *available
at* http://www.reuters.com/article/2012/02/29/libya-Surt-idUSL5E8DT1WF20120229.

[48] Jon Donnison, *Surt and Misrata: A tale of two war-torn Libyan cities,* BBC, Dec. 20, 2011,
available at http://www.bbc.co.uk/news/world-africa-16257289.

[49] *Libya: Transitional Council Failing to Secure Weapons,* HUMAN RIGHTS WATCH,
Oct. 25, 2011, *available at* http://www.hrw.org/news/2011/10/25/libya-transitional-council-
failing-secure-weapons.

controlled detention facilities.[50] After the fall of Sirte, thousands of men were arrested, many of whom had played no role in the conflict but were swept up in the campaign of detentions.[51]

The population in Sirte also complained of neglect and a lack of assistance from the interim government. The city's infrastructure had been severely damaged during the war and many homes were destroyed. There were also reports of house raids in Sirte conducted by *thuwar* after the end of the war, with the city's residents being targeted in revenge attacks.[52]

The city did begin to see some promising advancements, such as the General National Congress elections that took place peacefully on 7 July 2012.[53] There were no reports of violence in the lead-up to the elections in Sirte, unlike other parts of Libya that witnessed violent resistance to the election process.

3. ILLUSTRATIONS OF THE VIOLATIONS

3.1. *Unlawful Killing*

(a) *Qadhafi Forces*

As a Qadhafi stronghold, Sirte was the site of several detention centers used to hold *thuwar* and suspected *thuwar* supporters detained in other theaters of military operations during the conflict.[54] While there are a number of documented incidents of torture and ill-treatment being carried out by Qadhafi forces in these detention centers,[55] there are no such documented cases of unlawful killings.

(b) Thuwar *Forces*

The CoI reported on cases of unlawful killings carried out by *thuwar* forces in Sirte. In one notable case, the CoI gathered evidence and testimonies

---

[50] *See infra* Sec. 3.3. *See also* Mark Urban, *Post-revolution Surt a breeding ground for unrest*, BBC, Feb. 21, 2012, *available at* http://www.bbc.co.uk/news/world-17116657.

[51] *See infra* Sec. 3.2. *See also Id.*

[52] Oliver Holmes, *FEATURE-Tense reconciliation begins with Libya's Saharan tribes*, REUTERS, Nov. 9, 2011, *available at* http://www.reuters.com/article/2011/11/09/libya-tuareg-idUSL6E7M83L220111109.

[53] *See* Ch. V, Sec. 6. *See also Libyans celebrate free vote despite violence*, REUTERS, July 7, 2012, *available at* http://www.reuters.com/article/2012/07/07/us-libya-elections-idUS-BRE86412N20120707.

[54] *See infra* Sec. 3.2. *See also* Ch. V, Sec. 2.3.

[55] *See infra* Sec. 3.3.

regarding the execution of suspected Qadhafi soldiers and loyalists that took place in October 2011 at the Mahari Hotel in Sirte. According to the CoI

> Local residents told the Commission that a large number of bodies (estimates ranging from 65 to 78) were discovered on 21 October 2011 at the Mahari Hotel – the day after the end of hostilities in Sirte and the capture and killing of Muammar Qadhafi.[56]

During its visit to the site, the CoI documented evidence suggesting the presence of several *thuwar kata'ib* in the hotel. They were

> ...the Tiger Brigade (*Katibat Al-*Nimer), the Support Brigade (*Katibat Al-Isnad*), the Jaguar Brigade (*Katibat Al-Fahad*), the Lion Brigade (*Katibat Al-Asad*), and the Citadel Brigade (*Al-Qasba*).[57]

Deaths also occurred in detention facilities controlled by *thuwar* forces. The CoI documented 12 such cases. The victims were identified as agents of Qadhafi's security forces or Tawerghans.[58]

Regarding the death of Qadhafi's son, Mu'tassim, the CoI examined video footage which showed him alive, and then in the custody of *thuwar* after having been captured. However, the CoI has not been able to gather any accounts or obtain any report on the circumstances of his death and is, therefore, not able to confirm that the death of Mu'tassim Qadhafi was an unlawful killing.[59]

i. The Tawerghans

As in other areas where the *thuwar* took control, particularly in the region between Misrata and Sirte, Tawerghans were subjected to arrests, torture, other forms of ill-treatment and killings at the hands of *thuwar* groups.[60] The CoI was informed, for instance, about the execution in October 2011 of 17 captured Tawerghans at the hands of *thuwar* from Misrata.[61] The CoI also reported the killing of a Tawerghan man who had been a soldier with the Qadhafi forces, captured and shot in Sirte in October 2011 by *thuwar* from Misrata.[62] In another incident, a Tawerghan man died in custody as

---

[56] Report of the International Commission of Inquiry, advance unedited version (Mar. 2, 2012), *supra* note 25 at ¶ 215.

[57] *Id.* at ¶ 216.

[58] *See infra* Sec. 3.6. *See also* Report of the International Commission of Inquiry, advance unedited version (Mar. 2, 2012), *supra* note 25 at ¶ 31.

[59] Report of the International Commission of Inquiry, advance unedited version (Mar. 2, 2012), *supra* note 25 at ¶ 34.

[60] *See supra* Secs. 2.3, 5.3, 7.3 & 9.3. *See also Id.* at ¶ 58.

[61] *Id.* at ¶ Annex I, ¶ 429.

[62] *Id.* at ¶ Annex I, ¶ 220.

a result of torture by *thuwar* from Misrata in January 2012 when, according to survivors, the victim was taken from his cell and never returned.[63] Also a former soldier, the victim had been detained in Sirte and held in various detention centers.

On 16 April 2012, the body of a Tawerghan man who had been killed in detention was delivered to his family. The body showed signs of torture. The man had allegedly been arrested in October 2011 outside of Sirte after fleeing the fighting in the city. He was detained by Misrata *thuwar* and died in custody in a facility reportedly under the authority of the Misrata Security Committee.[64]

3.2. *Arbitrary Detentions and Enforced Disappearances*

(a) *Qadhafi Forces*

Several NGOs collected evidence of *thuwar* fighters and suspected opposition supporters being arbitrarily detained in Sirte. Physicians for Human Rights (PHR) recorded cases where interviewees reported their relatives had been detained in other cities, particularly from the east, before being transferred to Sirte.[65] PHR took the testimony of one individual who stated that he had been arrested in Ajdabiya on 17 March 2011, and driven through the night to Sirte with 26 other detainees and held incommunicado for three weeks. He was kept in a cell with 15 other men, in a detention facility with approximately 150 total detainees.[66]

One witness who spoke with Amnesty International reported that he had been arrested on 18 March 2011 by Qadhafi forces in Brega and taken to a detention facility in Sirte where he shared a cell with detainees from various *thuwar* controlled cities.[67] Other witnesses gave accounts that

---

[63] *Id.* at Annex I, ¶ 232.

[64] Amnesty International, 'We are not safe anywhere', Tawarghas in Libya 5 (June 8, 2012), *available at* http://www.amnesty.org/en/library/asset/MDE19/007/2012/en/514d579a-3e2b-4f89-ba8b-6f17d479c617/mde190072012en.pdf.

[65] Physicians for Human Rights, Witness to War Crimes: Evidence from Misrata, Libya 18 (Aug. 2011) [hereinafter "Witness to War Crimes"], *available at* https://s3.amazonaws.com/PHR_Reports/Libya-WitnesstoWarCrimes-Aug2011.pdf; Amnesty International, Libya: Detainees, Disappeared and Missing 9 (Mar. 29, 2011), *available at* http://www.amnesty.org/en/library/asset/MDE19/011/2011/en/569f0509-c3db-433f-b023-89aea68dde8e/mde190112011en.pdf.

[66] Physicians for Human Rights, Witness to War Crimes, *supra* note 65 at 12.

[67] Amnesty International, The Battle for Libya: Killings, disappearances and torture 66 (Sept. 2011) [hereinafter "The Battle for Libya"], *available at* http://www.amnesty.org/en/library/asset/MDE19/025/2011/en/8f2e1c49-8f43-46d3-917d-383c17d36377/mde190252011en.pdf.

their relatives were taken by Qadhafi forces from Bin Jawad in early March 2011 and reportedly transported to the Al-Sa'idi Katiba military compound in Sirte.[68] Amnesty International also reported that during the conflict, *thuwar* supporters were allegedly taken to the military police barracks for detention in Sirte.[69]

(b) Thuwar *Forces*

Thuwar forces carried out sweeping arrests in the aftermath of battles in which they had prevailed in Sirte as in the rest of Libya. Persons suspected of working in the Qadhafi regime, or persons from areas believed to have either supported Qadhafi, were arrested and held for extended periods without charge.[70] Following their victory in Sirte, the NTC forces detained and interrogated a number of Libyans and foreigners in the city.[71]

i. *The Tawerghans*

Witnesses told the CoI that armed members of the Qaria al-Mujahda *thuwar* from Misrata came to a farm in Sirte in mid-September 2011, where several Tawerghan families were living. They arrested eight men without giving reasons for their arrest and without informing their families where they were taking the men.[72]

3.3. *Torture and Other Forms of Ill-treatment*

(a) *Qadhafi Forces*

Detention facilities in Sirte were used during the conflict by Qadhafi forces for interrogation and torture, often carried out by intelligence agents with the aim of extracting information about *thuwar* movements in other theaters of the conflict.[73] Amnesty International reported that detainees held

---

[68] *Libya: Campaign of enforced disappearances must end*, AMNESTY INTERNATIONAL, Mar. 29, 2011, *available at* http://www.amnesty.org/en/news-and-updates/report/libya-campaign-enforced-disappearances-must-end-2011-03-29.

[69] THE BATTLE FOR LIBYA, AMNESTY INTERNATIONAL, *supra* note 67 at 58.

[70] Report of the International Commission of Inquiry, advance unedited version (Mar. 2, 2012), *supra* note 25 at Annex I, ¶ 256.

[71] Ian Black, *Gaddafi loyalists face torture, human rights groups warn*, THE GUARDIAN, Oct. 21, 2011, *available at* http://www.guardian.co.uk/world/2011/oct/21/gaddafi-loyalists-torture-human-rights.

[72] Report of the International Commission of Inquiry, advance unedited version (Mar. 2, 2012), *supra* note 25 at Annex I, ¶ 428. For more on arbitrary arrests and enforced disappearances carried out during the conflict, *see* Ch. V, Sec. 2.3.

[73] For more on the interrogation and torture of prisoners in detention centers run by Qadhafi's intelligence services, *see infra* Sec. 3.4.

in Sirte and Tripoli claimed to have been tortured and mistreated, especially upon arrest and during the initial period of detention. Several stated they had been shot at after they were arrested.[74]

Amnesty International spoke with a witness who stated that he had been arrested by members of Qadhafi's Internal Security Agency (ISA) and held in military police barracks in Sirte where he was handcuffed and blindfolded. Guards beat the detainee with rifle butts, pressed scalding hot rifle barrels on his skin and suspended him by his arms, which were tied behind his back.[75] There were numerous other accounts of detainees who were blindfolded during interrogation in Sirte. Some detainees were forced to sign pledges to defend the Qadhafi regime and denounce the opposition movement.[76]

(b) *Thuwar Forces*

Amnesty International documented the use of torture by *thuwar* forces in detention facilities in and around Tripoli, including in Sirte.[77] Detainees held in Sirte reported that they were beaten with chains, bars and wooden sticks, and electrocuted with live wires and suspended in uncomfortable positions.[78] Media reports also indicate that individuals captured during the battles for Sirte near the end of the conflict were tortured and interrogated for information regarding the tactics and movements of the Qadhafi forces.[79]

i. *The Tawerghans*
Tawerghans were targeted by *thuwar* in Sirte for attacks that included violations of torture and ill-treatment.[80] The CoI documented a case of four Tawerghan men arrested, detained and tortured in Sirte in late December 2011 by *thuwar* from Misrata. As in several other cases across Libya, the Tawerghan men were tortured by *thuwar* forces and coerced into confessing to crimes of rape in Misrata. The men told the CoI that

---

[74] The Battle for Libya, Amnesty International, *supra* note 67 at 65.

[75] *Id.* at 66.

[76] *Id.*

[77] Amnesty International, Militias threaten hopes for New Libya 6 (Feb. 16, 2012), *available at* http://www.amnesty.org/en/library/asset/MDE19/002/2012/en/dd7c1d69-e368-44de-8ee8-cc9365bd5eb3/mde190022012en.pdf.

[78] *Libya: 'Out of control' militias commit widespread abuses, a year on from uprising*, Amnesty International, Feb. 15, 2012, *available at* http://www.amnesty.org/en/news/libya-out-control-militias-commit-widespread-abuses-year-uprising-2012-02-15.

[79] Black, *Gaddafi loyalists face torture, human rights groups warn, supra* note 71.

[80] Report of the International Commission of Inquiry, advance unedited version (Mar. 2, 2012), *supra* note 25 at Annex I, ¶ 430.

> In the course of their detention, in various locations over the course of two weeks, the men were reportedly stripped, kicked in the back, hit with baseball bats, beaten with wooden sticks and electric cables, and handcuffed at the ankles and wrists for days.[81]

The CoI reviewed medical reports as well as photographs of the four victims that detailed the extensive physical trauma that the men had experienced, and noted that the men still showed visible injuries.[82]

3.4. *Attacks on Civilians, Civilian Objects, Protected Persons and Objects*

(a) *Qadhafi Forces*

There were attacks against civilians carried out by Qadhafi forces reported in the first months of the conflict. The CoI gathered testimony from a witness who reported that his house was raided by Qadhafi forces in April 2011. The man had been interviewed in a refugee camp in Tunisia, appearing on television condemning the violence committed by the Qadhafi forces in the Nafusa Mountains region. He returned to find his home in Sirte looted and ransacked.[83]

HRW reported that during the final fight for Sirte in September and October 2011 Qadhafi forces fired on the vehicles of civilians trying to flee the city.[84] There were also reported cases of members of the Qadhafi forces removing their uniforms and shooting at civilians.[85] Médecins Sans Frontières estimated that 10,000 civilians were trapped and living in dire conditions in Sirte in October. Reports indicate that the Qadhafi forces in these areas used civilians as human shields and prevented them from escaping.[86]

(b) Thuwar *Forces*

During the final battle for Sirte, *thuwar* forces used indiscriminate weapons that caused civilian casualties, and carried out heavy destruction of civilian

---

[81] *Id.* (internal citations omitted).

[82] *Id.*

[83] *Id.* at Annex I, ¶ 719.

[84] *Libya: Protect Civilians in Surt Fighting*, HUMAN RIGHTS WATCH, Oct. 12, 2011, *available at* http://www.hrw.org/news/2011/10/12/libya-protect-civilians-sirte-fighting.

[85] Farmer, *Gaddafi's final stronghold falls: Libyan forces conquer Surt, supra* note 9.

[86] Peter Beaumont, *Gaddafi loyalists hold out in last desperate resistance at Surt, as families flee*, THE GUARDIAN, Oct. 16, 2011, *available at* http://www.guardian.co.uk/world/2011/oct/16/libya-sirte-families-flee-gaddafi.

buildings in the city.[87] The CoI found that the *thuwar* used Grad rockets and heavy machine-guns, leaving dozens of buildings uninhabitable.[88] Numerous buildings showed evidence of shells consistent with fire from 106mm recoilless rifles and 107mm rocket artillery, using both High-Explosive Anti-Tank rounds and High-Explosive Squash Head rounds.[89] The CoI noted that some of the buildings were likely used by the Qadhafi forces and were therefore legitimate targets. However, the widespread damage indicated that the shelling was of an indiscriminate nature. Mortars were also widely used by *thuwar*.[90] HRW documented evidence that during the battle for Sirte the civilian population lived without water and electricity and that *thuwar* repeatedly shelled and fired barrages of Grad rockets at residential neighborhoods in the city.[91]

The use of indiscriminate weapons was not the only form of attacks on civilians and civilian objects documented in Sirte. Misratan *thuwar*, in particular, targeted those suspected of supporting the Qadhafi regime for acts of retribution.[92] HRW reported that Misratan fighters engaged in looting private property and torching the homes of families suspected of supporting the regime.[93] Media reports similarly indicate widespread looting and destruction of private property by *thuwar* after taking control of Sirte, including the theft of furniture and cars.[94] There are also reports that *thuwar* set up checkpoints at which they stole the property and cars of people trying to leave the city.[95] These reports correspond to accounts documented by the CoI of residents of Sirte who fled the town due to the intensifying fighting, and upon return found their homes looted.[96]

---

[87] *See* Ch. II, Sec. 3.3.

[88] Report of the International Commission of Inquiry, advance unedited version (Mar. 2, 2012), *supra* note 25 at Annex I, ¶¶ 575–81.

[89] *Id.*

[90] *Id.*

[91] HUMAN RIGHTS WATCH, *Libya: Protect Civilians in Surt Fighting, supra* note 84.

[92] Daniel Williams, *The Murder Brigades of Misrata*, HUMAN RIGHTS WATCH, Oct. 28, 2011, *available at* http://www.hrw.org/news/2011/10/28/murder-brigades-misrata.

[93] HUMAN RIGHTS WATCH, *Libya: Protect Civilians in Surt Fighting, supra* note 84.

[94] Al-Shalchi, *Libya: Anti-Gaddafi Fighters Loot, Burn Homes In Sirte, supra* note 34.

[95] *In Gaddafi's hometown, residents accuse NTC fighters of revenge*, REUTERS, Oct. 16, 2011, *available at* http://www.reuters.com/article/2011/10/16/us-libya-Surt-looting-idUS-TRE79F2DL20111016.

[96] Report of the International Commission of Inquiry, advance unedited version (Mar. 2, 2012), *supra* note 25 at Annex I, ¶ 53.

3.5. *Prohibited Weapons*

(a) *Qadhafi Forces*

There were reports of unexploded and abandoned ordinance causing contamination in the areas around Sirte.[97] Remnants of Type-84 anti-vehicle submunitions were found in Sirte by the Swiss Foundation for Mine Action (FSD) after the conflict.[98]

3.6. *Targeting Specific Groups*

(b) Thuwar *Forces*

i. *The Tawerghans*

As noted above, members of the Tawerghan community were targeted for attacks in Sirte by *thuwar* groups from Misrata during and in the wake of the September and October 2011 fighting.[99] Tawerghans were arrested, detained, tortured[100] and in some cases executed.[101]

3.7. *The Use of Children and Their Treatment in Armed Conflict*

(a) *Qadhafi Forces*

The CoI visited detention centers and interviewed three detainees under the age of 18 who had fought with the Qadhafi forces before being detained by the Misrata *thuwar*.[102] One of the minors was from Sirte, where he reported the Qadhafi regime had an office used to recruit volunteers to fight.[103]

4. THE ROLE OF NATO

As was the case in other parts of Libya, the NATO campaign played a definitive role in the success of the *thuwar* operations in Sirte. The early

---

[97] *Libya: Mine Action*, LANDMINE & CLUSTER MUNITION MONITOR, Updated Dec. 17, 2012, *available at* http://www.the-monitor.org/custom/index.php/region_profiles/print_theme/1955#_ftnref2.

[98] *Id.*

[99] Report of the International Commission of Inquiry, advance unedited version (Mar. 2, 2012), *supra* note 25 at Annex I, ¶ 427.

[100] *Id.* at Annex I, ¶ 430.

[101] *Id.* at Annex I, ¶ 429.

[102] *See infra* Sec. 3.11.

[103] *See also Id.* at Annex I, ¶¶ 701–702. For more on the use of children in the conflict, *See* Ch. V, 2.12.

strikes in March 2011 targeted the Libyan Air Force and Navy facilities in and around Sirte, with the aim of weakening the regime's military power in the region. On 19 May, NATO began heavily attacking Qadhafi forces by air, destroying naval carriers in the ports of Tripoli, Khums and Sirte.[104] Throughout the month of March, NATO forces heavily targeted the Libyan Air Force, severely damaging its deployment and operational capability. The strikes involved targeting important installations such as the Maʿatiga air base in Tripoli and the Gurdabiyya air base near Sirte.[105] Strikes in the region continued in the early months of the conflict, and on 6 May, NATO reportedly destroyed approximately 20 FROG-7 missile launchers and 20–30 SCUD canisters near Sirte.[106]

Near the end of the conflict, strikes in September and October 2011 were critical to the ability of the *thuwar* forces to take the city. NATO also conducted controversial airstrikes in Sirte that resulted in civilian casualties, however. HRW gathered evidence that a civilian home was hit on 16 September, when NATO attacked an apartment complex called ʿImara al-Ta'min.[107] A pregnant woman and a young man were reportedly killed. Several persons were also injured, including one four-year-old girl who suffered shrapnel wounds from the strike.[108]

In another incident on 16 September, an airstrike destroyed two pick-up trucks in Sirte belonging to Qadhafi forces, reportedly killing 30 individuals gathered on the street.[109] According to NATO, the military vehicles had been firing into civilian areas and authorization was given to engage them when they were clear of the populated area.[110] The CoI found that

---

[104] Vira &. Cordesman, The Libyan Uprising, *supra* note 7 at 29.

[105] *Id.* at 30.

[106] *Whatever Happened to Libya's Scud-Bs?*, International Institute for Strategic Studies 23, Mar. 2011, *available at* http://www.iiss.org/whats-new/iiss-voices/?blogpost=154; David Cenciotti, *Operation Unified Protector (was Odyssey Dawn) explained (Day 39–42)*, The Aviationist, Apr. 30, 2011, *available at* http://theaviationist.com/2011/04/30/operation-unified-protector-was-odyssey-dawn-explained-day-39-42/; *RAF destroys Qaddafi rocket launchers*, UK Ministry of Defence, May 9, 2011, *available at* http://www.global security.org/military/library/news/2011/05/mil-110509-ukmod01.htm; Vira &. Cordesman, The Libyan Uprising, *supra* note 7 at 35.

[107] The transliteration of this place name was adopted from the reference. Human Rights Watch, Unacknowledged Deaths, *supra* note 24 at 53.

[108] *See* Ch. III, Sec. 6.2. *See also* N.Y. Times, *Errant NATO strikes in Libya: 13 Cases*, *supra* note 23.

[109] *See* Ch. III, Sec. 6.2.

[110] Letter from Paul Olson to Philippe Kirsch, Chair of the International Commission of Inquiry (Feb. 15, 2012), *in* Report of the International Commission of Inquiry, advance unedited version (Mar. 2, 2012), *supra* note 25 at Annex II.

while the vehicles could be considered a legal target they were engaged within close proximity of civilian structures only 30 meters away.[111]

A week later, on 25 September, NATO carried out two airstrikes in central Sirte on the home of Salam Diyab – the brother of Brigadier General Musba Ahmad Diyab.[112] Neighbors and family members said the general and seven of his relatives were killed inside, but this could not confirmed.[113] Local residents told HRW that General Diyab was a senior military figure who commanded the Jeraf military base outside of Sirte and head of the Al-Shahid Muftah Spaya Katiba.[114] Although the site could have constituted a legitimate military target, HRW found that the loss of civilian life appeared disproportionate to the expected military gain.[115]

5. Conclusion

Sirte was the hometown of Qadhafi and its people were among his most steadfast supporters. The city saw very little protest during the initial stages of the conflict, and thereafter was primarily a launching ground for attacks on cities controlled by *thuwar* forces. Sirte was one of the last Libyan cities to hold out against the *thuwar*, and was the place where Qadhafi was killed. The battle for Sirte exacted a substantial toll on the civilian population and the city's infrastructure. Likewise, the aftermath of the battle saw serious violations against the civilian population and those suspected to have taken part in the fighting.

Ultimately, the final battle between the *thuwar* and regime forces in Sirte was highly destructive and bloody, leaving dozens dead on both sides. In this sense, it can be seen as a microcosm of the larger battle for Libya. Following the *thuwar* victory a sense of jubilation rose in the streets of Sirte, as both civilians – who had suffered weeks of siege – and *thuwar* celebrated the official end of the war. While the final battle for Sirte marked the end of official hostilities, it did not mark the beginning of a peaceful transition. Violations persisted in Sirte, alongside discontent

---

[111] Report of the International Commission of Inquiry, advance unedited version (Mar. 2, 2012), *supra* note 25 at Annex I, ¶ 96.

[112] *See* Ch. IV, 6.2. *See also* Human Rights Watch, Unacknowledged Deaths, *supra* note 24 at 47.

[113] N.Y. Times, *Errant NATO strikes in Libya: 13 Cases*, *supra* note 23; Human Rights Watch, Unacknowledged Deaths, *supra* note 24 at 47.

[114] The transliteration of this name was adopted from the reference. Human Rights Watch, Unacknowledged Deaths, *supra* note 24 at 48.

[115] Human Rights Watch, Unacknowledged Deaths, *supra* note 24 at 50.

and resentment among a population that had received special treatment under Qadhafi.[116] The city had experienced serious destruction, and many in Sirte blamed the NTC for failing to help the city rebuild. In many ways, the challenges in Sirte represented the plethora of post-conflict problems that arose in the wake of Qadhafi's death.

The fighting during the conflict and in the aftermath of the death of Qadhafi involved serious violations committed by both sides in Sirte. *Thuwar* forces were involved in the deaths of members of the Qadhafi forces and suspected loyalists. The incident at the Mahari Hotel in Sirte is one of the most notable incidents of all the theaters of military operations of summary executions of Qadhafi supporters and loyalists being carried out by *thuwar* forces

There are reported cases of arbitrary detention and enforced disappearances in Sirte. Qadhafi forces used detention facilities in the city to hold *thuwar* fighters and supporters detained in the region as well as in other cities. As the battle progressed and *thuwar* gained more ground in Sirte, there were several reports of abduction, arbitrary detention and enforced disappearances at the hands of the *thuwar*.

Torture was used by the Qadhafi forces to extract information and to intimidate opposition. Qadhafi's ISA is reported to have been responsible for torture and ill-treatment in Sirte. Blindfolding, handcuffing and beating detainees are some of the documented abuses against suspected *thuwar* fighters and supporters. *Thuwar* also engaged in acts of torture, particularly after securing Sirte in the wake of the death of Qadhafi.

Reports indicate that Qadhafi forces used civilians as human shields by hiding themselves in residential areas and preventing civilians from leaving the area. Qadhafi forces used violence and threats to intimidate residents into staying in the area, where they were subjected to direct attack by *thuwar*. In doing so, Qadhafi forces intentionally placed civilians in harm's way.

Reports also indicate that *thuwar* shelled and fired volleys of Grad rockets at residential neighborhoods. While there are reports that Qadhafi forces were stationed in some of these neighborhoods, the attacks were conducted from several kilometers away and with weapons that can only be used indiscriminately. *Thuwar* forces also destroyed property, carrying out acts of arson, looting and theft in the aftermath of the battle.

---

[116] *Gaddafi 'remains in the hearts' of Surt*, BBC, Feb. 9, 2012, *available at* http://news.bbc .co.uk/today/hi/today/newsid_9694000/9694560.stm.

Tawerghans were particularly targeted by *thuwar* forces and were victims of torture and murder.

The use of prohibited weapons, primarily landmines, was reported in Sirte. Qadhafi forces used mines to halt *thuwar* advances in the region, and there are reports of Type-84 anti-vehicle submunitions found in Sirte in the wake of the conflict.

Reports also indicate the extensive NATO airstrikes in and around Sirte, noting that several strikes hit non-military targets causing civilian casualties, including a residential home belonging to a regime general and an apartment building. On the basis of the available information, it can reasonably be concluded that NATO air strikes hit *thuwar* and civilian targets, causing numerous casualties.

TABLE OF AUTHORITIES

Books

ALI ABDULLATIF AHMIDA, THE MAKING OF MODERN LIBYA: STATE FORMATION, COLONIZATION, AND RESISTANCE (Albany, USA: SUNY Press, 2d ed., 2009)

YUSUF AKSAR, IMPLEMENTING INTERNATIONAL HUMANITARIAN LAW (New York, USA: Routledge, 2004)

ESAM AL-AMIN, THE ARAB AWAKENING: UNDERSTANDING TRANSFORMATIONS AND REVOLUTIONS IN THE MIDDLE EAST (American Educational Trust, 2013)

M. CHERIF BASSIOUNI, CRIMES AGAINST HUMANITY: HISTORICAL EVOLUTION AND CONTEMPORARY APPLICATION (Cambridge, UK: Cambridge University Press, 2011)

——, CRIMES AGAINST HUMANITY IN INTERNATIONAL CRIMINAL LAW (The Hague, The Netherlands: Kluwer Law International, 2d rev. ed. 1999)

—— ET AL., THE CHICAGO PRINCIPLES ON POST-CONFLICT JUSTICE (Chicago, USA: International Human Rights Law Institute, 2008), *available at* http://www.law.depaul.edu/centers_institutes/ihrli/pdf/chicago_principles.pdf

——, 1–2 DOCUMENTS ON THE ARAB-ISRAELI CONFLICT: EMERGENCE OF CONFLICT IN PALESTINE AND THE ARAB-ISRAELI WARS AND PEACE PROCESS (M. Cherif Bassiouni ed., Ardsley, USA: Transnational Publishers, 2005)

——, 1 INTERNATIONAL CRIMINAL LAW: INTERNATIONAL CRIMES (Leiden, The Netherlands: Martinus Nijhoff, 3d rev. ed. 2008)

——, INTRODUCTION TO INTERNATIONAL CRIMINAL LAW, SECOND REVISED EDITION (Leiden, The Netherlands: Martinus Nijhoff, 2d ed., 2013)

——, THE ISLAMIC CRIMINAL JUSTICE SYSTEM (Dobbs-Ferry, USA: Oceana Publications, 1982)

——, THE *SHARĪ'A* AND ISLAMIC PUBLIC LAW IN TIME OF PEACE AND WAR (Cambridge, UK: Cambridge University Press, forthcoming 2014)

M. CHERIF BASSIOUNI & EDWARD WISE, AUT DEDERE AUT JUDICARE: THE DUTY TO EXTRADITE OR PROSECUTE IN INTERNATIONAL LAW (Dordrecht, The Netherlands: Martinus Nijhoff Publishers, 1995)

BLACK'S LAW DICTIONARY 996 (St. Paul, US: West, 9th ed. 2009)

CHARLES T. CALL, WHY PEACE FAILS: THE CAUSES AND PREVENTION OF CIVIL WAR RECURRENCE (Washington, USA: Georgetown University Press, 2012)

ANDREW CLAPHAM, HUMAN RIGHTS OBLIGATIONS OF NON-STATE ACTORS (Oxford, UK: Oxford University Press 2006)

SHANE DARCY & JOSEPH POWDERLY, JUDICIAL CREATIVITY AT THE INTERNATIONAL CRIMINAL TRIBUNALS (Oxford, UK: Oxford University Press, 2011)

GERALD I.A.D. DRAPER, THE RED CROSS CONVENTIONS OF 1949 (New York, USA: Praeger, 1958)

THE MIDDLE EAST STRATEGIC BALANCE 2002–2003 (Kam Ephraim & Yiftah S. Shapir eds., Tel Aviv, Israel: Center for Strategic Studies at Tel Aviv University, Dec. 28, 2009)

CUSTOMARY INTERNATIONAL HUMANITARIAN LAW (Jean-Marie Henckaerts & Louise Doswald-Beck eds., Cambridge, UK: Cambridge University Press, 2d ed. 2013)

HANS KÖCHLER, THE SECURITY COUNCIL AS ADMINISTER OF JUSTICE (Vienna, Austria: International Progress Organization, 2011)

W. THOMAS MALLISON & SALLY MALLISON, THE PALESTINE PROBLEM IN INTERNATIONAL LAW AND WORLD ORDER (Essex, UK: Longman, 1983)

LUIS MARTÍNEZ, THE LIBYAN PARADOX (New York, USA: Columbia University Press, 2007)

HILAIRE MCCOUBREY, INTERNATIONAL HUMANITARIAN LAW (Brookfield, USA: Gower Pub. Co., 1990)

MARC LYNCH, THE ARAB UPRISING: THE UNFINISHED REVOLUTIONS OF THE NEW MIDDLE EAST (Public Affairs, 2012)

LIBYA: A COUNTRY STUDY (Helen Chapin Metz ed., Washington, USA: Federal Research Division, Library of Congress, 1989)

ALISON PARGETER, LIBYA: THE RISE AND FALL OF QADDAFI (New Haven, USA: Yale University Press, 2012)

JEAN PICTET, 1–4 COMMENTARY ON THE GENEVA CONVENTIONS OF 12 AUGUST 1949 (Geneva, Switzerland: International Committee of the Red Cross, 1952)

JEAN PICTET, DEVELOPMENT AND PRINCIPLES OF INTERNATIONAL HUMANITARIAN LAW (Dordrecht, The Netherlands: Martinus Nijhoff Publishers, 1985)

DAVIDE RODONGO, FASCISM'S EUROPEAN EMPIRE: ITALIAN OCCUPATION DURING THE SECOND WORLD WAR (Cambridge, UK: Cambridge University Press, 2006)

COMMENTARY ON THE ADDITIONAL PROTOCOLS OF 8 JUNE 1977 TO THE GENEVA CONVENTIONS OF 12 AUGUST 1949 (Y. Sandoz et al. eds., Dordrecht, The Netherlands: Martinus Nijhoff Publishers, 1987)

IBRAHIM SHIHATA, THE POWER OF THE INTERNATIONAL COURT TO DETERMINE ITS OWN JURISDICTION: COMPETENCE DE LA COMPETENCE (The Hague, The Netherlands: Martinus Nijhoff Publishers, 1965)

THE MIDDLE EAST STRATEGIC BALANCE 2004–2005 (Zvi Shtauber & Yiftah S. Shapir eds., Brighton, UK: Sussex Academic Press, 2009)

GEOFF SIMONS, LIBYA: THE STRUGGLE FOR SURVIVAL (New York, USA: St. Martin's Press, 1996)

ACCOUNTABILITY FOR ATROCITIES: NATIONAL AND INTERNATIONAL RESPONSES (Jane Stromseth ed., Ardsley, USA: Transnational Pub, 2003)

DIRK VANDEWALLE, A HISTORY OF MODERN LIBYA (Cambridge, UK: Cambridge University Press, 2006)

DIRK VANDEWALLE, LIBYA SINCE 1969: QADHAFI'S REVOLUTION REVISITED (New York, USA: Palgrave Macmillan, 2008)

LIESBETH ZEGVELD, THE ACCOUNTABILITY OF ARMED OPPOSITION GROUPS IN INTERNATIONAL LAW (Cambridge, UK: Cambridge University Press, 2002)

JOURNAL & BOOK ARTICLES

Georges Abi-Saab, *Wars of National Liberation in the Geneva Conventions and Protocols*, 165 RECUEIL DES COURS 353 (1979)

Christian F. Anrig, *Allied Air Power over Libya*, 91 AIR AND SPACE POWER JOURNAL 89 (Winter 2011), *available at* http://www.airpower.au.af.mil/digital/pdf/articles/winter2011/11-VA-Anrig.pdf

J.M. Asketell & S.M. Ghellali, *A palaeogeologic map of the pre-Tertiary surface in the region of the Jifarah Plain: its implication to the structural history of Northern Libya, in* 6 THE GEOLOGY OF LIBYA, THIRD SYMPOSIUM ON THE GEOLOGY OF LIBYA, HELD AT TRIPOLI 2381 (M. J. Salime, et al. ed., Amsterdam, The Netherlands: Elsevier, 1991)

Louis Aucoin, *Building the Rule of Law and Establishing Accountability for Atrocities in the Aftermath of Conflict*, 8(1) WHITEHEAD J. DIPL. & INT'L REL. (Winter/Spring 2007), *available at* http://blogs.shu.edu/diplomacy/files/archives/04-Aucoin.pdf

M. Cherif Bassiouni, *The "Arab Revolution" and Transitions in the Wake of the "Arab Spring"*, UCLA JOURNAL OF INTERNATIONAL LAW AND FOREIGN AFFAIRS. (forthcoming 2013)

——, *Combating Impunity for International Crimes*, 71 U. COLO. L. REV. 409 (2000)

——, *Introduction, in* A MANUAL ON INTERNATIONAL HUMANITARIAN LAW AND ARMS CONTROL AGREEMENTS (M. Cherif Bassiouni ed., Ardsley, USA: Transnational Publishers, 2000)

——, *The Future of Human Rights in the Age of Globalization, in* 40 DENVER J. INT'L L. & POL'Y 22 [PERSPECTIVES ON INTERNATIONAL LAW IN AN ERA TIME OF CHANGE] (Anjali Nanda and Alissa Mundt eds., 2012)

——, *Legal Control of International Terrorism: A Policy-Oriented Assessment*", 43 HARV. INT'L L.J. 83 (2002)

——, *The New Wars and the Crisis of Compliance with the Law of Armed Conflict by Non-State Actors*, 98 J. CRIM. L. & CRIMINOLOGY 711 (2008)

——, *The Normative Framework on International Criminal Law: Overlaps, Gaps, and Ambiguities in Contemporary International Law*, in 1 INTERNATIONAL CRIMINAL LAW 469 (M. Cherif Bassiouni ed., Leiden, The Netherlands: Martinus Nijhoff, 3d ed. 2008)

——, *The Perennial Conflict between International Criminal Justice and Realpolitik*, 22 GA. ST. U. L. REV. 541 (2006)

——, *"Terrorism": Reflections on Legitimacy and Policy Considerations*, in VALUES AND VIOLENCE: INTANGIBLE ASPECTS OF TERRORISM 233 (I.A. Karawan et al. eds., Dordrecht, The Netherlands: Springer, 2008)

M. Cherif Bassiouni & Douglass Hansen, *The Inevitable Practice of the Office of the Prosecutor*, in HUMAN RIGHTS & INTERNATIONAL CRIMINAL LAW ONLINE FORUM (2013)

M. Cherif Bassiouni & Benjamin Ferencz, *The Crime Against Peace*, in 1 INTERNATIONAL CRIMINAL LAW: CRIMES 167-97 (M. Cherif Bassiouni ed., 1986)

ANTHONY BELL & DAVID WITTER, INSTITUTE FOR THE STUDY OF WAR, 1 THE LIBYAN REVOLUTION: THE ROOTS OF REBELLION (Sep. 2011), *available at* http://www.understandingwar.org/sites/default/files/Libya_Part1_0.pdf

——, 2 THE LIBYAN REVOLUTION: THE ROOTS OF REBELLION 24 (Sept. 2011), *available at* www.understandingwar.org/sites/default/files/Libya_Part2_0.pdf.

ANTHONY BELL ET AL., INSTITUTE FOR THE STUDY OF WAR, 3 THE LIBYAN REVOLUTION: STALEMATE & SIEGE (Oct. 2011), *available at* http://www.understandingwar.org/sites/default/files/Libya_Part3_0.pdf

——, INSTITUTE FOR THE STUDY OF WAR, 4 THE LIBYAN REVOLUTION: THE TIDE TURNS (Nov. 2011), *available at* http://www.understandingwar.org/sites/default/files/Libya_Part4.pdf

The Current Elements of Command Responsibility Under International Law, in 3 INTERNATIONAL CRIMINAL LAW: INTERNATIONAL ENFORCEMENT 467 (M. Cherif Bassiouni ed., Leiden, The Netherlands: Martinus Nijhoff, 3d rev. ed., 2008)

Gerald I.A.D. Draper, *Wars of National Liberation and War Criminality*, in RESTRAINTS ON WAR: STUDIES IN THE LIMITATION OF ARMED CONFLICT (Michael Howard ed., Oxford, UK: Oxford University Press, 1979)

Churchill Ewumbue-Monono, *Respect for International Humanitarian Law by Armed Non-State Actors in Africa*, 864 INT'L REV. RED CROSS 905 (2006)

JESSE FRANZBLAU, INFORMATION CONTROL AND HUMAN RIGHTS: TRANSFORMING GOVERNMENT ARCHIVES INTO TOOLS FOR CIVIL SOCIETY, 13 MICHIGAN JOURNAL OF PUBLIC AFFAIRS 4 (Spring 2012), *available at* http://www.mjpa.umich.edu/uploads/2012/franzblau.pdf

Joan F. Hartman, *Derogation from Human Rights Treaties in Public Emergencies*, 22 HARVARD INT'L. L. J. 1 (1981)

Jean-Marie Henckaerts, *Study on Customary International Humanitarian Law: A Contribution to the Understanding and Respect for the Rule of Law in Armed Conflict*, 857 INT'L REV. RED CROSS (2005)

Hanspeter Mattes, *Challenges to Security Sector Governance in the Middle East: The Libyan Case* (Geneva Centre for the Democratic Control of Armed Forces conference paper presented 12–13 July 2004), *available at* http://www.dcaf.ch/Event-Attachement/Challenges-to-Security-Sector-Governance-in-the-Middle-East-the-Libyan-Case

Mohamed Megerisi & V.D. Mamgain, *The Upper Cretaceous-Tertiary formations of northern Libya*, in 1 THE GEOLOGY OF LIBYA: SYMPOSIUM ON THE GEOLOGY OF LIBYA 67 (M.J. Salem & M.T. Busrewil ed., New York, USA: Academic Press, 1980)

Diane F. Orentlicher, *Settling Accounts: The Duty to Prosecute Human Rights Violations of a Prior Regime*, 100 YALE L.J. 2537 (1991)

Alison Pargeter, *Qadhafi and Political Islam In Libya*, in LIBYA SINCE 1969: QADHAFI'S REVOLUTION REVISITED 83 (Dirk Vandewalle ed., New York, USA: Palgrave McMillan 2011)

Mehrdad Payandeh, *The United Nations, Military Intervention, And Regime Change In Libya*, 52 Va. J. Int'l L. 355 (2012)

Syracuse Institute for National Security and Counter Terrorism, Syracuse University, Libya in Conflict Appendix C (2012), *available at* http://insct.syr.edu/uploaded Files/insct/publications/Mapping%20the%20Libyan%20Conflict%20-%20INSCT.pdf

Leo Van den Hole, *Towards a Test of the International Character of an Armed Conflict: Nicaragua And Tadic*, 32 Syracuse J. Int'l L. & Com. 269 (Spring 2005)

Varun Vira & Anthony H. Cordesman, Center for Strategic and International Studies, The Libyan Uprising: An Uncertain Trajectory (June 20, 2011), *available at* http://csis.org/files/publication/110620_libya.pdf

Barbara F. Walter, *Does Conflict Beget Conflict? Explaining Recurring Civil War*, 41 J Peace Res. 3 (May 2004)

NGO Reports and Statements

Tariq Abdell, *Iraq's political sectarianism: National Reconciliation and the Oil Curse*, Iraq Business news, Oct. 10, 2010, *available at* http://www.iraq-businessnews.com/2010/10/01/iraqs-political-sectarianism-national-reconciliation-and-the-oil-curse

Fred Abrams, *For Libya to end the violence, it needs to shut down the militias*, Human Rights Watch, June 18, 2013, *available at* http://www.hrw.org/print/news/2013/06/18/libya-end-violence-it-needs-shut-down-militias?origin=from_home

Tani Marilena Adams, Woodrow Wilson Center, Chronic Violence and its Reproduction: Perverse Trends in Social Relations, Citizenship, and Democracy in Latin America (Sept. 2011), *available at* http://www.wilsoncenter.org/sites/default/files/Chronic%20Violence%20and%20its%20Reproduction_1.pdf

Ademola Abass, *Assessing NATO's Involvement in Libya*, United Nations University, Oct. 27, 2011, *available at* http://unu.edu/publications/articles/assessing-nato-s-involvement-in-libya.html

Rang Alaaldin, *Libya: Defining its Future*, LSE IDEAS!, *available at* http://www2.lse.ac.uk/IDEAS/publications/reports/pdf/SR011/FINAL_LSE_IDEAS__LibyaDefiningItsFuture_Alaaldin.pdf

Amnesty International, Arms Transfers to the Middle East and North Africa: Lessons for an Effective Arms Trade Treaty (2011), *available at* http://www.amnesty.org/en/library/asset/ACT30/117/2011/en/049fdeee-66fe-4b13-a90e-6d7773d6a546/act30117201ien.pdf

——, The Battle for Libya: Killings, disappearances and torture (Sept. 2011), *available at* http://www.amnesty.org/en/library/asset/MDE19/025/2011/en/8f2e1c49-8f43-46d3-917d-383c17d36377/mde19025201ien.pdf

——, Detention Abuses Staining the New Libya (2011), *available at* http://www.amnesty.org/en/library/asset/MDE19/036/2011/en/e1c30d0f-8ec3-4368-8537-03f1bb15a051/mde19036201ien.pdf

——, Europe: Now it is Your Time to Act (Sept. 2011), *available at* http://www.amnesty.org/en/library/asset/MDE03/002/2011/en/dc59ca51-da8a-4c37-a30a-56daaf33f57f/mde03002201ien.pdf

——, Libya: Detainees, Disappeared and Missing (Mar. 29, 2011), *available at* http://www.amnesty.org/en/library/asset/MDE19/011/2011/en/569f0509-c3db-433f-b023-89aea68dde8e/mde19011201ien.pdf

——, Libya – Disappearances in the besieged Nafusa Mountain as thousands seek safety in Tunisia (May, 2011), *available at* http://www.amnesty.org/en/library/asset/MDE19/020/2011/en/aed13a1a-07b4-434b-bb28-0c0aa1d53069/mde19020201ien.pdf

——, Libya: Rule of Law or Rule of Militias? (July 2012), *available at* http://www.amnesty.org/en/library/asset/MDE19/012/2012/en/f2d36090-5716-4ef1-81a7-f4b1ebd082fc/mde19012201en.pdf

——, MILITIAS THREATEN HOPES FOR NEW LIBYA (Feb. 16, 2012), *available at* http://www
.amnesty.org/en/library/asset/MDE19/002/2012/en/dd7c1d69-e368-44de-8ee8-cc9365b-
d5eb3/mde190022012en.pdf

——, MISRATAH UNDER SIEGE AND UNDER FIRE (May 6, 2011), *available at* http://www
.amnesty.org/en/library/asset/MDE19/019/2011/en/4efa1e19-06c1-4609-9477-feof-
2f4e2b2a/mde19019201en.pdf

——, 'WE ARE NOT SAFE ANYWHERE', TAWARGHAS IN LIBYA (June 8 2012), *available at*
http://www.amnesty.org/en/library/asset/MDE19/007/2012/en/514d579a-3e2b-4f89-
ba8b-6f17d479c617/mde190072012en.pdf

——, *Amnesty International Says "Out of Control" Libyan Militias Are Committing Widespread Abuses Against Suspected Al-Gaddafi Loyalists, Including Torture and Killings,*
AMNESTY INTERNATIONAL, Feb. 16, 2012, *available at* http://www.amnestyusa.org/news/
news-item/amnesty-international-says-out-of-control-libyan-militias-are-commiting-
widespread-abuses-against-su

Analysis: Libyan minority rights at a crossroads, INTEGRATED REGIONAL INFORMATION
NETWORKS, May 24, 2012, *available at* http://www.irinnews.org/report/95524/Analysis-
Libyan-minority-rights-at-a-crossroads

*The Assassination of judges in Libya undermines justice and threatens the foundation of
the rule of law,* THE ARAB CENTER FOR THE INDEPENDENCE OF THE JUDICIARY AND THE
LEGAL PROFESSION (ACIJLP), June 18, 2013

Conflict Analysis: Zawiya, Libya (as of 08 March 2011), UNITED NATIONS INSTITUTE FOR
TRAINING AND RESEARCH, Mar. 23, 2011, *available at* http://reliefweb.int/sites/reliefweb
.int/files/resources/7308EDFFF4FDA0478525785D00702BF7-map.pdf

Both sides in Libya conflict must protect detainees from torture, AMNESTY INTERNATIONAL,
Aug. 25, 2011, *available at* http://www.amnesty.org/en/news-and-updates/both-sides-
libya-conflict-must-protect-detainees-torture-2011-08-25

Giorgio Cafiero, *Beyond Libya's election,* FOREIGN POLICY IN FOCUS, July 18, 2012, *available
at* http://www.fpif.org/articles/beyond_libyas_election

CAMPAIGN FOR INNOCENT VICTIMS IN CONFLICT, LIBYA: PROTECT VULNERABLE MINORITIES
& ASSIST CIVILIANS HARMED (Nov. 2011), *available at* http://www.civicworldwide.org/
storage/documents/civic-ri%20libya%20report%202011%20final.pdf

The Carter Center Finds Libya's Tabulation Process Credible, CARTER CENTER, July 18, 2012,
available at http://www.cartercenter.org/news/pr/libya-071812.html?gclid=CMme_4zD2
LICFYqV3godyWEAFw

Constitution Building and Legal Reform, LAWYERS FOR JUSTICE IN LIBYA, *available at* http://
www.libyanjustice.org/our-programmes/constitution-building-and-legal-reform

ANTHONY H. CORDESMAN, CENTER FOR STRATEGIC AND INTERNATIONAL STUDIES, THE
NORTH AFRICAN MILITARY BALANCE: FORCE DEVELOPMENTS IN THE MAGHREB (Mar. 28,
2005), *available at* http://csis.org/files/media/csis/pubs/050328_norafrimibal%5B1%5D
.pdf

Divided We Stand: Libya's Enduring Conflict, INTERNATIONAL CRISIS GROUP, Sept. 14, 2012,
available at http://www.crisisgroup.org/~/media/Files/Middle%20East%20North%20
Africa/North%20Africa/libya/130-divided-we-stand-libyas-enduring-conflicts

Document – Libya: Militias threaten hopes for new Libya, AMNESTY INTERNATIONAL, *available at* http://www.amnesty.org/en/library/asset/MDE19/002/2012/en/608ac5a8-95d0-
4a3b-89de-b4a1b585feee/_Toc317144515

Draft Libyan Electoral Law 2012 – English Translation, LIBYAN PROGRESS, *available at* http://
www.libyanprogress.org/articles/draft-libyan-electoral-law-2012-english-translation/

Egypt: The Trial of Hosni Mubarak, Questions and Answers, HUMAN RIGHTS WATCH, May
2012, *available at* http://www.hrw.org/news/2012/05/28/egypt-qa-trial-hosni-mubarak

James Elder, *Libya: Nine-year-old boy, injured in Misrata fighting, reflects risks facing Libyan
children,* RELIEF WEB, Apr. 25, 2011, *available at* http://reliefweb.int/node/398930

Anas El Gomati, *Why Libya's 'Isolation Law' Threatens Progress,* CARNAGIE ENDOWMENT,
May 22, 2013, *available at* http://carnegieendowment.org/2013/05/21/why-libya-s-
isolation-law-threatens-progress/g5g2

Diana Eltahawy, Women who defied al-Gaddafi regime not spared from brutal jails, AMNESTY INTERNATIONAL, Sept. 5, 2011, *available at* http://livewire.amnesty.org/2011/09/05/women-who-defied-al-gaddafi-regime-not-spared-from-brutal-jails

Christina M. Fetterhoff, *Ríos Montt Genocide Trial Tests Durability of Domestic & International Legal Protections,* CENTER FOR HUMAN RIGHTS AND HUMANITARIAN LAW, Apr. 16, 2013, *available at* http://hrbrief.org/2013/04/rios-montt-genocide-trial-tests-durability-of-domestic-international-legal-protections

MICHAEL JOHN GARCIA, CONGRESSIONAL RESEARCH SERVICE, WAR POWERS LITIGATION INITIATED BY MEMBERS OF CONGRESS SINCE THE ENACTMENT OF THE WAR POWERS RESOLUTION (June 22, 2011), *available at* http://www.fas.org/sgp/crs/natsec/RL30352.pdf

Anas El Gomati, *Why Libya's 'Isolation Law' Threatens Progress,* CARNAGIE ENDOWMENT, May 22, 2013, *available at* http://carnegieendowment.org/2013/05/21/why-libya-s-isolation-law-threatens-progress/g5g2

Anton Hammerl, COMMITTEE TO PROTECT JOURNALISTS, Apr. 5, 2011, *available at* https://cpj.org/killed/2011/anton-hammerl.php

HUMAN RIGHTS WATCH, DELIVERED INTO ENEMY HANDS: US-LED ABUSE AND RENDITION OF OPPONENTS TO GADDAFI'S LIBYA (Sept. 2012), *available at* http://www.hrw.org/sites/default/files/reports/libya0912webwcover_1.pdf

——, PUSHED BACK, PUSHED AROUND: ITALY'S FORCED RETURN OF BOAT MIGRANTS AND ASYLUM SEEKERS, LIBYA'S MISTREATMENT OF MIGRANTS AND ASYLUM SEEKERS (Sept. 19, 2009), *available at* http://www.hrw.org/sites/default/files/reports/italy0909webwcover_0.pdf

——, UNACKNOWLEDGED DEATHS: CIVILIAN CASUALTIES IN NATO's AIR CAMPAIGN IN LIBYA (May 2012), *available at* http://www.hrw.org/sites/default/files/reports/libya0512webwcover.pdf

——, WORLD REPORT 2013: LIBYA (February 2013), *available at* http://www.hrw.org/world-report/2013/country-chapters/libya

Hundreds of unexploded devices destroyed in Ajdabiya, MINES ADVISORY GROUP, June 9, 2011, *available at* http://reliefweb.int/node/419314

ICC: Libya's Bids to Try Gaddafi, Sanussi, HUMAN RIGHTS WATCH, May 13, 2013, *available at* http://www.hrw.org/news/2013/05/13/qa-libya-and-international-criminal-court

Internal Displacement Monitoring Center, *Increasing reports of internal displacement,* RELIEF WEB, Apr. 21, 2011, *available at* reliefweb.int/node/397844

International Criminal Justice Program, *Libya: NPWJ Raises Awareness about Transitional Justice and Reconciliation in Sirte,* NO PEACE WITHOUT JUSTICE, May 17, 2013, *available at* http://www.npwj.org/ICC/Libya-NPWJ-Raises-Awareness-about-Transitional-Justice-and-Reconciliation-Sirte.html

INTERNATIONAL CRISIS GROUP, TRIAL BY ERROR: JUSTICE IN POST-QADHAFI LIBYA (Apr. 17, 2013), *available at* http://www.crisisgroup.org/~/media/Files/Middle%20East%20North%20Africa/North%20Africa/libya/140-trial-by-error-justice-in-post-qadhafi-libya.pdf

——, HOLDING LIBYA TOGETHER: SECURITY CHALLENGES AFTER QADHAFI (Dec. 14, 2011), *available at* http://www.crisisgroup.org/~/media/Files/Middle%20East%20North%20Africa/North%20Africa/115%20Holding%20Libya%20Together%20--%20Security%20Challenges%20after%20Qadhafi.pdf

INTERNATIONAL COMMISSION ON INTERVENTION AND STATE SOVEREIGNTY, THE RESPONSIBILITY TO PROTECT (Ottawa: ICISS, 2001), *available at* http://responsibilitytoprotect.org/ICISS%20Report

THE INTERNATIONAL INSTITUTE FOR STRATEGIC STUDIES, THE MILITARY BALANCE 2009 (June 2009), *available at* http://www.iiss.org/publications/military-balance/the-military-balance-2009.

INTERNATIONAL LEGAL ASSISTANCE CONSORTIUM, REPORT OF THE INDEPENDENT CIVIL SOCIETY FACT-FINDING MISSION TO LIBYA (Jan. 9, 2012), *available at* http://www.ilac.se/download/reports_documents/mission-reports_documents/LIBYA_FF_REPORT_111221.pdf

January 2013 Monthly Forecast, SECURITY COUNCIL REPORT, Dec. 21, 2012, *available at* http://www.securitycouncilreport.org/monthly-forecast/2013-01/libya_2.php

Journalists kidnapped by Misrata brigade were reporting on the racist lynchings of Tawerghans, GLOBAL CIVILIANS FOR PEACE, Mar. 7, 2012, *available at* http://global civiliansforpeace.com/2012/03/07/journalists-kidnapped-by-misrata-brigade-were-reporting-on-the-racist-lynchings-of-tawerghans

Journalists under attack in Libya: The tally, COMMITTEE TO PROTECT JOURNALISTS, *available at* http://www.cpj.org/blog/2011/05/journalists-under-attack-in-libya.php

Amanda Kadlec, *Disarming Libya's Militias*, CARNEGIE ENDOWMENT, Feb. 16, 2012, *available at* http://carnegieendowment.org/sada/2012/02/16/disarming-libya-s-militias/90fa

Eric Knecht, *The Questionable Campaign Behind Libya's Political Isolation Law*, THE ATLANTIC COUNCIL, May 8, 2013

Libya, MAX PLANCK INSTITUTE FOR COMPARATIVE PUBLIC LAW AND INTERNATIONAL LAW, *available at* http://www.mpil.de/ww/en/pub/research/details/know_transfer/constitutional_reform_in_arab_/libyen.cfm

Libya: Abandoned Weapons, Landmines Endanger Civilians, HUMAN RIGHTS WATCH, Apr. 5, 2011, *available at* http://www.hrw.org/news/2011/04/05/libya-abandoned-weapons-landmines-endanger-civilians-0

Libya: Abu Salim Prison Massacre Remembered, HUMAN RIGHTS WATCH, June 27, 2012, *available at* http://www.hrw.org/news/2012/06/27/libya-abu-salim-prison-massacre-remembered

Libya: Amend New Special Procedures Law, HUMAN RIGHTS WATCH, May 11, 2012, *available at* http://www.hrw.org/news/2012/05/11/libya-amend-new-special-procedures-law

Libya and the ICC: What Next?, OPEN SOCIETY FOUNDATIONS, Nov. 21, 2011, *available at* http://www.opensocietyfoundations.org/voices/libya-and-icc-what-next

Libya: Arrests, Assaults in Advance of Planned Protests, HUMAN RIGHTS WATCH, Feb. 17, 2011, *available at* http://www.hrw.org/news/2011/02/16/libya-arrests-assaults-advance-planned-protests

Libya: At Least 370 Missing From Country's East, HUMAN RIGHTS WATCH, Mar. 30, 2011, *available at* http://www.hrw.org/news/2011/03/30/libya-least-370-missing-countrys-east

Libya: Bolster Security at Tawergha Camps, HUMAN RIGHTS WATCH, Mar. 5, 2012, *available at* http://www.hrw.org/news/2012/03/05/libya-bolster-security-tawergha-camps

Libya: Campaign of enforced disappearances must end, AMNESTY INTERNATIONAL, Mar. 29, 2011, *available at* http://www.amnesty.org/en/news-and-updates/report/libya-campaign-enforced-disappearances-must-end-2011-03-29

Libya: Cease Arbitrary Arrests, Abuse of Detainees, HUMAN RIGHTS WATCH, Sept. 30, 2011, *available at* http://www.hrw.org/news/2011/09/30/libya-cease-arbitrary-arrests-abuse-detainees

Libya: Civilians at risk amid new mine threat, AMNESTY INTERNATIONAL, May 25, 2011, *available at* http://www.amnesty.org/en/news-and-updates/libya-civilians-risk-amid-new-mine-threat-2011-05-25

Libya: Commanders Should Face Justice for Killings, HUMAN RIGHTS WATCH, Feb. 22, 2011, *available at* www.hrw.org/en/news/2011/02/22/libya-commanders-should-face-justice-killings

Libya Constitutional Declaration, WIPO RESOURCES, *available at* http://www.wipo.int/wipolex/en/details.jsp?id=11248

Libya: Contact Group Should Press Rebels to Protect Civilians, HUMAN RIGHTS WATCH, July 15, 2011, *available at* http://www.hrw.org/news/2011/07/15/libya-contact-group-should-press-rebels-protect-civilians

Libya: detainees, disappeared and missing, AMNESTY INTERNATIONAL, Mar. 29, 2011, *available at* http://www.amnesty.org/en/library/asset/MDE19/011/2011/en/5a97c7df-aee8-4830-9f2b-d54f805d2dc1/mde190112011en.html

Libya: Detainees killed by al-Gaddafi loyalists, AMNESTY INTERNATIONAL, Aug. 26, 2011, *available at* http://www.amnesty.org/en/news-and-updates/libya-detainees-killed-al-gaddafi-loyalists-2011-08-26

Libya: Make Urgent Justice System Reforms, HUMAN RIGHTS WATCH, Dec. 22, 2011, *available at* http://www.hrw.org/news/2011/12/22/libya-make-urgent-justice-system-reforms

Libya: Mass Grave Yields 34 Bodies, HUMAN RIGHTS WATCH, Sept. 14, 2011, *available at* http://www.hrw.org/news/2011/09/14/libya-mass-grave-yields-34-bodies

Libya: Militia Should Transfer Journalists to State, HUMAN RIGHTS WATCH, Feb. 27, 2012, *available at* http://www.hrw.org/news/2012/02/27/libya-militia-should-transfer-journalists-state-0

Libya: Militias Terrorizing Residents of 'Loyalist' Town, HUMAN RIGHTS WATCH, Oct. 30, 2011, *available at* http://www.hrw.org/news/2011/10/30/libya-militias-terrorizing-residents-loyalist-town

Libya: Mine Action, LANDMINE & CLUSTER MUNITION MONITOR, updated Dec. 17, 2012, *available at* http://www.the-monitor.org/custom/index.php/region_profiles/print_theme/1955#_ftnref2

Libya: MSF Forced To Evacuate from Zintan, MEDECINS SANS FRONTIERS, May 27, 2011, *available at* http://www.doctorswithoutborders.org/press/release.cfm?id=5287

Libya: much-needed humanitarian aid reaches Misrata, INTERNATIONAL COMMITTEE FOR THE RED CROSS, May 9, 2011, *available at* http://www.icrc.org/eng/resources/documents/news-release/2011/libya-news-2011- 05-09.htm.232

Libya: No Impunity for 'Black Saturday' Benghazi Deaths, HUMAN RIGHTS WATCH, June 14, 2013, *available at* http://www.hrw.org/news/2013/06/13/libya-no-impunity-black-saturday-benghazi-deaths

Libya: Opposition Arbitrarily Detaining Suspected Gaddafi Loyalists, HUMAN RIGHTS WATCH, June 5, 2011, *available at* http://www.hrw.org/news/2011/06/05/libya-opposition-arbitrarily-detaining-suspected-gaddafi-loyalists

Libya: Opposition Forces Should Protect Civilians and Hospitals, HUMAN RIGHTS WATCH, July 13, 2011, *available at* http://www.hrw.org/news/2011/07/13/libya-opposition-forces-should-protect-civilians-and-hospitals

Libya: 'Out of control' militias commit widespread abuses, a year on from uprising, AMNESTY INTERNATIONAL, Feb. 15, 2012, *available at* http://www.amnesty.org/en/news/libya-out-control-militias-commit-widespread-abuses-year-uprising-2012-02-15

Libya: Protect Civilians in Sirte Fighting, HUMAN RIGHTS WATCH, Oct. 12, 2011, *available at* http://www.hrw.org/news/2011/10/12/libya-protect-civilians-sirte-fighting

Libya: Pursuing al-Gaddafi – the legal questions answered, AMNESTY INTERNATIONAL, Aug. 25 2011, *available at* http://www.amnesty.org/en/news-and-updates/libya-pursuing-al-gaddafi-%E2%80%93-legal-questions-answered-2011-08-25

Libya: Red Crescent volunteers and medical personnel in danger, Operational Update No 05/11, INTERNATIONAL COMMITTEE FOR THE RED CROSS, May 17, 2011, *available at* http://www.icrc.org/eng/resources/documents/update/2011/libya-update-2011-05-17.htm

Libya: Reject 'Political Isolation Law', HUMAN RIGHTS WATCH, May 4, 2013, *available at* http://www.hrw.org/news/2013/05/04/libya-reject-political-isolation-law

Libya: Revoke Draconian New Law, HUMAN RIGHTS WATCH, May 5, 2012, *available at* http://www.hrw.org/news/2012/05/05/libya-revoke-draconian-new-law

Libya: Rocket Attacks on Western Mountain Towns, HUMAN RIGHTS WATCH, May 27, 2011, *available at* http://www.hrw.org/news/2011/05/27/libya-rocket-attacks-western-mountain-towns

Libya: Secure Unguarded Arms Depots, HUMAN RIGHTS WATCH, Sept. 10, 2011, *available at* http://www.hrw.org/news/2011/09/09/libya-secure-unguarded-arms-depots.

Libya: Security Forces Fire on 'Day of Anger' Demonstrations, HUMAN RIGHTS WATCH, Feb. 18, 2011, *available at* http://www.hrw.org/news/2011/02/17/libya-security-forces-fire-day-anger-demonstrations

Libya: Security Forces Fire on Protesters in Western City, HUMAN RIGHTS WATCH, Feb. 26, 2011, *available at* http://www.hrw.org/en/news/2011/02/26/libya-security-forces-fire-protesters-western-city

Libya: Security Forces Kill 84 Over Three Days, HUMAN RIGHTS WATCH, Feb. 19, 2011, *available at* http://www.hrw.org/en/news/2011/02/18/libya-security-forces-kill-84-over-three-days

Libya: Slow Pace of Reform Harms Rights, HUMAN RIGHTS WATCH, Feb. 26, 2013, available at http://www.hrw.org/news/2013/02/06/libya-slow-pace-reform-harms-rights

Libya: State of the Transformation Process, MAX PLANCK INSTITUTE FOR COMPARATIVE PUBLIC LAW AND INTERNATIONAL LAW, *available at* http://www.mpil.de/ww/en/pub/research/details/Know_transfer/libyen.cfm

Libya: Stop Arbitrary Arrests of Black Africans, HUMAN RIGHTS WATCH, Sept. 4, 2011, *available at* http://www.hrw.org/news/2011/09/04/libya-stop-arbitrary-arrests-black-africans

Libya: supporting medical services in disputed areas, INTERNATIONAL COMMITTEE OF THE RED CROSS, Sept. 15, 2011, *available at* http://www.icrc.org/eng/resources/documents/update/2011/libya-update-2011-09-15.htm

Libya: Tawergha Residents Terrorized by Militias, HUMAN RIGHTS WATCH, Oct. 27, 2011, *available at* http://www.hrw.org/features/libya-tawergha-residents-terrorized-militias

Libya: Transitional Council Failing to Secure Weapons, HUMAN RIGHTS WATCH, Oct. 25, 2011, *available at* http://www.hrw.org/news/2011/10/25/libya-transitional-council-failing-secure-weapons

Libya urged to investigate whether al-Gaddafi death was a war crime, AMNESTY INTERNATIONAL, October 21, 2011, *available at* http://www.amnesty.org/en/news-and-updates/libya-urged-investigate-whether-al-gaddafi-death-was-war-crime-2011-10-21

Libya Weekly Report 2 April, 2012, JOINT MINE ACTION COORDINATION TEAM, Apr. 2, 2012, *available at* http://reliefweb.int/report/libya/joint-mine-action-coordination-team-%E2%80%93-libya-weekly-report-2-april-2012

Libya: 10 Steps for Human Rights: Amnesty International's Human Rights Manifesto for Libya AMNESTY INTERNATIONAL, Sept. 25, 2012, *available at* http://www.amnesty.org/en/library/asset/MDE19/017/2012/en/234877c1-0d9b-4917-af8f-82f3a9bdc730/mde190172012en.pdf

Libya: 19 Suffocated in Gaddafi Detention, HUMAN RIGHTS WATCH, Sept. 9, 2011, *available at* http://www.hrw.org/news/2011/09/09/libya-19-suffocated-gaddafi-detention

Libyan Constitution Deadline Extended, PROJECT ON THE MIDDLE EAST DEMOCRACY, June 28, 2012, *available at* http://pomed.org/blog/2012/06/libyan-constitution-deadline-extended.html

Libyan leader must end spiralling killings, AMNESTY INTERNATIONAL, Feb. 20, 2011, *available at* http://www.amnesty.org/en/for-media/press-releases/libyan-leader-must-end-spiralling-killings-2011-02-20

Libyan paramedics targeted by pro-Gaddafi forces, AMNESTY INTERNATIONAL, Mar. 4, 2011, *available at* http://www.amnesty.org/en/news-and-updates/libyan-paramedics-targeted-pro-gaddafi-forces-2011-03-04

Libyan public institutions and NGOs draft '10 Steps to End Torture', THE WORLD ORGANIZATION AGAINST TORTURE, Apr. 25, 2013, *available at* http://www.omct.org/events/libya/2013/04/d22233

Live Wire, *Families rent asunder by deaths and disappearances in Misratah*, AMNESTY INTERNATIONAL, May 21, 2011, *available at* http://livewire.amnesty.org/2011/05/21/families-rent-asunder-by-deaths-and-disappearances-in-misratah

——, *Pain and loss hits every family in Misratah*, AMNESTY INTERNATIONAL, May 25, 2011, *available at* http://livewire.amnesty.org/2011/05/25/pain-and-loss-hits-every-family-in-misratah

Lynching in Bengasi, HUMAN RIGHTS INVESTIGATIONS, July 17, 2011, *available at* http://www.humanrightsinvestigations.org/2011/07/17/lynching-in-benghazi

MAX PLANCK INSTITUTE FOR COMPARATIVE PUBLIC LAW AND INTERNATIONAL LAW, LAW N°04-2012 ON THE ELECTION OF THE NATIONAL GENERAL CONGRESS, *available at* http://www.mpil.de/shared/data/pdf/the_election_law_libya.pdf

May 2013 Monthly Forecast, UN SECURITY COUNCIL REPORT, May 2013, *available at* http://www.securitycouncilreport.org/monthly-forecast/2013-05/libya_4.php?print=true

BRIAN MCQUINN, SMALL ARMS SURVEY, ARMED GROUPS IN LIBYA: TYPOLOGY AND ROLES (June 2012), *available at* http://www.smallarmssurvey.org/fileadmin/docs/H-Research_ Notes/SAS-Research-Note-18.pdf

Karim Mezran and Duncan Pickard, *Libya's Constitutional Process: Moving Forward?*, THE ATLANTIC COUNCIL, Apr. 22, 2013, *available at* http://www.acus.org/viewpoint/libya's-constitutional-process-moving-forward

Misrata Local Council Response to Human Rights Watch, HUMAN RIGHTS WATCH, Apr. 11, 2012, *available at* http://www.hrw.org/news/2012/04/11/misrata-local-council-response-human-rights-watch

Monitoring Elections, CARTER CENTER, *available at* http://www.cartercenter.org/countries/libya-peace.html

NATO urged to investigate civilian deaths during Libya air strikes, AMNESTY INTERNATIONAL, Aug. 10, 2011, *available at* http://www.amnesty.org/en/news-and-updates/nato-urged-investigate-civilian-deaths-during-libya-air-strikes-2011-08-10

Jed Odermatt, *'New Wars' and the International/Non-international Armed Conflict Dichotomy*, INTERNATIONAL INSTITUTE FOR HIGHER STUDIES IN CRIMINAL SCIENCE, *available at* http://www.isisc.org/portal/images/stories/PDF/Paper%20Odermatt.pdf

Open letter condemning Laws 37 and 38, LAWYERS FOR JUSTICE IN LIBYA, May 9, 2012, *available at* http://www.libyanjustice.org/downloads/Letter%20re%20Laws%2037%20 and%2038.pdf

PALESTINIAN CENTRE FOR HUMAN RIGHTS (PCHR), ARAB ORGANIZATION FOR HUMAN RIGHTS (AOHR) & INTERNATIONAL LEGAL ASSISTANCE CONSORTIUM, REPORT OF THE INDEPENDENT CIVIL SOCIETY FACT-FINDING MISSION TO LIBYA (Jan. 2012), *available at* http://www.pchrgaza.org/files/2012/FFM_Libya-Report.pdf

PHYSICIANS FOR HUMAN RIGHTS, 32ND BRIGADE MASSACRE: EVIDENCE OF WAR CRIMES AND THE NEED TO ENSURE JUSTICE AND ACCOUNTABILITY IN LIBYA (Dec. 2011), *available at* https://s3.amazonaws.com/PHR_Reports/Libya-32nd-Brigade-Massacre.pdf

——, WITNESS TO WAR CRIMES: EVIDENCE FROM MISRATA, LIBYA (Aug. 2011), *available at* https://s3.amazonaws.com/PHR_Reports/Libya-WitnesstoWarCrimes-Aug2011.pdf

PROJECT ON MIDDLE EAST DEMOCRACY, POMED'S BACKGROUNDER: PREVIEWING LIBYA'S ELECTIONS (July 5, 2012), *available at* http://pomed.org/wordpress/wp-content/uploads/ 2012/07/Previewing-Libyas-Elections.pdf

Al-Qaddafi's Forces Carry Out Indiscriminate Attacks in Misratah, AMNESTY INTERNATIONAL, May 8, 2011, *available at* http://www.amnesty.org/en/for-media/press-releases/ al-Qaddafi%E2%80%99s-forces-carry-out-indiscriminate-attacksmisratah-2011-05-08

Morgan Lorraine Roach & Jessica Zuckerman, *MANPADS on the Loose: Countering Weapons Proliferation in North Africa and the Sahel*, THE HERITAGE FOUNDATION, Nov. 5, 2012 *available at* http://www.heritage.org/research/reports/2012/11/manpads-countering-weapons-proliferation-in-north-africa-and-the-sahel

Kenneth Roth, *The Day After, in* HUMAN RIGHTS WATCH WORLD REPORT 2013 (Feb. 2013), *available at* https://www.hrw.org/sites/default/files/wr2013_web.pdf

Donatella Rovera, Live Wire, *Revenge killings and reckless firing in opposition-held eastern Libya*, AMNESTY INTERNATIONAL, May 11, 2011, *available at* http://livewire.amnesty .org/2011/05/13/revenge-killings-and-reckless-firing-in-opposition-held-eastern-libya

Donatella Rovera, *Mines pose new danger as Libya battles rage on*, AMENSTY INTERNATIONAL, Apr. 6, 2011, *available at* http://livewire.amnesty.org/2011/04/06/mines-pose-new-danger-as-libya-battles-rage-on

ROYAL UNITED SERVICES INSTITUTE, ACCIDENTAL HEROES: BRITAIN, FRANCE AND THE LIBYA OPERATION, AN INTERIM LIBYA CAMPAIGN REPORT (Sept. 2011), *available at* http://www .rusi.org/downloads/assets/RUSIInterimLibyaReport.pdf

Rule of law in armed conflicts project RULAC, *Qualification of armed conflicts*, GENEVA ACADEMY OF INTERNATIONAL HUMANITARIAN LAW AND HUMAN RIGHTS, *available at* http://www.geneva-academy.ch/RULAC/qualification_of_armed_conflict.php

Periodical Articles

——, *Trial of Qaddafi spy chief resumes – and is postponed – for third time*, Libya Herald, July 11, 2012, *available at* http://www.libyaherald.com/2012/07/11/trial-of-qaddafi-spy-chief-resumes-and-is-postponed-for-third-time/

——, *Two more Qaddafi figures set to go on trial on 10 September*, Libya Herald, Sept. 6, 2012, *available at* http://www.libyaherald.com/2012/09/06/two-more-regime-figures-set-to-go-on-trial-on-10-september/

Sami Aboudi, *UPDATE 1 – NATO strike kills at least 16 in Brega – Libyan TV*, Reuters, May 13, 2011, *available at* http://af.reuters.com/article/energyOilNews/idAFLDE74C1GL20110513

Abu Yahya al-Libi, al Qaeda deputy leader, killed in U.S. drone strike, CBS News, June 5, 2011, *available at* http://www.cbsnews.com/8301-202_162-57447601/abu-yahya-al-libi-al-qaeda-deputy-leader-killed-in-u.s-drone-strike/

Lutfi Abu-Aun, *Russia: arming Libya rebels is "crude violation"*, Reuters, June 30, 2011, *available at* http://www.reuters.com/article/2011/06/30/us-libya-idUSTRE7270JP20110630

Richard Adams, *Libya's turmoil – Friday 25 February*, The Guardian, Feb. 25, 2011, *available at* http://www.guardian.co.uk/world/blog/2011/feb/25/gaddafi-libya-live-blog

Richard Adams et al., *Libya uprising – Thursday 10 March*, The Guardian, Mar. 10, 2011, *available at* http://www.guardian.co.uk/world/blog/2011/mar/10/libya-uprising-gaddafi-live

After a day of intense fighting, anti-Gadhafi forces pull back, CNN, Sept. 16 2011, *available at* http://articles.cnn.com/2011-09-16/world/libya.war_1_anti-gadhafi-moammar-gadhafi-Surt

Amir Ahmed, *Libyan rivals clash; at least 11 killed*, CNN, Oct. 18, 2012, *available at* http://edition.cnn.com/2012/10/17/world/meast/libya-violence/index.html

Hamid Ould Ahmed, *Rebels say 16 dead in Misrata, hospital attacked*, Reuters, Mar. 23, 2011, *available at* http://www.reuters.com/article/2011/03/23/us-libya-misrata-strikes-idUSTRE72M8BY20110323

Spencer Akerman, *Libya: The Real U.S. Drone War*, Wired, Oct. 20, 2011, *available at* http://www.wired.com/dangerroom/2011/10/predator-libya/

Ranj Alaaldin, *Libya should embrace federalism*, The Guardian, Mar. 28, 2012, *available at* http://www.guardian.co.uk/commentisfree/2012/mar/28/libya-federalism-regions-revolution

Al-Baghdadi Al-Mahmoudi fears unfair trial in Libya, Libya Herald, June 2, 2012, *available at* http://www.libyaherald.com/2012/06/02/baghdadi-al-mahmmoudi-fears-unfair-trial-in-libya/

Alleged Killer of Abdel-Fattah Younis Escapes Jail and Blast Damages Military Building in Benghazi, Tripoli Post, Aug. 1, 2012, *available at* http://www.tripolipost.com/articledetail.asp?c=1&i=8927

Al Jazeera staffer killed in Libya, Al Jazeera, Mar. 12, 2011, *available at* http://www.aljazeera.com/news/africa/2011/03/201131219235952376.html

Craig Allen et al., *Errant NATO Airstrikes in Libya: 13 Cases (Brega)*, N.Y. Times, Dec. 16, 2011, *available at* http://www.nytimes.com/interactive/2011/12/16/world/africa/nato-air-strikes-in-libya.html?ref=africa#page/rebel-convoy

——, *Errant NATO Airstrikes in Libya: 13 Cases (Mizdah)*, N.Y. Times, Dec. 16 2011, *available at* http://www.nytimes.com/interactive/2011/12/16/world/africa/nato-airstrikes-in-libya.html#page/warehouses

——, *Errant NATO strikes in Libya: 13 Cases (Surman)*, N.Y. Times, Dec. 16, 2011, *available at* http://www.nytimes.com/interactive/2011/12/16/world/africa/nato-airstrikes-in-libya.html?ref=africa#page/warehouses

——, *Errant NATO Airstrikes in Libya: 13 Cases (Surt)*, N.Y. Times, Dec. 16, 2011, *available at* http://www.nytimes.com/interactive/2011/12/16/world/africa/nato-airstrikes-in-libya.html?ref=africa#page/apartment-building

——, *Errant NATO Airstrikes in Libya: 13 Cases (Tripoli)*, N.Y. Times, Dec. 16, 2011, *available at* http://www.nytimes.com/interactive/2011/12/16/world/africa/nato-airstrikes-in-libya.html?ref=africa#page/missile-depot

Karen Allen, *Hundreds of Libyan prisoners freed*, BBC, Nov. 5, 2011, *available at* http://www
.bbc.co.uk/news/world-africa-15604542

——, *Libyan factions in deadly clashes near Zawiya*, BBC, Nov. 14, 2011, *available at* http://
www.bbc.co.uk/news/world-africa-15726099

Tarek Amara, *Libyan mountain refugees tell of fearsome assault*, REUTERS, Apr. 26, 2011,
available at http://www.reuters.com/article/2011/04/26/us-libya-mountains-idUSTRE73
033E20110426

——, *Libyan mountain town facing starvation: residents*, REUTERS, May 2, 2011, *available at*
http://af.reuters.com/article/libyaNews/idAFLDE7411M020110502

——, *Libyan refugees tell of border fight, fear revenge*, REUTERS, May 1, 2011, *available at* http://
www.reuters.com/article/2011/05/01/us-libya-tunisia-border-idUSTRE7402PH20110501

——, *Pro-Gaddafi forces clash with Tunisian military*, REUTERS, Apr. 29, 2011, *available at*
http://af.reuters.com/article/topNews/idAFJOE73S00320110429

——, *Rebels seize Libya-Tunisia border crossing: witnesses*, REUTERS, Apr. 21, 2011, *available at* http://www.reuters.com/article/2011/04/21/us-libya-tunisia-border-idUSTRE
73K32K20110421

Tarek Amara & Mariam Karouny, *Gaddafi Forces Shell West Libya's Misrata, 25 Dead*, REU-TERS, Mar. 18, 2011, *available at* http://uk.reuters.com/article/2011/03/18/us-libya-misrata-bombard-idUKTRE72H4L520110318

Kenneth Ang, *84 protesters killed in Libya*, ALLVOICES, Feb. 19, 2011, *available at* http://www
.allvoices.com/contributed-news/8240740-deaths-in-libya-protest-rise-to-84

Anti-government protests, clashes, spread to Libya, AP, Feb. 16, 2011, *available at* http://
abclocal.go.com/wpvi/story?section=news/national_world&id=7961876

Peter Apps, *Analysis: Libya rebel killing takes shine off opposition gains*, REUTERS, July
29, 2011, *available at* http://www.reuters.com/article/2011/07/29/us-libya-killing-idUSTRE76S46W20110729

——, *Factbox: Libya's key cultural, tribal divisions*, REUTERS, Feb. 22, 2011, *available at*
http://us.mobile.reuters.com/article/topNews/idUSTRE7294TD20110310?feedType=RSS
&feedName=topNews

Armed battles in Libya city streets, PRESS ASSOCIATION, Aug. 13, 2011, *available at* http://www
.independent.ie/breaking-news/world-news/armed-battles-in-libya-city-streets-2847757
.html

Assaults on Misurata, Ajdabijah and Zintan, THE TRIPOLI POST, Mar. 23, 2011, *available at*
http://www.tripolipost.com/articledetail.asp?c=1&i=5664

'Astonishing' to end Musa Kusa sanctions, THE INDEPENDENT, April 14, 2011, *available at*
http://www.independent.co.uk/news/world/politics/astonishing-to-end-musa-kusa-sanctions-2267796.html

At conference, UN envoy highlights importance of reconciliation process in Libya, UN
NEWS CENTRE, Dec. 12, 2012, available at http://www.un.org/apps/news/story.
asp?NewsID=43754#.URTP02cryAo

At Least Six Are Killed as Libyan Militias Clash on Coastal Highway Near Tripoli, N.Y. TIMES,
Nov. 14, 2011, *available at* http://www.nytimes.com/2011/11/14/world/africa/six-dead-as-libyan-militias-clash-near-tripoli.html

At least 30 killed in Libya as Gadhafi forces fight to take back rebel-held town, HAARETZ, Mar.
4, 2011, *available at* http://www.haaretz.com/news/world/at-least-30-killed-in-libya-as-gadhafi-forces-fight-to-take-back-rebel-held-town-1.347213

Samer al-Atrush, *Kadhafi's forces have rebels in retreat*, AFP, Mar. 10, 2011, *available at*
http://news.smh.com.au/breaking-news-world/kadhafis-forces-have-rebels-in-retreat-20110310-1bpvw.html

Fatima AzZahra, *Misrata and Tawargha*, FEB 17TH, Nov. 13, 2011, *available at* http://feb17.
info/editorials/op-ed-misrata-and-tawargha

Tara Bahrampour, *Libyan rebels struggle to explain rift*, THE WASHINGTON POST, Apr. 2, 2011,
available at http://articles.washingtonpost.com/2011-04-02/world/35231483_1_khalifa-haftar-haftar-and-younis-abdul-fattah-younis

Tara Bahrampour & Greg Jaffe, *Libyan rebels push toward Gaddafi's home town*, THE WASHINGTON POST, Mar. 29, 2011, *available at* http://www.washingtonpost.com/world/libyan-rebels-push-toward-sirte-gaddafi-sends-reinforcements/2011/03/28/AFedisoB_story.html

Duraid Al Baik, *Tension running high as Tripoli braces for attacks*, GULF NEWS, Feb. 17, 2011, *available at* http://gulfnews.com/news/region/libya/tension-running-high-as-tripoli-braces-for-attacks-1.768282

Battle at army base broke Gadhafi hold in Benghazi, WASHINGTON POST, Feb. 25, 2011, *available at* http://www.washingtonpost.com/wp-dyn/content/article/2011/02/25/AR2011022505021.html

Battle for Libya: Gaddafi troops engage Zawiya rebels, BBC, Mar. 5, 2011, *available at* http://www.bbc.co.uk/news/world-africa-12654670

Battle for Tripoli, THE WASHINGTON POST, Aug. 21, 2011, *available at* http://www.washingtonpost.com/world/battle-for-tripoli/2011/08/21/gIQA3CG9UJ_graphic.html?tid=sm_twitter_washingtonpost

Battle for Tripoli: pivotal victory in the mountains helped big push, GUARDIAN, Aug. 22 2011, *available at* http://www.guardian.co.uk/world/2011/aug/22/battle-for-tripoli-libya-gaddafi

David Batty & Warren Murray, *Libya military action*, THE GUARDIAN, Mar. 19, 2011, *available at* http://www.guardian.co.uk/world/blog/2011/mar/19/libya-live-blog-ceasefire-nofly

David Batty, *Libyan children suffering rape, aid agency reports*, THE GUARDIAN, Apr. 23, 2011, *available at* http://www.guardian.co.uk/world/2011/apr/23/libyan-children-suffering-rape

BBC journalist describes release from Rixos hotel, BBC, Aug. 24, 2011, *available at* http://www.bbc.co.uk/news/world-africa-14654958

Jonathan Beale, *Libya Conflict: NATO's man against Gaddafi*, BBC, June 26, 2011, *available at* http://www.bbc.co.uk/news/world-europe-13919380

Peter Beaumont, *In the chaos of Surt, anti-Gaddafi fighters are killing each other*, THE GUARDIAN, Oct. 14, 2011, *available at* http://www.guardian.co.uk/world/2011/oct/14/Surt-fighters-shoot-own-side

Peter Beaumont, *Libya Rebels and Government Sources Locked in Battle for Bin Jawad*, THE GUARDIAN, Mar. 6, 2011, *available at* http://www.guardian.co.uk/world/2011/mar/06/libya-rebels-government-battle-bin-jawad

Peter Beaumont & Mark Tran, *Libya protests break out after Friday prayers*, THE GUARDIAN, Mar. 4, 2011, *available at* http://www.guardian.co.uk/world/2011/mar/04/libya-protests-gaddafi-tripoli

Benghazi hospitals struggle to treat war-wounded, INTEGRATED REGIONAL INFORMATION NETWORKS, Apr. 13, 2011, *available at* http://reliefweb.int/node/396013

Belgium probes arms sales to Qadafi regime, EXPACTICA BELGIAN NEWS, Feb. 21, 2011, *available at* http://www.expatica.com/be/news/belgian-news/belgium-probes-arms-sales-to-kadhafi-regime_131541.html

Benghazi opts for township government, BBC, Feb. 26, 2011, *available at* http://news.bbc.co.uk/today/hi/today/newsid_9408000/9408121.stm

Benghazi votes to be recounted, IRISH EXAMINER, July 15, 2012, *available at* http://www.irishexaminer.com/breakingnews/world/benghazi-votes-to-be-recounted-559185.html

Annie Benard, *Libyan Transitional Leader Urges Reconciliation, Using Symbolism of Tripoli Site*, N.Y. TIMES, Sept. 12, 2011, *available at* http://www.nytimes.com/2011/09/13/world/africa/13libya.html

J. Benitez, *National Composition of NATO Strike Sorties in Libya*, ATLANTIC COUNCIL, Aug. 22, 2011, *available at* http://www.acus.org/natosource/national-composition-nato-strike-sorties-libya

The Berber Rising: The "Other Arab Spring", BROOKS FOREIGN POLICY REVIEW, Feb. 20, 2012 *available at* http://brooksreview.wordpress.com/2012/02/20/the-berber-rising-the-other-arab-spring

Michael Birnbaum, *France sent arms to Libyan rebels*, WASHINGTON TIMES, June 29, 2011, *available* at http://articles.washingtonpost.com/2011-06-29/world/35235276_1_nafusa-mountains-hans-hillen-libyan-rebels

Robert Birsel, *Clashes as Libyan rebels try to press Gaddafi stronghold*, REUTERS, Aug. 25, 2011, *available at* www.jpost.com/Headlines/Article.aspx?id=235376

Nancy Bisdsall & Arvind Subramanian, *Saving Iraq from its Oil*, 83(4) FOREIGN AFFAIRS, July/Aug. 2004

Jim Bittermann, *French helicopters keep up pressure on Qadhafi*, CNN, June 15, 2011, *available at* http://www.youtube.com/watch?v=oHNnyHShq30

Ian Black, *Abdullah al-Senussi: a trial of strength between the ICC and Tripoli*, THE GUARDIAN, September 5, 2012, *available at* http://www.guardian.co.uk/world/2012/sep/05/abdullah-senussi-trial-icc-tripoli

——, *Benghazi's moment of joy as Libya's tyranny ends*, THE GUARDIAN, Oct. 23, 2011, *available at* http://www.guardian.co.uk/world/2011/oct/23/benghazi-joy-end-libya-tyranny

——, *Gaddafi buried in secret desert location*, THE GUARDIAN, Oct. 25, 2011, *available at* http://www.guardian.co.uk/world/2011/oct/25/gaddafi-buried-libya-desert

——, *Gaddafi loyalists face torture, human rights groups warn*, THE GUARDIAN, Oct. 21, 2011, *available at* http://www.guardian.co.uk/world/2011/oct/21/gaddafi-loyalists-torture-human-rights

——, *Heavy fighting in former stronghold as Gaddafi's forces stage counterattacks*, THE GUARDIAN, Feb. 24, 2011, *available at* http://www.guardian.co.uk/world/2011/feb/24/muammar-gaddafi-libya-offensive

——, *Libyan forces predict fall of rebel-held Benghazi 'within 48 hours'*, THE GUARDIAN, Mar. 17, 2011, *available at* http://www.guardian.co.uk/world/2011/mar/16/libya-benghazi-gaddafi-48-hours

——, *Liyan rebels receiving anti-tank weapons from Qatar*, THE GUARDIAN, Apr. 14, 2011 *available at* http://www.guardian.co.uk/world/2011/apr/14/libya-rebels-weapons-qatar

——, *Muammar Gaddafi's 'trophy' body on show in Misrata meat store*, THE GUARDIAN, October 22 2011, *available at* http://www.guardian.co.uk/world/2011/oct/21/muammar-gaddafi-body-miorata-meat-store

——, *Qatar admits sending hundreds of troops to support Libya rebels*, THE GUARDIAN, Oct. 26, 2011, *available at* http://www.guardian.co.uk/world/2011/oct/26/qatar-troops-libya-rebels-support

Edmund Blair, *Gaddafi troops retreating westwards – Libyan rebels*, REUTERS, Mar. 27, 2011, *available at* http://www.reuters.com/article/2011/03/27/libya-east-westwards-idUSLDE72Q07F20110327

Bloodshed as tensions rise in Libya, BBC, Feb. 19, 2011, *available at* http://www.bbc.co.uk/news/world-middle-east-12513941

William Booth, *In war-torn Libya, no pause for Ramadan*, THE WASHINGTON POST, Aug. 1, 2011, *available at* http://www.washingtonpost.com/world/middle-east/in-war-tornlibya-no-pause-for-ramadan/2011/08/01/gIQA82pNoI_story.html

Julian Borger et al., *Battle for Tripoli: pivotal victory in the mountains helped big push*, THE GUARDIAN, Aug. 22, 2011, *available at* http://www.guardian.co.uk/world/2011/aug/22/battle-for-tripoli-libya-gaddafi

——, *Gaddafi family deaths reinforce doubts about Nato's UN mandate*, THE GUARDIAN, May 1, 2011, *available at* http://www.guardian.co.uk/world/2011/may/01/gaddadi-family-deaths-reinforce-doubts

Feras Bosalum, *Six Libyan soldiers killed in Benghazi violence*, REUTERS, June 15, 2013, *available at* http://www.reuters.com/article/2013/06/15/us-libya-attack-benghazi-id USBRE95E04Y20130615

Youssef Boudlal & Peter Graff, *Explosions in Tripoli, rebels seize Libyan town*, REUTERS, June 6, 2011, *available at* http://www.reuters.com/article/2011/06/06/us-libya-id USTRE7270JP20110606

Owen Bowcott, *Saif Gaddafi should go on trial in Libya, war crimes tribunal told*, THE GUARDIAN, May 1, 2012, *available at* http://www.guardian.co.uk/world/2012/may/01/saif-gadaffi-trial-libya-icc

Kate Brannen, *U.S. Still Hunting for Missing Libyan MANPADS*, DEFENSE NEWS, Feb. 2, 2012, *available at* http://www.defensenews.com/article/20120202/DEFREG02/302020009/U-S-Still-Hunting-Missing-Libyan-MANPADS

British Military Officers to be sent to Libya, BBC, Apr. 19, 2011, *available at* http://www.bbc.co.uk/news/uk-13132654

Ben Brown, *Libya: Rebels take Ras Lanuf, Brega, Uqayla, Bin Jawad*, BBC, Mar. 27, 2011, *available at* http://www.bbc.co.uk/news/world-africa-12873434

David Brunnstrom, *NATO worried by Libya armed groups, offers security help*, REUTERS, Sept. 27, 2012 *available at* http://www.reuters.com/article/2012/09/27/us-un-assembly-nato-libya-idUSBRE88Q1YO20120927

Mohamed Bujaneh, et al., *Abdul Jalil will stand trial "very soon" in connection with Younis murder*, LIBYA HERALD, Dec. 16, 2012, *available at* http://www.libyaherald.com/2012/12/16/abdul-jalil-will-stand-trial-very-soon-in-connection-with-younis-murder

Marc Burleigh, *Battle for Brega rages after Kadhafi forces ambush*, AFP, Apr. 3, 2011, *available at* http://news.smh.com.au/breaking-news-world/battle-for-brega-rages-after-ambush-20110403-1ctek.html

——, *Libyan rebels push towards Tripoli, promise new oil exports*, AFP, Mar. 27, 2011, *available at* http://www.thejakartaglobe.com/afp/libyan-rebels-push-towards-tripoli-promise-new-oil-exports/431978

——, *Snipers, cluster bombs panic Libya's Misrata*, AFP, Apr. 11, 2011, *available at* http://news.smh.com.au/breaking-news-world/snipers-cluster-bombs-panic-libyas-misrata-20110418-1dlhb.html

Giorgio Cafiero, *Beyond Libya's election*, FOREIGN POLICY IN FOCUS, Jul. 18, 2012, *available at* http://www.fpif.org/articles/beyond_libyas_election

Greg Campbell, *Gadhafi forces push towards western gate*, USA TODAY, Apr. 8, 2011, *available at* http://usatoday30.usatoday.com/news/world/2011-04-08-libya_N.htm

Nick Carey, *Gaddafi war crimes in Misrata widespread: report*, REUTERS, Aug. 30, 2011, *available at* http://www.reuters.com/article/2011/08/30/us-libya-misrata-warcrimes-id USTRE77T0J520110830

——, *Libya rebels boost firepower with homemade weapons*, REUTERS, July 12, 2011, *available at* http://www.reuters.com/article/2011/07/12/us-libya-misrata-weapons-idUSTRE76 A38N20110712

——, *WRAPUP 1 – Italy calls for political solution in Libya*, REUTERS, July 11, 2011, *available at* http://www.reuters.com/article/2011/07/11/libya-idUSLDE76A1NC20110711

——, *WRAPUP 1 – Libyan rebels take new villges [sic] in Western Mountains*, REUTERS, June 15, 2011, *available at* http://www.reuters.com/article/2011/06/15/libya-idUSLDE75 E29K20110615

——, *WRAPUP 1 – Rebels dismiss election offer, NATO pounds Tripoli*, REUTERS, June 16, 2011, *available at* http://www.reuters.com/article/2011/06/16/libya-idUSLDE75F25S20110616

——, *Zawiyah's heart a ghost town after rebel advance*, REUTERS, June 12, 2011, *available at* http://www.reuters.com/article/2011/06/12/us-libya-zawiyah-idUSTRE75B2HJ20110612?fe edType=RSS&feedName=topNews

Nick Carey & Peter Graff, *Fighting in Zawiya shuts Libya road to Tunisia*, REUTERS, June 11, 2011, *available at* http://www.reuters.com/article/2011/06/11/us-libya-idUSTRE7270JP20110611

Severine Carrell & Chris Stephen, *Abdullah al Senussi extradition unites Lockerbie relatives*, THE GUARDIAN, September 5, 2012, *available at* http://www.guardian.co.uk/uk/2012/sep/05/abdullah-senussi-extradition-lockerbie-relatives

Mary Casey & Jennifer Parker, Middle East Daily Brief, *Jibril's centrist party wins Libya's elections*, FOREIGN POLICY, July 18, 2012, *available at* http://mideast.foreignpolicy.com/posts/2012/07/18/jibril_s_centrist_party_takes_libya_s_elections

David Cenciotti, *Operation Unified Protector (was Odyssey Dawn) explained (Day 39–42)*, THE AVIATIONIST, Apr. 30, 2011, *available at* http://theaviationist.com/2011/04/30/operation-unified-protector-was-odyssey-dawn-explained-day-39-42/

——, *Photo: Unexploded MBDA PGM-500 500-lb guided bomb "Hakim" blown at Zintan, Libya*, THE AVIATIONIST, July 12, 2012, *available at* http://theaviationist.com/tag/uae-air-force/#.UMDQkJPjlAE

Louis Charbonneau & Hamuda Hassan, *France defends arms airlift to Libya rebels*, REUTERS, June 30, 2011, *available at* http://www.reuters.com/article/2011/06/29/us-libya-idUSTRE7270JP20110629

Amy Chew, *Oil-rich town of Ras Lanuf a major battleground*, THE STAR ONLINE, Mar. 10, 2011, *available at* http://thestar.com.my/news/story.asp?file=/2011/3/10/nation/8224848&sec=nation

C.J. Chivers, *Can you Name this Cluster Bomb?*, N.Y. TIMES, Feb. 1, 2012, *available at* http://atwar.blogs.nytimes.com/2012/02/01/can-you-name-this-cluster-bomb/?scp=1&sq=dpicm&st=cse

——, *Hidden Workshops Add to Libyan Rebels' Arsenal*, N.Y. TIMES, May 3, 2011, *available at* http://www.nytimes.com/2011/05/04/world/africa/04misurata.html

——, *Inferior Arms Hobble Rebels in Libya War*, N.Y. TIMES, Apr. 20, 2011, *available at* http://www.nytimes.com/2011/04/21/world/africa/21rebels.html

——, *Land Mines Descend on Misurata's Port, Endangering Libyan City's Supply Route*, N.Y. TIMES, May 6, 2011, *available at* http://www.nytimes.com/2011/05/07/world/africa/07libya.html

——, *Libyan Rebels Accused of Pillage and Beatings*, THE N.Y. TIMES, July 13, 2011, *available at* http://www.nytimes.com/2011/07/13/world/africa/13libya.html

——, *Looted Libyan Arms in Mali May Have Shifted Conflict's Path*, N.Y. TIMES, Feb. 7, 2013, *available at* http://www.nytimes.com/2013/02/08/world/africa/looted-libyan-arms-in-mali-may-have-shifted-conflicts-path.html

——, *With Help From NATO, Libyan Rebels Gain Ground*, N.Y. TIMES, May 9, 2011, *available at* http://www.nytimes.com/2011/05/10/world/africa/10libya.html

C.J. Chivers & Eric Schmitt, *In Strikes on Libya by NATO, an Unspoken Civilian Toll*, N.Y. TIMES, Dec. 17, 2011, *available at* http://www.nytimes.com/2011/12/18/world/africa/scores-of-unintended-casualties-in-nato-war-in-libya.html

C.J. Chivers, et al., *In Turnabout, Syria Rebels Get Libyan Weapons*, N.Y. TIMES, June 21, 2013, *available at* http://www.nytimes.com/2013/06/22/world/africa/in-a-turnabout-syria-rebels-get-libyan-weapons.html

Martin Chulov, *Battle for Brega could mark start of real war in Libya*, THE GUARDIAN, Mar. 3, 2011, *available at* http://www.guardian.co.uk/world/2011/mar/02/libya-civil-war-bregga

—— et al., *Libya: Fierce day of raids and clashes signals shift towards civil war*, THE GUARDIAN, Mar. 4, 2011, *available at* http://www.guardian.co.uk/world/2011/mar/04/libya-rebels-civil-war-gaddafi

——, *Libya: the importance of Zawiya to the rebels*, THE GUARDIAN, Aug. 18, 2011, *available at* http://www.guardian.co.uk/world/2011/aug/18/libya-rebels-zawiya-tripoli-assault

Child soldiers sent by Gaddafi to fight Libyan, CHANNEL 4 NEWS, Apr. 23, 2011, *available at* http://www.channel4.com/news/child-soldiers-sent-by-gaddafi-to-fight-libyan-rebels

City's huge arsenal a test for new Libyan rulers, REUTERS, Dec. 7, 2011, *available at* http://www.reuters.com/article/2011/12/07/libya-misrata-weapons-idUSL5E7N72IH20111207

Clampdown in Libyan capital as protests close in, AP, Feb. 23, 2011, *available at* http://www.washingtontimes.com/news/2011/feb/23/libyan-protesters-defiant-after-gadhafi-speech/

Clashes as rebels deny Libyan counter-offensive claim, Mar. 6, 2011, AFP, *available at* http://www.timesofmalta.com/articles/view/20110306/local/clashes-as-rebels-deny-libyan-counter-offensive-claim.353429

Clashes between Libyan Militia kills 2, SEATTLE TIMES, Nov. 13, 2011, *available at* http://seattletimes.nwsource.com/html/nationworld/2016749284_apmllibya.html

Clinton holds talks in Tripoli with Libya's interim authority, BBC, Oct. 18, 2011, *available at* http://www.bbc.co.uk/news/world-africa-15360308

David Cloud, *U.S. begins using Predator drones in Libya*, L.A. TIMES, Apr. 22, 2011 *available at* http://articles.latimes.com/2011/apr/22/world/la-fg-gates-libya-20110422

Ian Cobain, *Libyan dissidents launch action against UK government over rendition*, THE GUARDIAN, June 28, 2012, *available at* http://www.guardian.co.uk/world/2012/jun/28/libyan-dissidents-action-government-rendition

Margaret Coker, *Length of Libya's standoff hinges on leader's militia*, WALL STREET JOURNAL, Aug. 24, 2011, *available at* http://online.wsj.com/article/SB10001424053119033279045765 2664236989320.html

Col. Gaddafi's family French lawyer to sue NATO through ICC, DIGITAL JOURNAL, Oct. 29, 2011, *available at* http://digitaljournal.com/article/313579#ixzz27Ui0FkMa

Conditions in Libya deteriorating, AL JAZEERA, Mar. 4, 2011, *available at* http://www.aljazeera .com/indepth/spotlight/libya/2011/03/201134162742713130.html

Congress Threatens To Cut Off Funding For War In Libya; Obama Weighs US Troop Withdrawal From Afghanistan: Today's Q's for O's WH – 6/20/2011, ABC NEWS, June 20, 2011, *available at* http://abcnews.go.com/blogs/politics/2011/06/congress-threatens-to-cut-off-funding-for-war-in-libya-obama-weighs-us-troop-withdrawal-from-afghani

CORRECTED – Gun battles in Libya's Nalut kill 8-rebes, REUTERS, June 18, 2011, *available at* http://www.reuters.com/article/2011/06/18/libya-violence-idUSLDE75H04B20110618

Court reopens investigation into Younis killing, LIBYA HERALD, June 1, 2012, *available at* http:// www.libyaherald.com/2012/06/01/court-reopens-investigation-into-younis-killing/

Michael Cousins, *Party Profile: Union for the Homeland*, LIBYA HERALD, July 4, 2012, *available at* http://www.libyaherald.com/?p=10516

Alan Cowell, *France and Italy Will Also Send Advisers to Libya Rebels*, N.Y. TIMES, Apr. 20, 2011, *available at* http://www.nytimes.com/2011/04/21/world/africa/21libya.html

Alan Cowell & Ravi Somaiya, *France and Italy will also send advisers to Libya rebels*, N.Y. TIMES, Apr. 20 2011, *available at* http://www.nytimes.com/2011/04/21/world/africa/21libya. html?pagewanted=all&_moc.semityn

Rob Crilly, *Libya: Gaddafi loyalists 'using prisoners as human shields to protect Sirte'*, THE TELEGRAPH, Sept. 11, 2011, *available at* http://www.telegraph.co.uk/news/worldnews/africaandindianocean/libya/8755935/Libya-Gaddafi-loyalists-using-prisoners-as-human-shields-to-protect-Sirte.html

——, *Libya: tribe pledges to arrest rebels it believes were behind murder of opposition military commander*, THE TELEGRAPH, Aug. 26, 2011, *available at* http://www.telegraph .co.uk/news/worldnews/africaandindianocean/libya/8725413/Libya-tribe-pledges-to-arrest-rebels-it-believes-were-behind-murder-of-opposition-military-commander.html

——, *Libya: the battle for control of Sirte*, THE TELEGRAPH, Aug. 25, 2011, *available at* http:// www.telegraph.co.uk/news/worldnews/africaandindianocean/libya/8723027/Libya-the-battle-for-control-of-Sirte.html

Adrian Croft & Maria Golovnina, *Western, Arab nations say Gadhafi must go*, REUTERS, Apr. 13, 2011, *available at* http://www.thestar.com/news/world/article/974198--western-arab-nations-say-gadhafi-must-go

Ivo H. Daalder and James G. Stavridis, *NATO's Victory in Libya: The Right Way to Run an Intervention*, 91 FOREIGN AFFAIRS 2, Mar./Apr. 2012, *available at* http://www.foreign affairs.com/articles/137073/ivo-h-daalder-and-james-g-stavridis/natos-victory-in-libya.

Borzou Daragahi & David Zucchino, *Libyan rebels show signs of life*, L.A. TIMES, Mar. 24, 2011, *available at* http://articles.latimes.com/2011/mar/24/world/la-fg-libya-fighting-20110325

Deadline for Libyan towns' surrender passes, CNN, Sept. 10, 2011, *available at* http://www .cnn.com/2011/WORLD/africa/09/09/libya.war/index.html

Deadly clashes in Libyan border town, AL JAZEERA, May 16, 2012, *available at* http://www .aljazeera.com/news/africa/2012/05/201251620515544315.html

Deadly faction clashes erupt in Libya, AL JAZEERA, Nov. 13, 2011, *available at* http://www .aljazeera.com/news/africa/2011/11/20111113415595598501.html

Derna judge murdered outside courthouse, LIBYA HERALD, June 16, 2013, *available at* http:// www.libyaherald.com/2013/06/16/35028/

Jay Deshmukh, *Violence mars eve of key Libya election*, AFP, July 6, 2012, *available at* http://
reliefweb.int/report/libya/violence-mars-eve-key-libya-election

Disarming Libya's militias, BBC, Sept. 28, 2012, *available at* http://www.bbc.co.uk/news/
world-middle-east-19744533

Doctors operating without anesthesia in Misrata hospital, CNN, Mar. 24, 2011, *available at*
http://edition.cnn.com/2011/WORLD/africa/03/24/libya.hospital.scene/index.html

Doctors report 17 dead in Libyan city of Zawiya, CNN, Feb. 25, 2011, *available at* http://www
.cnn.com/2011/WORLD/africa/02/24/libya.protests/index.html

Jessica Donati, *Libya's Waha Oil faces tough task to fix war damage*, REUTERS, Oct. 2,
2011, *available at* http://www.reuters.com/article/2011/10/02/us-libya-oil-waha-idUSTRE
79117S20111002

—— et al., *UPDATE 1 – Oil shipments delayed as strikes shut Libyan ports*, REUTERS, July
6, 2011, *available at* http://www.reuters.com/article/2012/07/06/libya-strikes-ports-
idUSL6E8I67ZD20120706

Jon Donnison, *Surt and Misrata: A tale of two war-torn Libyan cities*, BBC, Dec. 20, 2011,
available at http://www.bbc.co.uk/news/world-africa-16257289

Dorda trial opened – and adjourned, LIBYA HERALD, June 5, 2012, *available at* http://www
.libyaherald.com/2012/06/05/dorda-trial-opened-and-adjounred/

Kate Doyle, *Guatemala's Genocide on Trial*, THE NATION, May 22, 2013, *available at* http://
www.thenation.com/article/174488/guatemalas-genocide-trial

Mark Doyle, *Libyan rebels make most significant advance in the west*, BBC, July 7, 2011 *available at* http://www.bbc.co.uk/news/world-africa-14074069

Kimberly Dozier, *Benghazi Suspects Identified by FBI, But no Arrests Made Yet*, AP,
May 21, 2013, *available at* http://www.huffingtonpost.com/2013/05/21/benghazi-
suspects_n_3314153.html

Iain Drewry, *Tornado's Top Guns' 3,000 mile mission to hammer tyrant's military machine*,
THE DAILY MAIL, Mar. 21, 2011, *available at* http://www.dailymail.co.uk/news/article-
1368259/Libya-Tornado-Top-Guns-3-000-mile-mission-hammer-Gaddafis-military-
machine.html

Alexander Dziadosz, *East Libya rebels organize, head towards oil town*, REUTERS,
Apr. 1, 2011, *available at* http://www.reuters.com/article/2011/04/01/us-libya-east-id
USTRE7301AG20110401

——, *Libya rebels beat rapid retreat east under fire*, REUTERS, Mar. 30, 2011, *available at*
http://www.reuters.com/article/2011/03/30/libya-east-retreat-idUSWEA174420110330

——, *Libya rebels push towards oil port*, REUTERS, Apr. 6, 2011, *available at* http://www
.reuters.com/article/2011/04/06/us-libya-east-idUSTRE7351SU20110406

——, *Libyan rebels fear fresh attack on Ajdabiyah*, REUTERS, Apr. 18, 2011, *available at* http://
uk.reuters.com/article/2011/04/17/uk-libya-idUKLDE71QoMP20110417

——, *Libyan rebels regain ground near oil port*, REUTERS, Apr. 6, 2011, *available at* http://
uk.reuters.com/article/2011/04/06/uk-libya-east-idUKTRE7351ZO20110406

——, *Rebels flee east Libya oil town under rocket fire*, REUTERS, Apr. 5 2011, *available at*
http://www.reuters.com/article/2011/04/05/us-libya-east-idUSTRE73424J20110405

——, *Tank burns at Libya's biggest oil terminal*, REUTERS, Aug. 30, 2011, *available at* http://
www.reuters.com/article/2011/08/30/us-libya-oil-tanks-idUSTRE77T1JZ20110830

Alexander Dziadosz & Edmund Blair, *Aircraft, blasts heard in direction of Libya
town*, REUTERS, Mar. 30, 2011, *available at* http://af.reuters.com/article/libyaNews/
idAFWEA16692011030

William Edwards, *Violent protests rock Libyan city of Benghazi*, FRANCE 24, Feb. 16, 2011
available at http://www.france24.com/en/20110216-libya-violent-protests-rock-benghazi-
anti-government-gaddafi-egypt-tunisia-demonstration

Egyptians arrest suspected terror leader in connection with Benghazi consulate attack, LIBYA
HERALD, Dec. 8, 2012, *available at* http://www.libyaherald.com/2012/12/08/egyptians-
arrest-suspected-terror-leader-in-connection-with-benghazi-consulate-attack

Election in Libya Proceeds as Federalist Protesters in the East Try to Disrupt Voting, TRIPOLI
POST, July 7, 2012, *available at* http://www.tripolipost.com/articledetail.asp?c=1&i=8760

Elections in Libya: 7 July General National Congress Elections – Frequently Asked Questions, LIBYA HERALD, June 30, 2012, *available at* http://www.libyaherald.com/?p=10175

Mohamed Eljarh, *Jalil ordered not to leave country*, LIBYA HERALD, Dec. 12, 2012, *available at* http://www.libyaherald.com/2012/12/12/jalil-order-not-to-leave-country

Mike Elkton, *In Benghazi, brutal memories fuel opposition*, USA TODAY, Mar. 3, 2011, *available at* http://usatoday30.usatoday.com/news/world/2011-03-03-libya-unrest_N.htm

Maha Ellawati & Nihal Zaroug, *Younis murder judge orders Jalil to appear in Benghazi court*, LIBYA HERALD, Nov. 9, 2012, *available at* http://www.libyaherald.com/2012/11/10/younis-murder-judge-orders-jalil-to-appear-in-benghazi-court/

Andrew England & Javier Blas, *Libya rebels fight to keep oil lifeline open*, FINANCIAL TIMES, Apr. 7, 2011, *available at* http://www.ft.com/intl/cms/s/0/711c6cd6-6146-11e0-ab25-00144feab49a.html#axzz2MmfaFCq7

Adam Entous, Siobhan Gorman & Margaret Coker, *CIA Takes Heat for Role in Libya*, THE WALL STREET JOURNAL, Nov. 1, 2012, *available at* http://online.wsj.com/article/SB100014 24052970204712904578092853621061838.html

Amatai Etzioni, *The Lessons of Libya*, 92 MILITARY REVIEW 45, 49 (Jan.–Feb. 2012)

Evidence of 'mass execution' in Tripoli, AL JAZEERA, Aug. 25, 2011, *available at* http://www .aljazeera.com/news/africa/2011/08/2011825124849190250.html

Ex-Libya PM al-Baghdadi al-Mahmoudi 'jailed in Tunisia', BBC, Sept. 22, 2011, *available at* http://www.bbc.co.uk/news/world-middle-east-15022757

Excluded from cabinet, Libya's Berbers fear isolation, AL ARABIYA NEWS, Nov. 28, 2011, *available at* http://english.alarabiya.net/articles/2011/11/25/179187.html

Exclusive: At bay, captured Libyan spy chief defiant, REUTERS, September 11, 2011, *available at* http://www.reuters.com/article/2011/09/11/us-libya-spy-idUSTRE78A3PR20110911

Explosions, planes heard in Tripoli; rebels seize border crossing, CNN, Apr. 21, 2011, *available at* http://articles.cnn.com/2011-04-21/world/libya.fighting_1_nato-commander-nato-military-official-moammar-gadhafi

Factbox: Latest developments in the Libyan conflict, REUTERS, Aug. 27, 2011, *available at* http://www.reuters.com/article/2011/08/27/us-libya-nato-idUSTRE77Q0T720110827

Leila Fadel, *After The War, A Bitter Feud Remains In Two Libyan Towns*, NPR, May 29, 2013, *available at* http://www.npr.org/blogs/parallels/2013/05/29/186927435/after-the-war-a-bitter-feud-remains-in-two-libyan-towns

Leila Fadel & Simon Denyer, *Libyan rebels targeted in airstrikes despite no-fly zone, rebels say*, THE WASHINGTON POST, Apr. 7, 2011, *available at* http://articles.washingtonpost .com/2011-04-07/world/35262954_1_ajdabiya-government-attacks-libyan-rebels

Leila Fadel & Steve Hendrix, *Libya's rebels hold back Gaddafi's forces*, THE WASHINGTON POST, Mar. 3, 2011, *available at* http://www.washingtonpost.com/wp-dyn/content/article/ 2011/03/02/AR2011030207023.html

Kareem Fahim, *Accused of Fighting for Qaddafi, a Libyan Town's Residents Face Reprisals*, N.Y. TIMES, Sept. 23, 2011, *available at* http://www.nytimes.com/2011/09/24/world/africa/ accused-of-fighting-for-qaddafi-tawerga-residents-face-reprisals.html

——, *Clashes and Car Bombing Highlight Insecurity Across Libya*, N.Y. TIMES, Nov. 4, 2012, *available at* http://www.nytimes.com/2012/11/05/world/africa/clashes-car-bombing-highlight-insecurity-in-libya.html

——, *Libya Rebels Threaten a Supply Line to the Capital*, N.Y. TIMES, Aug. 15, 2011, *available at* http://www.nytimes.com/2011/08/15/world/africa/15libya.html

——, *Libyan rebels show division after setbacks*, N.Y. TIMES, Apr. 4, 2011, *available at* http:// query.nytimes.com/gst/fullpage.html?res=9C06EEDF1639F937A35757C0A9679D8B63

——, *Qadhafi Forces Given Deadline to Surrender*, N.Y. TIMES, Aug. 30, 2011, *available at* http://www.nytimes.com/2011/08/31/world/africa/31libya.html

——, *Rebel leadership in Libya shows strain*, N.Y. TIMES, Apr. 1, 2011, *available at* http:// www.nytimes.com/2011/04/04/world/africa/04rebels.html

Kareem Fahim & David D. Kirkpatrick, *Airstrikes Clear Way for Libyan Rebels' First Major Advance*, N.Y. TIMES, Mar. 26, 2011, *available at* http://www.nytimes.com/2011/03/27/ world/africa/27libya.html

Kareem Fahim & David D. Kirkpatrick, *Attacks by government forces in Libya deal setback to rebel advance*, N.Y. TIMES, Mar. 7, 2011, *available at* http://www.nytimes.com/2011/03/08/world/africa/08libya.html

——, *In Libya, fierce fight near site of refinery*, N.Y. TIMES, Mar. 10, 2011, *available at* http://query.nytimes.com/gst/fullpage.html?res=9503E4D71F3FF933A25750C0A9679D8B63

——, *Libyan government presses assault on oil refinery in east and city in west*, N.Y. TIMES, Mar. 8, 2011, http://www.nytimes.com/2011/03/08/world/africa/08libya.html

——, *Rebel Advance Halted Outside Qaddafi Hometown*, N.Y. TIMES, Mar. 29, 2011, *available at* http://www.nytimes.com/2011/03/29/world/africa/29libya.html

——, *Rebels Retake Libyan City As Airstrikes Clear a Way*, N.Y. TIMES, Mar. 27, 2011, *available at*, http://www.nytimes.com/2011/03/27/world/africa/27libya.html

Kareem Fahim & Mark Mazzetti, *Rebels' Assault on Tripoli Began With Careful Work Inside*, N.Y. TIMES, Aug. 22, 2011, *available at* http://www.nytimes.com/2011/08/23/world/africa/23reconstruct.html

Mariam Fam et al., *Gaddafi strikes rebels in west as battles rage in oil ports*, THE WASHINGTON POST, Mar. 4, 2011, *available at* http://www.washingtonpost.com/wp-dyn/content/article/2011/03/04/AR2011030402184.html

Emma Farge, *Libya oil flows, foreign workers wait*, REUTERS, Sept. 23, 2011, *available at* http://www.reuters.com/article/2011/09/23/us-libya-oil-idUSTRE78M1TW20110923

——, *Libya sees oil output at pre-war levels in 15 months*, REUTERS, Aug. 30, 2011, *available at* http://www.reuters.com/article/2011/08/30/us-libya-oil-noc-idUSTRE77T3DM20110830

——, *Libyan oil refinery attack 'isolated incident': NOC*, REUTERS, Sept. 15, 2011, *available at* http://www.reuters.com/article/2011/09/15/us-libya-oil-noc-interview-idUSTRE78E32E20110915

Paul Farhi, *Libyan rebel advance traps journalists inside hotel*, THE WASHINGTON POST, Aug. 22, 2011, *available at* http://www.washingtonpost.com/lifestyle/style/libyan-rebel-advance-traps-journalists-inside-hotel/2011/08/22/gIQAX91VXJ_story.html

Ben Farmer, *Gaddafi's final hours: Nato and the SAS helped rebels drive hunted leader into endgame in a desert drain*, TELEGRAPH, Oct. 22, 2011, *available at* http://www.telegraph.co.uk/news/worldnews/africaandindianocean/libya/8843684/Gaddafis-final-hours-Nato-and-the-SAS-helped-rebels-drive-hunted-leader-into-endgame-in-a-desert-drain.html

——, *Gaddafi's final stronghold falls: Libyan forces conquer Sirte*, THE TELEGRAPH, Oct. 20, 2011, *available at* http://www.telegraph.co.uk/news/worldnews/africaandindianocean/libya/8838122/Gaddafis-final-stronghold-falls-Libyan-forces-conquer-Sirte.html

Zainab Fattah & Tamara Walid, *Libya rebels seek ceasefire as US vows to withdraw jets*, BLOOMBERG BUSINESSWEEK, Apr. 1, 2011, *available at* http://www.bloomberg.com/news/2011-04-01/libya-rebels-seek-cease-fire-after-u-s-vows-to-withdraw-its-fighter-jets.html

Benoit Faucon, *Libya's Zueitina Oil Co Restarts Production – NOC Head*, DOW JONES NEWSWIRES, Oct. 18, 2011, *available at* http://english.capital.gr/News.asp?id=1306932

FBI in Benghazi to investigate consulate killings as hunt for attackers narrows, THE GUARDIAN, Oct. 4, 2012, *available at* http://www.guardian.co.uk/world/2012/oct/04/fbi-investigate-benghazi-consulte-attack

Lee Ferran, *American Killed in Libya was on Intel Mission to Track Weapons*, ABC, Sept. 13, 2012, *available at* http://abcnews.go.com/Blotter/glen-doherty-navy-seal-killed-libya-intel-mission/story?id=17229037#.UMn536VpKfQ

Issam Fetouri, *Eastern Libya defies Tripoli to create autonomous council*, REUTERS, Mar. 6, 2012, *available at* http://www.reuters.com/article/2012/03/06/libya-east-federalism-idUSL5E8E64JK20120306

Max Fisher, *Libyan militia's failed security at Benghazi*, THE WASHINGTON POST, Nov. 2, 2012, *available at* http://www.washingtonpost.com/blogs/worldviews/wp/2012/11/02/libyan-militias-failed-security-at-benghazi/

Mary Fitzgerald, *Frontline surgeon says morale of anti-Gadafy forces high*, IRISH TIMES, June 7, 2011, *available at* http://www.irishtimes.com/newspaper/world/2011/0607/1224298498069.html

——, *The Syrian Rebels' Libyan Weapon*, FOREIGN POLICY, Aug. 9, 2012, *available at* http://www.foreignpolicy.com/articles/2012/08/09/the_syrian_rebels_libyan_weapon

Jeffrey Fleishman, *Battered Libyan fighters try to keep spirits up*, L.A. TIMES, Mar. 12, 2011, *available at* http://articles.latimes.com/2011/mar/11/world/la-fg-libya-east-20110312

Derek Henry Flood, *Taking charge of Libya's rebels: an in-depth portrait of Colonel Khalifa Haftar*, 2 MILITANT LEADERSHIP MONITOR 3, Mar. 2011, *available at* http://mlm.jamestown.org/single/?tx_ttnews%5Btt_news%5D=37724&tx_ttnews%5BbackPid%5D=567&no_cache=1

Rebecca Fordham, *Libyan Kids Maimed by War Remnants*, AL JAZEERA, June 7, 2011, *available at* http://english.aljazeera.net/indepth/features/2011/06/20116674436348565html

Former Libyan officials stand trial in Tripoli, XINHUANET, Dec. 11, 2012, *available at* http://news.xinhuanet.com/english/photo/2012-12/11/c_132033134_2.htm

Hadi Fornaji, *Egyptian Court Blocks Qaddaf al-Dam Extradition*, LIBYA HERALD, Apr. 3, 2013, *available at* http://www.libyaherald.com/2013/04/03/egyptian-court-blocks-qaddaf-al-dam-extradition

——, *Grand Mufti tells Tawerghans not to return home on Tuesday*, LIBYA HERALD, June 23, 2013, *available at* http://www.libyaherald.com/2013/06/23/grand-mufti-tells-tawerghans-not-to-return-home-on-tuesday

——, *Human Rights Watch demands fair treatment for Mahmoudi*, LIBYA HERALD, July 6, 2012, *available at* http://www.libyaherald.com/2012/07/06/human-rights-watch-demands-fair-treatment-for-mahmoudi/

——, *Tripoli International Airport Still Held by Zintan Brigade*, LIBYA HERALD, Mar. 25, 2012, *available at* http://www.libyaherald.com/2012/03/25/tripoli-international-airport-still-held-by-zintan-brigade

Four Italian Journalists abducted in Libya, FOX NEWS, Aug. 24, 2011, *available at* http://www.foxnews.com/world/2011/08/24/italy-4-italian-journalists-abducted-in-libya

Four Italian Journalists held by Qaddafi loyalists, CORRIERE DELLA SERA, Aug. 25, 2011, *available at* http://www.corriere.it/english/11_agosto_25/italian-journalists-held-libia_c8f40a5a-cf04-11e0-9639-95c553466c70.shtml

France airdropped arms to the rebels, BBC, June 29, 2011, *available at* http://www.bbc.co.uk/news/world-africa-13955751

France gives Libya rebels arms but Britain balks, AFP, June 29, 2011, *available at* http://www.google.com/hostednews/afp/article/ALeqM5gst8wAKgJwnMvBWiTl9EQ1Zpylmg?docId=CNG.041943dc452c61a507ee986061b49f2d.1031

Sheera Frankel, *Syrian rebels squabble over weapons as biggest shipload arrives in Libya*, THE TIMES, Sept. 14, 2012, *available at* http://www.thetimes.co.uk/tto/news/world/middleeast/article3537770.ece

Christian Fraser, *Libya conflict: US officials met Gaddafi envoys*, BBC, July 19, 2011, *available at* http://www.bbc.co.uk/news/world-africa-14195476

Colin Freeman & Sean Rayment, *Libya: British Forces Fire Missiles at Gaddafi*, THE TELEGRAPH, Mar. 19, 2011, *available at* http://www.telegraph.co.uk/news/worldnews/africaandindianocean/libya/8393128/Libya-British-forces-fire-missiles-at-Gaddafi.html

From voice said to be Gadhafi, a defiant message to his foes, CNN, Sept. 1, 2011, *available at* http://articles.cnn.com/2011-09-01/world/libya.war_1_moammar-gadhafi-national-transitional-council-libyan-people

Fugitive Baghdadi Mahmoudi 'starving to death', LIBYA HERALD, Mar. 9, 2012, *available at* http://www.libyaherald.com/2012/03/09/fugitive-baghdadi-mahmoudi-starving-to-death/

A guide to Libya's new political landscape, THE GUARDIAN, Sept. 1, 2011, *available at* http://www.guardian.co.uk/commentisfree/2011/sep/01/libya-political-landscape

Gaddafi blames unrest on al-Qaeda, AL JAZEERA, Feb. 24, 2011, *available at* http://www
.aljazeera.com/news/africa/2011/02/2011224143054988104.html

Gaddafi buried in secret location, THE GUARDIAN, Oct. 25, 2011, *available at* http://www
.guardian.co.uk/world/2011/oct/25/muammar-gaddafi-buried-libya

Gaddafi Dead: Family May File War Crimes Complaint, HUFFINGTON POST, Oct. 26, 2011,
available at http://www.huffingtonpost.com/2011/10/26/gaddafi-dead-war-crimes-
family_n_1033458.html

Gadhafi defiant as rebels claim to take 'revolution' inside Tripoli, CNN, Aug. 21, 2011, *available
at* http://edition.cnn.com/2011/WORLD/africa/08/20/libya.war

Gaddafi deploys forces as world raises Libya pressure, ASHARQ ALAWSAT, Mar. 1, 2011, *available at* http://asharq-e.com/news.asp?section=1&id=24331

Gaddafi family Tree, BBC, October 20, 2011, *available at* http://www.bbc.co.uk/news/world-
africa-12531442

Gaddafi forces accused of 'massacre' as battles rage, AFP, Mar. 6, 2011, *available at* http://
www.timesofmalta.com/articles/view/20110305/local/gaddafi-forces-accused-of-
massacre-as-battles-rage.353261

Gaddafi forces attack Libyan oil facility, AL JAZEERA, Sept. 12, 2011, *available at* http://www
.aljazeera.com/news/africa/2011/09/201191281455351413.html

Gaddafi forces flee rebels sweeping west to Sirte, AFP, Mar. 27, 2011, *available at* http://www
.timesofmalta.com/articles/view/20110327/local/gaddafi-forces-flee-rebels-sweeping-
west-to-sirte.356923

Gaddafi forces hit back at revolt, INDEPENDENT IE, Feb. 24, 2011, *available at* http://www
.independent.ie/breaking-news/world-news/gaddafi-forces-hit-back-at-revolt-2554397
.html

Gaddafi forces hit rebels east and west, THE AUSTRALIAN, Mar. 5, 2011, *available at* http://
www.theaustralian.com.au/news/world/gaddafi-forces-hit-rebels-east-and-west/story-
e6frg6so-1226016290063

Gaddafi forces launch offensive, AL JAZEERA, Mar. 11, 2011, *available at* http://www.aljazeera
.com/news/africa/2011/03/2011310412288563247.html

Gaddafi forces move east, bombard rebels with rockets, REUTERS, Mar. 30, 2011, *available at*
http://www.reuters.com/article/2011/03/30/libya-east-advance-idUSWEA16462011033o

Gadhafi forces shell oil town as troops advance, AP, Mar. 13, 2011, *available at* http://www
.huffingtonpost.com/2011/03/13/libya-gaddafi-forces-shell-brega_n_835032.html

Gaddafi forces still at Tunisia border – witness, REUTERS, Apr. 28, 2011, *available at* http://
af.reuters.com/article/libyaNews/idAFLDE73R2C820110428

Gaddafi foreign minister arrested, AL JAZEERA, Aug. 31, 2011, *available at* http://www
.aljazeera.com/news/africa/2011/08/2011831191145878877.html

Gaddafi Funeral Video: Footage Claims To Show Secret Ceremony, HUFFINGTON POST, October 26, 2011, *available at* http://www.huffingtonpost.com/2011/10/26/gaddafi-funeral-
video_n_1032728.html

'Gaddafi loyalists' and Libya NTC Tripoli battle ends, BBC, Oct. 15, 2011, *available at* http://
www.bbc.co.uk/news/world-africa-15319952

Gaddafi loyalists launch offensive, AL JAZEERA, Mar. 11, 2011, *available at* http://www
.aljazeera.com/news/africa/2011/03/201131041228856242.html

Gaddafi loses more Libyan cities, AL JAZEERA, Feb. 24, 2011, *available at* http://www.aljazeera
.com/news/africa/2011/02/2011223125256699145.html

Gaddafi 'remains in the hearts' of Surt, BBC, Feb. 9, 2012, *available at* http://news.bbc.co.uk/
today/hi/today/newsid_9694000/9694560.stm

Gaddafi son needs surgery on gangrenous fingers: doctor, REUTERS, Nov. 24, 2011, *available at*
http://www.reuters.com/article/2011/11/24/us-libya-saif-health-idUSTRE7AN1VW20111124

Gaddafi stronghold Bani Walid falls, THE GUARDIAN, Oct. 17, 2011, *available at* http://www
.guardian.co.uk/world/2011/oct/17/libyan-rebels-capture-bani-walid

Gaddafi uses, for the first time, a suicide bomber against combatants, ENNAHAR ONLINE,
Oct. 6, 2011, *available at* http://www.ennaharonline.com/en/international/7404.html

Gaddafi's death may be war crime: ICC prosecutor, REUTERS, Dec. 16, 2011, *available at* http://
www.reuters.com/article/2011/12/16/us-libya-icc-idUSTRE7BF0882011216

Gaddafi's forces battle rebels for Brega, AL JAZEERA, Apr. 1, 2011, *available at* http://www
.aljazeera.com/news/africa/2011/03/2011331142051984358.html

Gaddafi's forces withdraw from Kikla, 150 km SW of Tripoli, XINHUANET, June 15, 2011, *available at* http://news.xinhuanet.com/english2010/video/2011-06/15/c_13931305.htm

Gaddafi's New Forces: The Teenagers and Women Keeping Libya's Rebels from Taking Tripoli, TIME, July 8, 2011, *available at* http://www.time.com/time/world/article/
0,8599,2081970,00.html

Gaddafi's son had fingers 'cut off', THE AUSTRALIAN, Nov. 24, 2011, *available at* http://
www.theaustralian.com.au/news/world/gaddafis-son-had-fingers-cut-off/story-
e6frg6so-1226204095145

Rania El Gamal, *In Gaddafi's hometown, residents accused NTC fighters of revenge*,
REUTERS, Oct. 16, 2011, *available at* http://www.reuters.com/article/2011/10/16/us-libya-
sirte-looting-idUSTRE79F2DL20111016

——, *Libya ends public showing of Gaddafi's body*, REUTERS, Oct. 25, 2011 *available at* http://
www.reuters.com/article/2011/10/25/us-libya-gaddafi-body-idUSTRE79N2HW20111025

——, *Rebels clash with Gaddafi loyalists in rebel-held east*, REUTERS, July 31, 2011, *available at* http://www.reuters.com/article/2011/07/31/us-libya-idUSTRE76Q76620110731

Gabriel Gatehouse, *Battle of wills over control of Libya's border crossings*, BBC, Mar. 2, 2012,
available at http://www.bbc.co.uk/news/world-africa-17233519

——, *Benghazi's bid for Cyrenaica autonomy divides Libyans*, BBC, Mar. 10, 2012, *available at*
http://www.bbc.co.uk/news/world-africa-17316264

——, *Misrata votes for brighter Libyan future*, BBC, Feb. 20, 2012, *available at* http://www
.bbc.co.uk/news/world-africa-17107048

Afaf Geblawi, *Libya and France Sign 168-Million_Euro Arms Deal*, AFP, Aug. 2, 2007, *available at* http://www.spacewar.com/reports/Libya_And_France_Sign_168_Million_Euro_Arms_
Deal_999.html

Michael Georgy, *Captured Libyan soldiers say army morale is low*, REUTERS, July 29, 2011,
available at http://www.reuters.com/article/2011/07/29/us-libya-morale-idUSTRE76R4
KD20110729

——, *Libya rebels say they hold gains south of capital*, REUTERS, Aug. 7, 2011, *available at*
http://uk.reuters.com/article/2011/08/07/uk-libya-idUKTRE76Q30I20110807

——, *Libya's Zawiyah on edge after rebel capture*, REUTERS, Aug. 15, 2011, *available at* http://
www.reuters.com/article/2011/08/15/us-libya-zawiyah-scene-idUSTRE77E3R020110815

——, *Libyan rebels fly flag over key town near Tripoli*, REUTERS, Aug. 14, 2011, *available at*
http://www.reuters.com/article/2011/08/14/us-libya-idUSTRE77A2Y920110814

——, *Libyan Rebels Say They Have Tripoli Surrounded*, REUTERS, August 15, 2011, *available at*   http://news.nationalpost.com/2011/08/15/libyan-rebels-take-strongest-position-yet-
on-road-to-tripoli

——, *Rebels attack last Gaddafi Western Mountain stronghold*, REUTERS, July 30, 2011,
available at http://www.reuters.com/article/2011/07/30/us-libya-westernmountains-id
USTRE76T0XB20110730

——, *Rebels blame Libya air strike on mistake by NATO*, REUTERS, Apr. 7, 2011, *available at*
http://www.reuters.com/article/2011/04/07/us-libya-east-strike-idUSTRE73625
W20110407

——, *WRAPUP 1 – New pressure on Gaddafi on foreign, rebel fronts*, REUTERS, July 27, 2011,
available at http://www.reuters.com/article/2011/07/27/libya-idUSLDE76Q1QJ20110727

Michael Georgy & Maria Golovnina, *Rebels repel Gaddafi assault on Libya oil port*,
REUTERS, Mar. 11, 2011, *available at* http://in.reuters.com/article/2011/03/11/idINIndia-
55498020110311

Syed Murtaza Gheblehzadeh, *Air strikes resume as outgunned Libyan rebels scatter*, AFP,
Mar. 30, 2011, *available at* http://www.brecorder.com/top-news/1-front-top-news/9443-
air-strikes-resume-as-outgunned-libyan-rebels-scatter.html

Andrew Gilligan, *Gaddafi's ghost town after the loyalists retreat*, THE TELEGRAPH, Sept. 11, 2011, *available at* http://www.telegraph.co.uk/news/worldnews/africaandindianocean/libya/8754375/Gaddafis-ghost-town-after-the-loyalists-retreat.html

——, *Libya: Nato air strike 'kills 11 imams'*, TELEGRAPH, May 13, 2011, *available at* http://www.telegraph.co.uk/news/worldnews/africaandindianocean/libya/8513402/Libya-Nato-air-strike-kills-11-imams.html

——, *Libya: rebels celebrate seizing Misurata airport*, THE TELEGRAPH, May 11, 2011, *available at* http://www.telegraph.co.uk/news/worldnews/africaandindianocean/libya/8508488/Libya-rebels-celebrate-seizing-Misurata-airport.html

Maria Golovnina, *Libyan rebels blame West for lack of cash*, REUTERS, June 18, 2011, *available at* http://www.reuters.com/article/2011/06/18/us-libya-idUSTRE7270JP20110618

——, *Rebels control Libya town of Zawiyah*, REUTERS, Feb. 27, 2011, *available at* http://www.reuters.com/article/2011/02/27/us-libya-protests-zawiyah-idUSTRE71Q10Q20110227

——, *WRAPUP 2 – Libya fighters amass near pro-Gaddafi town*, REUTERS, Sept. 7, 2011, *available at* http://www.reuters.com/article/2011/09/08/libya-idUSL5E7K74ST20110908

Maria Golovnina and Mohammad Abbas, *Gaddafi forces step up attack on western rebel town*, REUTERS, Mar. 5, 2011, *available at* http://www.reuters.com/article/2011/03/05/us-libya-protests-idUSTRE71G0A620110305

Peter Graff, *China meets Libya rebels in latest blow to Gaddafi*, REUTERS, June 3, 2011, *available at* http://www.reuters.com/article/2011/06/03/us-libya-idUSTRE7270JP20110603

——, *Divisions hamper Libyan rebel fighters' advance*, REUTERS, July 14, 2011, *available at* http://www.reuters.com/article/2011/07/14/libya-rebels-weakness-idUSLDE76D16920110714

——, *Heavy casualties reported in Libya fighting*, REUTERS, July 16, 2011, *available at* http://www.reuters.com/article/2011/07/16/us-libya-idUSTRE76E0M720110716

——, *NATO helicopters ratchet up pressure on Gaddafi*, REUTERS, June 4, 2011, *available at* http://www.reuters.com/article/2011/06/04/us-libya-idUSTRE7270JP20110604

Peter Graff & Mussab Al-Khairalla, *Anticipation in Tripoli as net tightens on Gaddafi*, REUTERS, June 8, 2011, *available at* http://www.reuters.com/article/2011/06/08/us-libya-tripoli-idUSTRE7573F720110608

Peter Graff & Suleiman Al Khalidi, *Benghazi Anti-Militia Protest: Libyan Protesters Drive Islamist Militia from Country's 2nd Largest City*, REUTERS, Sept. 22, 2011, *available at* http://www.huffingtonpost.com/2012/09/21/libya-militia-protests-benghazi_n_1905288.html

Peter Graff et al., *Libya rebels say they retake western village*, REUTERS, July 13, 2011, *available at* http://www.reuters.com/article/2011/07/13/libya-village-idUSLDE76C1IG20110713

David A. Graham, *Inside Gaddafi's Compound*, THE DAILY BEAST, Aug. 23, 2011, *available at* http://www.thedailybeast.com/articles/2011/08/23/gaddafi-s-compound-inside-bab-al-azizya.html

George Grant, *Benghazi local election results announced – woman candidate wins most votes UPDATE*, LIBYA HERALD, May 21, 2012, *available at* http://www.libyaherald.com/benghazi-local-election-results-announced-2

George Grant, *Elections Analysis: So who are they and what do they actually stand for?*, LIBYA HERALD, June 30, 2011, *available at* http://www.libyaherald.com/?p=10156

——, *Supreme Court strikes down Law 37*, LIBYA HERALD, June 14, 2012, *available at* http://www.libyaherald.com/2012/06/14/supreme-court-strikes-down-law-37

George Grant & Ashraf Abdul Wahab, *Baghdadi Al-Mahmoudi refutes allegations of torture in TV interview*, LIBYA HERALD, July 1, 2012, *available at* http://www.libyaherald.com/2012/07/01/baghdadi-al-mahmoudi-refutes-allegations-of-mistreatment-in-tv-interview/

Alan Greenblatt, *Leaders Of The Libyan Opposition Emerge*, NPR, Mar. 14, 2011, *available at* http://www.npr.org/2011/03/15/134452475/leaders-of-the-libyan-opposition-emerge

Guardian journalist held in Libya, PRESS ASSOCIATION, Mar. 10, 2011, *available at* http://www.independent.ie/breaking-news/world-news/guardian-journalist-held-in-libya-2575277.html

Marie-Louise Gumuchian, *Libya says building case against Gaddafi son: ICC prosecutor*, REUTERS, Apr. 21, 2012, *available at* http://www.reuters.com/article/2012/04/21/us-libya-icc-idUSBRE83K09J20120421

——, *Protesters storm Libya election office in Benghazi*, REUTERS, July 1, 2012, *available at* http://www.reuters.com/article/2012/07/01/us-libya-elections-idUSBRE8600H520120701

——, *Shootout erupts at Tripoli foreign worker compound*, REUTERS, Nov. 22, 2011, *available at* http://www.reuters.com/article/2011/11/22/us-libya-shooting-idUSTRE7AL1MR20111122

——, *UPDATE 2 – Protest-hit Libyan oil terminals reopen – NOC*, REUTERS, July 8, 2012, *available at* http://www.reuters.com/article/2012/07/08/libya-elections-oil-idUSL6E8I822 O20120708

——, *Wrangling hampers Libyan drive to try Gaddafi son*, REUTERS, Apr. 29, 2012, *available at* http://www.reuters.com/article/2012/04/29/us-libya-saif-idUSBRE83S06K20120429

Gunfire heard in Libyan town of Zawiyah, REUTERS, Aug. 13, 2011, *available at* http://af.reuters.com/article/libyaNews/idAFL6E7JD07B20110813

Gunfire hits protesters in Libya, INDEPENDENT IE, Feb. 25, 2011, *available at* http://www.independent.ie/breaking-news/world-news/gunfire-hits-protesters-in-libya-2556477.html

Gunman attacks Libyan polling station, one dead, THE AUSTRALIAN, July 8, 2012, *available at* http://www.theaustralian.com.au/news/breaking-news/gunman-attacks-libyan-polling-station-one-dead/story-fn3dxix6-1226420111171

Gunmen attack Tunisian consulate in Benghazi, REUTERS, June 18, 2003, *available at* http://www.reuters.com/article/2012/06/18/us-libya-gunmen-tunisia-idUSBRE85H1V620120618

G8 summit: Sarkozy offers Libya's Gaddafi 'options', BBC, May 26, 2011, *available at* http://www.bbc.co.uk/news/world-europe-13564999

Mahmoud Habboush, *Battle between Tripoli, Misrata militias kills 4*, REUTERS, Jan. 3, 2012, *available at* http://www.reuters.com/article/2012/01/03/us-libya-rebels-clash-id USTRE8021FP20120103

——, *Libyan Islamists rally to demand sharia-based law*, REUTERS, Jan. 20, 2012, *available at* http://www.reuters.com/article/2012/01/20/us-libya-sharia-rallies-idUSTRE 80J23G20120120

——, *Two killed and 36 hurt in Libyan clashes*, REUTERS, Jan. 25, 2012, *available at* http://in.reuters.com/article/2012/01/15/libya-militia-idINDEE80E0102012015

Diaa Hadid & Michelle Faul, *U.S. reaches out to Libya rebels amid airstrikes*, AP, May 24, 2011 *available at* http://www.msnbc.msn.com/id/43140642/ns/world_news-mideast_n_africa/#.ULeOROOe9AG

Hand over Saif Gadhafi, court tells Libya, CNN, Apr. 5, 2012, *available at* http://articles.cnn.com/2012-04-05/africa/world_africa_libya-saif-gadhafi_1_moammar-gadhafi-saif-al-islam-gadhafi-zintan

Thomas Harding, *Col Gaddafi killed: convoy bombed by drone flown by pilot in Las Vegas*, THE TELEGRAPH, Oct. 20, 2011, *available at* http://www.telegraph.co.uk/news/worldnews/africaandindianocean/libya/8839964/Col-Gaddafi-killed-convoy-bombed-by-drone-flown-by-pilot-in-Las-Vegas.html

Luke Harding, *Gaddafi's daughter files "war crimes" lawsuit related to NATO air strike that killed relatives*, GLOBAL POST, June 8, 2011, *available at* http://www.globalpost.com/dispatch/news/regions/middle-east/110607/muammar-gaddafi-daughter-lawsuit-war-crimes-assassination-n

——, *Gaddafi's family escape Libya net to cross into Algeria*, THE GUARDIAN, Aug. 29, 2011, *available at* http://www.guardian.co.uk/world/2011/aug/29/gaddafi-family-escape-libya-algeria

——, *Libya elections: polling station raids mar first vote since Gaddafi's death*, THE GUARDIAN, June 7, 2012, *available at* http://www.guardian.co.uk/world/2012/jul/07/libya-elections-polling-raids-vote

Luke Harding et al., *Abdullah al Senussi: spy with secrets of Lockerbie bombing sent back to Libya*, THE GUARDIAN, Sept. 5, 2012, *available at* http://www.guardian.co.uk/world/2012/sep/05/abdullah-al-senussi-lockerbie-libya

Andrew Harding, *Libya: Misrata breathes as Gaddafi siege lifted*, BBC, May 17, 2011, *available at* http://www.bbc.co.uk/news/world-africa-13421646

Thomas Harding, *Libya: RAF fears over missile shortages*, THE TELEGRAPH, Apr. 20, 2011, *available at* http://www.telegraph.co.uk/news/worldnews/africaandindianocean/libya/8463799/Libya-RAF-fears-over-missile-shortages.html

Abdulsattar Hatitah, *Libyan Tribal Map: Network of loyalties that will determine Gaddafi's fate*, ASHARQ ALWASAT, Feb. 22, 2011, *available at* http://www.asharq-e.com/news.asp?section=3&id=24257

Abigail Hauslohner, *Rumors from an Encircled Town: The Fate of Ajdabiyah*, TIME WORLD, Mar. 15, 2011, *available at* http://www.time.com/time/world/article/0,8599,2059229,00.html

——, *US-backed force in Libya face challenges*, THE GUARDIAN, Nov. 13, 2012, *available at* http://www.guardian.co.uk/world/2012/nov/13/libya-middleeast

Heavy Fighting in Libya as rebels advance toward capitol, AP, Mar. 6, 2011, *available at* http://www.independent.co.uk/news/world/africa/heavy-fighting-in-libya-as-rebels-advance-toward-capital-2233947.html

Kat Higgins, *Libya, Gaddafi Gunships Fire on Rebels*, SKY NEWS, Mar. 6, 2011, *available at* http://news.sky.com/story/841639/libya-gaddafi-gunships-fire-on-rebels

Tim Hill, *Muammar Gaddafi son killed by NATO air strike – Libyan government*, THE GUARDIAN, May 1, 2011, *available at* http://www.guardian.co.uk/world/2011/may/01/libya-muammar-gaddafi-son-nato

Evan Hill, *Libyan rebels get organized*, AL JAZEERA, Apr. 19, 2011, *available at* http://www.aljazeera.com/indepth/features/2011/04/201141942947854663.html

——, *Rebel push stalls outside of Ras Lanuf*, AL JAZEERA, Mar. 10, 2011, *available at* http://www.aljazeera.com/indepth/spotlight/libya/2011/03/2011310131427537949.html

——, *Under Qadhafi's Eyes*, AL JAZEERA, Apr. 17, 2011, *available at* http://www.aljazeera.com/indepth/features/2011/04/20114171045914762.html

Oliver Holmes, *Enraged Benghazi residents feel ignored, forgotten*, REUTERS, Jan. 22, 2011, *available at* http://www.reuters.com/article/2012/01/22/libya-benghazi-anger-idUSL5E8CM0DK20120122

——, *Excluded from Cabinet, Libya's Berbers fear isolation*, REUTERS, Nov. 25, 2011, *available at* http://af.reuters.com/article/libyaNews/idAFL5E7MO0KJ20111125

——, *FEATURE-Tense reconciliation begins with Libya's Saharan tribes*, REUTERS, Nov. 9, 2011, *available at* http://www.reuters.com/article/2011/11/09/libya-tuareg-idUSL6E7M83L220111109

Oliver Holmes & Philippa Fletcher, *Zintan's hold on Saif al-Islam reflects Libya divisions*, REUTERS, Nov. 20, 2011, *available at* http://www.reuters.com/article/2011/11/21/us-libya-zintan-idUSTRE7AK08720111121

Oliver Holmes & Taha Zargoun, *Gunmen kill five in Libyan refugee camp: hospital staff*, REUTERS, Feb. 6, 2012, *available at* http://www.reuters.com/article/2012/02/06/us-libya-violence-idUSTRE81526T20120206

Holy grails – Libya loses control of its MANPADS, JANE'S INTELLIGENCE REVIEW, Apr. 15, 2011

John Hooper & Ian Black, *Libya defectors: Pilots told to bomb protesters flee to Malta*, THE GUARDIAN, Feb. 21, 2011, *available at* http://www.guardian.co.uk/world/2011/feb/21/libya-pilots-flee-to-malta

Bradley Hope, *Qaddafi cousin: Egypt sold me out for aid*, THE NATIONAL, Mar. 15, 2013, *available at* http://www.thenational.ae/news/world/middle-east/qaddafi-cousin-egypt-sold-me-out-for-aid

Nick Hopkins, *Nato reviews Libya campaign after France admits arming rebels*, THE GUARDIAN, June 29, 2011, *available at* http://www.guardian.co.uk/world/2011/jun/29/nato-review-libya-france-arming-rebels

Adam Housley, *Arms shipments traveled from Libya to anti-Assad fighters, sources say*, FOX NEWS, Dec. 6, 2012, *available at* http://www.foxnews.com/politics/2012/12/06/arms-shipments-traveled-from-libya-to-anti-assad-fighters-sources-say/

How Saif al-Islam was captured, BBC, Nov. 20, 2011, *available at* http://www.bbc.co.uk/news/world-middle-east-15805583

Ben Hubbard & Ryan Lucas, *Libyan rebels say airstrike killed 13 of their own*, AP, Apr. 2, 2011, *available at* http://usatoday30.usatoday.com/money/topstories/2011-04-01-2450814691_x.htm

John Hudson, *U.S. Intelligence Takes the Blame for the Government's Mixed Messages on Libya*, THE ATLANTIC WIRE, Sept. 28, 2012, *available at* http://www.theatlanticwire.com/global/2012/09/us-intelligence-takes-blame-governments-mixed-messages-libya/57416/

Mohamed Hussein, *Libya crisis: what role do tribal loyalties play?*, BBC, Feb. 21, 2011, *available at* http://www.bbc.co.uk/news/world-middle-east-12528996

ICC backs down on Saif Gadhafi trial demand, CNN, Nov. 23, 2011, *available at* http://edition.cnn.com/2011/11/23/world/africa/libya-icc/index.html?iref=allsearch

ICC delegation visits colleagues held in Zintan, Libya, BBC, June 12, 2012, *available at* http://www.bbc.co.uk/news/world-africa-18419756

In Gaddafi's hometown, residents accuse NTC fighters of revenge, REUTERS, Oct. 16, 2011, *available at* http://www.reuters.com/article/2011/10/16/us-libya-Surt-looting-idUSTRE79F2DL20111016

John Irish, *Qaeda links to militants in Libya envoy attack: U.S. general*, REUTERS, Nov. 16, 2012, *available at* http://articles.chicagotribune.com/2012-11-14/news/sns-rt-us-mali-usa-libyabre8ad13c-20121114_1_mali-crisis-qaeda-links-aqim

Farrag Ismail, *Egypt border tribes declare support to Libya revolt*, AL ARABIYA, Feb. 24, 2011, *available at* http://www.alarabiya.net/articles/2011/02/24/139018.html

Leela Jacinto, *Rebel Benghazi to get ambassador*, FRANCE 24, Mar. 11, 2011, *available at* http://www.france24.com/en/20110310-France-NTC-national-transitional-council-embassy-Libya

Alastair Jamieson, *US Ambassador Chris Stevens was 'courageous and exemplary'*, *Obama says*, ABC NEWS, Sept. 12, 2012, *available at* http://worldnews.nbcnews.com/_news/2012/09/12/13826542-us-ambassador-chris-stevens-was-courageous-and-exemplary-obama-says

Greg Jaffe & Karen DeYoung, *U.S. deploys low-flying attack planes in Libya*, THE WASHINGTON POST, Mar. 28, 2011, *available at* http://www.washingtonpost.com/world/us-deploys-low-flying-attack-planes-in-libya/2011/03/26/AF9grPqB_story.html

Randa Jamal, *Libya Head of the United Nations in Libya, Ian Martin, visits Al-Zawiya*, RELIEF WEB, Nov. 17, 2011, *available at* http://reliefweb.int/node/459924

Rana Jawad, *Libyans celebrate their freedom as they mourn the dead*, BBC, Sept. 1 2011, *available at* http://www.bbc.co.uk/news/world-africa-14752785

Jon Jensen, *Reporter release tempered by news of colleagues death*, THE GLOBAL POST ONLINE, May 19, 2011, *available at* http://www.globalpost.com/dispatch/news/regions/africa/110519/libya-journalist-death-anton-hammerl-james-foley-clare-gillis

Mark John & Diana Abdallah, *Anti-poll protesters burn Libyan ballots in Benghazi*, REUTERS, July 7, 2012 *available at* http://www.reuters.com/article/2012/07/07/us-libya-elections-protest-idUSBRE86604920120707

Mark John & Andrew Roche, *UPDATE 3 – Libya's Jibril in election landslide over Islamists*, REUTERS, July 12, 2012, *available at* http://www.reuters.com/article/2012/07/12/libya-elections-idUSL6E8ICDCU20120712

Sam Jones, *Guardian journalist freed at captivity in Libya*, THE GUARDIAN, Mar. 16, 2011, *available at* http://www.guardian.co.uk/media/2011/mar/16/guardian-journalist-freed-captivity-libya

Barbara Jones & Ian McIlgorm, *The Battle of Benghazi: City seemed lost to Gaddafi forces but was retaken by rebels*, DAILY MAIL, Mar. 20 2011, *available at* http://www.dailymail.co.uk/news/article-1368030/Libya-Benghazi-lost-Gaddafis-forces-retaken-rebels.html

Journalists Trapped Inside Tripoli Hotel, 9NEWS WORLD, Aug. 22, 2011, *available at* http://news.ninemsn.com.au/world/8288763/journalists-trapped-inside-tripoli-hotel

Kadhafi uses air strikes, artillery on rebel-held town, AFP, Mar. 8, 2011, *available at* http://www.timesofmalta.com/articles/view/20110309/world/gaddafi-uses-air-strikes-and-artillery-on-rebel-held-town.353842

Tarik Kafala, *'Cleansed' Libyan town spills its terrible secrets*, BBC, Dec. 12, 2011, *available at* http://www.bbc.co.uk/news/magazine-16051349

Jonathan Kar, *The Benghazi Emails: Talking Points Changed at State Dept.'s Request*, ABC, May 15, 2013, *available at* http://abcnews.go.com/Politics/benghazi-emails-talking-points-changed-state-depts-request/story?id=19187137#.Ub_QF-ioUdU

Jomana Karadsheh, *Libyan rebels move into Syrian battlefield*, CNN, Jul. 28, 2012, *available at* http://www.cnn.com/2012/07/28/world/meast/syria-libya-fighters

Souhail Karam et al., *Libyan troops defect near rebel-held Misrata*, REUTERS, Mar. 12, 2011, *available at* http://www.reuters.com/article/2011/03/13/libya-misrata-attack-id AFLDE72B0AO20110313

Zeina Karam et al., *Gaddafi Showers Strategic Oil Port With Rockets*, THE HUFFINGTON POST, Mar. 11, 2011, *available at* http://www.huffingtonpost.com/2011/03/10/libya-drives-rebels-out-ras-lanuf_n_834055.html

Mariam Karouny, *Gaddafi's forces shell west Libya's Misrata*, REUTERS, Mar. 18, 2011, *available at* http://www.reuters.com/article/2011/03/18/us-libya-misrata-bombard-idUSTRE 72H27Y20110318

——, *Zawiyah becomes ghost town as army ring tightens*, REUTERS, Mar. 10, 2011, *available at* http://www.reuters.com/article/2011/03/10/us-libya-zawiyah-city-id USTRE7296P420110310

Mussab Al-Khairalla, *Qatari plane supplies ammunition to Libyan rebels*, REUTERS, Aug. 6, 2011 *available at* http://www.reuters.com/article/2011/08/06/libya-rebels-ammunition-idAFLDE77505S20110806

Kidnapped Italians freed as rebels seek to consolidate hold, IBT, Aug. 25, 2011, *available at* http://www.ibtimes.com/articles/203712/20110825/kidnapped-italians-freed-as-rebels-consolidate-hold-on-tripoli.htm

Kidnapped Italian Journalists freed in Libya, VOA, Aug. 24, 2011, *available at* http://www.voanews.com/content/article-4-kidnapped-italian-journalists-freed-in-libya-128375738/144287.html

Tom Kington, *Italian Journalists kidnapped in Libya*, THE GUARDIAN, Aug. 25, 2011, *available at* http://www.guardian.co.uk/world/2011/aug/25/italian-journalists-kidnapped-libya

David D. Kirkpatrick, *Government Issues Order to Disband Libya Forces*, N.Y. TIMES, Sept. 23, 2012, *available at* http://www.nytimes.com/2012/09/24/world/africa/libya-orders-unauthorized-militias-to-disband.html

——, *Libya Democracy Clashes With Fervor for Jihad*, N.Y. TIMES, June 23, 2012, *available at* http://www.nytimes.com/2012/06/24/world/africa/libya-jihadis-offer-2-paths-democracy-or-militancy.html

——, *Libya Putting $2 Billion into Egypt's Central Bank*, N.Y. TIMES, Mar. 24, 2013, *available at* http://www.nytimes.com/2013/03/25/world/middleeast/libya-putting-2-billion-into-egypts-central-bank.html

——, *Libyan Violence Threatens to Undercut Power of Militias*, N.Y. TIMES, June 9, 2013, *available at* http://www.nytimes.com/2013/06/10/world/africa/libyan-violence-threatens-to-undercut-power-of-militias.html

——, *Libyan Woman Struggles to Tell Media of Her Rape*, N.Y. TIMES, Mar. 27, 2011, *available at* http://www.nytimes.com/2011/03/27/world/middleeast/27tripoli.html

——, *Lone Suspect Held in Benghazi Attack is Freed in Tunisia*, N.Y. TIMES, Jan. 8, 2013, *available at* http://www.nytimes.com/2013/01/09/world/africa/lone-suspect-held-in-benghazi-attack-is-freed-in-tunisia.html

——, *Political Islam and the Fate of Two Libyan Brothers*, N.Y. TIMES, Oct. 6, 2012, *available at* http://www.nytimes.com/2012/10/07/world/africa/political-islam-and-the-fate-of-two-libyan-brothers.html

——, *Spy Chief for Qaddafi Is Extradited to Libya*, N.Y. TIMES, September 5, 2012, *available at* http://www.nytimes.com/2012/09/06/world/africa/senussi-qaddafi-spy-chief-is-extradited-to-libya.html

——, *Western Libya Earns a Taste of Freedom as Rebels Loosen Qadhafi's Grip*, N.Y. TIMES, June 25, 2011, *available at* http://www.nytimes.com/2011/06/26/world/africa/26libya.html

David D. Kirkpatrick & Kareem Fahim, *Allies count on defiant streak in Libya to Drive Out Qaddafi*, N.Y. TIMES, Mar. 30, 2011, *available at* http://www.nytimes.com/2011/03/30/world/africa/30libya.html

—— et al., *Allies Open Air Assault on Qaddafi Forces in Libya*, N.Y. TIMES, Mar. 19, 2011, *available at* http://www.nytimes.com/2011/03/20/world/africa/20libya.html

The Khamis Al Qaddafi Brigade killed 135 soldiers who refused to shoot protestors, AL ARABIYA, Feb. 24, 2011, *available at* http://www.alarabiya.net/articles/2011/02/24/138976.html

Khamis Gaddafi 'killed during fighting in Bani Walid', THE GUARDIAN, Oct. 20, 2012, *available at* http://www.guardian.co.uk/world/2012/oct/20/khamis-gaddafi-killed-bani-walid-muammar

Jeffrey Kofman et al., *Gadhafi Compares Himself to Queen Elizabeth, Says Libya's Youth are on Hallucinogens*, ABC, Feb. 24, 2011, *available at* http://abcnews.go.com/Politics/moammar-gadhafi-speech-blames-libya-uprising-al-qaeda/story

Korva Koleman, *Gadhafi Using Foreign Children As Mercenaries In Libya*, NPR, Mar. 3, 2011, *available at* http://www.npr.org/blogs/thetwo-way/2011/03/03/134223827/gadhafi-using-foreign-children-as-mercenaries-in-libya

Ulf Laessing et al., *Gaddafi's former No. 2 defects – Libya rebels*, REUTERS, Aug. 19, 2011, *available at* http://www.reuters.com/article/2011/08/19/libya-defection-jalloud-idUSL5E7JJ3V820110819

Mark Landler & Steven Erlanger, *Obama Seeks to Unify Allies as More Airstrikes Rock Tripoli*, N.Y. TIMES, Mar. 22, 2011, *available at* http://www.nytimes.com/2011/03/23/world/africa/23libya.html

Karin Laub, *Gadhafi forces try to block Libyan rebel advance*, AP, Aug. 15, 2011, *available at* http://www.katu.com/news/national/127736888.html

——, *Gadhafi's troops use hospital as base, doctors say*, AP, Aug. 16, 2011, *available at* http://www.msnbc.msn.com/id/44164314/ns/world_news-mideast_n_africa/#.Tz4acLEkKf5

——, *Rebels poised to cut off Tripoli*, AP, Aug. 16, 2011, *available at* http://www.boston.com/news/world/africa/articles/2011/08/16/rebels_poised_to_cut_off_tripoli

Peter Layton & Kimberley Layton, *Long summer of civil war in Libya*, DEFENCE FOCUS, Aug. 29, 2011, *available at* http://www.academia.edu/1350056/A_long_summer_of_civil_war_in_Libya

Charles Levinson, *Rebel Leadership Casts a Wide Net*, WALL STREET JOURNAL, Mar. 10, 2011, *available at* http://online.wsj.com/article/SB10001424052748704629104576190720901643258.html

Charles Levinson & Muneef Halawa, *Libya rebels battle for key oil town*, WALL STREET JOURNAL, July 19, 2011, *available at* http://online.wsj.com/article/SB10001424052702304567604576454294028527696.html

Aidan Lewis, *Misrata: City under siege*, BBC, May 10, 2011, *available at* http://www.bbc.co.uk/news/world-africa-13118724

David Lewis & Adama Diarra, *Insight: Arms and men out of Libya fortify Mali rebellion*, REUTERS, Feb. 10, 2012, *available at* http://www.reuters.com/article/2012/02/10/us-mali-libya-idUSTRE8190UX20120210

Jon Leyne, *Libya protests: Gaddafi regime shaken by unrest*, BBC, Feb. 21, 2011, *available at* http://www.bbc.co.uk/news/world-middle-east-12523669

The liberated east – Building a new Libya – Around Benghazi, Muammar Qaddafi's enemies have triumphed, THE ECONOMIST, Feb. 24, 2011, *available at* http://www.economist.com/node/18239900

Libya crisis: Thursday 24 March, THE GUARDIAN, Mar. 24, 2011, *available at* http://www
.guardian.co.uk/world/blog/2011/mar/24/libya-crisis-live-updates

Libya Economic Indicators, ECONOMY WATCH, *available at* http://www.economywatch
.com/economic-statistics/country/Libya

Libya election helicopter 'shot near Benghazi', BBC, July 6, 2012, *available at* http://www.bbc
.co.uk/news/world-africa-18740803

Libya election: High turnout in historic vote, BBC, July 7, 2012, *available at* http://www.bbc
.co.uk/news/world-africa-18749808

Libya ex-PM al-Baghdadi al-Mahmoudi on trial in Tripoli, BBC, Dec. 10, 2012, *available at*
http://www.bbc.co.uk/news/world-africa-20668492

Libya: Forced to rape in Misrata, BBC, May 23, 2011, *available at* http://www.bbc.co.uk/news/
world-africa-13502715

Libya forces 'open fire' at funeral, AL JAZEERA, Feb. 19, 2011, *available at* http://www.aljazeera
.com/news/africa/2011/02/201121981665897.html

Libya forces try to halt rebel move toward capital, SUN STAR, Mar. 7, 2011, *available at*
http://www.sunstar.com.ph/breaking-news/2011/03/07/libya-forces-try-halt-rebel-move-
toward-capital-143492

Libya: Flights resume at Tripoli airport after seizure, BBC, June 5, 2012, *available at* http://
www.bbc.co.uk/news/world-africa-18335015

Libya follows deadly crackdown with mass arrests, AFP, Apr. 19, 2011, *available at* http://
www.google.com/hostednews/afp/article/ALeqM5i9oXPftOIEQ29EuNroc-jJkjxoXg?docI
d=CNG.30a7eb6de98a36de2dbb441ffee98187

Libya Free Elections In Misrata First Since Fall Of Gaddafi, AP, Feb. 20, 2012, *available at*
http://www.huffingtonpost.com/2012/02/20/libya-free-elections-misrata_n_1289156.html

Libya: Gaddafi forces detain and beat BBC Arabic team, BBC, Mar. 10, 2011, *available at* http://
www.bbc.co.uk/news/world-africa-12695077

Libya: Gaddafi loyalists mount onslaught, BBC, Mar. 11, 2011, *available at* http://www.bbc
.co.uk/news/world-africa-12708687

Libya: Gaddafi troops take rebel oil port of Ras Lanuf, BBC, Mar. 12, 2011, *available at* http://
www.bbc.co.uk/news/world-africa-12721908

Libya gunmen end occupation of parliament building, BBC, Nov. 2, 2012, *available at* http://
www.bbc.co.uk/news/world-africa-20178222

Libya holds 32 'Gaddafi loyalists' over Tripoli attack, BBC, Aug. 20, 2012, *available at* http://
www.bbc.co.uk/news/world-africa-19314714

Libya ICC lawyer Melinda Taylor and colleagues fly out, BBC, July 2, 2012, *available at* http://
www.bbc.co.uk/news/world-africa-18683786

Libya: Jalil faces Abdel Fattah Younes questions, BBC, Nov. 7, 2012, *available at* http://www
.bbc.co.uk/news/world-africa-20241092

Libya: job done?, THE GUARDIAN, Feb. 17, 2012, *available at* www.guardian.co.uk/
commentisfree/2012/feb/17/libya-torture-human-rights-abuses

Libya Live Blog, AL JAZEERA, Aug. 2, 2011, *available at* http://blogs.aljazeera.com/topic/
libya/libya-aug-2-2011-1650

Libya Live Blog, AL JAZEERA, Aug. 20, 2011, *available at* http://blogs.aljazeera.com/topic/
libya/libya-aug-21-2011-0017

Libya Live Blog, AL JAZEERA, Aug. 21, 2011, *available at* http://blogs.aljazeera.net/liveblog/
libya-aug-21-2011-1407

Libya Mass Grave Near Bin Jawwad Unearths 170 Bodies From Gaddafi Conflict, HUFFINGTON
POST, Mar. 5, 2011, *available at* http://www.huffingtonpost.com/2012/03/05/libya-mass-
grave-bin-jawwad_n_1322187.html

Libya: Misurata hospital damaged in fighting, THE TELEGRAPH, Mar. 24, 2011, *available at*
http://www.telegraph.co.uk/news/worldnews/africaandindianocean/libya/8405273/
Libya-Misurata-hospital-damaged-in-fighting.html

Libya: NTC deputy chief Abdel Hafiz Ghoga resigns, BBC, Jan. 22, 2012, *available at* http://
www.bbc.co.uk/news/world-africa-16671590

Libyan NTC troops and Gaddafi loyalists clash in Tripoli, BBC, Oct. 14, 2011, *available at* http://www.bbc.co.uk/news/world-africa-15314365

Libya opposition arrests senior leader, AL JAZEERA, July 28, 2011, *available at* http://www.aljazeera.com/news/africa/2011/07/2011728144624965299.html

Libya opposition launches council, AL JAZEERA, Feb. 27, 2011, *available at* http://www.aljazeera.com/news/africa/2011/02/2011227175955221853.html

Libya protesters storm Benghazi voting office, AL JAZEERA, July 1, 2012, *available at* http://www.aljazeera.com/news/africa/2012/07/201271184122330197.html

Libya protests: Benghazi 'returning to normal', BBC, Feb. 25, 2011, *available at* http://www.bbc.co.uk/news/world-africa-12575784

Libya protests: Death in al-Bayda as unrest spreads, BBC, Feb. 17, 2011, *available at* http://www.bbc.co.uk/news/world-middle-east-12500476

Libya protests leave 24 dead, says rights group, BBC, Feb. 18, 2011, *available at* http://www.bbc.co.uk/news/world-africa-12502657

Libya protests: massacres reported as Gaddafi imposes news blackout, THE GUARDIAN, Feb. 18, 2011, *available at* http://www.guardian.co.uk/world/2011/feb/18/libya-protests-massacres-reported

Libya protests: 84 killed in growing unrest, says HRW, BBC, Feb. 19, 2011, *available at* http://www.bbc.co.uk/news/world-africa-12512536

Libya: RAF Tornados destroy Libyan missile launchers, BBC, May 8, 2011, *available at* http://www.bbc.co.uk/news/uk-13325389

Libya rebel-held city on guard, fears for supplies, REUTERS, Mar. 3, 2011, *available at* http://www.reuters.com/article/2011/03/04/us-libya-zawiyah-idUSTRE7230892011.0304

Libya rebels 'capture key supply route town of Ghazaya', BBC, July 28, 2011, *available at* http://www.bbc.co.uk/news/world-africa-14321751

Libya rebels claim 'Misurata is free', AL JAZEERA, Apr. 23, 2011, *available at* http://www.aljazeera.com/news/africa/2011/04/20114231251998645.html

Libya rebels close in on Gadhafi, MSNBC, Aug. 20, 2011, *available at* http://www.msnbc.msn.com/id/44202953/ns/world_news-mideast_n_africa#.T_FR0PW5koI

Libya rebels eye Brega oil installations, AL JAZEERA, Aug. 13, 2011, *available at* http://www.aljazeera.com/news/middleeast/2011/08/201181215510690602.html

Libya rebels gain ground in east as council meets, AFP, Mar. 5. 2011, *available at* http://www.timesofmalta.com/articles/view/20110305/local/libyan-rebels-gain-ground-in-east-as-council-meets.353258

Libya rebels launch offensive on strategic town of Ghezaia, REUTERS, July 28, 2011, *available at* http://af.reuters.com/article/libyaNews/idAFL6E7ISoBL20110728

Libya rebels on edge as Kadhafi rages, AFP, Feb. 27, 2011, *available at* http://213.158.162.45/~egyptian/index.php?action=news&id=15494&title=Libya%20rebels%20on%20edge%20as%20Gaddafi%20rages

Libya: Rebels press Gaddafi on three fronts as southern tribe revolts, SCOTSMAN, June 12, 2011, *available at* http://www.scotsman.com/news/libya_rebels_press_gaddafi_on_three_fronts_as_southern_tribe_revolts_1_1691903

Libya rebels say plan attack on western mountain town, REUTERS, July 27, 2011, *available at* http://www.reuters.com/article/2011/07/27/libya-ghezaia-idUSLDE76Q1OK20110727

Libya rebels storm Tripoli's Abu Salim district, REUTERS, Aug. 25, 2011, *available at* http://af.reuters.com/article/commoditiesNews/idAFLDE77O0SH20110825

Libya rebels take control of Zawiyah oil refinery, REUTERS, Aug. 18, 2011, *available at* http://www.trust.org/alertnet/news/libya-rebels-take-control-of-zawiyah-oil-refinery

Libya rebels take Garyan, south of Tripoli-witness, REUTERS, Aug. 18, 2011, *available at* http://af.reuters.com/article/libyaNews/idAFLDE77H09I20110818

Libya rebels take casualties in Zliten advance, AFP, July 10, 2011, *available at* http://www.google.com/hostednews/afp/article/ALeqM5i9jbd5tDAHv4Zfe_9ADI_jFShTYw?docId=CNG.a51e0ccb6c8ecb11fbc3a0a97df80911.361

Libya revolt as it happened: Monday, BBC, Mar. 21, 2011, *available at* http://news.bbc.co.uk/2/hi/africa/9417359.stm

Libya Revolt as it happened: Monday, BBC, Mar. 6, 2011, *available at* http://news.bbc.co.uk/2/hi/africa/9417359.stm

Libya revolt as it happened: Monday, BBC, Mar. 22, 2011, *available at* http://news.bbc.co.uk/2/hi/africa/9432055.stm

Libya revolt spreads to Tripoli, AL JAZEERA, Feb. 21 2011, *available at* http://www.aljazeera.com/news/africa/2011/02/201122131439291589.htmls

Libya: Rival militia spray bullets and grenades in Tripoli, BBC, Nov. 5, 2012, *available at* http://www.bbc.co.uk/news/world-africa-20202065

Libya says Nato air strike kills dozens south of Zlitan, BBC, Aug. 9, 2011, *available at* http://www.bbc.co.uk/news/world-africa-14464400

Libya Seeking Arms Deals, DEFENSE INDUSTRY DAILY, Mar. 4, 2012, *available at* http://www.defenseindustrydaily.com/the-french-connection-libya-seeking-arms-deals-04417

Libya seizes tanks from pro-Gaddafi militia, BBC, Aug. 24, 2012, *available at* http://www.bbc.co.uk/news/world-africa-19364536

Libya stages back-to-back rallies in face of world condemnation, AP, July 17, 2011, *available at* http://www.news889.com/news/world/article/255217--libya-stages-back-to-back-rallies-in-face-of-world-condemnation

Libya: the fall of Tripoli – Wednesday 24 August 2011, THE GUARDIAN, Aug. 24, 2011, *available at* http://www.guardian.co.uk/world/middle-east-live/2011/aug/24/libya-rebels-take-gaddafi-compound-live-updates

Libya: Tight security after Tripoli unrest, BBC, Oct. 16, 2011, *available at* http://www.bbc.co.uk/news/world-africa-15325186

Libya to appeal ICC ruling to hand over Gaddafi's son, REUTERS, June 2, 2013, *available at* http://www.reuters.com/article/2013/06/02/us-libya-icc-gaddafi-idUSBRE9510FK20130602

Libya to disarm Tripoli by year end, AL JAZEERA, Dec. 7, 2011, *available at* http://www.aljazeera.com/news/africa/2011/12/20111262350566641.html

Libya: UK Apache helicopters used in NATO attacks, BBC, June 4, 2011, *available at* http://www.bbc.co.uk/news/uk-13651736

Libya: UN official voices concern as fighting blocks aid delivery in West, UN NEWS CENTRE, May 12, 2011, *available at* http://www.un.org/apps/news/story.asp?NewsID=38352&Cr=Libya&Crl

Libya: UN Secretary-General urges immediate end to attacks against civilians, UN NEWS CENTRE, May 11, 2011, *available at* http://www.un.org/apps/news/story.asp?NewsID=38348&Cr=libya&Cr1=

Libya unrest: Deadly clashes in battle for Zawiya, BBC, Mar. 4, 2011, *available at* http://www.bbc.co.uk/news/world-africa-12652613

Libya unrest: Entering Zawiya, BBC, Mar. 11, 2011, *available at* http://www.bbc.co.uk/news/world-africa-12720968

Libya: Zintan withdrawal rare success for rebels, 3 NEWS, Mar. 24, 2011, *available at* http://www.3news.co.nz/Libya-Zintan-withdrawal-rare-success-for-rebels/tabid/417/articleID/203851/Default.aspx

Libya's Berbers feel rejected by transitional government, DEUTSCHE WELLE, Nov. 8, 2011, *available at* http://www.dw.de/libyas-berbers-feel-rejected-by-transitional-government/a-15515687-1

Libya's congress gives new PM ultimatum to name government, REUTERS, Sept. 26, 2012, *available at* http://www.reuters.com/article/2012/09/26/us-libya-government-idUSBRE88P1U320120926

Libya's defeated Islamists, AL JAZEERA, Jul. 18 2012, *available at* http://www.aljazeera.com/indepth/opinion/2012/07/20127187155487377.html

Libya's Elections under Threat, AFP, July 3, 2012, *available at* http://reliefweb.int/report/libya/libyas-elections-under-threat-enar

Libya's ex-justice minister forms interim government in Benghazi, HAARETZ, Jan. 25, 2013, *available at* http://www.haaretz.com/news/world/libya-s-ex-justice-minister-forms-interim-government-in-benghazi-1.345892

Libyan militias accused of torturing detainees, The Guardian, Feb. 16, 2012, *available at* http://www.guardian.co.uk/world/2012/feb/16/libyan-militias-detainee-torture-amnesty-international

Libyan militias engage in battle, Belfast Telegraph, Nov. 13, 2011, *available at* http://www.belfasttelegraph.co.uk/news/world-news/libyan-militias-engage-in-battle-16076585.html

Libyan militia storm election office in Benghazi as violence spreads, The Guardian, July 1, 2012, *available at* http://www.guardian.co.uk/world/2012/jul/01/libyan-militia-storm-election-office

Libyan People's Hall on fire as protesters riot, Ria Novosti, Feb. 21, 2011, *available at* http://en.rian.ru/world/20110221/162699766.html

Libyan police clash with armed group in Benghazi, AFP, June 5, 2012, *available at* http://www.moroccoworldnews.com/2012/06/43035/libyan-police-clash-with-armed-group-in-benghazi

Libyan rebel advance halted, Sirte blasted by NATO jets, AFP, Mar. 28, 2011, *available at* http://www.heraldsun.com.au/news/victoria/libyan-rebel-advance-halted-sirte-blasted-by-nato-jets/story-e6frf7lf-1226029688023?from=public_rss

Libyan Rebel Chief: 'The End is Near for Gaddafi', Sky News, Aug. 20, 2011, *available at* http://news.sky.com/home/world-news/article/16053368

Libyan rebel-held city on guard, fear for supplies, Reuters, Mar. 3, 2011, *available at* http://www.reuters.com/article/2011/03/04/us-libya-zawiyah-idUSTRE72308920110304

Libyan rebel sharpshooters take aim at Kadhafi, AFP, Mar. 27, 2011, *available at* http://www.cumhuriyet.com/?im=yhs&hn=228608

Libyan rebels brought up short, vow to put Kadhafi on trial, Sakapfet, *available at* http://headlines.sakapfetstore.com/item/world_news/english/mar282011/libyan_rebels_brought_up_short_vow_to_put_kadhafi_on_trial.jsp

Libyan rebels claim victory in battle for Brega, BBC, July 18, 2011, *available at*, http://www.bbc.co.uk/news/world-africa-14180293

Libyan rebels close on key Gadhafi stronghold, AP, Mar. 28, 2011, *available at* http://www.independent.co.uk/news/world/africa/libyan-rebels-close-on-key-gaddafi-stronghold-2255180.html

Libyan rebels 'disappointed' by NATO, Al Jazeera, Apr. 6, 2011, *available at* http://www.aljazeera.com/news/africa/2011/04/201145191641347449.html

Libyan rebels fall back after failed advance on eastern oil town, AP, July 15, 2011, *available at* http://www.globaltvbc.com/libyan+rebels+fall+back+after+failed+advance+on+eastern+oil+town/305737/story.html

Libyan rebels fight for Zawiya, take Zlitan, AP, Aug. 19, 2011, *available at* http://www.cbc.ca/news/world/story/2011/08/19/libya-rebels-zawiya.html

Libyan rebels flee oil port battle, The Independent, Mar. 9, 2011, *available at* http://www.independent.ie/breaking-news/world-news/libyan-rebels-flee-oil-port-battle-2573356.html

Libyan Rebels Form 'Interim Government', Al Jazeera, Mar. 22, 2011, *available at* http://english.aljazeera.net/news/africa/2011/03/201132219394486231o.html

Libyan rebels give 4-day ultimatum to Gadhafi forces, Voice of America, Aug. 30, 2011, *available at* http://blogs.voanews.com/breaking-news/2011/08/30/libyas-rebels-give-4-day-ultimatum-to-gadhafi-forces

Libyan rebels near Ajdabiya 'killed in Nato air strike', BBC, Apr. 7, 2011, *available at* http://www.bbc.co.uk/news/world-africa-12997181

Libyan rebels on run, NATO strike kills 2 fighters, AFP, Apr. 7, 2011, *available at* http://173.254.58.56/~islamtri/2011/04/07/libyan-rebels-on-run-nato-strike-kills-2-fighters.html

Libyan rebels push towards Tripoli, promise new oil exports, AFP, Mar. 27, 2011, *available at* http://www.channelnewsasia.com/stories/afp_world/view/1119188/1/.html

Libyan rebels pushed back from Brega, Al Jazeera, June 19, 2011, *available at* http://www.aljazeera.com/news/africa/2011/07/201171922526752203.html

Joseph Logan, *Russia joins western chorus for Gaddafi to go*, REUTERS, May 27, 2011, *available at* http://uk.reuters.com/article/2011/05/27/uk-libya-idUKTRE74E1I420110527

—— et al., *Tripoli armed group says arms spreading to regions*, REUTERS, Sept. 24, 2011, *available at* http://www.reuters.com/article/2011/09/24/libya-weapons-idUSL5E7KO0TQ20110924

Ernesto Londono, *Fear for Libya's Roman Ruins*, THE WASHINGTON POST, June 15, 2011, *available at* http://articles.washingtonpost.com/2011-06-15/world/35236134_1_misrata-khums-rebel-spokesman

——, *In Libya, rebels gaining in the west*, THE WASHINGTON POST, July 6, 2011, *available at* http://www.washingtonpost.com/world/middle-east/in-libya-rebels-gaining-in-the-west/2011/07/06/gIQAmNvA1H_story.html

Dario Lopez, *Heavy gunfire in Tripoli as rebels close in*, 3 NEWS, Aug. 21, 2011, *available at* http://www.3news.co.nz/Heavy-gunfire-in-Tripoli-as-rebels-close-in/tabid/417/articleID/222904/Default.aspx

Christian Lowe, *Call for election boycott in Libya's turbulent east*, REUTERS, May 3, 2012, *available at* http://www.reuters.com/article/2012/05/03/libya-vote-boycott-idUSL5E8G3I7Q20120503

——, *Thousands rally in Libya against autonomy for east*, REUTERS, Mar. 9, 2012, *available at* http://www.reuters.com/article/2012/03/09/libya-east-autonomy-idUSL5E8E9AWK20120309

——, *UPDATE 1 – Government building on fire in Libyan capital*, REUTERS, Feb. 21, 2011, *available at* http://af.reuters.com/article/commoditiesNews/idAFLDE71K0OP20110221

Christian Lowe & Francois Murphy, *Libyan tribes protest at new government line-up*, REUTERS, Nov. 23, 2011, *available at* http://www.reuters.com/article/2011/11/23/us-libya-idUSTRE7AL0JM20111123

Christian Lowe & Taha Zargoun, *Rival militias wage turf war near Libyan capital*, REUTERS, Dec. 3, 2011, *available at* http://www.reuters.com/article/2011/12/03/us-libya-militias-idUSTRE7B20L620111203

Ryan Lucas, *Libyan rebels close on key Gadhafi stronghold*, AP, Mar. 28, 2011, *available at* http://www.aolnews.com/2011/03/28/libyan-rebels-close-on-key-gadhafi-stronghold-of-sirte

——, *Libyan rebels retreating after Gadhafi onslaught*, AP, Mar. 29, 2011, *available at* http://www.washingtontimes.com/news/2011/mar/29/libyan-rebels-retreat-after-gadhafi-onslaught/

Ewen MacAskill et al., *Libya: Six injured as US team botches rescue of downed airmen*, THE GUARDIAN, Mar. 22, 2011, *available at* http://www.guardian.co.uk/world/2011/mar/22/libya-downed-airmen-rescue

Alastair Macdonald & Oliver Holmes, *Special Report: Libya – divided it stands*, REUTERS, Dec. 16, 2011, *available at* http://www.reuters.com/article/2011/12/16/us-libya-future-idUSTRE7BF0MG20111216

Donald MacIntyre, *Gaddafi's men try to obliterate traces of massacre in Zawiya*, THE INDEPENDENT, Apr. 6, 2011, *available at* http://www.independent.co.uk/news/world/africa/gaddafis-men-try-to-obliterate-traces-of-massacre-in-zawiya-2263670.html

Glynnis MacNichol, *REPORT: U.S. Drone Responsible for Initially Hitting Qaddafi Convoy*, BUSINESS INSIDER, Oct. 20, 2011, *available at* http://www.businessinsider.com/us-drone-killed-qaddafi-2011-10

Anne E. Mahle, *Justice & The Generals The Yamashita Standard*, PBS, *available at* http://www.pbs.org/wnet/justice/world_issues_yam.html

Mahmoudi will not get fair trial in Libya claims Tunisian human rights president, LIBYA HERALD, June 11, 2012, *available at* http://www.libyaherald.com/2012/06/11/mahmoudi-will-not-get-fair-trial-in-libya-claims-tunisian-human-rights-president/

Ibrahim Majbari, *Armed clashes erupt after federalist rally in Libya*, AFP, Mar. 6, 2012, *available at* http://reliefweb.int/report/libya/armed-clashes-erupt-after-federalist-rally-libya

Militia gunmen besiege Libyan Foreign Ministry, demand resignations, RT, Apr. 28, 2013, available at http://rt.com/news/libya-foreign-ministry-riot-532/

Militia hands over Tripoli airport to government, REUTERS, Oct. 10, 2011, *available at* http://www.reuters.com/article/2011/10/10/libya-tripoli-airport-idUSL5E7LA3QV20111010

Peter Millership, *UPDATE 1 – Libyan rebels take oil town of Ras Lanuf- rebels*, REUTERS, Mar. 4, 2011, *available at* http://www.reuters.com/article/2011/03/04/libya-port-id USLDE72320420110304

Mohammed el-Megarif elected as Libya's interim president, THE GUARDIAN, Aug. 10, 2012, *available at* http://www.guardian.co.uk/world/2012/aug/10/mohammed-el-megarif-libya-president

More deaths in Kufra reported, THE LIBYA HERALD, June 29, 2012, *available at* http://www.libyaherald.com/2012/06/29/more-deaths-in-kufra-reported/

Colin Moynihan, *Libya's U.N. Diplomats Break With Qaddafi*, N.Y. TIMES, Feb. 21, 2011, *available at* http://www.nytimes.com/2011/02/22/world/africa/22nations.html

MSF: Libya torture 'completely unacceptable', BBC, Jan. 26, 2012, *available at* http://www.bbc.co.uk/news/health-16751785

Muammar Gaddafi killed as Surt falls, AL JAZEERA, Oct. 21 2011, *available at* http://www.aljazeera.com/news/africa/2011/10/20111020111520869621.html

Mubarak appears in fresh trial over protesters death, AFP, May 11, 2013, *available at* http://www.nation.co.ke/News/africa/Mubarak-appears-in-fresh-trial-/-/1066/1849126/-/q57wvzz/-/index.html

Rebecca Murray, *Libya's Tebu tribe hopes for lasting peace*, AL JAZEERA, Dec. 3, 2012, *available at* http://www.aljazeera.com/indepth/features/2012/11/20121118115735549354.html

Dan Murphy, *Battles erupt in key cities, moving Libya close to civil war*, CHRISTIAN SCIENCE MONITOR, Mar. 4, 2011, *available at* http://www.csmonitor.com/World/Middle-East/2011/0304/Battles-erupt-in-key-cities-moving-Libya-closer-to-civil-war

——, *In disorganized surge, Libya's rebels push west along shifting front line*, CHRISTIAN SCIENCE MONITOR, Mar. 5, 2011, *available at* http://www.csmonitor.com/World/Middle-East/2011/0305/In-disorganized-surge-Libya-s-rebels-push-west-along-shifting-front-line

——, *Libya test for NATO starts at Ajdabiya*, CHRISTIAN SCIENCE MONITOR, Mar. 25, 2011, *available at* http://www.csmonitor.com/World/Middle-East/2011/0325/Libya-test-for-NATO-starts-at-Ajdabiya

——, *Qaddafi air strikes intensify, unnerving Libya rebels*, CHRISTIAN SCIENCE MONITOR, Mar. 8, 2011, *available at* http://www.csmonitor.com/World/Middle-East/2011/0308/Qaddafi-air-strikes-intensify-unnerving-Libya-rebels

——, *Qaddafi strikes back at Libya rebels' western advance*, CHRISTIAN SCIENCE MONITOR, Mar. 6, 2011, *available at* http://www.csmonitor.com/World/Middle-East/2011/0306/Qaddafi-strikes-back-at-Libya-rebels-western-advance

Francois Murphy, *Libya will try Gaddafi's son fairly: ICC prosecutor*, REUTERS, Nov. 24, 2011, *available at* http://www.reuters.com/article/2011/11/24/us-libya-icc-idUSTRE7ANoQY20111124

——, *Libya will try Gaddafi's son fairly: ICC prosecutor*, REUTERS, Nov. 24, 2011, *available at* http://www.reuters.com/article/2011/11/24/us-libya-icc-idUSTRE7ANoQY20111124

Francois Murphy & Ali Shuaib, *Local commander made Libya Defense Minister: NTC source*, REUTERS, Nov. 21, 2011, *available at* http://www.reuters.com/article/2011/11/22/us-libya-idUSTRE7AIoG820111122

——, *Libya's NTC unveils new government line-up*, REUTERS, Nov. 22, 2011, *available at* http://www.reuters.com/article/2011/11/22/us-libya-idUSTRE7ALoJM20111122

Francois Murphy et al., *From east to west, Libyans cheer Gaddafi capture*, REUTERS, Nov. 19, 2011, *available at* http://www.reuters.com/article/2011/11/19/us-libya-saif-mood-id USTRE7AIoQY20111119

Musa Kusa traced to Qatar Resort, THE GUARDIAN, October 23, 2011, *available at* http://www.guardian.co.uk/uk/feedarticle/9909309

Houda Mzioudet, *Five Tunisians Abducted by a Libyan Armed Group*, TUNISIA LIVE, Apr. 7, 2012, *available at* http://www.tunisia-live.net/2012/04/07/37967

Andrew North, *Libya: US to Deploy Armed Drones – Robert Gates*, BBC, Apr. 22, 2011, *available at* http://www.bbc.co.uk/news/world-africa-13166441

Richard Norton-Taylor, *Jack Straw accused of misleading MPs over torture of Libyan dissidents*, THE GUARDIAN, Oct. 10, 2012, *available at* http://www.guardian.co.uk/world/2012/oct/10/jack-straw-torture-libyan-dissidents

Richard Norton-Taylor & Chris Stephen, *Libya: SAS Veterans helping NATO identify Gaddafi targets in Misrata*, THE GUARDIAN, May 31, 2011, *available at* http://www.guardian.co.uk/world/2011/may/31/libya-sas-veterans-misrata-rebels

Richard Norton-Taylor & Nick Hopkins, *Libya warned smugglers are looting Gaddafi's guns*, THE GUARDIAN, Sept. 2, 2011, *available at* http://www.guardian.co.uk/world/2011/sep/02/west-warns-smugglers-looting-libya-arms

Lin Noueihed, *Fighting rages in Libya's Western Mountains*, REUTERS, May 2, 2011, *available at* http://www.reuters.com/article/2011/05/02/us-libya-idUSTRE7270JP20110502

——, *Libyan leader's son Saif al-Arab killed in NATO strike*, REUTERS, Apr. 30, 2011 *available at* http://www.reuters.com/article/2011/04/30/us-libya-attack-idUSTRE73T2HV20110430

Lin Noueihed & Tarek Amara, *Libya angers Tunisia as war briefly crosses border*, REUTERS, Apr. 28, 2011, *available at* http://www.reuters.com/article/2011/04/28/us-libya-idUSTRE7270JP20110428

NTC will investigate allegations of crimes against pro-Gadhafi forces, official says, CNN, Oct. 30, 2011, available at http://edition.cnn.com/2011/10/30/world/africa/libya-militias

Obama directs $25M to support Libyan rebels, CBS NEWS, Apr. 26 2011, *available at* http://www.cbsnews.com/2100-250_162-20057689.html

Obama ups pressure, Interpol issues global alert on Gaddafi, AFP, Mar. 5, 2011, *available at* http://www.thedailystar.net/newDesign/news-details.php?nid=176475

Official Final Election Results in Libya Show Liberals got 62 percent of Votes, THE TRIPOLI POST, July 17, 2012, *available at* http://www.tripolipost.com/articledetail.asp?c=1&i=8837

One killed at polling station in Libya, SBS, July 8, 2012, *available at,* http://www.sbs.com.au/news/article/1667040/One-killed-at-polling-station-in-Libya

Opposition forces close in on Gaddafi stronghold, INDEPENDENT, Oct. 4, 2011, *available at* http://www.independent.co.uk/news/world/africa/opposition-forces-close-in-on-gaddafi-stronghold-2365188.html

Panetta: Terrorist carried out consulate attack, CBS, Sept. 28, 2012, *available at* http://www.cbsnews.com/8301-202_162-57522061/panetta-terrorists-carried-out-consulate-attack/

Alison Pargeter, *Libya and Islamism: the deeper story*, OPENDEMOCRACY, Aug. 7, 2012, *available at* http://www.opendemocracy.net/alison-pargeter/libya-and-islamism-deeper-story

Joe Parkinson, *NATO allies reject Libyan cease-fire offer*, WALL STREET JOURNAL, May 27, 2011, *available at* http://www.shabablibya.org/news/nato-allies-reject-libyan-cease-fire-offer

Paula Broadwell claims about Benghazi attack dismissed as 'baseless' by CIA, THE GUARDIAN, Nov. 12, 2012, *available at* http://www.guardian.co.uk/world/2012/nov/12/paula-broadwell-benghazi-cia-petraeus

Nicholas Pelham, *The Battle for Libya*, N.Y. REVIEW OF BOOKS, Apr. 7, 2011 *available at* http://www.nybooks.com/articles/archives/2011/apr/07/battle-libya

Thomas Penny & Partick Donahue, *Libya Rebels seek cease-fire after U.S. vows to withdraw jets*, BLOOMBERG, Apr. 1, 2011, *available at* http://www.bloomberg.com/news/2011-04-01/libya-rebels-seek-cease-fire-after-u-s-vows-to-withdraw-jets-by-tomorrow.html

Jeremy Peters, *Freed Times Journalists Give Account of Captivity*, N.Y. TIMES, Mar. 21, 2011, *available at* http://www.nytimes.com/2011/03/22/world/africa/22times.html

Scott Peterson, *Qaddafi likens Western airstrikes to 'Hitler's campaigns'*, CHRISTIAN SCIENCE MONITOR, Mar. 29, 2011, *available at* http://www.csmonitor.com/World/Middle-East/2011/0329/Qaddafi-likens-Western-airstrikes-to-Hitler-s-campaigns

Tom Pfeiffer, *UPDATE 1 – Libya rebels say Gaddafi forces retreat in east*, REUTERS, July 18, 2011, *available at* http://www.reuters.com/article/2011/07/18/libya-east-id USLDE76H0MR20110718

Duncan Pickard, *Libya's constitution controversy*, FOREIGN POLICY, Sept. 5, 2012, *available at* http://mideast.foreignpolicy.com/posts/2012/09/05/libyas_constitution_controversy

Elizabeth Pineau & John Irish, *France provided weapons, food to Libya rebels*, REUTERS, June 29, 2011, *available at* http://www.reuters.com/article/2011/06/29/us-libya-france-weapons-idUSTRE75S22P20110629

Sarah Posner, *UN rights office calls for investigation into Gaddafi killing*, JURIST, Oct. 21, 2011, *available at* http://jurist.org/paperchase/2011/10/un-rights-office-calls-for-investigation-into-gaddafi-killing.php

Post-war Tripoli port back in business, airport ready, REUTERS, Sept. 2, 2011, *available at* http://www.reuters.com/article/2011/09/18/us-libya-port-idUSTRE78H1UU20110918

Mitch Potter, *Rebels quash Gadhafi raid*, THE STAR, Mar. 2011, *available at* http://www .thestar.com/news/world/article/947638--the-star-in-libya-rebels-quash-gadhafi-raid

Elisabetta Povoledo, *Italy Closes Consulate in Benghazi After New Attack*, N.Y. TIMES, Oct. 15, 2012, *available at* http://www.nytimes.com/2013/01/16/world/africa/italy-closes-beng-hazi-consulate-after-ambush-attempt.html

Power Brokers – Qatar and the UAE take center stage, JANE'S INTELLIGENCE REVIEW, Dec. 21 2011, *available at* http://articles.janes.com/articles/Janes-Intelligence-Review-2012/Power-brokers--Qatar-and-the-UAE-take-centre-stage.html

Profile: Khamis Khaddafi, BBC, Sept. 4, 2011, *available at* http://www.bbc.co.uk/news/world-africa-14723041

Profile: Sirte, BBC, Sept. 18, 2011, *available at* http://www.bbc.co.uk/news/world-africa-12885322

Pro-Gvernment [sic] Forces Launch Large-Scale Offensive in Bid to Regain More Positions, THE TRIPOLI POST, Mar. 11, 2011, *available at* http://www.tripolipost.com/articledetail .asp?c=1&i=5574

Pro-Gaddafi forces use more civilian facilities, ANTAR NEWS, July 27, 2011, *available at* http:// www.antaranews.com/en/news/74160/pro-gaddafi-forces-use-more-civilian-facilities

Solane Pyne, *Video: Decoding Gaddafi's death*, GLOBALPOST (Oct. 21, 2011), *available at* http://www.globalpost.com/video/5678826

Q&A: Rebel spokesman Abdelbaset Abumzirig, AL JAZEERA, Apr. 24, 2011, *available at* http:// www.aljazeera.com/news/africa/2011/04/20114240556575343.html

Qadhafi Blames Uprising on Al-Qaeda, AL JAZEERA, Feb. 24, 2011, *available at* http://www .aljazeera.com/news/africa/2011/02/2011224143054988104.html

Qadhafi losing firm grip on Western Libya too, AP, Apr. 26, 2011, *available at* http://www .cbsnews.com/2100-202_162-20057593.html

Qatari weapons reaching rebels in the Libyan Mountains, REUTERS, Mar. 31, 2011, *available at* http://www.reuters.com/article/2011/05/31/us-libya-weapons-idUSTRE74U3C520110531

Sudarsan Raghavan, *Niger Resists Libyan demands for extradition of Moammar Gaddafi's playboy son*, THE WASHINGTON POST, July 3, 2012, *available at* http://articles.washington post.com/2012-07-03/world/35489060_1_gaddafi-loyalists-saif-al-islam-gaddafi-moammar-gaddafi

Sudarsan Raghavan & Leila Fadel, *Military helicopters reportedly fire on protesters in Libya*, THE WASHINGTON POST, Feb. 21, 2011, *available at* http://www.washingtonpost.com/wp-dyn/content/article/2011/02/20/AR2011022004185.html?sid=ST2011022004212

Sean Rayment, *How the Special Forces Helped Bring Qaddafi to His Knees*, THE TELEGRAPH, Aug. 28, 2011, *available at* http://www.telegraph.co.uk/news/worldnews/africaandindian ocean/libya/8727076/How-the-special-forces-helped-bring-Gaddafi-to-his-knees.html

Adam Rawnsley, *Gadhafi's Loose Weapons Could Number a 'Thousand Times' Saddams*, WIRED, Aug. 25, 2011 *available at* http://www.wired.com/dangerroom/2011/08/gadhafis-loose-weapons-could-be-1000-times-worse-than-saddams/

Rebel forces in Libya's western mountains issue call for help, CNN, May 18, 2011, *available at* http://edition.cnn.com/2011/WORLD/africa/05/17/libya.war

Rebels battle Gaddafi forces in western Libya, AL JAZEERA, June 12, 2011, *available at* http:// www.aljazeera.com/news/africa/2011/06/2011612155350821500.html

Rebels clear landmines, advance on Brega, UPI, July 18, 2011, *available at* http://www.upi
.com/Top_News/World-News/2011/07/18/Rebels-clear-land-mines-advance-on-Brega/
UPI-80801310987369

Rebels come under heavy fire in push to Gaddafi's heartland, THE INDEPENDENT, Mar. 7,
2011, *available at* http://www.independent.co.uk/news/world/africa/regime-hits-back-
as-rebels-push-on-to-gaddafis-heartland-2234232.html

Rebels deny Gaddafi troops on Benghazi outskirts, REUTERS, Mar. 17, 2011, *available at* http://
af.reuters.com/article/libyaNews/idAFWEA926720110317

Rebels make further advances, GULF NEWS, Mar. 7, 2011, *available at* http://gulfnews.com/
news/region/libya/rebels-make-further-advances-1.772651

Rebels Repel Assaults By Loyalists in Libya, N.Y. TIMES, Apr. 28, 2011, *available at* http://www
.nytimes.com/2011/04/29/world/africa/29libya.html

Rebels retreat from Libyan oil port amid barrage, AP, Mar. 11, 2011, *available at* http://www
.aolnews.com/2011/03/11/rebels-retreat-from-libyan-oil-port-amid-barrage

Rebels say Gaddafi, not British, attacked oilfield, REUTERS, Apr. 7, 2011, *available at* http://
af.reuters.com/article/topNews/idAFJOE7360AU20110407

Rebels stuck at Bin Jawad on way to Gaddafi hometown, AL AHRAM, Aug. 24, 2011, *available
at* http://english.ahram.org.eg/NewsContent/2/8/19649/World/Region/Rebels-stuck-at-
Bin-Jawad-on-way-to-Gaddafi-hometo.aspx

Report: Fighter jet shot down in Bengazi, CNN, Mar. 19, 2011, *available at* http://www.cnn
.com/2011/WORLD/africa/03/18/libya.civil.war/index.html

Paul Reynolds, *UTA 772: The Forgotten Flight*, BBC, August 19, 2003, *available at* http://news
.bbc.co.uk/2/hi/uk_news/3163621.stm

Xan Rice, *Libyan families flee Gaddafi forces in Ajdabiya as civilian death toll rise*, THE
GUARDIAN, Apr. 17, 2011, *available at* http://www.guardian.co.uk/world/2011/apr/17/
libya-attacks-ajdabiya-misrata-brega

——, *Libyan rebels pay a heavy price for resisting Gaddafi in Misrata*, THE GUARDIAN, Apr.
21, 2011, *available at* http://www.guardian.co.uk/world/2011/apr/21/libyan-rebels-heavy-
price-misrata

——, *Muammar Gaddafi's forces come under fire from the west*, THE GUARDIAN, June 12,
2011, *available at* http://www.guardian.co.uk/world/2011/jun/12/muammar-gaddafis-
forces-under-fire

James Risen et al., *U.S. Approved Arms for Libya Rebels Fell Into Jihadis' Hands*, N.Y. TIMES,
Dec. 5, 2012, *available at* http://www.nytimes.com/2012/12/06/world/africa/weapons-
sent-to-libyan-rebels-with-us-approval-fell-into-islamist-hands.html

Rival Libya militias fight gunbattle in capital, REUTERS, Feb. 1, 2012, *available at* www
.reuters.com/article/2012/02/01/libya-tripoli-battle-idUSL5E8D14QS20120201

Rival militia briefly holds Libya Islamist chief, REUTERS, Nov. 24, 2011, *available at* http://
www.reuters.com/article/2011/11/24/libya-belhadj-airport-idUSL5E7MO46X20111124

Nic Robertson, *Concern grows over jihadist numbers in eastern Libya*, CNN, May 15, 2012,
available at http://edition.cnn.com/2012/05/15/world/africa/libya-militants/index.html

——, *Rebels battle Gadhafi forces in Libyan mountains*, CNN, May 21, 2011, *available at*
http://edition.cnn.com/2011/WORLD/africa/05/21/libya.zintan

——, *War crimes court leaves Gadhafi probe to Libya*, CNN, Dec. 20, 2011, *available at*
http://articles.cnn.com/2011-12-20/africa/world_africa_libya-gadhafi-death_1_moammar-
gadhafi-saif-al-islam-gadhafi-sirte

—— et al., *Libyan official: U.S. drones seeking jihadists in Libya*, CNN, June 7, 2012, *available
at* http://security.blogs.cnn.com/2012/06/07/senior-libyan-official-u-s-deploying-drones-
as-concerns-rise-over-al-qaeda-in-eastern-libya/

—— et al., *Pro-al Qaeda group seen behind deadly Benghazi attack*, CNN, Sept. 13, 2012,
available at http://edition.cnn.com/2012/09/12/world/africa/libya-attack-jihadists/index
.html

Matt Robinson, *Heavy fighting as Libyan rebels try to push out*, REUTERS, June 17, 2011, *available at* http://www.reuters.com/article/2011/06/17/us-libya-idUSTRE7270JP20110617

——, *NATO war-lite means Libyan rebels must improvise*, REUTERS, May 25, 2011, *available at* http://www.reuters.com/article/2011/05/25/us-libya-westernmountains-idUSTRE 7402T920110525

——, *New Libyan leaders juggle demands, grievances*, REUTERS, Dec. 23, 2011, *available at* http://www.reuters.com/article/2011/12/23/libya-mood-idUSL6E7NN1X920111223

——, *WRAPUP 1 – Gaddafi rockets dent sense of security in Misrata*, REUTERS, June 21, 2011, *available at* http://www.reuters.com/article/2011/06/22/libya-idUSLDE75K23920110622

Josh Rogin, *Musa Kusa gets his money back*, FOREIGN POLICY, April 4, 2011, *available at* http://thecable.foreignpolicy.com/posts/2011/04/04/musa_kusa_gets_his_money_back

Nicholas Rushworth, *France Under Fire for Arming Rebels*, FRANCE 24, July 3, 2011, *available at* http://www.france24.com/en/20110701-france-arms-libya-rebels-un-resolution-russia-juppe-diplomacy-military

Russia set to sell $2B in arms to Libya, UPI, Jan. 27, 2010, *available at* http://www.upi.com/Business_News/Security-Industry/2010/01/27/Russia-set-to-sell-2B-in-arms-to-Libya/UPI-76051264611600

Missy Ryan & Rania El Gamal, *Libyans start Ramadan fast amid conflict, divisions*, REUTERS, Aug. 1, 2011, *available at* http://www.reuters.com/article/2011/08/01/us-libya-idUSTRE76Q7662011080

Ayman al-Sahli, *Libya interior minister calls time on rogue militias*, REUTERS, Mar. 10, 2012, *available at* http://www.reuters.com/article/2012/03/10/us-libya-militias-idUSBRE 8290DA20120310

Saif al-Islam's gangrenous fingers need amputating, TELEGRAPH, Nov. 25, 2011, *available at* http://www.telegraph.co.uk/news/worldnews/africaandindianocean/libya/8916912/Saif-al-Islams-gangrenous-fingers-need-amputating.html

Saif al-Islam Gaddafi to be tried in Libya in August, BBC, June 17, 2013, *available at* http://www.bbc.co.uk/news/world-africa-22945159

Heba Saleh et al., *Rebels claim to have Qadhafi surrounded*, FINANCIAL TIMES, Aug. 25, 2011 *available at* http://www.ft.com/cms/s/0/511e84f4-ce57-11e0-99ec-00144feabdco .html#axzz2JyKzKMh8

Henry Samuel & Nabila Ramdan, *Gaddafi's daughter thrown out of Algeria after she 'set fire to presidential residence'*, THE TELEGRAPH, Apr. 2, 2013, *available at* http://www .telegraph.co.uk/news/worldnews/africaandindianocean/libya/9967203/Gaddafis-daughter-thrown-out-of-Algeria-after-she-set-fire-to-presidential-residence.html

Satellite images appear to show destruction of Libya mosque, CNN, Mar. 22, 2011, *available at* http://www.cnn.com/2011/WORLD/africa/03/21/libya.zawiya.mosque/index.html

Charlie Savage & Thom Shanker, *In Libya, Scores of U.S. Airstrikes Followed Handoff to NATO*, N.Y. TIMES, June 20, 2011, *available at* http://www.nytimes.com/2011/06/21/world/africa/21powers.html

Scott Sayare, *Berber Rebels in Libya's West Face Long Odds Against Qaddafi*, N.Y. TIMES, Apr. 24, 2011, *available at* http://www.theglobeandmail.com/subscribe.jsp?art=1995361

Paul Schemm, *Battle at army base broke Gadhafi hold in Benghazi*, THE WASHINGTON POST, Feb. 25, 2011, *available at* http://www.washingtonpost.com/wp-dyn/content/article/2011/02/25/AR2011022505021.html

——, *Libyan warplanes strike rebels at oil port*, AP, Mar. 7, 2011 *available at* http://www .businessweek.com/ap/financialnews/D9LQHEPOo.htm

Lisa Schlein, *People in Battle-Torn Libya Facing Critical Shortages*, VOICE OF AMERICA, June 7, 2011, *available at* http://www.voanews.com/english/news/People-in-Battle-Torn-Libya-Facing-Critical-Shortages-123354293.html

Paul Schemm & Bassem Mroue, *Protesters Hit by Hail of Gunfire in Libya March*, AP, Feb. 25, 2011, *available at* http://abclocal.go.com/wpvi/story?section=news/national_world&id=7979856

Eric Schmitt, *U.S. to Help Create Libyan Commando Force*, N.Y. TIMES, Oct. 15, 2012, *available at* http://www.nytimes.com/2012/10/16/world/africa/us-to-help-create-libyan-commando-force.html

Eric Schmitt & Steven Lee Myers, *Surveillance and Coordination with NATO aided Rebels*, N.Y. TIMES, Aug. 21, 2011, *available at* http://www.nytimes.com/2011/08/22/world/africa/22nato.html

Eric Schmitt et al., *Attack in Libya was Major Blow to CIA Efforts*, N.Y. TIMES, Sept. 23, 2012, *available at* http://www.nytimes.com/2012/09/24/world/africa/attack-in-libya-was-major-blow-to-cia-efforts.html

Adam Schreck, *Libya says NATO airstrike killed 9 civilians*, AP, June 19, 2011, *available at* http://www.seattlepi.com/news/article/Libya-says-NATO-airstrike-killed-9-civilians-1429866.php

——, *NATO boosts airstrikes on military targets in Libya*, REUTERS, July 3, 2011 *available at* http://www.boston.com/news/world/africa/articles/2011/07/03/nato_boosts_airstrikes_on_military_targets_in_libya

Score-settling after Libya's war casts shadow, AP, Oct. 29, 2011, *available at* http://www.guardian.co.uk/world/feedarticle/9920407

Ashish Kumar Sen, *Gadhafi lays siege to west mountain towns*, THE WASHINGTON TIMES, Apr. 16, 2011, *available at* http://www.washingtontimes.com/news/2011/apr/17/gadhafi-lays-siege-libyan-mountain-towns/

Kim Sengupta, *NATO strike force in Libya enjoys quick success with Apache gunships*, THE GUARDIAN, June 5, 2011, *available at* http://www.guardian.co.uk/world/2011/jun/05/nato-libya-apache-gunships-success

——, *Top Libyan rebel commander shot dead*, THE INDEPENDENT, July 29, 2011, *available at* http://www.independent.co.uk/news/world/africa/top-libyan-rebel-commander-shot-dead-2328028.html

Anthony Shadid, *Libya Struggles to Curb Militias as Chaos Grows*, N.Y. TIMES, Feb. 8, 2012, *available at* http://www.nytimes.com/2012/02/09/world/africa/libyas-new-government-unable-to-control-militias.html

——, *Libyan forces rout rebels as west's effort for no-flight zone stalls*, N.Y. TIMES, Mar. 15, 2011, *available at* http://www.nytimes.com/2011/03/16/world/africa/16libya.html

——, *Qaddafi Forces Bear Down on Strategic Town as Rebels Flee*, N.Y. TIMES, Mar. 10, 2011, *available at* http://www.nytimes.com/2011/03/11/world/africa/11libya.html

Rami al-Shaheibi, *Libya's Tripoli Airport Attacked by Disgruntled Militia*, AP, June 4, 2012, *available at* http://www.huffingtonpost.com/2012/06/04/libyan-militia-takes-control-of-tripoli-airport_n_1567976.html

Rami Al-Shaheibi, *Rival Libyan militia clash near military base*, USA TODAY, Nov. 13, 2011, *available at* http://www.usatoday.com/news/world/story/2011-11-13/libya-militias/51184224/1

Hadeel Al Shalchi, *Discontent Rules in cradle of Libya Revolution*, REUTERS, July 7, 2012, *available at* http://www.reuters.com/article/2012/07/07/us-libya-elections-cradle-id USBRE8660DS20120707

——, *East Libyans threaten to stop oil to press govt*, REUTERS, Mar. 27, 2012, *available at* http://www.reuters.com/article/2012/03/27/libya-east-oil-idUSL6E8ER9WR20120327

——, *Libya: Anti-Gaddafi Fighters Loot, Burn Homes In Sirte*, AP, Oct. 5, 2011, *available at* http://www.huffingtonpost.com/2011/10/05/libya-gaddafi-fighters-looting_n_997154.html

——, *Vote in Libya's Benghazi tests support for autonomy*, REUTERS, May 19, 2012, *available at* http://www.reuters.com/article/2012/05/19/libya-benghazi-council-idUSL5E8GJ1BJ 20120519

Hadeel Al-Shalchi & Rosalind Russell, *Rocket damages Red Cross office in Libya's Benghazi*, REUTERS, May 22, 2012, *available at* http://www.reuters.com/article/2012/05/22/us-libya-redcross-bomb-idUSBRE84L0OB20120522

Shattered Gaddafi town says forgotten in new Libya, REUTERS, Feb. 29, 2012, *available at* http://www.reuters.com/article/2012/02/29/libya-Surt-idUSL5E8DT1WF20120229

Eman El-Shenawi, *Tripoli quick to deny rebel capture of strategic port town as fighters claim victory*, AL ARABIYA, Aug. 13, 2011, *available at* http://english.alarabiya.net/articles/2011/08/13/162174.html

Ghaith Shennib, *Libyan wartime leader Jalil faces questioning over killing*, AL JAZEERA, Nov. 2, 2012, *available at* http://af.reuters.com/article/worldNews/idAFBRE8A61FP20121107

———, *Rival Libya militias battle on streets of Tripoli*, REUTERS, Nov. 4, 2012 *available at* http://www.reuters.com/article/2012/11/04/us-libya-attack-idUSBRE8A30642012104

Ruth Sherlock, *The headless corpse, the mass grave and worrying questions about Libya's rebel army*, THE TELEGRAPH, July 20, 2011, *available at* http://www.telegraph.co.uk/news/worldnews/africaandindianocean/libya/8650436/The-headless-corpse-the-mass-grave-and-worrying-questions-about-Libyas-rebel-army.html

———, *Libyan rebels launch the final push for Surt and their crowning victory*, THE TELEGRAPH, Oct. 7, 2011, *available at* http://www.telegraph.co.uk/news/worldnews/africaandindian-ocean/libya/8813811/Libyas-rebels-launch-the-final-push-for-Surt-and-their-crowning-victory.html

Ruth Sherlock & Damien McElroy, *Nato lacks firepower to ensure collapse of Gaddafi regime, experts claim*, THE TELEGRAPH, June 24, 2011, *available at* http://www.telegraph.co.uk/news/worldnews/africaandindianocean/libya/8597107/Natolacks-firepower-to-ensure-collapse-of-Gaddafi-regime-experts-claim.html

Philip Sherwell, *Gaddafi and rebel forces in heavy clashes in town of Zawiya*, THE TELEGRAPH, Mar. 5, 2011, *available at* http://www.telegraph.co.uk/news/worldnews/africaandindi-anocean/libya/8363927/Gaddafi-and-rebel-forces-in-heavy-clashes-in-town-of-Zawiya.html

Harriet Sherwood, *Nato must send in troops to save Misrata, say rebels*, THE GUARDIAN, Apr. 16, 2011, *available at* http://www.guardian.co.uk/world/2011/apr/16/libya-muammar-gaddafi

Ali Shuaib, *Anti-Gaddafi fighters demand role in the new Libya*, REUTERS, Nov. 19, 2011, *available at* http://www.reuters.com/article/2011/11/19/us-libya-government-fighters-id USTRE7AI0W320111119

———, *Armed groups clash in turf war near Tripoli airport*, REUTERS, Dec. 11, 2011, *available at* http://af.reuters.com/article/topNews/idAFJOE7BA02P20111211

———, *Gaddafi-era officials go on trial accused over Lockerbie case*, REUTERS, Sept. 10, 2012, *available at* http;//uk.reuters.com/article/2012/09/10/uk-libya-trials-idUKBRE 8890YK20120910

———, *Libya militia hands Tripoli airport control to govt*, REUTERS, Apr. 20, 2012, *available at* http://www.reuters.com/article/2012/04/20/libya-airport-idUSL6E8FKF0P20120420

———, *UPDATE 1 – Refugees of Libya revenge attacks plan to go home*, REUTERS, Dec. 14, 2011, *available at* http://www.reuters.com/article/2011/12/14/libya-tawargha-return-id USL6E7NE4W620111214

Ali Shuaib & Hadeel Al Shalchi, *ICC lawyer meeting Gaddafi son detained in Libya*, REUTERS, June 9, 2012, *available at* http://www.reuters.com/article/2012/06/09/us-libya-icc-idUSBRE8580FH20120609

Ali Shuaib et al., *More than 100 killed in west Libya clashes in a week*, REUTERS, June 20, 2012, *available at* http://www.reuters.com/article/2012/06/20/us-libya-clashes-toll-idUSBRE85J1F620120620

Marlise Simons, *Hague Judge Faults Acquittals of Serb and Croat Commanders*, N.Y. TIMES, June 14, 2013, *available at* http://www.nytimes.com/2013/06/14/world/europe/hague-judge-faults-acquittals-of-serb-and-croat-commanders.html

Luis Sinco, *Journalists visit prisoners held by rebels in Libya*, L.A. TIMES, Mar. 23, 2011, *available at* http://framework.latimes.com/2011/03/23/journalists-visit-prisoners-held-by-rebels-in-libya/#/0

Six killed in attacks on army in Benghazi, LIBYA HERALD, June 15, 2013, *available at* http://www.libyaherald.com/2013/06/15/four-killed-in-attacks-on-army-in-benghazi/

Liz Sly et al., *France fires first shots against Libya after Qadhafi's forces enter Bengazi*, THE WASHINGTON POST, Mar. 18, 2011 (updated Mar. 19, 2011), *available at* http://www.wash-ingtonpost.com/world/us-allies-prepare-military-action-against-libya-as-gaddafi-forces-continue-attacks/2011/03/18/ABLAOfs_story.html

Dominique Soguel, *Libyans in historic vote amid tensions in east*, AFP, July 8 2012, *available at* http://reliefweb.int/report/libya/libyans-historic-vote-amid-tensions-east

Steven Sotloff, *Libya's New Crisis: A Wave of Assassinations Targeting its Top Cops*, TIME WORLD, Nov. 26, 2012, *available at* http://world.time.com/2012/11/26/libyas-new-crisis-a-wave-of-assassinations-targeting-its-top-cops

Zoubeir Souissi, *Pro-Qadhafi forces clash with Tunisian military*, REUTERS, Apr. 29, 2011 *available at* http://www.reuters.com/article/2011/04/29/libya-tunisia-idAFLDE 73S0Y020110429

Special forces swoop on Libya to pull Britons to safety, DAILY TELEGRAPH, Feb. 26, 2011, *available at* http://www.telegraph.co.uk/news/worldnews/africaandindianocean/libya/8349896/Special-forces-swoop-on-Libya-to-pull-Britons-to-safety.html

Richard Spencer, *Libya: last act of bloody vengeance by Khamis Brigade*, THE TELEGRAPH, Aug. 28, 2011, *available at* http://www.telegraph.co.uk/news/worldnews/africaandindianocean/libya/ 8728597/Libya-last-act-of-bloody-vengeance-by-Khamis-Brigade.html

——, *Libya: Saif al-Islam vows to continue the war and retake Tripoli*, THE TELEGRAPH, Aug. 31, 2011, *available at* http://www.telegraph.co.uk/news/worldnews/africaandindianocean/libya/8734174/Libya-Saif-al-Islam-Gaddafi-vows-to-continue-the-war-and-retake-Tripoli.html

——, *Libyan cleric announces new party on lines of 'moderate' Islamic democracy*, THE GUARDIAN, Nov. 10, 2011, *available at* http://www.telegraph.co.uk/news/worldnews/africaandindianocean/libya/8879955/Libyan-cleric-announces-new-party-on-lines-of-moderate-Islamic-democracy.html

——, *US consulate attack in Benghazi 'disrupted major intelligence operation'*, THE TELE-GRAPH, Sept. 24, 2012, *available at* http://www.telegraph.co.uk/news/worldnews/africaandindianocean/libya/9563831/US-consulate-attack-in-Benghazi-disrupted-major-intelligence-operation.html

Douglas Stanglin, *Gadhafi vows to attack Bengazi and "show no mercy"*, USA TODAY, Mar. 17, 2011, *available at* http://content.usatoday.com/communities/ondeadline/post/2011/03/gadhafi-vows-to-retake-benghazi-and-show--no-mercy/1#.UM4OInPjlAE

Statements on the Attack in Benghazi, N.Y. TIMES, Sept. 27, 2012, *available at* http://www.nytimes.com/interactive/2012/09/27/world/africa/administration-statements-on-the-attack-in-benghazi.html

Joe Sterling, *Libya picks armed forces chief*, CNN, Jan. 5, 2012, *available at* http://edition.cnn.com/2012/01/04/world/africa/libya-army-chief/

Christopher Stephen, *Libya bomb attack hits French embassy in Tripoli*, THE GUARDIAN, Apr. 23, 2013, *available at* http://www.guardian.co.uk/world/2013/apr/23/libya-bomb-attack-french-embassy

——, *Libya sees claims of beatings and human rights abuses as elections near*, THE GUARD-IAN, June 3, 2012, *available at* http://www.guardian.co.uk/world/2012/jun/03/libya-security-force-kidnapping-surgeon

——, *Libyan military prosecutor shot dead in Benghazi*, THE GUARDIAN, June 22, 2012, *available at* http://www.guardian.co.uk/world/2012/jun/22/libyan-military-prosecutor-shot-benghazi

——, *Libyan rebels advance on Gaddafi's home town*, THE GUARDIAN, Aug. 24, 2011, *available at* http://www.guardian.co.uk/world/2011/aug/24/libya-rebels-advance-gaddafi-home-town

——, *Libyan rebels launch major offensive to capture key towns*, THE GUARDIAN, July 28, 2011, *available at* http://www.guardian.co.uk/world/2011/jul/28/libya-rebels-launch-major-offensive

——, *Libyan rebels push towards Brega backed by Nato air strikes*, THE GUARDIAN, July 18, 2011, *available at* http://www.guardian.co.uk/world/2011/jul/18/libya-rebels-brega-nato

——, *Libyan rebels storm prime minister's office*, THE GUARDIAN, May 8, 2012, *available at* http://www.guardian.co.uk/world/2012/may/08/libyan-rebels-storm-prime-minister-office

——, *Qadhafi Files Show Evidence of Murderous Intent*, THE GUARDIAN, June 18, 2011, *available at* http://www.guardian.co.uk/world/2011/jun/18/gaddafi-misrata-war-crime-documents

Chris Stephen, *Misrata rebel forces seize arms after routing pro-Gaddafi troops*, THE GUARDIAN, July 31, 2011, *available at* http://www.guardian.co.uk/world/2011/jul/31/misrata-rebels-seize-gaddafi-arms

Christopher Stephen & Peter Beaumont, *Libyan leader vows to keep nation together by force*, THE GUARDIAN, Mar. 7, 2012, *available at* http://www.guardian.co.uk/world/2012/mar/07/libya-vows-nation-together-force

Christopher Stephen & Luke Harding, *Libya's former PM Mahmoudi 'tortured' on forced return to Tripoli*, THE GUARDIAN, June 27, 2012, *available at* http://www.guardian.co.uk/world/2012/jun/27/libya-mahmoudi-tortured-return-tripoli

Christopher Stephen & Afua Hirsch, *Libya Faces Growing Islamist Threat*, THE GUARDIAN, Apr. 28, 2013, *available at* http://www.guardian.co.uk/world/2013/apr/28/libya-mali-islamist-violence-tripoli

Christopher Stephen & Nick Hopkins, *Libya rebels frustrated by NATO's safety-first strategy*, THE GUARDIAN, June 8, 2011, *available at* http://www.guardian.co.uk/world/2011/jun/07/libya-rebels-nato-strategy

Christopher Stephen et al., *Tripoli facing three-sided advance by Libyan rebels*, THE GUARDIAN, Aug. 19, 2011, *available at* http://www.guardian.co.uk/world/2011/aug/19/tripoli-facing-advance-libya-rebels

Morgan Strong, *News Summary from the US/International Press on the Libyan Crisis*, THE TRIPOLI POST, Mar. 8, 2011, *available at* http://tripolipost.com/articledetail.asp?c=1&i=5544

——, *News Summary from the US/International Press on the Libyan Crisis*, THE TRIPOLI POST, Mar. 10, 2011, *available at* http://tripolipost.com/articledetail.asp?c=1&i=5558

——, *News Summary from the US/International Press on the Libyan Crisis*, THE TRIPOLI POST, Mar. 13, 2011, *available at* http://tripolipost.com/articledetail.asp?c=1&i=5587

——, *News Summary from the US/International Press on the Libyan Crisis*, THE TRIPOLI POST, Mar. 17, 2011, *available at* http://tripolipost.com/articledetail.asp?c=1&i=5618

——, *News Summary from the US/International Press on the Libyan Crisis*, THE TRIPOLI POST, Mar. 23, 2011, *available at* http://www.tripolipost.com/articledetail.asp?c=1&i=5661

Alex Sundby, *Ambassador Warned Libya was 'volatile and violent'*, CBS, Oct. 19, 2012 *available at* http://www.cbsnews.com/8301-250_162-57536446/ambassador-warned-libya-was-volatile-and-violent/

Surt fighter indignant at level of city's destruction, THE DAILY STAR LEBANON, Oct. 20, 2011, *available at* http://www.dailystar.com.lb/News/Middle-East/2011/Oct-20/151711-Surt-fighter-indignant-at--level-of-citys-destruction.ashx#axzz1bKo54RwM

Syria, Libya and Middle East unrest, THE GUARDIAN, May 9, 2011, *available at* http://www.guardian.co.uk/world/middle-east-live/2011/may/09/syria-libya-middle-east-unrest-live

Syria, Libya and Middle East unrest, THE GUARDIAN, May 18, 2011, *available at* http://www.guardian.co.uk/world/middle-east-live/2011/may/18/libya-syria-middle-east-unrest

Adam Tanner & Souhail Karam, *Six Killed in Libyan Town Shelling: Rebel*, REUTERS, Mar. 25, 2011, *available at* http://www.reuters.com/article/2011/03/25/us-libya-misrata-fighting-idUSTRE72O63720110325

Abeer Tayel, *Libya rebels capture Qaddafi's Tripoli compound, hoist flag & smash statue*, AL ARABIYA, Aug. 23, 2011, *available at* http://english.alarabiya.net/articles/2011/08/23/163724.html

Alan Taylor, *DIY weapons of the Libyan rebels*, THE ATLANTIC, June 14, 2011, *available at* http://www.theatlantic.com/infocus/2011/06/diy-weapons-of-the-libyan-rebels/100086

Ishaan Tharoor, *With Roman Ruins Under Threat, Libya's Ancient Past Presses Against Its Present*, TIME WORLD, June 14, 2011, *available at* http://world.time.com/2011/06/14/with-roman-ruins-under-threat-libyas-ancient-past-presses-against-its-present

Thousands of Libyans flee remote western area: report, REUTERS, Apr. 18, 2011, *available at* http://www.reuters.com/article/2011/04/18/us-libya-mountains-clashes-idUSTRE 73H6WL20110418

Timeline: Saif al-Islam detained, say officials, REUTERS, Nov. 19, 2011, *available at* http://www.reuters.com/article/2011/11/19/us-libya-events-idUSTRE7AI0HV20111119

Lorianne Updike Toler, *Libya's shortened constitutional timeline and why it should be extended*, LIBYA HERALD, Oct. 9, *available at* http://www.libyaherald.com/2012/10/09/libyas-shortened-constitutional-timeline-and-why-it-should-be-extended/

Mohammed al Tommy, *Bomb targets U.S. mission in Libya's Benghazi*, REUTERS, June 6, 2012, *available at* http://www.reuters.com/article/2012/06/06/us-libya-attack-us-idUSBRE8550GX20120606

——, *British envoy's convoy ambushed in Libya, two wounded*, REUTERS, July 11, 2012, *available at* http://www.reuters.com/article/2012/06/11/us-libya-attack-britain-idUSBRE85 AoTV20120611

——, *Courthouse bomb in Libya's Benghazi injures one*, REUTERS, Apr. 27, 2012, *available at* http://www.reuters.com/article/2012/04/27/us-libya-explosion-idUSBRE83QoEU 20120427

——, *Hundreds rally in Benghazi against militia*, REUTERS, Apr. 7, 2012, *available at* http://in.reuters.com/article/2012/04/06/libya-protest-idINDEE8350DZ20120406

——, *Protesters shut Libya's Agoco office for day*, REUTERS, Apr. 23, 2012, *available at* http://www.reuters.com/article/2012/04/23/libya-oil-protest-idUSL5E8FNBHI20120423

——, *Protesters storm Libyan government HQ in Benghazi*, REUTERS, Jan. 21, 2011, *available at* http://www.reuters.com/article/2012/01/22/us-libya-ntc-benghazi-idUSTRE80K0 OC20120122

——, *UPDATE 1 – Libya police put end to protest at oil firm Agoco*, REUTERS, May 9, 2012, *available at* http://www.reuters.com/article/2012/05/09/libya-agoco-idUSL5E8G92 XU20120509

Mark Tran et al., *Libya uprising – live updates*, THE GUARDIAN, Feb. 21, 2011, *available at* http://www.guardian.co.uk/world/blog/2011/feb/21/arab-and-middle-east-protests-middleeast

Tripoli facing three-sided advance by Libyan rebels, THE GUARDIAN, Aug. 19, 2011, *available at* http://www.guardian.co.uk/world/2011/aug/19/tripoli-facing-advance-libya-rebels

Tripoli hit by NATO airstrikes in heaviest bombing yet, NDTV, May 24, 2011, *available at* http://www.ndtv.com/article/world/tripoli-hit-by-nato-airstrikes-in-heaviest-bombing-yet-107799

Troops sent to quell clashes in western Libya, BBC, June 17, 2012, *available at* http://www.bbc.co.uk/news/world-africa-18474834

Tunisia accuses armed Libyans of kidnapping 80 nationals, AFP, Apr. 17, 2011, *available at* http://english.alarabiya.net/articles/2012/04/17/208438.html

Tunisia extradites Gaddafi's last PM to Libya, AL JAZEERA, June 25, 2012, *available at* http://www.aljazeera.com/news/africa/2012/06/2012624135853340329.html

Truth and Reconciliation Conference Makes Recommendations on Way Forward for Libya, THE TRIPOLI POST, Dec. 19, 2012, *available at* http://www.tripolipost.com/articledetail .asp?i=9649&c=1

Twelve men face execution by Libyan militia for allegedly being gay, DAILY MAIL, Nov. 26, 2012, *available at* http://www.dailymail.co.uk/news/article-2238812/Twelve-men-face-execution-Libyan-militia-allegedly-gay.html

UAE Air Force on the offensive in Libya, ARABIAN AEROSPACE, Aug. 24, 2011, *available at* http://arabianaerospace.aero/uae-air-force-on-the-offensive-in-libya.html

UK diplomat's convoy attacked in Libya, AL JAZEERA, June 11, 2012, *available at* http://www.aljazeera.com/news/middleeast/2012/06/201261115212735 6825.html

UK eases travel recommendations for Libya, REUTERS, Sept. 15, 2011, *available at* http://www.reuters.com/article/2011/09/15/us-libya-britain-travel-idUSTRE78E3T320110915

UK journalists held in Libya after Welsh mistaken for Hebrew, BBC, Mar. 20, 2012, *available at* http://www.bbc.co.uk/news/uk-wales-17444890

UK to update Libya travel advice, REUTERS, Sept. 15, 2011, *available at* http://www.reuters .com/article/2011/09/15/libya-britain-travel-idUSL5E7KF2A220110915

UN convoy targeted in explosion in east Libya-source, REUTERS, Apr. 10, 2011, *available at* http://www.reuters.com/article/2012/04/10/libya-explosion-idUSL6E8FA3SS20120410

UN rights chief condemns violence against protesters in Middle East, North Africa, UN NEWS CENTRE, Feb. 18, 2011, *available at* http://www.un.org/apps/news/story.asp?NewsID=375 67&Cr=protests&Cr1

UN sanctions on Libya to cost Russia US$4 Billion, RT, Feb. 27, 2011, *available at* http:// rt.com/news/russia-arms-export-libya

Unprecedented protests have taken place in Libya, AL JAZEERA, May 30, 2011, *available at* http://blogs.aljazeera.com/topic/libya/libya-may-30-2011-2350

UPDATE 1 – EU sanctions on Libyan ports seen lifted on Friday, REUTERS, Aug. 31, 2011, *available at* http://www.reuters.com/article/2011/08/31/libya-eu-sanctions-idUSLDE77U0EH20110831

UPDATE 1 – Libya rebels say Gaddafi forces retreat in east, REUTERS, July 18, 2011, *available at* http://206.132.6.105/article/libyaNews/idAFLDE76H0MR20110718

UPDATE 1 – Libyan rebels fight for Tripoli airbase – activist, Reuters, Aug. 20, 2011, *available at* http://af.reuters.com/article/libyaNews/idAFLDE77J0692011820

UPDATE 1 – NATO strike kills at least 16 in Brega – Libyan TV, REUTERS, May 13, 2011, *available at* http://af.reuters.com/article/energyOilNews/idAFLDE74C1GL20110513

UPDATE 2 – Gaddafi's son will get fair trial – Libyan PM, REUTERS, Nov. 19, 2011, *available at* http://www.reuters.com/article/2011/11/19/libya-saif-pm-idUSL5E7MJ1062011119

UPDATE 2 – Rebels, Gaddafi forces skirmish over "ghost town", REUTERS, Mar. 11, 2011, *available at* http://af.reuters.com/article/commoditiesNews/idAFLDE72A1WR20110311

Mark Urban, *Libya: Is a breakdown in order forcing NGOs out?*, BBC, Jan. 27, 2012, *available at* http://www.bbc.co.uk/news/world-16761200

Mark Urban, *Post-revolution Surt a breeding ground for unrest*, BBC, Feb. 21, 2012, *available at* http://www.bbc.co.uk/news/world-17116657

Uprising in Libya: Survival Hinges on Tribal Solidarity, SPIEGEL ONLINE, Feb. 23, 2011, *available at* http://www.spiegel.de/International/world/0,1518,747234,00.html

Up to 10 killed in Libyan clashes at Ras Lanuf: doctor, IPOT NEWS, Mar. 5, 2011, *available at* http://www.ipotnews.com/index.php?jdl=Up_to_10_killed_in_Libyan_clashes_ at_Ras_Lanuf__doctor&level2=&level3=&level4=international&news_id= 437294&group_news=ALLNEWS&taging_subtype=BANKING&popular=&search=y&q=

Gert Van Langendonck, *In Qaddafi's hometown, signs of trouble for Libya*, THE CHRISTIAN SCIENCE MONITOR, Oct. 25, 2011, *available at* http://www.csmonitor.com/World/Middle-East/2011/1025/In-Qaddafi-s-hometown-signs-of-trouble-for-Libya

Tom Vanden Brook, *Gadhafi promises 'long war' after allies strike Libya*, USA TODAY, Mar. 20, 2011, *available at* http://usatoday30.usatoday.com/news/world/2011-03-19-libya_ N.htm

Martin Veal & Missy Ryan, *Gaddafi forces, rebels fight over Zawiyah*, REUTERS, Aug. 13, 2011, *available at* http://uk.reuters.com/article/2011/08/13/libya-idUKLDE77C01F20110813

'Vehemence to violence' in Benghazi, BBC, Feb. 24, 2011, *available at* http://news.bbc.co.uk/ today/hi/today/newsid_9406000/9406270.stm

Mathieu von Rohr, *Settling Old Scores – Tribal Rivalries Complicate Libyan War*, SPIEGEL ONLINE INTERNATIONAL, July 26, 2011, *available at* http://www.biyokulule.com/view_ content.php?articleid=3695

Farah Waleed, *Extradited Qaddafi regime figures flown into Tripoli*, LIBYA HERALD, Mar. 26, 2013, *available at* http://www.libyaherald.com/2013/03/26/extradited-qaddafi-regime-figures-flown-into-tripoli

——, *Qaddaf Al-Dam implicated in disappearance of Mansour El-Kikhia*, LIBYA HERALD, Mar. 28, 2013, *available at* http://www.libyaherald.com/2013/03/28/qaddaf-al-dam-implicated-in-disappearance-of-mansour-el-kikhia

Portia Walker, *More than 1,000 Libyans Missing from Misurata*, THE WASHINGTON POST, June 4, 2011, *available at* http://www.washingtonpost.com/world/middle-east/more-than-1000-libyans-missing-from-misurata/2011/05/30/AGmuw2IH_story.html

——, *Qatari military advisers on the ground, helping Libyan rebels get into shape*, THE WASHINGTON POST, May 12, 2011 *available at* http://articles.washingtonpost.com/2011-05-12/world/35233351_1_rebel-council-libyan-rebels-rebel-army

Vivienne Walt, *Benghazi's Real Scandal: Why is the Libyan Investigation Such a Mess?*, TIME WORLD, Nov. 15, 2012, *available at* http://world.time.com/2012/11/15/benghazis-real-scandal-why-is-the-libyan-investigation-such-a-mess/

——, *Conflicting Priorities Imperil Effort to Gather Up Gaddafi's Discarded Arms*, TIME, Nov. 15, 2011, *available at* http://www.time.com/time/world/article/0,8599,2099549,00.html

——, *Gaddafi gets his revenge: The Price of Rebellion*, TIME, Mar. 17, 2011, *available at* http://www.time.com/time/world/article/0,8599,2059596,00.html

——, *How did Gaddafi Die? A Year Later, Unanswered Questions and Bad Blood*, TIME WORLD, Oct. 18, 2012, *available at* http://world.time.com/2012/10/18/how-did-gaddafi-die-a-year-later-unanswered-questions-and-bad-blood/

——, *Libya's Disaster of Justice: The Case of Saif al-Islam Gaddafi Reveals a Country in Chaos*, Time, June 28, 2013, *available at* http://world.time.com/2013/06/28/libyas-disaster-of-justice-the-case-of-saif-al-islam-gaddafi-reveals-a-country-in-chaos/#ixzz2YdNkb6oK

Joby Warrick & Liz Sly, *U.S. envoy Chris Stevens arrives in Libya to help opposition fighters*, THE WASHINGTON POST, Apr. 6, 2011, *available at* http://www.washingtonpost.com/world/us-envoy-arrives-in-libya-to-help-opposition-fighters/2011/04/05/AFTIV6lC_story.html

Bruno Waterfield, *Libya: British military advisers set up 'joint operations centre' in Bengazi*, THE TELEGRAPH, May 18, 2011, *available at* http://www.telegraph.co.uk/news/worldnews/africaandindianocean/libya/8521977/Libya-British-military-advisers-set-up-joint-operations-centre-in-Benghazi.html

Frederic Wehrey, *Libya's Militia Menace*, FOREIGN AFFAIRS, July 12, 2012, *available at* http://www.foreignaffairs.com/articles/137776/frederic-wehrey/libyas-militia-menace?page=show

Were The Libya Attacks A Failure of the Obama Administration?, ABC NEWS, Sept. 14, 2012, *available at* http://abcnews.go.com/Politics/video/libya-attacks-failure-obama-administration-17238467

Kathryn Westcott, *Muammar Gaddafi's presidential bolt-hole*, BBC, May 1, 2011, *available at* http://www.bbc.co.uk/news/world-africa-12831594

Tom Westcott, *"We won't use these weapons": militiamen at Justice Ministry siege*, LIBYA HERALD, May 1, 2013, available at http://www.libyaherald.com/2013/05/01/we-wont-use-these-weapons-militiamen-at-justice-ministry-siege/

——, *Transitional Justice: perspectives from and for young Libyans*, LIBYA HERALD, Mar. 17, 2012, *available at* http://www.libyaherald.com/2013/03/17/transitional-justice-perspectives-from-and-for-young-libyans

William Wheeler, *Libya's purge of former Gaddafi officials reveals growing power of militias*, GLOBAL POST, June 4, 2013, *available at* http://www.globalpost.com/dispatches/globalpost-blogs/groundtruth/libya-political-isolation-law-militias

Kim Willsher, *Gaddafi's daughter sues over deadly Nato air strike*, THE GUARDIAN, June 7, 2011, *available at* http://www.guardian.co.uk/world/2011/jun/07/gaddafi-daughter-sues-nato-air-strike

Tony White, *A chronology of NATO's involvement in Libya*, ROYAL CANADIAN AIRFORCE, Apr. 12, 2011, *available at* http://www.rcaf-arc.forces.gc.ca/v2/nr-sp/index-eng.asp?id=12783

Cajsa Wikstrom, *Calls for weekend protests in Syria*, AL JAZEERA, Feb. 4, 2011, *available at* http://www.aljazeera.com/news/middleeast/2011/02/20112217164967912.html

Kim Willsher, *Gaddafi's daughter sues over deadly Nato air strike*, THE GUARDIAN, June 7, 2011, *available at* http://www.guardian.co.uk/world/2011/jun/07/gaddafi-daughter-sues-nato-air-strike

Patrick Wintour & Kim Willsher, *G8 Summit: Gaddafi Isolated as Russia Joins Demand for Libyan Leader to Go*, THE GUARDIAN, May 27, 2011, *available at* http://www.guardian .co.uk/world/2011/may/27/g8-gaddafi-libya-russia

WRAPUP 1 – Deadlock in Libya exposes international rifts, REUTERS, Apr. 26, 2011, *available at* http://www.reuters.com/article/2011/04/26/libya-idUSLDE73P2022011o426

WRAPUP 2 – Libya says NATO air strike hits major oil field, REUTERS, Apr. 6, 2011, *available at* http://af.reuters.com/article/libyaNews/idAFLDE7352B62011o406

WRAPUP 3 – Libya rebels say they are advancing on Brega, REUTERS, Aug. 6, 2011, *available at* http://www.reuters.com/article/2011/08/06/libya-idUSLDE77504222011o806

WRAPUP 4 – Libyan rebel commander killed by allied militia, REUTERS, July 31, 2011, *available at* http://www.reuters.com/article/2011/07/30/libya-idUSLDE76S1K32011o730

WRAPUP 5 – Gaddafi govt says in talks, rebels say he must go, REUTERS, July 4, 2011, *available at* http://www.reuters.com/article/2011/07/04/libya-idUSL6E7I40402o11o704

WRAPUP 10 – Gaddafi forces step up attack on western rebel town, REUTERS, Mar. 5, 2011, *available at* http://www.reuters.com/article/2011/03/05/libya-idUSLDE72400F2011o305

Yearender: Uncertainties haunt Middle East, North Africa after sweeping unrest, NEWS XINHUANET, Dec 18, 2011, *available at* http://news.xinhuanet.com/english/world/2011-12/18/c_131313145_2.htm

April Yee, *Production resumes at Libya's largest refinery*, THE NATIONAL, Sept. 4, 2012, *available at* http://www.thenational.ae/business/energy/production-resumes-at-libyas-largest-refinery

Rob Young, *Libya's commercial hub recovers slowly*, BBC, *available at* http://www.bbc.co.uk/news/business-16366285

Sami Zaptia, *Political Isolation Law passed overwhelmingly*, May 5, 2013, LIBYA HERALD, *available at* http://www.libyaherald.com/2013/05/05/political-isolation-law-passed-over whelmingly/

Nihal Zaroug, *Justice Ministry seized by SSC; minister and staff ejected*, THE LIBYA HERALD, Mar. 31, 2013, available at http://www.libyaherald.com/2013/03/31/moj-building-sieged-by-armed-members-of-the SSC/

Zawiyah in rebel hands, but under siege, AFP, Mar. 5, 2011, *available at* http://www.news24 .com/Africa/News/Libya-Zawiyah-in-rebel-hands-but-under-siege-2011o305

Ariel Zirulnick, *Libya's rebels stage bold offensive in oil town of Brega*, CHRISTIAN SCIENCE MONITOR, July 18, 2011, *available at* http://www.csmonitor.com/World/terrorism-security/2011/0718/Libya-s-rebels-stage-bold-offensive-on-oil-town-of-Brega

Zlitan: Gaddafi forces say they control key town, BBC, Aug. 4, 2011, *available at* http://www .bbc.co.uk/news/world-africa-14413157

David Zucchino, *Air attacks put Libya town on edge*, L.A. TIMES, Mar. 9, 2011, *available at* http://articles.latimes.com/2011/mar/09/world/la-fg-libya-ras-lanuf-2011o309

———, *In Libya, rebel casualties tell the story behind fight for key city*, L.A. TIMES, July 19, 2011, *available at* http://articles.latimes.com/2011/jul/19/world/la-fg-libya-rebels-wounded-2011o719

———, *Kadafi's troops defending Surt force rebels to retreat 100 miles*, L.A. TIMES, Mar. 30, 2011, *available at* http://articles.latimes.com/2011/mar/30/world/la-fg-libya-counterattack-2011o330

———, *Libya forces, rebels locked in battle for Port Brega*, L.A. TIMES, July 20, 2011, *available at* http://articles.latimes.com/2011/jul/20/world/la-fg-libya-fighting-2011o720

Ariel Zirulnick, *Libya militias clash in longest sustained fighting since Qaddafi's fall*, CHRISTIAN SCIENCE MONITOR, Nov. 14, 2011, *available at* http://www.csmonitor.com/World/terrorism-security/2011/1114/Libya-militias-clash-in-longest-sustained-fighting-since-Qaddafi-s-fall?utm_source=feedburner&utm_medium=feed&utm_campaign=Feed%3A +feeds%2Fcsm+%28Christian+Science+Monitor+%7C+All+Stories%29

David Zucchino, *Libyan rebels appear to take leaf from Kadafi's playbook*, L.A. TIMES, Mar. 24, 2011, *available at* http://articles.latimes.com/2011/mar/24/world/la-fg-libya-prisoners-2011o324

——, *Libyan rebels' ragtag army left in disarray*, L.A. TIMES, MAR. 13 2011, *available at* http://articles.latimes.com/2011/mar/13/world/la-fg-libya-rebels-20110313

——, *Mistakes costing Libyan rebels: untrained fighters miss opportunities and waste ammunition*, L.A. TIMES, Mar. 8, 2011, *available at* http://articles.latimes.com/2011/mar/08/world/la-fg-libya-rebels-20110308

Suliman Ali Zway & Kareem Fahim, *Libyan Protesters Besiege Militant Group in Benghazi*, N.Y. TIMES, Sept. 21, 2012, *available at* http://www.nytimes.com/2012/09/22/world/africa/pro-american-libyans-besiege-militant-group-in-benghazi.html

4 dead as anti-Gadhafi forces, tribesmen clash, INQUIRER NEWS, Dec. 13, 2011, *available at* http://newsinfo.inquirer.net/110103/4-dead-as-anti-gadhafi-forces-tribesmen-clash

9/11 anniversary: Ayman al-Zawahiri confirms June death of Abu Yahya al-Libi, THE TELEGRAPH, Sept. 11, 2012, *available at* http://www.telegraph.co.uk/news/worldnews/september-11-attacks/9534938/911-anniversary-Ayman-al-Zawahiri-confirms-June-death-of-Abu-Yahya-al-Libi.html

18 killed in Benghazi demos Friday, NOW LEBANON, Feb. 19, 2011, *available at* http://www.nowlebanon.com/NewsArchiveDetails.aspx?ID=242231

20 reported dead Friday in Libya as thousands take to streets, CNN, Feb. 19, 2011, *available at* http://edition.cnn.com/2011/WORLD/africa/02/18/libya.protests/index.html

37 dead as Gaddafi regime hits back, PRESS ASSOCIATION, Mar. 4, 2011, *available at* http://www.independent.ie/breaking-news/world-news/37-dead-as-gaddafi-regime-hits-back-2565656.html

4,000 Gaddafi supporters in Libya prisons, THE VOICE OF RUSSIA, May 11, 2012, *available at* http://english.ruvr.ru/2012_05_11/74362355

UN DOCUMENTS

Ban Ki-moon, *Statement on Libya*, UNITED NATIONS, Mar. 16, 2011, *available at* http://www.un.org/sg/statements/?nid=5141

Conference on Truth and Reconciliation in Libya Concludes with Recommendations on the Way Forward, UN SUPPORT MISSION IN LIBYA, Feb. 8 2012, *available at* http://unsmil.unmissions.org/Default.aspx?tabid=3543&ctl=Details&mid=6187&ItemID=807743&language=en-US

Final report of the Panel of Experts established pursuant to resolution 1973 (2011) concerning Libya, U.N. Doc. S/2013/99 (Mar. 9, 2013)

Human Rights Council Resolution, HRC Res. S-15/1, UN Doc. A/HRC/RES/S-15/1 (Feb. 25, 2011)

Invitation to the Palestine Liberation Organization to participate in the efforts for peace in the Middle East, GA Res. 3375, U.N. Doc. A/RES/3375 (Nov. 10, 1975)

Letter dated 23 March 2012 from the Chairman of the Security Council Committee established pursuant to resolution 1970 (2011) concerning Libya addressed to the President of the Security Council (S/2012/178), U.N. Doc. S/PV.6768 (May 10, 2012)

Libya Response Situation Report No. 68 18 December 2011, U.N. OCHA, *available at* http://northafrica.humanitarianresponse.info/sites/default/files/20111218_SituationReport68.pdf

Misrata Factsheet, UN OFFICE FOR THE COORDINATION OF HUMANITARIAN AFFAIRS, Apr. 24, 2011, *available at* http://ochanet.unocha.org/p/Documents/Misrata%20Factsheet%20%2024%20April%202011_FINAL.pdf

More civilians flee Libya's Western Mountains, new aid reaches the east, UNHCR, Apr. 26, 2011, *available at* http://www.unhcr.org/cgi-bin/texis/vtx/search?page=search&docid=4db6dcf29&query=ajdabiya

Navanethem Pillay, *Establishing Effective Accountability Mechanisms for Human Rights Violations*, UN CHRONICLE, Dec. 31, 2012, *available at* http://www.un.org/wcm/content/site/chronicle/home/archive/issues2012/deliveringjustice/establishingeffectiveaccountabilitymechanisms

Press Release, *Hopes of Libyan People 'Must not be Dashed' Assembly President Says, As Secretary-General Voices 'Grave Concern' at Ongoing Violence against Civilians*, Mar. 1 2011, *available at* http://www.un.org/News/Press/docs/2011/ga11050.doc.htm

Press Release, *High Expectations for Quick Progress in Libya Strain Political System, but Given 'Terrible Legacy', Transitional Team Should Be Praised, Security Council Told*, UNITED NATIONS, May 10, 2012, *available at* http://www.un.org/News/Press/docs/2012/sc10644.doc.htm

Press Release *Outraged Secretary-General Calls for Immediate end to Violence in Libya*, UNITED NATIONS, Feb. 22, 2011, *available at* http://www.un.org/News/Press/docs/2011/sgsm13408.doc.htm

Report of the International Commission of Inquiry on Libya to investigate all the alleged violations of international human rights law in the Libyan Arab Jamahiriya, U.N. HRC. 17th Sess., U.N. Doc. A/HRC/17/44, final version (Jan. 12, 2012)

Report of the International Commission of Inquiry on Libya to investigate all the alleged violations of international human rights law in the Libyan Arab Jamahiriya, U.N. HRC. 19th Sess., U.N. Doc. A/HRC/19/68 (Mar. 2, 2012)

Report of the Secretary General and Head of UN Mission to Libya, UNITED NATIONS, U.N Doc. S/PV.6807 (July 28, 2012)

Report of the Secretary-General on the United Nations Support Mission in Libya, U.N. Doc. S/2011/727 (Nov. 22, 2011)

Report of the Secretary-General on the United Nations Support Mission in Libya, U.N. Doc. S/2012/675 (August 30, 2012)

Responsibility of States for Internationally Wrongful Acts, 2 YEARBOOK OF THE INTERNA-TIONAL LAW COMMISSION, 2011, U.N. Doc A/56/10 (2011)

Secretary-General, *Report of the Secretary-General's Panel of Experts on Accountability in Sri Lanka*, Mar. 31, 2011, *available at*: http://www.un.org/News/dh/infocus/Sri_Lanka/POE_Report_Full.pdf

Security Council Committee Established Pursuant to Resolution 1970 (2011) Concerning Libya, *List of Individuals Subject to the Measures Imposed by Paragraph 15 of Resolution 1970 (2011) (the Travel Ban) and/or Paragraph 17 of Resolution 1970 (2011) or Paragraph 19 of Resolution 1973 (2011) (the Assets Freeze)*, UNITED NATIONS, Apr. 2, 2011, *available at* http://www.un.org/sc/committees/1970/pdf/List%20of%20Individuals%20and%20Entities.pdf

Security Council, SC Res. 82 (1950), June 27, 1950, UN Doc. S/RES/83 (1950)

Security Council, SC Res. 84 (1950), July 7, 1950, UN Doc. S/RES/84 (1950)

Security Council, SC Res. 678 (1990), Nov. 29, 1990, UN Doc. S/RES/678 (1990)

Security Council, SC Res. 688 (1991), Apr. 5, 1991, UN Doc. S/RES/688 (1991)

Security Council, SC Res. 713 (1991), Sept. 25, 1991, UN Doc. S/RES/713 (1991)

Security Council, SC Res. 733 (1992), Jan. 23, 1992, UN Doc. S/RES/733 (1992)

Security Council, SC Res. 743 (1992), Feb. 21, 1992, UN Doc. S/RES/743 (1992)

Security Council, SC Res. 794 (1992), Dec. 21, 1992, UN Doc. S/RES/794 (1992)

Security Council, SC Res. 918 (1994), 17 May 1994, UN Doc. S/RES/918 (1994)

Security Council, SC Res. 929 (1994), June 22, 1994, UN Doc. S/RES/929 (1994)

Security Council, SC Res. 940 (1994), July 31, 1994, UN Doc. S/RES/940 (1994)

Security Council, SC Res. 955 (1994), Nov. 8, 1994, UN Doc. S/RES/955 (1994)

Security Council, SC Res. 1132 (1997), Oct. 8, 1997, UN Doc. S/RES/1132 (1997)

Security Council, SC Res. 1272 (1999), Oct. 25, 1999, UN Doc. S/RES/955 (1999)

Security Council, SC Res. 1313 (2000), Aug. 4 2000, UN Doc. S/RES/1313 (2000)

Security Council, SC Res. 1270 (1999), Oct. 22, 1999, UN Doc. S/RES/1270 (1999)

Security Council, SC Res. 1944 (2010), Oct. 14, 2010, UN Doc. S/RES/1944 (2010)

Security Council, SC Res. 1970 (2011), Feb. 26, 2011, UN Doc. S/RES/1970 (2011)

Security Council, SC Res. 1973 (2011), Mar. 17, 2011, UN Doc. S/RES/1973 (2011)

Security Council, SC Res. 2016 (2011), Oct. 27, 2011, UN Doc. S/RES/2016 (2011)

Security Council, S.C. Res. 2095, Mar. 14, 2013, U.N. Doc. S/RES/2095 (2013)

Statement by UNICEF Executive Director Anthony Lake on situation of children in the Middle East and North Africa, UNICEF, Apr. 20, 2011, *available at* http://www.unicef.org/media/media_58332.html

UNITED NATIONS INTER-AGENCY MISSION, MISRATA: 10 TO 14 JULY 2011, UN OFFICE FOR THE COORDINATION OF HUMANITARIAN AFFAIRS (2011), *available at*: http://reliefweb.int/sites/reliefweb.int/files/resources/Full_report_157.pdf

UNITED NATIONS SUPPORT MISSION IN LIBYA (UNSMIL), TRANSITIONAL JUSTICE-FOUNDATION FOR A NEW LIBYA (Sept. 17, 2012), *available at* http://unsmil.unmissions.org/LinkClick.aspx?fileticket=8XrRUO-sXBs%3D&tabid=3543&language=en-US

UNHCR REPORT UPDATE 27, HUMANITARIAN SITUATION IN LIBYA AND NEIGHBOURING COUNTRIES, June 3, 2011, *available at* http://reliefweb.int/sites/reliefweb.int/files/resources/Full_Report_1059.pdf

UNHCR warns of increased risk of mass displacement in Libya, UNHCR, Mar. 18, 2011, *available at* http://reliefweb.int/node/392568

UNRIC Library Backgrounder: Libya, UNITED NATIONS REGIONAL INFORMATION CENTRE, *available at* http://www.unric.org/en/unric-library/26483

UNSMIL Mandate, UN SUPPORT MISSION IN LIBYA, *available at* http://unsmil.unmissions.org/Default.aspx?tabid=3544&language=en-US

Update No. 22 on the humanitarian situation in Libya and the neighbouring countries, UNHCR, Apr. 28, 2011, available at http://www.unhcr.org/cgi-bin/texis/vtx/home/opendoc PDFViewer.html?docid=4dba71b612b&query=lanuf

US CABLES AND DOCUMENTS

Barack Obama, President, United States of America, *Remarks by the President in Address to the Nation on Libya*, Mar. 28, 2011, *available at* http://www.whitehouse.gov/the-press-office/2011/03/28/remarks-president-address-nation-libya

Christopher M. Blanchard, CONGRESSIONAL RESEARCH SERVICE, LIBYA: BACKGROUND AND U.S. RELATIONS (Aug. 6, 2008), *available at* http://fpc.state.gov/documents/organization/109510.pdf

——, CONGRESSIONAL RESEARCH SERVICE, LIBYA: UNREST AND U.S. POLICY (Sept. 29, 2011), *available at* http://fpc.state.gov/documents/organization/175868.pdf

Bill Gortney, U.S. Department of Defense News Briefing, *Libya Operation Odyssey Dawn*, Mar. 28, 2011

Carter Ham, Hearing to Receive Testimony on U.S. Transportation Command and U.S. Africa Command In Review of The Defense Authorization Request For Fiscal Year 2012 and The Future Years Defense Program, Testimony before Senate Armed Services Committee, Apr. 7, 2011, *available at* http://www.armed-services.senate.gov/Transcripts/2011/04%20April/11-26%20-%204-7-11.pdf

Libya 2012 Country Report on Human Rights Practices, UNITED STATES DEPARTMENT OF STATE, Apr. 19, 2013, *available at* http://www.state.gov/documents/organization/204585.pdf

Press Release, Office of the Press Secretary, The White House, Remarks by the President on the Situation in Libya, Mar. 18, 2011, available at http://www.whitehouse.gov/the-press-office/2011/03/18/remarks-president-situation-libya

Senate Armed Services Committee, *Hearing to receive testimony in U.S. Transportation command in review of the defense authorization request for fiscal year 2012 and the future years defense program*, Apr. 7, 2011, *available at* http://www.armed-services.senate.gov/Transcripts/2011/04%20April/11-26%20-%204-7-11.pdf

Senate Resolution, S. Res. 85, 112th Cong. §§ 2, 3, 7 (as passed by Senate, Mar. 1, 2011). Referenced in James C. Ho and Trevor W. Morrison, Editors, 1 J.L.: Periodical Laboratory of Leg. Scholarship 260, Apr. 1, 2011

Testimony of U.S. AFRICOM Commander General Carter Ham, SENATE ARMED SERVICES COMMITTEE, Apr. 7, 2011, *available at* http://www.armed-services.senate.gov/Transcripts/2011/04%20April/11-26%20-%204-7-11.pdf

U.S. Central Intelligence Agency, secret cable, *Terrorism Review*, COUNTERTERRORIST CENTER, June 1995, *available at* http://www.foia.cia.gov/docs/DOC_0000918468/DOC_0000918468.pdf

U.S. DEPARTMENT OF STATE, OFFICE OF THE INSPECTOR GENERAL, ACCOUNTABILITY REVIEW BOARD (ARB) REPORT ON THE SEPTEMBER 11TH ATTACK IN BENGHAZI (Dec. 18, 2012), *available at* http://www.state.gov/documents/organization/202446.pdf

U.S. Embassy in Tripoli, Confidential Cable, *SE Gration's Meeting with Abdulla Sanussi on Rebel Unification Efforts*, Nov. 1, 2009, *available at* http://www.telegraph.co.uk/news/wikileaks-files/libya-wikileaks/8294672/SE-GRATIONS-MEETING-WITH-ABDULLA-SANUSSI-ON-REBEL-UNIFICATION-EFFORTS-TRIPOLI-00000873-001.2-OF-002.html

U.S. Embassy in Tripoli, Confidential Cable, *Tribal Violence in Kufra*, Nov. 16, 2008, *available at* http://www.telegraph.co.uk/news/wikileaks-files/libya-wikileaks/8294878/TRIBAL-VIOLENCE-IN-KUFRA.html

U.S. Embassy in Tripoli, Press Release, *The United States and Libya Conduct Military Maintenance Training Seminar*, n.d., *available at* http://libya.usembassy.gov/news-events/news-from-the-embassy2/the-united-states-and-libya-conduct-military-maintenance-training-seminar.html

U.S. Embassy in Tripoli, Secret Cable, *Libya Interested in U.S. Weapons, More Ambivalent on Other Military Cooperation*, Dec. 31, 2008, *available at* http://wikileaks.org/cable/2008/12/08TRIPOLI992.html

U.S. Embassy, Secret Cable, *Saif al-Islam's Staff Reaches out on Pol-Mil Relations*, Dec. 14, 2009, *available at* http://www.telegraph.co.uk/news/wikileaks-files/libya-wikileaks/8294701/SAIF-AL-ISLAMS-STAFF-REACHES-OUT-ON-POL-MIL-ISSUES.html

U.S. Embassy in Tripoli, secret cable, *Libya's National Security Council: Experiencing Growing Pains*, Dec. 23, 2007, *available at* http://www.telegraph.co.uk/news/wikileaks-files/libya-wikileaks/8294769/LIBYAS-NATIONAL-SECURITY COUNCIL-EXPERIENCING-GROWING-PAINS.html

U.S. Embassy in Tripoli, Secret cable, *UK Denies Licenses for Export of Kalashnikovs to Libya, GOL Potentially Seeking Alternative Sellers*, THE TELEGRAPH, Nov. 6, 2008, *available at* http://www.telegraph.co.uk/news/wikileaks-files/libya-wikileaks/8294874/U.K.-DENIES-LICENSE-FOR-EXPORT-OF-KALASHNIKOVS-TO-LIBYA-GOL-POTENTIALLY-SEEKING-ALTERNATIVE-SELLERS.html

U.S. Embassy in Tripoli, Secret Cable, *What Passes for Political Ferment in Libya*, Oct. 26, 2009, *available at* http://www.telegraph.co.uk/news/wikileaks-files/libya-wikileaks/8294667/WHAT-PASSES-FOR-POLITICAL-FERMENT-IN-LIBYA.html

U.S. State Department, Remarks by Andrew J. Shapiro, *Addressing the Challenge of MANPADS proliferation*, Feb. 2, 2012 *available at* http://www.state.gov/t/pm/rls/rm/183097.htm

NATO DOCUMENTS

Ivo Daalder, U.S. Ambassador to NATO, *Remarks to the Press on Libya and Operation Unified Protector*, NORTH ATLANTIC TREATY ORGANIZATION, Sep. 8, 2011, *available at* http://nato.usmission.gov/libya-oup-90811.html

Fact Sheet, North Atlantic Treaty Organization, Operation Unified Protector Final Mission Stats, NORTH ATLANTIC TREATY ORGANIZATION, Nov. 2, 2011, *available at* http://www.nato.int/nato_static/assets/pdf/pdf_2011_11/20111108_111107-factsheet_up_factsfigures_en.pdf

Joint press briefing on events concerning Libya, NORTH ATLANTIC TREATY ORGANIZATION, Apr. 12, 2011, *available at* http://www.nato.int/cps/en/natolive/opinions_72290.htm

NATO and Libya: Commitment to protecting the Libyan people, NORTH ATLANTIC TREATY ORGANIZATION, Mar. 28, 2012, *available at* http://www.nato.int/cps/en/natolive/topics_71652.htm

NATO and Libya, Operation Unified Protector: Ending the Mission, NORTH ATLANTIC TREATY ORGANIZATION, available at http://www.nato.int/cps/en/natolive/topics_71652.htm%E2%80%8E

NATO and Libya: Operational Media Update, NORTH ATLANTIC TREATY ORGANIZATION, Apr. 7, 2011, *available at* http://www.nato.int/nato_static/assets/pdf/pdf_2011_04/20110402_110402-oup-update.pdf

NATO and Libya: Operational Media Update, NORTH ATLANTIC TREATY ORGANIZATION, Apr. 8, 2011, *available at* http://www.nato.int/nato_static/assets/pdf/pdf_2011_04/20110408_110408-oup-update.pdf

NATO and Libya: Operational Media Update, NORTH ATLANTIC TREATY ORGANIZATION, Apr. 28, 2011, *available at* http://www.nato.int/nato_static/assets/pdf/pdf_2011_04/20110428_110428-oup-update.pdf

NATO and Libya: Operational Media Update, NORTH ATLANTIC TREATY ORGANIZATION, June 25, 2011, *available at* http://www.nato.int/nato_static/assets/pdf/pdf_2011_06/20110626_110626-oup-update.pdf

NATO and Libya: Operational Media Update, NORTH ATLANTIC TREATY ORGANIZATION, June 29, 2011, *available at* http://www.nato.int/nato_static/assets/pdf/pdf_2011_06/20110630_110630-oup-update.pdf

NATO and Libya: Operational Media Update, NORTH ATLANTIC TREATY ORGANIZATION, July 6, 2011, *available at* http://www.nato.int/nato_static/assets/pdf/pdf_2011_07/20110706_110706-oup-update.pdf

NATO and Libya: Operational Media Update, NORTH ATLANTIC TREATY ORGANIZATION, July 7, 2011, *available at* http://www.nato.int/nato_static/assets/pdf/pdf_2011_07/20110707_110707-oup-update.pdf

NATO and Libya: Operational Media Update, NORTH ATLANTIC TREATY ORGANIZATION, July 26, 2011, *available at* http://www.nato.int/nato_static/assets/pdf/pdf_2011_07/20110726_110726-oup-update.pdf

NATO and Libya: Operational Media Update, NORTH ATLANTIC TREATY ORGANIZATION, July 28, 2011, *available at* http://www.nato.int/nato_static/assets/pdf/pdf_2011_07/20110728_110728-oup-update.pdf

NATO and Libya: Operational Media Update, NORTH ATLANTIC TREATY ORGANIZATION, Aug. 9, 2011, *available at* http://www.nato.int/nato_static/assets/pdf/pdf_2011_08/20110809_110809-oup-update.pdf

NATO and Libya: Operational Media Update, NORTH ATLANTIC TREATY ORGANIZATION, Aug. 13, 2011, *available at* http://www.nato.int/nato_static/assets/pdf/pdf_2011_08/20110814_110814-oup-update.pdf

NATO and Libya: Operational Media Update, NORTH ATLANTIC TREATY ORGANIZATION, Aug. 14, 2011, *available at* http://www.nato.int/nato_static/assets/pdf/pdf_2011_08/20110815_110815-oup-update.pdf

NATO and Libya: Operational Media Update, NORTH ATLANTIC TREATY ORGANIZATION, Aug. 15, 2011, *available at* http://www.nato.int/nato_static/assets/pdf/pdf_2011_08/20110816_110816-oup-update.pdf

NATO and Libya: Operational Media Update, NORTH ATLANTIC TREATY ORGANIZATION, Aug. 17, 2011, *available at* http://www.nato.int/nato_static/assets/pdf/pdf_2011_08/20110818_110818-oup-update.pdf

NATO and Libya: Operational Media Update, NORTH ATLANTIC TREATY ORGANIZATION, Aug. 18, 2011, *available at* http://www.nato.int/nato_static/assets/pdf/pdf_2011_08/20110819_110819-oup-update.pdf

NATO and Libya: Operational Media Update, NORTH ATLANTIC TREATY ORGANIZATION, Aug. 19, 2011, *available at* http://www.nato.int/nato_static/assets/pdf/pdf_2011_08/20110820_110820-oup-update.pdf

NATO and Libya: Operational Media Update, NORTH ATLANTIC TREATY ORGANIZATION, Aug. 21, 2011, *available at* http://www.nato.int/nato_static/assets/pdf/pdf_2011_08/20110821_110821-oup-update.pdf

Press briefing on Libya, NORTH ATLANTIC TREATY ORGANIZATION, May 17, 2011, *available at* http://www.nato.int/cps/en/natolive/opinions_74411.htm

Press briefing on Libya, NORTH ATLANTIC TREATY ORGANIZATION, May 20, 2011, *available at* http://www.nato.int/cps/en/natolive/opinions_74542.htm

Press briefing on Libya, NORTH ATLANTIC TREATY ORGANIZATION, May 27, 2011, *available at* http://www.nato.int/cps/en/natolive/opinions_74826.htm

Press briefing on Libya, NORTH ATLANTIC TREATY ORGANIZATION, June 10, 2011, *available at* http://www.nato.int/cps/en/natolive/opinions_75263.htm

Press briefing on Libya, NORTH ATLANTIC TREATY ORGANIZATION, June 14, 2011, *available at* http://www.nato.int/cps/en/natolive/opinions_75403.htm

Press briefing on Libya, NORTH ATLANTIC TREATY ORGANIZATION, June 20, 2011, *available at* http://www.nato.int/cps/en/natolive/opinions_75263.htm

Press briefing on Libya, NORTH ATLANTIC TREATY ORGANIZATION, June 21, 2011, *available at* http://www.nato.int/cps/en/natolive/opinions_75652.htm

Press briefing on Libya, NORTH ATLANTIC TREATY ORGANIZATION, July 7, 2011, *available at* http://www.nato.int/cps/en/natolive/opinions_76163.htm

Press briefing on Libya, NORTH ATLANTIC TREATY ORGANIZATION, July 12, 2011, *available at* http://www.nato.int/cps/en/natolive/opinions_76355.htm

Press briefing on Libya, NORTH ATLANTIC TREATY ORGANIZATION, July 14, 2011, *available at* http://www.nato.int/cps/en/natolive/opinions_75403.htm

Press briefing on Libya, NORTH ATLANTIC TREATY ORGANIZATION, July 19, 2011, *available at* http://www.nato.int/cps/en/natolive/opinions_76568.htm

Press briefing on Libya, NORTH ATLANTIC TREATY ORGANIZATION, June 20, 2011, *available at* http://www.nato.int/cps/en/natolive/opinions_75263.htm

Press briefing on Libya, NORTH ATLANTIC TREATY ORGANIZATION, June 21, 2011, *available at* http://www.nato.int/cps/en/natolive/opinions_75652.htm

Press briefing on Libya, NORTH ATLANTIC TREATY ORGANIZATION, July 26, 2011, *available at* http://www.nato.int/cps/en/natolive/opinions_76680.htm

Press briefing on Libya, NORTH ATLANTIC TREATY ORGANIZATION, Aug. 2, 2011, *available at* http://www.nato.int/cps/en/natolive/opinions_76803.htm

Press briefing on Libya, NORTH ATLANTIC TREATY ORGANIZATION, Aug. 9, 2011, *available at* http://www.nato.int/cps/en/natolive/opinions_77137.htm

Press briefing on Libya, NORTH ATLANTIC TREATY ORGANIZATION, Aug. 10, 2011, *available at* http://www.nato.int/cps/en/natolive/opinions_77137.htm

Press briefing on Libya, NORTH ATLANTIC TREATY ORGANIZATION, Aug. 16, 2011, *available at* http://www.nato.int/cps/en/natolive/opinions_77212.htm

Press briefing on Libya, NORTH ATLANTIC TREATY ORGANIZATION, Aug. 19, 2011, *available at* http://www.nato.int/cps/en/natolive/opinions_77137.htm

Press briefing on Libya, NORTH ATLANTIC TREATY ORGANIZATION, August 23, 2011, *available at* http://www.nato.int/cps/en/natolive/opinions_77362.htm

Press briefing on Libya, NORTH ATLANTIC TREATY ORGANIZATION, Sept. 13, 2011, *available at* http://www.nato.int/cps/en/natolive/opinions_77984.htm

Press briefing on Libya, NORTH ATLANTIC TREATY ORGANIZATION, Oct. 18, 2011, *available at* http://www.nato.int/cps/en/natolive/opinions_79613.htm

Press briefing on Libya, NORTH ATLANTIC TREATY ORGANIZATION, Oct. 24, 2011, *available at* http://www.nato.int/cps/en/natolive/opinions_79851.htm

Statement by the NATO spokesperson on Human Rights Watch report, NORTH ATLANTIC TREATY ORGANIZATION, May 14, 2012, *available at* http://www.nato.int/cps/en/SID-5040B041-666DF7DC/natolive/news_87171.htm

Prosecutor v. Stanišić and Simatović, Case No. IT-03-69-T, Trial Judgement (Int'l Crim. Trib. For the Former Yugoslavia, May 30, 2013)

Prosecutor v. Strugar, Case No. IT-01-42-T, Trial Judgement, (Int'l Crim. Trib. For the Former Yugoslavia, Jan. 31, 2005)

Prosecutor v. Tadić, Case No. IT-94-1-A, Appeals Judgement (Int'l Crim. Trib. for the Former Yugoslavia, July 15, 1999)

Prosecutor v. Tadić, Case No. IT-94-1-I, Decision on the Defence Motion for Interlocutory Appeal on Jurisdiction (Int'l Crim. Trib. For the Former Yugoslavia, Oct. 2, 1995)

Prosecutor v. Tadić, Case No. IT-94-1-I, Separate Opinion of Judge Li on the Defence Motion for Interlocutory Appeal on Jurisdiction (Int'l Crim. Trib. For the Former Yugoslavia, Oct. 2, 1995)

Prosecutor v. Tadić, Case No. IT-94-1-I, Separate Opinion of Judge Sidhwa on the Defence Motion for Interlocutory Appeal on Jurisdiction (Int'l Crim. Trib. For the Former Yugoslavia, Oct. 2, 1995)

Questions of Interpretation and Application of the 1971 Montreal Convention arising from the Aerial Incident at Lockerbie (Lib. v. U.S.), Provisional Measures, 1992 ICJ 114 (Apr. 14, 1992)

Regina v. Bow Street Metropolitan Stipendiary Magistrate (No. 1), *ex parte* Pinochet Ugarte, [1998] 3 W.L.R. 1456 (H.L.), *reprinted in* 37 I.L.M. 1302 (1998)

Regina v. Bow Street Metropolitan Stipendiary Magistrate, *ex parte* Pinochet Ugarte (No. 2), [1999] 2 W.L.R. 272 (H.L.), *reprinted in* 38 I.L.M. 430 (1999)

Regina v. Bow Street Metropolitan Stipendiary Magistrate, *ex parte* Pinochet Ugarte (No. 3), [1999] 2 W.L.R. 827 (H.L.)

Situation in the Republic of Kenya, Case No. ICC-01/09-01/11-307, Decision on the Application by the Government of Kenya Challenging the Admissibility of the Case Pursuant to Article 19(2)(b) of the Statute (Int'l Crim. Ct., Aug. 30, 2011)

Situation in Libya, Case No. ICC-01/11-01/11, Application on behalf of Aisha Gaddafi for leave to submit amicus curiae observations concerning her brother – Saif al-Islam Gaddafi (Int'l Crim. Ct., Dec. 31, 2012)

Situation in Libya, Case No. ICC-01/11-01/11, Application on behalf of the Government of Libya pursuant to Article 19 of the ICC Statute (Int'l Crim. Ct, 1 May 2012)

Situation in Libya, Case No. ICC-01/11-01/11, Decision on the conduct of the proceedings following the "Application on behalf of the Government of Libya relating to Abdullah Al-Senussi pursuant to Article 19 of the ICC Statute" (Int'l Crim. Ct., Apr. 26, 2013)

Situation in Libya, Case No. ICC-01/11-01/11, Decision on the admissibility of the case against Saif Al-Islam Gaddafi (Int'l Crim. Ct., May 31, 2013)

Situation in Libya, Case No. ICC-01/11-01/11, Decision on the postponement of the execution of the request for surrender of Saif Al-Islam Gaddafi pursuant to article 95 of the Rome Statute (Int'l Crim. Ct., June 1, 2012)

Situation in Libya, Case No. ICC-01/11-01/11, Document in Support of the Government of Libya's Appeal against the "Decision on the admissibility of the case against Saif Al-Islam Gaddafi" (Int'l Crim. Ct., June 24, 2013)

Situation in the Libyan Arab Jamahiriya, Case No. ICC-01/11-01/11, Prosecutor's Application Pursuant to Article 58 as to Muammar Mohammed Abu Minyar GADDAFI, Saif Al-Islam GADDAFI and Abdullah AL-SENUSSI (Int'l Crim. Ct., May 16, 2011)

Situation in Libya, Case No. ICC-01/11-01/11, Public Redacted Addendum to the Urgent Report Concerning the Visit to Libya OPCD (Int'l Crim. Ct., Mar 5, 2012)

Situation in the Libyan Arab Jamahiriya, Case No. ICC-01/11, Warrant of Arrest for Abdullah Al-Senussi (Int'l Crim. Ct., June 27, 2011)

Situation in the Libyan Arab Jamahiriya, Case No. ICC-01/11, Warrant of Arrest for Muammar Mohammed Abu Minyar Gaddafi (Int'l Crim. Ct., June 27, 2011)

Situation in the Libyan Arab Jamahiriya, Case No. ICC-01/11, Warrant of Arrest for Saif Al-Islam Gaddafi (Int'l Crim. Ct., June 27, 2011)

Trial of General Tomoyuki Yamashita, Case No. 21 (United States Military Commission, Manila, Oct. 8–Dec. 7, 1945)

Velásquez-Rodríguez case, Judgement of July 29, 1988, Inter-Am. Ct. H.R. (ser. C) No. 4 (1988)

INTERNATIONAL LAW DOCUMENTS

African Charter on Human and Peoples' Rights, 21 I.L.M. 58 (June 27, 1981)

ASSEMBLY OF STATES PARTIES, INTERNATIONAL CRIMINAL COURT, ELEMENTS OF CRIMES 5 (2011), *available at* https://www.legal-tools.org/doc/3c0e2d/

Charter of the International Military Tribunal – Annex to the Agreement for the prosecution and punishment of the major war criminals of the European Axis (Aug. 8, 1945)

Chemical Weapons Convention, 1974 U.N.T.S. 137 (Jan. 13, 1993)

Convention against Torture and Other Cruel, Inhuman or Degrading Treatment or Punishment, G.A. res. 39/46, U.N. Doc. A/39/51, 1465 U.N.T.S. 85 (Dec. 10, 1984)

Convention on the Elimination of All Forms of Discrimination against Women, G.A. Res. 34/180, U.N. Doc. A/34/46, 149 U.N.T.S.13 (Dec. 18, 1979)

Convention on the Non-Applicability of Statutory Limitations to War Crimes and Crimes Against Humanity, G.A. Res. 2391 (XXIII), U.N. Doc. A/7218, 754 U.N.T.S. 73 (Nov. 26, 1968)

Convention on the Prevention and Punishment of the Crime of Genocide, 78 U.N.T.S. 277 (Dec. 9, 1948)

Convention on the Prohibition of Military or Any Other Hostile Use of Environmental Modification Techniques, G.A. Res. 31/72, 1108 U.N.T.S. 151 (May 18, 1977)

Convention on the Prohibition of the Development, Production and Stockpiling of Bacteriological (Biological) and Toxin Weapons and on Their Destruction, 1015 U.N.T.S. 163 (Apr. 10, 1972)

Convention on the Prohibition of the Use, Stockpiling, Production and Transfer of Anti-Personnel Mines and on their Destruction, 2056 U.N.T.S. 211 (Sept. 18, 1997)

Convention for the Protection of Cultural Property in the Event of Armed Conflict, 249 U.N.T.S. 240 (May 14, 1954)

Convention on the Rights of Persons with Disabilities, G.A. Res. 61/106, U.N. Doc. A/61/49, 2515 U.N.T.S. 3 (Dec. 13, 2006)

Convention on the Rights of the Child, G.A. Res. 44/25, U.N. Doc. A/44/49, 1577 U.N.T.S. 3 (Nov. 20, 1989)

Convention on the Prohibition of the Development, Production, Stockpiling and Use of Chemical Weapons and on their Destruction, 1974 U.N.T.S. 45 (Jan. 13, 1993)

Convention on the Prohibition of the Use, Stockpiling, Production and Transfer of Anti-Personnel Mines and on their Destruction, 36 I.L.M. 1507 (Sept. 18, 1997)

Declaration of Basic Principles of Justice for Victims of Crime and Abuse of Power, G.A. Res. 40/34 (Nov. 29, 1985)

Definition of Aggression, GA Res. 3314 (XXIX), UN Doc. A/RES/3314 (Dec. 14, 1974)

Duties of States in the event of the outbreak of hostilities, GA Res. 378 B (V), UN Doc. A/RES/378 B (V) (Nov. 17, 1950)

First Optional Protocol to the International Covenant on Civil and Political Rights, G.A. Res. 2200A (XXI), U.N. Doc. A/6316 (1966), 999 U.N.T.S. 302

Formulation of the principles recognized in the Charter of the Nurnberg Tribunal and in the judgment of the Tribunal GA Res. 177 (II), UN Doc. A/RES/177 (Nov. 21, 1947)

General Treaty for Renunciation of War as an Instrument of National Policy, 46 Stat. 2343, 94 L.N.T.S. 57 (Aug. 28, 1928)

Geneva Convention on Asphyxiating Gases. Protocol for the Prohibition of the Use in War of Asphyxiating, Poisonous, or other Gases and Bacteriological Methods of Warfare, June 17, 1925, 26 U.S.T. 571, 94 L.N.T.S. 65, *reprinted in* 25 AM. J. INT'L L. 94 (1931)

Geneva Convention Relative to the Treatment of Prisoners of War (Third Geneva Convention), 75 UNTS 135 (Aug. 12, 1949)

Geneva Convention Relative to the Protection of Civilian Persons in Time of War (Fourth Geneva Convention), 75 UNTS 287 (Aug. 12, 1949)

International Conferences (The Hague), *Hague Convention (IV) Respecting the Laws and Customs of War on Land and Its Annex: Regulations Concerning the Laws and Customs of War on Land*, Oct. 18, 1907 at Preamble

International Convention against Apartheid in Sports, 1600 U.N.T.S. 161 (Dec. 10, 1985)

International Convention on the Elimination of All Forms of Racial Discrimination, G.A. Res. 2106 (XX), 660 U.N.T.S. 195 (Dec. 21, 1965)

International Convention on the Protection of the Rights of All Migrant Workers and Members of Their Families, U.N. Doc. A/RES/45/158, 2220 U.N.T.S. 3 (Dec. 18, 1990)

International Convention against the Recruitment, Use, Financing and Training of Mercenaries, G.A. Res. 44/34, U.N. Doc. A/RES/44/34, 2163 UNTS 96 (Dec. 4, 1989)

International Covenant on Civil and Political Rights, G.A. Res. 2200A (XXI), U.N. Doc. A/6316, 999 U.N.T.S. 171 (Dec. 16, 1966)

International Covenant on Economic, Social and Cultural Rights, G.A. Res. 2200A (XXI), U.N. Doc. A/6316, 993 U.N.T.S. 3 (Dec. 16, 1966)

International Convention on the Suppression and Punishment of the Crime of Apartheid, G.A. Res. 3068, U.N. Doc. A/9030, 1015 U.N.T.S. 243 (Nov. 30, 1973)

Optional Protocol to the Convention on the Elimination of All Forms of Discrimination against Women, U.N. Doc. A/RES/54/4, 2131 U.N.T.S. 83 (Oct. 6, 1999)

Optional Protocol to the Convention on the Rights of the Child on the Involvement of Children in Armed Conflict, U.N. Doc.A/RES/54/263, 2173 U.N.T.S. 222 (May 25, 2000)

Peace through Deeds, GA Res. 380 (V), UN Doc. A/RES/380 (V) (Nov. 7, 1950)

Principles of International Law Recognized in the Charter of the Nürnberg Tribunal and in the Judgment of the Tribunal, 2 YEARBOOK OF THE INTERNATIONAL LAW COMMISSION 97 (1950)

Protocol on Prohibitions or Restrictions on the Use of Mines, Booby-Traps and Other Devices as amended on 3 May 1996 (Protocol II), 1342 U.N.T.S. 168 (May 3, 1996)

Protocol on Prohibitions or Restrictions on the Use of Incendiary Weapons (Protocol III), 1342 U.N.T.S. 171 (Oct. 10, 1980)

Rome Statute of the International Criminal Court, 2187 U.N.T.S. 90 (July 17, 1998)

Rome Statute of the International Criminal Court Association of State Parties Resolution, Res. RC/Res. 6, UN Doc. RC/Res. 6 (June 11, 2010)

Second Optional Protocol to the Convention on the Rights of the Child on the Sale of Children, Child Prostitution and Child Pornography, U.N. Doc. A/RES/54/263, 2171 U.N.T.S. 227 (May 25, 2000)

Second Protocol to the Hague Convention for the Protection of Cultural Property in the Event of Armed Conflict, 2253 U.N.T.S. 212 (Mar. 26, 1999)

Standard Minimum Rules for the Treatment of Prisoners, E.S.C. Res. 663 C (XXIV) UN Doc. E/3048, July 31, 1957, *amended by* E.S.C. res. 2076, UN Doc. E/5988 (May 13, 1977)

Statute of the International Criminal Tribunal for the Former Yugoslavia, S.C. Res. 827, U.N. Doc. S/RES/827 (May 25, 1993)

Statute of the International Criminal Tribunal for Rwanda, S.C. Res. 955, U.N. Doc. S/RES/955 (Nov. 8, 1994)

Statute of the International Court of Justice, 156 U.N.T.S. 77 (June 26, 1945)

Statute of the Special Court for Sierra Leone, S.C. Res. 1315, U.N. Doc. S/RES/1315 (Jan. 16, 2001)

St. Petersburg Declaration Renouncing the Use, in Time of War, of Explosive Projectiles Under 400 Grammes Weight (Nov. 29/Dec. 11, 1868), *reprinted in* 1 AM. J. INT'L L. SUPP. 95 (1907)

United Nations, Charter of the United Nations, 1 UNTS XVI (Oct. 24, 1945)

Uniting for Peace, GA Res. 377, UN Doc. A/RES/377(V) A (Nov. 3, 1950)

OTHER

وزير العدل يستعرض خطة عمل الوزارة في الفترة القادمة, MINISTRY OF JUSTICE, Dec. 4 2012, available at http://www.aladel.gov.ly/main/modules/news/article.php?storyid=490

AFP, *Kadhafi forces flee rebels sweeping west to Sirte*, YOUTUBE (Mar. 27, 2011), *available at* http://www.youtube.com/watch?v=KPNd5UIBOrs

Ajdabiya, WOLFRAMALPHA, *available at* http://www.wolframalpha.com/input/?i=adjabiya

AlJazeeraEnglish, *Battle for Libya, Opposition Fighter Jet Shot Down*, YOUTUBE (Mar. 19, 2011), *available at* http://www.youtube.com/watch?v=-nUrxp74Hgg

M. Cherif Bassiouni, *Chronicles Of The Egyptian Revolution Of 25 January 2011: Egypt Update 17* (June 2012), *available at* http://t.co/WtpdQzo6

Benghazi, WOLFRAMALPHA, *available at* http://www.wolframalpha.com/input/?i=Benghazi

BLU-109/I-2000/HAVE VOID, GLOBALSECURITY.ORG, *available at* http://www.globalsecurity.org/military/systems/munitions/blu-109.htm

Brega, WOLFRAMALPHA, *available at* http://www.wolframalpha.com/input/?i=brega%2C+libya

Chair's Statement by William Hague, London Conference on Libya 2, Mar. 29, 2011, *available at* http://www.nato.int/nato_static/assets/pdf/pdf_2011_03/20110927_110329_-London-Conference-Libya.pdf

Country Profile: Libya, U.S. LIBRARY OF CONGRESS – FEDERAL RESEARCH DIVISION (Apr. 2005), *available at* http://lcweb2.loc.gov/frd/cs/profiles/Libya.pdf

Documents on Libyan Arab Jamahiriya, OFFICE OF THE HIGH COMMISSIONER FOR HUMAN RIGHTS, *available at* http://ap.ohchr.org/documents/dpage_e.aspx?c=104&su=110

Foreign Secretary on Musa Kusa's resignation, UK FOREIGN AND COMMONWEALTH OFFICE, March 31, 2012, *available at* http://www.fco.gov.uk/en/news/latest-news/?view=News&id=576566082

Google search "2 March A/HRC/19/68", GOOGLE, *available at* https://www.google.com/search?q=2+March+A%2FHRC%2F19%2F68&aq=f&oq=2+March+A%2FHRC%2F19%2F68&sourceid=chrome&ie=UTF-8#q=2+March+A/HRC/19/68&oq=2+March+A/HRC/19/68&sourceid=chrome&ie=UTF-8&pws=1&bav=on.2,or.r_qf.&bvm=bv.45921128,d.ZGU&fp=840023518346be54&biw=1440&bih=735

Information about Libya, UNITED STATES EMBASSY, TRIPOLI, LIBYA, *available at* http://libya.usembassy.gov/libya2.html

ICC Weekly Update, INTERNATIONAL CRIMINAL COURT, *available at* http://www.icc-cpi.int/NR/rdonlyres/9316F88E-EA95-4952-A619-3E56B6ED9CD3/284915/ED143_ENG.pdf

The Interim National Council, TEMEHU, *available at* http://www.temehu.com/ntc.htm

INTERPOL issues Red Notice for Assaadi Gaddafi at Libya's request, INTERPOL, Sept. 29, 2011, *available at* http://www.interpol.int/News-and-media/News-media-releases/2011/PR080

Jamahiriya Security Organization (JSO), GLOBALSECURITY.ORG, *available at* http://www.globalsecurity.org/intell/world/libya/jso.htm

Al-Khums, ENCYCLOPEDIA BRITANNICA ONLINE, *available at* http://www.britannica.com/EBchecked/topic/317074/Al-Khums

Khums, WOLFRAMALPHA, *available at* http://www.wolframalpha.com/input/?i=al+Hums%2C+Libya

Lakomtube, *Viagra and Condoms with Soldiers in Ajdabiya*, YOUTUBE (Mar. 27, 2011), *available at* http://www.youtube.com/watch?v=tYmdyy1kRoo

Laser Guided Bombs, FEDERATION OF AMERICAN SCIENTISTS, *available at* http://www.fas.org/man/dod-101/sys/smart/lgb.htm

Libya, OFFICE OF THE HIGH COMMISSIONER FOR HUMAN RIGHTS, *available at* http://www.ohchr.org/en/countries/menaregion/pages/lyindex.aspx

Libya, Intelligence, Haiat amn al Jamahiriya – *Jamahiriya Security Organization*, GLOBALSECURITY.ORG, *available at* http://www.globalsecurity.org/intell/world/libya/jso.htm

The Libyan Air Defense System: Libya's Surface to Air (SAM) Missile Network, CENTRE FOR RESEARCH ON GLOBALIZATION, GLOBAL RESEARCH, Mar. 21, 2011, *available at* http://www.globalresearch.ca/the-libyan-air-defense-system-libya-s-surface-to-air-missile-sam-network/23841

Libyan Air Force, GLOBALSECURITY.ORG, *available at* http://www.globalsecurity.org/military/world/libya/af.htm

Libyan Arab Jamahiriya, Country Profile: Human Development Indicator, UNITED NATIONS DEVELOPMENT PROGRAMME, *available at* http://hdrstats.undp.org/en/countries/profiles/LBY.html

Libyan Navy – Modernization, GLOBALSECURITY.ORG, *available at* http://www.globalsecurity.org/military/world/libya/navy-modernization.htm.

Libyan Penal Code of 1953 (Nov. 28 1953), *available at* http://archive.org/details/Libyan PenalCodeEnglish

Libyan People, TEMEHU, *available at* http://www.temehu.com/Libyan-People.htm

Libyan politician questioned by British police over rendition allegations, LEIGH DAY & CO SOLICITORS, July 19, 2012, *available at* http://www.leighday.co.uk/News/2012/July-2012/Libyan-politician-questioned-by-British-police-ove

Libyan Proud, *Zawiyya Hospital Aftermath of 11/06/2011*, YOUTUBE (June 12, 2011), *available at* http://www.youtube.com/watch?feature=player_embedded&v=EV5Kpvva9GM

Libyan Tribes – alphabetical list and by East West, WORLD VIEW FROM OFF THE STRIP, Feb. 26, 2011, *available at* http://www.sandraoffthestrip.com/2011/02/26/libyan-tribes-in-alphabetical-order-and-by-east-or-west

M Gee, *Blood & Guts Gaddafi Beaten To A Pulp as Part of Celebrations*, YOUTUBE (Oct. 21, 2011), *available at* http://www.youtube.com/watch?v=1chIX37laso&feature=related

Mi-17, GLOBALSECURITY.ORG, *available at* http://www.globalsecurity.org/military/world/russia/mi-17-specs.htm

Mi-24 HIND, Mi-25 HIND D, Mi-35 HIND E, GLOBALSECURITY.ORG, *available at* http://www.globalsecurity.org/military/world/russia/mi-24-specs.htm

M40 106mm Recoiless Rifle, GLOBALSECURITY.ORG, *available at* http://www.globalsecurity.org/military/systems/ground/m40rclr.htm

Milan, GLOBALSECURITY.ORG, *available at* http://www.globalsecurity.org/military/world/europe/milan.htm

MINISTRY OF FOREIGN AFFAIRS, www.aladel.gov.ly/main/modules/sections/category.php?start=0&categoryid=17

Misrata, WIKIPEDIA, *available at* http://en.wikipedia.org/wiki/Misrata

Misratah, WOLFRAMALPHA, *available at* http://www.wolframalpha.com/input/?i=Misratah&lk=1&a=ClashPrefs_*City.*Misratah.Misratah.Libya--

miusrata17miusrata, مصراته في حمزة كتيبة, YOUTUBE (Apr. 20, 2011), *available at* http://www.youtube.com/watch?feature=player_embedded&v=XK2UqU6Qprs

North Africa Pipelines map – Crude Oil (petroleum) pipelines – Natural Gas pipelines – Products pipelines, COUNTRIES OF THE WORLD, May 6, 2008, *available at* http://theodora.com/pipelines/north_africa_oil_gas_products_pipelines_map.html

Port Marsa El Brega, WORLD PORT SOURCE, *available at* http://www.worldportsource.com/ports/LBY_Port_Marsa_El_Brega_665.php

Press Release, *The African Union High-Level Ad Hoc Committee On Libya Convened Its 5th Meeting In Addis Ababa Press release*, AFRICAN UNION, May 26, 2011, *available at* http://www.au.int/en/sites/default/files/Press%20Release%20ad%20hoc%20committee%205th%20Meeting%2026%20MAy%202011.pdf

Press Release of Dec. 2009, EGYPTIAN EMBASSY, *available at* http://www.egyptembassy.se/press/23dec09.pdf

Press Release, *Libye: point de situation opération Harmattan n°1*, FRENCH MINISTRY OF DEFENSE, Mar. 25, 2011, *available at* http://www.defense.gouv.fr/operations/autres-operations/operation-harmattan-libye/actualites/libye-point-de-situation-operation-harmattan-n-1

Press Release, *UK Ministry of Defense, UK military liaison advisory team to be sent to Libya*, Ministry of Defence, Apr. 19 2011, *available at* http://www.mod.uk/DefenceInternet/DefenceNews/DefencePolicyAndBusiness/UkMilitaryLiaisonAdvisoryTeamToBeSent-ToLibya.htm

RAF destroys Qaddafi rocket launchers, UK Ministry of Defence, May 9, 2011, *available at* http://www.globalsecurity.org/military/library/news/2011/05/mil-110509-ukmod01.htm

Ras Lanuf – Harbour, Tracks 4 Africa, *available at* http://tracks4africa.co.za/listings/item/w185925

RAS LANUF OIL Airport Private Jet Charter Flights and Air Charter Service, Stratos Jet Charter Services, *available at* http://www.stratosjets.com/jet-charter-airports/Libya/RAS-LANUF-OIL

Revolutionary Guard, Globalsecurity.org, *available at* http://www.globalsecurity.org/intell/world/libya/rg.htm.

RPG-7, RPG-7V, Rocket Propelled Grenade, GlobalSecurity.org, *available at* http://www.globalsecurity.org/military/world/russia/rpg-7.htm

R-11/SS-1B SCUD A/ R-300 9K72 Elbrus/SS-1C SCUD-B, Federation of American Scientists, *available at* http://www.fas.org/nuke/guide/russia/theater/r-11.htm

Sirte, WolframAlpha, *available at* http://www.wolframalpha.com/input/?i=sirte

S-5 (57mm) Aircraft Rockets (Russia) (Russian Federation), Air-launched rockets, Jane's Intelligence Review, *available at* http://webcache.googleusercontent.com/search?q=cache:http://articles.janes.com/articles/Janes-Air-Launched-Weapons/S-5-57-mm-air-craft-rockets-Russia-Russian-Federation.html

Tripoli, WolframAlpha, *available at* http://www.wolframalpha.com/input/?i=tripoli

Two Benghazi tribes support Gaddafi-Libyan TV, Reuters, Mar. 16, 2011, *available at* http://www.reuters.com/article/2011/03/16/libya-tribes-tv-idUSLDE72F1YA20110316

Type-63 107mm Rocket Laucher, Federation of American Scientists, *available at* http://www.fas.org/man/dod-101/sys/land/row/type-63-r.htm

The World Factbook: Libya, Central Intelligence Agency, *available at* https://www.cia.gov/library/publications/the-world-factbook/geos/ly.html

John L. Wright, *Tripoli*, Encyclopedia of the Modern Middle East and North Africa (2004), *available at* http://www.encyclopedia.com/topic/Tripoli.aspx

Zawiyya Hospital Aftermath of 11/06/2011, Amara, *available at* http://www.universalsubtitles.org/en/videos/P2F7mQoXiJTw/en/117282

ZU-23 23mm Antiaircraft Gun, Federation of American Scientists, *available at* http://www.fas.org/man/dod-101/sys/land/row/zu-23.htm

9K51 BM-21 GRAD (HAIL), Federation of American Scientists, *available at* http://www.fas.org/man/dod-101/sys/land/row/type-63-r.htm

INDEX

OTHER